A FACSIMILE OF

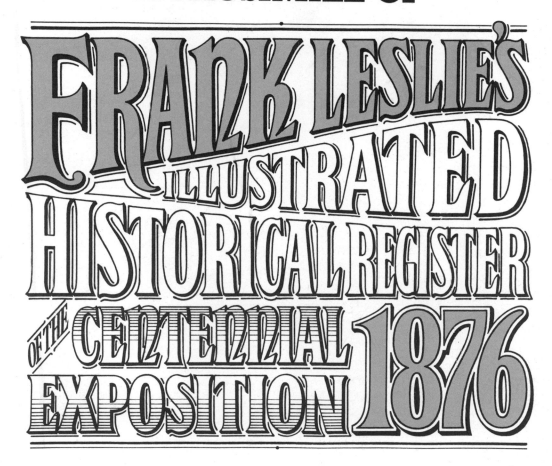

FRANK LESLIE'S ILLUSTRATED HISTORICAL REGISTER OF THE CENTENNIAL EXPOSITION 1876

with a new introduction by Richard Kenin

PADDINGTON PRESS LTD

THE TWO CONTINENTS
PUBLISHING GROUP

Richard Kenin is an American historian and writer now living in
England. He was born and raised in Portland, Oregon,and attended Reed
College and the University of London. He was awarded a Doctorate of
Philosophy in Modern History at Magdalen College in the University of
Oxford.

Dr Kenin is the U.K. representative for the Smithsonian Institution's
Bicentennial program.

Frank Leslie's Illustrated Historical Register of the Centennial
Exposition 1876 with a new introduction by Richard Kenin.
© Paddington Press Ltd. — 1974.
Printed in the United States of America.
ISBN   0-8467-0022-0
Library of Congress Catalog Card No. 73-15026
PADDINGTON PRESS LTD
Two Continents Publishing Group, 30 East 42nd St., N.Y.C., N.Y. 10017

INTRODUCTION
by Richard Kenin

T he most stupendous and successful competitive exhibition that the world ever saw"—that is how *Leslie's Historical Register* described the Philadelphia Centennial Exposition of 1876. As the United States celebrates its Bicentennial we can learn much from the grand Philadelphia Exhibition, and of all the works published for that celebration none equalled the *Leslie Register* for both illustrative entertainment and historical insight.

To call the Philadelphia Exposition the greatest of all such shows was quite a boast for America's one hundredth birthday party coming, as it did, at the end of a quarter century of major international exhibitions throughout the transatlantic world.

The mania for such shows began with the London Crystal Palace Exhibition of 1851 and spread enthusiastically to Ireland, France, Germany, Russia, Denmark, Spain, and Austria, culminating in the great Vienna Exposition of 1873, which ran for 210 days and welcomed over ten million visitors.

America had not been altogether out of the mainstream of such activity during those twenty-five momentous years. The New York Exhibition of 1853, the Buffalo World's Fair of 1869, and the expositions at Louisville and Cincinnati in 1872 all had received some praise and were to prove important trial runs for the grand Philadelphia extravaganza of the Centennial year.

However, with the passage of time, the importance of the Philadelphia Exposition has diminished in folk memory. The famous 'White City' of the Chicago Fair of 1893 is enshrined as a seminal font of contemporary American tastes and interests, but little thought is given today to the exhibition which, more than any other in our history, opened the eyes of America to the vistas of international commercial competition and cooperation.

In the handbook published by the exposition directorate is a keynote phrase that governed the general thinking of the time. The chairman of the commission wrote, "What better method of celebrating our Country's birth to freedom than by a grand exhibition which shall contain the BEST THAT WE CAN DO?" With such a thought in mind, planning went forward, and no idea was considered too grandiose or bizarre as to be beyond attempt. Everything was to be the newest, the biggest, and the best available, and this was a value system the American people

were to adopt whole-heartedly and were never to lose in the years that followed.

Certainly, there was a 'theory of expositions' that governed all of the planning of the Philadelphia Centennial. A world's fair was considered analagous to an ecumenical council. It was a microcosm which showed the world in miniature. Everything of value the world was thought to possess was to be represented in due proportion. Not only the industries, but the arts, sciences, and social lives of all peoples were to be on show for the instruction of the millions of American visitors whose attendance was anticipated.

No one seriously thought that such an undertaking would prove extremely lucrative. On the contrary, most were sure that heavy losses would have to be sustained. However, it was felt that the direct and indirect benefits to the people arising from such an exhibition were so great as to outweigh mere monetary considerations. America was rapidly coming of age, and many thought the time was ripe for the country to assume its rightful place of equality among the family of nations.

The genesis of the Philadelphia Centennial Exposition can be traced most properly to an 1866 article written in the *Anglo-American Times and Continental Gazette* by General Charles B. Norton, who was one of the American Commissioners to the Paris Exhibition of 1867. General Norton was greatly impressed not only by the magnitude of the Paris show, but also by the favorable impression of French achievements that was created in the minds of France's continental neighbors. He argued that a grand exhibition was the best way for the American people to make their presence felt in the international community, and no occasion was more fitting than the Centennial celebration of the nation's independence.

Norton's idea received a great deal of support in the years that followed, and on March 3, 1871 Congress formally adopted the plan by setting up the United States Centennial Commission. Unfortunately, the commission was plagued by bureaucratic inefficiency, and, just over a year later, Congress felt it was necessary to establish an ancillary body, the Centennial Board of Finance, to insure that the project would not collapse before it began. The

Board of Finance issued $10 million in capital stock which was to be taken up by the States on a quota basis. This was to be the primary source of funding for the Exposition and was considered theoretically adequate based on the cost figures of the Vienna Exhibition which totaled $9.8 million. Congress, in its enabling legislation, explicitly declared that the national government would not be held responsible for any debts incurred by the Centennial; consequently, it was necessary that the States support the endeavor strongly if the Exhibition was to meet its much vaunted expectations.

The Board of Finance, a very private body of twenty-five directors, sixteen of whom came from Pennsylvania and knew each other personally, was confident that adequate funds would be available. However, competition with the already-established Centennial Commission, which was national in character, proved a major stumbling block resulting in mass resignations between 1872 and 1876 as well as very little financial support from several of the States. Eight States subscribed less than $100 in Centennial stock, including one of the thirteen founding members of the Union.

Consequently, it was left to a small group of States, which felt they had an essential interest in the Exposition, to provide much of the cash that would be necessary for its success. Of the $2.2 million in stock which was eventually taken up, fully $1.7 million came from Pennsylvania and the balance from New York, New Jersey and the New England States. However, this was still an insufficient amount, so Pennsylvania and Philadelphia together subscribed an additional $2.5 million to get the venture off the ground. With only $4.7 million pledged, it was clear that the federal government would have to take an active part, and eventually an additional $5 million flowed out of government channels in a manner that was all too typical of the Grant administration. The idea that the Centennial would be a joint project of all the States had not succeeded, and it was left to the central government to try and patch things up.

In spite of continuing financial and bureaucratic difficulties, the organizers of the Centennial Exposition never lost their almost messianic faith in the success and purpose of the venture. Unbounded enthusiasm was evident in every public statement of the commission, and during the first weeks of 1873, positive steps were actually seen to be taken. On the 25th of February the Centennial Commission met at the Philadelphia Academy of Music for its first public convocation. On the following Fourth of July the grounds of Fairmount Park in Philadelphia were transferred to the commission by the authorities of the city and actual building was commenced.

Thirty-eight foreign nations accepted invitations to participate in the Exposition in spite of Secretary of State Hamilton Fish's lack of active support for the venture. While it was true that many European States played only a perfunctory role at Philadelphia, the emerging nations of Latin America and the Orient participated to the fullest extent possible and were instrumental in making the venture a success.

Within a few months of the commencement of building Philadelphia began to take on a distinctly cosmopolitan air. Hundreds of Japanese laborers were seen working alongside bearded Russians in white tunics and Turks gorgeously attired in red velvet jackets and baggy trousers. Dozens of foreign languages could be heard in the streets of the city, and the smells of foreign cooking rose from the laborers' temporary housing on the grounds of Fairmount Park.

Fully one third of all the exhibits erected at the Exposition came from abroad via a fleet of United States warships which had been sent from port to port collecting the arts and manufactures of those nations participating. As thousands of parcels and hundreds of cages containing strange and wonderful creatures appeared in Philadelphia every day became a parade day, and the excitement which these activities generated was infectious.

The full magnitude of the Exhibition began to take shape as buildings went up. The site at Fairmount Park encompassed over 230 acres, 50 acres of which were covered by buildings. Over 189 structures were in the process of erection, and it was rapidly becoming clear that the Philadelphia Centennial had the potential to outdo even the Vienna Exhibition of 1873 which had been the most spectacular to date.

The organizers of the Exhibition decided to test the enthusiasm of the populace by staging a trial run on July 4, 1875, the 99th anniversary of the signing of the Declaration of Independence. A commemorative program at Fairmount Park was so successful that few came away with doubts as to the inevitable popularity of the glorious celebration that was to begin the following year. Over 200,000 people attended the 99th anniversary and demonstrated their whole-hearted support for the venture.

The build-up of public emotion continued in the months that followed and reached a peak on New Year's Eve 1876 when the Centennial year was ushered in with a great display of popular sentiment. Throughout the day the bells of Philadelphia's churches were rung, and cannon were fired at five minute intervals. In the evening, all the houses of the city were lit by candle light, and Carpenters' Hall, where the First Continental Congress met, was brightly illuminated by gas jets spelling out the inscription, "THE NATION'S BIRTHPLACE".

Independence Hall was a scene of great public attention as thousands milled outside the building. Masqueraders and parades of bands wound their way through the crowds and precisely at, midnight, the Mayor of Philadelphia raised the old colonial flag of Pennsylvania.

The crowd had grown to an estimated 100,000 whose cheers drowned out the martial music that had been composed for the occasion. The bells of the State House pealed out the number 1,7,7,6 followed by 1,8,7,6 and then one hundred single chimes for the years of the Centennial. The newly erected 21,000 pound Centennial chimes burst forth with patriotic music, and red and blue lights were struck on all sides of the square. A pyrotechnic display illuminated the night with designs of the heads of the founding fathers, and public emotion was at such a high pitch that dozens of individuals fainted and required medical attention. So great was the public response that it was feared in some quarters that the actual opening of the Centennial would be anticlimactic, but this was to prove a worry without foundation as subsequent events demonstrated.

May tenth had been designated as the official opening of the Exposition, and in the months leading up to that day, activity on the exhibition grounds grew furious with preparations. Private police and fire patrols were established with a compliment of men drawn from all the States of the Union. Telegraphic and postal communications were set up in Fairmount Park, and the Exposition was formally linked with Philadelphia by three steam railway lines, four lines of horse cars, a line of omnibuses, and dozens of roads. A narrow, double-gauge railway was built around the perimeter of the park, and, for all practical purposes, a city within a city had been constructed in just a few short months.

When opening day finally arrived, the grand plaza of the fairgrounds was filled with nearly 200,000 people. Four thousand guests were seated on the platform in front of the Memorial Hall awaiting the commencement of formal ceremonies. Thirteen national anthems were played, and as President Grant's party made its way to the platform, the orchestra struck up a march composed especially for the occasion by Richard Wagner.

It was unfortunate that much of the program was both pompous and time-consuming. The crowd had to sit through an extremely long and boring 'Centennial Cantata' written by Sidney Lanier which could hardly be heard by a large proportion of the audience. Many of the speeches were fullsome beyond belief, and the crowd began to evidence signs of noisy impatience. Yet all lapsed into silence when, at 11:45 A.M. General Hawley, the Chairman of the Centennial Commission, rose and presented President Grant. As the chief executive began his speech there were few shouts of approval. Instead, a dour silence that could hardly be called respectful fell over the audience. William Dean Howells, writing in *The Atlantic* noted, "The President of the United States came, spoke and went without applause. A few scattered cheers made more apparent the silent indifference with which he was received. Let the truth be told in spite of reporters: there were more groans and hisses as he finished his address."

So rocked had the President's administration become with scandal, corruption, and illegal practice that the Centennial Commission which, in its early stages, had been designed to celebrate the accomplishments of that same administration, was now only too anxious to have the President finish his ten minute speech, declare the exhibition open, and then depart from public view. However, the crowd was only temporarily silent. They seemed determined not to let the public appearance of the President spoil their day. As soon as Don Pedro, the Emperor of Brazil and the only head of state to appear personally at the ceremony, was introduced, cheering once again began in full measure.

Once President Grant had been dispatched, the audience was again in good spirits, and at a signal from General Hawley, the American flag was unfurled, accompanied by a rendition of the Hallelujah Chorus and a salute of 100 cannon fired from nearby George's Hill. The official party then proceeded into the Machinery Hall, where the great Corliss engine was put into motion thus starting all the mechanical exhibitions housed in the building. The Centennial Exhibition had now truly begun, and the grounds at Fairmount Park although not absolutely complete in all aspects, were thrown open to the millions of Americans who came to Philadelphia for the celebrations.

The average visitor to the Exposition could not help but be awed by the sheer size of everything. The Main Exhibition Building, dominated by huge bronze statues of Pegasus at its entrance and galvanized iron eagles in each interior corner, was a vast transparent glass palace covering twenty-one acres with a central nave almost 1700 feet long. The adjoining Art Building, constructed in modern renaissance style, was capped by a 150 foot dome surmounted by a colossal figure of Columbia. In both buildings, band music was constantly heard, and numberless fountains rose and fell for the entertainment of the spectator.

In the Machinery Hall, where all manner of new things could be found, the Corliss engine, which required fifteen million pounds of stone and five million feet of lumber for its superstructure, dominated the entire proceedings. In that building the word 'automation' was breathed for the first time in America. Wherever one looked one could see new labor-saving devices, alternate fuels for energy consumption, unique engine complexes, and a variety of technical innovations ranging from pressurized soda fountains to I. L. Baker's Celebrated Sugar Pop-Corn Machine. The great Krupp cannon, brought from Germany, stood on one side of the main aisle opposed by a considerable array of European armaments, and the very position of these shiny brass weapons cast a somewhat ominous glow over the building.

Under the 'Mauresque' architecture of the Horticultural Hall and the great Gothic parallelogram of the Agricultural Building, thousands of species of plant and animal life were exhibited. Whole windmills were set up next to a giant aquarium containing 35 tanks full of hundreds of species of sea life which most visitors had never seen before.

The United States Government Building, covering four-and-one-half acres, was divided up among the Departments of War, Navy, Treasury, Interior, and the Smithsonian Institution. The official theme of the government exhibition was a demonstration of the functional and administrative facilities of the federal bureaucracy in time of peace and its resources in time of war. However, there was also an unpleasant side to this exhibition which manifested itself as an official justification for the slaughter and anticipated extermination of the Indian tribes whose lands were then up for grabs. Photographs of menacing savages together with examples of the 'primitiveness' of Indian life were all shown in great detail.

The exhibition nonetheless must have succeeded in its purpose, for as clever a man as William Dean Howells came away with the impression that the government's program was certainly justified. Howells wrote that the Red Man, as he appeared in effigy and photograph, was a hideous demon whose malign traits could hardly inspire any emotion softer than abhorrence. "In blaming our Indian agents for malfeasance in office, perhaps we do not sufficiently account for the demoralizing influence of merely beholding these false and pitiless savage faces; moulding flour and corrupt beef must seem altogether too good for them."

In addition to the official buildings, over two hundred special edifices were constructed for particular exhibits. Several foreign countries erected their own pavilions, the most important being those set up by England, Japan, Egypt, Turkey, and Australia. It has already been noted that whereas many European countries only made half-hearted attempts to provide comprehensive exhibits, the emerging nations of the world spared no effort to impress the Americans with their skills and wares. Great Britain alone among European powers made a concerted effort to participate fully; still she only spent $250,000 on her exhibits and those of her colonies and dominions, while Japan expended over $600,000 on what was acknowledged as one of the finest and most aesthetically pleasing exhibitions on the grounds. The Japanese exhibit launched the earliest of the recurring waves of oriental interest in the United States and established a powerful ingredient in American decorative taste that has grown and prospered over the years.

For most American visitors, a trip to Fairmount Park was the grand world tour they could never hope to have. Dozens of foreign restaurants, bakeries, and sweet shops lined the boulevards of the Exposition grounds. The Tunisian cafe celebrated the dexterity of the belly dancer, and the Turkish coffee house allowed gentlemen the novelty of smoking strange but delightful substances which "removed the burdens of worry from the mind and enlarged the vistas of sentimental pleasure." Such substances were, of course, legal in 1876.

Buildings devoted to the carriage and wagon industry, the brewers' craft, photography, printing, shoes and leather, and glass manufacture catered to the visitor of specialized interests. At the same time, the Hunters' Camp, the New England Kitchen, and relics of George Washington satisfied an ever-increasing passion for Americana among the populace.

The Education Department, with its emphasis on care for the physically and mentally handicapped, was of great interest to the public spirited, middle-class ladies of the late nineteenth century. Most particularly, the crowds were fascinated by new Swiss methods of preserving society from the infection of hereditary taint by its members. The science of genetics was achieving considerable notoriety in European journals, and the Philadelphia Exposition provided a major venue in the United States for these new methods of social engineering.

However interesting each building and exhibit was, the Exposition did not rely entirely on their individual or collective merit. It was rather the case that excitement and attendance built up from peak to peak based on the various special days of celebration. There were the individual State days which drew tens of thousands of loyal visitors to gubernatorial receptions and parades and such 'monumental' events as the crowning of the Queen of Love and Beauty. The pavilions erected by certain States became local centers of interest for a brief period of time, but activity passed on a daily basis from one building to another.

Certainly one of the most interesting of these 'Days' was November seventh, which was designated as Woman's Day. The Ladies Centennial Committee, organized in twenty-seven States by Mrs. E. D. Gillespie, erected a 30,000 square foot building at Fairmount Park "to show what has been effected in the past by the brains and hands of women and to prove there are higher aims and nobler ends than can be obtained by devotion to the needle." Consequently, the women's exhibit showed little relating to home economy or domestic science but concentrated, instead, on women as major contributors to the cultural life of society. The women also organized all the musical events throughout the Centennial and managed the demonstration experimental schools for young children. Woman's Day at the Centennial was not just a formal occasion; it was also symbolic of the growing strength of the suffragette movement, and many of the names associated with the Ladies Committee were later to become prominent in the national campaign to improve womens' rights.

Woman's Day was one of the most interesting at the Exposition, but in terms of excitement, it could not hope to compete with the celebrations that took place on the Fourth of July when the entire Centennial program reached its zenith in the minds of the public. It was natural that the venue for this event shifted back to Independence Hall in Philadelphia. The venerable Richard Henry Lee of Virginia emerged on the balcony of the hall holding the orig-inal draft of the Declaration of Independence. The old man read out the document slowly and with great dignity before an estimated crowd of 200,000. As he finished, a great shout rose from the crowd, and Lee turned the document around so that the words would be visible to everyone. The cries of the multitude rose to new heights, but there was no merriment or exuberance of a trivial nature; instead one observed "a universal expression of gladness and rejoicing."

America was coming to the end of the Reconstruction Era, and many hoped that the Centennial would act as a binding institution to heal the wounds that had so badly torn the fabric of the nation. In a letter to Robert E. Lee, President Grant remarked, "The animosities which attended the war are dying out. We shall soon celebrate their funeral in the Centenary." From the reaction of the people in Philadelphia on the Fourth of July, this prediction appeared to be coming true. In spite of the mischievous activities of Grant's administration, which had done so much to destroy the confidence of the people in the very institutions of government whose preservation had cost the nation so dear, the crowd still held an almost pious reverence for the relics of the Revolution which soared beyond the corrupting power of any individual politician.

The Fourth of July was naturally the high point of the Centennial, and most activities thereafter seemed somewhat anti-climactic. On Friday, November 10, 1876 President Grant arrived in a pelting rain and declared the Exposition closed. Most people were unaware of his presence and were much more concerned with the unfurling of the old flag of John Paul Jones, which was the last symbolic act of the Centennial Commission. The great Corliss engine in Machinery Hall was silenced, and as all the mechanical exhibits became still, the crowds drifted away from Fairmount Park, though it took several days for everyone to be convinced that the grand show was really coming to an end.

The Philadelphia Exposition attracted almost ten million visitors during its six months' existence. On average, 62,000 people arrived every day, though attendance occasionally skyrocketed on special occasions such as Pennsylvania Day when almost 275,000 people crowded into Fairmount Park. Faced with such an enormous mass of humanity, it is not surprising that commercial entrepreneurs took full advantage of the occasion.

Visitors to the fairgrounds were inundated with every sort of souvenir and guidebook imaginable, but none could quite compare with the profusely illustrated *Leslie's Historical Register of the Centennial Exposition*, which was compiled as a great retrospective view of the entire celebration. In every way, the *Leslie Register* emerged as the most entertaining and informative of all the materials produced for the Centennial. No other popular publication could hope to be as fullsome, and Leslie's undoubted success was due primarily to the nature of his publishing empire.

Frank Leslie, born Henry Carter, was a small, abstemious, hardworking Englishman who had shown an early gift as a wood engraver. His success on the staff of the *Illustrated London News* eventually led him to become head of that periodical's picture department. For six years he explored the then new field of illustrated journalism and in 1848, having mastered the fundamentals of his profession, he emigrated with his family to New York where he formed an association in the publishing business with P. T. Barnum.

In 1854, Leslie set up his first independent publishing venture by producing *Leslie's Ladies' Gazette of Fashion.* This was followed by a number of publications including the great *Frank Leslie's Illustrated Newspaper,* a landmark publication in the history of American printing.

The *Illustrated Newspaper* began in 1855 as a repository of sensational woodcuts of brawls, crimes, train collisions, mine disasters, gory battles, and sinking ships. Leslie could produce shocking illustrations of violent scenes within 24 hours of their occurrence by dividing his woodblock illustrations into a number of sections, assigning each bit of work to a different engraver, and then placing the entire block together for printing. Leslie pioneered this method of journalistic illustration, and, at its best, the *Illustrated Newspaper* was a serious competitor to the publications of his long-time rivals, the Harper brothers.

Leslie's method of illustration was applied to his *Historical Register of the Centennial* and was to prove highly successful, for as Chairman of the Board of State Commissioners to the Exposition, Leslie could have his artists placed at advantageous points to view every single activity as it was prepared and carried into execution.

When Leslie divorced his first wife and subsequently married Miriam Squier, the 38-year-old spouse of the editor of the *Illustrated Newspaper,* he took a step that was to have far-reaching effects not only on his personal life but on his publishing empire as well. The second Mrs. Leslie was a notable personality in her own right and soon emerged as the editor of several of the Leslie magazines and books. She was a staunch suffragette who eventually left her entire estate of two million dollars to the Women's Rights Movement, and her influence on the content of many Leslie publications is easily discernable. This was particularly true of the *Historical Register of the Centennial,* where the activities of the women's organization was given a considerable amount of space, and where her protégé, Joaquin Miller, the 'poet of the Sierras', was allowed several pages to publish his "Song of the Centennial," a poem of dubious merit at best.

Regardless of Mrs. Leslie's special editorial interests, the *Historical Register* did satisfy everyone's desire to know the most minute details surrounding the Centennial Exposition. The book did not attempt to be just a history of one particular exhibition but rather an encyclopedia of all previous world's fairs by including a vast amount of historical, descriptive, and statistical information on the agriculture, manufactures, and commerce of the world —at least this was the avowed intention of the publishers.

The Leslies' motto was "never shoot over the heads of the people" either in price or content for theirs were books for the unsophisticated. Of course, the beneficial result of such a policy for the modern reader is all too clear. Whereas sophisticated journals such as *Scribner's* and *The Christian Review* took much for granted in their reportage of the Centennial, the Leslies left nothing to chance. Everything was presented both visually and in highly descriptive detail, giving the modern reader an absolutely clear impression of mid-nineteenth century American and international tastes and styles. By looking through the *Leslie Register,* one quickly becomes enwrapped not just by the content but also by the spirit of the Centennial; the uninhibited patriotic emotion which was evident on so many occasions, sweeps across the pages of *Leslie's Register* with few thoughts save pride in national purpose.

The Leslies, who had an official and financial stake in the Centennial, were undeniably proud of the success of the Exposition. Their book is highly interesting not only for what it emphasizes but also for what is distinctly understated.

As has been said, the American people were slowly moving away from the Era of Reconstruction, and everyone wanted to forget the divisive horrors of the Civil War. Indeed Joaquin Miller's "Song of the Centennial" begins with the phrase "Peace on earth and harvest time! Hail the day, but heal the scars!" It was hoped that the Centennial would act as a unifying force in this effort, yet for many the appearance of the black man at Fairmount Park was an uncomfortable reminder of the Civil War. Consequently, the statue of the freed slave, a piece of sculpture that was only tolerated at the Exposition with great reluctance, was the only reminder in the entire exhibition that this recently emancipated sector of the community even existed. Further, the history of the labor movement, which had aroused great interest at the Paris and Vienna Exhibitions, was passed over in complete silence at Philadelphia. Labor relations in 1876 were also politically controversial, and nothing of such a nature was allowed to dilute the themes of unity and national purpose.

We have already spoken of the role of women in the Centennial, and this was no more clearly emphasized than in the symbolic scene portrayed on the cover of the *Leslie Register.* All of the dominent figures depicted allegorically are women, while the only male presented is subordinate both physically and racially in terms of the value-system of the time. The only black present is certainly not American by dress, and the sexual orientation of that individual is even somewhat dubious. It is perhaps most interesting that the role of women was the only controversial issue which appeared in the *Leslie Register.* Almost all references to President Grant are omitted, though Leslie does remark that the Centennial was undertaken at a time of great national stress and managed providentially to overcome the obstacles set up by Administration activity.

The Centennial Exposition was not just an excuse for popular merriment. It was a watershed in American history when the nation, in the midst of a period of rapid growth, paused for a moment to re-examine the first principles—moral, social, and political—in its foundation. Also, in a wider context, the Exhibition was a popular exploration of the genius which inspired man's great material progress in the later part of the nineteenth century.

As the United States celebrates its Bicentennial we can derive much inspiration and enthusiasm from the great Philadelphia Exposition of one hundred years ago. America is again seeking to bind the wounds of a divisive war. Our political problems have again raised fundamental questions about the stability of our institutions. The positions of the Black, the Indian, and the American woman are in the forefront of national attention. Beyond our borders competitive nations like the Japanese continue, as they did in 1876, to provide significant challenges for the American economy.

Leslie's Historical Register of the Centennial raises a number of salient questions regarding the course which our Bicentennial should take. Consequently, a careful review of its text and illustrations should not only prove to be a most entertaining exercise in historical nostalgia, but also a provocative introduction to the activities surrounding our own two hundredth anniversary of the signing of the Declaration of Independence.

Frank Leslie's

Historical Register

OF THE UNITED STATES

Centennial Exposition,

1876.

Embellished with nearly Eight Hundred Illustrations drawn expressly for this Work by the most Eminent Artists in America.

INCLUDING ILLUSTRATIONS AND DESCRIPTIONS OF ALL PREVIOUS INTERNATIONAL EXHIBITIONS, AND CONTAINING MUCH USEFUL INFORMATION, AND STATISTICS OF THE FOREIGN COUNTRIES REPRESENTED AT THE EXPOSITION.

Edited by Frank H. Norton,

Assisted by Scientific Men in the different Departments of Art,
Manufactures, Mechanics, Agriculture.

NEW YORK:
FRANK LESLIE'S PUBLISHING HOUSE.
MDCCCLXXVII.

INTRODUCTION.

THE design of FRANK LESLIE'S HISTORICAL REGISTER OF THE CENTENNIAL EXPOSITION has been, as was indicated in its Prospectus —"To furnish a permanent, truthful, and beautiful Chronicle of the Congress of Nations assembled in friendly competition in Philadelphia in 1876," and to "afford a complete history of exhibitive effort in the past, and an artistic and discriminating Record of the Great Centennial, the entire work illustrated in the highest style of art, and forming altogether a magnificent Memorial of the Colossal Exhibition in Fairmount Park."

The intention thus set forth was conscientiously undertaken, and has been carried out on a scale of liberal consideration for the presumed requirements of the public, which, it is believed, has never before characterized any similar publication.

The great works illustrating the Exhibitions of London and Paris are only to be obtained at a cost far exceeding the purse of the ordinary book-buyer ; the present publication, on the contrary, is within the reach of every one. The foreign works to which we allude have considered, in their descriptive and illustrative efforts, only selected subjects. FRANK LESLIE'S HISTORICAL REGISTER comprises history, description,. and illustration of all "World's Fairs" whatsoever—while to the Centennial it has given a degree of minute attention which includes nearly every detail of structure and exhibit. Finally, the HISTORICAL REGISTER presents, in connection with the subject immediately under consideration, a vast amount of historical, descriptive, and statistical information, which renders it, in fact, a comprehensive Encyclopedia of the Agriculture, Manufactures, and Commerce of the World.

The Centennial Exposition was, in itself, the culminating effort of a century of grand achievements. Presenting a panorama of the intellectual and industrial results of a hundred years of toil, it stands before humanity as a vast and complete exemplification of the progress of the past—to be utilized as a picture of experience for the benefit of the future.

To the millions of visitors to the Centennial Exposition, it would seem that some record should be desirable which might perfect for them the memory of happy days passed at Fairmount, and of the wondrous exhibition of human development in skill, industry, and intelligence there displayed before them.

To these it is hoped that FRANK LESLIE'S HISTORICAL REGISTER will come in the guise of an intelligent and discriminating friend—noting down and describing for their benefit the incidents and objects which they most desire to remember ; and, while affording instruction, presenting also a fund of interesting and entertaining reminiscence, which shall serve to recall out of the past the almost magic beauty and wondrous completeness of the Champion Exhibition of the World.

Lavishly illustrated by the pencils of the best living artists, the HISTORICAL REGISTER offers its services to the public as the only complete and permanent record of the magnificent events it chronicles, and the industrial works it describes.

FRANK LESLIE'S

HISTORICAL REGISTER

OF THE

CENTENNIAL EXPOSITION.

THE EXHIBITIONS OF THE WORLD.

HE international exposition of our time is the culmination of a long series of steps in competitive exhibition. The best method, therefore, of arriving at a just conclusion as to the merits of our own labors in this direction is by comparison, and we purpose for this reason to lay before our readers some examination of the history and progress of international exhibitions from first to last. The whole subject of competitive exhibitions is one not unworthy the consideration of the reader, and, as it seems not inappropriate at this time to extend even further our investigations, we will seek to trace the record of such exhibitions from the most recent inter-national examples, away back to the more remote and simple illustrations among the ancients.

FAIRS.

The word "fair" comes to us either from the Latin *forum*—a market-place, or *feriæ*—holidays. The Romans established such marts as these in all their provinces. In those days the difficulties of transportation precluded frequent markets, such as are obtained in our time with perfect facility; and, furthermore, these institutions were deemed serviceable in the earlier stages of society, and in rude and inland countries, where, in the absence of shops, it was necessary that something of this character should be established for the benefit both of merchants and of the general public. In fact, so generally was the usefulness of fairs admitted, that it became customary for Governments to grant certain privileges to them and special facilities were afforded them for the disposal of property. To give them still greater importance, and, as it were, to "kill two birds with one stone," these were originally associated with religious festivals or holidays.

This practice has come down even to our day, the fairs of Europe being commonly fixed for some saint's day or other religious festival. In England, no fair or market could be held in ancient times but by a grant from the crown, with the provision, also, that no two fairs should interfere with or impede each other. Various laws and enactments were made in reference to fairs. One of these was peculiar. A *bona-fide* sale made in the fair on market day transferred the property to the vendee, no matter how vicious or illegal the title of the vendor might be. Under

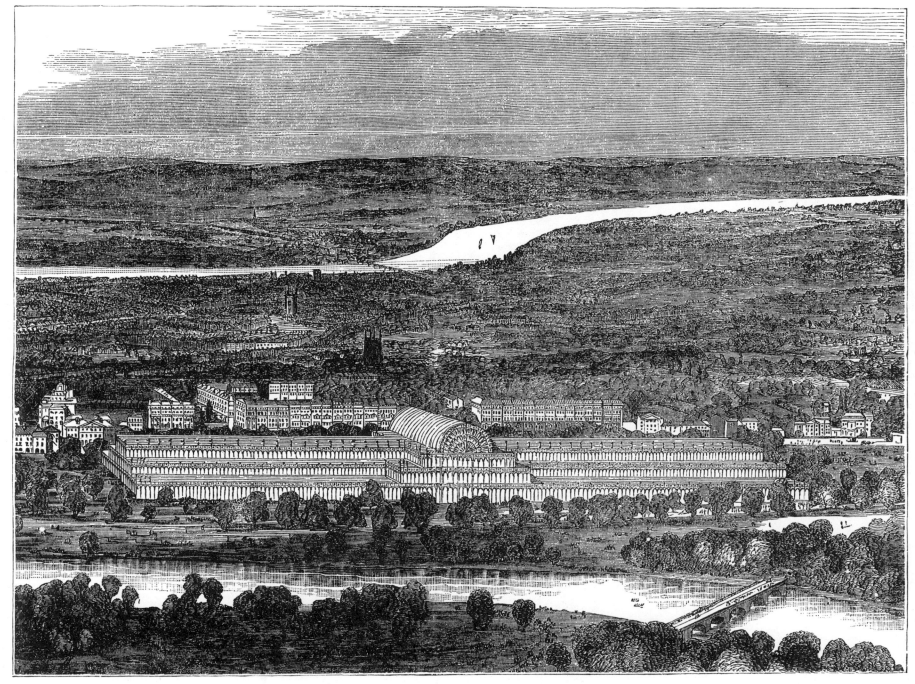

BIRD'S-EYE VIEW OF THE CRYSTAL PALACE, LONDON, 1851.

JEWELS BELONGING TO THE EAST INDIA COMPANY DISPLAYED AT THE LONDON EXHIBITION, 1851.

any circumstances, the claim of the buyer was good against any one except the king. And the better to exclude injustice during these gatherings, a court was commonly held at the same time and place with them, this court being called *pie-poudre*, in allusion to the dusty feet of the suitors.

At this court, accounts—as to contracts, purchase, and sale—were considered, as also the just weight and measure provided. A very important species of these fairs in England, and, indeed, on the Continent, was the cattle-fair, of which instances occurred at least once a year in different places—Exeter, Norwich, Norfolk, Carlisle, for instance. The great St. Bartholomew Fair was formerly one of great importance, and was one of the most interesting features of London life. As early as the time of William the Conqueror, there was established at St. Giles's Hill, near Winchester, England, a fair which was apparently instituted for the purpose of adding to the revenues of the Bishop of Winchester. In the time of Henry III. this fair extended to sixteen days, and its jurisdiction covered a space of seven miles. The law concerning it provided that within the fair district any one who sold goods individually forfeited their price to the bishop; this continuing as late as 1512.

The most important fair on the continent of Europe was formerly that of Beaucaire, in France. So highly was this market considered that, in 1314, Philip of France complained warmly to Edward II. that the merchants of England had desisted from frequenting them, to the great loss of his subjects, and entreated his brother-monarch to persuade the merchants of his dominion to return to their former custom.

The most important German fairs have been those of Frankfort-on-the-Main, Frankfort-on-the-Oder, and Leipsic, the latter being more particularly a book-fair, and very celebrated. The Easter fair at Leipsic has been

CANADIAN TIMBER TROPHY AT THE LONDON EXHIBITION, 1851.

LONDON EXHIBITION, 1851—TRANSEPT.

commonly visited by the entire book trade of Germany, and sometimes continued three weeks.

In Italy, the most noted fair is that of Sinigaglia, a seaport in the province of Ancona, at the mouth of the Misa. This fair still exists, lasting from the 20th of July until the 10th of August. It is attended by English, French, Germans, and others. In Hungary, the most important fair is that of Pesth, which is the centre of Hungarian commerce.

But undoubtedly the most remarkable fair known to us is that of Nijni-Novgorod, the foremost commercial and manufacturing town in Russia, at the confluence of the Oka and the Volga, seven hundred and fifteen miles from St. Petersburg, with which city, since 1862, it has been connected by railway. Here is conducted a great annual fair, officially opened on the 27th of July; but, owing to the slow arrival of goods, it is generally delayed in regard to its actual business for several days. At the time of this fair, the different nations are classified in shops, on the plan of the Oriental bazaar. Thus, Chinese, Persians, Armenians, Europeans, and others, are found in their respective quarters. Many of the transactions here are conducted by barter. Tea is perhaps the chief article of commerce, being brought from Kiachta; silks, etc., from China and India; and cloths, hides, morocco, etc., from Russia. Indigo, jewels, and innumerable other articles of luxury and for common use, are represented.

Meanwhile, huge craft throng the rivers, between which the town lies, varying from the great, Oriental-looking barges to the little canoes which convey passengers across the river. The little steamers tow long strings of barges after them. The close of the fair is proclaimed by the lowering of the flag over the governor's residence, and a procession of ecclesiastics, in long robes, bearing banners, etc., marching through the streets, proclaiming their blessing on the business that has been done and on the tradespeople interested. The strange conglomeration at this scene of the natives of all countries, and the votaries of all religions, forms a scene not to be met with in any other part of the world. The value of the goods disposed of during this fair is great, and seems to be continually on the increase. In 1697 it amounted to £14,000. One hundred and sixty years later (1857), it had increased to £14,000,000. In 1863 the value of sales amounted to £16,760,000. The town where this fair takes place is very ancient, having been founded in 1221 as a stronghold against the Bulgarians. Its prosperity dates from the year 1817, when the great fair was removed thither from Makarief, when a fire broke out in the latter place and destroyed the greater portion of the stores. The population of the town is about 50,000, but during a fair it increases to upward of 290,000.

In 1873, during the progress of the fair, the place was visited by the Duke of Edinburgh, who remained one week, and was entertained by the governor-general of the provinces. The duke is the first member of the royal family of England who has penetrated so far into the interior of Russia.

Among Eastern fairs the most important has been that held at Mecca during the season of the pilgrimages. Of late this fair has declined in importance, but is still considerable. At Hurdwar, on the Ganges, a locality chiefly important for the annual Hindoo pilgrimage for the purpose of ablution—the season comprising the end of March and the beginning of April—a great fair takes place at this time. In ordinary years the attendance here amounts to between two and three hundred thousand; but on the occasion of every twelfth year, which is for some reason of special importance, the visitors number about 2,000,000. It is of considerable importance to the rest of the world that from these "twelve years' fairs" usually date the most serious visitations and epidemics of the Asiatic cholera, which will be found in their appearance in the United States to appear at this distance of time from each other: as, for instance, 1832, 1843, 1854, and 1866.

The ancient Greeks held fairs in conjunction with popular assemblages for political purposes, as was the case in Rome. They were introduced into France as early as the fifth century; the great fair of St. Denis being instituted by Dagobert in 629, that of St. Lazare by Louis VI., and those of Aix-la-Chapelle and Troyes about 800; in 960 they were established in Flanders. Fairs for the sale of slaves were quite common in Germany, and in the north of Europe generally, in 1071, and were even encouraged in England by William the Conqueror. Slaves were also sold at the fair of St. Denis, in France, and French children were taken away to foreign countries in exchange. This trade, however, was prohibited through the influence of Bathilda, a wealthy freed-woman. This fair of St. Denis was continued till 1777, and was made attractive by the exhibition of a piece of wood taken from the "true cross," which, of course, all Paris went to see.

In the year 1789 most of the great fairs in France were abolished, and permanent markets took their place. But the fair of Beaucaire still continues, its sales amounting to four or five million dollars annually. This fair is held from July 1st to July 28th, and merchants come to it even from so far as Persia and Armenia there being as many as 100,000 people sometimes in attendance. Here the chief articles of commerce are silks, wines, oil, almonds, and other fruit, wool, and cotton. In Holland there are annual fairs of importance at Amsterdam, Rotterdam, and other cities. As has always been the case at all of these gatherings, they are the scene of a vast variety of side shows, spectacles, cheap theatrical representations and jugglery exercises, and other amusements for the edification of the visitors, who thus combine business with pleasure. Fairs are less frequent in Italy, Spain, and Portugal than in other parts of Europe; that of the 15th of May, however, at San Isadro del Campo, is still of importance, being held at the period when the annual pilgrimages draw crowds to that locality.

The fairs of Leipsic date from the twelfth century, and are the most frequented of any in Germany. The principal articles of trade are silk, cloth, cotton, china, glass, earthenware, drugs, hides, leather, breadstuffs, dyestuffs, colors, oils, alcohol, coal, and paper. Easter is the customary season for the booksellers' trade-sale and settling of accounts; but the exhibition of books formerly connected with fairs has fallen into disuse.

AMERICAN FAIRS.

On the American continent fairs date from an early period. In ancient Mexico, where there were no shops, they very frequently attracted large crowds, and a particular quarter of the city was allotted to each trade. The traffic at these fairs was carried on partly by barter, and partly by means of a currency comprised indifferently of quills filled with gold dust, bits of tin, T-shaped, and bags of cacao, each containing a specified number of grains. Fairs were regularly held at Azcapazalco, near the capital, where slaves were sold, and at Tascala were held great pottery fairs. The most important fair, however, was held in the city of Mexico, the number of visitors being estimated at 40,000 or 50,000.

In Peru the Incas instituted fairs for facilitating agricultural exchange. They took place three times a month in some of the most populous places, the trade being altogether by barter.

At Puerto Bello, now a small seaport town on the northern shore of the isthmus, four miles north of the town of Panama, was formerly held a great fair under the Spanish rule. The produce of the west coast was stored at Panama until the Spanish fleet was due at Puerto Bello, when a remarkable scene occurred at the latter place, to which these were then transported. Tents and huts were erected, and the place was at once transformed from a mud village to an enormous camp.

Among the goods exposed, the products of Spain were oil, wine, cloths, silks, etc., which were exchanged for gold, silver, logwood, and other articles, which were sent back to Spain on the vessels when they returned. In 1739, during the war between England and Spain, the locality of this fair was stormed by Admiral Vernon, and has since fallen into decay.

BAZAAR.

The bazaar of the East is essentially a fair, where articles are placed in practical competition. The word is derived from the Persian, and means *market*. In Turkey, Egypt, Persia, and India, portions of towns are exclusively appropriated to the bazaars, which consist of a connected series of streets and lanes, sometimes vaulted, with high brick roofs, domes, or cupolas. The porches of these vast markets are commonly lined with small shops, in which goods of little value are exposed for sale. The shops of the bazaars are nothing more than little closets, six feet square and eight or ten feet high, entirely open in front. The owner usually sits cross-legged on the floor or counter, with his goods about him, arranged for his convenience as to movement. It is said that the Persian, Armenian, and Jewish shopkeepers of the bazaar are more obliging than the Turks, and more anxious to obtain custom; but the greater portion of customers prefer to deal with the latter, who seem to be more honest in their business methods. Trade commences here with daylight and ends at sundown. The bazaars are well watched and generally secured by means of strong outer gates. Larcenies in these establishments are almost unknown, and shopkeepers do not hesitate to leave their places unguarded during brief absences. Various portions of the bazaar are assigned to different

LONDON EXHIBITION, 1851—END VIEW.

CORK EXHIBITION, 1852.

trades. Nearly all the bazaars are supplied with khans, or coffee-houses, to which the merchants resort after each trade (a fashion not entirely unknown even in Europe and this country). It is said that in Constantinople ladies sometimes provide for their private purse by embroidering handkerchiefs and other needlework, the result of their labors being sold in the bazaars. Women, however, are rarely seen in the bazaars, except those of the lower class. Men resort there for conversation, and to pass away the time, as well as for actual business.

NATIONAL AND STATE INDUSTRIAL EXHIBITIONS.

FROM the idea of the great fair undoubtedly sprung that of the Industrial Exhibition. The first being held for profit only, and being, in fact, only vast periodical markets for barter and exchange, it not unnaturally came to be thought that the same process could be made use of for exhibitive and competitive purposes. It was not, however, until a comparatively recent period that this idea was put into actual working order, and for much of the use to which it has been applied, and for the chief advantages which have been derived from it, we are indebted to the "London Society of Arts." This society was organized in 1753 by one William Shepley, an English drawing-master, a brother to the Bishop of St. Asaph, and its first meeting was held in March, 1754, at a coffee-house in Covent Garden, and continued to be held at such places for twenty years, when a building was erected for it in the Adelphi, on the site of the palace of the Bishop of Durham. From its inception this society was patronized by the nobility of England, some nobleman of high rank being always elected president; and this continued until 1845, when Prince Albert took the chair.

The influence of this society upon the arts and

manufactures of Great Britain has been enormous. By a judicious system of prizes, native ingenuity and inventions were encouraged, and some of the most prominent artists and others in England owe their rise to such encouragement on the part of the Society of Arts.

Among these may be mentioned the names of Flaxman, Landseer, Allan Cunningham, Mulready, Millais and others. In particular, every effort was made on the part of the society to encourage invention in its application to the arts and manufactures. Among other means for advancing civilization, it may be mentioned that the society promoted

earnestly the improvement of the fishery trade and commerce in the British colonies, besides all kinds of arts, sciences and manufactures; and to this course London owes at present its magnificent daily supply of fish.

A fact interesting to Americans, in connection with the early history of the "Society of Arts," is given in its records, to the effect that, on November 27th, 1755, Benjamin Franklin wrote a letter from Philadelphia to the society, in which he remarked that he would esteem it a great honor to be admitted a corresponding member of the society, and, though it was not required that corresponding members should bear any part of the expenses of the society, yet he desired that he might be permitted to contribute twenty guineas to be applied in premiums.

In 1849 the Society organized an annual exhibition of articles of utility, invented, registered, or patented during the previous twelve months, and these exhibitions have been continued ever since. While this was being done in London, a similar movement was being made in the city of Munich, Bavaria, where an Industrial Exhibition was conceived in 1849, but was kept back by political disturbances until 1854, when it took place. To this any contributions were invited, the exhibitors being principally from Austria, Prussia, Saxony, and other countries. The building which contained the exhibition was in the form of a cross, constructed of iron, glass and wood. The length of the main building was 800 feet; the main transept 280 feet, height 87 feet; space occupied, 244,814 square feet. There were 6,800 exhibitors, and the cost of the building was 880,000 florins. But if the Industrial Exhibition, as an institution, probably owes its existence to the valuable influence of the London "Society of Arts," it is to France that we must look for the first actual illustration of this idea of public competition in manufactures and arts.

The first Industrial Exhibition, in fact, was held in Paris

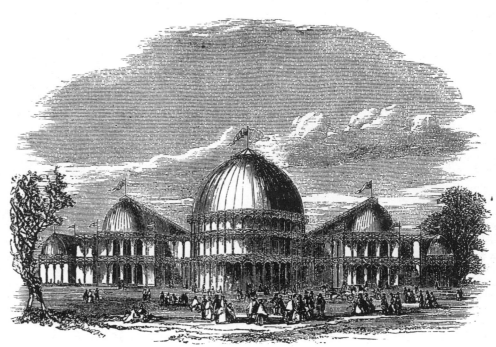

DUBLIN EXHIBITION, 1853.

in 1798, and comprised, chiefly, specimens of arts and manufactures loaned by their owners. This display led to another during the same year, and the apparent utility and evident success of both these prompted the more extended exhibitions under the Consulate, in 1801 and 1802. Thereafter it was intended that these exhibitions should be triennial, but on account of interruptions from political causes they were irregular. In England local exhibitions were held in Manchester, Leeds, Birmingham, and other cities, in 1828, 1837, 1839 and 1849. In Ireland the Royal Society of Dublin began a series of triennial exhibitions of Irish manufactures in 1829. Similar representations were held in Ghent in 1839, in Berlin in 1832, and Vienna in 1835. In 1852 a particularly successful exhibition of Irish arts and manufactures was held at Cork, and in 1861 a very important exhibition of the industries of Holland was held in Haarlem, besides others at Nantes, in France, and Florence, in Italy. In 1863 an International Exhibition was held at Constantinople for the display of Turkish products, and, though this was not important in the general sense of the word, it was rendered attractive by the display of beautiful jewels from the imperial palace and seraglio. In 1864 there was an exhibition in Amsterdam for the display of Dutch industries, and in the same year local shows of this character were held at Malta, Calcutta and Lucknow, as also a combined Spanish and French exhibition at Bayonne. The South London and North London Working Classes Industrial Exhibitions began in 1864. One of these was very important, having 934 exhibitors and 200,000 visitors during the eighteen days in which it was open. It netted a clear profit of £4,000. In 1865 there was an industrial exhibition at Oporto, confined to Portuguese manufactures; and the same year New Zealand contributed an exhibition at Dunedin.

At about this time, also, there took place at Cologne a combined exhibition by Germany, Holland, and Belgium,

NEW YORK EXHIBITION, 1853.

MUNICH EXHIBITION, 1854.

principally agricultural; and also an interesting display of fishing-tackle, and implements, at Boulogne. Meanwhile, exhibitions were being held at Birmingham, Nottingham, Preston, Manchester, and other English towns, while in Vienna 613 prizes were distributed among 1,025 exhibitors, and a clear profit was made of 2,000 florins. The idea continued to spread, and, in 1866, Sweden, Norway, Denmark, and Finland combined in a competitive display of Scandinavian industry. This exhibition took place at Stockholm, the principal manufactures shown being those in iron, steel, wool and earthenware. The same year there occurred an exhibition at Melbourne, where 3,360 exhibitors offered articles from South Australia, Victoria, New Zealand, New South Wales and Queensland. The Brazilian Exhibition, which took place first at Pernambuco, and afterward at Rio Janeiro, consisted mainly of raw products. In 1867, a very curious exhibition was made at Havre, where everything concerned in the fisheries was exhibited, including fishing-boats and all appliances for curing fish, making fishermen's clothes, etc. A still more important one was held there in 1868, comprising the display of marine engines, nautical instruments etc. Similar exhibitions took place during 1867 and 1868 at Agra, in India, at St. Petersburg, Ghent, and Berlin, while, in 1870, another was given at St. Petersburg, displaying Russian progress in the manufacture of steel guns, armor-plate, rails, locomotives, etc. During this year, also, an Intercolonial Exhibition was held at Sydney, New South Wales, which was important for its display of raw products and preserved meats. In 1871, a series of annual exhibitions was commenced by the "Italian Industrial Association" at Milan. This year, also, there was an exhibition at Lima, in Peru, of the industries of the South American Pacific States, and one at Cordova, of Argentine industries, and of foreign implements adapted to develop local resources. A similar display took place at Bogota in the following year.

In the United States, Industrial Exhibitions have long been a feature in the progress of State industry. The most important of these being those of the American Institute, in New York, founded in 1828. For many years the annual exhibitions of the Institute were in part agricultural and partly horticultural; but lately they have been chiefly devoted to the industries and arts, and open to exhibitors from all parts of the Union. These have constantly increased in magnitude and importance, and have acquired the largest available locality in the city of New York for their display, including Castle Garden and the Crystal Palace, the latter of which was burned, in 1858, during the progress of one of the American Institute Fairs, and all its contents destroyed. Of late years the exhibitions have been held in the premises known as the "Rink," near "Central Park," which has been purchased by the Institute. This association has a fund of $75,000 in Government bonds and loans and city real estate, with an annual rental of $12,000. These fairs are generally profitable. The Franklin Institute, of Philadelphia, was founded at about the same time with the American Institute, and publishes a valuable journal. In Cincinnati, the local association has held five annual exhibitions, and the "Mechanics' Institute, of San Francisco," ten; Baltimore, Boston and Buffalo have also had successful local Industrial Exhibitions, and for many years nearly all the County and State Agricultural Societies have held fairs and offered prizes.

It is undoubtedly to the enterprise and success noted in these exhibitions, that the displays on a grander scale to which we may now direct attention, owe their origin. Thus, by succeeding steps of energy and originality, the present class of Exposition has been made practicable.

INTERNATIONAL EXPOSITIONS, OR WORLD'S FAIRS.

RETURNING to the valuable services of the "London Society of Arts" to the cause of industry, we find that the first "World's Fair," which took place in the Crystal Palace, London, owed its existence to the efforts of that society. We have before alluded to the election of the Prince Consort to the Presidency of this Society, and it was by his labors chiefly that the exhibition, which we have now to describe, was made the crowning feature of the career of this organization. In an address before the society, in 1849, Prince Albert declared that the time had now come for a great exhibition, "not merely national in its scope and benefits, but comprehensive of the whole world." In accordance with this suggestion, efforts were made in the direction indicated, and, as a result, a Royal Commission was issued January 3d, 1850, and the Queen headed a subscription-list with £1,000. The building, popularly known as the Crystal Palace, was erected in Hyde Park, from designs by Sir Joseph Paxton, being composed, excepting the flooring and joists, wholly of glass and iron. This was in 1851, the first idea of the exhibition having been broached by the Prince Consort at a meeting of several gentlemen, members of the "Society of Arts," at Buckingham Palace, two years before. The Prince then laid before his hearers the plan of a grand collection of various products, to take place in London in 1851, for the purpose of "exhibition, competition, comparison, instruction and encouragement." He also suggested that contributions should be classed in four great groups or divisions: raw materials, manufactures, merchandise and mechanical inventions, works of sculpture and plastic art. These suggestions were afterward carried out almost to the letter. The Society of Arts adopted the scheme, and pushed it forward with great earnestness. Visits were made to many

districts at home, and inquiries among foreign countries, looking toward the great result desired. Important meetings were held in London, and the most cordial spirit was displayed by the merchants, bankers, and traders of the metropolis, while in the provinces the same sentiment prevailed to an unexpected extent.

Subscriptions were rapidly offered, and the entire necessary guarantee fund was soon contributed. The main difficulty which now presented itself was with reference to the character of the building required. Concerning this, it may be remarked, that Paxton's model was, in fact, a most felicitous inspiration, the general characteristics of which have governed the construction of all exhibition buildings ever since. Paxton's idea was founded on that of a splendid conservatory, which he had recently erected at Chatsworth for the Duke of Devonshire. His plan took the commissioners by storm, and was at once adopted, and the building erected in accordance with it. This building was 1,851 feet long, and 408 feet wide, with an extension on the north side 936 feet long and 48 feet wide. The height of the central portion was 64 feet, and that of the transept in the centre 108 feet. The entire area was about nineteen acres, and the site chosen—Hyde Park—was fortunate in every particular, of position, accessibility and locality. The materials in the building were iron, glass and wood. The quantities employed were: wrought-iron, 550 tons; cast-iron, 3,500 tons; glass, 900,000 superficial feet; wood, 600,000 feet; total area of ground covered, 772,784 square feet, and that of the galleries, 212,100 in addition. The galleries were nearly a mile in length, and the total cubic contents of the building 33,000,000 feet. The building was commenced September 6th, 1850, and was completed February 3d, 1851. It cost £176,000, and was opened May 1st by the Queen in person. The Exhibition closed October 11th, the number of visitors amounted to 6,107,000, averaging 43,536 daily. The greatest number on any one day was October 8th, 109,760—93,000 being present at one time.

After the payment of all expenses, the surplus fund from the exhibition was £150,000. The number of exhibitors exceeded 17,000, of which 6,566 were foreigners. The building was sold after the close of the exhibition for £70,000. No record was kept of the articles exhibited.

The foreign exhibitors occupied two-fifths of the space, and took away three-fifths of the honors. In merchandise, metal, glass and porcelain Great Britain took the lead; in miscellaneous manufactures, textile fabrics and fine arts, foreign exhibitors led. In raw materials foreigners took nearly four times as many prizes as the natives. One of the principal attractions was the Koh-i-noor, the great crown diamond of England. This exhibition demonstrated one important fact, which was that the great mass of the population, even including the educated, were in ignorance of the true character and importance of the relations of the arts to manufactures.

The Crystal Palace was purchased by a company, and transferred to Sydenham, where it was erected on an enlarged plan, and reopened by the Queen, June 10th, 1854, since which time it has been devoted to horticultural shows, monster concerts, etc.

DUBLIN INTERNATIONAL EXHIBITION, 1853.

THIS exhibition owed its origin to Mr. William Dargan, who advanced £80,000 for expenses. The building was 425 feet long, 100 feet wide, 105 feet high, and, with adjoining smaller halls, cost £48,000. It was opened by

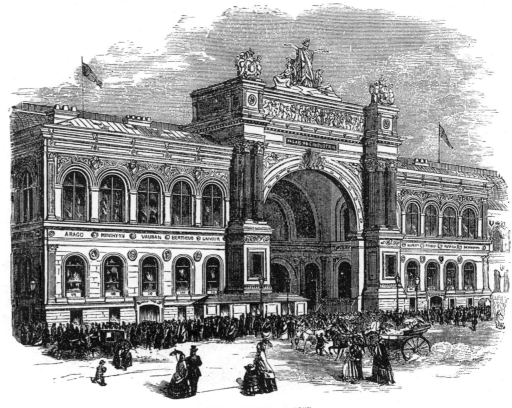

PARIS EXPOSITION, 1855.

INAUGURATION OF THE PARIS EXPOSITION—THE EMPEROR AND EMPRESS ARRIVING AT
THE ENTRANCE ON THE QUAI D'ORSAY.

the Lord-Lieutenant of Ireland on May 12th, 1853, and remained open until October 29th. The value of its contents at the height of the exhibition was estimated to be £500,000, of which the fine arts represented £200,000. Up to that period no finer collection of paintings had ever been gathered together in the kingdom. The exhibition was exceedingly popular, being visited by 1,150,000 people; but it was not financially successful. This failure is believed to have been occasioned by the circumstance that the prevailing character of the exhibition was too high for that of the people. It was neither national nor representative in its nature, and, therefore, it did not arouse Irish sympathy, nor stimulate Irish industry, since it neither participated in the one, nor represented the other.

NEW YORK CRYSTAL PALACE EXHIBITION, 1853.

THE American Industrial Exhibition of 1853 was purely a private enterprise, whereas that of London, in 1851, had been indorsed and sustained by the Government, court, and aristocracy, while the Queen in person took in it the liveliest interest, and the Prince Consort was its technical head. The "New York Exhibition," on the contrary, received no indulgence from any source, excepting that the Crystal Palace was made a bonded warehouse, and no duties were charged on goods imported for the exhibition. On January

INTERIOR VIEW OF THE FRESH WATER AQUARIUM AT THE PARIS EXPOSITION.

3d, 1852, the Corporation of the City of New York granted a lease for five years of the piece of ground known as "Reservoir Square," on two conditions. First, that the building to be erected thereon should be composed of iron, glass and wood; secondly, that the entrance-fee to the proposed exhibition should not exceed fifty cents. On March the 2d, a charter of incorporation was granted for the "Association for the Exhibition of the Industries of all Nations," this being by enactment of the Legislature. The main provisions of this charter set forth that the capital should be $200,000, with permission to increase to $300,000, power to award prizes, authority to occupy any real estate granted to the company, etc. As an illustration of the narrow-minded idea and policy of legislators, it may be remarked that this charter was not easily obtained, objection being made to it, as it was "hostile to domestic industry." The following was the Board of Directors of the company: Mortimore Livingstone, Alfred Pell, August Belmont, Alexander Hamilton, Jr., George Schuyler, Albert J. Anderson, Henry R. Dunham, W. C. Wardell, Jacob A. Westervelt, James A. Hamilton, Samuel Nicholson, Philip Burrowes, Johnston Livingstone, Charles W. Foster, Theodore Sedgwick, William W. Stone, William Whetten, John Dunham, William Kent, Watts Sherman, J. W. Edmunds, J. J. Roosevelt. Of this Board, Theo-

dore Sedgwick was elected president, and William Whetten secretary. A call for subscriptions to stock being issued, the latter was taken up by more than 150 individuals and firms, Messrs. Duncan, Sherman & Co., being the agents. The cooperation of European manufacturers was obtained by appointing proper agents; and Sir Joseph Paxton, who had designed the London Crystal Palace, was called upon to furnish the plans for that of New York. The form of the ground selected preventing the adoption of this plan, one was selected from a number offered. The one selected was designed by Messrs. Carstensen & Gildemeister. Work was commenced the latter part of August. On October 30th, 1852, the first column of the building was placed with appropriate ceremonies, in the presence of the Governor of the State of New York, and other notabilities. This building was two stories in height, the first being in the form of an octagon, and the second that of the Greek cross. In the centre was a dome 148 feet high. The four corners were octagon-shaped, and each front had two towers seventy feet high, supporting tall flagstaffs. The construction of iron columns, girders, etc., was similar to that of the London Crystal Palace; but the plan of the dome was original with the architects. The main building covered 170,000 square feet, and an additional one 33,000 square feet. This latter building was composed of two stories, and was 21 feet broad and 450 feet long, lighted from above, the sides being closed up. It was used for pictures, and was connected with the main building by two one-story wings, in which were refreshment-rooms. The ceilings of this building were of glass, sustained by iron pillars, there being 45,000 square feet, each way being 16 by 38. The prevailing style of architecture was Moorish; the decorations Byzantine; the ceilings were painted in blue, white, red and cream-color. There were three entrances 147 feet wide; the central aisle was forty-one and the side aisles fifty-four feet in width. The dome was one hundred feet across. The Crystal Palace was formally opened on July 14th, 1853, but was not then entirely completed, and only a few of its complement of articles were in. In the immediate vicinity of the locality were found the usual complication of side-shows, speculators, crowds, etc., throughout the period of the exhibition. Among the notables who were present at the opening, a few may be mentioned as follows: President Pierce; Jefferson Davis, then Secretary of War; Caleb Cushing, the Attorney-General; Honorable S. P. Chase; Major-General Scott; John C. Wall; Commodores Stewart and Boorman; Horatio Seymour, Governor of New York; George F. Post, Governor of New Jersey; Howell Cobb, Governor of Georgia; Archbishop Hughes; Bishop

Wainright; Judges Betts, Edmunds, Oakley, Roosevelt and others. Lord and Lady Ellesmere and daughters; General Almonte, Minister from Mexico, and M. De Sartiges, French Minister; Senor Deosma, Peruvian Minister; Mayor Westervelt and others. On the evening of the day it opened, a grand banquet was given at the Metropolitan Hotel, which was attended by the President of the United States and members of his Cabinet, and about six hundred invited guests. The classification of articles in the Crystal Palace was in four sections. One in raw materials, the second in machinery, the third in manufactures, the fourth in fine arts. The Crystal Palace was employed for various uses after the closing of the industrial exhibition, until 1858, when, on the occasion of an exhibition by the American Institute, it took fire, and was totally destroyed with all its contents. The fire began in the lumberroom, used for the storage of benches and other furniture, and although it might, at first, have been extinguished with a pitcher of water, yet, in less than half an hour, the flames had reduced the entire building to a shapeless mass of ruins. Once started, the fire ran along the pitch-pine floors as though they were so much tinder, and scarcely allowed time for the throng of visitors, who were present, to save themselves, before the whole building fell into ruins.

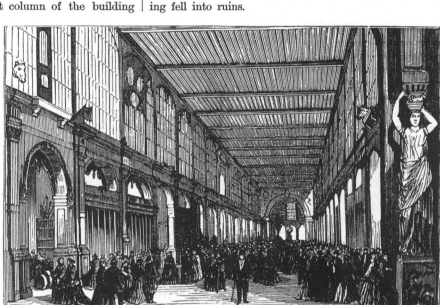

THE GRAND VESTIBULE OF THE PARIS EXPOSITION.

PARIS INTERNATIONAL EXPOSITION, 1855.

THIS exhibition, which was founded on the plan of that in London, in 1851, was organized with the understanding that the Government was to bear the entire cost over receipts, and have the appointment of the Commission. The building was erected in the Champs Elysées, of glass, stone, and brick; it was 800 feet long, 350 feet wide, and comprised, also, other additional buildings for machinery, painting, etc. In the main building goods were arranged and classified according to the countries from which they came, on the plan of the London exhibition. Numerous small structures were erected for special articles—as carriages, agricultural implements, etc. The spaces in the open ground about the building were also devoted to certain articles. The cost of the building was $5,000,000; the opening ceremony took place May 15th, 1855, and was presided over by the Emperor Napoleon and Empress Eugenie. The building remained open until November 5th, being visited at one time by Queen Victoria and Prince Albert—this being the first visit of an English sovereign to Paris since Henry V., who passed Christmas there in 1422. This exhibition was kept open on Sundays, and the entire number of visitors was 4,533,464. The number of exhibitors from France and her colonies was 10,691; of foreign exhibitors, 10,608, representing nearly 53 countries and 22 colonies. The exhibition was very successful as a

THE IMPERIAL PAVILION IN THE PARK OF THE PARIS EXPOSITION.

THE CHIME OF BELLS IN THE PARK AT THE PARIS EXPOSITION.

grand display, and of course a vast amount of money was expended in Paris by the strangers who came there, and this may be reasonably considered to have been ample compensation for the financial failure of the exhibition itself. Of the medals awarded, France took the largest number, 9,790 ; England next, 1,568 ; then Austria, 362 ; the smallest number being awarded to the United States, 140. These awards were for industry, arts, and miscellaneous manufactures. Of the medals awarded in fine arts, 1,000 were taken by French artists, the larger number of the remainder going to England.

LONDON INTERNATIONAL EXPOSITION, 1862.

IT was originally intended that the Crystal Palace Exhibition, of 1851, should have been the first of a decennial series, but the Italian War postponed the next exhibition for a year. As early as 1860, a Charter of Incorporation was issued by the Crown and Royal Commissioners, under the Presidency of the Prince Consort, a guarantee fund of £451,000 was readily formed, the Prince Consort himself subscribing £10,000 of this amount.

The death of Prince Albert, which occurred December 14th, 1861, besides being a profound blow to England, and a loss felt by the whole civilized world, was a most serious and deplorable occurrence in its relation to the forthcoming exhibition. To Prince Albert, entirely, the scheme of international exhibitions, in its final manifestation, is undoubtedly owing, and he, more than any other person in England, had labored for the advancement of industry and for the interests of the laboring classes. The loss of his counsel was sadly felt by the Royal Commission ; but the progress of the exhibition was not detained—the building was erected at South Kensington from plans furnished by Captain Fowkes, Royal Engineer, constructed of brick, glass and iron, and covering an area of 1,400,000 square feet, or sixteen acres of ground. The structure was 1,200 feet long and 560 wide, with additional annexes. Compared with that of Sir Joseph Paxton, this building is said to have been a wretched shed. The exhibition was opened with due ceremony on May 1st, 1862, the Duke of Cambridge presiding. It continued open 177 days, during which time there were 6,211,103 visitors, the largest number on any one day being 67,891, on October 30th, and the daily average 36,329. The entire sum received by the Commissioners was £459,631, which was entirely absorbed by the expenses, leaving a slight deficit to be covered. This loss was wholly due to the great cost of the building, which was intended to be permanent, but was subsequently demolished, and the material used in the construction of the Alexandra Palace, which was destroyed by fire, June 9th, 1873. There were at this exhibition 17,861 foreign exhibitors, who took 9,344 prizes ; of the balance, British and Colonial exhibitors took 4,071 prizes.

PARIS INTERNATIONAL EXPOSITION, 1867.

THIS exhibition was originated by an imperial decree of June 22d, 1863, in which was announced the fact that an exhibition would be held in 1867, at Paris, and that it was designed to be more completely universal in its character than any of its predecessors.

With a view to this intention, notice was given far in advance of the time, to give ample opportunity for mature consideration and reflection, and for the arrangement and carrying out of the necessary preparations. A second decree followed in 1865, appointing the Imperial Commission, and forming agencies at home and abroad. The Commission consisted of sixty members, including three from England—Lord Cowley, Earl Granville, and Mr. Richard Cobden. The Champs de Mars was placed at the disposal of the Commissioners by the Government, and thereupon was erected a one-story building, of oval shape, in which the entire exhibition was included. This building comprised vast series of concentric ovals, inclosed within the main outer building, and having within the innermost of the series a pavilion open to the air, encircled by a colonnade. The main building was 1,550 feet long, and 1,250 feet wide, covering eleven acres, while the entire area built upon was thirty-five acres, and seventy acres surrounding were partly laid out as a garden, sprinkled with all sorts of small buildings, including model cottages, restaurants, theatres, and even places of worship. The classification was as follows : First floor, works of art ; second, models of the liberal arts—such as printing, surgical, scientific and other instruments, etc. ; third to household goods ; fourth, clothing ; fifth, raw materials ; sixth, machinery ; seventh, cereals. From the centre, avenues radiated like spokes in a wheel through the ovals, and spaces between these avenues were assigned to the different countries, so that visitors making a tour of each oval could compare the productions in each class of the different countries. The exhibition was formally opened by the Emperor Napoleon, April 1st, 1867, and closed in like manner October 31st. There were 50,226 exhibitors and 10,200,000 visitors ; 12,944 medals and grand prizes of honorable mention were given, of which the United States exhibitors received three grand prizes, seventeen gold medals, sixty-six silver, and ninety-four bronze. The exhibition building cost about $4,000,000, of which the Government paid $2,500,000. The receipts for admission, etc., were $2,000,000, and there resulted, as was claimed, a profit of $600,000.

LONDON INTERNATIONAL EXHIBITION, 1871.

THIS was the third of the originally proposed decennial series of English exhibitions, and the first of a newly proposed annual series, each to be devoted to specified branches of industry. It was opened on May 1st, 1871, and closed September 30th. One million one hundred and forty-two thousand persons visited this exhibition, there being 4,000 fine art and 7,000 industrial, entries on the part of exhibitors — thirty-three foreign countries being represented. There were no prizes, and the receipts of the exhibition equaled its expenses. The second of the new series took place in 1872, and was devoted to arts connected with printing, paper, music and musical instruments, jewelry, cotton goods and fine arts. This was followed by the third annual exhibition in 1873, which made a feature

of cooking, and its apparatus. A school of cookery was opened in the exhibition, and lectures given. The exhibition remained open from April 14th to August 15th, and was attended by 31,784 persons.

MOSCOW EXHIBITION, 1872.

THE great Russian exhibition was organized by the Moscow Polytechnic Society, under the patronage of the Russian Government. It was on a large scale, and admirably managed. Its various buildings occupied a space of two English miles. In its arrangement the greatest skill was shown ; its classification is said to have been the best and most scientific which has ever yet been attempted. Each special group of objects had separate buildings.

VIENNA INTERNATIONAL EXHIBITION, 1873.

THIS, the grandest exhibition of the kind ever yet attempted (to be excelled only by the United States Centennial Exhibition of 1876), was opened May 1st, 1873, by the Emperor of Austria, in the Prater of Vienna. The prizes were distributed August 18th, and the exhibition closed October 31st. It should be observed, with regard to this exhibition, that its progress was marked by unforeseen difficulties of a most serious nature—the prevalence of a severe cholera epidemic and a financial crisis operating together to militate against its success. The main exhibition building was constructed of brick and glass, and was 2,985 feet long, 82 feet wide, and 52½ feet high to the central dome. Opening from this were 32 transverse galleries, 250 feet long and 49 feet wide—the entire structure presenting a form not unlike that of the spine of a fish with its lateral projecting bones. There was beside this a machinery annex, built with brick, 2,614 feet long, 155 feet wide, besides a large fine-art hall and numerous smaller buildings. The transverse sections were devoted to the

EXTERIOR OF THE FRESH-WATER AQUARIUM AT THE PARIS EXPOSITION.

different countries in the order of their geographical position. About sixty acres were covered by the buildings ; the average of daily visitors was 40,000 ; the main building, with the court between, and galleries, covered 230,000 square yards. In its classification this exhibition followed, nearly, the plan of those of London and Paris. There were 643 exhibitors from the United States, and these took 349 prizes, of which the International Bureau at Washington, the Lighthouse Board of the United States, the State of Massachusetts and city of Boston, for school system, and the School of the Smithsonian Institute, of Washington, received grand diplomas of honor. The entire number of exhibitors was about 42,584, this being exclusive of Oriental countries, the total number of visitors to the exhibition being 7,254,687. The cost of the exhibition was more than $12,000,000. The original Government appropriation was $3,000,000, with the provision that it would not be exceeded, and, as the receipts barely paid running expenses, there was a deficit of about $9,000,000. Added to the causes of this failure, to which we have already alluded, should be mentioned the inadequate accommodation furnished to visitors by the city of Vienna, and the extravagant cost of living. The Viennese seemed to think that the entire world was about to visit their city for the purpose of being plucked, and acted accordingly. The result of this greed and rapacity will probably deter other localities from a similar course in the future.

This closes our brief abstract of the history of industrial effort in the direction of public exhibitions. In prefacing this with a sketch of the entire history of exhibitive progress in the world, we have desired to indicate what seems to have been a natural drift of progress in this direction.

From the public markets, fairs and bazaars, which date back among ancient times, and which were designed in the period of difficult transportation to facilitate barter and exchange, down to the international exhibition of our day, which is purely exhibitive and not of a trade character, we find a series of legitimate steps, always advancing in the

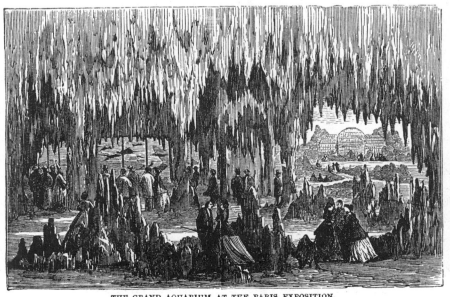

THE GRAND AQUARIUM AT THE PARIS EXPOSITION.

same direction and tending toward the same grand result — the spread of knowledge among the different peoples of the earth concerning the advancement made by each in industrial labor, in the arts of design, and in the culture and adaptation of the earth's products to the necessities of mankind. In the earlier stages of this progress it was necessary to offer inducements to enable the gathering of large numbers of people from distances wide apart, and therefore the purchase and sale of goods exhibited were particularly a feature of the occasion. But as the world became richer, transportation freer, and the minds of men more widespreading in the ambitious thirst for knowledge, the necessities for this feature no longer existed, and it was found that visitors, by reason of this, would travel vast distances only to see and not to purchase the products of the ingenuity and constructive skill and industry of their fellow-men. In the Centennial Exposition of 1876, it is to be hoped that we shall witness the culmination of all the better features of international ex-

PREPARATIONS FOR THE PARIS EXPOSITION—ARAB WORKMEN DECORATING THE PAVILION OF THE BEY OF TUNIS.

With a view to lay before the American people and the world in general a complete and authentic record of the

in importance to none of the same character which the world has ever witnessed. With this design, we shall first proceed to offer a history of the Centennial Exposition from its inception to the time of the present publication. Such a history, as will be seen, offers a liberal quantity of material, and, as well, numerous subjects full of interest for detailed illustration. The gradual struggle into being of an enterprise so vast, affords, even in its most minor particulars, indications of the almost superhuman energy exercised in its conduct. In the episodes and incidents connected with this history will be therefore found a fund of pleasant fact for the consideration of the reader. From this point it is intended to complete the history of the United States Centennial Exposition by a "Historical Register" or "Record" of the result of its efforts, to lay before the world, at a glance, a complete panorama of American industrial progress during the past century·

As early as the year 1866 occurred the first suggestions of an American celebration, to take place in 1876, with a view

THE EMPRESS EUGENIE'S PAVILION AND GRAND CONSERVATORY AT THE PARIS EXPOSITION.

COURT IN THE PALACE OF THE BEY OF TUNIS AT THE PARIS EXPOSITION.

hibitive effort, and while presenting all the best features of previous exhibitions, avoid the errors and imperfections which have too frequently detracted from their success.

CENTENNIAL EXPOSITION.

THE history of this enterprise is that of a gigantic undertaking, whose origination is attributable to no one mind, but was seemingly the outgrowth of the spontaneous "happy thought" of the entire American people — an undertaking commenced and pursued in the face, not only of innumerable difficulties reasonably to be expected, but also against very many which were totally unforeseen — an undertaking which met with a degree of opposition on the part of the press, and in many other influential quarters which had been certainly unlooked for — an undertaking, finally, which, despite all the antagonism it has aroused and all the obstructive elements by which it was met, has been pursued to complete fruition with unexampled excellence of judgment, fertility of resource, and energy of patriotic determination.

origin and progress of this magnificent conception, it is designed to collate from the official authorities every fact of

TUNISIAN CAFÉ IN THE BEY'S PALACE AT THE PARIS EXPOSITION.

importance bearing thereupon, and as well to set down each detail which shall seem to be illustrative of an event second

of commemorating the first centennial of American freedom and national unity. In this connection we may properly give the following extract from the Report of the United States Centennial Commission to Congress, February, 1873:

"Early in 1866, General Charles B. Norton, a United States Commissioner to the Paris exhibition, published an article in the *Anglo-American Times and Continental Gazette*, in which he strongly recommended the celebration of the one hundredth anniversary of our independence by an international exhibition. These views of General Norton were presented to the American Institute, New York, by Hon. D. S. Gregory, but no immediate action was taken.

"Professor John L. Campbell, of Wabash College, Crawfordsville, Indiana, addressed an interesting and suggestive communication on the subject to the Hon. Morton McMichael, at the time mayor of Philadelphia.

"In 1869, Colonel M. Richards Muckle, of Philadelphia, advanced the suggestion that a grand musical festival should be the distinguishing feature of the celebration."

Occasional hints toward some national display to commemorate our Centennial appeared in the newspapers of the day; and, at last, even the character of the proposed celebration was dimly indicated. Such allusions began gradually

TUNISIAN BARBER-SHOP AND CAMEL-STABLE AT THE PARIS EXPOSITION.

TURKISH BATHS AT THE PARIS EXPOSITION.

A TURNER AT WORK AT THE EGYPTIAN BAZAAR, PARIS EXPOSITION.

THE EGYPTIAN TEMPLE IN THE PARK, PARIS EXPOSITION.

to fasten themselves upon the minds of thinking men with something of a definite nature; and, in 1871, the Franklin Institute of Philadelphia concentrated the various crude notions which were afloat concerning the whole matter in a petition to the municipal authorities of Philadelphia for the use of Fairmount Park as a locality wherein to celebrate our national centennial. The result of this petition was the appointment of committees from the Philadelphian Councils to entertain the proposition; and this was speedily seconded by the Pennsylvania Legislature, which memorialized Congress to the following effect: "To take such appropriate action as will carry into effect the celebration of the centennial anniversary of American independence at the city of Philadelphia, . . . by an international exhibition of arts, manufactures and products of the soil and mind." This memorial was duly placed before Congress, and the scheme generally advocated by committees from the Pennsylvania Legislature, the Philadelphia Councils and the Franklin Institute, with the mayor of Philadelphia.

At once opposition was made to the plan suggested, on the part of representatives from other localities, who affected to consider the claims of these for selection, in place of Philadelphia, as equally good at least with those of the latter city. But on June 16th, 1870, the Committee on Manufactures and that on Foreign Affairs, of the House of Representatives, visited Philadelphia. Here arguments were adduced, in favor of the proposed choice of locality, sufficient to impress the minds of these representatives with the views entertained by those who had made the suggestion; and the committee returned to Washington with a report in favor of the advantages of Philadelphia for the purpose, and recommended it being made the scene of the proposed exhibition.

It was not, however, until March 3d, 1871, that Congress passed the following Act, creating the United States Centennial Commission:

An Act to provide for celebrating the One Hundredth Anniversary of American Independence, by holding an International Exhibition of Arts, Manufactures and Products of the Soil and Mine, in the City of Philadelphia, and State of Pennsylvania, in the year eighteen hundred and seventy-six.

WHEREAS, The Declaration of Independence of the United States of America was prepared, signed, and promulgated in the year seventeen hundred and seventy-six, in the City of Philadelphia; and whereas it behooves the people of the United States to celebrate, by appropriate ceremonies, the centennial anniversary of this memorable and decisive event, which constituted the fourth day of July, Anno Domini seventeen hundred and sev-

enty-six, the birthday of the nation; and whereas it is deemed fitting that the completion of the first century of our national existence shall be commemorated by an exhibition of the natural resources of the country and their development, and of its progress in those arts which benefit mankind, in comparison with those of older nations; and whereas no place is so appropriate for such an exhibition as the city in which occurred the event it is designed to commemorate; and whereas as the exhibition should be a national celebration, in which the people of the whole country should participate, it should have the sanction of the Congress of the United States: therefore,

SECTION 1. *Be it enacted by the Senate and House of Representatives of the United States of America in Congress assembled,* That an exhibition of American and foreign arts, products, and manufactures, shall be held, under the auspices of the Government of the United States, in the City of Philadelphia, in the year eighteen hundred and seventy-six.

SEC. 2. That a Commission, to consist of not more than one delegate from each State and from each Territory of the United

EGYPTIAN HOUSE AND STABLES CONSTRUCTED IN THE PARK OF THE PARIS EXPOSITION.

States, whose functions shall continue until the close of the exhibition, shall be constituted, whose duty it shall be to prepare and superintend the execution of a plan for holding the exhibition; and, after conference with the authorities of the City of Philadelphia, to fix upon a suitable site within the corporate limits of the said city, where the exhibition shall be held.

SEC. 3. That said Commissioners shall be appointed within one year from the passage of this Act, by the President of the United States, on the nomination of the governors of the States and Territories respectively.

SEC. 4. That in the same manner there shall be appointed one Commissioner from each State and Territory of the United States, who shall assume the place and perform the duties of such Commissioner and Commissioners as may be unable to attend the meetings of the Commission.

SEC. 5. That the Commission shall hold its meetings in the City

of Philadelphia, and that a majority of its members shall have full power to make all needful rules for its government.

SEC. 6. That the Commission shall report to Congress, at the first session after its appointment, a suitable date for opening and for closing the exhibition; a schedule of appropriate ceremonies for opening or dedicating the same; a plan or plans of the buildings; a complete plan for the reception and classification of articles intended for exhibition; the requisite custom-house regulations for the introduction into this country of the articles from foreign countries intended for exhibition; and such other matters as in their judgment may be important.

SEC. 7. That no compensation for services shall be paid to the Commissioners or other officers provided by this Act from the Treasury of the United States; and the United States shall not be liable for any expenses attending such exhibition, or by reason of the same.

SEC. 8. That whenever the President shall be informed by the Governor of the State of Pennsylvania that provision has been made for the erection of suitable buildings for the purpose, and for the exclusive control by the Commission herein provided for of the proposed exhibition, the President shall, through the Department of State, make proclamation of the same, setting forth the time at which the exhibition will open and the place at which it will be held; and he shall communicate to the diplomatic representatives of all nations copies of the same, together with such regulations as may be adopted by the Commissioners, for publication in their respective countries.

In accordance with this Act, the Commission was at once appointed by the President of the United States upon the nominations of the governors of the several States and Territories—the following being the

UNITED STATES CENTENNIAL COMMISSIONERS.

Alabama, James L. Cooper; *Arizona,* Richard C. McCormick, John Wasson; *Arkansas,* Geo. W. Lawrence, Alexander McDonald; *California,* John Dunbar Creigh, Benj. P. Kooser; *Colorado,* J. Marshall Paul, N. C. Meeker; *Connecticut,* Joseph R. Hawley, Wm. Phipps Baker; *Dakota,* J. A. Burbank, Solomon L. Spink; *Delaware,* H. F. Askew, J. H. Rodney; *District of Columbia,* J. E. Dexter, Lawrence A. Gobright; *Florida,* John S. Adams, J. T. Bernard; *Georgia,* George Hillyer, Richard Peters, Jr.; *Idaho,* Thomas Donaldson, C. W. Moore; *Illinois,* Frederick L. Matthews, Lawrence Weldon; *Indiana,* John L. Campbell, Franklin C. Johnson; *Iowa,* Robert Lowry, Coker F. Clarkson; *Kansas,* John A. Martin, George A. Crawford; *Kentucky,* Robert Mallory, Smith M. Hobbs; *Louisiana,* John Lynch, Edward Penington; *Maine,* Joshua Nye, Charles P. Kimball; *Maryland,* James T. Earle, S. M. Shoemaker; *Massachusetts,* George B. Loring, William B. Spooner; *Michigan,* James Birney, Claudius B. Grant; *Minnesota,* J. Fletcher Williams, W. W. Folwell; *Mississippi,* O. C. French; *Missouri,* John McNeil, Samuel Hays; *Montana,* J. P. Woolman, Patrick A. Largey; *Nebraska,* Henry S. Moody, R. W. Furnas; *Nevada,* Wm. Wirt McCoy, James W. Haines; *New Hampshire,* Ezekiel A. Straw, Asa P. Cate; *New Jersey,* Orestes Cleveland, John G. Stevens; *New Mexico,* Eldridge W. Little, Stephen B. Elkins; *New York,* N. M.

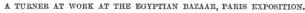

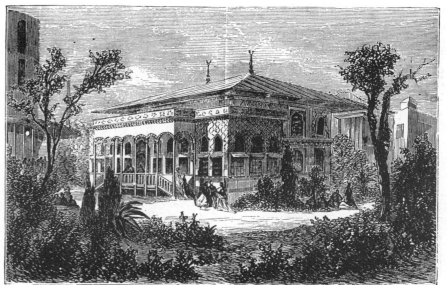

OTTOMAN SECTION, PARIS EXPOSITION—KIOSQUE OF THE BOSPHORUS.

TURKISH MOSQUE AND PALACE OF THE PASHA OF EGYPT IN THE PARK, PARIS EXPOSITION.

OPENING OF THE PALAIS DE L'INDUSTRIE. PARIS. 1855.

TURKISH PAVILION AT THE PARIS EXPOSITION.

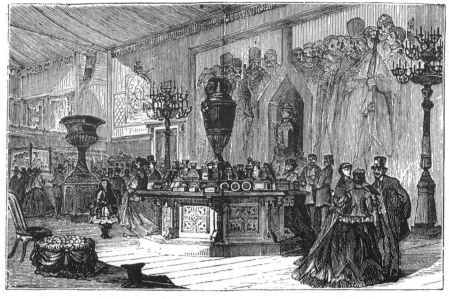

PRINCIPAL COMPARTMENT OF THE RUSSIAN SECTION, PARIS EXPOSITION.

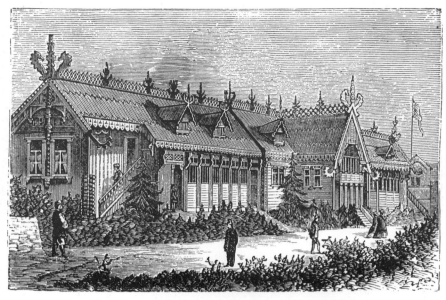

RUSSIAN STABLES IN THE PARK OF THE PARIS EXPOSITION.

Beckwith, Charles H. Marshall; *North Carolina*, Samuel F. Phillips, Jonathan W. Albertson; *Ohio*, Alfred T. Goshorn, Wilson W. Griffith; *Oregon*, James W. Virtue, Andrew J. Dufur; *Pennsylvania*, Daniel J. Morrell, Asa Packer; *Rhode Island*, George H. Corliss, Samuel Powel; *South Carolina*, William Gurney, Archibald Cameron; *Tennessee*, Thomas H. Coldwell, William F. Prosser; *Texas*, William Henry Parsons, John C. Chew; *Utah*, John H. Wickizer, William Haydon; *Vermont*, Middleton Goldsmith, Henry Chase; *Virginia*, Walter W. Wood, Edmund R. Bagwell; *Washington Territory*, Elwood Evans, Alexander S. Abernethy; *West Virginia*, Alexander R. Boteler, Andrew J. Sweeney; *Wisconsin*, David Atwood, Edward D. Holton; *Wyoming*, Joseph M. Carey, Robert H. Lamborn.

From these appointments the following organization was completed:

ORGANIZATION.

President: JOSEPH R. HAWLEY. *Vice-Presidents:* ALFRED T. GOSHORN, ORESTES CLEVELAND, JOHN D. CREIGH, ROBERT LOWRY, ROBERT MALLORY. *Director-General:* ALFRED T. GOSHORN. *Secretary:* JOHN L. CAMPBELL. *Assistant Secretary:* DORSEY GARDNER. *Counselor and Solicitor:* JOHN L. SHOEMAKER.

Executive Committee: DANIEL J. MORRELL, Chairman, *Pennsylvania*; ALFRED T. GOSHORN, *Ohio*; E. A. STRAW, *New Hampshire*; N. M BECKWITH, *New York*; JAMES T. EARLE, *Maryland*; GEORGE H. CORLISS, *Rhode Island*; JOHN G. STEVENS, *New Jersey*; A. R. BOTELER, *West Virginia*; R. C. MCCORMICK, *Arizona*; JOHN LYNCH, *Louisiana*; JAMES BIRNEY, *Michigan*; CHAS. P. KIMBALL, *Maine*; SAML. F. PHILLIPS, *North Carolina*. *Secretary:* MYER ASCH, *Philadelphia*.

Fine Arts.—Superintendence of the Fine Art Department and building, including allotment of space to Exhibitors:

A. T. GOSHORN, *Director-General*.

JOHN L. CAMPBELL, *Secretary*.

PHILADELPHIA, *March*, 1875.

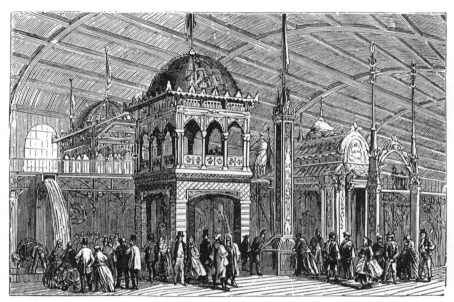

THE UNITED STATES MACHINERY DEPARTMENT AT THE PARIS EXPOSITION.

In view of the fact that only annual meetings of the members of the Centennial Commission were deemed advisable, it was provided that the prosecution of the detailed work of

the exhibition should be in charge of the Executive Committee mentioned above, and which should hold monthly meetings. Further, a subdivision of labor was judiciously effected by the organization of "bureaus of administration"; thus simplifying and systematizing all the manifold duties of preparation and organization. But the Act of Congress, incorporating the Centennial Commission, explicitly provided that no expenses should be incurred for which the Government should be held responsible. It therefore became necessary to organize a qualified body, in whose hands all the financial concerns of the general organization should be placed, and which should be sufficiently empowered to enable the collection of the necessary funds for the proper carrying out of the "Centennial" idea in such ways and by such provisions as should seem best calculated to answer the purpose. Accordingly, on June 1st, 1872, Congress passed the following:

An Act relative to the Centennial International Exhibition to be held in the City of Philadelphia, State of Pennsylvania, in the year eighteen hundred and seventy-six.

WHEREAS, Congress did provide by an Act entitled "An Act to provide for the celebrating the one-hundredth anniversary of American Independence, by holding an international exhibition of arts, manufactures, and products of the soil and mines, in the City of Philadelphia, and State of Pennsylvania,

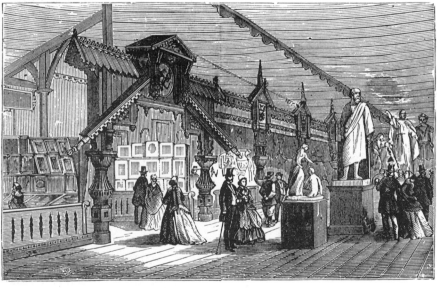

RUSSIAN STREET IN THE PARIS EXPOSITION.

MODEL OF A RUSSIAN HOUSE AT THE PARIS EXPOSITION.

BUREAUS OF ADMINISTRATION.

Foreign.—Direction of the foreign representation: DIRECTOR-GENERAL.

Installation—Classification of applications for space—allotment of space in Main Building—supervision of special structures: HENRY PETTIT.

Transportation.—Foreign transportation for goods and visitors—transportation for goods and visitors in the United States—local transportation—warehousing and customs regulations: DOLPHUS TORREY.

Machinery.—Superintendence of the Machinery Department and building, including allotment of space to Exhibitors: JOHN S. ALBERT.

Agriculture.—Superintendence of the Agricultural Department, building and grounds, including allotment of space to Exhibitors: BURNET LANDRETH.

Horticulture.—Superintendence of Horticultural Department, Conservatory and grounds, including allotment of space to Exhibitors: CHARLES A. MILLER.

THE MOORISH PAVILION IN THE PRUSSIAN SECTION OF THE PARK, PARIS EXPOSITION.

in the year eighteen hundred and seventy-six," approved March third, eighteen hundred and seventy-one, for the appointment of commissioners to promote and control the exhibition of the national resources and their development, and the nation's progress in arts which benefit mankind, and to suggest and direct appropriate ceremonies by which the people of the United States may commemorate that memorable and decisive event, the Declaration of American Independence by the Congress of the United Colonies, assembled in the City of Philadelphia, on the fourth day of July, Anno Domini seventeen hundred and seventy-six; and whereas, such provisions should be made for procuring the funds requisite for the purposes aforesaid as will enable all the people of the United States, who have shared the common blessings resulting from national independence, to aid in the preparation and conduct of said international exhibition and memorial celebration under the direction of the commissioners of the United States: Therefore

Be it enacted by the Senate and House of Representatives of the United States of America in Congress assembled, That there is hereby created a body corporate, to be known by the name of the Centennial Board of Finance, and by that name to have an incorporate existence until the object for which it is formed shall have been accomplished; and it shall be competent to sue and be sued, plead and be impleaded, defend and be defended, in all courts of law and equity in the United States; and may make and have a corporate seal, and may purchase, take, have, and hold, and may grant, sell, and at pleasure dispose of all such real and personal estate as may be required in carrying into effect the provisions of an Act of Congress, entitled "An Act to provide for celebrating the one hundredth anniversary of American Independence, by holding an international exhibition of arts and manufactures, and products of the soil and mine, in the City of Philadelphia, and State of Pennsylvania, in the year eighteen hundred and seventy-six," approved March third, eighteen hundred and seventy-one, and all acts supplementary thereto; and said Centennial Board of Finance shall consist of the following-named persons, their associates and successors, from the States and Territories as herein set forth.

Sec. 2. That the said corporation shall have authority, and is hereby empowered, to secure subscriptions of capital stock to an amount not exceeding ten million dollars, to be divided into shares of ten dollars each, and to issue to the subscribers of said stock certificates therefor under the corporate seal of said corporation,

ORIENTAL DIVISION, PARIS EXPOSITION—GENERAL VIEW OF THE JAPANESE SECTION.

quota, according to its population; after which period of one hundred days, stock not taken may be sold to any person or persons or corporation willing to purchase the same.

subscribed for stock, to be held in the city of Philadelphia, for the purpose of electing a board of directors to consist of twenty-five stockholders, whose term of office shall be one year, and until their successors shall have been qualified; at which meeting those who may be present in person or by proxy, of whom one hundred shall constitute a quorum, shall be competent to organize and elect said officers. The said board of directors, and every subsequent board, shall be chosen by the stockholders out of a list of one hundred stockholders, selected and nominated by the United States Centennial Commission. Nine members of the board of directors shall constitute a quorum for the transaction of business, but no election or change of officers shall take place unless at a meeting of the board of directors, at which a majority shall be present.

Sec. 5. That the said board of directors shall elect, from its own number, a president and two vice-presidents, whose term of office shall be one year, and until their successors shall have been duly qualified, and shall appoint a treasurer, a secretary, and such other officers as may be required to carry out the purposes of the corporation; which elected and appointed officers shall hold their respective offices during the pleasure of the board, receiving such compensation as the board may prescribe. And the board shall also adopt such by-laws, rules, and regulations for its own government and for the

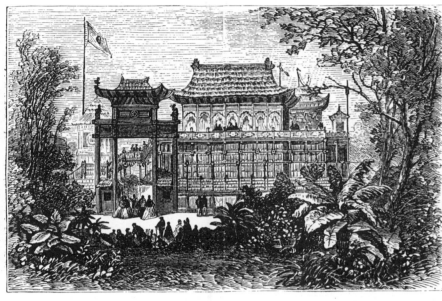

VIEW OF THE CHINESE QUARTER IN THE PARK OF THE PARIS EXPOSITION.

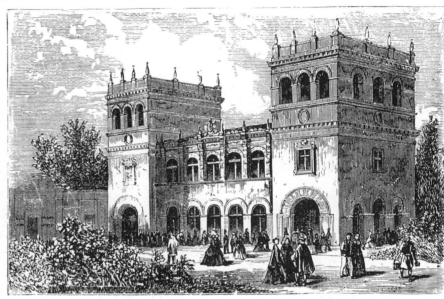

THE SPANISH PAVILION AT THE PARIS EXPOSITION.

which certificates shall bear the signature of the president and treasurer, and be transferrable under such rules and regulations as may be made for the purpose. And it shall be lawful for any municipal or other corporate body existing by or under the laws of the United States, to subscribe and pay for shares of said capital stock; and all holders of said stock shall become associates in said corporation, and shall be entitled to one vote on each share. And it shall be the duty of the United States Centennial Commission to prescribe rules to enable absent stockholders to vote by proxy. The proceeds of said stock, together with the receipts from all other sources, shall be used by said corporation for the erection of suitable buildings, with their appropriate fixtures and appurtenances, and for all other expenditures required in carrying out the objects of the said act of Congress of March third, eighteen hundred and seventy-one, and which may be incident thereto. And the said corporation shall keep regular minutes of its proceedings, and full accounts, with the vouchers thereof, of all the receipts and expenditures, and the same shall be always open to the inspection of the United States Centennial Commission, or any member thereof.

Sec. 3. That books of subscription shall be opened by the United States Centennial Commission, under such rules as it may prescribe; and an opportunity shall be given, during a period of one hundred days, to the citizens of each State and Territory to subscribe for stock to an amount not exceeding its

Sec. 4. That after the expiration of said period of one hundred days, the United States Centennial Commission shall issue a call for a meeting by publication in one or more newspapers published at the capital of each State and Territory, not less than thirty days prior thereto, of the corporators and all others who may then have

THE PORTUGUESE PAVILION IN THE PARIS EXPOSITION.

government of its officers as may be deemed expedient: *Provided*, That the same shall not be inconsistent with any act of Congress or the rules adopted by the United States Centennial Commission.

Sec. 6. That as soon as the board of directors shall have been duly organized, as provided for in Section 5 of this act, it shall be the duty of the United States Centennial Commission to deliver to the said board all stock subscription-books, with the papers and records of any kind in its possession pertaining to the same.

Sec. 7. That the grounds for the exhibition shall be prepared and buildings erected by the said corporation in accordance with the plans, which shall have been previously adopted by the United States Centennial Commission, and the rules and regulations of said corporation, governing rates for "entrance" and "admission" fees, or otherwise affecting the rights, privileges, or interests of the exhibitors, or of the public, shall be fixed and established by the United States Centennial Commission; and no grant conferring rights or privileges of any description connected with the said grounds or buildings, or relating to said exhibition or celebration, shall be made without the consent of the United States Centennial Commission; and said commission shall have power to control, change or revoke all such grants, and shall appoint all judges and examiners, and award all premiums.

Sec. 8. That the Centennial Board of Finance shall have authority to issue bonds, not in excess of its capital stock, and

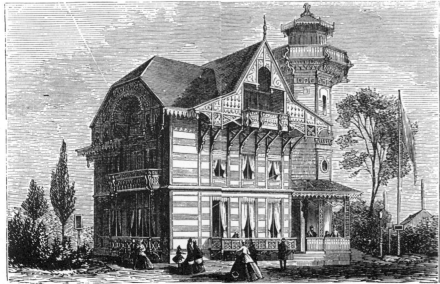

THE WAASER CHALET IN THE PARK, PARIS EXPOSITION.

MONSTER STEEL GUN MADE BY KRUPP OF ESSEN, AT THE PARIS EXPOSITION.

DISTRIBUTION OF PRIZES IN THE PALAIS DE L'INDUSTRIE, PARIS, 1867.

secure the payment of the same, principal and interest, by mortgage upon its property and prospective income.

Sec. 9. That it shall be the duty of the Secretary of the Treasury of the United States, as soon as practicable after the passage of this Act, to cause to be prepared, in accordance with a design approved by the United States Centennial Commission and the Secretary of the Treasury, a sufficient number of certificates of stock to meet the requirements of this Act; and any person found guilty of counterfeiting, or attempting to counterfeit, or knowingly circulating false certificates of stock, herein authorized, shall be subject to the same pains and penalties as are or may be provided by law for counterfeiting United States currency; but nothing in this Act shall be so construed as to create any liability of the United States, direct or indirect, for any debt or obligation incurred, nor for any claim, by the Centennial International Exhibition, or the corporation hereby created for aid or pecuniary assistance from Congress or the Treasury of the United States, in support or liquidation of any debts or obligations created by the corporation herein

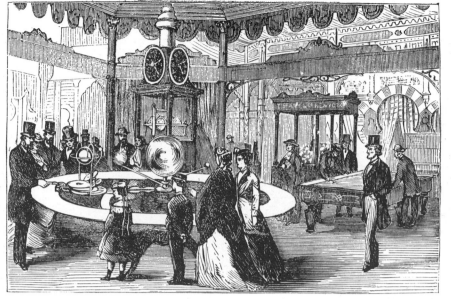

THE UNITED STATES SECTION AT THE PARIS EXPOSITION.

holders, *pro rata*, in full satisfaction and discharge of its capital stock.

Under the above Act the "Centennial Board of Finance" was organized, and, as now constituted, is as follows:

CENTENNIAL BOARD OF FINANCE.

President: John Welsh, *Philadelphia.* *Vice-Presidents:* William Sellers, *Philadelphia;* John S. Barbour, *Virginia.* *Secretary and Treasurer:* Frederick Fraley. *Auditor:* H. S. Lansing. *Financial Agent:* William Bigler.

Directors: Samuel L. Felton, Daniel M. Fox, Thomas Cochran, Clement M. Biddle, N. Parker Shortridge, James M. Robb, Edward T. Steel, John Wanamaker, John Price Wetherill, Henry Winsor, Amos R. Little, John Baird, *Philadelphia;* Thomas H. Dudley, *New Jersey;* A. S. Hewitt, William L. Strong, *New York;* John Cummings, *Massachusetts;* John Gorham, *Rhode Island;* Charles W. Cooper, William Bigler, *Pennsylvania;* Robert M. Patton, *Alabama;* J. B. Drake, *Illinois;* George Bain, *Missouri.*

AMERICAN MACHINERY DEPARTMENT AT THE PARIS EXPOSITION.

TEMPLE OF XOCHICALCO IN THE PARK, PARIS EXPOSITION.

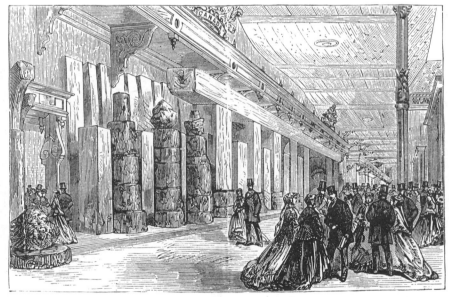

THE CANADIAN SECTION AT THE PARIS EXPOSITION.

THE NOVA SCOTIAN SECTION AT THE PARIS EXPOSITION.

authorized: *And provided,* That nothing in this Act shall be so construed as to override or interfere with the laws of any State; and all contracts made in any State for the purposes of the Centennial International Exhibition shall be subject to the laws thereof: *And provided further,* That no member of said Centennial Board of Finance assumes any personal liability for

any debt or obligation which may be created or incurred by the corporation authorized by this Act.

Sec. 10. That as soon as practicable, after the said exhibition shall have been closed, it shall be the duty of said corporation to convert its property into cash, and, after the payment of all its liabilities, to divide its remaining assets among its stock-

Of course, the first and more immediately important duty of the "Board of Finance" was to conclude, after careful computation, on an estimate of the sum of money necessary to carry out the intentions of the "Centennial Commission." The conclusion reached fixed upon the

MODEL HOUSE FOR WORKMEN AT THE PARIS EXPOSITION.

ENGLISH COTTAGE AT THE PARIS EXPOSITION.

COSTUME FIGURES IN THE SOUTH AMERICAN DEPARTMENT, PARIS EXPOSITION.

THE VENEZUELA DEPARTMENT, PARIS EXPOSITION.

sum of $10,000,000 as adequate for all the purposes of the exhibition. In accordance with this estimate, and with a view to giving every citizen of every State an opportunity to become interested in and connected with this great national exhibition, a quota was now established of a ratio of subscription for the several States, and every effort was made, through the public press, special circulars, and selected agents, to bring about such an interest as would lead to a popular subscription sufficiently large to absorb the capital stock, the ratio of each State being fixed as follows:

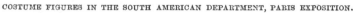

No.	State or Territory.	Population.	Quota in Shares.	Quota in Dollars.
1	New York	4,382,759	113,666	$1,136,660
2	Pennsylvania	3,521,951	91,341	913,410
3	Ohio	2,665,260	69,123	691,230
4	Illinois	2,539,891	65,871	658,710
5	Missouri	1,721,295	44,641	446,410
6	Indiana	1,630,637	43,587	435,870
7	Massachusetts	1,457,351	37,796	377,960
8	Kentucky	1,321,011	34,260	342,600
9	Tennessee	1,258,520	32,639	326,390
10	Virginia	1,225,163	31,774	317,740
11	Iowa	1,194,020	30,937	309,670
12	Georgia	1,184,109	30,710	307,100
13	Michigan	1,184,059	30,708	307,080
14	North Carolina	1,071,361	27,785	277,850
15	Wisconsin	1,054,670	27,353	273,530
16	Alabama	996,992	25,854	258,540
17	New Jersey	906,096	23,499	234,960
18	Mississippi	827,922	21,472	214,720
19	Texas	818,579	21,230	212,300
20	Maryland	780,894	20,252	202,520
21	Louisiana	726,915	18,852	188,520
22	South Carolina	705,606	18,300	183,000
23	Maine	626,915	16,258	162,580
24	California	560,247	14,530	145,300
25	Connecticut	537,454	13,939	139,930
26	Arkansas	484,471	12,565	125,650
27	West Virginia	442,014	11,464	114,640
28	Minnesota	439,706	11,404	114,040
29	Kansas	364,399	9,450	94,500
30	Vermont	330,551	8,573	85,730
31	New Hampshire	318,300	8,255	82,550
32	Rhode Island	217,353	5,637	56,370
33	Florida	187,748	4,869	48,690
34	District of Columbia	131,700	3,417	34,170
35	Delaware	125,015	3,242	32,420
36	Nebraska	122,993	3,190	31,900
37	New Mexico	91,874	2,383	23,830
38	Oregon	90,923	2,359	23,590
39	Utah	86,786	2,251	22,510
40	Nevada	42,491	1,102	11,020
41	Colorado	39,864	1,034	10,340
42	Washington	23,955	621	6,210
43	Montana	20,595	534	5,340
44	Idaho	14,999	389	3,890
45	Dakota	14,181	363	3,680
46	Arizona	9,658	250	2,500
47	Wyoming	9,118	236	2,360
		38,558,371	1,000,000	$10,000,000

Up to December 15, 1875, the actual amounts subscribed for the purposes of the Centennial were as follows:

Total stock subscriptions (*reliable*)	$2,357,750

In which are included

New Jersey	$100,000
Delaware	10,000
Connecticut	10,000
New Hampshire	10,000
Wilmington, Del.	5,000
	$135,000

Gifts, concessions, and interest	$230,000
Further receipts from concessions	100,000
Appropriation by Pennsylvania	1,000,000
Appropriation by Philadelphia	1,500,000
	$5,187,750
Amount still required to prepare for Opening up to May 10, 1876	1,537,100
	$6,724,850

By which it will be seen that the original estimate of $10,000,000 was found to be much more than sufficient for the necessities of the Exhibition.

The following table will display the cost of other international exhibitions:

Place.	Year.	Acres.	Cost.
London	1851	20	$1,464,000
New York	1853	5¾	500,000
Paris	1855	30	4,000,000
London	1862	24	2,300,000
Paris	1867	40½	4,596,763
Vienna	1873	50	9,850,000
Philadelphia	1876	60	6,724,350

The following nations have appropriated the sums set against their names for defraying their own expenses at the Centennial:

Great Britain, with Australia and Canada (gold)	$250,000
France and Algeria	120,000
Germany	171,000
Austria	75,000
Italy (Government, $38,000; Chamber of Commerce, $38,000)	76,000
Spain	150,000
Japan	600,000
Belgium	40,000
Denmark	10,500
Sweden	125,000
Norway	44,000
Netherlands (ample provision).	
Brazil	150,000
Venezuela (all expenses).	
Ecuador	10,000
Siam	100,000
Argentine Confederation (owns all goods exhibited)	63,000

A primary difficulty, which at once presented itself in the way of collecting subscriptions for stock, was the financial crisis of 1873; and this, with the difficulty of carrying out a working system through the agency of the banks, induced the adoption of a different plan, and the following "Board of Revenue" was established, with a view of operating through the labor of voluntary auxiliary boards, organized in different sections of the States and Territories:

CLEMENT M. BIDDLE, *Chairman*, Philadelphia; WILLIAM BIGLER, *Financial Agent*, Pennsylvania; EDMUND T. STEEL, AMOS R. LITTLE, JOHN WANAMAKER, DANIEL M. FOX, JAMES M. ROBB, JOHN BAIRD, Philadelphia; THOS. H. DUDLEY, New Jersey; JOHN CUMMINGS, Massachusetts; WILLIAM L. STRONG, New York; GEORGE BAIN, Missouri; C. B. NORTON, *Secretary*.

Chiefly through the medium of the energetic and comprehensive action of this Board, the entire aggregate of the sums subscribed for carrying on the labors of the "Centennial Commission" was accumulated. But, as we have already observed, the labors of these and other agents operating for the Centennial were rendered especially arduous and difficult on account of the opposition which the enterprise met with in different quarters in the first years of the undertaking. This opposition at first took the form of objection to the locality chosen for the exhibition. Jealousies on this account sprang up, and very soon manifested themselves through the Press and otherwise. Boston, New York, and other cities laid claim to the honor of selection for the purpose in hand, and for a time this claim was argued with considerable determination and such force as could be gained for it through the occurrence of historical events or other incidents. It was finally, however, conceded that the selection of Philadelphia as the scene of our Centennial memorial was just, wise, and propitious.

But this conclusion did not allay the slight irritation which had been manifested, but which now directed itself toward other objections. One of the most prominent of these regarded the proposed international character of the exhibition, and was generally based upon the idea that, for one reason or another, foreign nations would refuse to compete with Americans in the exhibition of their products and manufactures; while, in the case of Great Britain, it was especially alleged that the circumstances concerning British connection with our national brotherhood were of a character to preclude the hearty co-operation of that nation in our proposed jubilee. These latter objections, however, soon fell to the ground in the face of the almost unanimous acceptance by foreign powers of the invitation of the President, as offered in his proclamation, and in the subsequent note to foreign ministers, which documents were couched as follows:

PROCLAMATION

BY THE PRESIDENT OF THE UNITED STATES.

Whereas, by the Act of Congress approved March third, eighteen hundred and seventy-one, providing for a National Celebration of the one hundredth anniversary of the Independence of the United States, by the holding of an International Exhibition of

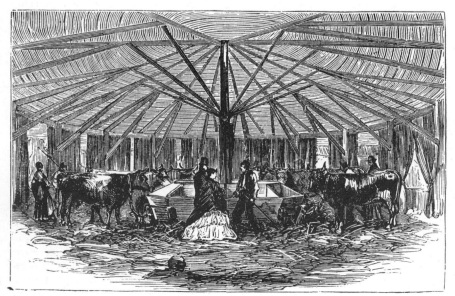

MODEL COW STABLES AT THE PARIS EXPOSITION.

FOWL HOUSE, GUINEA PIG CAGE, AND SHEEP HOUSE AT THE MODEL FARM, PARIS EXPOSITION.

Arts, Manufactures, and Products of the Soil and Mine, in the City of Philadelphia, in the year eighteen hundred and seventy-six, it is provided as follows:

"That, whenever the President shall be informed by the Governor of the State of Pennsylvania that provision has been made for the erection of suitable buildings for the purpose, and for the exclusive control by the Commission herein provided for of the proposed Exhibition, the President shall, through the Department of State, make proclamation of the same, setting forth the time at which the Exhibition will open, and the place at which it will be held; and he shall communicate to the diplomatic representatives of all nations copies of the same, together with such regulations as may be adopted by the commissioners, for publication in their respective countries;"

And whereas, His Excellency the Governor of the said State of Pennsylvania did, on the twenty-fourth day of June, eighteen hundred and seventy-three, inform me that provision has been made for the erection of said buildings and for the exclusive control by the Commission provided for in the said Act of the proposed Exhibition;

And whereas, the President of the United States Centennial Commission has officially informed me of the dates fixed for the opening and closing of the said Exhibition, and the place at which it is to be held;

Now therefore, be it known that I, ULYSSES S. GRANT, President of the United States, in conformity with the provisions of the Act of Congress aforesaid, do hereby declare and proclaim that there will be held, at the City of Philadelphia, in the State of Pennsylvania, an International Exhibition of Arts, Manufactures, and Products of the Soil and Mine, to be opened on the nineteenth day of April, Anno Domini, eighteen hundred and seventy-six, and to be closed on the nineteenth day of October, in the same year.

And in the interests of peace, civilization, and domestic and international friendship and intercourse, I commend the Celebration and Exhibition to the people of the United States; and, in behalf of this Government and people, I cordially commend them to all nations who may be pleased to take part therein.

In testimony whereof I have hereunto set my hand and caused the seal of the United States to be affixed.

Done at the City of Washington, this third day of July, one thousand eight hundred [Seal] and seventy-three, and of the Independence of the United States the ninety-seventh.

U. S. GRANT.
By the President:
HAMILTON FISH,
Secretary of State.

(Form of Note sent by the Secretary of State to Foreign Ministers.)

DEPARTMENT OF STATE,
Washington, July 5, 1873.

SIR: I have the honor to inclose, for the information of the Government of ———, a copy of the President's Proclamation, announcing the time and place of holding an International Exhibition of Arts, Manufactures, and Products of the Soil and Mine, proposed to be held in the year eighteen hundred and seventy-six.

The Exhibition is designed to commemorate the Declaration of the Independence of the United States, on the one hundredth anniversary of that interesting and historic national event, and at the same time to present a fitting opportunity for such display of the results of Art and Industry of all nations as will serve to illustrate the great advances attained, and the successes achieved, in the interest of Progress and Civilization, during the century which will have then closed.

In the law providing for the holding of the Exhibition, Congress directed that copies of the Proclamation of the President, setting forth the time of its opening and the place at which it was to be held, together with such regulations as might be adopted by the Commissioners of the Exhibition, should be communicated to the Diplomatic Representatives of all nations. Copies of those regulations are herewith transmitted.

The President indulges the hope that the Government of ——— will be pleased to notice the subject, and may deem it proper to bring the Exhibition and its objects to the attention of the people of that country, and thus encourage their co-operation in the proposed celebration. And he further hopes that the opportunity afforded by the Exhibition for the interchange of national sentiment and friendly intercourse between the people of both nations may result in new and still greater advantages to Science and Industry, and at the same time serve to strengthen the bonds of Peace and Friendship which already happily subsist between the Government and people of ——— and those of the United States.

I have the honor to be, sir,
With the highest consideration,
Your obedient servant,

———

In response to these documents, which were circulated throughout all civilized countries by means of our official agents, the following named countries accepted the invitation of the President:

1. Africa (Orange Free State); 2. Argentine Confederation; 3 Austria; 4 Belgium; 5. Brazil; 6. China; 7. Ecuador; 8. Egypt; 9. France; 10. German Empire; 11. Great Britain and Colonies; 12. Canada; 13. New South Wales; 14. South Australia; 15. Victoria; 16. Guatemala, Salvador; 17. Honduras; 18. Japanese Empire; 19. Liberia; 20. Mexico; 21. Netherlands; 22. Norway; 23. Peru; 24. Russia; 25. Sandwich Islands; 26. Siam; 27. Spain; 28. Sweden; 29. Switzerland; 30. Tunis; 31. Turkey; 32. Venezuela.

Following, we give a list of the Commissioners appointed by the respective Governments of these countries:

ARGENTINE CONFEDERATION, South America: Ernesto Oldendorff, *President;* Julio Victorica, *Secretary.* And nine Commissioners.

AUSTRALIA, VICTORIA, QUEENSLAND, NEW ZEALAND, ETC.: Sir Redwood Barry, *President;* J. Collins Levey, Esq., *Secretary.* And eleven Commissioners.

AFRICA, ORANGE FREE STATE: Charles W. Riley, Consul-General.

BELGIUM: Alfred Simonis, Member of the House of Representatives and Manufacturer; E. Sadoine, General Director of the Iron Works; Ch. De Smet, Manufacturer; President of the Industrial and Commercial Society. And fourteen Commissioners.

BRAZIL: Gaston d'Orleans, Conde d'Eu, *President;* Viscount de Jaguary, *1st Vice-President;* Viscount de Bonn-Retiro, *2d Vice-President.* *Members:* Viscount de Souza Franco; Joaquin Antonio de Azevedo.

CANADA: Hon. Luc. Letellier de St. Just, Minister of Agriculture; Hon. Robert D. Wilmot, Senator; Hon. Edward G. Penny, Senator; F. W. Glen, Esq., Ottawa; T. Perrault, Esq., *Secretary.*

CHINA: Edward B Drew, Gustav. Dietring, J. L. Hammond, Commissioners of Customs; Charles Hannen.

ECUADOR: Edward Shippen, Esq., Consul, Philadelphia; Gabriel Obarrio, J. J. Ribon, J. M. Muñoz, J. R. de La Espriella, New York.

FRANCE: A. L. De la Forest, Consul-General, New York; Ravin d'Elpeux, Vice-Consul, Philadelphia; Cat. Apnfrye, French Legation, Washington. FRENCH LOCAL COMMITTEE IN PARIS: Oscar de Lafayette, *President;* Laboulaye, Wolowski, Dietz Monin, *Vice-Presidents;* Flotard, Bonnet, *Secretaries;* A. Caubert, *Agent.*

GERMANY: Dr. Jacobi, Government Counsellor, *President.* And nine Commissioners.

GREAT BRITAIN: P. Cunliffe Owen; Colonel Sanford.

GUATEMALA, SALVADOR: Don Vincente Dardon, Minister Plenipotentiary, Washington.

HONDURAS: Governor Don Francisco Bardales; General Don E. de Salignac; Don José Maria Fiollos; Don Juan Ramon Valanzuela.

JAPAN: Giro Yano, *Agent,* Japanese Legation, Washington.

LIBERIA: J. L. Payne, Esq., Monrovia; Edward O. Morris, Esq., Consul, Philadelphia.

MEXICO: Don Romero Rubio, *President;* Eduardo E. Zarote, *Secretary;* Gabriel Mancera. And nine Commissioners.

NETHERLANDS: Dr. E. H. Von Baumhauer, *President;* Mr. C. Maysken, Haarlem, *Secretary;* Mr. L. Westergaard, Consul, Philadelphia; Mr. R. C. Burlage, Consul-General, New York. And eleven Commissioners.

NORWAY: Herman Baars; Wm. C. Christopherson.

PERU: Hon. Manuel Freyre, Minister Plenipotentiary, Washington; Fred. L. Barreda, Edward Villena, Charles Nacy.

SWEDEN: A. Bergstrom, *President;* C. Juhlin Darnfelt, *Secretary* Stockholm; L. Westergaard, *Agent,* Consul, Philadelphia. And thirteen Commissioners.

SANDWICH ISLANDS: Hon. S. G. Wilder, Minister of the Interior; Hon. J. U. Kawainui; S. U. F. Odell, Chargé d'Affaires and Consul-General, New York.

SPAIN: Don Emilio Castelar, *President;* Don José Emilio de Santos, General Commissioner, Philadelphia; Don Antonio Mantilla, Minister Plenipotentiary, Washington; Don Ricardo Palomino, Consul, Philadelphia; Don Alfredo Principe, Vice-Consul, Philadelphia. And fifty-eight Commissioners.

VENEZUELA: Leon de la Cova, Consul, Philadelphia; Dr. Adolphus Ernst, Professor, University of Caracas.

It will thus be seen that the main objections to the Centennial were met by the inexorable logic of events, and shown to be without just foundation in fact. This important battle having been won, it became, nevertheless, obvious to the "Board of Finance" that much difficulty would remain in the way of gathering together the enormous sum of money required for the organization of the exhibition. With a degree of fidelity to their own idea, however, which is unexampled, and with a lavish generosity equally unexpected, the State of Pennsylvania and the City of Philadelphia gave earnest of the force of their purpose, and the intensity of their determination to achieve success in the face of no matter what obstacles, by at once drawing with extraordinary liberality upon their own resources, and thus placing before the American people an example most praiseworthy in itself, and which certainly should have been more generally followed than was unfortunately the case.

With a design toward the encouragement of the collection of souvenirs of the Centennial, the "Board of Finance" issued a handsome medal of bronze and silver, with an appropriately commemorative inscription, and also an elaborately engraved certificate of stock subscription, it being conceived that both these articles would be eagerly sought for by the public in general, and their remunerative sale would add something to the fund for general expenditures, and so, by the different means adopted for the purpose, the "Board of Finance" succeeded in collecting very nearly the entire amount required for the expenses of the Centennial.

The manner in which this large fund was expended should properly come next under our consideration. By the original system of organization, the government and direction of the Centennial were vested in two Boards, as has already been mentioned. These were the "Centennial Commission," and the "Centennial Board of Finance." The division of duty, and its allotment between these two bodies, were as follows: The "Centennial Commission" had entire charge of everything concerning the exhibitive character of the Exposition. They conducted all correspondence with individuals, organizations, and Governments, at home and abroad, looking toward the exhibition by these of all products, works of art, or manufactured articles, when the buildings should be completed. Here

SOUTH KENSINGTON (LONDON) INTERNATIONAL EXHIBITION, 1871.

EXPOSITION OF ART AND INDUSTRY AT MADRID, SPAIN, 1871.

THE KING OPENING THE EXHIBITION OF INDUSTRY AND ART AT COPENHAGEN, JUNE 13TH, 1872.

also was placed the duty of allotting space, assigning each exhibitor to his appropriate department, and, in fact, generally superintending and supervising the Exposition as such. The "Centennial Board of Finance" had charge of all interests involving expenditures of money, as well as all the plans and arrangements for collecting the same.

Thus, in the hands of this latter important body was placed the duty of directing the construction of the buildings necessary for the exhibition; and to a description of these magnificent structures, erected upon a scale of unprecedented grandeur even in buildings of this character, we will now proceed to direct the attention of the reader.

As has been heretofore remarked, the land obtained for the purposes of the Centennial Exposition is comprised in Fairmount Park, the largest public park in proximity to a great city in the world. This park contains 3,160 acres, of which 450 were enclosed for this exhibition, besides which allotment provision was made for the exhibition of stock, and a farm of forty-two acres, arranged for the test of plows, mowers, reapers, and other agricultural machinery. The Centennial grounds, lying on the west bank of the Schuylkill river, extend over elevated land, while "George's Hill," at one extremity, offers not only a magnificent view of the entire exhibition territory, but also an admirable presentation of the great city beyond. Concerning the locality, it may be observed that in the opinion of Baron Schwarz-Senborn, the Director of the Vienna Exposition, this is larger and better adapted for the purpose in every particular than has been the case with regard to any former exhibition. The exhibitive space of the Exposition proper comprises five buildings: 1. Main Exhibition Building; 2. Art Gallery; 3. Machinery Hall; 4. Horticultural Hall; 5. Agricultural Building. But, beside these, there were erected numerous other and similar buildings by State direction, or on the part of foreign and other exhibitors, of which description will be given hereafter.

I. Main Exhibition Building.

This building is constructed in the form of a parallelogram, extending east and west, 1,880 ft. in length, and north and south, 464 ft. in width. The larger portion of the structure being one story in height, showing the main cornice upon the outside at 40 ft. from the ground, the interior height being 70 ft. At the centre of the longer sides of the building are projections 416 ft. in length, and in the centre of the shorter sides are also projections 216 feet in length. In these projections in the centre of the four sides are located the main entrances, which are provided with arcades upon the ground floor, and façades extending to the height of 96 ft. The east entrance forms the principal approach for carriages, the south entrance being the principal approach for street-cars, the ticket-offices being located upon the line of Elm Avenue, with covered ways providing for entrance into the building itself.

The main portal on the north side is arranged to com-

municate directly with the Art Gallery; and the main portal on the west side gives the main passage-way to Machinery and Agricultural Halls. Upon the corners of the building are four towers, each 75 ft. in height; and, in order to obtain a central feature for the building as a whole, the roof over the central part, 481 ft. square, is raised above the surrounding portion; and four towers, 48 ft. square, and rising to a height of 120 ft., have been introduced at the corners of the elevated roof.

The areas covered are as follows:

	Square feet.	Acres.
Ground floor	872,320	20.02
Upper floor, projection	37,344	85
Upper floor, towers	26,344	60
Total	936,008	21.47

The general arrangement of the ground plan of this building develops a central avenue or nave 120 ft. in width and extending 1,832 ft. in length, this being the longest avenue of that width ever introduced into an exhibition building. On either side of this nave is an avenue 100 ft. wide by 1,832 ft. in length, and between the nave and side avenues are aisles 48 ft. wide, and on the outer sides of the building similar aisles 24 ft. in width.

There are also three cross avenues or transepts, viz., a central transept 120 ft. in width by 416 ft. in length, and one on either side of 100 ft. by 416 ft., and aisles between of 48 ft.

The main promenades through the nave and central transept are each 30 ft. in width, and those through the centre and side avenues and transepts, 15 ft. each. All other walks are 10 ft. wide, and lead at either end to exit doors.

The foundations consist of piers of masonry. The superstructure is composed of wrought-iron columns, supporting wrought-iron roof trusses. In the entire structure there are 672 columns—the shortest 23 ft. and the longest 125 ft. in length. Their aggregate weight is 2,200,000 lbs. The aggregate weight of iron in the roof trusses and girders is 5,000,000 lbs. A peculiarity of the building consists in the fact that the columns and trusses are so designed as to be easily taken down, and erected again upon another site. The sides of the building, for the height of 7 ft. from the ground, are finished with brickwork in panels between the columns; and at the vestibules variegated brick and tile have been introduced.

The building standing nearly due east and west, the light is obtained almost entirely by side-lights from the north and south sides. Small balconies or galleries of observation are provided in the four central towers at the height of the different stories, these being attractive places from which excellent views of the interior can be obtained.

A complete system of water supply for the protection against fire, and for sanitary purposes, has been introduced into the structure. The offices for foreign commissions are arranged along the sides of the building in the side aisles. The design of this building is to enable all exhibitors to have an equally fair opportunity of exhibiting

their goods to advantage, the light being uniformly distributed, and each of the spaces devoted to the exhibition located upon one of the main thoroughfares.

This building cost $1,600,000.

II. The Art Gallery and Memorial Hall.

This building, which was designed from the first to be a permanent appendage to the City of Philadelphia, in which should be stored its art treasures, has been located with admirable design on an eminence in the great "Lansdowne Plateau," and commands a magnificent view of the city, looking toward the south. As this eminence is 116 ft. above the surface of the Schuylkill river, which lies a short distance from it, a charming prospect of the beautiful stream and also a fine view of the building from the river itself, are among the advantages of its situation in Fairmount Park.

The building is elevated on a terrace 6 ft. above the general level of the Plateau, and is built in the modern Renaissance style of architecture, the materials being granite, glass, and iron. No wood has been used in its construction, and it is thoroughly fire-proof. It is 365 feet in length, 210 ft. in width and 59 ft. in height, over a spacious basement 12 ft. in height, surmounted by a dome. The main front looks southward, on which side is the main entrance, consisting of three colossal arched doorways of equal dimensions; there is a pavilion at each end, and two arcades, each 90 ft. long and 40 ft. high. The doors are each of iron, and are relieved by bronze panels with the coats-of-arms of all States and Territories. The main cornice is surmounted by a balustrade with candelabras at either end. The dome rises from the centre of the structure 150 ft. in height, built of glass and iron, and of unique design, with a colossal bell, from which the figure of "Columbia" rises with protecting hands.

A figure of colossal size also stands at each corner of the base of the dome, typifying the four quarters of the globe. The main entrance opens on a hall 82 ft. long, 65 ft. wide, and 53 ft. high, decorated in the modern Renaissance style. On the farther side of this hall, three doorways, each 16 ft. wide and 25 ft. high, open into the central hall, 83 ft. square, and surmounted by the dome rising to a height of 80 ft. From its eastern and western sides extend the galleries, each 98 ft. long, 84 ft. wide, and 35 ft. high. These galleries admit of temporary divisions for the more advantageous display of paintings.

The centre hall and galleries form one grand hall, 287 ft. long and 85 ft. wide, capable of holding 8,000 persons—nearly twice the dimensions of the largest hall in the country. From the two galleries doorways open into two smaller galleries, 28 ft. wide and 89 ft. long, these again opening into private apartments on the north and south, forming two side galleries 210 ft. long.

All the galleries and the central hall are lighted from

CELEBRATION OF THE COMPLETION OF THE EXPOSITION BUILDING AT VIENNA, 1873.

above, the pavilions and central hall being designed especially for the exhibition of sculpture. This building cost $1,500,000.

III. MACHINERY HALL.

The arrangement of the buildings located this structure west of the intersection of Belmont and Elm Avenues, at a distance of 542 feet from the west front of the Main Exhibition Building, and 274 ft. from the north side of Elm Avenue. The north front of the building being upon the same line as the Main Exhibition Building, already described, a frontage is thus presented of 3,824 ft. from the east to the west ends of the exhibition buildings, upon the principal avenue in the grounds.

This building is arranged to consist of a main hall 360 ft. wide by 1,402 ft. long, with an annex on the south side of 208 ft. by 210, the entire area covered by the main hall and annex being 558,440 sq. ft., or 12.82 acres. Including the upper floors, the building, as completed, provides fourteen acres of floor space.

The arrangement of the ground-plan of this building comprised two main avenues, 90 ft. in width by 1,360 ft. in length, with a central aisle between and an aisle on either side. At the centre of the building, a transept extends 90 ft. in

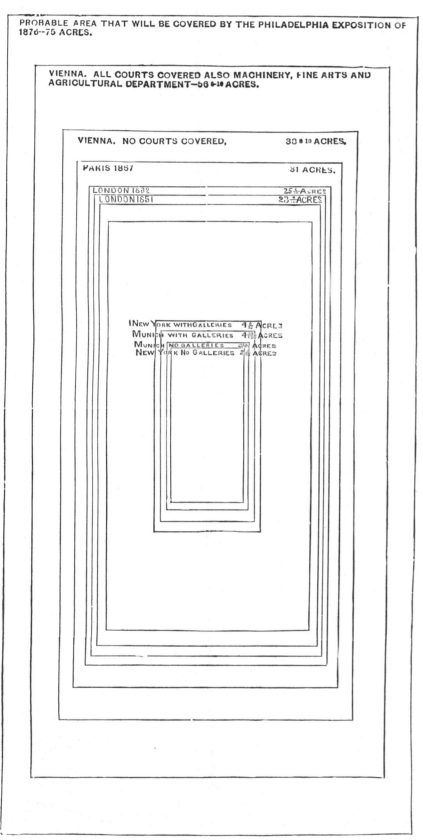

COMPARATIVE SIZE OF BUILDINGS.

width, forming an annex for hydraulic machines. The foundations of this building consist of piers of masonry, the superstructure of solid timber columns supporting roof-trusses, the outer walls being built of masonry to the height of 5 ft., and above that composed of glazed sash placed between the columns.

The construction of this building admits of the most complete shafting, the facilities in this respect being very superior. In the annex for hydraulic machines is built a tank 60 by 106 ft., allowing for a depth of water of 10 ft. At the south end of this arrangement is made for a water-fall 35 ft. high by 40 ft. wide.

This building cost $792,000.

A few figures having reference to the material used in the construction of the Machinery Hall will not be uninteresting to the reader, and will give some faint idea of the vast quantity of material absorbed in the buildings of the Exposition. There were used in this building 5,000,000 ft. of lumber; 500,000 lbs. of cast iron; 750,000 lbs. of wrought iron; 20,000 lbs. of nails and spikes; 700,000 sq. ft. of tin roofing; 175,000 sq. ft. of American glass, weighing 150,000 lbs., the average size of pane being 24 x 32; 15,000,000 lbs. of stone; 225 men were employed daily on the erection of this building, which was commenced on April 13th, 1875, and finished in about five months.

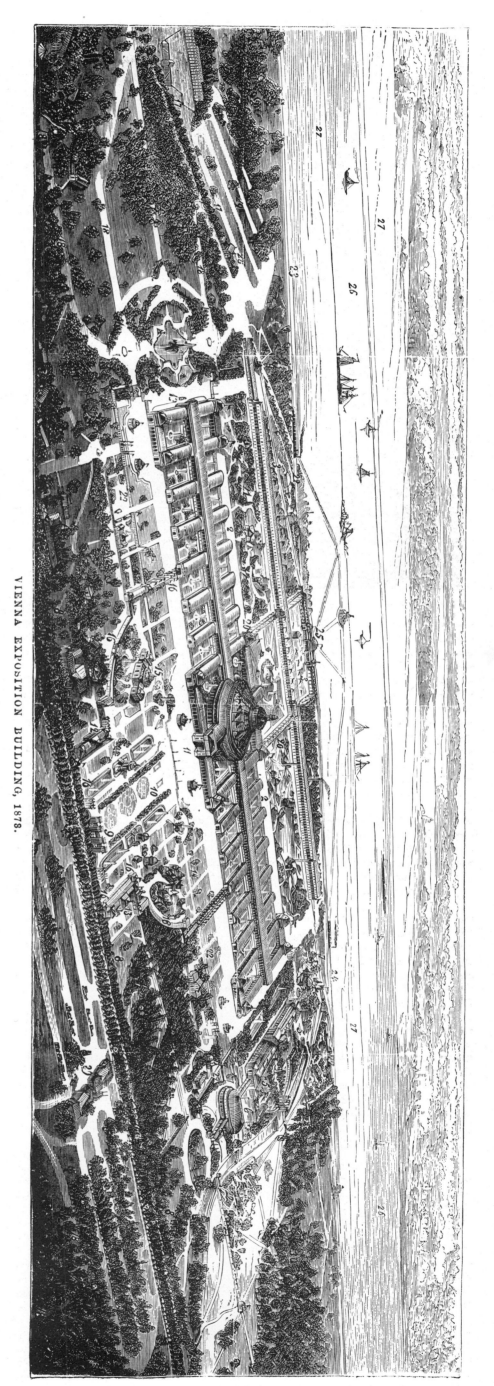

VIENNA EXPOSITION BUILDING, 1873.

MACHINERY HALL AT THE VIENNA EXPOSITION.

IV. HORTICULTURAL HALL.

To the city of Philadelphia is owing the special instance of liberality, which provided that the Horticultural Building of the exhibition should be so constructed as to remain a permanent feature of Fairmount Park. It is located on the Lansdowne Terrace, a short distance north of the Art Gallery, and has, like the latter, a commanding view of the Schuylkill River and a portion of the city. The design is in the Mauresque style of architecture of the twelfth century, the principal materials, externally, being iron and glass. The length is 383 ft., the width 193 ft., and the height to the top of the lantern 72 ft.

The main floor is occupied by the central conservatory, 230 x 80 ft., and 55 ft. high, surmounted by a lantern 170 ft. long, 20 ft. wide, and 14 ft. high. Running entirely around this conservatory, at a height of 20 ft., is a gallery 5 ft. in width. On the north and south sides are four forcing-houses for the propagation of young plants; each house is 100 by 30 ft., and covered with a curved roof of iron and glass. From the vestibules, at the centre of the east and west ends, ornamental stairways lead to the internal galleries of the conservatory, as well as to the four external galleries, each 100 by 10 ft., which surmount the roofs of the forcing-houses. These external galleries are connected by a fine promenade, formed by the roofs of the rooms on the ground floor, and having a superficial area of 1,800 sq. yds.

INTERNATIONAL INDUSTRIAL EXHIBITION AT BUFFALO, N. Y., OCTOBER 6TH, 1869.

STATE INDUSTRIAL EXPOSITION AT LOUISVILLE, KENTUCKY 1872.

CINCINNATI EXPOSITION, 1872

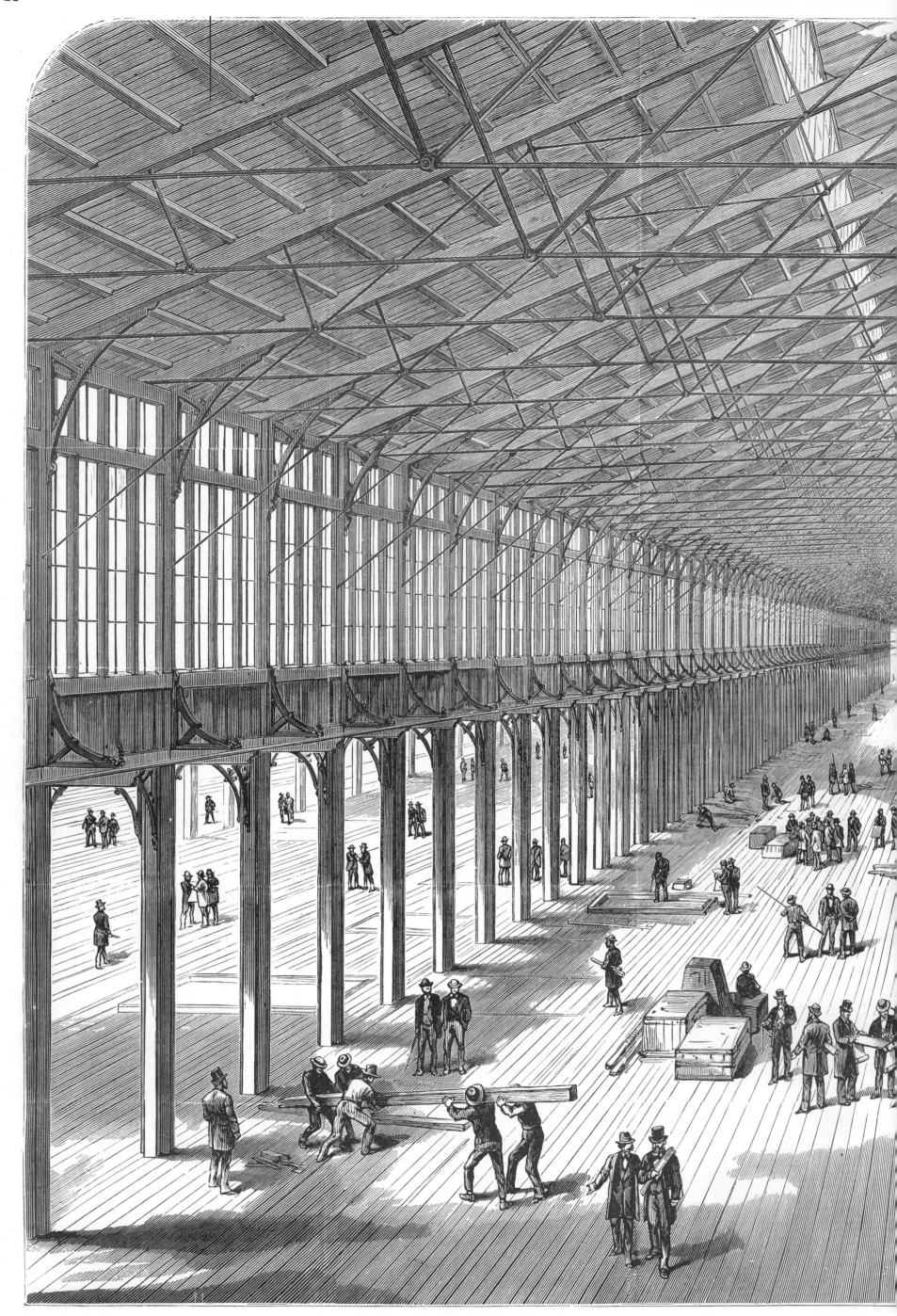

INTERIOR VIEW OF THE MACHINERY BUILDING, WHILE IN PROC

COMPLETION. AT THE INTERNATIONAL EXHIBITION, PHILADELPHIA.

THE CENTENNIAL—SOME OF THE ORGANIZERS OF THE CELEBRATION.

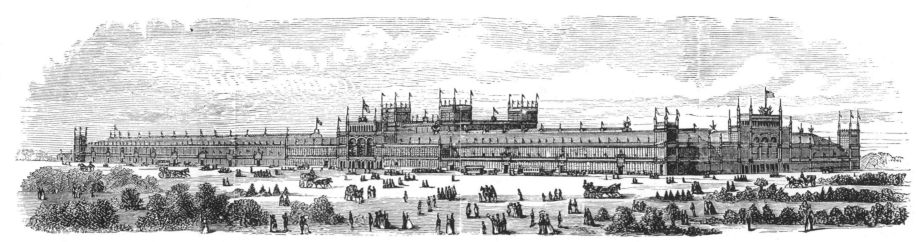

MAIN EXHIBITION BUILDING.

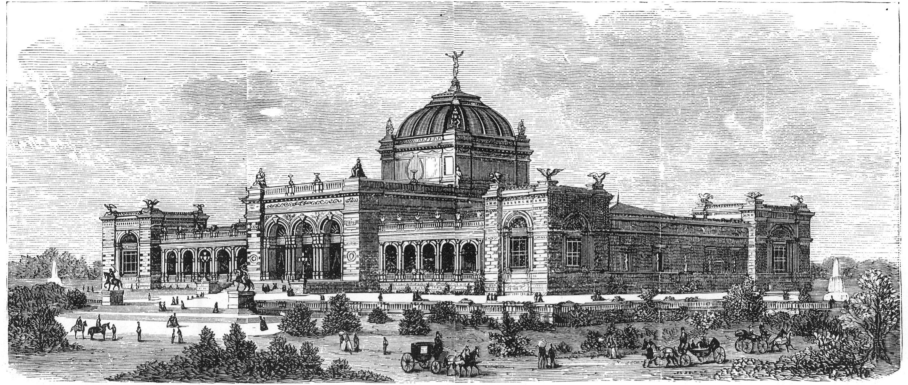

ART GALLERY.

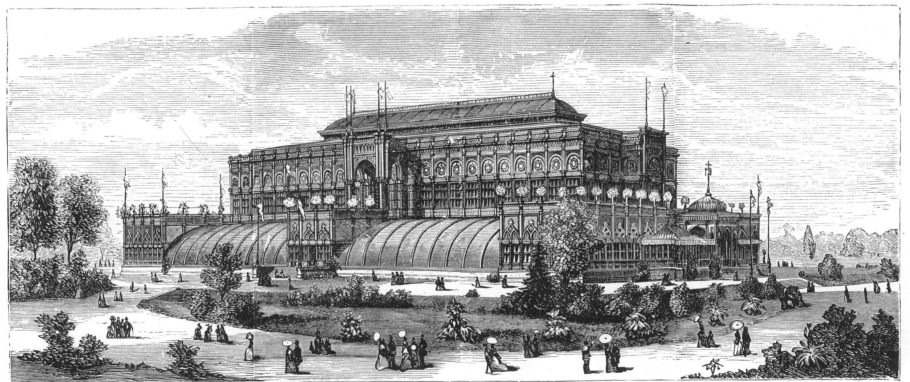

HORTICULTURAL HALL.

AGRICULTURAL BUILDING.

THE BUILDINGS FOR THE CENTENNIAL EXPOSITION AT FAIRMOUNT PARK, PHILADELPHIA.

MEETING OF THE CENTENNIAL COMMISSION AT THE ACADEMY OF MUSIC, PHILADELPHIA, FEBRUARY 25TH, 1873.

The east and west entrances are reached by flights of blue marble steps from terraces 80 x 20 ft., in the centre of each of which stands an open kiosque 20 ft. in diameter. At the angles of the main conservatory are eight ornamental fountains. Beside this principal building, a number of structures have been erected for various horticultural purposes, while the surrounding grounds are arranged for outdoor planting.

This building cost $251,937.

V. AGRICULTURAL BUILDING.

This structure, standing north of the Horticultural Building, and on the eastern side of Belmont Avenue, has been built on a plan illustrating a novel combination of materials, the latter being wood and glass. This combination consists simply of a long nave, crossed by three transepts, nave and transept being composed of Howe-trussed arches of a Gothic form, the nave being 826 feet in length and 100 ft. in width.

The ground-plan of this building forms a parallelogram, 465 by 630 ft., covering a space of seven and a quarter acres. In its immediate vicinity provision is made for space for the exhibition of horses, cattle, sheep, swine, poultry, etc. The arrangement of the ground-plan of the Agricultural Building includes four main avenues; one running north and south through the centre, 786 ft. long by 70 ft. wide, the remaining three running east and west, each 472 ft. long. By these avenues the building is divided into four sections, the four main avenues with 12 aisles forming an admirable arrangement for exhibition, each section containing four spaces, 184 ft. long and 42 wide, for the exhibition of goods, making sixteen in all, covering 117,760 sq. ft. of ground.

The ground enclosed for the site of all the exhibition buildings comprises 236 acres, the boundaries of the enclosure being as follows:

THE STATUE OF COLUMBUS AT FAIRMOUNT PARK, PHILADELPHIA.

South, Elm Avenue from Forty-first Street to Fifty-second Street; west, the Park Drive to George's Hill with the concourse; north, Belmont Avenue Drive from George's Hill to the foot of Belmont; and east, Lansdowne Drive from Belmont to Forty-first Street. The whole of the exhibition being enclosed, thirteen entrances are established along the boundary drive.

The following figures are of interest in connection with the situation plan:

Area of grounds, 236 acres; lineal feet enclosed, 16,000; number of entrances, 13; dimensions of Main Building, 1,880 ft. by 464 ft.—20 acres; Art Gallery, 210 ft. by 365 ft. — 1¾ acres; Machinery Building, 360 ft. by 1,402 ft.—14 acres; Horticultural Hall, 160 ft. by 250 ft. —1¼ acres; Agricultural Building, 540 ft. by 820 ft.—10 acres; United States Government Building, 360 ft. by 300 ft.—1½ acres; Offices of the Administration, 80 ft. by 324 ft. — ¾ acre; avenues and walks, 7 miles; length of horse railway, 4 miles; length of railroad tracks inside the grounds for the delivery of material and goods, 3¼ miles.

Among our illustrations will be found one showing, by a simple system of diagrams, the comparative size of the international buildings of the world, by which it will be seen that the Centennial Exposition buildings cover a very much larger area of ground than any other.

As a general rule, the various States organized local Centennial commissions, the better to enable the proper representation of State products and manufactures. Some of these Commissions obtained permission to erect buildings for their own use upon the Centennial grounds; and we shall have occasion to describe and illustrate certain of these hereafter. The duty of these local Commissions, as defined by the Centennial Commission, appears to be as follows: first, to disseminate information regarding the exhibition; second, to secure the co-operation of industrial, scientific, agricultural, and other associations in their districts; third, to appoint co-operative local committees representing the different industries in their districts; fourth, to stimulate local action on all measures intended to make the exhibition successful and a worthy representation; fifth, to encourage the display of all articles suitable for the exhibition; sixth, to distribute documents, issued by the Commission, to manufacturers and others in their districts interested in the exhibition; seventh, to render assistance in furthering the financial and other objects of the exhibition, and to furnish information on subjects referred to them.

With a view to the better encouragement of exhibitors,

bers of this body will be appointed by the Commission of each country and in conformity with the distribution and allotment to each, which will be hereafter announced. The Judges from the United States will be appointed by the Centennial Commission.

Third.—The sum of one thousand dollars will be paid to each commissioned Judge for personal expenses.

Fourth.—Reports and awards shall be based upon merit. The elements of merit shall be held to include consideration relating to originality, invention, discovery, utility, quality, skill, workmanship, fitness for the purposes intended, adaptation to public wants, economy and cost.

Fifth.—Each report will be delivered to the Centennial Commission as soon as completed, for final award and publication.

GENERAL DIRECTIONS FOR EXHIBITORS FROM THE UNITED STATES.

1. The Exhibition will be held at Fairmount Park, in the City of Philadelphia, and will be opened on the 10th day of May, 1876, and closed on the 10th day of November following.

2. Applications for space and negotiations relative thereto should be addressed to the Director-General, International Exhibition, Philadelphia, Penn.

3. Exhibitors will not be charged for space.

A limited quantity of steam and water power will be supplied gratuitously. The quantity of each will be settled definitively at the time of the allotments of space. Any power required by the

TRANSFER, BY THE PHILADELPHIA AUTHORITIES TO THE CENTENNIAL COMMISSION, JULY 4, 1873, OF THE GROUNDS AT FAIRMOUNT PARK.

the Director-General of the Centennial issued a system of awards, which, with the general directions for exhibitors from the United States, may properly find place here:

SYSTEM OF AWARDS.

First.—Awards shall be based upon written reports attested by the signatures of their authors.

Second—Two hundred judges shall be appointed to make such reports, one-half of whom shall be foreigners and one-half citizens of the United States. They will be selected for their known qualifications and character, and will be experts in departments to which they will be respectively assigned. The foreign mem-

Sixth.—Awards will be finally decreed by the United States Centennial Commission, in compliance with the Act of Congress, and will consist of a diploma with a uniform Bronze Medal and a special report of the Judges on the subject of the Award.

Seventh.—Each exhibitor will have the right to reproduce and publish the report awarded to him, but the U. S. Centennial Commission reserves the right to publish and dispose of all reports in the manner it thinks best for public information, and also to embody and distribute the reports as records of the Exhibition.

A. T. GOSHORN, *Director-General.*

JOHN L. CAMPBELL, *Secretary.*

exhibitor in excess of that allowed will be furnished by the Commission at a fixed price. Demands for such excess of power must also be settled at the time of the allotment of space.

4. Exhibitors must provide, at their own cost, all show-cases, shelving, counters, fittings, etc., which they may require; and all countershafts, with their pulleys, belting, etc., for the transmission of power from the main shafts in the Machinery Hall. All arrangements of articles and decorations must be in conformity with the general plan adopted by the Director-General.

Special constructions of any kind, whether in the buildings or grounds, can only be made upon the written approval of the Director-General.

VISIT OF NEW YORK AND NEW ENGLAND MERCHANTS TO THE CENTENNIAL GROUNDS AT PHILADELPHIA, MAY 11TH, 1875.

UNITED STATES CENTENNIAL EXHIBITION—1776-1876—CERTIFICATE OF CAPITAL STOCK ISSUED BY THE CENTENNIAL BOARD OF FINANCE

HEADQUARTERS OF THE NEW YORK STATE CENTENNIAL BOARD AT FAIRMOUNT PARK, PHILADELPHIA.

5. The Commission will take precautions for the safe preservation of all objects in the Exhibition; but it will in no way be responsible for damage or loss of any kind, or for accidents by fire or otherwise, however originating.

Favorable facilities will be arranged by which exhibitors may insure their own goods.

6. Exhibitors may employ watchmen of their own choice to guard their goods during the hours the Exhibition is open to the public. Appointments of such watchmen will be subject to the approval of the Director-General.

7. Exhibitors, or such agents as they may designate, shall be responsible for the receiving, unpacking, and arranging of objects, as well as for their removal at the close of the Exhibition.

8. The transportation, receiving, unpacking, and arranging of the products for exhibition will be at the expense of the exhibitor.

9. The installation of heavy articles requiring foundations should, by special arrangement, be begun as soon as the progress of the work upon the buildings will permit. The general reception of articles at the Exhibition buildings will be commenced on January 1, 1876, and no articles will be admitted after March 31, 1876.

10. Space not occupied on the 1st of April, 1876, will revert to the Director-General for reassignment.

11. If products are not intended for competition, it must be so stated by the exhibitor, and they will be excluded from the examination by the International Juries.

12. If no authorized person is at hand to receive goods on their arrival at the Exhibition building, they will be removed without delay, and stored at the cost and risk of whomsoever it may concern.

13. Articles that are in any way dangerous or offensive, also patent medicines, nostrums, and empirical preparations whose ingredients are concealed, will not be admitted to the Exhibition.

14. The removal of goods will not be permitted prior to the close of the Exhibition.

15. Sketches, drawings, photographs, or other reproductions of articles exhibited, will only be allowed upon the joint assent of the exhibitor and the Director-General; but views of portions of the building may be made upon the Director-General's sanction.

16. Immediately after the close of the Exhibition, exhibitors shall remove their effects, and complete such removal before December 31, 1876. Goods then remaining will be removed by the Director-General and sold for expenses, or otherwise disposed of under the direction of the Commission.

17. Each person who becomes an exhibitor thereby acknowledges and undertakes to keep the rules and regulations established for the government of the Exhibition.

Special regulations will be issued concerning the exhibition of fine arts, the organization of international juries, awards of prizes, the sale of special articles within the buildings, and on other points not touched upon in these preliminary instructions.

18. An Official Catalogue will be published in four distinct versions—viz., English, French, German, and Spanish. The sale of catalogues is reserved to the Centennial Commission.

19. Communications concerning the exhibition should be addressed to "The Director-General, International Exhibition, 1876, Philadelphia, Penn."

The Centennial Commission reserves the right to explain or amend these regulations, whenever it may be deemed necessary for the interests of the Exhibition.

A. T. GOSHORN, Director-General.
Philadelphia, July 4, 1874.   JOHN L. CAMPBELL, Secretary.

"THE WATER BABIES"—A GROUP IN MARBLE FOR THE CENTENNIAL EXHIBITION AT PHILADELPHIA, BY MARSHALL S. GOULD OF BOSTON, MASS.

In the meantime, it became obvious that certain further action on the part of the Executive Department of the United States Government would be fruitful of good service to the Centennial Exposition; and, accordingly, and with a particular view towards a representative exhibition of the Government in the Exposition, the President issued the necessary orders and made the requisite appointments. The documents which follow will be found to contain these, as also the Act of Congress authorizing the President to extend a cordial invitation to the Governments of foreign nations to be represented at and take part in the International Exposition; the Act authorizing the preparation, at the United States Mint, of medals commemorating the one-hundredth anniversary of the first meeting of the Continental Congress, and the Declaration of Independence; the Act admitting free of duty articles intended for the International Exhibition; and the regulations governing the importation of this class of goods, issued by the Secretary of the Treasury.

EXECUTIVE ORDER

BY THE PRESIDENT OF THE UNITED STATES.

Whereas it has been brought to the notice of the President of the United States that in the International Exhibition of Arts, Manufactures, and products of the Soil and Mine, to be held in the City of Philadelphia, in the year 1876, for the purpose of celebrating the one hundredth anniversary of the Independence of the United States, it is desirable that from the Executive Departments of the Government of the United States in which there may be articles suitable for the purpose intended, there should appear such articles and materials as will, when presented in a collective exhibition, illustrate the functions and administrative faculties of the Government in time of peace, and its resources as a war power, and thereby serve to demonstrate the nature of our institutions and their adaptation to the wants of the people. Now, for the purpose of securing a complete and harmonious arrangement of the articles and materials designed to be exhibited from the Executive Department of the Government, it is ordered that a Board, to be composed of one person to be named by the head of each of the Executive Departments which may have articles and materials to be exhibited, and also of one person to be named in behalf of the Smithsonian Institution, and one to be named in the behalf of the Department of Agriculture, be charged with the preparation, arrangement, and safekeeping of such articles and materials as the heads of the several Departments and the

1. Carpenters flooring the Main Building. 2. Painters at work in Machinery Hall. 3. Arrival of a monster gun for the Government Building. 4. Hoisting a girder in the Main Building. 5. Making roads on the Centennial grounds. 6. Workmen coming down to dinner. 7. Sodding the grounds around Horticultural Hall. 8. Carrying a girder to the transept of the Main Building. 9. A Centennial "Boss."

SCENES AND INCIDENTS ATTENDING THE PROGRESS OF THE WORK ON THE CENTENNIAL BUILDINGS.

Commissioner of Agriculture and the Director of the Smithsonian Institution may respectively decide shall be embraced in the collection; that one of the persons thus named, to be designated by the President, shall be chairman of such Board, and that the Board appoint from their own number such other officers as they may think necessary, and that the said Board when organized shall be authorized under the direction of the President to confer with the executive officers of the Centennial Exhibition in relation to such matters connected with the subject as may pertain to the respective departments having articles and materials on exhibition, and that the names of the persons thus selected by the heads of the several departments, the Commissioner of Agriculture, and the Director of the Smithsonian Institution, shall be submitted to the President for designation.

By order of the President:

(Signed)   HAMILTON FISH,

                       Secretary of State.

WASHINGTON, *January 23, 1874.*

In accordance with the above order, the President appointed a Board composed of a representative from each of the Executive Departments of the Government, except the Department of State and the Attorney-General's Department; but including the Department of Agriculture and the Smithsonian Institution. The Board is composed as follows:

War Department.—Col. S. C. LYFORD, Chairman, *Ordnance Bureau.*

Exposition to be held at Philadelphia, under the auspices of the Government of the United States, in the year eighteen hundred and seventy-six; *Provided, however,* That the United States shall not be liable, directly or indirectly, for any expenses attending such Exposition, or by reason of the same.

Approved, June 5, 1874.

ACT RELATING TO CENTENNIAL MEDALS.

AN ACT to authorize medals commemorating the One Hundredth Anniversary of the first meeting of the Continental Congress, and the Declaration of Independence.

Be it enacted by the Senate and House of Representatives of the United States of America in Congress assembled, That medals with appropriate devices, emblems, and inscriptions, commemorative of the Centennial Anniversary of the Declaration of Independence be prepared at the Mint at Philadelphia for the Centennial Board of Finance subject to the provisions of the fifty-second section of the Coinage Act of eighteen hundred and seventy-three, upon the payment of a sum not less than the cost thereof, and all the provisions whether penal or otherwise of said Coinage Act against the counterfeiting or imitating of coins of the United States shall apply to the medals struck and issued under the provisions of this Act.

Approved, June 16, 1874.

to admit free of duty articles intended for the International Exhibition of Eighteen Hundred and Seventy-six," provides as follows:

"*Be it enacted by the Senate and House of Representatives of the United States of America in Congress assembled,* That all articles which shall be imported for the sole purpose of exhibition at the International Exhibition to be held in the City of Philadelphia in the year 1876, shall be admitted without the payment of duty or of customs fees or charges, under such regulations as the Secretary of the Treasury shall prescribe: *Provided,* That all such articles as shall be sold in the United States or withdrawn for consumption therein at any time after such importation shall be subject to the duties, if any, imposed on like articles by the revenue laws in force at the date of importation: *And provided further,* That in case any articles imported under the provisions of this Act shall be withdrawn for consumption, or shall be sold without payment of duty as required by law, all the penalties prescribed by the revenue laws shall be applied and enforced against such articles and against the person who may be guilty of such withdrawal or sale."

In pursuance of the provisions of this Act the following regulations are prescribed:

First. No duty or customs fees or charges being required on any such importations, a new form of entry is prescribed, which will be employed in all cases at the port where such goods are received.

HEADQUARTERS OF THE WOMEN'S CENTENNIAL EXECUTIVE COMMITTEE, 903 WALNUT STREET, PHILADELPHIA—MRS. E. D. GILLESPIE RECEIVING REPORTS FROM SUB-COMMITTEES.

Treasury Department.—Hon. R. W. TAYLER, *1st Controller of the Treasury.*

Navy Department.—Admiral THORNTON A. JENKINS, *U. S. Navy.*

Interior Department.—JOHN EATON, *Commissioner of Education.*

Post-Office Department.—Dr. CHAS. F. McDONALD, *Chief of Money-Order Department.*

Agricultural Department.—WM. SAUNDERS, *Superintendent of Propagating Garden.*

Smithsonian Institution.—Prof. S. F. BAIRD, *Assistant Secretary of the Smithsonian Institution and U. S. Fishery Commissioner.*

WM. A. DE CAINDRY, *Secretary of Board.*

This Board has been charged with the duty of perfecting a collective Exhibition that shall illustrate the functions and administrative faculties of the Government in time of peace and its resources as a war power.

INVITATION TO FOREIGN GOVERNMENTS.

Whereas, at various International Exhibitions which have been held in foreign countries, the United States have been represented in pursuance of invitations given by the Governments of those countries, and accepted by our Government, therefore,

Be it enacted by the Senate and House of Representatives of the United States of America in Congress assembled, That the President be requested to extend, in the name of the United States, a respectful and cordial invitation to the Governments of other nations to be represented and take part in the International

ACT RELATING TO DUTIES ON FOREIGN ARTICLES.

AN ACT to admit free of duty articles intended for the International Exhibition of Eighteen Hundred and Seventy-six, provides as follows:

Be it enacted by the Senate and House of Representatives of the United States of America in Congress assembled, That all articles which shall be imported for the sole purpose of exhibition at the International Exhibition to be held in the City of Philadelphia in the year eighteen hundred and seventy-six, shall be admitted without the payment of duty or of customs fees, or charges, under such regulations as the Secretary of the Treasury shall prescribe; *Provided,* that all such articles as shall be sold in the United States or withdrawn for consumption therein, at any time after such importation, shall be subject to the duties, if any, imposed on like articles by the revenue laws in force at the date of importation; *And provided further,* That, in case any articles imported under the provisions of this Act, shall be withdrawn for consumption or shall be sold without payment of duty, as required by law, all the penalties prescribed by the revenue laws shall be applied and enforced against such articles and against the persons who may be guilty of such withdrawal or sale.

Approved, June 18, 1874.

REGULATIONS

Governing the Free Importation of Goods for the International Exhibition of Eighteen Hundred and Seventy-six, at Philadelphia.

TREASURY DEPARTMENT,

            Washington, D. C., Oct. 3, 1874.

An Act of Congress approved June 18, 1874, entitled "An Act

Second. The ports of New York, Boston, Portland (Me.), Burlington (Vt.), Suspension Bridge (N. Y.), Detroit, Port Huron (Mich.), Chicago, Philadelphia, Baltimore, Norfolk, New Orleans and San Francisco, will alone constitute ports of entry at which importations for said Exhibition will be made free of duty.

Third. All articles designed for such Exhibition must be forwarded, accompanied by an invoice or schedule of the numbers, character, and commercial value of each shipment, which statement shall be attested before a Consul of the United States, or a civil magistrate of the country in which they are produced or from which they are shipped to the United States. Such verified bill of contents and values must be transmitted in triplicate, one copy to the Collector of Customs at the port where it is desired to make entry, which will be retained for the files of his office; one copy to some duly authorized agent, either of the owners, or of the Foreign Commission of the country from which shipment was made, which agent must in all cases be recognized by the Director-General of the Exhibition, who will, by virtue of that authority, verify the goods and make entry; and one copy to the Collector at the port of Philadelphia, and all packages and enclosures containing goods destined for such Exhibition must be plainly and conspicuously marked with the words "For the International Exhibition of 1876, at Philadelphia."

Fourth. All goods arriving so marked and represented, either at the time of arrival or at any time while remaining in the custody of the Collector of Customs at the port of arrival on general order, will, when entered at the port of arrival, be delivered without examination to such recognized agent or agents, to be by him or them forwarded from the port of arrival by bonded line of transportation to Philadelphia, there to be delivered to the custody of the Collector of that port.

Fifth. Entry for warehouse will be made for all such transported packages on arrival at the said port of Philadelphia, and original entry for warehouse will be made for all goods directed by first shipment to Philadelphia. Warehouse entry having been made, the packages will be held in the custody of the said Collector until the Exhibition building, or some building erected by and in the custody of the officers controlling the said Exhibition, and suitable for secure custody as a warehouse under the authority of the United States, is ready to receive them.

Sixth. Separate and complete records of all packages so transmitted and received by the Collector at Philadelphia will be made by the Storekeeper at the port of Philadelphia in a book prepared for the purpose, in which will be entered, so far as known, the owner's name, the agent's name representing the articles, the country from which shipped, the date of such shipment, the name of the importing vessel, and the date of arrival, the general description and value of the goods, and the specific marks and numbers of the packages. Such record will also be kept in duplicate by a Special Inspector of Customs who, under the direction of the Secretary of the Treasury, shall be appointed to identify, forward, and care for packages so properly marked, and intended in good faith for the Exhibition, but which may not be properly represented by an owner or agent.

Seventh. When the said Exhibition building, or a warehouse suitable for secure custody of articles intended for the Exhibition, duly authorized for receiving bonded goods, shall be ready to receive articles then in the custody of the Collector of the port of Philadelphia, descriptive permits, in duplicate, shall be issued by the said Collector to the Storekeeper of the port, directing the delivery of packages as required by the owner or agent, or by the officers of the said Exhibition—one copy of which permits shall be preserved by the said Storekeeper, the second copy to be delivered with the goods to a proper officer of the customs stationed at the said Exhibition building or warehouse, to be there kept as a record of goods entered for such Exhibition in addition to the duplicate required to be kept in a book of proper form as before referred to. And all packages shall be opened in presence of an officer of the customs, who shall verify the contents from and upon such descriptive list, correcting and completing it as the facts may require.

Eighth. In case of receipt by the Collector at Philadelphia of packages imperfectly described or verified, or in regard to which information may be received questioning the good faith of the persons forwarding the same, he said Collector may direct an examination, in proper form, for the purpose of determining the question, and if, on conference with the Director-General, the goods are found to have been forwarded not in good faith for said Exhibition, they will be charged with duty according to their value and classification, and held by the said Collector, subject to appeal to the Secretary of the Treasury, to await proper claim and payment of duty by their owners.

Ninth. All charges for transportation, drayage, and freight, accruing on goods arriving for the said Exhibition, will be required to be paid by the owner or agent at the time of their delivery into the custody of the Collector of Customs at Philadelphia, or if on packages of small bulk or weight, not accompanied by the owner or agent, or consigned to a Foreign Commissioner, and not exceeding $5 in amount, will be charged against the goods as so delivered into the custody of the Collector at Philadelphia, to be paid with other charges subsequently accruing before the permit is issued for their delivery to the Exhibition building; and on all packages exceeding fifty pounds in weight, half-storage, as provided by regulation for the storage of ordinary merchandise in the public warehouse at the port of Philadelphia, will be charged against the goods received and stored therein from the time of receipt to the time of delivery to the Exhibition building. No fees for entry, permit, or other official act, and no duties will be charged upon or against such packages until after their withdrawal from such Exhibition, for sale, at its close or during its continuance.

Tenth. All articles received and entered at such Exhibition in the manner hereinbefore provided may, at any time consistently with the regulations controlling said Exhibition, be withdrawn for sale or delivery to other parties than the owner or agent concerned in their importation, on payment of the duties properly accruing on said goods according to the laws in force at the time of the importation thereof; and for the purpose of assessment and determination of such duties, and for proper identification of the articles, an officer of the Appraiser's Department of the port of Philadelphia shall be detailed to make due examination of the articles so withdrawn or sold, verifying them by the record of their introduction, and charging upon a proper form, to be prepared for such purpose, the said rate and amount of duty; and on payment of the duty so charged, but without fee or other expenses, the owner or agent shall receive a permit for their removal from the Exhibition.

Eleventh. Articles designed to be returned to the foreign country from which the same were imported, or to be removed from the United States, will, at the close of the Exhibition, or at such time as shall be directed by the officers of such Exhibition, be verified by the customs officer in charge at the Exhibition, re-enclosed, duly marked, and forwarded, under permit of the Collector at Philadelphia, to any other port for export, or may be directly exported from Philadelphia. Export entries for such use will be prepared, corresponding to the import entries under which the goods were originally received.

Twelfth. A Special Inspector of Customs will, under the direction of the Secretary of the Treasury, report at intervals to the Collectors of the ports of Philadelphia and of New York, or of such other ports as he may be directed to visit, for the purpose of applying the regulations herein provided.

[Signed,] B. H. BRISTOW, *Secretary.*

MRS. E. D. GILLESPIE, PRESIDENT OF THE WOMEN'S CENTENNIAL EXECUTIVE COMMITTEE.

GENERAL REGULATIONS FOR FOREIGN EXHIBITORS.

1. The Exhibition will be held at Fairmount Park, in the City of Philadelphia, and will be opened on the 10th day of May, 1876, and closed on the 10th day of November following.

2. All Governments have been invited to appoint Commissions for the purpose of organizing their departments of the Exhibition. The Director-General should be notified of the appointment of such Foreign Commissions before January 1, 1875.

Full diagrams of the buildings and grounds will be furnished to the Foreign Commissions on or before February 1, 1875, indicating the localities to be occupied by each nation, subject, however, to revision and readjustment.

3. Applications for space and negotiations relative thereto must be conducted with the Commission of the country where the article is produced.

4. Foreign Commissions are requested to notify the Director-General, not later than May 1, 1875, whether they desire any increase or diminution of the space offered them, and the amount.

5. Before December 1, 1875, the Foreign Commissions must furnish the Director-General with approximate plans showing the manner of allotting the space assigned to them, and also with lists of their exhibitors, and other information necessary for the preparation of the Official Catalogue.

Products brought into the United States, at the ports of New York, Boston, Portland (Me.), Burlington (Vt.), Suspension Bridge (N. Y.), Detroit, Port Huron (Mich.), Chicago, Philadelphia, Baltimore, Norfolk, New Orleans, and San Francisco, intended for display at the International Exhibition, will be allowed to go forward to the Exhibition buildings, under proper supervision of customs officers, without examination at such ports of original entry, and at the close of the Exhibition will be allowed to go forward to the port from which they are to be expected. No duties will be levied upon such goods, unless entered for consumption in the United States.

6. The transportation, receiving, unpacking, and arranging of the products for exhibition will be at the expense of the exhibitor.

7. The installation of heavy articles requiring special foundations or adjustment should, by special arrangement, begin as soon as the progress of the work upon the buildings will permit. The general reception of articles at the Exhibition buildings will commence on January 1, 1876, and no articles will be admitted after March 31, 1876.

8. Space assigned to Foreign Commissions and not occupied on the 1st of April, 1876, will revert to the Director-General for reassignment.

9. If products are not intended for competition, it must be so stated by the exhibitor, and they will be excluded from the examination by the International Juries.

10. An Official Catalogue will be published in four distinct versions—viz., English, French, German, and Spanish. The sale of Catalogues is reserved to the Centennial Commission.

The seven departmnets of the classification which will determine the relative location of articles in the Exhibition—except in such collective exhibitions as may receive special sanction—and also the arrangement of names in the Catalogue, are as follows:—I. Mining. II. Manufactures. III. Education and Science. IV. Art. V. Machinery. VI. Agriculture. VII. Horticulture.

11. Foreign Commissions may publish Catalogues of their respective sections.

12. Exhibitors will not be charged for space.

A limited quantity of steam and water power will be supplied gratuitously. The quantity of each will be settled definitively at the time of the allotment of space. Any power required by the exhibitor in excess of that allowed will be furnished by the Centennial Commission at a fixed price. Demands for such excess of power must also be settled at the time of the allotment of space.

13. Exhibitors must provide, at their own cost, all show-cases, shelving, counters, fittings, etc., which they may require; and all countershafts, with their pulleys, belting, etc., for the transmission of power from the main shafts in the Machinery Hall. All arrangements of articles and decorations must be in conformity with the general plan adopted by the Director-General.

Special constructions of any kind, whether in the buildings or grounds, can only be made upon the written approval of the Director-General.

The Centennial Commission will take precautions for the safe preservation of all objects in the Exhibition; but it will in no way be responsible for damage or loss of any kind, or for accidents by fire or otherwise, however originating.

14. Favorable facilities will be arranged by which exhibitors or Foreign Commissions may insure their own goods.

15. Foreign Commissions may employ watchmen of their own choice to guard their goods during the hours the Exhibition is open to the public. Appointments of such watchmen will be subject to the approval of the Director-General.

Foreign Commissions, or such agents as they may designate, shall be responsible for the receiving, unpacking, and arrangement of objects, as well as for their removal at the close of the Exhibition; but no person shall be permitted to act as such agent until he can give to the Director-General written evidence of his having been approved by the proper Commission.

16. Each package must be addressed "To the Commission for [*Name of Country*] at the International Exhibition of 1876, Philadelphia, United States of America," and should have at least two labels affixed to different but not opposite sides of each case, and giving the following information:

17. (1) The country from which it comes; (2) name or firm of the exhibitor; (3) residence of the exhibitor; (4) department to which objects belong; (5) total number of packages sent by that exhibitor; (6) serial number of that particular package.

18. Within each package should be a list of all objects.

19. If no authorized person is at hand to receive goods on their arrival at the Exhibition building, they will be removed without delay, and stored at the cost and risk of whomsoever it may concern.

20. Articles that are in any way dangerous or offensive, also patent medicines, nostrums, and empirical preparations whose ingredients are concealed, will not be admitted to the Exhibition.

21. The removal of goods will not be permitted prior to the close of the Exhibition.

22. Sketches, drawings, photographs, or other reproductions of articles exhibited, will only be allowed upon the joint assent of the exhibitor and the Director-General; but views of portions of the building may be made upon the Director-General's sanction.

23. Immediately after the close of the Exhibition, exhibitors shall remove their effects, and complete such removal before December 31, 1876. Goods then remaining will be removed by the Director-General and sold for expenses, or otherwise disposed of under the direction of the Centennial Commission.

24. Each person who becomes an exhibitor thereby acknowledges and undertakes to keep the rules and regulations established for the government of the Exhibition.

Special regulations will be issued concerning the exhibition of fine arts, the organization of international juries, awards of prizes, and sales of special articles within the buildings, and on other points not touched upon in these preliminary instructions.

25. Communications concerning the Exhibition should be addressed to "The Director-General, International Exhibition, 1876, Philadelphia, Pa., U. S. A."

The Centennial Commission reserves the right to explain or amend these regulations, whenever it may be deemed necessary for the interests of the Exhibition.

A. T. GOSHORN, *Director-General.*

JOHN L. CAMPBELL, *Secretary.*

Philadelphia, July 4th, 1874.

Following these we give an official list of directions to foreign exhibitors, as issued by the Director-General of the Exposition, and also the special regulations governing the Exhibition of Fine Arts:

SPECIAL REGULATIONS

Governing the Exhibition of Fine Arts at the International Exhibition of Eighteen Hundred and Seventy-six, at Philadelphia.

First. The Exhibition will be opened on the 10th day of May, 1876, and closed on the 10th day of November following.

Second. Works of Art will be admitted for exhibition, whether previously exhibited or not.

Third. Applications for space and negotiations relative thereto must be conducted with the Commission of the country of which the applicant is a citizen.

Fourth. No charge will be made for space.

Fifth. The admission of foreign works of Art to the Exhibition, except those referred to in Rule IX., will be left to the Commission appointed by the respective Governments.

Sixth. Foreign packages for this department must be marked "Art Department," and addressed to the Commission for [*Name of Country*] International Exhibition, Philadelphia, U. S. A.

Seventh. The works of foreign artists will be placed in the care of the Commission of the country to which they belong

Eighth. Works of foreign artists, belonging to residents of the United States, will be admitted on the approval of the Committee of Selection, for exhibition in a special gallery.

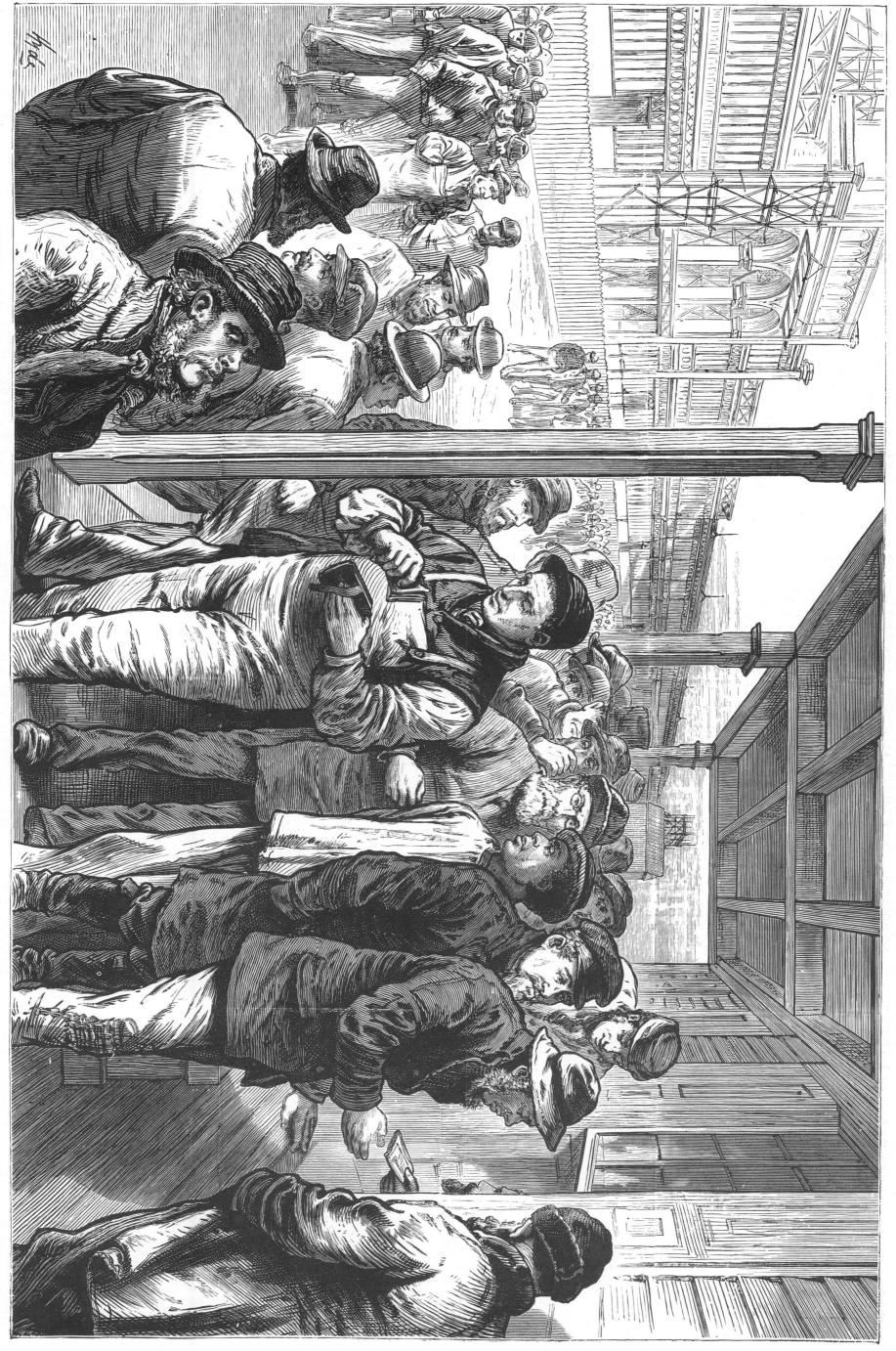

PAYING OFF WORKMEN AT THE CONTRACTORS' BUILDING, ON THE CENTENNIAL GROUNDS, IN FAIRMOUNT PARK.

THE PENN STATUE FOR FAIRMOUNT PARK.

Ninth. Foreign Commissions will transmit to the Director-General prior to March 1st, 1876, information concerning the works of Art to be exhibited by their citizens that may be necessary for the preparation of the Official Catalogue.

Tenth. The installation of works of Art admitted to the Exhibition will be under the supervision of the Commissions of the country to which they belong.

Eleventh. All works of Art must be of a high order of merit, and those produced by citizens of the United States will be admitted to the Exhibition only on the approval of the Committee of Selection.

Twelfth. Packages forwarded by exhibitors in the United States, for admission to this department, must be marked "Art Department, International Exhibition, Philadelphia." There must be also attached to the outside and inside of each package a label giving the name and address of the exhibitor, and the title and number of articles in the package.

Thirteenth. All pictures, whether round or oval, should be placed in square frames. Excessive breadth in frames or projecting mouldings should be avoided. Shadow boxes will not be allowed to project more than one inch beyond the frame. Glass over oil paintings will not be permitted.

Fourteenth. Works of Art intended for sale will be so designated in the Official Catalogue.

Fifteenth. All works of Art must be in Philadelphia prior to April 1st, 1876, and, after having been admitted under the rules, shall not be removed before the close of the Exhibition.

Sixteenth. Each person presenting works of Art for admission thereby agrees to comply with the special rules established for this department and the general rules for the government of the Exhibition.

A. T. GOSHORN, *Director-General.*
JOHN L. CAMPBELL, *Secretary.*
March 1st, 1875.

The stock certificate of the Centennial Exposition, to which we have already referred, as an appropriate *souvenir* of the occasion, was engraved in the United States Treasury Engraving Department, and is a remarkably fine specimen of that class of work. The design is pyramidal, America forming the apex, with Fame and Art, personified, sitting at her feet. The busts of Washington and Grant on either side, typical of the commencement and end of the century. America is represented as welcoming the representatives of foreign nations, who bear samples of their national industries and resources. Independence Hall and the National Capitol are in the background. Beneath the former stand Fulton and Fitch, with their steamboat models, and under the latter, Franklin and Morse, with electrical and telegraphic instruments. On the right, facing the figure of America, is Howe offering his sewing-machine, also a shipwright with a model of a clipper. The Freedman, Continental, and Federal soldiers and mechanics form a group on the right, and a farmer, miner, trapper and Indian, with evidences of their labor, on the left. In the centre of the base is Trumbull's painting of "The Signing of the Declaration of Independence," on the right of which is exemplified Progress—a busy manufacturing city in contrast with a neglected windmill. To the left of the base is represented Civilization—combining the railroad, telegraph, steamship, and reaping-machine, in contrast with a Conestoga wagon, mail-rider,

sailing-vessel, and a laborer with a sickle. The legend in the body of the certificate was engraved by a new and ingenious process, and is most creditable, as is also the printing, the Department evidently being determined to make the work worthy of the nation and the grand commemorative occasion.

With this illustrative memorial may properly be classed the Centennial Medal, struck at the Mint at Philadelphia in accordance with the Act of Congress already given. The description of this medal is as follows: The design of the obverse represents the Genius of American Independence rising from her recumbent position, grasping with her right hand the sword with which to enforce her demands, and raising her left to the thirteen stars, which, indicating the original colonies or States, are blazing in the firmament. Beneath is the date 1776. The reverse displays the Genius of Liberty, with the now ornamental sword buckled to her girdle, the Stars and Stripes at rest in her right hand, while with the other she extends a hand to the Arts and Sciences to do honor to the date 1876, which is inscribed upon the platform. These medals have been struck in bronze, silver, and other metals.

The classification of articles to be exhibited at the Centennial Exposition is simple and comprehensive. It embraces the following ten departments :

1. Raw Materials—Minerals, Vegetable and Animal.
2. Materials and Manufactures used for Food or in the Arts, the results of extractive or combining processes.
3. Textile and Felted Fabrics — Apparel, Costumes and Ornaments for the person.
4. Furniture and Manufactures of general use in Construction and in Dwellings.
5. Tools, Implements, Machines and Processes.
6. Motors and Transportation.
7. Apparatus and Methods for the Increase and Diffusion of Knowledge.
8. Engineering, Public Works, Architecture, etc.
9. Plastic and Graphic Arts.
10. Objects illustrating the efforts for the Improvement of the Physical, Intellectual and Moral Condition of Man.

These departments are subdivided into groups and classes, to facilitate the arrangement and display of the various articles placed on exhibition.

A still more comprehensive classification than this is found in the following table of seven grand divisions :

Departments.	Buildings.	Acres covered.
1. Mining and Metallurgy.		
2. Manufactures	Main Building	21.47
3. Education and Science.		
4. Art	Art Gallery	1.5
5. Machinery	Machinery Building	14
6. Agriculture	Agricultural Building	10
7. Horticulture	Horticultural Building	1.5
Total		48.47

The list of special buildings erected outside of those belonging to the Centennial Exposition proper is led by that of the United States Government, which covers four and a half acres, and in which space will be occupied by representative exhibitions from the War, Treasury, Navy, Interior, Post Office, and Agricultural Departments, and the Smithsonian Institution.

The Women's Centennial Executive Committee—an offshoot of the Centennial Commission, comprising lady members from all the different States—raised $30,000 for the erection of a special pavilion in which to exhibit women's work as a specialty. It should be here recorded that the labors of the ladies who have interested themselves

GIUSEPPE DASSI, ITALIAN COMMISSIONER TO THE CENTENNIAL INTERNATIONAL EXHIBITION AT PHILADELPHIA.

in the Centennial have been unremitting, judicious, and arduous, while their result will unquestionably reflect credit upon their taste, energy, and industry.

Besides the United States' national buildings, other nations have erected similar structures, prominent among these being those constructed by the Governments of England, Germany, Austria, France, Egypt, and Japan. Finally, many of the States have followed this example, notably : Pennsylvania, New York, New Jersey, Ohio, Indiana, Illinois, Michigan, Massachusetts, Connecticut, New Hampshire, Missouri, Kansas, Virginia, West Virginia, Nevada, Wisconsin, Iowa, and Delaware. Still further, many trades and industrial associations and special industrial interests are provided for in separate buildings. Among these are the photographers, the carriage-builders, the glass-makers, cracker-bakers, boot and shoe manufacturers, besides a number of individual exhibitors.

Altogether, the total number of special buildings may probably be set down at from two hundred to two hundred and fifty. As an evidence of the eagerness with which space was applied for, it may be mentioned that 333,300 sq. ft. had been demanded as early as the 1st of October, 1875, by American exhibitors only. In the machinery building alone there were 1,000 American exhibitors, 150 English, and 150 from other European countries, being about two hundred and fifty more than entered the Vienna machinery exhibition. For the art exhibition the same earnest desire for space was manifested from the first; applications from abroad calling for more than four times the exhibiting area afforded by the great Memorial Hall. One very generous and admirable arrangement was that of the Secretary of the Navy, by which a United States war vessel called at convenient European ports to collect and transport to the exhibition the works of American artists resident in Europe. Among the ports designated were Southampton for England, Havre for France, Bremen for Germany, and Leghorn for Italy.

A peculiar feature of the Exposition period may be noted in the promised gathering of numerous Orders and Fraternities at Philadelphia at this time. Among these may be mentioned the Grand Lodge of Pennsylvania, Independent Order of Odd Fellows ; Grand Encampment, Independent Order of Odd Fellows ; Grand Lodge, United States, Independent Order of Odd Fellows ; Grand Commandery, Knights Templars ; Grand Army of the Republic ; Presbyterian Synod ; Caledonian Club ; Portland Mechanic Blues ; Welsh National Eisteddfodd ; Patriotic Order, Sons of America ; a National Regatta ; the Life Insurance Companies ; National Board of Underwriters ; Agricultural Societies ; 2nd Infantry Regiment N. G. of California ; Philadelphian Society ; Methodist Episcopal Church · Cincinnati Society ; California Banner Society ; American Dental Convention ; Catholic Total Abstinence Union of America ; Independent Order of B'nai Berith ; National Alumni Association ; Salemen's Association ; 5th Maryland Regiment ; American

NEW JERSEY STATE BUILDING.

WORKMEN ASPHALTING THE WALKS AND BLASTING OUT THE STUMPS OF TREES IN THE CENTENNIAL GROUNDS.

INDIANA STATE BUILDING.

SWEDISH SCHOOL-HOUSE.

Pomological Society ; Maltsters Association of the United States ; Army of the Cumberland ; Humboldt Monument Association ; Christopher Columbus Monument Association ; Board of Trade ; Convention International Typographical Corps ; Life Association of the United States Centennial Legion ; National Medical Congress ; Old Volunteer Fire Department of Philadelphia : and many others.

The arrangements on the part of the Centennial management for the exhibition of live stock and general agricultural improvements display careful thought and judgment. This exhibition is set down to occupy the months of September and October, 1876, fifteen days being devoted to each class. Horses, mules, and asses from September 1st to the 15th ; horned cattle from September 20th to October 5th ; sheep, swine, and goats from October 10th to the 25th ; the animals, except breeding stock and fat and drafting cattle, to be of pure blood and highly meritorious. It is, of course, important that the world should see the best we can show, while it is probable the competition will be between some of the finest specimens of stock in the world.

A temporary exhibition of poultry is arranged from October 25th to November 10th in the coops and boxes in which they are forwarded. They must be fed and attended by the exhibitors, pure breeds only being accepted. Concerning this, it is desirable to establish a permanent exhibition lasting during the six months of the Exhibition.

The arrangement for the exhibition of agricultural machinery contemplates a separate department from that of other machinery in a section of Agricultural Hall of ten acres. Here are to be displays of mechanical devices and implements used on the farm. Cotton gins, sugar presses, thrashers, fanning mills, plows (both for animal and steam power), reapers, mowers, and hay rakes are to be tested in the field. The elements of merit are to consist of originality, utility, quality, skill, workmanship, fitness for the purpose intended, adaptation for public wants, and economy in cost.

In addition to the ordinary live stock, it has also been concluded to hold a show of sporting and non-sporting dogs from October 1st to 15th, the animals to be of pure blood and high merit. Exhibitors to provide food and attendance.

Fish, and all the processes used in their propagation and culture, are also among the articles to be exhibited, the Commissioners of Fisheries of the various States being requested to take such concert of action as shall secure a full exhibition of this new and important national industry.

Concerning fruit, the following circular displays the intention of the Commission : "The display of pomological products will cover the entire period during which the Exhibition will be opened, though varying in importance and extent. For instance, berries and other small fruits will be included in this department, and of these there will be certain classes, as strawberries

from the South, ready for exhibition on the opening day, and a variety and quantity will be presented.

"It will be perceived that the most important display will be made during September and October. The classification of fruits will be according to their species and variety, all of similar character being assembled together, that a more satisfactory conclusion may be reached as to their respective merits from different soils and States. All grapes will be in one position ; the same with apples, pears, and the entire list of wild fruits and nuts. Many being perishable fruits —as the products of the tropics, such molded in wax and plaster, will be acceptable. Exhibitors may be assured that the proper arrangement will be made for the united interests of pomological science. It is hoped that the pomological societies of the several States, and individual cultivators generally, will co-operate, with a view to place before the world a creditable evidence of the resource and capacity of our country in respect to fruit culture and products." The space set apart for the pomological contributions is the centre hall of the Agricultural Building, and is the most prominent in the whole building.

A bird's-eye view of the entire Centennial grounds, taken from the summit of George's Hill, presents a picture of such magnificent proportions, and representing such a tremendous development of energy and industry, as to create in the mind of the beholder a reasonably fair estimate of the expression of these qualities which he beholds spread out before him.

Immediately beneath him, and on his right, extends the great machinery building, running from the extreme western end of the grounds to the point where Belmont and Elm Avenues nearly unite.

Following on the 1,402 ft., which represent the length of the building, the eye next meets the even grander proportions of the Main Exhibition Building, which completes, with its 1,880 ft., the almost unbroken line of exhibition space of 3,824 ft. A little to the left of this, again, the observer sees the superb Art Building itself, an architectural structure unexcelled in the beauty of its lines and the general character of its execution ; and as an executive effort offering a most praiseworthy and creditable example of the architectural taste and capacity of this country. Further north of the main building, and to a point about opposite to its extreme western end, standing on the eastern extremity of Fountain Avenue, is the beautiful Mauresque structure, Horticultural Hall, which, with the Art

Building, is destined to give permanent value and beauty to this portion of Fairmount Park. North of the Horticultural Building and on the eastern side of Belmont Avenue, and about midway between the reservoir and the river, we perceive the oddly-shaped Agricultural Building, with its surrounding grounds. Scattered about among these mammoth structures are the minor buildings of the Exposition, while the grounds, intersected with broad avenues, and beautified by shade-trees, present, in every particular, a most charming and interesting scene.

On February 11th, the United States Senate passed the House Bill appropriating $1,500,000 for the uses of the United States Centennial Commission, for the expenses of the Exposition ; on the 16th the Bill was signed by the President. By the provision of this Bill the United States become preferred creditors of the Centennial Commission.

SKETCH OF THE EARLY HISTORY OF AMERICAN INDUSTRY.

BEVERLEY, in his "History of Virginia," in 1705, refers thus to the dependence of the colonists upon other nations to supply their wants : "They have their clothing of all sorts from England, as linen, woolen, and silk, hats, and leather ; yet flax and hemp grow nowhere in the world better than here. Their sheep yield good increase, and bear good fleeces, but they shear them only to cool them. The mulberry-tree, whose leaf is the proper food of the silkworm, grows there like a weed, and silkworms have been observed to thrive extremely, and without hazard. The very furs that their hats are made of, perhaps, go first from thence. The most of their hides lie and rot, or are made use of only for covering dry-goods in a leaky house. Indeed, some few hides, with much ado, are tanned and made into servants' shoes ; but at so careless a rate that the farmers do not care to buy them if they can get others, and sometimes, perhaps, a better manager than ordinary will vouchsafe to make a pair of breeches of deerskin. They are such abominable ill-husbands, that though their country be overrun with wood, they have all their wooden-ware from England ; their cabinets, chairs, tables, stools, chests, boxes, cart-wheels, and all other things — even so much as their bowls and birchen-brooms — to the eternal reproach of their laziness."

The first vessel ever constructed in North America by Europeans was called the *Onrest*, and was built in 1614 at Manhattan River. She was 16 tons burthen, with 38 ft. keel, 44½ ft. in length, and 11½ ft. wide. In her, Captain Wilkinson, in 1616, discovered the Schuylkill River, and explored nearly the entire coast from Nova Scotia to the Capes of Virginia. The Massachusetts colony built their first vessel at Salem. She was launched, curiously enough, on the 4th of July, 1631, and christened by Governor Winthrop, to whom she belonged, *The Blessing of the Bay.*

HEADQUARTERS OF THE JAPANESE COMMISSION. ERECTED BY NATIVE WORKMEN.

INTERIOR OF THE CENTENNIAL BUREAU OF INSTALLATION—ALLOTTING SPACE TO EXHIBITORS.

The want of money was so great in the colony that corn was made a legal tender for debts.

In 1642 there arrived at Plymouth a carpenter and salt-maker, who had been sent out by the Plymouth Company. This salt-maker made several unsuccessful attempts at his business of salt-making at Cape Ann and at Cape Cod; while the ship-carpenter died, after building only two small vessels.

The saw-mill is said to have been introduced into Massachusetts in 1633, some years before it was used in England. Even as late as 1767, a saw-mill was destroyed in the latter country by the mob, because it was supposed to be destructive to the work of the sawyers. As late as 1663, England depended chiefly upon Holland for its sawn lumber. In 1641 the General Court of Massachusetts passed an Act to the effect that there "should be no monopolies but of such new inventions as were profitable to the country, and that for a short time only." Under this provision sawing came in and paid a certain royalty. Saw-mills were erected by the Dutch in New York as early as 1633, and were also used there for grinding-mills. Of course, the introduction of saw-mills gave a great impetus to house construction. Whereas, before this, buildings were mere huts or wigwams, now they began to be more carefully fashioned. These two important industries, house-building and ship-building, had already been established as early as 1633. But house-building thus far was only by means of wood as a material. The first brick-kiln in New England was set up in Salem, Mass., in 1629. Before this, even the chimneys had been made of wood, coated with clay. In the first year of the settlement of Jamestown, Va., the fort, storehouse, with all its surplus supplies, and most of the rest of the town, were burnt down by fire, originating in a wooden chimney. The same fate, from the same cause, befell, in Plymouth, the storehouse within a month of its being finished. In Boston, a fire in 1641 was occasioned by the same cause, and thereafter the use of wooden chimneys and thatched roofs was forbidden by Governor Dudley. The first brick house built in Massachusetts is said to have been erected in 1628. In 1692 all buildings of a certain size were ordered by the Massachusetts General Court to be built of stone or brick, and to be roofed with slate or tiles.

In New York, bricks were early imported from Holland, and the style of the houses was in imitation of those of Amsterdam. Brick-making was introduced by Governor Stuyvesant. Bricks were made at the Van Rensselaer estate, below Albany, before they were at New York. Between 1630 and 1646, bricks were sold at fifteen florins a thousand.

Earthenware, which was said to equal that made at Delft, was early manufactured on Long Island. The daily wages of carpenters was about 80 cents, and those of day-laborers 40 cents a day. Nails were worth about 16 to 20 cents per ℔ of 100 nails. At the beginning of this century, a house was still standing in New Castle, in which Governor Lovelace entertained Fox in 1672. The Manor House, built by William Penn, near Pennsborough, was constructed of bricks brought from England. This house cost its owner £5,000.

In the Southern cities, wood was the material chiefly used in domestic architecture.

In a work called "Wonder-workings," published in 1651, the industries of the New England colonies are referred to, the author mentioning the trades of tanning and shoe-making, and the great ability and industry in the latter.

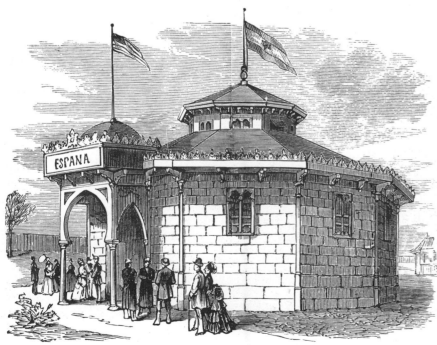

QUARTERS OF THE SPANISH CORPS OF ENGINEERS.

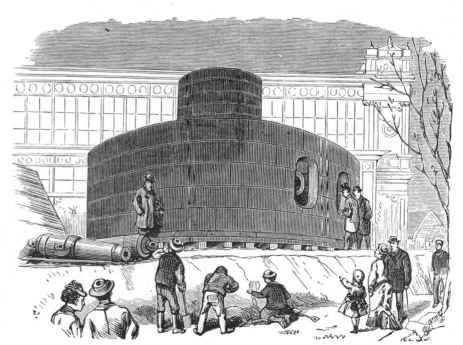

MODEL MONITOR-TURRET.

SCENE IN FRONT OF THE GOVERNMENT BUILDING ON THE CENTENNIAL GROUNDS, FAIRMOUNT PARK.

INTERIOR OF THE JAPANESE WORKMEN'S TEMPORARY QUARTERS.

He mentions also, among other trades, cartmakers, glovers, furriers, and tillers. In 1697, the Assembly of the United Colonies of Connecticut passed laws fixing the prices for tanning and for hides, as also those for which shoemakers were permitted to make shoes.

The first cattle ever brought to America are said to have been introduced by Columbus in his second voyage in 1493. In 1553, cattle were carried by the Portuguese to Nova Scotia and Newfoundland, and are said to have increased there very rapidly. In 1609, hogs, goats, sheep, and horses were introduced into Virginia; and the following year another stock of cattle was brought thither from the West Indies. In 1649, the cattle of Virginia, including bulls, cows, and calves, were estimated to number 20,000, with 200 horses and 3,000 sheep, 5,000 goats, and many swine, many of which were exported to New England, where the diversities of industries made them more valuable. In the *Plymouth* the first cattle were introduced in 1624. In 1626 twelve cows were sent to Cape Ann, and in 1629 thirty more were sent. The Indians and the wolves were very destructive to the animals of the colony, and yet the increase of this stock was very rapid. In New York domestic cattle were imported from Holland by the West India Company in 1625. In 1627 a cow was worth there £30, and a yoke of oxen £40. New Jersey was provided with cattle from New York, and their increase here soon made this province one of the storehouses for the supply for the States of Pennsylvania, Delaware, and New York. In 1627 Pennsylvania was supplied with neat cattle by the Swedish West India Company.

In Pennsylvania, in 1697, among the trades in vogue, were tanners, glovers, shoemakers, bookbinders, and carriagemakers.

Stone was not used as a building material in the colonies until 1752, when King's Chapel, in Boston, was built of a Braintree granite. The Dutch of New York put stone on the free list in 1640, to encourage its introduction from abroad—when it might have been had by the quarrying close by, in New Jersey. Quarrying at Quincy, Mass., began early in the present century, and the first railroad in the country was built from these quarries, three miles from the Neponset River, in 1827. It was a horse-railroad, designed for the transportation of this stone for shipment. American marbles were first used for making busts in Philadelphia in 1804. The Portland, Conn., quarry of brown freestone or sandstone has been worked for more than a century, and stone is now taken from that quarry at a depth of more than two hundred feet below the Connecticut River. In these quarries were often seen fossil footprints of gigantic birds, some with the footprints measuring sixteen inches in length and ten in width, and the tracks from four to six feet apart. The stone from here is extensively used in New York, whole streets of residences in the upper part of the city being built either of the solid stone or of brick faced with stone veneering.

In 1805, a company was incorporated in Pennsylvania for obtaining slate supplies in Northumberland County. Since then other companies have been incorporated in Pennsylvania, New York, and Maryland. The quarries on the Piscataqua River, forty miles above Bangor, in Maine, were opened in 1839.

CLOTHS.

In regard to the manufacture of cloths, in the early days of the settlements of the colonists, the distaff and spindle appear to have been used, though these were soon superseded by the spinning-wheel. In those days, England sought by every means in her power to suppress the industries of her colonies. But, despite the restrictions she placed upon the exportation of cloths made in America, the manufacture continued. In the early part of the last century, a public meeting was held in Boston, at which a committee was appointed to report upon the propriety of establishing spinning-schools for the instruction of children in the town. This resulted in the erection of a large brick building upon Tremont Street, emblematically decorated with a figure upon its façades of a woman spinning. At its opening an immense crowd gathered, the women of Boston coming in large numbers, carrying their spinning-wheels, and displaying their dexterity in using them. In 1837, a tax was laid upon private carriages and other luxuries, for the benefit of this spinning-school.

During the War of Independence the population was dependent for supplies of clothes upon home exertions. After the invention of the spinning-jenny by Hargraves, and of the spinning-frame by Arkwright, it was for a long time impossible to obtain these implements in America, so jealously did England prevent their exportation. It has been said that models of

THE BRITISH GOVERNMENT BUILDINGS.

1. Japanese workmen preparing their meals. 2. The chief workman and his assistant consulting their books and charts. 3. Bringing joists and timber from Machinery Hall. 4. Erecting the Japanese dwelling-house. 5 Mortising.
6. Sawing. 7. Using the adz. 8. Around the fire.

ERECTION OF THE JAPANESE BUILDINGS ON THE CENTENNIAL GROUNDS, IN FAIRMOUNT PARK.

Arkwright's machines, small enough to be concealed in a trunk, were seized by the Customs authorities and confiscated. Despite these precautions, however, to prevent the spread of the use of the machinery, the business was promoted in the United States by the establishment of a cotton factory at Beverley, Mass., in 1787. Some of the handkerchiefs made here were still in existence a few years ago, and were of a remarkably fine and solid texture. Possibly specimens of these may turn up at the Centennial. Of Arkwright's machines, the first used were in a mill at Pawtucket, R. I., which commenced operations in 1790.

Plymouth is still extant. Indeed, the quantity of chests, bedsteads, chairs, and bureaus which are *said* to have been brought over by the *Mayflower*, would load a fleet of full-sized steamships. For the first few years after the settlement of the colonies, all the best furniture — chiefly of mahogany, though sometimes of oak — was imported. Among the first pieces made in this country were economical articles, such as tables hung against the walls, which, when not in use, might be turned down, thus saving considerable space. These, of course, were made of native woods. After a while our West India trade led to the im-

try people, in Massachusetts for instance, to erect forges in chimney corners, and in Winter, in the evenings when little work could be done, to make quantities of nails—even the children taking part in this industry. These manufacturers took the rod-iron from the merchant, and returned him the nails.

About 1776, Jeremiah Wilkinson, of Cumberland, R. I., engaged in manufacturing hand-cards used in spinning, found the price of tacks so high, owing to the Revolution and to the time and labor necessary to their manufacture by the hand process, invented a process for cutting them

PLACING COLOSSAL STATUES AT THE BASE OF THE DOME OF MEMORIAL HALL.

In 1810, such a mill, supplied with cotton machinery, was erected near Philadelphia. The first cotton-mill ever built in the world, which combined all the requisites for making finished cloth from raw cotton, is said to have been erected in Waltham, Mass., in 1813.

• FURNITURE.

Our ancestors obtained the most of their house furniture, naturally enough, from England; and some of the furniture brought over by the settlers at Jamestown and

portation of mahogany, which was worked up solidly and in veneers into high-backed, uncomfortable chairs, tall bedsteads, huge bureaus, and side-boards, containing enormous closets, etc. Afterward came rosewood from the West Indies and South America, and furniture began to be made, for those who could afford to purchase it, from this beautiful material.

NAILS.

The first nails made in the United States were manufactured by a hand process, and it was common for the coun-

with a pair of shears, and the heading them in a vise. A machine for cutting and heading nails was invented about 1790, by Jacob Perkins, of Newburyport. It was patented in 1795, and is said to have been able to turn out 10,000 nails a day. In 1786 a machine was invented by a citizen of Bridgewater, Mass., for cutting tacks and nails. This machine made, in 1815, 150,000,000 tacks. A son of its inventor patented, in 1807, a machine for making and heading tacks, which turned them out at the then very wonderful speed of 60,000 per day.

1. Artillery salute at Belmont.   2. "A penny, please!"   3. Dedicating the site of the Hebrew Monument to religious liberty.   4. Military review at Belmont.   5. Centennial Fountain.   6. Going to the Centennial Buildings. 7. Going to the Park.   8. Children's Concert in Machinery Hall.   9. Ceremonies at the site of the Columbus Monument.   10. Balloon Ascension.   11. Fireworks.   12. Breaking ground at Agricultural Hall. 13. Review of the Schuylkill Navy.   14. Ceremonies at the site of the Humboldt Monument.   15. "Lemonade, ice-cold!"

CELEBRATION OF THE NINETY-NINTH ANNIVERSARY OF THE DECLARATION OF INDEPENDENCE AT FAIRMOUNT PARK

APPEARANCE OF AGRICULTURAL HALL WHILE IN PROCESS OF CONSTRUCTION.

In 1789, Samuel Briggs, of Philadelphia, memorialized the State Legislature of Pennsylvania and General Congress on the subject of a machine for making nails, screws and gimlets, and deposited with them, in a box, a model of his nail-machine. In August, 1794, he, with his son, received the first patent for a nail-making machine issued by the United States. A second patent of the same kind was granted in February, 1797, to Thomas Perkins, in Philadelphia.

GLASS.

The introduction of the manufacture of glass in the United States was contemporaneous with the settlement of the country. With the establishment of the first colony in Jamestown, in 1607, some of the colonists brought over with them "trials" of pitch, tar, glass, frankincense, and soap ashes. The first glass manufactory was set up in the woods about a mile from Jamestown, Va.

In 1621 a fund was subscribed to establish a factory of glass beads, to be used as currency in the trade with the Indians for furs.

In the settlements of Massachusetts, the first establishment of a glass manufactory is said to have been made at Germantown, near Braintree. Glass bottles alone were said to have been made here, and the business was carried on until the Revolution, when the buildings were destroyed by fire. In 1639 a glass-house was established at Salem, and the Court granted several acres of ground adjoining the house for the purpose of aiding the enterprise. In 1641 the Court further authorized the authorities of Salem to lend the proprietors £30, to be deducted from the next town-rate, and to be paid by the borrowers if the work succeeded. Bottles and inferior kinds of glass were made here.

The use of glass was not common in the old country, and, of course, not in the colonies. In 1752 the General Court of Massachusetts passed an Act granting the sole privilege of making glass in the province to Isaac C. Wesley. In New York some little glass was manufactured, and a glass-house is named as existing in Philadelphia in 1683. The business did not, however, assume any importance in the country before the Revolution, although glass was one of the articles taxed by the mother country. Lord Sheffield, writing to England, says, "There are glass-works in Pennsylvania, and glass is made in New Jersey; but there is no quantity of glass made in America as yet but bottles."

In 1788 the New York Legislature voted a loan of £3,000, for eight years, to the proprietors of a glass factory near Albany, which, in 1797, became the Hamilton Glass Factory, and was exempted from taxation by the State for five years. In Pittsburgh, which is at present the most important centre of the production of glass in this country, the first factory was begun in 1795. Among the papers of General O'Hara, whose name was given to the great O'Hara

ADORNING THE TOWERS OF THE MAIN BUILDING.

Glass-works at Pittsburgh, was found at his death a memorandum, "To-day we made the first bottle, at a cost of $30,000."

POTTERY.

In colonial times, wooden dishes and pewter platters were used almost entirely; and the grandmothers of the present generation took as great a pride in keeping their pewter dishes brilliantly polished as is now felt in having gold and silver in the same condition. In fact, it is only within this century that china and porcelain have come into general use. Potters, however, came out from England with the first settlers, both with the Plymouth and Virginia colonists. The Dutch, too, in their settlements in New York and the adjacent country, introduced the making of pottery; and such manufactories were established in the different colonies. An extensive bed of kaoline was discovered in 1810, and a company was organized for the purpose of making porcelain. In 1819, the manufacture of fine porcelain was commenced in New York, and in 1827 a manufactory in Pennsylvania brought this industry to an extensive and successful point of development.

The first factory in this country of American Queen's ware was set up in 1825; and even at that time our manufactures were claimed to be second only to those of France.

HATS.

Among the industries of America, the manufacture of hats has always held a prominent position. As early as 1662, the colonial government of Virginia offered a premium of ten pounds of tobacco for every hat made in the province. In 1672, some hatters in Massachusetts attempted to obtain from the General Court the exclusive privilege of the manufacture. Protection was early applied to the raw material of this manufacture. In 1675, the exportation was prohibited, and, in 1704, the hat-makers were given leave to introduce a bill for the prohibition of the exportation of goods for the manufacture of felt; and, in 1731, the felt-makers of London complained to Parliament that the foreign markets were supplied from America, and therefore they petitioned to have the export of hats from America into foreign markets prohibited. In consequence, a special committee was appointed to examine the subject, and reported that in New England and New York as many as ten thousand hats were weekly made and exported to all parts. Parliament enacted that "no hats, or felts, dyed or un dyed, finished or unfinished, shall be put on board any vessel, or in any place for exportation from thence to any other place whatever, under pain of forfeiture thereof," and the offender was likewise to pay £500 for every such offence. This remained in force until abrogated by the Revolution. Its effect, however, though intended to be the destruction of the manufacture of hats in the colonies, failed in that direction, as large manufactories were still maintained and the goods imported.

FOREIGN VISITORS TO THE CENTENNIAL EXPOSITION—OFFICERS OF THE SPANISH ENGINEER CORPS PROMENADING CHESTNUT STREET, PHILADELPHIA.

After the successful termination of the Revolution, the business increased steadily, and before 1800 was carried on in every State of the Union. By the census of 1810, returns were made of the manufacture of hats to the value of $4,323,744. In 1831, a convention estimated the hat manufacture at fifteen millions yearly.

SILK.

Silk culture was proposed by James I. on the settlement of Virginia, and that monarch sent supplies of silkworms' eggs from his private stores to the colony. This industry

another to Lord Chesterfield, and the third was the dress of Mrs. Harvey.

In 1837, in a report of the Congressional Committee on Manufactures, it was stated that it had been found practicable to raise mulberry-trees and silkworms in the United States. One specimen of the *moris multicalis* would sustain sufficient silk-worms to raise 120 lbs of silk, worth $640. The New England States were all of them engaged in the manufacture, and the Governments of these encouraged the industry by bounties. In all the States much interest was felt in the subject.

THE EXPRESS BUSINESS.

One of the most remarkable industries ever prosecuted in any country—of neither an agricultural or a manufacturing character — certainly deserves a place in this sketch.

The express business is a vast transportation agency, which, from the smallest possible beginning, has in less than half a century extended its Briarean arms over this entire country, and has even reached across oceans to most distant lands, prosecuting with perfect safety, celer-

PLACING THE COLOSSAL BRONZE STATUES OF PEGASUS IN FRONT OF MEMORIAL HALL.

was not, however, confined to Virginia; but every one of the colonies became interested, and more or less silk was raised in all, from Massachusetts to Georgia. In 1788, the President of Yale College wore at the commencement of the college a silk gown made from materials raised and woven in Connecticut. Various specimens of silk were raised, one of which is an entire dress in the possession of Mrs. Harvey, of South Carolina, which was made from a piece of silk manufactured from silk raised near Charleston in 1755, and from which three dresses were made, one of which was presented to the Princess Dowager of Wales,

In 1838 the speculation in mulberry-trees culminated, the excitement in this horticultural mania having risen to a height never before equaled, except by that of the John Law Mississippi scheme in France, or the great "Tuber" excitement in England and Holland. Single mulberry-trees sold at $10 each, and everybody went wild over the business. A grand revulsion followed, and most of the nurseries were abandoned or destroyed. Two years later, *moris multicalis* trees, healthy and well branched, were offered at three cents each, and even at that price found no buyers.

ity, and economy a trade of the greatest possible importance to commerce and civilization.

In 1839, William F. Harnden, of Boston, at the instance of some friends, advertised that he would make regular trips as a messenger between Boston and New York, by the Providence Railroad, and the steamboat from there to New York, and would take personal charge of such small packages or orders as should be entrusted to him. In accordance with this announcement, Harnden made his first trip on the 4th of March, 1839, being freighted with a few packages of books from booksellers, some orders, and certain

DECORATING THE MAIN BUILDING.

amounts ot money from the brokers, in Southern and Western bank-notes, to exchange and deliver. From this time Mr. Harnden found himself engaged in a constantly increasing and lucrative business. He made contracts with the railroad and steamboat companies, increased the frequency of his trips, and, with a masterly display of shrewdness, at once gained the favor of the Press by bringing them matter in advance of the mails. The advantages of this system were promptly recognized by the mercantile interests of the two cities, and soon his business increased to such an extent that it became necessary to organize it on a larger scale.

About the same time that Mr. Harnden started his enterprise, a similar express was commenced by Alvin Adams, and another, designed to connect Boston and New York by the Northern and Western lines. In the beginning of this undertaking, a carpet-bag was sufficient for the accommodation of the entire business; and from this has grown the vast Adams Express business with its immense capital, its trains of cars, armies and relays of assistants, and widely-extended business connections.

The foreign express business was established in 1840 by an agent visiting England. The following year it was extended to Philadelphia and Albany. A year or two later, the line was commenced between Philadelphia and Washington, and a third express from Boston and New York by the New York and Fall River line. From Albany to Buffalo, thence to other cities of the West, express lines were established by the different firms of Wells & Co., Wells, Fargo & Co., etc. In 1849, Adams & Co. extended their line to California, and, in 1852, Wells, Fargo & Co., theirs. In 1854, Adams & Co., Harnden Express Co., Kinsley & Co., and Hoey & Co., were consolidated in the Adams Express Co., whose capital was $1,200,000. At present, the entire capital invested in the business is supposed to be in the neighborhood of thirty million dollars.

LADIES' SHOES.

The manufacture of ladies' shoes in this country began early in colonial times, and the town of Lynn, in Massachusetts, has been distinguished for this branch of industry almost from the landing of the Pilgrims. The first shoemakers in Lynn are said to have been Philip Kertland and Thomas Bridges, in 1635. At first, women's shoes were made in Lynn of woolen cloth or neat leather only. A pair of white silk were made for the wedding-day and preserved afterward. In 1750, the report of the excellence of the shoes made gave an impetus to the business, which soon became the most important industry in the town. Until quite recently, shoes, both for men and women's wear, were made entirely by hand, and generally by individual workmen, working independently of one another. The shoes were made with sharp toes and wooden heels covered with leather. These were made until about 1800, when they were discarded for leather heels.

The shoemakers' shop of the olden time was generally from four to twelve feet square, and was occupied by berths, as the space for the workmen was called, these berths being, in fact, shoemakers' benches.

The first invention of any importance in this branch of industry was the pegging-machine. Pegged shoes, made by hand, were manufactured in large quantities a long time before the invention of this machine; but the machine was confined to coarser work. The next important invention was the last-machine, which was invented by Elias Howe, and patented in 1846. Prior to this, ladies' shoes were bound by hand; but these improvements revolutionized this department of industry. Another important invention was the McKay sewing-machine, an invention for stitching the uppers and soles together.

In 1870, Lynn produced 187,530 cases of boots and shoes,

of sixty pairs each, being 11,250,000 pairs, valued at $17,000,000.

COMBS.

The manufacture of combs is one of more importance than might at first be supposed, and has been a considerable industry in the United States for more than a century. The colonists imported their combs from England, but in 1759 the first iron comb manufactory in the country was in existence at West Newbury, in Massachusetts, where the business is still extensively carried on. In the same year, a manufactory in Pennsylvania advertised combs at wholesale and retail. In 1793, there was a comb factory in Boston, and two or three in Leominster, Mass. The first machine for making combs was patented by Isaac Tryon in 1798. As the importation of combs almost entirely ceased, the domestic manufacture was proportionately increased. In 1809, three manufactories were established in Connecticut.

At first the teeth were cut singly by a fine steel saw; but in 1814 one of the Leominster manufacturers secured a patent of a saw that would cut all the teeth at one operation. Another patent was granted to a Philadelphia manufacturer in 1818.

The invention of vulcanized India-rubber, and experiments in hard rubber, resulted in the discovery that this was one of the best and cheapest materials for making combs; and very superior and highly-finished combs are now made extensively of this material.

CARDS.

The construction, by machinery, of cards used in the manufacture of cotton and woolen cloths is one of the novelties of modern industry; and the machine with which this difficult and delicate process is performed is an American contribution to industrial progress. During the colonial period of our history, these cards were manufactured by hand-labor, and were an important branch of industry, continuing in use until this century. In 1775, Anthony Niles, of Norwich, Conn., set up a manufactory for making wires to be used in the manufacture of cards, and the Assembly

granted him a loan of £300 for four years. In 1777, Oliver Evans invented a machine for manufacturing cards, which is said to have produced them at the rate of three hundred a minute. In 1788, a firm in Boston commenced their manufacture with machinery, which it is said was invented by Evans. In 1784, a machine was invented which cut and bent the teeth, and was capable of producing 86,000 in an hour.

At first dog-power was used for cutting the teeth by machinery. The dog ran six machines, each of which cut twelve pounds in a day. These teeth were put up in boxes and distributed among many persons, who stuck the teeth into the cards and returned them complete.

ARTILLERY.

The manufacture of artillery had commenced in the colonies as early as 1664, when cannon and cannon-balls were cast in Massachusetts. In 1748, a factory at Bridgewater made guns of from 3 to 42-pounders. During the Revolution, cannon, cannon-balls, and shell were made in Massachusetts, Rhode Island, Connecticut, New Jersey, Pennsylvania, and Maryland. William Denning made a very effective wrought-iron gun of iron staves, hooped and boxed and breeched like other cannon. In 1810 there were several factories in the country which cast shot and shell, and in Richmond, Va., three establishments were constructed, each of them able to turn out pieces of artillery at the rate of three hundred a year. In 1813, a brass foundry at Watervliet made cannon by contract. Up to 1857, about 300,000 cannon and other implements of war had been cast in this country.

WALL-PAPER.

The first mention of wall-paper manufactured in this country was in 1765, but within ten years of that date there were manufactories of wall-paper in New Jersey, Pennsylvania, Massachusetts, and other States. In 1789, the manufacture of this article in Philadelphia had reached the production of 16,000 pieces a month—a quantity which would scarcely be a day's work in some establishments now. The paper of domestic manufacture, however, was of inferior quality.

The first patterns with glazed grounds were made in the United States in 1824; and soon after this the very best French designs began to be imitated here.

At first the paper was made in sheets, not more than 30 inches in length, and the printing was done by hand, block after block, each of the different colors used being printed in succession. The introduction of new paper-making machines, however, gave the rolls a length of from 1,000 to 2,000 yards, and from 20 to 40 inches in width. In 1843, an American machine was invented for printing in two colors; and, ten years later, one for six colors; while now there are machines that will print twenty and more colors at one operation.

JEWELRY.

Providence is the chief seat of this great industry, although it is prosecuted very heavily in a number of other towns in Connecticut and Rhode Island.

As early as 1810, a jewelry manufacturer, of Providence, was reported as employing over 100 workmen, with an annual production of $100,000. At present that city gives employment in this business to nearly 2,000 men and women.

IRON.

The manufacture of iron in the colonies dates from a period very soon after the first settlements. In 1620, there were iron-works at Falling Creek, in the Jamestown

PAINTING THE ORNAMENTS FOR THE TOWERS.

1. Visit of the Centennial Committee of the Stock Exchange, the Board of Fire Underwriters, and the Representatives of the Banks of New York City to Memorial Hall.　2. Address of Rev. Mr. Musgrove from the pedestal of the Witherspoon Monument.　3. Statue of Witherspoon.　4. Oration of Rev. Mr. Adams, in Machinery Building.　5. Painting the galvanized iron eagles for the corners of Memorial Hall.

SCENES AND INCIDENTS ON THE CENTENNIAL GROUNDS, FAIRMOUNT PARK, MONDAY, NOVEMBER 15th, 1875.

ARCHITECTS PREPARING PLANS AND DRAWINGS OF CENTENNIAL BUILDINGS AT THE ARCHITECTS' HEADQUARTERS.

River. In the following year the entire company were massacred by the Indians, except a young boy and girl, who managed to escape. This unfortunate event stopped the manufacture of iron in that locality, and it was not there revived until the year 1712.

In 1663, the General Court of Massachusetts granted certain persons the sole right and privilege of making iron for twenty years, allowing them the use of certain lands on which to set up their furnaces and forges. It is stated that the first factory established in that State was erected in Lynn. The village about the works was called Hammersmith, after the place of the same name in England, and from which many of the workmen here had emigrated. Operations were continued here for more than a century. The first article of iron said to have been cast in this country was made at these works, and was a small iron pot, capable of holding about a quart.

In 1750, there were in existence in this country three iron-mills and one furnace. Rolling-mills were chiefly employed in making nail-rods to be worked up by hand. The description of a furnace erected in 1794, in the town of Carver, Mass., mentions that ten forges were there employed for making bar-iron from scraps, to the extent of 200 tons annually. The furnace was 20 ft. high and 8 ft. wide. The blast was produced by two bellows, each 22 ft. long and 4 ft. wide, and driven by a water-wheel. Every six months, two or three blasts, continuing for sixteen or eighteen weeks, were made, each producing about 1,600 tons of hollow ware and other articles. This furnace produced, in addition, iron cylinders for slitting-mills, potash-kilns, stoves, large hammers, cannon-balls, and a great variety of machinery for mills. During the continuance of the Revolution, the increased demand for iron in the manufacture of weapons

of all kinds and for domestic consumption, together with the total stoppage of all foreign supplies, caused an enormous increase in the production of this commodity.

CORDAGE.

The manufacture of cordage was one of the first industries that early engaged the attention of the colonists. In the occupations laid out in London, in 1620, for the Virginia settlers, especial mention is made of the manufacture of cordage from hemp, flax, and especially from "silk-grass," which was said to be superior for the purpose; and, by enactment, every family was required to cultivate it. The thin hemp of New England, which the Indians used, soon attracted the attention of the Puritan settlers, who employed it; and, in the year 1629, hemp-seed for cultivation was received from the mother country. It was, however, thirty years later before the colonists of Massachusetts and Connecticut took any decided step in the matter of raising hemp, especially for cordage for ship-rigging, although John Harrison had made cordage in Boston as early as 1631, and

John Heyman was authorized to make ropes and lines in Charleston in 1662. The business soon spread rapidly through the colonies, and, in the year 1698, there were several ropewalks in Philadelphia.

Providence and Newport were also early engaged in the manufacture of cordage, and in 1730 had several manufactories in operation. In 1794, Virginia, as well as Maryland, had more ropewalks than any two of the Northern and Eastern States.

A spinning and twisting mill for making cordage was patented in the United States in 1804. In 1808, the Massachusetts manufacturers petitioned Congress for duty on the imported articles, though much of the flax worked into cordage came from abroad. In 1810, the domestic manufacture of cordage of all kinds was claimed to be fully equal to the home demand; and, besides the many manufactories on the Atlantic coast, Kentucky had at that time fifteen ropewalks. In 1811, though the country was still importing immense quantities of hemp from abroad, and principally from Russia, the Secretary of the Navy, in a report, advised an annual appropriation for hemp for the use of the navy.

There was in use at this time, in this country, a machine in which the threads were passed through perforated iron plates, and through iron tubes, of different dimensions, for various sizes of ropes. In 1834, a new machine was introduced in New York, which spun rope-yarn from hemp, without the usual *hatcheling* process, and thus saved from 8 to 10 per cent. of the material. And so, from the earliest manufacture of cordage, rapid progress has been made—from the use of horse-power to that of steam-power—until the latest improvements enable the largest ropes to be made as well as the smallest twine, and a single establishment can make all the rigging for the use of the largest ship.

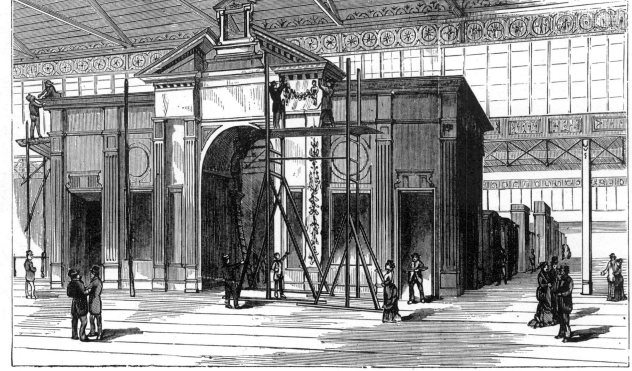

SPANISH PAVILION.

THE CONNECTICUT STATE BUILDING.

THE OHIO STATE BUILDING.

PAPER.

The first paper-mill in America, of which we have any account, was erected at Roxborough, near Germantown, in Pennsylvania, as early as the year 1693. This was fifty years after printing had been introduced into the colonies, but only five or six years after a proclamation had been issued by the English Government for the establishment of the first manufactory of white paper in England. This establishment was built by an ancestor of David Rittenhouse—whose family in Holland had long been engaged in the manufacture of paper—and William Bradford, the first printer in Philadelphia. All papers were made here until the paper-mill was carried away by a freshet. In 1728, Bradford, when Government printer in New York, owned a paper-mill in Elizabethtown, in New Jersey, which was probably the second of the kind erected in the colonies—unless the one upon Chester Creek, in Delaware County, Penn., should be so classed. This mill in Delaware County shortly after came into the possession of Mr. Wilcox, and his descendants continued the manufacture of paper by the old hand-process. From this mill the press of Benjamin Franklin was supplied with paper; and, during the Revolution, all the bank-note paper used for the printing of the Continental currency was made here by the hand-process. In 1829, the old mill was taken down and replaced by another, in which paper has continued to be made in the same way.

Benjamin Franklin himself, as was natural, was always greatly interested in the establishment of paper-mills; and after the Revolution, in 1787, he stated that he had been personally concerned in the erection of eighteen of them. In 1769, Pennsylvania, New Jersey, and Delaware are said to have had, together, 40 paper-mills—6 of these being within the present limits of the city of Philadelphia—and the entire number producing annually $100,000 worth of paper of various kinds and qualities.

In 1787, there were 63 mills in operation in all the States. Forty-eight of these were in Pennsylvania, producing, altogether, paper to the value of $250,000 annually.

The first patent for improvement in the process of paper-making, in the United States, was granted to John Carnes, Jr., of Delaware, in April, 1793, for an improvement connected with the molds. The second, in March, 1794, was granted to John Biddis, of Pennsylvania.

It is stated that the first paper-mill in Massachusetts was built in 1717, and that, three years later, the quantity of paper manufactured there was estimated to be worth £200. Another statement made is, that the first paper-mill in Massachusetts was built in 1730, by Daniel Henchman, a bookseller and publisher in Boston. Benjamin Faneuil, Thomas Hancock, and others, were induced to enter into this industry, by being specially encouraged by the terms of the license, which was granted them by the General Court. As was the case with nearly all colonial interests, the English paper merchants, learning, in 1732, that this mill was in successful operation, complained to the British Board of Trade of it, as being an infringement of their business. This mill was built at Milton, a town about seven miles from Boston, and continued in successful operation until the time of the Revolution, though with one or two interruptions from lack of experienced workmen.

The manufacture of paper during the last century, however, although it constantly and steadily increased, never equaled the demand. One of the causes of this was the difficulty of obtaining the necessary supply of rags. In order to stimulate the industry, the American company of booksellers, in 1804, offered gold and silver medals for the greatest quantity and best qualities of printing and wrapping papers made from other material than rags.

Meanwhile, in New York and New England both, the people were urged to preserve their rags, by advertisements and patriotic appeals in both prose and verse; added to which inducements, a considerable price per pound had doubtless something to do with the matter.

Steam-power was first applied in the United States to the manufacture of paper in 1816. The introduction of the Fourdrinier machines has greatly facilitated the manufacture of paper, and made the production of modern times quite able to satisfy the increased demand caused by the wonderful industrial demands of this century.

STOCKINGS AND KNITTING-MACHINES.

Felt, in his "Annals of Salem," gives a list of articles to be exported to New England in 1629, among which are eight hundred pairs of stockings, two hundred of which were to be Irish, and one hundred pairs of knit stockings. The prohibition of the exportation of knitting-frames from the mother country forced the colonists to depend entirely upon hand-labor for stockings and other articles of hosiery. Naturally enough, this labor fell to the women; and up to the present century the chief supply of hosiery for the

WOMEN'S PAVILION, ON BELMONT AVENUE, NEAR THE HORTICULTURAL GROUNDS.

VISCONDE DE JAGUARY, FIRST VICE-PRESIDENT.

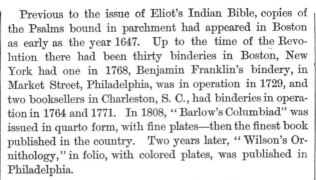

VISCONDE DE BON-RETIRO, SECOND VICE-PRESIDENTE.

inland population of the country was produced by women's fingers in such moments of leisure as they could find during the long Winter evenings. In the year 1662, the Assembly of Virginia voted a premium of 50 ℔s. of tobacco—at that time serving as legal currency in the colony—for every dozen pairs of woolen or worsted stockings. Just before the Revolution, the same State offered 50 ℔s. for every five hundred pairs of men's and women's stockings produced. The knitters of coarse woolen stockings in Pennsylvania received, as a premium, in 1698, half-a-crown a pair. But, notwithstanding the prohibition by the English Government of the exportation of stocking-frames—which, by the way, were invented by William Lee, in England, in the sixteenth century—knitting by their aid was introduced into the colonies a considerable time before the Revolution, the machine being probably brought over by the Germans.

The earliest mention of them is found in the *American Weekly Mercury* for 1723. In 1776, the Committee on Safety, in Maryland, appropriated the sum of £300 to the establishment of a stocking manufactory. Before this, however, the "Society of Arts," in New York, offered a prize of £10 for the first three stocking-looms of yarn set up that year, £5 for the next three, and £15 for the first stocking-loom made in the province. In 1794, a Newark man petitioned Congress for a higher duty to be imposed on hosiery, or for some other protection to that industry.

In the census, taken in 1810, the returns from ten States and Territories reported a manufacture of 481,399 pairs of stockings, valued at $572,742. Of this quantity, Virginia had made almost one-half, the balance being divided between the other States.

In 1831, Timothy Bailie, of Albany, succeeded in applying power to the old stocking-frame, by this means making it a power-loom. This had been repeatedly tried in England, but had been as often abandoned as an impossibility. From this time the industry became changed from a domestic to a factory manufacture.

BOOKBINDING.

The first bookbinding ever done in the colonies was done by John Ratliffe, an Englishman, who is said to have come over for the express purpose of binding Eliot's Indian Bible, printed at Cambridge, Mass., in 1661 and 1663; and Ratliffe was able to bind only a single copy in a day.

The first book printed in Boston was printed in 1676. The early provincial governors generally prohibited printing, as the art, even at that time, was looked upon as a means of disseminating heresies and libels. From 1684 to 1690, several books were published in Boston; in 1686, publications were made in Philadelphia, and, in 1693, in New York.

Previous to the issue of Eliot's Indian Bible, copies of the Psalms bound in parchment had appeared in Boston as early as the year 1647. Up to the time of the Revolution there had been thirty binderies in Boston, New York had one in 1768, Benjamin Franklin's bindery, in Market Street, Philadelphia, was in operation in 1729, and two booksellers in Charleston, S. C., had binderies in operation in 1764 and 1771. In 1808, "Barlow's Columbiad" was issued in quarto form, with fine plates—then the finest book published in the country. Two years later, "Wilson's Ornithology," in folio, with colored plates, was published in Philadelphia.

MANUFACTURE OF SALT.

It has been stated that this manufacture was the earliest in American history, since the colonists of Jamestown, Va., established salt-works in 1620, and as early as 1633 began to send salt to Massachusetts. In 1689, salt was made in South Carolina, and, indeed, since the earliest settlement of the country, it has been produced all along the Atlantic coast from sea-water, in large quantities, by boiling, or natural evaporation—especially during the Revolution, and during the war of 1812, when foreign importations were difficult.

After the Revolution, salt-making by solar evaporation became a very important business on Cape Cod. No less than thirty of the States and Territories are believed to have salt springs. Those of Southern Illinois were worked by the French and Indians in 1720. The Kentucky salt-works were used before 1790. The first salt manufactured in the State of Ohio was in 1798, and the first in Western

HIS HIGHNESS GASTON D'ORLÉANS, PRESIDENT.

Pennsylvania in 1812. It is said that the State of New York now produced more than one-half of the entire domestic supply of this article.

PLOWS.

One of the first persons to make a plow in this country was Thomas Jefferson, who attempted to solve the mathematical problem of the true surface of the mold-board. In the year 1793, Mr. Jefferson had several plows made after his patterns, and used them on his estates in Virginia. The first American after Mr. Jefferson, who made plows for common use, was a farmer, living in New Jersey, by the name of Charles Newbold. He invented the first cast-iron plow made in America. Mr. Newbold is said to have spent upward of $30,000 in trying to introduce his plow, but was forced to abandon it on account of the objection made by farmers, at the time, that the cast-iron plow poisoned the land. It is, perhaps, not generally known that, in about 1836, Daniel Webster invented a plow 12 to 14 inches deep, cutting a furrow 24 inches wide. This plow is still in existence. It is 12 ft. long, the mold-board being of wood,

fitted with thin iron strips. The beam is 28 inches from the ground. Concerning this plow, Mr. Webster remarked:

"When I have hold of the handles of my plow, with four pair of cattle to pull it through, and hear the roots creak and the stumps fall under the ground, and observe the clean, mellow surface of the plowed land, I feel more enthusiasm over my achievement than comes from my encounters in public life at Washington."

GRIST AND FLOUR MILLS.

It is said that the first mill in New England was a wind-mill, near Watertown, Mass., which was taken down in 1632, and was rebuilt in the vicinity of Boston. This mill was removed from its original position because it would not grind but with a westerly wind, and it was therefore set up in the locality known as Copp's Hill, in 1633. The first wind-mill set up in Rhode Island was built, in 1663, at Newport. In New York, the first wind-mill was a horse-mill, which was built, in 1626, on the site now occupied by Trinity Church. A horse-mill also stood for many years on the north side of South William Street, near the corner of Broad.

A wind-mill once stood in the locality now occupied by the present Hall of Records, in the New York City Hall Park.

The Swedes had a wind-mill on the Delaware in 1643, but it appears to have been comparatively little used. This was in the vicinity of Philadelphia. In Virginia, in 1649, were in operation four wind-mills and five water-mills. The first water-mill known in New England is supposed to have been built in 1633, in Dorchester, Mass., and the second, in the same year, at Lynn. The first water-mill erected in the Plymouth colony was put up in January, 1633, and was engaged in grinding corn for the whole colony. The first grist-mill in operation in Pennsylvania was built by Colonel John Pointz, the Governor of New Sweden, in 1643. This was the most ancient water-mill—earlier than any other in Pennsylvania, New Jersey, or Delaware—and stood near the Blue Ball Tavern, where the holes in the rock which supported the posts of the framework are still to be seen. The stream on which it was built is Cobb's Creek, a tributary of Darby Creek, which empties south of Tinicum, of which place Colonel Pointz had a grant from Queen Christina of Sweden. A few years following, a number of corn-mills were erected, at Wissahickon, by the German and English families who had settled in Germantown and Roxborough.

BREWING.

Wine and beer making were among the earliest industries in the colonial part of our history. At the time of the settlements of the American colonies, tea, coffee,

COMMENDADOR FRANCISCO ANTONIO GONZALVES.

CONSᴼ F. J. MARC HOMEN DE MELLO.

COMMENDADOR J. A. DE AZEVEDO, SECRETARY.

MEMBERS OF THE BRAZILIAN COMMISSION TO THE CENTENNIAL EXPOSITION.

and chocolate were almost unknown in England, their place being supplied with fermented liquors.

Ale and beer were originally made without hops, which were first raised in England in 1524. Of course, the early emigrants to America followed the tastes and desires of their ancestors, and brought their previous habits with them. The Court of Assistance, in 1629, mindful of this fact, sent among the outfits to New England, in addition to four hundred-weight of hops, forty-five tons of beer to the Plymouth colony. John Yenny, who came to Plymouth in 1623, was

Massachusetts, set up a malt-house in that State. The practice of using Indian corn was doubtless of American origin, and was probably derived from the Indians, who made artificial drinks from several native products, including maize.

Beer, in 1667, was sold in New England at one penny-ha'penny per quart; and, not very many years after this, beer and distilled spirits were made and exported from New England to the West Indies, Newfoundland, and other of the Continental colonies, in considerable quantities. In

cipal authorities took measures to prohibit the tapping of beer during service, under penalty of £25 for each offence, and of confiscation under the *Schoutfiscall*. Besides, the offender was not allowed to tap beer again for three months following.

In 1644, when New York was harassed by wars with Indians, John Kieft and his council imposed a tax of two guilders on each barrel of beer tapped by the tavern-keepers, and four stuyvers on each quart of Spanish wine. The Swedes, who were among the first settlers in Pennsylvania

ARRIVAL OF A LARGE SPECIMEN OF THE "PHŒNIX SYLVESTRIS," OR EAST INDIAN WILD DATE PALM, AT HORTICULTURAL HALL.

a brewer by trade, and a proprietor of one of the early established corn-mills. In 1639, the General Court of Massachusetts decided that no person should brew beer, malt, or other drink for sale at wholesale or retail, unless specially licensed by the Court and on payment of £100. By the same Act, the Court licensed Captain Sedgwick to brew beer during the pleasure of the Court. This seems to be the earliest mention of a brew-house.

Ten years later, there were six public beer-houses in Virginia. In 1640, John Appleton, one of the first settlers in

New York, in 1633, the Dutch West India Company, through their director, Wouter Van Twiller, caused the erection of a brewery upon a farm, which extended from the present Wall Street limits westward as far as Hudson Street. Its site was the north side of what is now known as Bridge Street, between Broad and Whitehall.

The distillation of brandy commenced in 1640—probably the first instance of its manufacture in the colonies. In the following year, drunkards had become so alarmingly prevalent, particularly on the Sabbath-day, that the muni-

and Delaware, made beer and brandy, and also brewed small beer from Indian corn. The brewing was done by the women mainly, as is customary in Sweden and in other parts of Europe.

The Dutch had several breweries in 1662. William Penn built a splendid mansion-house on his manor at Pennsborough, attached to which was a malt-house, brew-house, and bakery, all under one roof. This brew-house was standing not many years ago. About the first brewery in Baltimore was set up in 1744. In Virginia, as has already

HEADQUARTERS OF THE PENNSYLVANIA STATE COMMISSIONERS.

been mentioned, there were six public brew-houses in 1649, but most of the families brewed their own beer. The old custom of having the beer for the household brewed by the women appears to have been brought over by the colonists.

Peach brandy was, during colonial times, a household manufacture of considerable value, and much of it was exported. Breweries were established in the Carolinas, and distilleries were common. The manufacture of beer was also common in all parts of Virginia. Pale ale and porter were first made in this country about the year 1774.

MANUFACTURE OF WINE.

The early colonists found the vine growing wild in the woods, often climbing the loftiest trees. Even the earliest narratives of the Norse voyagers to America speak of the quantity and variety of the vines; and a portion of the continent was called by them "Vineland." As early as 1610, however, mention is made of the French sent over to Virginia for the sole purpose of making preparations to plant vines, which were there as common as brambles in the woods. A sample of wine made from native grapes was sent over in 1612. In the year 1621, a company sent thither a number of French vine-dressers, with a large supply of plants and cuttings from European vines. They reported the locality as far excelling their country, the vines growing in great variety and abundance all over the land. These Frenchmen were not, however, successful, although, previous to the massacre in 1622, they succeeded in making a small quantity of wine.

Wine of good quality was made in Virginia in 1649, or earlier, by a member of the Council. In New England, Governor Winthrop planted a vineyard by 1630; and the use of Governor's Island, in Boston Harbor, was granted in 1633, on condition that the grantee plant there a vineyard—which he did in 1634—and pay a hogshead of wine yearly. Vines were sent in the year 1642 to the New Netherlands, by Van Rensselaer, for the use of his colony on the Hudson, but they were all of them killed by the frost. In the Carolinas, the cultivation of the wine-grape was a prominent object in the settlements about the year 1670, under a grant from Charles II. to the Earl of Clarendon and others. The proprietors of these sent over vines and competent persons to arrange them. This attempt, however, was unsuccessful; as was also the second attempt, made in 1679. About the year 1690 King William sent large numbers of persecuted French refugees into Virginia. These attempted the manufacture of wine, and were partially successful. Wherever the Huguenots settled in America they planted vineyards.

William Penn seems to have cherished very warmly the hope of introducing the manufacture of wine into his State, and on a portion of his own property in the northwestern part of the city of Philadelphia, toward the Schuylkill River, a vineyard was planted by his direction on the mountain known as "Vineyard Hill." In order the better to conduct the business, he imported a competent person from France, and sustained him at considerable expense. It is generally believed that he was not rewarded by any success in the venture, and he abandoned the enterprise in 1695.

On the settlements in Georgia, the last

colonists of the original thirteen States, in 1732 attempts were made to produce wine, and a number of foreign vine-dressers were sent thither by the trustees of the provinces. The project was, however, at length abandoned.

It will thus be seen that the efforts to introduce successful wine manufacture in the colonies were regarded with interest abroad and at home, and the disappointment at the want of success following each attempt was seriously felt.

CLOTH MANUFACTURE.

Owing to the difficulty in the way of a continued and steady intercourse with England, and there being twenty to thirty thousand people inhabiting the colonies to be clothed, the attention of the colonists was turned at an early period of their settlement to the manufacture of their own woolen and linen cloths. The earliest order of the Court, which we find, was made by the Massachusetts Assembly in 1640, when the magistrates and deputies of the several towns were required to investigate the facilities existing for spinning and weaving, and what course it might be well to take for teaching boys and girls in the spinning and weaving of yarn, and of carding wool. A description of cloth, for the manufacture of which this act of the Court was designed to prepare the way, was a mixture known as fustian, dimity, etc. In the same year, 1640, an order of the Court offered a bounty on every shilling's worth of linen, woollen, and cotton cloth made in the colonies. Under this order, in 1641, certain persons were granted a bounty for their manufacture, which appears to have been the first sample of cloth ever made in the country. This was probably a coarse description of linen. In 1642 the different towns of New England agreed to take cotton-wool in certain quantities, and the price was fixed by two inspectors in each town being appointed to arrange this. In 1644 the first regular or systematic attempt at the manufacture of cloth, particularly woolen, was made by a company of Yorkshiremen, who were settled at Rowley, in Massachusetts, between Ipswich and Newbury. Here was built the first fulling-mill erected in the colonies, and this

appears to have been the first place in which woolen cloth was made in New England.

At this time cotton was obtained from Barbadoes, while hemp and flax were grown native. This very early effort of the young community to become independent in the manufacture of clothing derives peculiar incident from the fact that it involves the earliest mention of the use by the European population in America of the material cotton. Clothing manufacture, however, made but slow progress in the other colonies. In 1713 there was but one clothier established in Connecticut, and much of the cloth was worn unsheared and unpressed. Among the settlers of New Sweden fairs were established in 1686, where woolen and linen products are said to have been exhibited and sold; and three years before this, William Penn, in a letter to the "Free Society of Traders," refers especially to the manufacture of linen in the State of Pennsylvania. A variety of linen and woolen stuffs are mentioned as the manufactures of the Germans in Pennsylvania in 1698, such as druggets, serges, etc., and it is stated that the pay of Germantown tailors was twelve shillings per week and their diet.

In 1650, in Virginia, a Captain Matthews was a great cultivator of hemp and flax, which he also manufactured into cloth. Silk and cotton had also already been attempted there, and had been recommended to the attention of the planters. Several vegetable dye-stuffs had all been tested. In 1662 the Assembly of Virginia enacted several laws for the promotion of all industries, and particularly in the relation of cloth. Flaxseed was ordered imported from England to be distributed to each county. Two pounds of tobacco were offered for every pound of flax or hemp prepared for the spindle; three pounds for every article of linen cloth; and five pounds for every article of woolen cloth. Every titheable person was required to produce here two pounds of dressed flax or hemp. After the year 1684 another law was enacted in Virginia for the encouragement of the manufacture of linen and woolen cloth. The first fulling machinery was erected in Virginia in 1692, during the administration of Andros, who particularly recommended the encouragement of the growth and manufacture of cotton. His successor, however, opposed the raising of cotton, and asked Parliament to prevent it. This fact warrants the presumption that at this time the amount of manufactured goods in the colonies was such as to injuriously affect the importation of English goods.

In 1708 a member of the Council of New York wrote to the British Board of Trade that he had labored to divert the Americans from going on with their linen and woolen manufactures. He said, further, that they were all so far advanced that three-fourths of what they used were made among them—especially the coarse sort—and if some effectual means of stopping it be not found, they will carry it on a great deal further, and perhaps in time produce our manufactures at home.

In 1706 it was stated that the great scarcity, in the colonies, of woolen goods, which then sold at 200 per cent. advance on the cost, had forced the colonists to set up a very considerable manufactory for stuffs, kerseys, linsey-woolseys, flannels, buttons, etc., by which the importation of these goods was soon decreased £50,000 per annum. The descriptions of cloth

LOST IN WONDER.

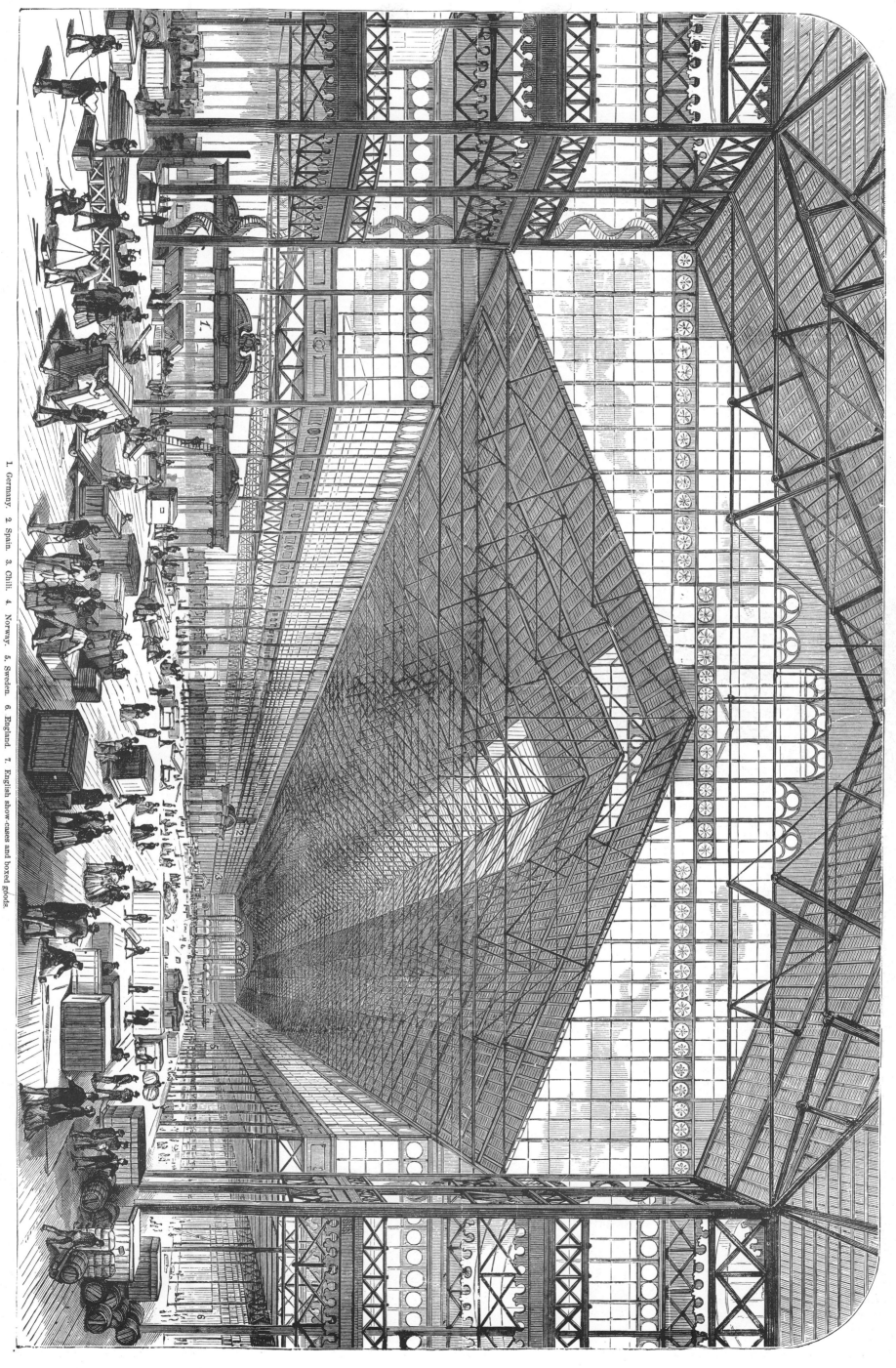

INTERIOR OF THE MAIN BUILDING SHOWING THE VARIOUS PAVILIONS AND SHOW-CASES CONSTRUCTED AND IN PROCESS OF ERECTION.

1. Germany. 2 Spain. 3. Chili. 4. Norway. 5. Sweden. 6. England. 7. English show-cases and boxed goods.

BUILDING THE CIRCULAR RAILWAY.

PLANTING EVERGREENS IN FRONT OF HORTICULTURAL HALL.

made at this time in America were chiefly those mentioned above, and generally they were the coarser kinds. Cotton was regularly imported in small quantities, chiefly from the Barbadoes, and occasionally, also, from Smyrna and other places to which trade had extended, and was made into fustians and other similar stuffs. But linen then subserved nearly all the purposes for which cotton is now employed, and hence the attention given to the cultivation of flax and hemp. The linens made at that time were for the most part of a very coarse texture. The kerseys, linsey-woolseys, serges, and druggets consisted of wool combined with flax and tow, and these formed the outer clothing of a large part of the population of the country. Hempen cloth and linen of different grades of fineness, from the coarsest tow cloth to the finest Osnaburg of Holland, constituted the principal wearing apparel, outward and inward, at most times. The under garments and the table-linen were almost entirely supplied from the serviceable products of the household industry. As the implements of manufacture then in use were comparatively rude, and many modern processes of manufacture and finish were as yet unknown, the fabrics, whether woolen or linen, were more remarkable for service than for elegance. The material

COUNTRY VISITORS—THE NOON LUNCH.

was usually grown upon the farms of the planters; and the breaking and hackling being done by the men, while the carding, spinning, weaving, bleaching and dyeing were performed by the wives and daughters of the planters, these useful products of the household were an object of pride and emulation with all thrifty families.

The dress of the apprentices and laborers in the last century almost invariably comprised shirts of Ozenbrig, made of hemp and flax, and varying in price from one shilling to one shilling and sixpence per yard, and vests and breeches of the same. Coats, or doublets, and breeches of leather or buckskin, and coats also of kersey, drugget, frieze, etc.; felt hats, coarse leather shoes, with buckles of brass and wooden heels, and coarse yarn or worsted stockings, were the common outward habiliments of that class of home manufacture. The differences of rank were pretty clearly defined, and the dresses of the middle and wealthier classes generally corresponded with the tastes of each. With the former class, domestic fabrics were much worn, and particularly the finer class of Osnaburg and Holland, and cloths of mixed and unmixed wool, such as they possessed the means either of making or of purchasing. They also frequently used imported broadcloths, which, however, were often worn white or undyed. The dresses of the rich consisted of the woolen manufactures of England, and the linens of Ireland. Scot-

land, and the Continent. Even silks, which were then much in vogue, formed quite a considerable part of their clothing, where it was permitted; and the price of a good farm was sometimes paid for a fashionable outfit.

Cottons and calicoes, introduced into America about the latter part of the seventeenth century, were for a time rendered very cheap here by an Act of Parliament passed in the year 1721, at the instance of wool manufacturers, by which the wearing of painted or dyed cotton goods was prohibited — excepting blue cloaks, muslins or fustians.

About the year 1719 a considerable improvement was made in the manufacture of linen in this country, by a number of Protestant people from the north of Ireland. The principal body of these emigrants were from the vicinity of Londonderry, in Ireland — to the number of sixteen families — and they settled in New Hampshire, where they commenced the raising of flax and the manufacture of linen.

In 1728 Sir William Keith presented a plan of government for the colonies to the King, which was referred to

THE GUIDE-BOOK BOYS.

THE LATEST ATTRACTION.

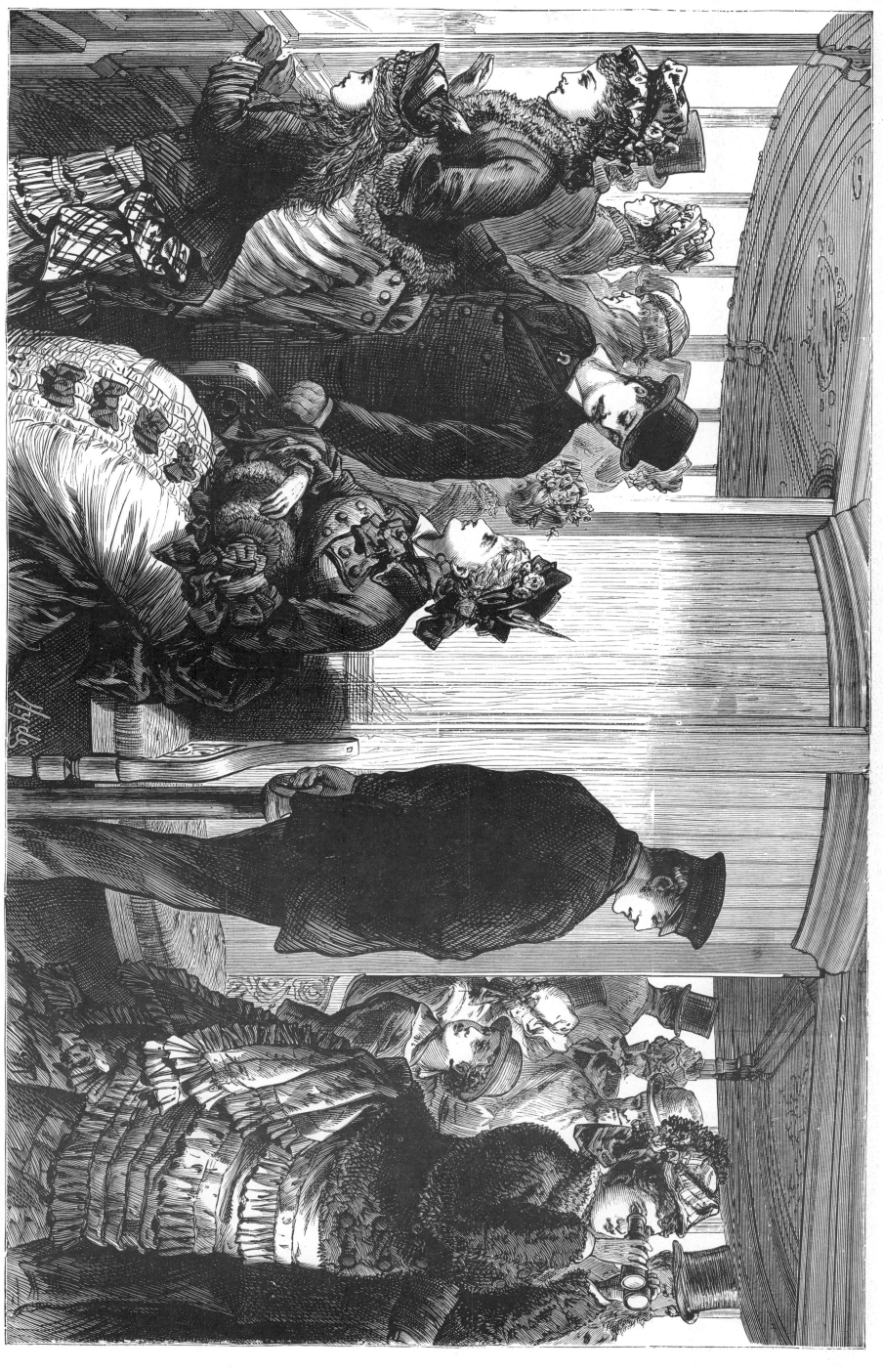

A RIDE IN THE ELEVATOR ON BELMONT HILL, FAIRMOUNT PARK—TAKING A BIRD'S-EYE VIEW OF THE EXPOSITION BUILDING.

OPENING OF THE CENTENNIAL YEAR AT PHILADELPHIA—RAISING THE OLD COLONIAL FLAG ON INDEPENDENCE HALL.

UNPACKING ARTICLES FOR THE ENGLISH DEPARTMENT.

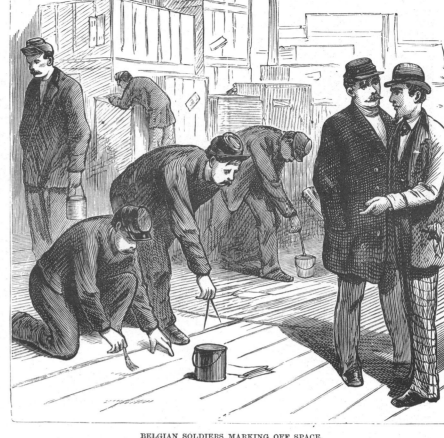

BELGIAN SOLDIERS MARKING OFF SPACE.

six commissioners of trade. After recommending the same exclusive policy as to the commerce of the country, he points out the advantages derived from them. He shows that the luxuries of the colonists are daily increased, they consuming great quantities of English silks, haberdashery and printed and woven goods of all sorts, and a considerable quantity of East India goods. A report made to the House of Commons by the Board of Trade on Colonial Industries, in 1731, stated that in the American colonies the settlers had fallen into the manufacture of woolen cloths and linen cloths, but for the use of their own families only; that the very high price of labor rendered it impracticable for them to manufacture such articles at less than twenty per cent. dearer than that exported from England; that the greater part of the clothing worn in the province of Massachusetts Bay was imported from Great Britain, and sometimes from Ireland; that there were a few hat-makers, only in the maritime towns; that there were no manufactures in New York worth mentioning, nor in New Jersey; that the chief trade of Pennsylvania lay in the importation of provisions, no manufactures being established, and their clothing and utensils for their houses all imported from England; that in Massachusetts Bay some manufactures were carried on, as brown holland for women's ware, which lessens the importation of cloaks and some other sorts of East India goods.

Concerning the woolen manufacture, the country people, who used to make the most of their clothing out of their wool, did not then make a third part of what they wore, but they were mainly clothed with British manufactures. It is believed, however, that this report fell considerably short of a correct statement of the extent to which domestic manufactures were even at that time carried on in the colonies. There were excellent reasons why the truth should not have been made known in England, and it is

alleged that it was with the greatest difficulty that the officers of the Government were able to procure true information concerning the trade and manufactures of the American colonies.

Meanwhile, in the Southern States of Carolina and Virginia, scarcely any progress had yet been made towards the

THE VENDER OF CENTENNIAL FLAGS.

supply of their own clothing; while Georgia made scarcely any progress in the mechanical arts before the Revolution. In Virginia it is stated that the profits of the tobacco culture were exceedingly large, while all their clothing was received from England. Hides were very plentiful, and were suffered to lie and rot—and that man was considered a rare economist who made a pair of leather breeches from the deerskins which abounded.

There is mention made, however, in 1721 of a coarse stuff for servants' wear, known by the name of Virginia cloth. An article of that name is mentioned as having been brought to great perfection in that State after the war. It was generally woven by the women of the country, and being brought to town, it was much sought after for the use of slaves, it being considered much superior to anything of the kind imported.

Up to 1763 it does not appear that any material advances were made towards the introduction of the manufacture of cloth. Great Britain and her colonies were then principally occupied with wars with the French and Indians; and, while commerce and the fisheries grew, this industry was totally neglected. The importations of English manufactures continued to augment with the constantly growing wealth and luxury of the people to the full extent of their ability to purchase. Large quantities of woolens, druggets, serges, flannels, Scotch plaids, and hosiery were imported, with linens of English, Scotch, Irish, and Dutch manufacture, and India goods, including silks. The cheaper and coarser kinds, particularly of woolens, were for the Indian trade and for negro wear. Gold and silver, and fine Flanders laces, French cambrics and chintzes, for the use of the planters' families, swelled the importations to a large sum.

Some efforts were continued to be made to work up the wool which the sheep supplied, but not in sufficient

THE JUDGES' PAVILION.

CENTENNIAL WORKMEN AT DINNER.

THE TRANSPORTATION OF FOREIGN GOODS TO THE MAIN BUILDING.

1. Main Building. 2. Custom House. 3. Judges' Pavilion. 4. Machinery Hall. 5. Catholic Temperance Fountain. 6. Spanish Building. 7. Japanese Building. 8. British Building. 9. New York State Building.

UNLOADING, FROM THE "VATERLAND," OF A PORTION OF THE MACHINERY FOR THE BELGIAN DEPARTMENT.

quantities for home consumption. Although in the main, the colonists were simple and frugal in their habits, yet the progress in luxuries of all kinds was sufficient to cause a rapid increase in general trade and commerce. In 1749 a society was formed in Boston for promoting industry and frugality.

COTTON.

Cotton seeds were first planted in the American colonies in 1621. In the provinces of Carolina the growth of the cotton plant was introduced in 1666. In 1736 it was grown in Maryland, and four years afterwards it was cultivated in Cape May. It was, however, not cultivated, except as a garden plant, until after the Revolutionary war, although at the commencement of the war one party is said to have had thirty acres under cultivation. A small shipment of cotton was made in the year 1754, and in 1770 three more, amounting to ten bales in the aggregate. In 1784 eight boxes, about to be shipped to England, were seized on the ground that so much cotton could not be produced in the United States. By some parties it was thought that this came from the West Indies, and that the first American cotton was exported in 1790. It is, however, known that Sea Island cotton was raised in Georgia, and the first successful crop of this famed variety was raised in Carolina in 1790. The excellent quality of this cotton enabled it to command much higher prices than any other. In 1836 it sold at 36 cents per pound, while other cotton brought only 22 cents.

The success in this venture caused many to engage in its cultivation, and some of the largest fortunes in South Carolina were then rapidly accumulated. The region adapted to it was, however, limited, and the amount raised in 1805 was not exceeded by the crops of 1832, being eight million pounds.

It was not until the year 1786 that expectations were held of the United States becoming ere long a great cotton-producing country. To encourage the production of the article, which promised soon to become a source of revenue, Congress was induced in 1789 to impose a duty of three cents a pound on foreign cottons then obtained from the West Indies and Brazil. The "gin" invented by Whitney in 1793 gave an impulse to the cultivation of cotton, and conferred on the plantation States a benefit scarcely to be estimated in money. This enabled the planters to clear for the market, by the labor of one man, 30,000 ℔s. of cotton.

On the 22d of February, 1775, a company, called the "United Company of Philadelphia for Promoting Manufactures," was formed, and books were opened for subscrip-

tions. The first general meeting was held at Carpenters' Hall on the 16th of March, and Dr. Rush was elected president. The object of this organization was to establish American manufactures of woolens, linens, and cottons, with a view to the exclusion and supercedure of British goods. The managers of the company established a manufactory at the corner of Market and Ninth Streets, Philadelphia, where they had a spinning-jenny then newly imported from England, and employed in spinning and other work four hundred women. Two years later this company contracted with Congress to make woolen cloth for the army.

It is related as an incident showing the condition of clothing among the soldiers of our army at this period, that General Lafaytte, being at Baltimore, was invited to attend a ball there. He went as requested, but instead of joining in the amusements of the evening, he addressed the ladies present as follows: "You are very handsome; you dance very prettily; your hall is very fine; but my soldiers have no shirts." The appeal was irresistible; the ball broke up; the ladies went home and to work, and in a few days a large number of shirts were prepared by the fair hands of Baltimore for the gallant defenders of their country.

The increased attention which had been given to wool-growing during the war and to cotton in the South, created a desire to secure the improved machinery by which England was being rapidly enriched. By 1780 spinning-jennys were beginning to be imported by subscription; and on the 30th of April of that year, in the Worcester (Mass.) *Spy* it was announced: "On Tuesday last the first piece of corduroy manufactured in this town was taken from the loom." Shortly after this cotton manufactories began to make their appearance in various parts of New England, and the industry of cloth manufacture may be said to have become fairly established in the United States.

CENTENNIAL REGATTAS.

It is believed that the Schuylkill will present at different periods of the Exhibition the most remarkable display of boating ever witnessed. Nearly all the chief organizations in the United States will participate, and clubs are expected from England, France and Canada. Among the races are: First, the International Race, open to all regularly organized boat-clubs throughout the world, to be rowed in accordance with the rules of the "International Amateur Rowing Association of the United States"; the prizes to be a piece of plate each for fours, for pairs, double and for single sculls; and, in addition, medals to be pre-

sented to each man rowing in the race, to be all gold for the winning crew; for the second crew, silver; and the remainder of bronze. Second, the International Club Race of four-oar shells, the prizes to be a piece of plate, with a gold medal to each member of the winning crew; open only to undergraduates. Third, the International Graduates' Race, for four-oar shells, open only to graduates of colleges or universities, the prizes being a piece of plate and a gold medal to each member of the winning crew. No person will be allowed to row in both the International Club Race and the International Graduates' Race.

ILLUSTRATIONS
OF THE
CENTENNIAL EXPOSITION

CENTENNIAL TEA PARTY IN THE NATIONAL CAPITOL.

One of the first and most important Centennial anniversaries was that of the destruction of tea in Boston harbor, December 16th, 1773, which was celebrated by a grand tea party in the Rotunda of the Capitol at Washington. Congress, at the previous session, had passed a joint resolution of both houses giving to the Centennial Tea Party Association the use of the Rotunda for the occasion. Of course the novelty of devoting the Government buildings to this purpose attracted general attention, and the place was crowded with ladies and gentlemen, clad in the picturesque costume of a hundred years ago.

The Capitol Rotunda was originally designed for public ceremonials, but was never before used for the purpose, except once, under the presidency of John Quincy Adams, when there was an exhibition of American manufactures held in it. For the occasion of which we speak it was tastefully decorated, and canopied with flags extending from the dome, 180 feet above the paved floor, down to the series of historical pictures which adorn the walls. In the centre was a large American flag, made of California silk, which was displayed at the Vienna Exposition. Around the Rotunda on the floor were tables, above which were banners displaying the armorial bearings of the thirteen original States, and small silk flags with the names of all the States and Territories decorated the walls. On one side was a rural temple for the sale of American fruits, flowers, and wines. A miniature ship, managed by small boys in sailor costumes, who sold packages of tea, attracted cons'derable attention. The ladies in attendance at the tables disposed of large quantities of tea at one dollar a cup —the purchaser having the privilege of retaining the cup and saucer. This was the first of these gatherings, which have since been quite frequent all over the country.

THE 99TH 4TH OF JULY.

On the 4th of July, 1875, the Philadelphians celebrated the close of the 99th year since our national independence by a grand celebration at Fairmount Park, when it was estimated that over 200,000 people participated in the ceremonies. The day opened with a salute from the battery on George's Hill, followed by a review of the first division National Guard of Pennsylvania. After this the ground was broken for the Jewish monument to "Religious Liberty," which was followed by the unvailing of a statue of America, which now surmounts the dome of Memorial Hall. After this there was a concert by 3,500 school children in Machinery Hall, each of the singers holding a bouquet and a flag, while the hall was magnificently decorated with bunting. Later, the ground was broken by the Italians for their monument to Christopher Columbus. In the afternoon, a celebration with addresses, etc., took place, followed by breaking ground for the Catholic Temperance Fountain, and that by a grand vocal and instrumental concert in Machinery Hall. The ceremonies of the day closed with a review of the Schuylkill navy, and in the evening there was a fine display of fireworks. Three balloon ascensions were made during the day.

INCIDENTS IN THE CONSTRUCTION OF THE CENTENNIAL BUILDINGS.

Of course the employment of thousands of men at Fairmount in the construction of the Centennial buildings could not be devoid of incidents of interest, and many of these have been found sufficiently important for illustration. The very avocations of the workmen, the manner in which they perform their duties, are instructive, and even at times amusing. Here we see hundreds of carpenters scattered like flies about the floor of the main building, placing boards and nailing them ; there, painters, mounted on scaffolding, are decorating the ceilings and walls, or sending pails of paint up and down by ropes ; again a monster gun is arriving, and being placed in position. The labor of hoisting one of the great girders of the main building, employing a number of men, is plainly displayed by the artist, as also that of rolling the roads on the Centennial grounds, also done by workmen. The manner in which the workmen come down from the labors on the scaffoldings to obtain their dinner, by

sliding down ropes, is a somewhat amusing incident, while the picture of a Centennial boss will be recognized as a not unfamiliar figure on the grounds during the past few years.

A group of men with large wooden implements, sodding the grounds around Horticultural Hall, and another group carrying one of the iron girders from one point to another, will be found in our illustrations.

THE PENN STATUE.

One of the most important of the statues to be placed in Fairmount Park is that of William Penn, by Mr. Bailie, of Philadelphia. It will be of bronze, thirty feet high, the Quaker being represented in the act of explaining the original plan of the city, which rests upon the stump of a tree at his left hand. This statue will be placed in the park, and there remain until the public buildings on Broad and Market Streets are completed, when it is to be permanently set upon the dome. As this will be 500 feet above the sidewalk, this figure of W. Penn will be the highest specimen of terminal architecture in the world.

THE WATER BABIES.

A very charming piece of sculpture to be exhibited at the Centennial is by Marshal G. Gould, a young sculptor not yet of age, who has been for the last three years studying with his father Thomas R. Gould, in Florence. The design of the work presents two naked children, who have taken shelter in a shell. One of them is asleep, and is clasped in the arms of the other, who appears as its protector. The figures are the size of infant life, and the whole is being sculptured out of a single block of marble in Florence. The work is described by those who have seen the original design in plaster as presenting the most charming illustration of the subject selected.

THE BRAZILIAN COMMISSION.

Brazil has taken a lively interest in the Centennial from its inception. On September 26th of last year the *Semana Illustrada*, a paper published at Rio de Janeiro, devoted its entire space to the illustration, explanation, and advocacy of the Exposition at Philadelphia, urging the Brazilian people to interest themselves in it, and otherwise indicating the prevalent favorable opinion of the enterprise in Brazil. From this paper we obtain the portraits of the Brazilian Commissioners, presenting the following distinguished personages : His Highness Gaston d'Orleans, Conde d'Eu (President of the Commission), Visconde de Jaguary, Visconde de Bon Retiro, F. J. Marc conde de Jaguary, Visconde de Bon Retiro, F. J. Marc

Homem de Mello, Commendado, Francisco Antonio Gonçales, Commendador J. A. de Azevedo.

THE CENTENNIAL NEW YEAR'S.

Special celebrations of New Year's Day, 1876, occurred in all parts of the country. The ringing of bells and firing of cannon in all the great cities ushered in the Centennial year in most praiseworthy manner. In Philadelphia, however, the event was held with more than ordinary enthusiasm. On the night of the last day of the year 1875, by special request of the Mayor, the houses in Philadelphia were illuminated, and, despite the fact that the weather was dark, stormy, and disagreeable, the city presented a most brilliant appearance. The streets were thronged with people until a late hour of the night, while the illuminations made a complete blaze of light everywhere. Every building in the city connected with revolutionary history was appropriately illuminated. At the southwest corner of Seventh and Market Streets stands a brick building which, in 1776, was a fashionable boardinghouse, and where Thomas Jefferson wrote the Declaration of Independence. On this occasion it was blazing with light and covered with appropriate inscriptions. Carpenter's Hall, where the first Continental Congress met, was also illuminated, and inscribed "The Nation's Birthplace," in gas jets. Christ's Church was lighted from basement to steeple-top, while its bells rang out a merry welcoming peal—the same bells that ushered in the first year of the century. Independence Hall was the great scene of attraction, the streets in the vicinity being jammed with people, during the whole evening, and until after midnight. Masqueraders, in groups and singly, threaded their way among the crowd ; drums, fifes, horns, and trumpets sounded ; processions of clubs and military paraded, and at precisely twelve o'clock the Mayor raised the old Colonial flag at the head of the flagstaff of Independence Hall, amid the cheers of a hundred thousand people. The State House bells struck 1,7,7,6, then 1,8,7,6 and 100 taps in quick succession. The State Fencibles fired thirteen rounds from Independence Square, which was succeeded by rapid file-firing from another regiment, continued for fifteen minutes. Red and blue lights were burned by hundreds, and calcium lights and fireworks from the State House completed the celebration.

THE WOMEN'S PAVILION.

A noble monument of the energy and patriotism of the women of America is the Women's Centennial Pavilion in Fairmount Park, which was built under the supervision of the Women's Centennial Committee. The pavilion is

RECEPTION AND EXAMINATION OF JAPANESE GOODS BY CUSTOM-HOUSE OFFICIALS.

located on Belmont Avenue, near the Horticultural grounds, and covers an area of 30,000 square feet. It is formed by two naves intersecting each other, each 64 ft. in width and 192 ft. long. At the end of these there is a porch 8 by 32 ft. The corners formed by the two naves are filled by four pavilions, each 48 ft. square. The whole structure is built of wood, in a modern and ornate style of architecture, and is roofed over by segmental trusses. In the centre, which is raised 25 ft. higher than the rest of the

immediately stop the car and hold it in position. To the east the Delaware River is seen winding its way along the borders of Pennsylvania and New Jersey, with the Delaware Bay lying far away in the distance; north and west one sees towns and villages, fields and meadows. Closer at hand the entire city of Philadelphia is spread out like a bird's-eye view, while, immediately beneath, Fairmount Park, with the elegant Centennial buildings, appears like a charming garden.

116 ft. On the side of the building are seven commodious committee rooms, and in the front are three other spacious rooms. Two stairways give access to a gallery 10 ft. wide, running round three sides of the main hall.

The Phœnix Sylvestris Palm Tree.

A specimen of the East India wild date palm, or Phœnix Sylvestris, on exhibition at Horticultural Hall, twenty feet in width by thirty feet in height, will be one of the

JAPANESE WORKMEN LAYING THE FOUNDATION OF THE JAPANESE BUILDING.

building, is an observatory, with a cupola on top, making the entire height of the building 90 ft.

The Centennial Elevator.

On Belmont Hill, in Fairmount Park, stands the Sawyer Observatory, 185 feet high in itself, and 410 feet above the level of the Schuylkill River. This observatory is a straight shaft, the summit of which is reached by an elevator car, which is raised or lowered by eight wire cables, and this is prevented from falling, should the cables give way, by steel columns acting on perpendicular rods, which would

The Judges' Pavilion.

This building, which is intended for the use of the judges and committees who are to award the prizes at the Exposition, covers a space of 152 by 113 feet, is built of wood and plaster, and highly ornamented. In the centre is a large hall, 59 by 78 ft., containing a platform and speaker's desk. A corridor, 10 ft. wide, runs entirely around this, and separates it from another hall 28 by 59 ft. By an arrangement of partitions rendering them movable, these two rooms can be thrown into one large hall, 59 by

curiosities of the Exhibition. It belongs to a class of hardy palms, similar to that from which the dates of commerce are obtained. It is a native of Africa and Tropical Asia, and is common throughout the East Indies. The specimen in question is said to be one of the most magnificent ever brought to this country.

Loading the Big Gun.

An interesting incident in connection with the Centennial furnishes a good subject for illustration. One of the great guns forming a portion of the display of ordnance of the United States is represented having an infant seated in its muzzle, laughing gleefully at the group of ladies and gentlemen who have placed her there.

THE PENNSYLVANIA STATE BUILDING.

This building, which is located on Belmont Avenue, near the United States buildings, was built by the State for the headquarters of the Pennsylvania State Commission under an appropriation of $15,000. It is a wooden building, in Gothic style, 98 by 55 ft. in dimensions. It is

active labor and earnest enthusiasm during the past three years. The Women's Centennial Committee was organized February 15th, 1873, with Mrs. Elizabeth Duane Gillespie as its president. The original number of this committee was thirteen, symbolical of the original States. Subcommittees were organized in every ward in the city, while prominent ladies in other States were added to the original organization, forming a most efficient body, extending throughout the entire country, and whose work has been most important and effectual.

tapering points with wing-shaped heads. These they carry in small wicker baskets, hung to a sash worn around the waist. Their plane is a flat tool, an inch and a half thick, which they draw towards them, instead of pushing from them, as with us. The saw is shaped like a cleaver, with a thin blade, and with small and sharp teeth. The adz differs from our own in having a peculiar twist to the handle. The chisel is a short piece of steel of a semi-circular shape, with a short handle. The Japanese show great facility in handling these tools, and are by no means

GRAND TROPHY IN THE EAST END OF THE MAIN BUILDING, ILLUSTRATING THE GROWTH OF THE AMERICAN FLAG.

surrounded by a piazza, 6 ft. wide, and is ornamented with a central tower, and two smaller octagonal towers. The height of the top of the central tower is 65 ft. The main hall is 30 by 50 ft., on the right of which are two rooms intended for ladies' and gentlemen's parlors, being fixed up with dressing-rooms and other conveniences.

THE WOMEN'S CENTENNIAL COMMITTEE.

The headquarters of the Women's Centennial Committee at 903 Walnut Street has been the locality of considerable

JAPANESE TOOLS.

The Japanese are quite as peculiar in their tools and implements as they are in every other incidental of their life. They use an ink line instead of a chalk line, for instance. The apparatus for this is a case, in the centre of which is a sponge, which may be saturated with any color. The line is made to pass through this, and a pointed peg at the end holds it in place. The Japanese seldom use nails, and those they do use are of a peculiar construction, having

such clumsy workmen as their implements might lead us to suppose.

THE GREAT CORLISS ENGINE.

The grand power which is to keep in motion the mechanical part of the Exposition is the Corliss engine, situated in the centre of Machinery Hall. This engine is of fifteen hundred-horse power, but is capable of doing the work of twenty-five hundred horses if necessary. It is from Providence, Rhode Island, and weighs some seven hundred tons. Sixty-five cars were required to transport it, and some of its sections were so heavy that the cars on which they were placed had to be of extra strength. For many weeks pickax men and masons were employed upon its deep, cemented foundation, while the strong, firm timbers, by which its several parts were hoisted in place, swarmed with workmen nearly to the ceiling. This engine furnishes power to all the machinery in the building. Miles of shaft lead away from it down along the aisles from end to end. Of these are eight main lines, four on each side of the central transept, where the engine stands, extending lengthwise. Seven have a speed of 120 revolutions, and one a speed of 240 revolutions a minute. Counter-shafts are introduced into the aisles at different points. The power is transmitted by the *spur-gear* fly wheel, 30 ft. in diameter, weighing 56 tons ; the jack-wheel, 10 ft. in diameter on the main shafting, which, being run under the floors to the pulleys, the power is transmitted thence to the eight main lines of shafting above the floor, aggregating one mile in length, from which the machinery of the Exhibition derived its power. These made about 35 revolutions per minute, and for driving them there were 20 Corliss boilers, capable of developing 1,400 horse-power, and of standing a pressure of 100 pounds to the square inch.

PROGRESS OF CONSTRUCTION.

The appropriation by Congress of one and a half million dollars to the purposes of the Exposition gave fresh impe-

THE TERMINALS.

tus to the work upon the grounds at Fairmount Park, and this was rapidly displayed in the completion of the erection of the numerous minor buildings devoted to the objects of the display.

Meanwhile, the city began rapidly to assume a more varied and cosmopolitan aspect than it had ever before presented. The arrival of the members and employés of the different foreign missions—including the British, Belgian, Spanish, Swedish, French, German, Japanese, Turkish, etc.—introduced new elements among the promenaders on Chestnut Street, occasioning that thoroughfare to present daily an appearance of renewed brightness and vitality, while, at Fairmount Park, the new arrivals were constantly seen engaged in the erection of the various National Buildings and in other necessary avocations.

NEW JERSEY STATE BUILDING.

This building is 94 ft. long by 57 ft. wide, two stories in height, with attic and observatory. It has been erected on a very pleasing model, presenting many gables and ornamented with red tiles. Built of cross-beam timbers, the first story is filled in with paneling painted a light color, the rest of the exterior being covered with tiles. It has a square tower, 85 ft. high, and porches, verandas, balconies, gables and dormor-windows innumerable, the whole arranged in a most picturesque manner, and designed to offer the most pleasing appearance. Within, the arrangements are made in the most convenient and admirable manner, including a fine stairway leading to the tower, from which an excellent view can be had of Fairmount Park and its delightful environs.

SPANISH SOLDIERS PAINTING ORNAMENTS FOR THEIR PAVILION.

SPANISH BUILDING.

The Spanish Pavilion in the Main Building, situated about half-way between the centre transept and the west entrance on the centre nave, has been from the moment of its commencement an object of interest. Emblazoned and very elaborately ornamented, the inclosure is 46 ft. in height, constructed of wood and canvas, painted, carved and gilded in rich and ornate style, having a grand doorway in the centre, and two grand portals handsomely decorated. The central entrance, surmounted by a massive pediment broken in the centre, is ornamented with a painting representing Spain in the act of disclosing the Western Hemisphere to the assembled nations. Below this, the portraits of Columbus, Isabella, Cortez, Pizarro, De Soto and other prominent personages in the history of Spanish discovery. The doorway is hung with heavy folds of silk curtains, displaying the Spanish national colors—red and yellow. These, surmounted by a grand trophy of shields, helmets, and standards, present a very neat and elegant appearance.

INDIANA STATE BUILDING.

The headquarters of the State of Indiana, located on State Avenue, near Belmont Avenue, is peculiar and original in its construction, 65x65 ft. in dimensions, with an extension in the rear of 33x14 ft. The front building is 30 ft. in height to the top of the lantern. It is octagonal in shape, and built of ornamental woodwork, inclosing large plate-glass, a portion of which is said to be the largest in America, being 18 ft. high by 8 ft. 2 inches in width. A tasty veranda is built around three sides of the structure. The interior, handsomely finished with wainscoting and paneling, contains committee-rooms, parlors, post-office, telegraph and other offices.

THE SWEDISH SCHOOLHOUSE.

Sweden, being noted for her educational facilities, and particularly for the admirable construction of her schoolhouses, has always, in international exhibitions, made a special point of this species of exhibit. Under the direc-

tion of the Government, the schoolhouses of Sweden are more carefully constructed in a sanitary point of view than are those of any other country. At the Vienna Exposition, a Swedish schoolhouse was erected which cost 6,000 crowns. That at Fairmount cost 25,000, and the building, although plain and simple in appearance, is a most interesting feature of the Exposition. It has been erected between the Jury Pavilion and Memorial Hall, near the west end of the Main Building, and is a fac-simile of the best common schoolhouse of Sweden, except that it is not divided into two rooms, as is customary, but is formed in order to obtain advantages for displaying school-furniture, apparatus, etc. It is one and a half stories in height, constructed of native wood, and erected by Swedish workmen. A peaked roof everhanging the sides is a feature of the method of construction ; the entire building is carefully finished, all the wood being either oiled or polished, and no nails being exposed. The windows are arched, the sashes swinging upon hinges. It is one of the prettiest buildings on the grounds.

* * * *

The last days of constructive effort on the grounds at Fairmount, prior to the opening, continued to be marked by the same energy and industry which had characterized the proceedings from the beginning. On every side, companies of brawny men having the word "terminal" marked on the bands of their caps, were busy unloading goods—these embracing cases and crates of all sizes, hogsheads, machinery, etc.—placing them on trucks, rolling the various packages into the building, and disposing them in the respective sections. In some in-

A CAUTIOUS EXHIBITOR.

stances, the exhibitors, feeling annoyed by the premature inspection of their wares, screened themselves behind canvas coverings, while arranging their goods for public display.

Of course, the operations of the foreign mechanics attracted much attention and interest, these being specially directed toward the French workmen, on account of the peculiar character of the tools which they employed, and also toward the Spanish department, where soldiers were engaged in various manipulations connected with their duties.

A rather amusing and certainly useful feature of the Exposition was the "broom brigade"; a squad of men and boys kept constantly employed in the buildings, sweeping up the *débris* after the workmen, cleaning the windows, carrying off the refuse in huge wheelbarrows constructed for that particular purpose.

The arrival of goods at the Exposition Buildings awakened much interest, and aroused the curiosity of all those who were permitted to be present and observe it. Considerable amusement was occasioned among the bystanders on the uncovering of the statuary intended for the Art Department, as the figures were gradually unvailed.

The transportation of heavy boxes of goods, and that of immense masses of stone, as displayed in our illustrations, was also a never-ending fund of interest. A process which did not fail to attract a crowd was the erection of the interesting model of the city of Paris. This remarkable miniature structure presented the topography of the famous city, with the Seine, bridges, public buildings, hotels, Arc de Triomphe,

FRENCH CARPENTERS AT WORK.

GUIDE-BOOK BOYS.

Place de la Concorde, Colonne Vendôme; in fact, a miniature fac-simile of the beautiful city. Another object of interest was the Centennial Letter Box, by means of which preparations were made for the convenience of all nations in the matter of postal communication. On this letter-box, inscriptions in all languages explained the purpose of the receptacle in a manner easily to be understood. Such boxes, distributed throughout the grounds and buildings illustrate the care which was taken by the Centennial authorities to offer all the facilities possible.

MASSACHUSETTS STATE BUILDING.

This fine structure occupies one of the most prominent positions within the inclosure. It is built after the style of houses common in colonial times, and of course presents a rather quaint-looking appearance that could not fail to attract general attention. A steep roof, the rear twice as long as the front, is a peculiarity making the rear wall considerably shorter than the front one. The building is one and a half stories in height, with dormer-windows, and light fancy verandas over the entrance. Over the main entrance there is a shingled covering. The building is lathed and plastered outside and in, the timbers painted a deep-brown, giving an appearance of paneling.

CHILIAN COURT.

Each of the different foreign nations devoted time, labor and expense in fitting up respectively their quarters in the Main Building in a style at once commodious and pleasant. The Chilian Government has not fallen short of the others in this regard. The portion inclosed and devoted to the uses of that South American State is situated near the west entrance of the Building. It is arranged in two rows of handsome cases, having a pavilion at each end in ornamental woodwork, attractively painted and decorated. This is naturally one of the most pleasing departments of the Exposition. In all former exhibitions and international displays, Chili has made a creditable showing, but inferior to what has been done in connection with the Centennial.

TURKISH COFFEE HOUSE.

Near the bazaar of the Syrians from Jerusalem is erected the Turkish "Khavé," or Coffee House, where two Constantinople citizens direct smoking and coffee-drinking in genuine Ottoman style, visitors being served by legitimate Turks in full costume. This building has been erected by American carpenters, under the direction of Turkish overseers.

KANSAS STATE BUILDING.

The State of Kansas has erected a large structure near the "Women's Pavilion" and the New Jersey Building, occupying a spot of ground 132 x 123 ft. Elaborately designed, this building is an honor to the State which directed its construction and to those engaged in building it. In form it is an ornamental cottage, having a large circular hall in its centre. From this radiates commodious apartments, attached to which are numerous large rooms intended for private offices.

SITE OF THE EXPOSITION.

A view of 240 acres, more or less, occupied by the Centennial Exposition, as it appeared at the time of the opening, was certainly calculated to impress the eye-witness with a just idea of the immensity of the undertaking which has been carried through by the Centennial Commission. Standing on George's Hill, where perhaps the most comprehensive view can be obtained, the eye first meets the magnificent proportions of Machinery Hall, running east and west, extending nearly from the extreme western end of the grounds to the point where Belmont and Elm Avenues intersect each other. Carrying the eye beyond this point—and at this distance the line seems unbroken—stretches the vast length of the Main Exhibition Building, giving an entire and nearly unbroken covered space for exhibition of 3,824 ft. in length, and between

FINISHING THE TOP OF A SHOW-CASE.

centre he sees the beautiful structure known as Memorial Hall, and which is really the Art Gallery of the Exposition, built in the modern Renaissance style of architecture, and admirably proportioned and surmounted by a beautiful dome, from whose apex rises the colossal statue of Columbia, springing 150 ft. from the ground. This building is, in the chasteness and symmetry of its architecture, an immediate relief from the more formal lines of the Main and Machinery Buildings. Situated on a considerable elevation in the Lansdown Plateau, overlooking the city in the distance and the beautiful river at its feet, no more charming spot could have been chosen for this prominent building.

Gazing still further north, and at a point about opposite the extreme western end of the Main Building, the eye now meets the Horticultural Building, also designed to remain a permanent ornament to Fairmount, and which, being built in the Mauresque style of architecture of the twelfth century, is still more ornate and picturesque than those structures already seen. Nearly 400 ft. in length, 200 ft. in width, and 72 ft. in height, this little and beautiful edifice, devoted entirely to plants and flowers, is one of the most interesting and pleasing features of the entire view.

Finally, the chief system of structures is completed by the Agricultural Building, north of the last-mentioned and on the eastern side of Belmont Avenue. Midway between this and Machinery Hall is the building for the Exhibition of the United States Government.

The eye, taking in the numerous smaller edifices erected for the use of the different States, for the exhibition of special trades and manufactures, for the convenience and accommodation of the visitors to the Exposition, or for the display of private enterprise, industry and energy,

THE "BROOM BRIGADE" GOING THE ROUND.

400 and 500 in breadth. Yet this line is not in the least monotonous, as the tall towers in the centre and at either end of the Main Exhibition Building produce a striking and effective interruption of the distance, without interfering with its continuity or magnificence. Both these buildings lie between the two main thoroughfares of the Centennial Grounds, the Avenue of the Republic and Elm Avenue.

As the spectator on George's Hill carries his eye a little to the northward of the Main Building, and at about its is filled with a vision of architectural exercise and industrial excellence which has probably never been excelled in any one locality in the world. The special purpose and character of these minor buildings are described elsewhere. Of those not thus specified, there should be mentioned the following:

THE CARRIAGE AND WAGON BUILDING.

This building is located northwest of Memorial Hall. It is built of wood and iron, and lighted principally by

UNCOVERING STATUES.

THE FIRST GERMAN ARRIVAL.

HOLLAND SOLDIERS ARRANGING GOODS.

POLISHING A VASE IN THE GERMAN DEPARTMENT.

skylights, is 345 ft. long and 230 wide. On each of the four sides are entrances, with offices attached to each entrance. One side of this structure is devoted entirely to carriages, railway cars, omnibuses and wagons. The exhibits in this department by American manufacturers number more than 100; those of the English nearly 50; of France 36; Germany and Italy also exhibit.

BREWERS' BUILDING.

This building is 200 ft. by 80, and contains all the machinery used in brewing, with samples of lager-bier, Rochester and Milwaukee bier, English pale ale, stout and porter, Philadelphia and New York ales, with a large exhibit from the best breweries in Europe.

ARKANSAS STATE BUILDING.

This building is octagonal in shape, covering an area of 5,000 square ft., the columns being placed in a circle of 82 ft. in diameter, the ceiling spherical, with an octagonal dome over all, the top being 50 ft. above the floor line.

THE CENTENNIAL PHOTOGRAPHIC COMPANY'S BUILDING.

The Centennial Photographic Company, which has the concession of all photographs made within the precincts of

CONSTRUCTING THE CHILIAN COURT IN THE MAIN BUILDING.

the Exhibition, have a building on the east side of Belmont Avenue, just north of the western end of the Main Exhibition Building. It is built of wood and plaster, highly decorated, is one story high, and situated on a terrace 3 ft. above the ordinary grade, has a vestibule, reception-room, gallery 22 ft. square for the exhibition of

photographs; public and private offices, dressing-rooms, etc., are included in its scope.

GLASS MANUFACTURE.

Messrs. Gillender & Sons have erected a handsome building wherein will be represented, in actual working order, this highly interesting and important industry, and all the processes of glass melting, blowing and manufacturing will be exhibited in all their various branches, in active operation.

SHOE AND LEATHER BUILDING.

This building is 160 ft. wide, 314 deep, forming a parallelogram, constructed of wood, glass and iron. The interior presents an open space, 256 ft. long by 160 wide. The roof is supported by columns, 16 ft. apart. The central section is a curve 80 ft. wide, of the Howe-truss pattern, over which, 59 ft. above the ground, is a Louvre ventilator, 20 ft. wide, running the entire length of the building. The flag-staffs are 80 ft. high, and the pavilions, respectively, 20 and 30 ft. in height. Within, an aisle, 15 ft. wide, runs through the centre of the building from end to end, having on either side two aisles, 10 ft. wide, running parallel with it. Across the centre is an aisle 10 ft. wide, ending in sliding-doors, which lead to

ERECTING THE CORLISS ENGINES IN THE SOUTH TRANSEPT OF MACHINERY HALL.

Machinery Hall on the north, and to Elm Avenue on the south. The east and west sections of the ground-floor have aisles 14 ft. wide. On the right and left of the main entrance, stairways lead to the second-floor, in front of which are galleries 8 ft. wide, which give an unobstructed view of the lower floor. A hall, 16 ft. wide, divides the second story into two parts, and leads to the balcony facing Belmont Avenue, giving a commanding view of all the buildings on the grounds. On either side of the hall are ladies' and gentlemen's parlors, and on the

ft. each, and 8 spaces of 190 square ft. each. The walls of the building furnish 5,320 ft. more, making in all 18,360 square ft. The entire exhibitive space is 20,000 square ft., furnishing an opportunity for the exhibition of photographs such as has never before been witnessed.

DELAWARE STATE BUILDING.

This is located on State Avenue, north of the British Government Buildings, and opposite the New York State Commission Building. It is built in the Swiss Gothic

and High Schools, with their furniture, fittings, apparatus, etc.; academies and seminaries with pictures of buildings, cabinet collections, etc.; normal schools; views of buildings and grounds, models and charts; institution for the blind, apparatus for teaching; orphan schools; music buildings, charts, etc.; Sunday-schools, with materials, maps, charts, forms and models.

NEW YORK STATE BUILDING.

This building is 60 ft. long and two stories high, with

TURKISH COMMISSIONERS AND THEIR GUIDE INSPECTING THE UNLOADING OF HEAVY MACHINERY.

first floor various rooms for the accommodation of exhibitors and those employed in the building.

PHOTOGRAPHERS' HALL.

The photographic profession throughout the United States have combined to procure the erection of this Building, which will contain the specimens of photographs exhibited by the different nations. The building occupies a space 258 ft. long by 107 ft. wide. The interior furnishes 28 hanging screens, 48 spaces of 240 square

style of architecture, and entirely of woods native to the State. The first floor is used for reception-rooms, the second floor being devoted to business purposes.

PENNSYLVANIA EDUCATIONAL HALL.

This building is situated north of the Art Gallery, fronting the Lansdowne Drive. It is octagonal in shape, 148 ft. by 100 ft., and contains 32 alcoves for exhibitive purposes, a large assembly-room and reception-room. The exhibits will include Kinder Garten; Primary, Grammar

a French roof, having in the centre a graceful tower, from the top of which a charming view of the grounds can be enjoyed. Around three sides of the building is a tasteful piazza, 15 ft. wide. Within are offices for the State Centennial Board, reception-rooms for visitors from New York, private rooms for ladies, and all modern improvements for the comfort of exhibitors and guests. This is a beautiful specimen of modern architecture, designed and constructed under the direction of skilled artists. The following are the Commissioners for the State of New York:

HANGING THE DRAPERY IN THE NETHERLANDS DEPARTMENT.

area of over 4,000 square ft., is three stories in height, and is carefully adapted to the purpose it is intended to subserve. It is located at the west end of Machinery Hall, and will contain, among other interesting exhibits, the press on which the Declaration of Independence was first printed.

THE NEWSPAPER BUILDING.

On a line between the United States Government Building and Machinery Hall is the structure devoted to the exhibition of newspapers and periodicals, each exhibit

A CENTENNIAL LETTER-BOX.

MOVING HEAVY CASES IN THE MAIN BUILDING.

no additional fees, all the buildings being free for the entrance of any visitor. A force of 600 uniformed policemen, carefully organized and well disciplined, is distributed throughout the grounds to preserve order and protect the buildings and exhibits. There is also a large and efficient Fire Department, provided with steam fire-engines, and ready at a moment's notice on an emergency. Besides this, the telegraphic and postal communication system of the Exhibition has been perfected under the most excellent and

Frank Leslie, *President;* John Murdock, Alonzo B. Cornell, Felix Campbell, Jackson S. Schultz; and Thomas McElrath, *Secretary.*

MICHIGAN STATE BUILDING.

This structure is built in a highly ornamental style of architecture, finished in the most attractive and liberal manner, and is well worth the examination of visitors.

THE WORLD'S TICKET AND INQUIRY OFFICE OF COOK, SON & JENKINS.

It is erected on a triangular piece of ground, on Belmont Avenue, near Machinery Hall. In the centre is a hall 60 ft. in diameter, and there are also numerous offices and waiting-rooms for the accommodation of visitors. Here also will be found a staff of officials in the employ of the exhibitors.

CAMPBELL PRESS BUILDING.

In this building, erected in the interest of the press of the country, will be seen the process of running a complete newspaper, a job-printing office, as well as the various articles manufactured by the exhibitors, whose liberality has procured the erection of the structure. It covers an

being presented in an alphabetical arrangement of partial files, and bearing suitable labels.

THE DAIRYMEN'S ASSOCIATION BUILDING.

Located near the Horticultural Hall, under the shade-trees of this peculiarly attractive structure, modeled after the favorite resort of Maria Antoinette, the Petti Tria Non is a most pleasing object. It is 50 ft. wide, 100 ft. long, in the midst of the ground, prettily laid out and ornamented with fountains and statues.

The American Restaurant, Paris Restaurant, Singer Sewing Machine Building and others, complete the private and State structures.

ADMINISTRATION.

The uniform price of admission to the Centennial Exposition is 50 cents. The seemingly unnecessary exaction that this sum should be paid in each case in a single stamp has been abolished, and hereafter the ordinary custom will be observed.

There are thirteen entrances to the Exposition, and the admission fee once paid and the grounds entered, there are

judicious management, and will be found entirely competent to all the necessary uses of those who may have to employ these important facilities.

The restaurants, including the American, Southern, German, Sudreaux, Trois Frères, Hebrew, Vienna Bakery and Coffee-house, and Turkish Coffee-house—all these, after the first vagaries as to charges, will be found to have settled down to a set method of compensation and a suitable cuisine.

The facilities for transportation to the Exposition have never been equaled on any previous occasion of the same character. Being connected with Philadelphia by three lines of steam-railway, four lines of horse-cars, and a line of omnibuses, Fairmount Park has peculiar advantages. The Pennsylvania Railroad and the Reading Railroad are constantly dispatching trains from their chief terminal stations, while the street-car lines are running their vehicles without cessation. As all roads are said to lead to Paris, so in Philadelphia and the surrounding country all roads lead to the Centennial, while each road is utilized to the fullest extent of human skill in the matter of transporting the largest number of human beings in the shortest possible time. Within the grounds a double narrow-gauge railway

TRUCKING HEAVY BLOCKS OF STONE.

MACHINERY HALL ON A RAINY DAY.

makes the circuit of the inclosure, having stations adjoining all the principal buildings. The cars are open at the sides and are drawn by dummy-engines. Passengers pay five cents at the gates leading to the station-platform, and can ride the entire length of the line, about four miles, or get off at any stopping-place.

The transfer companies run omnibuses to Chestnut Street and the principal hotels, fare 50 cents; while another company runs vehicles between Fairmount Park and the foot of Market Street for 25 cents fare.

of the numerous hotels which have been recently erected. It should be generally understood that the Centennial Exposition cannot be seen without time and some exercise of judgment. It is estimated that a week is the least time it should be allowed, while two weeks is only a fair period to devote to a thorough examination of all the features of the Exposition. Ordinarily speaking, an allowance of $5 a day may be made to cover all expenses of visiting the Centennial Exposition. Of course there are means of economizing on this, while those with more extravagant tastes

the latter in extent being as large as the other two, and this by Australasia, India and the other colonies of Great Britain. Next is the department of Canada, and then that of Great Britain itself, which brings one to the centre of the transept. Proceeding, we come now upon the space allotted to France and her colonies, following which are Switzerland and Belgium; then Brazil, the Netherlands, Mexico and a portion of the United States of America, which, however, occupies the entire opposite side from the eastern end up to the centre of the transept. On this side,

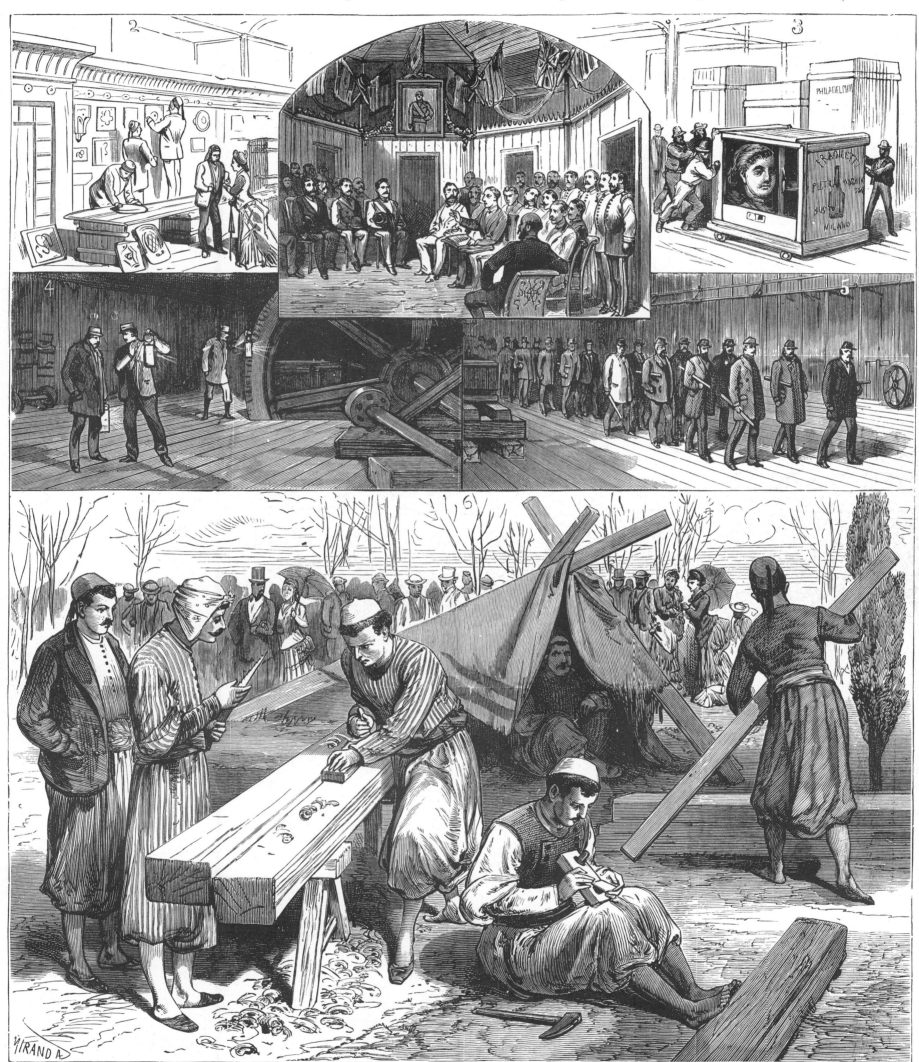

1. Spanish Commissioners Celebrating the Birthday of Cervantes.   2. Decorating the Egyptian Department in the Main Building.   3. Transporting the Washington Statue in Sections to the Italian Department.
4. Firemen Patrolling Machinery Hall in the Night.   5. Centennial Policemen—the Patrol Relief.   6. Turkish Mechanics Erecting a Bazaar.

SCENES AND INCIDENTS OF THE EXPOSITION PREPARATIONS.

The Pennsylvania Railroad put in operation a new schedule on the opening day of the Exposition. By this the company runs daily (Sunday excepted) from New York to Philadelphia numerous express and accommodation trains direct to the grounds and return. A uniform reduction of 33 per cent. below the regular rates has been made.

In securing lodgings in advance through the agencies, a friend should be employed to select a locality in order to be near the Exposition. Those intending to remain only a few days will promote their comfort by sojourning at one

can exceed the amount to their full desire. Hotel board rates from $2 to $5 per day. Board can be obtained in private houses all the way from a dollar a day up.

THE MAIN BUILDING.

INSTALLATION PLAN.

The visitor entering the Main Building from Machinery Hall finds on his left, next to the entrance, the space allotted to Italy. This is followed by Norway and Sweden,

the southern, following the United States toward the Machinery Hall, is: first, the space of the German Empire; next, that of Austria and Hungary; then Russia, Spain and Portugal; next, Egypt, Turkey, Tunis and the Sandwich Islands, with an additional allotment to Sweden and Denmark. Following this are Japan and China, which brings us to Chili, Peru and the Orange Free States of Africa, when we have made the entire circuit of the building and find ourselves again at the entrance facing the eastern end of Machinery Hall.

OPENING OF THE CENTENNIAL EXPOSITION, MAY 10TH, 1876—SCE

THE GRAND PLAZA IN FRONT OF MEMORIAL HALL.

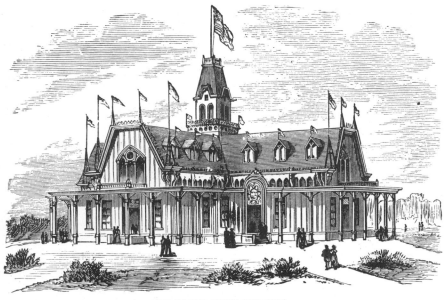

THE KANSAS STATE BUILDING.

THE MASSACHUSETTS STATE BUILDING.

The principal approach for carriages to the Main Building is at the east entrance; that at the south entrance being mostly used for visitors arriving by the street-cars. The north entrance leads to the Art Galleries of the Memorial Hall, and annex.

The Main Building presents the display of the various manufactures, and the nations exhibiting are represented here. With the exception of Tunis, the Sandwich Islands, Peru and the Orange Free States, the different nations have exhibiting space on the central aisle, and this promenade, of course, affords the most attractive treasures in the collection. Some of the departments have been handsomely ornamented with architectural fronts, or are entirely inclosed. In the centre of the transept is a circular music-stand, while in various parts of the building are showy structures devoted to soda-water.

The entire number of buildings on the Centennial Grounds, as published in the list of the official record of the Commission, and including soda-water stands, popcorn stands, restaurants, wind-mills, cloak-rooms, and all other structures for accommodation or display, is 189.

OPENING OF THE EXPOSITION.

The morning of May 10th—the day most important in the annals of the Centennial Exposition—opened gloomily. The air was damp and the sky was overcast, but a little later on, in time enough before the hour fixed for the ceremonies at Fairmount Park for every one to be apprised, the sky brightened, and by eight o'clock the day was brilliant and beautiful.

The grounds were opened at nine o'clock, and even at that hour the neighborhood of the gates was crowded with thousands of persons awaiting admission. According to the programme of the Commission, the first admitted were the invited guests, and these entered at the southern entrance of the Main Building. The guests were there in large numbers, and on entering these passed through the Main Building and out at the northern side, under the great platform erected for the use of the orchestra and chorus, and thence to the platform in front of Memorial Hall set apart for them. Each guest was provided with a diagram of the platform, on which was indicated, in red ink, the position assigned to every holder of a platform ticket. Upon the latter there was a plan of the grounds, and also a programme of the exercises. These arrangements avoided confusion, and greatly added to the comfort of the visitors. After the guests came the crowd, and soon their number increased by thousands

in the space between the two halls, and outside of that framed in by ropes for the accommodation of the immediate ceremonies of the occasion, until the assembled mass was estimated by careful observers to reach as many as 200,000 persons, inclosed in the space of nearly a half of a mile in length and 750 ft. in breadth. Even the two pedestals and the bronze figures which supported the Pegasus statues were crowded over, each by 30 or 40 persons, who had climbed on the bronze backs of the horses and clung to their wings, or perched upon the heads of the figures. The number of guests upon the platform was considered to amount to as many as 4,000 persons. They included the high official dignitaries of the country, members of the Cabinet, Senators and Congressmen, Supreme Court Judges, all in full dress; general officers of the Army, and Admirals and Commodores, subordinate officers, staff-officers, etc., in uniform; the diplomatic corps, in full court-dress, their breasts covered with decorations; and numerous ladies elegantly costumed—the whole creating a varied and vivid picture of humanity in its most attractive phases.

On the arrival of popular personages and those well-known to the assembled crowd, loud cheers rent the air. This happened in the cases of General Sherman, General Hancock, General Philip Sheridan, Hon. J. G. Blaine, Secretary Bristow, and many others. At a little past ten o'clock the Emperor and Empress of Brazil arrived at the platform, Dom Pedro being loudly cheered on his way, an attention which he repeatedly acknowledged. The appearance of the soldiers amassed in the crowd, as occasion required, to restrain the latter from inroads upon the rope which separated them from the inclosed space, gave color to the dark picture of the human beings without.

The ceremonies commenced by the performance at the hands of Theodore Thomas's magnificent orchestra of a series of thirteen national airs:

1. The Washington March.
2. Argentine Republic (Marche de la Republica).
3. Austria. Gott erhalte Franz, den Kaiser.
4. Belgium. La Brabançonne.
5. Brazil. Hymno Brasileira Nacional.
6. Denmark. Volkslied—den tappre Landsoldat.
7. France. La'Marseillaise.
8. Germany. Was ist des Deutchen Vaterland?
9. Great Britain. God Save the Queen.
10. Italy. Marcia del Re.
11. Netherlands. Wie neerlandsch bloed.
12. Norway. National Hymn.
13. Russia. National Hymn.

At eleven o'clock, following the completion of the international music, the orchestra performed the "Wagner Inauguration March," written for the occasion by the celebrated German composer, of which the capable musical critic of the New York *Tribune* says: "No praise which has been lavished upon this noble composition overstates its merit, and we are greatly disappointed in the taste of our countrymen if it do not soon become one of the most popular of Thomas's concert pieces." And again: "It is a purely original work; perhaps one of the most original things Wagner has written since Tristan."

After the performance of the Wagner March, Bishop Simpson arose and offered the following prayer, the vast assemblage listening with uncovered heads:

Almighty and everlasting God, our Heavenly Father. Heaven is Thy throne and the earth is Thy footstool. Before Thy majesty and holiness the angels vail their faces, and the spirits of the just made perfect bow in humble adoration. Thou art the creator of all things, the preserver of all that exist, whether they be thrones, or dominions, or principalities, or powers. The minute and the vast atoms and worlds alike attest the ubiquity of Thy presence and the omnipotence of Thy sway.

Thou alone art the sovereign ruler of nations. Thou raiseth up one and casteth down another, and Thou givest the kingdoms of the world to whomsoever Thou wilt. The past with all its records is the unfolding of Thy counsels and the realization of Thy grand designs. We hail Thee as our rightful ruler, the king eternal, immortal, and invisible, the only true God, blessed forevermore.

We come on this glad day O Thou God of our fathers, into these courts with thanksgiving, and into these gates with praise. We bless Thee for Thy wonderful goodness in the past, for the land which thou gavest to our fathers, a land vailed from the ages, from the ancient world, but revealed in the fullness of time to Thy chosen people, whom Thou didst lead by Thine own right hand through the billows of the deep, a land of vast

LAYING OUT THE MODEL OF THE CITY OF PARIS.

extent, of towering mountains and broad plains, of unnumbered products and untold treasures.

We thank Thee for the fathers of our country, men of mind and of might, who endured privations and sacrifices, who braved multiplied dangers rather than defile their consciences, or be untrue to their God, men who laid on the broad foundations of truth and justice the grand structure of civil freedom.

We praise Thee for the closing century, for the founders of the Republic, for the immortal Washington and his grand associates; for the wisdom with which they planned, and the firmness and heroism which, under Thy blessing, led them to triumphant success. Thou wast their shield in hours of danger, their pillar of cloud by day, and their pillar of fire by night. May we, their sons, walk in their footsteps and imitate their virtues.

We thank Thee for social and national prosperity and progress, for valuable discoveries and multiplied inventions, for labor-saving machinery relieving the toiling masses, for schools, free as the morning light for the millions of the rising generation, for books and periodicals scattered like leaves of Autumn over the land, for art and science, for freedom to worship God according to the dictates of conscience, for a church unfettered by the trammels of State.

Bless, we pray Thee, the President of the United States and his constitutional advisers, the Judges of the Supreme Court, the Senators and Representatives in Congress, the Governors of our several Commonwealths, the officers of the army and navy, and all who are in official position throughout our land. Guide them, we pray Thee, with counsels of wisdom, and may they ever rule in righteousness. We ask Thy blessing to rest upon the President and members of the Centennial Commission, and upon those associated with them in the various departments, who have labored long and earnestly, amid anxieties and difficulties, for the success of this enterprise.

May Thy special blessing, O Thou God of all the nations of the earth, rest upon our National guests, our visitors from distant lands. We welcome them to our shores, and we rejoice in their presence among us, whether they represent thrones, or culture, or research, or whether they come to exhibit the triumphs of genius and art, in the development of industry and in the progress of civilization. Preserve Thou them, we beseech Thee, in health and safety, and in due time may they be welcomed by loved ones again to their own, their native lands.

Let Thy blessing rest richly on this Centennial celebration. May the lives and health of all interested be precious in Thy sight. Preside in its assemblies. Grant that this association in effort may bind more closely together every part of our great Republic, so that our Union may be perpetual and indissoluble. Let its influence draw the nations of earth into a happier unity. Hereafter, we pray Thee, may all disputed questions be settled by arbitration, and not by the sword, and may wars forever cease among the sons of men.

May the new century be better than the past. More radiant with the light of true philosophy, warmer with the emanations of a world-wide sympathy. May capital, genius, and labor be freed from all antagonism by the establishment and application of such principles of justice and equity as shall reconcile diversified interests and bind in imperishable bands all parts of society.

GENERAL T. SAIGO, CENTENNIAL COMMISSIONER FROM JAPAN.

We pray Thy benediction especially on the women of America, who for the first time in the history of our race take so conspicuous a place in a national celebration. May the light of their intelligence, purity, and enterprise shed its beams afar, until in distant lands their sisters may realize the beauty and glory of Christian freedom and elevation. We beseech Thee, Almighty Father, that our beloved Republic may be strengthened in every element of true greatness, until her mission is accomplished by presenting to the world an illustration of the happiness of a free people, with a free church in a free State, under laws of their own enactment, and under rulers of their own selection, acknowledging supreme allegiance only to the King of kings and Lord of lords. And as Thou didst give to one of its illustrious sons first to draw experimentally the electric spark from heaven, which has since girdled the globe in its celestial whispers of "Glory to God

in the highest, peace on earth and good will to men," so to latest time may the mission of America, under divine inspiration, be one of affection, brotherhood, and love for all our race. And may the coming centuries be filled with the glory of our Christian civilization.

And unto Thee, our Father, through Him whose life is the light of men, will we ascribe glory and praise, now and forever. Amen.

When the prayer was ended, the following hymn, by John Greenleaf Whittier, the music by John K. Paine, of Massachusetts, was sung, with organ and orchestral accompaniment, with magnificent effect:

Our fathers' God! from out whose hand
The centuries fall like grains of sand,
We meet to-day, united, free,
And loyal to our land and Thee,
To thank Thee for the era done,
And trust Thee for the opening one.

Here, where of old, by Thy design,
The fathers spake that word of Thine,
Whose echo is the glad refrain
Of rended bolt and falling chain,
To grace our festal time, from all
The zones of earth our guests we call.

Be with us while the new world greets
The old world thronging all its streets,
Unvailing all the triumphs won
By art or toil beneath the sun;
And unto common good ordain
This rivalship of hand and brain.

Thou, who hast here in concord furled
The war flags of a gathered world,
Beneath our Western skies fulfill
The Orient's mission of good will,
And, freighted with love's Golden Fleece,
Send back the Argonauts of peace.

For art and labor met in truce,
For beauty made the bride of use
We thank Thee, while, withal, we crave
The austere virtues strong to save,
The honor proof to place or gold,
The manhood never bought nor sold.

O! make Thou us, through centuries long,
In peace secure, in justice strong;
Around our gifts of freedom draw
The safeguards of Thy righteous law;
And, cast in some diviner mold,
Let the new cycle shame the old!

PRESENTATION SPEECH BY MR. JOHN WELSH.

Mr. John Welsh, President of the Centennial Board of Finance, then presented the buildings to the United States

VISITORS PASSING THROUGH THE TURNSTILES.

RECEPTION, AT PHILADELPHIA, OF GOVERNOR RICE OF MASSACHUSETTS, ON MAY 9TH.—THE PROCESSION LEAVING THE BERKS STREET DEPOT.

Centennial Commission being frequently applauded while speaking. He said:

MR. PRESIDENT AND GENTLEMEN OF THE UNITED STATES CENTENNIAL COMMISSION: In the presence of the Government of the United States, and of the several distinguished bodies by whom we are surrounded, and in behalf of the Centennial Board of Finance, I greet you.

In readiness at the appointed time, I have the honor to announce to you that, under your supervision, and in accordance with the plans fixed and established by you, we have erected the buildings belonging to us, and have made all the arrangements devolving on us necessary for the opening of the "International Exhibition." We hereby now formally appropriate them for their intended occupation; and we hold ourselves ready to make all further arrangements that may be needed for carrying into full and complete effect all the requirements of the acts of Congress relating to the Exhibition.

For a like purpose, we also appropriate the buildings belonging to the State of Pennsylvania and the City of Philadelphia, erected by us at their bidding, to wit: Memorial Hall, Machinery Hall and Horticultural Hall. These and other substantial offerings stand as the evidence of their patriotic co-operation. To the United States of America, through Congress, we are indebted for the aid which crowned our success.

In addition to those to which I have just referred, there are

other beautiful and convenient edifices, which have been erected by the representatives of foreign nations, by State authority, and by individuals, which are also devoted to the purposes of the Exhibition.

Ladies and Gentlemen : If in the past we have met with disappointments, difficulties and trials, they have been overcome by a consciousness that no sacrifice can be too great which is made to honor the memories of those who brought our nation into being. This commemoration of the events of 1776 excites our present gratitude. The assemblage here to-day of so many foreign representatives uniting with us in this reverential tribute is our reward.

We congratulate you on the occurrence of this day. Many of the nations have gathered here in peaceful competition. Each may profit by the association. This exhibition is but a school: the more thoroughly its lessons are learned, the greater will be the gain; and, when it shall have closed, if by that study the nations engaged in it shall have learned respect for each other, then it may be hoped that veneration for Him who rules on high will become universal, and the angels' song once more be heard:

"Glory to God in the highest,
And on earth, peace, good will toward men."

General Hawley then arose, and said that the President of the Centennial Commission accepted the great trust confided by the Board of Finance.

THE CANTATA.

At 11.35 the following cantata by Sidney Lanier, of Georgia, was rendered with very great effect:

From this hundred-terraced height
Sight more large with nobler light
Ranges down yon towering years;
Humbler smiles and lordlier tears
Shine and fall, shine and fall,
While old voices rise and call
Yonder where the to-and-fro
Weltering of my Long-Ago
Moves about the moveless base
Far below my resting-place.

Mayflower, Mayflower, slowly hither flying,
Trembling westward o'er yon balking sea,
Hearts within Farewell dear England sighing,
Winds without But dear in vain replying,
Gray-lipp'd waves about these shouted, crying
No! It shall not be!

Jamestown, out of thee—
Plymouth, thee—thee, Albany—
Winter cries Ye freeze: away!

Fever cries, Ye burn: away!
Hunger cries, Ye starve: away!
Vengeance cries, Your graves shall stay!

Then old Shapes and Masks of Things,
Framed like Faiths or clothed like Kings
Ghosts of Goods once fleshed and fair,
Grown foul Bads in alien air—
War, and his most noisy lords,
Tongued with lithe and poisoned swords—

Error, Terror, Rage and Crime,
All in a windy night of time
Cried to me from land and sea,
No! Thou shalt not be!
Hark!
Huguenots whispering yea in the dark,
Puritans answering yea in the dark!
Yea, like an arrow shot true to his mark,
Darts through the tyrannous heart of Denial.
Patience and Labor and solemn-souled Trial,
Foiled, still beginning,
Soiled, but not sinning,
Toil through the stertorous death of the Night,
Toil, when wild brother-wars new dark the Light,
Toil, and forgive, and kiss o'er and replight.

Now Praise to God's oft-granted grace,
Now Praise to Man's undaunted face,

tion of the natural resources of the country and their development, and of its progress in those arts which benefit mankind," and ordered that an exhibition of American and foreign arts, products, and manufactures should be held, under the auspices of the Government of the United States, in the City of Philadelphia, in the year 1876. To put into effect the several laws relating to the Exhibition, the United States Centennial Commission was constituted, composed of two Commissioners from each State and Territory, nominated by their respective Governors and appointed by the President. The Congress also created our auxiliary and associate corporation, the Centennial Board of Finance, whose unexpectedly heavy burdens have been nobly borne. A remarkable and prolonged disturbance of the finances and industries of the country has greatly magnified the task: but we hope for a favorable judgment of the degree of success attained. July 4, 1873, this ground was dedicated to its present uses. Twenty-one months ago this Memorial Hall was begun. All the other 180 buildings within the inclosure have been erected within twelve months. All the buildings embraced in the plans of the Commission itself are finished. The demands of applicants exceeded the space, and strenuous and continuous efforts have been made to get every exhibit ready in time.

By general consent the Exhibition is appropriately held in the City of Brotherly Love. Yonder, almost within your view, stand the venerated edifice wherein occurred the event this work is designed to commemorate, and the hall in which the first Continental Congress assembled. Within the present limits of this great park were the homes of eminent patriots of that era, where Washington and his associates received generous hospitality and

GENERAL GRANT DECLARES THE EXHIBITION OPEN.

At 11:55 A. M., amid great applause, President Grant accepted the trust confided to him by the authorities of the Centennial in the following speech:

MY COUNTRYMEN: It has been thought appropriate, upon this Centennial occasion, to bring together in Philadelphia, for popular inspection, specimens of our attainments in the industrial and fine arts, and in literature, science and philosophy, as well as in the great business of agriculture and of commerce.

That we may the more thoroughly appreciate the excellences and deficiencies of our achievements, and also give emphatic expression to our earnest desire to cultivate the friendship of our fellow-members of this great family of nations, the enlightened agricultural, commercial and manufacturing people of the world have been invited to send hither corresponding specimens of their skill to exhibit on equal terms in friendly competition with our own. To this invitation they have generously responded; for so doing we tender them our hearty thanks.

The beauty and utility of the contributions will this day be submitted to your inspection by the managers of this Exhibition. We are glad to know that a view of specimens of the skill of all nations will afford you unalloyed pleasure, as well as yield to you a valuable practical knowledge of so many of the remarkable results of the wonderful skill existing in enlightened communities.

One hundred years ago our country was new and but partially

PRESIDENT GRANT AND PARTY LEAVING THE RESIDENCE OF GEORGE W. CHILDS, ESQ., TO ATTEND THE OPENING CEREMONIES.

Despite the land, despite the sea,
I was: I am: and I shall be—
How long, Good Angel, O how long?
Sing me from Heaven a man's own song!

" Long as thine Art shall love true love,
Long as thy Science truth shall know,
Long as thine Eagle harms no Dove,
Long as thy Law by law shall grow,
Long as thy God is God above,
Thy brother every man below,
So long, dear Land of all my love,
Thy name shall shine, thy fame shall glow!"

O Music, from this height of time my Word unfold:
In thy large signals all men's hearts Man's Heart behold:
Mid-heaven unroll thy chords as friendly flags unfurled,
And wave the world's best lover's welcome to the world.

PRESENTATION TO THE PRESIDENT.

At 11:48, A. M., began the presentation speech by General Hawley, turning the Exhibition Buildings over to the President of the United States. General Hawley said:

MR. PRESIDENT: Five years ago the President of the United States declared it fitting that "the completion of the first century of our national existence should be commemorated by an exhibi-

able counsel. You have observed the surpassing beauty of the situation placed at our disposal. In harmony with all this fitness is the liberal support given the enterprise by the State, the city, and the people individually.

In the name of the United States you extended a respectful and cordial invitation to the Governments of other nations to be represented and to participate in this Exhibition. You know the very acceptable terms in which they responded, from even the most distant regions. Their Commissioners are here, and you will soon see with what energy and brilliancy they have entered upon this friendly competition in the arts of peace.

It has been the fervent hope of the Commission that during this festival year the people from all States and sections, of all creeds and churches, all parties and classes, burying all resentments, would come up together to this birthplace of our liberties, to study the evidence of our resources; to measure the progress of a hundred years; and to examine to our profit the wonderful products of other lands; but especially to join hands in perfect fraternity, and promise the God of our fathers that the new century shall surpass the old in the true glories of civilization. And furthermore, that from the association here of welcome visitors from all nations, there may result not alone great benefits to invention, manufactures, agriculture, trade and commerce, but also stronger international friendships and more lasting peace.

Thus reporting to you, Mr. President, under the laws of the Government and the usage of similar occasions, in the name of the United States Centennial Commission, I present to your view the International Exhibition of 1876.

settled. Our necessities have compelled us to chiefly expend our means and time in felling forests, subduing prairies, building dwellings, factories, ships, docks, warehouses, roads, canals, machinery, etc., etc. Most of our schools, churches, libraries, and asylums have been established within a hundred years. Burdened by these great primal works of necessity, which could not be delayed, we yet have done what this Exhibition will show, in the direction of rivaling older and more advanced nations in law, medicine and theology; in science, literature, philosophy and the fine arts. While proud of what we have done, we regret that we have not done more. Our achievements have been great enough, however, to make it easy for our people to acknowledge superior merit wherever found.

And now, fellow-citizens, I hope a careful examination of what is about to be exhibited to you will not only inspire you with a profound respect for the skill and taste of our friends from other nations, but also satisfy you with the attainments made by our own people during the past one hundred years. I invoke your generous co-operation with the worthy Commissioners to secure a brilliant success to this International Exhibition, and to make the stay of our foreign visitors—to whom we extend a hearty welcome—both profitable and pleasant to them. I declare the International Exhibition now open.

The President was loudly cheered, the Emperor of Brazil rising in his seat and joining in the demonstration by waving his hat.

OFFICIAL TOUR OF THE BUILDING.

At 12 o'clock, at a signal from General Hawley, the American flag was unfurled from the Main Building, the Hallalujah Chorus was rendered with orchestral and organ accompaniment, and a salute of 100 guns was fired from George's Hill, together with the ringing of chimes from different parts of the ground. During the performance of the chimes the Foreign Commissioners passed from the platform into the Main Building and took places in the general aisle before their respective departments; after which, President Grant, accompanied by the Director-General, Goshorn, followed by the guests of the day, also passed into the Main Building, and thence to Machinery Hall, and from there to the Judges' quarters, where a reception by the President was held. The procession, headed by the President, after passing through the Main Exhibition Building, passed to the Machinery Hall, where the President assisted by Dom Pedro, at 1:22 P. M., put in motion the great engine, thus starting all the machinery in that building. This closed the formal ceremonies of the day. The following was the order of the procession as it passed through the Main Building:

The President of the United States
and Alfred T. Goshorn, Director-General.
The Chief-Justice of the United States.
The President of the Senate.

The Governors of States, and Territories.
The Senate of the United States.
The House of Representatives.
The General of the Army, and Staff.
The Admiral of the Navy, and Staff.
The Lieutenant-General of the Army, and Staff.
The Vice-Admiral of the Navy, and Staff.
The General Officers of the Army, and Staffs.
The Rear-Admiral and Commodores of the Navy, and Staffs.
Officers of the Army and Navy.
Military and Naval Officers of Foreign Governments.
Consuls-General and Consuls of Foreign Governments.
Judges of the United States Courts and Officers of the
United States Executive Bureaus.
Officers of the United States Coast Survey.
Officers of the Smithsonian Institution.
The Boards of Judges of Awards of the Exhibition.
The Supreme Court of Pennsylvania.
The Legislature of Pennsylvania.
The Judiciary of Pennsylvania.
The Board of State Supervisors of Pennsylvania.
The Boards of State Revenue of Pennsylvania.
The Mayor of Philadelphia.
The Mayors of Cities.
The Select and Common Councils of Philadelphia.
The State Centennial Boards.
The Women's Centennial Commission.
The Advisory and Co-operating Committees, and Boards of
Commissioners.
The International Regatta Commissioners and the Committee of
the International Rifle Association.
Officers of the City Department of Philadelphia.

Miss Lilly was born in 1792. The doll's eyes still move, and it continues to wear the finery in which it crossed the ocean, to show the ambitious dames of the young Republic how their Parisian sisters dressed.

TEXTILE FABRICS:
THEIR ORIGIN AND HISTORY.

THE progress of the arts and manufactures as displayed in the exhibits of textile fabrics in the Centennial Exposition is a subject of interest to the world at large. For this reason, and before considering the actual display of these exhibits at Fairmount, we devote some space to the consideration of the past history of this important branch of manufacture.

SILK.

While there are many references in the Scriptures which have been taken by different translators and commentators to have the meaning of silk, there is yet no absolute account of any use of the article, or any clear mention of it, in the Bible. In certain Hebrew books, the "Targum" for instance, this fabric seems more clearly designated, but it has been decided by some of the best scholars that there is no mention of silk in the Old Testament, and that it was unknown to the Hebrews in ancient times. The first gar-

BISHOP SIMPSON INVOKING A BLESSING UPON THE EXHIBITION.

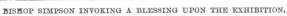

PRESIDENT GRANT DECLARING THE EXHIBITION OPEN.

The Speaker of the House of Representatives.
Joseph R. Hawley, President of the Centennial Commission.
John Welsh, President of the Board of Finance.
Daniel J. Morrell, Chairman of the Executive Commitee
of the Commission.
John L. Campbell, Secretary of the Commission.
Frederick Fraley, Secretary of the Board of Finance.
The Cabinet.
The Supreme Court of the United States.
The Diplomatic Corps.
The Foreign Commissions,
[which successively took positions immediately after the
Diplomatic Corps, as the latter passed the foreign
sections of the Main Building.]

The Centennial Commission.
Chiefs of Bureaus of the Administration.
The Board of Finance.
Henry Petit and Joseph M. Wilson, Engineer and Architect
of the Main Building and Machinery Hall.
H. J. Schwartz, Wood Architect of Memorial Hall and
Horticultural Hall.
Joseph H. Windrim, Architect of Agricultural Hall
and of the Government Building.
Richard J. Dobbins, Contractor for the Main Building
and Memorial Hall.
Philip Quigley, Contractor for Machinery Hall and
Agricultural Hall.
Aaron Doane, Contractor for the Government Building.
The Board of the United States Executive Department.
The Women's Centennial Executive Committee.
The Fairmount Park Commission.

During the day the display of flags throughout the city was magnificent, nearly every house being ornamented to some extent in this manner, while many were completely covered from roof to cellar with bunting. The principal business streets of the city vied with each other in their efforts to display the largest number of flags of all nations, Chestnut being conspicuous in this particular, while the display at Independence Hall was really superb, and the *Public Ledger* building exhibited flags from every one of its innumerable windows. Throughout the principal streets were to be seen regiments and companies of soldiers, while throngs of gayly-dressed ladies and children made the scene exceptionally charming and beautiful.

THE CENTENNIAL DOLL.

NEWPORT, R. I., contributes to the Centennial a doll believed to be the oldest in the country. It is made of wax, is about ten inches high, and has grown yellow with age, until it looks frightfully like a corpse. It boasts of the following history: It was imported from Paris as a model of the fashions of the day, and was bought in Philadelphia by the Hon. Benjamin Bourne, of Bristol, who was a Member of Congress from 1790 to 1796. The doll was given to his niece, Miss Lilly C. Turner, daughter of Dr. Turner, a surgeon in the Revolutionary Army.

ments worn were, undoubtedly, made from the leaves of trees and vegetables. After this the sheep furnished the first fabric, as there is mentioned in the Hebrew books a dress manufactured from wool, called the *simla*—an upper garment consisting of a piece of cloth about six yards long, and two or three wide, in shape not unlike our blankets. In the course of time various other garments came into use, as mentioned in several other parts of Scripture. The materials of which these garments were usually made seem to have been linen, or woolen, or the natural skin of animals. The first reliable mention of the manufacture of silk is found in the Chinese records, and ascribes it to the period of 1703 B. C., which would make Hoong-Ti, who is alleged to have been the inventor or discoverer of this culture, contemporary with Joseph, when Prime Minister over the Land of Egypt. In a Chinese work upon the culture of the mulberry and the rearing of silkworms we read as follows:

"From the translation of M. Stanislas Julien, the lawful wife of the Emperor Hoong-Ti, named Si-Ling-Chi, began the culture of silk. It was at that time that the Emperor Hoong-Ti invented the art of making garments. This great prince was desirous that Si-Ling-Chi, his legitimate wife, should contribute to the happiness of his people. He charged her to examine the silkworms to test the practicability of using the thread. Si-Ling-Chi had a large quantity of these insects collected, which she fed herself in a place prepared for that purpose, and discovered not only the means of raising, but also the manner of reeling, the silk, and of employing it to make garments. It is through gratitude for so great a benefit that posterity has deified Si-Ling-Chi, and rendered her particular honors under the name of 'The Goddess of Silkworms.'"

The first ancient author who affords any evidence respecting the use of silk is Aristotle, who refers to Panphile, daughter of Plates, as reported to have first woven in Cos; but as, long before the time of Aristotle, a regular trade

the world's history. They evidently existed in Egypt at the time of Joseph, 1,700 years before the Christian era, and two centuries later the Hebrews carried with them, on their departure from that ancient seat of civilization, the arts of spinning, dyeing, weaving, and embroidery. The women of Sidon, before the Trojan War, were especially celebrated for their skill in embroidery; and Homer, who lived 900 B. c., mentions Helen as being engaged in embroidering the combats of the Greeks and Romans. According to Pliny, Semiramis, the Syrian Queen, was be-

a distaff and spindle, and to the present day the distaff is used in India, Egypt, and other Eastern countries. Spinning among the Egyptians, as among our ancestors of no very distant age, was a domestic occupation in which ladies of rank did not hesitate to engage. The term "spinsters" is yet applied to unmarried ladies of every rank, and there are persons yet alive who remember to have seen the spinning-wheel as an ordinary piece of furniture in domestic economy. In Homer's pictures of domestic life we find the lady of the mansion superintending the labors of her

PRESIDENT GRANT AND THE EMPEROR OF BRAZIL STARTING THE GREAT CORLISS ENGINE IN MACHINERY HALL.

had been established in the interior of Asia, bringing its most valuable productions, and especially those which were most easily transported, to the shores opposite this flourishing island, it is quite probable that the raw silk was brought to the coast from the interior of Asia, and there manufactured.

The arts of spinning and weaving, which rank next in importance to agriculture, having been found among almost all the nations of the old and new continents—even among those little removed from barbarism—are not unreasonably supposed to have been invented at a very remote period of

lieved to have been the inventor of the art of weaving. Minerva, in some ancient statues, is represented with a distaff, to intimate that she taught men the art of spinning. This honor is given by the Egyptians to Isis; by the Mohammedans, to the son of Japheth; by the Chinese, to the consort of their emperor, Yao; and by the Peruvians, to Mamaela, wife of Manc Capac, their first sovereign.

Paintings representing the gathering and preparation of flax have been found on the walls of ancient sepulchres at Eleithuis and Benihassan, in Upper Egypt. The instrument used for spinning in all countries, in the earliest times, was

servants, and using the distaff herself. Her spindle, made of costly material and richly ornamented, and the wool dyed of some bright hue to render it capable of being touched with aristocratic fingers, remain an appropriate present which the Egyptian Queen, Alcandra, made to the Spartan Helen whose skill in embroidery and every species of ornamental work was as much celebrated as her beauty. The distaff was generally about three feet in length, commonly a stick or reed, with an expansion near the top for holding the ball. It was usually held in the left arm, and the fibres were drawn out from the projecting ball, being at

OPENING OF THE EXPOSITION, MAY 10TH BY PRESIDENT GRANT—SCENE IN THE ROTUNDA OF MEMORIAL HALL.

the same time spiral, and twisted by the forefinger and thumb. The thread so produced was wound upon the spindle until the quantity was as great as it could carry. The spindle was made of some light wood or reed, and was generally from eight to twelve inches in length. At the top, a slit or catch, to which the thread was fixed so that the weight of the spindle might carry the thread down to the ground as fast as it was finished. Its lower extremity was also inserted into a wheel made of stone or metal, or of some heavy material, which both served to keep it steady and to promote its rotation. The spinner every now and then gave the spindle a fresh gyration by a gentle touch, so as to increase the twist of the thread. Whenever the spindle reached the ground, the thread spun was then taken out of the slit or clasp, and wound upon the spindle. The clasp was then closed together, and the spinning of a new thread commenced. In India, women of all castes prepared the thread for the weaver, spinning on a piece of wire or a very thin rod of polished iron, with a ball of clay at one end.

The Parthian war, and the increased intercourse between the Roman Empire and the kingdoms of the East, were the means of introducing every kind of silken goods into more general use. In the time of Horace silken webs were worn at Rome only by women who aimed at being notorious. The Emperor Caligula had silk curtains attached to his throne, and wore silk as a part of his dress when he appeared in public. Under the early emperors it is probable that silk was obtained in considerable quantities for the wardrobe of the emperors, where it was preserved from one reign to another, until in the year 176 Marcus Aurelius Antoninus, in consequence of the exhausted state of his treasury, sold at public auction in the forum of Trajan the imperial ornaments, together with the golden and silken robes of the emperors.

The use of shawls and tunics of silk was, except in the case of extravagant Caligula, confined to the female sex. As to this emperor, Suetonius tells us that he often went into public wearing bracelets and long sleeves, sometimes in the garment of silk. At a very early period the use of dyeing had been carried to a great degree of perfection in Phœnicia. The method of dyeing woolen cloth of purple was, it is stated, at first discovered at Tyre. This art, the most celebrated among the ancients, appears to have been brought to a degree of excellence of which we can form but a very faint idea. It is mentioned by Byzantian historians that before silkworms were brought to Constantinople in the middle of the sixth century, no person in that capital knew that silk was produced by a worm, which is considered good evidence that none were reared so near to Constantinople as the island of Cos. Josephus says that the Emperors Titus and Vespasian wore silk dresses when they celebrated at Rome their triumph over the Jews. Pliny dissuades the virtuous and prudent wife from wearing silk, and Martial alludes to the employment of persons for preserving the garments of silk and other precious metals belonging to the emperors. Pausanius mentions an interesting circumstance —the breeding of silkworms within doors, in houses adapted both for Summer and Winter. It is remarkable that in China the worms are now reared in small houses, a practice which long prevailed in that country.

Among the valuable and curious effects of the Emperor Commodus, which, after his death, were sold by his successor, Pertinax, was a garment with a woof of silk of a bright yellow color, the materials of which are more beautiful than if the material had been interwoven with threads of gold. In about the third century silk became exceedingly dear, owing to the victories of the Persians, which at that time cut off all direct communication between the silk-producing countries and the Western World. In the fourth century the art had been acquired of preparing silk by covering the thread with gold, and with this gold thread a woof was made from which robes for important purposes, as installations, were made. In India, silk was more common. The article in its raw state, as well as woven, was conveyed down the Indus to the coast of the Ery-

RECEPTION OF THE EMPEROR AND EMPRESS OF BRAZIL IN THE WOMEN'S PAVILION.

threan Sea, and also brought to the great mart of Barygaca, on the Gulf of Cambay, near the modern Surat. Tyre appears to have been the only city of antiquity which made dyeing its chief occupation and the staple of its commerce. There is little doubt that purple, the sacred symbol of royal dignity, was a color discovered in that city, and that the use of the dye contributed to the city's opulence and grandeur. The Tyrian dye was used to stain both wool and silk. The introduction of silkworms in Europe, took place about A. D. 530, when two monks, arrived from India, learning that Justinian was desirous that his subjects should no longer purchase raw silk from the Persians, went to him and informed him as to the nature and process of silk manufacture, offering to furnish him with eggs of the silkworm. The Emperor having promised the monks a reward, they returned to India and brought the eggs to Byzantium, where, having hatched them by burying them in warm soil, the monks fed the silkworms with the leaves of the black mulberry, and thus enabled the Romans henceforth to obtain raw silk in their own country.

Silk shawls had long been manufactured in the Phœnician cities of Tyre and Berytus. During the Persian wars the manufacturers put up the prices of their goods, when it was determined by the Emperor that the silk-manufacture should be carried on thereafter solely by the imperial treasurer. By this means the Emperor and Empress amassed great wealth, while the silk trade was ruined in Byzantium and Tyre. By the middle of the sixth century silk was used in adorning church vestments, and is mentioned specially in connection with the church of St. Sophia, at Constantinople. It is uncertain when silk was first introduced into England, though existing documents prove it to have existed there by the end of the sixth century. The usual dress of the earliest French kings seems to have been a linen shirt, and drawers of the same material, next to the skin. Over these, tunics, probably of fine wool, which had a border of silk, ornamented sometimes with gold or precious stones. Charlemagne, we are informed, wore such a tunic or vest, with a silken border, about the year 970, when silk was in common use in England or in Britain. Kenneth, King of Scotland, paid a visit in London to Edgar, King of England, and the latter king, to evince his friendship, bestowed upon his illustrious guest silks, rings and gems, together with 100 ounces of gold.

The breeding of silkworms, however, in Europe, appears to have been confined to Greece from the time of the Emperor Justinian until the middle of the twelfth century. The manufacture of silk was also very rare in other parts of Europe, being probably practiced only as a recreation and an accomplishment for ladies; but in the year 1148, Richard I., King of Sicily, having taken the cities of Corinth, Thebes, and Athens, thus got into his power a great number of silk-weavers, took them away with the implements and materials necessary for the exercise of their art, and forced them to reside at Palermo. In twenty years from this forcible establishment of the manufacture, the silks of Sicily are described as having attained a decided excellence; as being of diversified patterns and colors, some fanciful, interwoven with woolen tastefully embellished with figures, and others adorned with gold. From Palermo the manufacture of silk extended itself throughout all parts of Italy and into Spain. By the fourteenth century it had been carried into Venice, Florence, Milan, and even into Germany, France, and Great Britain. Although this was the first silk manufactured in those countries, there is ample evidence that silk was known to the inhabitants of France and England as early as the sixth century. This is manifest from the use of words for silk appearing in several of the northern languages at this time. The Danish kings began to use silk in appending the waxen seals to their charters. Silk, in the form of velvet, may now be seen on some ancient armor in the Tower of London. As early as the fourteenth century silk was used in the binding of books, while the ancient Catholic vestments were embroidered in silk with extreme beauty. The art of embroidery seems to have attained a higher degree of perfection in France than in any other country in Europe. Embroiderers formerly composed the great portion of the working population, and laws were specially confirmed for their protection. They were formed into a company as early as 1272. Since its introduction into Europe, silk-culture has always formed a great branch of industry in Italy, Turkey, and Greece, and it has continued to be cultivated to some extent in France, Spain, and Portugal.

The introduction of silk into France is assigned to Louis XI., who in 1480 obtained workmen from Genoa, Venice, and Florence, and established a manufactory at Tours, which did not prosper, so that in the reign of Francis, a new importation of workmen had to be obtained from Milan. These, about the year 1521, were established at Lyons, which has ever since been the seat of silk manufacture in France. The increased supply and more general use of silk in England which followed on the successful progress of the manufacture in France, seem to have awakened the alarm of the rulers in that country lest the silk trade should suffer from the importation of goods. In the reign of Mary, 1504,

PRESIDENT GRANT AND PARTY PASSING THROUGH A LINE OF SAILORS TOWARD THE MAIN BUILDING.

OPENING OF THE EXPOSITION, MAY 10TH—SCENE IN HORTICULTURAL HALL.

THE EMPEROR AND EMPRESS OF BRAZIL VISITING THE BRAZILIAN DEPARTMENT ON THE DAY OF THE OPENING OF THE EXPOSITION.

that whoever should wear silk in any form should be imprisoned during three months and forfeit ten pounds. In the first year of James I. this law was repealed. The trade in silk carried on by the merchants of Antwerp was very extensive, yet none of the costly goods were retained for their own wear. They sold the finest of their own cloths to France, and bought coarse cloth from England to wear themselves. On the taking of the City of Antwerp by the Duke of Parma, in 1585, the commercial law of the country was almost destroyed, and about one-third

mencement of the eighteenth century the silk machinery of England was still very defective, the best machinery being in existence in Italy. In fact, this machinery was introduced into England by the dishonorable bribing of workmen connected with the mill at Piedmont, to allow an emissary secretly to make an inspection. The information was brought to England at the risk of the lives of the conspirators, who obtained it in 1717, when a famous silk-mill was erected on the Derwent, at Derby, which excited great astonishment at the time. It was five stories

value of about £6,500,000 sterling. It requires 1,600 worms to raise a pound of silk. The silk manufactories of Great Britain are chiefly located in Spitalfields (London), and Macclesfield, Coventry, and Derby. The dyeing is done chiefly at London, at Nottingham, and at Manchester, and considerable quantities of silk goods are sent from India, to be printed in patterns at London and other parts of England.

Concerning the introduction and progress of this industry in America, an account has already been given on

THE CHINESE COURT—CELESTIAL EXHIBITORS EXPLAINING THEIR WARES.

part of the manufacturers took refuge in England, and gave a powerful impulse to manufacture there. In 1666 it was stated that no fewer than 40,000 individuals in England were engaged in this trade. Thus the English manufacturers thus steadily progressed, notwithstanding the fact that the importations of foreign silk, with occasional exceptions, were quite free. In 1685 the evocation edict of France drove hundreds of thousands of the industrious people of France to seek protection in other countries. Some 50,000 came to England. At the com-

high, and one-eighth of a mile in length. Rapid improvements were made in the English machinery and manufacture, and in the year 1842 the value of British silk goods exported to France amounted to about $1,000,000. The great Exhibition in London, in 1851, displayed the vast advance made in that country in this manufacture.

The quantity of silk raised in the world is enormous. Great Britain imports, in the unmanufactured state, about 12,814,700 pounds, valued at £10,000,000 sterling, and, in addition to this, manufactured silk goods to the

page 38, in the "Sketch of the Early History of American Industry."

WOOL.

Of the materials employed by the ancients for making cloth, by far the most important was the wool of Europe. In examining the history of this industry we are first struck with the fact, as a result of careful research, that the sheep is not a native of Europe, but has been introduced there by man. In fact, it is generally conceded by zoologists that the whole race of domesticated sheep found their origin in the elevated regions of Central Asia, and we are therefore not surprised to learn that from the earliest times the inhabitants of Tartary, Persia, Mesopotamia, Syria and Palestine, and North Arabia, have been addicted to pastoral employments. The tribe of wandering Arabs which still frequent those countries are descendants of progenitors who led the same lives years ago, and whose habits and manners are preserved to the present day, with scarcely the slightest change. Herodotus, Strabo and others speak of sheep, and other early writers refer to shepherds and herdsmen wandering through uncultivated fields employed in attending herds and flocks. These, however, were strangers to the use of woolen garments, being clothed in skins and furs. Damascus supplied the materials of wool, and Syria was generally noted for its breeding of sheep and wool products. The Arabs appear from the earliest times to the present day to have bestowed no less attention upon sheep than upon their horses. The Phœnicians, however, did not employ themselves in breeding and pasturing sheep. The narrow strip of territory which they occupied at the eastern extremity of the Mediterranean was in general too densely populated to be adapted to this purpose. Their activity and enterprise were directed toward commerce and other channels, and they supplied them-

were forbidden to be buried in woolen cloth, or to use it in the temples, yet Herodotus states that on ordinary occasions they wore a garment of white wool over their other linen shirts, and also used wool for embroidering. At the southeastern extremity of Circassia, on the northern declivity of Mount Elborus, there still exists a mountain clan, consisting of rather more than 250 families, which retain the manners and habits of their ancestors 2,500 years ago. It is said of them that they are the most cultivated in Caucasus, and surpass their neighbors in refinement of manners. Their dress is chiefly made of woolen goods, which they deftly weave from the produce of their flocks. The region they occupied was at a distance of from 40 to 80 miles from the coast, to which they always resorted for commercial purposes. These people, in the earliest times, were noted for their fine wool and for the carpets and shawls which they produced from it. Their valleys are distinguished by beauty and fertility, and are still occupied by numerous herds of cattle and vast flocks of sheep and goats. In fact, there can be no doubt that the use and management of sheep were known from the earliest times in nearly the whole of Asia Minor, and that the woolen manufacture, in a primitive way, was carried on by the inhabitants, and to a very large extent. From Asia Minor,

Romans during their domination, and, finally from Africa, by the Moors, who maintained a footing for nearly eight centuries. The large sheep of the plains have long wool, often of a brown or black color. The sheep of the mountains, downs, and arid plains have short wool, of different degrees of fineness and different colors. The most important of these latter breeds is the Merino, now the most esteemed and widely diffused of all the fine-wooled breeds of Europe. Pliny mentions a breed of sheep with red wool, produced in the district adjoining the River Gaudalquiver. Martial, a Spaniard by birth, frequently alludes to Spanish sheep, and especially to the various natural colors of their wool, which was much esteemed, as it was manufactured without dyeing. Seven of his epigrams refer to this subject. Estramadura is still famous for its wool. There the Spanish flocks hybernate, and are conducted every Spring to pasture in the mountains of Leon and Asturias. It may be remarked here that sheep have always been bred principally for the weaver, not for the butcher, and that this has been more especially the case in ancient times and in Eastern countries, where the act of killing a sheep for food, except on solemn or extraordinary occasion, was regarded with feelings little short of aversion. The Arabs rarely diminished their flocks by using them for

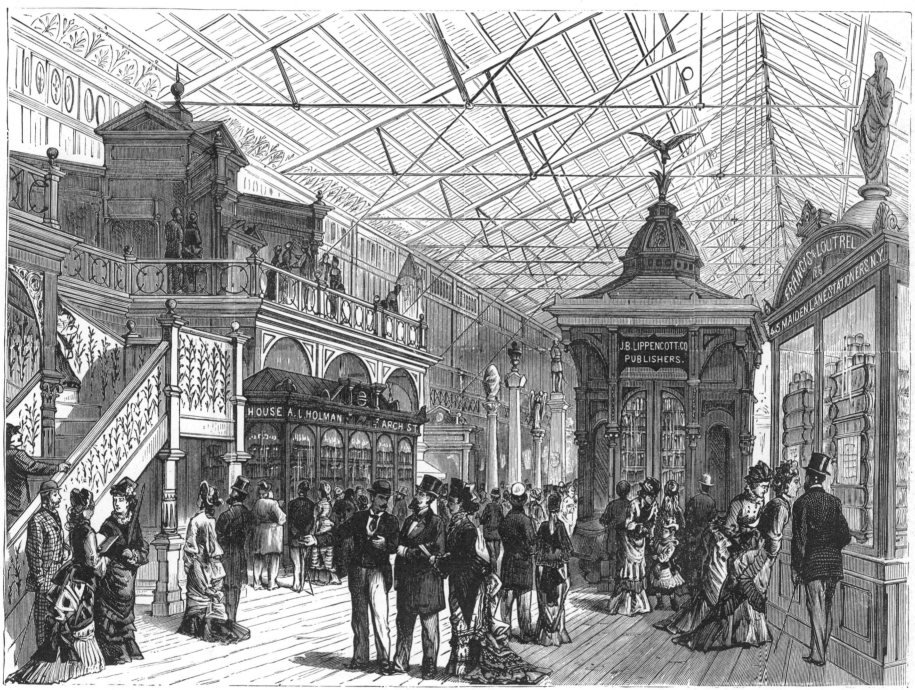

THE BOOK DEPARTMENT.

selves from foreign countries with wool for their celebrated manufactories. On the other hand, the Hebrews, who were the immediate neighbors of the Phœnicians, were altogether an agricultural and pastoral people. It is impossible to conceive a more striking difference in manners and institutions than that which must have presented itself to the traveler in very ancient times, when he passed from the deserts of Arabia and Idumuida to the richly populated and cultivated plains of Egypt. The wandering tribes of the former locality were forbidden by a positive law to till the ground or to construct settled habitations, and they lived on the produce of their flocks, which they continually led from place to place, in the pursuit of pasture adapted to the season of the year. The Egyptians, on the contrary, appear to have been originally under a prohibition of exactly the opposite kind, since they cultivated the ground with care, excelled most other nations in all the arts of life, and produced the most splendid proof of their architectural skill, but were not allowed to keep flocks of sheep and goats. Although it is shown by early writers that sheep were bred in Egypt, it is also in evidence that their number was very limited. What was produced must have been consumed in the country. For although the cheap material for the clothing of Egyptians was linen, and they

sheep-herding and wool-growing and manufacture spread into Greece, from Athens into Italy, and so into Central Europe. There is no reason, however, to suppose that the ancient Germans had any great skill in sheep-breeding. In France, too, the wool, where it is mentioned, is spoken of as of a coarse kind, more like hair than wool, and chiefly produced in Provence.

Cæsar relates that the ancient inhabitants of Britain had cattle, which is presumed to include sheep, the breed of which was improved greatly by both the Belgians and the Saxons. The people of Kent, who were of Belgic origin, and more refined than the original Britains, attained earlier great excellence in the arts of spinning and weaving, although their productions were only of a coarse description. Of all the countries in Europe, Spain has been the longest distinguished for the excellence of its wool. This fine country, more varied in its surface and natural productions than any other region of like extent in Europe, produces a great variety of breeds of sheep from the larger of the richer plains to the smaller races of the higher mountains, and more arid. The different races of sheep were introduced into Spain first from Asia by the early Phœnician colonists; then from Africa by the Carthagenians during their brief possession; next from Italy by the

food, but lived chiefly from dates, bread, milk, etc., or whatever they received in exchange for their wool. A lamb or kid, roasted whole, is a favorite at Aleppo, but seldom eaten except by the rich. Many Arabs have a sheep-shearing, and perhaps kill a lamb and treat their relatives and friends with it, together with new cheese and milk, and nothing more. Among the Mohammedans, sheep are sacrificed on certain days, as a festive and at the same time a religious ceremony. These ceremonies are of great antiquity, and derived from Arabia. On the pilgrimage to Mecca, every one is required to sacrifice a sheep. The spinning and weaving of wool was well-known in the time of Moses, and was extensively practiced by the ancient Greeks and Romans, and when the latter people made conquest of Britain, they probably introduced these arts into the island. The Romans are said to have had a factory at Winchester for supplying cloth to the Roman army. It is related that the mother of Alfred the Great was skilled in the spinning of wool, and instructed her daughters therein; but the origin of woolen manufacture, as a national employment, is supposed to date in England from the time of William the Conqueror, when a number of Flemings, being driven out of their territory by the incursion of the sea, came to England and endeavored to obtain the patronage of the queen, who was a native of their country. In this they were successful, and were established in their trade as weavers under royal patronage. By the close of the reign of Henry II., the manufacture of wool had been extended to many parts of the kingdom, and several companies of weavers were formed in various counties, paying to the king for the privilege of carrying on their trade. Under this reign the use of Spanish wool was prohibited under pain of forfeiture of the goods. In the reign of Edward III., numerous Flemish wool manufacturers were invited to England, and, as a result, followed the production of wool fustians, baizes, broadcloths, kerseys, friezes, and serges in large quantities. The cruelty of the reigning Duke drove from the continent a number of industries, which increased the prosperity of the woolen trade of England. Wool soon became so much esteemed that it sold at a very high price in foreign markets, and was often used instead of money; and it is related that in 1342, when gold was scarce, the king sent a large number of sacks of wool

land, numbers were skillful in the manufacture of wool and improved lighter textures; a large supply of fine cloth was produced; a greater number of sheep were bred; and the trade generally revived.

The total annual importation of wool into England in 1872 was 137,507,126 pounds. The estimated produce of home-grown wool in 1871 was 144,985,712. The introduction of cotton machinery in a modified form became of great importance to manufacturing processes. The chief seat of the woolen manufacture in England is in Yorkshire, though it is also carried on to a considerable extent in other parts of the kingdom. Woolen cloth, formerly woven by hand, is now manufactured chiefly by power-looms. Some of the British colonies are very important wool-producing countries, Australia, in this respect standing far in advance of all other countries whatever, though California is not far behind. The Australian wool is in general a beautiful, short, silky staple, well adapted for the manufacture of soft, pliable and elastic fabrics. The breed has

including alpaca lustres, umbrella and parasol cloths, mohairs, lustres, etc. In 1865 the exportation of worsted stuffs from England was valued at £13,361,000, of which a very considerable amount went to France. The worsted manufacture has increased rapidly of late years, and this may be ascribed to the greater simplicity of the processes, to the recent introduction of combing machines, and especially to the introduction of cotton warps in 1835, which not only cheapened the goods but vastly increased their variety.

THE HUNTERS' CAMP.

HALF-WAY between Memorial and Horticultural Halls is a picturesque ravine, the most romantic spot within the Centennial Grounds. It begins near the centre of the latter, and runs east, growing broader and deeper until it opens out upon the Schuylkill. It is crossed within the grounds by three bridges, of which the central one is 90 ft. above

THE HUNTERS' CAMP IN LANSDOWNE RAVINE.

to Cologne to redeem King Philip's crown, which was pawned there for £2,500. The long-wooled sheep of England soon became celebrated, and the fleece was in large request throughout Europe. The system of monopolies established in the reign of Henry VIII., which restricted the manufacture of certain articles to particular towns, was very injurious to the woolen trade. However, at the end of this reign, the introduction of the spinning-wheel, about the year 1530, caused some revival in the manufacture, and in the reign of Elizabeth it shared in the general prosperity of the country. Although the English were skillful in the weaving and dressing of cloth, yet the art of dyeing and finishing, once well-known to them, had been lost amidst the destructions of the kingdom. It was, therefore, the custom to send white cloths into Holland to be dyed and dressed. In the year 1667, however, a dyer came from the Netherlands with his workmen, and under the patronage of the Government, instructed the English manufacturers in its art, so that they soon became independent in this respect. In the year 1685, at the revocation of the edict of Nantes, among the many thousand workmen who sought refuge in Eng-

sprung from three merino lambs and five ewes taken out in 1797. The most costly of all wools is obtained from the Thibet goat, and is found next to the skin, under the thick hair of the animal, and from it the far-famed Cashmere shawls are made. There are two great classes of manufactories using wool as a raw material. In the one, where carded wool is employed, the goods are called woolen fabrics; in the other, where combed wool is used, the goods are called worsted fabrics. In all the manufactures of wool they have received the greatest advantage from the spinning-jenny, the mules and the power-loom. The term worsted is said to have derived its origin from a village of that name in Norfolk, where this manufacture was first carried on. Stuffs under this name are classified according to the materials of which they are composed, viz.: 1. Fabrics composed entirely of wool; 2. Fabrics composed of wool and cotton; 3. Fabrics composed of wool and silk, including the rich Irish poplins, coburgs, damasks, etc.; 4. Fabrics composed of wool, silk, and cotton, such as vestings, cravats, shawls, scarfs, barèges; 5. Fabrics composed of alpaca and mohair, mixed with cotton or silk,

the bottom of the ravine. From end to end of the latter a stream of clear water, having its source in Centennial Lake, descends in alternate cascades and gentle falls, being also fed by rills leaping down the rugged, but verdant and thickly-wooded, hillsides. Just beneath a point near the central bridge, and on the northern bank of the stream, is the Hunters' Cabin, which is among the most attractive novelties of the Exhibition. It is built of logs, in the "salt-box" style, and entirely open in front. Not only is it a fac-simile of the abode of a Western hunter or trapper, but within and around it are all the paraphernalia that a pushing and ingenious pioneer would be likely to provide. Inside, standing against the walls, or hung on pegs, are fishing-tackle, a panther's head, the horns of Rocky Mountain rams, hides of huge black bears, buckskin coats, leggins and moccasins, captured from Indians, a snow-white hide of a polecat (the only one of such a color known to have ever been seen in the United States), stuffed prairie-chickens and ducks, and a score of other curious trophies. There are also several stalwart fellows—practical hunters—in the buckskin garb of their profession. They lounge on the rough log couch, smoke, dress skins, cook and eat, thereby illustrating their manner of living in the West. Just outside the cabin is a campfire, kept constantly burning; a rough table, upon which the frugal repast is spread; and a cord hammock, hung from two trees. Occasionally a hunter springs into this, to show how he can sleep out of reach of snakes and vermin. Near by are some deer and a black bear, tethered to trees; and in the stream below a dam is constructed, upon the waters of which float several canoes. In these the men in buckskin practice rowing, and show how fish are gulled and the beaver caught.

JOHN WELSH,

CHAIRMAN OF THE BOARD OF FINANCE.

MR. JOHN WELSH is a native of Philadelphia, and now about seventy years of age. He was for many years a member of the firm of S. & W. Welsh, general shipping and commission merchants, Delaware Avenue, near Walnut Street. His reputation as a business man and executive officer was, at the time of his election, of the highest character, and during his service, now almost three years in extent, he has proven himself eminently qualified for the responsible position. On the 3d of March last, in his capacity as Chairman of the Board, and with Mr. Fraley, the Treasurer, he signed a bond of $500,000 for the faithful disbursement of the Congressional appropriation of $1,500,000. The best evidence of the high esteem with which both himself and Mr. Fraley are held by their fellow-citizens was shown in the eagerness of the most prominent and wealthy men to affix their names to the bond as sureties. The services of one hundred gentlemen were accepted, and the bond, as now filed, represents security at least ten times greater than the amount appropriated.

THE CHINESE COURT.

THE Chinese section is, next to the Japanese, the most curious in the Main Building. Its attraction, however, is owing more to the extreme gaudiness of the structure which incloses it than to any extraordinary interest possessed by its contents. The section is 148 ft. in length and 38 in width, the structure inclosing it being of the pagoda style of architecture, and evidently its Mongolian decorators first used up all the colors of a peacock's tail and of the rainbow, and then, as though regretting that they had not ten or eleven more different styles of rainbow to imitate, had recourse to their fertile invention for other shades. The pavilion (if it may be so called) was constructed in Canton in sections, and is, doubtless, to-day, the most gaudy building between Hudson's Bay and Cape Horn. The structures forming the entrances—of which there are three: one in front on the grand nave, and two on the western side —rise high above the rest of the pavilion, and are overtopped only by the pagoda or joss-house, and the towers seen inside. All these are of the pagoda style, which is familiar to every one who has seen a tea-caddie painting. The showcases are arranged in circles, their contents being principally pottery, porcelain, bronzes, carved wood-work, chasings on silver, inlaid-work, and silks. In appearance, the showcases are in keeping with the curious pavilion inclosing them.

NEW ENGLAND KITCHEN.

BETWEEN Horticultural and Agricultural Halls is a deep and wooded valley, which lacks only ruggedness and skipping streams of water to be fully as picturesque as Lansdowne Ravine. Near the summit of the hill, on the southern side of this valley, and snugly nestled among the tall trees which are now in the freshness of renewed life, is a quaint structure of that style of architecture which characterized the backwoodman's cot in Vermont or Connecticut one hundred years ago. It is called the New England Log Cabin. In connection with it is a building of familiar architecture, and called the New England Modern Kitchen. Taken together, they are designed to exhibit a comparison between the manner of carrying on culinary operations and attending table a century ago, and that of doing the same things at present in the Eastern States. A combination of quaint architecture, antiquated furniture, and the epochal costumes of the attendants, gives one a pleasing view of life in New England a century

ago. There is a chair that was brought from Old England in the second ship that landed on our coast; and another, made in Danvers, Mass., over 200 years ago, which has descended from the family of Governor Endicott. Underneath a clock, said to have been made 168 years ago, is John Alden's writing-desk, which was brought over in the *Mayflower*. The fire-place is a glimpse of history in itself. Hanging over the fire on the crane are two of the oddest-looking kettles, said to have come from England in the *Cardwell*. On the mantel are the tinder-box, the crane-lamp, and other ancient articles, above which hang the old flint-lock musket and powder-horn. At the side of the fire-place is a small but neat spinning-wheel, which, according to Mrs. General Cunningham, was brought to this country in the *Mayflower*. Years ago it was thrown aside as useless, but when the Centennial movement began to extend its influence over the country, a Miss Tower took hold of it, burnished it up, and put it in condition to be operated on by her, much to the amusement of the visitors. Alongside of the wheel is a chest of drawers, said to be 200 years old, an assertion its appearance fully justifies the truth of. At the other side of the hearth hangs a saddle, made 170 years ago, and a sample of the kind used entirely by the gentility

JOHN WELSH, CHAIRMAN OF THE BOARD OF FINANCE OF THE UNITED STATES CENTENNIAL COMMISSION.

of that day. Against the walls hangs a commission granted to Lieutenant-Colonel Nathan Barrett, from John Hancock, first Governor of Massachusetts, in 1781. Also pendent is a sword worn by Colonel Barrett, in the memorable Concord fight of April 19th, 1775, when he was only a captain. A pewter platter, said to have been made a century ago, is suspended beside a canteen of the Revolution and a wooden plate, filled with marks of time, but which originally formed a portion of a fashionable young lady's wedding outfit. On an old-fashioned sideboard is arrayed the china-ware in vogue during the Revolution, with its peculiar figured plates and many-colored cups and saucers. Here is a silver teapot used by the Marquis de Lafayette during his residence in Boston, alongside of which is a saltcellar brought to this country in the *Mayflower*.

THE BOOK DEPARTMENT.

THE American Book Association conceived and successfully executed an artistic and novel design for displaying books of science, art, or literature, published in the United States. Instead of arranging that each firm should exhibit in a separate showcase, as is done by exhibitors of all other interests in the Main Building, the Association constructed

in the southeastern corner of the building an elegant platform about 75 ft. in length and 30 ft. in width, from which arise iron pillars, supporting a second floor, corresponding in every respect with the one below. The construction of the iron stairways ascending to the second floor is extremely elaborate, as is also that of the showcases on each floor. The whole is divided into as many sections as there are exhibitors in the Association, at the top of each section being the name of the exhibitor in chaste gilt letters. Most of the leading book firms in each city of the United States are represented.

SWEDEN AT THE EXHIBITION.

THE kingdom of Sweden has shown greater liberality in regard to providing for her Centennial show, in proportion to her population, than any other country. Parliament having voted the sum of $125,000 for expenses, exhibitors in Sweden have only had to deliver their goods at the nearest railway-station, and they were forwarded to Stockholm, expenses of ocean transportation to the coast and show-cases being provided for by the Government.

The Swedish school-house erected on the Centennial grounds, near the Art Building, is a *fac-simile* of the best common school-houses in the country, and displays all the furniture and apparatus customarily used. The Swedish school-house at Vienna cost 6,000 crowns, while that at Philadelphia will cost 25,000 crowns, or about $7,000. In her art department, Sweden has one hundred paintings by her best artists. The machinery department presents numerous recent inventions of value and importance, including the new mitrailleuse lately adopted by the Governments of Russia, Italy and Denmark, and also an ingenious machine for cutting corks, two or three steamengines, and a railway locomotive.

A small iron steamboat, used for canal navigation in Sweden, is exhibited. The Swedish collection also displays farm products, a beautiful variety of fishes in glass jars, and agricultural machines and implements, including a reaper of novel construction and Swedish plows. The great iron and steel industries of that country are fully represented, as well as her woolen goods and fabrics of silk, cotton, and linen. In the manufacture of matches there is an extensive display, while the celebrated potteries of Gustafsverg and Roestand have sent admirable specimens of porcelain and majolica ware. Paper and cardboard made from pinewood are among the interesting specialties of this country, while peasant-life in the different provinces of the kingdom is displayed by means of thirty costumed figures of life-size, modeled from paintings by different artists. Among the minerals shown are a number of articles of a fine red granite, which material takes as high a polish as the well-known Scotch granite; the manufactures, too, of the beautiful porphyry found in Elfdale, in the province of Dolarne, are represented by a table belonging to the kingdom, which cost $10,000.

There are also shown a number of rare books upon the early settlement of America, among which is one printed in Stockholm, in 1696, in the language of the Indians, who inhabited this country upon the Swedish settlement on the Delaware. Finally, the meteorite, weighing 10,000 pounds, attracts the notice of scientific men.

In the Swedish Section, probably the most striking objects of interest to the casual observer are the admirable groups of costumed figures illustrating peasant life. They are models in plaster; the faces and hands are painted, so that they are exceedingly lifelike. The costumes have all been actually in use by peasants, having been purchased directly from the wearers. The artist who made the figures is Professor Lödermann, of Stockholm, a sculptor of great reputation. Such great care has been taken to secure absolute correctness in detail, that when the hand of one of the figures was broken in transit, it was supplied by a cast taken from the hand of a Swedish girl in the employ of the Commission. Most of the groups were made up from paintings. The expression of the countenances and the attitude of the figures are remarkably natural. One of the most admirable of these groups is that represented in our illustration, in which a Laplander in his sledge is shown. The sledge is drawn by a reindeer, and the driver is stopping to chat with a fur-clad woman, carrying a baby slung to her neck in a sort of trough—a thoroughly national characteristic.

OPENING CEREMONIES IN THE MAIN BUILDING—THE PRESIDENT

RTY BEING INTRODUCED TO THE FOREIGN COMMISSIONERS.

EXTERIOR OF THE NEW ENGLAND KITCHEN.

INTERIOR OF THE NEW ENGLAND KITCHEN.

MISCELLANEOUS ITEMS

The Italian Exhibit.

ITALY'S contributions to the Centennial are in charge of the Central Committee formed in Florence, the members of which act in concert with the ministers of agriculture, industry, and commerce. This committee consists of the following gentlemen: Giuseppi Dassi, *President;* Professor Salvatore Mazza, *Vice-president;* Francisco Barzoghi, Vespasiano Bignanie, Luigi Bianchi, Baron Eugeni Cantoni, Giovani Spertini, Giacomi Cottaodori, *Secretaries.* The articles exhibited include, first, representations of painting and sculpture, of which there are a large number. Then filigree work from Genoa, mosaic from Rome, glass from Venice, lava from Pompeii, and corals from Naples; also oil, wine, liquors, cheese, rice, macaroni, dried fruits, porcelain, and terracotta.

Native Pacific Coast Woods.

A fine collection of Pacific coast woods has been made for the Centennial, and to these have been added select similar in most respects to those which are contained in the drifts of the Old World, embracing separate heads or scrapers of palæolithic man. The order of the foremost is thus given: Brick, earth, and underlying, grayish clay, nine feet; seam of rounded gravel of a reddish hue, four feet; deposit of fine bluish sand formed from gravel, twelve feet; a bed of gravel and bluish pebbles, four feet; alternate seams or beds of compact sand, gray, and as far as known, four feet. The flints from the lower bed of gravel appear to have been worked chiefly from the bluish-looking pebbles that lie so conspicuously in the same bed. After being washed and dried, they assume that glossiness which, it is said, belongs exclusively to implements from the drift. These discoveries are considered at the Smithsonian as among the most important bearing upon the pre-historic man of this Continent.

Spain at the Centennial.

The Centennial Commission for Spain has charge of all articles sent from Spain, Cuba, and the Philippine Islands. The articles include ancient and modern paintings, manufactures of iron, wood, cotton, and wool, and the various fantry (1793), North Carolina; the Washington Light Infantry (1807), South Carolina; the Clinch Rifles (1836), Georgia. Each company carried the colors of the State it represented, and the whole command comprised a Light Battery and Squadron (two companies) of Cavalry, and ten companies of Infantry.

Australian Ferns.

From California, the extent of whose variety in animal and vegetable products is almost exceptional among countries, we have a collection of Australian ferns, ranging from three to eight feet in height—an evidence of the fact that these delicate plants may be transplanted safely from long distances.

North Carolina as an Agricultural State.

It is a fact little known to the general public, but which has doubtless been demonstrated in the course of the Centennial Exposition, that North Carolina is the only State in the Union in which every article enumerated in the century's statistics is produced. Her great diversity of soil and climate enables her to yield a variety of productions almost endless; among others are cotton, tobacco, rice,

THE BANKERS' PAVILION.

specimens of Mexican woods, representing 425 varieties, all of which are exhibited under the auspices of the Southern Pacific Railroad Company. Among the samples are white, black, colored, and gray walnut. All these woods are susceptible of a very fine polish. There is also a sample of engravers' wood, called minela, a kind which is extensively used both in this country and in Europe. Then there is a class of ship-building wood, called fecomate, said to be equal in strength and durability in water to the best live oak. Specimens of lance-wood, formerly used for spears by the savage tribes of Mexico, and now used in the manufacture of flutes and other musical instruments, are exhibited. The collection also embraces many samples of nesquite, linolu, blood-wood, avelina, prinda verea, grandillo (or rosewood), aiotispa (or yellow rosewood), cabano (mahagony for veneering), linolu (scented), and hulagean, beautiful in grain and susceptible of the highest polish.

Geological Exhibit.

In displaying the geological character of at least a portion of the United States, the drift deposits along the north side of the James river are shown from a bluff recently laid open by excavation.

Among these, in the lower beds of gravel, are war-flints kinds of wine peculiar to Spain, segars and sugar from Cuba, and, in fact, all products and manufactures illustrative of the peculiarities of Spanish life and Spanish industry. By these exhibits it is hoped by the Spanish Commissioners to show the world that the late civil war in Spain affected only the Basque provinces and Catalonia, and that all the other portions of the Spanish peninsula are peaceful, industrious, and prosperous.

The Centennial Legion.

This organization, which represents the oldest military corps existing in the original thirteen States of the Union, was organized under three sections: From New England, from the Middle States, and from the South. The New England battalion was led by the Boston Light Infantry, presided over by the Honorable Josiah Quincy, as *President,* and the Honorable R. C. Winthrop as *Vice-president.* The Middle States battalion was led by the Old Guard of New York, under Major-General G. W. McLean, President of the New York Stock Exchange, and the Southern battalion was organized by the Washington Light Infantry. In the South the following commands were duly enrolled: The Norfolk Light Artillery Blues (1828), Virginia; Fayettville Independent Light In- Indian corn and wool, rye, barley, oats, potatoes, together with all kinds of fruits (except the tropical), and grapes of all species, including the Scuppenong, Catawba, Lincom, Isabella, and others.

United States Government Exhibition.

The building erected by the United States Government in the grounds of the Centennial Exposition covers two acres in extent, and cost about $30,000. In this the War Department alone occupies about 12,000 square feet, besides outside buildings. This department sends contributions from its different bureaus—the Engineers, Quartermasters, Ordnance, Medical, Signal. The Engineer Bureau exhibits maps, charts and engravings, illustrating the system of river and harbor improvements, also models of some of the works, samples of building-stone, pontoon bridges and pontoon wagon-trains, mining tools and models of lighthouses. The Ordnance Bureau displays a complete set of gun-making machinery in operation, as also the parts of the Springfield rifle and carbine, various small arms, apparatus for determining the velocity of projectiles, and a twenty-inch Rodman gun, weighing more than 100,000 pounds. Besides these, there is an immense variety of projectiles, fuses, powders, etc. A peculiar feature of the ordnance display consists of a series of figures, showing the appearance and dress of the American soldier during the Revolutionary period, the War of 1812, the Mexican War, the War of the Rebellion, and at the present time.

The Medical Department contributes a post hospital and twenty-four beds ; one wing of which has been fitted up for actual service, so that if necessary it can be used as a hospital of the Centennial Exposition. There is also presented a very complete series of medical apparatus, as used in the army, including medicines and medical and surgical instruments, hospital stores, hospital clothing, railroad-cars for the transportation of the sick and wounded.

In the Quartermaster's Department may be seen the clothing from every branch of the service, from an early date to the present time, all articles of camp equipage, including musical instruments from each arm of the service, army wagons and harness, etc.

The Signal Bureau furnishes a full signal-train with nine wagons, a complete outfit of international and Government signals, and an assortment of thermometers, anemometers, and all other meteorological apparatus. The entire machinery of this office is exhibited, including its method of making the daily weather maps, etc.

CATHOLIC FOUNTAIN MEDALS.

Besides the fountain erected on the Centennial grounds by the Catholic Total Abstinence Union, the same organization ordered medals to be struck, commemorating the occasion and the gift. This medal is about the size of the United States silver dollar, and is struck in copper, and gilded. It has on the obverse a representation of the fountain, with the inscription, "Centennial Fountain, Fairmount Park, Dedicated to American Liberty, July 4, 1876, Philadelphia." On the reverse is the badge of the society, with the inscription, "Erected by the Catholic Total Abstinence Union of America."

CENTENNIAL ICE-BOATS.

One of the Ice-boat Clubs has had constructed an ice-boat for exhibition at the Exposition. She is sloop-rigged, built of clean white pine, the side-pieces being cased with black walnut, ornamented with gilt beading. The centre keelson is strengthened with a black walnut truss ; the deck is of narrow, closely-jointed strips of red cedar and spruce, while the iron work throughout is all handsomely nickel-plated.

THE WOMEN OF AMERICA AND THE EXPOSITION.

The liberality, industry, and perseverance of American women in the cause of our Centennial Exposition are subjects of just pride to every American citizen, not only in Philadelphia, but throughout the country. They have manifested the most untiring interest in the occasion, while their devotion to the work which they have set themselves has been beyond praise. Not only did they readily supply the sum of $30,000 for the construction of the woman's pavilion — for which purpose contributions were made by the women of Florida, Massachusetts, Rhode Island, Connecticut, Maine, New Jersey, District of Columbia, Ohio, Kansas and Pennsylvania —not only this, but, in all, $100,000 had been contributed from this source prior to December 1st, 1875, and added to the funds of the general ex-

PASSENGERS' WAITING-ROOM OF THE PENNSYLVANIA RAILROAD DEPOT, JERSEY CITY.

hibition. The object of the women's department is to exhibit the highest types of woman's work, and, if possible, to enlarge the sphere of her usefulness and profit in the future. It therefore displays several specimens of sculpture, painting, literature, engraving, telegraphy, lithography, education and invention, as also the finer kinds of needlework, lacework, etc. Short biographical sketches of eminent women of the United States have been collected in a volume, and a volume of American Cookery has been published, the women of each State contributing receipts. Charitable institutions, carried on by women, are shown through the medium of figures and historical narratives.

FROM NEW YORK TO THE EXHIBITION.

SCENES ALONG THE PENNSYLVANIA RAILROAD.

THE Pennsylvania Railroad Company, being the leading line for passenger and freight traffic to the Exposition, some account of its condition and facilities, as well as the route over which it passes, may not be uninteresting.

This road has now under control 6,615 miles of road, being the best track-bed in the United States. At the mammoth depôt at Jersey City nearly 200 trains arrive and depart daily, about half of these being passenger trains.

Jersey City is a port of entry, and has a population of 82,000, of which more than 50,000 are natives, the balance foreigners. Within its limits are located 333 manufacturing establishments, employing a capital of $11,718,400, and a working force of 5,624 hands. On this basis, the annual receipts from manufactures amount to nearly $25,000,000.

The Pennsylvania Railroad Company, always progressive, is constantly devising and executing improvements, many of these in Jersey City, along the river front and in

its vicinity, being very extensive and important. The new passenger depôt, complete in every detail, is 620x228 ft. in dimensions. Access from the ferry-boats is gained by a passage of 40 ft. in width by 228 ft. in length, from which open the general waiting-rooms, including ticket-offices and restaurants. A ferry-house, 40x120 ft., contains large and comfortable rooms and offices, and includes every necessary accommodation for the public. Over these are the rooms devoted to the uses of the superintendents and other officials. Within the depôt, and extending through it, are 12 railway tracks for the use of passenger trains only.

The freight business is conducted at what is called Harsimus Cove, a short distance north of the passenger depôt. Here are stock-yards, 1,300x225 ft. in dimensions, attached to which is an abattoir 225x200 ft., and also a water slip 180 ft. wide and 1,500 ft. long, a pier 200x1,500 ft., and at the rear of the latter, a grain elevator 600x100 ft. There is also a water slip extending the entire length of this pier, and freight sheds 1,000x125 ft., a grain pier and covered shed 500x60 ft., with reserve places for warehouses 500x25 ft. ; and besides all these, tracks connected with floats on which the cars are transferred to barges and carried across the river, to and from New York. By this convenient device, cars are loaded at New York, and towed to the Jersey City terminus, where they are landed and attached to the trains.

The cutting through of an extra tunnel in the Bergen Hill rocks was a most important improvement, giving room for the exclusive accommodation for freight, leaving the main tracks only for passengers.

The traveler on his way from New York to the Centennial, by the Pennsylvania road, passes through Newark, as the first city of importance, this being 9 miles from Jersey City. Newark was originally settled by New Englanders, who emigrated from Connecticut about 1666, being invited thither by the first Governor of the province. It is related that the site of the town was originally purchased from the Indians, who received therefor the following articles : 3 trooper's coats, 1,850 fathoms of wampum, 20 hoes, 50 double hands of powder, 100 bars of lead, 20 axes, 10 guns, 20 pistols, 10 kettles, 10 swords, 4 barrels of beer, 50 knives, and 10 pairs of breeches. The name is supposed to have been given to the city by the Rev. Mr. Pearson, who settled in 1667, being a native of Newark, England. Its population is above 125,000. The Passaic River affords great facilities to the vast manufacturing interests of the city, which may be termed the Birmingham of America.

Thirteen miles further on the traveler reaches New Brunswick, formerly the terminus of the old Camden and Amboy Railroad, which became a portion of the great Pennsylvania Central, having consolidated in 1872. This city has a population of about 17,500, and a manufacturing capital of about $4,250,000 invested, annually producing an average of $5,375,000. New Brunswick is quite a thriving city, and has a commodious passenger and freight depôt.

Nineteen miles beyond New Brunswick, the train enters the city of Princeton, settled about 1700. Princeton is chiefly noted for its college, of which the main building is called Nassau Hall, and was erected in 1756. This is an interesting locality in a patriotic sense, as the Continental Congress held its sessions in the library-rooms of this

NEWARK, NEW JERSEY.

FROM NEW YORK TO THE EXHIBITION—SCENES ALONG THE ROUTE OF THE PENNSYLVANIA RAILROAD.

college in 1783, when compelled to leave Philadelphia.

Trenton, the capital of New Jersey, situated on the left bank of the Delaware, 57 miles from Jersey City, was first settled about 1680, but did not receive its present name until nearly a hundred years later, when it was thus denominated, in honor of Colonel William Trent, at that time Speaker of the Assembly. In 1790, it was selected as the capital of the State, and two years later incorporated. Trenton is memorable for having been the scene of the celebrated retreat of Washington with his army, after the disastrous reverses on Long Island. This occurred on the 8th of December, 1776, when, in the midst of ice and in the depth of Winter, the ragged soldiery crossed the Delaware from Trenton to the Pennsylvania side, while the Hessians, unable to follow, went into camp on the Jersey shore. On the morning of the 26th, the American troops recrossed, surprised, and completely routed their opponents, capturing nearly 1,000

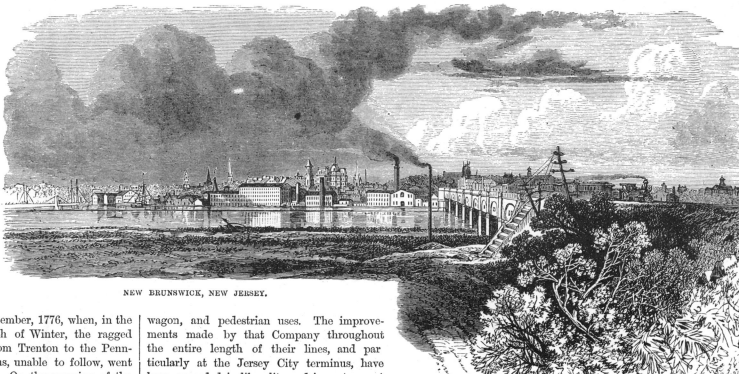

NEW BRUNSWICK, NEW JERSEY.

THE DEEP CUT AT BERGEN HILL, NEAR JERSEY CITY.

men. During the prevalence of yellow fever in Philadelphia, in 1793, the Government officers removed to Trenton; and in 1798, President Adams temporarily had his official residence there. It has a population of over 23,000. Its manufacturing establishments employ about $5,000,000 invested capital, and 5,100 hands.

The Pennsylvania Railroad Company have erected in Trenton a commodious passenger and freight depôt, and have spanned the river with a bridge designed for railroad,

wagon, and pedestrian uses. The improvements made by that Company throughout the entire length of their lines, and particularly at the Jersey City terminus, have been exceeded in liberality and importance at Philadelphia. Arriving at the latter city, the traveler passes over the mammoth and picturesque Girard Avenue bridge crossing the Schuylkill, from which point he obtains an excellent view of the Exposition Buildings, while, on descending from the train, he finds himself facing the entrance to the grounds. Here a special branch line accommodates the Centennial traffic, and still further exhibits the enterprise and energy of this remarkable company.

The systematic and judicious manner in which this great railroad corporation have specially catered for the Centennial traffic is deserving of all praise. Special Centennial trains arrive and depart at almost every hour in the day, and these being designed particularly for the accommodation of those persons who desire to visit the Exposition, no pains are spared by which this desideratum can be accomplished.

Pullman Palace Cars are attached to every train, and the mere knowledge that the unwonted tourist can be relieved of all annoyance of changing cars, and be deposited at the very gates of the Exposition after a rapid and entirely comfortable ride, is one of the most agreeable and satisfactory features of a visit to the Centennial Exposition. In every particular of its administration in this emergency — in its provision for the comfort of its patrons, in the liberality of its reduced rates, and in the conscientious regard which it pays to speed and safety combined, as well as comfort, this company has given its aid in making the great Centennial display at Fairmount in every possible way worthy of its occasion and sentiment. The Pennsylvania Railroad Company have also established a regular line of steamships, plying between Philadelphia and Liverpool, includ-

PRINCETON COLLEGE, NEW JERSEY.

ing already four first-class iron vessels, built of American materials and by American artisans.

THE TURKISH BAZAAR.

THE romantic banks of the Centennial Lake are noted for the curious buildings clustered upon them. Of these, the most remarkable are the Syrian Bazaar and the Turkish Bazaar and Café. The latter is a frame structure, displaying a rich variegation of color and a general appearance decidedly Moorish. The interior accommodates the Bazaar on one side, the rest of the building being devoted to the use of smokers and coffee-drinkers. The latter portion is furnished with chairs and round tables, the walls being hung with pipes, including the chibouques and nargiles. These are always ready for customers. But the chief attraction of the place is the coffee—clear as amber, black as ebony, and fragrant as the perfume of "Araby the Blest." The picturesque costumes of the country are worn by the attendants, all but one of whom are males. When coffee is called for, one of the Turkish attendants places a heaped spoonful of ground and browned Mocha in a little silver dipper of about the capacity of a coffee-cup, adds a little sugar, fills up with hot water from a diminutive boiler, stirs the mixture, and holds it over the glowing charcoal until it almost reaches the boiling-point. It is then ready for drinking, and a more invigorating beverage could not be desired. Our illustration shows the manner of cooking the coffee, and of decanting it from the long-handled dippers into the customers' cups. The tent in the upper corner of the page is the private apartment of the attendants. On the lower portion are seen the cashier's desk and the Bazaar.

NATIONAL COSTUMES.

THE different costumes seen at every point formed a very attractive part of the Exhibition. Here we noticed the picturesque attire of the Turk, the Chinese of higher grade—which is quite different from the shiny sack and sabots of Ah Sin, the washerman, that are now so familiar to our eyes. These national costumes

THE BRIDGE OVER THE DELAWARE RIVER AT TRENTON, NEW JERSEY.

FROM NEW YORK TO THE EXHIBITION—SCENES ALONG THE ROUTE OF THE PENNSYLVANIA RAILROAD.

THE WOMAN'S PAVILION.

would have been more frequently seen but for the extremely rude gazing which the wearers were subjected to by the curious eyes of the vulgar. That enterprising and sensitive people, the Japanese, for instance, donned the American fashions—from plug hats to patent leather boots; and from a rear elevation the Japs might have been mistaken for genuine Americans. This vulgar curiosity prevented a great many foreigners from appearing in their national dress, and as a consequence, the grounds did not present that picturesque appearance they should.

people, and is certainly one of the most popular of living sovereigns. Nor do we think that his popularity will be in any way diminished when it is known that the government defrayed the entire cost of the magnificent Russian display at Philadelphia. The whole collection was arranged for between October, 1875, and February, 1876; nothing was prepared for show, and everything exhibited may be looked upon as having represented Russia in her every-day dress. To a citizen of the United States this display ought to have been specially interesting, for there is no country in Europe

anticipated in making known to our citizens what, under the skillful guidance of wise men, like Peter the Great and his successors, has been accomplished by the Muscovite nation. Take, for instance, one branch of the display—the specimens of the pupils' work in the Stroganoff Central School of Technical Drawing, and the Art and Industrial Museum of Moscow. This latter museum, opened in 1868, consists of an artistical, a historical, and an industrial section. It received an honorable mention at the Vienna Exhibition in 1873, and the gold medal at the Polytechnical

LAPLANDER IN HIS SLEDGE, IN THE SWEDISH DEPARTMENT.

THE RUSSIAN EXHIBIT.

The visitor to the Russian section must be impressed with the belief that no effort had been spared to render the exhibit worthy of the mighty Empire it represents. *Bozhe tsara hraini,* "God save the Emperor," is the refrain of the Russian national hymn, and well may every subject of the Czar desire for the present ruler of that vast Empire long life, health, and happiness. Alexander II., by his many enlightened acts, has endeared himself to the hearts of his

at all approaching Russia in extent, and the relations between our own vast Republic and the Empire ruled over by the Czar have, for many years past, been of the most friendly character.

We venture to say that the first impression of the visitor on entering the Russian department was one of mingled surprise and admiration. No one who has not visited Russia would imagine that in that northern clime arts and science, industry and mechanics were so far advanced, but from the display here made truly great results may be

Exhibition of Moscow in 1872. It sent to Philadelphia a large collection of pottery from the studios for painting on china and delf.

There were jugs, dishes, pitchers, vases for flowers, tumblers, salt-cellars, and flagons, all in true Russian style; then there were tiles of glazed clay, very creditably executed, and also some alabaster moldings, embracing the Russian styles of the eleventh, twelfth, thirteenth, fourteenth, fifteenth and sixteenth centuries. The books published by the museum comprise histories of Russian

THE TENT.

THE CASHIER'S BUREAU.

THE GUESTS' COFFEE-ROOM.

MAKING COFFEE IN TURKISH STYLE.

THE BAZAAR.

THE PAVILION.

THE TURKISH PAVILION, AND SCENES THEREIN.

ornaments and decorations, Russian popular embroidery, and the original Stroganoff book of image facial paintings. The Stroganoff School of Technical Drawing was established in 1860, with a view of forming an intelligent class of designers and ornamenters for the work of manufactories and industrial establishments. Two hundred scholars are taught there in the preparatory and special classes, and the whole course of study extends over five years. Among the 740 pupils taught there since the commencement, there are many men who have become distinguished in their profession ; and, commencing with 1861, the pupils have received medals and honorable mention at every exhibition at which their productions have been displayed.

The collection of drawings sent by the Stroganoff pupils on this occasion consists of linear drawings, perspective sketches of flowers, Russian and Greek ornaments, landscapes, and calligraphy. The student will here observe specimens of every kind of drawing, from the elementary exercises to drawing from plaster figures and from nature, while drawing as applied to commercial purposes forms quite a prominent feature of the display. Let us, ere proceeding, state that the Stroganoff Central School of Technical and Drawing and the Art and Industrial Museum of Moscow are to all practical intents and purposes one and

elegant and costly cases of black walnut have been erected, aisles between these giving ample opportunity for the visitor to move about at ease and examine their contents.

There are 595 exhibitors in this department, and the display comprises everything conceivable in leather, as well as all the tools used in its manipulation. The exhibits are arranged in admirable order, being classified systematically, and thus enabling the visitor to follow the processes of the manufacture from their very beginning to their culmination in the most delicately finished work in the different departments.

Commencing, then, at the western and following the side of the south wall, we come first upon a few skins of animals having the fur on, and designed probably only to enable the spectator to commence at the very beginning. Next appear the exhibits of sole-leather, this particular exhibition being said to be the finest ever made, and comprising 118 exhibits of three different processes. Passing slowly along, we presently come upon a display offered by Messrs. Schultz, Southwick & Co., at the centre of the south side.

Here an ornamented structure, having two horns gracing its summit, contains specimens of sole-leather from eight different tanneries, including the Keystone, Scotia, Nich-

Here are specimens of satchels, Russia leather pocket-books, shoes with diced and fluted leather, invented by a Philadelphian ; goat-skins for shoes, and in one case of these a fat sheep, stuffed, and exhibiting a peculiarly long and fine fleece. Lynn makes a fine display in all departments, and especially in goat-skins prepared in a superior manner.

Rubber goods are included among the exhibits, and there are cases of rubber medical goods, gas-bags, rubber bath-tubs, gloves, etc. The Goodyear Company make an extensive display, including such articles as have been already mentioned, and besides these, toilet cases, rubber tubing, cuspidores, toys in great variety, chest-protectors, etc. There are also rubber shoes and boots from Providence, R. I., rubber-cloth of the finest quality, life-preservers, babies' teething-rings, and finally a specimen of the *caoutchouc* tree, and some rubber-milk in a glass jar, precisely as drawn from the tree in Panama, Guiana and Ecuador.

After examining an exhibit of rubber-coats as fine as silk, we come back to leather, and the consideration of some magnificent specimens of hand shoe and boot making, varied by embroidered work in gold and silver thread. Next to these are heavy shoes and boots, with double soles and uppers, and ladies' gaiters and children's shoes in

THE RAILROAD BRIDGE ACROSS THE SCHUYLKILL RIVER AT WEST PHILADELPHIA—THE FIRST GLIMPSE OF THE EXPOSITION BUILDINGS.

the same institution. This institution has set itself the task of reviving the ancient Russian art of ornamentation, freeing it from all foreign materials, cultivating a taste for the beautiful among the people, and bringing back the art of facial image painting to that original, pure type taken from the Greek. In this task a large measure of success has already been attained, as every visitor to the Exhibition will probably acknowledge.

THE SHOE AND LEATHER BUILDING.

EXTENDING along the southern side of the machinery building in an easterly and westerly direction, and east of the machinery annexes, is the building devoted to the exhibits of those in the shoe and leather trade. This building is 560 x 314 ft. in dimensions, and has the widest span between posts, being 80 ft. of floor space, of any building on the grounds.

Entering this building at the western end, a very brilliant and pleasant *coup d'œil* is presented. Across the roof are stretched tri-colored strips of canvas or muslin, while at either end a trophy of flags is displayed. On the floor

olson, Caledonia, Wilcox, etc. There is, of course, a considerable sameness in the display of sole-leather with which this portion of the building is filled ; but we now presently come upon cases containing other manufactures and applications. Here are specimens of split leather as fine as broadcloth ; fancy colored enameled leather, comprising all the colors of the rainbow, grouped as prettily as could be done with ribbons. Here are cases containing the different dressings used for leather, and here others devoted to alligator skins alone. The cases themselves are ornamental works, many exceedingly artistic. They are in oak, black walnut and other woods, with plate-glass fronts. Now we came upon fancy skivers for satchels and trunks, buckskin for different uses, and even a case devoted to horse-hide leather. Then there are specimens of bark, etc., notably the exhibits from Cleeve W. Hooper & Sons, Bermondsey and Leadenhall Market, London. One case displays mammoth specimens of boots, having soles two inches thick. A few sole-leather trunks and valises from St. Petersburgh, as well as some specimens of stamped leather of very fine quality from the same locality, bring us to the extreme eastern end, and we turn and go back.

endless variety, and of every style and quality Fancy shoes in different colored leather, enameled and stamped, are a favored exhibit, and display the best improvements made in these goods of late years. There are also, rather incongruously, displayed here a large exhibit of ten soldiers representing veterans of 1776, the New York Seventh Regiment, and other varieties. Fancy satin shoes, in different color and of the finest make and fabric, are to be seen in numbers. There is also a liberal display of infants' shoes, gilt and bronzed. Then there are shoes with tassels, and shoes with buckles, wooden shoes from Chicago, gaiters in leather and other materials for children, elegant riding boots with spurs, and delicate bridal boots in white satin, besides high-heeled shoes like those worn by our grandmothers, ornamented with bright buckles.

Edinburgh and London both send fine displays of tanned leather, and from Mainz and Bordeaux there are some specially excellent exhibits of fine work. A very handsome case in black and gold from Wilson, Walker & Co., Leeds, England, contains fine leather fabrics, and particularly binders' materials, including Levant morocco, which is made from sealskin.

Edwin C. Burt, the well-known manufacturer of ladies'

shoes, has two handsome cases, illustrating his specialty and displaying very beautiful specimens in leather, satin, and other materials. His exhibits are located in the centre of the building, on the south side of the nave.

An interesting display of top-boots, prairie boots, and other large wear is sent from Boston; and a very showy case, black and gold, filled with fine work in ladies' and children's wear, from Syracuse. Six exhibits, each under glass, and placed on a gilded pedestal, from a New York house, include really superb specimens of manufacture in ladies' shoes, being made of silk and satin, embroidered with much gilding and gilt buttons, in all respects very beautiful. A very rich display of fine ladies' work comes from Moses How, of Haverhill, Massachusetts. As for slippers, there are a sufficiency—slippers with rosettes and slippers without rosettes; gilt slippers, silvered slippers; embroidered, strapped and needle-worked slippers in all colors and every variety of shape; fine quilted satin slippers—in fact, every imaginable species of the article.

On the northern side of the building we find exhibits of shoe manufacturing goods, such as lastings, linen thread, drills, bindings, etc., as well as tools, button-hooks, ornaments, rosettes, buttons, heel-stiffening, resembling dentists' plates for the jaws, etc. From Auburn, Maine, there is a good display of fine work in heavy men's wear. Newark, New Jersey, has a very large display of the best work, including everything from top-boots to gold-embroidered slippers, and all of the best quality, material and workmanship.

And this brings us to the harness department, which is extremely large and very varied. Here Newark is also prominent, exhibiting fine ornamental harness in gilt and plated work, bridle-rings, fancy mountings, gilt and plated collars, patent bits, all very tasty and ornamental. Here are sleigh-bells, in clusters and strings, and here an exhibit of the curious celuloid work from the Newark factory, displayed in various articles, in harness material, having much the appearance of ivory, and seemingly well adapted to those purposes. Next we come upon heavier harness, including collars, blinders, traces and reins, also spurs—some of which are of the Mexican species and very dangerous-looking. Here are harness-makers' tools, files, various tools for ornamental work, stamping, etc.

Entering again upon the shoe department in our progress, we come upon boot-stretchers and lasts, these latter made of metal or wood, in considerable variety, some being presented in process of use in the actual boots themselves. A fine display from Lynn offers every possible kind of shoe and last materials, etc. The New York manufacturers are lavish in heavy harness, saddles, collars, traces, and complete sets, many heavily mounted, embossed and otherwise ornamented. There is a larger show of harness dressing from Boston, and from Philadelphia a goodly display of saddlery, whips, etc. A very handsome fancy set of harness from Washington occupies a special case. Another contains elegant whips, these being from Philadelphia, and mounted in mother-of-pearl, gold, silver, etc.

Shoe-making machinery from Boston, Lynn, and elsewhere occupies a considerable space, and displays the processes of manufacture in actual operation.

A fine display of harness-makers' tools, beautifully finished, is exhibited by Newark. A number of heavy sewing-machines for leather-work, and rossing machines used by the tanners in grinding and cutting bark, with other mechanisms, bring us back to the western end, and to the trunk and bag department, which is mainly by itself.

Here is found every imaginable variety of trunk, satchel, valise, toilet-case, portmanteau, etc., and those in morocco, sole-leather, Russia leather, enameled leather and other materials. There are traveling-bags with toilet-cases attached, Saratoga trunks, of the latest, largest and most complete pattern; pocket-books in every kind of leather, shawl-straps, all sorts of patent devices for fastening and locking trunks, etc., and an especially excellent show of trunks, satchels, valises and toilet-cases from New York.

The display of rubber goods is completed at one end of this department by exhibits of rubber belting and hose; and among the machines are power-punches, wax-thread machines, sand-paper machines, shoe upper machines, and finally the entire exhibition concludes at the northeastern end with a very large and brilliant exhibit of "Challenge" and other blacking, presented with artistic adjuncts of life-size metal statuary and bas-reliefs. In fact, the show of blacking is one of the most notable exhibits in the building.

ART-POTTERY FROM ENGLAND.

From Lambeth, near London, a remarkably fine exhibition of art-pottery may be seen at the Exposition, embracing, in round numbers, at least, a thousand objects. Many pieces are small, being services and vessels for table and household use, but all of them are examples of designs made and executed by the firm which sends them. A new application of an old discovery in the art of glazing pottery is exhibited in this collection. This process was originally made in Flanders and Germany, and there is a tradition that the first pieces were produced in the Low Countries at the very beginning of the fifteenth century. The principal centre of its production was, however, in Germany, Bayreuth, Massfeld, Nuremberg, and Ratisbon, but the best samples were from the neighborhood of the Lower Rhine, where the glaze most fit for that class of pottery was easily to be found. Here, in fact, for the first time in Europe, the body of the ware was produced, vitrified by the high temperature to which it was submitted, and also with the remarkable peculiarity that it was glazed by volatilization of common salt thrown into the oven when the temperature had reached its climax, two processes the combination of which had never before been procured.

This ware varies in color, some being almost white, and

CIGAR EXHIBIT OF MESSRS. KERBS & SPIESS, NO. 35 BOWERY, NEW YORK.

other of a light-gray hue, the last being the most esteemed when the effect was heightened by blue or purple grounds. The shapes were generally elaborate, adorned with moldings, and nriched with embossed ornaments, some of which were designed by distinguished artists. The decline of this ware began with the seventeenth century, since which time the material has been only used for ware of the costliest kind. It is only recently that it has been successfully revived at Lambeth. Of this and other forms of pottery quite an interesting collection is produced from this section, including cups, vases, bowls, etc. Many of these are ornamented by etchings, the work of lady artists trained in the Lambeth school. In such cases the choice of subjects is left entirely to the artist, and these run through all classes of natural history, chiefly horses, oxen, dogs, cats, birds, and humanity, forming a broad variety of the exercise of the etching-tool. Some of these illustrations present subjects from child-life, and are accepted to be exceedingly beautiful. Besides minor works, there are a number of choice exhibits in terra-cotta. Prominent among these is a pulpit of stone and terra-cotta, with subject-panels representing subjects from the Bible; also a church-font of massive proportions, with stone-ware panels on the eight sides, with subjects taken from child-life as associated with our Saviour. The stone basin of this font is one of the largest known, having upon its edge birds in the same material, the whole being sustained by a central shaft of stone, with figured panels and painted polished stone pillars.

CONCESSIONS.

The sale of concessions—for the sale of victuals, drink, and other things on the Centennial grounds—has amounted to $450,000. The privilege of printing and selling the official catalogue was sold for $100,000. The American, French, German and Hebrew restaurants, and the *Trois Frères Provenceaux*, each pay $6,000. Ten *cafés* will bring in about $45,000. Milk, Vienna bread, candy, and other such privileges, bring from $3,000 to $5,000 each, and pop-corn, $7,000. The sale of soda-water rights brought $52,000; cigars and tobacco, $18,000; rolling chairs, $40,000. All beer pays a royalty of three dollars a barrel. The Departments providing comforts of toilet, etc., pay $16,000.

UNITED STATES GOVERNMENT BUILDING.

This building, of which a description will be found in another portion of this work, and in illustration of which we give a number of cuts, has a central nave running through it longitudinally east and west, crossed by a transept nearest the eastern end.

Beginning at the west end and on the north side of the nave in our examination, we find ourselves at first in a department allotted to the exhibits furnished by the Smithsonian Institution, which has been enabled to make a very handsome exhibition by means of its offer to take charge of articles furnished by different states and individuals, providing that at the close of the Exposition these shall become the property of the Institution. The first portion of this display is geological and mineralogical, beginning with a fine collection of native marbles, white and colored, a large portion of which is from Vermont, from West Rutland, Rutland, Sutherland Falls and other places. From Quarryville, Hawkins County, Tennessee, a handsome exhibit is made in variegated brown and white marble, very like the Italian. It may be observed here that there are 121 different kinds of marbles exhibited by Tennessee alone. Here are also square blocks of granite, shell, limestone, etc., and near the wall a soapstone model of the celebrated Comstock Lode and Sutro Tunnel of Nevada. We now observe specimens of mineral wool made from the slag of blast furnaces, and next a very handsome display of exhibits of petroleum, coal and coal products, including crude oil, residuum, gasoline, naphtha, etc.

The cases along the wall contain specimens of minerals and ores in great variety. The town of Roxburgh, Connecticut, exhibits one case containing an exhibit of iron ore. Along the floor by the wall are ranged specimens of coal, large and small, from Rhode Island and West Virginia, and in the same vicinity is a considerable exhibit of specimens of fire-brick from New York.

Next, a handsome glass case contains a fine display from the State of Pennsylvania, including copper ore, magnetic ore, copper sulphuret, copper pyrites, copper-bearing silicate, and the same is treated with other products. There are also malachite, crystallized copper, cement copper, and ingot copper.

We next come upon ponderous specimens of zinc ore, emery rock, and samples of spelter from the State of New Jersey; and next, iron blooms and iron wire made by petroleum fuel. A case of copper ores and large specimens of sulphureted copper ore exhibited by Vermont, and specimens of emery and emery-rock by the town of Chester, Massachusetts. Newbury, Massachusetts, sends specimens of *verd antique;* New York State contributes bluestone; and Massachusetts sends specimens of new red sandstone.

A noticeable exhibit is a case containing fine polished stones, agates, porphyry, etc. Connecticut displays very handsome specimens illustrating the manufacture of steel, ax-heads, etc., while from New Jersey we have zinc ores in large specimens, and from New York glass cases containing iron ores, with charcoal and other materials used in smelting and blasting. A large specimen of nickel ore from Pennsylvania is particularly noticeable.

The next case in order contains a considerable variety, including copper pyrites and other minerals, cobalt ores and other products from Pennsylvania, and a beautiful specimen of cobalt-ammonia-sulphate. Here are also German silver in wire, etc., fine specimens of crystallized blue vitriol, nickel in the rough ore, pure, wrought and cast, with specimens of nickel-plating. From Chester County, Pennsylvania, we have specimens of graphite. A fine exhibit of tin-lined pipe is prominent just here, ranged in a monumental cone on a pedestal.

Next, the entire half of the building north of the nave is crossed by a mammoth exhibit from Tennessee. The Tennessee display is entirely owing to the liberality of an individual, the State not having contributed anything in the way of an appropriation.

General J. T. Wilder, of Chattanooga, who sent a very handsome exhibit to the Vienna Exhibition, is the originator of the present display. This includes iron-ores, red hematite, brown hematite, magnetic iron-ore, which is manufactured into iron in one process, and into Bessemer steel in two; also, hammered iron. A most interesting exhibit is a specimen of meteoric iron found on a farm in Greene County, Tennessee, and which weighs 293 pounds. Another curiosity is a specimen of coal found at Rockwood, Tennessee, and taken from a seam 104 ft. 5 in. in thickness. There are also specimens of native woods in small blocks, including 52 different kinds, all found on one farm in Greene County, Tennessee. The ores are from the Chattanooga mineral district, there being 40 kinds of iron ore. The locality where this is found is peculiarly fortunate, as it furnishes calcareous spar, carbonate of lime in large quantities, which can be used for flux. It is stated that these ores can be transported to the furnaces at the small cost of $1.75 per ton.

Pittsburg, Pennsylvania, sends a fine exhibit, illustrating the manufacture of crucible steel, including pin wire, broom wire, etc. Missouri furnishes cases of iron, zinc and lead ores, coal, limestone, sandstone and other minerals, making a very handsome collection. North Carolina has a fine display of minerals in small specimens in glass cases. These include soapstone, marble, mica, calcine, plaster, gypsum and sandstone. Virginia and West Virginia exhibit specimens of sandstone (fireproof), stalactites from the "Fountain Cave," gypsum, iron-ore, and a peculiarly fine display of West Virginia coal. South Carolina exhibits a curious collection of fossil teeth, including fossil horse-teeth, and a tooth of a tapir taken from the Stone River. Michigan is represented by a magnificent collection. Here are large specimens of specular iron-ore, hard hematite and granular ore, magnetic ore, beautiful specimens of copper ores, and rock showing the crystals of copper, copper as extracted from the ore, native silver and silver ore. This display fills four cases, and is introduced at the nave by a ponderous specimen of native copper.

The display furnished by Montana is in a case ornamented with deer-heads and horns, and includes a large and varied collection of minerals, comprising crystallized ores and different kinds of stone for building purposes. Oregon, Arizona, and Utah exhibit gold and silver ores in a large variety of specimens. Colorado has also a rich display of these ores. An upright black-walnut case, labeled "Nevada" in gilt letters, contains a most interesting collection, including silicified wood, chalcedone in numerous specimens, sandstone, silver ore, lead ore, and gold ore, showing free gold—these specimens being peculiarly rich. Idaho also exhibits largely in gold and silver ores and products and ingots. The Nevada exhibit is particularly rich in specimens from the Comstock Lode and the Reese River district, and also offers a very fine exhibit of native sulphurets, wulfenite, etc.

Four glass cases include the contributions of California, comprising gold and silver ores, with all the materials used in their disintegration—giant-powder, fuses, and other appliances and processes.

We now leave the mineral department, and enter that devoted to the products of the sea—this, in fact, being the marine display of the Navy Department of the United States Government. It commences with a collection of specimens of *algæ* from California, Colorado, Massachusetts, Rhode Island and their waters, ranged on both sides of a long screen and including the ordinary *eel* grass, as it is called, kelp, and very many other interesting and beautiful species. Next are cases containing seamen's clothing in oilcloth and rubber; next to which is a case in which are ranged a large number of articles illustrating the habits and customs of the American Indians. Here are various Indian implements and weapons, game-bags,

spears, dog-whips, saddles covered with skins, spears from the *Navajos*, of Mexico, snow spectacles from the Esquimaux and other natives of Arctic America, snowshoes from *Carriboo*, a pack-saddle, once the property of a Sioux, shot-pouches heavily ornamented with bead-work, powder-horns and flasks from the Apaches, Comanches, Sioux, etc.

The north wall of the building at this point and for a length of about 150 ft. is covered to a height of 8 ft. with a splendid collection of framed photographs illustrating American sea, river and lake fish taken from actual specimens. This is, in all respects, a most remarkable and interesting collection, and it is doubtful if there has ever been exhibited one comprising so many different specimens or so largely illustrating this branch of natural history.

The next cases contain exhibits of Winchester and Colt arms, Maynard rifle, Remington fowling-pieces, six-shooting rifles and shotguns with powder-flasks, bullet-molds, and all the paraphernalia of sport of this character. A curiosity in this collection is a flint-lock gun, formerly the property of Sir John Franklin. The next case, properly enough, illustrates the art of angling, and contains angling-rods of every conceivable variety, pickerel, gudgeon, salmon and bass, down to the most delicate and exquisite

ALFRED T. GOSHORN, ESQ., DIRECTOR-GENERAL OF THE CENTENNIAL EXPOSITION.

trout rod. At this point we meet with a stuffed figure representing a hunter clad in a waterproof suit, short coat filled with pockets, breeches and gaiters, and having a pole at his back and extending over his head, at the top of which is suspended a lantern.

The marine display proper opens here with a case containing models of fish-weirs, salmon-weirs, fish-slides, fish-pots of wicker-work, lobster-pots, etc.; while contiguous to it is a display upon which are box-traps, woodchuck and bear-traps, models of grouse-snares, bird-traps, models of gilnet, etc. The exhibit of models of boats in this department is curious and interesting, comprising *kijaks* in large variety, Chesapeake oyster canoe, birch-bark canoe, fore-and-aft schooners, Nantucket harbor-boats, Adirondack boats, model of Lake Erie Pound boat, fishing-schooner, Cape Ann seine boat, Nantucket dory, Alexandria Bay boat, Lake Pound steamer, portable boat, etc. Here are also models of full-rigged ships, barks, clippers, steamers, lobster-boats, Whitehall boats, New England surf-boats, ship's yawl, several wooden canoes of a kind used at Sitka, and a raft of *tule* grass. These exhibits are set off by glass cases containing specimens of beautiful feather-work in fans and flowers, chiefly from the birds of Florida.

Here are also representations of manufactures in whalebone, showing the bone-fibre, brushes, bed stuffing, corset sticks, surgical instruments, canes, etc. There is also an exhibit of brushes, from the coarsest bristle to the finest peacock tail, and there are feather-dusters, paint-brushes, shaving-brushes, etc.

Returning northward to the wall again, the screen is seen upon which are displayed various marine implements and appurtenances, such as boat-anchors, boxes, swivels, trawls and other articles in wood and metal. Here we see cases containing shells of the Pacific, hawk's-bill turtle, to show the material of a handsome set of tortoiseshell jewelry—necklace and locket, earrings, brooch and sleeve-buttons—to illustrate the manufacture.

Next is a case of horn for manufacturing purposes, with combs, sets of jewelry and other articles prepared from it. Here are also alligators' teeth carved and mounted, and other marine ivory, painted and otherwise ornamented; an elephant's tusk and a fossil tusk; and this brings us to the magnificent display of imitations of saltwater fish—these being in most cases life-size and colored to perfection.

Here is the sleeper shark, 9 or 10 ft. long; next the gigantic butterfly rae, 4 ft. long; the seine fish, an unsightly object, 5 ft. in length; the great torpedo or cramp fish, 5 ft. long and 3 ft. broad; the sting-rae, dog-fish, sturgeon, skate, monk-fish, gar-pike, sword-fish, paddle-fish, mackerel, shark, cat-fish, dusky shark, conger eels, shad, white fish, cod-fish, drummer-fish, muscalonge, red bass, pompano, red snapper, angler, and several hundred others, large and small, too numerous to mention. In other cases are a fine collection of walrus tusks, polished and scrimshawed, as it is called by the sailors. There are also neat carvings from these in chains, cane-handles, napkin-rings, sleeve-buttons and studs.

Six large cases are devoted to a quite remarkable collection of oyster-shells, including pearl oyster-shells, showing the formation of the pearl with the products of pearl, shell, and mother-of-pearl, manufactured into buttons, studs, etc. Here is also a collection of specimens of sponges. Quite an interesting exhibit is made of river mussel shells as used in ornamental work, and there are also specimens of small sea-shells used in road-making. An interesting feature is a collection of specimens of ship's timbers, showing the ravages of the ship-worm.

Returning north again, we come once more upon tackling for ships and boats, boat-hooks, boat-fittings, small fog-horns, sailor's *palms* or thimbles, needles, grappling-gear, and a case of decoys for bird-shooting.

The articles from Alaska are quite numerous, including spears, arrows and other weapons used by the natives. The fishing-gear for deep sea fishing includes trawl-lines, cod hand-lines, mackerel lines, bone hawks from Alaska, and from these through every conceivable kind of fishing line and produce, from the finest to the largest, from the clumsy shark-hook and gear to the smallest Limerick trout-hooks and hair-lines, trawling-spoons, very beautiful fly-hooks of every conceivable species of fly, reels of all sizes and materials. After these is a collection of harpoons and spears from Alaska, seal's bladder buoys, the curious "throw stick" used in rabbit-hunting by the *Moqui* Indians, which is, in fact, the boomerang; rope and hide lariats, hand-nets, harpoons of all kinds, harpoon-lines made from elkskin; fish-spears, etc.

The collection of knives used by fishermen is in itself a very curious exhibit. It comprises broad knives for cutting blubber, the throating or ripping-knife, halibut knife, mackerel splitting knife, clam knife, clam chopper for bait, hand mince-knife for mincing blubber, and lances for the pursuit of the swordfish, whale, and other large sea-prey.

Next are cases containing starfish, crabs, sea-urchins, gigantic prawns, clam-shells, mussel-shells, and the curious *hiqua* shell strung and used as money in the Indian trade. A large case contains bottles in which are shrimp, craw-fish, the small octapoos or cuttlefish, sea hair and preservations of Iceland moss and dye-stuffs from marine plants, etc. Among the curiosities at this point is a pair of boots made by a Broadway shoemaker, and which claims to be manufactured from the skins of men. Here are alligator boots also, and boots from the boa, exhibiting the peculiar marks of that reptile. Then there are dressed rattlesnake skins, sturgeon skins, and ladies' satchel, slippers, and cigar case made from alligator hide ; a coil and rope manufactured from cow-hide, a doll's head made of raw hide, and looking quite equal to those made of china or papier-mache.

Here is also a sea lion's throat manufactured into a parchment pouch designed for valuable papers. The specimens of fish-oils and glycerine are numerous, and include black fish oil, *menhaden*, porpoise, sperm whale, codliver, shark, sunfish, grampus and seal, with spermaceti can-

gear, including coil of rope, harpoons, immense jaw-bones of the whale, whale-lines, and specimens of whalebone.

We now come to a large and very fine collection of skins of animals. These include buffalo-skins, mountain-sheep (bighorns), bareback deer, caribon, mule deer, marmot, deerskin and rabbit skins, specimens of dressed skins of rattlesnake, sturgeon, eel, alligator and white whale ; the woodland caribon, peccari, prong-horn antelope, *blees-bok*, duck tanned sheepskin, lambskin, imitation buckskin from the American bison, etc.; moleskin, musk-

wolf, coyote, lynx, ocelot, panther, and even the common house cat.

Next is a collection including stuffed animals, among the larger of which are the Polar bear, American deer, puma or cougar, brown bear, grizzly, peccari, caribon, mountain goat, American elk, American mountain sheep, antelope, a splendid pair of musk-oxes, a group of fur seals, sea-lions, harpy seals, hooded seals, elephant seal, manatee-leopard ; and cases containing rabbits, horses, wild cats, lynxes, foxes, squirrels, raccoons, weasels, minks, skunks, wolver-

THE INDIAN DEPARTMENT, IN THE UNITED STATES GOVERNMENT BUILDING.

dles, isinglass made from the cod, etc. The canned specimens include lobster, clams, oysters, Russian caviar, sturgeons, turtles, anchovies, eels ; and there are also specimens of smoked herrings, pickled herrings, and smoked sprats.

Here are some more very handsome specimens of shell work, including baskets and other articles, and a little further on, a display of barnacles, sea-snails, slugs, *beche de mer*, oysters, crabs and a collection of sponges. Then there are models of fish-trays, and a display of seal fishing-

rat, black woodchuck, white bearskin with fur, and fine specimens of other furs, including the black bear, grizzly, common seal, hooded seal, harpy seal, square-flapper, banded, and other seals. Of the fur-seals there are several fine specimens from the North Pacific and South Sea.

There are also large robes made from the feathers of the brown pelican, goose, swan, grebe and other birds.

Still other skins are the opossum, sea-otter, American otter, skunk, wolverine, brown mink, fine marten or American sable, silver, black, red, and white fox, black

ines, woodchucks, and many other small animals, all admirably prepared and placed in lifelike attitudes.

This brings us to the transept ; and the first article which we observe is a case containing a model of a whaler, with whale fishery illustrated by whales diving, one having a bolt in his jaws, another being harpooned, while the various processes of skinning, etc., are being conducted on a miniature ship.

On a table near by are specimens of hatching-cans, and models of a lobster-house, fishing-smack, and menhaden oil factory, Nantucket salt mill and menhaden steamer, with seine-boats, etc.

Next is a collection of real boats, nets, etc., including Adirondack boat, paper canoe, curious Indian canoe—bullet-shaped—made of skins, a portable folding-boat, wooden canoe, bark canoes, skin canoes, etc. Right here also is a remarkable group of imitations of sea-fish, some of them being life-size. These include black fish, striped porpoise, sow-fish, bow-head whale in miniature, sword-fish, life-size, and others. Specimens of a bait-mill and fish-dresser bring us to several refrigerators filled with large fish—sturgeon, bass, etc.—concluding this portion of the exhibition.

TREASURY DEPARTMENT.

Crossing the transept on the north side of the United States building, we enter the United States Revenue Bureau of the Treasury Department. Here are framed specimens of all the engraved stamps used in the Treasury Department, as also specimens of articles requiring Internal Revenue stamps, such as tobacco, snuff, canned fruits, etc., while several large barrels of spirits which have passed the Revenue officers are exhibited, having upon them the necessary official stamps and brands.

There are also exhibited specimens of hydrometers, showing the specific gravity of liquors, and other instruments used in the Revenue service. Next comes the

BUREAU OF ENGRAVING AND PRINTING,

where are seen large frames containing specimens of Treasury notes and bonds, ranging all the way from $10,000 to fractional currency. An exhibit is also made of proof impressions of all the vignettes used in this department. In a very handsome case are collected specimens of the national medals and coins exhibited by the United States Mint, and contiguous to these are framed illustrations of national architecture, as represented in public buildings such as post-offices, custom-houses, etc., in different cities, with a large plaster model of the public buildings in Nashville, Tennessee, containing the post-office, custom-house, and court-house.

LIGHTHOUSE DEPARTMENT.

This brings us to the Lighthouse Department, which is exceedingly interesting and full in its exhibits. The first and most prominent objects which attract the eye are the lighthouse lanterns, of which there are several, including the first, third, and fourth orders. The largest of these is a flash-light, revolving by clockwork. Lard oil is now used exclusively in the lighthouses, and specimens of this are given, as well as of the lamps used in the lanterns, and also smaller lanterns, including the river lights employed on Western rivers, and a range of leading lights used in channels where a certain range must be kept. A large map, about 14 ft. square, shows the United States lighthouse stations, and there are also framed illustrations, photographic, etc., of the different lighthouses on the coast. Two models in wood display the foundations of the South-

west Pass Lighthouse, Louisiana, and the Minots Ledge Lighthouse. There are also models of two lighthouses—one being at Chicago—which are about five and eight feet in height, respectively. Other smaller models display different styles of lighthouses, and there is a model of a cofferdam and caisson used in building them.

THE COAST SERVICE DEPARTMENT

exhibits models of signals, and also numerous instruments, including the theodolite, vertical circle, synthetic telescope, equation apparatus, hydrographic sextant, self-registering tide-gauge, sounding-rods, specimen cups, thermometers for soundings, etc.

WAR DEPARTMENT.

We now enter the division allotted to the War Department, and first explore that section devoted to the exhibits

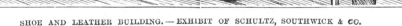

SHOE AND LEATHER BUILDING. — EXHIBIT OF SCHULTZ, SOUTHWICK & CO.

of the Signal Service Bureau. Here, as in the department last examined, we observe numerous instruments, including the anemograph, which gives daily record of the direction of the wind; the rain-gauge, which gives the amount of rainfall; the velocity anemograph, which records the velocity of the wind; self-registering thermograph, etc. Here are exhibited the processes of printing the "Probabilities," and weather maps, copies of which are printed here daily and given away to visitors. The various processes of giving and obtaining signals are fully illustrated in this department, including specimens of heliographs for communicating signals by sun-flashes, signal rockets and pistols, an entire kit or case for signal equipments, signal flags, mortars, foot torches, flying torches for night service, fieldglasses, etc., with models of signal stations, battery wagons for field telegraphy, cautionary signal-lanterns, etc. Next

to these comes the Engineer Corps Department, in the extreme northwest corner of the building.

Here is a fine model of a sounding machine of Colonel J. M. Macomb; numerous specimens of buoys, as used in actual service; specimens of stone employed in military engineering, being about 150 varieties; model of a United States steam-drilling scow; models of military bridges—some extended, some packed in wagons—pontoon bridges, and a very interesting model illustrating the operations of General Newton at Hell Gate. By a simple arrangement, the exposed surface of the rock which is to be exploded at this point is lifted several inches, showing the operations beneath, and clearly defining the methods to be used in its destruction. Next to this are seen the apparatus for field photography, and an exhibition under water, illustrating operations in submarine mining. Then we come upon an apparatus for operating and testing torpedoes, models of gabions, etc., used in harbor improvement; a large collection of working models of cribs, an iron shipping and landing pier, and the Delaware breakwater; counterpoised gun-carriage, triangulation station for surveying, sea-coast battery with counterpoised gun-carriage, dredge-boat used in improving the mouths of the Mississippi, dry dock derrick, etc.—all models.

A collection of handsomely bound reports of explorations, commissions to the War Department, models illustrating river improvements; framed photographs, maps, charts, etc., illustrating geographical and other surveys, complete the collection exhibited in this department.

We now encounter a large collection of military saddles and horse-gear, and scattered about among these, and, indeed, through all the War Department, are figures representing different army costumes, including the Continental uniform; that of Morgan's Rifles, 1776; Washington's Life Guards, 1776; and all the costumes from 1800 down to the present time—these being exhibited on life-size figures, and representing all arms of the service, including cavalry, and even horses without riders.

There are also models of army tents, various tools used in campaigns, and the various fabrics employed in the manufacture of army clothing.

Here are two interesting machines, one being a standard screw machine, which manufactures the screws used in Government shoes; and A. Worth's Inclosed Traveling Cut Machine, for cutting out any kind of garment or portion of it, the knife, which works on the jointed arm, formed somewhat on the principle of the human arm, cutting through twenty-six thicknesses of woolen cloth at once with perfect ease and accuracy, following a chalk-line drawn for the pattern.

We now enter the exhibition of artillery, shell, and other projectiles belonging to the Ordnance Department. Here are army powder-wagons, caissons, cannon of all calibres and of every make, as well as models of the same, from the Gatling gun to the mountain howitzer. A fine collection of models of shells, artillery, etc., will be found on a large table facing the nave.

It should be observed that all the departments of the United States Government are ornamented by oil portraits, many of them fine works of art, representing distinguished personages connected with them—the War Department being thus illustrated by portraits of Secretaries of War and prominent army officers.

In the Ordnance Department is a model of a 15-inch Rodman gun, accompanied by all the various appurtenances for its use. Here may also be seen a specimen of a sharpshooter's rifle on a tripod, and near this every variety of projectile, including shrapnel, grape and canister, and from these to a thousand-pound 20-inch shot.

From this point to the extreme eastern end of the building the space is chiefly occupied with machinery representing on one side the manufacture of guns as conducted at the Springfield Armory; and on the other that of cartridges from the Frankfort Arsenal, Philadelphia. In this latter department some dozen machines placed side by side complete the perfect cartridge through its stages, from the thin disk of copper, with which the operation commences, to the final placing of the priming and bullet within it. As

Complete in every particular, from keel to topmasts, with her entire armament and 22 miniature guns. The model is about 35 ft. in length. Next is a model of the French line-of-battle ship *Dante*, built about the year 1600—a very admirable representation of a class of ships in vogue at that time. A section of a model of a double-bottomed iron-clad, and one of an iron-clad ram, are the next in order. Also a small model of the French frigate *Didon*, comprising the hull alone. This exhibit includes also a model in frame of the sloop-of-war *Antietam*, showing the construction of a sloop-of-war. This is made to scale, each part being numbered.

This section closes with the model of a boat with apparatus for lowering, hoisting, and securing, and also for detaching and attaching. Two forms of hoisting-tackle conclude this portion of the Exhibition.

A considerable space of this department is occupied by specimens of naval artillery and projectiles, equipments, cordage, implements, etc., while racks along the wall are filled with Remington carbines and other small arms, with and without single band, and revolvers are displayed on a shelf beneath. A miscellaneous and rather heterogeneous collection of naval material of all kinds fills several tables in

of the Mississippi, these being displayed on the wall, next to which are various cases containing naval ordnance, fuses, etc., flanked by a 32℔ steel gun, mounted on a wooden carriage.

It should be observed that the various uniforms current in the Naval Department at different periods are illustrated here, as is the case in the War Department, by stuffed figures upon which they are displayed. These include sailors armed and unarmed, and in position for the performance of different duties.

Here are also to be seen in glass-cases, displayed on tables, the various instruments used in navigation, including sextants, compasses, spy-glasses, binocular glasses, artificial horizons, aneroid barometers, etc., with head lanterns, cabin lights, sounding apparatus, deep sea leads, ships' pinnacles, and a curious apparatus designed to illustrate the action and the force of projection and gravity in determining the *trajectory* of the shot.

More models of ships, dry docks, blocks of wood made from parts of different men-of-war, and extensive collections of blocks of various designs, and very fine oil portraits of different distinguished officers of the Navy, are to be found in this vicinity. A collection of charts is next in

ARRIVAL OF THE EMPLOYES OF THE SINGER MANUFACTURING COMPANY AT THE SINGER BUILDING ON THE CENTENNIAL GROUNDS, JUNE 22D.

these machines are in operation at certain hours of the day, this most interesting process can be witnessed by every visitor.

A number of ingenious and neatly-made models will be seen near this point, representing the entire mechanism used in gunmaking. Near this are some exhibits of ancient artillery, including the breech-loading cannon of the sixteenth century, a relic of the Spanish occupation of Mexico; also several Revolutionary 6-pounders presented by Lafayette, a Whitworth gun, Vavasseur gun, and Hotchkiss gun.

After pausing to look at some more figures in uniform, we examine a fine display of muskets ranged along the wall and in racks, including every variety of gun known to the service, breech-loading or otherwise, flint-lock, blunderbusses and other quaint-looking old weapons. Behind these, on shelves, are displayed small arms in every variety. This completes our examination of the northern side of the United States building.

NAVY DEPARTMENT.

Commencing at the southeast corner, and working westward, we first encounter a series of models of ships, the most important of which is a full-rigged and completely equipped model of the United States sloop-of-war *Antietam*,

the centre, from metal cannon to gun-swabs, ship's lanterns, sections of bridges, candle-molds, and cartridge-boxes. A glass-case contains a number of specimens of gun-locks of various models, flint and others. A collection of curiosities displays boarding-caps, boarding-axes, bowie-knives, old Roman cutlasses, fragments of shell, cutlass of Paul Jones, used by him on the ship *Bon Homme Richard*, and an Enfield rifle taken from the sunken monitor *Keokuk*.

Here are also samples of powders, fuels, schooners, rockets, submarine water-fuses, cartridges, etc. Here are also two cases with very pretty models of gun-carriages, guns and mortars, and specimens of tompions, with shot of various calibre.

This brings us to the exhibit of the torpedo department, which includes samples of the various materials used at the United States Station, Newport, R. I. Following these are the electric machines and other implements used in discharging torpedoes; and next, specimens of the torpedoes themselves, including the great "fish" torpedo, about 12 ft. in length; the Harvey torpedo, the spar torpedo, and Barbour's torpedo.

Contiguous to the torpedo department are found several sectional models of monitors, sloops-of-war, and other armed ships, including one of the old side-wheel steamships

order, and specimens of canvas flagging hung about at intervals.

A very interesting and complete collection is given in a glass-case by itself, being that of Captain Charles F. Hall, and representing his three expeditions to the Polar regions. This includes the log of the *Polaris*, Captain Hall's flag, instruments, photographs, and Esquimaux curiosities.

The remaining exhibits of the Naval Department are found displayed in a case containing various books of accounts, blankets, etc., used in the department, with specimens of stationery, etc. Here are also exhibited all the various medical stores and surgical instruments required on shipboard during long voyages, showing the entire fit-out of a first-class man-of-war. With these, and a very large show of cordage, cables of rope and chain, heavy iron tacklings, and other fittings and furnishings for ships, and with an exhibit of marine galleys, etc., the display of the Naval Department closes.

POST OFFICE DEPARTMENT.

In this portion of the Exhibition is illustrated the entire postal system of the United States, with all its necessary appurtenances, methods and processes. These commence with the exhibition of a case containing mail-bags of leather and canvas, and samples of the fabrics used in the manufacture. A large map on the wall, about 10 ft. square, presents the chief line of railway mail service, while smaller post-route maps illustrate other features of postal service. Specimens of marking stamps, mail-boxes, stamped envelopes, blank forms for postmasters, mail-locks, scales, and a collection of U. S. postage stamps of all denominations, are seen. Bound volumes of post-route maps, postal cards, registered packages and letter envelopes are also displayed.

For curiosities, there are the commission of Dr. Benjamin Franklin, first Postmaster-General of the United States; and the journal of Hugh Finlay, ostensibly sent out by the British Government in 1774 to examine into the post-routes and post-offices of the country, but really, as is believed, for the purpose of manufacturing evidence sufficient to warrant the dismissal of Dr. Franklin from his position. These two volumes, both manuscripts, are exhibited securely locked in cases.

The display of the Post-office Department closes with a full post-office in running order, including money-order office, registered letter department, etc., being duly authorized by the United States Government for use during the continuance of the Centennial Exposition.

This brings us to the transept again, on the opposite side of which, still turning westward, we enter upon the display of the Patent Office, beginning with the Agricultural Department.

Commencing at the extreme south, we find upon the walls various maps, charts, and tables illustrating, by statistics, the agricultural condition and proportion of farm areas in the United States. Here there is a large and very comprehensive exhibition of various native woods, displayed in sections, and including numbers of woods indigenous to the country, among which are to be found the aloe, palmetto, agave, yucca-tree of Arizona, California cactus, and the *pritchardia*, or recently discovered palm, from Southern California. With sections of trees are also given framed specimens of leaves and fibrous growth, these being pressed and dried. Drawings of fungi, colored by hand and neatly framed, follow, illustrating all of those of the United States — and these, with magnified illustrations of fibre,

seeds, and other parts of plants, close this portion of the display.

The museum exhibit of the Agricultural Department includes cases of stuffed birds, very handsomely prepared, and specimens representing fruits and vegetables, with a considerable collection comprising many interesting and some very valuable specimens. Specimens of the growth of cotton, flax, and other fibrous plants, with samples of manufacture of the same, fill some tall cases, as also paper stock in various stages of preparation, and giving illustrations of the manufacture of paper. Here are also a collection of specimens of fruit, which is very large and varied, as well as of very artistic manufacture, and which illustrate all the different varieties of the indigenous fruits of the earth.

The wool exhibit is large and varied. That of Indian corn in the ear is also considerable, and displays some magnificent specimens. With this exhibit commences a general display of grains, which are shown in glass jars, and evidently cover the entire field of these products. With these are shown specimens of soils and subsoils, illustrating their influence on the growth of plants in different localities.

This brings us to the liquid products from vegetable growths, including ales, beers, wines, cider, and spirits— also maple sugar, beet sugar, resins, gums; and next, to the exhibit of barks, ferns, and other preserved leaves; and

finally, to the display of preserved fruits, dried fruits, and vegetables.

With a small exhibit of tobacco, snuffs, and some few specimens of oils, the Agricultural Department closes.

The Mechanical Department.

The mechanical exhibits of the Patent Office Department include all patent inventions in every branch of mechanics, displayed in their models. These commence with mechanisms used in metal-working, of which there are two large cases, and continue through the departments of metallurgy, printing and stationery, clay, stone, railways, pneumatics, harvesters, wood, civil engineering, electricity, navigation, textile fabrics, agricultural implements, architecture, ice, gas, guns, hydraulics, vehicles, leather, hoisting, and steam —these being the different departments under which the articles patented are classified.

Of course, as every branch of manufacture and constructive effort in mechanism is illustrated in this display, it would be impossible, except on the basis of a mere catalogue, to give any idea of the articles, which number thousands, and include every imaginable invention and improvement which has been made in the United States during the last eighty-six years in the various departments, the first patent having been granted on July 31st, 1790, to Samuel Hopkins, for making pot and pearl-ash.

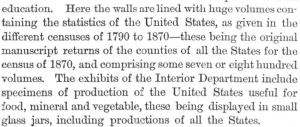

THE EXHIBIT OF PUMPS BY MESSRS. W. & B. DOUGLAS, OF MIDDLETOWN, CONN.

In the centre of the collection of patents are seen bound volumes of all the reports, including that photo-lithographed from the first volume, and running from 1790 to 1836. Among the more curious exhibits are the Howe sewing machine; the Morse telegraph, patented April 16th, 1845, and the model of that patented April 11th, 1846, being an improvement; the original model of the Whitney cotton gin, patented March 14th, 1794; the first steam fire engine invented in the United States, by Alexander B. Latta, patented April 10th, 1853; the first steam hammer, invented by James Nasmyth, and patented on the 10th of April, 1843; and the Adams power printing press, one of the first to which steam was applied, patented March 2d, 1836. As most of these models are manufactured by skilled mechanics, they represent in every particular the exact construction and working of the articles themselves. This is illustrated particularly in the case of a cotton-gin which cleans the cotton with the facility and perfection of a full-sized gin, although it is only a model about a foot square.

Among the patented machines used in wood construction are to be found models of saws, planing machines, barrel-making machines, etc. Among those representing the manufacture of textile fabrics are various sorts of cotton mills, weaving machines, power looms, spinning-jennies, and bonnet-frame machines. In agriculture, the display is, of course, endless; plows, harrows, reapers, mowers, fences,

butter-workers, cheese-presses, cider-mills, feed-racks, sheep-racks, and innumerable other articles. The display in civil engineering includes railroads, railway bridges, viaducts, machinery for well-boring; and in electricity, all kinds of batteries for telegraphy, with the various parts of these as individually patented. In navigation there are models of boats and parts of boats, wheels, screws, capstans, and a variety of other things. In architecture, every imaginable form of building, and material used in construction, as patented—and curious features in roofs, odd inventions in window and door-frames, stair-cases, locks, hinges, etc. The improvements in the product of ice since the first exportation of that article from the lakes have been numerous and important, and in many ways are displayed in the collection of patented articles illustrating this subject. These include machinery for getting out ice, refrigerators, ice-cream freezers, and machines for the manufacture of ice-cream by the use of steam artificial ice machines. And so on to the various other departments the observer can wander, viewing at a glance the progress of manufacture and invention in each of them, including everything since the first patent was granted to Samuel Hopkins, in 1790.

Interior Department.

The exhibition of the Interior Department commences with that portion which is within the jurisdiction of the 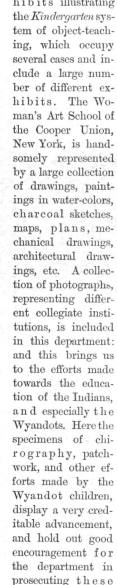 United States Bureau of Education, and begins with exhibits illustrating the *Kindergarten* system of object-teaching, which occupy several cases and include a large number of different exhibits. The Woman's Art School of the Cooper Union, New York, is handsomely represented by a large collection of drawings, paintings in water-colors, charcoal sketches, maps, plans, mechanical drawings, architectural drawings, etc. A collection of photographs, representing different collegiate institutions, is included in this department: and this brings us to the efforts made towards the education of the Indians, and especially the Wyandots. Here the specimens of chirography, patch-work, and other efforts made by the Wyandot children, display a very creditable advancement, and hold out good encouragement for the department in prosecuting these attempts at Indian education. Here the walls are lined with huge volumes containing the statistics of the United States, as given in the different censuses of 1790 to 1870—these being the original manuscript returns of the counties of all the States for the census of 1870, and comprising some seven or eight hundred volumes. The exhibits of the Interior Department include specimens of production of the United States useful for food, mineral and vegetable, these being displayed in small glass jars, including productions of all the States.

The collection of Indian curiosities is large, and comprehends a very curious and instructive exhibit, including pottery, bead and wampum-work, carvings, costumes, domestic utensils, and household implements of a very curious and uncommon collection, illustrating games in vogue among the different tribes of Indians, among which are to be found various gaming sticks, dice, and packs of quaintly painted cards. Some very handsome specimens of bead-work are shown here. Indian masks, pipes, tobacco-pouches, the collection of these last being large and most interesting, in every variety of stone as to the pipes, ornamented with carvings, in many cases quite artistic and representing a rather high degree of art idea. Several interesting specimens of basket-work, including water-tight trays and glasses, are exhibited, made by the Pueblo and Navajo Indians. Also hats and caps of different materials, the handiwork of the Indians, and leggins as well.

VIEW OF THE MAIN BUILDING, LOOKING DOWN THE CENTR

SLE FROM THE ORGAN LOFT IN THE EASTERN GALLERY.

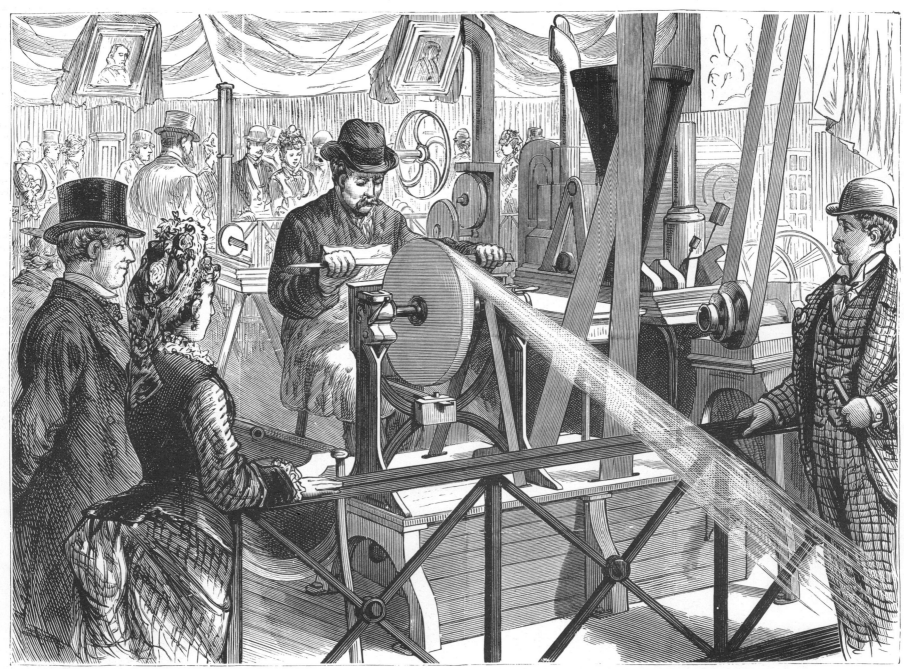

MANUFACTURING ARMS IN THE GOVERNMENT BUILDING—BURNISHING BAYONETS.

A superb collection of bows, arrows, and other weapons of war, some very curious wooden idols from British Columbia, head-dresses, jewelry, and ornaments; various skins and robes are manufactured into garments; buck-skin hunting - shirts, trimmed with wampum; women's dresses of sheepskin and wampum; ax-heads and arrow-heads of flint and other stone—all form a perfect museum of American archæology. A very curious exhibit is that of models of the mounds of Wisconsin, formed in the shape of different animals. This Indian collection is one of the finest which has been brought together, and will readily repay the careful observation of those who are interested in the manners, customs, and implements of the aborigines of America.

The collection of the Department of the Interior ends with a series of gigantic models presenting the conformation of the land in different parts of the country, notably in the Territories of the West — Arizona, Colorado, Utah, etc. This completes the account of the contents of the United States Government Building, excepting the nave, in which are placed large objects which could not be conveniently disposed of elsewhere.

Among these, the first exhibit represents the manufacture of steel from the ore to the completion of crucible steel, and finished boiler-plates, some remarkably fine specimens of files, axes, ice-chisels, etc.

Next to these is an exhibit of Kanawha coal from the Kanawha County, W. Va. This is followed by a second iron and steel exhibit from Troy, N. Y., and this by gigantic specimens of silver and other ores. Then comes a mammoth "dug-out," sixty feet long and eight feet beam, made from one log by the natives of British Columbia. At the point of junction between the nave and the transept there is an exhibit of coal, certainly the largest ever made, being forty-three feet in height. This is surrounded by marble and other minerals in large specimens, bales of cotton, and other smaller exhibits.

Without the United States Buildings are several articles too large to admit of their being placed within it. Besides numbers of the larger cannon exhibited by the Ordnance and Navy Departments, there is an iron turret, armed and equipped, which

is placed near the eastern entrance of the building, and attracts considerable attention. There is also a lighthouse, with a flash (revolving) light, which is lighted up at night.

INDIAN CURIOSITIES.

Among the curious specimens from the National Museum of the Smithsonian Institute exhibited in the United States Government Building, and to which we have alluded elsewhere, are the "totem posts," so called, of the Indians of the Northwest coast. These Indians inhabit that portion of the Pacific Coast lying between Oregon and Alaska, and the rude carvings, of which we give a full-page illustration, and which will be doubtless mistaken for idols by most of those who see them, are really a species of genealogical work, the carvings being designed to perpetuate the pedi-

NICHOLAS MULLER'S SONS' EXHIBIT OF BRONZE GOODS.

gree of those using them. As is well-known, it is a custom among all Indian warriors to take to themselves some name indicative either of a trait of character or of some incid nt in their lives. Such are Walk-in-the-Water, Sitting Bull, White Antelope, Red Dog, Red Jacket, Black Hawk, Spotted Tail, Bear Stand Up, Crazy Horse, Scabby Head, Black Moccasin, Red Cloud, Swift Bear, etc. It is, however, peculiar to the Indians of the Northwest Coast to keep a family record by cutting "totems" in tall posts of cedar. These posts are not worshiped as idols, though it is understood that they are in some sense considered, from a superstitious standpoint, as possessing some power to protect those occupying the house in front of which they stand.

The "totem posts" pictured in our illustration belong to the Mukah Indians, who are chiefly engaged in fishing. These tribes are noted for their artistic attainments, and are greatly in the habit of making such carvings as these.

OUR ILLUSTRATIONS.

A CIGAR EXHIBIT.

A very good specimen of the most artistic designs in exhibition cases displayed in the Centennial Exposition is represented in our illustration. It is that of the firm of Kerbs & Spiess, cigar manufacturers, at No. 35 Bowery, New York City, and is in the Agricultural Building.

This case is both elegant and solid in its design and structure. Its form is hexagonal. It is constructed of ebony, and stands eighteen feet in height and ten feet in width. Within, it is lined throughout with satin trimmings; it is surmounted by an eagle and two handsomely wrought figures, while on either side are figures of large carvings of dragons elaborately formed of bronze, each of them holding in one of its claws a handsome card-receiver. This work was executed by a French artist, and is highly creditable in its design and execution. The case contains boxes filled with various brands and styles of cigars manufactured by Messrs. Kerbs & Spiess, these being artistically arranged in order around a circular framework which supports them.

CENTRAL TRANSEPT OF THE MAIN BUILDING.

A marked and beautiful architectural feature of the Main Building of the Centennial Exposition is found in its centre, where, for an area of 184 ft. square, the roof is elevated above the surrounding portion, and where four towers, 48 ft. square at the base, and rising to the height of 120 ft., are prominent objects, and present, in their circular form, an agreeable change from the strict parallel outlines of the rest of the building.

In the double-page illustration by which we depict this portion of the building, there is presented a wide view. Here are located the following departments: Northeast, France; northwest, Great Britain and Ireland; southeast, United States; southwest, Germany. The open area made by the space occurring where the nave and main transept of the building intersect at this point contains in its centre a circular platform 35 ft. in diameter, and raised 4 ft. from the floor, designed as a music-stand, and frequently occupied by a band discoursing the latest and most popular musical compositions. In the rear of the stand, as seen in the illustration, is a German exhibition of pottery and earthenware statuary. The French section at this point presents a fine exhibit of silks. The United States department is made prominent by exhibits in gold and silverware and jewelry, belonging to the Messrs. Tiffany & Co., of New York, and the Gorham Manufacturing Company.

DIRECTOR-GENERAL GOSHORN.

The Director-General of the Centennial Exposition, and the master-spirit of the entire display, is Mr. Alfred T.

THE TURKISH BAZAAR.

Behind the Pennsylvania State Building is a large octagonal structure, having three entrances opening upon verandas. This building is the Turkish Café and Bazaar, and we give an illustration representing a scene within it which will be recognized as characteristic by those who have seen it. The interior of the building is furnished with divans along the sides, covered with blue and straw-colored plush, having in front of them circular tables. The windows are hung with handsomely embroidered curtains, and in two of the corners of the room will be seen a number of pipes, including the Turkish *chibouque* and the Persian *narghile*, or water-pipe. The establishment is served by native Turks, clad in their national costume, and these furnish visitors with coffee and pipes, the former being served in small cups inclosed in silver holders, while the latter, supplied with Turkish tobacco, may be obtained by those desiring them.

The entire scene, with its surroundings, is curious and interesting. The picturesque costumes of the attendants include the red fez caps, red tunic, yellow sash, and blue or brown silk trowsers. On one side of the apartment are two waiting-rooms for ladies, which are furnished with lounges and ottomans and hung with Turkish tapestry. At the sides are small bazaars, where are sold rich costumes, carpets, pipes, swords, daggers, hilts, and other articles.

WASHINGTON RELICS IN THE UNITED STATES BUILDING.

An interesting historical feature of the exhibition made by the United States Government, and one to which we

garden engines, pump chains, hydrants, etc. Their works were founded in 1832, and they have repeatedly obtained the highest medals at public exhibitions, including the Universal Exhibition of Paris in 1867, and that of Vienna in 1873. The manufactories of this firm are at Middletown, Connecticut, and they have branch warehouses at Nos. 85 and 87 John Street, and 197 Lake Street, Chicago, Illinois.

The reputation of the Douglas Pump, on account of its convenient form, its thorough adaptability, and its general excellence for use either in domestic service or for factories, railways, ships, steamers, quarries, or mines, is, beyond cavil, the highest of any. So much is this the case, that it is even alleged that foreign manufacturers do not hesitate to foist imitations of this valuable article on the public.

THE SINGER BUILDING.

The great Singer Sewing Machine Manufacturing Company has upon the Centennial Grounds a large and beautiful building which attracts general attention. This enormous company represents a capital of $27,000,000, and employs in the manufacture of its machines 4,000 persons. Desirous of affording their employés an opportunity of witnessing the Centennial Exposition, the Singer Company gave these an excursion to Philadelphia on the 22d of June, 1876. Six trains on the Pennsylvania Railroad and Central Railroad of New Jersey, comprising seventy-six cars in all, carried more than 4,000 persons in the employ of this firm, leaving New York, Elizabethport, and Newark at various times between 5.30 and 6.30 A. M. The excursionists reached Philadelphia at half-past nine o'clock, and marched in a body, preceded by a band of music, to the

HOWES, BABCOCK & CO.'S EXHIBIT OF GRAIN-CLEANING MACHINERY.

Goshorn, who was born in Cincinnati in 1834, graduated at Hamilton College twenty years later, and who, preferring the profession of law, was admitted to the Bar in 1856. Mr. Goshorn did not, however, continue in his chosen profession; but entered into manufacturing business, by becoming proprietor of a large white-lead establishment in Cincinnati.

Entering actively into politics, he was for some time a member of the City Government, and of the local Board of Trade, and as a member of the Executive Committee of the latter organization interested himself in the Industrial Exhibition held in Cincinnati in 1870, of which he was made president, and of which, in its succeeding representative exhibitions, he continued to retain the management. In 1873 Mr. Goshorn was appointed to represent the State of Ohio in the United States Centennial Commission; and immediately after was called to the general direction of the Exposition.

During the year 1873 Mr. Goshorn repaired to Vienna, and there devoted much time and thought to the consideration of the Austrian International Exhibition. On his return to America he entered actively upon the duties of his important post, and soon displayed in his administrative ability, his executive power, and the wisdom of his judgment, as well as the comprehensiveness of his acquaintance with the subject, a capacity which amply fulfilled the expectations felt in his appointment. It is only justice to say that to Mr. Goshorn's admirable qualities are due very much of the success of the exposition, and that to his guidance is greatly owing its progress to the perfection of excellence which it has certainly achieved.

desire to give special prominence, is a case which contains the Washington relics. These relics have been collected chiefly from members of the Custis and Lee families, many of them having been heretofore stored at Arlington, in the old Custis mansion, over the Long Bridge from Washington. One of our illustrations displays the contents of this case, which include the actual wardrobe and service used by General Washington while occupying his position as Chief of the American Army. Here are the coat, breeches, and vest which the General actually wore when, at Annapolis, in 1783, he resigned his commission as General-in-Chief. Here are also Washington's dress-sword, his rude iron-bound treasure-chest, his camp-chest, with its certainly unostentatious service of plate, spoons, cups, cans, bowls, and other articles for the table, a dinner set of china presented to Martha Washington by General Lafayette, a portmanteau marked "Yorktown," counterpanes worked by Lady Washington in her youth, and the compass used by the General when he was a surveyor and before the Braddock expedition. There is certainly no exhibit in the entire exposition which is so calculated to rouse our feelings of national pride and to thrill our hearts with memories of the days of '76 as is this one.

A PUMP EXHIBIT.

Our illustration presents a view of an exhibit of pumps displayed in the pump annex of the Machinery Building by W. & B. Douglas, of Middletown, Connecticut. This firm is the oldest and most extensive establishment engaged in the manufacture of pumps in the world, their manufactures including, besides ordinary pumps, hydraulic rams,

New Jersey building, where they were addressed by General Hawley, President of the Centennial Commission, and Mr. Welsh, of the Board of Finance. Here also Mayor Towles, of Elizabeth, presented the excursionists with a banner in the name of his city, where the Singer Manufacturing Company's works are located.

The entire body then marched to the Singer Pavilion, the moment of their entrance into which having been chosen by our artist for his illustration. At noon a magnificent banquet was given to the guests of the Singer Manufacturing Company, at the Restaurant Lafayette—this including statesmen, editors, the Centennial Commission, and others. The total cost of the excursion was $15,632, exclusive of the loss of the services of the employés.

No business conducted on a less enormous scale could afford such a donation as this; but the Singer Manufacturing Company sold in the year 1875 nearly 200,000 machines, and pays dividends of $10,000,000 capital, while the entire number of its employés amounts to upwards of 50,000 persons. It has 41 domestic offices, over 500 sub-offices in this country, and 31 in England, Ireland, Scotland, Germany, Russia, Spain, France, South America, Cuba, Canada, and Australia. It employs more than 1,800 traveling agents in the United States, and has 316 canvassers in the city of New York alone.

THE EUREKA WHEAT-CLEANER.

The above illustration represents a scene in Machinery Hall, displaying the powerful and beautiful mechanism of the Eureka Grain-cleaning Machinery of Messrs. Howes,

Babcock & Co. The wheat-cleaning machines of this firm received the highest medal at Vienna, and have the honor of holding the only gold medal given by the Royal Agricultural Society of England in 1869.

AMERICAN FIREARMS.

The display of Messrs. Remington in the Main Building is a very prominent feature of the locality where it is situated. The frontage of their case is about twenty-six feet in length, comprising an elegant show-case on a neatly carpeted platform, the whole inclosed by a bronze railing.

Here are to be seen a fine collection of the Remington revolvers, sporting rifles, military arms, a very handsome Creedmoor rifle, beautiful specimens of their shot-guns, long-range rifles, military rifles with sabres, short black rifles called "civil guards," they being used by the municipal police of Spain and Cuba. Between the cribs of cases is a large star composed of Remington cartridges, having on either side trophies formed by a combination of sabres and

muskets. Below these are sixteen different kinds of pistols of Remington manufacture. Another portion of the exhibit presents samples of every part of the military rifle in various stages of manufacture. The sign which denominates this exhibit is peculiar and original in its design. The board is three feet in height, and the name of the firm is displayed in nickel-plated revolvers laid upon purple velvet. The top of the exhibit is surmounted by an American eagle, surrounded by the flags of those governments which use the Remington rifles. This entire display of arms is arranged in the most artistic manner, and is well worthy the consideration of the curious in such matters for this reason, and still more for the real beauty and merit of the articles themselves.

AMERICAN BRONZES.

A very creditable competition with European manufacturers in the matter of bronzes is made by the Messrs. N. Muller's Sons, of No. 8 Cortlandt Street, New York, whose exhibit in the Main Building will be found to repay

examination. It is located near the book publishers' structure, and comprises fine bronze inkstands, thermometers, and other articles, in whose design elegance and novelty are combined with utility. Our illustration gives a very good view of this handsome exhibit in its massive case, surmounted by a tasty monogram.

GOLD PEN EXHIBIT.

A very beautiful exhibit in gold pens, pencil-cases, etc. is made by Messrs. Aiken, Lambert & Co., of No. 12 Maiden Lane, New York, and is illustrated in our engraving. The exhibit is contained in a graceful and elegant ebony case, finished with gold, the canopy of which is supported by four massive pillars in the form of barrel-pens, each being clasped by a closed hand. Below is a combination of show-cases, surmounted by a pedestal, resting upon which is an eagle. These show-cases contain specimens of the workmanship of these manufacturers, including gold pen and pencil cases finished in Roman, enamel, carving, and red

AMERICAN VISITORS SMOKING CHIBOUQUES IN THE TURKISH BAZAAR.

gold; small pencils and toothpicks, of gold, pearl, ivory and fancy woods, tipped with gold; pens of all sizes, including those under the special terms of leviathan, mammoth, Spencerian, etc. The summit of the canopy of this unique case is surmounted by a globe having a symbolical purpose. The entire display, though comparatively small, is very beautiful and interesting.

THE CENTENNIAL ADMINISTRATION.

Chiefs of the Executive Bureaux.

THERE are ten gentlemen comprised in the heads of the various executive bureaus of the Centennial Exposition, and of these we give portraits of six, including Mr. John Sartain, Chief of the Art Bureau; Mr. David G. Yates,

DAVID G. YATES.

Chief of the Bureau of Admissions; Mr. John L. Shoemaker, of the Law Bureau; Mr. H. J. Schwarzmann, Architect-in-Chief; Mr. Thomas Cochran, Chief of the Bureau of Grounds, Plants, and Buildings; and Captain John S. Albert, Chief of the Machinery Bureau.

Mr. Cochran has been connected with the Centennial movement from its organization, and to him is due the general plan of the grounds and buildings; besides which, his personal influence in securing legislation and donations has been of the greatest value and importance. Mr. Cochran was born in Mercersburg, Pa, in 1832, was a lawyer and State Legislator, his specialty being the subject of Taxation, concerning which he has written largely, his works being translated into several foreign languages. For many years he was Chairman of the Board of Local Taxation at Philadelphia.

Mr. Yates has had an arduous and most difficult position to fill in his charge of the Department of Admissions; and that he has filled it with universal satisfaction is a high compliment to his patience, judgment and courtesy. This gentleman was born in Philadelphia, in 1835, and, after studying the art of portrait-painting, finally adopted that of engraving, and established himself in this business in New York in 1856. At the beginning of the war he accepted a position in the pay department of the United States Treasury in Washington; but after two years returned to the business of engraving in Philadelphia. To Mr. Yates we are indebted for the engravings of the structures which

JOHN L. SHOEMAKER.

CAPTAIN JOHN S. ALBERT.

have become so popular, and which were made before they were erected.

Mr. Shoemaker, the Solicitor of the Commission and Board of Finance, has been devoted to the service of the Exposition from the beginning, and his influence and personal character have been important adjuncts in its success. To him has been due much of the liberality afforded by Philadelphia to the enterprise, while his legal judgment in his professional relations with the boards controlling the Exposition has been constantly relied on throughout the progress of the work. Mr. Shoemaker is a Philadelphian, about forty years of age, and is highly esteemed as a lawyer and as a man.

The Chief Architect of the Exhibition is Mr. Schwarzmann, who was born in 1843, in Munich, and is the son of the celebrated Bavarian fresco artist. Educated at the Munich military academy, he served in the Bavarian army in 1866, but in the following year came to this country. He was employed as landscape architect in laying out Fairmount Park, the Zoological Museum, and other grounds in Philadelphia; and in 1873 visited the Vienna International Exhibition, in behalf of the Fairmount Park Commissioners. Mr. Schwarzmann was the author of the plans which were finally adopted for Memorial and Horticultural Halls, and also the designer of the Judges' Hall, Women's Pa-

JOHN SARTAIN.

vilion, Pennsylvania State Building, German and Brazilian Pavilions, the annexes to the Main Building and Art Gallery, the Photograph Building, and numerous other small structures on the grounds. He has also had charge of the water and gas supply, laying out of the walks, and other important duties.

Captain Albert, the able and reliable Chief of the Bureau of Machinery, has had a most important position to fill—that of superintending and directing the organization of the entire machinery, whose completeness and perfection of movement are the pride of all those concerned in the Exposition. Captain Albert was born in Brooklyn, in 1835, and in 1855 was appointed third assistant engineer in the United States Navy. He was promoted rapidly, and in 1861 became chief engineer. During the war he was with the Gulf Squadron, and at one time in the blockade service off Charleston, S. C. After the close of the war he became Inspector of Government work at New York, having under his jurisdiction all the steam machinery, monitors, iron

vessels, etc., located there. In 1868 and 1869 he was sent by the South Pacific Squadron as Fleet Engineer, and later became a member of the Board of Examiners for the promotion of naval engineers. In 1875 he received leave of absence from the Government service to accept his appointment as Chief of the Bureau of Machinery tendered him by the Centennial Commission, since which time he has devoted himself with skill and judgment to the arduous duties of his position.

Mr. Sartain, Chief of the Art Department, was born in London in 1808. He studied engraving, and as early as 1828 began to devote himself to the development of the *mezzo-tinto* style of engraving, by which he is best known. In 1830, he came to Philadelphia, and some years later started the *Sartain Magazine*, a monthly art journal, for which he engraved the plates, and through which his name

H. J. SCHWARZMANN.

became known throughout the country. Mr. Sartain has been long appreciated as a gentleman of fine art taste and culture, and his appointment to his present important post has been generally accepted as appropriate—a judgment which the thoroughness of his work has fully confirmed.

THE OLD WINDMILL IN AGRICULTURAL HALL.

Near the western end of Agricultural Hall a very interesting and quaint exhibit is made by Messrs. George V. Hecker & Co., the flour manufacturers of New York, which includes a collection of their various manufactures, ranged about an antiquated structure attracting considerable attention. This is a reproduction of a gristmill in use among our ancestors, and of which there are at present few, if any, left in the country. The motive power of this machine is the wind operating upon huge fans hung upon the outside of the mill. Within is a small room where are the various plans for making flour, similar in construction to those in use a century ago.

Among the samples displayed in the Hecker exhibit are the self-raising flour, extra Croton flour, Manhattan flour, farina, American flour, cracked wheat, and numerous other products of their mills. Another pleasant feature of this exhibition is found in the actual use of the products here displayed in the manufacture of griddle-cakes on the spot, these being made and cooked in the presence of the visitors, who are invited to partake of them. The cakes are made from Hecker's self-raising flour.

THOMAS COCHRAN.

THE CENTENNIAL ADMINISTRATION.—CHIEFS OF THE EXECUTIVE BUREAUX.

UNITED STATES GOVERNMENT BUILDING.

(Continued from page 109.)

Even after a reasonably complete examination of the collection of exhibits in the United States Building, one finds numerous articles of importance to have been forgotten, and is reminded of cognate things which are deserving of mention. For instance, as to the Lighthouse Board exhibit, it is worth mentioning that there are 953 lighthouses erected on the Atlantic, Pacific and Lake Coasts of the United States. Of these, 46 are of the first order; 28 of the second; 67 of the third; 190 of the fourth; 125 of the fifth; and 179 of the sixth order, ranging according to size, the latter being the smallest. Then there are 38 reflector-lights, and 280 State-lights, beside 53 steam fog-signals. The steam fog-signal close beside the United States Building makes itself heard at various times during the day, producing a voluminous and not very pleasing sound, which generally attracts the attention of all new-comers, and occasions considerable questioning as to its nature and intention. Perhaps the furthest distance a light can be seen is in the case of a lighthouse on the Pacific Coast, which stands on a bluff, about 480 feet above the sea level, and whose light is said to be seen at a distance of 28 nautical miles.

The Department of Agriculture of the United States Building, of which we have already given a description, is particularly worthy of notice, in that it displays by actual presentment the different varieties of fruit and grain, where they attain the perfect state, and in what sections the same are of inferior quality and growth, thereby affording the farmer, or those wishing to emigrate, knowledge which it would be quite impossible to obtain but by years of personal experience. The collection of maps, charts, and drawings exhibited by Mr. J. R. Dodge, Chief Statistician of this department, is very complete and important. By these charts the exact production of wheat in each State, *per capita*, for instance, is given, and this is followed through other grains and products. Another chart shows the aggregate value of the crops in this country, the most valuable being corn, and the least buckwheat. The total consumption of corn during the years from 1870 to 1874 is shown to have been about a thousand million bushels. There are also charts showing the value of farm lands by counties in the United States, the price that is paid for farm labor in the different States, the wine-producing States, and those in which cotton, hemp, flax, wool, and silk are grown, with the amount of each. Nearly all the hemp of the country is raised in Kentucky; while Texas, New Mexico, and the Western States raise most of the wool.

GOLD PEN EXHIBIT OF MESSRS. AIKIN, LAMBERT & CO., OF NEW YORK.

In the collection of articles illustrating the Department of Natural History there is a case exhibiting the different insects which are injurious to plants, and including the insect in all its various stages of development, from the egg upward. Here are also seen those insects which are hurtful to forest-trees, and the best modes for their extermination are exhibited. Again, the moth and other insects injurious to the household are presented. Even the birds are classified with regard to their uses and abuses as to the agriculturist. A very simple and ingenious method of presenting these has been adopted by painting the perches white where the birds are beneficial, and black if they are injurious. As the only method for discovering these facts, with regard to birds, is by dissection, it is easy to see that much time and care have been applied to this service. The specimens of birds shown number 500.

The display of fruits is deserving of careful consideration. These fruits are made of plaster-of-paris, and painted in exact imitation of nature. There are 3,000 specimens of fruits and vegetables. Emigrants from one part of the country to another can ascertain, by examination of this collection, what is best suited to the climate and soil of that portion of the country to which they intend to emigrate. It is noticeable that from this collection the peach is absent, the reason being that specimens of this fruit have not as yet been prepared, owing to the extreme delicacy of its color, and the rapidity and care necessary in the workmanship. This fruit will, however, be hereafter added to the collection.

In the collection of the tobacco exhibits, all varieties are represented from twenty States, some being of so fine a quality as to be worth, wholesale, $4 per pound. This grade comes from Virginia, considered the best tobacco-producing State in the Union. There are 100 samples. The light-colored is largely made into smoking tobacco, the dark into cigar-wrappers and fine-cut chewing, and the very black, being sweetened by molasses and other foreign substances, is made into plug.

The display of cereal grains comprises 800 samples, each kind of grain being ranged together so as to compare that of one with another. One hundred samples of Indian corn are exhibited, one ear from New York State being seventeen inches in length.

Of wool there are 300 specimens, the most of it being very fine and fleecy. The goods into which this wool is transformed by manufacture are also exhibited. Two hundred specimens of cotton from the South are shown, with the system of manufacture, and a number of miscellaneous fibres from the Far West, which have not yet been utilized. There are also on exhibition fine linen and other kinds of paper, and the materials from which they are made. There are 100 specimens, among which is a wasps' nest of genuine paper.

The 5,000 models in the Patent Office are picked specimens from 150,000 at Washington. Applications are perpetually being made there for patents of the wildest description. One genius is said to have wanted a patent for a machine to bore through the earth; another for a huge illuminator, which, hung over great cities, should dispense with the gas and the moon; and a third for an apparatus to make spirits—of the rapping kind—visible to mortals. The Martha Washington china, presented to her by Lafayette, Washington's camp-service, and a portion of his clothing, were placed in the Patent Office for safe-keeping, which will account for their figuring in the present exhibition in that department. Formerly the Patent Office was the only fire-proof building in Washington. One article which excites considerable interest is a model of a plan for lifting vessels over shoals, which was designed by Abraham Lincoln. One of the most interesting features in the Post Office Department is the Centennial Envelope Folding-press. This machine is the same as is used by the United States Stamped Envelope-works. It gums, prints, folds, and counts 2,500 envelopes per hour, being operated by a lady, and apparently without either manual or mental labor.

The collection of the woods of the United States in the southern wing of the building is most complete. Each tree is represented by a section of its trunk, about two feet in length, sawed longitudinally, the under surface being planed, showing the color and density of the wood. In the arrangement, one piece is placed with the bark outward, while the other is shown with the planed surface outward, with the leaves, flowers, and fruits of the tree placed in a frame above. This collection embraces specimens of all the principal varieties of trees, including some thirty species of oak, about the same of pine, thirteen of walnut and hickory, eleven of ash, nine of maple, seven of magnolias, etc. It is a noticeable fact that nearly all deciduous trees—such as birch, maple, and oak—are found in the Eastern part of the United States, while the *coniferæ*, or pines, are the prevailing varieties in the Western part. Of the thirty species of oaks, only about six are found West of the great plains. Sections of the "big trees" of California are shown, cut wedge-shaped, from four to five feet in diameter. Also specimens of the California nutmeg tree, of which only four species are known. This tree is an evergreen, and is valued chiefly for its ornamental use. It produces a nut about the size of a walnut, which resembles a nutmeg, from which fact the tree derives its name. The yucca-tree is very abundant in Arizona, and one species is thus described: "At the height of six or eight feet it divides into a few long branches, each of which terminates with tough, sharp bayonet-like leaves, about nine inches in length. The wood of this tree is made into paper." Another variety of the yucca bears a cluster of fig-like fruit, which is pleasant to the taste, and, when fresh, is much valued by Indians, being dried by them and preserved in the form of cakes. The leaves are used for cordage. The fibre is also woven by some tribes into saddle-blankets, and is even used in making clothing materials. The whole genus is endogenous—that is, they attain their growth by accretions made within the stem already formed, and not externally, as in all other trees except the palms; and there is no perceptible difference between the bark and the inside of the wood. With regard to the Indian collection, it may be remarked that a stranger to the habits and customs of this curious people can learn more about them in this section than he could in any other way, except by living with them. Here are concentrated the habits and traditions of tribes scattered thousands of miles apart. Every article is carefully labeled, and the studious observer will here find much to repay him.

The photographic collection representing the Powell Expedition is very full, displaying native villages, inhabitants, ruins, domestic avocations, etc. The social economy of the Alaskan Indians is quite fully displayed by the collection illustrating that nationality.

The United States Government Building and contents have been contributed by the Government of the United States at a cost of about $500,000, its object being, in the words of a writer on the subject, "to display such articles and material as will, when presented in a collective exhibition, illustrate the functions and administrative faculties of the Government in time of peace, and its resources as a war power, and thereby serve to demonstrate the nature of our institutions and their adaptations to the wants of the people." The same writer further describes it as a "scientific panorama of the Republic, beginning with the flint arrows and stone implements of Arizona, and running down to the mighty ordnance which bids defiance to every foe. There is scarcely a question that can be asked of the United States as a nation that cannot be answered here. Its fruits and flowers; its animals; its fish; its topography; its agricultural resources; its machines; its system of education, postal-service, and military strength — all are presented palpably to the eye and touch." That this is only a fair delineation of the fullness of this collection will be admitted on carefully considering it, while it will also be conceded that the United States Government display is one of the most interesting as well as the most important of any in the Centennial Exposition.

AGRICULTURAL HALL.

This building runs north and south. Entering the nave at the southern end, and turning to the left, we find ourselves in the German Department. Here, facing the nave, a stupendous structure is devoted to the exhibition of wines of Messrs. Sohnlein & Co. Surmounted by four mammoth bottles as samples of the display, an artistic and comprehensive arrangement presents to the gazer bottles in dozens and hundreds of Rhenigan, Mosel, Baden, and other districts. This whole presentment is grand, ornate and stupendous.

Moving toward the north we next have exhibits of Bavarian beer, representing different makers, of which there is a suitable display in shelved cases. Specimens of large barrels, labeled "cherry-juice" are next met, and a fine show of cordials and liqueurs from Breslau, Königsberg, Dantzig, Cologne, etc. One case offers a choice collection of preserved ginger, and other condiments from the East Indies, essences and extracts of different kinds in quaint-looking jugs and bottles; another displays tobacco and cigarettes of German manufacture. Now we see a mammoth trophy of scythes. This is four-sided, about 15 ft. high and 6 ft. square, and has probably 200 different blades displayed upon it. These scythes are mostly short, and very much broader than those in use in this country. This exhibit is duplicated by another of the same style, but larger, a little distance from it.

Halfway down the department we come upon the exhibits of Austro-Hungary. Here are, first, a collection of Hungarian wines, then a case of specimens of wool, very fine in texture, and specimens of Hungarian woods, highly polished, showing the natural grain, and offering a considerable variety. An exhibit of pickles, liqueurs, essences, and extracts, and we come to a table upon which are displayed hops in glass vases, representing the product of Styria, Moravia, Hungary, etc. Here is also a table covered with boxes of sardines or some other preserved fish. A small case, with glass top, contains wool and specimens of potash gained from wool by washing. Various grains, flour and meal, vinegar and extracts, are offered as exhibits from Buda-Pesth. The Transylvania Wine Company exhibit a good display of wines, and there are some specimens of hemp and flax, and some very fine specimens of

FRANCE.

Next succeeding the German department is that of France. This opens on the nave with a display of Bordeaux and other wines. Immediately behind this, arranged on the sides of a three-sided partition, are a series of colored illustrations of French vegetation, being pictures of vegetables of all species of the natural size. After this comes an exhibit of Cognac, in bottles and barrels, including that of the celebrated firm of Otard, Dupuy & Co. A considerable show of dried grain and grasses, with small bags of grain and beans, occurs here. Next, a series of large upright cases presents a very fine and elaborate display of preserves in bottles, cans, and jars, including fruit, mushrooms, and various kinds of common vegetables, truffles, *bœuf à la mode,* jellies, confections, mustard, sardines, and boxes of candied fruits, exquisitely prepared. This display includes not only the usual articles of this sort seen in our confectionery stores, but whole mushmelons and apples of the largest size. The preparation of vegetables, such as beans, peas, asparagus, and artichokes, are veritable triumphs; another French specialty is seen in the pickled meats, put up in glass, with a variety of

of loaf-sugar, refined, and near it a pretty show of fine confectionery, from the old house of "*Au Fidèle Berger,*" of Paris, founded in 1720. This brings us to the exhibit of the great house of E. Mercier & Co., of Epernay, specimens of whose wines (champagne) are exhibited, with the mechanism displaying the various processes employed in the manufacture, such as for uncorking the bottles at the stage of manufacture when the sediment that settles on the cork is blown out by the force of the gas generated by the wine, and for recorking, after filling with a preparation of sugar and brandy—the final operation in the process of champagne-making. At this point, reversing our steps to return to the nave, we observe various exhibits of cement, hydraulic lime, Portland cement, etc. Next are specimens of wine of Amboise, and sundry small models of different implements, and specimens of wood-paving; after these is a large collection of grindstones, of different sizes, and scales and steelyards of various models. A small space contains *pâtés* and cognac, and two or three others are filled with specimens of siphons for mineral-waters, many of them very beautiful. We now come upon a large and handsome display of machines employed in the manufacture of gas for soda and mineral-waters, with various con-

THE OLD MILL IN AGRICULTURAL HALL.

honeycomb from near Prague, in Bohemia, with a hive and breeding-boxes.

From Leopold Sandpickler, of Görz, near Trieste, we have a very brilliant display of preserved fruits—certainly one of the finest we have ever seen—including numerous varieties, many of them preserved whole. Here are mineral waters from Pullna, Bohemia, and other places, and curious exhibits of what is called "egg-powder preserve," designed to take the place of eggs, and sent by S. Berg, of Cracow.

A table next attracts our attention covered with Bosnia prunes, nuts like English walnuts, a liqueur distilled from prunes; and curiously enough, a large glass-jar of cantharides or Spanish flies, brilliant in their vivid green hue. A small case of cigarettes from Dresden and Warsaw, and a larger one, making a fine display of cigars, from Rauenberg, are the next exhibits, and next to these is a trophy of sugar, and then a very fine display of candies and confectionary, from Cologne, in a large upright case, the exhibit of the Brothers Stollwerck.

A view of the exhibit of curled hair from H. Stein & Co., Frankfort-on-the-Main, and the large case containing a specialty of Rhenish mustard, from Theodore Moshopf, of Fahr, near Neuwied, Germany, complete our brief glance at this department.

vegetables, including calf's head, crabs, etc. The wines of Bordeaux, Burgundy, and the Champagne country are largely exhibited. Of champagne there are present exhibits from about twenty exhibitors. A large map of the Champagne country, with a border of pictures of wine-sellers and wine-establishments, is seen further on. Quite a display is made of wines, brandies, liqueurs, etc., of the *Société Anonyme.* An interesting feature right here is an ornamental exhibit of macaroni and vermicelli, from Messrs. Marge Fils, of Lyons. Here, also, occurs the display of the products of Algiers, including alfa, olive-oil, iron-ore, vermicelli, and other pastes, dried fruits, etc. Next come more brandies and more wines. Vermouth, champagne, wines from the Gironde, *sirops, pâté de foie, canard,* truffles from Perigord; "chambery" from Savoy; liqueurs from Alsace, and "*Sirop d'oranges rouges de Malte.*" A case containing specimens of *curaçoa* and other cordials is seen here; and next to it cognac-brandies of E. Dubois & Co. Two large cases represent the manufactures of a number of French houses in preserves of all kinds, being a very handsome and creditable display, and peculiarly so in candied fruits. The *Compagnie Française d'Alimentation* exhibit a large number of their preparations in pressed and concentrated meats, fruits, vegetables, etc., for soups. Directly behind this is a fine exhibit

trivances for the better production of coffee as a beverage. This brings us to the outer line of the French exhibition, where we are again met by a display of wines, etc., from a number of manufacturers. Among the products should be mentioned sardines, sausages, Roquefort-cheese, mustard in great abundance, and beet-sugar. The well-known chocolate establishment of Menier makes a handsome and at the same time instructive display of the cocoa-bean and the pod in all its various preparations, accompanied by photographs of exterior and interior views of their works. Almost the only agricultural machinery shown is a number of riddle-sorters for cleaning grain. These are revolving tubes of metal, perforated with holes of different sizes, set at an inclination, and worked either by hand or power. The riddle can be changed so as to adapt the machines for fine seeds, for the larger grains, or for peas, beans, or coffee. Among the millstones, and apparently a new invention, is a bolting-stone, which is said to effect acceleration in grinding, avoid excessive heat, and great economy in motive-power. Slates are cut through the stone, and in them are inserted wire-bolting cloths of about two inches in width. The Portland cement is exhibited by two companies. Here is seen a heavy apparatus for testing the cohesive strength of the bricks made from the cement, which are found to endure a direct strain of from 1,500 to 1,700

INTERIOR VIEW OF THE POST-OFFICE AISLE.

pounds. There is also a large tank of cement, in which the bricks are immersed, to prove that water has no effect upon them, and a block which has been immersed sixteen years in the sea is still solid.

NETHERLANDS.

Intersecting the eastern side of the French department is the portion allotted to the Netherlands. This commences with a circular structure, in which is a collective exhibition of wines, liqueurs, etc., chiefly from Amsterdam. This includes Noyaux, Fleur d'Orange, Stoughton, Club-house, Curaçoa, Anisette, etc., and also Schiedam, Geneva, and other gins. Next to this exhibit is another, chiefly of gins, and beside that a very large exhibition by the Dutch Agricultural Society, of grains of the Hague, displayed in glass jars of different sizes, in all about 200. Here are also fine specimens of wheat and other grains in the stalk ; also peat or turf, and about twenty-five specimens of the different kinds of native woods. A collection of hyacinths, crocuses, and other bulbs, and some boxes containing specimens of native hemp are also to be seen here. This exhibit concludes with a dozen specimens of Dutch cheese under glass. Next is quite a show of preserved vegetables, meats, etc., in cans and bottles, and a number of large glass jars containing beet-root sugar. An exhibit of beeswax and dried peas comes next, and beside this a handsome case, displaying fabrications in chocolate confectionery, etc. A very fine show of cigars follows, a case of fine feathers from Rotterdam, linseed-oil and cakes from Dordrecht ; and next some illustrations of the manufacture of bent wood and cordage. A very pretty model of a schooner is seen here, of which the mainmast is observed to be very far astern, the sails and flag being silk. This is from Scheveningen. A quaint and clumsy square-built sloop is also shown in a

model. Next, there are specimens of manufactured cork, lubricating-oil for sewing-machines, etc., and preparations of chocolate confections from Amsterdam. More Dutch cheeses, fine specimens of blue Dutch flax and flaxseed, tobacco in the leaf, hops, specimens of native vegetables, wooden shoes, etc., complete this department.

BRAZIL.

Among the foreign nations represented in the Agricultural Building, Brazil is justly credited with making one of the finest and most interesting displays, embracing all the varied products of the country and its provinces, the exhibits of coffee, sugar and cotton being especially large and fine. It should be remembered that of the immense territory of Brazil, covering 3,200,000 square miles, barely one-fifth is cultivated, with only forty-six inhabitants for each league, there being, according to the last census, 17,454 agricultural establishments in thirteen provinces. The space occupied by Brazil in the Agricultural Building comprises about 4,250 square feet, and is inclosed by a low Moorish railing, and overhung with a forest of the national

colors, interspersed with festoons from the hides of the boa and other wild and domestic animals, contrasting agreeably with the whitewashed roof of the gigantic hall. The first object which attracts attention is a large temple about twenty feet in height, and as many square, formed of samples of raw cotton of the numerous provinces. The effect is quite pretty, and the design original. The cotton is arranged in a lattice of graceful arches, with here and there large tufts of raw manilla, hanging upon rods of iron, made in imitation of branches, giving the appearance of huge wheat-blossoms. In the centre of the space formed by the temple is a pyramidal stand, formed of several hundred glass vases, containing over one hundred specimens of coffee, in various stages of preparation. Forming a low wall around the base of the inclosure are numerous packages of cotton, some of them of superior quality and neatly exhibited. The exhibit of tobacco is very full, embracing over thirty varieties, exclusive of the manufactured cigars, snuff, etc. Here are rolls of twisted tobacco, tall columns of cigarettes in showy wrappers, hundred-weights of cigars, and near these is the great amphitheatre of long-necked bottles of aguardiente, whiskys, brandies and wines. Immediately in the rear of the display of cotton and coffee is an inclosure 60 ft. long by 40 wide, containing exhibits of woods and miscellaneous goods. From the top of the inclosure hang the skins of tigers, leopards, deer, otter, lions and serpents, giving the place an attractive appearance. The specimens of wood comprise three or four hundred, and afford a fit commentary on the value and importance of the Brazilian forests—an importance not only represented by its gigantic trees, but also by the value which each of them possesses in relation to the arts, to house and ship-building, to food and to medicine. Among the woods, of course, are

MAMMALIA DEPARTMENT.

UNITED STATES GOVERNMENT BUILDING.

WHALING APPARATUS.

WASHINGTON RELICS.

prominent mahogany, iron-wood, ebony, and rosewood. A number of immense pine nuts are also included in the collection, together with several specimens of woods curiously variegated. There are said to be over one thousand kinds of wood in Brazil. Those exhibited are arranged so as to show specimens with the bark on, the natural color of the wood, and also varnished. In extent and variety, they excel any other collection in the exhibition. A large upright case contains the exhibits of silk-cocoons, some of the colors being very gorgeous, though the display is not as full as that made by some other nations. The collection of sugars comprises about fifty varieties, contributed by exhibitors from various provinces. The export of this product last year aggregated over $15,000,000. India-rubber and other valuable products are represented by numerous exhibitors in various stages of manufacture, and of different qualities. Then there are exhibits of flax, sugar-cane, vegetable-fibres, used for filling mattresses, and numerous specimens of fibres made of the bark of the palm and other trees. Some of these fibres are soft and pleasant to the touch, and they are said to be a source of considerable revenue. The exhibits of wines, liquors and cordials, with rums and vinegars, are large, and near these are samples of preserved fruits, sweet-meats, chocolates, etc. Of beans, Brazil sends ninety varieties, of all colors and sizes, arranged in glass jars, and properly labeled. Beside these are many specimens of wheat, flour, tapioca, arrowroot, oatmeal, and rice-flower. The exports from Brazil last year amounted to $118,267,641. Of this amount in round sums there were: coffee, $64,000,000; sugar, $15,000,0000; cotton, $14,000,000; hides, $8,000,000; india-rubber, $5,000,000; mate, a kind of cheap tea extensively used throughout South America, $2,000,000; and diamonds, $1,000,000.

ITALY.

The Italian agricultural display is located in the southeastern corner of the structure, and is tastefully arranged. It includes exhibits—the greater number being wines and liquors—from about 300 exhibitors. The space is partly inclosed by glass cases, containing various articles on exhibition, while in the centre a number of stands of a pyramidal shape are filled with hundreds of bottles of wines and liquors of every kind. On the floor around the sides of the section are the plows, cultivators and other farming implements in use among the Italian farmers—none of these, how-

ever, equaling our own manufactures in this line. The display of olive-oil and that of macaroni are, as might be expected, very rich and full. They are shown in various styles and as manufactured by different firms. There are also full exhibits of dried and preserved meats, fish and fruits. In this department the preparation of bologna-sausages will attract attention as especially fine, some samples being six feet in length. Then come the oils of all kinds, arranged in a high glass case, near which is a wooden stand, handsomely ornamented in gilt, and with bunches of artificial flowers, and upon it are placed samples of the best of wines, liquors, etc. After these are drugs, chemicals, and pharmaceutical preparations and colognes. The latter are contained in fancy bottles, whose varied colors make a very attractive appearance. Hundreds of jars contain samples of wheat, rice, nuts, barks, etc., while in glass cases are exhibited specimens of different minerals, the largest being iron ores. The exhibits of sumac are quite noticeable, comprising a number of cases, and near these are specimens of dye-stuffs, guanos, glues, etc. There are also several large cakes of castile soap, each weighing hundreds of pounds, together with a number of boxes of fancy soaps. The display of hides, leather, boots and shoes, and belting, is large, as is also that of other ornamental goods. The specimens of hemp and hempen goods are particularly fine. There are also numerous exhibits of candied-fruits, confections, citrons, and other similar goods. At different points of the section are shown stalks of grain of different kinds, and numerous stalks of corn, with the dry ears still attached. The Italian Exhibition is a valuable and useful one, and doubtless gives a fair idea of the agricultural products of that country. The largest portion of the space occupied, however, is devoted to wines and liquors. Of the forest products, besides sumac,

already mentioned as in considerable quantity, there are manna, sweet-almonds, hazelnuts, pistachios, and numerous other nuts; in pomology, olives, lemons and oranges, from Salerno and Syracuse; agricultural products, besides those already mentioned; exhibits of rice from Modena and Novara. In fish, there are sardines, in oil, from Leghorn, and eels from Bologna. The animal and vegetable products are, of course, the largest. These comprise articles not already named: cheese, glue and honey from Bologna and Palermo; wax from Venice and Milan; preserved and dried meats from Genoa and Milan; paste for soup from Syracuse and Leghorn; tomato-sauce and preserved tomatoes from Bologna, Salerno and Parma; dried figs and candied fruits from Palermo; flour-paste from Naples, and wines from Naples, Leghorn, Palermo, Brescia, Syracuse, Sicily, Florence, Modena; vermouth from Alexandria, Turin, Marsala; extract of tamarind from Milan, and chocolate and confectionery from Rome and Turin. From Pisa we have biscuits, as well as cakes from Rome and Pistoja. The agricultural machinery includes plows, harrows, plowshares, hand-reaping machines, and butter-machines, coming from Ancona, Cremona, Venice, Pisa, Parma, and Bologna. A very interesting exhibit in agricultural engineering is the plan of General Garibaldi's system of irrigation relative to the river Tiber, which is exhibited by Quirico Filopanti, of Bologna.

SPAIN.

The Spanish section, surrounded with a wall of yellow wood, and entered under a lofty gothic portal, is a wonderful museum of wines, oils, spices, fruits, grains, woods, tobaccos, skins, and nuts—all from Spain and her colonies. On the floor lie huge logs of mahogany and rosewood, almost as heavy as so much iron. Festoons of tobacco-leaves and sheaves of grain surround the pillars. Upon shelf rising above shelf stand bottles and jars in orderly array, filled with every imaginable article. Among the wines are many excellent varieties unknown outside of the Peninsula. Cuba sends her cigars and tobacco, the Havana cigar-makers exhibiting in a row of light mahogany cases mounted upon standards. From the Philippine Islands come manilla and hemp; and all the provinces of the mother country send something of interest.

AQUARIA.

Among the many attractive displays in the Agricultural Building that of the

ARTILLERY AND ORDNANCE.

UNITED STATES GOVERNMENT BUILDING.

UNIFORMS OF THE AMERICAN ARMY AND NAVY, 1876.   EXTERIOR VIEW OF THE UNITED STATES GOVERNMENT BUILDING.   UNIFORMS OF THE AMERICAN ARMY AND NAVY, 1776

collection of aquaria on the west side of the building is not the least interesting. This collection has been arranged with regard not only for the interest of fish-breeders, but for the gratification of the public and the study of the naturalist. The collection is being constantly changed by deaths and accessions; but at the time of this writing is contained in thirty-five large tanks and aquaria, one tank alone being 23 ft. long by 7 wide and 4 deep. These are divided into three classes: Those for salt-water specimens, those for fresh, and the third for cold-water fish. To supply salt-water, a tank capable of holding some 10,000 gallons has been built outside the building, and water brought from the Atlantic by rail. Fresh water, of course, is plentiful, but to keep cold-water fishes properly the water, before reaching the aquarium, passes through a coil of pipe packed in a box of ice. Among the specimens in one aquarium are crabs, including the king-crab, or horse-foot. Another is filled with terrapins. In the largest tank were formerly a number of green turtles, the heaviest weighing over three hundred pounds. These, however, died. About a dozen specimens of toad-fish, some very fine fresh-water eels, drum-fish and rock-bass are among the larger fish. Specimens of graylings

from Michigan, and the Oswego bass, or Southern chub, will be interesting to the Eastern people. A curious-looking creature is pleasantly entitled "a hell-bender," and is ugly and repulsive-looking enough. This one is twelve or

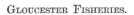

FISH DEPARTMENT.

fifteen inches long, and has legs or fins, four in number, having four fingers each. A peculiarity of the animal is that these limbs may be removed and in less than a year will grow again. There are also long-finned chubs, suckers,

black-gill sunfish, large black bass and moon-eye fish, or lake herring. In one aquarium are hundreds of specimens of little California salmon, eggs of which were sent from California by the United States Commission, and hatched at Marietta, Pennsylvania. It is designed to increase this collection from time to time with fish from other waters than our own, including the Gulf of Mexico and the Caribbean Sea.

GLOUCESTER FISHERIES.

The exhibit of the Gloucester fisheries is the most interesting one of its kind in the Exhibition, and contains by far the most complete representation of the industry, inasmuch as it gives a correct idea of the growth, from very insignificant proportions to their present gigantic position, of fisheries of the largest fishing-port in the world. Since 1830 there have been lost out of these fisheries 1,590 fishermen and 333 ships. In 1873, 31 Gloucester vessels sailed out to return no more, and 174 fishermen were lost.

In the vicinity of the aquarial department, in a corner of the Hall, the town of Gloucester has erected a tank 23 by 12 ft., filled with water in which accurate models of the fishing fleet of the old and new times are afloat, illustrating the different branches of the fisheries. In one corner is the old "cob"

MINERAL DEPARTMENT.   LIGHTHOUSE DEPARTMENT.

UNITED STATES GOVERNMENT BUILDING.

KINGSFORD'S OSWEGO STARCH EXHIBIT IN AGRICULTURAL HALL.

THE WILSON SEWING-MACHINE COMPANY'S EXHIBIT IN MACHINERY HALL.

wharf of Revolutionary years, with its primitive appliances, and the odd, quaint-looking "pinkies" lying beside it. Opposite it is a model of the massive and endurable pile-wharves, such as are built in Gloucester in 1876, ten times as large as the old ones. On this the fishermen are shown at work packing mackerel. All the appliances of fishing-wharves are exhibited, while arranged about in a little harbor are models of all the various improvements in the fishing craft, from 1800 down to the present time. One of these models is that of the old *Manchester*, a famous fisher in her day, built about the beginning of this century, and still in existence, and in the carrying trade somewhere "down East." The "bankers" that go to George's Bank, the "seiners" and the "market boats," are all shown, while the setting of the mackerel seine is displayed in a practicable model. In addition to the exhibit of this tank, there is also here a very fine collection of objects belonging to the fisheries, and of curiosities collected during voyages. There is also on exhibition a curious substance resembling branch coral, said to have been fished up in 150 fathoms of water by a "banker." Here, too, are to be found all the appliances belonging to the fishing vessel of the present day, furnishing a contrast to those employed by its rude prototype of a century ago. Gloucester maintains her position as first among the fishing ports. Every year more and more direct trade comes to her, and she still controls her market, even on the Pacific coast, sending great quantities of fish to Sacramento. This very year she has even begun to export fish to Sweden. A little volume can be had in which a full account of the fisheries, dating from 1623, is contained, at which time an English company sent out a vessel with the mission of founding a settlement on the rocky coast near Cape Ann. This exhibit is altogether complete and admirable, and does not appear to have been duplicated by any other State.

KANSAS AND COLORADO BUILDING.

This is among the largest and most attractive of the State buildings in the Centennial Grounds. Kansas refused to conform to the rigid classification directed by the United States Centennial Commission, and, failing to secure space for her exposition in one of the main buildings, erected a separate one. Here Colorado, being duly admitted a State, has been allotted one-fourth of the entire exhibition space afforded. The two States—formerly one territory, separated now by only an imaginary line—have still intimate commercial relations, Kansas producing breadstuffs and meats for consumption in the mining districts of Colorado, in exchange for the gold and silver in the latter. Colorado occupies the west wing of the building; the Atchison, Topeka and Santa Fé Railroad Company, sixteen feet of the east wing, while Kansas occupies all the rest. The building is in the form of a Greek cross, in the centre, and from the cupola of which is suspended a bell ingeniously constructed out of grains in the stalk, grasses and broomcorn brush, while the tongue consists of a bell-shaped gourd, suspended at the end of a longitudinal club-gourd, over 6 feet long by about 2 inches in diameter. This bell is 8 feet 9 inches across the bottom, and 8 feet 6 inches in height, and is in the same proportion and bears the same inscription as the old Liberty Bell in Independence Hall: "Proclaim liberty throughout all the

THE PAPER COLUMN OF BYRON WESTON, DALTON, MASS., IN THE MAIN BUILDING.

land, unto all the inhabitants thereof." (Lev. xxv., 10.) "By order of the Assembly of the Province of Pennsylvania, for the State House in Philadelphia." There are forty-two flag-staffs on the building, there being flags for forty-one, which have been generously contributed by the ladies of Leavenworth. These flags consist of the national colors of the United States and those of foreign governments exhibiting, the same to be added, at the close of the exhibition, to the Centennial collections, and returned to the State House at Topeka, for preservation in the Museum of the State Board of Agriculture, there to remain as a souvenir of the kindly co-operation of the ladies of Leavenworth. At the north end of the building, twenty-four feet from the floor, is a transparency, "The great seal of the State of Kansas," from which rays of golden grain radiate, alternated with a background of cotton and hemp, the latter a staple in Southern Kansas. Immediately under this there is an attractive collection of vegetable-casts resting on a projection. Suspended from this projection is a well-drawn map, in colors, of Kansas, 24 by 13 feet. From the floor to the map is a receding grain-stand with ten shelves, supporting over 1,000 samples in glass jars, which contain an exhaustive display of wheat, rye, corn, barley, oats, buckwheat, sorghum, extract of beans, and an oil manufactured from the same, and tobacco, the seeds of hemp, flax, broom-corn, millet, Hungarian grass, timothy and red clover, hazel, pecan, and peanuts, soils, fire-clay, yellow and red ochre, mineral-paints, plaster-of-paris, potters'-clay, hydraulic cement, salt, etc. The labels on these jars

give the names of the contents, and where and by whom grown or collected. By reference to the large map the locality is easily determined. The space of about 14 feet on either side of the map, and between it and the two sides, is devoted to corn of wonderful growth. The stalks are from 15 to 18 feet high, containing from one to three ears each, some of which are as much as 14 inches in length. Arranged along the walls on either side in glass cases, will be seen an attractive exhibit of wild and cultivated grasses and grains in the stalk. Here are wheat cut from fields said to yield from 40 to 60 bushels to an acre; corn, from 40 to 100; oats, from 50 to 75; timothy, 2¼ tons; clover and millet, 4; blue-grass, from 2 to over 3 feet in height; 14 varieties of wild-grass, varying in height between 6 inches and 10 feet. In one case there is a display of silk ribbons and silk cocoons, the latter raised from eggs imported from Japan, and exhibiting the noticeable increase in size of the succeeding generas raised in the Kansas. Silk culture in this young State has already reached a prominent position. The remainder of the display in this building comprises a collection of valuable building-stones, sent from nearly every county in the State, between forty and fifty different kinds of wood, a collection of stuffed birds, including about 300 species, a fine entomological collection, extensive exhibition of fossils, gold-ore, coal, etc. Attached to the building is a reading-room provided with Kansas and Colorado papers, and a bureau of information for the convenience of the people of those States.

ARGENTINE CONFEDERATION.

The space allotted to the Argentine Confederation is located about one-third of the way from the eastern end of the building, on the southern side, and between Chili and Portugal. It comprises 58 exhibits in arboriculture and forest products; 59 agricultural products; 63 in land-animals; 63 in water-animals, fish-culture, and apparatus; 63 in animal and vegetable products; 68 in textile substances of vegetable or animal origin, and 69 agricultural, engineering and administration. The collection of woods, natural and polished, and of ornamental articles manufactured of, and representing, native woods, is very large and varied. Many of the different species are formed into canes, frames, racks and other pretty articles, although a very large number of the exhibits are simply of sections of the wood represented. The provinces from which exhibits are gathered are San Juan, Santa Fé, Cordova, Salta, Jujui, Catamarca, La Rioja, Tucuman, Mendoza, San Luis, Corrientes, Buenos Ayres, Santiago del Estero, Entre Rios. The woods include the carob-tree, chica-wood, lignum-vitæ, laurel-bark, and tanning materials; quina-quina, Lata incense-wood, yareta, viscote-wood, cactus, cebil-bark for tanning, chanar-chanar bark for cleaning cloths, curupay guazu, caaroba-wood, curromamuel-wood, black acacia, cochineal and dyeing materials; turpentine, carob and mandubay-wood, cocoanut bark, sacanza, jumo for making soap, indigo-plant, mbui-wood for dying silk and wool, sarsaparilla, myrrh, the seed of yareta (a resinous plant), cherimolia-seed, mistol, malingasta-nuts and tusca-seeds. The agricultural products represent, including, first: the principal grains, wheat, barley, rice, and corn; lima-beans, lentils, maize, grasses, straw, the maté-herb, lucern-seeds, canary-seed,

CAZADE, CROOKS & REYNAUD'S EXHIBIT OF OTARD, DUPUY & CO'S BRANDIES.

peas, melons, sugar-cane, tobacco, onion-seed, potatoes, wheat in stalks, Spanish peas, Indian paper manufactured from tobacco, cigars, etc. ; sweet-potatoes, esparto-grass, mandioca (for making starch), chipa-bread, tapoyua (used as a food), mustard, beet-root, carrots, lettuce, cabbage, red and sweet oca-oxalis, coffee, cumin and anice ; maté-herb packed in tapir-skin, pigeons stuffed with maté, herbs packed in wolf-skins, cloves, chocolate, araza (a spice), extract of beans, flax and spurge, seed of the Jerusalem artichoke, seed of the palmachristi. The collection of prepared land-animals, insects and reptiles, includes forty-one, comprising several exhibits—of birds : the hawk, woodpecker, wild sandpiper, the humming-bird, the gull, etc. ; a number of prepared skins of the tern-tern, ostrich, partridge, chimango craw-birds, etc. ; nests of the hornero and the boyero, a wild bird of Gualeguachu. There are also a stuffed wild-cat of Balcarce ; a stuffed mouse, fox, lynx ; a number of vipers, rattlesnakes, coral-viper, and skins of vipers ; a dissected guana (South American lizard), and a number of insects ; spiders with their silken cocoons, etc.

There are also exhibits of shells from Santa Fé, Corrientes, San Juan fishing lines, the baskets, etc. The

mestic cat-skin, said to be a cure for rheumatism; tanned and colored kid skins for gloves, lizard leather for gaiters, wild-boar skins, goat, ricuyna and ai-ai skins, tiger, alpaca, gray fox, swan, fox, ferret, ampalagua, sea wolf, coatia, horse, rabbit, carpincho, llama, lina, merino and river wolf skins. In fruits, nuts, and sweetmeats, there are oranges, peaches, plums, melons, watermelons, and quinces; sweetmeats, dried peaches, preserved lemons, peeled raisins, citron, cocoanuts, grapes and quinces, almonds, dried apples and figs, musk grape, raisins, preserved olives, coyote sweetmeat, candied quinces, and yatay palm cocoanuts. There are a number of preserved meats, such as pickled partridges, pickled tongues, salt meats, salt tongues and beef, dried mutton and beef, and gelatine. Several exhibits are made of flour, bran, mandioca starch, corn-meal, grits, macaroni, vermicelli and vermicelli cheese. There is one exhibit of Peruvian bark from the province of La Rioja. Buenos Ayres sends biscuits and crackers, and the province of Santa Fé, peanut oil.

The textile exhibits include cotton and cotton-pods, chaguar thread, and bark ; yuchan fibre ; bristle-rope and fabrics for sieves ; ropes made of caraguata-bark ; feather-grass, chord thread, hemp, spun flax and flax-straw, alpaca,

Many of the woods exhibited are parasites. From quite a number various dyes are extracted. The comandá-guazai is used in making carriages, and is very highly valued. The price of these woods is about fifty cents per square yard. Then there is canelon, whose ash is used in soap-factories ; the chanar, which produces a fruit similar in form to an olive, and is also used in making spirits ; the espinello, from which is made the guayaibi, a very handsome wood, the centre of which is of a fine purple color, and is much used for furniture ; the ceibo, whose bark is used for tanning hides. The exhibit of tapacho-wood is in the form of a book, containing samples of silk and woolen textures, dyed with an extract from the wood. There is also a tablet in which are inserted several kinds of wood, having in the centre a photographic view of the exhibitor's steam saw-mills. Twelve palms are exhibited in the form of a book, and are very durable. They cost from $16 to $20 per hundred. There are several woods, such as quillay and tomatillo, which are used instead of soap for cleaning cloths. A specimen of cebil-bark, used for tanning, measures two-and-a-half yards, being half the circumference of the tree. A very interesting exhibit is the yareta-

CAZADE, CROOKS & REYNAUD'S EXHIBIT OF FOREIGN CHAMPAGNES, CORDIALS, WINES, ETC.

animal and vegetable products furnish the largest list of articles exhibited. The Parana Commission, province of Entre-Rios, exhibit sponges, shad oil, leather skins, ostrich feathers, sausage, domestic beer, lemonade and wine. The Provincial Commission, province of Salta, exhibit cheese, honey and wax, dried peaches and nuts, wheat flour, mandioca and wheat starch, sugar-cane syrups, aguardiente brandy, and a number of skins of the lion, chinchilla, viper, etc. Quite a number of private exhibitors send specimens of cheese and skins of animals, the latter including lion, hare, fox, buck, and otter, with heron skins, condor and ostrich feathers, sheep skins, wild boar, deer, weasel, wolf, and other skins and hides. Of wines, there are cherry liqueur and chacoli, quavirami liqueurs, sugar-cane and orange juices, white wine, Indian fig syrup, Querocilla mead, sugar-cane brandy, cognac, orange wine, anisette and nonogasta syrup, carob mead, cognac bitters, grape, lemon, currant, banana and peach syrups, hesperedina bitters, banana balm, bitter-sweet tonic, Chevilcoy beer, Chartreuse and Kerman liquor, Trinidad wine ; quince, gin and ratifia liquors; vanilla liquor, cocoa extract, lime liquor, sugar-cane brandy and vermouth. Besides the skins already mentioned, there are those of the sea-lion, ox, colt, lamb, aguara, vermingo skin from Lalaguna de Los Padres, do-

wool, fleece of Angora goat, fleece of Negretti lamb, merino wool, and silks spun and in cocoons ; horse-hair, cow-hair and hair-ropes. The province of Buenos Ayres furnishes one implement, the model of a pump, and from the same province are several exhibits of artificial manure, charcoal and tallow. Among the curiosities of the Argentine Republic exhibits are several walking-sticks, some of which are made of different kinds of wood ; racks, one being composed of twenty-five different species of wood ; cigar-cases of oak and chica-wood. The number of the different kinds of wood exhibited is very large, and the names of most of them are not translated, and are unknown to us. Of those with which we are acquainted, there are the poplar, mulberry, orange, pear, apple, pine, walnut, weeping-willow, apricot, cherry, rosewood, cinnamon, acacia, oak, palm and laurel. Some of the native woods are very curious and interesting, both in their appearance and uses. The mandupa produces a fruit similar in form to that of a pear ; the tata-yuba is highly valued for furniture ; the incienso and the perteribi are used for building purposes ; the quebracho is also employed in building and has the peculiarity of petrifying on being buried or placed under water ; the palode de leche produced a substance like gutta-percha or india-rubber.

fungus, found in great quantities in several places among the mountains of Rioja, and grows to an enormous size. It is very combustible, on account of the quantity of resin it contains, and is also classified as a medical plant. A curious exhibit is that of guano of the mountain bird called guancho. This is composed of a kind of gum or resin, and is used by the natives in cases of broken or fractured bones, being mixed with grease when splints are required. The yerba-maté comes chiefly from the province of Corrientes, and sells at about $2.50 per araba of twenty-five tons. Specimens of this herb are shown as prepared for camp-travelers. The tobacco exhibit comes from six or seven different provinces.

THE FIRST INTERNATIONAL EXHIBITION.

A RETROSPECT.

THE Centennial Exposition having completed the first half of its period of existence, it may not be useless or uninteresting to present such information as will enable our readers to draw a modified comparison between its results thus far and those of the English exhibition of 1851. That Exhibition, as has been heretofore stated,

THE INSTRUCTION OF CHILDREN IN THE KINDERGARTEN COTTAGE, UNDER THE AUSPICES OF THE WOMAN'S DEPARTMENT.

opened on the 1st of May and closed on the 15th of October, the time occupied being two weeks less than that allotted to our own. The official catalogue of the London Exhibition was not ready, in a perfect edition, until the 30th of April, notwithstanding 10,000 catalogues, properly made up and stitched, were delivered at the Building on the morning of the 1st of May, together with two copies, elegantly bound in morocco, with gilt edges, and lined with silk, for presentation to Her Majesty the Queen and

nary Exhibition and social gathering, while famine and pestilence were confidently expected as the inevitable consequence of the assembling of such vast multitudes in one city. Quite the reverse of all this lugubrious condition was, however, the case. London exhibited a wonderful degree of order and good-humored accommodation for the crowds, and power to provide for their wants. While the general health of the metropolis is said to have been good beyond the usual average, it was found that it was

police were entirely unaided by soldiery, and simply managed, through the necessary increase and discipline of their own numbers, to keep the peace of the city. Enormous excursion trains daily poured in their thousands and tens of thousands without disturbing the unanimity of the residents. It was said that, throughout the season, there was more unrestrained and genuine fellowship and less formality and customary ceremonial than had ever been known in English society. It was like an assembling for a gigantic

SCENE IN A TUNISIAN CAFE—THE SCARF DANCE.

Prince Albert. This official catalogue consisted of 320 pages, and was sold for one shilling. Translations in French and German were also sold at two shillings and sixpence each. At the opening there were about 25,000 persons present in the Building. Throughout the whole period of the great Exhibition the state of the metropolis occasioned wonder and admiration on the part of all who visited it. Previous to the opening there had been predictions made that confusion, disorder and demoralization, even actual revolution, would result from this extraordi-

not even necessary for any special steps to be taken on the part of the authorities for the housing of guests. Such were the hospitalities exercised, the contrivances made, and the extensive arrangements due to private enterprise, that these, taken in conjunction with the shortness of the visits and the rapidity of the succession of guests, enabled the city to comprehend within her limits a very large assemblage of visitors, in addition to her own formidable population, then numbering 2,500,000.

In conducting order in the public thoroughfares the

picnic, where all felt at liberty to roam at will, and all were disposed to yield something to the novelty of the occasion. Country parties actually picnicked in the open air, crowds having brought provisions in large baskets. Numbers of the working people received holidays, and through the generosity, and at the expense, of their employers, visited the Exhibition. Eight hundred agricultural laborers, in their peasant's attire and decorated with rosettes of colored ribbons, assembled from districts in Surrey and Sussex, and went to London by special train, conducted by their

CONCERT IN THE MAIN BUILDING—VIEW

E CENTRAL TRANSEPT. LOOKING SOUTH.

clergymen. As has been the case with the Centennial Exposition, numerous large firms in the north of England sent the people of their establishments to view the Exhibition in Hyde Park. An eminent agricultural implement maker in Suffolk sent all his people in two hired vessels, provided with sleeping-berths, cooking apparatus and every comfort. These vessels, drawn up to the wharf at Westminster, furnished homes to the excursionists during their stay in London, and strict rules were enforced as to returning

school children visited the exhibition, of whom 2,700 were in the building in one day.

This system and general sanction of the undertaking by employers, with the gradual increase in the number of general visitors, affected, of course, in a remarkable degree the railways throughout Great Britain. Trains containing 1,000 persons were common. Trains of 2,000 and 3,000 were not infrequent, and one immense train from Bristol brought etc. 5,000 persons. The total receipts of the

signed in one vertical column to the Pacific Ocean, the depth of which is estimated at about six thousand feet, the last edition would still have formed a lonely peak, rising to the height of Chimborazo or Cotopaxi, or eighteen hundred feet above the level of the sea. Another very abstruse calculation was to the effect that if the whole number of catalogues sold had been raised into a vertical pile, it would have exceeded the height of St. Paul's Cathedral fifty times. It was further discovered

THE KRUPP GUN IN MACHINERY HALL.

to the vessels at night. Several admirable plans were arranged by gentlemen of fortune for affording their dependents an opportunity of sharing the festivals of the year. One, in particular, organized by the Duke of Northumberland, and conducted at his expense, provided, by printed directions, for the employment of each day and hour, so that the 150 persons who availed themselves of this guidance were able to see in one week most of the principal objects of attraction in the metropolis. Nearly 44,000

railways having their termini in London, are said to have been £800,000 more during the Exhibition than the corresponding receipts of the previous year. To meet the wants of this array of visitors, a great number of guides, hand-books, etc., of the great Exhibition were brought out, as has been the case in Philadelphia, and those of London met with remarkable success, as have our own. Several curious calculations were made on the sale of the official catalogue. One was, that if all the editions had been con-

that the number of catalogues sold was equal to about one-fifth of the estimated number of printed volumes issued from the printing press within the first three centuries after the discovery of the use of printing. The actual number of catalogues really sold was upward of 300,000, and the paper required for their manufacture weighed 118 tons, and the type 70,000 pounds. Another curious suggestible fact connected with the Exhibition is that the total number of letters on the subject received by the Executive

Committee amounted to 37,000. During the twenty-four weeks of the Exhibition more than 6,000,000 of persons visited the building, the numbers rising immensely toward the close after some previous fluctuation. The opening month did not bring the amount of provincial and foreign visitors expected, and at the end of May the price of admission was lowered, when the attendance was greatly increased. The daily average during May was upwards of 19,000, but by the end of July this average had increased to upwards 50,000, and the entire mean of the daily average was 43,311, the highest number of admissions being in the

FIELD HEADQUARTERS OF THE CHAMPION MOWING AND REAPING MACHINES.

CONTEST OF THE CHAMPION MOWING MACHINE FOR THE SUPREMACY OVER ALL OTHER MOWERS, AT EDDINGTON, PA., JUNE 27TH.

last week of the Exhibition, when about 518,277 persons visited it. The daily average for that week was 86,379. It is estimated that, allowing for a fair average of visits to each person, there were actually upwards of 3,000,000 of different visitors to the Great Exhibition of 1851 during its existence. As some guide for judgment concerning the Centennial Exposition it may be remarked that, from the opening in London on the first of May, 1851, until the middle of June, the number steadily rose; then some abatement, but as the closing period approached, the concourse became as no occasion had previously witnessed, the four last shilling days, October 6, 7, 8 and 10, presenting an average of 100,000

THE CHAMPION REAPING MACHINE IN OPERATION IN THE WHEAT-FIELD AT SCHENCK'S FARM, JULY 6TH.

COMPETITIVE TRIALS OF THE CHAMPION MOWING AND REAPING MACHINES.

per diem. Some interesting figures are given of the provisions consumed at the several refreshment stalls within the Exhibition, as follows: Bread, 52,000 loaves; small loaves, rolls and biscuits, 120,000; plain buns, 870,000; Bath buns, 930,000; cakes, 220,000; cakes sold by the pound, 50,000 pounds; meat and rolls, 80,000; ham, 70,000 pounds; beef, tongue, etc., 260,000 pounds; rough ice, 800,000 pounds; salt, 8,000 pounds; milk and cream, 65,000 quarts; tea, coffee and chocolate, 21,000 pounds; lemonade, soda-water and ginger-beer, 1,900,000 bottles. The Exhibition had its own post-office, electric tele-graph and branch bank, its little army of police, its *cafés* and *table d'hôtes*. There were upwards of 900 persons in official employ, and, exclusive of these, 264 attendants at the re-freshment stalls, and about 1,000 exhib-itors' attendants. The highest temperature was on the 26th of June, when at 4 P.M. the thermometer reached 97 degrees. The glass ends of the building at the en-trance were removed on the 2d of July, when the thermo-meter came down from 74.4 to 66.6. After that 73.4 was about the maximum. The number of ex-hibitors in the Lon-don Exhibition of 1851 was about seven-teen thousand. There were thirty-four juries, each consisting of an equal number of British subjects and foreigners, empowered to call in the aid of associates, who acted as advisers only, without a vote. Each jury had its own chairman, deputy chairman, and reporter. The chairmen of several juries formed the council, whose duties were to determine the conditions upon which the different prizes should be awarded. Two medals were awarded: one, a prize medal, being given wherever a certain standard of excellence in production and workmanship had been attained; the other being conferred for some improvement in the value of an invention or application. The former medal was awarded by the juries; the latter by the council of chairmen upon recommendation of the jury. The number of prize medals awarded was 2,918; the number of council medals, 170; the total number, including a very extensive list of honorable mentions, was 5,084. Of that gross number, 3,000 distinctions were granted to foreign exhibitors, and 2,039 to exhibitors from Great Britain.

This delineation of the statistics, and otherwise, results of the first great International Exhibition a quarter of a century since, will furnish food for interesting and instructive reflection as to the application of past experience to the situation in Philadelphia. It is not unlikely that the great increase in the business of the London Exhibition, noticed as having occurred during the last three months of its existence, will be paralleled in the history of our own Centennial.

MONUMENT TO JOHN WITHERSPOON.

CONCERNING the statue to the memory of John Witherspoon, D.D., LL.D., the corner stone of which was laid November 16th, 1875, the following will be pertinent: Dr. Witherspoon was born in Scotland, February 5th, 1722, and died in Princeton, N. J., September 15th, 1794. He is chiefly known as President of Princeton College in 1768, and as one of the signers of the Declaration of Independence. It is also said that he was a lineal descendant, on the mother's side, of John Knox.

He was educated at the University of Edinburgh, and in 1745 was ordained minister. He was present as a spectator at the Battle of Falkirk, January 17th, 1746, and was taken prisoner, but was released after a short confinement. In 1776 Dr. Witherspoon was a member of the Provincial Congress of New Jersey, and of the Continental Congress at Philadelphia. For some time previous to

W. F. MURPHY'S SONS' BLANK BOOK EXHIBIT IN THE MAIN BUILDING.

his death he was totally blind. An incident is related of him which shows the influence of the man. When the Declaration of Independence was on its passage in the Continental Congress, and the result was doubtful, the scale is said to have been turned in a great measure by a speech of Dr. Witherspoon. In the course of that speech he said: "There is a tide in the affairs of men—a nick of time. We perceive it now before us—to hesitate is to consent to slavery. That noble instrument on your table, which insures immortality to its author, should be subscribed this very morning by every pen in this house. For my own part, of property I have some, of reputation more; that reputation is staked upon the issues of this contest, that property is pledged, and although these gray hairs must

soon descend into the sepulchre, I had infinitely rather they should descend at the hands of the executioner than desert at this crisis the sacred cause of my country." The statue of Dr. Witherspoon is of bronze, 12 feet high, on a pedestal also 12 feet high, constructed of Quincy granite. The site upon which it is placed is an elevated lawn, just east of the Art Gallery, including 475 feet north and south, and 325 feet east and west, around which Lansdowne Drive sweeps in almost three-fourths of a circle. The cost of this monument will be about $25,000.

THE FLORAL EXHIBITION.

THE Horticultural Grounds at Fairmount comprise forty acres, covering the whole of a sugar-loaf-shaped hill, situated near the centre of the Exposition inclosure. The entire space, exclusive of walks, borders and building sites, has been allotted to various parts of the world which make extensive exhibits in ornamental gardening, and of the trees, shrubs, and plants of commerce. Many of the trees indigenous to the United States are represented, as also plants recently introduced into this country from Japan, China, and other Oriental countries. In the place set apart for the display of ornamental gardening there are several thousands of flowering, and perhaps as many foliage plants, arranged in the different ornamental styles of gardening—carpet, bed, ribbon, geometrical, etc.

The building, exclusive of the main hall and the four green-houses, is divided into compartments for the individual exhibits of florists and gardeners. On the north and south sides are the two greenhouses, each 30 x 100 ft. in size, heated by hot water, and specially intended for the exhibition of choice plants of commerce, tropical and other exotic productions. The Main Hall is 80 x 230 ft. in size, and is ornamented by a handsome marble fountain in the centre, surrounded by statuary and specimens of ceramic art. This large building is also heated by hot water conveyed through pipes, about four miles of four-inch iron pipe being used.

A large number of the most attractive decorations of the Conservatory have been received as donations from the Congressional Joint Library Committee, the Agricultural Department of the Government, and from prominent private citizens.

EXHIBIT OF GREENFIELD & STRAUSS, CONFECTIONERS, IN MACHINERY HALL.

Song of the Centennial

BY JOAQUIN MILLER

The Minstrel Sings:

1.

Peace on earth and harvest time!
Hail the day, but heal the scars!
Heavens blue, yon bannered stars
Blending in the far sublime,
Sing Peace on earth and harvest time!

2.

Peal the cannon! clang the bell!
Wave the banners! Bow and pray.
Turn in gratitude to-day
To mighty men who fought and fell—
To Him who doeth all things well.

3.

Peace on earth and harvest time!
The farmer sings; the battle-field
Bears on her breast a gleaming shield
Of corn that clangs in rippled rhyme—
Lo! peace on earth and harvest time!

"*The turbulent soul
Of the Arab Sheikh, that defies control.*"

Orator, pointing to the Flag:

I.

Yon stars stand sentry at the door of dawn ;
Yon bars break empires.   Kings in vain
Shall rave and thunder at freedom's fane,
Till the stars leave heaven and the bars be gone.
Then wave, O flag, like the waves of the sea ;
Curve as the waves curve, wild and free,
And cover the world.   Exult in the sun,
But thunder and threaten where the black storms run ;
And the years shall be yours while the eons roll ;
Ay, yours till the heavens be rolled as a scroll.

II.

O glitter bright harvest of stars and gleam !
O rise in the heavens and run before
And bring us the Wise of the East as of yore,
When the good shepherds studied the stars in a dream.
O triumph, my beauty ! exult in the air,
High-throned over all, while the brave and fair
Sit down by the rivers of peace to rest.
And scream, O eagle ! exult and scream—
O scream as you never have screamed before,
And flutter your pinions from shore to shore.

Minstrel to the People:

III.

Hark ! ho ! To the movement of men as when
The good shall gather on the judgment day !
The world is astir ! The wide highway
Has blossomed with beauty and with manly men
Hark ! ho ! Since an hundred years ago,
'Tis the year of all years to be young once more ;
To come to the front proud soul'd as of yore,
In the face of men, in the sun's full glow,
Hark ! ho ! To the boom of gun and of bell,
And the brave land answers us—All is well.

" *Come ! sit by their rivers where they rest, and you
Shall hear them sing from the sudden canoe.*"

IV.

'Tis the year of all years to be young, O man !
O man of South-land, or Alaska clan.
When Liberty keepeth her natal day,
'Tis a time to feast, and to kneel and to pray.
'Tis the hundredth year of the Samson's youth !
Now what do you bear in your brave, hard hands,
O men of freedom, of God, and of truth,
From the four far corners of the uttermost lands ;
From the ultimate West and the uttermost East,
To grace in the tents at the world's great feast ?

V.

The People:

Why, we bring plenty, and we bring peace.
Borne high in the hand, blown far in the air,
And fair as that banner of stars set there,
Are the signs we bear to the world.   And these
Are the fruits we bring to the land's great feast.
From the rock-built bank of the sea of the East,
From the great gold shore of the vast West sea,
Why, we bring love to the world, and we
Have spread in the tents by the rivers here
The full ripe fruits of an hundred year :

VI.

Ripe fruits of the bough, rich fruits of the brain,
The South red rose and the roses of snow ;
The fruits from the mountain, the fruits from the plain,
Red grapes of the North and Los Angelo.
Then ores that the gnomes of the earth conceal ;
Then iron things, and sharp things of steel ;
Then the red-mouthed orators, men of war,
That mounted the bastions and battle car,
And turned to the glittering face of the foe,
And spake, just an hundred years ago.

VII.

Minstrel :

O good, fair women, are the gifts ye bear,
O sweet, brave men, is the feast in store,
And all is well and the world is fair
And a braver old world than ever before ;
But the great, grand things of the vast West land,
The glories that thrill and that stir the blood,
The men of the land, the land, the flood,
They come not borne in any man's hand,
Or image of them ; and of these I sing,
And these be the gifts of the feast I bring.

VIII.

A woodman's mattock, his rifle, and then
A lone, low cabin, half hidden from view ;
Then a toil-grimed face from the bowed-down few,
As they grappled the forest ! God, it was hard,
That strife on the border ; but this the reward !
Lo ! these, O people, were the heroes when
The battle's edge redden'd the whole east land,
And men held musket and plow in hand,
And watched the furrow and watched the foe,
The heroes ! an hundred years ago.

IX.

I bring from the land of flocks and of herds,
From broad, fertile fields of measureless land,
From lands of untamable beasts and of birds,
From lands of the Gulf and of Rio Grande,
The tall Texan Ranger, the mate of wild men.
With blade in his hand he is blazing the way
For the world to come after.   He does not say,
Nor yet quite comprehend.   But finally, when
The New World is finished, 'twill be written that he
Was no dull worker in its destiny.

X.

The Lone Star that rose from the Mexican seas,
And rode in the morn of the tropical West
Over gray San Jacinto, still shines in the trees,
Where foliage is freshest, and fruits are the best.
Here roves the Ranger.   He is strong, he is free.
As the storms of the Gulf.   Lo ! the majesty
Of manhood is his.   The turbulent soul
Of the Arab Sheikh, that defies control,
How it tides and swells in this half-tamed man
As he turns like a king or a Tartar Khan ·

The Ranger :

" I'm one uv them fellers as fought with ole Hood.
I reckon, by golly, yer might recoleck
Them lean, ragged Rangers. . . . Not 'ligiously good.
They'd cuss, and the like.   So ?   Then I speck
They've writ up a book 'bout that tussle with Hood.

" What ! you fit us ? you ! Lord ! Thar stood you'ns,
A long blue line uv blazin' red hell.
Then Hood gave a whoop, and down on the blue'ns ;
Then back rolled the gray'uns, then, God, sich a yell !
And, cats and black dogs ! it was hot then for you'ns. . . .

' We won it that day. Lord ! Every blue cuss. . . .
Shucks ! Let a man brag. That's all that we've go .
Yer needn't to straddle and make sich a muss. . . .
The bare right to brag uv the fight that we fought,
That's all that we got . . . . Thar ain't much left to us.

" . . . Centennial, eh ? Say ! Tell 'em that fight . . .
W'y, uv course the rebs won.   But then, don't you see,
No matter who won, or, or which 'uns was right,
'Twas a reg'lar ole American victory ;
And a reg'lar ole he-American fight.

" Me reconstructed ?   Gen'ral Jackson ! save us
From men you can lick like dogs till they love you. . .
But thar's the ole flag that our gran'fathers gave us,
And, never may other flag flutter above you . . .
Liquor ! Well, here's to ole Abraham . . . Davis !"

XI.

I bring you a lofty and a lordly fir,
Unshorn of a limb, and mantled in moss
And the clouds that tangle his tops across,
From the north Columbia where the cyclones stir.
From the dark, from the edge of the world, I bring,
High borne in heaven on her seas of air
A wide-winged, dolorous swan to sing.
By the cloudy capes, you may hear her, where
She dwells in the clouds, as if riding on
The windy waters of the Oregon.

"*My bride my trusty rifle is,
My babe my bowie-knife.*"

XII.

My dark-brow'd cedars of Ochoco
I bring you.   Weird levels of shadowy land,
Lo ! endless lie upon either hand ;
The moccasined red men come and go ;
They gallop the watered and wood-locked land
Below white columns and cones of snow,
That round and top to the arch of the skies. . . .
The red man is looking his last.   He dies !
The Saxon is sheathing his knife.   The plain
Is fertile from blood, and will bloom again.

XIII.

I bring you, from nearest to heaven ; I bring
From the bastion of Titans their cloud-set tents.
O whiter indeed than the swan's white wing.
Mighty indeed as God's battlements.
The snowy cones of mine Oregon ;
They break from the high-held crest of woods,
They start from the terrible solitudes
Where the dead nights lie.   They do come upon
The edge of heaven in their awful grace,
And do make God's portal their abiding-place.

XIV.

I bring you my people from the deeps of fir,
By the wide still waters and the windy vales ;
A pastoral people of dreams and of tales,
Of stories of wonder that thrill and stir
The blood as they sit by the bright cabin fire.
See ! They part the deep woods, peep forth, retire,
Abashed, but with laughter, to the lovely breast
Of sweet Mother Nature, as her babes, to rest.
Come ! sit by their rivers where they rest, and you
Shall hear them sing from the sudden canoe ;

"A ghostly king
Stretched forth a red hand to the peaks of snow."

Oregonian sings:

"Mi-ka ti-ka cluch-a-man,
Ni-ka ti-ka cu-i-tan,
Live! for life is but a span,
Love! for love is life, O man,
Sailing on the Oregon.

"Hi! They say they have a show. . . .
Shall we rest or shall we go?
They have not one peak of snow
Like yon seven in a row
Rounding in my Oregon.

"Go, exhibit if you will;
Here, with herds on ev'ry hill,
We will rest and feast our fill.
Cha-co mit-lite, ni-ka til,
Wood and wave of Oregon.

"Wave your banners, keep your feast,
Elder brothers of the East;
Here is Lethe, here is peace,
Lands and herds and fat increase,
Sku-kum tum-tum, Oregon.

"Show your prowess, keep your feast,
Elder brothers of the East;
Rest we here! Yet, sound the drum
When the days of trouble come,
And you shall hear from Oregon."

XV.

I bring you from regions bound round by room,
The Lord of the Plains—the buffalo bull.
His horns fall a-rest. He stretches his length.
His high shoulders heave and his dark brows gloom
His sinews are knotted. His brisket sweeps full.
His vast mane tumbles with gathering strength.
His black eyes blaze. His swift tail snaps
As it whips in the air. His black hoof taps
Right light on the sand. He quivers, and he
Is shaking the earth with his majesty.

XVI.

I bring you the rover of the vast, lone plain.
The skin-clad hero scarce keeps his seat
As his steed beats the air with his black bare feet.
He drowns his hand in his flood of mane;
The wild steed neighs to his mates in the wind;
He vaults, he plunges—the world is behind!
The world it is his—space, room, are his own!
His bright steel his sceptre—his black steed his throne:
The spurned dust rises, the sharp hoofs ring.
He rides. As he rides you may hear him sing:

The Hunter sings:

1.

"I ride, I reign the leveled plain;
I chase the buffalo.
Good-by—I give my steed the rein,
I ride as winds may blow.

2.

"My mates are bold and bearded men,
My songs the tempest shrill—
The panther screaming in the glen,
The war-whoop on the hill.

3.

"My bride my trusty rifle is,
My babe my bowie-knife—
'Tis but a copper's toss if this
Be not my last of life.

4.

"And yet I sleep with babe and bride
Below God's rounded wall,
As soundly and as satisfied
As if in guarded hall.

5.

"The morn may wake to mortal strife,
The day may lay me low;
Yet I shall die with babe and wife—
Good-by—lift hands—I go!"

XVII.

I bring you the red man. Nay! I bring
But the beck'ning ghosts of the warriors that were. . .
We stood on the mountain of fire. The air
Was heavy with shadows. A ghostly king
Stretched forth a red hand to the peaks of snow,
Saying, "These are mine. These are mine,
Through ages that follow, to threaten and shine
And recall my achievements. The red man must go,
But Shasta remains." . . . He turned from his post,
And moved down the land like a shadowy ghost.

XVIII.

Despise not his story. The last of his race
Once stood in the twilight of wood, and told
Of the melting of stars and the making of gold,
As he gathered his blanket and looked in my face:
"In the days of my fathers, my mother, the earth,
Gave birth to the moon. She trembled abed,
And men were fearful to death and fled
In canoes to the sea. Then, after the birth,
Looking back as they rode on the sea and afar,
They saw flames leaping till they touched a star.

XIX.

"The flames touched heaven, and then leapt through
And melted a star into rain till it fell
And scattered a shower of shot as of hell,
And sowed the land as your sowers do.
Ay! Sowed it with death. Hist! Listen to me:
The earth lay still lay in her lodge at morn,
And the flames drew back, for the moon was born;
But, oh, the plague as they rode on the sea!
For the star that melted had made the gold
That led the Saxon to our last stronghold."

XX.

I bring from the mighty untracked domain
The Pimo palms that fan Mexico.
I bring you black steeds that do wheel and blow
In clouds and unbridled along the plain.
I bring you the ruins that wrestle with Time,
The gray Casse Grande that rise sublime,
From burning red sands where the savage roams;
A homeless people and peopleless homes!
The mild-eyed Aztec, his flocks of snow,
His arts of three thousand years ago.

XXI.

I bring the Sierras, where the sunlight like gold.
Sifts down through depression and high heaving wood
Behold the Vaquero! How dashing and bold
In his broad sombrero! The solitude
Of far forked heights is broken with song,

"The surly leviathan there that rides
The curled swift waters."

As he cheerily urges his train along.
Up! up through the clouds, to the turbulent height
Of the lone miners' town. Up, up through the night
The brave mules clamber in line, and they cling,
And you hear him shout, as you hear him sing:

The Muleteer sings:

"Uppa! mula! mucha, caro,
Senorita, monte, faro—
Nights must be,
But lights may burn
Oh, bide for me,
For I return.

"Ki! Muchaco! Yaup! Lolita!
Some one's waiting, Senorina—
Nights must be,
And storms must blow,
But love fears neither
Night nor snow."

XXII.

I bring you the river of earth that divides
The wide middle-world; and the men thereon;
The surly leviathan there that rides
The curled swift waters; that turns upon
His keel as a strong man turns on his heel.
My whole soul thrills as I see the king
At wheel or fire. His arms are bare.
His breast is opened. It is black with hair
And the smoke of battle. Behold, I bring
This man to the feast, and I crown him king.

XXIII.

A new and black brother, half troubadour,
A stray piece of midnight, comes grinning on deck.
Lo! beauty and valor! The song of the shore,
The "Hail Columbia!" falls faint and far.
We come upon night and her sentinel star—
The thousand bright banners have dimmed to a speck.

"Behold the Vaquero! How dashing and bold
In his broad sombrero!"

The black man has mounted a keg. From
  his throne
He thrums his banjo. Come! let us alone.
Ay, let us be careless! The next hundred
  year,
Wherever it brings us, will not bring us here·

The Negro sings:

"Gwine down to de Quaker ball,
We white folks and de niggers all,
Gwine to dat Centeni-awl.
Oh, fight for de Union!

Chorus:

"Gwine to dat Centeni-awl,
  Centeni-awl, Centeni-awl;
  Gwine to dat Centeni-awl;
  To fight for de Union!

"Don't know jis whot it's all about,
I'se gwine down to see 'em out,
For I kin shake a heel an' shout.
Oh, fight for de Union!

"Hat an' boots I'se gwine down
To dat ole Pensi-quaker town,
An' camp upon de battle-groun',
Oh, fight for de Union!

Bully boy, wid hat bent in,
Lots o' time an' lots o' tin,
Shoutin' for de flag dat win,
Oh, fight for de Union!

"Stoga boots an' stove-pipe hat,
Standin' collar, an' plenty o' dat;
Sweet potatoes an' 'possum fat,
Oh, fight for de Union!"

XXIV.

From the salt-flood floors of the Golden
  Gate,
Where the sea shows his teeth like a
  dog in wait,
I bring you for Commerce a handful of
  sand—
A handful of sand that sinewy men
Have sifted from cañon and gorge and glen.
In this was she nourished—grown tall and free,
Till her ships went forth to the farthermost land,
And girdled the earth with golden estate,
And made or unmade the monarchs to be,
From the gold of the sand by the vast West sea.

"*A new and black brother, half troubadour,
A stray piece of midnight comes grinning on deck.*"

XXV.

Lo! rock-rent Nevada! The heaved land is sown
With cinder and boulders. 'Tis the torn battle-field
Of the Titans of Saturn. Here fell the shield
Embossed in chased silver. Yonder was thrown
The gold-headed javelin. . . Hark! Engine and wheel!
Behold! from yon chimneys roll columns of smoke.
The furnaces gleam. You may hear the stroke,
The clashing and clanging of pick and of steel—
The steel in the heart of the ribb'd earth hurled,
And a song sounds up from the deeps of the world:

"*We are battling with the gnomes,
We have gripped them in their homes.*"

Miners sing:

1.

'In the earth and underground,
Full a half a mile below,
Where the days may never come,
Where the nights may never go,·
Where the smoky gnomes are found
Just a level mile below
We are moleing through the ground.

2.

"We are marching underground,
Full a hundred thousand strong;
You may hear our armor sound,
You may hear our battle-song.
There is clash of pick and tine,
There is movement in the mine,
We are marching underground.

3.

"We are fighting underground.
Now a thud, a smell of powder—
Louder now, and—louder, louder
Till the deeps be deaf with sound.
We are battling with the gnomes,
We have gripped them in their homes,
We are bleeding underground.

4.

"We shall conquer underground,
We shall pillage castle, palace,
We shall plunder plate and chalice,
Where the busy gnomes abound;
We shall rise with shouts of joy,
We shall come, like Greeks from Troy,
From the battle underground."

Orator to the People:

XXVI.

Oh, wondrous the wealth, prodigious the
  powers!
Unbound the dominion, and matchless the
  love!
And this the inheritance! This, then, is
  ours;
Reached down, as yon stars are reached
  down, from above.
Then rise in your places. Rise up! Let us
  take
A great oath together as we gather us
  here,
At the end and beginning of an hundred
  year,
For the love of Freedom, for Liberty's
  sake—
To hand the Republic on down, undefiled,
As we have received it, from father to child.

XXVII.

The past is before us. Its lessons are ours;
The cycles roll by, and beckon, and cry—
"Lo! there fell Babylon; fell, eaten away
With lust and luxury. Her thousand towers,
Her temples, her gardens, are dust to-day,
And the wild-fox burrows where her portals
  lie.
Lo! Greece died here, devoured by strife
Of kings she had cradled and nurtured to
  life.
Lo! there proud Rome, in imperial flight,
Fell down from the sun to the darkness of
  night.

XXVIII.

Oh, let us live pure in the flush-tide of life;
Be patient in valor as the solemn years roll.
Oh, let us not strive too much in the strife,
But bridle ambition and invoke control.
Come, turn us from luxury, dash down the
  wine,
And walk by the waters. So live, that men
Who shall stand where we stand, in the foot-
  prints of Penn,
By the same broad city, in the same sun-
  shine,
Shall say of us all, just a century hence,
"They were worthy, indeed, the inherit-
  ance."

The People sing a Song of Peace:

1.

The grass is green on Bunker hill,
  The waters sweet in Brandywine;
The sword sleeps in the scabbard still,
  The farmer keeps his flock and vine;
Then, who would mar the scene to-day
  With vaunt of battle-field or fray?

2.

The brave corn lifts in regiments
  Ten thousand sabres in the sun,
The ricks replace the battle-tents,
  The bannered tassels toss and run.
The neighing steed, the bugle's blast
These be but stories of the past.

3.

The earth has healed her wounded breast,
  The cannons plow the field no more;
The heroes rest! Oh, let them rest
  In peace along the peaceful shore!
They fought for peace, for peace they fell;
  They sleep in peace, and all is well.

4.

The fields forget the battles fought,
  The trenches wave in golden grain
Shall we neglect the lessons taught
  And tear the wounds agape again?
Sweet Mother Nature, nurse the land,
  And heal her wounds with gentle hand.

5.

Lo! peace on earth. Lo! flock and fold,
  Lo! rich abundance, fat increase,
And valleys clad in sheen of gold.
  Oh, rise and sing a song of peace!
For Theseus roams the land no more,
And Janus rests with rusted door.

"*Lo! peace on earth.*"

AGRICULTURAL HALL.

(Continued from page 117.)

JAPAN.

The southwest corner of the Agricultural Building is devoted to Japan. This department, beginning with an exhibit of tobacco, in leaf, pressed and cut, is followed by a frame of illustrations done in colors by hand, presenting is made illustrating the manufacture of silk in cocoons and reel. A number of hides are displayed, dressed with the fur on, presenting specimens of some twenty different animals. From the province of Totomi there is a small exhibit of fibres; and from that of Setzu an exhibit of cotton in a raw state and in all stages of preparation. A display of hemp, ramie, jute and China grass fibres completes this portion of the Japanese department. A very pretty exhibit is made of the different kinds of native dye-woods, number-

without the bark, in its natural condition, and varnished. These specimens number about one hundred.

VENEZUELA.

The Venezuela department includes a considerable exhibition of native grains, including the coffee bean; quite a show of preserved fruits; barks used for medicinal purposes and for dyeing; oils, balsams, etc. Added to these are specimens of wax, soaps, and native wines and cordials.

JULY 4TH, 1876.—THE CENTENNIAL CELEBRATION IN PHILADELPHIA—RICHARD HENRY LEE, OF VIRGINIA, READING THE DECLARATION OF INDEPENDENCE AT INDEPENDENCE SQUARE JULY 4TH.

the cultivation of tea, and the various growths of the plant. At this point commences the exhibit of Japanese teas in boxes and in jars of wood, metal, and pottery, with a large number of glass bottles filled with small samples of tea. There is a small display of wicker-work, baskets, mats, etc., fishing-nets of different patterns, and fishing-rods of bamboo in a considerable quantity, some of them being highly decorated. A small collection of insects injurious to vegetation is displayed, with models of the mulberry-tree, a model of a Japanese house, etc. A very handsome display

ing twenty exhibits; and next are several specimens of the skins of fish, dressed after a peculiar manner. There is a small display of preserved fish and meat, the latter of hams. There is an exhibit of isinglass, and a number of exhibits of sugars, starch, Japanese candies, preserved fruits, and bottles of mulberry wine, lemonade punch and other native drinks. From Tokio there is quite a collection of sauces, for meat or fish, prepared from fermented grain. The display of native Japanese woods is quite full and very handsomely presented, including specimens of leaves, of wood

The celebrated Angostura bitters are here in full force. The textile fabrics are displayed to some extent, and there is a very ingenious-looking piece of mechanism for measuring in the manufacture of clothing. Dyes, wax-fruits, chocolate, an exhibit of boots and shoes of a very tasteful appearance, and a small exhibit of blank books, complete this collection. A compliment is paid to America in the exhibit of a large specimen of artistic work in human hair—a figure supposed to represent Liberty accompanying Washington. This is exhibited by Antonio Guzman Blanco.

NORWAY.

The department of Norway is situated immediately behind that of Brazil, and its exhibits are presented in an ornamental shape, the cases containing the different articles being very prettily constructed and artistically decorated. In the centre is quite a show of confectionery, bottles of punch and liqueurs. Next to this is an exhibit of native woods, showing sections of trunks of trees, planks, battens, staves, cornices, etc. Behind this is a display of grains, stuffed birds, canned meats, Norwegian pale ale, hides, and condensed milk. The display of butter of various manufacture is quite large. The Christiania Preserving Company exhibits a large number of specimens of preserved meat, poultry, game, fish, soup meats, etc. There is one case devoted to tobacco and cigars, and several to aqua vitæ and other preparations of spirits. One custom of the country is represented by a stuffed figure presenting a passenger on a reindeer-sledge, a man in life-size, being heavily coated and wrapped in furs, and a reindeer rather undersized, in a very natural position. But decidedly the most interesting portion of the Norwegian display is comprised in the exhibition of fish and of fisheries. This is quite in the northwest corner of the building, and occupies a space of about fifty feet square. In this are a collection of glass jars exhibiting specimens of the different fish native to the country, models of some larger specimens, models of fishing-boats, boxes and jars containing preserved fish, and including red herrings, cods, haddocks, white herrings, fish-oil, fish-roes, salted and dried cod, oysters, etc. There are also exhibited fishing glue, caviar, fishing oil, preserved salmon, lobsters, etc. A Norwegian fishing sled with implements is also displayed. There are several specimens of leather and belting, one exhibit of butter, and one of preserved old cheese. Fish guano and Norwegian artificial manure are also exhibited; and, in addition to the models of fishing-boats, a model of a fisherman's hut. Besides these, there is a large collection of fishing-tackle, including nets of the very largest species, model of an ice-house, salt herrings in boxes. In fact, a large and most complete and instructive collection of articles, illustrating one of the most important industries of Norway.

INDIA RUBBER EXHIBIT OF SOUTH AND CENTRAL AMERICA.

A short distance from the department last described, a space of about twenty-five feet square is given up to exhibits of india rubber, including the rubber-tree in several varieties, and the gum in different conditions, india rubber milk, dry leaves, and various other products, these being exhibited by brokers in the South American trade, and including exhibits from Guayaquil, Panama, Carthagena, Honduras and other South and Central American countries, besides specimens from Mexico, Madagascar, Mozambique, and the western countries of Africa, Assam, East Indies, etc.

PORTUGAL.

The Portuguese exhibition is extensive and varied. Naturally it presents its chief force in its display of wines: muscatel, grape, port, etc. Besides the wines, there are considerable exhibits of brandies, liqueurs, syrups, etc., after which come the exhibits of grains and seeds, beans of innumerable varieties, the whole being comprised in about a thousand glass jars of various sizes and shapes, making a very handsome and complete display of this class of agricultural products. The display of canned fruits and vegetables is also unexpectedly large and full, and comprises all imaginable articles in this line. There is also a considerable display of cheese, and a very full exhibit of olives, as also of indigenous nuts, dried fruits, honey and

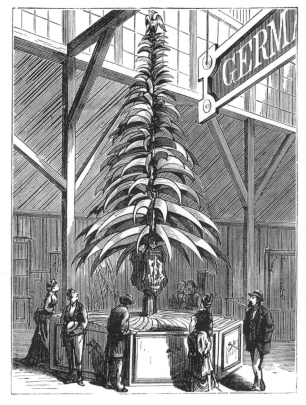

MONUMENT OF SCYTHE BLADES.

biscuits. The exhibition of confectionery is quite showy, including dried fruits, candies and preserves of various kinds. The Portuguese exhibition closes with an exhibit of hides and a full representation of native seeds in bottles. But the space allotted to Portugal and filled by that country does not end here. On the southern wall of the building, east of the nave, and on a line with the Japanese department, is a very full display of fibrous materials, arranged in glass vases, and including the products of hemp, flax, wool, cotton and silk in cocoons and skeins. Next to this is a long line of bottles, many hundreds in number, containing exhibits in olive oil. Fronting these exhibits are those of the various Portuguese colonies, including Goa, Mozambique, St. Thomas, Principe, Cape Verde, Macao. These exhibits include the production of the countries specified, comprising specimens of native woods, gums, grains, seeds, nuts and tobacco. A trophy of arms, axes, spears, javelins, clubs, etc., presents a bristling appearance. A number of cocoanuts, preserved fruits and vegetables, and a specimen of a gigantic fungus growth, complete this department.

SPAIN.

The department of Spain is next to that of Portugal, and includes also the various colonies; the West India Islands,

Philippine Islands, etc. The spectator is at once struck with the largeness and wealth of this department. Naturally, the display of tobacco in its various forms, and particularly cigars of the finest manufacture, is large and imposing. This would be expected, but the surprising feature of the Spanish department is the extent of its exhibits in unexpected directions; as, for instance, in the matter of grains and nuts the display far exceeds anything else of the same character in the entire exhibition. In that of fibres it is no less complete, the exhibits showing unusual care and taste in their selection and display. In the products of olive, both in the fruit and the oil, there is a full and handsome representation. Wines and liqueurs are represented to a considerable extent, although not in comparison with those of Portugal. It is to be regretted that, no catalogue having been prepared of the Spanish department, the investigator is left to his own resources in examining it.

RUSSIA.

Immediately behind Spain, and extending to the west wall of the building, is the department of Russia, whose exhibits commence with a number of agricultural machines and implements, including the reaping-machine, thrashing-machine, winnowing and sorting-machine, asparagus-digger, etc. Beside these is a considerable display of soap, including two large cases of Castile soap. Next to this, in a frame, are specimens of sealing-wax, artistically arranged; also a case containing samples of Portland cement, and some very beautiful specimens of cocoons, raw and flossed silk. Specimens of mineral colors and samples of pottery come next, and in the centre a curious little roof-structure is hung with a miscellaneous collection of domestic articles in use in Russia, including lanterns, tea-urns, a cradle, harness, brushes, toys, musical instruments, china-ware, religious paintings on panel, and a great many other articles not peculiar to Russia. A large case contains albumen, phosphates, sulphate of copper, and other chemicals, neatly presented in glass jars. Next to this is a case specially devoted to an exhibit of ink of different colors, and next a very beautiful exhibit of refined beet-root sugar. Then comes a case containing chocolate and other confections, preserved fruits, nut-candies, etc. Next, another case with exhibits of sugar in loaves, cut and granulated. Near to these exhibits last mentioned are a number of cases in which is displayed tobacco in various forms, the well-known Russian cigarette being present in large quantities. There are, also, however, exhibits of apparently well-made cigars. Following these is a case containing wax candles and specimens of wax imitation fruits, which brings us to some samples of manufactures in chiccory and wheat flour. A large case of liqueurs and extracts next attracts our attention, beside which is another containing confectionery and cakes. We then come upon an exhibit of garments made of various furs and skins, including astrakhan, lamb's wool and others. The display of wool and fibrous material is very large, and includes samples from most of the wool-growing districts of Russia. There are here, also, specimens of silk manufactured from the worm and the cocoon up to skeins of raw silk, and exhibits in flax and hemp innumerable. In fact, the display of wool and flax, staple products of Russia, may be considered one of the chief points of the agricultural exhibition of that country.

Next to this, perhaps, the exhibits of grains, seeds and beans are the most extensive and representative. Nearly in the centre of the Russian department is a group of trunks or boxes, a kind commonly used by the Russians, being made of wood and metal, some of them being considerably larger than the Saratoga trunk. Something of a show is made by the Russians in basket-

THE BRAZILIAN COTTON PAVILION.

OBJECTS OF INTEREST IN AGRICULTURAL HALL

work, but considerably more in very pretty constructions in birch bark; a few specimens of native woods in the form of books, backed with the bark, and labels thereupon, with the name of the wood, are to be seen in a case facing the end of the Spanish department, next to which is a case containing artificial honey and honeycomb, and next to that a bee-hive. Russia furnishes a very full show of preserved fruits and berries, dried, including strawberries, whortleberries, raspberries, etc., beside which are some specimens of coffee in large glass jars, dried peas, lentils, anise, cedar-nuts, walnuts, Spanish nuts, filberts, prunes, more honey, more preserved fruits and isinglass. This brings us to the display of canned meats, fish, etc., and of distilled brandies, liqueurs, wines, balsam, etc., to which may be added mention of two cases which occur here, containing samples of leaf tobacco, with two cases containing specimens of leggins, over-boots, caps, and other fabrications in felting, with a few scarfs in fancy colored materials.

Among the forest products are specimens of various kinds of trees growing in the forests and steppes of Russia. Samples of larch-wood, larch and cedar combs, gall-nuts, willow-bark for tanning skins, fir and pine seeds, and reproductions of sixty-two varieties of apple-trees peculiar to the Isle of Waylaam, on the Ladoga Lake. The agricultural products exhibited consist of red wheat, rye, barley, oats, timothy-grass, India millet, maize, buckwheat, vetch, red clover, and luzern. Concerning the cigarette manufacture, one establishment is mentioned, situated at Rostov, on the Don, which employs 500 workmen, and manufactures 25,000,006 of cigarettes annually, of the value of 1,500,000 rubles; but this is exceeded by a manufactory in St. Petersburg and one in Warsaw, which employs 1,600 workpeople, men and women, and whose manufacture is valued at 1,700,000 rubles per annum. The tobacco used for these cigarettes is Bess-Arabian, Virginian, Caucasian, Crimean and native. Chiccory is manufactured to a considerable extent in Russia, as is also fig-coffee and chocolate. Among the seeds displayed are linseed, wild rape-seed, Odessa, beet-root seed and mustard-seed. The Russian caviar is exhibited, and isinglass made from the sturgeon. The sugar manufactories of Warsaw employ as many as 500 to 600 workmen, each manufacturing sugar to the value of 2,500,000 rubles annually. One of these employs 1,000 workmen, and another makes to the amount of more than 4,000,000 rubles worth per annum. The wines exhibited by Russia include white grape-wine, sweet muscatel wine, Kakhetian wine, and others of better known brands; corn brandies of different kinds are exhibited, and punch, imperial, raspberry and cherry. One beer manufactory at St. Petersburg employs 250 workmen, and manufactures beer to the amount of 600,000 rubles per annum. A

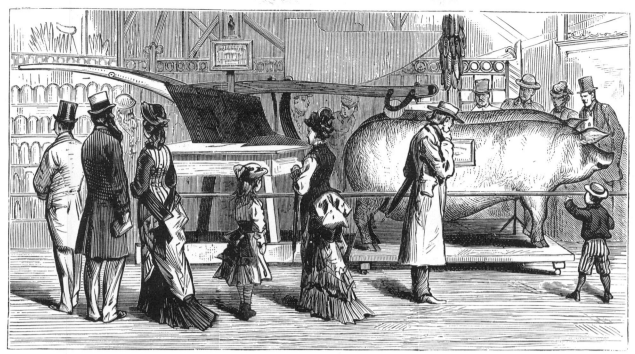

DANIEL WEBSTER'S PLOW.

confectionery in Moscow, which exhibits sugar-candy, marble fruit, preserves, and gingerbread, employs 600 workmen, and its manufacture is worth over a million of rubles per annum. It should be mentioned that a ruble is worth about seventy-eight cents, gold. The Agricultural Museum of St. Petersburg exhibits a collection of samples of cotton and cotton seeds from Turkestan. The flax and hemp come from Riga, Kazan, and St. Petersburg. The wool, which includes merino, Spanish, Russian and Negretti breeds, is from Moscow, Poltova, Warsaw, Odessa and St. Petersburg. The silk is from Kief and Moscow. Of the machines and implements, the asparagus-digger, invented by the exhibitor, Albert Benkowski, is from Warsaw, as are also reaping-machines, thrashing-machines, and winnowing and sorting machines. The phosphatic and other manures come from St. Petersburg, from a manufactory established in 1859, employing 100 workmen.

ENGLAND.

Returning now to the southern end of the building, on the eastern side of the nave, we enter the department allotted to Great Britain and her colonies. Here we begin with specimens of manufacture in iron wire, netting, screens, etc., for fences and for mining and other purposes. The next exhibit is Staffordshire ware, both plain and ornamental. It is quite full enough to give one an adequate idea of the peculiar quality and characteristics of this manufacture. Some of the specimens are exceedingly beautiful, very tastefully ornamented, as is the case, also, with samples of toilet sets. Next are some burr mill-stones for wheat-grinding, and smaller stones for fine-edged tools, an exhibit of terra-cotta, chimney-shafts, scouring-bricks, more manufactures in terra-cotta from Sussex, England, some of them being quite ornamental; some specimens of pottery from Devonshire; and this brings us to an exhibit of sheep and garden-shears from Sheffield; edgetools used in agriculture, from Mell's Iron Works, in Somersetshire; an exhibit of Tennent's ales, and one of East India ale from the Punjaub, are all the British liquors that we meet here. The next exhibit is of a filter as used in water-tanks; and the next a filter-press for clarifying liquids. The display now begins to be exceedingly miscellaneous, including cement for glass and crockery, etc.; specimens of cocoa, baking-powders, crackers, desiccated milk, extracts of meat from Australia, Scotch oatmeal; a special exhibit of the London celebrated chocolate menier; a magnificent upright cabinet containing mustard from a factory established 134 years ago; more oatmeal, ginger-ale, cowslip-wine, Bindell & Co.'s and Coope & Co.'s ales from Burton-on-Trent; barrels and bottles of pale ale from Newark-upon-Trent, are exhibited by Richardson, Earp & Slater. We come now to the first transept, in the centre of which stands Aveling & Porter's road and farming locomotive and wagon, both being exceedingly ponderous pieces of mechanism; an exhibit of iron wire from the Norfolk Iron Works, Norwich, England, comes next, which completes the exhibits of Great Britain.

BRITISH COLONIES: VICTORIA, NEW ZEALAND, NEW SOUTH WALES AND SOUTH AUSTRALIA.

Victoria displays a large number of specimens of her native woods. New Zealand exhibits specimens of wool, and the South Australia Commissioners at Adelaide send a reaper, some ax-handles from South Australia, iron ores, a model of an improved ore-dresser. And we now come to the department of

CANADA.

The Canadian agricultural exhibition begins with a very full and varied display of grains, beans, peas, etc., in glass

jars and boxes under glass. Following this are exhibits of wool, and next is a very interesting collection illustrating the entomology and ornithology of Canada. The flora of Canada is illustrated in dried specimens exhibited in portfolios under glass. Here also is a small exhibit of Canada-manufactured tobacco, canned meats and fish, and an exhibit of Canada salt comes next, after which is presented an exhibit of macaroni from Montreal, and also from the same city a considerable display of buckwheat, oatmeal, wheat, and cracked wheat flours. The Montreal brewery makes a fine show of ales and porters, and from Hamilton are several very fine fleeces, carefully prepared and of beautiful texture. Hams and sides of bacon come next, with more canned articles, including every imaginable eatable, game-pie, hunter's-pie, venison-pie, Oxford sausages, boiled fowl, lamb-chops, curried fowl, soups, truffled fowls, hashed mutton, pigeons, mutton-chops, beefsteak-pie, etc. From Victoria, British Columbia, are some exhibits of dried fish, cranberries, different kinds of oil, boxes of wool, vinegar, wooden pails, and manufactured tobacco. Quite a prominent exhibit in this department is the tick-destroyer for sheep. The fisheries of Canada are illustrated by dried specimens in boxes and others in spirits, besides canned fish in a variety. We now come upon the display of New Brunswick woods, arranged upon a high partition, topped with a moose-head and a pair of snow-shoes, as an appropriate ornament. These woods include forest woods, shrubs, etc., evergreen and deciduous trees indigenous to the province of New Brunswick, used for shipbuilding, constructional, cabinet, and ornamental purposes. These comprise sixty-seven specimens, accompanied with foliage and cone. Victoria and New Westminster, British Columbia, also exhibit cranberries. In Nova Scotia there are six cases of stuffed birds, one pair of cariboo, two cariboo-heads, two moose-heads, and one black bear. From Ontario there are stuffed birds. Ontario sends flax and Victoria wool, and the Canadian Commission make a display of Indian wool from British Columbia. The agricultural machines and implements include plows, a very fine one being the Yeankle plow—almost entirely manufactured of steel—from Ontario. Ontario, in fact, sends the most agricultural implements, although from St. John there are a mower, hay-rake, thrasher, hay-cutter, and potato-diggers. From Charlottetown, P. E. I., there is a potato-digger, and from Halifax a horizontal churn. One potato-digger has five rows of steel blades, nine in each row. This, called the Dominion-Howe's mower and reaper, manufactured by Sawyer & Co., of Hamilton, Ontario, discharges the overflow of grain by the movement of a lever under control of the driver, and seems generally well-fitted to its purpose. There are also grain-

THE MAHOGANY AFRICAN.

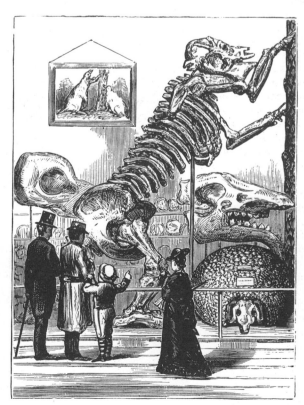

ANTEDILUVIAN RELICS FROM THE MUSEUM AT ALBANY.

OBJECTS OF INTEREST IN AGRICULTURAL HALL.

THE KANSAS AND COLORADO BUILDING.

crushers, fanning-mills, horse-rakes, root-cutters, both for power and hand, cheese-presses, etc. From St. Catherine's there are exhibited refrigerators, and from Barie, Ontario, a sleigh and snow-plow.

DENMARK.

Denmark occupies only a single space in the Agricultural Building, its chief agricultural exhibition being in the Main Building. A small space here, lying between Sweden and

these products to the Exposition. Besides these, there are iron ore, logwood, robes of a native chief, a canoe about fifteen feet long, and hammocks. Quite a thriving trade is done in the building in coffee and palm soap.

SWEDEN.

The Scandinavian countries are allotted a space in the Agricultural Building on the west side, about one-fourth of the distance from the southern end of the building, with a

only a very short period of Spring and Autumn. The packing is all done by hand. These anchovies are exported from Sweden to Denmark, Germany, Russia, and Finland. The operatives engaged in the manufacture receive—men, thirty cents per day, and women fifteen to seventeen cents per day. The production during 1874 amounted to $1,670 gold. The raw materials used for the production were 6,000 firkins of sprats. The refuse, skin and bones, is composted and used as a fertilizer. Besides

THE STATUE OF "THE FREED SLAVE" IN MEMORIAL HALL.

Norway, contains some exhibits of spirits, beer and bitters, some canned butter, grains, and a model of a milk refrigerator.

LIBERIA.

Quite a little display is made by the far-off Republic of Liberia, a territory comprising about 600 miles in length of coast land on the West Coast of Africa, and having a population of about 700,000, of whom about 20,000 are emigrants from America. Liberia exports palm oil, palm nuts, arrow-root, coffee, ivory, and sugar, and has sent specimens of all

small space at the extreme northwestern end devoted to a fishery exhibit. The first exhibits to which our attention is drawn consist of glass jars and bags of seeds, and grain, some fishing-nets, and some dried grain in small sheaves. There are also to be seen specimens of flour, and boxes of preserved anchovies. The oyster anchovies, which are to be found here, unlike the common anchovies, are packed with spices, and have not before been exhibited at any International Exhibition. The manufacture was first commenced in 1845. The time of catching extends through

anchovies, the fish exhibition includes mackerel of the fattest and best quality, which are cleaned and then preserved with a mixture of sugar, salt, and white pepper, after which they are smoked in the smoke from juniper-sprigs, when they are cut into small slices and packed in sweet-oil. So economical is this fish-preservation, that the heads, fins, roes, etc., are sold cheaply to the poorer population. Besides these, there are boneless herring and Swedish sardines, also put up in cans. The collection of fishes from the fresh waters and coasts of Sweden is exhibited,

THE MISSISSIPPI STATE BUILDING.

including seventy-seven species preserved in glass jars and spirits of wine. Of fishing-nets there are those in use for the capture of herrings, mackerel, flounder, for salmon and lake-fishing, and for cod, of different models. There are also shown cod and flounder lines, and, indeed, a complete collection of hook and fishing-gear, with grapnels, buoys, etc., as used by Swedish fishermen when fishing on the North Sea and the Cattegat. Several models of fishing crafts are displayed, including the bank fishing-vessel as used on the banks of the North Sea, mackerel-boats, herring-boats, skiffs for fishing in smaller lakes, and others for transporting living fish in Stockholm, and boats used for fishing and traveling on the Lapland rivers. From Leidedorff, fishing implements are displayed. They are manufactured at Stockholm. The greater part of the articles manufactured for this establishment are made by home-work. Among the strictly agricultural products of Sweden are exhibited wheat, rye, barley, oats, including specimens of these grains raised at Ava, the most northern agricultural school on the earth, located only forty-eight English miles south of the North Polar circle. Beans, peas, and vetches, dried for food, are also exhibited. From Stockholm is exhibited tobacco, grown near that city. Tobacco-raising in this locality was started in 1856. Samples of snuff are also shown, manufactured on the spot. Among the specimens of native woods exhibited are sections of fir-timber grown at 67 north latitude. Illustrating the manufacture of leather there are exhibited calf-skins, cow-leather, horse-leather, patent leather leggins, patent leather uppers, etc. The raw materials used are Buenos Ayres, Para, Pernambuco and Swedish hides, kid, calf, goat and sheepskins. The exports go to Germany, Silesia, and the Netherlands. There are some exhibits of confections and preserved fruits, and preserved vegetables. Of liqueurs a prominent exhibit is Swedish punch, an article which is consumed principally in the country, but some of which is exported to Germany, Denmark, Norway, Brazil, and the Southern States of North America. This punch is manufactured from arrack, put up in glass bottles. A novel exhibit is that of spirits manufactured from lichens. This species of alcohol is manufactured from reindeer moss, which grows in immense quantities in the northern countries. The discovery which established the manufacture was only made in the year 1868. A few specimens of biscuit are exhibited which can be kept for half a year without changing. The machinery exhibit includes patent steel plows, and plows with molded shares and shafts of steel. There are also scythes of different models, and one mower. The collection of drawings, illustrating the construction of peasant-cottages and other dwellings for workingmen's farm-houses, and barns, dairies, stables, pigsties, sheepfolds, tool-houses, etc., concludes the exhibition of Sweden.

United States.

Although the agricultural exhibits of the United States exhibitors occupy fully half of the Agricultural Building, the American public have been so familiarized with their character through State and other fairs, that any precise description of most of the articles would be a work of supererogation in this place, and we shall therefore only refer to these exhibits generally, and in accordance with the classification employed in the arrangement of the building. Beginning with arbor culture and forest products, we have the fine collection of conifera of the Pacific Coast, illustrating the native woods of that locality very fully. North Carolina, Indiana, Pennsylvania, Iowa, New Jersey and Wisconsin have full exhibits in this line. The State of Michigan offers a magnificent display of native woods, in sections of gigantic trees and in specimens of timber in the rough and dressed. Ohio sends white pine lumber; Oregon medicine-roots and barks; Massachusetts offers burnetized lumber for bridges, wharves, railroads, and other positions where wood is liable to decay; North Carolina sends cedar and cypress shingles; Maine basswood panels; Virginia ground sumac; New York various elastic gums, and New Orleans southern moss. The Michigan display is a collective exhibit from the Michigan State Agricultural College. Pomology is the next subject in order, and this at the present writing has not been very fully illustrated, but will doubtless be later in the season, a building having been specially constructed and devoted to the purpose of pomological exhibits. At present there are wax models of apples, pears, and other fruit from Iowa, cranberries from various portions of New Jersey, apples from the Michigan Pomological Society at Detroit, pecan-nuts from New Orleans, etc.

In agricultural products strictly, the display is, of course, large and varied. Some exhibits, as is the case in the State of Massachusetts, are collective and very largely representative. Besides corn, wheat, barley, rye, oats, buckwheat, peas, beans, grasses, and the various vegetables exhibited by the different States, there are also straw for the manufacture of straw-goods from Pennsylvania, field and garden seeds, grasses and tobacco from the seed-farms of D. Landreth & Sons, Philadelphia, the production of their seed-farms in Pennsylvania, New Jersey, Virginia and Wisconsin. The State of Oregon sends native and cultivated grasses and grass-seeds, with grain in the sheaf and in the sack. The State of West Virginia has a collective exhibit, including grass and agricultural products, tobacco, wheat, corn, oats, barley and rye. From Georgetown, South Carolina, there is an exhibit of Carolina rice. From one establishment in New York there are 200 varieties of potatoes exhibited. The display of tobacco is really superb, including Perique from New Orleans, plug, leaf, and smoking tobacco from Durham, North Carolina, and snuff, cigarettes and cigars from all the other leading manufactories, and including all the prominent brands. Richmond (Virginia) and Louisville (Kentucky) are largely represented, while the well-known house of Gail & Ax, of Baltimore, makes a handsome display of smoking and fine-cut chewing tobacco, snuffs, etc., in a pagoda-like structure. Messrs. Kerbs & Spies, of New York, have a very handsome exhibit of cigars, which has been illustrated and described in another portion of this work. From West Springfield, Massachusetts, we have exhibits of Connecticut seed-leaf tobacco, and from Detroit, Michigan, cigars of home manufacture. The tobacco-growers of Penn's Manor, Morrisville, Pennsylvania, send an exhibit in sweated tobacco. This tobacco, known as Duck Island, is grown in Bucks County, Pennsylvania, and adjoining islands, and is very highly considered.

After tobacco, there are exhibits of coffee, spices, mustard, peas, field and garden seeds, tree, shrub and apple seeds from New Jersey, New York, Connecticut, Minnesota, Maryland and other States.

The display of land-animals should appropriately commence with mention of that interesting relic, "Old Abe," the live "war-eagle," which was carried for three years, during the war of the Rebellion, by the Eighth Regiment of Wisconsin Volunteers. "Old Abe" occupies a prominent position on a perch set up on the west side of the nave, and is the observed of all observers. He is perfectly tame, although he has not in the least lost any of his fire, but overlooks the sale of his photograph and biography, which goes on to a considerable extent beside him, with entire satisfaction and equanimity. Next to "Old Abe," the most interesting exhibit is that of Ward's Natural Science Establishment of Rochester, New York, which makes a very fine display of skeletons, articulated and stuffed animals and reptiles, including the giraffe, dromedary, moose, grizzly bear, American elk, wild cat, etc., all handsomely preserved and placed in life-like positions within glass cases. The Michigan State Agricultural College of Lansing, Michigan, exhibits a collection of useful and injurious birds and insects. Philadelphia has quite a display of stuffed birds, and the land department of the Central Pacific Railroad Company has also a similar exhibit. A taxidermist of Aurora, Illinois, sends a collection of stuffed birds artistically arranged, representing the gathering of the nations at the Centennial. A Philadelphia house has an exhibit of stuffed Hamburg fowls with their young. The Academy of Natural Science of Allentown exhibits birds with their nests and eggs, and a few quadrupeds; Wisconsin birds and animals are also displayed. From Delaware there comes a collection of insects, and Miss Nellie Brown, of Philadelphia, has an exhibit illustrating the process of hatching and rearing silkworms without mulberries. In this connection it should be stated that the exhibits of live stock at the Centennial Exposition occur as follows:

Horses and dogs from September 1st to 14th; neat cattle from September 21st to October 4th; sheep from October 10th to 18th; swine from October 10th to 18th; poultry from October 27th to November 6th. The displays of competitive agricultural products were set down originally to occur as follows: Pomological products and vegetables from May 16th to 24th; strawberries from June 7th to 15th; early grass butter and cheese from June 26th to July 6th; early Summer vegetables from June 20th to 24th; honey from June 20th to 24th; raspberries and blackberries from July 3d to 8th; Southern pomological products from July 18th to 22d; melons from August 22d to 26th; peaches from September 4th to 9th; Northern pomological products from September 11th to 16th; Autumn vegetables from September 19th to 23d; cereals from September 25th to 30th; potatoes and feeding-roots from October 2d to 7th; grapes from October 10th to 14th; Autumn butter and cheese from October 17th to 21st; nuts from October 23d to November 1st; Autumn honey and wax from October 23d to November 1st. In water-animals, fish-culture and apparatus, we have already alluded to the display of aquaria, and that of the Gloucester fisheries. Beyond these we have from Philadelphia stuffed fish, American and imported leeches, fish-tackle, aquarium-tanks and glue, bamboo fly-rods, trout-rod and case, and a parlor aquarium. San Francisco sends preserved salmon; Chicago glue and Russian isinglass; Massachusetts fishing-lines of linen, cotton and silk in all sizes; New York a very fine show of fishing-rods, reels, lines, flies and fishing-tackle; New Jersey the combination hatching-box; Michigan fishing and hatching apparatus.

The animal and vegetable products, of course, comprehend a very large variety of articles, and include exhibits from every State and every principal town in the Union. Quite a show is made in glue, gelatine, neat's foot oil, lard oil, refined lard, stearine and other similar products, chiefly from New York and Philadelphia. Honey, wax, and

THE WEST VIRGINIA STATE BUILDING.

EXHIBIT OF DOMESTIC CHAMPAGNES BY THE PLEASANT VALLEY WINE COMPANY OF HAMMONDSPORT, N. Y., IN AGRICULTURAL HALL.

candles are exhibited from Pennsylvania, Illinois, and New Jersey. In hermetically sealed canned and preserved fruits, vegetables and meats, there are innumerable exhibits from all parts of the country, including canned and preserved fruits and potted meats from Dover, Delaware, which location is specially celebrated for these articles. Baltimore sends canned oysters and vegetables; New Jersey, preserved cranberries and canned tomatoes; New York, condensed milk, coffee and cocoa, extract of beef, canned fruits, flavors, tomatoes, walnut and mushroom sauces, desiccated cocoanut. From Chicago there are pickles, preserved jellies, sauces and canned goods; from Portland, Oregon, canned salmon, and from Portland, Maine, canned meats, soups, fish and vegetables. Baltimore and New York exhibit hams, lard, and lard oil, breakfast bacon, and beef tongues, shoulders, etc.; Cincinnati also makes a fine display of various preservations of pork. New Jersey makes a special display of hominy, samp-corn, flour from corn grown on the Monmouth and Princeton battle-fields, graham flour, wheaten grits, etc. Hecker & Co., of New York, exhibit their self-raising flour, farina and wheaten grits. Their interesting exhibit of an old-fashioned windmill, located in the nave of the building, has been already illustrated and described. Starch is exhibited by New York, Ohio, Pennsylvania, and Illinois; maple sugar by Vermont; and beet-sugar by Boston, Mass. Vinegar and cider from New York and Pennsylvania are fully displayed; a cider-mill in operation, manufacturing a very excellent article, which is sold on the premises, being a noticeable feature. The exhibition of native wines is quite astonishing when it is remembered that only a few years ago a bottle of good American wine was a thing almost unknown. The grand exhibition of this article in the agricultural department is especially creditable. California and Ohio are chiefly remarkable for their exhibits in this direction, and the display of their wines is large and varied. Besides these, Hammondsport, N. Y., sends champagne, still wines, and brandies. Detroit, Michigan, exhibits native grape wines, currant and elderberry wines. St. Louis offers sparkling and still wines, and New Jersey and Iowa native grape wines. From Centre Island, New York, comes an exhibit of apple wine; and from Fremont, Ohio, extract of barley malt; rye and bourbon whiskies are exhibited in a large variety by various States. Concerning the California vintage, some interesting statements are made. This vintage is always in October, from the 15th to the 30th, when the grapes, as soon as they have been gathered and brought to the press, are stripped from the stems, the stems thrown aside, and the grapes fall from the stripping-machine into a mill, which breaks the grapes without crushing the seeds; from this mill the grapes fall on the press, from which the juice passes directly through india-rubber pipes into the casks arranged on the lowest floor to receive it. There the juice ferments and is drawn

off three times the first year, twice the second year, and once only the third year, and always in January. The third year the wine is bottled in the month of February, and is not offered for use until six months later, or about September. In order to enable visitors to the Exhibition to appreciate the qualities of the wine of California, an enterprising San Francisco manufacturing establishment has a lunch-counter near the north entrance, where a half-bottle of native wine with lunch is served up for one dollar. Confectionery and chocolate preparations make a notable show in the Exhibition, Philadelphia, Boston and New York carrying off the palm in this display. The exhibit of Henry Maillard of bonbons, chocolate, and ornamental confectionery should be specially noticed in this connection. It is situated next to Ward's display of stuffed animals, and makes a very handsome presentation. Crackers, cakes, biscuits, ship-bread, etc., are exhibited from Philadelphia, Trenton, N. J., Cincinnati, Ohio, Seneca Falls, N. Y., Cambridge, Mass., and other localities.

The display of textile substances consists of cotton, hemp and flax, oakum, wool and woolen fabrics, china-grass, hair, moss, horsehair and bristles. Raw and dressed cotton and cotton-plants are exhibited by the States of Georgia, Arkansas, Louisiana, Tennessee, Mississippi, Missouri and South Carolina. Wool is exhibited from Vermont, Oregon, New Hampshire and Ohio.

Decidedly, the largest exhibition in the Agricultural Building consists of machines, implements, and processes of manufacture used in agriculture. These include every imaginable machine and implement, and in them the United States certainly excels all the rest of the world. Indeed, so far as the Centennial Exposition is concerned, the competition in this department is hardly noticeable. Every State sends agricultural implements and machines, including shovels, spades, plows, harrows, cultivators, hoes, rakes, sowers, forks, farm engines, corn-shellers, root-cutters, hay-rakes, grain-cradles, harvesters, cotton-seed planters, cotton gins, thrashing-machines, etc., too numerous to mention in detail. Besides, there are machines for stripping tobacco, berry and fruit baskets, and a cultivator with an attachment for eradicating potato-bugs (rather a curious exhibit), wheelbarrows, common seed-planters, churns, drainage-tools, cider-mill, meat-cutter, and a curiosity in the way of a spade used by a soldier in Washington's army at Valley Forge, exhibited by George Griffith, of Philadelphia; apple-parers, peach-parers, cherry-stoners, feed-cutters, portable engines, all sorts of agricultural knives, sickles, scythes, etc., are found here without number. The implements on exhibition are in all cases finished with great beauty and elegance, and to the practical farmer this portion of the exhibition cannot fail to prove most interesting and instructive. The space occupied by the agricultural implements and machinery is the largest devoted to any one branch exhibited in the Exposition. There is no process in the agricultural or farming business which is not illustrated here by specimens of actual tools employed in them in the latest and most improved styles. No amount of description in a work of this character could do equal justice to the exhibitors in this department, and it has been deemed wisest to refrain from comparative commendation altogether. It is unlikely that any agricultural district in this country will fail to send its full quota of visitors to the Exposition, and to these

the farming classes must refer for information concerning our progress in this manufacture.

Agricultural engineering and administration comes next in the classification. This department includes such articles as ditch-machines, stump-pullers and rock-lifters, road-scrapers, post-hole diggers, rollers, and other similar machinery, with fertilizers, farm-carts, beehives, bird-cages, windmills, poultry coops, kegs and barrels, sugar evaporators, ornamental iron and bronze work, etc. Philadelphia and New Jersey exhibit largely in this line; and New York and Ohio are next in importance as exhibitors. Under the head, Tillage and General Management of Farms, a miscellaneous collection of exhibits is made, including horse and cattle food, devices for training and educating horses, food for cage-birds, and a considerable display of horseshoes and nails, and horseshoe machinery. A working model for making horseshoes by machinery is a notable exhibit and well worthy of examination. In this machine a bar of annealed iron is passed through two rollers, which act as automatic feeders, being kept in constant pressure on the bar by an attachment to the acting lever, which, working on a cam, cuts off the bar just the necessary length of iron to make one horseshoe. At the moment of cutting off, the bending tongue catches the piece cut off and carries it into the first die, which gives the shape and form to the shoe. It then passes on to another roll on a shaft called the creasing shaft, on which is a die, to which the creases are attached, and by means of which the creasing of the shoe is produced, while at the same time the holes for the nails are pierced. Here is then a finished shoe for the horse or mule, which is only to be heated and fitted by the local blacksmith before being used. One great advantage which this machine possesses is, that any shoe of any shape, size or pattern can be made upon it. A plaster-cast pattern of the shoe is carefully taken, and this plaster-cast is used instead of the ordinary wooden pattern for making the sand mold in which the iron die is to be cast. As soon as the horseshoe comes from the second die (plenty of water always dropping from the machine), it is carried off on an endless chain, and about the time it arrives there is comparatively cool. This completes our examination of the United States department and of the Agricultural Building.

In many respects the American exhibits in this building best express the progress of the United States in the past century. We have hitherto been a very practical people. Indeed, it is only within a few years that we have, to any great degree, cultivated æsthetic tastes and begun to make our mark in the world of art. It is therefore that our advancement in those directions, which are generally grouped together in our display in the Agricultural Building, is actually a fair exponent of our real progress. As already remarked, we have met with but little competition at Philadelphia in the adjuncts of agriculture; and, doubtless, this is because the means for such competition do not exist. It

THE TIVOLI BEER EXHIBIT IN AGRICULTURAL HALL.

1. Gloucester Codfish-boat.   2, 3. Norwegian Fishing-boats.   4, 5. Swedish Fishing-boats.   6. Swedish Scoop.   7. Swedish Row Boat.   8. Swedish Oar.   9. Norwegian Oar.   10. Norwegian Rudder.   11. Swedish Anchor.

EXHIBITS OF FISHING CRAFT IN AGRICULTURAL HALL.

will not be uninteresting in this connection to view succinctly the statistics of the world in this great branch of human effort.

AGRICULTURAL STATISTICS

UNITED STATES.

THERE is almost no country on the face of the earth so admirably adapted for agricultural purposes as the United States. The area of the country in 1867 was 1,956,740,480 acres. This is exclusive of the Territory of Alaska, which in itself comprises 370,000,000 of acres. The mountain ranges, the Appalachian chain toward the east, the Rocky Mountains in the centre, and the Sierra Nevada in the west, divide the United States into four great regions; the Atlantic Slope, the basin of the Mississippi and Missouri, the country between the Rocky Mountains and the Sierra Nevada, and the Pacific Slope. The rivers of the United States are of vast magnitude and importance. Of those flowing east and south, the principal are the Mississippi and Missouri, which, with their tributaries, the Ohio, Arkansas, Red, Yellowstone, and Nebraska, give to the interior an extensive inland navigation, and the facility of commu-

valuable timber still exist in the Eastern States, such as beach, birch, maple, oak, pine, spruce, elm, ash, walnut; and in the South live-oak, magnolia, palmetto, cypress, etc. Apples, pears and plums flourish in the North; peaches, melons and grapes in the Middle States; pineapples, pomegranates, figs, almonds and oranges in the South. Maize is grown from Maine to Louisiana, and wheat throughout the Union; tobacco as far North as Connecticut, and in the Western States south of Ohio. Very little cotton is raised north of 37 degrees, though it does grow as far north as 39. Rice is cultivated in South Carolina, Georgia, Louisiana, and as far north as St. Louis, Missouri. Sugar-cane grows as high as 33 degrees, but does not thoroughly succeed beyond 31. Vines and the mulberry grow in various parts of the Union; oats, rye, and barley throughout the North and the mountainous parts of the South; and hemp, flax and hops in the Western and Middle States.

The following are a few figures from the ninth census, 1870, giving some idea of the annual productions of agriculture: Spring wheat, 112,549,733 bushels; Winter wheat, 175,195,893 bushels; Indian corn, 760,944,549 bushels; rice, 73,635,021 pounds; tobacco, 262,735,341 pounds; cotton,

regions. Gold and silver exist in the States and Territories west of the Rocky Mountains in large quantities. Gold has also been found in Virginia, the Carolinas, Georgia and Tennessee. Quicksilver, zinc, manganese, with lime and building-stone, are the other chief mineral products. The value of such products (1870), in round numbers, is as follows: Anthracite coal, $39,000,000; bituminous coal, $35,000,000; copper, $5,000,000; gold, $10,000,000; quartz, gold and silver bearing, $17,000,000; iron ore, $13,000,000; lead, $736,000; petroleum, $20,000,000. The American manufacturing establishments of the Union in 1870 numbered 252,148, employing 2,053,996 hands; wages, $775,000,000; total products, $4,232,325,442. The growth of the railway system in the United States is from 23 miles in operation in 1830 to 72,623 miles in operation in 1874. The gross earnings in 1874 of these roads were about $520,000,000, the dividends paid, $67,000,000. The total length of the telegraph lines in January, 1875, were 75,000 miles; length of wires, 165,000 miles; number of offices, 6,172; number of messages transmitted during the year 1874, 13,700,000.

GREAT BRITAIN.

The area of Great Britain and Ireland is 78,411,520

NEW JERSEY.—THE NEW LINE TO PHILADELPHIA—THE BRIDGE OVER THE DELAWARE AT YARDLEYVILLE.

nication includes the entire continent The principal rivers flowing into the Atlantic are, the Hudson, Delaware, Susquehanna, Potomac, Savannah and St. Johns. Into the Pacific Ocean flow the Columbia, Sacramento and Colorado. The area of the water basins is as follows: Rivers flowing into the Pacific, 644,040 square miles; into the Atlantic, 488,877 square miles; into the Gulf of Mexico, 1,683,825 square miles, of which three-fourths are drained by the Mississippi and Missouri Rivers. The coast-line on both oceans is 13,200 miles in length, excluding the numerous bays and sounds; on the great northern lakes 3,600 miles Of course in a country extending through 24 degrees of latitude and nearly 60 of longitude, the climate varies considerably. In the north, along the British frontier, the Winters are very severe, and as far south as Pennsylvania and New Jersey the thermometer falls below zero. Yet in these latter States it rises in Summer to more than 100 degrees Fah., the mean annual temperature of Albany being 49 degrees, of Philadelphia 54, of Natchez 65, and of Florida 72. It is remarkable that the temperature along the Pacific is much higher than in corresponding latitudes of the eastern coast, that of Sitka ranging at times as high as at Charleston, South Carolina.

The Mississippi Valley is very fertile. Vast forests of

3,011,996 bales; Irish potatoes, 143,337,473 bushels; wine, 3,092,369 gallons; hay, 27,316,048 tons; wool, 100,102,387 pounds; and sugar from cane, 87,043 hogsheads. Of dairy products there are made in round numbers, 514,000,000 pounds of butter, and 53,000,000 pounds of cheese. The cash value of the farms in the United States in 1870 was $9,262,803,861. of farm implements and machinery, $336,878,429; of live-stock, $1,525,276,457; total estimated value of all farm productions, $2,447,538,658; the value of orchard products, $47,335,189; products of market-gardening, $26,719,229. There were at the same time (1870), 8,690,219 horses, 28,074,582 cattle, 28,477,951 sheep, and 25,187,540 hogs. Anthracite coal is found most extensively in Pennsylvania, also in Western Virginia, and in the eastern portion of Ohio and Illinois. The oil-wells of Pennsylvania contain inexhaustible stores of mineral oil or petroleum; salt-springs exist in New York, Virginia, Pennsylvania and the Western States; iron is found in the coal measures of Pennsylvania, Ohio, Virginia and Tennessee; iron ore also abounds in the Northwestern States; a large proportion of the ore found in the northeastern part of the United States is magnetic; lead is found in Missouri, Wisconsin and Illinois, and large deposits of copper in Michigan and the Lake Superior

acres. Except on the west and north, it is for the most part a level country, so cultivated as to be highly productive. In the other districts its mineral wealth in iron, tin, lead, copper and coal, makes abundant amends for their agricultural poverty. In the year 1874, the value of pig-iron raised in England was £16,476,372. The total value of the metals produced amounted to £20,000,000. The aggregate value of all the minerals and metals obtained in the United Kingdom in 1874 was £67,834,313. The climate of Great Britain is mild and equable in a remarkable degree. The Winters are considerably warmer and the Summers colder than in any other place of equal latitude. The mean temperature of England is 49.5 degrees. Very few species of plants or animals are peculiar to Great Britain. The flora resembles that of Germany. The soil of Great Britain is almost exclusively devoted to the production of bread-stuffs, and grass-roots, etc., as food for domestic animals. The total extent of the land returned in 1872 under all kinds of crops was 31,004,773 acres in Great Britain; 15,746,547 acres in Ireland; 88,573 acres in the Isle of Man, and including the Islands of Jersey, Guernsey, Alderney, etc., making the total of the United Kingdom 46,869,326 acres. The number of horses was 2,715,000; the total number of

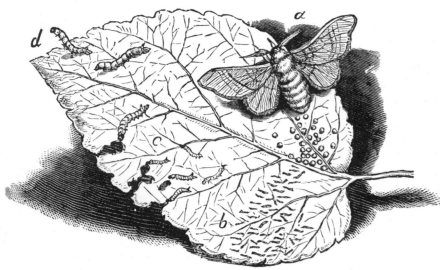

a. THE MOTH LAYING EGGS—LIFE-SIZE. b. SILKWORM ONE DAY OLD—LIFE-SIZE. c. SILK-
WORM THREE DAYS OLD—LIFE-SIZE. d. SILKWORM SEVEN DAYS OLD—LIFE-SIZE.

cattle was 9,718,000; sheep, 32,246,000; pigs, 4,178,000. In the textile industries in 1874, there were 7,294 factories, employing 1,006,675 hands. On the 1st of January, 1875, there were 16,448 miles of railway open in the United Kingdom. The total length of the postal telegraph wires at the end of 1874 was 107,000 miles.

NEW SOUTH WALES.

The total area of New South Wales is 206,999,680 acres. This colony extends over 11 degrees of latitude, and its climate is very various; in the northern districts, which are warmest, its tropical or Summer heat occasionally rising to 120 degrees. At Sydney, the mean temperature of the year is about 65 degrees. The Summer here lasts from the end of December to the first of February. Sometimes the rain almost fails for five or six months in succession; at other times it descends in continuous torrents, causing the rivers to rise to an extraordinary height. Cotton is produced as far south as latitude 32, beyond which the climate is more temperate, and is fit to produce all the grain products of Europe. Immense tracts of land, admirably adapted for agriculture, lie in the southwest, while in the north tobacco and sugar-cane are grown. Pine-apples, walnuts, lemons, citrons and other tropical fruits are also produced. In the cooler regions of the south peaches, apricots, oranges, grapes, pears, pomegranates and melons are grown in perfection, sometimes in such abundance that the pigs are fed with them. Wheat, barley and oats are also grown. In 1875 New South Wales had 22,872,882 sheep, 856,609 horned cattle, 346,691 horses, and 219,958 pigs. The total area of land under cultivation at that date embraced 469,957 acres. In 1874 there were twenty-eight coal mines working, the value of whose product was estimated at £786,152.

The gold mines of New South Wales cover a vast area. The gold export of 1873 was valued at £773,439 in gold-dust and bar, and £2,151,168 in gold coin. New South Wales possesses 436 miles of railway, and 8,000 miles of telegraph wires.

NEW ZEALAND.

The total area of the British colony of New Zealand is about 64,000,000 acres. It consists of three principal islands — North, South, and Stewart Islands, and several small islets, including Chatham Island and the Auckland Islands. The mountains are mostly covered with evergreen forests of luxuriant growth, and occasionally with treeless, grassy plains. Extensive and rich valleys and sheltered dales abound in the North Island and in the east of the South Island, and there are extensive plains adapted for agriculture and cattle-breeding. Water and water-power are found in great abundance in the colony. Its streams are short, and not navigable for more than 50 miles above their mouths. About one-fourth of the surface of New Zealand consists of dense forest tracts, one-half of excellent cultivable lands, and the remainder of waste lands and rugged mountain regions. The average temperature is remarkably even. January is the hottest month, and June the coldest. All the grains, grass, fruits and vegetables grown in England are cultivated in the colony with perfect success, while the vine is cultivated in the open air, and maize and sweet potatoes grow successfully in certain portions. The entire area under crop in February, 1875, was 1,788,800 acres in wheat, oats, barley, potatoes and grass. The live-stock of the colony consisted in 1874 of 99,859 horses, 494,917 cattle, 11,704,853 sheep, 123,921 pigs. In the year 1874 the value of the yield of gold was $7,526,655, the average yield of the gold-fields since 1862 having been about $11,000,000 per annum. The principal product of the colony is wool, the export of which in 1874 was valued at $14,173,475.

VICTORIA.

The British colony of Victoria comprises the southeast corner of Australia, where its territory projects furthest into the cool southern latitudes. The area of the colony is 56,446,720 acres. The climate is healthful and agreeable. The average temperature at Melbourne is 57.6 degrees—about the same as that of Marseilles, Nice, and Madrid. The usual Summer heat is from 65 to 80 degrees, although it occasionally rises higher. In 1875 there were 1,011,776 acres under crops of wheat, oats, barley, potatoes, hay and forage; the total number of horses was 180,254; milch cows, 241,137; horned cattle, 717,251; sheep, 11,221,236; pigs, 137,941. The manufactories of Victoria employed 25,000 persons, and the number at work in the gold-fields December 31, 1874, was 45,151. The total exports of wool in 1874 were valued at £6,373,641. The export of gold, exclusive of specie, was £4,053,288. Victoria had, in 1875, 457½ miles of railroad open for traffic, and 427 more in the course of construction. In 1874 there were 4,464 miles of telegraph wires.

SILKWORM SPINNING A COCOON.

SOUTH AUSTRALIA.

This colony embraces 25 degrees of latitude through the centre of the continent of Australia from the Southern to the Indian Ocean, and is bounded on the east by the colonies of Victoria, New South Wales, and Queensland, and on the west by the colony of Western Australia. Its area is 585,427,200 acres, being about one-third of the area of the United States of America. Its chief exports are wool, wheat, and copper. In 1875 these exports were valued at £4,442,100. The colony contains about 6,000,000 of sheep, 200,000 head of horned cattle, many thousands of horses, and a few hundred camels. In 1872 South Australia erected 1,973 miles of telegraph wire across her territory, and at the cost of £350,000 connected Australia with India and Europe.

QUEENSLAND.

This colony occupies the whole of the northeastern portion of Australia. Its entire area comprises 433,920,000 acres. Unlike almost every other portion of Australia, Queensland is correctly described as "a land of rivers and streams." These rivers find an outlet in the many large and beautiful bays and estuaries on the eastern seaboard. One of these, Moreton Bay, receives the waters of five rivers, which are always navigable. The longest tidal river in Queensland is the Fitzroy, which drains an area of not less than 50,000,000 of acres, and receives as tributaries several large streams flowing for hundreds of miles from the northwest, west, and southwestern parts of the interior. The banks of the rivers are usually well suited for cultivation, in many places consisting of very rich alluvium, brought down from the mountains. A great mountain range runs north and south, parallel to the sea-coast, at a distance from it of from 50 to 100 miles. Beyond this dividing range the country presents features of great beauty and fertility. Vast plains from 60 to 80

a. DOUBLE-LATTICE FRAME FOR THE WORMS TO SPIN UPON. b. CASE SHOWING PROGRESSIVE DAILY GROWTH OF WORMS.

MOTHS EMERGING FROM COCOONS.

COCOONS AND CHRYSALIS—NATURAL SIZE.

GLASS JARS OF COCOONS.

THE BRAZILIAN SILKWORM EXHIBIT IN MACHINERY HALL.

LOOSENING THE OUTER FIBRE OF THE COCOONS.

miles across stretch out. They are level and unbroken by a single tree, but covered with luxuriant grass. These are well watered with a network of streams, which trickle from the slopes of the mountain range. The soil of this locality is admirably adapted for tillage. The land is lightly timbered, is cleared with little labor, and is peculiarly adapted for a growth of wheat of the finest quality. The yield per acre has sometimes been as much as 50 and even 60 bushels to the acre, of 63 pounds to the bushel. Indian corn and other cereals, as well as all the European fruits, grow here luxuriantly. The climate of Queensland is said to closely resemble that of Madeira. The growth of cotton and of sugar has been attempted in recent years, and both industries are reported to be rapidly advancing. At the end of 1873 there were 9,663 acres under cotton, and 14,495 acres under sugar-cane, the entire acreage under cultivation being 64,218 acres. The live-stock at the end of 1873 numbered 99,243 horses, 1,343,093 cattle, and 42,884 pigs. It is estimated that there are at present about 17,000,000 sheep in the colony. The gold produce in 1873 was valued at £555,310. The principal articles of export of the colony are gold, wool, tin, ore, and raw cotton. At the end of 1873 there were 218 miles of railway open for traffic. There were also 3,609 miles of telegraph wires.

TASMANIA.

Tasmania, formerly known as Van Diemen's Land, is an island, 100 miles southeast of Australia. Its total area is 16,778,400 acres, the total area under cultivation being 326,486 acres. The most important articles of strictly agricultural produce is wheat, which is produced for the English market, and the export of this grain for the year 1874 was valued at about half a million of dollars. The number of horses in Tasmania in 1874 was 23,208, cattle 110,450, and sheep, 1,714,168. Most of the wool produced is merino. The export of this article during the year 1874 amounted to 5,050,920 pounds, representing the value of £350,713. The mining industry for many years was confined to gold and coal, but of late tin, iron, and salt have attracted attention. The principal timber trees of Tasmania are blue-gum, white-gum, swamp-gum, and peppermint-tree. Other useful woods are the acacia, blackwood, myrtle, sassafras, iron-wood, cherry, white-wood, pink-wood, and native pear. Bark is largely exported. Hops are also extensively cultivated. The principal animals are the kangaroo, wallaby, opossum, and bandicoot, the skins of which are all valuable for tanning purposes, the fur being highly esteemed as rugs, etc. The chief industries are brewing, milling, jam-making, tanning and coopering.

CAPE OF GOOD HOPE.

This colony lies south of the Orange Free States, from which it is divided by the Orange River. On the south it is bounded by the Indian Ocean, and on the west by the Atlantic. Its area is 128,670,000 acres. The mean temper-

ature of the year at Cape Town is about 68 degrees. Among the articles of export, wool is the most important, being valued at £3,600,000. Among the other leading articles of export are copper-ore, feathers, and sheepskins. The sheep-farms are of very great extent, and comprise each from 3,000 to 15,000 acres and upward. Those in tillage are comparatively small. The number of horses in the colony in 1875 was 207,318; draught oxen, 398,825; other cattle, 698,681; wooled sheep, 10,064,289; other sheep, 944,050; angora goats, 972,733; common goats, 2,122,808; pigs, 110,489; ostriches, 22,257.

CANADA.

The Dominion of Canada consists of the provinces of Ontario, Quebec, Nova Scotia, New Brunswick, Manitoba, British Columbia, and Prince Edward's Island. The entire area of the Dominion is 2,230,129,280 acres. The St. Lawrence River drains an area of 565,000 miles. The principal rivers are the Ottawa, about 450 miles long; the St. Lawrence, nearly 400 miles in length; and the Saguenay, 225 miles long. A great part of Canada, more especially along the Lake Superior shores, produces minerals, such as iron, zinc, lead, copper, silver, gold, cobalt, manganese, gypsum, granite, sand-stone, millstone, salt, and marbles of nearly every imaginable color. Considerable portions are heavily covered with timber, chiefly with pine, and are but little adapted for cultivation. The neighborhood of the Gulf of St. Lawrence is of importance for its yield of fish, the land being comparatively worthless. Thus the area for profitable production of ordinary cereals cannot materially exceed 25,000,000 acres. This cultivable track increases regularly in width and fertility from its commencement on the Lower St. Lawrence to the shores of Lake Huron. Below Quebec is seen the primeval forest,

SPINNING SILK THREAD.

The climate of Canada is subject to great extremes of heat and cold, the thermometer ranging between 102 deg. above and 36 below zero. The statistics of Canada which we employ refer only to the provinces of Ontario, Quebec, New Brunswick and Nova Scotia. In these provinces the yield of coal in 1871 was 671,000 tons; of iron ore, 129,000; of gold, 23,000 ounces; of silver, 70,000 ounces; of crude petroleum, 13,000,000 gallons — all in round numbers. The statistics of agriculture are as follows: Wheat, 17,000,000 bushels; oats, 42,000,000 bushels; hay, 3,818,000 tons; buckwheat, 3,800,000 bushels; corn, 3,800,000 bushels; potatoes, 48,000,000 bushels; turnips, 25,000,000 bushels. The principal items of fur are 500,000 muskrats, 150,000 minks, 50,000 beavers, 20,000 of moose, cariboo and deer, 18,000 martens, 37,000 seals, 13,000 foxes, 6,000 otters, and 2,500 bears. In manufactures the total value of the products was $221,617,773; the number of hands employed, 187,942; the amount of yearly wages, $40,851,009. The statistics of the fisheries are as follows: Vessels, 991; men, 6,984; boats, 16,876; men, 25,876; shoremen, 46,471. The leading items of the product of the fisheries were 682,631 quintals of cod, 120,213 quintals of haddock, 417,300 barrels of herring, 77,925 barrels of mackerel, 2,491 gallons of cod-liver oil, and 676,403 gallons of other fish-oils. The exports for 1874 amounted to $89,851,528, chiefly to the United States and Great Britain. At the end of 1874, Canada had 4,020 miles of railway, and 1,120 miles in course of construction.

FRANCE.

France Proper comprises 129,024,000 acres of land. Her foreign possessions, including Algeria, cover 296,850,280 acres. In the present sketch we shall confine ourselves to the Republic of France.

There are four great mountain-chains belonging to France—the Pyrenees, the Cevenno-Vosgian chain, the

REMOVING THE OUTER FIBRE.

Alps, and the Sardo-Corsican range. The grand watershed of France is the Cevenno-Vosgian chain, which determines the course of the four great rivers—the Seine, the Loire, the Garonne, and the Rhone. The entire extent of river navigation in France amounts to 5,500 miles, while the 99 larger canals extend over a course of 2,900 miles. France is peculiarly rich in mineral springs, of which there are said to be nearly 1,000 in use, and whose waters are an important element in the wealth of the country. Nearly fifty per cent. of the entire average of France is in arable land; four per cent. in vineyard; eighteen per cent. in meadow lands; and ten per cent. in cultivated lands.

France possesses one of the finest climates in Europe, though very considerable diversities of temperature are to be met with, ranging from an annual mean of 50 deg. at Dunkirk to 62 deg. at Toulon. The following are the statistics of agricultural production for 1869, in hectolitres of 2¾ bushels: Wheat, 108,000,000; rye, 24,000,000; barley and oats, 90,000,000; maize, 10,000,000; potatoes, 100,000,000. The production of beet-root sugar amounted in 1872–73 to 418,000 tons. The average yearly produce of the vineyards of France is estimated at about 1,000,000,000 of gallons, of which one-seventh is made into brandy.

The principal forest-trees are the chestnut and birch on the central mountains, the oak and cork-tree in the Pyrenees, and the fir in the Landes. About one-seventh of the entire territory of France is still covered with wood. Turf taken from the marshy lands is extensively used, more especially in the rural districts, for fuel.

According to the census of 1866—the most recent in regard to animals—there were in France 3,312,637 horses, 518,000 asses, 350,000 mules, 12,733,000 horned cattle, 36,386,000 sheep, 5,500,000 swine, and 1,680,000 goats. There were 3,000,000 beehives, valued at about $5,000,000. Poultry is estimated at $9,000,000, and the eggs and feathers at $7,000,000 annually.

The chief mineral products of France are coal and iron, and 250,000 men were employed in mining them in 1868. The yield of coal in 1868 was about 13,000,000 tons. During the same year there were about 150 iron mines in operation. Other metals are worked, but to little advantage. The annual produce of salt is about $1,250,000; and from its quarries of granite and free-stone, marbles, sands, lithographic-stones, millstones, etc., France derives about $8,000,000 annually. The value of the chief products of French industry is as follows (annual): Linen fabrics, $50,000,000; cotton fabrics, $130,000,000; woolen fabrics, $190,000,000; silk fabrics, $200,000,000; mixed fabrics, $60,000,000; jewelry, watchmaking, $7,000,000; gilt wares, $2,000,000; minerals, mines, salt, etc., $120,000,000; articles of food, as sugar, wines, etc., $73,000,000; skins, leather, oils, tobacco, $110,000,000; bone, ivory, isinglass, etc., $6,000,000; chemical products, $16,000,000; ceramic arts, $19,000,000; paper, printing, $12,000,000; forests,

GATHERING FIBRES INTO THREADS.

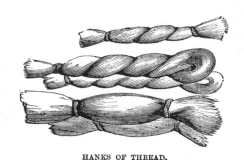

HANKS OF THREAD.

THE BRAZILIAN SILKWORM EXHIBIT IN MACHINERY HALL.

1, 3, Norge Costume.　2, 4, Wingaker Costume.　5. A Laplander.　6. Skone Costume.　7. Orsa Costume.　8. Swedish Costume.　9. The Infant's Death.

SWEDISH CHARACTER GROUPS IN THE MAIN BUILDING.

fisheries, $19,000,000. In 1874 there were 12,886 miles of railroad in operation in France, and about 75,000 miles of telegraph wire.

GERMANY.

The area of Germany is estimated at 133,120,000 acres. The country presents two very distinct physical formations—first a range of high table-land, occupying the centre and southern parts of the country, interspersed with numerous ranges and groups of mountains; and, second, a vast, sandy plain, which extends from the centre of the empire north to the German Ocean, and which includes about 62,000,000 acres of land. Germany is drained by the Danube, the Rhine, the Weser, the Elbe, the Oder, and the Vistula. Numerous lakes occur throughout the country, but none of great size, but the canals are both frequent and important. Mineral springs are common, and many of them very valuable. The climate of Germany is quite equable, the mean annual temperature varying only between 43 deg. at Königsberg, and 48 deg. at Frankfort-on-the-Main.

Germany is rich in mineral products, among which the most important are silver, iron, salt, and coal. The number

AUSTRO-HUNGARY.

The Empire of Austria and Kingdom of Hungary combined, and of which Francis Joseph I. is at once Emperor and King, occupy an area of 154,318,720 acres. Of this three-fourths are mountainous or hilly, being traversed by three mountain chains, viz.: the Alps, Carpathians, and Sudetes. The chief plains of the Austrian Empire are the great plains of Hungary—of which these in the eastern part are traversed by the Danube and the Theiss—and the plains of Galicia. The leading rivers having navigable tributaries are the Danube, the Vistula, the Elbe and the Dniester. The climate of Austria is generally favorable, but from the extent and diversity of surface it presents great varieties. In the warm southern regions, rice, olives, oranges and lemons ripen, and wine and maize are produced anywhere. In the middle temperate region the vine and maize thrive to perfection. In the northern portion grain, fruit, flax, and hemp are raised successfully. The mean temperature ranges between 44 deg. at Lemberg

magne, in which a crop of Winter wheat is followed by one of Summer grain, and that by fallow. In Hungary the Magyar adheres to his primitive husbandry; the German and Sclave are adopting improved methods. Rice is cultivated in the Bannat, but not enough for the consumption. Potatoes are raised everywhere, and in elevated districts are often the sole subsistence of the inhabitants. Horticulture is carried to great perfection, and the orchards of Bohemia, Austria Proper, Tyrol, and many parts of Hungary, produce a profusion of fruit. Great quantities of cider are made in Upper Austria and Carinthia, and of plum brandy in Sclavonia. In Dalmatia oranges and lemons are produced, but not sufficient for the requirements of the country; twice as much olive-oil is imported as is raised in the monarchy. In the production of wine Austria is second only to France. With the exception of Galicia, Silesia, and Upper Austria, the vine is cultivated in all the provinces; but Hungary stands first, yielding not only the finest quality of wine, but four-fifths the amount of the whole product of the empire. The average entire product of the empire is about 680,000,000 gallons. Flax is cultivated almost universally, and white hemp in a number of

THE VICTORIA COURT, IN THE BRITISH COLONIES DEPARTMENT, IN THE MAIN BUILDING.

of persons employed in mining operations in Germany in 1870 was 204,585; the yield of the different minerals was: Coal, 35,000,000 tons; iron ore, 3,000,000 tons; zinc, lead, and copper, 700,000 tons.

The value of the leading products of industries in metals was about $20,000,000.

The vegetable products of Germany include all the ordinary cereals, which are largely imported. Hemp and flax are also important products, while the vine is a still greater element of the wealth of the country, being cultivated chiefly in the districts watered by the Danube, Rhine, Main, Neckar, and Moselle rivers. The hops of Bavaria have a high reputation, and the chiccory grown in that country, and in the district between the Elbe and the Weser, finds its way all over Europe as a substitute for coffee. The average yield of the cereals is as follows: Rye, 250,000,000 bushels; oats, 240,000,000 bushels; wheat, 100,000,000 bushels; barley, 90,000,000 bushels. The average potato crop amounts to 90,000,000 bushels; beets, 3,000,000 tons; tobacco, 35,000 tons.

According to the last enumeration in Germany of live stock, there were 3,500,000 horses, 15,000,000 cattle, 30,000,000 sheep, 8,000,000 swine, and 2,000,000 goats. The wool crop for 1869 amounted to 27,500 tons. The

in Galicia, and 58 deg. at Trieste. In its raw products Austria is one of the most favored countries of Europe, and its mineral wealth is not surpassed by any other European country: it is only recently that Russia has exceeded it in the production of gold and silver. Except platina, none of the useful metals are wanting. Gold is found chiefly in Hungary and Transylvania; quicksilver in Idria, Hungary, Styria, etc.; tin in Bohemia alone, copper in many districts, zinc in Cracow and Carinthia, lead in Carinthia, iron in almost every province of the empire. Of metals and minerals there were produced in Austria in 1867: Coal, 108,000,000 cwt.; iron, 5,000,000 cwt.; copper, 47,000 cwt., etc. Many gems are found in various parts of the empire, including the opal, garnet, carnelian, agate, beryl, jasper, ruby, sapphire, topaz, etc.

The annual product of rock-salt is above 3,000,000 cwt., and that from salt springs as about as much more. Sixteen hundred mineral springs are enumerated, some of them of European reputation. The vegetable productions are exceedingly various. Grain of all kinds is cultivated most abundantly in Hungary, Bohemia, Moravia, Silesia and Galicia. Agriculture is not, however, as yet far advanced; the prevailing system is still what is called the three-field system introduced into Germany by Charle-

districts. Tobacco is raised in great quantities, particularly in Hungary. Bohemia raises hops of the first quality, and the indigo plant has been lately cultivated successfully in Dalmatia. Austria produces about a quarter of a million of silk cocoons annually. The silk trade is very extensive in the Tyrol.

In 1851 the number of horses in Austria was estimated at 3,300,000; cattle, 10,410,484; sheep, 16,801,545; goats, 2,275,000; and swine, 7,401,300. Nearly three-fourths of the population are engaged in husbandry. The cotton industry in Austria has risen greatly in value of late; the annual value of the silk industry is about 60,000,000 florins; the manufacture of tobacco is a state monopoly, producing a revenue of 58,126,000 florins per annum: the salt monopoly secures about 19,000,000 florins. The length of railways in Austria at the end of 1875 was about 10,000 miles; that of telegraph wires in 1874, 77,502 miles.

NETHERLANDS.

The Kingdom of the Netherlands has an area of 8,721,280 acres. The land is generally low, much of it being under the level of the sea, rivers and canals, especially in North and South Holland, Zealand, the southern part of Guelderland and Friesland. Along the west coast

HENRY PETTIT.

the lowlands are protected from the sea by a line of sand-hills or *dunes*, and where that natural defense is wanting, strong dikes have been constructed to keep back the waters, and these are maintained at great expense, under the direction of special engineers who have charge of them. A hilly district stretches from Prussia through the eastern part of Utrecht into the country between the Maas and the Waal. This tract is of a light sandy soil, and well watered.

The greater portion of the north is very fertile, the lowlands and Zealand being adapted for pasture and cattle, and the light soil for cereals and fruits.

The chief rivers are the Rhine, Maas and Scheldt, which have also important branches. Waterways are more numerous than in any other European country, the immense tracts of meadow land being girdled by large canals and cut in all directions by smaller ones for drainage and communication.

The climate of the Netherlands is variable, chilly cold often succeeding high temperature, inducing various forms of fever and agues In Summer the thermometer sometimes rises above 80 deg., and even to 90 deg., in the shade, and a Winter of great severity usually occurs every five years.

The farms are generally small and well cultivated. The leading agricultural products of Zealand are wheat and madder. In South Holland madder, hemp, butter, and cheese. In North Holland butter and cheese are extensively made, and cattle, sheep and pigs reared and exported. The horses of certain districts are of first-rate quality Fruit is abundant, and in several provinces much attention is paid to bees. In Haarlem tulips and hyacinths are much cultivated, realizing a large annual amount.

Game is plentiful, and forms an article of export, including deer, pheasants, partridges, wild ducks, snipe, plover and hare.

The chief manufactures are linen, woolen, cotton and silk fabrics, paper, leather, glass, etc. Leyden and Tilburg are famed for woolen blankets, wool-dyed pilot, fine cloths and friezes. Linens and rich damasks are the specialty of one district, and calicoes, shirtings, drills and table-cloths of others. Good imitation Smyrna and Scotch carpets,

and carpets of hair and wool, are manufactured ; also yarns, dyed silks and silk stuffs, leather, glass and firearms. Sugar-refining is largely carried on at Amsterdam, Rotterdam and Dordrecht, from all of which places it is exported to Russia, the Levant and other countries of Europe. The chief motive power is the windmill, which forms a never-failing element in the scenery, though of late years steam is becoming more general.

Fishing in inland waters, and also on the coast of Scotland, is vigorously pursued. In 1872, 108 vessels were employed in the herring fishery in the North Sea, and the take was valued at about $400,000, that on the Netherland coast at $250,000, while in the Zuyder-Zee, additional, about 180,000,000 herrings were taken. The anchovy take, almost exclusively in the Zuyder-Zee, amounted to about $900,000.

At the beginning of the year 1875 there were 1,200 miles of railway open for traffic, the length of telegraph wires at the same time being about 10,000 miles.

DENMARK.

The area of Denmark is 9,313,920 acres. The chief pursuits are agriculture, cattle-breeding, navigation and fishing, about one-fourth of the population being engaged in these industries. The annual yield of grain may be calculated at about 100,000,000 bushels, besides 200 barrels of potatoes, beans, etc. About three-fourths of the whole country is under cultivation.

The raising of horses and cattle is quite an important industry. The statistics of live stock are, in round numbers, as follows : Horses, 300,000 ; cattle, 1,250,000; sheep, 1,900,000 ; hogs, 450,000.

The exports consist mainly of grain, flour, horses, cattle,

CHARLES B. NORTON.

hogs, pork, butter, wools, hides and skins, brandy, train oil, etc. There are large mills, sugar refineries, iron foundries, machine-shops, distilleries, tanneries, etc., and flour-mills can be found in all sections of the country.

The length of railways in the kingdom at the end of 1874 was about 800 miles, and of telegraph wires about 6,000.

FRANCIS WALKER.

Cattegat, the Skager-rack, the North Sea, the Atlantic and Arctic Oceans, and thus completely separated from the mainland, with the exception of the northeastern part. The entire peninsula embraces an area of 188,160,000 acres.

Sweden is generally less mountainous than Norway, about 8 per cent. of its area being considered to lie upwards of 2,000 feet above the level of the sea. Of the entire area of the kingdom, a third part does not lie 300 feet above the level of the sea, and it is within the low-lying districts that the cultivated parts of the country are found, as well as the largest plains.

Next to Finland, Sweden is the best irrigated country in Europe, as here lakes and rivers cover an area of 14,428 English square miles, with a seacoast of 1,500 English miles.

The climate of Sweden is mild in comparison to its high latitude, an effect attributed to the influence of the Gulf Stream. There are dense forests, and barley and rye mature in the province of Nordland, while its most southern part lies in the same latitude as the highest fields of Greenland, and its northern in that of barren Iceland. The variation of the mean annual temperature of the entire kingdom is between 34 and 46 degs. The farmer's worst enemy is the frost, which in a single clear night, perhaps after a warm Summer day, will destroy his brightest prospects ; but it is hoped that the increase of tillage and drainage will mitigate its severity, if not prevent it. They are very rare in the central and southern parts of Sweden.

Mining is one of the most important departments of Swedish industry, and the working of the iron mines in particular is making constant progress by the introduction of new machinery.

In 1873 there were raised about 20,000,000 cwt. of iron ore, and the manufactured steel amounted to 1,290,907 cwt. There were also raised 1,660 lbs. of silver, 26,152 cwt. of copper, and 645,631 cwt. of zinc ore. There are large veins of coal in various parts of Sweden, but no systematic working of them has yet taken place.

The principal articles of cultivation are, in addition to the various cereals, potatoes, hemp, flax, tobacco and hops, which are generally grown in sufficient quantities for home consumption.

The forests are of great extent, covering nearly one-

BURNET LANDRETH.

SWEDEN.

Sweden and Norway, united under one king, form the Scandinavian country, whose shores are washed by the waters of the Gulf of Bothnia, the Baltic, the Sound, the

CHARLES H. MILLER.

DOLPHUS TORREY.

THE CHIEFS OF THE EXECUTIVE BUREAUX OF THE CENTENNIAL EXPOSITION.

fourth of the whole surface, the birch, fir, pine and beech being of great importance, not only for the timber, tar and pitch which they yield, but also for their supply of charcoal and fire-wood. The common fruit-trees—apple and pear—grow as far north as 60 deg.

Cranberries and other berries abound in all parts of the country.

In 1870 there were in Sweden 428,446 horses, 1,965,800 horned cattle, 1,780,000 sheep and goats, and 354,303 swine.

At the end of September, 1875, the total length of railways open for traffic was 2,237 English miles. All the telegraphs, with the exception of those of private companies, belong to the State, the total length being 10,980 English miles.

NORWAY.

The area of Norway and Sweden is about equally divided, that of Norway comprising 77,938,560 acres. Only 1 6-10 per cent. of the whole area can be cultivated, natural pastures occupying about 1 5-10 per cent., forests about 20 2-10 per cent., mountains, glaciers, lakes, rivers, etc., about 76 7-10 per cent. The whole of the Peninsula consists of a connected mountain mass, which, in the southern and western parts of Norway, constitutes a continuous tract of rocky highlands, with steep declivities dipping into the sea, and here and there broken by narrow tracts of arable land.

The peculiar physical character of Norway necessarily gives rise to great varieties of climate. The influence of the sea and the Gulf Stream, and the penetration into the interior of deep inlets, greatly modify the severity of the climate of the western shores. In Norway Proper, the Winters, as a rule, are long and cold, and the Summers, which rapidly follow the melting of the snows in the months of April and May, are warm and pleasant.

The principal cereals cultivated are oats, barley, corn, rye and wheat. The yearly produce is about 11,160,000 bushels, besides 14,100,000 barrels of potatoes. The value of the harvest amounts to about $16,000,000 per annum. The products of agriculture and cattle-breeding being insufficient to supply the wants of the country, considerable quantities of them are imported.

The forests cover more than one-fifth of the area. They supply considerable quantities of timber, the average annual exports of these being about $16,000,000.

The fisheries of Norway employ about 27,000 men, and yield about $16,000,000 per annum. They are of great importance, and not only yield one of the most valuable articles of home consumption, but, at the same time, prove one of the most profitable sources of foreign exportation. Fish are caught in almost every stream and lake of the interior, as well as in the *fjords* of the coast, and in the bays and channels which encircle the numerous islands about the long sea line of Norway. These fish are principally cod and herring. Codfish and dried salt-fish are exported to Spain and Italy, herrings to the Baltic ports.

The principal articles of exports were, in 1873: the products of the fisheries, $11,600,000; of forestry, $15,800,000; of agriculture and cattle-breeding, $1,300,000; metals and minerals, $1,800,000.

Norway had, in 1875, 150,000 horses, 950,000 oxen and cows, 1,710,000 sheep and goats, 110,000 pigs, and 102,000 reindeer. The value of the annual product is about $25,000,000.

Norway has 304 miles of railways, and 147 miles of canals.

ITALY.

The superficial area of Italy is 72,113,280 acres, of which 57,542,740 acres are productive soil. The physical aspect presented by the surface is diversified in the extreme. Northern Italy is, for the most part, composed of one great plain—the basin of the Po, comprising all Lombardy and a considerable portion of Piedmont and Venice,

bounded on the northwest and partly on the south by different Alpine branches.

Throughout Central Italy the great Apennine chain gives a picturesque irregularity to the country, in the highland districts of

THE CARPET-BAG BATH-TUB, IN THE MAIN BUILDING.

EXHIBIT OF PARLOR ORGANS BY GEORGE WOODS & CO., CAMBRIDGEPORT, MASS., IN THE MAIN BUILDING.

Naples reaching an appearance of savage grandeur. Along the extensive coast-plains, as well as in the sub-Apennine valleys, a brilliant flora and vegetation impart a noble character of beauty to the scenery. The great plains of Italy are those of Lombardy, of Piedmont, the Venetian Plains, the plain of the Roman Legations, the plain of the Campo Felice, on which stands Vesuvius, the Apulian Plain, and the long, narrow Neapolitan Plain 100

"OLD ABE," THE WISCONSIN WAR EAGLE.

miles in length and 24 in breadth, stretching along the Gulf of Torrente.

The great majority of the rivers of Italy are only navigable for small-boats or barges. By far the most important is the Po, which rises on the borders of France, flows into the Adriatic, and has numerous tributaries.

The canal system of Italy is most extensive in the north. Nine principal canals in Lombardy administer to the irrigation of the plains and to the purposes of commercial communication, contributing in no small degree to the prosperity of the district. Venice comprises 203 navigable and 40 minor canals. Piedmont is intersected by 253 canals, extending over a length of about 1,000 miles. This system of water-communication was early carried to a high degree of efficiency in Italy, and is of incalculable service in the agricultural districts.

The mineral and thermal springs of Italy are innumer-

able, and possess a great variety of curative and sanitary properties.

In the northern provinces the climate is temperate, salubrious, and frequently severe in Winters. In the centre it assumes a more genial and sunny character, while the heat of the southern extremity is almost of a tropical intensity. The drawbacks of Italy's climate are the *tramontana* or mountain wind; the deadly *sirocco*, which blights all nature at seasons along the western coast; and the malaria or noxious miasmata which issues from the *maremma* of Tuscany, the pontine marshes of the Venetian lagoons, generating pestilential fevers and aguish diseases in the Summer season. The mean annual temperature of the country ranges between 55 at Milan and 60 at Sardinia.

Staple products of Italy are corn, wine, raw silk, rice, olives and fruits. Hemp, flax and cotton are also largely grown. The sugar-cane is successfully cultivated in the two Sicilies. Agriculture, except in the north, is in a very backward condition. It is calculated that only two-thirds of the area of the kingdom capable of production are cultivated, and that the rest lies waste. Of lands capable of cultivation, more than half is devoted to the cultivation of cereals, mainly wheat. The average crop is insufficient for the supply of the country.

As to the wines of Italy, those of Naples are esteemed the best. Small quantities of the famous *Lachrymœ Christi* are exported, while the Sicilian wines of Marsala form a considerable item of export.

The best oil and olives are furnished by Tuscany, Lucca and Naples.

Silk is chiefly manufactured in the northern provinces, the cultivation of the mulberry and the rearing of the silkworm forming in Lombardy the main industry. Oranges, lemons, almonds, figs, dates, melons and the *pistachio* are grown and largely exported. The sea and fresh-water fisheries are considerable. The Mediterranean furnishes immense quantities of tunny-fish, anchovies, sardines and mackerel.

The total length of railways open for traffic in 1874 was 4,607 English miles. The length of telegraph lines was 12,622 English miles.

JAPAN.

Japan Proper comprehends four large islands, viz.: Niphon (the Japanese mainland), Sikok, Kiusiu and Yesso. The empire, however, includes about 3,800 small islands and islets, besides four larger ones. These islands appear to be of volcanic origin, that part of the Pacific on which they rest being affected by volcanic action, earthquakes occurring very frequently in Japan, although certain parts of the country are exempt. Japan has been called the "Land of Mountains"; but although these are very numerous, and many volcanic, they are of moderate elevation, and rarely attain the limits of perpetual snow. The country generally is of moderate elevation, with fertile valleys, picturesque landscapes, and a coast indented with magnificent and commodious harbors.

The soil is productive, rich in mineral wealth, and teeming with every variety of agricultural produce.

June, July and August are the months of rain in Japan, this sometimes descending in torrents. The months of October and November are pleasant and genial. The Summers are very hot, and the Winters in the northern parts extremely cold, the thermometer rising to 96 in the shade in the former, and sinking to 18 below in the latter season. Hurricanes and waterspouts are frequent, and about the change of the monsoons, typhoons and equinoctial gales frequently sweep the seas.

The country is rich in minerals, gold, silver, iron, sulphur, and especially copper, abounding. There are also large quantities of coal.

Amongst the most remarkable of the vegetable production is the camphor-tree, the varnish or lacquer, the paper mulberry-tree, the vegetable wax-tree, the tea-shrub, the tobacco-plant and the rice-plant. The principal manufactures are those of silk and cotton.

The first line of railway, from Yokohama to Yeddo, 17 miles long, was open for traffic on the 12th of June, 1875. Since that time 20 more miles of road have been opened, and 27

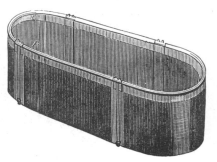

THE CARPET-BAG BATH-TUB, IN THE MAIN BUILDING.

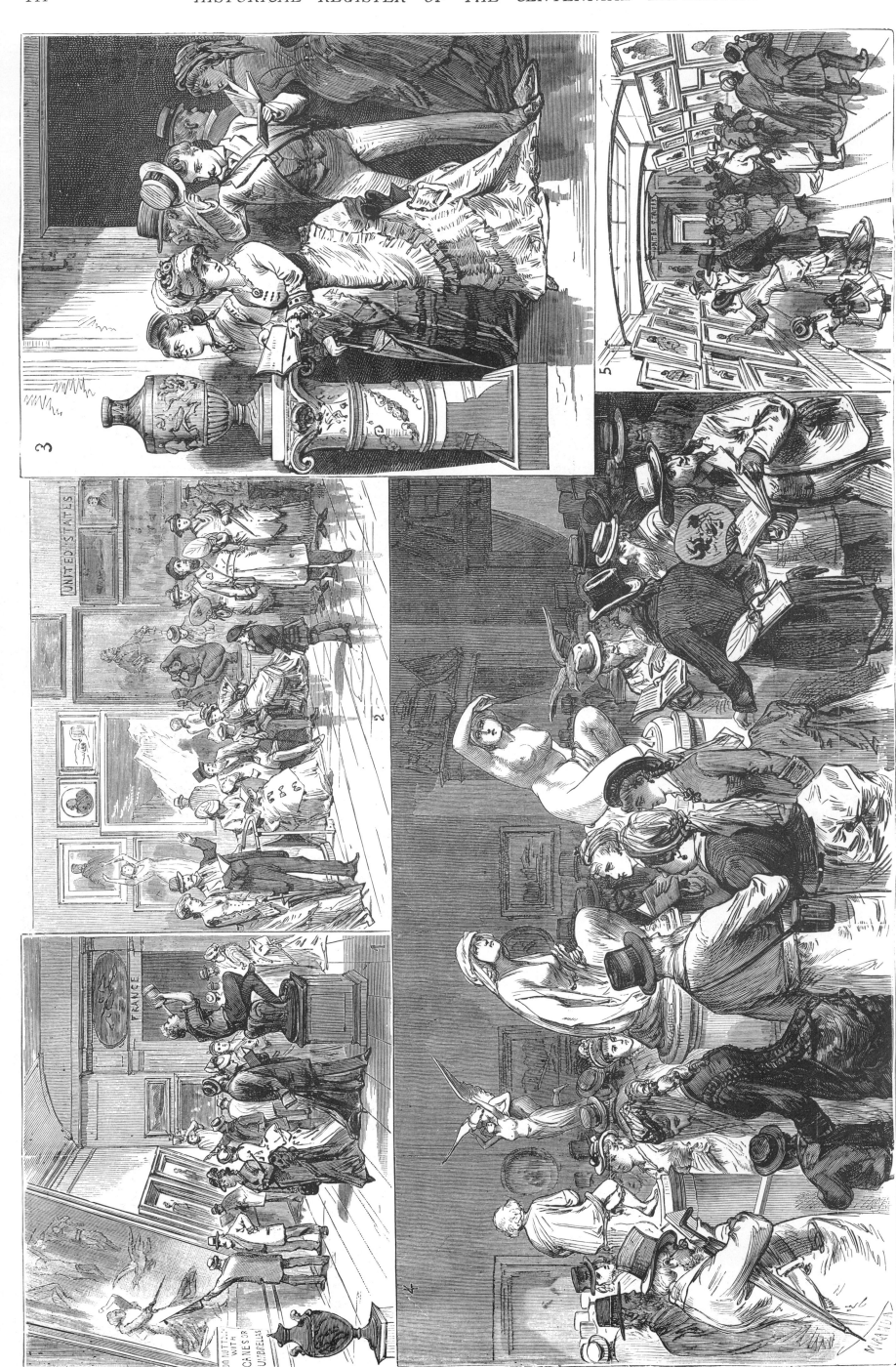

1. The French Gallery.   2. The United States Gallery.   3. Visitors Taking Notes.   4. Italian Sculpture.   5. The Corridor of the Annex.

CHARACTER SKETCHES IN MEMORIAL HALL AND THE ANNEX.

1. Cossack at Close Quarters.   2. After the Fight.   3. The Skirmisher.   4. Attacked by Wolves.   5. The Falconer.   6. The Jealous Foal.

THE RUSSIAN BRONZES IN THE MAIN BUILDING.

FRANK LESLIE'S PAVILION ON THE LAKE.

are in process of construction. The length of telegraph lines open or in construction was 1,755 miles in 1873, and 3,516 in 1874.

BRAZIL.

The area of Brazil is 1,984,000,000 acres, while her coast line is nearly 4,000 miles in length. Much of the territory inland is covered with mountains. The country is watered by a number of rivers, particularly in the north and south. The Amazon, Rio Negro and Madeira are the principal of these.

The soil is varied, and it is rich with productions of all kinds. Its arborial vegetation, in particular, surpasses that of the rest of the world. In 1867 there were exhibited in the Paris Exposition 400 specimens of different kinds of wood from Brazil; and Agassiz related that he saw 117 different kinds of wood, all valuable, from a piece of land not half a mile square. There are nearly 400 species of palm alone, all valuable, and some necessary to the existence of the natives. The Indians obtain from them food, drink, raiment, buildings, hammocks, cordage, cooking utensils, tools, fishing tackle, hunting implements and medicines.

Countless herds of wild cattle range the meadow land of the southern provinces, while horses, asses, sheep and cattle multiply rapidly.

The valuable products include in the north coffee, cotton, cocoa, cautchouc, sugar and tobacco; in the south hides, tallow, horn, etc.; and from the middle districts drugs, diamonds, gold-dust, dyes, rice, manioc, tapioca, spirits and rose-wood. Their total value in the three years from 1870 to 1872 average £34,000,000 per annum. Besides these products, the wine and olive are cultivated to a limited extent in the southern provinces. Rice is an important article of cultivation in several provinces, and is easily raised anywhere in the empire. In 1871 the value of the cotton exported was $24,000,000. Four-fifths of the coffee used in the United States, and more than one-half of that in the entire world, comes from Brazil. Bahia and Pernambuco are the great cane-growing provinces, and sugar-refining is carried on extensively there. In 1870 and 1871 the quantity of sugar shipped from Pernambuco amounted to over a million tons.

The best land in Brazil, especially that used for cotton culture, is very costly, and growing dearer every day. The difficulty of communication is a chief reason why thousands of square miles of the richest soil have continued for ages to remain unexplored and uncultivated.

The scarcity of labor in Brazil is severely felt, and inter-

feres with the production of its most important staples. It is believed that with a sufficient labor system cotton could be produced in Brazil in successful competition with the whole world.

The tea plant of China has been introduced, but hitherto with indifferent success.

The empire possessed, at the end of 1873, railways of the total length of 714 English miles open for traffic. There were others of an aggregate length of 397 miles in course of construction at the end of June, 1874. At the beginning of the year 1874 the telegraph lines extended to the length of 3,375 miles.

ARGENTINE REPUBLIC.

This Confederation, formed by a federal union of fourteen Provinces and three large Territories, covers an almost unbroken plain with an area of 768,000,000 acres. The chief exports are wool, hides, salt beef and tallow. Its resources embrace all products of the tropical and temperate zones, as may be seen by the description of its exhibits.

The farming stock of the republic is estimated at about 15,000,000 horned cattle, 4,000,000 horses and 80,000,000 sheep, whose aggregate value cannot fall much short of $200,000,000 gold, yielding about $50,000,000 export produced per annum.

At the end of the year 1873 there were 664 miles of railway open for traffic and 642 miles in course of construction, these being mainly at the expense of the State. There were, besides, at the end of 1873, railways of a total length of 1,997 miles sanctioned by the Government, including an international line from Buenos Ayres to Chili, of 894 miles. At the end of September 1873, the total length of telegraph wires in the republic was 8,267 miles.

LIBERIA.

The Republic of Liberia, which makes quite an enterprising display in the Agricultural Building, is situated on the west coast of Africa, and extends along 520 miles of the coast. An English colony is on the Sierra Leone, at the mouth of the San Pedro, while its most interior settlement is thirty miles from the seaboard.

All tropical productions are raised in Liberia, many of them the entire year, being dug every month for use. The lima-bean and egg-plant are indigenous, and of several varieties. Fruits grow in a wild state and under cultivation. Oranges are especially fine. Nowhere is a better quality of sugar-cane produced, and Liberian coffee is said to be the richest known, always commanding the highest market price. Ginger, ground-nuts, pepper and indigo are

mainly raised by the settlers. Palm-oil is made by the natives; ivory, cam-wood, gums and hides are valuable articles for exportation from Liberia.

The climate is uniformly sultry and moist, and the heat is not excessive, the thermometer ranging between 71 and 82 deg. as the highest points.

The manufacture of palm-oil, soap and indigo has only recently been commenced in Liberia, and the introduction of improved and patented machinery, and that of a steamer on the St. Paul's River, have stimulated both the production and transportation of articles for export.

SPAIN.

The Kingdom of Spain occupies an area of 125,459,840 acres, including the Balearic and the Canary Islands. An immense plateau occupies the central regions of Spain, rising to the height of 2,000 to 3,000 feet, and comprising upward of 90,000 square miles, or about half the entire area of the country. Numerous ranges of mountains, including the Pyrenees, the Sierra Morena, the Sierra Nevada, and others, break the country in different directions.

The climate, owing to the superficial configuration, is exceedingly varied. In the northwest provinces it is damp and rainy during the greater part of the year. At Madrid Winters occur of great severity, while the south and east provinces are warm in Winter and exposed to almost tropical heat in Summer.

The vast mountains of the country, affording for the most part only scanty crops of herbage, are utilized as pasture grounds, and divided into large farms; but in the warm plains, especially where water is abundant, the farms are smaller.

A great advance has been made in the department of the agricultural and mineral resources of Spain within the last ten years, and chiefly in mining. Lead, copper and tin are abundant; there are large deposits of good coal and iron ore. The quicksilver mines of Almaden have been long celebrated and are still worked.

The principal exports are wine, dried fruits, flour, green fruits, olive oil, wool, grain, cork, seeds and salt.

The length of railways in operation in January, 1875, was 3,810 English miles, and 1,264 miles in course of construction. The length of telegraph wire on the 1st of January, 1875 was 16,950 miles.

PORTUGAL.

The area of Portugal, including its insular appendages, is 23,906,400 acres. Its principal mountain ranges and rivers are, with few exceptions, mere western prolongations of those of Spain. The valleys are very numerous, and by their great fruitfulness present a great contrast to the barren and rugged mountains which inclose them. The largest rivers are the Guadiana, the Minho and Douro, the Tagus and the Mondego.

Portugal has salt marshes on the coast, whence large quantities of salt are annually obtained by evaporation. Mineral springs are abundant in many parts of the country, but hitherto these have been almost deserted.

The diversified conditions of the surface of the country produce corresponding diversities of climate, so that while snow falls abundantly on the mountains, it is never seen in southern districts, where Spring comes with the New Year, and harvest is over by mid-summer. Rain falls abundantly, especially on the coast, from October to March, and, as a general rule, the climate is healthy in the elevated districts of the southern provinces, but malaria and fevers prevail in low flat lands and near the salt marshes. The mean annual temperature at Lisbon is 61 degrees.

The natural products correspond to the diversity of the physical and climatic conditions; for while barley, oats and wheat, maize, flax and hemp are grown in the more elevated tracts, rice is cultivated in the low lands, the oak in the northern, the chestnut in the central, and the cork, date and American aloe in the southern parts; while every species of European and various kinds of semi-tropical fruits and vegetables are grown in different parts of the country. The soil is generally rich, but agriculture is nearly everywhere neglected, being scarcely made subservient to the wants of the population.

The cultivation of the vine and the olive are almost the sole branches of industry. From the former is derived the rich red wine familiarly known as port, from its being shipped at Oporto, "the port."

The mineral products include gold, antimony, lead, copper, marble, slate, coal, iron and salt.

The total length of railways in Portugal at the commencement of 1875 was 523 English miles. There were in 1872, 1,944 miles of telegraph wires.

RUSSIA.

The Empire of Russia, extending over a large portion of the northern regions of the globe, includes 5,068,800,000 acres. European Russia consists of a vast plain bordered with mountains. The districts in the southwest of Russia, between the Vistula and the Pruth, are covered by hilly ranges from the Carpathian Mountains. The plain of

European Russia naturally divides itself into three tracts or zones, each of which differs from the others in the nature and quality of its soil. The northern zone extends between the Arctic Ocean and the Ural Baltic table-land; the middle zone between the Ural Baltic and the Ural Carpathian table-land; and the southern between the Ural Carpathian table-land and the Black and Caspian Seas.

The soil of the northern zone is marshy, and the climate inclement. In the middle part of the middle zone the soil is partly heavy, covered with mold, and toward the north sandy. Beyond the Oka luxuriant meadows abound, and on the east beyond the Volga, this tract forms an extensive valley, covered with a thick layer of mold and abundance of woods. The southern zone consists of steppes extending along the shores of the Black and Caspian Seas.

The mean temperature varies between 32 and 58 deg. The climate is in general healthy.

Russia is an eminently agricultural country, although only a comparatively small portion is under cultivation. The system of husbandry in practice is what has already been described as the three-fallow system. In the south and southeast, however, a system of agriculture peculiar in Russia is in operation, called the fallow system, which consists in raising three or four consecutive crops on the same land, and afterward allowing it to lie fallow for five or six years, after which it begins to grow feather-grass, which is considered a token of returning fertility. The chief cereals are wheat, barley and oats. Buckwheat and rye are grown in the south, and from these—especially from rye—the staple food of the inhabitants is made. Hemp and flax are extensively cultivated, and the oil extracted from the seeds of the former is an indispensable article of the peasant's household, being used for food during the fasts, which extend over about half the year. Tobacco crops cover about 16,000 acres. Beet root and maize are also cultivated, and there are numerous vineyards in the Crimea, Bessarabia and along the Don. An area of 486,000,000 acres is covered with woods. Timber is the chief article of internal commerce, and is floated down the rivers from the well-wooded districts to those which are destitute of wood.

There are about 30,000,000 head of cattle in Russia, 18,000,000 horses, 10,000,000 sheep, of which upward of 1,000,000 are of the fine merino. Besides these animals, there are camels in the south of Russia, reindeer in the north, and hogs and poultry are everywhere abundant.

The fisheries of the Caspian and Black Seas and the Sea of Azov and their tributaries are important. The herrings,

codfish and salmon, caught in abundance in the White Sea, constitute the chief resources of the inhabitants of the adjoining districts.

Bee culture is very general in Russia. Silkworms are reared chiefly in the Caucasus.

The total length of railways at the end of the year 1874 was 13,227 English miles. The length of telegraph wires was 58,675 miles.

AMERICAN RAILROAD FREIGHT BUILDING.

NORTH of the Avenue of the Republic, and east of Photograph Hall, stands a building in which is fully illustrated the American system of fast freight lines. It is in a retired situation, hedged around by the wire fences of the narrow-gauge railroad, and therefore escapes the notice of many visitors, but it contains one of the most interesting exhibits on the grounds. The building is 45 ft. long by 22 ft. wide, with two wings, each 12 ft. long and 10 ft. wide. It is filled with models giving an excellent idea of the mode of obtaining and shipping petroleum, and of transporting and handling grain and other freights.

The building has the general appearance of an ordinary railroad freight-depot—in miniature, of course, when compared with the mammoth edifices of our giant railroad corporations, but still retaining that look of practicability and substantiality which characterizes such structures. Much of the material employed in the building will hereafter be used in car-construction.

In the centre of the building a shelf or counter extends entirely around the walls, on which the ingenious models are arranged. On the counter lines of railroad-tracks are laid, over which run miniature cars and engines, fully illustrating the methods of boarding, unloading, weighing and transporting freights.

The Empire Transportation Company's grain-elevator at Erie, Pennsylvania, is represented by a working model that stands in the northeastern corner of the building. This model is about 6 ft. long, 6 ft. high, and 4 ft. deep. The company owns large elevators at Erie, the largest of which has a capacity of 250,000 bushels in 47 bins, and a transfer capacity of 100,000 bushels in each 24 hours. The one taken as a model has an aggregate storage capacity of 100,000 bushels of grain in 31 separate bins, and a transfer capacity of 75,000 bushels. A 9 ft. long representation of the lake propeller *Japan*, which is an iron screw steamer of 1,429 tons freight capacity, and accommodations for 150

1. General Hawley Receiving Governor Bedle. 2. Mr. Browning's Oration. 3. Governor Bedle's Speech in the New Jersey Building.

"NEW JERSEY DAY," AUGUST 24TH.

THE SCHUYLKILL RIVER RACECOURSE, SELECTED FOR THE INTERNATIONAL ROWING MATCHES.

THE FIRST HEAT OF SINGLES.—THE START.—P. C. ACKERMAN, ATALANTA, N. Y.; R. H. ROBINSON, UNION SPRINGS, N. Y.; C. P. TASKER, CRESCENT, PHILADELPHIA.

first-class and 500 immigrant passengers, can be seen at the wharf of the model elevator. From the hold of the vessel the little elevator lifts its cargo of flaxseed (representing wheat), and transfers it into the freight-cars on the track alongside. Near by is a Fairbank's railroad scale, on which the cars are weighed before and after being loaded. Further along the track is also a working model of a railroad track scale, with a "dead-rail" running over it continually without affecting the running portions. At the other end of the counter is shown the method of transporting, handling and storing grain at tide-water. Here is a model of the Pennsylvania Railroad Company's freight-depot at Pier 38, North River, New York. Barges for transferring trains of freight-cars, the wharves, buildings for storage, and appliances for handling grain, are all represented.

In the east wing of the building are models showing the method of obtaining and shipping petroleum. The oil is pumped from the well into wooden tanks, from which it is pumped or allowed to flow into large storage tanks situated at points conveniently situated for collecting the oil from a number of wells. From these tanks pumps force the oil through "pipe-line" to iron tanks, on the line of the railroad. These tanks are raised a sufficient distance above the level of the track to permit the oil to run from them into iron cars. The model tank cars are beautifully nickel-plated. The originals consist of a wrought-iron boiler on trucks, each having a capacity of 3,600 gallons. The boiler is fitted with a man-hole, expansion dome, valves, etc. These tanks, as well as the pipe-lines, have to be constructed of the best materials and in the most workmanlike manner, to prevent leakage, as there are few liquids so difficult to hold in any receptacle as petroleum and its products.

A model of an oil-depot at Communipaw is also given, showing the extensive warehouses provided for the storage of barreled oil, and illustrating the manner of unloading bulk-oil from the tank-cars and loading it into bulk-boats, which carry from 48,000 to 50,000 gallons, or from 1,000 to 1,500 barrels each, by means of the boats between the refineries and the yards. Large iron tanks are sunk in the ground beneath the level of the railroad tracks. Between the rails runs a trough, which leads to the tanks. The train of oil tank-cars is run over the troughs, and on the valves in the bottom of the cars being opened, the oil is allowed to run into the trough, and thence to the underground tanks. From here it is pumped into large tanks above ground, from which it runs through hose into the holds of the bulk-barges which carry it to the refineries. In the western wing of the building is another working model, 10 by 12 ft. in dimensions, by which is illustrated the method of obtaining and shipping petroleum.

It shows a hilly country with a creek flowing through the centre, and flowing and pumping wells around it—the latter provided with a model pump at work pumping crude oil, the former discharging a stream of petroleum into a tank. A well is also shown in process of boring, displaying the derricks, engines, tools, etc. In another place men are seen erecting a derrick for boring a well. There is also exhibited a blacksmith's shop, with men at work repairing tools, etc. In the front portion is shown the railroad

THE FINISH OF THE FIRST HEAT OF FOURS.—ATALANTAS, N. Y. CITY, FIRST; BEAVERWYCKS, ALBANY, N. Y., SECOND; YALE COLLEGE, NEW HAVEN, CONN., THIRD.

OPENING RACES OF THE REGATTA OF THE NATIONAL AMATEUR ASSOCIATION, ON THE SCHUYLKILL RIVER, AUGUST 22D.

1. The Hell Gate Obstructions.   2. The Shaft at Hallett's Point.   3. Bed Rock below the Water Line.   4. The Excavations, showing the present Supports of the River-bottom.

MODEL OF THE EXCAVATIONS AT HELL GATE, HALLETT'S POINT, OPPOSITE NEW YORK CITY, EXHIBITED IN THE UNITED STATES GOVERNMENT BUILDING.

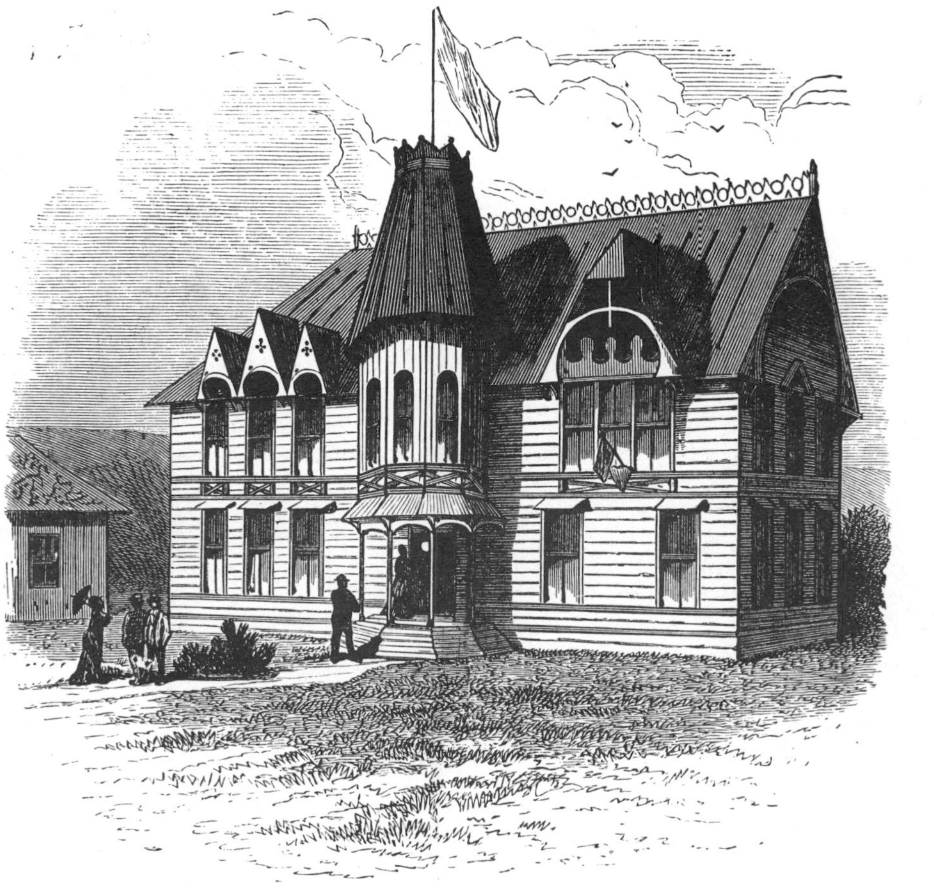

THE DELAWARE STATE BUILDING.

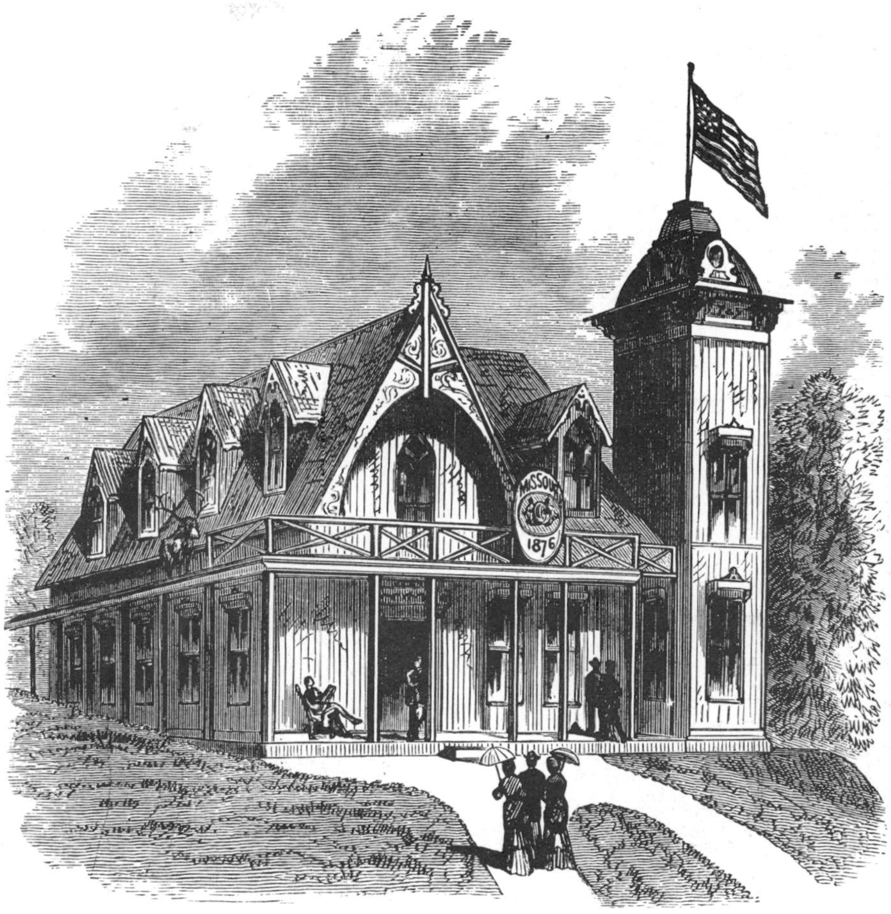

THE MISSOURI STATE BUILDING.

station at Franklin, Venango County, Pennsylvania, with the oil-works, passenger-station, tanks with pipe and racks for loading petroleum into the cars, and the railroad track, with a locomotive and train of cars. There is a large number of moving figures, about three inches long, of men employed in various work about the oil-wells and buildings. All the portions of this model work perfectly by means of a small steam engine. In addition to the working models above described, there are shown specimens of the equipment of cars. There is a complete freight track, full size, and samples of car-wheels made by different manufacturers; also axles bent cold into various shapes, to show the excellence of the material from which they are made. There are also complete models of cars; the box or house-car for the transportation of grain, flour, boxed meats, wool, cotton, etc.; the rack-car for the transportation of oil in barrels, lumber, railroad iron, iron pipe, coal, and similar heavy freights; the flat, or gondola car for the movement of heavy stone blocks, iron castings, etc.; and the butter and egg car, which is a box-car with double-lined top, bottom and sides, and an ice-chest in each end for refrigerating the contents of the car. There are also on exhibition models of couplers, car-doors and frames, seal-locks, springs, bolts, etc., some of the latter being full-sized specimens. The wall space above the counter is occupied on one side with an outline map showing some of the principal rail and water-routes between the Atlantic and Pacific seaboard cities. There is also a map of the pipe-line system of Western Pennsylvania, a map and profile of a line of levels through Butler, Clarion, and Armstrong Counties, and a large number of photographs. As an annex, and adjacent to the Main Building, several hundred feet of railway have been laid, on which a handsome working model of a locomotive engine, one-fourth size, draws a train of similar proportioned model freight-cars. A neat, ornamental shed protects the engine and train when not in service. The locomotive is a beautiful piece of steam machinery, complete in every portion, and works perfectly.

INTERNATIONAL REGATTA.

The boating season on the Schuylkill River opened on the 23d of August, by the Annual Regatta of the National Amateur Association, the course being from the Falls Bridge to Rockland Landing, just above the Reading Railroad Bridge, a distance of exactly a mile and half, as measured on the ice. The course is a beautiful one, so far as picturesque scenery is concerned, and it has the special merit of lying low down in a valley, sheltered from the wind by bold banks, so that the water is seldom disturbed. Its defects are a bend in the last half-mile, and the narrowness of the stream—the latter making it unsafe to start more than three four-oared shells at once. Where there are a number of competing crews, it is, therefore, necessary to row in heats, the winning crew in each heat alone having place in the final decisive contest.

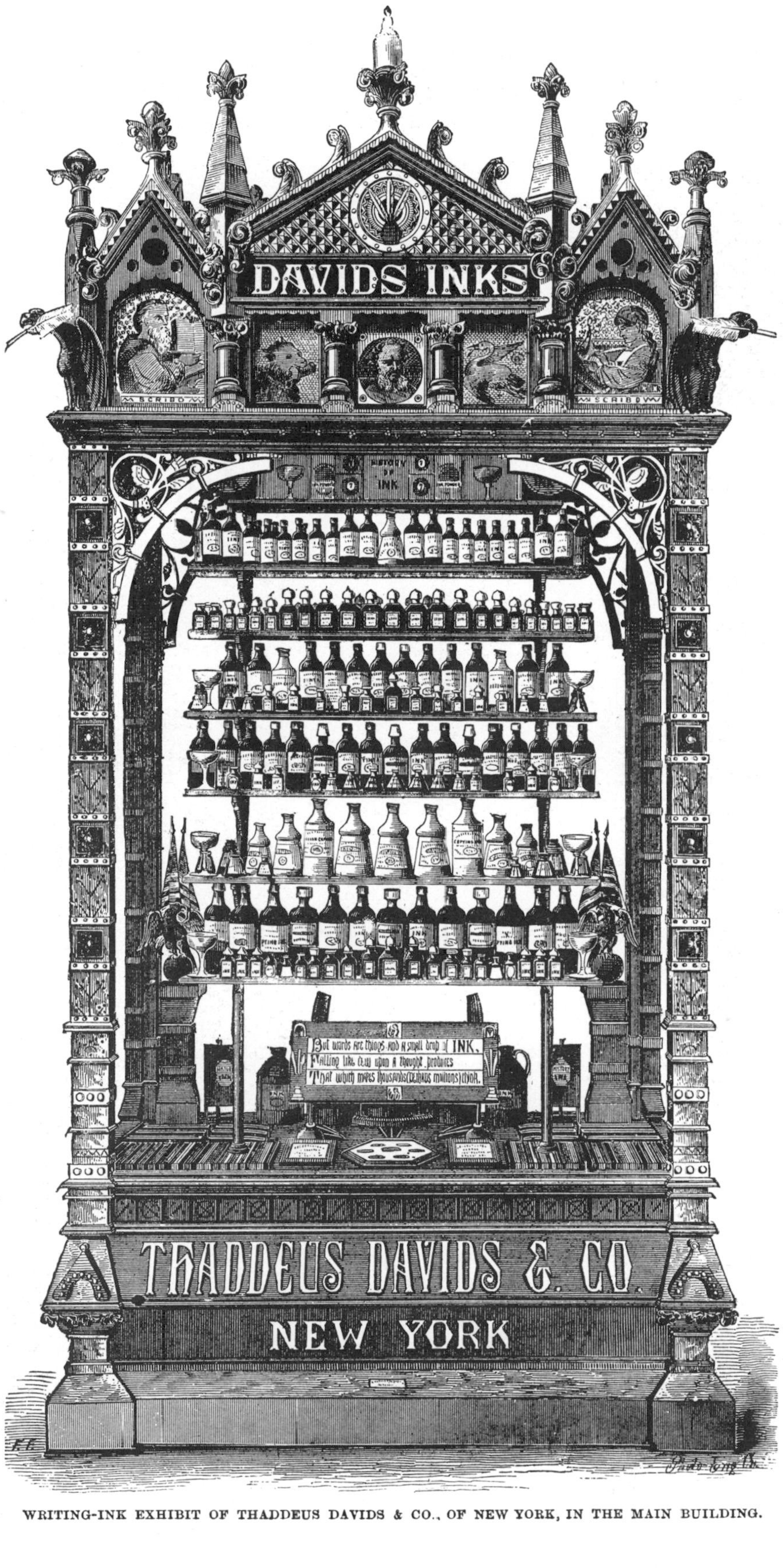

WRITING-INK EXHIBIT OF THADDEUS DAVIDS & CO., OF NEW YORK, IN THE MAIN BUILDING.

In the Amateur races the Atalantas won the first heat and the Columbias the second, placing them both in the final heat, which was pulled between them on the 24th, when the Columbias won the heat.

These preliminary races having been won, the next event in order was the International Rowing Regatta—four oars—the first ever held, which commenced on the 28th. The following is a list of the crews and positions, the latter being drawn for by lot, and forming the programme for the first day:

First Heat, 2 o'clock p. m.—Eureka Boat Club, Newark, N. J.; Argonautas Rowing Association, Bergen Point, N. J.; and Dublin University Boat Club.

Second Heat, 2:45 p. m.—Vesper Boat Club, Philadelphia; Yale College Crew; Crescent Boat Club, Philadelphia.

Third Heat, 3:30 p. m.—Columbia College Crew, New York; Elizabeth Boat Club, Portsmouth, Va.; Quaker City Boat Club, Philadelphia.

Fourth Heat, 4:15 p. m.—Beaverwyck Rowing Club, Albany, N. Y.; Falcon Boat Club, Burlington, N. J.; Duquesne Boat Club, Allegheny City, Pa.

Fifth Heat, 5 p. m.—Pennsylvania Boat Club, Philadelphia; Watkins Boat Club, Philadelphia; Malta Boat Club, Philadelphia.

Sixth Heat, 5:45 p. m.—London Rowing Club, England; Northwestern Rowing Club, Chicago; Atalanta Boat Club, New York.

Seventh Heat, 6:30 p. m.—First Trinity College Crew, Cambridge, England; Oneida Club, Burlington, New Jersey.

In the seven heats seventeen crews took part, three having withdrawn. The weather was delightful, and crowds were assembled to view the contests. The result of the first heat was: Eureka 9:29½, Dublin 9:36¼, Argonautas 9:42; of the second, Vespers 9:43¾, Crescents 9:46½; third heat, Columbia 9:11, Elizabeth 9:20½; fourth heat, Beaverwycks 9:14; fifth heat, Watkins 9:06¼. In the sixth heat the London Rowing Club, said to be the best amateur crew in English waters, was entered to pull against the best two American crews, one of which, however, the Atalantas, withdrew at the last moment on account of the illness of one of the men, leaving only the Northwestern crew of Chicago, holder of the American championship, to race with the great London four. This was a tremendous race in speed, power, and intense interest. It was won by the London crew: time, London, 8:55; Northwesterns, 8:59¼. In the seventh and closing heat, the Cambridge University Crew of England were matched with a raw club from Burlington, New Jersey, and beat easily. The time was: Cambridge 9:06¾; Oneidas, 9:53¼.

THE CENTENNIAL REGATTA.—THE LONDON CREW WINNING THE SIXTH AND LAST HEAT OF THE FOUR-OARED, SHELL RACE, AUGUST 28TH, 1876.

NORTHWESTERN ROWING CLUB : Charles T. Corning, *Stroke* ; John Killoran ; James Jerome ; W. B. Curtis, *Bow.*   LONDON ROWING CLUB : J. Howell, *Stroke* ; A. Trower ; F. S. Gulston ; R. H. Labat, *Bow.*

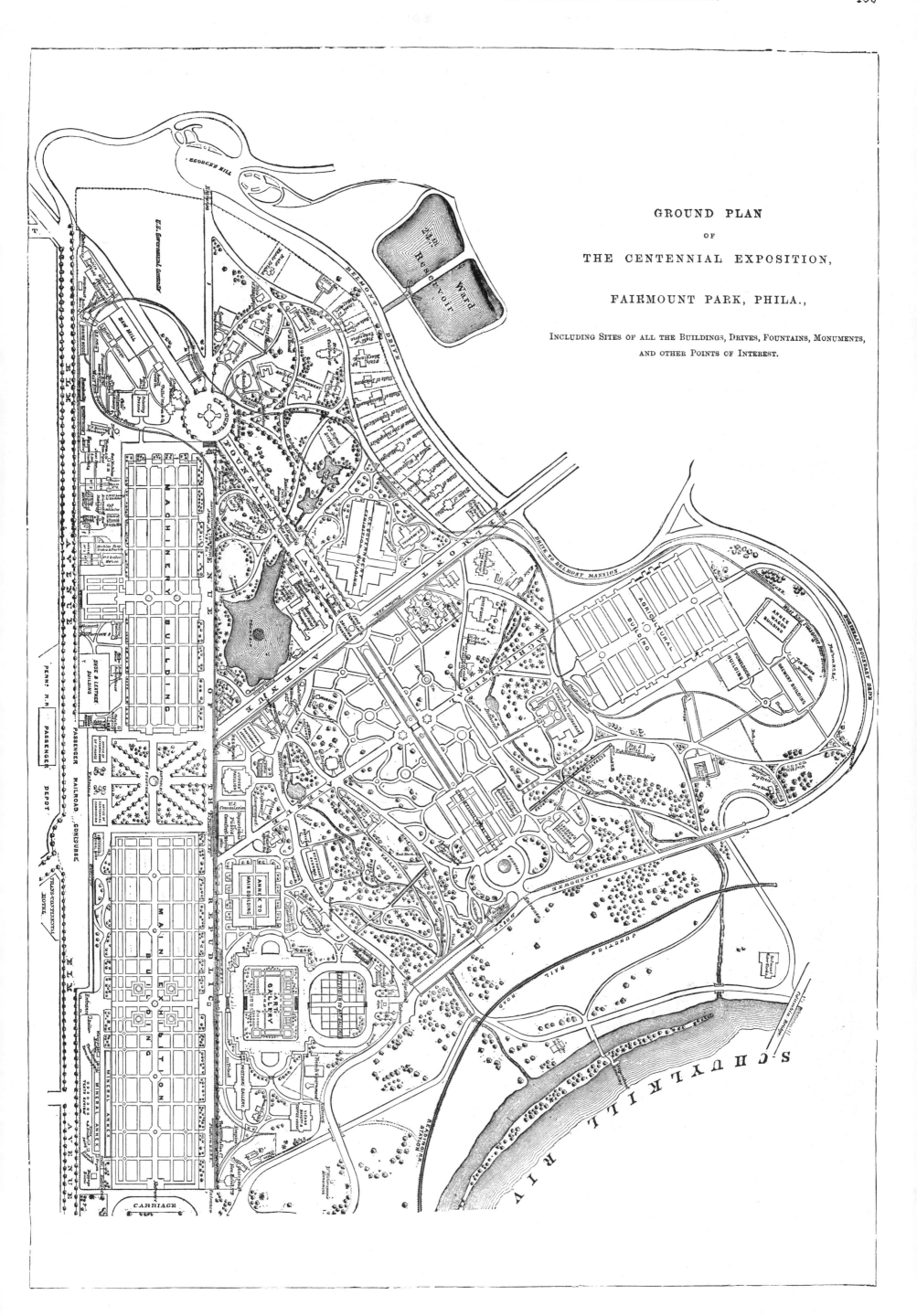

GROUND PLAN

OF

THE CENTENNIAL EXPOSITION,

FAIRMOUNT PARK, PHILA.,

INCLUDING SITES OF ALL THE BUILDINGS, DRIVES, FOUNTAINS, MONUMENTS, AND OTHER POINTS OF INTEREST.

On the second "International" day, the first heat was won by the Beaverwycks: time, Beaverwycks, 9:07; Eurekas, 9:13. In the next heat, the Columbias, who were to have pulled, drew out of the race, leaving the

held to be quite liberal on the part of gentleman-oarsmen. This plan consisted in forcing the Yale crew to take the London boat's water or risk a foul. The result was that the Londoners won by about five feet. Time, London, 8:51½; Yale, 8:52¼. By this splendid pull Yale beat the time of the Northwesterns of the day before, and won the right to being considered the best amateur four in America.

By this time the Centennial Regatta had been acknowledged generally to be a decided success, and some of the

THE JURY OF AWARD ON AN INSPECTION TOUR IN THE WINE VAULTS OF AGRICULTURAL HALL.

Watkins crew to row against the Cambridge (Trinity) boys. In this heat Cambridge stopped rowing, one of her men being taken ill, and Watkins rowed on to the finish, making time, 9:01¾, beating their own time of the day before.

The last and greatest race of the day, and, in fact, the greatest of all the four-oared contests, brought Yale in competition with the splendid London crew. The race was magnificently rowed, though considerable dissatisfaction was felt with the London crew for using a system of jockeying, which, although allowable by the strict rules, was not

English oarsmen did not hesitate to say that the Schuylkill was the best water they had ever rowed in. And so the third day was ushered in amid a general feeling of satisfaction, to which the fact that now was to occur one of the most interesting of all the events did not fail to add its quota of interest.

The single-scull heats did not attract much attention throughout the regatta, and least of all on this third day. But when the Watkins four-oars put in an appearance and pulled down to the start, followed by the Londoners and the Beaverwycks, a dense crowd had collected, and every-

1. Struggle between the London and Yale Crews at the Finish, August 29th. 2. The Finish on August 30th—The Beaverwycks Victorious—Scene from the Grand Stand.

THE INTERNATIONAL FOUR-OARED REGATTA ON THE SCHUYLKILL RIVER.

body was on the alert. The positions were : Beaverwycks at the west, London in the middle, and Watkins east. The race was desperate from the start, the Watkins boat taking the lead, London next, and Beaverwycks gradually drawing up, and at length reaching the lead, which they held to the end, the distance between theirs and the London boat being only four feet, Watkins being about three lengths behind. This race gave the Beaverwycks the great prize of a handsome silver cup, valued at $1,000, while each member of the crew received a gold medal, and each member of the second crew (London) received a silver medal. The time of this race was : Beaverwycks, 9:06 ; London, 9:06½ ; Watkins, 9:16.

The programme for August 31st was as follows :

At two P. M. the first trial heat of single sculls between F. E. Yates and C. E. Courtney, of the Union Springs, and H. Gourley and F. Pleasanton, of the Quaker City Club.

At a quarter to three the second heat, between W. G. Thomas of the Pennsylvania; J. B. Mingus, of the Vesper; J. McCartney, of the Friendship; and Ed. Mills, Jr., of the Atalanta.

At half-past three, first trial heat for pair-oared shells—(red) Nautilus, W. Walsh and E. D. Roache; (white) London, J. Howell and A. Trower; (blue) Atalanta, W. H. Downs, and J. E. Eustis; (green) Argonautas, E. Smith and F. C. Eldred.

At fifteen minutes past four, second trial heat for pair-oared shells—(red) Northwestern, Corning and Curtis; (white) London, Labatt and Gulston; (blue) Northwestern, Killoran and Smith.

The international regatta continued from day to day, the single scull races attracting little attention, comparatively speaking, and even the pair-oared contest rousing no enthusiasm. The amateur races concluded on the afternoon of the 1st of September. The day's racing began with double-scull contests, the final heat being won by the Northwestern Club, two selections of the club running against two of the Atalanta's. The race of this day was between the four-oared crews of Yale, Columbia, and Trinity College, Cambridge. Owing to various misfortunes in the Cambridge crew, their boat got out of the race, and Yale won against Columbia by three lengths in 9 minutes 10¾ seconds. The regatta closed on September 6th, with the final heats for professional prizes. The match between the Halifax fishermen and the famous London Four was contested with spirit, and the race was awarded to London. The last match was for pair-oars between two of the London Four and two Boston men, the latter winning. This closed the series of contests.

WOMEN'S PAVILION.

This building stands near the United States Government Building. It is 208 feet square, and was originated and paid for by the women of America, its cost being $30,000. Its contents are exceedingly varied, all, however, possessing the feature of having been exclusively the contribution and work of the women from different parts of the world. It is

to be observed that while the building contains a very large display of needlework, and what would be ordinarily anticipated from women, there is also much more of the artistic and utilitarian offered in various directions, of a character which would scarcely be looked for from this source. A considerable collection of paintings in oil is arranged together, comprising many specimens of considerable merit, although possibly none of the very highest character. The drawings are, as a rule, more deserving of praise. The modeling, of which there are several exhibits, is creditable, and one instance in this line is deserving of high encomium. This is a medallion head in high relief, modeled from common butter, and representing an ideal subject, entitled "The Dreaming Iolanthe." In considering this work, the difficulties attached to the employment

THE CANADIAN LUMBER EXHIBIT.

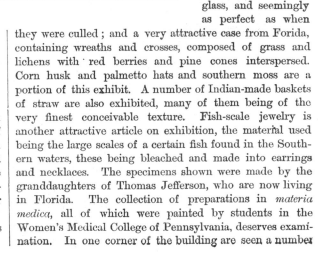

of such material should be taken into account, while it must be conceded that, whatever material the artist employs, the work itself is one exhibiting a high degree of talent, a fine ideal feeling, as well as exceeding delicacy and brilliancy of manipulation. An unexpected exhibit is that of many articles of furniture, large and small, including bedsteads, secretaries, etc., elaborately carved by hand by women. A number of these are from Cincinnati, the School of Design of that city making quite a wonderful exhibition in this direction, a particular instance being a case which will compare favorably with anything of this character in the entire exhibition. There are also from this same organization a large number of exhibits in the decorative arts other than carving, particularly in painted china, the subjects of which are selected from flowers, leaves, single heads, groups of figures, etc., all of them displaying remarkable taste.

A very beautiful carved bedstead is thus described : "It is made of walnut, inlaid with ebony, the carving being the work of two young ladies, the head panels representing latice-work, from which hang trumpet-flowers. On the posts are carved lilies and poppies, and above the central decorations, at the head, are two panels, upon which are painted clusters of morning-glories, closed for the night. The foot-board is ornamented with carving of some flowers opening under the rising of the morning sun." It should be observed that the design is poetic, and symbolical as well as artistic. A child's bedstead near this is made of Spanish mahogany, inlaid with ebony, and beautifully carved, having upon its foot-board many amusing scenes from "Mother Goose." The Royal School of Needlework of England has made many contributions, including work done by members of the Royal family. A satin skirt, closely embroidered, from a design by the Princess Louise, wife of the Marquis of Lorne, is the property of Queen Victoria. Near this is a case in which are a considerable number of etchings from the hands of Queen Victoria herself. Many of these display very fine art-feeling and a decided talent. It is noticeable, perhaps, that her best work displays itself in homely, domestic and social scenes and incidents, rather than where she has attempted more ornate and severe subjects. The display of lace and embroidery is large and very valuable. The ladies of Brazil have contributed extensively in this direction. Some lacework and certain embroidered cushions will well repay careful observation. A home piece of embroidery is a quilt sent by a lady from Alabama. It is white and rose-colored satin. On the white ground are embroidered 1,500 roses and rosebuds, in each of which there are from 500 to 900 stitches. Seven thousand skeins of silk were used in this work, and a lady was engaged upon it eighteen months. A very pleasing exhibition of wax flowers and fruits is made, and will be found on the eastern side of the building. Some representations of forest leaves are exquisitely natural. Near these are specimens of real flowers, preserved under glass, and seemingly as perfect as when they were culled ; and a very attractive case from Forida, containing wreaths and crosses, composed of grass and lichens with red berries and pine cones interspersed. Corn husk and palmetto hats and southern moss are a portion of this exhibit. A number of Indian-made baskets of straw are also exhibited, many of them being of the very finest conceivable texture. Fish-scale jewelry is another attractive article on exhibition, the material used being the large scales of a certain fish found in the Southern waters, these being bleached and made into earrings and necklaces. The specimens shown were made by the granddaughters of Thomas Jefferson, who are now living in Florida. The collection of preparations in *materia medica*, all of which were painted by students in the Women's Medical College of Pennsylvania, deserves examination. In one corner of the building are seen a number

1. Ironwood Man.   2. Bronze Dog.   3. Bronze Teapot.   4. Vase.   5. Mandarin Procession.   6. Priest.   7. Stork.   8. Bronze Vase.   9. Ivory Pagoda.   10. Flower Boat.   11. Bamboo Chair.   12. Carved Bedstead

CURIOSITIES IN THE CHINESE DEPARTMENT IN THE MAIN BUILDING.

of carpet-weaving machines, presided over by ladies, and where the processes in this manufacture may be duly witnessed in full operation. Quite a number of labor-saving machines of women's invention are displayed near these, most of them being for domestic use. The engine which runs the machines for carpet-weaving, as well as others for spinning cotton and manufacturing worsted, is managed by a woman engineer—certainly an anomaly in mechanics. A life-preserving mattress, invented by a lady from the State of New York, is an important exhibit. There are several dolls exhibited, with doll-dresses and decorative articles, and a large number of children's garments, exquisitely embroidered. Also bridal costumes of trousseaux, etc. This collection, illustrative of woman's work, has been decried by many writers, yet on careful inspection it displays very much that is worthy of the highest commendation, and in its entirety will compare favorably with any other special exhibition on the grounds. It should be considered with regard to it that the entire effort was only commenced at a very late period, and that it was prosecuted by the women under a good many disadvantages without outside assistance.

Among the foreign countries contributing to the collection in this building besides Brazil, is Japan, which furnishes a case containing a number of very beautiful and interesting articles, and several exhibits in painted ware placed on the walls. There are also exhibits from the Scandinavian countries, and a large and very fine one from Canada, containing among other articles a number of very carefully and beautifully made models of public institutions, charitable and others, in the Dominion. A novel and seemingly important improvement in the manufacture of women's undergarments is exhibited here, the design being to remove the weight of the clothing from the hips and suspend it from the shoulders. The idea has been heretofore explained in public at certain women's meetings in New York and Boston, and is considered by the medical faculty very important in its relation to health. Another interesting exhibit in this connection is that of a number of articles used in electro-magnetic treatment for chronic diseases, and which are exhibited by Mrs. Elizabeth J. French, of Philadelphia, a pioneer of a quarter of a century ago in the scientific treatment of diseases by electricity.

THE "KINDERGARTEN."

Close by the Women's Pavilion, and forming, as it were, an annex of that building, is a little cottage, where are shown, under the auspices of the Women's department, actual methods of education in use in the infant school system of Froebel, termed the "Kindergarten." Here the system is developed, and can be seen on certain days of the week, illustrating its working with eighteen little children from three to six years of age, taken from the "Northern Home for Friendless Children." The business of this school is conducted by Miss Burritt, the furniture and

material being contributed by Mr. Steiger, of New York. Miss Burritt commenced her labors in this direction last Winter in the Northern Home for Friendless Children of Philadelphia, and by the suggestion of Mrs. Gillespie, the head of the women's movement, the sum of $1,500, raised by the Rhode Island committee of the women's building, was devoted to the erection of this little cottage. Here these little children go through the regular daily exercises of the Kindergarten system, and to those who may be interested in the novel and beautiful feature of a child's education nothing can be more charming than a visit to this school. Friederich Froebel introduced this new method of teaching into his native country of Germany in 1837, giving it the name of Kindergarten (children's garden), certainly a most happy effort at nomenclature. The idea involves a large, well-ventilated, well-lighted and pleasant room, opening upon a garden where should be combined a playground for general enjoyment, a large garden-plot, and smaller plots for each child old enough to cultivate one. Here the little ones should be taught to plant and cultivate flowers, useful vegetables, and even trees, and to surround these with such birds as encourage a kindly treatment, and which can be brought to make their home there. Usually from three to five hours are passed in these gardens.

Froebel's system did not contemplate corporal punishment, exclusion from a game or from the garden being considered sufficiently severe treatment. He devised a number of games and exercises for use in his course of instruction, and also six "gifts," which are now used in the Kindergarten. These gifts consist of soft balls of different colors—with strings attached to them—cubes, cylinders, wooden balls, cubes divided for the construction of buildings and other objects, and many other articles, the whole being intended to convey the meaning of form, color, size, motion, individual and other qualities to the infant mind.

Froebel died in 1852. During his life more than fifty Kindergartens were established in Germany, Belgium, and Switzerland.

Although no government has yet introduced the system in the public schools in the United States, these schools have become quite numerous in New York, Washington, Philadelphia and Boston, Miss E. P. Burritt having been perhaps more instrumental than any other in popularizing them. It is likely that the exhibition of the Kindergarten at the Centennial will introduce the system into many cities where it is at present unknown.

THE BREWERS' BUILDING.

THE Brewers' Building stands in the extreme northeastern corner of the grounds, and directly east of Agricultural Hall. The structure is 96 feet wide by 272 feet long, with a centre tower having an elevation of 60 feet, and wings of 28 feet.

In addition to the main hall a building has also been provided for the storage of malt liquor for exhibition and competition, 70 feet by 80, with double walls, the extension being divided in three compartments. One compartment, 25 by 80 feet, is for the storage of ale in bulk; another of the same dimensions for malt liquor on draft, and the centre compartment, 20 by 80 feet, over which is an icebox to hold four feet in depth of ice, is for the storage of lager beer. The uniform temperature for the middle compartment is 45 deg., and of the two side compartments 56 deg. In the centre of the building is a brewery in operation, and near it are models, one representing a brewery in the olden time, and the other one of more modern style. Forming the mechanism of brewing as exemplified in this building are a huge copper tun, immense wooden vat, with all the machinery, pipes,

THE JAPANESE TOILET MIRROR IN THE MAIN BUILDING.

pumps, etc., attached, which usually appertain to the manufacture. Arranged in different parts of the building are exhibits of the different kinds of mechanism used by the brewer, including patent rinsers, one of which is represented in operation within a glass barrel; and in fact here can be followed all the processes of the beer manufacture from the actual growth of the hops—that indispensable plant being trained on the outside of the building and exhibited in its natural condition. There are, according to the latest returns, in the United States, in active operation, 2,600 breweries, producing annually for consumption, in round numbers, 285,000,000 gallons of malt liquors, not including numerous private breweries. By far the majority of these establishments have been erected during the last twenty-five years. It is stated that not one of the present structures was in existence in the first year of our independence, and but one or two in the first year of this century.

The largest quantity of malt liquors produced in a year by a single brewery is 4,225,000 gallons. It is curious to notice the number of trades more or less dependent upon brewing. From the agriculturist the brewer obtains his barley for malt, and other cereals for fodder, and hops. In 1874 there were 1,580,626 acres of land under cultivation with barley, producing nearly 32,552,500 bushels, valued at about $30,000,000; barley yielding, next to potatoes and tobacco the highest value per acre, and being the seventh agricultural staple article of the country, and nearly $7,000,000 higher in value than tobacco. Of hops, the last agricultural census reports a total production in the United States of 25,456,669 pounds. From the arboriculturist the brewer obtains his oak, cedar, and pine for barrels, vats, etc., and other timber for building purposes. The business of the maltster, supplying malt to the brewers, is extremely large, employing a capital of about $14,000,000, and having under operation nearly 400 malthouses, valued at more than $10,000,000, employing 2,500 men, whose annual wages amount to more than $1,000,000. The entire capital invested in breweries

EXHIBIT OF FINE FURS OF F. BOOSS & BRO., NEW YORK, IN THE MAIN BUILDING.

is about $89,000,000. The number of men employed in breweries and malthouses is about 13,500, whose annual wages amount to nearly $7,000,000. The process of making beer is described as follows: "A certain quantity of malt-barley is taken and ground. It is then mashed with hot water, the sweet liquor or wort extracted, a proper amount of hops being added. The whole is then boiled until the preserving quality, as well as the aroma of the hops, is obtained. It is then allowed to cool, and afterward fermented with yeast to produce the small quantity of alcohol it contains and to give it life. Lager beer contains 91 per cent. water, 5 per cent. malt extract, 3½ per cent. alcohol, the remainder being carbonic acid, etc. It is said that from 40 loaves of fresh bread, weighing two pounds each, alcohol equal to one bottle of port-wine may be extracted.

CENTENNIAL ADMINISTRATION.
Chiefs of Bureaux.

CONTINUING our sketches of the official heads of the departments in the Centennial Administration, we will proceed to give brief accounts of the chiefs of the following bureaux: Transportation, Installation, Agriculture, Horticulture, Awards, and the Press department.

Captain Dolphus Torrey, chief of the Bureau of Transportation, is forty-two years of age, a native of Central New York and a citizen of Philadelphia. He was engaged in the war, at first as a private soldier in the 2d Ohio Infantry, and afterward as a captain in the 20th Ohio Regiment. Having been largely engaged in the railroad business,

particularly in the transportation department, he was selected to take charge of this important branch of the Centennial administration.

It is a fact, in this connection, that American exhibitors delayed sorting their goods so long that they endangered their presentation at the time undertaken by the Centennial Commission. Had it not been for the administrative ability and quick executive capacity of Captain Torrey, there is no doubt that a very serious state of embarrass-

FRANCIS BERGER, COMMISSIONER FROM LUXEMBOURG.

ment would have preceded the opening. For a month before the opening all the railroads leading to the Exhibition were choked up with laden cars. The duty of disentangling this slough, and of facilitating and placing the goods, belonged to the Captain, and he was so successful in accomplishing his arduous task that the Centennial Commission passed a special vote of thanks for his efficiency. The best confession of the appreciation of Captain Torrey's services is found in the fact that both the Pennsylvania Railroad Company and the Pullman Palace Car Company have availed themselves of these.

Henry Pettit, chief of the Bureau of Installation, an engineer and architect of the Main Building and Machinery Hall, has been employed as engineer in the construction department of the Pennsylvania Railroad Company, and his talent as an inventor has been made use of by that company in the construction of their bridges. Mr. Pettit studied at the University of Pennsylvania, and though still a young man, being only thirty years of age, ranks high as an engineer. In 1873 he was sent to the Vienna Exhibition by the Centennial Commission, with directions to report on its engineering features. It was only by request that Mr. Pettit was permitted by the Pennsylvania Railroad Company to accept the engagement with the administration of the Centennial Exposition. Here at once he made himself felt, and although in the plans for the Main Building and Machinery Hall he had many competitors, his were adopted, and the erection of these two principal structures was superintended by him. To Mr. Pettit, in his position as chief of the Bureau of Installation, is due the admirable and systematic arrangement of the exhibits of all countries in the Main Building.

Burnett Landreth, chief of the Bureau of Agriculture, has a large practical knowledge of the agriculturist's business, being a member of the firm of Landreth & Sons, widely known as seed-raisers. Mr. Landreth has extensive farms on the Delaware and elsewhere, which have acquired a national reputation. He is a graduate of a Polytechnic College, served during the war, and as chief of the Bureau of Agriculture is generally esteemed.

Charles H. Miller, chief of the Bureau of Horticulture, was born in London about forty years ago, and learned his business as a scenery and landscape gardener in his native country. For the last twenty years he has been a resident of Philadelphia, and is a member of the firm of Miller & Hayes, of Germantown. The condition of the grounds about the Horticultural Building, and the fine taste displayed in the arrangement within the Horticultural Hall, are sufficient evidence of the administrative and professional capacity of Mr. Miller.

General Francis A. Walker, chief of the Bureau of Awards, is a general so distinguished as a statistician that his name need only be mentioned to give testimony to the qualification held by the official in charge of the Bureau of

RELICS AND CURIOSITIES IN THE PERUVIAN AND ARGENTINE DEPARTMENTS, IN THE MAIN BUILDING.

Awards. This position involves no common acquirements. The responsibility of chief of the International Jury of Awards, comprising 225 individuals—half Americans and half Europeans,—will be at once conceded. For this position probably no more eligible person could have been selected than General Walker. Born in Boston, July 2d, 1840, he graduated twenty years later from Amherst College with high honors. After studying law for a few months, he entered the army in 1861, and served until 1865, during the last two years as Assistant Adjutant-General. At different times he was upon the staff of Generals Couch, Warren and Hancock. For the next two years General Walker was employed as classical instructor at Williston Seminary, Mass., and during the year 1868 was connected with the editorial staff of the *Springfield Republican.* In the following year General Walker was appointed chief of the Bureau of Statistics; in 1870 he superintended the census, and in 1871 was Commissioner of Indian Affairs, in addition to the last-named position. In 1872 he accepted the professorship of political economy and history in the Sheffield Scientific School of Metallurgy, retaining the office of superintendent of the census without salary. General Walker has published three quarto volumes toward the ninth census, and is the author and compiler of numerous other important statistical works, his "Statis-

been gained by any other similar exhibition. This has been particularly the case in Europe, where these illustrations have been widely circulated. General Norton has had charge of the issue of all the tickets to the Press, and his kind and courteous management of this rather onerous duty has secured for him many friends.

OUR ILLUSTRATIONS.

MODEL OF THE EXCAVATIONS AT HELL GATE, N. Y.

In our description of the United States Government Building we made some allusion to the model there exhibited, representing the excavations recently prosecuted at that spot so dangerous to navigation known as "Hell Gate," off Hallett's Point, and opposite New York city. A more extended description of our illustration of this model will be in order.

The scale of the model is 12½ feet to the inch, the model being made of plaster, and topographically correct. It presents a view of the bed of the river, raised in such a manner as to show at once the surface, the surroundings of the land and water, and the submarine excavations, cover-

galvanic batteries, each of which would explode from 17 to 20 charges. These batteries were to be operated from a bomb-proof chamber at a distance of 300 feet southeast of the main shaft. All the batteries were to be brought into action at the same time by an ingenious method, and when a complete circuit was formed, the entire 3,500 charges would be set off together, and utterly destroy the great plateau of rock which has made Hell Gate so dangerous to navigators.

CHINESE ARTICLES IN THE MAIN BUILDING.

Several illustrations of articles selected from the Chinese section in the Main Building include the following: A carved representation of a pagoda, the tower in miniature, is 4½ ft. high, is made of ivory, and has ten stories, each story surrounded by the peculiar and well-known Chinese roof. The tower is hexagonal and slightly pyramidal. At each edge is a round support, running from top to bottom. From the four corners of each of the ten roofs are suspended balls. The pagoda stands on the centre of the ivory base representing a plot of ground inclosed by a fence of ivory posts supporting carved ivory panels. In the plot about it are forty trees, heavily laden with fruit, while miniature Chinese are scattered about beneath them. This piece consists of many pieces united by dovetailing

JAPANESE DEPARTMENT—THE GRASSHOPPER SCREEN, IN THE MAIN BUILDING.

tical Atlas of the United States," of 1874, being alone a work of the highest grade in its line. General Walker received a medal of the first class of the Geometrical Congress, at Paris, in 1875, and is an honorary member of the Statistical Society in London.

General Charles B. Norton is chief of the Bureau of the Press Department. An official report of the United States Centennial Commission has given to this gentleman the credit of having, in 1866, first publicly proposed the Centennial Exposition. In 1853 General Norton was a juror of the New York Exhibition, and in 1867 United States Commissioner to the Paris Exposition, having in these positions gained a large experience in exhibition administration. He was called to Philadelphia by the Executive Committee of the Centennial Commission in 1873, and was put in charge of the Press, the entire publicity of the enterprise being placed in his hands. Having a wide knowledge of both the American and foreign Press, and a large administrative capacity, General Norton's services have been found to be of the greatest value to the Centennial Board of Finance, under whose general-direction he has operated. His reports and suggestions have always been considered with respect, and in many cases adopted; and the systematic plan conceived by him of advertising the Exposition by the publication of well-designed views of the buildings has been found to develop a better and more extended knowledge of the enterprise than has ever

ing an area of nearly three acres. The arrangements made by General Newton to surmount the engineering difficulties which presented themselves in undertaking the enterprise of blasting out this enormous mass of solid rock were: First, he built the coffer, as represented in the illustration, designed to exclude the water; next, a shaft was sunk, tunnels from which extended in radial lines, these being crossed at right angles, by leaving at the points of action natural pillars of solid rock, of which there were 172, each eight feet square, but varying in height between 10 and 20 feet. All the tunnels between these piers were then cleared out, and in the surface of the rock 3,500 holes, ranging in depth from 3 to 11 feet, of the uniform diameter of 3 inches, were bored in an upward direction. In these holes were to be placed the explosive materials—dynamite where the rock was hardest, and vulcan powder where it was easiest to blast—in the explosion of which the grand result was to culminate. As the floor tunnel slopes upward from a depth of 32 to 40 feet below water, and the depth of the water required for navigation is only 26 feet at mean low water, sufficient room would be furnished, after the explosion and the subsequent dredging, for the largest ships known on the voyage to and from Europe. It is estimated that there were about 70,000 cubic yards of rock to be exploded, each charge being expected to break up about 20 cubic yards. The whole was to be exploded by means of about 200 of Grove's

and other mechanical devices, but without the use of nails, screws, or pins. The whole is exquisitely engraved, and its price, $600, is certainly not unreasonable when the time and labor of its construction are taken into consideration.

A bronze vase of porcelain, and standing 2½ feet in height, is the next object which we illustrate. The design is quaint, the bowl being supported on the backs of three water-hens, each standing on a polished vessel of bronze. This vase is said to be over 1,100 years old, and its price is $1,250.

A bamboo reclining-chair is another curiosity. The back is movable at will, and various devices for the convenience of the occupant exist in this peculiar piece of furniture.

A figure two feet in height, carved in iron-wood, is worth noticing. It represents a man standing on a tree-stump, clinging to it with both hands. This piece of carving is executed very carefully, and is cheap at $40. A set of wood carvings represents a procession supposed to be accompanying a Mandarin, or high-caste Chinaman, who is at the rear, being carried in a sedan-chair by four coolies. The procession includes men carrying flags, drawn swords, musical instruments, etc. An arched bedstead is shown, in which the support for a mattress is woven of cords made from the inner bark of a native tree, and covered with rattan. Resting on the ends of the bed, and completely covering the whole, is an arched canopy, wherein a wooden frame-work, elaborately carved, supports a silk gauze cover, curiously painted with various figures. Other interesting objects are two finely carved ivory flower-beds and a bronze figure, supposed to resemble a hideous species of the dog, and of the kind of art-work executed in China over fifteen hundred years ago. Other smaller articles in bronze and porcelain need no particular description.

Swedish Character Groups.

There is perhaps no special class of articles exhibited in the Main Building which has been more generally inspected than the groups of life-size figures exhibited in the Swedish Department. These figures illustrate peasant life in Sweden. They are the work of a noted Swedish sculptor—Professor Töderman—of the Royal Academy of Fine Arts in Stockholm. The coloring and costuming of these figures are admirably true to life, and their grouping and attitudes artistic, and at the same time natural. The peculiar scene about the little cradle of the dead baby attracts special attention. The grouping which illustrates the old-time play of pulling a flower to pieces with some such refrain as "He loves me, he loves me not," etc.—reminiscence of Marguerite and Faust, by-the-way—will be found in the Women's Pavilion.

Ink Exhibits of Thaddeus Davids & Co.

A very interesting and characteristic display of stationery, and chiefly of ink, mucilage, sealing-wax, etc., is made by the great house of Thaddeus Davids & Co., of New York, in the Main Exhibition Building.

The case containing the exhibit is constructed of native woods. The woods employed are black walnut and maple, all highly polished. Four square columns, rising on a massive base, support the upper case, on each of whose four topmost corners is a griffin, carved by hand in black walnut and holding in its mouth a gold quill pen. Other graceful columns, with carved capitals and veneering shafts, support the gables and pinnacles, dividing the front and rear into panels. This case is inclosed in plate-glass. The interior has gold-plated standards supporting shelves of highly polished boards of maple, on which are placed the inks and other articles exhibited. To the art-taste of its makers, Messrs. William H. Kirk & Co., of Newark, N. J., every credit is due. In the centre and front of the case, lying on blue satin, in Russia leather, are seven silver and bronze medals, which have been obtained by Messrs. Davids at previous exhibitions. Jugs of writing-fluid and black writing-ink; copies of the history of ink, compiled by the senior member of the firm; eighteen different classes of sealing-wax, beautifully arranged; with lawyer's pounce, wafers, mucilage, ink, papers, etc.—these represent the exhibits of Messrs. Davids & Co., who have a high and deserved reputation for the character of their goods, and

H. MAILLARD'S EXHIBIT OF CONFECTIONERY, IN AGRICULTURAL HALL.

whose display is in all respects a worthy and creditable exhibit.

Canadian Building.

The character of this building, which stands in front and a little at one side of the English Commissioners' Buildings, is not only novel in itself, but admirably characterizes the chief product of the country to which it belongs. Although symmetrical in its outline, it is roughly formed of boards, logs, and in fact lumber and timber of every conceivable shape, and so arranged as to make a very full and faithful exhibit of the forest products of the Dominion. It is certainly the most original structure among all the individual buildings, and the one showing most purpose and intention in its mere design and construction.

Tivoli Beer.

The Berlin Tivoli Beer Company, whose exhibit in the Agricultural Hall we illustrate, is an immense establishment, whose brewery manufactures about 300,000 barrels of liquor in the Winter months only, while in its malt-kilns 20,000,000 pounds of barley are annually prepared. This beer is well known in America, and has a high reputation among those who drink imported lager.

The Judges Testing Wine.

The scene illustrated represents the testing of wine in the French Department by the Judges. This illustration quite reminds one of Hasenclever's celebrated picture of the "Wine-tasters," which was exhibited in New York some years ago at the Dusseldorf Gallery, and formed a part of the loan exhibition at the National Academy of Design during the present Summer. Similar scenes might probably be witnessed quite frequently in the different sections exhibiting in Agricultural Hall, as the various wines exhibited have all been tested pretty freely by the Judges during the continuance of the Exhibition.

The Freed Slave.

This illustration represents the life-size bronze figure which faces the rear entrance of Memorial Hall, and which is an ideal presentment of a freedman, made such by the Emancipation Proclamation of January 1st, 1863. The work is by an Austrian artist, named Pezzicar, of Trieste. The figure is strongly characteristic, though a little exaggerated, in order to present more obviously the elements

which are identified with the situation. The attitude is impressive and full of vital force. The face shows exhilaration and joy in a high degree. It having been complained that the marked protrusion of the chest in the figure is anatomically incorrect, the objection has been answered in the catalogue of the Austrian Art Department, by reference to a theory of Lessing, presented in the present case in the following words: "That, as the slave is, in this instance, supposed to be the highest embodiment of the feelings of all other slaves, it was necessary to express this by intensifying the effect. Viewed in this light, the height of the chest, although not strictly in accordance with anatomical truth, is justified in an artistic sense."

Russian Bronzes.

The exhibition of bronzes by Felix Chopin, of St. Petersburg, should be carefully inspected. They comprise first, a representation of a Cossack wiping his sword on his horse's mane, after having just slaughtered a Turk. The second figure is a Cossack standing in his stirrup, firing backward, designed to display the remarkable horsemanship of this peculiar race. Next is a sledge drawn by three horses, while hungry wolves watch them from the road. The next is a single figure of a horse, exquisitely designed. "The Jealous 'Foal'" is another, which represents a boy milking a mare, while the foal bites him vindictively in the back. Still another shows a Russian falconer, sitting on his horse and letting loose a falcon from his hand.

The Silkworm Exhibit.

The silkworm exhibit in Machinery Hall represents the progress of silk from the cocoon to the finished thread, as displayed in the Brazilian Department of this portion of the Exhibition, and as cultivated under the auspices of the Imperial Agricultural Institute at Rio Janeiro. The moth of the silkworm is about an inch long, of a pale-yellow color, and the females are inactive, and die a few hours after depositing their eggs, which are about the size of a mustard-seed. In warm, dry weather the young emerge from these in a few days, and immediately begin to eat ravenously. When full-grown they are three inches long, of a light-green color. The product of an ounce of eggs is said to eat upward of 1,200 pounds of mulberry-leaves, and furnish 120 pounds of cocoons. The various processes by which the silk is obtained from the cocoon, and the methods used in preserving and caring for the worms, are exhibited in our illustrations.

Yardleyville Railroad Bridge, on the New Line between New York and Philadelphia.

The new railroad route to Philadelphia, which opened on May 1st, and is known as the Bound Brook Line, has become quite popular during the Centennial excitement, and will doubtless gain sufficient favor in the present year

SILVER PRIZE CUP WON BY THE BEAVERWYCK CREW, IN THE INTERNATIONAL FOUR-OARED RACE ON THE SCHUYLKILL RIVER, AUGUST 30TH, 1876.

SOLID SILVER PRIZE CUP PRESENTED BY GEORGE W. CHILDS, ESQ., CONTESTED FOR BY THE INTERNATIONAL COLLEGE FOURS ON THE SCHUYLKILL RIVER.

to become permanently successful. This road is graded throughout for a double track, has substantial iron bridges, and is laid with steel rails and stone ballast. Its stock comprises new and powerful engines, comfortable and convenient cars, finished with all due elegance, and, in fact, all the appliances which modern art and science have made available for railway uses.

Our illustration presents a view of the bridge at Yardleyville, New Jersey, which is one of the engineering triumphs of the country. This bridge, with its approaches, is 4,000 feet long, and was built by the North Pennsylvania and the Delaware and Bound Brook Railroad Companies, the dividing line being the middle of the Delaware River. It first crosses the Belvidere division of the Pennsylvania Railroad and the Raritan Canal feeder, which lie here side by side, by means of two 60-feet spans, and by a draw-span of 182 feet, all made of wrought iron, and measuring 19 feet between the trestles. Beyond these, extending westward to a distance of 622 feet to the river, is a timber trestle, the bridge in turn being 1,448 feet long, supported on eight sandstone, ashlar pillars, and two abutment piers of combined ashlar and rubble. Six of the piers are in the river, the rest on a solid cobblestone substratum.

vantages. At Bergen Point the road crosses Newark Bay by a bridge, fully a mile in length, to Elizabeth. A little distance beyond this, the "All Rail Line to Long Branch" diverges from the main line.

From Elizabeth the road passes through pleasant villages, including Roselle, Cranford, Westfield, Fanwood, and Plainfield. From this point the section of country traversed by the road is full of Revolutionary reminiscences, many marches, skirmishes, and battles having occurred on this historic ground. Just beyond Plainfield is Washington Rock, associated with the great chief whose name it bears, from having been the lookout station used by him during the campaign. On the plains beneath this occurred a skirmish between the troops of Sir William Howe and Lord Sterling. A little further on, the road passes through Bound Brook, diverges from the main line of the Central Railroad of New Jersey, crosses the Raritan River, and runs off southwesterly to the Delaware River, a distance of twenty-seven miles.

Here is a fertile and well-watered farming country, pleasant to look upon, and interesting to one thoroughly acquainted with its history during the period of the Revolution. It was at Rock Hill, a few miles southeast of

was under the immediate supervision of the committee selected by the Agricultural Board, and Mr. Coleman, a prominent and practical agriculturist of England, was chosen chairman of the committee.

All the celebrated machines of the country were entered for competition, and the experiments were thorough and complete. Each machine was submitted to the most difficult tests to which they are subject in their ordinary work. The implement known as the "Champion" was victorious, drawing the remarkable light draught of 131 pounds, the lightest on record. We have already illustrated the scene of this contest and the victory of the "Champion" machine.

This harvester is the invention of Mr. W. N. Whitely, of Springfield, Ohio, and dates back to 1852, when the inventor received his first patent. They are manufactured at Springfield, Ohio, at the factories of Warder, Mitchell & Co., "Champion" Machine Company, and Whitely, Fassler and Kelly, where nearly 40,000 were produced for the centennial year. The factories cover thirteen acres, and give employment to 2,500 operatives. One of the severe contests was to cut rolled grass, and the "Champion" successfully cut the rolled grass from the heavy rain-storm of the

THE FIRE OPPOSITE THE EXPOSITION BUILDINGS, SEPTEMBER 9TH—THE MAIN BUILDING IN PERIL.

The distance from rail to low water is 72 feet. The nine spans of which the bridge is made up measure in length as follows, from the pier centres, and commencing at the eastern bank, viz. : One abutment span of 60 feet, one span of 198 feet, five spans of 200 feet each, one span of 120 feet, and one abutment span of 60 feet. These are entirely constructed of wrought iron, the chords being made of angle iron, riveted and latticed. The floor system is made of built lateral beams, tied together longitudinally by a series of built beams under each rail, and over the centre of each truss.

This bridge, however, although a remarkable feat in railway engineering, is but one feature of the road, which offers many others of convenience and pleasurable attribute both as regards the construction of the road itself and the advantages of its scenery.

The Bound Brook Line starts from the foot of Liberty Street, North River, N. Y., the passenger crossing the Hudson River upon one of the Central Railroad Company's spacious and comfortable ferry-boats, and being landed at the Jersey Central Station, where the Philadelphia train is in waiting.

The first six miles of road over which he passes skirt the western shore of the bay, and offer very pleasing scenic ad-

Hopewell, the next Jersey town, that Washington wrote and issued his farewell address to the American Army in 1783. Crossing Stony Brook, the road enters Pleasant Valley, passes through Pennington, and so on to Yardleyville, a short distance above which town Washington crossed the Delaware on the memorable Christmas in 1776, to attack the British in Trenton, the spires of which city can be seen quite plainly from the railroad bridge.

This bridge, which we have already described, was commenced December 1st, 1874, and a train passed over it January 10th, 1876. The scenery here is very charming, and the bridge itself, as well as being mechanically remarkable, is to the observer on either shore a most ornamental structure. After crossing the bridge the road enters the North Pennsylvania railroad division of the line, extending a distance of twenty-nine miles through a highly cultivated and beautiful farming country.

The Philadelphia depot of the new line is at Berks Street, with a branch running direct to the Centennial Grounds.

HARVESTING-MACHINES COMPETITIVE EXHIBITION.

This exhibition commenced on the 5th of July, at Schenck's Station, on the Philadelphia and Trenton Railroad, and the trials proved very interesting. The contest

previous week. The Champion Companies have in the Agricultural Hall a mowing-machine worth $8,000, composed of gold, silver and rosewood, said to rival in beauty and finish any piece of machinery exhibited.

FISHING-CRAFT IN AGRICULTURAL HALL.

In our general description of the articles in the Agricultural Building we have taken occasion to refer to models of fishing-boats sent by different countries. Our illustration shows a number of these. One from Norway is a broad sloop, without bowsprit, and having a straight, high sternpost, and which carries a square sail, the yard being held away from the mast by a curious collar. A smaller-sized Norwegian boat offers a peculiar style of steering apparatus. It is a solid piece of wood, run out from one side of the upper part of the rudder, to the extremity of which is made fast a pole by a movable joint. The rudder is made to change its position by moving this pole backward and forward.

An open six-oared boat from Norway has a high, upright stem and sternpost and curved rudder, and a sail like a square sail, but with a very short yard. The oars are fastened by ropes to a single thole-pin. The Chebacco boat is a two-masted, full-bowed craft, having sails fore and aft, but

EXHIBIT OF GANTZ'S "SEA FOAM" BAKING POWDER, IN THE MAIN BUILDING.

no jib. The stem rises perpendicularly, the stern being also carried up to form a trawling-point. Sail-boats like these, the bows, however, sharper, and the general beam narrower, are still to be seen on our lakes.

OREGON IN THE AGRICULTURAL BUILDING.

ONE of the most curious exhibits in the Agricultural Building is comprised in the Oregon collection, but was only added to it during the latter part of August. This is a chronological chart, about 22 ft. long by 2½ ft. wide, in which is presented systematically the entire history of the human race, including, as far as is practicable, the record of leading events of every nation from the earliest time to the present. Here are seen mutations of empires, kingdoms, republics and states; their manners, customs and dress; their progress in civilization and discovery; the inventions which have changed the face of nature and the fate of nations, such as the steam-engine, electric telegraph, etc.; the introduction of letters; the progress of language; the spread of literature; the names, nationalities, and distinguishing characteristics of eminent men; the names and dates of all important battles and other events; sovereigns and the duration of their authority; the area and population of each country, together with fac-similes of ancient coins, medals, illustrations and monuments, obelisks and implements of warfare and husbandry; alphabetical letters and hieroglyphics; evidences of the stone age, the iron age and the brass age; scenes depicting the progress of invention and the structure of ships; astronomy, and the size, distance and number of heavenly objects.

This chart not only shows the periods of occurrence of each event in history, but the relation of one to another. One of the chief features of the work is its systematic arrangement on a synchronous basis. Thus it shows that the founding of Troy and Athens were contemporaneous with the Egyptian bondage, and the founding of Thebes by Cadmus, who first introduced letters. Here it is also displayed that when Solomon was writing his "Proverbs," Homer was at work on the "Iliad"; that while Lycurgus was alive in Sparta, Queen Dido existed in Carthage, and Elijah was prophesying; that while Isaiah was extant, Romulus was founding Rome—and so on. This chart is in fact a very useful illustration of object-teaching, and is certainly a credit to the distant State of Oregon, from whence it comes.

THE DOG AND HORSE SHOWS.

THE competitive exhibition of dogs and horses opened at the Live Stock Exhibition Grounds on Belmont Avenue, a short distance from the Centennial Grounds proper, on September 4th. For the accommodation of the dogs, nine long sheds, with double rows of stalls, were provided, and here about 600 canines were exhibited; while in the extensive plot of ground within the barriers, numbers of horses were shown, being ridden or driven in procession every afternoon past the Judges' stand, and otherwise under inspection at all hours during the day.

The actual number of dogs recorded in the catalogue was 557, a large majority being English and Irish setters. Next to these in point of numbers were pointers and terriers, black-and-tan, Skye, fox, bull, Scotch, etc. A few fox-hounds and beagles, still less grayhounds, two or three bloodhounds, spaniels and mastiffs, three or four St. Bernards, a few Newfoundland dogs, half a dozen Siberian dogs, and as many Dalmatian or coach-dogs, Pomeranian or Spitz dogs, and poodles, made up the general classification.

To the outside observer there were so many setters, that the variety seemed less than it really was; yet the exhibition, as certainly the largest ever held in this country, should be considered a successful one. Some of the dogs bear a very high valuation, certain Irish setters of extraordinary blood being held at 200 guineas in gold.

The entries of horses comprised 270, of which 143 were from the United States, and the balance from Canada; of thoroughbred turf stallions fourteen were exhibited by the United States and five by Canada; thoroughbred mares, six by the United States, one by Canada; trotting stallions, thirty-nine by the United States and two by Canada; the remaining portion of the American exhibits included Percheron stallions and mares, Clydesdale stallions and mares, walking horses, match teams, ponies, one mule from Tennessee, 20¼ hands high, weighing 2,200 pounds; draught horses, and one pure bred jack, four and a half years old, 9¾ hands high, weighing 265 pounds. Canada's exhibits included, beyond those mentioned, saddle horses, agricultural horses and mares, heavy draught stallions and mares, roadster stallions and mares, carriage stallions, carriage mares, and match teams. This portion of the exhibition was visited by from 4,000 to 5,000 persons daily during its continuance.

Nearly all the Canadian horses, so-called, were imported from England or Scotland, or were the immediate progeny of imported stock, Canada producing no important distinctive breed. One of the imported stallions, Marquis, weighed 2,100 pounds, and another, Royal Tom, weighed about 2,200. Among the roadsters was one said to have been bred by the Emperor Napoleon III., and a few of the animals came from fine stock, one being the son of Voltigeur, and another a grandson of the famous Kentucky horse, Lexington.

Among the Pennsylvania horses the principal animals were imported or of imported breed. One Clydesdale stallion was 17 hands high, and weighed 2,260 pounds. A curiosity of the American exhibit was a beautiful Arabian horse, brought from a tribe of Bedouins. He was fifteen hands high, grayish-white in color, and very gracefully formed. The great Norman draught horses and the little Percheron breed offered a marked contrast to each other. The show of American horses pure was very slim. All the noticeable animals were of English or Scotch birth.

THE PHOTOGRAPHIC EXHIBITION.

NORTH of the Main Building, and east of the Memorial Hall, situated on the Avenue of the Republic, is the building devoted to the exhibits in photography. It is a one-story structure, comprising a single large hall, and having screens projecting from the side walls, forming alcoves for exhibition purposes. It is of ample size and elegantly arranged, and on the walls are specimens of photographic art from nearly every country where the art is practiced.

There are 287 exhibits in all, of which 136 are American, the remainder comprising specimens from London, Manchester, Leeds, Dublin, Tunbridge Wells, Leamington, Lincoln, Aberdeen, Cardiff, and other places in Great Britian; Montreal, Kingston, Toronto in Canada, and Paris, St. Petersburg, Berlin, Coblentz, Vienna, Carlsruhe, Mainz, Bremen, Munich, Frankfort, Venice, Geneva, Dornach, Breslau, Hamburg, Weimar, Christiana, Ghent, Stockholm, Upsala, Warsaw and Nice, on the continent of Europe; also from Japan and from Rio de Janeiro, Para and Buenos Ayres, in South America. American contributions include all the more noted photographers in New York, Philadelphia, Brooklyn, San Francisco, Baltimore, Washington, Cleveland, Ohio; Rochester, N. Y.; Boston, Cincinnati, Chicago; Helena, Montana; and other cities.

Besides the ordinary photographic apparatus and views which are exhibited, there are articles which may be termed the curiosities of photography, among which are photographs in pastelle, oil, and canvas, photographic transparencies for magic lanterns, graphoscopes, pyro-photographs on porcelain, etc. Then there is a collection of daguerreotypes, 25 years old, exhibited by a St. Louis photographer. Another exhibit is of character photographs, representing the seven ages of man; also laughing and crying babies, these being from Cincinnati. Then there are portraits of Indians, views of Yellowstone Park, stereoscopic views of the Yosemite Valley, views of the Holy Land, original designs of ferns, feathers, and mosses in photographic transparencies for door and window decoration, microscopic photographs for charms, and many others.

There are also exhibits of articles used in photography, including the dark tent, passe-partout, in velvet cases, specimens of albuminous and other paper, revolving stereoscopes, chemicals and lenses, photographic apparatus, camera-stands, glacé embossing-press, and a very interesting collection, from a Philadelphia photographer, of illustrations of photography from August, 1839, to May, 1876.

The leading American exhibitors are Bradley and Rulofson, of San Francisco; Sarony, Kurtz, and Howell, of New York; Watkins, of San Francisco; Brady, of Washington; Hazzard, Hovey, and Broadbent, of Philadelphia, and others.

The exhibits of Kurtz and Howell are particularly worth notice; the elegant black-walnut case exhibited by Mr. Howell being the same which he exhibited at the Vienna Exposition. Of the European photographs, perhaps those of Vienna and St. Petersburg are the most interesting. Among the photographs from Vienna there are many portraits of beautiful women, in the treatment of which every attribute and quality of the art seems to have been employed with success. An exceedingly handsome series of

EXHIBIT BY THE CORK DISTILLERIES CO. OF OLD WHISKY, IN AGRICULTURAL HALL.

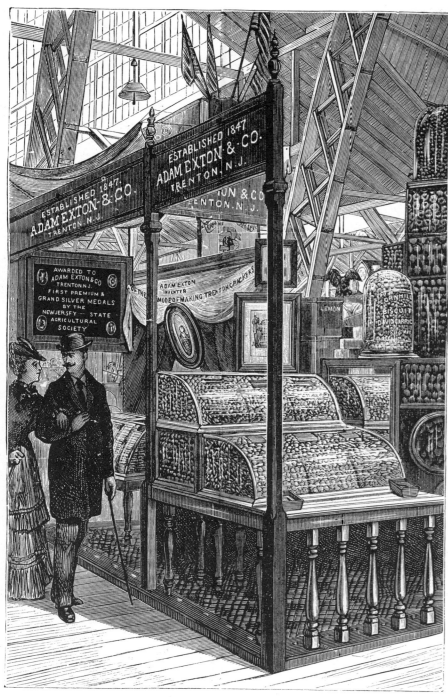

EXHIBIT OF ADAM EXTON'S CRACKERS, IN AGRICULTURAL HALL.

views of the Thousand Islands, and Northwestern scenery, including some elaborate studies of Minnesota Indians, made by a St. Paul photographer, pleasing views of the valley of the Saco and of Mt. Washington and the country about it, of Mt. Desert, or North Conway, Crawford Notch, Echo Lake, and Franconia, the canyons of Colorado and California, Lake George and the Upper Hudson, and a splendid display by Watkins, of San Francisco, of Pacific Coast views.

Altogether, the photographic collection is remarkably representative, and may be considered to offer perhaps as complete an exposition of the progress of the art, both in its work and in its mechanism, as could be got together. The exhibition is carefully and artistically arranged, and the whole display is entirely creditable to all who have been concerned in bringing it together.

BALTIMORE AND OHIO LOCOMOTIVES.

CLOSE beside the Maryland State Building are to be seen two locomotive engines, numbered 6 and 600, respectively. These are exhibited by the Baltimore and Ohio Railroad Company, and represent the engine of 1835 and that of to-day in juxta-position. It is most interesting to view these two pieces of mechanism side by side.

The old engine, with upright boiler, cylinders, and walking-beam, is very little like the superb structure beside it; and here can be seen at a glance, better than almost anywhere else, the vast improvements which have been made in locomotive construction during the forty-one years which have elapsed since No. 6 was built. The class of engines of which the latter is a specimen was designed and constructed by one Davis, of York, Pa., after the first proposal ever issued in the United States for locomotive engines. It was only in 1829 that Stevenson's "Rocket" developed the germ of the modern high-speed engine; and on the 4th of January, 1831, the Baltimore and Ohio Railroad Company issued an advertisement offering to pay the sum of four thousand dollars for the most approved engine which should be delivered upon their road for trial within five months, specifying certain conditions, such as that it should not exceed three and a half tons in weight, and capable of drawing upon a level road 115 tons, including the weight of the wagons, at the rate of 15 miles per hour. Four engines were produced in answer to this proposition, one of which was accepted by the company, and this engine was substantially like the exhibited engine No. 6, which superseded the others, and was known as the "Grasshopper" engine. Mr. Ross Winans, a well-known engineer of Baltimore, aided in the construction of this engine, and engine No. 6 has been at work continuously from 1835 until it was sent to the Exhibition.

The engine No. 600, which has been selected to represent the practice in locomotive construction at the present time, is a heavy-grade passenger-engine, combining great tractive force with high speed. Such engines are necessary in the difficult work of crossing the Alleghany Mountains, where there is a continuous grade of 116 feet per mile for a distance of 17 miles, upon which there are numerous curves of 600 feet radius. The fact that such a grade could be practically and economically overcome, without the employment of stationary power, was first demonstrated on this road, The railway over the Semmering Alp, from Vienna to Trieste, was subsequently constructed of corresponding grades, after the Austrian Government had sent its engineer to America to investigate the subject of steep gradients.

Engine No. 600 weighs 90,400 pounds. The boiler is double-riveted, and has a shell three-eighths of an inch in thickness, with steel fire-box. The cylinders are nineteen inches in diameter, with twenty-six inches stock. It is capable of hauling a passenger-train of six cars, including one Pullman car, up a grade of 116 feet to the mile, at a speed of 18 miles per hour, without the assistance of a helper.

No better means of comparing locomotive engines of the past and present could have been devised than in this very interesting exhibit.

THE WAGON AND CARRIAGE EXHIBITION BUILDING.

THE building devoted to the exhibition of wagons and carriages lies a little north of the western end of the Main Building, of which it is, in fact, an annex. This annex, although popularly recognized as the Carriage Building, has, in reality, a very large proportion of its space devoted to articles other than would be signified by this title, such as furniture, household utensils, stoves, hardware, willow-work, wooden-ware, etc. A display is made here of furnaces, ranges, registers, and other apparatus for heating buildings and for cooking purposes. There are also exhibits of refrigerators, coffee-mills, house-furnishing wooden-ware, fruit-jars, railroad refrigerator-cars, water-coolers, copper-ware in kettles, etc.; washing-machines, wringers, and ironing-boards; smoothing-irons, bath-tubs, copper boilers, cabinet wooden-work, earth closets, shutters, window-frames, doors, wainscoting, Venetian blinds, iron railings, wire-work, and cast-iron ornamental work, ventilating apparatus, illuminating tiles, and, in fact, all articles connected with domestic use and household fitting, excepting general household furniture, of which the only exhibits contained in this building are mattresses, chairs, and a few tables.

One interesting exhibit found here is that of Ethelbur Watts, of Philadelphia, and shows a portable bath-trunk, of which an illustration will be found elsewhere.

The hardware display is chiefly carriage hardware, including some very fine exhibits of carriage mountings in silver, oroide and gold plate. The basket-work and wicket-ware comprise baskets, cradles, work-stands, etc.

The carriages and other vehicles displayed include about 150 exhibits, of which about 40 are foreign, the remainder being from all parts of the United States. Of these latter, there are pleasure-carriages, coaches, landaulets, phaetons, coupés, rockaways, family, park and seaside carriages, road-wagons, buggies, track sulkies, broughams, top-wagons, dog-carts, and even velocipedes. Brewster makes a fine show, including a landau, town-coach, coupé, Victoria, and the celebrated Windsor wagon. There are also barouches, physicians' phaetons, cabriolets, track-wagons, children's carriages, spring and leaping horses, and an article from a Baltimore exhibitor which includes a sleeping-coach with a walking and nursery chair and vehicle all in one. Even hearses are not wanting, and quite a number of fine sleighs, particularly those from Portland, Maine, are exhibited.

The railway rolling-stock includes ordinary and narrow-gauge passenger-cars, parlor-cars, combined locomotive, baggage and passenger car from Boston, freight-cars, drawing-room cars, a hotel car exhibited by the Pullman Palace

Hungarian types is exhibited in this collection, and is well worthy of consideration and careful study. From Upsala, Sweden, there are many beautiful views of mountain-scenery, and a few studies from peasant life. There are quite a number of good Norwegian exhibits; and although the largest photographic exhibition of France is in the Main Building, there are a number here from Paris which are very pleasing. Among the Japanese pictures are some of young women who certainly possess claims to beauty. The majority of these pictures are published by the Japan Photographic Association of Yokohama, and give a very clear representation of the manners and customs of the country. They include troops of beggars, processions of soldiery, acrobats and jugglers, pictures of old men, views of Japanese scenery, etc.

The Bible land views photographed in 1874 merit attention. They include views of Damascus, the Jordan, Lebanon, Baalbek, the Sea of Galilee, Mt. Carmel, Sinai, Moses' Rock, the Wells of Moses, the Sphinx, the tombs at Petra, Jerusalem and Gethsemane. There is also a collection of Arctic views exhibited by a Boston firm. They represent glaciers and ice mountains, a crew of Arctic explorers hunting Polar bears, an Esquimaux in his lodge of skins, another in his kajah, or canoe, a steamer surrounded by hummock ice, ice-fields, etc.

The English photographic display includes both portraits and landscape. Among the latter are a "View from Drummond Castle," "Hertford, North Wales," "Scene in a Highland Village," "Killarney," etc. One frame of portraits includes the Duke of Edinburgh, the Prince Imperial, Earl Russell, the Duke of Connaught, the Duke of Norfolk, and other distinguished personages.

Of our own notabilities there are represented the late Senator Sumner, Wendell Phillips, William Loyd Garrison, Longfellow, President Grant, Lincoln, the late Vice President Wilson, Prof. Morse, Daniel Webster, Bryant, and many others.

The portion of the Hall occupied by Canada presents a very varied and pleasing selection of photographic work. A great deal of it is richly colored, and illustrates Winter sports, such as mask balls in skating rinks, sledge parties, marches on snow-shoes, and pictures representing the lives of trappers and hunters amid the northern snows. Canada makes a very large display, which will compare favorably with that of any country.

Of American scenery, besides the numerous photographs of American public buildings and of important bridges— one of these, by-the-way, being a remarkably fine picture of the Portage bridge on the Erie railway—there are many

G. Q. RICHMOND, THE CENTENNIAL COMMISSIONER FROM COLORADO.

THE CATARACT IN MACHINERY HALL.

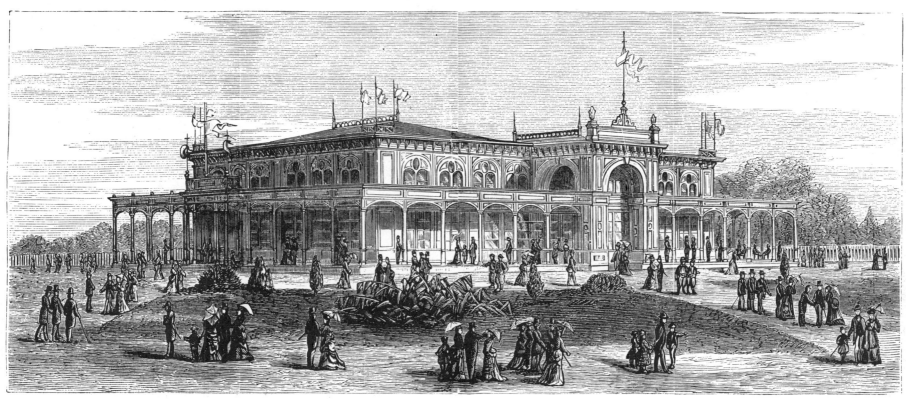

THE VIENNA BAKERY, ON THE CENTENNIAL GROUNDS.

Car Company, one and two-horse street-cars, and a large number of exhibits in car material and mechanism, including patent platforms, bumper-springs, couplings and lubricators, bell-punches and fare-registers, ventilating apparatus, hubs for wheels, etc. Finally, a Philadelphia house exhibits a model of an ice-boat.

Among the foreign exhibits, those of Great Britain are the most numerous and the most interesting. They come from London, Norwich, Manchester, Leamington and Coventry, and include landaus, barouches, coupés, broughams, park and road drags, phaetons, Whitechapel carts, four-in-hand drags, gig, char-à-banc, wagonette, dog-cart, and, finally, a child's perambulator, and two exhibits of bicycles.

Russia exhibits a Victoria from St. Petersburg, and a drosky from Warsaw; also a trotting-wagon and sledge with robe from Moscow, besides several exhibits of harness. Canada sends a cariole, phaeton, buggies, landaulet, double and other sleighs, including cutter and adjustable-back sleighs. From Italy there is an exhibit of street cabs. From Vienna a landau, with harness and saddlery; and from Germany, material, including axles, springs, etc.

John Robertson, of Sidney, New South Wales, makes the only wagon exhibit from that country. It is a Concord box, with new front, the wood-work and iron-work being of New South Wales material.

Among this collection there are certain noticeable exhibits which we will indicate. One of these is a lady's brougham, lined with rich green satin. In the front portion is a toilet-case of bird's-eye maple, and revolving mirrors so arranged that the whole can be drawn in out of sight. A light sleigh is shown, weighing only 80 lbs. It is colored in black, with lines of gold, and trimmed with dark-green velvet plush, and is intended for but one person. Another, similarly finished, for two persons, has dark maroon trimmings. A new feature is a small wire sieve on the dash-board to keep out snowballs and drift snow. A Canadian sleigh is colored maroon, and lined with maroon-colored cloth. It has bearskin rugs, and a novelty is an extension of the runners above the dash-board for 5½ feet. These are surmounted with horsehair plumes, dyed in solferino. From the ends of the dashboard hang silver bells.

A Cincinnati manufacturer exhibits a buggy with side-springs, by which it is claimed that these give greater ease of motion than the elliptic spring, while combining the advantages of a side-bar attachment.

Rochester sends an elaborately finished hearse in ebony, with rich gold mountings, and with the border about the windows inlaid with gold and silver plate. On either side, near the top, are crestings in silver. At the top is a handsome railing in gold and silver plate, divided into sections, and from each rise urns in gold plate, elaborately decorated. On the top, in silver, is the figure of Faith, supporting herself on a cross. The floor is

covered with mahogany, silver mounted, and on either side a railing with vases holding artificial flowers.

The road-wagon from Sidney, South Australia, which we have mentioned, has a body of unpainted wood, varnished. On one side is painted a kangaroo, and on the other a picture of an ostrich.

The railway carriages are, some of them, the most magnificent imaginable of such structures. The narrow gauge exhibit includes a boudoir and parlor car, called Dom Pedro II., and was built for the San Pablo and Rio de Janeiro Railway, of Brazil, and is to be used on state occasions. It is constructed in sections, so that it may be taken apart and stowed in the hold of a vessel. It was manufactured by the Jackson & Sharpe Company, of Wilmington, Del., and is furnished with Miller platforms and the Westinghouse brake. It will seat thirty persons. In the front portion of the car is a small boudoir. The carpet is drab-color, with delicate flowers, and the window-curtains of dark-green and gold. Near the centre is a table covered with crimson rep, on which are placed pictures of the Emperor of Brazil and his daughter, the Princess Imperial. There are also two handsome mirrors, and two cabinets—one to contain books and the other meats and fruits for luncheon—on which are placed gold-plated candelabras holding wax candles. The sides are inlaid with different woods, and the car is lighted from the top by small windows with stained glass. Adjoining the boudoir are two other rooms, one a reading, and the other a writing, room; the one fitted up in blue, and the other in crimson. Next to these is the ordinary apartment, with walnut chairs, cane-seated, and the sides beautifully inlaid with gold, walnut, mahogany, and ebony. The doors have panels of walnut and rosewood.

The exhibits of the Pullman Palace Car Company comprise two very handsome cars, combining all the comforts and conveniences for which they are famous. A feature of the highly ornamental decoration of these consists of inlaid work of bouquets of flowers, made of pieces of wood stained in different colors, and then inlaid, producing delicate and beautiful effects. The ceiling is lined with canvas, on which are painted leaves and flowers. The berths are arranged as is customary in these cars, so as to be closed up

in the day time and put entirely out of sight, with the exception of the portion of the frame which is shut up against the side of the car; when let down for the night, these are formed into comfortable beds, in two tiers, having rich hangings of crimson, blue and gold. When transformed into a dining-room, the apartment is broken up in little sections with a table and seats for four in each section. It is also fitted up with toilet-rooms with a number of handsome mirrors.

The refrigerator is a square box, hung underneath the car. The brakes are the Westinghouse patent, and on each side of the wheels is a large flange, which, should the car run off the track, will catch on the rail and prevent it from going further.

An exhibit from an inventor of Lincoln, Ill., illustrates the working of a new invention for coupling cars. It consists of a model of a train of cars, the coupling being done without the necessity, on the part of the brakesmen, of getting between the cars. The coupling apparatus consists of heavy steel draw-bars with hooks, which, when the cars come together, runs into a square hitch in the iron bull's-nose on the end of each of the cars. If it is so desired, by means of a very simple arrangement, the apparatus can be thrown out of gear, and in such a case, when the cars come together they will not couple. No springs are used, and the mechanism is at once simple and ingenious.

THE STATE BUILDINGS.

Arkansas Building.

The Arkansas Building lies west of that of Maryland. It is large, and contains much that is interesting. On the east and west of the entrance, ranged against the walls, are sheaves of wheat and oats, bundles of timothy and red top grass, and stalks of corn measuring six feet in height. The grains are well-formed and of good weight, while the hay and grass are luxuriant. There are sections of trees showing immense growth of timber, specimens of petrified wood, and large bolls of cotton. Near these are two counters containing various exhibits, both made of different kinds of Arkansas woods, beautifully inlaid, and handsome specimens of carpenter's work. One contains gigantic ears of corn, beans, barley, oats, dried grass, wheat, and oat-straw, raw cotton, brooms, specimens of work by the pupils of the State Institution for the Blind, wines and leathers.

Standing on the floor behind the counter is a box containing a cotton bush with bolls of cotton growing on it. On the other counter is a great variety of archæological remains, as tomahawks, stone pestles, darts, and other Indian relics, some of great antiquity. There are also specimens of

THE AMERICAN RESTAURANT, ON THE CENTENNIAL GROUNDS.

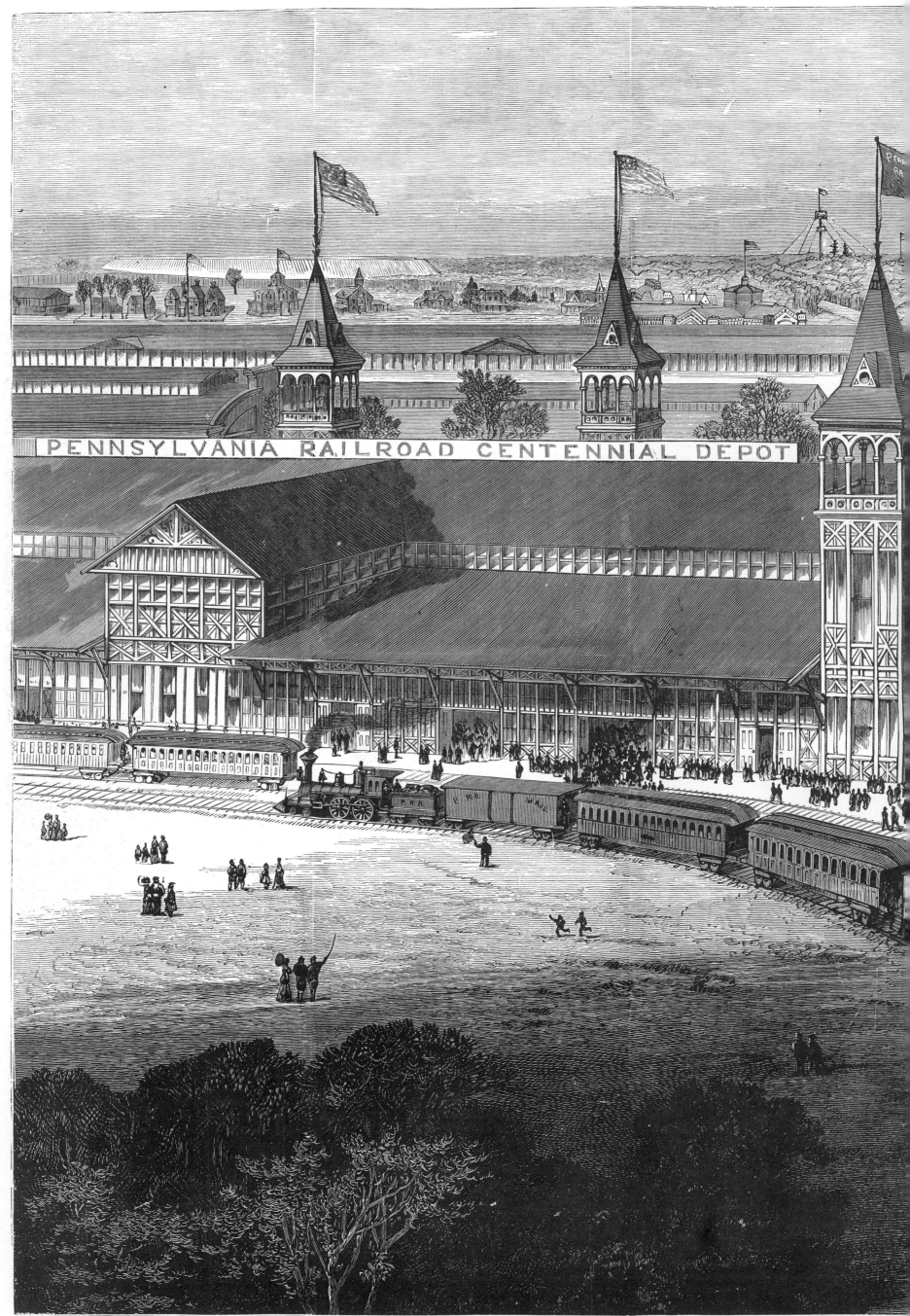

Shoe and Leather Building.   Pennsylvania Railroad Centennial Depot.   United States Government Building.

VIEW, LOOKING NORTH OF THE PENNSYLVANIA RAILRO

Machinery Hall.   Agricultural Hall.   Judges' Pavilion.   Horticultural Hall.   Main Building.

NTENNIAL DEPOT AND THE EXPOSITION BUILDINGS.

jewelry, made from smoked and clear quartz, minerals, and a cravat made of silk raised in Arkansas, and which was worn on the Fourth of July by Dr. G. W. Lawrence, the Centennial Commissioner from that State. Near the southeastern section of the building, the St. Louis, Iron Mountain and Southern Railway Company have erected a case containing specimens of novaculite, argentiferous Galena marble, magnetic iron, etc., found along their route.

CONNECTICUT BUILDING.

The large hall of this building, used as a general reception-room, contains a fine old-fashioned fire-place, surrounded with painted tiles. Above the mantel is the gun with which General Putnam is said to have killed the wolf, beside the portrait of Putnam himself. On the mantel is a portrait of Governor Ingersoll. There is an old-fashioned clock, and a sideboard with specimens of silverware manufactured in Connecticut. There is also a cottage organ, also manufactured in the State. In one corner is a blue banner, containing the names of the Presidents, the letters being cut out of wood from the famous Charter Oak; and in the opposite corner is the coat-of-arms of Great Britain, which hung above the chair of the Speaker of the House of Representatives. In addition to this is a section of the Charter Oak, and a wooden ham and wooden nutmegs of the same tree. Near the fire-place is a spinning-wheel.

INDIANA STATE BUILDING.

This consists of three sections. One of these is used as a general reception-room, and contains, in addition to slabs of native woods, a chair made of 100 pieces of wood from Elkhart County. Back of this is a lady's reception-room containing, in addition to the furniture, a large painting of the scenery of the Sierra Nevada, and some pictures in worsted-work. In the rear of the hall is a post-office and baggage-room, and on the right an office, in the rear of which is a reading-room with files of papers, maps, etc. The central hall rises clear to the roof, and on the walls are panels, on which are painted in large letters statistics of resources, population, etc., and the different counties and large towns.

MARYLAND BUILDING.

The Maryland Building stands north of the New York State Building, and is a small structure, but contains many very interesting articles. Among these are a collection of models of Chesapeake oyster-boats, with tongs and drags used in catching oysters. In the rear is a model of a fish-hatching house at Druid Hill Park, Baltimore, in which

EXHIBIT OF THE NEW YORK SLATE ROOFING COMPANY.

thousands of black bass, California salmon and trout are hatched annually and placed in the rivers of Maryland. Near by is a model of a Packing House, with wharf, boats, etc.

Arranged about the hall are cabinets containing oysters found in the Chesapeake and tributary waters. There is also a very beautiful collection of minerals, handsome marbles, sections of wood, and large pieces of coal. At each end of the hall is the escutcheon of the State, and on the walls are portraits of personages prominently identified with the history of Maryland, contributed by the Maryland Historical Society. Among these are Charles Carroll, of Carrollton, Samuel Chase, William Packer, Baron de Kalb, members of the Calvert family, and others. The first room on the left is an office, and contains a register. A piece of wood painted so as to closely resemble marble is here exhibited. In the adjoining room is a belt made of wampum by the Indians, and casts of the arms of Penn

and Lord Baltimore, as cut on the boundary stones of Mason and Dixon's Line, and a grant of land in Baltimore County to the Taylor family, by Lord Baltimore.

MASSACHUSETTS STATE BUILDING.

The construction of this building has already been described. The wainscoting is of unstained woods, and the rafters supporting the roof are left unclosed. On the right of the entrance is the Governor's reception-room, richly furnished, with paintings on the walls, a Japanese screen, and a number of other ornamental objects. The hall contains an organ, and a book-case filled with standard works. At the north end is an office with a register and post-office, and near it a small room where parcels, etc., may be left.

MISSISSIPPI STATE BUILDING.

This, although a small structure, is one of the most pleasing and original on the grounds. It is a log cabin, every foot of the timber used in the construction of which was sent from Mississippi, with carpenters to erect it. With its rough-hewn wood, its artistic windows, Gothic doorway and hanging moss from its eaves, its balconies formed of natural wood, it is a notable one among the State buildings.

There are comprised in this little building 68 different kinds of wood, not including the door-panels, which include 48 other varieties. The outside walls are of hickory and split logs with the bark on; the doors and window-frames are made of different varieties of pine, the whole being ornamented by natural curiosities in wood found in Mississippi forests, and the inner walls made of finely polished specimens of pine, some of which are quite beautiful, both in color and in marking. Hanging baskets, arched verandas and moss-hung porticoes complete the ornamental features of this characteristic structure.

WEST VIRGINIA BUILDING.

This is quite near the last-mentioned building, lying on the eastern slope of George's Hill. It covers about four times as much ground as that of the Mississippi Building, and, like that, is composed entirely of wood representing many native varieties. All about the plot of ground surrounding it are large blocks and masses of bituminous and other coal, native to this region. Within the buildings are found specimens of petroleum in various stages, sections of timber, and some objects illustrating children's work, including crayon drawings, compositions, etc. Contained in the West Virginia Buildings are a great variety of

"MASSACHUSETTS DAY." SEPTEMBER 14TH—RECEPTION BY GOVERNOR RICE.

CENTENNIAL RIFLE MATCH AT CREEDMOOR—THE FIRST DAY'S COMBINED PRACTICE OF THE FOREIGN AND AMERICAN TEAMS, SEPTEMBER 6TH, 1876.

specimens illustrating the timber production of the State, also iron and copper ores, specimens of petroleum, wines, agricultural products, limestone, marble, woodwork in axhelves, crockery manufactured at Wheeling, potter's clay, black flint, fire-clay, yellow ochre, mill-stone rock, etc. There is also a shield exhibited by George B. Crawford, of Wellsburgh, which is made of a number of pieces of wood, to show the great variety of timber in Berks County. It bears on its surface, cut in the wood, the names of the

ers' rooms, and ladies' parlors. In the latter are portraits of the survivors of Perry's victory on Lake Erie, framed with wood from the ship *St. Lawrence.* An extension is occupied as a reading-room, and contains files of the Ohio newspapers, register, etc.

ILLINOIS STATE BUILDING.

The building erected by the State of Illinois for the headquarters of the Illinois Commissioners to the Centen-

Tennessee has not erected any building, but has a large tent, in which she exhibits some very fine specimens of iron ores, coals and marbles of that section of the country. This tent lies between the Maryland and Ohio Buildings.

Iowa displays some worsted-work representing " Henry the Fourth on Shrewsbury Plain," a " Madonna," " Abraham and Hagar," and "Rebecca and Rowena."

The Rhode Island Building is also intended simply as

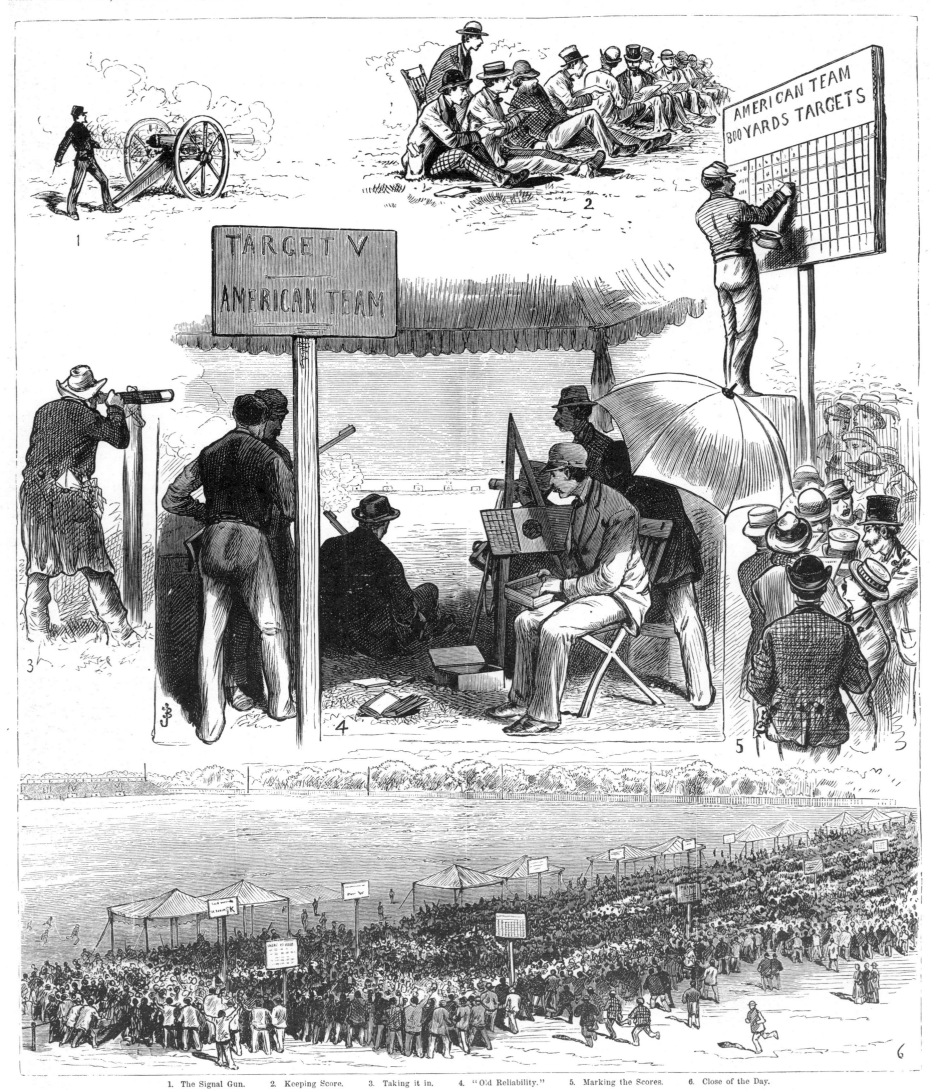

1. The Signal Gun.   2. Keeping Score.   3. Taking it in.   4. "Old Reliability."   5. Marking the Scores.   6. Close of the Day.

THE INTERNATIONAL RIFLE MATCH AT CREEDMOOR—THE FIRST DAY'S SHOOTING, SEPTEMBER 14TH.

Presidents of the United States, and of the signers of the Declaration of Independence. There is also a gigantic map of Berks County, maps of the State, and a map for the blind, prepared by H. H. Johnson, teacher in the West Virginia Institute for the Blind and Deaf and Dumb.

OHIO STATE BUILDING.

This State has erected a structure partly of stone, partly of wood. There are rooms on both sides of the central hall, occupied respectively as a general office, Commission-

nial was situated on State Avenue, north of the United States Government Building. It was a neat and serviceable structure, presenting a very pretty appearance. Its dimensions were 60 by 40 feet. We give an illustration of this building, representing its front on State Avenue.

THE REMAINDER OF THE STATES.

The remainder of the States have erected buildings, most of which are simply for the accommodation of residents visiting the Exposition.

headquarters, and contains reception-rooms and a register for visitors.

The New York State Building is elegantly furnished, probably with more costly articles than any other State building on the Grounds. It contains a few fine paintings, one of which is the Centennial picture, painted by John Phillips, of Chicago, representing a centenarian telling the story of the Revolution to a captain of the War of the Rebellion, and his wife, who holds an infant in her arms, completing the three generations. This is a notable work,

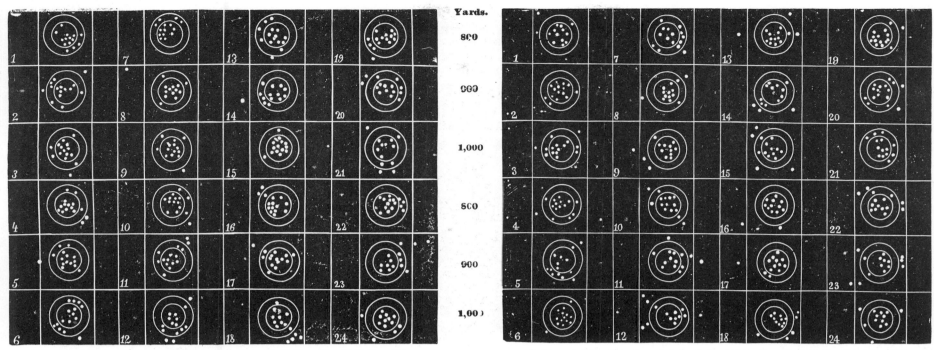

Yards.
800
900
1,000
800
900
1,000

Dakin, 1, 2, 3. Weber, 4, 5, 6. Fulton, 7, 8, 9. Rathbone, 10, 11, 12. Allen, 13, 14, 15. Gildersleeve, 16, 17, 18. Farwell, 19, 20, 21. Bodine, 22, 23, 24.

Rathbone, 1, 2, 3. Gildersleeve, 4, 5, 6. Bodine, 7, 8, 9. Farwell, 10, 11, 12. Weber, 13, 14, 15. Allen, 16, 17, 18. Dakin, 19, 20, 21. Fulton, 22, 23, 24.

DIAGRAM OF THE TARGETS OF THE AMERICAN TEAM, VICTORS IN THE INTERNATIONAL RIFLE MATCH.

and should have been in Memorial Hall. The New York Building contains a register, furnishes unlimited supplies of stationery to visitors, and has a post-office.

The California Building comprises one large room, handsomely finished, and in which are represented the native growths of wood, by long panels of each species fitted into the walls. In the rear of this apartment is a room devoted to the uses of the State Commissioners.

The Pennsylvania Building is designed to afford reception-rooms and a rendezvous for Pennsylvanians. Above the doorway is a keystone in gold, with the word "Pennsylvania" in black letters.

Delaware uses her State Building as a rendezvous, and offers files of the Delaware papers and a register.

New Hampshire has a reception-hall where a register is kept, and the walls are hung with views of New Hampshire scenery.

The Michigan Building is used solely as headquarters.

In the Wisconsin Building is a portrait of Joseph Creete, who died at Portage City, in 1866, and who is said to have been 141 years old; also a portrait of a squaw, who is said to have reached the astonishing age of 160 years.

The New Jersey Building is in the old style of half-timber and red-tiled architecture. Besides a reception-room, it contains a room for editors and reporters. There are no special exhibits in the New Jersey Building, but the red tiles which cover the exterior of the structure are illustrative of that class of products of the State.

IOWA AND HER AGRICULTURAL EXHIBITS.

THE State of Iowa is nearly rectangular in its form, its breadth from east to west being about 300 miles, and its length from north to south a little over 200 miles. Its most prominent cities are Davenport, Dubuque, Muscatine, and Keokuk, on the Mississippi, and Council Bluffs and Sioux City on the Missouri. The area of the State is about 35,000,000 acres.

Iowa possesses an almost uniform altitude, having no mountainous elevations. The most striking feature of its topography is the predominance of prairies. Timber is scarce, being only found skirting the streams on the bottom-lands, where, in many parts of the State, are to be found elm, linden, poplar, ash, black walnut and white oak trees. The climate is mild and healthful; in the northern counties, bordering on Minnesota, the Winters are occasionally very severe. The soil of this State is unsurpassed for richness and fertility; 95 per cent. of it is said to be tillable.

So much for the general characteristics of the Hawkeye State. A special feature of the display of Iowa in Agricultural Hall consists of specimens of its soil. These are inclosed in glass tubes, each six feet deep, taken from a number of counties in the State. Thirty-five counties are represented, and it is said that one of these specimens has been selected by the Swedish Commission to be forwarded to Sweden as a sample of the agricultural district where so many of her people have found a home.

The great staple crop of Iowa is Indian corn, of which

PRESENTATION OF PRIZES TO THE AMERICAN TEAM AT GILMORE'S GARDEN, SEPTEMBER 15TH—CHEERING THE FOREIGN TEAMS.

MAJOR-GENERAL THOMAS S. DAKIN.

COLONEL HENRY A. GILDERSLEEVE.

MAJOR HENRY FULTON.

the yield last year amounted to more than 136,000,000 bushels. A most interesting display is the magnificent pomological collection in wax, embracing over one thousand specimens of more than three hundred varieties of fruit, which are seen in the Agricultural Building. Specimens of the actual fruits will be displayed in the Fall pomological exhibition. Two hundred of these casts have been secured by the Japanese Commission, and will be sent to Japan at the close of the Exhibition. Of corn there are 74 varieties shown ; of wheat, rye, oats and barley, 80 ; 30 of grass and field seeds ; 200 of vegetable seeds ; 60 kinds of grass on the stalk ; and 65 or 70 varieties of timber seeds. All these exhibits are from one farm, and are intended as a sample of what may be grown on any farm in the State.

Iowa took the first prize given by the Butter and Cheese Association ; and 8,000 pounds a week of this butter are shipped to Philadelphia. An exhibit which is a curiosity is also found in the Agricultural Building, being a table composed of 3,983 pieces of Iowa woods. The design of the table consists of twenty-four arrows, the points of the largest six forming a six-pointed star in the centre, and six unstrung bows in the border ; presenting a most artistic surrounding. This work is the result of six months' labor by a resident of Iowa. One hundred and sixty varieties of Iowa woods are displayed in this department.

It may as well be mentioned here that Iowa has a collection of specimens of her mineral and geological wealth in the mineral annex to the Main Building, which is said to be one of the finest in the Exhibition. The geological stratification is shown by specimens of the various formations to the depth of 3,700 feet, embracing sections of the entire State. A sample of lead ore from the celebrated mines of Dubuque is shown, containing 97 per cent. of pure lead. Iowa also sends several samples of its coal, which is practically inexhaustible, underlying, as is computed, four million acres of the State.

Samples of building-stones, and relics of the moundbuilders, complete the mineral and archæological display of Iowa.

COL. LOPEZ FABRA AND THE TOLEDO BLADE.

COLONEL FRANCISCO LOPEZ FABRA was chief of the Spanish Centennial Commission, and it was under his administration that the magnificent exhibition of Spain was organized and arranged with a degree of success which made it one of the prominent features of the entire display.

Colonel Fabra has served for thirty-five years in the Spanish army, his administrative capacity and talent for organization having occasioned his frequent selection for duties requiring the exhibition of these qualities. For

COLONEL JOHN BODINE.

RANSOM RATHBONE.

twelve years prior to the Centennial Exhibition he had been at the head of certain important geographical works connected with the Post-Office Department. He is also a practical, scientific man, and in 1871 first put into operation in Spain the application of photography to printing, reproducing by this method the first edition of Cervantes's "Don Quixote," which was published in 1605. This phototype reproduction received an award in Vienna and also in Philadelphia. In 1873 Colonel Fabra was a member of the jury of the Vienna Exhibition. At the time of his appointment to the Commission at Philadelphia he filled in Barcelona the position of President of the Industrial

Section of the "Junta Provincial," and also of the "Ateneo Barcelonés."

Colonel Fabra was distinguished while in this country by the energy and earnestness with which he acquainted himself with the manners and customs of the people, and by the urbanity and business-like character of his administration. He traveled over a considerable portion of the country, employing his leisure time in this manner, the better to inform himself concerning our chief cities and towns and their inhabitants. In one of his journeys he visited the city of Toledo, Ohio, and in the course of his stay there called in at the office of the Toledo *Blade*, a journal chiefly known to the American public as being the original source of the humorous writings of Mr. D. R. Locke (Petroleum V. Nasby), who was at one time its editor, and is still a regular contributor. Colonel Fabra was impressed with the title of the "Blade," and after his visit to the office, and in consideration of the compliment paid to his own country by the selection of this title, he presented to the paper a genuine "Toledo blade," a magnificent weapon of the finest quality and workmanship, and the genuine production of the celebrated city whose name it bears. We give an illustration of this sword, whose description is as follows : Its form is of the double-edge pattern commonly seen in medieval pictures. At the hilt the blade is one and three-quarter inches wide, and a quarter of an inch thick, and tapers symmetrically to a sharp point. It is intended mostly for thrusting, but can be used with terrible effect as a broadsword. The length of the blade from hilt to point is 43 inches. Near the hilt the blade is neatly inlaid in gold, in arabesque patterns, and bears on one side the inscription, "Fabric de Toledo—1873." A two-handed steel hilt with an elaborately carved wrought guard, inlaid with gold, affords the means of handling the weapon, and makes the length altogether 65 inches, or more than four and a half feet. Although so large and long, so skillfully is it made that it can be poised and wielded with the greatest ease. The scabbard is of the finest Cordova leather, the tip and mouth-piece of fine steel, inlaid with gold. Accompanying

LIEUTENANT-COLONEL WILLARD B. FARWELL.

L. WEBER.

ISAAC LEROY ALLEN.

THE AMERICAN TEAM.

this gift was a letter addressed to the editor of the Toledo *Blade*, written in Spanish, and which, translated, reads as follows:

"I have had the honor to forward to the Director-General of the Philadelphia Exhibition the following communication:

"'The Press of the United States of America has spontaneously and without exception, with a generosity and courtesy worthy of all encomium, held only expressions of sympathy and eulogy for the Spanish portion of the Centennial Exposition. Therefore, desiring to leave to the entire press a testimonial of my appreciation and affection, I have selected for its representation the journal the Toledo *Blade*, on account of the name it bears, and the splendid city where it is published, as a representative, and have transmitted and presented, in the name of Spain, one of the best of the Toledo swords shown at the Centennial Exhibition, a modest offering symbolical not only of the confidence inspired by the high and wise institution to which it is dedicated, but also the firmness and temper of our good-will. God give you many years.

"'FRANCIS. LOPEZ FABRA,
"'*Royal Commissioner of Spain.*'"

After that of the Damascus blades, the sword-manufacture of Toledo is the most renowned in the world. It is probable that this manufacture was introduced into Spain by Arabs at the time of their conquest of the country, they having secrets in the art of forging steel which are as much a mystery to-day as ever. Indeed, though attempts were made to remove the manufacture from Toledo to Seville, the same processes which were employed at Toledo failed there to produce the same sword of steel, and for want of a better explanation of the cause of the failure, it was attributed to some peculiar excellence of the water in the Tagus in which those of the Guadalquivir were lacking. Swords are still made of as good qualities as ever.

Marvelous stories are told of these blades. In ancient times so sharp were they that they would cut a silk handkerchief in two as it was thrown in the air; while they would sever iron bars without losing their edge, and such was their exquisite temper that they could be tied into a knot, or rolled up like a watch-chain. The latter statement is undoubtedly true, since visitors at the Centennial had exhibited before them blades so rolled up and packed inside of a circular hole in a block.

COLONEL FRANCISCO LOPEZ FABRA, CHIEF OF THE SPANISH CENTENNIAL COMMISSION.

Islands. A rich display of the celebrated sword-blades of Toledo is to be seen here, as also quite a fine collection of engineering and other mathematical instruments. A number of war-weapons of the natives of the Spanish colonial countries may be also seen in this building. The collection of models includes also those of bridges and aqueducts, as well as quite a number of preparations in *papier-mache* or other similar material, illustrating the sub-

---

AUSTRIAN EXHIBIT OF ORNAMENTAL LEATHER.

THE Austrians compete fairly with the French in the manufacture of numerous little articles of stationery and personal ornament, among which those manufactured in leather attracted special attention, as exhibited in highly ornamented pavilions in the Austrian Department of the Main Building. This manufacture included portable writing-desks in great variety, pocket match-boxes, traveling candlesticks, bon-bon boxes, and numerous other fancy articles in leather. In one manufactory in Vienna there were produced, in 1875, ten thousand three hundred dozens of these articles in all varieties. Our illustration, on page 176, displays a pavilion filled with specimens of this manufacture.

THE SPANISH BUILDING.

THE Spanish Government Building is about 100 by 80 ft. in dimensions, and is devoted to the exhibition of articles representative of the Government works of Spain and its colonies, with other exhibits illustrating the advancement of the different phases of education. One side of the building is devoted entirely to a large collection of books, architectural designs and photographs, framed maps, charts, plans, etc. The collection of books is largely representative of recent Spanish literature in science and arts, as well as in history, poetry, the drama, theology, etc. Contiguous to this collection is the exhibition of the Spanish War Department, comprising models of fortifications, of artillery, pontoon-bridges, army-wagons, etc., with specimens of Spanish arms, cannons, sabres and small-arms. A very handsome steel model of heavy ordnance attracts considerable attention. A few stuffed figures exhibit the different costumes in use in the Spanish army. These exhibits occupy the entire centre of the hall, the remaining side being filled with specimens of Spanish woods, including many hundred varieties, among which cork is prominent. A collection of agricultural implements is ranged upon the walls, and there are stuffed birds and animals, a small collection of insects, specimens of gums, barks, a herbarium in six large folios, and a few musical instruments. Besides these, there is quite a display of medicinal barks, gums, resins, and preserved fruits from the Philippine

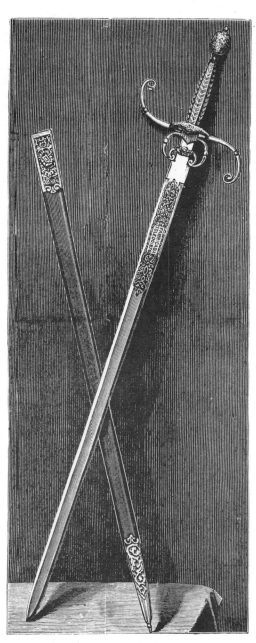

THE TOLEDO BLADE.

ject of anatomy. The walls all about are hung with photographs and maps in large numbers. A few models of boats, some with lateen-sails from the Philippine Islands, stand on a table near the centre of the hall. The army exhibition includes also military equipments, army-chests, harness, etc.; also a very pretty model of infantry barracks. Models representing the city and port of San Sebastian, with its fortifications, and those showing the battles of the Spanish forces against the Moors in Morocco during 1859 and 1860, are most interesting as illustrating military movements. Taken in connection with the splendid exhibits made by Spain in the Main Building and in Agricultural Hall, this collection is truly remarkable, and causes us to regret exceedingly the absence of a complete catalogue of the Spanish collection of articles in the Exposition.

The book exhibits comprise nearly 400 numbers, each of which includes a selection of separate works, contributed by publishers and authors, besides the institutions and Government departments.

Quite a variety of curious exhibits are made in decoration, including an inlaid table from Cuba, and specimens of mosaics in wood from Madrid.

Of the exhibits of woods, quite a number are from the Island of Cuba, including dye-woods, ornamental-woods, etc. Those from Spain comprise cork, pine, yew, oak, etc.

ITALIAN CHAISES.

VISITORS to the carriage annex to the Main Building will have noticed the two peculiar-looking cabs exhibited by the Kingdom of Italy. These cabs or chaises were somewhat like the "Hansom" cab of London, but different from it in certain particulars. The specimens exhibited were constructed of the finest materials, and in their linings, drapery and other ornamentation were made with due regard to beauty as well as to service.

FRENCH GOVERNMENT BUILDING.

A LITTLE to the west of Memorial Hall annex is a building erected by the French Government, and devoted in its contents to a display of models, charts, etc., illustrating the progress of engineering and important Government structures in France. The building itself is made of a framework of iron, with iron girders and rafters, and the walls filled in with brick. Some ornamentation has been made by the arrangement of black-faced bricks in diamond shapes. On each side of the entrance on the south front the wall is made of ornamental tiles, in white, blue and green, arranged in figures.

Entering the vestibule, we find it paved with encaustic tiles, arranged in a square pattern. In this vestibule are two lighthouse lanterns. The one in the right-hand corner is a catoptric light, to show different faces in different directions, so as to present the bearing to a vessel. In the left-hand corner is an electric light, with Fresnel glass. The interior of the building is one large hall, of which the sides and ceiling are paneled and elaborately painted. The centre of the roof, and from end to end, for a width of eighteen feet, is open, the canvas covering being painted in square panel-work designs. At the north end, facing the vestibule or entrance, is a large map of France, showing public roads and railways, harbors and anchorage grounds, the principal points being marked with brass-headed nails. This is in a massive frame, and surmounted by a trophy of flags. On the walls are hung pictures, plans and elevations of important public works, harbors, etc., with drawings of details of construction well arranged about the main hall, showing viaducts, iron and stone bridges, sections of engineering-work, etc. One of the pictures shows the side elevation of the stone bridge over the Seine, at Point-du-Jour. Near this is a picture of the viaduct of the Rocquefavour. Underneath this picture is a model of the same, on the scale of one-twenty-fifth of the actual size. It represents the first four arches of the viaduct on the left bank. This is built of stone, with double main arches springing from the same piers; and above the upper one a smaller span, sustaining the waterways. On each side of the structure are commodious roadways. The entire structure is faced with ashlar masonry, and the arches are semicircular.

On the east walls are plans, elevations, and details of the noted harbors of Marseilles, Bordeaux, Saint Jean de Luz, and also elevations, plans and sections of lighthouses. A fine view of the city of Marseilles is given, showing the public dry-docks, breakwater, and other works; a view of

Bordeaux, showing the public improvements, also very complete. There is here, too, a plan and elevation showing the iron jetties used in the improvement of the mouth of the river Adour, and also plans of the docks of San Jean de Luz, showing the manner of dredging; in both cases giving some of the more important details.

On the north side of the hall, besides the map of France, are elevations, plans and sectional views of lighthouses. These are very complete, and comprise perpendicular sections, showing the interior arrangements and the mode of construction. The lighthouse of La Palmyre is on an elevated piece of ground, constructed of iron, having three braces of tubular iron firmly anchored. There are also elevations, plans and details of several viaducts; and on the west wall are a number of plans, details and views of the reservoir St. Chemond, and a variety of maps. One of these latter is a geological map of France. There is also a map of a portion of the river Seine, and profiles of the Seine, and map of the Seine between Paris and Asnières, with details of construction, locks and machinery, and a map of the canal of the Lower Marne, with details of machinery used in the same.

Here is a plan of the immense depôt at Orleans, and above, a number of views of lighthouses on the French coast.

On two long tables, running the entire length of the hall, are a number of remarkably fine exhibits of models of bridges and other public works. Commencing on the right, as you go in, is a massive model representing a plan of the viaduct of Rocquefavour, in process of construction, and also representing the various machinery used to assist in raising and placing the heavy stones and other material. The whole is made to a scale of one-tenth actual size. From the surface of the ground springs a massive-looking trestle, which sustains a road and tramway for the lifting machines, which are worked by steam. From the top of the unfinished piers a bridge of wood, braced by saddle-braces of iron, is swung across. The manner of placing the stones is clearly defined.

The bridge of Arcola is shown in a beautiful model, made to a scale of one-twenty-fifth natural size. This bridge, which is of iron, is of a very handsome design, and has a single broad span. The roadway is suppported by twelve arched ribs, firmly braced together. The abutments are massive, of stone, and on each end of the bridge there is a broad roadway, though below the roadway of the bridge.

Here are also three arches of the viaduct of Dinan, made on a scale of one-twenty-fifth actual size. It represents a structure built entirely of masonry, with stone parapets. The bridge of Tarascon, over the Rhone, on the Lyons and Marseilles Railway, is finely modeled. This is an iron bridge, with double tracks, and has eight spans. The ribs of the arch are built solid, and the spandrels are open-worked. The abutments are of massive masonry, with semicircular enlargements on each side. Through these abutments are passageways, arched and faced with brick, set in cement. There is also here a small model showing the manner of

CASE OF AUSTRIAN ORNAMENTAL LEATHER GOODS.

connecting the spandrels to the arched ribs. On both sides of this table are arranged a fine collection of photographs of the different public works of France. Next we see a number of models, full and in section, of some of the principal lighthouses, selected to show the various constructions in stone and iron, and also a fine model of the port of Marseilles, showing the public buildings erected along the shore, the extensive system of dry-docks, having models of ships within them, as also in the main docks, and the rails and tramways. Here, too, are five models of different styles of buoys, some with beacons, and one with a bell inside of cage-work. There are also specimens of different kinds of oil-lamps used in the lighthouses, and the model of an iron buoy-boat, with bell and beacon.

Here are two models of iron lighthouses of Antioch and New Caledonia, made to a scale of one-twenty-fifth, the latter standing six feet in height. By this are placed two full-sized lights, one a Fresnel light with three-burner oil-lamp, and on the opposite side of the table a light with clockwork arrangement for flashing.

On the long table at the left, as we enter the hall, are models of the viaduct of Point-du-Jour, a massive stone structure about 100 feet in width, the upper part containing the waterway, about thirty feet wide. This is represented on a scale of one-twenty-fifth. The roadway beneath is spanned by one broad arch of five centres, and the superstructure has arches of semicircular form. There is a smaller model of this viaduct, having a roadway on each side of the superstructure. There is a model of two iron trestle piers of a bridge at Brest; a large model of another viaduct on the Limoges Railroad, of which the foundation courses are of stone, the piers being of tubular iron, braced with angular. The spans are made of iron trusses of lattice pattern.

On this table are models of a large siphon weir and dam of a reservoir; also a

reservoir for the supply of water to the town of St. Etienne; sections of two tunnels of the same, with machinery; also a lock of the port of Dunkerque, with gates and iron swinging-bridges, gates to the dam, and swing-valves. There are also two large models of a swing-bridge at Brest, and the model of a canal bridge over the Elbe.

On each side of the doorway as we enter the hall are engineering instruments and various implements used by the "Central Society for Saving Shipwrecked Persons," including guns for firing rockets and lines, floats, etc.

This collection is exceedingly complete, and in its particular department is unequaled in the Exhibition.

VISIT OF THE KNIGHTS-TEMPLARS TO THE EXPOSITION.

On August 29th the Grand Commandery of the Knights-Templars of the United States visited the Exposition in a full representation from all parts of the country. A delegation of Knights from Canada represented the Dominion, and it is doubtful if so large a gathering of the Order has ever occurred before in this country. The Knights were handsomely received by their Philadelphia compatriots, and marched in procession through the city, to the admiration of the thousands assembled to witness the demonstration.

Our artist has depicted the scene presented on the occasion of this procession, the locality represented being Broad Street, at the time when the column of Knights-Templars was passing the magnificent Masonic Temple.

The numerous organizations which took the occasion of the Centennial to hold meetings in Philadelphia gave opportunity by this action for their inspection and consideration by the hundreds of thousands of strangers who thronged the city. Probably none of these made a more satisfactory impression than did this fine representation of the Knights-Templars.

MEMORIAL HALL.

We have already given a description of Memorial Hall on page 20, and a view of the building on page 27.

The universal critical verdict upon this building places it in the front rank, architecturally, among the more ornate structures existing in this country. Erected at a cost of a million and a half dollars, with the design to afford a permanent art-repository for the City of Philadelphia, Memorial Hall is at once the best existing exemplification of the American art-idea in structure, and the most marked and

ITALIAN CHAISE.

emphatic illustration of the liberality of the city it adorns, and the State to whose generosity, conjointly with that of Philadelphia, it owes its existence.

The architect of Memorial Hall is Mr. H.J. Schwarzmann.

In the installation plan of this Building, the corridor between the front and rear entrances is devoted chiefly to the statuary of Italy, the United States, Great Britain,

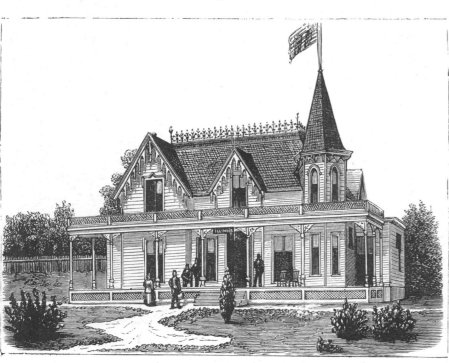

ILLINOIS STATE BUILDING.

VISIT OF THE GRAND COMMANDERY OF THE UNITED STATES KNIGHTS TEMPLARS TO THE EXPOSITION—THE COLUMN PASSING THE MASONIC TEMPLE IN BROAD STREET, PHILADELPHIA.

Germany and France. The eastern end of the building is allotted to the paintings of France, Germany and Austria; western, to the United States, Great Britain, Spain and Sweden; the northeast corner is devoted to France, the southeast corner to Germany, the southwest to the United States and Norway, and the northwest to Great Britain. The galleries in the rear of the building are allotted to Great Britain, Italy, Belgium, France, and the United States.

ITALY.

The larger portion of the art-exhibits of Italy is placed in the Art Annex, and will be referred to in detail in our description of that building. In Memorial Hall there are something over 100 exhibits, comprising sculpture and mosaic-work. The entire presentation of sculpture is highly interesting, and in this way creditable to the modern art school and genius of the country. In this department, however, one is struck with the lack of the more exalted efforts of inspiration, and with the prominence of simpler and more homely expressions of art than would possibly have been expected from Italy.

A number of the works in sculpture represent children in various attitudes, and illustrating various infantile pur-

the Annex, are three rooms communicating, devoted to Italian exhibits, and comprising one of the most interesting features of the exhibition. They consist of a collection of archæological curiosities, exhibited by Mr. Alessandro Castellani.

In the first room is a rare collection of antique marbles, conspicuous among which are the "Indian Baccchus," a figure of heroic size, which was found near Naples. The "Spinario," a Greek statue of the school of Pergamos; heads of Sappho, Tiberius, Alexander and Perseus, the latter of the school of Phidias, with the Emperor Augustus, and statues of Cupid and Psyche, the last two being of the school of Praxiteles, are here. In the same room are to be seen twelve toilet-caskets in bronze, some engraved with early Roman legends, these having been found in the tombs of Palestrina, near Rome.

In the second room is a remarkable and highly interesting collection of majolica-ware, comprising 350 pieces, arranged in chronological order. Of these, a few large pieces in dark-blue and gray, the work of the Arabs, appear to be handed down from the twelfth century. Above these are some fine specimens illustrating "lustre" made of clay. Next we notice the Della Robbia ware of the

turies of the factories of Central Italy is represented in Caffagiola, Faenza, Forli and Pisaro make. One piece of the first named ware is dated 1466, and is the earliest known specimen of this manufacture. The museum at Paris possesses a piece dated 1477, eleven years later than the one in Mr. Castellani's collection, which has heretofore been supposed to antedate all others extant. Among the Faenza specimens are some very beautiful pieces. A characteristic of this ware is the artistic blending of different shades of blue. On a groundwork of antique blue is traced a delicate scrollwork, toned off in some instances to a bluish-white, and in the centre is usually to be found a coat-of-arms or some historic subject.

Among the exhibits of majolica are found specimens of the famous lustre of the Italians, by Georgio Andrioli. This is a most interesting collection, representing as it does one of the lost arts of Italy. The manufacture was short-lived, extending only over the period between 1520 and 1540, when the secret died with its inventor. The chief charm of this work consists in its brilliant play of color, which almost seems to change as one looks upon it. The subjects are scriptural and mythological, but there are also plates which in those days lovers purchased as love-gifts.

"NEW YORK DAY," SEPTEMBER 21st — GOVERNOR TILDEN'S RECEPTION IN THE NEW YORK STATE BUILDING.

suits. The mere names of them will convey the idea we are advancing, such as "After School," "Simplicity," "Bashfulness," "First Sensation of Love," "Study and Work," "Youthful Amusement," "The Reader," "Peasant Girl," "The Little Teacher," "The Youth of Michael Angelo." Besides these, there are "The Odalisque," of Croff, Milan; "The Coquette," of Romani; "Dante," by Giberto; "Alexander von Humboldt," by Biganzoli; "Garibaldi," by an unknown artist; "A Vailed Girl," by Galli, of Milan; "The Bride," by the same; and "The Daughter of Zion Weeping over Jerusalem," by Salomi, of Florence.

These are all in Gallery A, at the entrance to the building. There are two pieces of sculpture representing Washington, one by Guarnerio, of Milan, the other by Gallandt, of Rome. "The Vailed Girl," by Brodzaki, of Rome, is particularly noticeable in the artifice displayed in the treatment of the marble. "Wearied with Play," by Braga, of Milan, and "The Sailor Boy," by Trojario, are both pleasing works of a simple character. "The Little Savoyard," by Galli, is characteristic, and "The Pompeiian Woman," by Tantardini, is a strongly conceived and carefully executed work.

In the rear of Memorial Hall, and on the right passing to

fifteenth century—the manufacture of Lucca and Andrea Robbia, who, it is supposed, were the first to discover and practice the art of tin-glazing. These two were uncle and nephew, and are said to have been equal in point of excellence of workmanship, their work consisting chiefly of earthenware medallions and bas-reliefs of white glaze. These medallions were used in the exterior decoration of churches and public buildings. Some idea of the durability of this material may be obtained from the fact that a terra-cotta medallion, eleven feet in diameter, which was fixed in an exterior wall in the vicinity of Florence fifty years before the discovery of America, after having endured the climatic influences for four centuries, was found to retain all its original beauty, brilliant color and fine appearance. This ware is now extremely rare, but several specimens are to be seen in this collection. Of these, perhaps the most characteristic is a bas-relief representing the Virgin in an attitude of adoration. On a groundwork of deep blue, the Madonna is presented kneeling before the infant Christ, with the Deity in a group overhead. The figures are painted white, offering a fine contrast to the rich blue of the background. Another specimen of this beautiful ware is in the form of a baptismal font.

The pottery of the fourteenth, fifteenth and sixteenth cen-

On one of this class there is a heart pierced through with Cupid's arrow, encircled with jets of flame, having above it a pair of clasped hands. The designs of Urbino, of the fifteenth and sixteenth centuries, show traces of the school of Raphael.

A very valuable piece in this collection is a plate on which is painted the portrait of Charles the Fifth of Spain, the work of one of the best artists of the manufacture, Arazio Fontana. On the absorption of the Duchy of Urbino into the Papal dominion, this factory was removed to Rome. The best artists, however, failed to follow, and the result was a visible decline in the style of workmanship, as is shown by some pieces of this ware which were manufactured after the removal of the factory to Rome, and in which there is a marked inferiority in drawing and finish.

The Abruzzo majolica brings us to the seventeenth and eighteenth centuries. A number of pieces of this are seen in a glass case in the centre of the room. Among these are to be especially mentioned a piece resembling a Greek vase, this having formed part of a blue-and-gold service presented to Pope Paul III. by the Duke of Urbino. There is also a piece of Medici porcelain, one of the earliest specimens known. It is one interesting feature of this collection that

"NEW YORK DAY," SEPTEMBER 21ST—REVIEW OF THE NEW YORK CITY POLICE BY GOVERNOR TILDEN.

THE INTERNATIONAL LIVE STOCK EXHIBITION IN THE EXPOSITION STOCK-YARD—THE AFTERNOON CAVALCADE.

many of the pieces are from services which originally belonged to the nobility of Italy, since they bear the arms of many of them. The coat-of-arms of Pope Leo X., with its six pills and three crowns, occupies the centre of a very large plate, and proclaims the subjection of Sienna, since before the conquest of Sienna the Medici coat-of-arms bore but five pills. These pills indicate the original profession of the Medici family — and we may as well interpolate here that this furnishes a well-founded theory of the origin of the three golden balls employed by pawnbrokers. The Medici became great bankers in Florence, and wherever their establishments were located these golden balls were exhibited as a sign. As pawnbroking became an attribute of the banking business during their time, it is not unreasonable to suppose that later individuals in that line of business adopted a sign which became familiarized in that connection.

In the third room devoted to this exhibition is a collection of jewelry and other ornaments covering a period of

collar being placed around the slave's neck, to the end that when found he should be restored to his owner.

Among the collection of jewelry mentioned is that found by Prince Torlonia, 350 B. C. The ornaments are in a perfect state of preservation, and consist of necklaces, chains, pins and earrings, which evince a chasteness of design and skill that may well challenge the admiration of the goldsmiths of the nineteenth century.

Conspicuous among the Roman ornaments of the first and second centuries is a necklace of amethyst, the connecting links being formed of crystals of beryl. Another necklace is formed of emeralds, crude in finish, as the art of cutting gems geometrically was not known at that period. Among the early Græco-Egyptian ornaments of the Ptolemaic period is a gold bracelet formed of an open-worked band of leaves and tendrils, having a clasp in the form of a vase, embellished with a delicate wreath of grape-leaves, and set with emeralds. Prominent in the case of personal ornaments of Charlemagne's time is a silver buckle,

exaggerated or unnatural, and the figures are full of vitality, while there is much in the composition of the work to attract favorable criticism. This picture is numbered 168 in the catalogue.

In this gallery is to be found also (No. 216) Rothermel's "Amy Robsart Interceding for Leicester," and Leutze's the "Iconoclast" (229), both well-known works. Here are paintings by several of the earlier American artists, beginning with the "Ariadne" of Vanderlyn (No. 150), and including Thomas Sully's portrait of his wife (199) and "Kenilworth Castle" (210), by Cole. Many of the best of our later artists are represented here, and generally in creditable works.

Here, for instance, is Eastman Johnson's "Catching the Bee" (143). Here is the interesting portrait of Shakespeare, by William Page, taken after the wax mask which was supposed to have been made from the face of the dramatist after death. This is numbered 154. Edward Moran has two pictures, both of strictly American interest, the one

EXAMINATION OF "MESSENGER' STOCK HORSES AT THE JUDGES' PAVILION, IN THE STOCK-YARD.

more than twenty centuries. Conspicuous among these is a case of engraved gems from Nineveh and Persepolis, with others, including cameos, representing the art in this direction of Etruria and Greece, and illustrating its rise, progress and decline in those countries from its earliest inception to the fifth century of the Christian era. Opposite this case is one in which are rings of gold, silver, amber, bronze, glass, stone and ivory, representing the interval between the earliest Tyrrhenian period and the end of the sixteenth century. Near these are other cases, in which are seen bronze and silver ornaments which were used by the Crusaders of the eleventh, twelfth and thirteenth centuries; gold ornaments of the Lombard style in the seventh century; collections of cupellated and uncupellated gold ornaments of Etruria, 700 years before Christ. In this collection there is a metal placque, which bears a Latin inscription, which, translated, reads: "Take me, and keep me and send me back to the farm of Maximian, the antiquarian." This placque is supposed to have been one of those which were used in those days attached to a collar for the purpose of identifying property in the slave, the

octagonal in shape, studded with pearls, sapphires and rubies.

In Gallery K, in the southwest corner of Memorial Hall, is a collection loaned by Pope Pius IX. It includes three pieces in mosaic, the first a basin of Florence, the second a Madonna, and the third a mosaic of Raphael's "Madonna de Seggiola." Besides these, there is a piece of tapestry representing the martyrdom of St. Agnes.

THE UNITED STATES.

The American pictures in Memorial Hall are divided between the Central Gallery, Gallery C, and Galleries X, Y and Z. On entering the long hall at the left, called Gallery C, one first notices Rothermel's extensive canvas of the "Battle of Gettysburg." This picture has been the object of considerable severe and not a little hostile criticism on the part of the Press; yet it is perhaps the best picture that Rothermel ever painted, and certainly seen under advantageous circumstances, or at least from the proper point of view as regards distance, it is not by any means a discreditable battle-piece. The composition is not

being (No. 165) "The Winning Yacht," and the other (No. 253) "Moonlight in New York Bay." J. H. Beard is represented here by one of his clever humorous creations, "The Attorney and his Clients"; and W. H. Beard by his well-known "March of Silenus," now owned by the Buffalo Fine Art Gallery. The first of these is numbered 166, the latter 262.

S. R. Gifford has here but one picture (178), "The Golden Horn." McEntee is seen in his "Saturday Afternoon" (182), a characteristic work.

At the North end of this gallery, directly beneath Hicks's well-known portrait of General Meade, is a charming landscape by Kensett (231), and entitled "Conway Valley, N. H." This is a refreshing picture, with a peaceful river flowing through the silent plain, upon which one gazes from the mountains in the foreground among gray rocks and noble trees. At the left, in the distance, are seen clouds full of promise of storm as they sweep around the tall summits of the mountains; but below, the sunlight still lingers, casting capricious gleams upon the grasses and the thickets, the winding pathways and rugged roads.

"BLIND MAN'S BUFF."

"THE FIRST STEP."

"THE ORPHANS."

"THE FORCED PRAYER."

THE STATUARY IN THE ART GALLERIES.

Near this is a pleasing landscape by James M. Hart (236), "A Summer Memory of Berkshire," the property of the Republican candidate for the Governorship of the State of New York, Mr. E. D. Morgan. This is a little pastoral, so stamped with the peculiar atmosphere of Western Massachusetts in Summer that it could be readily picked out from a hundred works as having been painted in that section. No. 239 is a portrait of Hackett as "Rip Van Winkle," by Henry Inman, near which is F. A. Bridgeman's "Nubian Story-teller" (238). This last-named painting represents the interior of a Turkish harem. Into the dull life of the women there now has crept a ray of light. The story-teller—a fantastically-dressed Nubian woman — has arrived, and, seated in a square in which a fountain plays, has commenced a recital. In one corner, upon a divan, near a low, latticed window, sits a beautiful woman over an embroidery-frame, and is listening intently ; another has thrown herself back in luxurious *abandon* on a couch, drinking in with parted lips and moistened eyes the poetic legend told by the mysterious woman. On the floor is a child that has left the toy camels, and also listens, with fear and wonder depicted on his infant features. A female slave, standing near a pipe-rack, hears the tale with an air of stolid incredulity. On the right, on another divan, is a group of beauties, one robed in green-and-white, holding a rose to her lips, a second fondling her child, and a third apparently off into dreamland.

Close by McEntee's picture hangs David Johnson's "Old Man of the Mountain, Franconia Notch, N. H." (221), a faithful and carefully studied work. W. Whittredge exhibits his "Twilight on the Shawangunk Mountains" (201), a picture somewhat theatrical in its manner of treatment, but full of interest in the composition, and showing care in the execution. Eastman Johnson exhibits, besides his "Old Stage Coach," his painting entitled "Milton Dictating to his Daughters" (259), a very careful study, the grouping in which is exquisite. The blind poet is shown seated in his arm-chair with one thin hand uplifted, as if to beat time to the measure of his verse, which one of his daughters is transcribing, while

"L'AFRICAINE."

the other, with her arms folded across the chair, gazes earnestly upon her inspired parent, seemingly enrapt by the charm of the beautiful, mystical story which he evolves from his vividly poetic imagination.

One of Johnson's best pictures is in the corridor, and is called "The Prisoner of State." The startling effect produced in this picture is mainly due to the remarkable manner in which the shadows in the background are handled. The picture shows a tall, robust man standing in a prison-cell near a grated window, which is higher than his own head. He supports himself by holding on with one hand to a ring suspended from the dungeon-ceiling by a rope. He is dressed in a long coat and reddish waistcoat and dark trowsers. There is nothing picturesque or eccentric or unusual in his attire to attract notice. The face, however, is so full of vitality and expression, that one seeks at once for its immediate cause, finding it in a little bird which has just alighted on one of the grate-bars of the window. The simple story is told pathetically and with true art.

No. 186, "Fishing-boats of the Adriatic," by Sanford R. Gifford, displays the peculiar charm of the wonderful sea, with its fringes of high and rugged mountains, its delicate effects of color, and its fleet of boats with stained and painted sails. Among Waterman's exhibits is "Gulliver in Liliput" (156), a picture which was exhibited at the National Academy of Design, N. Y., some years ago.

Mr. J. B. Irving is represented by "The End of the Game," a clever work, which presents this artist in his best manner (187). Bierstadt exhibits the "Settlement of California, Bay of Monterey, 1770" (207). Shattuck has a "Lake Champlain" (223), Sonntag his "Sunset in the Wilderness" (250), Schussele (252) "The Iron Worker," and Irving "Cardinal Wolsey and his Friends" (261).

In the Central Gallery, west, are found quite a number of works by the early American painters, among which "The

Mountain Ford," by Cole (33), a portrait by Gilbert Stuart (52), a landscape by Washington Alston (60), and a portrait of Alston when young, painted by himself (77), two portraits by Copley—one of these being John Adams—numbered 83 and 85, respectively, and the famous picture by Alston (86), "Spalatro's Vision of the Bloody Hand." Gilbert Stuart is also represented by the portrait of Chief-Justice John Jay (9). A picture deserving examination is McEntee's "October Afternoon" (128), a landscape tender in its distance, rich and romantic in the foreground, and infused with the delicate haze so peculiar to our Autumn. This painting is absolutely faithful to Nature as exhibited at this season in the Northern States.

Near this is "Spring," by Regis Gignoux (131), a landscape representing an orchard close, with low trees laden with blossoms, and happy, barefooted children straying over the green turf toward a low-roofed cottage, fancifully set off by a broken fence. Near McEntee's picture is R. Swain Gifford's "Egyptian Fountain" (124). Some Mohammedan travelers have arrived at a green spot where two palm-trees struggle up irregularly before the basin of an artistic fountain from which two camels are drinking. In front of the basin stands a figure clad in a long, red gown and white turban, and near him two Orientals silently contemplating the scene in the distance. The cactus and a few stunted bushes are all the vegetation exhibited. In the distance are two travelers mounted on camels, taking their way toward another village or fountain.

Just above this hangs one of Edward Moran's marine pictures, "Minot Ledge Light" (125). De Haas exhibits a number of pictures, the chief of these, perhaps, being his "Moonrise and Sunset" (25). This shows a headland, low and ragged, of barren rock, dun in color. At a little distance from it is a single tree, upon which the sea seems to have beaten until all its freshness and verdure have died out of it. Before us is the ocean, over which linger the warm rays of the declining sun, while in the still heated sky the moon is apparent, surrounded by a tremulous haze. Distant sails glide away, looking like ghosts on the horizon.

"PREPARING FOR BED."

"IL RINAPROVERO."

THE STATUARY IN THE ART GALLERIES.

George Bouton's "The Pilgrim's Sunday Morning" (20), the property of Mr. R. L. Stuart, of New York, is well known through engravings. The straggling procession on its way to church through the woods looks bleak and severe enough. Whittredge's "A Home by the Sea" (109), represents a vast plain stretching away to the flat coast, painted with great care and freedom from conventionality. On the left is a low-roofed cottage ; here and there on the plain are patches of garden and green grass and thicket. Beyond, but dimly seen, white sails are gliding along. Whittredge's other pictures are "The Window," "One Hundred Years Ago," "Platte River," and "The Woods of Ashakar."

No. 110, "Boats at Boulah, on the Nile," by R. Swain Gifford, a small Egyptian study, is full of vigor and thought. In the distance are seen the Pyramids, silent, colossal, incomprehensible. On the stream drift or skim merrily numbers of *dahabiahs*, while others crowd toward the ship, carried in by the currents.

Further on is Edwin White's "Sabbath of the Emigrant" (105), and near it the very charming picture by S. R. Gifford, "A View on Lake Geneva." Another good picture is by Cropsey, "Old Bonchurch, Isle of Wight" (39), an English landscape, in which the very grass is differ-

the Annex, and where can be seen a number of chromolithographic reproductions of water-color sketches by Mr. Thomas Moran, illustrating the Yellowstone region and that of the Colorado, as also oil-paintings by the same artist. Among these are views of the Hot Springs, Gardener's River, the Great Blue Spring, the Lower Geyser Basin, the Castle Geyser, Upper Geyser Basin, Lower Yellowstone range, Yellowstone Lake, Lower Falls and Sulphur Mountain, Head of Yellowstone River, Yellowstone National Park, the Mountain of the Holy Cross, Colorado, Summit of the Sierra Nevada, Valley of Babbling Waters, and the Great Salt Lake. The sketches are accurately executed and brilliant in color. The views of Yellowstone Park are the result of the Hayden expedition of 1871, which made this section of country known, and was followed by 3,000 square miles being set apart by Congress as a National Park. Mr. Moran accompanied this expedition, and his pictures are faithful reproductions of some of the finest and most startling of Nature's works. In one of these, Tower Falls, we have one of the peculiar features of the scenery. Tower Creek is a swift mountain torrent, tributary to the Yellowstone. Within a short distance of the river it breaks into rapids, and passing between high masses of rock it falls 150 ft. into a basin cut

A broad river, smooth and unruffled, flowing quietly into the middle of the scene, and then plunged into the labyrinth of rocks, tumbling over a precipice 200 ft. high, and flowing westward in a slow, deep current, disappears behind a black promontory. Where it falls upon the western promontory it is wholly in shade. A scanty growth of coniferous trees fringes the trunk of the cliffs overhanging the river. Barrenness is the whole sentiment of the scene."

In Gallery C there are four pieces of sculpture, "The First Rose," by Roberts, of Philadelphia (139) ; "Spring," by Bailly, of Philadelphia (140) ; "Honor Arresting the Triumph of Death," and "Ophelia," by Connelly, of Florence (141 and 142). Besides these, there are a number of important works in the Central Hall, Gallery B, where Mr. Connelly has no fewer than nine pieces, including the bust of Charles Sumner, and his "Diana Transforming Acteon" (1192 and 1194, respectively). The more important works in this gallery are Story's "Medea" (1184) ; Miss Foley's "Jeremiah" (1185), and "Cleopatra" (1201) ; Story's "Beethoven" (1206) ; Hazeltine's "Fortune" (1188), and "Lucia de Lammermoor" (1211). Mr. Palmer is represented here by a bronze statue of Robert Livingston (1213) ; Randolph Rogers by his "Ruth"

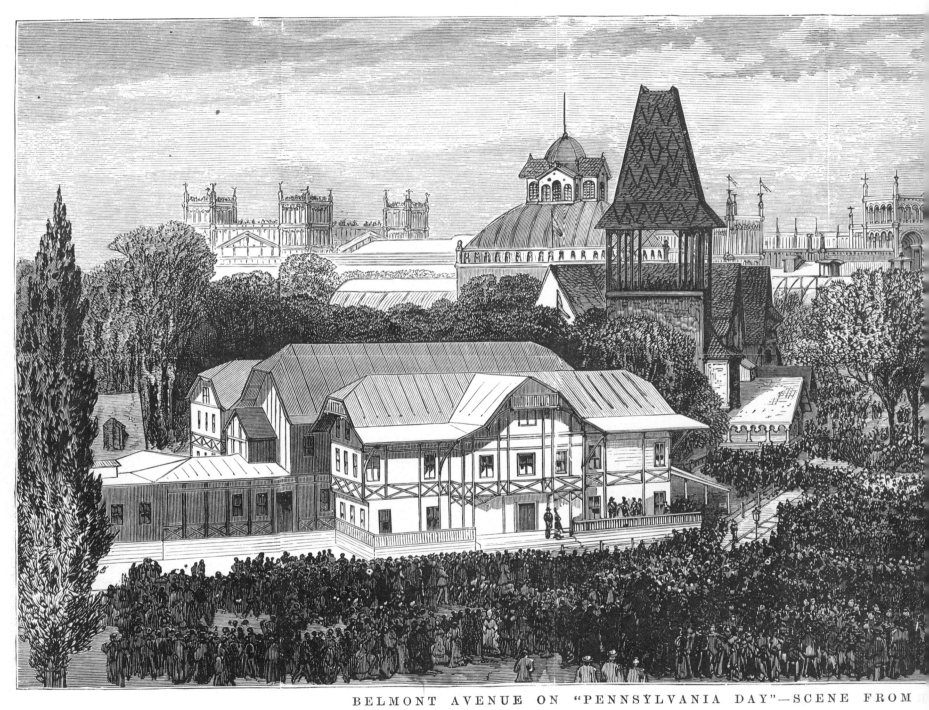

BELMONT AVENUE ON "PENNSYLVANIA DAY"—SCENE FROM

ent from that of America, being greener and riper. The old dilapidated church stands in a yard partially inclosed by a high stone wall, and filled with grass, protected by tall tombstones covered with inscriptions. Beneath shady trees a tall cross looms up ominously.

Samuel Coleman exhibits "The Merchants of Laghouat *en route* between Tell and the Desert, Algeria" (14) ; Durand has some "Studies from Nature" (19) ; Eugene Benson offers the "Sirocco, Venice" (22) ; A. F. Bellows has one of his charming works, the result of his English studies, "Sunday in Devonshire" (26) ; Huntington has a portrait (34) ; Kensett a "View near Northampton" (47) ; "The Strayed Maskers," by Benson (71), is a startling picture, and attracts much attention. A clever work by J. B. Irving is "The Bookworm" (101) ; this has been engraved and is well-known. Eastman Johnson's "The Old Kentucky Home" (118), will be recognized as an old favorite. It is a picture full of genuine interest to every American, although artistically it is by no means up to the excellence of the artist's later work ; the composition is faulty, the points of interest being diffused in several directions instead of being concentrated in one.

Visitors to Memorial Hall should not fail to pass some time in Gallery X, which lies very near the exit toward

in the solid rocks. The picture represents one of the towers at the brink of the fall. It stands like some gloomy sentinel, distantly outlined against the bright background of Sulphur Mountain, while at its base is the dark ground of the rushing torrent, capped with foam, where hidden rocks dispute its right of way.

Another important and interesting picture is that of the Holy Cross Mountain, the most northern peak of the Wasatch range in Colorado, and the only mountain of the name in the world. Its characteristic feature is a cross formed by snow-filled fissures crossing at right angles on the face of the mountain. It is of such remarkable size, and of such distinct contrast, that it can be seen at a distance of eighty miles. The perpendicular arm of the cross is 1,500 ft. in length, the horizontal arm 800 ft.

Another interesting view is that of the Great Falls of Snake River. These cannot be seen until within a mile of the base, when they suddenly burst into view with an indescribable grandeur and magnificence. Of these beautiful falls, Professor King, the geologist of the expedition, says :

"On all sides we find the horizon is as level as the sea. There we gaze upon a circular well, whose sharp sides are here and there battlemented in huge fortress-like masses.

(1217) ; Vinnie Ream exhibits her "Spirit of the Carnival," and "The West" (1218 and 1220) ; "Miriam" (1222), and the bust of Senator Morrill (1224). A charming figure also is Randolph Rogers's "Nydia, the Blind Girl of Pompeii."

In Gallery K, in the southwest corner of the building, are some twenty other works in sculpture. Among these is Miss Edmonia Lewis's ambitious effort, "The Death of Cleopatra" (1231) ; a single piece by Calverly, a bas-relief likeness of Peter Cooper (1230) ; two medallions of Mary and William Howitt, by Miss Foley (1234) ; the bust of a child, by Vinnie Ream, and some portrait busts, and a metal model of Independence Hall. There are also exhibited here some fine specimens of stained glass in arabesque designs.

In the west arcade, on the façade, are six sculptures by Eyre, of Florence, numbered from 1251 to 1256, the subjects being "Leda," "Rebecca," "Hercules and Antæus," "Ruth," "Juno," and "Genius of the Vatican." In the east arcade Mr. Eyre exhibits seven other works, numbered from 1257 to 1263.

It should be mentioned here that in the Central Hall, Gallery B, is exposed the original portrait by Gilbert Stuart, from life, of Washington, painted in 1796. This is the only picture from life by Stuart, except a portrait in the Boston Athenæum. Here is also exhibited a memorial altar by an Italian artist.

In Gallery Z there are a number of drawings, etchings, etc., by Darley, Thomas Moran, Edwin Forbes ("Life Studies of the Great Army"), Swain, Fabronius and others.

In Gallery Y there are a few oil-paintings, of which the most important are "Charity," by Merle (1296); the "Rabbit-Seller," by Meyer von Bremen (1297), and J. H. Beard's "There's Many a Slip," etc. (1299).

The collection of works of art exhibited by the United States in Memorial Hall is completed by illustrations of art applied, which are displayed in the second-story corridor, and Rooms 1, 2, 3, 4 and 5. Here are exhibited chromos, engravings, cameos, fine art works, frames containing specimens of stone gems and impressions of seals, a curiosity in the way of a frame composed of 15,000 pieces of wood constructed without nail, screw or glue, imitations of natural woods in wall-paper, and other artistic work in decorative paper, etc. In Room No. 1 is to be seen an inlaid show-case composed of 120,000 pieces of wood. In Room No. 2 are painted imitations of woods and of marbles, specimens of oak, walnut and rosewood graining, chromo-lithographs designed for crochet and

GREAT BRITAIN.

Hypercriticism has been busy with the English art exhibition as with other departments, and scarcely a just estimate can be formed of the works on view from the comments in the public press. The fact is, that stay-at-home Americans who are at all familiar with foreign paintings have derived that familiarity chiefly from experience of the French, Belgian and German schools, there having never been that interest displayed by American collectors in the works of British artists that has been shown with regard to those from the Continent, while but one representative exhibition of English paintings has ever been made in this country, and that was nearly twenty years ago, in New York, when we were permitted to see some of the works of a few of the best modern English artists. Taking all this into consideration, with the fact that no school of painting can more widely differ from another than does the modern English from those with which we are familiar, it will be seen that no snap-judgment formed on a cursory view of the present collection can be a just one. It is true that line engravings have, of late years, informed us of all that can be told in black and white concerning the more prominent recent English

always occasions of interest, and in the case of royalty become of universal interest. The present scene is specially attractive as rendered by the artist, in that many of the personages depicted are portraits, including Queen Victoria, who stands in a prominent position in a balcony, with her maids-of-honor behind her, though at some little distance. It is, in fact, this single figure of the then only recently widowed Queen which gives a pathetic and almost solemn interest to the picture. Excepting this, and the general atmosphere of aristocratic position, there is little in the work to attract favorable comment. Having sacrificed to the popular taste, we may now properly turn to the portrait of Sir Joshua Reynolds, by the great artist himself (148), which hangs in the corner of the opposite side of the gallery. This painting is familiar to most through engravings, and is certainly a most admirable specimen of the artist's style. The subject is dressed in picturesque costume; the pose is easy and unaffected, though withal somewhat pronounced; and the face is portrayed with the perfection of skill and care. Near to the Reynolds, on the same side, is Gainsborough's portrait of the Duchess of Richmond (51), loaned by Baron Lionel de Rothschild. It is a full-length figure, carefully painted, but, excepting for the artist's name and fame, is not attractive. A portrait

RTHERN ENTRANCE OF THE GROUNDS, LOOKING SOUTH.

embroidery, ornamental painting on glass, and pastelle drawing. In Room No. 3 are specimens of chromo-lithography, including a number of well-known pictures, the "Old Oaken Bucket," the "Changed Cross," etc., of some of which the original oil-paintings are also exhibited. Room No. 4 contains chromo-lithographs, painting and inlaying in mother-of-pearl on glass, specimens of artificial box-wood for wood-engraving, silhouettes, etc. In Room No. 5 are exhibited the competitive designs of the Centennial Buildings, 1361 in the Gallery.

We cannot leave this department without referring specially to the work numbered 202 in the catalogue (Gallery C), entitled only a "Portrait," and painted by Miss Anna M. Lea, of Philadelphia. There is a degree of daring in this artist's work so far removed from the ordinary conventional portraiture of the period as to be quite startling. There is not the slightest effort obvious in her execution, but there is such a defined purpose, and such evidence of grasp manifest in the handling, as to evince the possession of absolute genius. Details are indicated in such wise as to seem to be clearly defined, while ruling everything there is a forceful mastery of technique which causes this painting to quite stand out from among the rest in special prominence.

works. It is also true that the style of coloring in vogue in England offers a broad contrast frequently to the more brilliant method of the Paris *Salon*. Yet there is much to be conceded, perhaps, to difference of climate, and still more to difference of temperament, and it is something, surely, to have the opportunity of seeing the works of such artists—if only for their names' sake—as Sir Edwin Landseer, Wilkie, Frith, Ansdell, Gilbert, Faed, Elmore and Maclise, not to mention Sir Joshua Reynolds and Sir Thomas Lawrence, who are both represented.

The British collection in Memorial Hall is contained chiefly in Galleries B, D, L and Z, with the water-colors and engravings in the rear rooms of the building, overlooking the annex.

Of all of these galleries, certainly the most interesting is Gallery L, in the extreme northwestern corner of the building. Here are the important and valuable works loaned by the Queen of England and the Royal Academy, and to these we will first turn our attention.

The work which first and chiefly attracts notice in this room—although by no means the best or most important—is Frith's "Marriage of H. R. H. the Prince of Wales, in St. George's Chapel, Windsor, March 10th, 1863," numbered 47 in the catalogue. Weddings are

of the Queen in her coronation robes, by Sir George Hayter (63), is interesting on account of the subject, depicting her in the early bloom of her youth, when she ascended the throne, the idol of her subjects. At the left of Frith's large painting are several works deserving of special notice. One of these is Benjamin West's "Death of General Wolfe (184), well known by engravings; another is the "Rape of Ganymede," by William Hilton (67), which hangs above it. On the right of the Frith is "The Banquet Scene from Macbeth," by Daniel Maclise (107), remarkable in the attitudes and expressions of fear and surprise depicted in the faces of the various figures, and particularly in the admirable and effective method of introducing the ghost of Banquo, and in the incident of the spilled wine which flows from the goblet dropped from the nerveless hand of Macbeth. The figure of Lady Macbeth is full of self-poise and character, and the grouping is artistic and charged with purpose and consistency. The work by Sir Thomas Lawrence, the great rival of Reynolds in portrait-painting, "The Three First Partners of the Baring House" (33), is specially of interest to Americans from the fact that a citizen of Boston was at one time a partner in this firm.

Other works deriving importance mainly from the names

VISITORS ARRIVING ON THE PENNSYLVANIA RAILROAD IN PEACH-CARS.

THE STREET-CAR ACCOMMODATIONS.

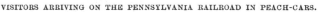

appended to them are Constable's "The Lock" (23); a "Landscape," by Creswick (29); Fuseli's "Thor Battering the Serpent of Misgard" (50), though this deserves attention on its merits ; "The Wood Ranger" (108), by Maclise; "The Village Buffoon" (118), by Mulready ; Opie's "Portrait of Hannah More" (124)—a most estimable work ; Clarkson Stanfield's "On the Scheldt" (157). Turner's "Dolbadden Castle, North Wales" (168)—very little, however, an exponent of Turner's mannerisms, which most made up that artist ; and Sir David Wilkie's "Reading the Gazette," and "Boys Digging for a Rat" (186–187), both of which are clever paintings, and the latter an admirably characteristic work by a great and renowned artist. Here may be concluded the survey of this gallery.

Returning to the corridor and going eastward, we stop at the entrance to Gallery D, the main exhibition-room of English paintings in this building—that is, so far as the size of the apartment and number of works is concerned. Here are gathered representative paintings by the more recent artists of Great Britain ; and here, with much that possesses little merit, there are not a few really fine and noteworthy pictures. Among the more important of these we may direct attention to the following : Alfred Elmore exhibits three works, numbered 38, 39 and 40. These are "Two Women shall be Grinding at the Mill," a rather clever work, but which apparently offers no indication of the remaining and emphatic words of the quotation—"the one shall be taken and the other left." "On the House-tops," by the same artist, is a graphic and even dramatic illustration of the Eastern custom—of our own days as in ancient times—of frequenting the flat roofs of the houses in the cool of the evening, for rest, gossip, and even scandal—as is pretty plainly evidenced by the group of dark-skinned maidens in the foreground, who are obviously

tearing a sister to pieces, after the amiable and still not infrequent habit of the sex. This idea of introducing a "situation" into a picture otherwise only illustrative of the customs of a people is a happy thought, and in this instance is well carried out. The last of Elmore's pictures, "Lenore" is the most striking, and is so peculiar in its treatment as to claim special consideration from the observer. It is the old ballad of Bürger, illustrated in weird and mysterious methods, and by a ghastliness of coloring peculiarly adapted to the subject. Two large pictures by Edward William Cooke are worth notice. One of these (24), is "The Goodwin Lightship," lent by Thomas Brassey, Esq., M. P., the celebrated English engineer ; the other represents "The Rescue of a Bark on the Goodwins," by a life-boat (25). Both these are carefully and strongly painted, and are excellent specimens of this class of marine subjects. Further, they are imbued with vitality, and full of the representative qualities which they should contain—the one expressing a graphic and comprehensive fact of general human interest, the other a melodramatic incident of the most marked and striking character—a rescue from shipwreck.

Frith's well-known picture, "The Railway Station," hangs in this room (48), but is not altogether an attractive work, and is one of those paintings which most certainly owe their fame and popularity to the engraver. Beside Frith's picture is one by S. Luke Fildes, "Applicants for Admission to a Casual Ward," before which we may properly pause for some degree of analysis. This, too, has been engraved, but here the coloring, though sombre and low in tone, harmonizes so consistently with the sentiment of the subject, that we find nothing lacking in that ; while the composition and the delineation of individual characteristics are deserving of the most favorable criticism. By

those who have read Greenwood's "Experiences of a Lambeth Casual," or, indeed, by any one thoroughly acquainted with Dickens's writings, this painting will be at once understood and appreciated. In the shadow of the cold, sleety night, a line of famished and frozen creatures waits before the door of the Casual Ward of a London "Union," or temporary poor-lodging, each one striving, with such patience as is practicable, to subdue for a moment physical pain and mental anguish, in view of the possible respite near them—if the ward be not over-crowded. Here is poverty in its most sorrowful as well as its most obnoxious shape. Honest, decent poverty, as well as besotted and degraded poverty, both dependent upon the same fragile hope—the same dubious sheet-anchor. A policeman, with lantern open, stands in the centre of the composition examining a paper which has been offered to his inspection by a frozen, miserable wretch, who has evidently passed through that pleasant preparation for his present situation termed "seeing better days." Ragged, curly-headed children, an honest-faced mechanic and his sick and starving wife, a sot from the gutters—these are some of the other characters, all of whom are pitiable and heart-rending objects enough. As a portraiture of one of the most dismal phases of "real life" in a great city, this painting is an absolute success.

Three portraits by Sir Francis Grant, one of the late Viscount Hardinge, one of Earl Russell, lent by the illustrious subject, and one entitled "Mrs. Markham," should be examined as specimens of one modern English school of portrait-painting. They are numbers 59, 60 and 61 in the Catalogue. "The Rape of Ganymede," by William Hilton, R. A., is a rather noticeable work, being somewhat richer in color and less constrained in composition than are many in this collection. Holman Hunt's portrait of himself also

SCENE IN FRONT OF THE PENNSYLVANIA STATE BUILDING.

THE HON. B. H. BREWSTER DELIVERING THE ORATION OF THE DAY.

"PENNSYLVANIA DAY" ON THE EXPOSITION GROUNDS, SEPTEMBER 28TH.

demands attention. It represents the painter of "The Light of the World" as a rugged and unconventional personage, but having a face full of strong characteristics, as might be expected. Sir Edwin Landseer is represented in this room by four works. Two of these (89, 90) are named "Study of a Lion"; they hang far above the eye-line, and might have been painted by Bispham, for all of special force displayed on them—which is not by any means asserting that Bispham could not have painted them better. But in "The Traveled Monkey" and "The Sick Monkey" (86, 87), the true genius of the greatest animal painter who ever lived clearly displays itself. The quaint humor and even satire of "The Traveled Monkey" is a lesson in morals and manners, as the execution of the work is a lesson in art. This is one of the paintings in Memorial Hall which it were worth a visit to Philadelphia—even from a goodly distance—to have seen. "The Sick Monkey" is quite of a different cast. If the other be caricature and satire, this is pure nature. The marvelous understanding of the character of his subject, the exquisite treatment of every incident of composition and drawing, are qualities in which Landseer stands unequaled, and which are admirably illustrated in the painting before us. Three paintings by Frederick

Rivière, in his method of treating this subject, has justly delineated the sorceress as a woman of marked personal attraction, combined with a manifest force suggestive of supernatural origin. She has assumed a position which indicates languid indifference and contempt, as the sentiments with which she contemplates the mass of hustling swine, walking and tumbling in the basin on whose edge she sits, clasping her knees and regarding them. Each individual hog of the drove has a personality, and one can fairly appreciate the human feelings of passionate attraction, rage, fear and shame which seem to express themselves in the attitudes and movements of the human creatures who have been thus transformed into these disgusting beasts, yet without being relieved of their human souls. This is a quite extraordinary work, and will repay study. One other painting by Rivière in the collection is called "War-Time" (152.) Other works in this gallery which should not be passed without notice are Wynfield's "The Death of Buckingham" (190); "Julian the Apostate Presiding at a Conference of Sectarians" (6), by Edward Armitage, lent by the Corporation of Liverpool; "The Siesta" (13), by Philip Calderon; "The Lock" (23), by Constable; a "Landscape," by Creswick (29); "The

milking. She has gathered daisies on her way, and her pail is half-filled with them. The figure is life-size and half-length, and contains much in its handling that is clever as well as grateful to the eye. Marcus Stone's "My Lady is a Widow and Childless" (160) is a work which tells its story without need for analysis. A peasant group in the garden in the foreground, occupied with impressions of family ties, and displaying these in pleasant little passages of affection, is seen by the stately and childless lady of the manor passing by in the distance—and thus the intention of the picture is solved.

"Little Sunshine" (16), painted by H. H. Canty, is a large painting, representing a little child walking along a country road, and carrying on her arm a basket of wild flowers. It is a pretty subject, simply and easily treated. "Convalescence," by Alma-Tadema (164), is a Roman or Pompeian subject, and is handled in this artist's characteristic manner. A young girl reclines upon a couch, to whom an aged woman reads from a lengthy roll of manuscript, while the slave, on her knees, blows a fire in a movable fireplace, to warm some broth or other decoction. In the background a long flight of marble steps leads to a corridor, and that to a conservatory behind. Four servants

"PENNSYLVANIA DAY"— RECEPTION BY GOVERNOR HARTRANFT IN THE PENNSYLVANIA STATE BUILDING.

Leighton, each widely differing from the other in character, next attract our attention: they are: "Summer Moon" (96); "Interior of a Jew's House, Damascus" (97); and "Eastern Slinger Scaring Birds in the Harvest Time—Moonrise" (98). This brings us round to Geo. H. Boughton's "God-speed" (8), which may be properly examined in connection with the portrait of the artist in rather a theatrical costume, by John Pettie (135), which hangs further along on the same wall. Near the former of these pictures is "The Disputed Toll" (62), by Heywood Hardy, wherein an elephant behind a toll-gate contemplates removing the obstruction with his trunk, while his keeper disputes the question of passage-money with the old toll-taker. "The Ibis Girl," by Edward J. Poynter (139), representing an Eastern maiden feeding a group of the sacred birds, is worth examination. Rivière's "Circe and the Companions of Ulysses" (151), which has only recently been engraved. Circe was a sorceress who lived in the island of Æea. When Ulysses landed there, Circe turned his companions into swine, but Ulysses resisted this metamorphosis by virtue of an herb called *moly*—

"Who knows not Circe,
The daughter of the Sun, whose charmed cup
Whoever tasted lost his upright shape,
And downward fell into a groveling swine?"
—MILTON.

Battle of Naseby" (53), a stirring war piece by Sir John Gilbert; Frederick Goodall's "Cairo Fruit-girl" (56); "The Lord Gave, the Lord Hath Taken Away," etc. (70), by F. Holl; "Travelers Waiting for the Darkness" (78), by Colin Hunter; "The Unwelcome Guest," by George Lance (85), and "Early Days" by John Everett Millais. Sir John Gilbert's "Battle of Naseby" being for sale, it is in order to hope that it may be purchased for one of our galleries—public or private. Millais's work is very little of the character we should expect from the painter of "The Huguenot Lovers." It represents a little girl, a portrait, seated on the ground holding a kitten in her lap. She wears a buff overdress and light-blue skirt, and has upon her head a quaint little muslin cap. The expression of the face is simple and childlike, the attitude is easy, the coloring is only passable. There is nothing here to recall Millais. This artist's portrait, by George F. Watts (177) will be viewed with interest. Most of the English paintings are delineations of rustic or domestic subjects. Mr. Fildes's "Betty" (46), relieves one pleasantly from the saddening influences of his larger work, "The Casual Ward" and its painful grouping of "applicants." This represents the typical English country maiden, hearty and handsome, with saucy eyes beaming with good nature, and her face radiant with enjoyment, as she lingers on her road to her

carry a litter filled with plants, and two or three figures standing about complete the composition, the accessories of which are a bronze shield upon the wall, a portrait of Marius Pomponius, and a bust hung with a wreath of flowers. Indeed, from the prevalence of flowers in this picture, one is led to believe that they are votive offerings intended for the restoration to health of the convalescent invalid. "The Stone-breaker," by H. Wallis (170), is a picture which created in London considerable talk when it first made its appearance, and is a representation of a master of the advanced ideas of the pre-Raphaelite school. The subject is simple enough; the old workman, having dropped his hammer, is represented as fallen asleep upon a mass of the fragments of a rock which he has been breaking. So sound is his repose that a stoat or weasel steps unscared across his limb. The merit of this work, according to the school to which it belongs, exists in the fidelity and close, almost microscopic, accuracy with which each individual fragment of stone, each leaf and shoot of grass, is delineated. There is evidence of hard and conscientious work here, and in the treatment of the background, where, a quite wonderful distance beyond, the river is depicted, displaying a breadth of ability which might have more worthily exercised itself than in compassing these minute and frivolous details. Calderon's "Desdemona" (12),

"PENNSYLVANIA DAY"—SCENE IN THE LOBBY OF THE TRANS-CONTINENTAL HOTEL.

represents the heroine seated in a chair before her mirror, immediately after her first preparations for retiring. The figure is carefully drawn, and the expression of languid reverie is well put. "Baith Faither and Maither" (43), by Thomas Faed, is a picture of eloquent pathetic sentiment. The old cobbler drawing a glove on the hand of his little motherless child, in preparation for her departure for school, conveys in his own personality, as depicted by this artist, the full meaning of the situation. The little child herself looks on, half amused and half surprised, at the clumsy though tender efforts of the father to supply by his devotion the attentions of the one who is lost. Three little schoolfellows, who have come to accompany her, stand a little behind the principal figures, and seem to appreciate the position of things. A little boy upon a stool holds a puppy in his lap, while a bright-eyed, rough-looking terrier sits beside him. The complement of rude accessories about the cobbler's shop appropriately complete the details of this very interesting work. "Out in the Cold" (109), by J. MacWhirter, represents a belated donkey shut out in the snow, and is well known by engravings. "In Memoriam" (158), by Mrs. M. E. Staples, a young maiden clad in black silk and lace, in an old-fashioned style, with blonde hair looped up with a black velvet band, is represented pressing her lips to a name carved in the bark of a big cherry-tree, whose stem her arm can only half encircle. The caressing attitude in which she stands, and the pathetic illustration of fidelity, render this picture worthy of notice. Edward J. Poynter exhibits two paintings, "The Golden Age" (140), and "The Festival" (141). These are antique subjects of the classical age, representing, the one, two half-naked peasants plucking pears from a tree, and the other, two females, in the drapery of the ordinary Roman costume, decorating the walls of the room with wreaths of flowers. "The Vintage Festival" (165), is still another work by Alma-Tadema, and one within the last two or three years well known through engravings. It is one of the most elaborate of this artist's efforts at depicting antique subjects with historical accuracy. W. Q. Orchardson exhibits two paintings (125–126), the first being entitled, "Prince Henry, Poins and Falstaff," and the second, "Moonlight on the Lagoons, Venice." Both these works show the influence of the modern French school of art, and are in consequence more interesting than some of those which are more exclusively British in treatment.

Water-Colors.—The collection of water-color paintings exhibited by Great Britain comprises 54 numbers, and many of these works are the best, perhaps, of any that have

been exhibited in this country of the English school of water-color paintings. No. 18, by Walter Goodall, "The Lottery Ticket," will attract attention for its excellence of composition and force of character. The group of persons have intermitted their noonday meal to listen to the reading of the list of the successful numbers drawn in a current lottery. The feeling of excitement and concentrated interest in the theme is well depicted in each of the faces represented. "Young England" (11), by A. D. Tripp, presents a little country lad, apparently of one of the Lake counties of England, who, in his rustic health and purposeful face, is a fair type of the characteristics of his race. "Winter" (27), by J. M. Jopling, is the picture of a pretty but serious, and a little careworn, face, charmingly lifelike, and presenting a purity of color and richness of tone quite equal to oil-painting. Another picture by the same artist, entitled "Flossy" (26), is a delicious little presentment of a child in full ball array, sitting in a rocking-chair, and holding in her arms a pet dog. She is apparently waiting for, or has just returned from, some festivity. One of the larger pictures in the collection is by Sir John Gilbert (14), and is entitled "Visit of King Francis the First of France, the Queen of Navarre, Madame d'Estampes, and the Cardinal of Lorraine, to the Workshop of Benvenuto Cellini." The pencil of this master is recalled in the marked differences of expression in the faces of the group, and in the easy grace with which the picture is composed. Mr. L. Alma-Tadema has three paintings in this exhibition. "The Picture" (43), is a powerful study by this original artist. The poses of the figures and the expression of rapt attention, inspired by the painting upon which they are supposed to be gazing, are admirably delineated. "The Three Friends" (44), is one of this artist's eccentricities. An ungainly child, a very natural dog and a lean and disreputable-looking cat, form the subjects of this painting. The child reclines upon a couch and holds a doll in its arms. Except that it is a fair exemplification of the peculiar manner of Alma-Tadema, this painting is not of much worth. "The History of an Honest Wife" (45), although quaint and characteristic, is far more meritorious than either of these others. It illustrates an ancient French legend, explanatory of a miracle supposed to have occurred in the reign of King Chilpéric. This work is a sort of triptych, the story being told in three divisions or partitions of the painting. It is admirably illustrative of Alma-Tadema's style, and is altogether a most interesting work. "Starring in the Provinces" (12), by A. D. Tripp, represents an organ-grinder and monkey, who are making a successful tour through a country village, and have halted

in front of a rustic cottage, where, accompanied by a scissors-grinder and surrounded by a group of children, they recall the days "when Music, heavenly maid, was young." "A Study" (24), by E. K. Johnson, represents a graceful young woman, who stands in a forest of shrubbery and vines, inhaling the scent of a wild rose with every appearance of sympathy and satisfaction in the act. The figure is charmingly drawn and pleasingly treated throughout, without the use of any brilliant coloring. "A Morass" (29), by J. Knight, represents a dull expanse of water and marsh; the man pushing off a boat into a narrow creek, and dull, leaden-gray clouds hanging over all, present a scene full of gloomy force. George Cattermole is represented by one picture, "The Death of Duncan" (6), which effectively illustrates the peculiar powers of this artist as a historical painter. Perhaps the best landscape in this part of the Exhibition is by A. P. Newton, entitled "Mountain Gloom, Glencoe" (35). It represents a pass or reef in the mountains, full of interminable shadows, and oppressed with a savage desolation which fully entitles it to its name.

Galleries Q, R, S and T of Memorial Hall are devoted to the exhibition of engravings, drawings and chromo-lithographs. Among the engravings are several noted pictures as, Maclise's "Play Scene in Hamlet," Rosa Bonheur's "Horse Fair," and "Highland Cattle," and Rivière's "Circe and the Friends of Ulysses," as also Holman Hunt's "The Light of the World," and Rivière's "Daniel in the Lions' Den." Several frames contain etchings, some of which are by members of the Etching Club; pictures from *Punch*, and specimens of engraved book and magazine illustrations. Gallery S is filled with architectural designs and representations of illuminated work. A very excellent collection is contributed by the South Kensington Museum of the Science and Art Department, and includes drawings by the pupils of the school in anatomy, fruit, flowers, portraits, architecture, etc. A very noticeable series in this part of the collection is that personifying the months by female figures in different attitudes.

SWEDEN.

The collection of art-works contributed by Sweden is placed in Gallery H, at the western end of Memorial Hall, and comprise a specimen of statuary by E. J. Börjeson, of Rome, entitled "The Ladies of the Lake," and something over a hundred oil-paintings, of which fifty are in Memorial Hall, and the remainder in the Annex. Speaking of the general Swedish collection of paintings in Memorial Hall, it is to be said that they do not impress one as possessing extraordinary merit, although certainly none of them are very bad, while a few are quite up to the ordinary standard of the Exhibition. "Birch Forest" (11 B), by Edward Bergh, is cleverly painted. "Market Day in Düsseldorf" (33 A) is quite as good a representation as such pictures generally are. "A Mother's Grief," by Miss W. Lagerholm (39), represents a young mother weeping over her dead infant, and is a most creditable work. The simple pose of the mourner on her knees before the cradle of the dead child is full of pathos. Much care is exhibited in this work in the painting of the tapestry and antiquated furniture, screen, rug, etc., in the apartments represented. A clever bit of coloring is seen in a small female head, entitled "Young Girl with Grapes" (54 A), by Miss Sophie Ribbing, of London. The largest and most prominent picture in the gallery, and one also very meritorious in its execution, is Höchert's "Burning of the Royal Palace in Stockholm during the Youth of Charles XII." (32). The hurried and alarmed flight of the inhabitants of the Palace before the hastening flames is represented with marked fidelity to what we may imagine must have been the situation. The massive carved work, which is all that can be seen through the smoke and glare, is carefully executed in all its details. Particular attention should be paid in this picture to the examination of the details and texture in the garments of the different individuals. "In the Spring" (61), by C. E. Skanberg, is a landscape with two figures representing a gentleman and lady walking through a forest. This work is executed with greater breadth than is altogether customary in landscape work. The subdued effects of light, filtering, as it were, through the dense foliage, is artistically contrasted with the deep shadows beneath. Another landscape by Edward Bergh (11 C), represents a Swedish waterfall with a mill and rustic bridge. This picture presents very decided marks of talent. The tumbling waters of the fall are represented with a most just idea of their natural appearance. The distance is well marked, and such foliage and grass as are seen are carefully painted. The thick mist shrouding the summit of a bold rock in the middle distance, and the swift-flying storm-clouds above, are excellently represented.

SPAIN.

The Spanish collection in Memorial Hall is contained in the gallery with that of Sweden, and includes "The Wounded Bull-Fighter" (plaster) by Nobas, of Barcelona, "The Massacre of the Innocents," in terra-cotta, by Domingo Talarn, and forty-four oil-paintings. In the collection, however, there is no representation of the modern school of Spanish art, of which Escosura is the most notable master. These paintings are full of interest, including, as they do, a veritable Murillo, a genuine Velasquez, and several large compositions of decided merit and interest. One of the most remarkable works in this gallery is by A. Vera, and is entitled "Burial of San Lorenzo at Rome" (40 L), and is the property of the Museum of Fine Arts of Madrid. The corpse of the dead saint is painted with an exactitude ot accuracy in the representation of death which is quite startling. "David's Victory over Goliah" (50 A), by Lucas Jordan, is the work of a renowned artist, and possesses merits peculiar to this master. "The Landing of Columbus," by D. Puebla (40 G), is a rather theatrical representation of the event it illustrates, but depicts the generally accepted popular version. The "Velasquez" (204), is a portrait, and is the property of the Countess Antonia Du Mazuel. As we seldom see a painting by this artist, it is not easy to criticise it in regard to his customary work. It is certain, however, that it possesses all the marks of genius in portraiture which are commonly attributed to Velasquez, with those special qualities of coloring which were peculiar to him. In landscape—which can be compared favorably with those of other countries represented in the Exhibition—is a painting by D. Carlos Häes (41 B), and is entitled "Reminiscences of the Pyrenees." While it presents a luxurious growth of verdure and foliage, carefully painted, there is a sympathy and force in the combination, and a purity of tone and atmospheric effect which are eminently creditable. The scene represents the mountains in the distance, and in the foreground the blank wall of a dwelling, embowered in foliage, beside which is a massive bridge over a single arch, the road crossing which is apparently a highway. A single figure leaning over the frail railing of the bridge is the only living object in the scene. The subject of the Murillo (42 D), is the "Crucifixion." Immediately above it is "The Trinity," by Alonso Cano (42 C); and below a triptych on wood by an unknown artist, and two works by Divino Morales, entitled "Madonna and Child," "The Holy Mother and Child" (on wood—fifteenth century), and "Saint Bruno," by an unknown artist, are in this immediate vicinity, and complete a collection of curious specimens of Spanish art of the earliest period. Another American subject is the "Landing of the Puritans in America," by A. Gisbert (51), a large canvas presenting the scene familiar to us by paintings. Right beneath this work is "The Two Friends," by Agrassot. It represents a little child who has fallen asleep beside a rock in a field, with her pet kid with bell and ribbon beside her. This is the only scene of this character in the Spanish collection. It is a simple, rural subject, treated with genuine feeling.

FRANCE.

The collection of French paintings in Memorial Hall is only representative in one particular—that is, of names of which no one, in this country, at least, has ever heard. There are, in fact, but one or two artists in the entire collection whose names are known to American picture-buyers, who in the Paris market are certainly the most liberal and the most frequent of any in the world. If it has been to introduce to our notice artists little known, this method of collecting the exhibition offered may be considered to have been politic, or rather would have been, had the selection been of a tempting character ; but, inasmuch as there is not a single great picture in the entire French collection, there is little to be said for it on this score. Neither the present generation of French artists of reputation nor the past is here illustrated. Not Meissonier, nor Frère, nor Rousseau, nor Delaroche, nor Horace Vernet—are any of them here: not any one, in fact, to represent the better art-work of France. Meanwhile, all of this being true, and this being our complete judgment with regard to the collection as a whole, there are, nevertheless, a number of pictures which are interesting, and some of which present to us artists which deserve to be known.

Beginning with the central gallery, east, we first note No. 2, by Lesrel, "A Nobleman—Reign of Louis XIII." The figure in this is carefully painted, the costume being elaborate, and delineated with every attention to detail, as witness the fine lace of the broad collar and about the wrists. A collection of swords, and small arms, helmets, etc., engraved and damascened, is presented upon the table, which is all the furniture of the room. These articles, as well as the elaborate cloth which covers the table, are also painted with due precision. "Storm—Entrance to the Harbor of Boulogne," by Veron (6), is successful in expressing by broad, general effects, rather than in minute detail, the situation suggested. The figures on the long pier projecting out into the water are very cleverly portrayed. In "Floral Offerings to the Holy Mother, Naples," by C. L. Blanc (5), there is some very excellent work, the faces being expressive and lifelike. "Melancholy," by Feyen Perrin (8), a solitary figure of a woman standing on the margin of a pool in the shade of twilight. The sentiment and coloring of this painting are of a better character than

"PENNSYLVANIA DAY"—THE RUSH FOR REFRESHMENT AT THE PUBLIC COMFORT BUILDING.

is the drawing, which, to say the least, is not exact. "Evening in the Harbor of Venice" (12), by A. Rosier, a moonlight scene, with the palace of St. Mark on the right, a large ship at anchor, and a solitary gondola gliding across the reflection of the moon on the scarcely-rippled waters. F. A. Bartholdi exhibits two pictures of American subjects (11, 15), "Old California" and "New California.' In one we have represented a group engaged in washing for gold. All about the scenery is bleak and dismal, the passionate

artist of No. 8, already noticed, contributes another work entitled "Antique Dance (16). In this a group of nude females are represented in saltatory attitudes, one of these having fallen to the earth either by reason of the eccentricity or the rapidity of her movements. There is good execution in this work, but a sameness of expression, and that of so serious a caste as to mar the general effect. Michel exhibits a painting entitled "Decameron" (21), the scene and costumes being Italian of the period of Boc-

by means simply of water, rocks and the stranded figure of a dead girl flung loosely upon the latter. Brunet-Houard contributes the picture of a miniature traveling circus (32), consisting of a wagon drawn by a large dog, containing a number of other dogs and monkeys, and beset by a following of altogether extraneous dogs of various breeds, which, by loud barking and general contemptuous behavior, express their distaste of this particular class of peripatetic exhibition, as a sort of reflection upon dog aristocracy. A

"PENNSYLVANIA DAY," SEPTEMBER 28TH—THE DISPLAY OF FIREWORKS ON GEORGE'S HILL—THE GEORGE WASHINGTON BUST.

thirst for wealth being symbolized in the eager efforts of the gold-seekers to gather it from the washings of the auriferous earth. In the companion picture we have what is possibly the same party, now extensive farmers, whose grain covers the land to the distant foot-hills, and about whose life is to be witnessed the contrast furnished by calm, domestic serenity, in place of the concentrated anxiety for gold depicted in the former picture. Both these works are more notable for their expression than for their execution, although there is some good work in both, the landscape rather than the figures. The

caccio. A young man is apparently declaiming to an interested gathering of listeners some of the interesting tales of the great story-teller. Hanoteau has a capital picture of a girl feeding hens (24); the time is Winter and the grounds snow-clad. Everything in this work is carefully and well done, from the peasant girl in her wooden-shoes to the poultry about her, the trampled snow and generally dismal wintriness of the scene. Antigua contributes a work entitled "The Shipwrecked" (26), in which with exceeding force and concentration of purpose he has, as it were, focalized the central interest which hangs about wrecked ships

picture by T. Gide, entitled "Studying" (40), is a small genre picture of the school of Meissonier, and is painted with care and skill. "Hélène at the Fountain," by A. Maignan (38), represents the partially nude figure of a girl seated on the brink of a fountain basin, having beside her a little repast of fruit and wine, and engaged in watching the magnificent peacock standing before her. F. M. Leyendecker, one of the few names in the collection at all familiar to us, is represented by a picture, "Still Life"—game-birds hung against the wall. The chief collection of French pictures is contained in Gallery E, a large room

"PENNSYLVANIA DAY"—THE PYROTECHNICAL NIAGARA.

next adjoining the central gallery. Schenck's "Sheep in a "Snow-storm" and "Sheep on the Heath" (44, 49), two companion pictures, are specimens quite up to the usual mark of the work of this excellent artist. Between these is a large canvas representing Mlle. Croizette, the popular actress of the Théâtre Français, Paris, on horseback, apparently on the beach at some watering-place. The face is expressive and quite charming, the figure graceful and the pose easy. The horse is well drawn, and the whole picture is more interesting than the ordinary class of portraits. "Visiting the Confessor," by Pallière (42), represents an amusing scene, where a fat old priest sits in his high-back chair, and receives the adoration of a number of young women visitors. Castiglione exhibits (47) "The Warrants," an English picture of the Cromwellian times, being apparently the arrest of a cavalier by an officer and his men. A very good specimen of Plassan is (5) "In front of a Looking-glass." A luxurious-looking blonde, half dressed, is represented trying the effect of pearls in her yellow hair. The flesh is well painted, and there is much care and attention to detail noticeable in the furniture and other articles of the room. Viger is represented by a picture entitled "Remember the Poor" (22), in which a very ripe and rather lavishly-displayed lady, dressed in the costume of the French Republic, stands at the foot of a staircase, holding in her extended hand a silken purse, supposed to indicate a plea for charity. This brings us to the western end of the gallery, where are exhibited nine tapestries, representing the Gobelin manufactories in Paris, Beauvais and Gobelin. Three of these are large figure subjects, the centre one representing Penelope sitting beneath a bust of Homer, looking for her lover, while she weaves her work and muses sadly. In light and shade coloring, and indeed all the attributes of this class of art, this work is truly wonderful. The delicate blending of the different colors, and the excellence of the modeling, are remarkable. The remaining figure-tapestries are two Watteau subjects, and are pleasing in design and brilliant in execution. Five other tapestries are representations of flowers, fruits and arabesques in panels, and are marvelously executed. Returning to the paintings, we are attracted by the enormous canvas of Clément, "The Death of Julius Cæsar" (63). Without possessing the gloomful force of Gérome's treatment of the same subject, this work is undoubtedly excellent. The figures are posed dramatically, and the interest of the spectator concentrates easily and forcibly upon the central point—the figure of the dying Cæsar. A very charming picture is "Repose" (62), by Perrault—a little gleaner fallen asleep amid her sheaves, her sickle on one side of her, and a basket of fruit, doubtless lunch for the farmers, on the other. The pose is easy and graceful, and the very pretty effect of the light coming through the trees and falling upon the face is accomplished with considerable skill. "The King's Entertainment," by P. C. Comte (73), represents a sick monarch—probably Louis XI.—amused into a passing

smile by the antics of some performing pigs. Two monks praying by the fire, and a group of courtiers, with the exhibitor of the entertainment, complete the personality of the work. This brings us to No. 76, Becker's "Rizpah Protecting the Bodies of her Sons from the Birds of Prey." A more utterly atrocious work than this it has rarely been our misfortune to see upon canvas. In sentiment, conception and execution it is equally deserving of censure. The leading figure, supposed to present an illustration of maternal affection and fidelity, is so positively hideous as to render it impossible to conceive of its being the habitation of any sentiment of a tender nature whatever. The hanging figures of the dead sons of Rizpah present the very nightmare of dissolution. An artist would have perhaps painted one or two of these figures, but only indicated the remainder, centring the interest where it properly belongs—in the suitable manifestation of maternal love depicted in the person of Rizpah; but this painter has violated all rules of sense and sensibility, and has therefore produced only a horrible, and unnecessarily horrible, manifestation of every idea but the one which ought to be indicated. The scriptural story of Rizpah runs in this wise: The Gibeonites, having seen their brethren slaughtered by Saul, claimed for reprisals the lives of his seven sons. To make up the seven sons, in order to gratify this scheme of revenge, David was forced to take the two sons of Rizpah, who had been one of Saul's concubines. Saul had been dead at this time about forty years, and Rizpah was probably about sixty years of age. Quoting from the Bible, ii. Samuel, chap. 21:

8. But the king took the two sons of Rizpah, the daughter of Aiah, whom she bare unto Saul, Armoni and Mephibosheth; and the five sons of Michal, the daughter of Saul, whom she brought up for Adriel, the son of Barzillai, the Meholathite.

9. And he delivered them into the hands of the Gibeonites, and they hanged them in the hill before the Lord; and they fell all seven together, and were put to death in the days of harvest, in the first days, in the beginning of barley harvest.

10. And Rizpah, the daughter of Aiah, took sackcloth, and spread it for her upon the rock, from the beginning of harvest until water dropped upon them out of heaven, and suffered neither the birds of the air to rest on them by day, nor the beasts of the field by night.

The scriptures leave the question of the after-disposition of the bodies somewhat doubtful, since it is stated therein that only the bones of Saul were collected and buried in the tomb of his fathers.

"King Morvan" (96), of Luminais, which hangs opposite Becker's work, is a prize picture from the *Salon* of Paris, and is a work of considerable merit, particularly in relation to the careful attention paid to the painting of the costumes of the three figures presented, and their accessories. A nude figure, in cabinet size, by Saintain (103), is entitled "Leda and the Swan," and contains good drawing and excellent flesh-coloring. Two mouse pictures, by Chevrier (94, 102), represent these little animals, in the one case gnawing a breviary

or prayer-book, and in the other caught in a mouse-trap, three of them at once. We now pass to Gallery Z, where are a few French paintings, some of which are worth noting. No. 167, by Munier, entitled "Refreshment," represents a youth and young girl, both of whom are clad in the airy costume which was popular in past ages, and in which the girl is giving her companion to drink from her two hands water which she has just taken from the spring. The flesh-coloring in this work is commendable. The drawing is only fair. Rather an interesting picture is that by Hirsch, "The Model" (165), which introduces us to the *atelier* of a sculptor, who is perceived modeling a life-size clay figure from the nude woman who poses before him in the character of a model. Some finished and unfinished busts, statues and bas-reliefs standing about, give a proper character to the locality. A picture by Notermann, a well-known name, called "The Auction Sale" (161), represents a monkey-auctioneer descanting on the merits of the pictures which he is selling, while monkey-buyers are bidding vociferously, and show that evidently intelligent anxiety for gems which one may witness in auctions frequented by the final development of this species. This is a thoroughly clever work, of a class seldom seen, and in the painting of which our well-known artist Beard is so successful. "A Monk," by Muraton (157), is worthy of examination, the head being powerfully drawn. "Going Home from the Fields" (133), by Delobbe, is a pretty rustic scene—a mother and little boy mounted on a donkey, the father trudging by their side. "The Flower Market at the Madelaine," by Morin (149), is a very good representation of a lovely and characteristic scene in Paris, the various figures and equipages making up an attractive and brilliant spectacle. Dumaresque's "Declaration of Independence, United States of America" (143), is interesting as showing the French idea of our forefathers. The figures of Jefferson and Franklin will be at once recognized. "Basket with Fruit," by Lays (142), is a capital picture of still life. The grapes, plums, raspberries, etc., with the leaves of these, are painted to the very life. Gallery I completes the French exhibition in Memorial Hall. On entering this room we are at once struck with the painting called "Salambo" (203), by A. de Cetner, which hangs near the door. It represents the life-size figure of a nude woman reclining upon a couch, and amusing herself with an anaconda or boa-constrictor, which is gamboling about her. The scenery is tropical, and the sculptured pillars sustaining the building in which the figure lies are manifestly Egyptian. The work is rich in color, and the figure exquisitely drawn and painted. The subject, however, is not agreeable. "The Flower Girl," by Glaize (176), represents a young woman fashionably dressed, with a face above the average in intelligence, but who, nevertheless, sits on the stone steps of a church, or other public building, with her lap filled with flowers, soliciting custom. It is, however, a very pleasing picture. An interesting historical picture illustrates an interview of Napoleon I. with Goëthe and Wieland. It is

"PENNSYLVANIA DAY"—THE ILLUMINATED FOUNTAIN ON THE LAKE.

PRESENTATION OF THE REPORT OF THE JUDGES OF AWARDS IN THE JUDGES' HALL, SEPTEMBER 27TH—GENERAL HAWLEY ANNOUNCING THE AWARDS.

1. Rocket and Lantern Rock.   2. Hand-Signal Light.   3. Hand-Pistol for Rope.   4. Small Brass Mortar for Rope.   5. Exterior of Building.   6. Buoys.   7. Howitzer for Firing Rope over a Ship.   8. Small Bomb.
9. The Lake Boat.   10. Interior of House.

THE BUILDING AND THE EXHIBIT OF THE UNITED STATES LIFE-SAVING SERVICE.

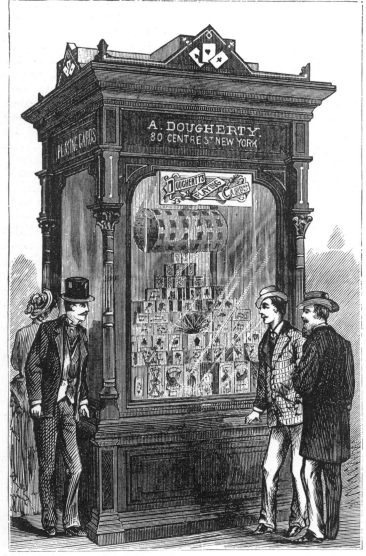

EXHIBIT OF DOUGHERTY'S PLAYING-CARDS, IN THE MAIN BUILDING.

TROMMER'S EXTRACT-OF-MALT EXHIBIT, IN AGRICULTURAL HALL.

by Hillemacker (178). The scene is occurring apparently in the Palace of the Tuileries, or at Malmaison, and a ball is going on in a large room, just out of which the interview takes place. "The Surrender of Yorktown," by Dumaresque (181), is as good a representation as such pictures usually are. "Checkmate," by Jacomin (190), is a very elaborately delineated representation of a game which is accompanied with drink and love-making, and military arms and costumes as accessories.

AUSTRIA.

On entering the Austrian department the eye is first impressed with a sense of richness of color, producing the sensation, however, rather of autumnal maturity than of the brilliancy of spring-time. Much of this impression is to be attributed to the superb work by Makart, which occupies half of the east side of gallery G, and is unquestionably the most notable picture in the entire exhibition. This work is entitled "Venice Paying Homage to Catarina Cornaro."

The story of this painting is told as follows: Catarina Cornaro was born a noble in Venice, in 1454; was married in her fifteenth year to King James, in Cyprus, and, in order to win the favor of that sovereign, was given, by the consent of her native city, the illustrious distinction, "Daughter of the Republic"; was dowered with an immense fortune, and accompanied to her island-home and throne by an imposing retinue of national vessels-of-war. This was in 1469. Three years later the king died, leaving his kingdom to his widow, and commended both it and her to the fostering care of the Venetian Republic. Protected by the presence of the fleet of Venice, and despite the protestations of the sister of her late husband, who laid claim to the throne, Catarina assumed the functions of sovereignty, but scarcely had her husband been peacefully laid in his grave before an insurrection arose. Her uncle and steadfast friend, Andrea Cornaro, was assassinated; her palace was placed in a state of siege, and she herself, with her infant son, was seized and imprisoned. The Venetian men-of-war in the harbor, however, came to her assistance, and dispersed and punished the insurgents. Having done this, the Venetians, who had long coveted Cyprus, now took possession of the island, and although the unfortunate queen still measurably retained her royalty, it was surrounded by such uncomfortable conditions that her life was made very miserable. For years this state of things continued, until at length the Council of Ten required her abdication. Unable to resist, Catarina surrendered her kingdom to Venice, and on the 14th of May, 1489, after a painful reign of seventeen years, embarked for her native city. Her homeward journey, however, was made even more triumphal than her outward had been. Everywhere along the route she was received with acclamations, and hailed as the benefactor of the Republic, and when her royal barge, magnificent with decorations, floated

in front of the palace, Doge and senators vied with each other in greeting her with the honors due to her rank, conducted her to a throne in the square of St. Mark's, and joined the leading citizens of Venice in offering to her homage and treasures. It is this scene which the painter has selected for his brush.

At the right, Catharine sits elevated on a sumptuous throne, having near her her women and courtiers. Before her, girls richly clad bring her offerings of flowers, fruits and jewelry. Further on arrive visitors of all races to pay homage. The costumes are superb, in velvet, cloth-of-gold and jewels. The composition is grand and comprehensive. Each figure is strongly individualized, and there is not one but is an adjunct of some importance to the general merit and intention of the picture. The contrasts of rich coloring are impressive; the queen is in white and gold, relieved by a background of rich crimson, while before her lighter colors tone down into umber and different shades of yellow and dead-red. The figures are all colossal, and there are forty of them represented. The picture measures about 25 feet by 10. The work of Robert Russ, "Mill near Mals, South Tyrol" (3), will attract attention as representing a peculiar feature of Tyrolean farm-life and scenery. "Girl with Fruit" (15), by John Canon, of Vienna, is quite Titianesque in the quality of its coloring. Indeed one would think, to look at the entire Austrian collection, that Austrian art owed more to Titian and Giorgione than to any other of the masters. An ideal female head and bust, by Amerling (8), displays some exquisite coloring, but the picture "Bathsheba," by A. George-Mayer, of Vienna (16), is not satisfactory. It is coarse in expression and lacks sentiment. It is also strained and conventional in drawing. An exquisite little bit of nude work is seen in the "Sleeping Nymph," by Lewis Minegerode (18). In the perfect abandonment of the pose, and in the exceptionally fine outlines, and truth to nature in coloring, this picture is a gem. "At the Sea" (23), by Augustus Schaeffer, presents only a desolate scene of moss-covered rocks and pools of water, with a dull-gray and white sky overhead, yet out of these slight elements the artist has made a picture full of beauty and originality of treatment. In No. 42, "Girl and Cat," by Francis Russ, we have a *genre* subject, treated with attention to detail worthy of the best modern French school. It is a garden scene, wherein, behind a screen, a table is spread for lunch, and near it a graceful girl stands petting a white kitten. In the background are foliage and flowers. "The Peasant Woman of Upper Austria," by Lafite (38), is a characteristic and powerful head. "Overwhelmed with Grief" (43), by Francis Stocker, is a work deserving of the heartiest commendation. Upon a bier, partially covered with flowers, and beside the head of which are two candles burning, is extended the corpse of a child, lightly covered with a vail, whose artistically painted transparency enables the infant's face to be seen beneath. Seated beside the bier, and resting upon the latter in utter abandonment, is the mother, whose face expresses the completeness of her bereavement. Eugene Felix's "Pan and Bacchantes" (62), a large work which faces the Cornaro, represents two nude female figures: the one reclining, the other embracing a bronze statue of Pan, to whose mouth she offers the libation of wine. Beside her a goat capers near an overturned vase of brass or bronze, while the whole is made effective by rich coloring in flowers and drapery. The figures are perfect in grace, and colored with a very just feeling for flesh. The composition is original and graphic. This is one of the most notable pictures in the Austrian collection. "Roman

Pomegranate-Seller," by Ralph Gevling (78), is a quite Murillo-like picture of a little black-haired boy with his basket of fruit before him, sitting on a stone step. Next to this is a portrait by Grabowski (79), wonderfully vigorous and lifelike, and which it would be difficult to equal in this country by anything short of the work of Elliott. "A Study"—female head—(88), by the Countess Eliza Nemes-Ransonnet, deserves more than passing attention. Being painted by a woman, it is yet entirely masculine in the strength of its treatment. The modeling is excellent, the lights and shades well thrown in, and the color of the complexion and hair, as well as the texture of the latter, most successfully treated. "View of a Dutch Town by Moonlight," by R. von Haanen (101), is a capitally executed landscape. A few straw-thatched dwellings apparently form the town; the narrow river running beside it, with woods in the distance, and the moon struggling through a dark cloud, being all there is of this very ably painted picture. "The Nun's Reverie," by G. A. Kuntz (104), represents a solitary nun, seated in a window embrasure, looking off into the distance. It is a simple subject, but treated with great sweetness of sentiment and purity and excellence of handling. "Siesta of an Oriental Woman," by A. Schönn (109), is another nude picture, the naked Oriental having fallen asleep while smoking her nargile, lying on the brink of a pool of water, into which it is not improbable she will be plunged presently. Behind her a black slave woman and a young Eastern woman converse eagerly together, the reclining figure being apparently the subject of their talk. "The Page," by John Canon (117), presents a young man of the medieval age, carrying a salver on which is a flask of wine. There is noticeable some very close and artistic work in this. Wertheimer's (121), "The Moor and his Horse," is a large picture hanging high above the eye-line, next to Makart's great work, and deserves a better position, being boldly and powerfully drawn, and nicely expressing the peculiar sympathy which is said to exist between Orientals and their steeds.

GERMANY.

The paintings exhibited in Memorial Hall by the Empire of Germany are comprised in the central gallery, east, and in Gallery F, the larger number and more important being in the latter department. The main American acquaintance with German art having been chiefly derived from experience of specimens of the Düsseldorf school, and of late years but comparatively few German works having been purchased or exhibited in this country, the first glance at the German pictures in Memorial Hall is certainly disappointing; and, in fact, it must be admitted that, with a few exceptions, this collection is as devoid of merit as of interest. On entering the large room in which most of the German pictures are collected, the eye is first attracted to the life-size portrait of Prince Frederick of Prussia —"Unser Fritz," Crown-Prince of Germany, who commanded the German Army at the great victory of Woerth, by C. Steffeck of Berlin (89). The painter has represented the Prince in a dark-blue uniform, mounted on a bay horse; behind are seen two soldierly figures, Marshal

Obverse.   Reverse.

THE PRIZE MEDALS.

Blumenthal and General Hartman. As a historical portrait this work is certainly full of merit, and may be considered an important and representative work in the latest school of German art, which, to say the least, is certainly not sympathetic. This fact is especially manifest in the "Capitulation of Sedan" (45), by Count von Harrach, of Berlin, which is very hard and woodeny, exaggerated, and, as is believed, not in agreement with the facts of the surrender. "Picnic in Asia Minor," by Eckenbrecher (114), is a decided improvement on these, both in artistic merit and in the quality of personal interest. It represents a party of Europeans picnicking in a grove of poplars and cypresses by the shores of the Ægean Sea. These are waited upon by Greek attendants, and at a little distance are seen a group of Turkish women muffled in their *yashmaks*, giving an Oriental character to the scene. This picture is full of fine feeling for color, the shades being warm, and the whole canvas vital and full of atmosphere. "Broken Flowers," by A. Schwarz (126), is still further an advance on the last in the qualities which make paintings appeal to the sympathy and the soul. A lady in modern costume, and apparently of the upper class, is seen standing alone among rushes and low underbrush on a river's bank ; a gray and threatening sky, with little of light to brighten the landscape, is over all. The figure is turned with the face away from the spectators, the hands clasped over the eyes, and the entire attitude one of sorrow, if not of remorse. The drawing of the form is admirable, the color artistic and sympathetic. The lady's costume, of purple-and-black, and the gray sky, give a sombre effect to the scene, which is only sufficiently relieved by the transparent green of the rushes. In every particular of artistic harmony of drawing, composition and coloring, this work seems nearly perfect. The expression of forlorn isolation is wrought up by the simplest means into a positive and vivid reality. It is gratifying to be able to commend in high terms this one really admirable work. "A Landscape," by R. von Poschinger, "The Environs of Munich" (61), is an agreeable picture of a river and green meadows, the latter dotted with trees, a few white geese visible, with a girl watching them, and above a bright, blue sky, marked with whitish-yellow clouds. This work is quite unlike the ordinary German landscape either of the present or past art-period. J. N. T. von Starkenborgk's "Harvest in Holland" (128), is another worthy landscape, representing a nooning in a wheat-field during harvest. The sheaves are gathered together, and under the shelter of one of these we see the reapers at their midday repast. The sky in this picture is admirably painted, a passing storm being indicated. In the background is a village. "Tobacco Gatherers," by the same artist (68), presents some fine effects of color. Andreas Achenbach, well known in this country as a Düsseldorf artist, has one picture entitled "Storm at Vlissingen, Holland" (112). This is a class of subjects in which this artist is at home, and in the present work we have all his mannerisms, none of which, fortunately, are objectionable. "Faust and Marguerite" prison scene (129), by A. Dietrich, of Dresden, is an imposing canvas, containing three figures : in front the girl in her mad scene, Faust, apparently horror-stricken at his situation and by his own remorse, and Mephistopheles in the background enjoying his opportunity. This is an ambitious work, but is scarcely treated in accord with the possibilities of the subject. The face of Marguerite, though certainly indicating aberration, is painful and unsatisfactory. "A Smoker" (88), by K. Dietlitz, of Berlin, is painted carefully and shows thorough precision of detail. It represents a native of Upper Bavaria enjoying the weed. "Oxen Plowing" (38), by E. Ockel, represents a team struggling up a hill-side, in which the animals are painted and drawn with a just appreciation of Nature, the landscape and sky being, however, unsatisfactory. "Penserosa," by G. Gräf (55), is a clever head, with the flesh-painting noticeable for its excellence of color and texture. The sentiment of this picture, in so far as it expresses the ideal, is not successful. The drawing is good. "Departure of Frederich V. from Prague after the Battle of the White Hills" (124), is a pretentious work, in which the composition is theatrical but effective. No. 125, by Schrader,

THE DAIRY ON THE CENTENNIAL GROUNDS.

is entitled "Queen Elizabeth Signing the Death-warrant of Mary Queen of Scots." In the treatment of this often-painted subject the artist is quite effective, and, through the most simple means, the Queen's face is expressive and thoughtful ; that of her counselor full of the urgency of the occasion. The artist has idealized Elizabeth quite beyond the historical truth concerning this period of her life. "Luther Intercepted," by Count von Harach (135), illustrates an incident in the life of the great Reformer, and represents him met with a warning by a mounted knight in armor, while on his journey in a rude wagon, and traveling by a by-road through the woods. The central point of interest—the figure of Luther—is admirably depicted for sustaining the immediate object of the artist, but beyond this the composition is complicated, and, if we may use such an expression, "huddled up." The figures, however, are strongly drawn, and the landscape accessories of trees and vivid green foliage well wrought in. No. 136, "Christ Appearing to Mary Magdalene," by Prof. Plockhorst, is a work in which the arrangement of the two figures emphasizes the intention of the artist by means of

broad contrasts of light and shade. The Christ, clad in a single garment of pure white, is dignified and impressive. The figure of Magdalene at his feet is only subordinate in its importance. This is one of the most worthy pictures in the room. "Mouth of the Thames," by Xylander (79). The merit of this picture lies only in an admirable treatment of the water and sky, with the effect of strong moonlight breaking through the clouds. Otherwise the work might have for its subject any other water, anywhere, as well as that indicated in the title. A couple of brigs, fully rigged, and under full sail, with studding-sails flying, and a solitary pilot-boat, tacking probably to get in-shore, give human interest and commercial life to the scene, which otherwise, with its tranquil waters and gentle-floating clouds, might seem void of these elements. "The Last Rehearsal previous to Going to the Singers' Festival" (69), by Ortlieb, is a very characteristic work. Though exaggerated somewhat, it will be recognized as presenting a just idea of a singing-school the world over. The eighteen works which we have indicated comprise all the one hundred and forty-five pictures in the German collection, which we deem worthy of a special mention.

NORWAY.

The larger number of the Norwegian pictures are in the Annex, but in Gallery K of Memorial Hall are a dozen works, some of which are worth examination. "Hans Gude," of Carlsruhe — considered one of the greatest Norwegian artists—was born in 1825, and is now at the head of the Carlsruhe Academy, Baden. He has two pictures, one, "A Fresh Breeze, Norwegian Coast" (1), and the other, "Calm, Christianiafiord" (5). These pictures are both for sale, the first for $5,000, and the second for $2,000. In the first, the green waves, sparkling under the rising breeze, and in the other, the more quiet water, touched softly with the shadows of clouds above, and reflecting distinctly the fishing-boats, and the rocky side of the fiord, are delineated with wonderful power. "Arbo's Day" (3) is also a clever work. It represents a youth riding forth into the night, mounted upon a white horse, and creating daylight by means of a blazing torch. "Peasants in a Wood," by A. Tidemand, who was the master of Gude, and probably the greatest artist Norway has produced, will at once attract the attention of any one who enters the gallery. "Midnight Sun in Norway," by Frantz Boe (4), is also a very striking work. Four of the artists represented in this room hail from Düsseldorf, three from Christiania, two from Carlsruhe, and one—Bennetter—from Paris ; his "Vikings at Sea" (2) being still another work which should be carefully examined.

RUSSIA.

The Russian collection in Memorial Hall is contained in Gallery M, on the north side of the building, and comprises sixty-three numbers of paintings and seven marbles. The most striking picture is "The Amulet-Seller," by Semiradsky (34), a large canvas containing three figures with appropriate composition for an Oriental interior. The scene represents a Nubian peddler of jewelry and ornaments recommending a specimen of his wares to a fair-skinned girl, who is listening intently to the description, and apparently revolving in her mind her opinion of the possible virtues of the offered charm. In the background a female slave, dark-skinned and clad in a drapery of golden yellow, holds a peacock-feather fan in one hand, and, while leaning languidly on the marble base of a statue, listens to the monologue going on before her. This composition is artistic and graceful, the coloring rich, without being gaudy, and the accessories of statuary, furniture and tapestry are painted with great skill and care. Immediately below this is a picture representing a Roman thermal, where a number of semi-nude females are seen standing or lounging about in various attitudes in the interest of health. Some of the flesh-painting in this work is passable, and the drawing is good, but, as a whole, the composition lacks vitality. The figures are too much posed for effect. Directly opposite this are two pictures, both of which are noticeable. The principal and larger of the two is entitled "Carnival Week in the Country," representing a race between two sledges, each driving three horses, according to the Russian

GEORGE MATHER'S SONS' EXHIBIT OF PRINTING INK, IN THE MAIN BUILDING.

"RHODE ISLAND DAY," OCTOBER 5TH—GOVERNOR LIPPITT'S RECEPTION ON THE STEPS OF THE RHODE ISLAND STATE BUILDING.

custom. This is by Svertchkoff (43). No. 46, immediately below it, represents "A Steamer in Floating Ice," and is a creditable work. The contrast between the color of the sky and the surroundings of broken ice and open water, where the steamer is plunging through, is broad and well sustained. No. 5, "Storm in the North Sea," and numbers 1, 4, 6 and 7, are by the same artist—Aivazowsky—and are illustrative of atmospheric effects, and in four instances under storm-influences. This artist evidently has an earnest and truthful feeling for Nature in her wilder phases, and has succeeded in portraying those with very marked success. No. 39, by Skirmund, represents "A Member of the Council of Ten, Venice," visiting a family group. The scene is, of course, Venetian, and the alarm and dismay of the party seated about the table taking their wine and food are very well depicted, although the entrance of the cause of their perturbation is rather more melodramatic than artistic. The attention to details of costume and interior decoration in this picture has been careful and studious. Another work by this artist (38) hangs near it, and represents "A Festival in the Palazzo Colonna, Rome" (sixteenth century). Here there is noticeable a little forcing for effects of attitude and grouping, while the same creditable care in details is also made obvious. "The Prisoner," by Silvanovitch (44), is a small cabinet picture representing the unhappy occupant of a cell seated where the sunlight from the only window can shine upon him. There is good expression in this work, equally in the face and attitude of the prisoner, and in the contrast produced by the interposition of the little light which penetrates the gloomy apartment. "The First Snow on a Plowed Field," by Clever (51). In this work very simple means have been used for producing an effective picture. The moon, just showing itself a little above the horizon and crossed by a passing cloud, shines upon the snow-sprinkled stubble scene, which could only be called a field by courtesy, and upon a few dozen rude thatched cottages, which make up the habitations visible. A single hare, darting across the foreground of the picture, presents the only living object depicted. The effect of the moonlight, projected from a sky black and dense, and thrown upon the fallen snow, is well given. No. 50, by Skirmund, is skillfully painted, but coarsely. It is entitled "A Family Party on the Balcony." The conception of this painting is puerile, but the drawing is good, and the details well worked out. "The Stepmother," by Yooravleff (17), is a *genre* subject, and is suggestively treated. A woman in the lower rank

of life holds her infant on her knee with one hand, while with the other she threatens the poor little waif, to whom she stands in stead of his lost mother. Of the landscape works of this collection, "Birch Forest" (19), by Baron Klodt, is carefully painted, and is a characteristic representation of this species of forest growth. No. 49, by Lagorio, "Along the Road from Tiflis to Akhaltzik," is a more ambitious work, and presents a romantic scene with decided skill and precision. The statuary of the Russian Department includes four pieces by Zengler, of Warsaw: "The Mother's First Joy," "Bashfulness," "Sophia" (in illustration of the poem by Mickieviecz), and a bas-relief in marble of the poet Mickieviecz. Two pieces, by Ryger, of Warsaw, are a "Bust of Washington," in marble, and a "Bust of Dr. Levitoux," in plaster-of-paris. These works are all interesting, but not remarkable.

BELGIUM.

The oil-paintings exhibited by Belgium are contained in the Annex. In Gallery O, Memorial Hall, there is, however, a collection of works in other departments of art which demand consideration. First among these are a dozen pieces of statuary in marble, all of which are clever, and two excellent. These two are (189), "The First Child," by Fraikin, which represents a young

EGYPTIAN WATER-JARS IN THE EGYPTIAN DEPARTMENT

mother, seated in her night-dress, nursing her infant. The sentiment of this work is pleasing, and the execution symmetrical and artistic. No. 190, by the same artist, "The Drone Bee," represents a little child in the attitude of trapping, with the skirts of its single garment, a huge bumble-bee, which is burying itself among the petals of a convolvulus. The stealthy movement and anxious interest displayed in the child's attitude and look produce a very pleasing and natural effect. A number of statues in terra-cotta are very clever, especially "The Little Mother" (180), "Winter" (182), "Summer" (183), each of which are admirably humorous in design and exquisite in execution. These are all by Polydore Comein, Brussels. Here are also several large pieces of artistic brass-ware, all by Labaer, of Antwerp, and all portraits. A miscellaneous collection of medals and medallions is contained in a frame, and includes several industrial medals awarded by different European countries. In decorated Faïence there are some sixty pieces, representing, however, only five artists—Dauge, De Mol, Miss Georgette Meunier, Edward Tourteau and François Xavier Volkaerts, all of Brussels. These represent chiefly mythological scenes, and, to those who are interested in this class of art-work, will prove attractive. Finally, this room exhibits a complete collection of the photographic representations of the works of the Belgian painter Wiertz, deceased, exhibited by the Royal Belgian Society for Photography. This collection presents the complete lifetime labors of an artist who, for weird imagination and marked originality of execution, stands entirely alone in the department of the grotesque and the horrible.

THE ART ANNEX.

THE arrangement of the Annex to Memorial Hall comprises its subdivision into forty-five rooms or galleries of different sizes. Of these, Numbers 1 to 4, 17 and 19 are devoted to the exhibits of Italy. Numbers 5, 15, 21 and 23 contain the Netherlands collection. Numbers 6, 8, 10, 12, 14, 16, 18, 20, 22, 24, 28, 30, 40, 42 and 44 include the pictures exhibited by the United States in this building. Norway, Denmark and Sweden have rooms Numbers 7 and 11; Argentine Republic, Chili and Mexico, rooms 9 and 27; France, Numbers 21, 32, 34 to 38, inclusive, 43 and 45; Belgium, 23, 33, 39 and 41; Spain, 25 and 31; Canada, 26; Portugal and Brazil, 27 and 29,

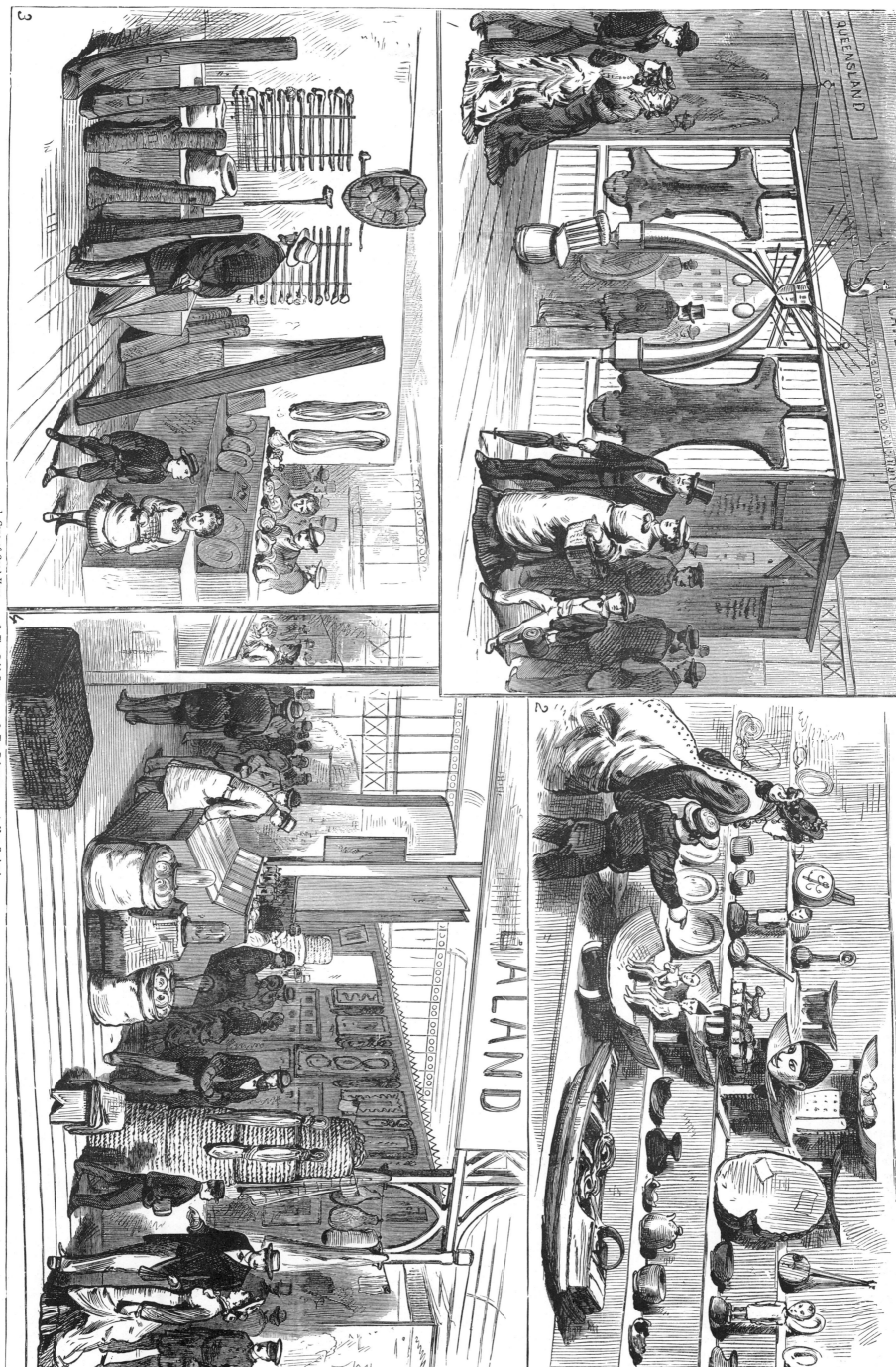

BRITISH COLONIAL EXHIBITS IN THE MAIN BUILDING.

1. Cape of Good Hope. 2. The Gold Coast. 3. The Bahamas. 4. New Zealand.

EXHIBITION OF NEAT CATTLE.—1. OXFORD GENEVA.   2. WINSORELLI: 3. DAIRYMAID.

ITALY.

The principal portion of the Italian exhibits is to be found in room No. 1, and comprises sculpture chiefly. We have already indicated the character of this portion of the contribution of Italy. Here are to be found a large number of those exquisite little figures, illustrating childhood in its various seasons and phases. Here, too, are others whose subjects are of a mythological or quasi-classical character. We will glance briefly at a few of these. No. 2, "Repentance," by Pietro Bernasconi. In this work the artist has succeeded in expressing in marble the sentiment which forms the subject of his effort. No. 50, "Angelica," and 51, "Psyche," are among the more notable ideal subjects—the first of these by Prof. Magni, the other by Pagani. "Death of Abel," by Miglioretti (48), is expressively and carefully sculptured. "Cleopatra," by Braga (43), presents the conventional idea, though, fortunately, not in the conventional attitude—expiring under the influence of the asp. Here she stands erect, resting one hand upon the shoulder of a slave, who has flung a piece of some heavy woven fabric beneath her feet, for her to tread upon, à la Sir Walter Raleigh. The Cleopatra type in this work is decidedly Nubian. No. 37, "Angelic Love," by Giulio Bergonzoli, very cleverly depicts an incident of those days when the angels fell in love with the daughters of men, the object in this instance being of a most human and womanly character, and presenting, to say the least, a feast of material graces for the regard of her angelic lover, possibly satiated with the too-pronounced purity of the females of his own race, if such there be. "The Youthful Hannibal" (35), by Epinay, is a bronze displaying the well-known incident of the boy-conqueror struggling with an eagle. "Fleeting Time" (15), by Barcaglia. This work represents a winged and bearded figure of an old man with hour-glass in hand,

pressing forward, though held back entreatingly by a young girl who thus struggles against futurity. The poise of this work is quite a marvel, as it seems almost impossible that the larger figure of Time should not outbalance and overthrow the group. The expression and attitude are alike wonderfully executed here, while the drapery is treated with a light and airy grace quite exquisite. The collection of paintings in this room includes only a dozen numbers. No. 95, by Alberto Gilli, "Arnoldo da Brescia and Pope Adrian IV.," a large historical work, painted with great force, the perspective effect indicated only by the two figures, being quite an extraordinary effort of skill in the art of mathematical drawing. "Galileo before the Tribunal of the Inquisition" (92), by Lodigiani, is a still larger canvas, presenting this well-known subject in a characteristic and expressive manner. "The School of Love" (91), by Prof. Tedesco, is quite a charming work of the modern type, representing two young girls in costumes of the present day, standing in easy attitudes in a garden or courtyard, and studying the actions of a pair of turtle-doves, doubtless with a view to the future application thereof. This work is full of grace and beauty, the coloring being effective, the drawing exact, and the composition simple but sufficient. The large work by Fumagalli (100), "Columbus conducted back to Spain as a Prisoner," while interesting as the representation of an incident having some connection with the early history of America, is not attractive as a painting. In drawing it is, to say the least, hard and unsatisfactory, while the composition is crude and inartistic. "A Cup of Tea," by Ernesto Giroux (103), is not improbably a portrait, since the subject is one which would not otherwise be likely to enlist the attention of an artist so clever as the painter of this evidently is. Under the bad light it is difficult to do it justice; but there is enough in it to make it an attraction even where it hangs. A large

collection of mosaics, some mounted in tables and others framed, presents a very complete idea of the merit and extent of Italian work in this direction in the present day. Gallery No. 3 contains a number of important pieces of sculpture. "Love's Net" (152), by Pereda, a life-sized figure of a woman, draping her body with a net; and 155, by Renato Peduzzi, entitled "Berenice," will probably first attract attention. In the latter work considerable power is manifested, and the treatment of drapery will be particularly noticed as artistic and careful. "L'Africaine," by Caroni, has been heretofore illustrated in this work. No. 160, "The Mirror of Love," and 163, "Girl at the Bath," the latter by Guarnerio, and the former by Cantalamessa, are fine illustrations of flesh-modeling. The walls of this department are hung with paintings, of which only a few require special notice. "Storm on the Coast," by Della Valle" (181), exhibits some fine wave-painting. "Landscape—A Park," by Formis (177), of Milan, is of the modern Italian school, and a meritorious sample thereof. The landscape is admirably painted, the coloring being pleasing, and the texture of the costume well considered. Altogether, this is a most interesting picture in the new style. No. 187, "A Refusal," by Palazzi, might doubtless and properly be termed a "Temptation"—at least the young woman, evidently a seamstress by trade, puts aside the jewels which are offered to her by an older female, who has decidedly the attitude of a temptress, with an expression quite indicative of the situation. The scene is well rendered. No. 188, a scene from "Robert le Diable," entitled "Evocation of Souls," by Fontana, is a weird and ghastly picture enough, the sheeted ghosts, in various conditions as to nudity, not, however, presenting themselves as altogether agreeable accessories to the painting. Hung lower, it would doubtless be possible to aver of this work that the landscape portion of the composition is well executed.

EXHIBITION OF NEAT CATTLE.—4. WEDDING-DAY.   5. CYMBELINE.   6. CROWN-PRINCE.   7. LILY DALE.   8. ROGER.

"Interior of the Choir of the Cathedral of Parma" (194), by Marchesi, is a carefully executed copy of carved wood, wainscoted, with cabinets and bronzes. This is a cleverly wrought picture. There are four figures presented, a priest and three chorister boys in full costume. "A Grandmother's Admonition," by Cammarano (195), is a pretty little domestic scene, charmingly painted. "Beware of a False Step" (211), by Prof. Gustaldi, is a work which will bear close examination so far as the execution is concerned, but in which the intention of the artist is at least doubtful. A young girl in masquerade attire appears to have been lured into some disreputable association, and to have awakened suddenly to the full appreciation of the dangers of a "false step."

These rooms—2 and 17—which are formed by a long and narrow hall, immediately facing the southern entrance, contain both paintings and sculpture. In the latter class the works are all of a simple and homely character, the larger number of the subjects being children in various attitudes. One which will have been interesting to Americans is by Prof. Zocchi, of Florence, and is entitled "Benjamin Franklin in his Youth" (222). It represents a lad about ten years of age, seated at a rude desk, made of board, propped upon books, and writing. He has on a work-apron, is seated on a pile of books, and has an intense and thoughtful expression in his face very suitable to the distinguished historical character represented, whether a likeness or not. Next to this work is another

where the inscription of "PAX VOBIS" on the wall forms an apt commentary on the scene. This is cleverly painted, and is a hint of the popular feeling in Italy on Church matters during late years. "The Harpist," by Mancinelli (264), has some good work in it, particularly in the treatment of the facial expression. "The Alpine Tourists" (279), has some good landscape work, while the grouping of the figures is free from stiffness, and the perspective and atmospheric effect show a capable and conscientious artist. Nos. 289 and 290, by Picchi, are entitled "The Ebony Frame, Florentine style (sixteenth century)." The ebony frame is artistic, the Florentine style satisfactory, the sixteenth century not obvious. Why these two pictures have not titles is not made manifest. One represents a game of chess between a seventeenth century cavalier and a priest, and the other a wine-drinking scene in a cellar. Neither of them is particularly excellent as a work of art, but there are very many other worse ones in the collection. In "The Anniversary" (288), by Bompiani, of Rome, a Roman lady is represented ornamenting a bust with wreaths of flowers. The face and figure of the fair devotee are very pleasing, particularly in contrast with the hideousness of the bust, the anniversary of whose subject she is remembering. "A Happy Morning" (311), by Michis, is a rather noticeable painting, representing a small boy clad in tatters, and having the general appearance of a chimney-sweep, reclining upon a floor of an apparently elegant apartment, and luxuriating in a cup of coffee and

certainly not less attractive in marble. The artist in this case has certainly conquered his subject. Not only is the figure admirably lifelike and graceful, the contours and modeling in general exquisite, but the sculpture has thrown into the face of Phryne an expression not only indicative of the position indicated by the title, but also of the very character and nature of the woman. The full, voluptuous, languid, and drooping eyes, and the very pose of the head, are all suggestive. If one must treat such subjects in marble, or with color, it is well that they should be treated with that truth to nature which is herein displayed. "The Last Days of Pompeii" (329), by Guarnerio, of Milan, like the statue of Nydia, already mentioned, illustrates a scene during the terrible catastrophe indicated. "Love is Blind," by Barcaglia (340), should be noticed for its anatomical accuracy and artistic modeling. To turn now to the paintings on the walls of Gallery No. 4, it is to be observed first that quite a number of them are copies—and very true copies, also—of works by old masters. These include Titian's "Flora," Carlo Dolci's "Magdalene," Titian's "Bella," Salvator Rosa's celebrated "Marine View"; "Madonnas," by Raphael and Perugino; Fra Angelico's "Angels"; "Beatrice Cenci," copy of Guido Reni; Correggio's "Madonna and Child," and the "Madonna" and "Fornarina" of Raphael. To those who are not familiar with these important works through engravings these copies will be interesting as studies. After these, there are but a half a dozen pictures which require notice.

EXHIBITION OF NEAT CATTLE.— 9. LUCY.   10. COSSACK.   11. DURHAM BULLS.   12. DRAUGHT CATTLE.   13. BUFFALOES.

representing the proverbial "Washington and his Hatchet," by Romanelli (224). The next subject is by Villa, of Milan, a "Girl Playing with a Bird" (225), a very original idea pleasingly expressed. Next are other children; "Dancing Faun," by Peduzzi (228), and then a statue entitled "Carnival," by Borghi, of Milan (230), which represents a girl, very lightly clad, holding a mask in her hands, the expression of whose face, however, is not as joyous as might be anticipated. The attitude is easy and the workmanship exquisite. "Once I was Rich," by Enrico Butti (233), a girl whose tattered clothing, despite the flounces, finely portrays the sentiment expressed in the title. The management of the drapery in this piece is most excellent, while the artist has given an expression to the face fully adequate to the subject of his text. More children; cupids; a little girl with a broom, a very pathetic little piece, entitled "A Wounded Friend," by Tantardini (242), representing a child of three or four years, nursing a wounded dog. "The Discarded," by Malfatti (243), is an effort to present the modern style of costume in sculpture. A young lady, of not quite life size, stands in a melancholy pose, crushing in her right hand a letter, which has evidently afforded the occasion for the work. The dress is all modern, and its silken texture is thoroughly well indicated in the handling. The position is easy and natural, and the expression of shock defined. With this we may conclude the consideration of sculpture in these rooms. The paintings in this department may be speedily dealt with. "During the Sermon" (257), by Michis, of Milan, shows two acolytes playing cards upon a bench in a vestry-room

a feast of grapes. It is decidedly a very clever work. "Offerings to the Lares" (324), by Scifoni, of Rome, an early Roman or Pompeiian subject, treated in the style of Coomans, and very ably treated withal.

From the last-named apartment we enter the centre of the building, Gallery 19, in which are nine pieces of sculpture. In the centre of the room, on a pedestal, is a large subject entitled "The Night of the 11th of October, 1492" (405), by D'Amore. It represents two men pointing emphatically and gazing eagerly in the same direction, the one having the left foot resting on a coil of rope, indicating that they are on shipboard. The two are probably Columbus and one of his officers. The subject is vigorously treated. "Boy Gathering Grapes" (407) is by an unknown artist. This work is elaborately developed, the boy being represented poised on one foot, his head thrown back and right hand extended upward, grasping a branch of a grape-vine, while in his other hand he holds a bunch of newly plucked grapes. The vine and fruit are very carefully sculptured, and the child is admirably modeled. "Silvia" (411), by Barzaghi, a girl half nude, leaning forward and fastening a flower in her hair, taken from a mass of flowers which she holds in her garment gathered about her waist. It is a pretty conceit and poetically handled.

Gallery No. 4 closes the Italian Exhibition in the Art Annex. Here are some twenty-five or thirty works of sculpture, of which a few deserve special notice. Of these "Phryne before the Judges," by Barzaghi (328), will first attract attention. It represents the old situation already so adequately represented on canvas by Gerome, and which is

"Buoso da Duero, the Betrayer of King Manfred of Sicily, Dying from Starvation at the Door of a Convent" (357), by Di Chierico, is a large canvas, and is a striking picture. The most of the work is taken up with the massive masonry of the entrance to the convent, whose iron doors, having just been opened, disclose to the view of the group of horror-stricken monks the figure of the betrayer lying upon his back on the steps, and lightly covered with a snow which has fallen during the night. The scene is a dramatic one and is very well depicted. Three works in sixteenth century frames are exhibited by A. Vertunni, of Rome, but are not numbered or comprised in the catalogue. The first of these is on a canvas about 8 feet by 4, and represents the ruins of Pæstum. In the foreground is a marshy pool, where a few of the rough cattle of that section have come down to drink. This is all in shade, and it is not until you reach the ruins of the temple, in the centre of the picture, that you see the light. The entire upper portion of the ruins, and the distance beyond, are warmed and mellowed by it in an exceedingly novel and striking manner. The artist's treatment of light and shade effects is original and most skillful. Over the ruined buildings hover large flocks of birds, possibly cranes, and in the distance a range of high hills looms through the hazy, warm atmosphere, and skirts the shores of the sea between. Next to this work is another by the same artist, representing the Pyramids; and beside this again, still another, presenting a portion of the lagoon of Venice, with two men tying their boat to a group of piles, probably preparatory to fishing. The two first of these works may be fairly considered among the best exhibited by recent Italian painters.

NETHERLANDS.

The Netherlands collection is generally a creditable one, and contains some works possessing peculiar merits. "The Widow" (50), by Verveer, represents a poor widow wood-gatherer crossing a field with her apron filled with wood, an infant clinging to her neck and a small child beside her, also laden with fagots. Near her walks an old man, also a fagot-gatherer, leaning upon his crutched stick, and having, evidently, an eye to the charms of the pretty, though poverty-stricken, young widow, with the toddling child beside, glancing at him askance, as though wondering to herself what kind of a stepfather he would make. This work shows the influence of the modern French school, and is handled after its best manner. No. 52, by W. C. Nakken, "Pack-horses in the Woods of St. Gatien, Normandy," represents a Winter scene with half a dozen horses standing beneath the eaves of a thatched cottage. Except a rough, wooden-shod peasant, who gives them fodder, there is no other living object to be seen; and the landscape, the ground being covered with snow, and the trees stripped of their foliage, is dreary enough. The horses are well drawn and closely copied after nature. The landscape is excellent, the bleak wintriness of the period being well shown. No. 54, "At Church," by Bisschop, presents a young woman seated in her pew in church, with her attention, however, evidently directed away from the ancient-looking prayer-book before her. The face is well painted, and is full of expression. The texture of the costume is carefully wrought. A figure of a woman in the background, with her head leaning against a wall, is unnecessary to the picture, and inartistic. "Scene in Kuilenburg" (55), by Koekkoek, represents a street-scene with people loitering about, a wagon laden with hay moving slowly along, occasional trees, a church tower in the distance, and on the sides of the street quaint old Dutch houses—all very carefully painted and true to fact. No. 58, "A Critical Moment," by Henkes, represents an incident of a child which has fallen into the water near a bridge, and is being mixed up with pieces of ice in a manner not very suggestive of a lengthened future for the unfortunate. A man has, however, leaped to her rescue, and, with the aid of two others in a boat, who hold him with a rope about his middle, is just about grasping the sinking child, furnishing the "critical moment" of the artist. A group of compassionate bystanders on the bridge above well displays the attitudes occasioned by such situations. The work is vigorously though accurately treated. "On the River-side," by Van Everdingen (62), is a pleasing landscape, showing a road running off into the background beneath trees, with the river lying placidly at its side, and

a single sail specking the blue and white sky above. No. 67, "After the Storm," by Israels, is an admirable painting, without regard to its title, which has no special reference to it. A woman sits in a doorway, with about an inch and a half of sky in sight, which is certainly dark enough to indicate a storm. An older woman stands beside her with folded arms, leaning against the wall, with a very wretched and hopeless expression on her face, which indicates quite as much of a storm within her. A little child sits beside her on a rude bench, eating. The painting of this picture is careful, and shows full capacity and appreciation. No. 69, by H. A. Van Trigt, entitled "Norwegian Women Bringing Children to be Baptized, and being Welcomed by the Clergyman," represents a baptismal scene, and is not particularly interesting, nor specially well painted, though considerable care has been taken in the faces of the principal figures. There is evidence of originality, however, in the work, although it is a "medal" picture. "The First Lesson in Swimming" (70), by Maris, represents a duck, evidently quacking loudly, having plunged into the water, and about to be followed by her entire brood of ducklings, one of which has already ventured. This picture, without minute attention to details, either of feathers or foliage, is true to nature and is quite full of vitality. Compared with the others, it should have had a medal, but has not got one. No. 76, by Miss Vos, a picture of "Still Life," is the only work of the kind in the room, and perhaps has received a medal on that account. Otherwise, it is not remarkable. "The Potato-Gatherers" (89), by Sadee, is quite the best painting in this gallery, and therefore has no medal. Like No. 50, it is a reflection from the French school, but

wonderfully good in the representation—so good, indeed, that there are but one or two French artists who could approach it. The subject is simple enough, only a dreary-looking potato-field with a little patch of dry brush on the left of the foreground; one peasant woman digging potatoes, and two others picking them up and transferring them to the basket and apron. In the distance, a church spire gives indication of a village. This is all there is of it; but the artist has so thoroughly imbued his work with a just and true sentiment, that it is specially worthy of notice. No. 90, by Mrs. Henriette Ronner, entitled "The Last Hope," represents a fleeing hare chased by four dogs, the latter being just in the act of crossing a brook, over which the hare, by means of a board, has successfully passed. This work is full of life and action, the animals being capitally drawn, the incident mentioned being perfectly executed. No. 93, by our own artist, Kruseman Van Elten, of New York, is a "Holland Landscape," and a very charming one. This artist is so well known, that it is only necessary to indicate his work to attract attention to it. No. 102, by Taanman, a sixteenth century scene, representing the "Sheriff's Hall in the Old Town Hall at Kampen," with an old carved chimney-piece and fire-place, and ancient furniture, well given. Two old-time state officials at a table covered with books and documents, and an attendant or page in waiting, are characteristic features. No. 105, by Heemskerk, represents a river scene near Amsterdam, with a storm brewing; a Dutch small-craft flying before the wind, with the city wharves, etc., in the distance. No. 106 is an illustration after Lafontaine's fable of "The Cat Pretending to have been Hanged." It is cleverly given, the deceitful cat being particularly well rendered.

In room 13 three sides are given up to four large paintings by Altmann, of Amsterdam, painted after Rembrandt and other masters, but offering nothing requiring notice. "The Nursery" (130), by Allebé, is a pretty little domestic scene, representing two small children watching a cat and her little kittens. Immediately beneath this picture is No. 131, by Ebersbach, called "Recreation," representing several ladies engaged in shooting at a mark, which is particularly noticeable from its being quite unlike in treatment any other painting which we have thus far met with in the Netherlands collection. It is handled in an airy and easy manner, yet with sufficient force, nevertheless, to make it quite an effective little work. No. 152, by J. C. Van Essen, "A Moment's Rest," deserves passing notice. An old peasant woman, wending her way homeward over snow-covered and frozen ground, has stopped for a moment to rest her tired bones, and is seated on a rude bench or log by the way-side. There is sentiment and quiet dignity in the face of the poor old creature, and enough poetry in it to interest some one who is appreciative, for it is marked "Sold."

"NEW HAMPSHIRE DAY," OCTOBER 12TH—GOVERNOR CHENEY ADDRESSING THE GUESTS FROM THE NEW HAMPSHIRE STATE BUILDING.

THE KING OF SIAM'S GIFT OF GOLD AND SILVER TO THE UNITED STATES, FOR EXHIBITION AT THE CENTENNIAL.

We now pass to Gallery 15. No. 4, by H. Koekkoek, of Amsterdam, "Beach on the French Coast," represents a stormy scene, the waves foaming and tossing, and black, lowering clouds flying rapidly across the sky, a schooner beached in the foreground, and a group of people, fishermen and others, engaged in unloading her, while in the distance a second schooner rushes in before the wind under shortened sail. No. 6, by Israels, "The Card-Players," is a large work, full of power, and handled with marked freedom of touch. The players comprise three men sitting about a table with pipes and liquor, while a woman, having a child in her arms, leans against a wardrobe near by. "Storm on the North Sea" (23), by H. W. Mesdag, is a work which consists of a sea and stormy sky, with a few gulls perceptible. It is a medal picture, and if we were to get at a distance from it of about one hundred and fifty yards, with a spy-glass, we might discover its merits; but the size of the room precludes this, and we fail to see them. "Early Morning" (27), by Apol. Here the judges stumbled on a good picture. The first faint glimmer of sunrise is making its appearance in the distance, and brightening up the scene, which comprises a forest on one side, and grass and underbrush on the other, with a little-used road between. It is thoroughly well painted, however, and deserves the medal accorded to it. There is nothing else in this department which requires attention.

The Netherlands collection concludes with a number of

1. Bridal Crown. 2. Drinking Vase. 3. Old style Tea-set. 4. Silver Drinking Cups. 5. Drinking Horn on Wheels. 6. Fur Robe, Shoes, etc. 7. Single Sleigh. 8. Feather Carpet. 9. Old-fashioned Chair. 10. Old-fashioned Carved Bedstead. 11. Old-fashioned Buffet. 12. Snow-shoes. 13. Three-gallon Tankard. 14. Modern Stove. 15. Arms. 16. Skates. 17. Sleigh, and method of using it as a Market-basket. 18. Snow-shoes. 19. Single Sulky.

THE NORWAY EXHIBIT IN THE MAIN BUILDING.

chromo-lithographs and photographs in Gallery No. 21, and some engravings in No. 23, both being a portion of the long hall which passes through the centre of the building from east to west.

UNITED STATES.

The United States pictures commence in Gallery No. 6. Marshall's Portrait, "Abraham Lincoln," should receive some consideration. No. 404, by S. R. Gifford, "Twilight in the Adirondacks." This picture is full of a lurid effect of light, which is peculiar to this artist. Cropsey's (405), "Old Mill," is a well-known picture, whose vivid and brilliant coloring reminds one rather of a transformation scene at the theatre than either of nature or art. No. 409, by Jerome Thompson, "The Old Oaken Bucket," is another familiar work, which has been chromoed, and is known by every one. "The Jealous Duchess" (412), by Vaini, exhibited in the Academy of Design in New York. The story of this unfortunate artist, who committed suicide while visiting Prof. Doremus, at his country-seat, near New York, will give special interest to this picture, which, however, contains sufficient merit to demand consideration. If it were not for the hideous countenance which the artist has given to the jealous and murderous wife, this work would be as attractive as it is excellent. The three pictures by Cole, "The Cross of the World— Youth, Manhood, and Old Age," will be gazed upon with

and the "Lair of the Sea-Serpent," Vedder has gone on improving in power and increasing in eccentricity. As he is still young, it is impossible to imagine what point he will reach in the end. No. 849, by H. Thouron, "Charlotte Corday—The Eve of her Execution," is a striking picture. Barring the little coarseness, it is very meritorious. "Virginia during the War" (852), by J. McEntee, is a desolate picture enough, and suggests rather than depicts the actual condition of the South during the period indicated. Willard's now celebrated picture, entitled "Yankee-Doodle," is known by the lithographs and engravings, and will be welcome here in the original.

We now come to Gallery 12, one side of which is occupied by a huge canvas by F. Pauwels, of Weimar, entitled "The New Republic." It is an allegorical piece, and, like the most of such works, exaggerated. Those who admire this class of works should examine it for themselves. Most of the paintings in this gallery are works by foreign artists, and loaned for the occasion. Prominent among these are Nos. 781 and 806, by Hans Makart, of Vienna, the painter of the celebrated Cornaro picture in Memorial Hall. The first of these works is entitled "Abundance of the Sea," and the second "Abundance of the Earth." In these two pictures the artist has permitted his imagination to run riot. Nude women, other women clothed and in their right mind, children, lobsters, conch-

is also the handling of the drapery. Another piece of statuary by M. S. Gould, called the "Water Babies," is a charming little work, which we have already illustrated and described.

In Gallery 14 there are five pieces of sculpture, one of which, "Christ in the Sepulchre," by Cusachs (500), is in plaster, and the others in marble. None of these requires special mention. Of the oil paintings we must first note Huntington's "Titian and Charles V." (454), in which the artist has exhibited his faculty for coloring to advantage, while the composition is pleasing and characteristic. "Lake George," by J. F. Kensett (458), is rather warm in tone and seemingly a little exaggerated in that particular, but is a pleasing representation of this artist's method. Just above is Whittredge's "The Pilgrims of St. Roche" (459), forming in the gloom of its sky and its shadows a broad contrast to the more brilliant work below. "San Giorgio, Venice" (461), by S. R. Gifford, is a good specimen of this artist's style in coloring and atmospheric effects. Eastman Johnson's "Bo-peep" (462), painted in 1872, is one of the very best of this artist's small works. It represents a young mother amusing her child by means of the game indicated in the title. The two lounge upon a sofa in a graceful and natural pose, the furniture in the apartment is carefully and exactly painted, and the tone of the work and the management of light and shade are

THE MINERAL ANNEX. — CHINESE DEPARTMENT.

some curiosity by those who are not familiar with this artist. "Bison at Bay" (441), by W. J. Hays, now deceased, is a good representation of the buffalo on the plains, the one given in this picture being chased by wolves.

Gallery 8 contains an exhibition of architectural drawings, a large collection of which is the work of Messrs. Schwarzmann and Kafka, artists of the Centennial Exhibition. In Gallery 10, "Neptune's Bridal" is a large work by Otto Seitz, of Munich (825), and is a gorgeous and glowing representation of Neptune and his fairy bride, seated on a throne of shell, drawn by sea-horses and surrounded by a group of mermaids with their nymphs and mermen, with flying cupids in the air, and music performed on conch-shells by the band. This work is large and showy, and there is some good figure-painting in it. Nos. 824 and 827, by Clementina Tompkins, "The Little Musician" and "An Artistic Début," represent two little black and brown-skinned boys, and are both interesting works. No. 836, Bierstadt's "Yosemite Valley," does not need description. Healy's Portrait — "Ex-President Thiers" (840), will attract attention for its subject and 838, Sully's portrait of his wife, will gain consideration on account of the artist. "The Greek Actor's Daughter" (842), by Vedder, is a quite remarkable work by a remarkable young artist, who unites in himself the idiosyncrasies of Gerome, Coomans, and Alma-Tadema, all in one. From his first pictures, "The Roc's Egg,"

shells, nautilus, magnificent drapery, oysters, sea-plants, etc., are mingled together in marvelous confusion, yet with the spirit and fire of genius impregnating the whole. This is the sea picture. The other, which is of land, presents naked babies, melons, apples and oranges, bare legs, kids, fruits of the vine and fruits of the tree—all in inextricable confusion, and displaying this artist's wonderful feeling for color and aptitude in composition. Here are some works set forth with a claim for authenticity, which makes one's hair stand on end: A "Judith," by Domenichino, for instance; "St. Francis in his Cell," of Murillo; "St. Jerome," of Albert Dürer; "St. Andrew Bearing his Cross," and "Christ Stilling the Tempest," by Andrea Del Sarto; "War Scene," by Wouvermans. Wherever all these old masters came from, or whether they are old masters, or only copies, we leave to those who choose to investigate. "The Crucifixion," by Vandyke, appropriately concludes this list of remarkable paintings. No. 777, by Cabanel, "Francesca di Rimini," is not a very striking or worthy picture. "Bridal Procession in Alsace" (791), by G. Brion, is one of those conventional paintings which are only interesting to a few. "Autumn" (790). The fact that the figure in this work is by Dubufe, and the sheep by Rosa Bonheur, is quite sufficient to render it interesting. In this room is a piece of sculpture by T. R. Gould, of Florence, entitled "The West Wind." The idea is a poetical one, and is prettily and cleverly sustained by the artist. The modeling of this figure is very creditable, as

highly artistic. It is an admirable specimen of *genre* painting. "The Great Trees, Mariposa Grove, California," by A. Bierstadt (473). This work is familiar to most of our art-students, and is a good illustration of the artist's style of handling colossal subjects, although this painting is much smaller than his other works. "The Shadow of a Great Rock in a Weary Land," by Oertel (482), is an allegorical subject in which an Oriental youth is represented reposing himself beneath a rock, which forms a part of an oasis, and beside which flowers grow luxuriantly. Beyond, the desolate desert, with a driving sand-storm, from which the wayfarer has just escaped, presents the contrast in which the allegory is contained. This work covers a large canvas, about 10 feet by 8, and is executed with evident earnestness and considerable merit. "Going to Church, Christmas Eve," by J. C. Thom (484), represents a village road seen in perspective, the ground covered with snow, and moonlight brightening the scene. Up the road come straggling parties of villagers on their way to church, an ancient, ivy-mantled edifice, whose portal alone, with a little of the walls, and a single lighted window, are all that is to be seen of it. This work is made more interesting than the nature of the subject would be presumed to have. "Morning at Narragansett," by A. T. Bricher (486), is a marine piece, representing a quiet beach with the surf tossing gently upon it, and the sun just above the horizon breaking the shadows.

Gallery No. 16 contains contributions of the American

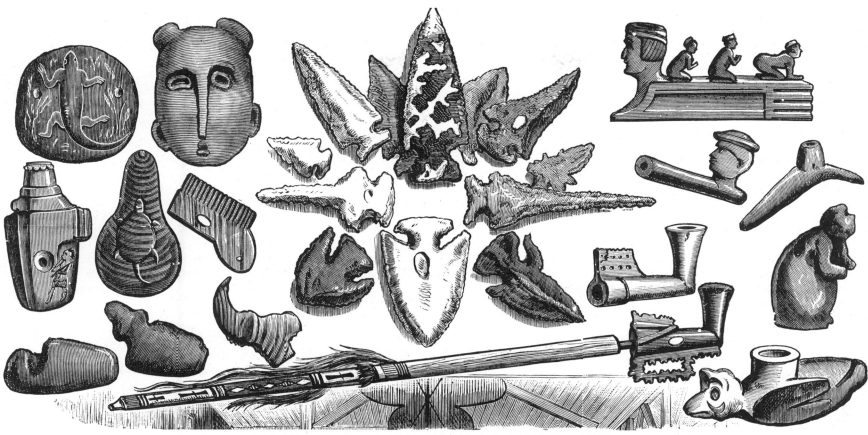

THE MINERAL ANNEX. — ARROW-HEADS AND STONE IMPLEMENTS.

Society of Painters in Water Colors, of New York. This association has in a few years risen to almost the first rank in water-color paintings, and the works exhibited here are generally a fair exponent of the merits of the artists represented. Glancing rapidly through the collection, we can only indicate a few of the more specially noticeable and meritorious works. No. 276, by Louis C. Tiffany, "The Old and New Mosques—Ali Hassimin and Sultan El Carmel, Cairo"—is a very admirable representation of Oriental architecture. "Lazy Life in the East—Gate of the Sub-Treasury, Tangiers" (277), by the same artist, displays the characteristics of the Ottomans in their every-day life, the costumes being carefully portrayed and the grouping easy and life-like. No. 283 is still another Oriental picture, but by Samuel Colman, the scene being in Algiers, and the subject the "Mosque of Sidi Hallui." Colman has made his mark in this class of paintings and the present work exhibits him at his best. "Normandy Girl Caught in a Shower" (287), by Geo. H. Boughton, is a capital representation of a French peasant, and a very bright and pleasing little picture. No. 288, by J. O. Eaton, "Out of Mischief," represents a curly-headed little boy of some three or four Summers lying fast asleep in his crib. It is a charming little domestic subject, exquisitely treated. "Mount Madison, N. H." (294), by William Hart, is one of the pleasing landscapes peculiar to this artist. "A Scrub Race on the Western Plains" (309), by James D. Smillie, is a lively and animated picture, in which, however, the horses are not drawn with that accurate regard to equine anatomy which might be desired. It is an illustration of the increased valuation put upon water-color pictures of late, as the price of this one is $1,500. "Romeo and Juliet" (318), by Alfred Fredericks, of New York, is one of the few figure subjects in the collection which can be commended. Our artists are by no means as successful, as a rule, in figure-painting, as they are in landscape, marine and architectural. Fredericks is, however, an exception to this rule, and the present work, although not one of his best, fairly displays his talent. "The Little Prisoner" is by J. O. Eaton (321). This artist

is most successful in treating children, and this work is quite excellent in the manner of its handling. A little chap cornered behind two chairs, which are tied together, is represented to be mourning his incarceration and chewing the bitter cud of melancholy and despair in the form of the corner of his little apron, while one hand behind his back displays children's most accustomed position, one phase of the changeable temperament of a child. "In the Darkling Wood" (327), by F. Hopkinson Smith, represents an avenue in the midst of a forest vanishing in perspective. In the foreground a still pool of water, and barricading that a mass of overthrown and moss-covered trunks of trees. This is quite the best work by this artist out of the several in the collection. The foliage and bark of the trees are painted with care and conscientious fidelity to nature. The distance is well presented, and the sense of breadth and expanse is demonstrated most appreciably. "Brace's Rock," by F. A. Silva (333), a marine containing the simple elements of rock, sky and water, painted with care and purpose. "Autumn Woods," by A. F. Bellows (332). Mr. Bellows has been as successful in water-color paintings as he has in oils. The work under our notice presents a group of young persons among the underbrush on the outskirts of a forest. The Autumn hues are carefully depicted, and the work is a creditable one. No. 342, "The Ferry," is another and—because containing more life—more attractive specimen by the same artist. William T. Richards exhibits "Paradise, Newport" (343), one of the largest of the water-color paintings exhibited, representing the quiet rural country, painted with that consideration for detail, which is a special part of Mr. Richards's artistic quality. "Gathering Water-Lilies," by A. T. Bricher (347), is quite one of the very best works in the room, if not the best. It represents a tranquil brook, resting, as it would seem, passively, in a pool beneath the shadow of large trees which skirt its side. In the middle distance a boat is shown, from which a girl leans forward to grasp the water-lilies, while another, behind her, holds the paddle with which she propels them through the water. Without the slightest appearance of effort there is artistic power to

be seen in this picture. "The Willow Wagon" (349), by A. F. Bellows, is doubtless a reminiscence of his English study and experience. It is a very charming landscape. Nos. 350 and 356 are by R. Swain Gifford. The first illustrates the Arabian Nights ideal of a "Roc's Egg," in which that remarkable ovum is placed in contrast with ordinary humanity, to the manifest disadvantage of the latter. The second picture, that of the "Venetian Companions," presents three gondolas gliding side by side along the surface of the lagoon, with Venice dimly seen in the distance. "The Old House on the Hill" (366), by Henry Farrer, is a better success than those who saw Mr. Farrer's first efforts in pre-Raphaelite art would have expected. It is a characteristic and creditable picture. "Evening, Long Island Sound" (375), is by Kruseman Van Elten; rich and luminous in color, and an ambitious effort, rather different from the customary work of this artist. "Egyptian Twilight" (378), by R. Swain Gifford, is a far better representation of the real merit of Mr. Gifford than are those to which we have just drawn your attention. There is a quiet charm about it, which is explained by his fidelity to its theme. "Sunday Afternoon in New England," by A. F. Bellows (383), is a characteristic portraiture of a familiar scene. The long village road, overhung by spreading elms, with the old-fashioned church, and the older-fashioned houses, forms a most exact representation of New England village scenery. One of the best of the few marines exhibited is by J. C. Nicoll, and is entitled, "On the Gulf of St. Lawrence" (387). Here there is conscientious and entirely satisfactory work, and the picture is in all respects attractive. "Columbia's Daughter," by Wm. Wallace Scott (389). Here is some exquisite flesh-painting, and there is altogether a delicacy and refinement of touch to be seen in this work which makes one wish for more ambitious efforts on the part of the artist. "Rome, Looking Down the Tiber," by Samuel Colman (397). This picture should also be ranked among the first-class water-colors. There is a breadth of effect, a rich combination of details, which is highly comprehensive, and well indicates the special merits of this very clever artist. The water-color

THE MINERAL ANNEX. — POTTERY, PETRIFACTIONS, ETC.

"STATE DAY" OF MARYLAND, DELAWARE AND VIRGINIA, OCTOBER 19TH. — THE TOURNAMENT AT GEORGE'S HILL IN THE AFTERNOON.

collection closes with 399, "Safely Landed" by A. F. Bellows. A young girl at the foot of a grand old tree leans forward over the brook beneath her, and with a twig succeeds in rescuing from the water a bird's nest filled with young, the mother, meanwhile, fluttering behind her floating offspring and eagerly watching the efforts toward their safety. This is a most charming work, and is an excellent study.

Gallery 18 forms a part of the transverse corridor in the transept, and contains framed specimens of engravings; also a considerable collection of painted china and glassware from the firm of Steele Bros., Philadelphia, from Hinrichs, of New York, and from Gay, of Philadelphia. Some specimens of china dinner-sets forming a portion of these exhibits are very artistic, and compare favorably with some of the foreign work in the Main Building.

Gallery No. 20, immediately next to this, contains very much the same class of works as that last mentioned. The decorated china is from Bevington & Co., of Philadelphia, and is more ambitious in design. There is also exhibited a considerable display of electrotype reproductions of medals and bas-reliefs from Augustus Haas, of New York.

Gallery No. 22 contains engravings on steel exhibited by Samuel and John Sartain, of Philadelphia; George E. Perine, A. B. Durand, W. E. Marshall, and M. Knoedler & Co., all of New York. There is also a collection of twenty-nine representations in plaster of the popular statuette subjects of John Rogers.

Gallery No. 24 contains specimens of bank-note engraving from the National and American Bank Note Companies; also a frame of the collection of notes and bonds of the Empire of Japan; specimens from the Continental Bank Note Company; and the collection of very wonderful specimens of steel-pen work, including quite marvelous copies from certain well-known paintings, the whole executed by F. W. H. Wiesehahn, of St. Louis. The corridor ends here with some illustrations of wood-carving, plaster ornaments for interior decoration, an ancient Hindoo idol supposed to be two thousand years old, and some other miscellaneous articles, including two colossal statues in plaster.

Gallery No. 28 contains a large number of paintings, all by Boston artists, of which quite a number need consideration. Nos. 896 and 904, by B. C. Porter, of Boston, entitled "Portrait" and the "Hour-Glass," are quite above the ordinary range of American figure-work in merit, and in this room stand out as prominent subjects for consideration. There is evinced in these works a profound

feeling for color and texture, the delineation of the latter being remarkable in its fidelity. The face painting is also excellent. The pose of the figures, particularly that of the portrait subject, is easy and natural. We confess never to have heard of this artist before, but his works should be esteemed highly. Four fish paintings, by W. M. Brackett (897 to 900), depict the progress of angling experience in which the noble king of fish, the salmon, is the victim. The entire course of struggle, from the rise to the catch, is capitally set forth, there being real animation and vitality presented in the movements of the unhappy fish. "Port of Antwerp" (906), by D. J. Elwell, of Boston, is a work which possesses considerable merit, and is treated with a breadth of understanding of this class of subjects which we do not always find in American artists. No. 910 is a portrait by Elizabeth Boott. This work, however, though not pleasing and hung too much out of range for good observation, seems to contain elements to indicate an artist of considerable capacity. "Sheep in Pasture" (924), by T. Robinson, presents these interesting animals in a favorable and natural light. No. 927, by W. E. Norton, "Fog on the Grand Banks." Any one who has experienced the situation shown in this picture, as has the writer of this, will at once appreciate the closeness of the fidelity shown by the artist in the scene represented, which as placed upon the canvas possesses more picturesqueness than might at first be anticipated. Nos. 931, 932, and 933 are portraits by the late Gilbert Stuart of "Fisher Ames," "Judge Story," and "Bishop Chevenix." They are interesting solely on account of the name of the artist. "Under the Oaks" (935), by E. M. Bannister, is quite a startling representation of a grove of old gnarled oaks, beneath which a shepherd watches a small flock of sheep browsing on the slight declivity which leads to a quiet pool in the foreground. These trees are painted with such wonderful closeness to nature as to fairly stand out from the gray-and-white background of the sky as though in relief. "Lake Champlain" (938), by Mrs. S. T. Darrah. There is nothing here to indicate Lake Champlain, or any other large body of water, but there is some good work in it, nevertheless. We will go back for a moment to 881, called the "Empty Nest," and which is by R. M. Staigg, of Boston—a very pleasing picture, and quite up to the high reputation of the artist. "In the Bay of Naples" (883, by F. D. Millet, is too realistic to be either artistic or pleasing. There is no disputing the anatomy and possibly the color, but this is not art. "Isaac of York—Ivanhoe" (895), by Washington Allston, would be interesting on account of the painter, if one could see it, which is impossible from

its being hung on the upper line, about ten feet from the floor.

Gallery No. 30 contains exclusively works by Philadelphia artists, notably 1037, Schussele's "Zeisberger Preaching to the Indians"; 1048, Rothermel's "Christian Martyrs in the Colosseum"; 1065, F. de B. Richard's "Campagna di Roma," and 1081, G. W. Pettit's "Cremation of Julius Cæsar." These are sufficiently described by their titles. 1039, by Thomas Moran, is an effort at brilliant effects of color which reminds one of Turner gone mad; 1040, "Natural Arch at Capri," by W. S. Haseltine; 1047, "Valley of the Rio Virgen, Utah," by Moran; and 1049, "Dream of the Orient," by the same artist—another Turneresque picture, will all bear examination. 1050, by Thomas Eakins, a portrait, gives evidence of some power, but is so badly hung that it is quite impossible to determine its merit. 1059 and 1068, by Anna M. Lea. Both, and more particularly the former, sustain us in the words we have already written concerning this artist. She certainly possesses a skill in the handling of flesh tints and the manipulation of textures which, so far as our knowledge and experience go, is quite unequaled by any other artist in this country. It should be considered that very little creditable American art-work has been done in the way of figure-painting. With the exception of Leutze, Huntington, Greene, Eastman Johnson, and a few others, no attempts which bear any special reputation have been made in this direction. It is, therefore, the more creditable and the more gratifying to be able to award such high praise as can conscientiously be given in the present instance. The first of her works in this gallery is entitled "A Patrician Mother"; the other, "Genevieve de Brabant." 1054, by P. F. Rothermel, "The Virtuoso," is rather a striking and characteristic picture by an artist whom it is the fashion to decry. "Drifting Snow" (1069), by Bonfield. This is a capital work, painted with real feeling, and understandingly. 1072, by Peter Moran, "Settled Rain," is also well painted and characteristic. The sheep, however, vary. They do not all look as sheepish as they might. 1076, by Rosenthal, represents a young monk observing the movements of two butterflies which have flown into the window of his cell. There are both good sentiment and good art here. 1070, by A. J. H. Way, of Baltimore, a pair of panel pictures, representing grapes, are very truthful. In the centre of this room is a large piece of sculpture, "Atala," by Randolph Rogers. It represents the chieftain stooping upon one knee, and holding seated upon the other a beautiful maiden of the period. Both these figures are more of the American

Indian type than that with which Atala might better be classified.

Gallery No. 40 begins with 988, by Charles Volkmar, Jr., "The Passing Shower." This is a large landscape, the scene of which is laid near Vichy, France. It is vigorously treated, the foliage being handled with skill, and the cloud effects and resultant shadows being treated with artistic care. 992, by Anna M. Lea, is a portrait of an elderly lady, seated in a high-backed old-fashioned chair beside a table, on which are cup and saucer, strongly suggestive of tea. One can be certain, on examining this work, that it is as excellent as a portrait as it is in its artistic workmanship. The work is strongly individualized, the expression being soulful and earnest. The same elements which go to make up the excellence of Miss Lea's painting exhibited in her other works is observable here. 1003, by Thomas Hill, "Home of the Eagle," and 1005, Bierstadt's "Mt. Hood, Oregon," are well-known works, and attract attention. 1024, by H. Herzog, of Philadelphia, "Norwegian Waterfall in Hallingdal," is a large painting, full of power, ideality, and conscientiousness. The scene is wild and romantic, and its elements, which might well be exaggerated, are so held within bounds as to furnish a truthful and at the same time gratifying picture.

Gallery 42. Over the collection in this room we will draw a vail of respectful concealment—at least so far as names and numbers are concerned. It is only necessary to observe that here are placed the atrocities of the Exhibition. It is creditable at once to the good sense and good taste of the Art Committee that, being forced to admit this collection by the fiat of their chief, they have wisely placed the responsibility where it belongs, in a printed label affixed to each of the more execrable compositions.

Gallery No. 44, in the extreme northwestern corner of the Annex, is surrendered to a collection of portraits by deceased artists of distinction, and a few pieces of sculpture, besides which a portion, separated from the main room by a screen, contains Catlin's colored representations of North American Indians. Among the oil portraits are the work of C. Wilson Peale, Benjamin West, J. Vanderlyn, William Dunlap, S. F. B. Morse, Thomas Sully, J. W. Jarvis, John Trumbull and Waldo. Some of the figures in marble in this room are prettily executed, notably 1178 and 1179, by R. H. Park, of Florence, entitled, "First Sorrow," and "Sunshine."

DENMARK.

Gallery No. 7. This room is at the extreme southeastern front of the Annex, on the right as you enter from Memorial Hall. Three sides of the apartment are devoted to the paintings contributed by the Kingdom of Norway, and the remaining side to those exhibited by Denmark. No. 1, by A. Andersen, of Copenhagen, "Winter Landscape," is well painted. The scene is particularly true to nature. No. 3, by C. Eckardt, "The Harbor of Genoa," has some good work in it. No. 6, by W. Hammer, "Fruit Under an Apple Tree," is chiefly remarkable for its size, though the plums and raspberries are certainly painted with great skill. Nos. 9 and 10, by A. Mackeprang, "Fox in the Chicken Yard" and "Fox and its Young," are very good specimens of animal painting.

NORWAY.

Of the Norwegian pictures, No. 15, by Jacobsen, of Düsseldorf, is a remarkable painting of a "Birch Forest," with a wide road passing through the middle and vanishing in the distance, and two figures in the foreground. "View from Dröbak, near Christiana," by Hans Gude (17). The distant hills in this work, and the sky, are well painted. The picture, however, as a whole, does not come up to the reputation of this artist. 23, by Knud Baade, "View on the Norwegian Coast," is a wild and romantic scene, seeming almost impossible in its character, but painted methodically and evidently with truth. 28, by J. J. Bennetter, representing a "Sea Fight between the Frigate *La Preneuse* and the Line-of-battle Ship *Jupiter*, off Le Banc des Aiguilles, 26th September, 1799," English and French men-of-war, is much the best picture in the room, and one of the best marines in the Exhibition. 29, by Otto Sinding, of Munich, "Ruth and Boaz," is a not unworthy representation of this favorite theme with artists who draw their subjects from the Scriptures. "Flowers" (47), by Frantz Bōe, shows some exquisite painting and is marked "Sold," and its future owner may congratulate himself on having a very pleasing and able work in this line of art. "Interior of a Monastery," by Vinc. St. Lerche (52), of Düsseldorf, represents three monks, one of whom, seated, is inspecting a china toy over wine and walnuts, in the discussion of which they have all been engaged. This is the only strictly *genre* picture in the collection of Norway. It is painted with such skill and such precision of character that one might wish for other examples from the same hand.

ARGENTINE REPUBLIC, CHILI, AND MEXICO.

Gallery No. 9, which is next to the right of the one we have just been considering, is devoted to the works of the Argentine Republic, Chili and Mexico. Among the paintings exhibited by the latter country are several which deserve attention. Quite a large number are religious, allegorical, or otherwise conventional subjects. No. 21, by Clavé, represents the death of "Isabel of Portugal," and is a work of no ordinary merit in historical painting. "The Withered Flower," by Ocaranza (18), is a very pleasing representation of a young girl standing with clasped hands, observing the broken blossom of a flower in a glass vase before her. The sentiment of this picture is very charming, and it is painted with considerable skill. "The Fisher Boy" (26), by Rodrigo Gutierrez, shows also decided ability. "The Morning Paper" (14), by Gargollo, is a very carefully executed little cabinet picture, representing a single figure of a man in a dressing-gown, with cigar in mouth, seated in an arm-chair in his library, reading the paper. This work is very small, and its execution is capital. There is flesh-painting in the head and hands which would not do discredit to the skill of Meissonnier himself. "Evil Presentiment" (16), by Gonzalez. This is also a small canvas, on which is painted the head and bust of a young girl, who leans upon her hand looking out over a window-sill, while she holds a letter which she considers thoughtfully, expressing the presentiment of evil in her countenance and attitude. This is a very charming work, handled with skill and taste. No. 8, "The Death of Abel," by Figueroa, is a powerful work in many respects. The position is effective, and the two figures are painted with a just conception of the idea which it is desired to have conveyed. "St. Charles" (4), by Salomé Pina, is an ambitious work of a religious character, painted evidently with some eager enthusiasm. No. 30, by Escudero, is a "Portrait of Benito Juarez, late President of Mexico," whose name, at least, is well known in connection with the numerous revolutions which have occurred in that unhappy country. In this picture the subject is handled vigorously, and we should suppose that the portrait was close. "The Young Sketcher" (29), by Montenegro, presents the entirely nude figure of a boy of some six or seven years of age, who stands before a canvas on which he is sketching some rude outline with a piece of chalk. The main interest of this picture lies in the anatomy and flesh-painting of the child's figure. These are excellently well handled. This entire collection of works from Mexico is contributed by the National Academy of that country.

BELGIUM.

Gallery No. 23 in the corridor contains one large oil-painting. One side of this department is devoted to the

"STATE DAY" OF MARYLAND, DELAWARE AND VIRGINIA, OCTOBER 19TH.—CROWNING THE QUEEN OF LOVE AND BEAUTY, IN THE JUDGES' HALL.

contributions of Belgium, consisting chiefly of engravings on steel from Brussels and Mons. There is also a drawing by Demannez (275), entitled "The Christian Martyr," a picture well known by the engravings. A very large oil-painting, by John Bernard Wittkamp, of Antwerp, called "Cruelty of Adolph toward his Father, the Duc de Guelders," will have interest for Americans, from the fact that the subject is furnished by the History of the Dutch Republic by our countryman, John Lothrop Motley. The horrible subject, which represents the old man dragged by a rope attached to the horse on which his son rides, is wrought out on the canvas with great skill, and is presented with true feeling and pathos.

While in this vicinity we will consider Galleries 25 and 27, which form the extreme eastern end of the corridor. Gallery 25 is divided between Sweden on the south side and Spain and Norway on the north. Among the Swedish pictures, of which there are a dozen, that which first attracts attention is "Odalisque," by Hugo Salmson, of Stockholm, a life-size nude figure, standing in front of a couch where curtains and draperies of green, blue, and crimson set off her figure to advantage. To such as are interested in this class of subjects Sweden's effort in this line—which of late seems to be exclusively the province of France—will be considered with interest. The Spanish pictures on the opposite side of this gallery are religious subjects. Norway contributes some clever colored drawings in book-work and a frame of photographs. Sweden has some water-color paintings and engravings. The extreme end of the corridor, Gallery 27, is divided between a large collection of engravings and photographs from Brazil, and a number of oil-paintings contributed by the Argentine Confederation.

The collection of Belgium is contained in rooms 33, 39, and 41. Beginning with Gallery 33, the first to which we would draw attention is No. 5, by Ernest Slingeneyer, "A Christian Martyr in the Reign of Diocletian." This work, which is well known by engravings, presents the figure of a sleeping youth, naked except his waist, and holding a small crucifix in his hand. Behind him the rude wooden door of his cell is about being opened by a brutal attendant of the amphitheatre without, whose galleries can be seen crowded with waiting spectators. At the right of the prisoner you catch a glimpse of the head of a fierce-looking lion, snarling as he contemplates the feast prepared for him. There is some false drawing in this work, but the composition is effective and dramatic, besides conveying a pathetic meaning peculiar to its subject. No. 8, Huygen's "Bouquet of Thorn-Blossoms," is very delicately and pleasingly painted. "Rebecca" (15), by De Keyser, of Antwerp, is conventional, but not lacking in interest as a skillfully painted figure. "Sea-Shore at Blankenbergh" (16), by Verhas, represents three little children digging in the sand on a beach, with a bathing-machine, barely indicated, close by. The little figures are capitally painted, their attitudes being actually those most natural to children. The green waves coming in upon the beach are painted a little too hard, perhaps, and, curiously enough, there is a pre-Raphaelite look in the whole picture. No. 19, by Cardon, "The Smoking-Room." The cavalier and a page, figures, and accessories, are drawn with care and attention to details. Nos. 20 and 34, by Robbe, are clever illustrations in the art of flower-painting, with a monkey thrown in, in the case of No. 20, which is entitled "The Destroyer." "Flemish Stallion" (29), Tschaggeny. This artist is known as a remarkable painter of sheep. In his present work he displays no less knowledge of the horse, nor less skill in the delineation of the more noble animal. No. 33, a cabinet picture by Roosenboom, represents a lady in the costume of the period. She is arrayed in black velvet and muslin, and seated in a crimson velvet armchair, having a little child in her lap, which clasps her neck with evident fondness. The picture is called "Mo-

GEORGE W. CHILDS, PROPRIETOR OF THE PHILADELPHIA "LEDGER."

therly Love," and is a good example of its kind. No. 38, by De St. Cyr, "Sentinel at the Entrance of the Harem," is a large work, presenting the single figure of an armed guard, seemingly a Nubian, who sits upon an ottoman and has his feet upon the skin of a tiger. Beside him is a heavy hanging curtain, which is interposed between the interior of a harem and its mysteries and the outside world. The figure of the Oriental soldier is strongly delineated, and the picture is a striking one. "Fire in the Stable" (43), by Charles Tschaggeny, is the striking and impressive incident of a superb horse in peril on the approach of the flames. The peculiar disposition to extreme terror always evinced by this animal under such circumstances is shown with great skill and marked dramatic power in this picture.

Passing from this room to Gallery 39, we continue the consideration of the Belgium collection. No. 44, by Miss Clemence Van den Broeck, is a "Flemish House in A.D. 1600." In this work there are painted with true Dutch or Flemish fidelity the usual accessories of an old-time Flemish kitchen. Every dish or other utensil is elaborately painted to its true pattern, and an amount of time and labor has been expended over the work which its import-

ance would scarcely demand. It is very clever and very truthful. No. 49, by Victor Lagye, "The Sculptor"—a careful and spirited painting—represents an interior of a sculptor's study and his work. No. 53, by Van Luppen, of Antwerp, "After the Rain—View from Anseremme, near Dinant," is the best landscape in the collection. In fact, there are not many landscapes exhibited. There is no warmth of color in this work, the hues being all deep-green, russet and gray, relieved a little by the thin streak of white, foaming water, which comes leaping and plunging down the hill to its base in the foreground of the picture: yet it is all the more natural, and worked out with a true feeling for nature's intention. No. 89, by Jean Portaels, of Brussels, is entitled "Deception," and represents a brunette lady, seated in a heavily upholstered chair, with a coronet visibly embroidered upon it. Deception is not clearly shown, but there is some good work in the painting of both the figure and the fabrics displayed. "The Little Sleeper" (95), by Lampe, is a capital work, and its textures of satin, velvet and brocade, are quite remarkable, and indicated with fidelity. The figures are well enough, but not specially meritorious.

The last of the Belgian pictures is contained in Gallery No. 41. "On the Road to Market" (126), by Plumot, is a beautiful little rustic piece with some distant landscape and rustic architecture. No. 135, by J. Stallaert, of Brussels, "The Cellar of Diomede—Scene at the Destruction of Pompeii," is a large canvas containing a number of figures, and presenting certain elements of interest, but by no means up to the importance of the subject in merit. Meanwhile there are pathetic incidents shown or suggested which display considerable wealth of idea. It is in the treatment of details that the artist is deficient. No. 152, "Byron's Parisina," by Wittkamp, apparently a work of real and special merit, but badly hung and impossible to consider closely. No. 155, "Sea-shore at Scheveningen," by Musin, is a vivid representation of a stormy sea-beach, and fishermen hurrying their barks to shore. "Waterwomen of Venice" (156), by Wulffaert. If the Venetian waterwomen are as pretty and as graceful as is here indicated, the demand for water in that charming city should be incessant. "Clytie," by Le Jendre (163), is an illustration of Ovid, and is a remarkable work, and the contrast afforded by the naked figure and the gray, gloomy rocks, on whose surface she is extended almost at full length, is original and striking. "Flowers" (165), by Raoux, is quite gorgeous in color, and well drawn, and, besides, affords a pleasing relief from the general lowness of tone of the Belgium pictures. No. 169, by Roosenboom, "The Gems," is an interior with two female figures, old furniture, bronze, etc., and cleverly rendered. "The First Ice of the Season" (174), by Ooms, represents a little boy evidently bemoaning a fall, and being consoled by his sister or sweetheart, while several other little children stand behind and jeer at him; a quaint-looking high-roofed village, with church, being seen in the background. No. 171, by Verheyden, is a "Landscape," and a good one, by an artist of deserved reputation and real merit.

SPAIN.

Gallery 31, which commences the list of contributions from Spain, contains a very heterogeneous collection of paintings, statuary, wood-carvings, terra-cotta, and bronze. Many of these are copies of the old masters, the reproductions of mural paintings from the Spanish cathedrals. The leading contributor appears to be Señor Rabada. His two paintings (29a and 29b) display considerable force and original methods of treatment. "Faun Playing a Flute" (54a), by Francisco Jover, is a large work, in which the sylvan scene and the characteristics of the mythological personage illustrated are well rendered. There are a few pictures here which depict the modern Spanish costumes and domestic incidents, which are moderately interesting. "Hunting Dogs" (39b), by Leopoldo Villamil. These dogs are splendidly painted. They are drawn with

MALACHITE CANDELABRUM IN THE RUSSIAN EXHIBIT, IN THE MAIN BUILDING.

TERRA-COTTA FOUNTAIN IN THE BRITISH EXHIBIT, IN THE MAIN BUILDING.

MALACHITE VASE IN THE RUSSIAN EXHIBIT, IN THE MAIN BUILDING.

great fidelity to nature, and colored to life. No. 34, by M o d e s t o Urgell, "The Village Graveyard." This is probably the best work in the room. It comprises only a little strip in the foreground of "God's Acre," with the spires of slender trees pointing heavenward, and all the rest. a gloomful, gray-and-white sky, with half a dozen curiously shaped gravestones scattered here and there to mark the character of the place. No. 58c, "Type from the Seventeenth Century," by José Ortiz, presents the full length figure of a Spanish cavalier, the figure. being about seven inches in height, painted with great minuteness, and very cleverly and accurately. No. 38, by Carlos Wade, of Cadiz, is of the later Spanish school, and is a characteristic work. 58a, by José Diaz Valera, is called "Venus" in the catalogue, but why Venus, any more than any other nude woman, it is difficult to imagine. Anatomically this particular nude woman appears to be correct, although there are effects of light and shade in the way of modeling the human flesh which appear to have been beyond this artist. The figure is represented as reclining on a low couch in an apartment wherein the walls seem to be decorated and hung with curtains. The treatment of the covering of the couch, which consists of linen, silk and lace, is perhaps the best work in the picture.

BRAZIL.

Gallery No. 29, next adjoining the one last described, contains about a dozen of Mexican pictures, the remainder of its contents being the contribution of Brazil. Of the Mexican works here, the "Savoyard Beggar-Boy," by Mrs. de Mayora (34), is perhaps the best. It is modest and unpretentious, and very truthful. Brazil displays three or four very large works, of which three represent sea-fights, incidents in the Paraguayan War, two of them being by Victor Meirelles de Lima, of Rio Janeiro. One of these, No. 7, which is about 16 ft. by 10, "The Brazilian Ironclad Fleet passing by Humaita," is a striking picture, in which the present Emperor, Dom Pedro, is shown standing at the bow of the flag-ship waving his cap as the fleet dashes through the very thickest of the fight, which is conducted from the Paraguayan side from rafts, small boats, disabled and dismantled vessels.

CANADA.

In Gallery No. 26 Canada displays one hundred and fifty-eight paintings in oil and water-color, including two portraits attributed to Vandyke, four to Sir Peter Lely, and one work entitled "Ship Firing a Salute," said to be by Vandervelde. These require no further notice at our hands. Of the Canadian pictures, quite a number are landscapes, representing local scenery, and others, heads of Indians. No. 15, by J. C. Forbes, "Beware," is a portrait exceedingly well executed. No. 19, by T. M. Martin, "A Whisky Ring," represents a party of rats, which have upset a whisky-bottle and broken it, and are getting themselves gloriously drunk on the contents. This is a capitally humorous picture, and is very well

MOSAIC RUG IN THE RUSSIAN EXHIBIT, IN THE MAIN BUILDING.

painted. The water-color collection in this gallery is of a higher class and really more deserving of praise than are the oil-paintings. Nos. 53, by Edson, 58, by Way, and 59, by Jacobi, will compare very favorably with anything in the American water-color exhibition, as will also 63, by Edson, entitled "Trespassers," representing stray sheep among sheaves of wheat. No. 74, by D. Fowler, "Hollyhocks," is gorgeously colored, yet not the least exaggerated. No. 117, by H. Sandham, "On the Godbout River," is a striking picture of very romantic, or rather impressive, scenery, with precipitous declivities, and in the distance hanging over a dark and turbid pool, which breaks into a dashing and rapid current, immediately before and immediately after. In the foreground the foliage peculiar to this latitude is carefully worked into the composition. No. 147, by Mrs. Schreiber, "Olivia." This is from the "Vicar of Wakefield," and is a very charming representation of the character conceived by Goldsmith. The girl, with a thoughtful expression on her countenance, is represented sitting at a window, which looks off on an English landscape, being engaged in the occupation of peeling apples, but has ceased her employment and dropped into a reverie.

MALACHITE CLOCK IN THE RUSSIAN EXHIBIT, IN THE MAIN BUILDING.

FRANCE.

The remainder of the French exhibits, completing the collection in the Art Annex, are contained in Galleries 32, 34 to 38 (inclusive), 43 and 45. Gallery 32, next to the corridor, and near the centre of the building, contains but few works specially noteworthy. No. 240, by Barrias, "Electra (Victor Hugo)," is an impressive and strong representation. There is something indeed majestic in the pose of the figure, which the surroundings in the background are artistically made to bring into due prominence. "Gale on the Nile during the Flood" (251), by N. Berchere, represents a boat lateen-rigged, being driven before the wind over the scarcely disturbed waters of the sacred river. This is a peculiar work, and will bear inspection. No. 258, "Alone in the House," by Couder. This picture depicts a magnificent floral display in a large vase of exotics, with a glass globe containing gold-fish beside it on

a handsomely carved table well painted. On the floor two kittens gambol about over a Prussian carpet, destroying such flowers as they are able to pull down, having made wreck of a costly fan, which lies broken upon the floor, and being now engaged in earnest efforts to topple over the jar of gold-fish. This is a pretentious work, but not more so than meritorious. The colors are vivid in the flowers and leaves, and the action of the scene is graphic with a touch of the humorous. No. 255, by O. P. Mathieu, "The Nymph Echo bewailing the Death of Narcissus." The Nymph is well enough portrayed in this picture, which is not, however, altogether admirable. The most important picture in this room is 268, "The Bather," by Jules Garnier. A tall and certainly graceful figure of a nude female, obviously of the better class, judging from her surroundings, stands beside a stone basin, clearly in the open air, and touches the water with her feet before she ventures to bathe in it. There is no disputing the excellence of art which has compassed this work. The figure is lifelike, exquisite in proportion, vivid and human in the reality of its flesh modeling. The face is not pleasing, but is characteristic of the situation. What there is of incidental surrounding about her is ably painted, not the least of this being a rather large-sized tortoise, which is about to plunge itself into the water. To those who are fond of the nude in art, this work certainly offers a congenial repast.

Galleries 34, 36 and 45 contain the French exhibits of water-colors, engravings and bronzes. It is impossible to devote time or space to the detailed consideration of the works here displayed. Many of them are deserving and some highly meritorious. Bartholdi's "Génie funèbre," a bronze figure in a crouching attitude, is admirably expressive of the sentiment involved. No. 483, by J. Cambos, "La Cigale," a graceful figure in bronze, represented leaning upon the stump of a tree, holding under one arm some kind of stringed musical instrument. The noticeable pictures of this room are 347, by Adan, "Scene of the Inquisition"; 349, by Zier, "Julia," quite a notable and powerful representation of a Roman scene; 352, by Antigna, "Fascination," representing the influence of a small serpent over a little girl, who stands naked, having just apparently removed her clothing for the purpose of bathing; 361, by Jundt, "The Hair Fair in Auvergne," an original and novel idea, worked into a rather picturesque and certainly well-executed painting; 365, by Rougeron, "Teasing"—a lady in full modern dress, lying upon a couch, and worrying a pet bird. One side of Gallery No. 37 is occupied by a full-length, life-sized portrait of Washington on horseback. This work is by R. Princeteau, of Paris. The canvas is about 10 ft. by 8 in dimensions, and the work is quite as well executed as portraits of this size and character usually are. 313, "The God of the Woods," by Maignan, represents the deity in the form of a

MALACHITE TABLE IN THE RUSSIAN EXHIBIT, IN THE MAIN BUILDING.

MALACHITE TABLE IN THE RUSSIAN EXHIBIT IN THE MAIN BUILDING.

half-naked boy, upon one finger a little lizard. 302, "The First Mourners," by Debat, being Adam and Eve bewailing over the body of Abel. "Cassandra," by Camorre (325).

In Gallery 38 the most notable works are Nos. 287, "Interior of a Forest," by Alexandre de Bar; 289, by Cherez, representing a gorge in the mountains of France, with a torrent plunging through it; 290, by Mathieu, "The Vanquished"; 291, by Jadin, a striking figure of a dead Sheikh; 293, "The Nymph Echo," by Tortez; 294, "The Friends of the House," by Monginet, an immense fruit and flower-piece with monkeys introduced; 303, "The Bather," by Perrault, a nude figure in a hammock, and a superb work withal, of which we have seen both photographs and engravings.

Gallery No. 43 completes the French collection with an exhibition of architectural designs sent by different artists from Paris, and with these we end our examination of the Art Gallery.

CUBA AT THE EXPOSITION.

The exhibits of the Island of Cuba at the Centennial were included in the Spanish departments in the Agricul-

surveyors' instruments, etc.; while mahogany is abundant and of a superior quality. Another important native wood is known as the Havana cedar, and is used for the inside of drawers and wardrobes, and particularly in the manufacture of cigar-boxes.

Humboldt enumerates five species of palm as indigenous to the island, and says further that "we might believe that the entire island was originally a forest of palms and wild lime and orange-trees."

There might have been made from Cuba an exhibit of birds of the most pleasing character, there being more than 200 distinct species on the island, many of them remarkable for the beauty of their plumage.

The population of Cuba in March, 1870, was 1,399,811. This included 763,176 whites, 363,288 slaves, and 288,927 free colored. The number of coolies at the same time was stated to be 34,420. The latter have increased largely of late, while the number of slaves, owing to the cessation of the slave-trade, has fallen off. Of course the insurrection in Cuba has resulted in a considerable decline in the fortunes of the island; but the crops of sugar and tobacco promise to be much greater in 1877 than ever before, and the benefit to the interests of the island will be correspond-

and deserves special mention and description in this record. This watch occupied more than two years in its construction, and in all its parts is made with an exactness of accuracy almost impossible to imagine.

Perhaps the best as well as the most amusing description of this astonishing timepiece is that written by Mark Twain (H. L. Clemens), and we cannot do better than quote it:

"I have examined the wonderful watch made by Mr. H. L. Matile, and indeed it comes nearer to being a human being than any piece of mechanism I ever saw before. In fact, it knows considerably more than the average voter. It knows the movements of the moon, and keeps exact record of them; it tells the day of the week, the date of the month, and the month of the year, and will do this perpetually; it tells the hour of the day, and the minute and the second, and even splits the seconds into fifths, and marks the division by stop hands, having two of the latter; it can take accurate care of two race-horses that start, not together, but one after the other; it is a repeater (wherein the voter is suggested again), and musically chimes the hour, the quarter, the half, and the three-quarter hour, and also the minutes that have passed of an uncompleted quarter hour, so that a blind man can tell the time of day by it to the

1. Crayon Drawings.　　2. Statuary.　　3. Mrs. Greatorex's Pen-and-Ink Drawings.

THE ART DEPARTMENT IN THE WOMAN'S PAVILION.

tural, Main and Spanish Government Buildings, and—except in the matter of cigars—were quite lost as to individuality. The display of cigars and cigarettes from the manufacturers of Havana was full, and of the very finest possible quality. This was seen in the handsome and comprehensive show made in the Spanish section of the Agricultural Building. But besides this, there were in the Spanish Government Building specimens of the native woods of Cuba, both those employed in construction and for ornamental purposes, which were in the highest degree interesting.

Cuba is noted for its forests of hardwood-trees of species specially valuable for their durability, hardness and toughness; and also for the remarkable beauty which they impart to the scenery. Here are varieties of timber which are unknown out of the West India Islands, and early in the eighteenth century their existence led to the establishment of shipbuilding among the Spaniards, while from 1724 to 1796 Havana was the great nursery of the Spanish Armada, 114 vessels of more than 4,000 guns being constructed there in that time.

Among the more valuable woods may be mentioned the lignum-vitæ; cocoa-wood, which is used in the manufacture of flutes; lance-wood, exported for carriage-shafts,

ingly important. The manufactures peculiar to Cuba are few, and this fact will account for her display at the Centennial being less noticeable than was the case with other countries of far less importance. One article of indigenous manufacture and use might have have been exhibited to advantage, but was not. This is the far-famed *volante*, the peculiar Cuban vehicle; which, with its low, straggling body and high wheels, always attracts so much attention from visitors to the island. It has very long shafts, thus keeping the mule or horse at a considerable distance from the carriage, while a *calisero*, or postilion, rides on the animal's back, instead of a driver on a seat. But the old-fashioned *volante* is gradually disappearing, except in the country towns of the island.

THE MATILE WATCH.

In the Swiss Department of the Main Building there were exhibited in the portion of the structure lying north of the nave, and allotted to scientific instruments manufactured in Switzerland, certain "precision watches" manufactured by H. L. Matile, of Locle. One of these was certainly a most remarkable specimen of human ingenuity,

exact minute. Such is this extraordinary watch. It ciphers to admiration. I should think one could add another wheel and make it read and write; still another and make it talk; and I think one might take out several of the wheels that are already in it, and it would still be a more intelligent citizen than some that help to govern the country. On the whole, I think it is entitled to vote—that is, if its sex is of the right kind."

The Matile Watch is valued at $1,400. It is inclosed in an extra heavy and solid gold case, and is a somewhat ponderous intrument. But as an illustration of patience, mathematical and mechanical ability, this watch is undoubtedly without an equal in the world.

THE INTERNATIONAL RIFLE MATCH AT CREEDMOOR.

On Tuesday, September 12th, commenced this series of rifle matches, under the auspices of the United States Centennial Commission and the National Rifle Association. The Irish, Scotch and Australian Rifle Teams had arrived in New York early in the month, and were formally received by the National Rifle Association, an amateur rifle club, on

THE VICTOR ROCK-DRILL, IN MACHINERY HALL.

September 4th, at the Fifth Avenue Hotel. The names of the gentlemen composing the teams are as follows : *Americans*—Messrs. Dakin, Farwell, Weber, Fulton, Gildersleeve, Rathbone, Bodine and Allen. *Irish*—Messrs. Johnson, Fenton, Rigby, Dyas, Pollock, Goff, Joynt, Milner and Leech. *Australian*—Messrs. Smith, Sleep, Lynch, King, Gee, Draper, Slade and Wardell. *Scotch*—Messrs. Boyd, Whitelaw, Mitchell, McVittie, Ray, Thornburn, Clark and Menzies. *Canadian*—Messrs. Mason, Bell, Murison, Adams, Gibson, Colton, Disher and Cruit. On Wednesday, the 6th of September, the members of the different teams, except the Canadian, met at Creedmoor for long-range practice, when the Irish made the best total, the Scotch the worst. The match commenced on September 12th with the short and mid-range contests. In the first match of 200 yards there were 164 marksmen, shooting ten rounds each at sixteen targets. In this match George Disher, Canadian, was the only foreign marksman who carried off the prize. In the mid-range competition there were 159 competitors, among whom were Messrs. Milner and Thynne of the Irish, Col. Gildersleeve and Mr. Rathbone of the American, and C. E. Overbaugh and H. S. Jewell of the reserves. At this range the Americans did exceedingly well, only one of the foreigners, Mr. Milner (Irish Team), carrying off the prize. H. S. Jewell won the first prize on a clean score of 50 points out of a possible 50. On the following day the first long-range match was held, five team entries being made—the American, Canadian, Scotch, Australian, and Irish. In this match the Americans led with 550 out of 600 possible, the Scotch and Irish tied at 535, the Australian was fourth at 531, and the Canadian was last at 521. The 900 yards range commenced at two o'clock and closed at four, the best individual score being made by McVittie (Scotch Team)—eleven bull's-eyes and six centres, 71. The team-scores showed that the Scotch had made 528, the Irish and Australian 524, the American 518, and the Canadian 476, the whole total for the two ranges being : Americans, 1,068; Scotch, 1,063; Irish, 1,059; Australians, 1,055; and Canadians, 997. The next match was the 1,000 yards range, and was finished at six o'clock by the Scots completing the total of 523 on the 1,000 yards, which made their grand total 1,586 ; the Irish tying them on the 1,000 yards, making a grand total of 1,582 ; while the Americans stood third at 1,577; the Australians fourth at 1,545 ; and the Canadians at 1,490. Dr. J. Mitchell (Scotch Team) made the extraordinary score of 14 bull's-eyes and an inner, scoring 73 out of the possible 75. On Thursday the shooting of long ranges was resumed, completing at 1:15 P. M., leaving the Scotch first; the Americans 9 points behind ; the Irish third, 18 points behind the Americans ; and the Australians 17 points behind the Irish. The Canadians were 129 behind the Scotch. The great contest of the day on the 1,000 yards was completed at four o'clock, and in this Mr. Milner, of the Irish team, made his 15 consecutive bull's-eyes, making what has never before been

made, either at match or practice, a perfect score at 1,000 yards. The Americans added a score of 509, making a grand total of 3,126, leading the field by 22 points. The Irish took the second place, 242, and headed the Scotch, who tied the Australians ; the Canadians being far in the rear. At the announcement of the victory of the American Team there was most enthusiastic applause, the members being mounted upon a table in full sight of the vast concourse of spectators, and congratulatory remarks being made by the captains of the different teams. On Friday evening, the 15th of September, Gilmore's Garden, in New York city, was crowded to its utmost capacity on the occasion of the presentation of the Creedmoor prizes. As the teams entered they were escorted to the boxes, decorated with the colors of the nation represented. After a special programme had been performed, Mayor Wickham and Gen. Hawley, the umpire, proceeded to the Americans' box and headed the procession of the teams to the platform upon which rested the great trophy, which has already been illustrated in this publication. Gen. Hawley presented the medals of the Centennial Commission to the members who won in the short-range matches, and then the trophy itself ; after which he presented each member of the team with a miniature copy of the trophy in gold and silver.

INTERNATIONAL LIVE-STOCK EXHIBITION.

Neat Cattle.

United States.—The exhibition of neat cattle, under the auspices of the Centennial Commission, commenced September 21st and closed October 4th. This department comes under the head of Group 30, in which the following gentlemen were judges : T. C. Jones, Delaware, Ohio ; William Birnie, Springfield, Mass. ; Warren Percival, Vassalborough, Maine ; M. Wilkins, Harrisburg, Oregon ; Colin Cameron, Lancaster, Pa. ; S. J. Lynch, Los Angelos, Cal. ; J. Milton Mackie, Great Barrington, Mass. ; Frank T. Anderson, Rockybriar, Va. ; James Moore, Harriston, Canada ; T. Duckham, London, England ; Gen. Horace Capron, Chicago, Ill. ; Ashbel Smith, M.D., Houston, Texas ; Henry C. Meredith, Cambridge City, Indiana. The classification of animals commenced with short-horn bulls, in which there were 18 entries, most of these from Easton, Pa. ; "Oxford Geneva" and "Mariner 2d" being notable exhibits from Winchester, Ky. The next class was short horn cows and heifers, in which there were 62 entries, the larger number of these being also from Easton, Pa. ; but there being some exhibits in this class from Poughkeepsie, N. Y., Winchester, Ky.; West Liberty, Iowa, and five of them being exhibited by Mr. George Grant, of Victoria, Kansas—a gentleman quite renowned for his stock-farm —these five exhibits being bred by Her Majesty the Queen of England. The next class was Hereford bulls, in which there were 9 entries, chiefly from Illinois and Maryland ; of Hereford cows and heifers there were 27 entries, also chiefly from Illinois and Maryland, although 5 came from Fairfield Centre, Maine ; of Devon bulls there were 16 entries, chiefly from New York and Pennsylvania, one eleven-

year-old red bull, "The Prince of Wales," being bred by Her Majesty the Queen of England, and imported by R. W. Cameron, Clifton, Staten Island, New York. There were 47 entries of Devonshire cows and heifers, quite a large number being entered by J. B. Anchor, Union Deposit, Pa. Several were from Connecticut, and a few from Michigan, and a large number comprised in this class being from the State of New York. Two entries of Holstein bulls were from Illinois and New Jersey. Three Holstein cows and heifers were from the same States ; one Guernsey bull, exhibited by Charles H. Muirheid, Titusville, N. Y., named "Milfred," No. 182 in the catalogue, five years old, fawn-and-white, sent from Liverpool, September 7th, 1872. Sire and dam both obtained prizes in the Royal Agricultural and other British shows. This was a magnificent animal, as was also a Guernsey heifer named "Test," five years old, fawn-color, exhibited by the same party. Of this class there were but 4 entries. Of Jersey bulls there were 173 entries, mostly from New Jersey and Pennsylvania. Of Alderney bulls but one entry, from Philadelphia ; of Ayrshire bulls there were 15 entries, and of Ayrshire cows and heifers, 46 entries. Miscellaneous entries were made of "Cupid 2d," a black and white Breton heifer, three and a half years old ; and two buffaloes and two heifers, natives of Kansas and Nebraska, caught on the plains and well broken. Of fat cattle there were 15 entries, the largest being a steer, eight years old, weighing 6,000 pounds, exhibited by W. W. Somers, of Tennessee ; three triplet-steers, "Tom," "Dick" and "Harry," 8 years and 8 months old, average weight, 3,200 pounds ; "General Grant," a Durham steer, contributed by James T. Branson, from Guthrieville, Pa., was seven years old, and weighed 4,000 pounds. Two three-quarter Hereford bulls, from six to seven years old, weighing, respectively, 5,200 and 5,100 pounds, were contributed by John Brooks, of Princeton, Mass. The draught cattle, chiefly Durham and Devon, included 13 numbers. Of Galloways there was one bull and four cows and heifers. Of herds exhibited—Ayrshire, Jersey and Galloway—there were 17 entries, completing the catalogue of the United States contributions, being about 500 entries altogether.

Great Britain.—This country contributed 6 entries, three being short-horn bulls, three cows and heifers. "Cymbeline," four years and six months old, a white bull, No. 464 in the catalogue, contributed by Benjamin St. John Ackers, of Gloucestershire, England, who, in fact, furnished all the British entries, is noted as having received

THE "MOHAWK DUTCHMAN" WOOD-SAWYER, IN MACHINERY HALL.

twenty-two prizes, and commendatory notices of which were posted in his stall. "Clovis" (466), two years and one month old, had received eight prizes. There were also shown among the British entries three prize-swine and a litter of five pigs.

Canada.—The most interesting of the exhibits of cattle were from Canada, comprising 105 entries of short-horns and Hereford bulls, cows and heifers; Devonshire bulls; Ayrshires, Alderneys and Galloway bulls, cows and heifers; two exhibits of fat cattle and eight herds. We may mention as among the more noted exhibits the following: "Duke of Cumberland," two years and seven months old, short-horn bull, roan, contributed by Thomas Boak, Hornby, Ontario; "Graceful," one year and nine months old, red heifer, contributed by Hodge & Ketchley, York Mills, Ontario; "Jessie" and "2d Duchess," of Grimsby, roan heifers, contributed by W. W. Kitchen, Grimsby, Ontario; "Harry," Hereford bull, two years and seven months old, bred by the exhibitor, George Hood, Guelph, Ontario; "Carrick Lad," Ayrshire bull, four years and six months old, red and white, contributed by William Rodden, Plantagenet, Ontario, who has taken eight first

In the exhibits of fat sheep the weight ranges from 200 pounds to above that figure. There were four exhibits of Angora goats, bucks, and four of does, one Angora goat, two years old, pure breed, weighing 125 pounds. Great Britain made fifty-six exhibits of Cotswolds, Oxford Downs—rams—South Downs, and long-wooled rams. Canada had twenty-nine exhibits of Lincolns, Leicesters, Cotswolds, and South Downs—rams and ewes. The American exhibits of swine numbered one hundred and eighty-one, including Berkshire boars and sows, large Yorkshires and small Yorkshires, Chester Whites, fat swine, Poland-China and Neapolitan. One exhibit of fat swine from Williston, Pa., was a pair of Chester Whites, four years old, male 1,000 pounds and female 800 pounds. Great Britain made four exhibits, all by Benjamin St. John Ackers, of Gloucestershire, England. These include one Berkshire boar and three Berkshire sows. Canada had twenty-six exhibits, comprising Suffolks, Berkshires, Chester Whites, and Yorks—boars and sows.

———

Our illustrations of the cattle show include thirteen selected specimens. No. 1 is "Oxford Geneva," one and a

OREGON.

Its Resources and its Position in the Centennial.

In a previous portion of this work we have referred to some extent to the progress of the State of Iowa, as manifested in its display at the Exhibition. We propose now to consider briefly the claims of Oregon upon our attention in the same direction. Oregon is the fourth State in size in the Union. Originally, and as a Territory, it extended from 42° to 49° north latitude, and from the Pacific Ocean to the Rocky Mountains, and included its present area and what are now the Territories of Idaho and Washington. The country embraced in Oregon was formerly within the dominions of Spain, subsequently claimed by France, as also by Great Britain, by reason of exploration and settlement, and was held for a period of years in joint occupancy by the United States and Great Britain. The name "Oregon" is supposed to have originated with the early Spanish voyagers, and to have been derived from the plant *origanum*, or wild marjoram, which exists abundantly in this State. Indian legends, however, say that Oregon means "The land of the setting sun." The geographical character of Oregon is varied, and includes soil and climates

I. L. BAKER'S CELEBRATED SUGAR POP-CORN EXHIBIT, IN MACHINERY HALL.

prizes and diplomas in the Dominion in two years, as the best bull of any age exhibited; "Viscount," one year and five months old, red and white, Ayrshire bull, by same exhibitor, took first prize at Montreal; "Tarbolton 2d," Ayrshire bull, six years and four months old, red and white, contributed by George Thompson, Bright, Ontario, the winner of three successive prizes at Ontario provincial exhibitions, weight 1,855 pounds; of fat cattle, "Lord Dufferin," exhibited by Satchel Bros., Ottawa, Ontario, weight 2,930 pounds.

Sheep, Goats, and Swine

The third stated display of live stock commenced on October 10th, and concluded on the 18th. It comprised sheep and goat and swine exhibits, being made by the United States, Great Britain and Canada in both departments. In part first, of sheep and goats, there were three hundred and fifteen exhibits from American exhibitors. These include rams and ewes, Lincoln and Leicestershire sheep, Cotswold, Oxford Downs, Shropshire Downs, South Downs, Merinoes and fat sheep, Angora goats, bucks and does, and one exhibit of slaughtered mutton. The largest number of exhibits was in Merinoes, of which there were eighty-two of rams, and one hundred and thirty-five of ewes, many of the exhibits being in pens of three and four.

half years, roan, exhibited by Benj. B. Groom & Son, Winchester, Kentucky, value $10,000. No. 2, same exhibitors, "Winsorelli," 3 years, roan, value $10,000. No. 3, exhibitor, Thomas L. McKeen, Easton, Pa., "Dairymaid," three years, white. No. 4, Benjamin St. John Ackers, Gloucestershire, England, "Wedding-Day" (English cow), two years eleven months old, roan. No. 5, same exhibitor, "Cymbeline" (English bull), four years six months, white, weight 3,000 pounds. No. 6, Catherine R. Bradley, of Champaign, Illinois, "Crown-Prince" (Holstein bull), three years three months, black-and-white. No. 7, exhibitor, George Hood, of Guelph, Ontario, "Lily Dale" (Galloway cow). No. 8, same exhibitor, "Roger" (Galloway bull), six years, eight months. No. 9, exhibitor, William Rodden, Plantagenet, Ontario, "Lucy" (Alderney cow, Canada), two years, eight months, fawn-and-gray with a little white. No. 10, exhibitor, William Crozier, Northport, N. Y., "Cossack," three years, dark fawn. No. 11, exhibitor, H. H. Duyskinck, Brick Meeting-house, Maryland (fat cattle), pair of Durham bulls, six years four months, 3,000 pounds each. No. 12, exhibitor, August Hamilton (Devon), draught cattle, one yoke of oxen, one year old, red, 1,600 pounds. No. 13, exhibitor, N. S. Wood, Pawnee City, New Brunswick, two buffaloes, natives of Kansas or Nebraska, caught on the plains, now well broken to the harness.

of every character. The State is traversed by three ranges of mountains, running parallel with the shore of the Pacific. These are the Coast Range, Cascade Range, and the Blue Mountains. The population of Oregon in 1875 was 104,920. Portland is the chief city, and Oregon City a promising manufacturing town. Salem, the capital, is beautifully laid out, in the Willamette Valley, has a population of about 5,000, and, though 130 miles from the sea, ships carrying 1,200 tons can come to its wharves and load direct for Liverpool. Oregon is noted for its magnificent scenery—Mount Hood, Jefferson, the Three Sisters, Diamond's Peak and others being some of the most remarkable mountains in the country. Oregon is rich in precious metals, about $30,000,000 having been taken from her mines when the first discovery of gold was made. Sheep-raising is the leading industry of the State, the crop of wool for 1875 having been nearly 2,000,000 pounds. In the same year there were cultivated about 600,000 acres of land, producing 5,000,000 bushels of wheat, 3,000,000 of oats, 300,000 of barley, about 200,000 tons of hay, 30,000 pounds of tobacco, 500,000 bushels of potatoes, etc. It is also a remarkable State for fruit-growing, the valley of the Willamette being celebrated as "The land of big red apples." This being the history and character of the State of Oregon, it is not remarkable that, since there was public enterprise, enough within its limits, to form a representative collection for the Exhibition in the Agricultural Department of the Centennial Exposition, this exhibition should be one of the most interesting and instructive displays. Such is the case. Such an agricultural show, coming from the most northwestern State of the Union, is as extraordinary as it is creditable to the enterprise and industry of those who are able to make it. Here are to be found every variety of the wild grasses, flowers, mosses and ferns of Oregon; heads and horns of her elk and antelope; skins of her mountain sheep, beaver, otter, sable, monkey and dark-gray wolf; her birds stuffed, from the American eagle to the red bird, including every variety of duck known to the sportsman. Here are also transverse sections of her trees—the red cedar, spruce, white, red and yellow fir. Three of these trees attained a monstrous size in Oregon, one being mentioned as 67 feet in circumference and 325 feet high. Here are also specimens of mountain oaks, including white oak, mountain mahogany, hemlock, cotton-wood, laurel, leather, yew, dogwood, maple (pronounced the most beautiful wood in the world), leather-curled maple, shittim, larch, black and white ash, tamarind, black and white thorn, etc.; also cherry, plum, and fruit-trees, showing a growth of 9¼ feet from the graft in a single year. Besides these, there are black and white walnut and hickory. Here, too, are samples of the cultivated grasses of Oregon, red and white clover, orchard grass, timothy and blue grass, the specimens being five feet high and upwards. Here is rye in stalk standing over 10 feet; oats 8 feet; every variety of grain—all of extraordinary size and yield. There is wheat from land neither plowed nor harrowed. Flax is pulled over five feet high and of fine quality. Dried fruits, as prepared for the markets of the world — apples, pears, plums, peaches and prunes, equal to any imported. There are specimens of wool of the Oxfordshire, Cotswold and Ulster breed, this staple being over a foot in length and of remarkable lustre. Specimens of salmon in barrels and cans from the Columbia River are exhibited, representing a trade of over $2,000,000 of gold per annum. Oregon makes a fine exhibit of iron ore and pig iron, of woolen goods, glue, leather, apple-butter, and of cider concentrated in such a way as to be sold by the yard, pound or pint, being the first time that commodity has been made a suitable article for shipment and trade. This curious result is produced by withdrawing from the cider itself 9 per cent. of water, by a simple mechanical process involving the application of heat, the residue being rolled up like a piece of leather or cloth, and undergoing no change until again dissolved in water. With this process cider can be sent anywhere, any length of time, remaining unchanged. Oregon has a great trade in lumber, sending it to California, South America, Australia, China and Japan, in all of which countries it is used for building purposes. At home red cedar is manufactured into shingles, weatherboards, house and furniture finishing; spruce into shingles and staves, which are shipped to California and South America. The most common and useful wood is the yellow fir, which is extensively used for street-planking, railroad and ship-building. In the Oregon exhibit at the Centennial is shown a piece of this yellow fir which was taken from the planking of a steamer, where it had been exposed for twenty years to the action of fresh and salt water, and yet is perfectly sound and without the slightest indication of decay. From this brief examination it will be seen that

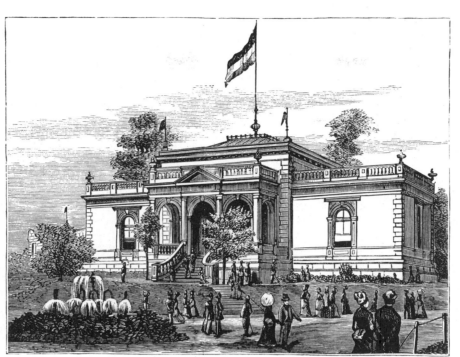

THE GERMAN EMPIRE PAVILION.

Oregon, which has not yet been a State twenty years, is entitled to the full appreciation as one of the most valuable and important, at least, of our Western Commonwealths.

UNITED STATES LIFE-SAVING STATION.

On the north side of the lake, and near the United States Government Building, is the small model station which has been erected for the purpose of exhibiting the appliances used in the United States Life-saving Service. On the lake itself are the American self-regulating and self-balancing life-boat and the Kansas life-raft. The life-boat weighs 4,500 pounds.

Entering the station on the right, from the lake side, the visitor sees a long wide-beam surf-boat, resting on the carriage used to run it along the beach to the nearest point to the wreck; and opposite to this, the cannon for throwing the line to the ship. This weapon throws a ball of 24 pounds, attached to a light line of 200 yards in length, to the wreck, and when this is caught by those on board, the shore end is fastened to an endless line with pulleys. The appliances are seen, and the gun-carriage is exhibited. The men on the beach are by this means able to pull on the line one after another until they send out hawsers. Another appliance used is the life-buoy, of oval shape, formed of cork and canvas. The surf-boat is for a sandy beach, and can be easily managed in an ordinary sea, while the life-boat is so constructed as to weather any storm. It has two decks. The upper deck connot possibly be sunk below the water line, and as the sea washes in, the water rushes out of the bottom through large tubes extending from deck to deck. The hull is of iron, and so heavy that if overturned it resumes its position, while the air-chambers are so distributed that to keep the boat submerged would be impossible.

The Kansas raft is shaped like two cigars strapped together, and weighs 400 pounds. Properly managed, it will ride every sea. Several kinds of mortars and cannons, and other appliances to meet the various exigencies which may arise, are also displayed at the station, and in the reception-room is a model which fully illustrates the method of throwing a line to a ship, running across the hawser and working perfectly.

Over the door leading to this department is a table showing that since the organization of the United States Lifesaving Service, in 1871, no less than 271 wrecks received assistance, and in these, 3,201 lives were imperiled, all of which were saved excepting 43. Five hundred and ninety-seven shipwrecked passengers received shelter after being landed. The aggregate number of days within which protection was extended was 1,882. In these wrecks property valued at $8,122,694 was endangered, and of this, more than two-thirds were saved

OUR ILLUSTRATIONS.

VICTORIA'S EXHIBITS IN THE MAIN BUILDING.

Our illustration presents a view of a portion of the Victoria section in the Main Building. Here are to be seen a fine collection of exhibits of minerals, ores, stone, and other mining products, besides manufactures in wood, pottery, textile fabrics and mechanisms; also stuffed animals and birds, and a long list of animal and vegetable products, including native wines, preserved meats, vegetables, and fruit, a fine display of wool and fleeces, and some very creditable articles in the way of furniture, clothing, jewelry, tools, cutlery, etc.

Among the mineral exhibits, and very prominent articles in the section, are fac-similes of gold ingots found in the

Victoria mines. One of these weighed 718 ounces, another 844 ounces, another 1,105, and still another 2,195. There are also specimens of gems and precious stones, including diamonds, blue sapphires, Oriental emeralds, rubies, aqua-marine, topaz, beryl, opal, garnets, tourmalines, etc.

JAPANESE TOILET MIRROR, ETC.

This illustration represents an elaborate toilet mirror, with its accompaniment of screens and carvings. In front of the mirror is a charmingly carved wooden model of a Japanese dwelling-house. On either side of it are screens with wood carvings of grotesque shapes, dragons, etc. The two bronzes represented are storks holding candelabras, and are considered among the finest representations of this class of art in the Exhibition.

SOUTH AMERICAN ARCHÆOLOGY.

Peru and the Argentine Republic display in the Main Building a fine collection of relics in pottery, etc., obtained from the mounds which exist in these countries. The pottery is generally of simple form, but is engraved with hieroglyphics and grotesque characters, to which no key has as yet been discovered. Fifty mounds in Peru have contributed toward this collection, and among the other articles found have been skeletons of Araucanian Indians, who are supposed to have existed about 1,500 years ago, and mummies of Incas who it is said became extinct at least 3,000 years ago. The Araucanian skulls have narrow, receding foreheads, high cheek-bones and projecting chins, forming a most repulsive presentment. The Incas' skulls, however, have foreheads broad and high, and very regularly-formed features. The skins of the mummies are black, leathery and shrunken. Those of an aristocratic position were buried in stone jars, while the lower orders were simply inclosed in cotton shrouds. Articles appertaining to the habits and customs of these people were buried with them: with females, such as knitted-socks, hard-wood needles and balls of cotton yarn; with warriors' rude weapons. Each corpse was also supplied with a piece of woven cloth to work in the spirit-land, with sacks of herbs, ears of maize, which were preserved by jars, which articles of medicine and food were to be devoted to the necessities which might arise during the journey about to be taken by the deceased. The Argentine Republic exhibits quite an archæological collection, which will be described fully with a general description of the Main Building.

EXHIBIT OF THE FURS OF F. BOOSS & BRO., IN THE MAIN BUILDING.

The exhibit illustrated comprises a fine representation of furs, including samples of all this class of articles at present fashionable. Here are sealskin sacks for ladies, some trimmed with chinchilla, and others with unplucked otter, and others without trimming. Here are also carriage-robes of beaver, red and white fox, black bear and wolverine; muffs and boas in Russian sable, silver-fox and other furs; articles for children in Russian chinchilla, seal, etc., and a remarkably fine, double-breasted sealskin overcoat for a gentleman, made in the most approved style of the period. This firm has a large establishment at 449 Broadway, New York.

ITALIAN SCULPTURE IN MEMORIAL HALL ANNEX.

As has been elsewhere remarked, Italian art in sculpture, at the present time, so far as its representation in our Exposition is concerned, achieves its best success in

MYER ASCH, ASSISTANT SECRETARY TO THE CENTENNIAL COMMISSION.

W. J. PHILLIPS, CHIEF OF CENTENNIAL TELEGRAPH BUREAU.

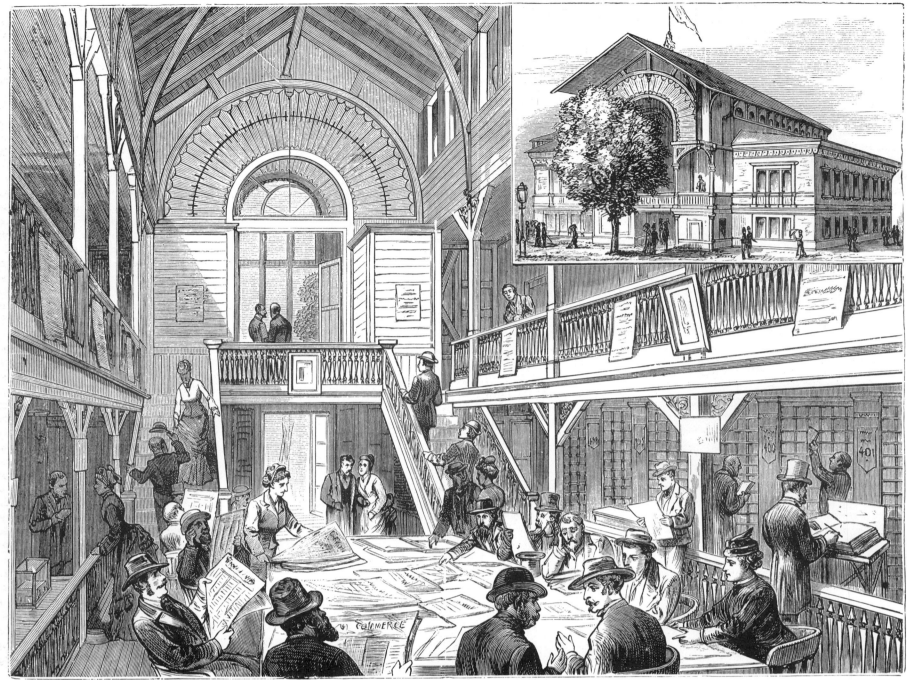

GEORGE P. ROWELL & CO.'S NEWSPAPER PAVILION.

representations of children and infantile subjects. Four such subjects have been illustrated by our artists. One of these is called "The Forced Prayer," No. 332 in the catalogue of the Italian collection, and is by Pietro Guanerrio, of Milan. The idea supposes a little boy weeping bitterly at being compelled to say his prayers, and the artist has most successfully developed this conception. This work took the first prize at Vienna, and was highly praised on all sides. "The First Step," by Trombetta, of Milan, No. 24 in the catalogue, explains itself. The anxiety expressed in the child's face and the accuracy of the mechanical action of the body are admirably displayed, and entitle this work to careful examination. "The Orphans," by Pereda, of Milan, represents two children, sister and brother, in a posture indicative at once of affection, protection and isolation; the sentiment of the group being most skillfully expressed. "Blind-Man's-Buff," by Barzaghi, No. 19, presents a young girl, blindfolded, reaching out, as it were, in fear of falling or stumbling against some one, as she seeks vainly for her hiding companions in the popular game.

CATARACT IN MACHINERY HALL.

In the centre transept of Machinery Hall, and immediately behind the Corliss Engine, is an exhibition of water-power, waterfalls, and scientific and powerful pumping, such as probably never was made before anywhere. This is located in a sort of a wing known as the Pump Annex. In our illustration the spectator is supposed to be standing at the dividing line between the Annex and the main structure, looking south. In the centre is a tank, 160 by 80 feet in dimensions, which is kept nearly full of water received by the Centennial Commission's own system of water-works, direct from the Schuylkill. At the further end of the tank is a cataract, 40 feet wide, the water being precipitated a distance of 40 feet, at the rate of 18,000 gallons a minute. The construction of this artificial fall is as follows: Supported upon iron pipes, which answer also the purpose of conduits, is a platform over which the water descends, and to which it is forced by powerful pumps, which are also on exhibition. On both sides of the tank are various forms of pumps exhibited, some of which, operated by steam, force water through pipes, at a distance above the tank in such way that the rushing streams from them shoot in parabolic curves into the waters below.

JAPANESE SCREENS.

The illustration represents one of the peculiar and characteristic subjects with which the Japanese decorate their screens. It exhibits a long line of green grasshoppers,

marching in single file on their hind legs, each carrying a species of flowers. In the centre of the line a high-caste grasshopper is carried along in a palanquin. The Japanese devote a great deal of time and thought to the decoration of their screens, and succeed in combining embroidery and painting with quite wonderful effects; the faces of figures and outlines of landscape being painted on a silk background, while costumes, animal structures, etc., are embroidered in relief. The larger-sized screens cost from $100 to $400, and the best pictorial art in Japan is devoted to their decoration; the wealthy and cultured Japanese enjoying the collection and exhibition of these articles in the same manner as does a merchant-prince in this country his gallery of paintings. In painting on silk, without the aid of the effect produced by embroidery, some very charming work is exhibited; a few small screens like that which we have illustrated, displaying the most quaint and original conception.

CRACKERS, BAKING-POWDER, CONFECTIONERY AND SLATE ROOFING.

There are in Agricultural Hall, as will have been noticed by most of the visitors to that interesting building, a number of exhibits of crackers put up in such ornamental shape as to be most attractive. Of these exhibits, that of Adam Exton & Co., of Newton, N. J., is deserving of consideration. Our artist has represented the pretty case, which contains the different kinds of crackers exhibited by this firm, including the "butter," the "water," the "oyster," the "plain wine," the "fancy wine," "constitution crackers," etc. On the walls of the section containing these exhibits are hung pictures of their inventor, Exton, and also of his patented cracker machine, together with the long list of his premiums, gold and silver medals, and other prizes, which have been given him at State Fairs since 1850. His factory dates back to three years previous to that time.

In this same locality, and close by the windmill, is the confectionery exhibit of H. Maillard. We have already referred to it in our general examination of Agricultural Hall. The compartment devoted to Mr. Maillard's exhibits is handsomely furnished in walnut, with carpets, mirrors, lounges, etc. The most conspicuous article on exhibition, as is seen in our illustration, is a huge spire-shaped monument of white sugar, nearly fifteen feet in height, and ornamented with historical figures and groups in sugar and chocolate, illustrating incidents in the history of the United States. These include the signing of the Declaration of Independence, the landing of the Pilgrim

Fathers, the capture of Fort Ticonderoga, side figures representing Sitting Bull and General Custer on horseback, etc. These figures are all made by hand. There are also two fine pieces of confectionery: the one a massive vase called the Medicis, of solid chocolate, weighing 200 pounds; the other a book of enormous size, containing 3,000 varieties of bon-bons and chocolate, made by Mr. Maillard, and appropriately entitled, "Une Voyage dans L'Isle des Plaisirs."

Leaving the Agricultural Hall for the Main Building, but still in the same line of exhibits, we note the display made by G. F. Gantz & Co., of New York. The illustration shows a handsome and elaborately carved walnut case, containing cans in which are the celebrated "Seafoam Baking Powders." These are neatly and artistically arranged, and the entire exhibit is surmounted by a glass jar, containing the sea-foam in full view, rising to the height of 15 or 20 feet.

Another of our illustrations, in quite a different department of manufacture, is that representing the building of the New York Slate Roofing Company, located near the annex to the Main Building. This Company manufacture a cheap but durable coating for roofs made by a combination of slate in the form of paint for the protection of roofing. One coat of this paint applied to shingle roofs fills all the holes, pores or cracks, warped or curved shingles, and makes the roof resemble slate in color and condition. It is claimed by the proprietors to be the only reliable paint made, which will effectually fill all leaks, in flat, shingle or other roofs, at the same time proving the most durable paint for metal surfaces. Many of our largest Government buildings, as also theatres, bridges, factories, foundries and corporations, use this roofing in preference to all others.

PORTRAIT OF G. Q. RICHMOND, OF THE CENTENNIAL COMMISSION FROM COLORADO.

Colorado being the "Centennial State," on account of having just been admitted into the Union, it is proper that the portrait at least of one of her Centennial Commissioners should be given in this publication. We have selected that of Mr. G. Q. Richmond, of Pueblo, Colorado. Born August 9th, 1845, in Kennebec County, Maine, at the age of sixteen he enlisted in the 61st Massachusetts Regiment, and served until the end of the war, at the close of which he was appointed to a position in the Treasury Department and although filling this, he continued his studies and actually passed through Columbia College, Washington, D. C., with high honors, and received a diploma of its

Law School. He practiced law in Washington City for three years, when he went West and took up his residence in Pueblo, Colorado, where he has recently by his own ability passed through the different grades of City and County Attorney, and is now a State Commissioner to the Centennial, in which position he has given his best effort towards making the exhibition of his State what it is, one of the most notable and interesting on the grounds.

FRANK LESLIE'S PAVILION.

At page 146 of this work will be seen a view of the pavilion erected by Mr. Frank Leslie, on the banks of the lake in the Centennial Grounds. The building is octagonal in shape, of very ornamental and artistic design, but comprises for use only one floor, where are the headquarters of the authorized representatives of Mr. Leslie's publishing establishment, as well as resident artists, to whom are due the illustrations of the HISTORICAL REGISTER. During the Summer this building has had the advantage of a cool position, while its locality, fronting obliquely on Belmont Avenue, the principal thoroughfare in the grounds, has made it one of the most noticeable objects among the numerous smaller buildings which go to make up the Exposition. Files of the numerous periodicals issued by Mr. Leslie have been kept in the Pavilion, and have been a constant source of attraction to passers-by.

CENTENNIAL RESTAURANTS.

We illustrate two of the restaurants on the Centennial Grounds — the Grand American and the Vienna Bakery. The American restaurant has been very popular during the time the Exposition has been opened, and has given excellent satisfaction. It is claimed to be the largest establishment for this purpose on the ground, having seating capacity for 5,000 guests. Its location is near Agricultural Hall, and its surroundings and the views from it are particularly beautiful. The Vienna Bakery is an establishment which cannot be too highly praised, and if its existence at the Centennial should do what it promises, it may effect a permanent improvement in American bread-making. The Viennese, who are said to be the best bread-makers in the world, will then deserve the hearty thanks of the future generations of Americans. The establishment where the Vienna bread has been first introduced into this country is a plain structure, in which the only articles served are coffee, ices, chocolate, and bread. Yet this building has been crowded to repletion during every day of the Exhibition, hundreds frequently waiting for opportunities to obtain a seat at one of the marble-top tables, and a chance at the limited but most excellent bill of fare. Messrs. Gaff, Fleischman & Co., who established the Vienna Bakery, design to locate branches, after the Exhibition is over, in the cities of New York and Philadelphia, with a view to introduce what is known as the "German Press Yeast," by the use of which it is claimed this wonderful bread can be manufactured by anybody. It is to be hoped that the firm will be eminently successful in their undertaking.

INTERNATIONAL REGATTA PRIZES.

Our illustration of the two principal prizes for the great Centennial Boat Races is from a photograph by Broadbend & Philips, of Philadelphia. These prizes are of solid silver, the manufacture of Messrs. Bailey & Co., and are valued respectively at $1,700. The larger one, presented by Mr. Geo. W. Childs, the proprietor of the Philadelphia *Ledger*, was presented to the winner of the intercollegiate race. It stands upon an ebony base, about three feet high, and is surmounted by a miniature statue of Victory holding a wreath. Two American Eagles, the British Lion, Liberty Bell, and other symbols, form a pretty ornament of this fine piece. The smaller prize was given to the winner of the international four-oared race. It represents an oval-shaped bowl, with a shell-boat running through it. On the sides are engraved views of the course on the Schuylkill and the boat-houses. The figure of Liberty, copied from that on the Capitol at Washington, surmounts the whole.

PORTRAIT OF MR. FRANCIS BERGER, COMMISSIONER OF LUXEMBURG.

The Grand Duchy of Luxemburg was declared neutral by the Treaty of London, May 11th, 1867, and placed under the sovereignty of the House of Orange and Nassau. The population of this little Grand Duchy numbers 210,000 souls, and the annual budget amounts to about a million and a half dollars. Its army consists of one battalion, its religion is Roman Catholic, and its language German or French. Meanwhile, it has a large number of railways, and is both agricultural and manufacturing by vocation. Some of its products are exhibited in the Exhibition, especially gloves, which have obtained a high reputation in Europe. In more practical products Luxemburg is also quite rich, producing annually 350,000 tons of pig-iron, and 1,600,000 pounds of ore. The King of Holland, Grand Duke of Luxemburg, has sent to Philadelphia, as delegate to represent the Grand Duchy at the Centennial, Mr. F. Berger, whose portrait we reproduce. This gentleman has filled several important positions in his own country, and has the reputation of being one of the most active and capable members of the Luxemburg Chamber of Deputies. It is to him that the Grand Duchy owes the creation of the National Bank, having a capital of 300,000,000 francs, issuing notes payable to bearer. He has been decorated with the Orders of France, Belgium, and of his own country.

THE CENTENNIAL AWARDS.

In the system of awards adopted by the Centennial Commission, a wide divergence has been made from the plan heretofore followed by international exhibitions. Thus it has been the custom to place the decision with regard to the comparative value and merit of articles in the hands of juries, who were required to render in the case of each class of articles a definite decision as to which was best, which second best, etc. For these relative merits, graduated medals were awarded. This plan, however, has never been altogether satisfactory. The jury system, in fact, both at the Paris Exhibition, in 1867, and that held in Vienna in 1873, resulted in universal disgust and dissatisfaction. Jealousies and intrigues were found to be a part of the programme, and the best judgment on the subject decided to do away with the system altogether. The Centennial Commission adopted the judicial system, one-half the judges being Americans and the other half foreigners, appointed by the different countries. The whole number of judges was 225, being about one-half that of the jurors at the Vienna Exhibition. Each American judge received $600, and the foreign judges $1,000, to cover necessary expenses. The *personnel* of the Board of Judges was of the highest character, and especially so in regard to the Chief, Gen. Francis A. Walker, a gentleman who brought to the duty apportioned to him not only scientific attainments of the highest rank, but first-class executive ability and wide experience.

The old system consisted in showing that one article was superior to the others, without designating in what particular the superiority consisted. Meanwhile, medals of four or five grades were awarded in gold, silver, bronze, etc., showing degrees of excellence. By the new system a uniform bronze medal was given, the real award consisting in the carefully discriminating report by the judges, showing

"WOMAN'S DAY," NOVEMBER 7TH—MRS. GILLESPIE'S RECEPTION IN THE WOMAN'S PAVILION.

the special merit for which the medal was given. The plan was, in fact, to give awards of medals of equal value for all articles considered by the majority of the judges having the groups under consideration which possess distinguished merit, and to plainly point out the character of the merit itself. None of these diplomas or medals is in itself better than any other.

It is desirable to make this fact very plain, as many exhibitors have announced themselves, by a public advertisement, as holding medals or diplomas of a higher rank than all others. Such is not, and by this system cannot be, the case. All are alike as far as the medals are concerned, the special differences in the articles honored being specifically mentioned in the diplomas.

The awards were made on the evening of October 4th, in the Judges' Hall on the Centennial Grounds, and in the presence of the foreign Commissioners and about 1,800 invited guests. Addresses were made by Commissioners Morrell and Goshorn, after which the President of the Centennial Commission presented the diplomas or awards to the Presidents of the different Foreign Commissions, and to Mr. Goshorn the awards of the successful exhibitors

a block of coal and a very fine exhibit of wool. The beautiful photographs from Sydney are also most attractive, while here, too, is an obelisk showing the amount of gold taken from the mines of this colony. Queensland has a smaller obelisk, representing the quantity of gold found in this colony since 1868. It amounts to sixty tons of gold, valued at $35,000,000. Here also are specimens of tin, copper, arrowroot, woods, oils, silks and botanical specimens. In production of tin Queensland actually exceeds that of gold, and immense quantities of both products are exported.

South Australia, Tasmania and New Zealand also make interesting exhibits.

CENTENNIAL MEDALS.

It is stated that about 12,000 medals have been awarded to successful exhibitors, being in the vicinity of one-fourth of the entire number. These medals are all bronze, four inches in diameter, the largest of the kind ever seen in this country. On the obverse is represented the Genius of America, holding a crown of laurels above the emblems of industry lying at her feet. Female photographs on the

well as American demand. For over half a century this firm has maintained its well-earned reputation for manufactures of the finest quality, and it is always adapting every new available discovery to aid the printer in the more perfect execution of his work. Messrs. George Mather's Sons received, for their exhibits, the highest medal at the disposal of the Commission of Jurors to the Centennial Exhibition, and the honor awarded to this firm is a guarantee of their successful past and their more pre-eminent future.

MESSRS. GEORGE P. ROWELL & CO.'S NEWSPAPER PAVILION.

The enterprising advertising agents, Messrs. George P. Rowell & Co., conceived and carried out a most original and useful idea when they established the Newspaper Building on the Exposition Grounds. Here visitors were offered a comfortable apartment 67 feet in length by 46 in width, and 33 in height, admirably lighted and ventilated, where they could write letters home, if that convenience was desired, or could examine any one of the 8,000 newspapers published in the United States, every issue of each journal being received during the Exhibition. The sys-

SCENE AT THE PASSENGER DEPOT OF THE NEW JERSEY CENTRAL RAILROAD.

of the United States. We have illustrated the scene of the occasion of this important transaction.

THE BRITISH COLONIES EXHIBIT IN THE MAIN BUILDING.

The section devoted to the British Colonial exhibit comprises a very considerable place on the nothern side of the nave of the Main Building, west of the transept. Chief among these colonies are, of course, the Australian group, which occupy one-third of the entire space allotted to the dependencies of Great Britain, Canada having one-half, and the remainder being given to India, the Cape of Good Hope, the Gold Coast, Jamaica, Bermuda, the Bahamas, Seychelles, Ceylon, British Guiana and Trinidad.

It is to the Australian exhibit, illustrated by our artists, that we wish to direct the attention of the reader in the present instance. Here are specimens of raw products, statistics of wealth, views of scenery, samples of minerals, textile fabrics, etc., and especially in the Victoria Court, the exhibits illustrating the gold product of that colony.

The five Australian colonies have produced since the beginning of gold mining in 1851, excluding Victoria, 17,996,834 ounces; while Victoria alone has produced 45,629,122 ounces, valued at more than $875,000,000. Most interesting exhibits in this connection are models representing the gross product of gold as well as other metals of enormous ingots. In the New South Wales exhibits are

outer zone, typifying America, Europe, Asia and Africa, are accompanied by appropriate symbols. On the reverse is a wreath of laurels, having in the exergue, "International Exhibition, Philadelphia, MDCCCLXXVI.," and within the wreath, "Awarded by the United States Centennial Commission."

EXHIBIT OF MESSRS. GEORGE MATHER'S SONS' LETTERPRESS AND LITHOGRAPHIC PRINTING-INKS, ETC.

This very unique exhibit (see page 195) is located on the southeastern side of the Main Building, and comprises samples of the various kinds of black and colored printing-inks for letterpress and lithographic printing, and also the varnishes and oils used in these trades. The samples of inks, varnishes and oils are neatly arranged upon shelves, while the unsurpassed specimens of printed work produced by the celebrated manufactures of Messrs. George Mather's Sons (60 John Street, New York) are disposed about the section in such a manner as to render them easily accessible to the most critical disciple of the ennobling art of Printing.

The finest illustrated newspapers, periodicals—(such as *Frank Leslie's Illustrated Newspaper, Frank Leslie's Historical Register of the Centennial Exposition,* and *Harpers' Weekly*)—and books published in this country are printed with this firm's inks, and such is the care and skill bestowed in their manufacture that they have secured a Foreign a

tematic arrangement of this multitude of journals was such that any paper could be found at a moment's notice; and as the attendants in charge were civil and courteous, it was a real treat and pleasure to submit one's self to their kind attentions.

Extending around the upper portion of the building were two galleries containing about thirty desks, supplied with pens, ink and paper gratis, while several private rooms, comfortably fitted up, offered an additional feature of convenience.

Of the 8,000 and over American newspapers, 6,235, or more than three-fourths, are weekly. The State of New York supplies 1,818, the City of New York alone furnishing more than 400. Next comes Pennsylvania with 738, including Philadelphia with her 160. After these follow Ohio, Iowa and Indiana, and next Massachusetts, with 350. California ranks fourth in the number of its dailies.

It is an interesting fact that during the last five years an average number of six new journals have been started in the United States every day; and yet the actual increase during that time has not been much over two thousand.

Messrs. George P. Rowell's establishment was largely patronized during the Exhibition, and very many visitors from a distance will hold in grateful remembrance the thoughtfulness which provided for them, constant news from home.

NORWAY EXHIBIT IN THE MAIN BUILDING.

Reference to our general article on the Norwegian exhibition will show the general character of the articles to be seen in this section. In our illustration there will be found sketches of several Norwegian drinking-cups, tankards and horns, a large silver drinking-vase, old silver cups of antique pattern, a drinking-horn on wheels, which is fully described in its proper place; a mammoth tankard of soft metal, three feet high, having a capacity of three gallons, etc.

THE DAIRY.

One of the most satisfying refreshment establishments on the Centennial Grounds is the Dairy, which is located on Landsdowne Ravine, between the Main Building and Horticultural Hall, one of the most picturesque spots in the entire area. The main building is about 360 feet in length, built of rough-hewn logs and grapevine branches in artistic style. It has two annexes, yet it is constantly crowded by its patrons. The special feature of the Dairy *menu* has been the richness and purity of its milk and cream, and the excellence of its butter. The bread dispensed is that of the Vienna Bakery; and other articles in the bill-of-fare are wheaten grits, pies, pastry, etc.

THE WITHERSPOON MONUMENT.

The engraving of the Monument of John Witherspoon will be found on page 49, and an account of the subject—one of the signers of the Declaration of Independence and President of Princeton College, 1768—on page 124. The monument stands outside the grounds, east of Memorial Hall, on Landsdowne Drive. It was unvailed with appropriate ceremonies on the appointed day. The statue was erected under a resolution of the General Assembly of the Presbyterian Church, at a meeting held at Cleveland, in 1875. On the present occasion a procession was formed and marched in the morning, from the Tabernacle Church, Princeton, where they were joined by the Synod of New Jersey to the Reading Railroad depot. There they embarked on the cars for the Centennial Grounds, and the site of the monument. The proceedings opened with prayer and read-

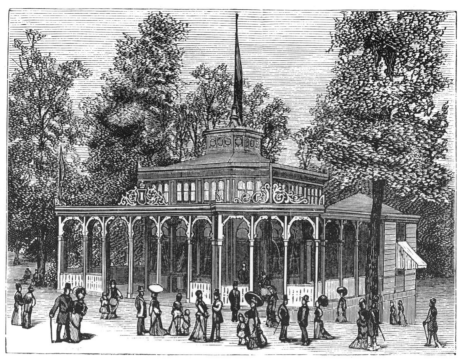

THE PORTUGUESE PAVILION.

ing of Scriptures, when the Rev. Henry C. McCook gave a history of the effort to erect the monument. This was followed by a hymn, the contents of the corner-stone and the inscriptions being then recited. The inscriptions are as follows: On the north side, "Of property I have some, of reputation more; that reputation is staked, that property is pledged on the issue of this contest; and although these gray hairs must soon descend into the sepulchre, I would infinitely rather that they should descend thither by the hand of an executioner than desert at this crisis the sacred cause of my country"; on the south side, "Proclaim liberty throughout all the land, unto all the inhabitants thereof.—Lev. 20 ch. 10 v."; on the east side, "John Witherspoon, D.D., LL.D., a lineal descendant of John Knox, born in Scotland, February 5th, 1722, ordained Minister in the Presbyterian Church, 1745; President of Princeton College, New Jersey, 1768 to 1794, the only clergyman in the Continental Congress a signer of the Declaration of Independence; died at Princeton, November 15th, 1794"; on the west side, "This statue is erected under the authority of a committee appointed by the General Assembly of the Presbyterian Church in the United States of America, July 4th, 1876." At the bottom is the following: "This

pedestal is the gift of the Presbyters of Philadelphia and vicinity." The statue was then unvailed by D. W. Woods, Esq., a grandson of Dr. Witherspoon, and after the singing of a hymn, his Excellency Joseph D. Bedle, Governor of the State of New Jersey, delivered the oration. The presentation of the statue to the Park Commission was made by the Hon. H. Ross Snowden, LL.D., and it was accepted by Mr. John Welsh. The thanks of the Park Commission were tendered by the Rev. Dr. George Hale. The doxology was announced, and the exercises were concluded with the benediction of Rev. James McCosh.

TROMMER'S EXTRACT OF MALT.

Among the numerous preparations of malt exhibited in the Brewers' Building is the one above named, a nutritive beverage said to combine sedative, tonic and alterative virtues. Malt extract is highly recommended by the medical faculty as a restorative of exhausted constitutions, it being exceedingly nutritious and most satisfactory in its digestion. A single dose of this extract is said to contain more of the important constituents of malt than is found in a pint of the best ale. In Germany the article is frequently employed in place of cod-liver oil in the treatment of pulmonary consumption. Our illustration displays the handsome exhibit herein described, the article being manufactured in Fremont, Ohio.

MINERAL ANNEX.

THIS is a long, low, narrow building, extending over about one-third the length of the Main Building, south of that structure, and near the eastern end. On entering this building at the western end, and after an exhibit of stone, we come upon a large collection of articles from China, which are apparently the overflow from the crowded Chinese department of the Main Building, since many of them are certainly not minerals or geological specimens.

First there are a number of articles in basket-work, some of them quite curious and pretty. Then there is a collection of specimens of native woods. After these, in a glass case, there is an exhibit of Indian ink in the small

THE FRENCH GOVERNMENT BUILDING.

cakes familiar to the frequenters of stationery stores, as well as in larger pieces. Then there are Chinese kites and balloons in different shapes of strange-looking insects and birds. Next come fabrics and some specimens of vegetable fibre, as well as some tobacco. There are quite a number of articles of straw, such as hats, matting, etc., with specimens of straw braid in different conditions of manufacture. Then come personal ornaments, combs and slippers, these being in cases. There are specimens of tea under glass, and next a long table covered with domestic tools, teapots, etc.

Perhaps one of the most pleasing and attractive exhibits in this collection is composed of images about a foot in height, made of papier-mache or some other similar material, and formed to represent different classes of society in China, the figures being in different attitudes and costumes. These little objects are very cleverly constructed, and admirably illustrate the peculiar dress of the country.

There are a few musical instruments, rather difficult to describe, some being like a combination of the guitar and banjo, others like tambourines. There are heavy Chinese shoes, and then more of the small figures already mentioned, including among them a number of birds, and groups of two or three figures together. Next, ranged against the walls, are seven or eight life-size representations of Chinese men and women in actual costumes. A very large collection of vegetable medicines is shown, obtained from different ports and provinces, such as Ningpo, Amoi, Newchang, and Chinkiang. Still more little figures, some of these peculiar by reason of having hideous masks, yet none of them more than a few inches in height. Then a few Chinese bamboo chairs, a number of models of Chinese junks and other native boats, some fur skins of native animals hung over a partition above, cases containing nuts and other vegetable products, grains, etc.; and a collection of the inevitable painted screens closes the Chinese exhibition in this building.

Now opens the mineral exhibit proper, arranged according to States. The exhibition of minerals of the State of

GILLENDER & SON'S GLASS-WORKS — EXTERIOR.

PENNSYLVANIA at this point includes only specimens of marble and coal, after which comes

DELAWARE.   Here is a large case of minerals, and there are also some exhibits of marble ores and granite

OHIO begins her exhibition with several fine specimens of coal, one of these being about fifteen feet high and four feet square. There are also large specimens of ores and minerals arranged on shelving, and some samples of manufactured bars and wrought iron. Next, a considerable show of pottery and fire-brick, limestone, salt, and a glass containing bromine. Then there is freestone, specimens of grain, etc., and a positively splendid collection, illustrating the Stone Age as elucidated through its relics in Ohio. This includes ax and arrow-heads, and a very fine collection of Indian pipes, beads, wampum, cork, shells and awls or punches. Some of the pipes are beautifully carved and polished. There are also a large number of discoidal and other stones from the mounds. One specimen exhibited here is a pipe presented to Captain Lewis, by a Mandan

chief. The bowl is of carved redstone, and the stem is of wood about three feet long, and an inch and a half broad, ornamented near the mouth-piece with what appeared to be horse-hair and wampum. This collection of Indian and other relics is very large and most interesting. It is exhibited by the State Archæological Association of Ohio.

INDIANA presents a very fine exhibit, including iron and other ores, specimens of pottery, fire-brick, oil-stone, hydraulic cement, kaolin or porcelain clay, rubber, sandstone, cannel coal, bluestone, limestone, etc.

MICHIGAN. Here we have a very handsome show of minerals, and native copper and silver. One peculiar and characteristic exhibit is an Indian birch-bark canoe from Lake Superior. There are also some Indian curiosities, and a very fine display of Lake Superior copper ore, bar and ingot copper, some of the specimens of copper ore and conglomerate being of enormous size. Then there is native metallic copper, stamped work, etc. Finally, we have a case containing a good show of specimens of Michigan gypsum; and another, of articles illustrating the Stone Age, as represented in this State.

WISCONSIN. In this State we have first a fine collection of pre-historic stone tools in upright cases, including ax and arrow-heads, pestles, cutting utensils, etc. Here are specimens of a number of different kinds of native stone, polished and plain; also brick, clay, and fire-brick. A very curious exhibit is a case of pre-historic copper tools and flints, arrow-heads, etc. The copper articles include knives, chisels and pointed tools, and are most interesting. There are also four large cases containing a general mineral display. Vegetable products, corn in the ear, grains, etc.— these latter being in a glass case—together with samples of manufactured iron and steel, complete the exhibit.

IOWA exhibits kaolin. There are here also several upright cases containing specimens of the geological strata of the State, from the Saint Peter's sandstone to the post-tertiary, lacustrine and drift strata. Among these are numbered the Potsdam sandstone, Trenton limestone.

MELTING-FURNACE.

THE GLASS-WORKS EXHIBIT OF GILLENDER & SON, PHILADELPHIA.

ENGRAVING GLASS.

Niagara limestone, etc. It is in the exhibition made by this State that we first meet a collection of the relics of the Stone Age and of the pre-historic inhabitants of that section of the country. This collection comprises ax-heads, arrow-heads, fragments of pottery, and even skulls, although these latter are of course, of a later period. Here is lead ore from Dubuque, a number of glass cylinders containing red and yellow ochre, sand and gravel, and a formidable column of coal, taken from the mines of an Iowa Coal Mining Company. The exhibition of the State of Iowa closes with two miniature freight-cars, in which is displayed a new patent coupling of considerable utility.

The exhibits in the Mineral Annex conclude with a display obtained from the second geological survey of Pennsylvania, including a large number of fine specimens. There are also some minerals from Illinois, grains, shells, etc., and a large mass of native sulphate of soda from the Laramie Plains, Wyoming Territory.

THE STATE DAYS.

New Jersey.

The system of State reunions at the various State Buildings on the Centennial Grounds commenced with that of New Jersey, on August 24th, 1876, when it is estimated about 50,000 persons went from New Jersey to the gathering at Philadelphia. Shortly after 11 o'clock, a committee of citizens of New Jersey met the Governor of the State at the Centennial Depot, and escorted him and his party to the Judges' Hall, where Hon. Abram Browning, the orator for the State, delivered an address upon the history and growth of his State. This was followed by a reunion at the New Jersey Building, on Belmont Avenue, where the immense audience were addressed by Gov. Bedle, Gen. Hawley and Mr. John Welsh. A formal reception was then held by Gov. Bedle, which continued until three o'clock, citizens of the State being presented to his Excellency.

Massachusetts.

Thursday, September 14th, was "Massachusetts Day." Gov. Rice, surrounded by his full staff, held a reception in the Massachusetts State Building, and a very large crowd, including about 50,000 from the "Bay State," col-

lected in that locality. During the reception the "Sons of Massachusetts," an organization of Massachusetts men resident in New York City, under the lead of Col. Frank E. Howe, presented to the State a handsome flag, which was received by the Governor, Mr. Nathan Appleton being the spokesman of the donors.

New York.

On Thursday, September 21st, "New York State Day" occurred, and attracted nearly 125,000 visitors. The rush from New York City was quite tremendous, and included a detachment of 650 police officers, headed by their superintendent, inspectors, captains, etc. At one o'clock Gov. Tilden arrived at the State Building, but long before that hour the crush in front of the house was so great that it was difficult to force a way through it. The Governor was enthusiastically received, and in return devoted an hour to promiscuous hand-shaking, after which he was introduced to the crowd outside by Gen. Hawley, and made a short speech. Gov. Tilden was supported during his reception by Col. Frederick A. Conkling, Frank Leslie, Jackson S. Schultz, A. B. Cornell, and Col. Pelton, a nephew of the Governor. After the reception, he made a short tour through the Grounds and principal buildings, and on returning to the State Building reviewed the New York City Police.

Pennsylvania.

But all the State days and all exhibition days whatsoever were eclipsed on Thursday, September 28th, when the "Pennsylvania State Day" occurred, and when the Centennial Grounds presented the wonderful and unheard-of spectacle of 250,000 people honoring at once the Industrial Exhibition, the State to which it was chiefly owing, and the United States, whose history and achievements it commem-

ANNEALING GLASS.

orates. The ceremonies of the day were divided between the Pennsylvannia State Building and the Judges' Hall, in which latter building Gov. Hartranft held a reception, when, after the singing of a Centennial Hymn, the audience was addressed by the Governor of the State; by Gen. Hawley, President of the Centennial Commission; Mr. John Welsh, President of the Board of Finance; and by Ex-Gov. Pollock and Ex-Senator Scott. Gov. Hartranft's personal reception occurred at the "Pennsylvania State Building," and was extremely flattering and gratifying. The Governor was accompanied from his hotel to the State Building by the Mayor of Philadelphia, the State Treasurer, and other important personages. In the afternoon a reception was held at the Judges' Hall, by the Woman's Centennial Executive Committee, when Mrs. Gillespie, the President, Mrs. Forney, Mrs. Wright, and other ladies of the Committee, were present, and Gen. Hawley, Col. Forney, Dr. Stebbins and other prominent citizens of Philadelphia were introduced. The occasion was enlivened by music from Theodore Thomas's unrivaled band. Still another reception took place at the Municipal Building, Mayor Stokley receiving. A peculiarity observable on this occasion was the arrival, in procession, of numerous employés of various manufacturing firms. The ceremonies concluded with a magnificent display of fireworks, when it is supposed as many people were assembled as during the day.

Rhode Island.

October 5th being selected as "Rhode Island Day" at the Centennial, there was present at the grounds a very fair show of wealth and beauty from "Little Rhody." The State Building on George's Hill was thronged by visitors; and at noon Governor Lippitt, preceded by his staff, entered the grounds and was escorted to the Rhode Island

HORIZONTAL BUFFING-MILL.

Building by Gen. Hawley, President of the Centennial Commission, and other prominent officials. To the assembled citizens President Hawley introduced the Governor of the State, who tendered the thanks of his State to the Centennial authorities and to the people of Philadelphia. Many thousands of people were afterwards welcomed by the Governor; and after this interchange of pleasantries and courtesies, the gubernatorial party visited the most prominent features of the Exhibition, and while examining the Corliss Engine, Mr. Commissioner Corliss was introduced to the distinguished visitors. "Rhode Island Day" will long be held in remembrance by the participators in the pleasures of the occasion.

New Hampshire.

Thursday, October 12th, was the day selected by the "Granite State" for the union of her sons at the Centennial. The State Building was gayly decorated with national and foreign colors, and thither Gov. Cheney and staff were escorted by the Centennial Commission, the Board of Finance, the Lexington Cadets, and Amoskeag Veterans, with the usual ceremonies. Several thousand persons assembled in front of the structure; the Amoskeag Veterans, in their picturesque Continental uniforms, being drawn up in a line before the Governor and staff; and then Gen. Hawley welcomed the Governor, who, in a few words, acknowledged his reception. Later in the day the Governor delivered an address, in which he reviewed the early history of New Hampshire, and the prominent part which she took in the Revolutionary War. He was followed by Prof. E. D. Sanborn, appointed orator for the day, who delivered a eulogy on those sons of New Hampshire who are remembered as heroes in the struggle for independence. Short addresses were made by prominent New Hampshire gentlemen, and the ceremonies concluded with the usual courtesies and an examination of the buildings and the grounds.

Southern Day.

On Thursday, the 19th of October, the States of Virginia, Delaware and Maryland, and the District of Columbia, united in a reception on the Centennial Grounds. The day selected was memorably important for two reasons.

GLASS-CUTTING FRAME.

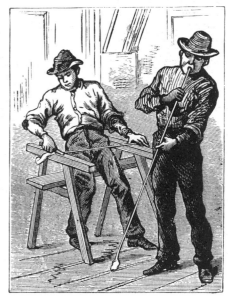

GLASS-BLOWING.

On that day, in 1774, the *Peggy Stewart*, freighted with tea, was burned in Annapolis harbor, Maryland, and on the same day, 1781, the surrender of Cornwallis at Yorktown occurred. the allied armies of the French and Americans being drawn up in two columns outside of Yorktown, with Washington and Rochambeau on horseback at their head, and between them, the conquered troops marched out, laying down their arms as they passed. The number of British was about 7,000, that of the French and Americans about 16,000.

On hearing the news Congress recommended a day of thanksgiving to be observed throughout the States, and Washington, the commander of the American forces, ordered the liberation of persons under arrest for any offense, that all might share in the general joy. Even to the present day it is customary in country militia musters for the soldiers to go through the form of the surrender, the occasion being called "A Cornwallis." Under the circumstances of these historical associations, and of the union of the Southern States named, the occasion at the Centennial was one of peculiar interest. The attendance on that day was the largest in point of numbers, excepting Pennsylvania Day, which has occurred during the Exhibition the total number of paying admissions being nearly 170,000. The official statement comprises 160,124, besides 1,240 cash admissions to the Live Stock Exhibition. It is estimated that at least 90,000 visitors were from the three States and the District of Columbia. At about 11 o'clock the State authorities of Delaware, and the city officials of Wilmington, reached the Exhibition Grounds, when they were received by the Centennial officials and escorted to the Delaware State Building. Here Gov. Cochran acknowledged the complimentary reception of Gen. Hawley, and addressed those present. He was followed by Hon. Wm. G. Whiteley, who gave a concise history of Delaware to the present day, stating, among other things, that the first iron steamship built in this country — the *Bangor* — was built at Wilmington, in 1844, since which time 442 iron vessels have been constructed there. At about noon the Maryland visitors were received at the gates in the usual manner, and escorted to the Maryland State Building. Here Gov. Carroll reviewed the Second Brigade of the Maryland National Guard, and addressed the people. He was followed by Gov. Denison, and Gov. Thomas Wilson, who were introduced as representatives of the District of Columbia, and who severally delivered eloquent addresses. Mr. J. G. Findlay, the orator for Maryland, spoke at considerable length on the history and resources of his State. At the Virginia State Building only informal gatherings took place. The number of Virginians present was estimated to be about 5,000. Those from West Virginia numbered about a thousand, who were to be found chiefly at the State Building near George's Hill. An interesting incident of the day's ceremonies was the arrival of members of the Society of Cincinnati, who paid their respects to the Centennial Commission, and were received by General Hawley in the Judges' Hall. But decidedly the great feature of the day's entertainment was the tournament which took place on George's Hill in the afternoon, and which was witnessed by about 75,000 people, fully half of whom were ladies. This class of festival is almost peculiar to Maryland and Virginia, although tournaments are occasionally given in other of the Southern States. Nothing of the kind had ever previously been seen so far North. There were fifteen knights, who represented the thirteen original States, the Union and the Centennial, and the objects for which they were gathered together was to ride over a course suitably laid out, and to compete for the prizes offered by thrusting spears through small rings hung at intervals of about fifty yards, the course being about 300 yards in length. At these intervals were arches 15 feet high by 10 or 12 wide, from the top hanging wooden rods ending in a piece of iron a foot or more in length, from each of which was suspended a small red ring about an inch and a half in diameter. The rules of the tournament demanded that each knight should ride at a full run, and that each knight's spear should be at least six feet long. As the rider must thrust his spear through the ring and carry it with him, the task was not so easy as it might appear, particularly as the rings chosen for this occasion were much smaller than is customary. The knights were H. Crozier, representing New Hampshire; E. H. McFarland, Jr., Massachusetts; ———, Rhode Island;

William P. Bryan, Connecticut; George V. Bacon, New York; C. D. Chapman, New Jersey; H. M. Perry, Pennsylvannia; R. L. Kane, Delaware; R. W. Hereford, Maryland; P. A. Scaggs, Virginia; J. M. Howard, North Carolina; F. Nelson Jarboe, South Carolina; C. A. Fox, Georgia; Charles White, Jr., representing the Centennial, and A. B. Suit, representing the Union. These gentlemen, however, were not citizens of the States they represented, except in the cases of North Carolina and New Jersey, the others being from Maryland and Virginia. The Judges appointed for the occasion were Col. Skinner, Dr. Morgan, C. S. Barton, Gen. Torbert and H. J. Smith. The result of the tournament was as follows: New Hampshire, 5 rings; Massachusetts, 1; Rhode Island, 4; Connecticut, 6; New York, 2; Pennsylvania, 3; New Jersey, 5; Delaware, 8; Maryland, 5; Virginia, 3; North Carolina, 3; South Carolina, 6; Georgia, 2; the Union, 2; Centennial, 6. Five prizes were contended for, and were won in the following order: First prize, Delaware; second prize, Centennial; third prize, Connecticut; fourth prize, South Carolina; fifth prize, Maryland. The ceremony of the day concluded in the evening at Judges' Hall,

GENERAL JOSEPH R. HAWLEY, PRESIDENT OF THE CENTENNIAL EXPOSITION.

which was gorgeously decked and brilliantly lighted for the occasion, the immediate attraction being the crowning of the Queen of Love and Beauty. Miss Parke P. Perkins, a beautiful brunette from Buckingham County, Virginia, was the Queen, and about her throne were grouped her maids-of-honor, Mrs. Ida Taylor, of Washington, and Ida Griffin, of Maryland. An address was delivered by Col. Stewart, when the knight of Delaware placed upon the Queen's head a handsome crown. A glee was sung by the Virginia Jubilee Singers, and the maids-of-honor were crowned by the other victorious knights, another glee followed, and the festivities closed with dancing.

UNVAILING OF THE COLUMBUS MONUMENT.

On "New Hampshire Day," October 12th, the Columbus Monument, on the Centennial Grounds, was unvailed by Governor Hartranft and Baron Blanc, Minister from Italy to the United States. This monument is one of the finest in Philadelphia. It is made of pure Italian marble, and is a notable specimen of modern sculpture. The entire work cost $18,000. It stands 22 feet high from the ground, the statue of Columbus being 10 feet high and the pedestal 12. The sculptor has represented Columbus as having arrived at middle age, costumed in the dress of his period, a tunic

and short cloak, trunk hose, a sword by his side, and on his breast a medal representing one presented to him by Queen Isabella. In his left hand he holds a chart, while his right rests upon a globe, upon which his attention is fixed. The figure is a little larger than life-size. Upon the four sides of the pedestal, which is also made of Italian marble, are sculptured scenes selected from the life and voyages of the great navigator, and an inscription announcing that the monument is presented by Italian citizens to the City of Philadelphia.

The ceremony of unvailing was impressive and pleasing. At about 3 o'clock P. M. Governor Hartranft arrived on the grounds, being escorted by the First and Second Regiments, Washington Grays, and other soldiery. Alonzo M. Viti, Honorary Consul of Italy, and a member of the Centennial Committee, made a few remarks; after which the monument was formally unvailed. Addresses were then made by Governor Hartranft, Baron Blanc, Mr. Finelli, of the Monument Association, and Hon. Morton McMichael. The orator of the day, however, was Chief-Justice Daly, of New York, who made a lengthy and most interesting address proper to the occasion. Commenting on the important connection of Italy with the discovery of America through the navigators John and Sebastian Cabot, Verrazano, and Vespuccius, he proceeded to consider the condition of commerce at the time of the discovery, in the later part of the fifteenth century. Next he referred at length to the geographical theories of Columbus, and the idea which he held to the day of his death, that the land which he had discovered was a part of the eastern shores of Asia. A concise description of the voyage followed, and the address concluded with a just and discriminating examination of the character of Columbus. In closing, Judge Daly alluded to a remarkable account of a dream of Columbus, and related a conversation held between the orator and Humboldt, in 1851, concerning it. In this dream Columbus hears a voice cry out: "Oh! fool, and slow to believe! Did God do more for Moses or David, than He has done for thee? He has made thy name resound throughout the earth. He has delivered into thy hands the keys of the gate of the ocean. He has given thee the Indies, the richest of the earth, to dispose of unto others. What did He more for the people of Israel? Turn to Him and acknowledge thine error! He has many a vast inheritance yet in reserve. Fear not to seek them, for the promises God has made to thee He has never broken!" Finally, Judge Daly made a pathetic allusion to the last scenes in the life of Columbus; his long and lonely journey upon a mule, when he was enfeebled by age and disease, across the rocky soil of the eastern Maduro, and the rude sierras of Toledo and Guadalajara, to Segovia, to make a last appeal, which was unsuccessful, and speedily followed by his death. He gave to Spain an empire, and she gave him, in return, simply a grave.

The statue of Columbus stands in the Centennial Grounds opposite the Sons of Temperance Ice-water Fountain, and near the United States Building. The ceremonies of unvailing were concluded by addresses on the part of distinguished Italians.

HORTICULTURAL HALL.

A VIEW of Horticultural Hall will be found on page 27 of this work, and one of the interior on page 82, and the description of the building may be read on page 22. The building extends east and west on Landsowne Terrace, the design being in the Moorish style of architecture in the twelfth century. The central conservatory is 22 feet by 80, 55 feet high, and has a garden-plot running the entire length, excepting promenades. Immediately in the centre is a handsome fountain, ornamented with small figures, tritons blowing horns; at the four corners immediately next to the central basin, are marble statues. This garden is planted with exotics, and particularly numerous tropical plants, including varieties of the palm, the flower-banana, and other horticultural rarities. All about the central conservatory is a gallery, in the northeastern end of which is an orchestron. At the western end, on the north side, a large room contains a number of very interesting articles, some of which are not, however, strictly horticultural. Among other exhibits, there is a fine display of wax fruit and flowers, in several cases. There are also exhibits of colored feather-work and artificial flowers in bouquets and baskets. Quite a pretty show is made in tasteful flower-baskets worked in straw, as also in hair-work, made into wreaths of flowers, etc., and framed. A large steamboat model, made of wire, for the reception of natural flowers, is a prominent object. One case contains bulbs; and another, preserves of natural flowers. There is also considerable rustic-work to be seen about this room. On the south side of the western end an exhibition-room displays all kinds of Warden-cases, small flower-pots, hanging-baskets in ornamented and painted tin and other materials. Some choice wreaths grace the exhibit, and on a table is a beautiful display of skeleton leaves, formed into bouquets, and shown under glass. Also, various ornamental straw baskets and other receptacles for flowers, and a goodly show of ornamental earthenware and terra-cotta flower-pots. Here, too, are some garden vases, terra-cotta and rustic-ware, and a large number of horticultural tools and implements. Finally, there are specimens of beans and seeds shown in glass jars, a case of bulbs, and a large case of colored grasses, and featherwork formed into bouquets, at the eastern end of the building. On the south side there is a room containing large garden stands for pots, and a great variety of styles of garden-vases in terra cotta. There are also some very handsome bouquetholders, made of ornamental paper and other materials. The room on the north side at this end is devoted to horticultural implements, flower-pots of all sizes and styles, some greenhouse boilers, and garden chairs and settees in iron. On either side of Horticultural Hall there are forcing-houses —each of them 100 by 30 feet in dimensions, and covered with curved roofs of iron and glass—for the propagation of young plants. In these houses have been displayed large numbers of plants, very few of which, however, in flower. Among the plants exhibited may be mentioned the eucalyptus, gladiolus, brencheyeasis, ferns, decorative and ornamental foliage plants, a very fine show of cacti, including the cactus of the Pacific Coast in large variety, and a large number of hot-house and conservatory plants. The Committee of the Congressional Library of the United States (Botanic Garden) exhibit a number of medicinal, tropical and semi-tropical plants, and the Agricultural Department of the United States, mahogany, cocoa, chocolate, guava, papaw, rose-apple, etc. From the Zoological Society of Philadelphia there is a specimen of the Australian fern-tree, and from Samuel M. Bines, one india-rubber tree. Miss Ann E. Merryweather, of Camden, New Jersey, sends an aloe. There are also orange-trees, bananas, datepalm, the wax-plant, century-plants, the sago-palm, etc. Then there is a fig-tree, numerous orchids, with variegated pine-apples, etc. The out-door exhibits in the Horticultural Department are numerous, and cover a considerable area of ground, extending westward from the building

nearly to the uncompleted Catholic Fountain. Over this extent of space, garden plots have been laid out and planted with every variety imaginable of flowering and brilliantly colored leaf plants, producing during the Summer months a variegated and most beautiful horticultural presentment. Numerous varieties of geraniums, verbenas, roses, dahlias, rhododendrons, kalmias, magnolias, azaleas, and others less known, are also exhibited. Rustic summer-houses, hanging-baskets, settees, chairs, rustic gates, stands, vases, wrought-iron railing, artificial stone-work in fountain-basins, vases, tiles, etc., terra-cotta vases, trellises, and, in fact, every conceivable species of ornament for gardens and summer-houses, are to be seen. The garden-tools exhibited include the Comstock sower, hand seed-

PROFESSOR WIDDOWS RINGING THE CHIMES IN THE TOWER OF MACHINERY HALL.

sower, portable sprinkler and fountain lawn-sprinkler, wheel-hoe, self-acting water-fountain, portable boilers, heating apparatus for green-houses, etc. For portable plants there are plant-stands, ferneries, window-boxes, revolving flower-stand with fountain attachment, drainer and evaporator with globe attachments, for pots, vases and hanging-baskets, combined aquarium, plant-stand, birdcage and fernery, and other conveniences.

THE ALLSOPP BREWERY EXHIBIT.

ALLSOPP'S ale is as well known throughout America as in England, and the display of specimens of this beverage in Agricultural Hall attracts considerable attention from the reputation of this great brewing establishment.

The ale breweries of the Allsopps are located at Burton-on Trent, and have long been recognized as among the most interesting and extensive industrial establishments in Central England. From time immemorial the town of Burton has been the famous brewing centre. Its pale ales are known throughout the world; and it is alleged that the excellence of it is due to the adaptation of the Burton waters for brewing purposes—a discovery said to have been made by the monks in the thirteenth century, at which early period the trade of malting was already carried on upon an extensive scale. As early as 1748 the Burton ales had a large sale in St. Petersburg.

The Allsopps date back to nearly half a century ago, and have been manufacturing ale ever since. The waters used by them in their manufacture are obtained from wells, some of the borings being more than 100 feet deep, and one of them 46 feet in diameter. They number eleven in all, their total supply of water being estimated at over 100,000 gallons per hour; and this tremendous production in the height of the brewing season is severely taxed.

The new brewery, maltings and cooperage buildings of the Allsopps cover an area of fifty acres, and the general offices alone of the establishment occupy the ground-floor of an entire block of buildings. The material of their buildings is chiefly brick and iron, on foundations of concrete. They have three great malting establishments: one at Burton, one at Beccles, and another at Grantham. They have, besides, ten smaller maltinghouses at Burton, and are further supplied by private firms.

Some idea may be formed of the magnitude of these works from the fact that the water is boiled in four enormous vessels, each holding 280 barrels, or 10,000 gallons, and capable of supplying together a constant supply of boiling water of one million gallons per week. Their fermentation facilities are close upon 9,000 barrels at one time. They employ a grand total of 4,294 union casks, holding four and a half barrels each, for the purpose of cleansing their ales. These casks hold an aggregate of nearly 700,000 gallons, and during the brewing season every one is fully employed.

The stores of the establishment cover an enormous area, and are capable of receiving about 10,000 barrels of ale. The firm have private railroad conveniencies, their lines extending from one end of Burton to the other, the road being over ten miles in extent, in which the firm employs three locomotives, while during each week as many as 5,000 railway-trucks pass in and out of their premises. The quantity of malt consumed amounts to thousands of tons, and the average number of employés, including those at the London and country agencies, is about 1,500.

This description of the business of a malt brewery on a large scale will be interesting to those readers concerned in the manufacture of ale.

REPUBLIC OF CHILI BUILDING.

MAIN EXHIBITION BUILDING.

Great Britain.

The space allotted to the United Kingdom of Great Britain and Ireland comprises about one-half of the entire Main Building lying on the north side of the nave and extending from the Canadian section east to the transept, or for about half of the space north of the nave and west of the transept.

It is almost impossible to give the slightest conception either of the magnitude, the comprehensive character, or the educational value, of the vast number of exhibits made by Great Britain. When taken in connection with her colonies and with the Dominion of Canada, which may fairly be considered in the same category in this instance, her display is colossal. Whether we consider this as representative of her industrial ingenuity or her magnificent and wide-spreading power, whatever view we may take of her exhibition, we cannot fail to admire and respect. Here we may not improperly quote a fluent writer on the subject, who says, in reference to the exhibits of Great Britain:

"She meets you everywhere. Go into the machinery department, and her engines are among the finest and most substantial ever made by human hands. In cotton goods she has no superior in the world; and it is esteemed no small compliment to stand with her in any of the marts of commerce. In silks she rivals the looms of Lyons, in carpets she is almost without a peer, in cutlery she is master of the situation, in silverware she need not fear to enter into competition with the artisans of any land, and in the million and one of smaller items that go to make up the business of the world, she displays an activity and grasp marvelous to behold. Go where you will, you see on great flags, 'Great Britain and Ireland,' 'Colonies' and 'Colonial Dependencies,' and when taken altogether, there is nothing that man produces or secures by his labor or his genius, his courage or his perseverance, but that she seems to have a part in it. The contributions of a single colony are superior to those of many nations. Every product from the equator to the pole is exhibited in some of her departments. No matter what any other nation puts on exhibition, she is there to rival them. Roam among the halls of the Art Gallery, and amid the aggregate gems of genius of the world, there are the paintings of Sir Joshua Reynolds, Turner, Landseer and the works of the multitude of the apostles of art which have made her name immortal."

Separating from this its hyperbole, and we have after all only a fair intimation of the breadth and importance of Great Britain's exhibits. Moreover, in those sent to our Exposition, there has been displayed a judgment and appreciation of the objects to be gained, which, besides being business-like, are in the highest degree wise and intelligent. For instance, at Paris and Vienna the English had an immense display of machinery; but in Philadelphia there are very few specimens of English mechanism. British inventors and manufacturers in this direction have been made aware that American machinery is more ingenious and more original than others, and that it defies competition. It is the same with jewelry. In Paris and Vienna, the British had a gorgeous display in this direction, while in Philadelphia there is little or none. This is doubtless for the reason that the American and English tastes in jewelry are quite diverse and opposite. England, therefore, while withholding many articles for the production of which she is justly celebrated, but in which America begins fairly to compete with her, makes, on the other hand, an unusually strong display in those branches in which she knows she cannot be beaten. Prominent among these are ceramics of all kinds, artistic furniture, crystal ware, some branches of cutlery and oil-cloths. Of the magnitude and variety of her exhibits of ceramics, it is quite impossible to give any fair idea. They comprise every imaginable kind of earthenware, from the most unpretentious pottery to the finest specimens of porcelain and majolica. Doulton's terra-cotta, or Lambeth faience, as it is commonly called, is represented as never anywhere before. By the side of immense utensils for manufacturing purposes are to be seen elegant dinner sets of the most ornate character, while the same faience is displayed as used with admirable effect in the decoration of furniture, walls and fire-places. The finer kinds of porcelain are represented in several very precious collections. There is a set of finely decorated Greek vases, modeled from specimens in the British Museum, certainly superior to anything of the same kind that was ever seen on this side of the water.

In the furniture line, certain London firms have sent out superb specimens of every style, whole rooms being fitted out with admirable effect; and the richness, solidity and exquisite taste of every one of the pieces of artistic furniture exhibited are unparalleled. It is the same with crystal ware and articles of cut glass; but if we except these branches of industry, and perhaps a few special classes of cutlery and certain varieties of textile fabrics, we may see for our satisfaction that there is scarcely any other manufactures in which we cannot fairly compete with Great Britain.

The exhibit of the British section begins with the famous Sheffield cutlery, of which the display is very large and very interesting. This includes razors, knives, daggers, scissors, dressing-case instruments, tools for mechanics, and among the more curious articles a newly invented set of tools for the economy of labor in carving stone and wood, so highly tempered as to cut the hardest stone, and a case of tools for iron, brass, hard woods, etc. There are also displayed among articles of hardware, handles, bolts, nails and castings from Birmingham, steel safe and locking apparatus, pneumatic signals, etc.

Next to the hardware and cutlery, come the scarcely less celebrated Nottingham laces, Irish poplins, Manchester towelings and prints, and Belfast linens. Lancashire and Yorkshire, Paisley, Glasgow and Belfast sent yarns, cotton in various stages, cotton fabrics, quilts and other bed-covers, brocades, cotton and linen damasks, dimities, muslins, dress fabrics, linen goods, consisting of shirtings, pillow-linens, sheetings, napkins, table-damasks, pocket-handkerchiefs, ladies' dress lawns, and a variety of other fabrics too numerous to mention—including, however, hand-painted cloths in imitation of tapestry, for wall decoration, from Edinburgh; patented floor-cloths and floor-coverings of various materials, with the highly esteemed Scotch floor oil-cloths.

The woven and felted goods of wool and mixture of wool come from Gloucestershire, Yorkshire, Leeds, London, Belfast, Dublin, etc. Among the exhibits are woolen cloths, meltons, beavers, twills, tweeds and woolen serges; woolen shawls in great variety, mauds and rugs for railway traveling, all-wool tweeds, made of Australian wool. There are also Irish poplins, Yorkshire alpacas, bombazines, crapes, etc., and finally a handsome display of carpets, including Brussels and Wilton, and rugs woven of wool, silk or cotton from India, Persia, Cashmere and Western Asia; Axminster carpets, woven in one piece; Durham Axminster, woven by hand power, tapestry for wall decoration, domestic hair-cloth for furniture covering, and other similar articles.

Next to these come the Doulton and Watts pottery from Lambeth. It is in the art classes of goods, ceramics and furniture, that the British section presents possibly the most striking collections among the European exhibits at Philadelphia. The principal display of pottery, porcelain, etc., occupies an enormous space in the main transept, besides having specimens in conspicuous places in the section elsewhere. That portion of the ceramic exhibition which represents Mr. Doulton, of Lambeth, comprises an immense display of the peculiar stone-ware to which he has given his name, and the terra-cotta, for which he has made the world-wide reputation. Here are heavy stone-ware articles, jugs, crucibles, stills, smelting-pots, terra-cotta ornaments, and particularly the ornamental pieces already referred to as Lambeth faience, including vases of graceful shape, tankards, drinking-cups, placques, etc. Here is a sort of temple built up with dark-blue stone-ware or ornaments, devoted to the exhibition of Doulton ware and the Lambeth faience. Conspicuous articles are a terra-cotta pulpit, showing the two characteristic colors of this ware—red and buff—with indigo ornaments. There are also small panels about four inches wide and twelve inches long, on which are exhibited in high relief scriptural groups and pulpit legends. The combination of useful and decorative pottery is peculiarly exhibited in the British section by several constructions representing the whole side of a room—one of the most conspicuous of these representing the application of the Doulton ware to fireplaces. There is a mantel-piece and mirror frame of terra-cotta, decorated, reaching to the ceiling. The hearth is tiled, and a parapet of terra-cotta around it serves as a fender. A beautiful little clock in brown and indigo stone-ware, and a few placques, vases, etc., on the mantel, complete the pleasing effect.

Mr. Doulton shows painted tiles inserted in the backs of chairs; and of the display of tiles of all sorts by different makers, the most beautiful and interesting are those of Minton & Co., of Stoke-upon-Trent, which perhaps is the largest and most varied collection. Here are chimney-pieces as large as the side of a small room, constructed entirely of tiles having figures of birds and flowers around the fireplace, and a large domestic scene over the mantel. A brilliant picture, four feet square, presents a water view. Others are single tiles, with allegorical figures of the seasons in black, outlined on a gold or silver ground.

Of other kind of porcelain, a rare collection is that of A. B. Daniell & Son. In the centre of their principal show-case stands the Prometheus vase, a superb piece of work about four feet high, having a bed of rich turquoise-blue. The figures of Prometheus and the vulture are on the cover, and the handles comprise chained figures in scale armor, the armor imitating the appearance of metal so exactly that one can scarcely believe it to be of china. The Greek vases, of which there are two pairs, are of a dark-bronze color, the chief decoration being a series of exquisite figures, representing on one pair the elements fire and water, and on the other a race between the Three Graces. One of these pairs of vases is priced at 380 guineas. Other remarkable articles in this collection are a set of Henry II. faience, a copy of some gems of the sixteenth century, a teapot of quaint design, imitations of old Limoges enamel, cups of Grecian antiques, pilgrim bottles, etc. The Staffordshire potteries, which are exhibited near these, embrace almost everything imaginable in China, including tile paintings and encaustic tiles for mural decoration. A specialty here is a very beautiful white ware, ornamented with large birds and leaves and ultramarine. A dinner set of this ware, comprising about one hundred pieces, cost $85 in currency. Among the majolica-ware are some pretty little strawberry-baskets, and among the bedroom china is a white-and-gold washstand with sunk basin, copied after one recently made for the Queen.

The display of furniture is arranged in such a way as to give a representation of a suite of rooms furnished and decorated in different styles and by different manufacturers. One firm furnishes five or six complete little rooms, with carpets and wall-hangings included. There is a dining-room set of carved oak, with sideboard; another of carved mahogany, several rooms with cabinet furniture in the English style of the eighteenth century, including an inlaid

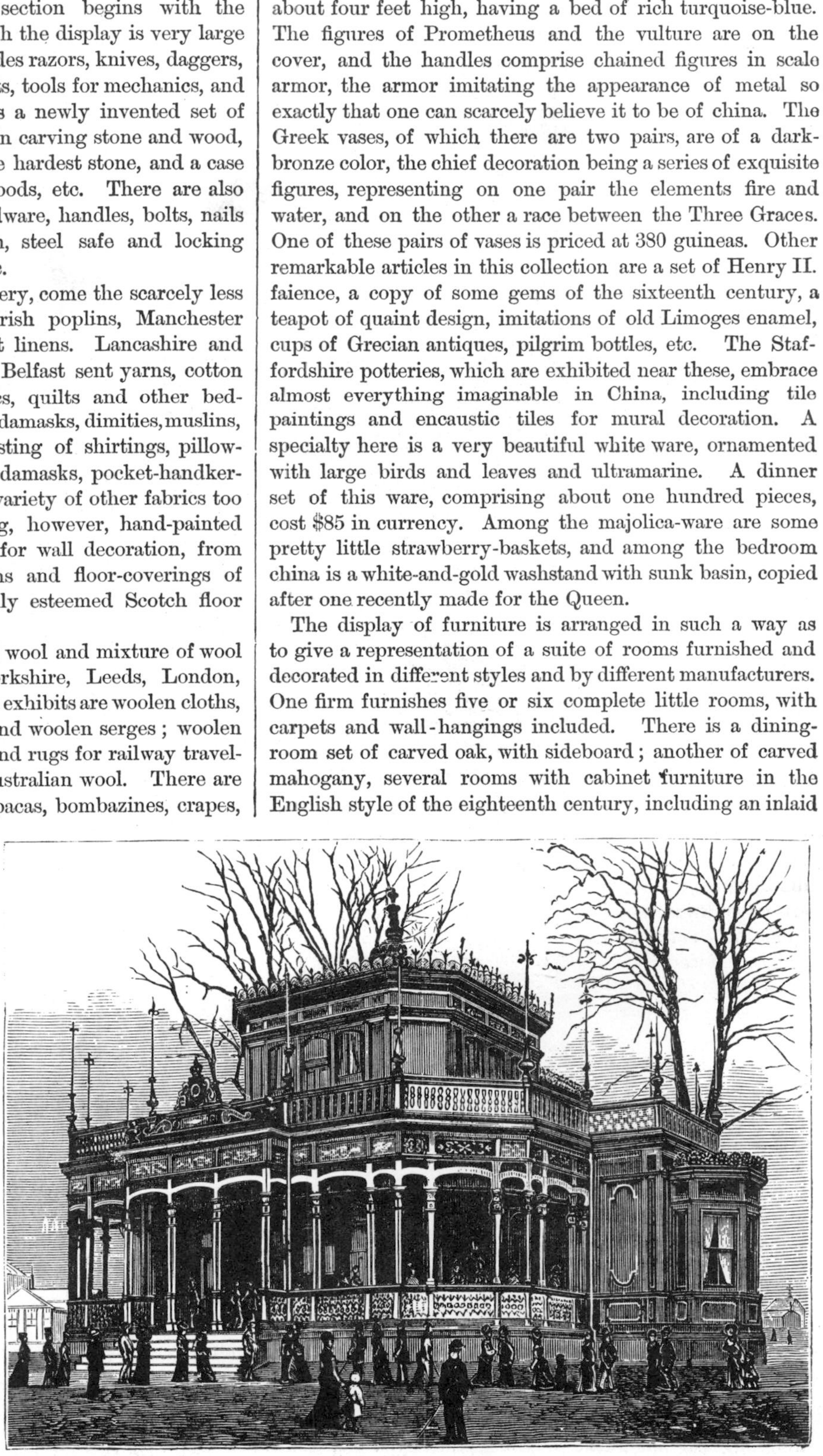
THE BRAZILIAN PAVILION.

mahogany sideboard, and secretary and writing-desk of the same material, side-tables of satin-wood, etc. A grand sideboard of dark oak, elaborately carved, exhibited by Cooper & Holt, of London, is an attractive exhibit. Another from Edinburgh is in stained wainscot with panels of embossed leather. Then there is a carved oak chair, small hanging cabinets of different styles, wall cabinets of oak, with base mountings and panels of real bronze; and finally there is a huge chimney-piece, forming the greater part of the end of a room, which is one of the most ornamental and artistic articles in the exhibition. The fireplace is of stone and marble, inlaid with tiles, birds and foliage, and four figures representing the Song, the Tale, the Jest and the Book, designed to be emblematic of fireside amusement. The framework is of carved oak, with mirrors and three painted panels, the subjects being Maternal, Conjugal and Filial Affection.

A quaint and curious exhibit from Exeter, England, is an oak chest made of beams nearly 600 years old, taken from the choir of Salisbury cathedral. It is about five feet long and four feet high, with iron mountings. In this connection should be mentioned the ornamental brass-work and other metal-work exhibited, including altar crosses, candlesticks, dishes, etc., for ecclesiastical purposes; also a door arranged as a dumb-waiter to hold a tray and lamp —though a similar exhibit to this can be seen in the Russian department. Finally, among the articles classed as "Furniture and Objects of General Use in Construction and in Building," are the exhibits of Elkington & Co., manufacturing silversmiths, of Regent Street, London, also Manchester and Birmingham.

The Elkingtons have a triangular court inclosed with black-and-gilt wood cases, at whose entrances stand mail clad figures of the size of life. Their exhibits include works of art in gold, silver, and other metals, *repoussé* works of art, gold and silver damaskeen works of art, solid silver and silver plate for domestic use, table plate relieved with electro-gold and oxidized silver, antique art treasures in metal from the South Kensington Museum, *cloisonnaie* and *champ leve* enamels on silver and copper, and bronze statuary. Chief among these works of Messrs. Elkington & Co., who were the inventors of electro-plate in 1840, are twelve complete dessert services in the leading and distinctive styles of ancient, renaissance and modern art, numerous varieties of enamel, gilt and oxidized silver and gilt bronze, and particularly the three remarkable works of art, the Helicon Vase, the Milton Shield and the Pompeiian Toilet. The vase or centre-piece is wrought out of silver by the *repoussé* process, the whole of the exquisite work being hammered out of the plate silver entirely by hand, and being further enriched with damaskeen tracery in gold and silver. It took six years to manufacture. The Milton Shield, of which the original was manufactured for the International Exhibition of Paris in 1867, and was purchased by the English Government for the South Kensington Museum, is designed and wrought

in the same manner as the last-mentioned. The subjects selected for illustration on this shield were taken from Milton's "Paradise Lost." The value of the original shield was $15,000; but electrotype fac-similes like the one exhibited are furnished for $100, duty free. The Pompeiian Toilet is a placque about twenty inches in diameter, especially made for this exhibition, and is the latest work by the same artist who designed and made the two foregoing specimens. It is of similar materials and wrought by the same process. The subject represents a Pompeiian lady at her toilet; and it is the opinion of the most competent judges that it has never been surpassed either in conception or in the delicacy of its manipulation. The value of this work is $7,500 gold.

The articles of glassware include exhibits from James

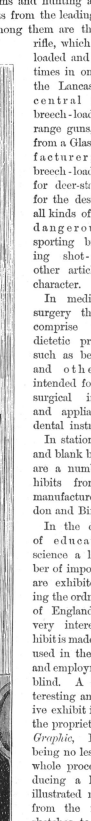

THE POPE'S EXHIBIT IN MEMORIAL HALL.

Green & Nephew, London, John Millar & Co., Edinburgh, and Alexander Jenkinson, also from Edinburgh, and comprise articles in table-glasses, cut and engraved, table decorations, flower-stands, new Venetian glasses, vases, finger-basins, etc., all in antique shapes, engraved jugs and goblets and wine-glasses.

The exhibits of silks and silk fabrics are handsomely displayed, many of them being in robes on lay-figures. Besides dress goods, are exhibits of embroidery and sewing-silks of all kinds, also goods for furniture and upholstery purposes, and in the same class of exhibits scarfs, shawls and all sorts of Summer fancy articles in this class of fabric.

One case from John C. McGee, Belfast, is devoted to a display of the Ulster coat in its pristine beauty.

In jewelry ornaments and traveling equipments there is a very large show, including fancy leather-work, national

costumes, ready-made clothing, church vestments, hats, caps, boots, shoes, millinery, etc. Special exhibits in jewelry and personal ornaments are the Scotch jewelry in gold and silver, with Highland ornaments and stones found in Scotland, such as pearls, cairngorms and pebbles, of which a very handsome display is made by James Aitchison, court jeweler by special appointment to H. I. M. the Emperor of Austria. Other interesting exhibits are the bog oak jewelry and ornaments displayed by a Belfast exhibitor, and the exhibition of Whitby jet in brooches, earrings, bracelets, necklaces and cameo ornaments, from London and Whitby.

The display of military arms and hunting and fishing implements comprises exhibits from the leading manufacturers of Great Britain. Among them are the "Soper" rifle, which has been loaded and fired sixty times in one minute; the Lancaster gun; central firing and breech-loading long-range guns, and rifles from a Glasgow manufacturer; patent breech-loading rifles for deer-stalking and for the destruction of all kinds of large and dangerous game; sporting breech-loading shot-guns, and other articles of this character.

In medicine and surgery the exhibits comprise medicines, dietetic preparations, such as beef extracts and other articles intended for the sick; surgical instruments and appliances, and dental instruments.

In stationery, paper and blank books, there are a number of exhibits from leading manufacturers in London and Birmingham.

In the department of education and science a large number of important maps are exhibited, including the ordnance maps of England; and a very interesting exhibit is made of articles used in the education and employment of the blind. A highly interesting and instructive exhibit is made by the proprietors of the *Graphic*, London, being no less than the whole process of producing a high-class illustrated newspaper, from the receipt of sketches to the final issue of printed sheets to the public. This, with an exhibition of the more prominent plates known to the readers of the London *Graphic*, forms a unique presentment, which received at Vienna, in 1873, the fine-art medal. From Dickinson & Higham, publishers, London, we have the hexaglot Bible, dedicated by special permission to Her Majesty the Queen, in a fine paper copy, handsomely bound in six royal quarto volumes, including the Hebrew, Greek, Syriac, English, German and French. A large number of educational books and appliances, such as drawings, color-boxes, mathematical instruments, books for wood-engravings, specimen sheets of printing, specimens of chromo-lithographs, fac-similes from ancient landscapes, and printed books, engravings, etc. These complete the educational exhibit.

The scientific and philosophical instruments displayed are numerous, and include many very important novelties, to which it is impossible to allude more directly in this place.

It is interesting to find an exhibit here from the house of Charles Frodsham & Co., the ancient house of John Arnold,

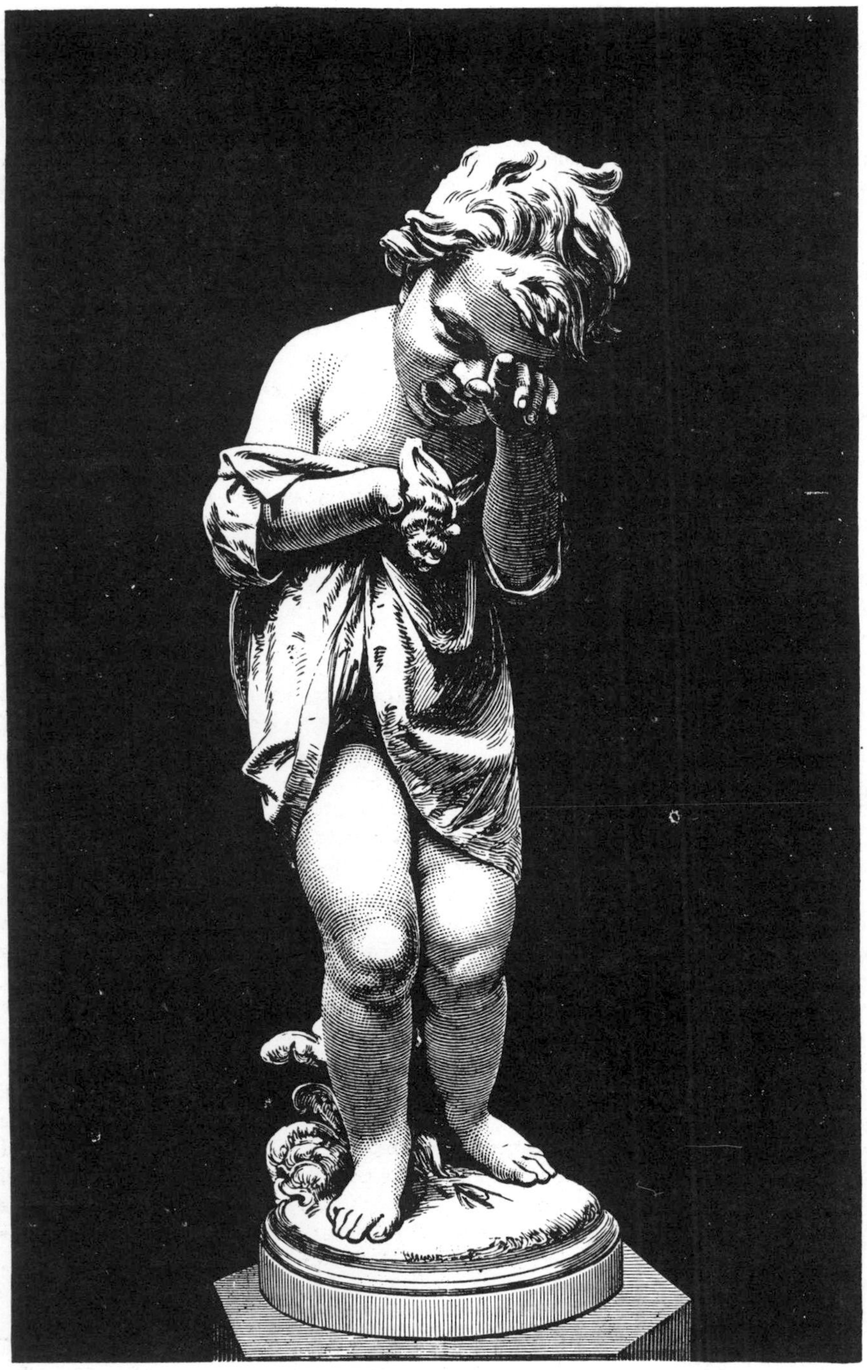

GRIEF.

the inventor of the marine chronometer, and to which was awarded by the Board of Longitude the Government prize of £3,000 for that important invention. Microscopes, magic-lanterns, watches, chronometers, musical instruments, including portable organs, violins, pianofortes, brass and wood instruments for bands and orchestras. These are a few of the articles exhibited in this department.

Games are represented by an exhibit of curling-stones from Canongate, Edinburgh, and another of balls played on scientific principles.

Drawings illustrating the Greenway method of hospital instruction of Henry Greenway, surgeon, Plymouth, England, are exhibited, and are important.

In chemicals, exhibits are made in all directions, from pastry and baking-powder and bleaching-powder to soaps, fluid magnesia, creosote, gelatine, drugs and perfumery, the latter including the exhibits of Eugene Rimmell, the well-known Paris and London perfumer and toilet-soap maker, and comprising extracts and essences, vaporizers, pomades, oils, hair-washes, cosmetics, toilet and shaving-soaps, etc.

This completes our description of the department of Great Britain, and which, meagre as it is, may give some idea of the comprehensive scope and the elaborate character in general of the Exhibition, which in some directions is certainly unparalleled.

CANADA.

The Dominion of Canada extends from the nave to the northern wall between Great Britain and her Colonies, and occupies about as much space as all the latter. The exhibits are divided in the Main Building into three departments: those illustrating mining and metallurgy, exhibits of manufactures, and those other which have reference to education and science.

The collection of minerals is large, and fully illustrative of the mineralogy of the entire Dominion, beginning with a collection of exhibits of gold and silver, presenting to some extent an illustration of the gold-fields and silver-mines of the Dominion, which are far more extensive and important than is generally supposed. We have, in continuation, specimens of copper pyrites and ore, magnetite, iron ores, antimony, galena, barytes and mica from Canada, from Victoria and Nova Scotia. There are also numerous specimens of coal from the mines of Nova Scotia, Cape Breton and Ontario, and even from Vancouver. A few exhibits of petroleum and albutite oil are also made. There are sandstones for building purposes, marble polished and in various colors, red granite, limestone, serpentine, granite, dolomite and jasper, amethyst and agates among the more costly stones. Specimens of artificial stone, lime and cement, clay for bricks, fire-brick, graphite, grindstone and lithographic stone complete this collection. Finally, in metal there is exhibited an ingot of silver from Silver Islet, Lake Superior, and there are iron-pigs and iron bars from Ottawa and Three Rivers, with Canadian axes, car-wheels, rolled iron plates, etc., from St. John, N. B. One very interesting specimen in this collection is an aerolite which was found in 1854, and before cutting weighed 370 lbs. It contains 6.35 per cent. of nickel. This specimen is sent from Madoc, Ontario. From St. Urbain Bay. St. Paul, Quebec, is sent a specimen of ilmenite from a bed forty feet thick. Specimens of specular iron ore are exhibited from Pictou County, Nova Scotia, the lode, so far as examined, ranging in thickness from ten to twenty feet. Specimens of bog-iron ores are shown, and these are of common occurrence in the provinces of Quebec and Ontario. Specimens of copper pyrites and copper ore are exhibited from Lake Superior, Ontario and Quebec, as also from Nova Scotia and New Brunswick, and zinc from Lake Superior. British Columbia sends also copper and lead, as well as silver, of which there are specimens in nuggets and ingots. Nuggets and grains of native silver have been found washing for gold in almost all parts of British Columbia. The gold exhibited comes from Frazer River. The yield of gold from the province of British Columbia has increased from $520,000 during six months of 1858, the year when it was first discovered, to $2,500,000 in 1875. The entire yield in eighteen years has been $38,166,970. Gold was first discovered in Nova Scotia in 1859; and in 1862 upwards of 7,000 ounces were obtained. Since that time the average annual yield for the province has been over 17,000 ounces, the average yield per ton being fourteen pennyweights twenty-one grains. This gold is remarkably pure, and sells for about $19.50 per ounce; but the official estimate is $18 per ounce. The amount per man employed has increased from $249 in 1862 to $660 in 1875.

A specimen of platinum is exhibited from British Columbia, also antimony from Quebec and New Brunswick, and bismuth from Ontario. The coals exhibited include anthracite as well as bituminous, the former from British Columbia. A column of coal from the Albion mines, Pictou County, Nova Scotia, three feet square at the base and twelve feet high, is a prominent exhibit. Specimens of albutite from New Brunswick are shown, being an extremely curious exhibit. This mineral has been regarded by some as a true coal, by others as a variety of jet, and by others as more nearly related to asphaltum. It differs from true coal in being of one quality throughout, in containing no traces of vegetable tissue, and it occurs as a vein and not as a bed.

The shipment of the Albert mines to the United States during twelve years has amounted to 154,800 tons, the price varying between $15 and $20 gold per ton.

Specimens of peat are also exhibited from Huntingdon and St. Hubert, Quebec. Peat occurs in great abundance in many places in the Dominion, but has never been worked much, except in a few localities south of the River St. Lawrence, and not far from Montreal. On the ground it sells for $3.50 per ton, and in Montreal at from $4 to $4.25 per ton.

Among the building-stones are found many specimens of the well-known Nova Scotia sandstone.

The department of manufactures from Canada is very large, including heavy furniture, mirrors, picture-frames, fabrics of wool and cotton, laces and embroideries, of which quite a display is made from Quebec and Halifax; furs, and a large display of hardware. The show of domestic ware and household utensils, saddlery and harness, boots and shoes, heavy cutlery and grinding tools, furs and fur-clothing, is very comprehensive. Ontario makes a creditable display of woolen goods, furs and clothing, stone china, iron castings in railings, etc., dry-goods and yarns.

A particularly interesting exhibit, both in the Main Building and in the Woman's Pavilion, and a specialty of Canadian ingenuity, is found in the models of public institutions, schools and other buildings. These are carefully and prettily constructed, and should be recognized as a Canadian specialty. A special exhibit has been made by the Province of Ontario in its educational department. The exhibit is divided into three parts: the first comprising reports of educational institutions, photographs of school-buildings, pupils' work, school method, etc.; the second, text-books for public and high schools, books relating to the profession of teaching; and part three, reading lessons, object lessons, maps, charts, globes, philosophical instruments, etc. The models for school-buildings are made to a proper scale for working, and with the ground-plan are used for reference by trustees requiring information respecting valuation, school accommodation, etc., previous to erecting new buildings. The exhibits of school-furniture include desks, model of gymnasium, blackboards, etc. Specimens of map and pencil drawings, as well as penmanship, are exhibited from Toronto, Hamilton, and other cities. The collection of books includes all those used under the educational system of Canada, as well as those devoted to the information and instruction of teachers, among which quite a number are on the kindergarten and object-teaching system. The school apparatus comprises maps, drawing materials, music and historical charts, and a very fine collection of globes, terrestrial and celestial, planetariums, geological cabinets, crystals in glass, flowers used in teaching botany, zoological specimens, etc. Ethnography is taught by the aid of busts of representative men celebrated in history, arts and science in different parts of the world. There are also anatomical and physical models, apparatus for instruction in chemistry, and numerous philosophical and other instruments giving instruction in meteorology, acoustics, optics, etc. The Canadian exhibit will be seen to have been large and comprehensive, and it in fact compares favorably with those of other countries.

INDIA.

The articles exhibited in the Indian department of the Main Building were selected from the Indian Museum in London. A large show of minerals and ores is made, chiefly from the Madras and Bombay Presidencies. These include the various iron ores which exist in great abundance throughout the Indian Peninsula, including the remarkable deposits of magnetic iron ore in the Madras Presidency, where there are beds from fifty to one hundred feet in thickness, which can be traced for miles. The ores include manganese, copper, lead, antimony, tin and gold. There are also exhibited specimens of arsenic, graphite, sulphur; and in ornamental minerals, cornelians, of which those from Cambay have been known since the time of the Romans; tourmalines, sapphires, garnets, etc. There are also samples of coal and clays, and other materials used in pottery. The chemical exhibits include salt, saltpetre, alum, borax, carbonate of soda, and sulphate of copper.

Indigo—one of the most important Indian contributions—is exhibited in four samples from four different parts of the country. The history of the commerce of this substance is curious. On its first introduction it came into competition with the old-fashioned *woad*, then used as the basis of a dye, and was received with bitter intolerance. In 1557 it was denounced by the Germanic Diet of Frankfort as the devil's dye; and as late as 1754 by an Imperial edict at Ratisbon. In England an edict was published against those who introduced it, and authorizing its seizure and destruction. This continued in force until the reign of Charles II.

The pottery exhibited includes water-jars, jugs, vessels, "hookah" bills, pitchers, etc., from Patna, Madras, Hydrabad, Allahabad and Bombay. There are also ornamental tiles from Hydrabad. There is a very handsome exhibition of metal utensils, including brass boxes, cups, copper water-utensils, a spitting-dish from Mirzapore, upright handing-swing and stand, lamps, some brass vessels with figures from Nepaul, copper rose-water sprinkler, mixed tin and brass plates from Patna, sweetmeat-plate from Calcutta, betal-plate, inlaid with silver, from Hydrabad, and a brass spoon from Madras.

The cotton fabrics include the famous Dacca muslins, and also a few specimens of muslin from Madras. Six carpets are shown, including one of Cashmere, two from Madras, one woolen carpet from Scinde, and two from Ferrahan, Persia. Three of these carpets are marked, respectively, $593, $661 and $1,016. They look to be about five yards square. The cashmere shawls, chuddahs, India scarfs, berenices, etc., were imported by Messrs. Farmer & Rogers, of Regent Street, London. They include a long gold shawl, a long cashmere shawl, square black and scarlet shawls with borders, long white Umritsir shawls with borders, long white chuddahs, white, blue, drab and scarlet chuddahs, fine India scarfs, black India scarfs, embroidered berenices, rich black gold striped berenices, and a rich black gold embroidered cloak. The shawls are marked $78, $172, $620, $697 and $850; the scarfs $25, $29, etc. There is a large show of raw silk, also pieces of Deccan silk, Burmah and Benares silk fabrics, and a piece of gold-and-crimson stripe from Chuddabad. A number of native garments are shown, both for males and females, including cashmere coat, silk dress, satin apron, child's dress, velvet shoes, embroidered with gold, and turbans with gold borders.

The embroidered fabrics and laces are very numerous. Here are shown coats embroidered with gold, silk scarfs embroidered with narrow gold ribbon, embroidered ribbons from Delhi, velvet bodice, embroidered, from Benares; linen coat, embroidered, from Bhurtpore; book-cover, embroidered with crimson velvet and gold, from Scinde; a dress with embroidered figures from Benares. The native laces include many exhibits in gold and silver, as well as white laces. The manufacture of lace in India is entirely of European origin, and the workers are mostly under European guidance. The textile manufactures of India are further illustrated by fifteen frames containing photo-lithographs, forming a portion of a good work now in process of preparation at the India Museum. This is to include thirteen volumes, containing 720 examples in actual material of the fabrics, eight large folio volumes of lithographic and chromo-lithographic plates, and thirty frames designed for exhibiting 240 of these plates suspended from the wall for examination.

A fine case of Indian jewelry in gold and silver is shown, and a collection of fans of palm-leaf with lace edging, talc, embroidered straw, ivory, peacock quill and sandal-wood. The collection of arms is very extensive and showy, including spears, some with pistols attached, some covered with green velvet, embroidered with gold; coat-of-mail, gauntlets, various arms covered with green velvet from Lahore, battle-axes, steel-head dagger, iron maces, swords with carved belt and ivory hilt, short sword with wooden scabbard, sword with horn handle, helmet with steel and brass rings from the Punjaub, match-lock mounted with silver and brass plate, and match-lock beautifully washed with gold from the Punjaub.

There is a considerable display of medicinal plants and gums, and of course of opium. The cultivation of the poppy-seed in India can be traced back to the sixteenth century. Opium is manufactured from the juice of the poppy, which is obtained by lancing in the months of February and March.

The show of wooden and basket ware, of papier-mache and of lacquer-work is large and handsome. The lacquer used is a mixture of alum, rosin and a certain preparation of sulphur and beeswax, which is applied to the article while the latter is rotated in a frame; after the lacquer is laid on the article is polished with bamboo and oil-rugs.

Several models of traveling vehicles are here exhibited, including covered passenger-cars, models of luggage-cars, and others, all from Bombay; also a state carriage from Poonah.

The carved black wood-work is very elaborate and handsome. There are also a carved sandal-wood model of a Hindoo temple, carved vases, idols of carved wood and stone, pith figures carved, illustrating the trades, such as barber, shoemaker and bird-seller; carved ivory boxes and horn drinking-cups. Inlaid work in India dates back only to about a hundred years, when it is supposed to have come from Persia; and even at this date the arms which were imported from the latter country are still preserved. There are now about fifty shops in Bombay carrying on this business, giving employment over one hundred people. The work is composed of ivory, horn, sandal-wood, ebony and tin, in imitation of silver. The articles exhibited are inlaid marble boxes, glove-boxes, card-baskets, caskets, etc.

Some miniature paintings on ivory, and others on mica, are also very handsome. There is a full display of native seeds, also of raw cotton, and a fine show of photographs of ruined temples and other scenes in India. A large case of musical instruments, and specimens of sculptured stones from the ancient temples, complete the exhibit of India.

New Zealand.

New Zealand was discovered in 1642 by the Dutch navigator, Tasman, who, however, did not land upon the shores. In 1769 it was first visited by Captain Cook, who explored its coasts. Subsequently, however, the country became a resort for whalers and traders. In 1840 the native chiefs ceded the sovereignty to the British crown.

The aborigines, called *Maoris*, are a branch of the Polynesian race, and a remarkable people. They have a tradition that their forefathers, some 600 years ago, came to New Zealand from Hawarka, which may have been Hawaii, in the Sandwich Islands, or Sarai, in the Navigator or Samoa group. These Maoris are not unlike the Highlanders of Scotland, being, like the latter, divided into clans. On June 1st, 1874, the Maoris and half-castes amounted to 46,016.

The colony of New Zealand consists of three principal islands, called respectively, the North, the Middle and the South or Stewart's Island. There are several small islets, mostly uninhabited, the chief of these being the Chatham and the Auckland Isles. The three principal islands extend in length 1,100 miles, but their breadth varies between 46 and 250 miles. The total area of New Zealand is about 64,000,000 acres. It has a healthy and salubrious climate, with a very equable temperature. The Summers are as cool as those of England, and the Winters as warm as those of Italy. The mean annual temperature at Auckland is nearly the same as at Rome.

The revenue of New Zealand in 1874 was £3,063,811; the imports of that year amounted to £8,121,112; the exports to £5,251,269. The form of government in New Zealand is as free as any in the British Dominions, the executive power being nominally vested in the Governor, appointed by the Queen, but actually the direction of affairs is conducted by the representatives of the people.

The changes of weather and temperature are very sudden, calms and gales, rain and sunshine, heat and cold, often alternating so frequently and suddenly as to defy previous calculation.

A very large number of the population of New Zealand are occupied in mining for gold, which for the last twelve years has formed one of the most important exports of the colony. The quantity exported up to 1874 amounted to about twenty-five million pounds sterling. Petroleum springs occur in various parts of the colony, but these are very little worked. In the entire colony about 12,000,000 acres of land are fitted for agriculture, the balance being adapted for pasturage. All kinds of domestic animals have been imported, and are now bred throughout the colony. Many of the more valuable trees of Europe, America and Australia have also been produced. All the European grasses and other useful plants produce returns equal to those of the most favored localities. Fruit is abundant all over New Zealand, oranges, lemons, citrons, peaches, apples, pears, grapes, apricots, figs and melons being found in abundance. The principal items of export are gold, wool, grain and flour, Kourie gum, hides and tallow, and preserved meats. New Zealand now stands third on the list of the British wool-producing colonies. The population of the colony on March 1st was estimated at 299,684.

As you enter the New Zealand section at the nave you are met by a fine display of photographs giving views of scenery in the different islands, photographs of Maoris and others, exhibiting the domestic life of the people. There are also views showing foliage, buildings, processes of gold mining, etc. Then there are a very large number of weapons, ornaments, garments and other articles, illustrating the life of the Maoris. Many of these weapons are made of whalebone, and some of them are quite elaborately carved. There are also stone weapons, wooden battle-axes, ornamented spears, flax mats, ornamented with red feathers of the *kaka*, or mounted parrot; others interwoven with feathers of the native wood-pigeon, one in particular intended as a gift to the President of the United States; also ancient fish-hooks tipped with human bone, carved pipes and calabash, neck ornaments of green stone, ear ornaments made of a shark's tooth, green stone ear-pendant, ancient stone ax and stone hatchet of ten generations back, and a Maori image with headdress and ear-ornaments of feathers.

A case of feather garments displayed is very curious and interesting. There are also fancy articles made from the feet and bones of sea-birds, muffs, collerettes, wristlets, etc., of feathers, skulls of Maoris, and finally there is a skeleton of a *moa*, a gigantic extinct bird, about eight feet in height, apparently of the ostrich species, with the model of an egg of the same. A good display of minerals is made, including coal, and there is also shown cordage, glue, canned meats, specimens of native woods, hides, and the celebrated Kourie gum. The *Phormium tenax*, or New Zealand flax, is displayed raw and manufactured.

The Agricultural exhibits include wheat, rye, barley, bread-beans, Canadian oats, and field-peas. There are also specimens of hops, and some hams and bacon. Among the minerals are building-stone, fire-clay, porcelain-clay, and also fire-bricks. Barks are shown from different trees which are used in tanning, and some employed for producing the red and brown colors used by the Maoris.

Jamaica.

Jamaica exhibits tobacco in the leaf, cigars and cigarettes; also rum and sugar. There is a case of articles made of lace bark, and another of ornaments made from the native "dagger-plant." Then there are baskets and fans from leaves, palm-leaf hats, shell-baskets, walking-sticks, tortoise-shell necklaces, hats made from the "dagger-plant," and from lace bark; also fans, flowers, baskets, etc., of the same, with earrings and brooch made of lobster-shell. Cocoanut-shell ornaments are also exhibited, razor-strops made from the stems of plants, ropes from Sisal hemp, bamboo baskets, specimens of native wood, lance-wood, cashew, pimento, olive, mahogany, cedar, lignum-vitæ, ebony, satin-wood, rosewood, logwood, mangrove, etc. Among the agricultural products exhibited are ginger, nutmegs, tobacco, tea, cocoa, coffee and chocolate. A number of cordials of orange, ginger, pimento, lime-juice, etc., are exhibited; and textile fabrics of Sisal hemp, China grass, coir, mohoe, trumpet-tree, and other plants.

Bermudas.

The Bermudas, or Summer's Islands, are a collection of about 100 small islands, situated on the western side of the Atlantic Ocean, at a distance of about 580 miles from the nearest land, viz., Cape Hatteras, of North Carolina. Fifteen or sixteen of these are inhabited, the largest, or Bermuda Proper, containing less than twenty square miles of land, and nowhere exceeding three miles in breadth. The climate has long been celebrated for mildness and salubrity. The islands produce arrowroot and an indigenous cedar well adapted for shipbuilding. Turtles are common; whales are occasionally taken in the neighboring waters. The inhabitants export largely certain articles, especially potatoes, onions, tomatoes and arrowroot, but they are dependent on foreign supplies for all the flour and most of the meat consumed.

Among the displays are an assortment of building-stones of various qualities, Bermuda potatoes and onions, sections of specimens of woods, conch-shells used by cameo-cutters, corals, sponges, corallines, sea-fans, arrowroot, articles made from the palmetto-leaf, etc. The show of algæ, corals, etc., is very fine. There is also a case of native point-lace, one of small articles made from Bermuda wood. A wreath of shell-work, walking-canes made from the exterior of the gru-gru palm, two inlaid tables of Bermuda wood and workmanship are noteworthy objects. There is a model of one of Her Majesty's floating docks. A few stalactites and stalagmites taken from submarine caves, some paintings and photographs of Bermuda scenery complete the display.

Bahamas.

This group is composed of about twenty inhabited islands, and an immense number of islets and rocks. The

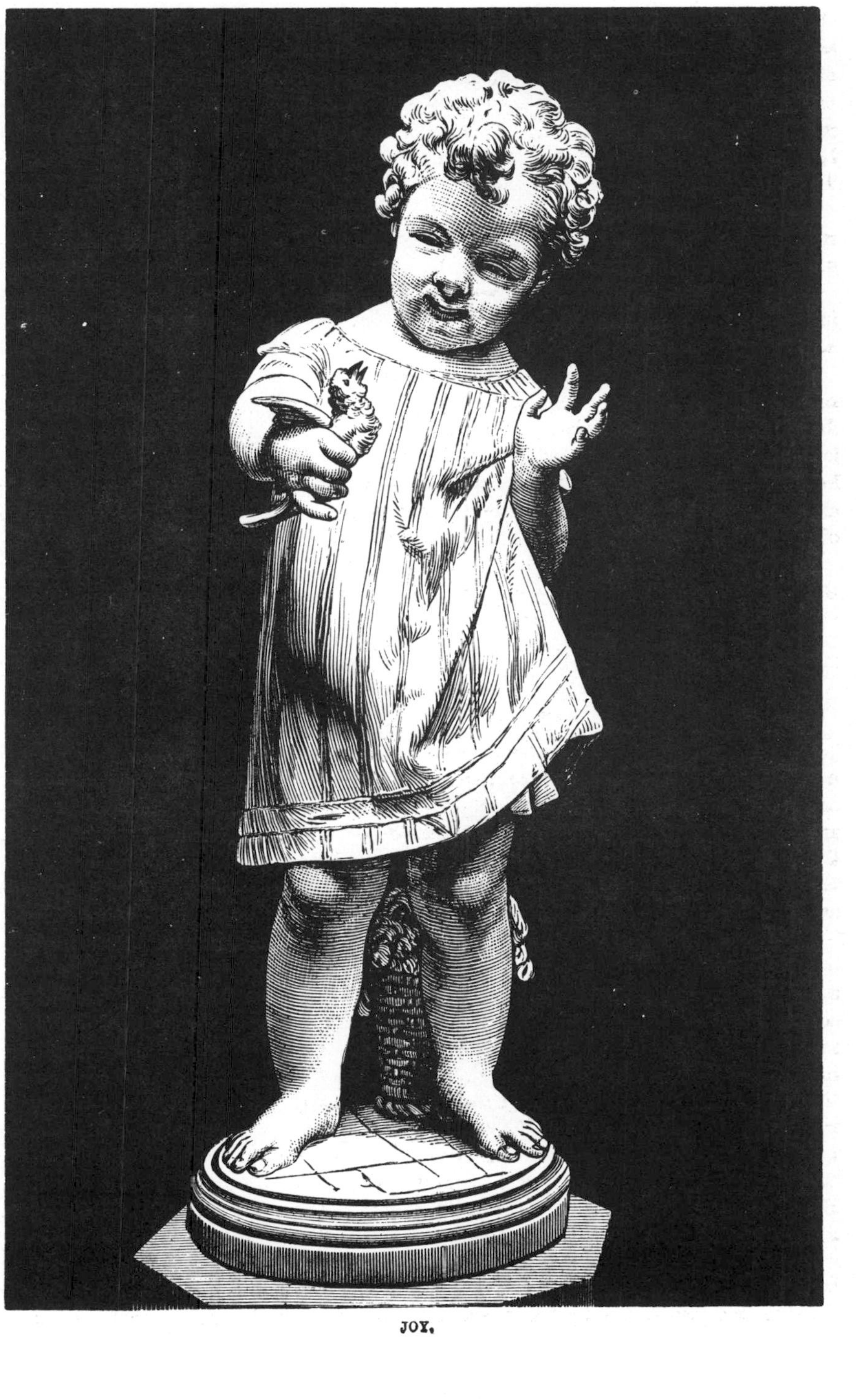

JOY.

principal island is New Providence, containing the capital, Nassau. San Salvador, one of these islands, was the first land discovered by Columbus on his voyage in 1492. Pineapples have been largely grown here, and are extensively cultivated. Salt and wood have also added to the exports. At the present time the staples are salt, fruit, sponge, barks, dye and furniture woods, guano, straw, tortoiseshell, fish-scale and shell-work. The specimens of native woods exhibited include mahogany, satin, cedar, cocoanut, green ebony, logwood, and brazinetto woods; also lignumvitæ, orange, and horse-flesh wood. Quite a number of walking-canes are exhibited, manufactured out of woods growing in the Bahamas, including crab-tree, cassava, black torch, lignum-vitæ, cocoanut, mahogany, sabin, iron, green ebony, saffron, cascarilla, wild lemon, tamarind, guava, and wild coffee woods. A dray is shown, manufactured out of nine different woods, also bread-platters, including three to be presented to Cornell University. Sponges are displayed in strings, and there is a very beautiful show of shells and shell-work, one case containing about one hundred varieties of small shells, valued at $100. Other cases contain shell-work, baskets, bridal-wreath, etc., and one displays a magnificent epergne of shells valued at $500. Tortoiseshell is

the West India Company in 1680, but was finally ceded to Great Britain in 1814. The area of the colony has been computed to be about 76,000 square miles. The exhibits in the Main Building include a number of specimens of sugar and rum, contributed by various sugar estates and plantations, specimens of silk grass, sweet-brier, monkey-apple and mahoe fibres, some rice-straw ornaments and a collection of starches, barks and other medicinal productions of the colony. A native curiosity is shown in the shape of a specimen of greenheart wood nearly one hundred years old.

GOLD COAST COLONY.

This colony in West Africa, comprising the British settlements on the Gold Coast and at Lagos, was constituted by a charter bearing date 24th July, 1874. The name is generally given to a portion of Upper Guinea, between 5 deg. and 4 deg. 20 min. east longitude, stretching along the Gulf of Guinea. The exhibits in this collection include articles of clothing, weapons and implements used by the natives, with specimens of oils made from African nuts and seeds, including palm-oil, ground-nut-oil, cocoanut-oil and gold dust, and gold ornaments comprising crosses, brooches, lockets, chains, bracelets, etc. A number of the Ashantee

natives. Some oyster-shells are shown from the south coast of the colony, skins of native animals, elephant tusks, a robe of skins of the jackal, skins of the hyena and cheetah or hunting leopard, antelope and rhinoceros skins, ostrich feathers and eggs, ostrich incubator, stuffed ostriches; with preserved lemons, citrons, bitter oranges, melons, Cape gooseberries; also Cape wines, wool, horns and native woods.

MAURITIUS, SEYCHELLES ARCHIPELAGO, CEYLON AND TRINIDAD.

The British Colonial section proper ends at the eastern end, with the colonies above named, whose exhibit comprises native products in general. For instance, the Strait settlements send silk floss, silk thread and silk lace, woods from Singapore, Madras, Bombay and Nangpo; nuts, grass, tea, coffee and spices from Singapore, and cotton and wool from the same island. Ceylon exhibits tin and plumbago, india-rubber, gutta-percha, coffee, spices, tobacco and cigars, kakao-de-mer, vegetable fibres and native woods; also straw hats and mother-of-pearl and other shells.

Mauritius makes a very fine display of native woods and samples of coffee, a large number of fibres, specimens of native sugar and articles made from the palmiste robes,

THE ROYAL BAKING POWDER COMPANY'S EXHIBIT, IN AGRICULTURAL HALL.

represented in pieces, with a hawk's-bill and logger-head turtle; one tortoise, polished, being priced $75. A case of tortoiseshell ornaments, including necklace, pin and earrings, bracelets, etc., is valued at $140. A set consisting of chain, charm, scarf-pin, solitaire and studs and vest-button, $50; a spoon and paper-knife at $10. All this work is manufactured by hand.

Some pretty mimosa bean-work is shown, including a set of jewelry and single articles. The mimosa grows well in the Bahamas. Various fibres are shown, including the plantain, banana, pineapple, aloe and Esparto grass. None of the Bahama fibres are at present utilized. It is stated, however, that they could be exported in large quantities. Specimens of the wild fig-tree and palmetto, made into rope, are also shown, as well as rope made out of the fibre of aloe. One case contains palmetto-work, including fans and hats; also a case of native salt, cascarilla, arrowroot, cassava starch, bees-wax and myrtleberry-wax are shown, as well as specimens of tobacco and coffee, native building-stones, and some bottles of preserved fruits and pickles.

BRITISH GUIANA.

This colony in South America extends from east to west about 200 miles, and includes the settlements of Demarara, Essequibo and Berbice. It was first partially settled by

and King Cofficalli cloths, with samples of iron, and specimens of cloth in the loom, slippers and Lagos sandals are exhibited, with goat-skins, fans, knife-sheaths, specimens of odoom, which is the building-wood of the country, and a desk and envelope-case of the same, made by the native workmen; a collection of specimens of native woods, models of canoes, carved and plain calabashes, musical instruments, Niger swords in ornamented leather scabbards, bows and arrows, and a specimen of white clay used in medicine, and also to chalk divorced wives. This clay is likewise used in law-suits to mark those who are successful, and at marriage ceremonies as an indication of purity. A number of native utensils, palm-oil ladles, palm-leaf hats, etc., complete the collection.

CAPE OF GOOD HOPE.

This colony makes a considerable display in minerals, ores, stone, and metallurgic products, including copper, saltpetre, coal, etc. There is also a display of native ornaments, including necklaces and bracelets, native aprons, headdresses, exhibits of skeleton flowers, work-box constructed of different woods, pots, baskets, vegetable barks, and medicines used by the Caffres, and native weapons, including Caffre assegais and a bushman's ax. A number of paintings, engravings, lithographs, photographs, etc., display the scenery, costumes and appearances of the

including slippers, cigar-cases, baskets and rugs. There are also a number of views taken in Mauritius, and types of the Chinese, Indian, Malagash and Mozambique inhabitants of Mauritius.

The Seychelles, or Mahé Islands, include a group comprising 50,120 acres, and are distant 940 miles from Mauritius. The Archipelago is subordinate to the Governor of Mauritius. The exhibit from Seychelles is most curious and interesting. It is particularly noticeable for the delicacy of the native work displayed, this work being made from the inner husk of the kakao-de-mer, of which curious nuts several are shown in the rough state and polished. They are in appearance a sort of twin cocoanut, larger and of a somewhat different shape from the ordinary cocoanut. The articles exhibited of this manufacture include baskets, hats, slippers, cigar-cases, watch-pockets, tea-cups and saucers, etc. There is also shown a kakao-de-mer wood walking-stick and other canes, a roll of Seychelles tobacco, and a parcel of cigars made from the same specimen of kakao, cloves, coffee, a sample of cotton, fine boxes of shell, samples of wheat, rum and cocoanut-oil, and pieces of hawk's-bill turtle-shell.

Trinidad makes an exhibit of native woods, including 236 varieties. Some of the more curious of these are the Lezard or Fill wood, the Indian teak, tropical almond,

INTERIOR OF PHOTOGRAPHIC HALL.

olive-wood, incense-wŏod, lance-wood, bread-fruit wood, lime-tree and cactus. A large number of native fibres are also exhibited—including that extracted from the husks of the cocoanut—brooms, brushes, bedding, etc. Then there are specimens of Angostura bitters, nutmegs, cloves, manioc, and a collection of baskets, including Indian baskets, miniature egg-baskets with mats, rice and coffee-pans, and small models of the cataures for carrying loads. Some baskets are shown, manufactured of the towel-gourd, presenting a very rude appearance.

1. MERINO RAM.   2. VERMONT RAM.

Orange Free State.

The Republican Orange Free State is situated on the northern boundary of the Cape Colony, and covers an extent of territory roughly estimated at about 70,000 square miles. It consists of extensive undulating plains, sloping from the great water-shed northward and westward to the Vaal and Orange Rivers. The courses of the larger rivers are extremely tortuous and hollow, their banks being precipitous and commonly lined with the water-willow, mimosa and other trees indigenous to this country. The streams are usually fordable, but during the Winter season become swollen and impassable.

The country is divided into fourteen districts, each of which has its chief town and capital, besides villages. In either district there are small ranges of hills, forming their water-sheds, in which the various streams take rise, and affording landmarks which are used as division lines of the various districts. The plains and table-lands are covered with grass, which in rainy seasons

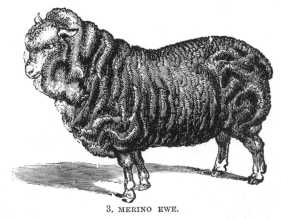

3. MERINO EWE.

level of the sea is about 5,000 feet, and the climate is generally salubrious, the Winters being cold, but dry, and the Summers warm and moist. The population of the

Republic is estimated at 75,000 white, and 25,000 colored or native. The form of Government is republican, the legislative power being placed in the hands of an assembly called

He is elected by the direct vote of all the burghers, and his election does not affect the positions of the other officials in the country. The State President is assisted by an Executive Council; but the entire control of the State affairs, internal as well as external, rests in his hands, with certain exceptions specified in the Constitution. The qualifications of the burghers include: First, that they shall be whites, and born in the State. Secondly, whites who have resided in the State during one year, and have fixed property to the amount of £150. Thirdly, whites who have resided in the State for three successive years, the two latter classes being obliged to furnish certificates of conduct and written acknowledgments to respect the laws of the State.

The constitutional Church of the Orange Free State is the Dutch Reformed. There is likewise a branch of the Anglican Church of South Africa, represented by a bishop and a numerous staff of clergy. The Wesleyan Methodist Church, the Evangelical Lutheran Church, and the Roman Catholic Church, are also represented in the Republic. A rough estimate fixes the number of farms throughout the country as between 6,000 and 7,000. The revenue of the State is raised by quit-rents on these farms, hire of the State lands, license, stamp duties, etc. The Orange Free State was formerly the occasional residence of marauding bands of Caffres and Bushmen rather than inhabited by any definite race, these wild tribes infesting it from time to time, there to secure pasture for their flocks, or to escape destruction from the hands of some stronger race. The present control of the country has only existed twenty years, and when it is considered that its revenues

4. COTSWOLD RAM.   5. SOUTH-DOWN EWE.   6. SOUTH-DOWN RAM.

becomes rank and luxuriant, affording excellent pasture for stock of all descriptions. In the southern and eastern districts this grass is burned off once a year, for the purpose of destroying the old crop, which rots by reason of rains, and becomes injurious to sheep and cattle. In the western districts the grass is rapidly becoming supplanted by a dwarfed bushy vegetable. The greater part of the Orange Free State is a grazing country, and though agriculture is everywhere attended to more or less, it is chiefly in the southern and eastern districts that it is carried on as the principal resource, these districts furnishing the grain which is brought into the markets of the others. The Republic has also considerable mineral wealth; coal of a very good quality, and in paying quantities, has been found, and diamonds, rubies and other precious stones have been discovered in various parts of the country. Formerly an immense variety of wild animals inhabited the Orange Free State, and even now the lion still frequents some sections; but, owing to the advanced civilization of the country, the larger animals, such as the elephant, rhinoceros, hippopotamus and giraffe are disappearing. Antelopes, however, roam the plains in countless numbers, while horses and cattle are plentiful, and the wooled sheep may be estimated by millions. Birds abound in great variety, including the ostrich, eagle, vulture, pelican, hawk, and various species of the crane, among the larger kinds. The staple articles of export from the Orange Free State are wool, skins, ostrich feathers, and, of late years, diamonds and other precious stones. The average height of the Orange Free State above the

the *Volks-raad*, whose members are elected for four consecutive years, the whole number of representatives being fifty-two, half retiring by rotation every two years, when a

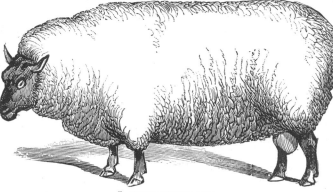

7. OXFORD-DOWN RAM.

new election takes place to fill the vacancies. The executive power in the State rests in a State President, whose term of office is five years, and who is eligible for re-election.

have increased in that time from about $100,000 per annum to $600,000, while a considerable import and export trade has been established, it will be admitted that the prosperity of the Orange Free State Republic presents a historical picture almost unprecedented. The exhibits of the Orange Free State are located south of the South Avenue, between columns two and five. These exhibits are so peculiar that they attract a great deal of attention, and have aroused considerable interest in the minds of visitors. Here are to be seen specimens of diamonds in the rough from the diamond-fields of the Orange Free State, accompanied by diamondiferous soil with diamond in it, and pebbles which accompany the latter. There are also copper and iron ore, magnesite, coal and kaolin; of woods there are represented the blue gum, mimosa and olive-wood, while several quite artistic and very interesting figures, carved from wood with a penknife, are seen, these being made of willow, of yellow wood and of deal, which is simply pine. There are Angora, blessbok and jackal karosses; then there are boots of native manufacture, baskets, harness made of white leather, and pipes manufactured by the natives, specimens of petrified wood, sumach, a collection of stuffed birds, and one of butterflies and other insects; tusks of ivory, horns of various specimens of the native deer, known under the names of blessbok, gemsbok, hartbeest, roorbok, wildebeeste, etc. There are also skins of the blessbok, koodoo cow and hartbeest, some of these being tanned. Then there are reins or thongs and girdles made of hides of the buffalo, bullock, eland, giraffe and gnu, as also shamboks; flexible rods, whips of

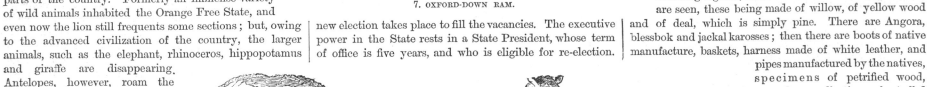

8. OXFORD-DOWN EWE.   9. SOUTH-DOWN RAM.   10. SOUTH-DOWN EWE.

PRIZE ANIMALS IN THE LIVE-STOCK SHOW--THE PRIZE SHEEP.

rhinoceros hides, and whips of giraffe hide. Ostrich feathers and other bird plumage in their natural state make a most interesting exhibition, and there are ostrich eggs, dried fruits, specimens of wool, washed and unwashed, and also mohair from the Angora goat. These articles are in charge of Mr. Charles W. Riley, Consul-General at Philadelphia, and Commissioner for the Orange Free State to the International Exhibition.

Peru.

Immediately contiguous to and north of the Orange Free State section is that devoted to Peru. The articles exhibited in this collection comprise a considerable number of antiquities, paintings in oil, some wood-carving, photographs, specimens of printing, artificial flowers and embroideries, gloves, straw hats, shoes and canes, the most of these being from Lima. A very good display is made of the minerals of Peru by the Special Commissioner to the Exposition from Lima. There are also specimens of sulphur, tar, petroleum, oil, soap and

1. BERKSHIRE BOAR.   2. SUFFOLK SOW.

arsenical silver ore, samples of porphyritic rock and specimens of fossils, samples of copper ore, crystallized red oxide, black copper, kaolin, cobalt, malachite, salt and sulphur ores, nitrate of soda and black polished porphyry, two very large rock crystals, native sulphur, alabaster with gold in sight, taken from the gold mine of Cachiyuyo, red hematite, samples of fossil coal, gray nickel, amethyst taken from a mine near Copiapo, sulphuret of lead, salt, galena, argentiferous galena, iron oxide and

mont of colored wools and lace color, two linen handkerchiefs, two doilies of Flemish thread, one rug, two counterpanes, or coverlets, crochet-work, samples of lace, embroidered blanket, two cushions with borders of Flemish thread, and a parasol with lace fringing. The "Nuns' House of the Good Shepherd" exhibits an embroidered handkerchief representing a palace of the Chilian Exposition. From Santiago there are a number of gypsum ornaments, card-baskets and samples of printing, lithography and binding.

In ceramics, the only exhibits consist of samples of enameled tiles for flooring. The Government of Chili contributes a map of the country, with plans of bridges and public buildings. A crucifix carved in wood is an artistic work; also a pen-drawing, being a portrait from life. Two medallion portraits in bronze are shown, as also a plaster portrait bust. The agricultural products exhibited by Chili include a very full show of grass, grown and exhibited by the Normal School Farm, as also beans, peas, lentils,

3. BERKSHIRE SOW.   4. BERKSHIRE BOAR.

candles of native manufacture. Something of a show in wood-work is made from the Penitentiary, and some articles in textile fabrics, including ponchas; tools, etc., and goods made from the vicuna texture. From the Department of the Amazon there are shown samples of vegetable silk; from the Bureau of Education of Lima, a map of Peru. The forest products exhibited include specimens of native woods, also nuts, olives and raisins. In strictly

cinnabar. There is a specimen of stone taken from the crater of the La Ternera volcano, also fossil impressions taken from the coal-pit of La Ternera, and feldspar, which by decomposition produces pumice-stone. From the copper foundries of Don Adolfo Lapostol, in the department of San José, province of Santiago, are shown a bar of copper and twelve samples of copper ore. This collection is large, varied, and very valuable, and presents an elaborate

garden-seeds, tree-seeds, 19 different varieties of potatoes—all from the same source. A collection of medicinal herbs, including 108 varieties, is exhibited, chiefly by the Departmental Junta of Victoria. The collection of woods exhibited by the Normal School Farm includes 51 species, and also a frame containing 78 specimens of different woods from the Department of Sontué. Quite a number of specimens of barks, cotton in the pod and ginned silkworm

5. BERKSHIRE BOAR.   6. SMALL YORKSHIRE SOW.   7. SMALL YORKSHIRE BOAR.   8. CHESTER SWINE.

agricultural products there are various kinds of grain, tobacco and cigars, rice, sugars and starch, and in manufactured articles other than these, rum, wines, brandies, Amazon bitters, olive-oil and castor-oil. Two of the departments send specimens of hides and skins, and a considerable display is made of cotton, wool and silk.

Chili.

The population of Chili in 1874 amounted to 2,400,000. The imports for that year were estimated at $38,417,729, and the exports at $36,540,659. The most important values in exports are in barley, flour, wheat and cattle. The value of the mining production for the same year was $16,562,974. The table of maritime movements shows arrivals and departures of about 12,000 ships of say 8,000,000 tons burden. The total of the Custom House revenues was $8,000,000. The exhibits in the Main Building from Chili lie north of those of Peru, and extend to the nave, side by side with those of the Argentine Republic. Much of the larger portion of this collection is composed of minerals, ores, stone and metallurgical products. These include very rich samples of native silver, silver ore, and

and complete display, illustrating the wealth of the country in this direction. Among the ornamental articles in stone there is shown a table-top of alabaster, one of marble with mosaic, and one of black marble, with views and a shield of the arms of Rome. There is also another ornament with garlands, and a cup with doves in the centre, of mosaic; a specimen of wood mosaic will also be found interesting. Quite a pretty display is made by the pupils of the Public College of Molina, including a loom and spindle, an assort-

cocoons, horse-hair, fleeces of common wool, etc., are also exhibited, and a number of samples of beeswax and honey are to be found here. Among the animals exhibited are the condor and the Chilian lion, stuffed, as also preserved fish and shell-fish. Finally, there is a display of national publications, including all the official reports of the Government, commercial statistics, etc., the Chilian codes of law at present in force, Reports of the Sessions of the National Congress from 1826, Annals of the University of Chili, a collection of the historians of Chili, text-books of instruction used in the National Institute and in the primary schools, scientific and literary periodicals and reviews, and a large collection of miscellaneous books, comprising several hundred volumes. Here may particularly be mentioned the Chilian Building, a small brick structure, lying west of Machinery Hall and near George's Hill, where is displayed the silver and gold amalgamating machinery exhibited by the Republic of Chili. This is a model in fac-simile of the amalgamating machine in use at Antofagasta, and is constructed on a scale, 1-6th of the original size. The model consists of three sections, including first the reduction and washing of ore, which is accomplished by means

9. CHESTER WHITE SOW, WITH LITTER.

PRIZE ANIMALS IN THE LIVE-STOCK SHOW—THE PRIZE HOGS.

of two vertical iron rollers, resting on an iron plate, which being kept in motion, produce the necessary friction to grind the ores, which are received in the iron cup containing the rollers, by means of self-feeders. The reduced ore is carried with the water, which is kept running upon it continually by means of pipes through gutters into the open tanks below, and there allowed to settle ; the water is then run off and the ore carried to the drying-shed. The second process is that of amalgamation. Here are twelve large and two small revolving casks, four upright tanks, containing a chemical solution, one washer, and one centrifugal machine. By this process the ore is freed from impurities, leaving the pure silver and quicksilver, the whole being carried into the centrifugal machine, where the quicksilver is separated from the silver, after which all remaining impurities are washed out into two smaller casks with boiling salt-water. The silver is then discharged and stamped into molds ready for section three. This section includes the quicksilver condenser and smelting-furnace. Here the final residuum of quicksilver is evaporated from the silver column by means of heat. In the Chilian Building the first and second section of this model are seen in motion. The entire model was exhibited in 1875 at the Chilian exhibition of Santiago, and cost $13,600, the cost of the actual machine being $230,000. According to the official report, the mining products of Chili during the years from 1842 to 1872 amounted to the sum of $201,826,240, of which more than $75,000,000 was silver in bars.

ARGENTINE REPUBLIC.

At the extreme western end of the Main Building, next to Chili, is the section containing exhibits of the Argentine Republic, extending from the nave to South Avenue. Here a very considerable exhibit is made of minerals and ores from the various provinces, these forming, in fact, the most important part of the Argentine display. A special collection of minerals, comprising 298 exhibits, including a number of fine specimens of native silver, malachite, copper, kaolin, nickel and other valuable minerals, is exhibited by William A. Treloar, and is valued at $3,000. The Provincial Commission of the province of Rioja exhibits silver ores, copper ore, porphyry. Francisco D. Aquilar makes a display of 388 exhibits, which he values at $1,000 for the collection. From the province of Catamarca we have an interesting, though small, collection of minerals, and some ancient stone-miners' hammers found in the abandoned mines of Ortiz. Samples of iron ore are sent from this province, and it is stated that the National Congress of the Confederation has passed a law authorizing the Executive to subscribe for shares in a proposed mining company to the amount of $100,000. The University of Cordoba displays garnet, limestone, pumice-stone, and other minerals. Six samples of copperas are exhibited from Patagonia, and a collection of stones from the shores of the rivers La Plata and Uruguay. There are also shown specimens of coal, anthracite, bituminous and semi-bituminous ; and from the province of Buenos Ayres samples of curious stone having herbs growing upon it. From Cordoba are specimens of marble, and from the province of San Luis a stone pestle used by the Indians for stamping maize ; also ash-pan for burning incense, made by the Indians, and an ash-tray. The province of Entre-Rios sends hydraulic stones, conglomerated shell and clay-stones, hydraulic lime and petrified wood ; also petrified oyster-shells, of which there are said to be large quantities in the province of Parana. Clays, kaolin, silex and other materials used in the manufacture of porcelain; glass, fire-bricks, etc., are displayed in considerable quantities. The chemical manufactures include citric acid, mineral salt, alum, salt-petre, and quite an exhibition made in soaps, glycerine, petroleum, tar and various medical articles.

Native porcelain and pottery are shown in flower-pots, bottles, jugs, dishes, mugs, coffee-pots, and other objects made by the natives, being held at pretty high prices. Twelve pieces, for instance, made by the Indians are valued

at $200. In glassware, there is but one exhibit, that from Buenos Ayres, a cruet-stand of cut glass. A most curious and unexpected article, one that would be rather looked for as the product of Yankee ingenuity and skill than as coming from one of the South American Republics, is called " El Enciclopedico del Rio de la Plata." This is a combination writing-table, wash-stand, dressing-case, etc., containing many other useful articles for convenience in domestic life, opening out, and displaying various compartments for the uses indicated. The article is priced at $600. The furniture exhibit also includes night-tables for bedrooms, of coco-wood, and algerroba-wood, a new system of Venetian-blinds and a carved arm-chair.

There are also shown ostrich-feather dusters, esparto matting, wooden dishes and trays, hammocks, ponchos, towels, shawls, napkins, table-cloths, these latter made of cotton grown and spun in the province of Tucuman ; also native wood and silver tankards, and cups made of stone. Woolen fabrics include ponchos, blankets, saddle-bags, rugs, coverlets, etc., dyed of different colors with native roots and plants.

Woven articles made by the Pampas Indians are rugs, garters, saddle-cloths and blankets, which, with two ponchos, blue with white spots, are interesting specimens of native

VESTIBULE OF MEMORIAL HALL.

manufacture. The vicuna articles include some quite costly. A vicuna shawl of natural colors is priced $400. Neckties and a purse are $10 each. A thick vicuna poncho is valued at $50, another $150, and a suit of clothes of the same fabric $250. Among these articles are also mufflers, cloaks, and finally a vicuna shawl, containing 6,600 warped threads, woven for the Philadelphia Exhibition, of which the price is 25 gold ounces. Native leather is represented by a pair of boots, price $16, another pair of "dandies," $10, and one pair at $6. A Buenos Ayres milliner sends three bonnets. One of these, a white bonnet, trimmed with blue feathers and flowers, is priced at $40 ; another, with green leaves and grapes, is priced $28. Straw hats are exhibited made from the leaves of the Yatay palm-tree. These hats are very much used in the province of Corientes, and are very durable. A pair of boots, made of snake-skin, is a curious exhibit from this section. This same province exhibits a flower made of hair, and a wreath of artificial flowers made of the pith of a native plant. A basket of flowers made of different kinds of seeds and grains is offered for sale at $100. Quite a number of articles in hair are displayed, one such exhibit of flowers being valued at $600. A pair of silver Indian earrings is exhibited by the province of San Luis, and a necklace and locket of gold,

representing the 14 Argentine provinces, comes from the province of Buenos Ayres, and is priced $800. Another ingenious structure, something similar to the " Enciclopedico " before mentioned, is exhibited by Eugenio Mataldi, of the province of Buenos Ayres. This is a traveling-trunk, which can be transformed into a sofa, writing-desk, table, dressing-case or chest of drawers. Several other trunks of raw-hide are exhibited, one from the province of Santa Fé being marked $48. The Indian articles displayed are always very curious, fifteen rings made by the Indians of the province of Corientes, and a work-box, being among these curiosities. A large collection of medicinal herbs or plants is exhibited by the provincial commissions of the different provinces. These include articles for every imaginable disease, from headache to asthma. Dentistry is represented by a case of artificial teeth, mounted in plates in imitation of gums, exhibited from Buenos Ayres. Horse-furniture, harness and saddlery are represented quite extensively. A saddle from Santa Fé is priced $45, a Mexican saddle made in San Juan, with girdle, stirrups, bridle, etc., very complete, is valued at $350 ; a whip made of horse-hair, a plaited lasso and a pair of boleadoras for hunting ostriches, are among the curiosities in this department. Lassoes are numerous, as are also pillions, horse-rugs and hobbles. Some pillions are made of ostrich feathers, others of horse-hair, and others of skins of native animals. This department completes its exhibition with quite a full display of Argentine books published in the different departments, and including educational works, statistics, historical books, atlases, maps, digests and compilations of laws, voyages and travels, poetry, reviews, medical books, etc. Two costumed figures, representing Argentine Gauchos, will have been noticed standing at the entrance to the section. Finally, there is a collection of antediluvian relics, including a tooth weighing four pounds and seven ounces, tail-joint weighing from 18 to 30 pounds, a shin-bone and a back-tooth, from what animals is not stated, the collection being valued at $200.

TUNIS.

The section devoted to Tunis lies south of South Avenue and immediately behind Denmark, Sweden and Turkey, and occupies 2,015 feet of space. The contributions to this department include minerals and ores, essences and flavoring extracts, pottery, porcelain, glass, household furniture, carpets, rugs, woolen blankets, shawls, woven silks, hangings, burnooses, embroideries, jewelry, national costumes, arms and accoutrements. Quite a number of interesting and characteristic articles have been contributed by his Highness Sidi Mahomed Essadok, Bey of Tunis, including jewelry, national costumes, a collection of the minerals and ores of Tunis, pottery and furniture. Specimens of ancient mosaics from Carthage form an interesting feature of the Tunisian collection. Several cases of arms, damascened, are to be seen, and the woven fabrics, including cloths of gold and silver, while there are a number of articles of filigree jewelry, and an Oriental saddle of velvet and gilded embroidery. A small alcove, divided off, is furnished like a Tunisian apartment, the furniture being rather tawdry than valuable. Among the more notable articles is a solid silver table set, including a salver, ten small coffee-cups of china, set in silver filigree, and a dish of filigree shaped like a cake-basket. Among the weapons are quite a number of very antique appearance. Some of these are sharply engraved and handsomely damascened. Certain articles of furniture are inlaid with pearl, and there are mirrors with pearl inlaid frames. The carpets and rugs exhibited, as well as the shawls and hangings, are rich and heavy. The Bey of Tunis also exhibited two Arabian tents, illustrating the domestic life and customs of the Arabian Sheikhs and Bedouins.

DENMARK.

Denmark lies south of the nave and between Sweden and Turkey. Among the articles of chemical manufacture

MOONRISE AT SUNSET. — From the Painting by M. F. H. De Haas.

exhibited are stearine candles, matches, varnish, double-distilled bay-spirit and oil of bay-leaves from St. Thomas, West Indies. A very pretty display of Danish pottery in black-and-red is made, ornamented with flowers, some articles being in Etruscan forms, and those from Wendrick and Son, Copenhagen, being specially elegant. A trophy of bottles of cherry cordial is quite a prominent exhibit, and there is a considerable show of playing-cards. A glass case fixed against the wall contains a suit of clothes apparently of very fine manufacture. In clothing there are also woolen goods from the Faroe Islands; and oil, clothing and gloves, also jewelry and ornaments, from Copenhagen. From the Faroe Islands there is likewise a collection of birds, feathers, eggs, etc. A very interesting ethnographical collection is sent from Copenhagen, illustrating the products, minerals, manners and customs of Greenland. This case includes weapons and tools used by the natives; clothing, furs, eider-down and skins, stuffed native birds and a model of a kajak. There is also a Greenland kajak of the usual size, with fish, spears, paddles, etc., and a stuffed figure placed in the centre to illustrate the method of using it.

TURKEY.

The Turkish section fronts on the nave, and lies between Denmark and Egypt, comprising the same space as the latter country, 5,022 feet. This section is more truly Oriental in its character, as we understand the Oriental, than any other. It begins, properly enough, with a large case of pipes—long chibouks with red clay bowls—native jewelry of gold and silver, and enameled small coffee-cups, cups of horn, amber sets, including brooches, sleeve-buttons, etc., strings of beads, and scented wood, etc. The display of opium, essences and gums is large, and is made with great care and discrimination, illustrating effectively these peculiar Oriental articles. Of the same character is the exhibit of attar-of-rose. This finest of all perfumes is nowhere made in such perfection as among the Turks. A bottle nine inches high and about four inches in diameter sells for $120 in gold, besides the duty; a little

bottle holding not much more than a gill is marked $50. The wines and liquors of Turkey are illustrated pretty completely, including brandy, muscat, Samos wines, etc. A case of curious green pottery is attractive, the forms of the articles being peculiar. There are also some black

STATUE, "FLYING TIME."

tea-sets, ornamented with what seems to be silver-foil. Turkish tobacco, and the fine Macedonian tobacco, are exhibited in bunches, bowls, casks, and in cigarettes. Opium is also displayed in masses wrapped in leaves. Curiously enough, a principal exhibit is a large case filled with rosaries, crosses, caskets, paper-knives and other articles made of olive-wood, and reported to have come from the Mount of Olives; although this is probably apocryphal, and the wood is likely enough to have come from Spain or some other southern European country. A case of native arms includes scimitars, guns, helmets, etc., all heavily engraved, and displaying very fine workmanship. There is a good show of rugs and carpets; also of Turkish shawls and other garments, the fez being prominent in numbers. Quite a large display is made of crude silk, wool and flax, including wool of various grades in small bags, silk in the rough, in skeins, etc., and cocoons classified in jars according to quality and color.

A variety of leather-work makes a very handsome show, and includes a display of prepared skins heaped up in the rear of the section. Here are also fine leather leggins, saddle-bags, belts, etc., and a variety of bead-work on leather, which is curious. Perhaps the prettiest collection of the department is a case of goods of carved mother-of-pearl, said to be manufactured in Bethlehem. The articles are all small, the largest being carvings of the pearl oyster-shell; the centre piece is a cross of native wood. The remaining articles are crosses, earrings, buttons, strings of beads, etc. The Turkish carpets deserve all praise. In some particulars they are pre-eminent, and are worthy of the high repute in which they are held all over the world. The vividness of colors and originality of design of these fabrics defy competition. The texture of the goods is among their strongest points. A few skins of animals are shown, including a tiger-skin. A number of domestic articles in brass and copper, including vegetable-dishes, water-jars, etc., are interesting as being peculiar to the country. The gauze fabrics of silks, with shining bands of gold or silver thread, alternating with gay stripes of scarlet, green and white, are strikingly Oriental, as are also the velvet jackets, heavy with gold bullion, the tissues of the mixed silk and cotton covered with gold embroidery, the scarlet table-spreads with intricate tracery of arabesques in gold threads and colored silks, and slippers of green and scarlet leather, with pointed toes. Fine Turkish towelings and gauze muslins, with heavy brocade goods, and a lavish amount of embroidery in various materials, complete the Turkish exhibit of fabrics, and with them we close our description of this section.

EGYPT.

The section devoted to Egypt lies between those of Turkey and Spain, and fronts upon the nave. It comprises 5,022 feet of space. Here is seen, on entering the section, a large display of native woods from Egypt and the annexed provinces, including the cotton-tree, and also samples of gums and materials for dyeing, and other vegetable articles for industrial purposes. There is also a very large case full of silk cocoons and manufactured silk, while cotton and tobacco are seen in considerable quantities, as well as specimens of sugar, and even of bread manufactured in that country. The minerals and building-stones of Egypt are exhibited in rough-hewn and polished specimens, including alabaster, limestone, lime-rock, clay, cement, plaster, sand, and materials for manufacturing porcelain and faience. The exhibits of metals include iron, gold-dust and solid rough gold pieces. A number of articles of Egyptian manufacture are exposed, and a large case of books, in the Arabic language, including school and text-books, newspapers and periodical literature, illustrate the educational system of the country. The Polytechnic School of Cairo sends a number of tools, and quite a display is made of articles of pottery from Assouan, Upper Egypt, showing the styles of Egyptian earthenware, with porcelain tiles and bricks from Lower Egypt, contributed by the National Museum. Specimens of majolica-ware of different designs, and porcelain, are contributed by Brugsch Bey, of Cairo. The National Museum also displays table-furniture, porcelain, solid gold and silverware, coffee-sets, and vessels of brass, utensils for kitchen use, and tinware. The clothing, jewelry and ornaments, traveling equipments, etc., are contributed by the National Museum, and include dress-goods for men's and women's wear, hats and boots, women's shoes, embroidered in velvet, silk, gold and silver; silk dress-trimmings and embroideries woven with gold and silver; turquoise jewelry and ornaments worn upon the person; fans, walking-canes, sun-shades, with pipes of all descriptions, and a historical collection of national costumes from Abyssinia and the Soudan. There is also, from the same source, an exhibition of swords, spears and dirks. A number of small articles are exhibited manufactured of shell, ivory and mother-of-pearl, including spoons, egg-cups, small coffee-cups, etc.; pipe-bowls of red clay and pipe-stems of perfumed jasmine are notable articles. The array of native weapons and accoutrements is very large. In furniture there are a number of magnificent pieces. One of these is a cabinet made of sycamore and acacia, inlaid with ivory and pearl. This is engraved by hand, both upon

THE SEGUR EXHIBIT, IN THE MAIN BUILDING.

wood and ivory, in highly finished style. The price of this piece of furniture is $2,500; a black-wood cabinet with mother-of-pearl inlaying is priced $4,000. A curiosity is a door made in a most peculiar manner, the figures which appear upon the face being pieces of wood inserted from the back in a manner quite unlike anything else in the exhibition, not being mosaic, or even of that character. It is stated that this kind of work is only made by one family in Egypt. Some of the fabrics exhibited here are truly magnificent. Velvet with heavy gold embroidery, wool, fancy silk, etc. A stuffed crocodile from the Nile, standing near the centre of the section, is a notable object, and a very curious inlaid gate of a mosque in Cairo, a very antique article, is another. Still another curiosity is a photographic copy of the Koran in a little volume about 1½ inches by ¾ of an inch in dimensions and ⅓ of an inch thick. Magnificent saddles, covered with velvet and gold embroidery, chibouks, with gold embroidery covering, narghiles of Bohemian glass, and large lanterns, complete the collection of Egyptian articles.

PORTUGAL.

The Portuguese section is south of South Avenue and immediately behind that of Egypt, and includes 3,590 feet of space. Decidedly the most important display in the Portuguese department is made in the direction of fabrics and woven goods of wool and silk, and in clothing, jewelry and ornaments. The exhibition of articles of filigree and jewelry is comprised in three large cases, and is of the finest possible character, comparing favorably with any similar exhibit in the Exhibition. In woven goods, commencing with those of the coarsest character, we find grass and straw mats; also marsh-reed matting, coarse fabrics of rushes, and plaited straw articles, manufactured from the Guinea aloe fibre, and all kinds of floor-matting from the coarsest quality to the finest article for the drawing-room. In cotton there are exhibited yarns and fabrics, bleached and unbleached, including canvas, toweling, counterpanes, embroidered table-cloths, cotton prints, handkerchiefs, etc.; and linen articles, such as towels, napkins, table-cloths, duck, linen yarns, striped linen counterpanes, and some very curious vases made of linen thread. Woolen cloths are exhibited from Saragossa, Lisbon, Oporto, etc., and include everything from plain flannel and coarse blankets up to fine poplins, and cassimeres and cloths. Silk is shown from a cocoon to the manufactured article, including raw silk, spun silk, twisted silk, woven silk, satin and gold damasks, figured silks, gold tissues, serges, satins, velvets, figured satin, handkerchiefs, brocatelles, fine samples of black velvet, fringes, braids, etc. All sorts of articles of clothing are exhibited, including colored petticoats, shawls, knitted hose, sashes, men's jackets, laces, crochet-work, artificial flowers, hats, gaiters, military boots and gloves, wooden shoes, peasants' shoes, reed and straw hats, cork hats, woolen caps, knitted stockings, etc. The show of pottery includes a number of articles in majolica, earthenware and faience, some of these being figures illustrating the costumes of the country. A peculiar exhibit is a number of small figures, about one foot in height, representing types of the national costumes, trades and avocations; a case of fine chinaware and one of musical instruments are also noticeable; and the display of minerals and native stones and marbles is very complete and important. One large case, filled with damask-work, cutlery, etc., is also not uninteresting. The display of books of an educational and

statistical character is quite large and important, as is also that of scientific and philosophical instruments, works upon engineering, maps, plans, models, bridges, charts, etc. The display of photographs is very handsome, including one of the King of Portugal, Dom Luis I., this collection showing a very creditable progress in the photographic art. The mineral exhibit from Portugal includes antimony ore, copper ore, iron ores, lead and zinc ores, manganese, tin ore, galena, iron pyrites, coal, limestones, marbles, slate, hydraulic cement, phosphate of lime, kaolin, whetstones, and pumice. The metallurgical products exhibited are gold and silver, bar and leaf; aluminium, platina and tin leaf, iron and tin ingots, and an exhibit of horse-shoes. Quite a number of mineral waters are exhibited from Lisbon, Oporto and San Miguel.

SPAIN.

The space allotted to Spain in the Main Building extends from the nave to the southern wall of the structure, and comprises 11,253 feet. Beginning at the wall of this section we find cases of clothing, toys, hats, large numbers of slippers and other miscellaneous articles, and a considerable display of cordage and straw-work cases, containing fans and articles in straw boxes, etc., and near by are a few models of the Philippine Islands small-craft in use by the natives of those islands. A case containing Spanish decorations and medals is seen here, and is peculiar and interesting. Next we come upon the exhibits of fabrics, which are wonderfully comprehensive, and in fact the finest show in the section. The cloths are peculiar in quality as well as in name. They include llama cloths, paten cloth, tricot, edredon, satin, corduroy, velvet, etc., chiefly from the provinces of Alicante and the city of Alcoy. Besides these are the more commonly known cloths, melton, tweeds, serges, flannels, etc., chiefly from Toledo and Barcelona. The number of shawls is enormous, in every variety and quality, including cases of the well-known and attractive blond-lace shawls for which Spain is so famous. The exhibits of muslins and prints of

BELGIAN CARVED PULPIT.

BOUCHÉ FILS & CO.'S EXHIBIT OF BITTER-WATER, IN THE MAIN BUILDING.

the patterns peculiar to the lower classes of the Spanish peasantry are quite wonderful in their extent and variety. In fact, they are innumerable, of every conceivable design, and interesting as displaying the distinctions of the Spanish people. Here a large case of women's corsets is conspicuous. A considerable show of carpets, hung from above, is also to be seen, and a fine display of blankets, floor-cloths, table-cloths and rugs. Next are the finer qualities of dress-goods, calico-goods, linens, underwear and embroidered work; and next a circular case containing the inevitable Spanish fan in every possible form and quality; woolen cloths for gentlemen's clothing, boots and shoes come next, and after these a truly magnificent display of silk and brocade goods and satins. A grand exhibition of shirts is made in two enormous cases from Barcelona and Catalonia, and a superb show of blond-laces also occurs here. The collection of shoe-coverings includes varieties little known in this country. There are sandals, boots and shoes, and slippers—"slip-shods," as they are called; riding-boots, clogs, sabots, sandals for women, and in fact every conceivable pattern of coverings for the feet. Hats and gloves are not wanting, kid-gloves being exhibited by the city of Seville, and hats from Havana, Cuba. Some very handsome articles of embroidery are exhibited, including embroidered pictures, church ornaments, embroidered altar-cloths, lithographed embroidery, sofa-cushions, handkerchiefs, while His Majesty the King of Spain exhibits embroidery made by the lay brothers of San Lorenzo. The straw-work peculiar to Spain is interesting, and includes a large variety of articles. There are baskets and needle-cases of straw, ladies' work-boxes covered with straw, glove-boxes of the same, straw hampers, match-boxes of straw, etc. There are also some specimens of human hair-work from Madrid, which are curious. In miscellaneous articles there are canes and cane-heads, combs of horn and tortoise-shell, cigarette-paper in quantities, playing-cards, toothpicks, case of filigree silver, cross and earrings of the same, and church ornaments exhibited by the President of the Women's Catholic Association of Madrid. In arms there are a hunting-knife, Arabian sword-blade, dagger-blade, a dagger from Toledo; a sword, dagger and shield from San Sebastian; pistols, etc. A collection of medals from Madrid may be classed among the miscellaneous art-objects. Returning to the natural products of Spain, we find minerals largely represented, including all the better known ores, cobalt, cinnabar, argentiferous lead, stalactites from the province of Burgos, yellow and red ochre, quicksilver, malachite, blue copper, nickel, and a large variety of specimens of coal and coke. The stones exhibited include alabaster, marble, granite and jasper; lava and volcanic products from Teneriffe, Canary Islands; serpentine, gypsum, spar, whetstones, grindstones and jet; a considerable display of ferruginous, sulphurous and other mineral waters from the various provinces. Quite a number of exhibits are made in tiles and pottery for flooring; and there is some very fine metallic-work, handsomely damascened, in vases, swords, boxes, etc., glass-bottles, china-ware and terra-cotta, including some specimens of china exhibited by His Majesty the King of Spain; mosaics from Seville and the province of Tarragona; Delft pitchers from Cordoba; antique vases from Murcia; and glass, chiefly from Barcelona, although some plate-glass and a crystal lantern are exhibited from the province of Santander. In furniture there is a dressing-table, a couch from Barcelona, and a dining-room sideboard from Madrid; wooden curtains from Havana are novel, and the articles manufactured from esparto-grass are also peculiar to Spain. In default of an English catalogue of the Spanish articles, and owing also to the fact that the Spanish catalogue, even, was very late in making its appearance, it is impossible to make a just showing of the really superb display in the

Spanish section. It is proper, however, to direct attention to the fact that perhaps the most interesting portion of this display is in the fabrics and laces, which we have been able only to barely mention.

RUSSIA.

The Russian section lies next to that of Spain, and between it and the Austria-Hungary department, and extends from the nave to the southern wall of the Main Building, comprising 11,802 feet of space. This section is in some parts one of the most interesting and important in the Main Building, and it must be conceded that although the Russian Government was slow in making up its mind to participate in the Centennial Exhibition, yet when it did decide, it acted with great energy and liberality. The Government undertook the payment of freight and insurance to and from Philadelphia, and all expenses of installation, including the purchase of show-cases. No part of the Exhibition has more richly repaid careful study; and this chiefly from the fact that the Russian display differs from those of England and France, no matter how magnificent these may be, in that it comprises works in the arts and manufactures hitherto totally unknown to Americans. A vast improvement in art-industry in Russia has taken place in late years, and it was only at the Exhibition of 1867 that this great country was able to make a display which could compete with the nations of Western Europe. All this progress has been owing to the School of Technical

THE BISON AT BAY.—FROM THE PAINTING BY W. J. HAYS.

Design, founded in Moscow in 1864, and which makes a fine exhibit in the Russian section, displaying the system of education employed, and the progress of its pupils, as illustrated in plaster casts, patterns for textile fabrics and wall-papers, and other art-works. It is in the richness and the magnificence of its exhibits that Russia strikes the observer as being superior to all other sections. Whether it be in the novel specimens of silverware or in the fine and elegant enameled-ware, the massive and costly articles of malachite, or the superb furs, it is all grand and illustrative of lavish wealth and liberality.

The cases of fur garments cannot be surpassed in the magnificence and value of the articles. Here is a Russian sable cloak, valued at $2,000; a blue foxskin cloak for $350; muffs of Thibet goat, blue-fox and sealskin; lynx, sable and marten coats, trimmed with sheepskin; a carpet of furs in mosaic; bearskins; ermine-skins; and on either side of the fur case two immense Russian bears standing on their hind legs, veritable "dumb-waiters." One holds in his paws an armful of sealskins worth from $30 to $45 a skin. Deer-horn chairs, upholstered, and tête-à-têtes of the same structure are here, and also a little foot-stool covered with foxskin with the fox's head prominent. Above the case are two stuffed martens.

The silks, brocades and tissue goods are rich and handsome, the most magnificent being the rich altar-cloths and materials for priest vestments, red velvets and flowers of gold, black satin embroidery with flowers and gold figures

woven with gold thread; silver cloths—altogether the heaviest and richest fabrics to be seen anywhere.

The Russian department opens at the nave with a beautiful show of gold and silver plated-ware and jewelry. Here are plain bands of gold, set on the edge with rows of pearl and turquoise. Here, too, are elaborate dishes in gold and silver, or heavily gilt; curious *repoussé* work, the figures of which are beaten out by hand from the under side, and any quantity of silver bowls lined with gold, silver cups and tankards, gold knife, cigar-cases, inkstands—in fact, all conceivable articles in ornamental work. Next to this is the show of malachite, jasper and lapis-lazuli. This is a peculiar Russian industry, the articles being manufactured from a variety of ornamental stones found in the Ural Mountains, although some of the stones used come from Labrador. Very few articles have attracted more attention than these. Here is a large mantel of malachite, with a mosaic front, comprising perhaps twenty different stones, with carved fruit-work, and which is valued at $6,500. Malachite vases, about 3½ feet high, each cut from a single block of stone, cost $4,500 a pair, while the smaller size, about 18 inches high, is valued at $650. The malachite and lapis-lazuli tables range in price between $100 and $1,000. A great variety of small articles are made of these stones, and are sold at very moderate prices. These include brooches, necklaces, bracelets, studs, sleeve-buttons, crosses, etc., in personal ornaments; clocks, paper-weights, small vases, etc. Among the striking ornamental exhibits in this section is a large circular plaque in high *repoussé* relief, representing the Adoration of the Shepherds. This is valued at $7,000. A Cossack chief mounting his horse, exceedingly spirited, and worked with microscopic and most minute detail, costs $1,670; and a cup with figures of peasants dancing, is valued at $1,070. One kind of work, which is quite common among the Russians, is novel in design and perfect in execution. It consists of a cake-basket of gold-and-bronze, on which lies a white damask napkin, which appears at first sight to be linen, but which is really silver, with the fibres and pattern of cloth imitated so perfectly that the illusion is complete. In some, this napkin has a colored border, and in others it forms the covering of a punch-bowl. None of the articles of this class in the Russian department show any signs of French or Italian styles, but are purely Muscovite and original in design and structure. The fabrics of silver and gold thread, heavily embroidered, surpass anything of the kind exhibited by the Oriental nations, which are supposed to excel in this work.

The dress silks, woolen goods, cotton and linen fabrics, rival those of France and England. Among these a most attractive and interesting collection of garments and table-spreads comes from Circassia, and is richly embroidered in silk and in gold-and-silver threads. Some specimens of work in carved woods are exhibited by an Industrial School in St. Petersburg, under government patronage. The most noticeable object in this collection is a peasant's chair in black-walnut, across the seat of which lies an imitation towel, made of some white wood; the handles are of the form of hatchets; at the back of the seat lie a pair of mittens, admirably carved, and in the frame is the characteristic motto, in the Russian language, "Go slow and you will go far." Returning to the malachite articles, it is to be observed that these rank among the special lions of the Exhibition with the London ceramics, Japan bronzes, and the China ivory carving. They took this position from the start, and persistently maintained it. Usually the malachite is used alone, although there is an exception in the case of two sideboards, where walnut-wood is used for the framework of the articles; the malachite is set in as panels, the effect being rich and peculiar. Malachite is in one sense a precious stone, since the larger pieces are very

THE FRENCH ART GALLERY, IN MEMORIAL HALL

valuable, while a similar amount in bulk, if broken up into a number of smaller articles, is worth comparatively little. This variation is caused by the scarcity, and the difficulty of mining the larger specimens. An interesting exhibit is a large lump of the material as it comes from the earth. The finest article on exhibition is a table with a top of solid malachite, having an urn of the same material suspended underneath, with the stone vases, priced at $2,400. Another smaller table is valued at $1,500. The sideboards just mentioned are held at $900 each. In the display of jewelry is a novel exhibition of gold ornaments in delicate gradations of red, produced by oxidation. One article which attracts much attention is a breast-pin made in the form of a rose-leaf, upon which has alighted a jeweled bee, the body being formed of a magnificent pearl, the head of rubies, and the wings of diamonds. A case of printed cotton goods, calicoes, chintz, etc., shows that Russia has attained a degree of excellence in this important manufacture not greatly differing from that of England, France or the United States. The fabric is good, the design artistic and graceful, and the coloring brilliant. There is also a good showing of linens and other Russian manufactures, including table-cloths, toweling, napkins, the famous "crash," and various other preparations of flax. Among these articles are some patterns of colored napkins, which have not yet been seen in the American market. The cases of velvet suits constitute a wonderful display, a magnificent royal purple cloak being the finest in the collection. Some of these are richly trimmed with fur. The braid-work exhibited in this section is much finer than anything of the sort elsewhere in the Exposition. The style is a close resemblance to the Turkish. A very pretty collection is made in articles of amber, including colored varieties in cigar-tubes, jewelry and beads. There is also a small but very choice collection of lacquer-boxes, adorned with miniature paintings. These are quite like the Japanese work. A surprising exhibit is a case of india-rubber goods. The Russian-American india-rubber Company of St. Petersburg was founded in 1860. The works are furnished with twelve steam engines of 700-horse-power, and employ 1,378 working-people, men and women. An American industry which has only recently been introduced in Russia, where it has met with remarkable success, is the manufacture of zinc, the product amounting to $5,000,000 per year. The pavilion containing this exhibit is of ebony, and very ornamental and attractive. There are cases of scimitars and other arms, and also surgical and other instruments. Pianos are not wanting, and there is even a billiard-table exhibited.

The display of minerals from Russia is extensive, and includes the usual varieties. Some of the mining works of Russia are quite enormous, those of Prince Demidof employing 11,000 men, of whom 4,500 are engaged in supplying the works with fuel and other materials. The collection of minerals, fossils and rocks natural to Russia are exhibited by the Mining School of St. Petersburg, while the administration of the mining district in Western Poland exhibits specimens of coal with plans of the pits. This district contains not only coal-pits, but also zinc-smelting works, iron-forges, and iron rolling-mills; and a mine explored in the Middle Ages. The present yearly produce amounts to 80,000 tons of coal, and large quantities of zinc, cast-iron and wrought-iron. Prince Demidof also exhibits clay, quartz, hearthstone and common brick, besides specimens of gold, platinum and native gold. Also cast-iron, manganese, pig-iron, raw copper, copper in ingots, bar iron, boiler-plates, ship-plates, steel in bars, etc. The Russian Rolling Manufacturing Company, exhibiting cast-iron and iron wire, was founded in 1872, and employs 1,000 men. The Armory Plate Works in the Government of Perm, founded in 1862, employs 680 men. These works exhibit specimens of iron plate and corrugated iron sheets. Stearine candles, glycerine, glue, tallow, linseed and other oils and soap are exhibited by a number of companies and manufactories. One chemical manufactory, founded in 1855, employs 1,000 workmen, and manufactures to the value of 3,500,000 roubles annually, a rouble being about seventy-five cents. Cosmetics, phosphorus matches, gunpowder and fire-proof bricks are among the manufactured articles exhibited. Enameled plates, vases, dishes, etc., are exhibited from St. Petersburg, the designs being in Russian, Byzantine and Arabian style. The Museum of

Fine Arts applied to Industry, attached to the Strogonoff School of Design of Moscow, sent articles in porcelain and faience, with designs in the Russian style; dishes, jugs, goblets, wooden cans, boxes, tea-pots, sugar-vases, etc. The malachite articles come from the establishment of Hessrich & Wöerful, of St. Petersburg. A cotton manufactory in Moscow, which exhibits calico and cotton yarns, was founded in 1847, and employs 2,000 workmen. A weaving manufactory in the Government of Moscow, exhibiting cotton stuffs, calicoes, etc., employs 2,150 men. Many such factories exist in Russia, employing anywhere from 300 to 1,500 workmen. One such manufactory making a special cloth prepared from camel's wool was founded in 1819, and employs 700 men, its annual product being valued at 200,000 roubles; another, making only shirt-fronts and silk ties in Warsaw, employs 500 workmen, and manufactures to the amount of a million roubles annually. A glove-factory in Moscow makes from 14,000 to 15,000 dozens of gloves, and employs 400 men. The articles of embroidery in gold come chiefly from the Moscow workshop founded in 1859, wherein the working-people are women, and number 120. There exists in Moscow a Society for the Encouragement of Women's Labor, which

STATUE, "LOVE'S MESSENGER."

exhibits embroidered linen handkerchiefs, table-cloths, towels, etc. The articles in amber come from Ostrolenko, in the Government of Lomza, and the establishment of Bernstein Brothers, founded in 1798. A very interesting exhibit comprises Russian national costumes, including kaftans worn by Russian ladies, and articles of dress for boys and girls from St. Petersburg. In military and other firearms there are infantry and cavalry guns, muskets, field-guns, cast-steel guns, rifles; daggers of silver, with niello, swords inlaid with gold and silver, damascened blades, yataghans, hunters' knives in silver setting, daggers in cast and damask steel. In medicines we have specimens of drugs exported from Russia, a collection of surgical instruments, apparatus for embalming, a veterinary surgeon's case, artificial teeth, india-rubber bands for stammerers; and, curiously enough, from Warsaw, "American drops and elixir for toothache." The display of cutlery and metallic apparatus is large, and includes knives of all sorts, scissors, needles, razors, bronze candlesticks, articles in bronze, models of the Czar and "Ivan," the great bell at Moscow, silver basin for water, articles in bronze, samples of wire, nails, tacks, bells, etc.; papier-maché articles are shown in albums, tea-caddies, portmanteaus, snuff-boxes, cigar and cigarette-cases, match-boxes, etc.; ornamental articles of

wood are seen, some of these being household utensils, wooden tureens, spoons, carved wooden toys, candlesticks, etc. As in other sections, there are here painted figures in clay representing Russian types. A collection of Russian coins and metals is exhibited. The articles in silver and bronze come chiefly from Moscow and St. Petersburg. They include tankards, goblets, pitchers, vases, cigar-cases, match-boxes and articles of church furniture, ornamented with enamel, chased and figure-work. A number of carvings in cypress-wood, representing the leading events related in the Holy Scriptures, form a curious and interesting exhibit. Other carvings in wood of heads and busts, and articles cut in bone, including a crucifix, brooch, thimble and models of furniture, are peculiar exhibits. In mosaic-work there are seen a butterfly on a box for stamps, very prettily constructed. Bronze articles come from St. Petersburg, including chandeliers, candelabra, lamps, etc.; bronze clocks, furniture for a chimney-piece, etc., are exhibited by Felix Chopin, of St. Petersburg, whose manufactory was founded in 1865, and employs 1,500 workmen.

AUSTRIA.

The department allotted to the exhibits of Austria and Hungary extends south of the nave to the south wall of the Main Building, and between the Russian and German sections, occupying 24,070 feet of space.

This collection commences with a magnificent show of glass-ware and a display of meerschaum pipes and amber, with which there is no competition. Here is to be seen the superb glass-ware of Bohemia in innumerable articles; these including manufacturing establishments never before shown in this country. The exhibits include colored, stained and white sheet-glass, plain cut glass, common glass vessels, wine-bottles, table-glass, mirrors cast and blown, Bohemian crystal hollow ware of all kinds, many of the articles colored and stained, and otherwise exquisitely decorated; also refined glass, sets of table service, vases, miscellaneous articles of fancy and ornamental glass, mounted with bronze, as vases, inkstands, cigar-plates, flagons, etc. Besides these articles, there are wreaths of glass pearls, and glass cylinders of crystal, all from Bohemia. These articles are exported to Germany, France, Belgium, Italy, South America, etc. The wreaths consist of plaits of glass pearls, and are used for ornamenting graves, on account of their beauty and durability. There are also exhibits of glass silk and spinnings, and small articles such as buttons and trinkets. This entire display is exceptionally brilliant and attractive.

Several cases of articles in meerschaum, one of which stands immediately upon the nave, have attracted great and persistent attention during the Exhibition. The firm exhibiting these is that of Ludwig Hartman and Eidam (which means son-in-law). Here a magnificent carved pipe is exhibited, valued at $600, and an amber flower-vase at $250. The most costly article in the case may be said to be absolutely unique. It is a chandelier constructed entirely of amber, and believed to be the finest piece of work ever made in this material. Upon this structure eight men labored for five months, while it took two years to obtain amber of the desired color for its manufacture. The value of the article is set at $8,000.

Beside the meerschaum pipes, there are others of French brier-wood, and still others of the Australian myoll, with amber mouth-pieces. Smokers' cases containing pipe, etc., made of walnut, are marked $25. This firm of Hartman, in Vienna, began trade in the year 1829 with one single turning-lathe, and has worked its way up to its present business, which is valued at 300,000 florins per annum, of which all but one-tenth is exported. The establishment employs one hundred operatives and uses steam power.

Next after the meerschaum comes the exhibition of china, porcelain and pottery, including reproductions after the antique, such as vieux Saxe, vieux Sèvres, ancient Vienna, Chinese and Japanese. One establishment exhibiting has been for thirty years engaged in reproducing antique porcelains after the most excellent models of the best periods. This establishment exhibited at the International Exhibition of New York in 1853. The business is conducted in Vienna, by Samuel Von Fischer, and it is related that Alexander Von Humboldt, in a letter addressed to the factory in the year 1857, expressed himself to the effect that in his extensive travels he never met with anything so perfect in its line as the productions of this porcelain-ware manufacturer.

The porcelain manufactory of Count Thun, in Bohemia, displays dinner-table, coffee and washing services richly decorated, and other porcelain articles in great variety. This manufactory was established in the year 1794, and until 1820 its production was confined to tobacco-pipes, cups and saucers and small articles; but after 1822, being chartered by the Government, it began to produce dinner and coffee services, and other articles for use and luxury. An average number of 400 workmen are employed, their daily labor being about ten hours. This establishment makes richly furnished services, furniture knobs, buttons and studs, and many other articles, to the value of about 250,000 florins per annum.

A manufacturer of Prague exhibits miscellaneous wares, including pyramidal chimney-stoves, enameled; also figures and pictures enameled in fire on clay slabs. This manufactory employs from fifty to sixty workmen. Handsome exhibits are made of embossed and otherwise ornamented leather goods, ormolu and other ornamental work in jewel-cases, card-receivers, etc.

In jewelry a very fine display is seen, including gold and silver, niello and enamel. Two cases are especially admirable in their contents of turquoises and garnets in jewelry, as also a case of garnets and carbuncles. Gold chain work is exhibited, also cut opals in some magnificent specimens, the Bohemian garnet articles being a specialty. A large case of imitation gems of great brilliancy and peculiarly excellent workmanship has attracted considerable attention.

In bronze there is a joint exhibition of manufacturers in Vienna, including candelabra, inkstands, candlesticks, vases, epergnes, writing-table furniture, photograph frames, fancy ornaments, etc., in large variety. The exhibition of mother-of-pearl articles is also considerable, and is a joint display on the part of Vienna manufacturers. It includes mother-of-pearl buttons and fancy articles of all sorts. A small case containing crystals set in ivory, also in buffalo-horn, is curious.

A specimen of wood-carving has also attracted much attention. It represents the Emperor Maximilian I. entering Vienna after the departure of the Turks in 1490. It is about 22 x 15 inches in dimensions, and is exquisitely carved—the number of figures of soldiers being very great, and the features being cut with the greatest exactness.

In the Austrian department is seen the largest show of chromos exhibited in the Exposition. Some of these are well known from having been seen in the picture-stores in our chief cities, and many of them are exquisite copies after fine paintings.

The show of gloves and articles of clothing is very large, the work in textile fabrics being generally highly creditable. One establishment in Vienna exhibits flowered shawls of great beauty. This manufactory was established in 1831, but did not commence making these shawls until 1852, since which time it has produced all varieties of flowered long-shawls and antique cloths, not only of wool, silk and cotton, but also of India and Cashmere wool. Later there have been added to its manufacture plain and brocaded cashmere shawls. Twelve designers are continually occupied in drawing patterns for shawls and embroidery. The number of operatives vary between 500 and 1,200, averaging about 1,000, and during the last five years these have produced 43,419 different shawls.

Other establishments exhibit dressing-gowns, gentlemen's wearing apparel of extra fine quality, one establishment at Prague being particularly noticeable in this direction. This concern was founded in 1834, and numbers among its customers several members of the Imperial family, as well as the nobility and gentry of Austria, and even patrons in Germany, Russia, and another employs 82 persons, and exports largely to Germany, its proprietor having been decorated by the Emperor of Austria with the Golden Cross of Merit, on account of the manufacturer's industrial endeavors. Still another Vienna house in the clothing business has branch establishments at Presburg, Bucharest, St. Petersburg, Moscow, Odessa, Warsaw and other cities, devoting itself to gentlemen's and boys' clothing. Such samples of clothing as are seen from Austrian houses fully bear out the high reputation of its manufactures.

Large displays of worsted yarns are made, also samples of quilted swan-skins, bleached cotton yarns, linen and cotton threads, table-linen, miscellaneous woolen fabrics, carpets, rugs and coverlets; likewise velveteens, silk and mixed silk manufactures, taffetas, gros-grain silk, velvets and embroideries, ribbons, velvet ribbons, lace-fringe and laces, and in fact every imaginable manufacture in fabrics. The kid gloves come chiefly from Prague, and include leather gloves and gloves of chamois or lamb-skin. One manufacturer employs 75 persons in cutting out and 600 females in sewing an average annual production of 21,600 dozens. The display of the joint exhibition of Vienna glove-makers is extensive and very fine.

In silk and felt hats, crushed hats, etc., and in fine boots and shoes, the exhibits are very commendable, as are also those in lace lappets, lace tippets, fans, handkerchiefs, covers for sun-shades and other lace articles. From Bohemia there are specimens of thread-lace, Chantilly lace, and from Galicia domestic hand-laces.

The bronze and leather fancy articles are chiefly from Vienna, including portable writing-desks in great variety,

JAPANESE VASE.

pocket match-boxes, traveling candlesticks, etc. One concern employs 44 operatives, and produced in 1875 10,300 dozens of articles.

Printing-paper, marble-paper, cigarette-paper, lamp-shades and lace papers are sent from Vienna. A fine show of musical instruments is made, both brass and string. Finally, and returning to the exhibit of Bohemian glass, particular attention should be directed to the exhibit of Count Harrach, of Bohemia, whose display of refined glass, fancy and ornamental glass, sets of table-service, vases, etc., is exquisite.

Mention should also be made of the bent-wood display of a Moravian firm, whose principal factories are at Wsetin and Vienna. The number of workmen employed by this concern is between three and four thousand, and 30,000 cubic metres of timber are worked up every year into about 500,000 pieces of furniture of all kinds, representing an average value of 1,300,000 florins, 85 per cent. of which are exported. The production of household furniture from bent-wood is an invention of Michael Thonet, Sr., a native of Boppart, on the Rhine, where he had a manufactory of furniture, and began in 1835 to apply the contrivance of bending wood to sundry parts of pieces of furniture, until he succeeded, after untiring assiduity and perseverance, in executing complete pieces of furniture of bent-wood. In 1850 he founded, with his five sons, the first manufactory of this kind in Vienna. The establishment of Thonet Bros. now has five manufactories in Moravia and Hungary, with branches at Vienna, Pesth, Berlin, Hamburg, Amsterdam, Brussels, Paris, London, New York and Chicago. They employ 4,500 persons, two-thirds of whom are females. Their factories produce 2,000 pieces of furniture per diem, and their articles have been distinguished at twenty-one exhibitions with first class medals.

A manufacturer of parquetry and veneers exhibits specimens of his works which are very pleasing and ingenious.

In the way of minerals the Austrian exhibit includes the common ores and metals, and also the manganese, specular iron, white lead and rough opals from Hungary. Of chemical manufactures there are volatile oils, medicines, glycerine and toilet soaps from Vienna; cosmetics and pomades and perfumes, these latter coming chiefly from an establishment in Prague, which dates back to 1777, and where, owing to the extensive use of machinery, only thirty men are employed, exportation being made to Holland, Germany, Denmark and England. There are also stearine, paraffine and artificial wax candles, soaps; manufactured oil extracted from the hazel; tapers, Christmas lights, thread wax, cobbler's wax and flower wax from cerecine, and artificial wax made at a manufactory near Vienna, which employs 400 persons, and manufactures very largely.

The well-known Pullna bitter waters are exhibited in clay jugs, as are also other mineral waters from Hungary and Austria. Altogether, it should be said of the Austria and Hungary exhibition, that in its specialties of Bohemian glass, meerschaum and amber and fine clothing, it offers attractions in fair competition with any other department in the Main Building.

GERMAN EMPIRE.

Next to Austria, and extending from that section to the transept, facing across the nave, the department of the German Empire occupies 27,705 feet of space. The exhibits in the German section are classified into departments: mining, chemical, manufacturing, book-trade and printing, clocks and musical instruments, etc.

The display of minerals is considerable, comprising joint exhibitions from different sections of country, some of which are extremely interesting. Among these should be mentioned the exhibits of raw amber, for ornamental and industrial purposes from Berlin and Königsberg, where the business was established in 1855, and employs nearly 3,000 workmen in dredging, diving and mining the article; the annual production being two thousand hundred weight. Pieces of amber with inclosed insects are curiosities in this line.

A very fine show is made of tufa as used in the manufacture of vases, aquaria, etc. There is also a show of flagstones, lithographic-stones, cement, mosaic, asphalt for paving, mill-stones, sandstone for polishing wood, and other varieties of stone. An exhibit is made of the celebrated Frederickshall bitter water by the proprietors of the springs at Frederickshall, which were discovered about thirty years ago.

The show of metals comprises iron, steel, stamped plate, rolled T iron 48 feet in length, iron ores, pig iron, iron-stone, lead ores, pyrites, cast-steel for tools and arms, copper and brass tubing, zinc, etc. The value of the iron manufacture of Germany is enormous, nearly equaling that of the United States, and the industry is found scattered all over the country. Exhibits of salt are made from the great deposits of rock and potassium salts of Stassfurt.

The chemical industry of Germany is illustrated to a fuller extent and in more minute detail than is the case with any other country, although the principal products of this industry in Germany, mineral acids, soda and bleaching-powders, are scarcely represented at the Centennial on account of the high duties on these products rendering their export from Germany to the United States impossible, while competition with England in this direction would scarcely prove successful. At present Germany produces, for instance, as much carbonate of potash as England and France taken together. For alkaloids it has a large number of establishments, and the exportation of chloral hydrate is of considerable importance. Essential oils, for the preparation of which this country has long

SANDWICH ISLAND BOAT.

been renowned, are represented by the products of a large number of famous establishments. Of mineral colors, ultramarine is by far the most important, and Germany exports four times as much of this as all other countries together, her annual production amounting to the value of $2,500,000. Germany is noted for her production of aniline colors, although the exhibition in this direction at the Centennial is small. Soaps, perfumes, toilet articles, glue, varnish and inks are exhibited with considerable freedom, these articles being largely exported to America. Paraffine candles form another German specialty in this department, as are also essential oils and essences, and of course the world-renowned cologne of Farina. A joint exhibition is made of metal foils and bronze powder from Bavaria, the two towns of Nuremberg and Fürth having more than 250 establishments engaged in this manufacture. This includes articles in fine rolled, or gold and silver plated, or colored copper wire, a branch of industry peculiar to Nuremberg since the end of the sixteenth century, and only found elsewhere in a few neighboring towns.

The present manufacturers of the Farina cologne are Johann Maria Farina and F. Maria Farina, both of the city of Cologne. The establishment dates from 1709.

The exhibition of porcelain-ware, though considerable, bears no comparison with that of other countries as already described. It includes vases, decorative vessels, plastic basket-work, white and colored porcelain-ware from a manufactory at Berlin, established in 1763, cups of antique German pottery and fancy objects, including enameled figures, painted pitchers and cups, Etruscan vessels, terra-cotta, majolica and other ware.

A joint exhibition is made of mirrors and plate glass from Fürth. The trade in these articles with the United States amounted in 1874 and 1875 to three-quarters of a million of dollars, and included framed looking-glasses, ground plate for industrial purposes, etc.

In furniture there is quite a display of carved work, including a carved table, a cigar-chest, a chair of antlers, also carving in wood and ivory from Görlitz, carved oaken sideboard, etc. An interesting display is made of ship furniture from Frankfort-on-the-Main, designed to prevent sea-sickness. In this line may also be mentioned billiard-tables and billiard-balls, work-tables and étagères, and a very large collection of finely painted wood statues, of scriptural and ecclesiastical subjects, etc.

The plated work includes tin-plated forks and plates, drinking-vessels mounted with tin ornaments, gold and silver galloons, laces, braids, fringes, flowers, etc.; frames for pictures and photographs, gas lustres and candelabra, bronzes, door-handles, lamps, house and kitchen utensils.

The exhibits in textile industry are very numerous, and although not especially attractive, are interesting as showing the progress in this important branch of German manufacture. It should be remembered that the manufacture of woolen cloth was developed at a very early date in Germany, and was prominent as far back as

the twelfth century. The wool product of the German Empire in 1873 amounted to 625,000 hundred weight. Germany manufactures cloths of all sorts, from the highest finish to the plainest quality. Specialties are buckskins of excellent quality, while the cloth manufacture of Blandenburg, Saxony and Silesia is of repute everywhere. Certain towns are renowned for military cloth, while others manufacture cloths for the East, and have a reputation for carriage-linings, as also for light tissues for ladies' dresses, large quantities of which are exported to China and Japan.

In worsted woolen yarn and in mixed fabrics Germany is also prominent, and by the annexation of Alsace, the country has been enriched by that province, in which wool-spinning is highly developed. The chief localities of this industry are Saxony, Silesia, the Rhine Provinces and Alsace. The principal market for these goods is America.

The Elberfeld cloth has a high reputation, and that town employs annually worsteds to the value of $5,000,000 in its manufacture. A joint exhibition of Elberfeld manufactures displays this industry fully.

The shawl manufacture is represented by Berlin, as is also the manufacture of plushes for dresses and caps, which is a Berlin specialty. The German cotton industry is situated principally in the Rhine Provinces, Westphalia, Saxony and Wirtemberg, but more in Alsace, which possesses no fewer than 2,100,000 spindles. The knitting yarns from Saxony, Bavaria and Alsace are especially noticeable. The linen industry is also fully exhibited, chiefly in that peculiar to Silesia, where it is carried on not only by power looms but also by hand-weaving. From this province comes also the fine damask which finds an extensive market in America.

The German silk production was estimated in 1872 to be valued at $38,000,000, its chief seat being in Rhenish Prussia. In passementerie and lace, especially that of Saxony, where are produced malines, guipure and valenciennes laces; in hosiery (and the export of Chemnitz hosiery to America is valued at about $4,000,000); in knitted and crochet fancy articles, and in gloves, the exhibits of Germany are important, and fully illustrate the extent of these manufactures. This is also the case in ladies' apparel, in which Berlin ranks next to Paris.

It is in its display of textile fabrics and manufactured clothing that Germany has achieved special prominence in the Exhibition. Special articles to be noticed besides those already mentioned are felts, imitation Smyrna carpets, chenille shawls, fine damask and towelings, and a particu-

larly beautiful and interesting show of gold-embroidered silks, which are marvelously fine and rich. A large case of cotton velvets, of all shades and colors, is a prominent and very showy exhibit. Kid and washed leather gloves, gauntlets, etc., of all colors, should be especially noticed.

In the exhibition of jewelry we may draw attention to the art of working agate into jewelry, which is an industry peculiar to the section of country about Oberstein and Idar. This manufacture employs about 3,000 persons, and finds its market chiefly in transatlantic countries. The exhibits include breast-pins, cuff-buttons, studs, polishing-stones, stones for pendulums, etc. The chief seats of the gold ware and jewelry manufacture are Hanau, Pforsheim, and Gmünd in Wurtemberg. The manufacture of jewelry in Hanau dates from the sixteenth century, when it was brought thither by the French and Dutch emigrants, and now employs a considerable part of the population, numbering about 20,000 souls. Here there are about 200 establishments, employing 2,000 workmen and working up about $1,250,000 worth of material annually. Pforsheim excels even Hanau in this production. It has 280 manufactories of gold ware, 150 smaller jewelry shops, and altogether employs 8,000 persons, its productions amounting to about $8,750,000 annually. The exhibits include gold and silver watch-chains and pendants, thimbles, spectacle-frames, hand-mirrors, bracelets, diadems, lockets, pens, Prussian Orders, articles of plated brass, writing-desk furniture, breast-pins, earrings, chains, etc.

Another German specialty is the manufacture of toys and small goods, in which trade Nuremberg and Fürth are the chief seats, the former possessing more than 100, the latter 50 houses, exporting about $1,000,000 per annum. The production goes back as far as the sixteenth century. These include articles of bone, ivory, shell, and horn, as well as wood, iron and tin. In only a few cases is the manufacture carried on upon a large scale; usually it is done in the family. The production of cameos, brooches, bracelets, pipes, etc., in this way is enormous; 200,000 dozen cameos, valued at $400,000, are made every year in these towns. For this end 750,000 horns, 200 hundred weight of ivory, and 100,000 hoofs are worked up. The exportation of toys and small goods to the United States in 1874–75 was $219,800. The exhibits include games, tin toys, rocking-horses, whistles, trumpets, children's swords, philosophical, mechanical and automatic apparatus, magnetic toys, tobacco-pipes, paper-knives, pen-holders, cigar-holders, brooches, cameos, breast-pins, earrings, studs, etc., some of tortoise-shell partly inlaid with gold; magic-lanterns, balls, dolls, some dressed for parties, others for promenade, others still in national costumes; goods of mother-of-pearl and sea-shell, and many other articles of the same character, are included in the great cases of the Nuremberg and Fürth exhibits.

The display of carved work in ivory and of toilet articles in this material is large and handsome. A considerable show is made in tools and cutlery.

A few bronzes are exhibited, those from the Count Stolberg-Wernigerod Works at Ilsenberg being of really fine quality and very interesting. They are artificial casts, comprising plate, basins, and other articles reproduced from notable works of art, especially those of Benvenuto Cellini. Two Berlin establishments exhibit bronze reproductions of monuments, statues, etc., including bronze eagles,

BLOWING MACHINERY, IN MACHINERY HALL.

BREWERS' HALL.--EXTERIOR OF THE BUILDING.

Corinthian pillars, vases, etc. A variety of musical instruments are in this department; time-pieces are also largely represented by a great number of clocks of all kinds, sizes and material.

As in the case of Austria, there is a handsome show of chromos, and the book-trade, for which Germany is celebrated, makes a very full joint exhibition of articles illustrative of this important industry, including exhibits of different methods of illustrating—such as xylography, engraving, lithography and color-printing, and photography as applied to book-making. The book exhibits come from Munich, Leipsic (which is the great German book centre),

BREWERS' HALL. — MAMMOTH VATS.

Berlin, Frankfort, Düsseldorf, Halle, Stuttgart and other principal cities, and include a great number of finely illustrated works in architecture and the fine arts, natural history, medicines, etc.

Nuremberg, besides its toys, has been an important seat of the manufacture of mathematical instruments since as far back as the fifteenth century. Single establishments make as many as 4,000 of these instruments per annum, and there are about sixty such shops in Nuremberg. The clock industry is similar. It is established chiefly in Schwarzwald, and dates from the end of the seventeenth century. The annual production amounts to about 1,800,000 clocks, of the value of nearly four and a half million dollars. About 14,000 persons are engaged in the industry.

The chief cities of the musical instrument manufactory are Berlin, Leipsic and Stuttgart, Hamburgh, Dresden and Munich. German organ-building is represented by Walcker and Co. The manufacture of string instruments is comprised in a joint exhibition. A special exhibit is that of mouth harmonicas, for which the Wurtemberg towns of Trossingen and Knittlingen are famous. This completes the description of the German section.

FRANCE.

East of the centre transept, and extending from the north wall to the nave, occupying the space of 43,414 feet, is the section devoted to France and her colonies, second only in extent among the foreign divisions to that allotted to Great Britain.

The collection of French exhibits commences at the transept on the nave with the exhibition of bronzes and silks, these latter being presented in an immense and elaborate display. A shrewd writer says of the French Exhibition that "if the Berlin porcelain was taken out of the German section, and the Elkington silver and porcelain, and the Doulton ware out of the English, in respect to beauty, the space occupied by these countries would rank with that of France very much as a potato-field does with a flower-garden." This criticism is both severe and precise. It is intended to indicate the peculiarly quick perception of beauty which is characteristic of the French people, and which is exhibited by them through the entire range of their manufactures, so that the construction of articles which on account of their uses are elsewhere entirely commonplace, is there elevated almost into a fine art. Thus the predominance of articles of real beauty, such as bronzes, porcelain, faience, laces, jewelry, etc., combined with the systematic and tasteful arrangement which obtains everywhere in the exhibition of the plainer and more simple wares and fabrics, make the French section a positive delight to people of cultivated taste.

It has been particularly noticeable that this department has been a favorite resort of ladies, and this is very easily explained, since nowhere else could be seen so many elegant things in the line most coveted by the fair sex. Shawls of the finest workmanship, silks in a profuse variety of color and pattern, rich brocades and velvets, exquisite embroideries, costly dresses heavy with flowers and real point-lace, silk stockings with lace inserted at the instep, the daintiest of shoes and slippers, jewelry, fans, ribbons, artificial flowers, and withal a thousand articles for the writing-desk, the mantel and the boudoir and table —here indeed were to be found a multitude of absolute conceits in every direction of manufacture, such as could not possibly, be devised or executed out of France.

The collective exhibit of the Lyons silk manufacturers, including contributions from perhaps forty or fifty different makers, presents a *tout ensemble* in this important and brilliant industry quite impossible to conceive without seeing it; while the advantage of presenting such an exhibition in combination over the plan of separate exhibitors is nowhere made so manifest as in this case. The exhibition is, in fact, the most imposing of the French department, including as it does silks, satins and velvets arranged with exquisite taste and presenting the very finest possible productions of the Lyons looms. Besides the ordinary dress goods

there are velvet and silk ribbons, foulards, embroidered silks, stuffs for church ornaments and upholstery, crepes, tissues, taffetas, and in fact all the possible combinations and preparations of silk.

In the direction of laces there are, besides thread-laces, which are marvels of beauty, and garments made from the most costly tissues of this character, specimens of Alençon which belonged to the Marquise de Pompadour in 1750. Here, too, are tissues of almost inconceivable fineness for robes and vails, gauze, barége, grenadine and other costly exhibits of this class. The peculiar work of the Jacquard loom is exhibited in silk portraits, including the inventor of the loom, President Lincoln, and other distinguished personages.

In bronzes, although some of the most celebrated of the Paris houses are not represented, there are fine pieces, copies of old works, by Marchand and others. One of the best statues is Bourgeoise's "Negro Snake-charmer," which gained for the artist the Prix de Rome in 1862, a prize which means two years' study in Rome at the expense of the French Government. Another work of this artist is the "Kabyle Laundress," which represents a half-nude woman stamping upon a pile of soiled linen, upon which she pours water from a pitcher. Two other figures represent Egyptian dancers holding musical instruments. Another good work is the "Boy and Tortoise," which received a gold medal at the Paris Salon last year. A nude boy, life-size, has discovered a tortoise, and is down on his knees on the rock, cautiously picking up the alarmed animal. One of the most costly and imposing art exhibits in the entire exposition is Marchand's monster mantel of black marble and bronze, 16 feet high and 11 feet wide. Its principal decorations are in *verd antique* and gilt bronze. Under the cornice and in front of a dead-black table, having a Pompeiian border in gold and colors, is a gilt statue of Minerva; and at either side of the fireplace a figure representing one of the Grecian sages. The price of this is $10,000. Another costly article is a large circular sofa, in the centre of which is a fountain in real antique marble, surmounted by a bronze candelabrum. The upholstery is green satin.

Some very handsome bronzes are also exhibited by Susse Frères, the chief piece of which is a colossal bust of Washington, cast in a single solid piece. The expression of this is noble and heroic. Another fine piece of work in this

BREWERS' HALL. — BOCK BEER.

collection is Gregoir's Group, a classical piece about two feet high, in which the texture of the skin of the two figures is worked out with microscopic minuteness. Here are also to be seen an enlarged copy of Pradier's "Atalanta," and Maigne's "Pointer and Pheasant." A very handsome mantel group by the Count of Nieuwerke represents the "Death of the Duke of Clarence," who is represented as being unhorsed by a French knight. The figures are in brass, and the armor and harness in nickel. The same firm exhibit clocks and slabs in hammered brass, and also some very handsome articles in onyx.

The Paris house of Kaffel exhibits a large variety of vases, tables, candelabra, flower-stands, etc., of gilt and silver bronze combined with porcelain and glass.

Next to the bronzes are the exhibits of porcelain, in which the most important display is made by Barbizet *Fil*, of Paris, who exhibits Palissy ware. Barbizet is the grandson of the man who discovered at Dijon, half a century ago, the secret of Bernard Palissy's method, and the processes used in the manufacture of the fifteenth and sixteenth century faience. The porcelain exhibits include numerous artistic articles, white, colored and decorated; and this department comprises also articles of decalcomanie on porcelain, and flowers, jewels, crowns and bouquets, represented in the same material. A large exhibit, both attractive and curious in this way, is that of carved figures for church decoration. These are life-size, gorgeous in color, and represent in some instances important groups illustrating scriptural subjects. One of these is the "Adoration of the Magi"; another, "The Good Samaritan."

There are also numerous church vessels in gilt and gold, and enameled crucifixes.

Among the exhibits of china, that of the house of Haviland & Co., of Limoges, is extensive, and presents articles

The exhibits of furniture are scarcely characteristic or illustrative of present styles. A large bookcase of heavily carved walnut in the Louis XV. style, costing $5,000, and a cabinet of ebony and lapis-lazuli in the style of Henri IV., marked $6,150, are prominent objects in this class; but, except some pretty tables and secretaries inlaid with porcelain tiles and a few gilt frame mirrors, with a wardrobe or two, rather elaborate, there is nothing of importance.

The collective exhibit of the French publishers is full, and both interesting and showy, including the names of Alfred Mame et Fils, of Tours; Delagrave, Jaoust, Gauthier, Villars, Hachette & Co., Guillaumin & Co., Morel, Renouard, the Collection of the Bibliothèque Charpentier and the Cercle de la Librairie, all these latter of Paris. The books exhibited in this collection have been presented in the best possible manner, under the direction of M. Terquem, the courteous and accomplished gentleman in charge of the interests of the French publishers at the exhibition.

Among the houses here represented are some dating back into the last century, while very many of them are from twenty-five to fifty years of age as business establishments. Among the books exhibited many are the most elaborate and magnificent specimens of the art which have been issued. Prominent among these are the works exhibited by the great house of Mame, founded at Tours in the commencement of the present century, and at present in the hands of M. Alfred Mame, who came

The Mame establishment comprises printing house, bindery and publication bureau. From its printing establishment go out 20,000 volumes every day. The binding portion of the establishment occupies three vast halls, independent of the numerous other apartments, where are deposited skins, paper and the other various materials necessary in binding. The capacity of the publication house amounts to several millions of volumes. Yet this is necessary to satisfy the great demands made upon this monster establishment. It should be said further of this house that it has received medals from the French Exhibition of 1849, the Great Exhibition of London in 1851, that at Paris in 1855, that at London in 1862, the grand

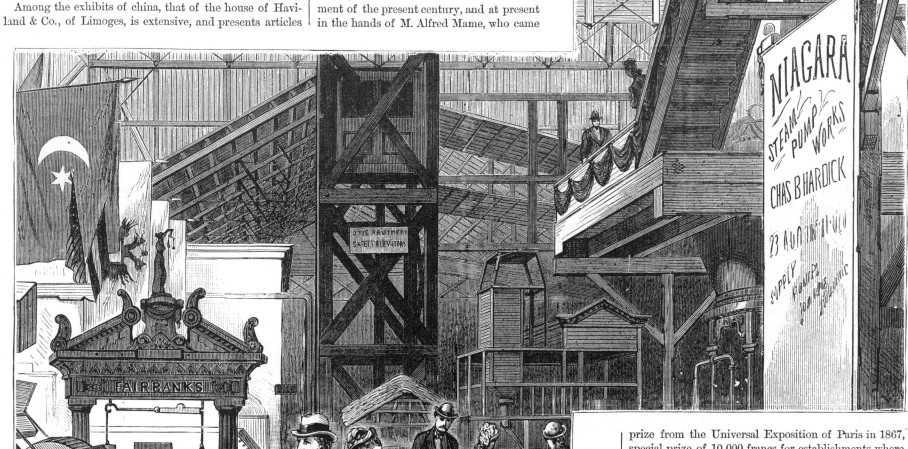

BREWERS' HALL. — INTERIOR OF THE BUILDING.

prize from the Universal Exposition of Paris in 1867, the special prize of 10,000 francs for establishments where the social harmony and well-being of operatives is especially considered, and finally, a diploma of Honor at the Exposition of Rome in 1870; and at the Exposition of Vienna, M. Alfred Mame, being out of competition, as a member of the jury, received the Cross of a Commander of the Legion of Honor.

The house of Hachette & Co., originally a classical bookseller's establishment, has for a quarter of a century added to its former business that of general literature. It is, however, chiefly famous for children's books and works of education, although many of the most celebrated French writers have gained added popularity from the publication of their works by this important establishment.

The establishment of Morel is noted for its magnificent works of art, prominent among which are the "History of Industrial Arts in the Middle Ages," by Lebarte, the "History of Russian Ornament from the Tenth to the Sixteenth Century," by Boutowsky, important and costly works of architecture by Viollet-le-Duc, including a Dictionary of French painters by this author; also the Basilewsky collection and that of Burgoyne. This house, in fact, should be considered among the more important in book-publishing the world over, since it is enabled to place before the public works so costly as to be beyond the means of minor establishments.

The house of Guillaumin publishes chiefly works of political economy, statistics, commerce and commercial law, etc., and is held in deserved esteem by savans in these directions.

Altogether, the French publication exhibits are to be mentioned as a specially beautiful, characteristic and important collection, which must have opened the eyes of the average American to possibilities in book-making hitherto unknown to him.

The photographic display near the book department

of great fineness and most elaborate and artistic treatment. The display of Aubusson and other tapestries offers several large, complicated and elaborately woven exhibits of great beauty. In the pottery department are two massive pieces designed to commemorate the Centennial itself. One is "1776," with a portrait of Washington and the names of the Signers of the Declaration of Independence, the Angel of Peace proclaiming the birth of a new nation; the other is "1876," with the Goddess of Liberty and the names and periods of service of the several Presidents at the top, and at the base agricultural products and mechanical implements, displaying the progress of the country.

into possession in 1845. This establishment is one of the largest in the world, while the works which it publishes are more magnificent in the style of their making than almost any that can be exhibited by other publishing houses. Among these should be mentioned "La Touraine," a superb folio, which received the highest prize at the Paris Exhibition of 1855; the Holy Bible, with illustrations by Gustave Doré; "Les Jardins," another splendid folio; "L'Imitation de Jésus-Christ," with superb engravings after Hallez; "Les Châteaux Historiques de France," and besides these the most luxurious editions of the principal authors in the French language belonging to the seventeenth century.

EXHIBIT OF THE SOCIETY FOR THE PREVENTION OF CRUELTY TO ANIMALS.

deserves mention as being comprehensive and largely illustrative of the best results at present attained in this art. To conclude our very meagre report of the French exhibition, we should mention the glove-case of Jouvin, and the considerable display of chemical manufactures, perfumes, medicines, etc.

On many accounts, and for various reasons which will occur to any one who has glanced through the foregoing summary, the French department is one of the most difficult to describe in a limited space, and certainly the most impracticable to receive justice in a briefly written account. After all, silks, laces, china and glass-ware, and most of all jewelry—of which we have said nothing—must be seen to be appreciated. It is only in the case of peculiar and conspicuous individual exhibits that description can be attempted. It may be concluded, however, that France, if she did not altogether do entire justice to herself in the exhibition in the Main Building, has at least done all that could be demanded for us in the beautiful and costly articles which she there brought together.

SWITZERLAND.

East of the French department, north of the nave, and occupying 6,646 feet of space, is the section devoted to the exhibits of Switzerland, ranged in a series of courts, inclosed by plain show-cases, painted drab, and without ornament. Beginning at the nave, these courts may be described as representing the following classification of exhibits, viz. : Watches, education, embroideries, textile fabrics, wood carvings and chemical products. At the rear of the section, by the north wall, is the office of the Swiss Commission, a pretty little one-story châlet, in the Swiss style of architecture.

Switzerland is 180 miles in length, and in its greatest width 130 miles. It is the most mountainous country of Europe. Its population in 1870 was 2,669,147. In sixteen of its cantons the German language is spoken by the majority of the inhabitants, the French in four, and the Italian in two. In the census returns to which we have just referred, 384,561 families speak German, 134,183 French, and 30,293 Italian. According to recent returns, there were five towns in Switzerland with more than 25,000 inhabitants, viz. : Geneva, the seat of the watch and jewelry industry, with 46,783 inhabitants ; Basle, the centre of the silk industry, having 44,834 inhabitants ; Berne, the political capital, with 36,000 ; Lausanne, 26,520 ; and Zurich, 1,199. The soil is pretty equally divided among the

population, it being estimated that four-fifths of the inhabitants are landowners, and 95,000 individuals supported either wholly or in part by agriculture. Meanwhile, the manufactories employ 216,468 persons, and the handicrafts 241,425. In the canton of Basle 6,000 persons are employed in the manufacture of silk ribbons, with a total annual production valued at $7,000,000. In the canton of Zurich 12,000 operatives work in silk floss to the value of about $8,000,000. The manufacture of watches and jewelry in the cantons of Neufchâtel, Geneva, Vaud, Berne and Solothurn employ 36,000 workmen, who produce annually 500,000 watches, three-sevenths gold and four-sevenths silver, valued at $9,000,000. In the cantons of St. Gall and Apenzell, 6,000 workers make $2,000,000 worth of embroidery annually.

The manufacture of cotton goods occupies upward of 1,000,000 spindles, 4,000 looms and 20,000 operatives, besides 38,000 hand-loom weavers. Switzerland is noted for its educational facilities, as in no other country is elementary instruction more widely diffused. Parents are compelled to send to school their children of from five to eight years, but not above that age. The number of clubs for scientific, literary, and musical and social purposes is remarkable. In St. Gall is the "Voluntary School for the

AMERICAN CARRIAGE.

Improvement of Merchants' and Artisans' Apprentices," which, starting from a Sunday drawing-school, was remodeled in 1860, and opened under its new name, being finally enlarged in its scope in 1863. Here are taught geometrical and free hand drawing, modeling in wood, clay, etc. ; arithmetic and bookkeeping, modern languages, geography, and history of commerce, etc. Pupils are received into this school after passing an examination and exhibiting school testimonials, having to pay the trivial amount of one franc for the Summer course and two francs for the Winter course, which goes toward defraying the expenses for writing and drawing materials furnished to the school. Another interesting and peculiar feature of the Swiss educational system is known as the "Swiss Unions of Young Merchants," which exist in almost every town of Switzerland. These unions are designed to improve young merchants in a mercantile point of view, as well as in general essentials ; and to promote good-fellowship and social intercourse among its members. An interesting and important feature of these organizations is the collecting of patterns and samples of works and raw materials for the purpose of acquainting the members with the products and manufactures, the commerce in which is to be, presumably, the business of their lives. During the last century watch-making has become the chief industry in the French-speaking cantons of Switzerland, and it is therefore natural that this great manufacturing interest should be given a prominent position in the Swiss section in the Main Building. The court containing the exhibits in this direction is the first which you enter from the nave. There are 45 exhibitors of watches, chronometers and parts of watches from the cantons where this is the chief industry. The exhibits include gold and silver watches and chronometers of different shapes, watch-hands, stems, detached parts of stem-winders, enameled watch-dials, precious stones and jewels for watch manufactories, movements, watches of platina and nickel, watch-springs, tempered steel for spirals, various complicated and precision watches, ladies' watches, etc., including also machines and tools appertaining to watchmaking. From the cheapest silver escapement up to elaborate pieces of mechanism, which strike the hour and the minute, and tell the day of the month and the phase of the moon, all are here. Here, too, are watches so small that they are inserted in finger-rings and in charms for ladies' chains, one watch being even contained in a gold pen-holder. This one has three dials each 3-16th of an inch in diameter, indicating the time, the day of the week, and the day of the month. Its price is $800. Watches set in gold rings, and a little larger than this one, cost about $300. The most valuable watch exhibited is priced $1,000, gold. This is an hour, quarter and minute repeater, has an independent second-hand, and a calendar of the day, month and year, and shows the changes of the moon. Watch-cases are displayed which are valuable as art-works, being engraved in the most artistic manner in gold of different colors. Watches are properly classed in the Swiss catalogue as scientific instruments, in which department there are also exhibited mathematical drawing instruments, hygrometer, thermometer, telegraph apparatus for controlling the speed of railway trains, regulator for electric clocks, transits, theodolites, level instruments, tower clocks, and a double dial clock for railway stations. The Swiss are celebrated for their music-boxes, and a number of these are exhibited, the largest of which plays thirty-six tunes, and is priced at $2,000; a small one, which plays only eight tunes, but combines with the ordinary music-box movement a drum and a chime of bells, is also valued at $2,000. A very pretty article in this line is a châlet of carved oak, containing a clock, a music-box and a singing bird. The next court in the Swiss department illustrates the subject of education, combined with those of engineering and architecture. Here every canton in the confederation is represented by school-books of all kinds, articles used in object-teaching under the Fröebel system, collections of minerals, plants, insects, plans, maps, atlases, photographs illustrating engineering matters, and in fact in this direction a vast variety of material of the highest value to the thoughtful student of that all-important subject—education.

Next come the laces and embroideries, including very beautiful work in curtains with raised patterns, and embroideries—of great ingenuity and elegance—upon white goods, silks, woolens and velvets. The curtains are marked at various rates, between $15 and $25, with the duty added. The silks of Zurich, straw goods, horse-hair braids, silk bolting cloths and cheap cotton fabrics come next, the latter finding their market chiefly in Oriental countries. Among the manufactured articles are hosiery, knitted jackets and undergarments, colored shirts, and straw-hats A considerable space is taken up with *passementerie* and cravats, edgings, machine embroidery, embroidered handkerchiefs, etc. The pretty carved wood from the Bernese Oberland is shown in a large variety in châlets, clocks, chessmen, box and mantel ornaments, as they are cut by hand in the cottages of the peasants in the Alps during the Winter season, when there is no out-of-door work that can be done. The woods employed in this industry are yew, linden, walnut, maple, pear, chestnut, cherry and oak. The art dates back for many generations, being handed down from parents to their children, it seeming to come natural to the Swiss to carve. The Swiss section concluded with a display of condensed milk, chocolate, aniline dyes and liqueurs. It should be mentioned that a very interesting special exhibition is made by a Board of Public Works in the canton of Berne, including maps, drawings, bound books, reports, etc., among which are maps of the canton of Berne, an album with eight photographic views showing the official residences of the district authorities, ancient castles and the town-hall of Berne, albums presenting sections of roads, bridges, blocks and coffer-dams, with recent works containing the police regulations and other laws of Berne, statistics of public works and their history, and various monographs on canals, bridges, etc.

Belgium.

Next to Switzerland is the section occupied by Belgium, comprising 15,358 feet of space. Belgium is the most densely populated country in Europe, the estimate being 404 to the square mile. About 58 per cent. of the inhabitants are Flemish, the rest Walloons and French, and 39,000 Germans in Luxemburg. Belgium is rich in minerals, which, next to agriculture, constitute the chief source of its national

THE TORCH OF LIBERTY.

prosperity. The number of hands employed in the coal-mines of Belgium is nearly 100,000. The fisheries are also valuable, and Belgium is famous for its horses. An immense industry is that of woolen manufacture, which in Verviers and its environs alone employs a population of 50,000 operatives. Here flannels, serges, camlets, carpets, flax fabrics, silks, velvets, fine laces, hosiery, hats, paper, etc., are extensively and profitably manufactured. The working of metals in iron, copper and tin is very important, the manufacture of cannon, firearms and locomotive engines being a special feature of the metallurgical industry of Belgium. The collective exhibition of Brussels and Valenciennes laces is very large and showy, including both black and white laces, guipure, magnificent fans in *point à l'aiguille*, ornamented with the arms of Belgium, and other exquisite fabrications in this material. Some fine pieces of carving, and massive and beautiful specimens of furniture are exhibited, the most important of these being a pulpit twelve feet high, richly embellished with delicate carvings in relief. This is illustrated on page 230. A massive Flemish chair of the sixteenth century, rich in tracings, is also a superb specimen of this work, and there are ornamental balustrades, heavy door-panels and costly suites of furniture, all of which are a fine illustration of Belgian art and ingenuity. The linen industry is largely illustrated, the show of linen goods, as also of fine blankets, being particularly noticeable. A large collection of polished, varnished, bronzed and enameled plate and wrought iron household utensils is also to be seen, while the display of firearms, including sporting pieces, rifles, guns, pistols, with hunting-knives, is likewise a fair presentation of this prominent Belgian industry.

In fact, the exhibition in metals is remarkable both for its extent and its completeness and excellence. It includes clamps, ferrules, rivets, forged nails, locks and nickel ware in great variety; bolts, chisels, screw-nuts, wire and tacks, etc., indefinitely. There is also a good representation of chemical products and manufactures, salts, crystals, etc. A large display is made of plate-glass, a monster mirror being a notable object. Plastic clays, earthenware, brick for glass furnaces, engraved and cut glass-ware, and variegated crystal dinner-services are also shown, and there is a case of fine brass musical instruments, and a considerable display of leather-work, boots and shoes, gaiters and slippers. The exhibition of kid gloves is considerable, and here we may properly allude to the kid-glove exhibit from the Grand Duchy of Luxemburg, which is contained in a large case standing at the south wall of the Main Building, between the sections of Russia and Austro-Hungary.

Returning to Belgium, we should refer more especially to the display of iron and iron ores, the exhibit including ornamental rough cast-iron patterns, rolled iron, iron wire, corrugated and galvanized sheet-iron for building, iron walls made by means of welding, Bessemer cast-steel, rolls, tires, axles, forged pieces in rolled bars, tramway rolls, copper-ware from the province of Namur, zinc and lead ore, and other articles illustrating this industry. From Liege we have white and colored clay pipes; from Charleroi white and colored window and unpolished and corrugated glass, with variegated rosettes engraved and cut; also colored and fancy window-glass, cathedral and stained glass, old glass, imitation samples of plate-glass at different stages of manufacture, etc. Several remarkable mantel-pieces, and Belgian mosaic marble panels for dining-room decoration, mosaic tables and other articles in marble are notable exhibits, and the Malines tapestries should not pass unnoticed. These include a portrait of Rubens, panel from Galliet, portrait in Arabian costume, eight panels together representing eight gods from Olympus, with their attributes, and a full-length painting of the style of Louis XIV. These are all carefully executed, and have attracted considerable attention. There has been much judgment displayed in the Belgian exhibition. Thus at the Vienna Exposition her exhibit in the mining industry was much larger and more comprehensive than at Philadelphia, although the latter gives a fair idea of the nature and value of Belgian iron. The reason for this difference exists in the fact that Austria presents a good market for Belgian iron, which is not the case with regard to the United States. The same thing, reversed, occurs in regard to laces. Austria manufactures her own laces, and the display of this manufacture at Vienna was by no means as large or as fine as that in our Main Building, since in this country we buy liberally from Belgium and pay high prices. The exhibition of laces in the Belgian section is ranked by experts among the chief attractions of the Main Building. Certainly there was almost nothing else in the Exhibition which attracted ladies so generally as these exquisite robes, shawls and handkerchiefs. Another Belgian specialty in art-manufacture is that of parquetry, or wood mosaic-work for floors, of which there are exhibited specimens, among the best of which is a fac-simile of the flooring of the dancing-room in the royal palace of Brussels. From Spa we have some very pretty paintings on wood in caskets, card-cases, paper-knives and jewelry in imitation of flowers, this being an art recently borrowed from the Swiss. A large display of sewing-machines is made in the Main Building by a Brussels firm. These are solid and strong, but do not compare favorably with the light and graceful American machines. A little Belgian schoolroom in the midst of the section is a curious enough exhibit, to which we shall refer hereafter in commenting upon the general subject of education.

Brazil.

The Brazilian department is situated between those of Belgium and the Netherlands, north of the nave, and includes a space of 6,897 feet. Brazil is by no means unacquainted with industrial

CURLING.—FROM THE PAINTING BY J. G. BROWN.

THE WHITE HILLS IN OCTOBER. — From the Painting by A. D. Shattuck.

exhibitions, four of these having been held in the capital of the Empire, Rio de Janeiro—the first in 1861–62, the second in 1866, the third in 1873, and the fourth and last commencing on December 2d, 1875, and closing January 11th, 1876. These were all inaugurated by His Majesty Dom Pedro, and were preceded by exhibitions in the capitals of certain provinces. Products selected by a jury of the capital from the empire were also sent to the International Exhibitions of London, Paris and Vienna. The Imperial Government is organizing general and special agricultural and other exhibitions, designing to regulate industrial exhibitions, in order to make them a permanent institution, and to erect a vast building adapted for the purpose. An association of exhibitors has been organized at Rio de Janeiro which has efficiently assisted the Brazilian Government in the last two exhibitions. Further, the Association for the Promotion of National Industry held a horticultural exhibition, the first of this character ever organized in South America, in 1871, and which was inaugurated by the Imperial Princess Regent, in the absence of the Emperor. A sufficiently large capital has been created to permit similar exhibitions being held annually.

It is especially flattering to the Centennial Exhibition that the Emperor of Brazil should have appointed as President of the Brazilian Commission to Philadelphia His Royal Highness Gaston d'Orleans, Count d'Eu, the son of the Duke de Nemours, and a Marshal of the Brazilian Empire, who has married the Princess Imperial of Brazil.

The exhibits of Brazil in the Main Building are classified into feathers, flowers and jewelry, education and science, manufactures, leather and hats, mining and metallurgy. The arrangement of the section is light, airy and elegant. Near the entrance are cases of costly books admirable in workmanship and rich in binding. The display of minerals, ores, building-stones and mining products contains specimens from all the different provinces, including marbles, some curious specimens of stalactites, samples of colored argillaceous clay, specimens of minerals showing gold and diamond formations, diamonds found on the banks of a river in the Province of Parana, where they are said to be very abundant, yellowish rock crystals, agates, alum—and for actual diamonds there were sent three weighing 23 karats, and valued at $15,000, and one cut diamond of the value of $8,000. The collection of agates, gems and precious stones, including specimens of gold and auriferous stones, gold-dust, etc., is considerable and interesting.

Mining engineering is illustrated by collections of geological photographs and maps.

The exhibits in manufactures begin with a display of chemicals, including essences, flavoring extracts, perfumery, toilet-soaps and pomades. Pottery and porcelain are illustrated by articles especially noteworthy for their elegance and the perfection of their workmanship. Some of these are terra-cotta vases, imitating the Etruscan style. In furniture an attractive exhibit is a complete set for the parlor, after the Brazilian style, manufactured of jacaranda and rose-woods, and containing one sofa, four arm-chairs and twelve chairs, all carved. There are also articles of furniture made by the inmates of the House of Correction of Rio de Janeiro. A secretary of cedar-wood and a small work-box inlaid with different woods are very handsome native specimens. One exhibitor sends chairs made from the genipapo, a native wood. This manufacturer employs about 120 workmen, using only Brazilian woods in his manufactory.

Some tortoise-shell boxes, straw articles, cups made from the gourd, varnished and colored, and others made of sassafras and other woods, with a curious collection of small artistic objects made from pine-tree-knots, are among the curiosities, as are also some carved cocoanut-shells. A number of hammocks trimmed with feathers, made in the provinces of Para and Amazonas, are sent from Rio de Janeiro.

A considerable exhibition is made of cotton goods and other fabrics, and though these are not up to the standard of English or American manufactures, they are interesting

as showing what has already been done in this important industry, and as indicating that with an abundant possession of the raw material, improvements may be readily made. Hats and caps make a considerable display, including a number of hats manufactured from different native reeds and grasses, and even from leather, besides the ordinary black beaver and silk-lined gray beaver and sheepskins, which display a very favorable condition of this trade. A large number of feather articles, including flowers, fans, ornaments, coiffures and insects mounted in gold, in which department Brazil has no rival in the world, presents this peculiar industry in a favorable shape.

Walking-canes, buttons, watch-chains, etc., made of cocoanut, are among the ornamental articles. Brooms, brushes, cordage, saddles, harness, whips and other articles in leather, are here in numbers.

The educational exhibition comprises specimens of writing, drawing and other handiwork; a collection of text-books and theses; a variety of educational books, and drawings and models made by the cadets in the Naval School of Rio de Janeiro; the books used in the lower and higher schools of the empire exhibited by the Instruction Board of Rio de Janeiro; specimens of book-binding; maps and charts; a collection of writings and drawings by the deaf and dumb; and geometrical figures, drawn by the blind boys of the Imperial Institute for the Blind of Rio de Janeiro. There is also a collection of Brazilian newspapers, reviews, and other periodicals, musical works, an exhibition of insects, a few philosophical instruments, one or two musical instruments, and a considerable exhibit of drawings, plans and profiles illustrating public works of Brazil. This collection closes with a display of medals and Brazilian coins.

The Netherlands.

The Netherlands section in the Main Building lies between those of Brazil and Mexico, north of the nave, and includes exhibits of its East India colonies, comprising in all the space of 15,450 feet. The Kingdom of the Netherlands is 195 English miles in length by 110 in breadth, being a little smaller than Switzerland, although it contains 1,000,000 more people. Allusion has heretofore been made in this work to the dikes of the Netherlands, the greatest of which are those of the Helder and of West Capell, on the east coast of Walcheren. These dikes and the national hydraulic works are in the charge of special engineers; and, as the public works of the Netherlands are numerous and important, the exhibition in the Main Building begins

WINTER TWILIGHT. — From the Painting by Geo. H. Boughton.

GENERAL VIEW OF THE SOUTH NAVE OF MACHINERY HALL.

EGYPTIAN WINDOW-CURTAIN.

at the nave with a very full display illustrating these by means of photographs, maps, charts and models exhibited by the Ministry of the Interior, the Channel Company of Amsterdam, the Chambers of Commerce and Industry, the Polytechnic School of Delft, and the Dutch Railroad Company of Amsterdam, which last sends a model of a railroad bridge and drawings illustrating it.

Among the models are some which are curiosities: one, exhibited by a citizen of Rotterdam, is a model of a cheap boarding-house; another, from The Hague, exhibited by an association for the improvement of workmen's buildings, is a model block containing lodgings for workmen.

The collection of mineral and mining products by the Netherlands is small, including only iron and cinnabar, some specimens of peat pressed by machinery, stones used for pavement, lithographic - stones, oil-stones, whetstones, grindstones, polishing material, granites, topazes, diamonds and corundum. In chemical manufactures there are soaps, oils, glue, a few colors and varnishes, an exhibit of cologne, turpentine, inks and wax.

No porcelain or pottery is exhibited except such of the latter as is comprised in tiles and other material for architectural purposes, and there are but few exhibits of furniture or such articles. What there are include picture-frames, lamps, mantels, chairs, and a few fancy articles. Some hangings, sofa-cloths, imitation Smyrna rugs, and a few cloaks, with a small exhibit of silks, comprise the exhibition of fabrics.

A large collective exhibition of books is made by the Netherlands Booksellers' Association, including works in all departments of literature, art and science, school-books, newspapers and periodicals. The subjects covered by these exhibits include works of bibliography, theology, geography and history, natural sciences, philology and general literature, the fine arts, juvenile books and a very large collection of educational works, including a number of Egyptian and Chinese books. The newspaper exhibition is complete, and includes specimens of papers dating back as far as 256 years ago, and representing most of the chief cities and towns of the Netherlands. Among these are a number of newspapers from Batavia, Surinam, and others of the Netherlands colonies. This entire collection is important and thoroughly representative, comprising exhibits from publishers and booksellers in Amsterdam, Rotterdam, Utrecht, The Hague, Dordrecht, Haarlem, Groningen, etc., to the number of 126 different establishments. The Netherlands colonies are represented by exhibits of lacquer and inlaid screens and cabinets, native woods, war weapons, furs and fabrics.

MEXICO.

The Mexican department is between that of the Netherlands and the United States exhibits, north of the nave, and comprises 6,503 feet of space. The Mexican exhibit is not of a collective system or official character; neither has it a historical aspect, by means of which might have been presented in progressive series the relics of the Aztec civilization, the state of the national industry when the country accomplished its independence, and its present products and manufactures. Instead of adopting such a plan as this, the Government of Mexico preferred to invite the producing and manufacturing classes to contribute to the exhibition, offering, at the same time, all the necessary facilities of remitting, placing and preserving their articles. It is unfortunate that the industrial classes of Mexico were rather lukewarm in answering to the liberal proposition which defrayed the expenses of transportation, placing, preserving and returning to owners the objects exhibited; and it is alleged that neither the best products of certain industries, nor any samples of others that have arrived at the highest degree of perfection in Mexico, have been sent to Philadelphia. For instance, the exhibits in the group of woolen and cotton fabrics in the Mexican department are cited as illustrating the first proposition, and the absolute lack of any exhibit in the line of saddlery, cabinet-making and fine hardware as a proof of the latter.

The population of Mexico is 8,743,000, of which a little more than one-third are Europeans and only one-fifth indigenous, the remainder being of mixed origin. On entering the Mexican department, what first attracts attention and is likely to hold it, is a huge circular mass of silver, weighing about 4,000 pounds and valued at $72,000. The next peculiar and notable exhibit is found in the display of beautiful polished slabs of variegated marble, in which green is the predominating color, with streaks and clouds running through the stone, bearing a strong resemblance to agate. The display of minerals and metallurgical products in general includes native gold and silver, mercury, iron, lead, copper and bismuth ores, specimens of meteoric iron from Chihuahua, one weighing 3,200 pounds, green sandstone, bituminous coal and wrought and cast-iron. Not many chemicals are exhibited, but these include indigo and essence of the eucalyptus, and some other specimens. In ceramics, pottery, etc., we have from the City of Mexico some vases in Aztec, Japanese, Egyptian and Chinese styles, and a few Indian vases. Fabrics are represented by woven cords, cotton yarns, a few specimens of cotton and waterproof clothing, chairs made from Mexican reeds, woolen goods and some native Indian dresses. An embroidered carpet, straw hats, specimens of gold and silver galloon come also under this head. In medicines there are certain medicinal plants and Indian drugs, specimens of the extract of sarsaparilla, Peruvian bark, etc. The various cities of Mexico, such as Pueblo, Mexico, etc., make a show of native wines and extracts, and display a few silk fabrics and stuffs,

EGYPTIAN SADDLE AND CLOAK.

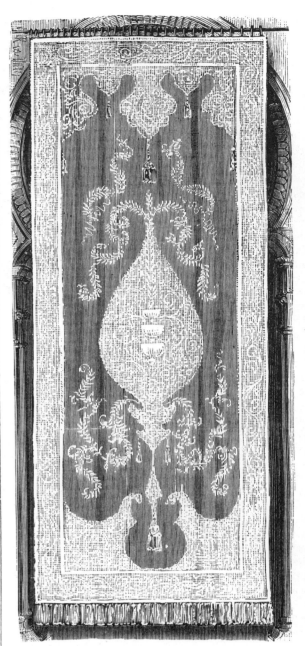

EGYPTIAN DOOR-CURTAIN.

woven of gold, resembling Oriental work. The ladies' shoes and a few fancy articles are made with some skill, but without much finish. The implements exhibited are, generally speaking, poor, but the mining tools are of a good quality. There is raw cotton on exhibition, which is not remarkable, however, for stability nor for strength. Exhibits are also made of Mexican maize or Indian corn, and samples of sugar and coffee. Samples of forest woods comprise a large number of varieties; among these are the *tepehuage, mezquite,* mahogany, scented cedar, and blackwood like the ebony, and the linaloe, which is a clear yellow-tinted wood, and is susceptible of a fine polish. The peculiarity of this wood consists in its delicate and very pleasant fragrance. This makes it very highly esteemed for toilet-boxes, it growing profusely in the States bordering on the Pacific coast. The palo-escrito is of the color and fineness of mahogany. The campeche-tree is well-known all over the world for its dyeing properties. Large quantities of precious and ordinary woods are exported from Mexico to Germany, France, United States, Spain and England. In 1873 the value of this exportation was something over a million of dollars. The Mexican Society of Natural History exhibits some native gums and resins, which are largely used in medicine and in the arts; one of these, known as copinole, is used by the manufacturers of varnishes. Large quantities of this material are collected in the State of Oaxaca, and it is sold in the City of Mexico at $1 a pound. A native resin is burned by the Indians as a perfume. Another is used for the preparation of illuminating gas and the manufacture of soap. A new elastic gum, called the *Durango caoutchouc,* is the product of a plant which flourishes in the State of Durango. Like the genuine india-rubber, it hardens with sulphur and receives a beautiful polish. The india-rubber-tree grows abundantly in Chiapas, Campeche and other localities near the Gulf of Mexico. The export of india-rubber in 1873 amounted to about $100,000.

Some very fine samples of tobacco from Vera Cruz are exhibited. The annual exportation of this amounts to about $150,000. Some small Mexican vases, etc., are shown, as also peculiar black-and-red native pottery. The agricultural exhibit in general is very large. Besides the trees, etc., already mentioned, we should refer to the specimens of coffee, vanilla, and fibres of the henequen, which is a species of agave used for cordage. It includes also a very large collection of indigenous plants of the Valley of Mexico, exhibited in six large volumes, collected by the National Preparatory School. These volumes contain 274 plants, besides 70 different ferns. A special and characteristic feature of the Mexican exhibit is the cactus-plant, and, in particular, that one upon which the cochineal insect lives. The Mexican exhibition includes specimens of cochineal from the State of Oaxaca, and also of carmine prepared from that material. Cochineal is sold at an average price of 32c. a pound. Specimens of vanilla-beans come from the State of Vera Cruz. The value of the exportation of this product for 1873 was about $500,000. As to coffee, it is alleged on good authority that in Mexico there exists the agricultural capacity to produce all the coffee that can be consumed in the United States, and of a quality equal to the best grown in any country. Inasmuch as the United States consumes more than one-third of the entire coffee crop of the world, which is estimated at 900,000,000 pounds, this fact, if it be a fact, is one of no little importance. In Mexico, coffee is cultivated with success at the elevation of 4,500 feet, and is found even still higher. On the eastern coast of Yucatan, coffee-trees of prolific yield are growing near the sea level, as well as in many other localities. The adaptability of Mexico as a coffee-producing country has been shown by more than fifty years of cultivation. That it has not assumed the first place in exportation is reasonably attributed to the same causes which have retarded all commercial and agricultural development in the country—i. e., to the political confusion and disorder. The exportation of coffee from Vera Cruz, however, increased from 672,000 pounds in 1871, to 5,373,000 pounds in 1875, the coffee exported from Vera Cruz being all grown in that State. The average price of land in the coffee-growing regions, reference being made to the Valley of Cordova, in the province of Vera Cruz, as a sample, has been between $5 and $10 per acre. The public or government lands can be taken up at from $20 to $25 per *caballeria*, a Spanish measure of about 105 acres. Wages are reported at 25c. per hand a day. Mexico for three centuries has been famous for its great production and exportation of silver, yet it is asserted that in coffee it possesses a far greater source of prosperity. Its natural capacity for this production is at least equal to that of Brazil, yet the value of the coffee exported from Brazil is more than three times as great as that of the gold and silver product of Mexico. The samples of coffee on exhibition are from Colima City, Cordova and San Luis Potosi.

ITALY.

The section devoted to the kingdom of Italy, in the Main Building, lies at the extreme western end of the building, extending from the transept near it to the wall, and lying opposite to the sections of the Argentine Republic and Italy.

In minerals Italy displays marble and alabaster, cement, limestone, lithographer's stone, sulphur, and a few specimens of metals, such as native iron, manganese, and manufactured iron wire. Quite a display of chemicals is made, sent from Naples, Turin, Palermo, Padua, Pisa, Milan, and other cities. This includes sulphurous products, sea and rock salt, cream of tartar, sodas, bicarbonate of potassium and sodium, and a large exhibit of manufactured articles, including soaps, olive-oil, varnishes, inks, perfumery, essences and extracts.

In furniture there are articles in ebony, metal and stone; and in fabrics, woven goods, yarns, etc., and a display comprising cotton goods from Turin; colored calicos from Pisa; linens from Salerno and Pisa, and woolen cloths from Messina, Naples, Modena, and Turin. Milan and Turin send raw, spun and woven silk; Messina, cocoons; and Milan, also silk velvets.

The wood-carving displayed is particularly artistic and excellent. Many of the articles, such as bedsteads, mirror frames, etc., are very valuable. An elaborately carved bedstead is priced $4,500. A very fine praying desk and chair, with beautiful decorative carvings and figures cut in basso-relievo, is marked $3,500. There is also a sort of wardrobe or closet for which $4,500 is asked. A

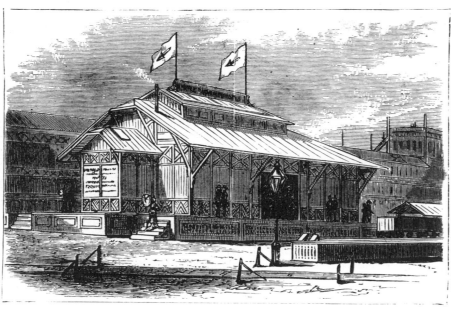

THE EMPIRE TRANSPORTATION CO.'S BUILDING.

number of fine mosaics are shown in this collection, though most of these articles are to be seen in the art collection in Memorial Hall. A table representing St. Mark's, at Venice, is noticeable. One small mosaic is priced at $5,000. Most of these are from Florence and Rome.

Venice glass makes a fine display, and Naples a large one of corals. Turin sends jewelry. A very interesting portion of this exhibition is found in the inlaid work in different-colored woods, displayed in the form of arabesques and even landscapes and figures. This art finds its perfection at Sienna. There are some examples of inlaid ebony and other dark woods and minerals, such as lapis-lazuli, marbles, malachite, onyx, etc. There are also a number of small bronzes, reproductions of antique statuettes. The terra-cotta figures, of which there are a number, attracted attention. They are designed for garden ornaments, and some of them are very clever. The candelabra, with sprouting figures of Nubians in gay-colored garments, are very pleasing and peculiar. In glass mosaics there are some satisfactory exhibits, the most remarkable being a landscape about 8 inches by 12 in dimensions, and marvelous in the beauty and accuracy of its coloring. One large case is filled with gold and silver filigree articles from Genoa.

In the jewelry collection, a heavy necklace of diamonds and rubies, set in silver, and a similar one of pearls,

surrounded with smaller diamonds and rubies on filigree, have attracted a great deal of attention, as has also a massive necklace of gold and sapphires, which was sold to the Empress of Brazil for $4,000. Some jewelry in the Etruscan style is exhibited by Signor Castellani, whose exhibition in Memorial Hall has been already described. The tortoise-shell and conch-shell work in ornaments is very fine and pleasing.

The collection of marbles includes more than 100 varieties displaying the most beautiful colors. Quite a remarkable article is a carved representation, in dark wood, of a fireplace so ingeniously devised that it presents, with marvelous skill, the appearance of ruin and dilapidation.

The Faenza Ceramic Company display a large number of carved pieces, vases, decorated and ornamental plaques, pitchers, ewers, pilgrim bottles and small ornamental objects. They have also one or two large pieces, a fireplace and toilet-stand elaborately ornamented. Most of these are the work of one man. One very excellent bit of work is a statuette of St. John, a copy from Donatello, which shows some fine molding and very beautiful enameling. An elaborate toilet-stand is a noticeable article. Another is a pilgrim bottle, decorated in two shades of blue, which is very graceful.

The best lustre-ware comes from Ancona, and is exhibited by Cesare Miliani, whose imitations of renowned ware are very close and successful. Reproductions of Urbino ware from Florence, by Torelli, are quite brilliant in color.

Useful articles exhibited include Leghorn hats, gloves, shoes, buttons, bed-spreads, etc. A Cremona violin, 171 years old, said to have belonged to Paganini, is exhibited, and is for sale at $1,000. Genoa velvets, which have a world-wide reputation, and of which there should be a suitable exhibition, are wanting, except in one meagre exhibit; and the same is the case with regard to Turin silks. There are some few laces from Venice and Como exhibited, and some embroidered pictures, and handkerchiefs from Milan. Straw hats and braided straw come from Florence and Bologna, chiefly. A few Sicilian costumes are exhibited, and some tortoiseshell work from Naples. Brescia sends a gun and some needle-gun barrels, and Messina specimens of shot, which are all we have of Italian weapons; medicine and surgery are represented by a powder and extract to prevent sea-sickness. In hardware we have a mechanical lock and bronze church bell, and a few tools.

The subject of education is illustrated by a number of scientific and educational works, maps, music, specimens of penmanship, etc. In scientific instruments there are a universal clock, electric batteries, telegraph instruments, and a cylindrical piano, with an instrument for writing notes as played.

A few articles of sculpture are shown in this section, including the following: "Cupid and Psyche," group, by Bazzanti, of Florence; "Surprise," bust, by Porcanai; a cupid of Michael Angelo; "David," by Torelli; "Traste Verino"—Roman costume, "After the Theatre," "Cio Ciara," "a Genzanese," these four by Garofoli, of Rome; and a fine statue of Dante, by Paoli Ricci, of Florence.

The Director of the Anatomical and Pathological Museum of Florence contributes a collection of microscopic, normal and pathological anatomical preparations. A plan for a tunnel is exhibited by Antino Linari, of Rome. A citizen of Turin shows a new idea for a pistol, and another of Naples offers a new system of disinfection. Maps are exhibited from Milan and Verona, including geographical map in reliefs, and a map of the world, in the form of a globe, besides other articles designed for use in the study of geography. An album containing specimens of stenography is exhibited by Prof. Luigi Periili, of Milan, and a

THE EMPIRE TRANSPORTATION CO.'S EXHIBIT

single newspaper, *La Donna*, is the contribution of Signor Beccari, of Bologna.

The articles of greatest interest and importance in the Italian section are certainly the carved furniture and mosaics, the work in terra-cotta, and a few of the ceramic specimens. In other directions it will be seen that the exhibits of Italy are surpassed by those of other countries.

CHINA.

The Chinese section in the Main Building has proved to be one of the most attractive in the entire exhibition, and compares favorably with that of Japan in the curiosity and interest which it excites. This section is third in numerical order from the western end of the building, and occupies an area of 8,844 square feet, extending south of South Avenue, between columns 5 and 11. The arrangement is comprised as follows: At the western end are the china-ware, furs and skins, and the trade collections; at the eastern side are the furniture, woodwork and carvings; in the centre are the silks and satins, the cloisonnés-ware and bronzes; and in the rear part, the office.

This section owes much of its importance and value to Hu-Quang-Yung, of Shanghai, an eminent Chinese, a pink-button mandarin, and said to be the wealthiest banker in the Empire, having branches of his business in every principal city and town in the country. He has a reputation both throughout Europe and Asia as a collector of ancient and valuable specimens of Chinese art. At the Exhibition he is represented by his nephew, Hu-Ying-Ding, a young man, and a mandarin of the blue-button, or fourth class, and who speaks English fluently. The special collection contributed by Hu-Quang-Yung comprises enameled and cloisonnés-ware and bronzes, which exhibits we shall consider hereafter. Quite a number of minerals are shown in this section, including native copper ore, galena, hard and soft coal, sulphur, tourmaline, auriferous rock and petrifactions. There are also building-stones, marble, slate, granite, etc.; fire-clay, talc, gypsum, chalk, lithographic-stones and graphite. In metals there are gold and silver-leaf, pig-iron, steel and tinfoil. Coal, both anthracite and bituminous, is found in large quantities all over the north

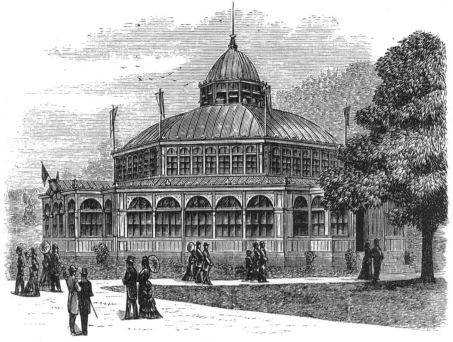

ARKANSAS STATE BUILDING. — EXTERIOR.

of China. It is estimated that the extent of these coal-fields is 87,000 square miles, but, owing to the lack of proper machinery and mining appliances, such mineral as has been extracted hitherto has been surface coal. In 1874 foreign steamboats consumed some 41,000 tons of this mineral. The native iron is used for making nails, tools, and every variety of foreign implements, but a considerable quantity of iron in different forms is imported into China from Europe, because, owing to the imperfect means of communication and transportation, and the system of manufacture followed by the Chinese, foreign iron can be furnished at less cost than the native article.

The chemicals exhibited include various vegetable oils, alum, soda, indigo, malachite, verdigris, copperas, arsenic, cinnabar, etc. It is, however, in its display of porcelain that the Chinese exhibition is chiefly remarkable. The largest quantity and the finest quality of porcelain produced in China is manufactured at the imperial potteries in the Province of Kiangsi. This is sent to all parts of the Empire, and has recently been largely exported to foreign countries. A special kind of china-ware, ornamented with the five-clawed dragon, is made there for use in the Impe-

rial household, and is sent annually to Pekin as tribute. In manufacturing it, the figures are traced in Indian ink, and then painted in water-colors, mixed with strong glue. The pieces are placed in a reverberating furnace about half an hour, and are taken out and washed when sufficiently cooled. There is an inferior quality, however, which is manufactured in large quantities, and forms one of the principal exports of Amoy. A vast quantity of pottery is also made, the difference between this and china-ware consisting in the kind of clay used, and in the finish. This ware is all kneaded and worked into paste, being formed by hand into the required shapes. Pottery is the article in its rough, brown state, whilst china-ware is glazed and painted; but the enameled and cloisonnés-ware to be seen in the Chinese collection are of a much higher stamp. Some of these specimens are from two to five hundred years old, and the art of making them has been lost for two centuries. A number of specimens of cloisonnés are made from jade, a very rare and valuable stone. Some of the plates of cloisonnés-ware are valued at $350, while a small piece of jade-stone, intended as a charm for a watch-chain, costs $150. A number of vases are very large, a pair of these being ornamented with gilt dragons and valued at $2,500. Among the Chinese articles of china-ware exhibited, are an earthenware elephant and pagoda, black-wood stand, and Indian with a gourd; vases of various colors, some of them "crackled"; teapots, flower-pots, rice-bowls, water-bowls, incense-bowls, snuff-bottles, and yellow cups with covers; a Chinese dinner service, 147 pieces; dessert service, 137 pieces; wash-basins, hand-basins, fruit-stamps, cuspedores, etc. There are also punch-bowls, toilet-bottles, card-receivers, ash-receivers, and a multitude of other articles, in all colors and sizes. Many of these are manufactured in the Kiangsi province, and are sent to Canton to be painted. A favorite design for china articles is found to be animal subjects. Thus we see candle-stands, elephant shape; other articles in the form of cats, dragons, etc. Many of the teacups are painted by hand. Occasionally the designs are classical; some have bamboos and vines or birds painted upon them. There are also porcelain stands and jugs, vases with metal lining,

ARKANSAS STATE BUILDING. — THE WOOD, COTTON, AND MINERAL EXHIBIT.

porcelain figures on stands, reptiles in porcelain, pomade-pots, and some specimens of glassware from Canton.

The collection of furniture displayed is rare and curious. Some of this is carved and ornamented with inlaid work in ivory and rare woods, in the most beautiful and artistic manner. Time certainly seems to have been an element which has not been considered in the construction of these articles. One bedstead is priced at $4,000. It is a master-piece of intricate and delicate carving. Another is covered with a canopy, presenting panels of silk embroidery with great nicety and beauty. The wood-carving is done chiefly in a peculiar black, close-grained wood, resembling ebony, which takes a deep polish and becomes an admirable wood for ornament. A parlor set, including a superb sofa, is specially noticeable. Buffets with shelves and doors are favorite articles. Fine centre-tables of the same material, having tops of native variegated marble, or painted china, resembling mosaic-work, are also found here.

The office of the Chinese Commission, in the rear section, is a structure about 8 feet high and 12 feet wide, covered with gilt carving, with panels of Chinese painting. Near by is an elaborately carved show-case, in which is exhibited a collection of antique china-ware, some of which is seven or eight hundred years old. A sideboard is seen, the top of which, being of wood, is carved into a fabric almost as delicate as lace. Among the carving is a Chinese Court of Justice, in which the judge is seen sitting, with fan in hand, at a desk, and before him kneeling criminals, some handcuffed with boards, and others with wooden yokes fastened about their necks. Other carvings represent mandarins with their attendants, some mounted on horses, and others on sedan-chairs. Near the main entrance is a show-case containing a variety of ivory carvings of the most delicate workmanship.

The collection of screens is very interesting, some of them being inlaid with porcelain tablets, others having carved black-wood frames; many of these screens being made of silk. The furniture also includes bamboo sleeping-chairs, in black-and-white rattan; armchairs in black-wood, enamel and marble; small tables or tea-poys in camphor-wood, red-wood and black-wood; lacquer writing-desks and couch for opium-smoking, inlaid with pearl; silk panel screens painted by hand with black-wood frames; one of these representing the growth and manufacture of tea, and the other the manufacture and use of silk. Some of the screens present historical scenes or Chinese romances, while others have birds or flowers painted upon them. There is a puzzle-table in seven pieces. There are carved book-cases and clothes-presses, washstands, brackets, boxes, arm-chairs, cabinets, etc. The lacquer-work comes chiefly from Foo-Choo and Canton, and includes chairs, sofas, dressing-tables, screens, chess-tables, what-nots, card-tables, mandarin-chairs, etc. In table furniture there are quite a number of articles of silver, including napkin-rings, cups, a silver cup with a dragon handle, another ornamented with grapes in relief, and still another with fish, silver claret-jug, salt-cellars, teapots, and an entire silver set, including teapot, coffee-pot, milk-jug, and sugar-bowl, in a bamboo pattern, from Canton. Carved picture-frames are exhibited, valued at from 75 cents to $4. Some of these are of sandal-wood. There are also rattan cradles, and child's chairs on wheels; likewise large sedan-chairs of bamboo—chair carried on poles by two men.

The interest always felt by the Chinese in toys, fans, painted screens—and, in fact, everything artistic which can serve to amuse—is in no particular made more evident than

WASHINGTON STATE CARRIAGE.

in the passion experienced by every Celestial for "lanterns." The display of artificial light through an ornamented and pictorial medium seems to be a part of the very existence of the Chinese. Lanterns form a portion of the belongings of every family, and appear at every festival, while the "Feast of Lanterns" is one of the most characteristic, gorgeous, and impressive institutions of the country, and probably attracts the largest crowd of any demonstration, whenever it occurs.

A number of lanterns are shown, which are, in fact, chandeliers made to hold lamps or candles, the light showing through sides of painted glass, rich in color. Some of these have silk sides, some are made of bone, and others of silk, richly embroidered. The lanterns all come from Canton. Some curious antique bronzes in the rear part of the section are noticeable, one of these articles being certified to be eighteen hundred years old. The bronzes include vases, bells, bowls, teapots, urns, and numerous articles in shape of animals. There are also bronze incense-dishes, antique bronze birds, censers and a pair of bronze idols from Pekin. In the manufacture of silk, China had for ages the monopoly of the world, and in some parts her silk manufactories are even yet unrivaled. The display of this article is a fair one, although not as complete as could have been expected. The grades of the goods exhibited are not familiar, and will repay inspection. The figures are large, beautifully worked, and the fabric has a solidity and firmness of appearance seldom seen in the products of other lands. There are also rich plain silks, as well as light semi-rugs, and a number of specimens of the famous Canton crapes.

The silk show is among the best of the Chinese section. Some of the silk is valued at $16 a yard in China. The manufacture of silk in China dates from a very remote antiquity. Popular tradition assigns its invention to the wife of the Emperor Hwang-Ti, B. C. 2602, while notices of the culture of the mulberry-tree and the rearing of silk-worms are found in Chinese books as far back as B. C. 1780. It has also been an industry enjoying the peculiar care of the Government, and in one province, where the mulberry-trees were nearly all destroyed during the occupancy of the Taeping rebels, mulberry-plants were

during five successive years imported by the local government from another province, and distributed gratuitously among the owners of land, while silk-cultivators were brought to teach the peasantry the art, which had been forgotten. The consumption of silk in China is enormous, as it is largely used as a staple for clothing by all but the poorest classes of the population. Among the exhibits of silk are raw yellow silk, raw white silk, cocoons, brown silk, etc. Then there are plain woven silks, lute-strings, sarce-nets, satins, serges, foulards, and tissues for hat and milli-nery purposes. The manufacture of silk piece goods, including satins, Chinese crapes, gauzes, etc., is confined to four provinces. In Shantung is manufactured a curious kind, known as "Shantung pongee," which, for its cheapness and durability, is much prized as an article of Summer clothing by both natives and foreigners, valued at $5 per piece of 22 yards. Then there are figured satins, camlets, brocade silks, pongees, shawls, handkerchiefs, etc., and striped gauzes, sashes of embroidered silk, scarfs, etc. But silk is not the only fabric in which China makes a satisfactory exhibit. For one thing, it has the faculty of making a fabric from asbestos, a fire-proof material, by weaving the fibre with cotton or hemp. Then the grass-cloth, which is a native specialty, is manufactured from the fibre of several plants, which are classed in China under the generic term of ma. The principal seats of the grass-cloth manufacture are the provinces of Kwang-Tung, Kaang-Si, Kiang-Si. That of Canton, Swatow, Kinkiang, has ports of shipment. There are many varieties and qualities of the article, varying in price from eight cents to one dollar and twenty cents per yard. The coarse kinds are exported in small quantities to Manilla and Singapore, where, as is the case in China proper, they are extensively used as materials for Summer clothing. A number of pieces of grass-cloth, white, blue and yellow, are exhibited, as also grass-cloth handkerchiefs, embroidered and plain. There is also a piece of cloth exhibited from South Formosa. Matting is another important manufacture of China. It has a texture made from reeds, the natural color of which is greenish-white. These are not bleached, but become white in use. To produce the different patterns, the reeds have to be dyed before being woven, the colors employed being red, yellow, green and a very dark-blue. The chief seat of the matting industry is the province of Kwang-Tung, and it is shipped from Canton to the United States and Great Britain, the average value being $4 per roll. Specimens of the patterns most in favor here are exhibited from Canton. A number of exhibits of cotton cloth and nankeen are made. Cotton cloth gets the name of "nankeen" from Nankin, where the manufacture is said to have been begun, and where the finer kinds are still produced. This manufacture, however, is carried on everywhere in China. Each piece of cloth is 28 Chinese feet long, and from one foot three inches to one foot four inches wide, and an industrious worker can make a piece in twelve hours. The cloths are of all colors, blue

THE BAILY GUN, IN THE INDIANA STATE BUILDING.

being most in favor. It is made in hand-looms, worked principally by women. One piece is sufficient to make a short jacket and a pair of trowsers, which are said to be twice as durable as those made of ordinary shirting, and are from Mantchooria. The clothing exhibits include stockings, bamboo undershirt, some women's and men's shoes, the women's shoes being small-footed, and valued at Canton at $1 per pair. There are also straw shoes, others of satin, caps from Mantchooria, and tanned ox-hides and moccasins The jewelry and ornaments include filigree-ware, silver bracelets, necklace, cross and earrings inlaid with kingfisher's feathers from Foo-Choo, a set of jewelry of gold,

NORMANDY GIRL IN A SHOWER. — FROM THE PAINTING BY GEO. H. BOUGHTON.

the value varies according to the weight, from 68 to 85 cents per piece.

There are exhibited a few rugs in different colors, some of which are camel's wool and others sheep's wool. These and some of silk and velvet and velveteen, cotton cloth, Spanish striped, felt and dried skin. Silk hats are valued at 47 cents each, and felt hats at 25 cents ; bamboo are sold at five cents a piece. There are also dog-skin and fox-skin pearl and coral complete, in an ivory box from Canton. A pair of bracelets, in ivory and gold, and earrings in the same materials. There are also gold anklets, pearl buttons, gold-plated ornaments for dressing the ladies' hair, from

Pekin, gold-plated bells for attaching to the collar of pet dogs, and one pair of guards, gold-plated, from Pekin. A fine display of fans includes some in ivory and paper, others ivory and feathers, ivory and bone, bone and silk, ivory and silver in lacquer, valued at $7; pearl, valued at $5; silk, in a silk box, from $1 to $1 50; lacquer and embroidered, in paper boxes, $3, and ivory, in sandal-wood boxes, from $3 50 to $21; ivory and silk is worth $15, and one tortoise-shell, carved, in a lacquer-box, costs $13. Paper fans sell at 25 cents at Swatow, and gauze fans, the cheapest, at 8 cents. Paper umbrellas are shown, valued at 20 cents each, and a number of boxes of silk and velvet artificial flowers, ranging from 82 cents to $44 per piece. The opium-smoker is cared for, and there are opium-pipes and pipe-bowls and pipe-bowl stands, smoking-trays, smoking-lamps, boxes, knives, scrapers, picks, and refuse, plate-copper boxes for opium, bamboo pipes from North Formosa, brass water-pipes and a set including a water-pipe case and stand, opium pipe-case and pouch for opium-box, valued at Shanghai, $4 14. Native curiosities are a coat, cap and pipe used by the North Formosa aborigines, ivory puzzles in lacquer-boxes, and kites of all sorts. Quite a number of articles are shown which are manufactures of leather, including trunks, dressing-cases, leather pocket-books, leather pouches, tobacco-pouches, fan-cases, etc. A marriage headdress and full suit of clothes of the Formosa country women of Chinese origin is valued at $47 80; a headdress of the "Pepohoan" woman of Formosa, with full suit of clothes, at $8 75; a bride's coronet costs $4 40 at Canton, and a complete set of theatrical properties is worth $100 at Amoy; a woman's satin dress costs $3 93; silk crape dresses—the material for which can only be obtained at Soo-Chow—are also exhibited.

Chinese paper is made chiefly from bamboo, but also from rice-straw, wheat-straw, cotton, hemp, the bark of the ailanthus, the stalks of reed, the refuse of silk cocoons. The chief centres of the paper industry are in the southern Yangtse provinces. Rice paper is used for artificial flowers, specimens of which are exhibited, as are also pictures, delicately painted on the same substances. There are, further, specimens of paper made from the bark of the mulberry-tree, and used by the wealthier classes in Mantchooria and North China, instead of glass, for covering windows, and also for making umbrellas. Paper-making is one of the chief industries of the kingdom of Corea, and the article finds its way into China by means of three annual fairs, which are held near the boundary between the two countries. Quite a large display of the different kinds of paper is made, and forms a very curious exhibit, including, besides packing-paper, writing-paper and cards, a number of specimens of enameled and colored wall-papers in imitation of leather, wood, etc. The display of Chinese weapons is not very large. In fact, it includes only one Chinese musket from Amoy, valued at $2 50, some bows and arrows used by the aborigines of Formosa, an Amoy sword, which costs $6 per dozen, and an Amoy knife used by the Chinese for decapitating criminals, valued at $4 per dozen. The collection of Chinese medicines and medicinal vegetables, fruits and animals is contained in the mineral annex, alluded to elsewhere. Some of these articles have very peculiar uses in China. For instance: cantharides is considered a specific in hydrophobia; the fruit of cardamom is supposed by the Chinese to increase knowledge by strengthening the stomach, with which the Chinese connect a person's disposition and mental capacity; the dried skin of a certain kind of orange is used as a sedative; dried aloe-flowers are used in pulmonary affections, and are also employed in cookery as a tonic or relish. The honeysuckle is given in cases of rheumatism, and the dogbane in diseases of the kidneys. Almonds are sedatives in the Chinese pharmacopœia, and cassia-buds a tonic and astringent. Melon-seeds are taken for coughs, colds and asthma, while the morning-glory root is used in severe dyspepsias. Pumpkins are said to possess soothing properties, and are used in cases of colics, spasms, etc. Quite a number

of vegetables are considered cures for consumption and remittent fever. The under-shell of the land-turtle is taken as a decoction by the old and weak, and as a stimulant, as is also mustard-seed. To oleanders are attributed rejuvenating and highly nutritive qualities. One vegetable, with a totally unpronounceable Chinese name, is employed to work off the effects of drunkenness. Fragments of fossil crabs, crushed and powdered, are considered a specific in affections of the eye. That most useful of vegetables, rhubarb, is indigenous to China, and, in former times, Canton was the only port from which the drug was exported. The Chinese dig the roots early in the Spring, before the leaves appear, cut them into long, flat pieces, dry them for two or three days in the shade, and then string them on cords. Turmeric is used for diseases of the skin; also as a yellow dye in the preparation of tobacco, and, mixed with indigo or Prussian-blue—a fact which will be interesting to Americans—it is employed to color green tea, as also to season curries. Another of the Chinese vegetables is used to bring out the eruption of smallpox, and also to color candles; while still another plant is found equally important in the curing of boils, and in strengthening the hair. From castor-oil beans the

Chinese express an oil which is used in the manufacture of candles. A very costly gelatine is made by boiling down deer-horns, after which it is employed as a tonic. One of the most important medicines in China, taken in spirits, is supposed to heal fractures of any kind. Petrified crabs are used for boils, sores, etc., snake-skin for smallpox, and caterpillar is employed in bronchial complaints; dried cow's gall is used as an expectorant; the refuse of tobacco mixed with straw as a stimulant, and cow's glue made from buffalo-hides, a sedative. There is, in fact, no end to the novel uses to which everything, mineral, animal and vegetable, is put in China. Glue seems to be peculiarly medicinal. That made from the tortoiseshell is a tonic, while that which is obtained from tiger's bones has also tonic properties, but is valued at the enormous price of $1,500 per picul (a weight of 133¼ pounds).

The Chinese salt scorpions, and then use them for smallpox. Ant-eaters' scales cure rheumatism, and with the peculiar facility which the Chinese possess for reversing the customary uses and appliances of civilized people, they do not employ leeches alive, but make a decoction of the article, dried, in water or spirit, and take it as a purgative, or apply it outwardly for bruises. Dried toads are considered a tonic, but are not expensive, as they are sold at two cents each. A tiger's skull is taken in

typhoid fever, ague and rheumatic headache. It is also taken by the person who has been bitten by a mad dog, as a preventive to hydrophobia. The article is valued at $150. Pearls are prescribed in affections of the heart and liver; also in deafness. All these different medicines are exhibited, and can probably be obtained by such as are anxious to venture on these novel modes of treatment. A description of the Chinese articles would be totally incomplete if no allusion were made to the gongs. Of these there are several exhibited, valued at from 50 cents for a hand-gong to $4 41 for a large article. Two of these are in black-wood frames, one called the "little soochow gong," valued at 85 cents. Besides these, which are classed as musical instruments, there are drums, a guitar having three strings, a two-string viol, a seven-string harmonica, a twenty-five-string lute; and then there is a dulcimer, a mouth-organ, a set of cymbals, tambourine, flute, violin, rattles, and wooden drum used by the Buddhist priests, and a set of fine brass instruments, including two trumpets and three clarionets, valued at Shanghai $3 36 for the lot. The collection of coins exhibited comes from Shanghai and Foo-Choo, and includes 1,236 specimens on seventy cards; four boxes, each containing sixty gold pieces, and the collection on thirty trays including 816 coins.

The collection of ivory carvings in small articles is very fine, comprising chessmen, cigar-stands, glove-boxes, jewel-boxes, six ivory cocktail-shakers; a set of thirteen ivory balls, one within the other; an ivory pagoda, already described and illustrated in this work; ivory flower-boat and black-wood stand, two feet long, very handsome; also a sandal-wood jewel-case, carved ebony jewel-case, ivory and tortoise-shell box, ivory cabinet, glove-stretchers, photograph-frames and card-cases. The acme in carving is reached by a set of twenty-one ivory balls, one within the other, on a black-wood stand. Some curious pictures in water-color and aquarelle on pith paper, are subjects illustrating the cultivation and manufacture of tea, occupations in the life of a Chinese lady, mandarins, landscapes, flowers and fruits, silk manufacture, gambling, the theatre, occupations of wealthy men, funeral procession, hunting scene, and one painting of the Buddhist purgatory, showing the eighteen punishments inflicted there. A number of Chinese relics are shown from the Imperial Summer Palace of Pekin, and the collection of curious articles may be closed with mention of a pair of bronze idols, also from Pekin.

SANDWICH ISLANDS.

The display from Hawaii is located immediately behind that of Tunis; and, for so young and so small a kingdom is most creditable. The chronology of Hawaii begins in 1716. In 1779 (February 14), Captain Cook was slain by the natives. English trading with the islands commenced seven years later, and though massacres occurred thereafter, and human sacrifices were not infrequent in religious ceremonies, it is a most remarkable fact in the history of these islands, and in the history of religion anywhere, that on June 26, 1822, the existing pagan system of worship was abolished, and 102 idols burned, by orders of King Kamehameha II., leaving the people without any established religion whatever.

Missionaries had reached Hawaii two years before, however, from Boston, and now they flocked thither in numbers, and many converts were made, though the morality of the natives does not seem to have been ever of a very elevated standard. Coffee and sugar-planting were begun in 1825. By 1844 the independence of the islands was established, and since then the little kingdom has had quite a flourishing existence, with a considerable foreign trade. The present monarch is King Kalakaua, who visited the United States in the Winter of 1874–5. The total population of the Hawaiian Islands, from a census taken December 27, 1872, appears to be 56,897, of whom 889 were Americans, 849 born in Hawaii of foreign parents, 619 British, 395 Portuguese, 224 Germans, 88 French, 364 other foreigners, and 49,044 natives. The chief city and capital of the

BELGIAN FURNITURE, IN THE MAIN BUILDING.

SUNKEN GARDENS ON FOUNTAIN AVENUE, LOOKING FROM HORTICULTURAL HALL.

kingdom is Honolulu, with about 15,000 population. The coffee exportation of Hawaii is very variable, having reached 415,111 pounds in 1870, while in 1872 it fell to 39,276 pounds, and in 1874 was only 75,496 pounds. The total amount of exportation of domestic products reached $1,622,455 in 1874, and averages about that figure during the past ten years. It is a curious fact that the quantity of spirits consumed in the kingdom, which amounted to 7,862 gallons in 1863, had increased to 21,212 gallons in 1873, though there was a slight falling off in the following year. The exports of Hawaii comprise sugar, molasses, rice, coffee, hides, wool, calf, sheep and goat skins, and tallow.

The Hawaiian exhibits in the Main Building comprise most of the special and more curious products of the kingdom. There is, for instance, quite a show of native feathers, these being displayed more particularly in the case devoted to the exhibit furnished by Queen Emma, widow of the late King Kamehameha V. Here are wreaths and festoons made by means of attaching these feathers in their natural colors to strings, and thus forming them into any desired shape. Here, there is also to be seen a small kapa, made from these feathers, in yellow-and-black, and which is very highly valued. Indeed a single wreath of this character costs $600.

It had been rumored that the state robe of the Hawaiian Majesty was among the contributions in this department, and much curiosity has been aroused to see this remarkable garment. The fact is, however, that the cloak or robe, which is also made of feathers, and is used only at coronations, or on other important state occasions, could not possibly be allowed to go out of the kingdom. The value of this unique garment is said to be several hundred thousand dollars, and the time and labor employed in its construction were something quite enormous. Some very attractive exhibits are made in manufactures of native Hawaiian woods. One large round table contains 36 varieties of wood, covering all those known to exist in the island, is beautifully inlaid in symmetrical figures, and is priced $250. Another table, containing only two different kinds of wood, but these very rare, is valued at $150. These woods are not the product of forest-trees but of small shrubs, and these only exist in very limited quantities, having been killed by blight or the ravages of some native destroyer. Other articles of wood construction are bowls of very pretty shape, some having covers, others without, and varying in size between a capacity of about a quart and that of several gallons. These sell at Honolulu at prices varying between $3 and $20, the natives buying them very eagerly whenever offered at the public auctions, which take place there periodically. Still further contributions of wood manufacture are a number of cans, some of which are made of cocoanut, and others of the same woods already described. Some very pretty articles are manufactured of a peculiarly fine white straw, resembling rice-straw, and of delicate and ornamental texture.

JAPAN.

The empire of Japan is governed by a supreme legislative and executive body, comprising the "Supreme Chamber," or "Great Council of State," over which His Majesty the Emperor presides in person, and which also includes the Prime Minister of State, the two great officers, and a number of councilors of state, with clerks, attendants, etc. Then there is the Deliberative Assembly, which has the privilege of investigating the action of the executive branch of the Government, and of reporting upon such action when found contrary to the laws and rules established, but which has no power to deliberate on the promotion or dismissal of officers. The officials and members of this Assembly are selected from among the members of the Imperial family and officers ranking above the fourth grade. Then there is a department for foreign affairs, which includes the diplomatic and consular services, a home department, war department, naval department, judicial department, and court of appeal—the court which unites the power of the French Court of Cassation with that of the American Supreme Court. The dependent principalities of the Government are administered by a ruler, secretaries, and a Deliberative Assembly.

The population of the empire amounts to 33,300,675 souls, according to the census of 1874. This number is almost equally divided between males and females, the predominance of the former over the latter being only about 500,000. The whole country is divided into nine large districts, which are subdivided into 85 provinces, in which three cities—two of which are capitals—and 59 chief towns have been designated. Tokio (Yeddo) is the capital of Japan and the seat of government of the empire. Its population is 595,905 inhabitants. A railroad communicates with Yokohama, and a telegraph extends to nearly all parts of the empire, and thence to Europe and America. Kiyoto, the western capital, has a population of 238,663. There are at present six ports open to foreign commerce: Yokohama, Osaka, Hiogo, Nagasaki, Nigata and Hakodadi.

The known history of Japan commences with the first year of the Japanese era, 660 B. C., since when the Imperial line has continued unbroken. The American treaty with Japan, which preceded all the treaties made between that country and the European nations, was effected in 1858, by means of the expedition under Commodore Perry. In the reign of the 121st emperor, who is now reigning, the controlling power of the government and the administration of affairs was assumed by him. Old customs, which had lasted for 700 years, were cast aside, as it were, in one day. The feudal system was abolished, and the monarchical form of government instituted. Many European and American arts and sciences have since been introduced, the youth of Japan have been sent abroad to America and to European countries to be educated; and it is stated that the present sovereign and his people are united as one family.

LAKE MAGGIORE. — FROM THE PAINTING BY S. R. GIFFORD.

in the promotion of progress and reform. The revenue of the empire, according to the last official report, was $81,552,294. The exports in 1875 amounted to about $20,000,000, and the imports to about $3,000,000. The Japanese army consists of the Imperial body-guard of 3,994 men, and of 37,812 men in garrison. The navy comprises 20 vessels, manned by 3,757 men.

The present reigning sovereign is Tenno Mutsu Hito, born November 3d, 1852. He was married on February 9th, 1869, to Haruko, daughter of a noble of the first rank, born May 29th, 1850. They have issue, one daughter, Shigheko, born January 25th, 1875. The parents of the Emperor are both living, and there are ten princes and four princesses of the Imperial family in existence.

Up to 1873 the empire of Japan had not participated to any great extent in the various European International Exhibitions. She, however, was worthily represented at the Vienna Exhibition. As early as June, 1873, the Government was officially informed by the Government of the United States concerning the Centennial Exhibition; and in November, 1874, our Government was officially notified that Japan would participate. The direction of the Imperial exhibition was intrusted chiefly to those who had attained experience at Vienna. The office was organized in January, 1875, at Tokio. It was decided to constitute the Imperial Commission as a department of that division of the Ministry of the Interior, and His Excellency Okubo was appointed President of the Commission, and General Sagio Vice-President.

The value of the goods sent to Philadelphia from Japan is estimated at $200,000. The Government has expended about $30,000 in forming a Government collection, and about $70,000 in making advances to various manufacturers to assist them in making a creditable display. In addition to this, a sum of $300,000 was appropriated for general expenses, which include even the traveling expenses of all such exhibitors as might wish to accompany their goods. Thus liberally endowed, the Japanese exhibition, so far as manufactures are concerned, was placed in the space allotted to the empire in the Main Building, lying near the western end, and extending south from the nave to the wall, having China on one side and Sweden on the other.

In the group of articles, we have at the entrance, in the centre, a bronze fountain. To the right of this is the exhibition of bronze-ware and cloisonné enamel; on the left Arita porcelain. Following on the right are cloisonné enamel ware, heavy furniture, lacquered furniture, straw and bamboo ware, lacquered utensils and cabinet work; behind which is placed the ancient copper and bronze ware; next, screens; then embroidered laces, silk fabrics and embroideries; behind this again, pictures, scientific and philosophical instruments, writing materials, books, reports, etc.; charts and maps; and at the wall, drugs and school-room furniture.

On the left, beginning at the nave, are first the specimens of Tokio porcelain and Satsuma faience. Behind this is the Satsuma ware, then the Kutani porcelain; after this, inlaid work in wood, bamboo ware; behind all this, a row of screens; then small objects of dress and adornments, toys and fancy articles, dried leathers, screens again, and at the wall, mineral ores, building-stones and mining products.

In the centre, commencing at the nave and behind the fountain, are the gold and silver-ware, historical collection of pottery and porcelain, bronzes, plastic art, earthenware,

ENGLISH FOUR-IN-HAND DRAG.

lacquered ware and small articles, weapons and coins. In the centre of the section is a large collection of lacquered ware; behind this, small ware and fancy articles, straw matting, lanterns, cotton rugs and other cotton goods.

The collection of minerals includes gold and silver, iron, copper, and, in fact, all the metals—manganese, alum, malachite, sulphur, etc. There are also exhibited coal, mineral oils, building-stones, limestone and samples of mortar. The minerals used in the manufacture of pottery and porcelain, including clay, kaolin and silex, are also exhibited, as are some specimens of mineral-waters, from the chemical laboratory of the city of Kiyoto. Quite a number of chemicals, vegetable oils, soaps, Japanese inks and indigo, form a further display.

The exhibition in ceramics includes flower-vases, tea-jars, tea-sets, coffee-sets, bonbonnières, censers, bottles, flower-pots, plates, brasiers, lamps, ornamental pieces, water-jugs, etc. The cloisonné enamel display includes the most of these articles. Of the vases one is 10 feet in height. These come from Tokio, Kiyoto and Arita. The ancient pottery and porcelain from Tokio includes pitchers, ladles, bottles, brasiers, and other objects.

The furniture is mostly lacquered-ware, and comprises utensils of all sorts, trays, lunch-boxes, chop-sticks, glove-boxes, jewel-cases, tea and coffee cups, incense-boxes, bureaus, toilet-tables, book-cases, backgammon-boards, sword-racks, poetry-boxes, screens, and even decanters, water-jugs, saddles and stirrups. Then there is lacquered furniture ornamented with incrusted mother-of-pearl shell, decorative objects, pictures on silks, painted screens, ornamental objects of rock crystal. There are walking-sticks ornamented with gold, lacquered chandeliers, and other articles too numerous to mention. In table furniture there are iron utensils imitated from ancient bronze ware, kettles, alcohol lamps. There are silver tea-sets, flower vases and jars; lacquered and decorated; a silver tea-kettle; and in miscellaneous articles, lanterns, bath-tubs, and even blinds. The vegetable fabrics contributed include mats of different sorts, canvas, cotton cloths, fancy and white cotton rugs and ramie cloth, as well as plantain fibre cloth and hemp cloth. The display of silks is large and very fine. Commencing with raw silk, there are fabrics made of gold and silver threads; fine dress silks, white, corrugated and dyed, fancy dress silks in different colors, also silk carpeting.

Then there are crapes dyed and figured, velvets, gauze; and, in manufactured articles, handkerchiefs and tobacco pouches.

The articles of clothing are not numerous, but under that head come some curious hats made of the *wistaria*. There is a large variety of fans, folding and non-folding, walking-canes, pin-cushions, table-cloths and shawls, embroidered silk carpeting and innumerable screens.

Quite a number of articles in crystal are exposed, including necklaces, earrings, buttons, ornamental images, etc., and a magnificent spherical crystal about five inches in diameter. The stationery articles include writing-brushes, specimens of paper, some of these being of plantain fibre and straw, thick colored and ornamented paper for writing, and wall-papers, some of which are made in imitation of leather.

The military articles include a coat of mail, swords, spears, halberds, bows and arrows. Under this class come also surgical instruments, dental instruments, and vehicles for the transportation of wounded soldiers.

A good display is made in bamboo work and straw, including trays, vases, baskets, book-cases and cabinets; also in rattan work and cardboard.

The bronzes include the large bronze fountain already mentioned—which is exhibited by the First Japanese Manufacturing Company of Tokio—bronze statuettes, vases, censers, candlesticks, basins, kettles, teapots, cups, etc.

In carved wood and ivory there are a number of very pleasing objects, including a miniature palace made of sandal-wood, carved and colored statuettes—some dressed in silk—ivory boats, a carved wooden bedstead, a set of bedroom furniture, and small ivory images carved at Tokio. The inlaid work comprises articles similar to those already named; and the silver ware includes enameled silver goblets, silver cake-box, silver vase, a kind of censer, and various decorative objects of this material. An enameled basin and some porcelain statuettes are also objects worthy of notice.

The silks exhibited are in rolls of 12 yards each. Two specimens are valued at $37 per yard.

Some of the cabinet-ware is very high-priced. Two small pieces are valued at $3,000; another, with carved drawers, $1,850, and a cabinet in this style of work is marked $5,000. A carved bedstead, with a beautiful silk covering and pillow-shams, is priced $1,000.

One specimen of bronze is valued at $2,500. The bronze-ware is in the highest degree artistic and beautiful, while being at the same time quaint and original in design. The bronze vases are of the most elaborate and intricate work, abounding in grotesque shapes of birds, beasts and human figures, mingled, and strikingly faithful reproductions of natural objects, familiar to every one.

It is claimed that to make a copy of one of the smallest of the objects in this collection would be beyond the skill of the best French artisans. The bronze-ware is of two kinds, the cheaper being cast, while the other is worked out by hand, with cutting and polishing instruments, with marvelous patience and skill. It is estimated that the work on one of the vases is equivalent to 2,250 days' steady labor of one man. When the fact is appreciated, the price asked, $2,000, does not seem extravagant. The ground color of the fine vases is a dark slate.

The grotesque in art, which seems to be a part of the very nature of the Japanese, is displayed in the most

ENGLISH CUTTER.

ENGLISH SPORTSMAN'S CARRIAGE.

marvelous conceptions imaginable, not only in the strange dragons and other unknown creatures delineated, but in caricatures of domestic life which are exceedingly comical. On one of the largest pieces there is a platform just above the base, surrounded by a procession of women, each carrying a gold or silver rose about twice as large as her head. Above, on the right, are a number of scenes, with male characters ; and above this on panels, in relief, are representations showing officials and high dignitaries. The handles are formed of dragons. In the case of one large vase, the handles are made by flocks of birds, which appear to be swooping down to alight on the mass of rocks at the base, regardless of a dragon just making his appearance.

The art of making these bronzes dates back two or three centuries ; and the manufacture is carried on in no fewer than sixteen places in the empire. The prices of the articles in the finer class of work run from $200 for a pair of small vases about 18 inches high to $2,500 for a single large piece.

Quite a number of urns and vases are from three to five feet in height. One urn, which is particularly noticeable, has a base in the shape of a twisted root, among the gnarled projections of which are crowded dragons, serpents and tortoises, while on the top perches an eagle. It is observed that the modern bronzes of the Japanese exhibit very plainly the effect of the active communication with the outside world, which has obtained for the past ten years ; since, although the ornaments resemble those of the antique, there is more strict attention paid to the lines of true artistic design, and what is lost in the grotesque is gained in the æsthetic.

The large bronze basin of the fountain at the entrance of the Japanese section presents a magnificent specimen of silver inlaying, all in handwork. Perhaps the most remarkable of all the bronzes is one which stands in the eastern case on the first platform from the fountain, and which has been purchased at the price of $3,800. The design of this is intricate. A grotto of perforated rock rests in a sea which is around its base, the drops of spray of which are not bronze, but silver, and in and through which fish are swimming, crabs crawling, and two enormous lizard-like dragons writhe themselves upward. Upon the top of the mass of rock rests the casket which forms the bed of the vase. It is about 18 to 20 inches square, with the most delicate raised work imaginable on its sides. On one of these is the ancient story of the spider and the fly ; on the opposite side a cat with golden eyes pursues a mouse. It is to this vase that are attached for handles the flocks of birds. These are joined to each other and are life-size—as are the other creatures represented.

Two other large and elaborately wrought vases rest upon the heads and trunks of elephants. A favorite connection between the bed of the vase and its foundation is a succession of serpents twining about each other. Sometimes

upright human figures support the bed of the vase, displaying evidences of the influence of European art. A striking exhibit in this department is a tall candelabra made of a sort of bronze, representing storks holding aloft broken branches in their bills. The workmanship displayed in the long, feathered plumes of the birds is very delicate. A common form is an idol mounted on some undomesticated animal, as a stag. These articles, as well as certain huge censers, bronze articles, etc., are of a lighter color than the modern bronzes, and are generally three or four hundred years old. One of these, a sort of pagoda mounted on the back of an animal something between a hippopotamus and elephant, has been purchased by President Hawley, of the Centennial Commission.

The mode of casting bronzes is as follows : The models

RUSSIAN HUT.

are done in wax, in which material everything down to the smallest feather of a bird's wing or the hair of a spider is elaborated with scrupulous care. Afterwards the wax model is painted all over with a coating of fine sand held together by a fireproof mucilage. This is done in succeeding coats, so as to fill the most minute space. Sometimes half a year is consumed in the work of painting the model three or four inches thick around the wax. When the model is thick enough and strong enough, the wax inside is melted away, the bronze is poured in, and the whole vase or statue is wrought in a single casting. The model is subsequently removed with the greatest possible care.

The bronze incense-burner with bird handles has been purchased by Professor Archer, of the British Commission, for the South Kensington Museum.

The entire display is said to be much finer than that made at Vienna. Indeed, one of the largest and costliest pieces here was intended for the Vienna Exhibition, but could not be finished in time, having occupied two men several years in the production. There Japan was represented by a few bronzes, and those of older date. The wonderful pieces now on exhibition have been mostly produced for the occasion.

The display of porcelain is only less beautiful and wonderful than that of bronze. This art was brought to high perfection in Japan long before it was known in Europe. The entire exhibit of both porcelain and pottery made by all the other countries in the world does not furnish so great a variety in styles and forms of ornamentation as is displayed by Japan alone. The finer of these works come from the manufactory at Arita. The Satsuma ware is large and costly. A pair of vases five feet in height are valued at $2,000 each. These stand on pedestals ornamented, in bamboo frames, in the style commonly known as the Greek border, but which is said to have been original in Japan. The vases have openwork receding arms, in the shape of bundle-wood bamboo sticks, beside a highly-pleasing commingling of grains and roots with gilt or white ground. Two vases of this ware have been presented to the Pennsylvania Museum and School of Industrial Arts. They are nearly two feet high, formed like jars, with covers on which appear tigresses with their young. Upon one of them a young ocelot is displayed.

Then there are vases with broad sea-like masses of gold on their sides, in which seem to swim huge turtles. Perhaps the most costly of these objects for their size which are to be seen are in the form of shells of enamelwork less than a foot in height. The price of these is $500 each.

Another great speciality of Japanese manufacture is the lacquered-ware, of which we have seen small specimens in the shops of our large cities ; but these give little idea of the possibilities of this class of work. From little cake trays which cost 50 cents to cabinets marked $1,000 and $1,500, there are an extraordinary variety of articles. It is stated that the art of lacquering has declined in the course of the last three centuries, and that the old masterpieces cannot now be duplicated, Here, for instance, is a cabinet 350 years old, heavily ornamented with engraved silver plates ; $5,000 is the price of it. Eight cases containing lacquered-ware include perhaps all the known varieties of ornamentation. Some of these date back as far as six centuries ago.

The designs of the older pieces are less grotesque than those of one or two hundred years old ; while they all have the delicacy of finish which makes this material its reputation. In one case there is a writing-table over 600 years old—believed to be over 700. It is about a foot and a half in height by two feet. Salvers 300 years old, lacquered

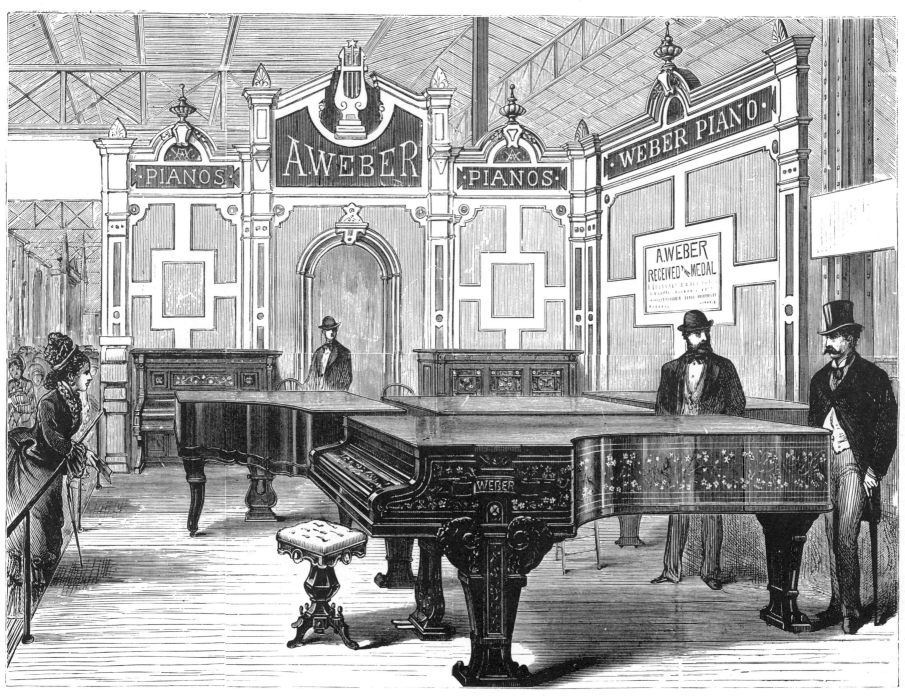

THE WEBER PIANO EXHIBIT, IN THE MAIN BUILDING.

pieces 600 years old, work-boxes, writing instruments, are all to be found in this collection. Much of the ware is inlaid with silver and mother-of-pearl, and it includes all the articles of utility or ornament for which it could possibly be employed. As in bronze, the display of lacquered-work is finer than that made in Vienna. The very perfection of *genre*, the spirit of ornamentation and beautiful combination of delicate colors are to be observed in these articles.

TIME-GLOBE, EXHIBITED IN THE MAIN BUILDING.

Gilded carvings enrich them, and sparks of the most vivid color flash from them. Overspreading all is the glossy, transparent varnish or enamel, which has never been successfully imitated by any other people. Here are cups and saucers of wood as light as cork and protected by varnish to a degree that they will withstand the hottest water. It has been remarked, and it is only fair to mention the fact, that in all the designs exhibited in Japanese art work, there appears no prevalence of the taste for the nude which obtains in Western, and as is assumed, more civilized nations. Whether this be a general fact in the history of all Japanese art is not stated. If it be, it is certainly cred-

itable both to the morals and honor of this remarkable people, and especially when we take into consideration the immediate contiguity of China, where the reverse is the case.

A curious and interesting exhibit is made of several exquisite little ivory cabinets, as also of vases made of sections of elephants' tusks, ornamented with lacquered-work. There is one exhibit of furniture in European frames which shows the capacity of the Japanese to excel the artisans of Western nations in their own business. The upholstered chairs are admirable; and there is a wardrobe in carved walnut which surpasses anything of the kind in the Italian court. The Japanese screens are among the most wonderful articles in their exhibition. In these the most astonishing effects are produced by combining embroidery with painting, the faces of the photographs being painted on a silk background, and the costumes, etc., brought out into relief. The prices are between $100 and $400.

The best decorative art in Japan appears to be devoted to the screens. In painting on silk the most artistic effects are produced in scenes from history and in *genre* sketches. Some of the smaller screens are designed apparently to be hung as pictures on the walls, and are beautifully quaint. One represents a long line of green grasshoppers marching in single-file, each carrying a flower. A black beetle leads the van, and a company of frogs sit by the road-side and watch the strange procession as it passes. The screens are all made on one general plan, usually in three divisions connected by hinges of metal, and of uniform size. The frames are of bamboo and the coverings of silk, cotton or paper.

In embroidery, the Japanese equal the world; and the work on the screens will be found to equal that displayed in the Woman's Pavilion. The delineation of small birds is exquisite.

Even the humbler kinds of screens are most interesting objects, being suggestive of Japanese manners and customs. These are covered with gilt paper of peculiar texture, the ornamentation consisting of patches of various material fastened thereon. The chief decorations are made in a primitive manner. The work is uniformly on a ground of silk, the designs being either painted, embroidered or quilted. The subjects of these delineate Japanese life are of all grades, from the recreation of the nobility to the toil of the lowest order of people, giving us clear ideas of the people, customs, industries, scenery and natural characteristics of Japan.

One process of ornamentation consists of the building up of figures by patient tailor work, layer after layer, of silken, woolen or other materials, these being sewed or glued upon each other.

In relation to the capacity of the lacquered-ware to resist wear and tear, it is stated that the French mail steamer *Nile*, on which were shipped back to Japan the articles shown at the Vienna Exhibition, was wrecked on the Japanese coast before she reached her harbor. This vessel actually sunk; yet, a year afterward, the articles were

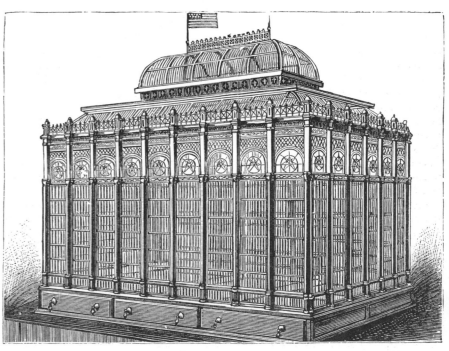

OSBORNE MANUFACTURING CO.'S BIRD-CAGE EXHIBIT, IN AGRICULTURAL HALL.

recovered, when the lacquered-work was found to be as good as when it went down into the sea.

The Japanese exhibit fewer of the elaborate carvings of ivory which are such an attraction in the Chinese departments; but their inlaying of ivory is exquisite.

One of the most instructive sections of the Japanese is the large pavilion near the southern entrance, on the inside of which is exhibited by small figures all costumes known in Japanese life, and the wild and domestic animals. Here can be seen the dress of all ranks, from the Mikado down to the beggar. Soldiers, merchants, laborers of all classes have their distinctive costumes, which no others are permitted to wear.

The peculiar little Japanese ponies, not until very recently broken to saddle, the pretty chickens, and numbers of other domestic animals, most of them possessing peculiar marks of isolated breeds, are also exhibited.

Among the wood and ivory carvings is a temple of wood very delicately cut, and filled with bas-reliefs of religious scenes and ornamented with dragons. This is made of sandal-wood. Several Japanese boats of various kinds, with the sailors cut out of ivory, are also exhibited; and three miniature skeletons made of a solid piece of ivory, with skulls, are scattered about the floor of one case, where at one end is a large flower-pot cut from an elephant's tooth and embossed with tinted figures representing hunting scenes.

The cases of silk embroidery are numerous, and the exhibits indescribably rich. Birds and animals of all possible varieties are here found transferred to elegant fabrics, making a most gorgeous and wonderful display. A large model of a Japanese pleasure-boat, double-decked, occupies a case by itself. The floor of the little cabin is covered with matting, and lacquered-work in rich colors makes a most gorgeous display. Near the collection of costumed figures is the space devoted to the Government exhibits of building-stones, metallic ores, coals, medicinal plants, grains, stuffed animals, wax fruits, ambulances, and a multitude of other objects.

The department closes with the educational section. Here a long table is filled with philosophical instruments of all descriptions, from the Archimedean screw to the spectroscope; the spaces on each side are occupied with maps, school-books, charts and geometrical figures, compositions in French, German and Japanese, written by pupils in the public schools, and school-apparatus. In addition to this are a number of pictures representing school-work of Japan, and contrasted with the pictures are to be seen the well-known Japanese paintings, proficient in outline, and not unnatural in color, but innocent of every idea of perspective.

Several very beautiful photographs on porcelain are exhibited in this section by a Tokio artist. Near by are many old paintings on paper and cloth; and finally, we have a collection of copper

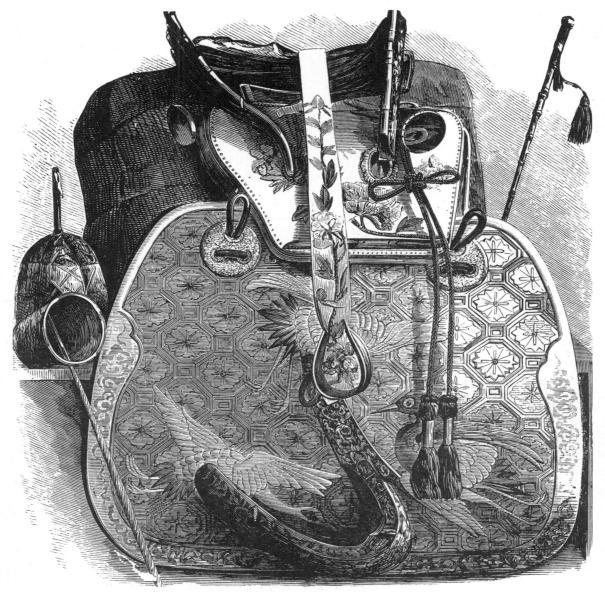

JAPANESE SADDLE.

plates used for printing Government bonds, revenue stamps, etc., samples of type, stereotyped plates, proof-sheets, and a number of books in Japanese, including a history of Japan, the Code Napoleon a collection of poetry, and—*mirabile dictu*—Buckle's "History of Civilization," in Japanese, with native binding.

Some facts in reference to the mining and manufacturing industries of Japan will not be uninteresting or inappropriate in this place. It is stated that mines were worked as far back as the latter part of the eighth century; and even now the system of working mines is changed but little from that in use in the earliest times. Miners use hand-tools—pick and hammer—and gunpowder has only been brought into use for blasting purposes quite recently. Silver-mines were worked in the province of Iwanni to an enormous extent a few years ago; but this was interrupted by violent earthquakes in 1872. The Ikuno mines were open some 300 years ago; and at the beginning of this

century they gave employment to some 4,000 miners. The most important coal-fields are in the northwest of the Island of Kioshiu. Rich seams have been found in the Island of Takashinia, about eight miles west of Nagasaki. This mine produced 78,000 tons in 1874. Petroleum is found to the northwest of Tokio, where oil was discovered 300 years ago. A natural combustible gas issuing from the ground in certain places has long been brought through pipes of bamboo into the houses and used for illuminating purposes. Oil, however, has only been used by the people of the country during the last forty-six years. Since then 508 wells have been sunk in one district, some of these wells being 600 feet deep.

Building-stones are not scarce, but are seldom used for houses, and mostly for foundations, gate-ways, sea-walls, etc. The graveyards and temples contain great numbers of stone monuments, and lanterns adorn the approaches to the temples. Marbles of different colors are found in several provinces. The smelting of iron is carried on in the old method in small furnaces 12 to 15 feet high, made of fire-clay. Improvements have recently been introduced, and a certain number of glass furnaces for smelting magnetic

ore have been built. Large smelting-works are about to be commenced in one province, the cost of which is estimated at $820,000.

The origin of Japanese industries and manufactures can be traced back to China and Corea; but these have been so much modified in every respect that the creations of Japanese artisans have a character of their own. As the country has been at peace since 1600, the industries have been developed extensively, particularly those connected with art. Of late years not only the Government, but private persons, have made great efforts to create large industrial establishments. Several paper-mills and cotton-mills, with steam and water power, are to be found in different places; glass furnaces have been built in Tokio, and the streets of Yokohama and a great part of Tokio are lighted by gas made from coal mined in one of the provinces. Several machine-shops and other manufactories have been established by the Government, and an arsenal at Yokohama is completely organized for the purpose of ship-building. The Government has special Boards with a view of promoting and developing newly-introduced industries, as in the case of pottery, the art of weaving, and making silken garments. These Boards are a very ancient institution. As to the invention of pottery, old Japanese legends attribute it to a period long before the commencement of the Japanese chronology, 660 B. C. Samples of earthenware made as early as 724 A. D. still exist in the empire. The beginning of the manufacture of real porcelain occurred late in the sixteenth century, since which time this art has been a prominent industry.

The most remarkable manufactures belonging to the

JAPANESE LACQUER-WORK BOXES.

class of stone pottery are the Satsuma and Awata, the latter being manufactured in the suburbs of Kiyoto. Both are made from a kind of porcelain clay. The old Satsuma ware was seldom made in large pieces, but comprised small dishes, saucers, teapots, etc. In later years vases of moderate size have been made, and some of these, of exceptional height and difficult workmanship, have been manufactured especially for the Philadelphia Centennial. The decoration is mostly composed of bright and flowery paintings, amongst which the chrysanthemum and peacock's tail take prominent places. It is further distinguished by the delicacy of outline and the fine red and green colors. More recently the Satsuma ware, and especially the vases, have been frequently imitated in Yokohama and Yeddo.

The Awata ware is distinguished by a more yellowish tint than the Satsuma. A peculiar kind of stone-ware, resembling, to a certain extent, the wedgewood, is made in the province of Ise, and called Banko y Aki, from the name of the inventor. The material used for this ware is a brown stone of such toughness that teapots and other small articles can be made extremely light and thin. It is decorated with paintings and opaque enamels. Of this ware, a tea-service was on exhibition.

The art of porcelain-making is conducted by methods the old fashion of sitting on the floor. The ordinary mats in Japanese houses are made of various kinds of brush, lined with rice-straw. These are more than an inch thick. They are all of the same size throughout Japan, six feet by three. As the rooms are usually of corresponding dimensions, the mats can be removed from one house to another, and will be found to fit, as also the ceiling, doors and windows, which are everywhere of the same dimensions.

The cotton industry is of comparatively recent origin in Japan. The plant is only said to have been introduced some 300 years ago. The Japanese loom resembles the common European loom of the last century in its construction.

Silk is the principal export from Japan, and constitutes three-fourths of the total merchandise exported, although the silk trade comprehends scarcely anything but raw silk and silkworms. The exhibition at Philadelphia proves, as it did at Vienna, that the manufacture of silk has taken a high degree of perfection. As early as 300 A. D., persons were sent to China for the purpose of engaging competent people to teach the art of weaving and producing silk goods.

A great variety of articles, such as taffetas, baréges, velvets, damasks, crapes and brocades are found of such excellence as to excite the admiration of foreigners. The of ivory, mother-of-pearl, etc. The umbrella is another article of necessity, whose enormous manufacture and cheapness are attributable to the prevalence of that useful plant, the bamboo.

NORWAY.

The Norwegian section lies north of the nave, extending to the northern wall of the Main Building, and between the spaces allotted to Italy and Sweden.

The mining and metallurgic industry of Norway is esteemed to be worth about $2,000,000 per annum, the product including pyrites, copper, iron, slate, silver and nickel. Of building-stones, especially fine granite, Norway possesses large quantities. Slates are found in different places, and also white and colored marbles. Traces of coal have also been discovered in different parts of the country, and these discoveries are now being pursued to some advantage. The exhibited mineral ores and building-stones from Norway include nickel, copper, silver and iron ores; also stones illustrating the different geological strata of the country, samples of various minerals, with all sorts of hewn stone for jetties, quays, dikes, fortifications, etc., flint millstones, the raw material of which flint-stone is made, brought from France, samples of slates, Norwegian emeralds found at a distance of 30 to 40 feet from the

THE INTERNATIONAL POULTRY EXHIBIT.

very similar to those employed in Europe, the machinery used, however, being of a very primitive kind. Kaga-ware is distinguished by a very fine gold ornamentation, generally on red, sometimes on black, grounds, showing open fields, flowers, birds, and personages, either traced in red or gold outlines or painted with transparent enamels.

The native furniture is generally of a very light and elegant construction, and can easily be moved in case of damage by fire, etc. The finest lacquered-ware is made in Tokio and Kiyoto. The cheaper articles are mostly manufactured in the interior. The art of lacquering is more than a thousand years old; and pieces made in those ancient times are still extant in the country. Lacquer is not merely used for small objects. Larger constructions are made of it, as the interior sills of temples, ceilings, columns, staircases, etc.

The art of carving lacquered-ware was introduced into Japan by Chinese artists. The carvings mostly represent flowers, birds, and human figures, in imitation of the Chinese. In inlaid-work, pieces of mother-of-pearl shell are selected, but are only made use of in moderation, to give variety to the gold paintings.

A most important article of house furniture in Japan is matting, as the people of the country continue to retain weaving establishments of Kiyoto are all located in one square of the town, and seldom contain more than twenty looms each. The loom on which the figured goods are woven is made on the principle of the old loom used in Europe previous to the invention of the Jacquard loom.

Jewelry and other small articles of personal adornment are only used by the women in Japan, and consist almost exclusively of ornaments worn in the hair. Latterly gold rings, chains and brooches have been made in imitation of foreign articles.

Among the principal articles of manufacture are fans; and every child is said to have one special holiday in the year when it is presented with all sorts of articles of the latter species. Great luxury is frequently displayed in dolls, or in small figures, richly dressed in silks and brocades, representing scenes of court-life, national legends, etc. Another class of children's toys consists of excellent imitations of animals. Of fans there are two kinds, the folding and the non-folding. The former is a Japanese invention, made in the seventh century, A. D. That this invention was afterward introduced into China from Japan is stated in Chinese books. The cheaper kind of fans are made of bamboo; others are manufactured of fine woods, tortoiseshell and ivory, with gilt paintings, incrustations shore of the Lake Mjosen in a quartz lode, and phosphate of lime.

There are also exhibits of silver in bars, and granulated silver, and iron in various conditions. The Cathrinholm Iron Works, a foundry of Frederickshal, exhibits iron specimens. These works were established in 1827, and manufacture boiler-bolts, chains, railway and armor plate, bells, axles, and other parts of machinery; also steel and iron wire, and bar and wrought iron. They employ 250 men, and find their chief market in Norway, although they do sell to England and the Continent, and also to America, Australia and Africa. These Works have never before exhibited at an international exhibition.

The manufactures of Norway include fish oil, matches, pottery and crockery, bricks, glass, furniture and textile fabrics, also the fabrication of filigree silver ornaments, and paper. Large manufacturing establishments are not yet common in Norway, but the domestic work throughout the country is of great value. Here the men make all their tools and furniture, and the women do all the work in the manufacture of clothing, such as spinning, weaving, sewing, etc. Specimens illustrating these latter industries are found in the Women's Pavilion.

The chemical manufacture illustrated by Norwegian

1 4. Buff Cochin Roosters and Hen.   2. Black-red Game Bantam.   3. Light Brahma Rooster and Hen.   5. Gold Sea-bright Bantam.   6 Bronze Turkey and Hen.   7. African Goose.   8. Wood-duck and Hen.   9. Muscovy Duck.
10. White and Gold Pheasants.   11. Rumpless Fowl.   12. Silver-Gray Dorking.   13. Sultan Rooster and Hen.   14. Black Poland.   15. La Fleche.   16. Derby Game Rooster.   17. Colored Leghorn.   18. Japanese Rooster.

THE INTERNATIONAL POULTRY EXHIBIT.

exhibits, include toilet soaps, Scandinavian ink, essences, perfumery and pomades, safety and phosphorus matches, percussion-caps and gunpowder. Matches, which now form an important industry in Norway, were not manufactured there until 1863, when the Nitedal Match Factory, near Christiania, was established. Other attempts in this direction had been previously made, but had been unsuccessful; but in 1865 this factory was able to produce more than the consumption of the country required, and entered into competition with the rest of the world. This success resulted in the founding of other establishments, and Norway now numbers 27 match factories. That at Nitedal only supplies safety-matches, and exhibited at Paris in 1867 and at Stockholm in 1866, obtaining medals in both exhibitions.

The exhibits of ceramics, pottery, porcelain, etc., as well as glass and glassware, come from Christiania, and include

most attractive. The most prominent articles in this collection are drinking-vessels, from the vast drinking-horn down to the flagons of various sizes, and silver mugs holding scarcely half a pint. One drinking-horn has a capacity of a gallon or more, and is set on golden wheels. At its base it ends in a large knob, where a crowing cock is placed. The mouth is finished with gold in a wide band, ornamented with a border of flowers, and in front nymphs and satyrs are placed, dancing.

A porcelain flagon, with a richly wrought silver lid, is a very handsome article in this collection. The porcelain is remarkably fine, ornamented with gilding and flowers. On the lid is a figure in high relief, representing a knight mounted. Another porcelain flagon, very small, has a graceful tracery of blue on a white ground, and a silver lid, with the date 1742. The silver drinking-cups are about the size and shape of ordinary tumblers, with simple designs

southern side of the nave, between Denmark and Japan, extending to the south.

The total population of Sweden in 1874 was 4,341,559. Norway and Sweden are united under one king, the government being a constitutional monarchy. The Swedish people are represented by a Diet, including the first and second chamber, whose members, who are not restricted except by the fundamental law of the kingdom, have the right to move whatever questions they think proper. The speakers or presidents of the houses are, however, appointed by the king.

Domestic industry has always had a prominent place in Sweden, owing to the fact that the distances between settled localities are great, and the inhabitants have been obliged to depend upon their own energies; and also because the long Winter evenings have compelled the inhabitants to seek suitable employment within doors. It is

NATIVE WEAPONS FROM THE PHILIPPINE ISLANDS.

painted and decorated porcelain, colored and decorative glass, and glass floats for fishing-nets.

In furniture and household articles the exhibits are also from Christiania. The fittings of the Norwegian section are the exhibit of a Christiania joiner, and Chr. Holst, head steward to His Majesty the King, contributes some arm-chairs, saloon-chairs, etc., from the Royal Villa, Oscarshal.

In fabrics there are shown cotton, yarns, shirtings, canvas, ginghams, dyed cotton fabrics, and net materials. The Fagerheim Net Company, of Berlin, is the only one in Norway which makes fishing-nets mechanically, and was only established in 1873. Christiania sends also an exhibit of Scandinavian jewelry, ornaments and traveling equipments, which are displayed in the Main Building, and of which we shall have more to say presently. These include ready-made linen, meerschaum pipes, carpets, furs, fur lining, and national costumes. Some interesting exhibits are made in the manufacture of paper from wood pulp, as also in asphalt paper for covering roofs.

The medicinal exhibits are represented chiefly by cod-liver oil, the chief specimens of this article being shown by Peter Moller, of Christiania, whose manufactories are situated in the Island of Lofoten. These are worked by steam-power, and can produce from 2,000 to 3,000 barrels of oil annually. When the oil is extracted and filled into barrels of tin or galvanized iron, it is sent to Christiania, where the bottling process takes place, being accomplished chiefly by girls. The oil is prepared according to the method originated by Peter Moller, who has received personal decorations at the hands of the King of Sweden, who conferred upon him the Swedish Order of Knighthood of Vasa, and the Norwegian Knighthood of St. Olaf, for his services in promoting a national branch of industry.

Some exhibits of cutlery and tools are made, including a collection of knives, with carved handles of walrus teeth, and wood, commonly carried by tourists of Norway, contributed by the Norwegian Tourists' Club, Christiania.

The Norwegian section is inclosed by a light framework of unpainted pine, with the Norwegian colors picturesquely draped. The most attractive exhibit of this country is placed near the nave, and is perhaps the most interesting, because unexpected. This is an exhibit of silver filigree, which includes jewel-boxes, bracelets, necklaces, earrings, diadems, bouquet-holders, silver belts, sprays of leaves, all of marvelous beauty and exquisite workmanship. One exhibit from P. A. Lie, of Christiania, includes a number of articles of tasteful design and perfect execution. Perhaps the most remarkable thing in this collection is a drinking-horn of silver and gold, placed on a base of ebony, its tip of golden fretwork, and the cover richly decorated, the crown of silver filigree, holding a harp. Underneath are figures carved in high relief, representing Scandinavian deities. The horn is upheld by a sturdy figure in silver, and the entire effect is artistic and satisfying.

The exhibits of antique jewelry and silver-ware of William Graham, a dealer in curiosities of Christiania, are

engraved or in *repousse*. There are also a sugar-bowl, salt-cellars and spoons. Most of these articles have the initials of former owners engraved upon them, and thus have doubtless associations of their own. There are several snuff-boxes, elaborately worked in *repoussé*, and a number of beautiful little vinaigrettes in the shape of hearts, or small horns, tipped with silver, belt clasps, chatelaines, earrings and finger-rings, all highly ornamented.

There is also a show of antique articles of hammered brass and copper; and the carved furniture is well worthy of examination. The largest piece is a buffet of oak, worthy 8 feet wide by 10 high. If this be really a buffet, the subjects designed upon it are strikingly inappropriate. These include the Nativity, the Adoration of the Magi, the Vision of Zacharias, the Circumcision, the Last Supper, and the Crucifixion; while upon the bars supporting the panels are carved heads of the apostles. The carvings are artistic and finely finished. Another piece is a bedstead, surmounted by a canopy, both richly carved. Here the panels are also illustrative of scriptural subjects. The canopy is upheld by small figures, supported by caryatides. The brass and copper-work includes a number of great plates with designs in *repoussé*, of scriptural subjects, and also antique brass candlesticks and candelabras.

The national costumes of Norway are shown by life-size figures, which are not only life-size, but life-like. These are in groups, illustrating manners and customs, as well as costumes. One of these groups includes three Laplanders, their dress of heavy woolens of the gayest colors, and their

CANADIAN SLEIGH.

headdresses curious and quaint. The man wears a hat which consists of a band about the forehead, surmounted by what appears to be a small cushion. The child is enveloped in skins. On another platform stand a bridal pair of rosy-cheeked peasants. The youth is bareheaded, but the bride wears a sort of marriage crown. In another inclosure, a Laplander sits holding the reins over a reindeer, while a woman beside him supports the baby.

Among the furs there are beautiful robes of eider-down, rugs made from the white and black bear skins, and robes pieced from the plumage of aquatic birds.

Sweden.

Sweden lies next to Norway, extending also from the nave to the north wall, and eastwardly to the British colonial section, with a narrow strip upon the opposite or

stated, however, that domestic industry is on the decline, owing to the reduction of prices and the greater perfection and tastefulness of the manufactures.

Among the industrial branches, that of weaving is still the most important, although the peasants do not now, as formerly, wear almost exclusively clothes made by their wives. In some districts they spin and weave fine linens, both plain and figured, for tablecloths; in others they make woolen cloths. These for market; but the industrial art is carried on in a great many places where the manufacture is intended for home use.

Smith and joiners'-work, and the manufacture of clocks, basket and straw-work, boots and shoes, are among the male employments. These methods of manufacture have developed the peddling system of commerce; but this, too, is falling off. Sometimes West Gothians or Svealanders are still met with, traveling about the country, offering for sale their home-woven cotton or woolen fabrics; or a Dalecarlian may be found far away from his home trying to dispose of a clock, or a Dalecarlian woman peddling her work even into Norway and Denmark, or as far as Germany or England.

The mining interest is most important in Sweden, which is very rich in ores, especially in iron ore, limited, however, to certain districts. There are also copper ore, native silver, cobalt, manganese, and coal, which has been mined in small quantities since the middle of the eighteenth century. There are inexhaustible supplies of granite in Sweden, and considerable marble, sandstone, fire-clay and cement. The precious metals are scarce, although gold and silver are both found in small quantities.

The manufacture of iron and steel is not yet large enough even to satisfy the necessities of the country itself.

The manufacture of earthenware is at present carried on in Sweden at the two china and faience factories, Röstrand and Gustafsberg, both near Stockholm, as also at Malmö and Höganäs, where porcelain stoves, common earthenware and bricks are made. The manufacture of earthenware employs about 1,200 persons, and the value of the product is about $750,000 gold per annum. The manufacture of porcelain stoves in Sweden, where such are almost exclusively used for the heating of dwelling-houses, is considerable. The tiles of the stoves are made from clay, coated with a brilliant glaze. This manufacture has been recently greatly improved, and there is quite a demand for it even from abroad.

The manufacture of glass for the year 1873 amounted to $786,000, the number of workmen employed being 1,670. Painting on glass has been introduced within the last half-year, and colored glass is likewise manufactured.

Sweden being extremely rich in forests, the timber industry occupies a very important place. Cabinet-makers' work is carried on partly as a domestic industry and partly in manufactories, as well as in workshops of prisons and poor-houses. As a domestic industry, the manufacture of furniture is practiced all over the country. The woods used

OUT ALL NIGHT. — FROM THE PAINTING BY J. H. BEARD.

are birch, elm, oak, mahogany, walnut, rosewood, etc.; the walnut being at present most in favor. It is obtained from Gottland and the most southern parts of Sweden.

Basket-work has of late attracted general attention in Sweden, and the production, chiefly of domestic industry, has been encouraged by various economical societies, which have established schools for instruction in this and in straw-work.

The manufacture of articles belonging to the clothing industry, such as wearing apparel, lace-work, embroideries, artificial flowers and the like, is insignificant; although it is practiced in small manufactories, and partly as a domestic industry. In some districts lace-making is still continued.

The Swedish department in the Main Building begins with a group of five figures, showing the costume of the country. They are represented standing by a deer, which has just been shot. Next there are cases of minerals with specimens of native marble cut into small blocks, and on the partitions, geological maps of the kingdom. Some fur-skins are next shown; and there is a specimen of a porcelain stove peculiar to the country. A case of manufactured furs and fur-trimmed clothing is next seen, and then a case of perfumes and toilet articles. Several large cases contain fabrics of wool and silk.

North of North Avenue, and extending the full width of the section, are the exhibits of Swedish iron and steel, including ores and heavy castings. The Swedish iron industry is promoted by an association composed of nearly all the iron-masters of Sweden, and which meets every three years in Stockholm. This association advances money to its members to assist them in extending their works, makes appropriations for experimenting and investigation, and in other ways extends a liberal protection over this manufacture. This association was founded in 1745. Its capital is more than $1,000,000 gold.

The iron ores exhibited include magnetic and specular iron ores. There are also exhibits of pig-iron, bloom and bar-iron, iron plate, armor, steel springs, axles, shafts and various forgings for machinery, etc. The Iron-Masters' Association has a collective exhibit covering pretty much the whole manufacture. The manufacture of bar-iron was commenced in 1856, pig-iron in 1872, and steel in 1874, in one manu-

factory contributing to this collective exhibit. The celebrated Dannemora mines exhibit Bessemer steel, ingots, steel bars and cast-steel ingots made from the Dannemora iron. Copper is also exhibited in plates, bars and ingots, with specimens illustrating its various stages of production. Brazen hardware is shown from the works established in 1611 by the Government on the estate of Skultuna.

Returning south from the metal exhibits, we find those illustrating the manufacture of paper and printed books, including wall, writing and wrapping paper. Next are chemicals and philosophical implements. In a case just here is seen a chessboard with a curious set of carved wood chessmen. Then there is a monument on which are displayed a large number of candles of different sizes. These are manufactured from stearine, oleine and glycerine. A show of fire-brick and large pottery comes next; and this brings us to a magnificent display of china, glass and porcelain at the nave. This exhibition includes many articles which in originality of form and beauty of coloring compare favorably with the best exhibited.

There is a species of majolica-ware shown here, which is extremely artistic and original in design. Its general

popularity is displayed in the fact that almost every article in the collection is marked "sold." This exhibit includes faience, china, porcelain and terra-cotta. Much of it has received medals at different continental exhibitions—those of Stockholm in 1866, Paris, 1867, Moscow, 1872, Copenhagen, 1872, and Vienna, 1873. Here are found faience, plain and decorated, majolica and Palissy, and in fact all the different varieties. It is interesting to know that in the manufactories where these wares are made, generous provisions are made for the welfare of the workmen employed, such as sick and burial funds, poor funds, Savings Banks, reading-rooms, libraries, Sunday-schools and other important educational and charitable institutions.

Glassware, plain and decorated, is shown; one factory, established in 1810, employing 224 laborers, whose wages average $33,500 gold per annum. This company has a church, school and hospital, and keeps a drug-store.

The Swedish section ends on the nave with a group of figures; but continuing north again, you meet with exhibits of furs, clothing, and a large case of safety-matches, brass-ware, a fair showing of cutlery, and a very large display of tinware. Outside of the section in the east are three large groups of costumed figures. The display of glassware is very handsome, and the carved wood, cabinet-work, etc., will attract attention.

Among the curious exhibits in furniture manufacture is a set in varnished pine, consisting of a table, sofa and four chairs, which can be folded together and are easily transported. There is also a writing-desk and a cigar-case in inlaid-work. A cabinet of Swedish birch-wood, veneered with birch veneer, is a very artistic article. A curiosity is a chair made from oak from a Swedish line-of battle ship sunk in 1676, and partly raised in 1870. It is stated that the wages of journeymen cabinet-makers is from $4 71 to $7 per week, and that this is 50 per cent. higher than two years ago.

Among the articles of gold and silverware, of which there are few, a silver drinking-cup, richly chiseled and adorned with medallions, is noticeable. The furs exposed are those of the kid, reindeer, moose, beaver, marten, sable, blue fox and otter, both dressed and in manufactured articles. The life-size figures dressed in national costumes are also exhibited,

WISCONSIN STATE BUILDING.

Wood pulp for paper-making, chemically manufactured, is quite an important article, one manufactory employing 110 workpeople. The product is exported to England, Germany and France.

Too much cannot be said in favor of the educational system of Sweden, and its lasting benefits to the growing youth of the country. In illustration of that system, we have a Primary Country Schoolhouse, with furniture, books, maps and apparatus for instruction, situated north of the Main Building, and illustrated and described elsewhere in this work. The framework for this building, which is 40 by 50 feet in dimensions, was imported from Sweden, and is exhibited by G. O. Wengström.

The space devoted to Sweden, extending from the nave to South Avenue, is given up to army equipments, army wagons, drawings, charts, plans, etc., illustrating engineering, and incloses four life-size figures in uniforms displaying the dress of Swedish soldiers of the different grades. These figures are wonderfully close in their resemblance to the actual human article—so much so, in fact, as to quite deceive visitors, who frequently mistook them for living beings.

Before closing our consideration of the Swedish industries, a few words may properly be said in reference to the iron manufacture beyond what we have already given. This industry has been in a state of uninterrupted development, not only as regards the quality of the iron produced, but also the amount of the production since the time of its inception. It is true, however, that its production has not increased in the same ratio as that of several other countries, although in 1870 it was one and a half times greater than in 1860.

Most of the deposits of iron ore in Sweden are confined to certain districts, in some of which, owing to the difficulty of transport and the extreme sparseness of population, it has not been possible to utilize them to any considerable extent. It is, however, the scanty supply of fuel which limits the iron production of Sweden; coal occurring only in a few districts, and this not of the best quality. Consequently the manufacturers are confined to the fuel which may be obtained from the forest and peat mosses, and to imported coal, for the working of their iron. It is, therefore, impossible that Sweden should become a large iron-producer, notwithstanding the value and importance, in quality and extent, of its ore-deposit. This being the case, the Swedes are devoting themselves to the production of iron of a superior quality, and are constantly seeking to improve this quality up to the very highest standard.

Swedish iron is distinguished generally by a much greater purity than that of its foreign competitors, which contains more phosphorus, sulphur, silicon and cinder. Swedish iron has long been in constant demand. It is, in fact, unnecessarily good for most purposes, for which an inferior and cheaper iron suffices. The iron ores consist principally of black ore or magnetite, and specular ore or hematite, which are so called to distinguish them from the other kinds of ores, viz.: lake and bog ores. The ores that are freest of phosphorus are in general employed in making steel; and as the Swedish iron consumed in England and elsewhere is made to serve in the manufacture of steel, the value of the Swedish varieties of iron depends chiefly on their freedom from phosphorus.

In the manufacture of malleable iron and steel, the method of refining most common in Sweden is that which is called the Lancashire process, carried on in small, closed furnaces, the product being obtained being afterward reheated in separate furnaces. In the Dalecarlian district, two work together in such a way that the bloom is produced in the one and reheated in the other.

The Bessemer method of refining has been in use in Sweden from its first origin. Indeed, a completely satisfactory Bessemer product was attained at an earlier period in Sweden than in England. The production of iron and steel has not hitherto been so great that the export has been equal to the import, one reason for this being that the Swedes do not go to the expense of Bessemer rails in the construction of their roads, but continue to use the cheaper puddle iron rails, which are imported.

The geological specimens, of which we have already spoken, and which are placed near the nave in the Swedish section, are an exhibition of the Geological Survey commenced in 1858, and include geological maps and papers published by the survey; 278 specimens of Swedish quaternary deposits, concretions, glacial shells, lake and bog iron ore, and 176 polished cubic specimens of Swedish rocks. One of the maps is 13 feet long and 10 feet in height. The rock specimens include limestone, green sand, white chalk, fire-clay, sandstone, red-clay, red sandstone, clay-slate, red-gneiss, alluvial sand, etc. There are also a large number of shells from the glacial deposits of Sweden.

In the districts about the west coasts of this country, entire and broken shells, inclosed either in glacial clay, or sand and gravel, are found in several places, and at heights varying from 90 to 500 feet above the level of the sea. Lake and bog iron ores are found in a great many of the Swedish lakes and bogs, and in many places deposits of this kind are still common. The polished cubic specimens are very beautiful, and include marble, granite, limestone, porphyry, garnet gneiss, a dull-green marble, clay-slate, trap-rock, etc.; these stones are extensively used for architectural and monumental purposes. There is a granite of a red color, which, when cut and polished, is very handsome. This has been used in the pedestal of the equestrian statue of Gustavus Adolphus II., in Stockholm, and also in the construction of the Strömsholm canal. The porphyries which come from Dalecarlia are used in the manufacture of urns, vases, columns, pedestals, tombstones, table-tops, dishes, plates, knife-handles and boxes. Another stone used for the same purposes is called phonolite, and sometimes serpentine. Altogether, the geological specimens of Sweden offer a subject of much interest and instruction.

STATUE, "VANITY."

British Austarlian Colonies.

The British colonial section, which is larger than any other foreign department in the Main Building excepting Great Britain, France and Germany, is located between Sweden and Canada, and extends from the nave to the northern wall of the building.

This section commences with *Victoria*, the most populous colony in Australia; a colony 420 geographical miles long and 250 broad—in fact about the size of Great Britain. Although Victoria is smaller than any other of the Australian colonies, its population is nearly as large as all the others put together—being, in round numbers, 820,000.

Victoria was first discovered by Captain Cook in 1770, but the first permanent settlement there did not take place until 1834. The discovery of gold, which took place in 1851, enormously increased the population and revenues of the colony; yet of the exports in 1874, while gold was about £4,000,000, the export of wool was valued at more than six and a quarter millions.

Melbourne, which is the metropolis, has a population of about 55,000, and is a large and prosperous city, containing more than 10,000 dwelling-houses. Taking in the suburbs, which extend for a radius of 10 miles and embrace 15 other towns or boroughs, the population in 1871 was 206,780. The second town in Victoria, according to population, is Ballarat, having about 50,000 inhabitants. The population on the gold fields in 1871 was 270,428. The imports into Victoria for the year 1874 were £17,000,000 in round numbers, and the exports about fifteen and a half millions. The whole quantity of gold raised in the colony from the period of the first discovery of gold to the end of 1874 is estimated at £177,656,709.

The number of scholars receiving instruction was in 1874, 238,592. The Melbourne Public Library was opened on the 11th of February, 1856, although the building is still unfinished. Its cost up to the end of 1874 was £170,990. It is a magnificent structure, containing, besides the public library, the National Gallery, the Industrial and Technological Museum, and a National Museum in a building attached to the Library. Free libraries, athenæums or literary institutions exist in most of the towns of the colony. These numbered 130 in 1874, and possessed 104,103 volumes. The total number of books in the Melbourne Library in 1874 was 83,231.

There are 32 general hospitals in Victoria, also 5 benevolent asylums, 7 orphan asylums, 4 hospitals for the insane, 9 industrial and reformatory schools, and 4 refuges for fallen women. In Melbourne there are also an asylum and school for the blind, and a deaf and dumb institution, an eye and ear hospital, and a children's hospital; also friendly societies, dispensaries, a sailors' home, and other charitable institutions.

Wages in Melbourne vary from $3 50 to $5 per week and rations for farm laborers; $3 to $4 with rations for laborers employed on ship stations; $2 50 to $3 per day for mechanics; and $1 50 per day to town laborers, this without rations. The weekly rent of a dwelling suitable for a mechanic and his family ranges, in the suburbs of Melbourne, between $2 and $4. In other towns it is lower.

Land is held in the colony under license during three years, within which period the licensee must reside on his selection at least two and a half years, must inclose it, cultivate one acre out of ten, effect substantial improvements to the value of about $5 per acre, 320 acres being the largest amount which any one person is allowed to select. The rent payable during this period is two shillings sterling per acre per annum, which is credited as part payment. At the expiration of the three years' license, provided the selector has complied with all conditions, he can either purchase his holding by paying up the balance of 14 shillings sterling per acre, or may convert his license into a lease extending over seven years, at an annual rent of two shillings per acre, which is also credited as a part payment of the fee-simple. On the expiration of this lease and due payment of the rent, the land becomes the freehold of the selector. The total extent of land sold since the first establishment of the colony is about 10,000,000 acres; the fee simple of the whole of which is secured to the purchasers. A further extent of land, amounting at the end of 1874 to about 5,650,000 acres, was in process of alienation under the system of deferred payments.

On entering the Victoria section of the Main Building, one is perhaps first struck with the stuffed specimens of native animals and birds, including the kangaroo, ému, native turkey, etc. Here are also fac-similes of gold nuggets found in Victoria. Among these is the "Welcome" nugget, found on the 11th of June, 1858, at Ballarat, 180 feet beneath the surface, the weight of which is 2,195 ounces. Another, the "Viscount Canterbury," was found at a depth of 15 feet from the surface, on the 31st of May, 1870, and weighed 1,105 ounces. Still another, the "Viscountess Canterbury," was found on the 3d of October, 1870, at 6 feet 6 inches below the surface, and weighed 134 ounces 10 pennyweights. Twenty-five of these nuggets are exhibited by the colonial government.

Some cases of insects and a large number of photographs of local scenes and buildings, specimens of artificial fruit, ornaments in jewelry, of native marble, cloths and shawls, some exhibits of pottery and basket-work are also to be seen here, and a large number of specimens of wool of different varieties, with skins of animals, hides, cordage, etc. There are also exhibited a large number of native war weapons, including the celebrated boomerang. Quite a collection of rocks, minerals and fossils, illustrative of the geological and mining resources of Victoria, is exhibited by the government, and a fine selection of gems, precious stones, including diamonds, blue sapphires, Oriental emeralds, rubies, aqua-marines, topazes, beryls, garnets and tourmalines are exhibited by J. I. Valesdale, of Melbourne.

There are also specimens of nickel ore, coal, marble, sandstone and granite among the minerals; and antimony, pig-lead and block-tin in metals. The pottery includes bricks, drain-pipes, vases, stone-pottery, jugs, fire-clay,

crucibles and caustic-tiles, vases, etc., with some specimens of glass-ware, and stained glass for windows.

In furniture there are tables of black-wood, sideboards, articles in basket-work, such as cradles, perambulators, basket-chairs, fur-stands; and there is a collection of pot-

to be seen here. The artificial or cultivated fruit include, beside the ordinary varieties, the *medlar, Loquat,* apricots, pomegranates, figs, *ran apples,* egg-apples and Cape gooseberries.

The next division is *Queensland,* the northeast section of Australia, and a colony of vast size, having nearly three times the area of Texas, with a seaboard equivalent to that of the United States from Maine to Louisiana. This colony is rich in minerals, and equally so as a farming country; extensive and valuable sugar-plantations existing in certain sections, while gold, silver, lead and copper abound, and the whole country is well provided with sheep, cattle and horses.

In the west are vast rolling prairies, large enough to accommodate either Germany or Austria, while the coast is dotted with beautiful islands, grassy and fertile, and is distinguished by picturesque beauties of reef, island, mountain and river.

In the Queensland section, one side is devoted to the colony from a geological point of view; the other is illustrative of its mining, pastoral, agricultural and other industries, including photographs, representations exhibiting the geological formation, as well as local scenes and native inhabitants. Among the minerals there is a trophy of tin, besides specimens of manganese, iron and antimony, an ingot of native copper, copper ores, gold-bearing quartz, building-stone, and a slab of polished malachite. There are also specimens of gold in nuggets, and tin and copper in nuggets. There are varieties of the soil, specimens of products, cassava, arrowroot, sweet-potatoes, flour, silk-cocoons, wheat, maize, barley, tobacco, etc. Sugar is a very important article of commerce, although as late as 1866 there was none grown there at all, while the yield for 1874 was 14,000 tons.

In the body of the court the exhibits are arranged in four groups, representing mining, agricultural, pastoral and miscellaneous products. There are exhibits of sugar which will enable the observer to see how far advanced this product is in quality in Queensland. The specimens of native woods exhibited include a great number of varieties. There are various specimens of pine, oak and cedar, including the swamp-oak, cypress pine, red-cedar, also the yellow wood, spotted tree, sweet and sour plum, orange and lemon, *balsam copaiva,* silver-tree, pulp wood, tamarind, tea-tree, yellow box, spotted gum, red mahogany, blue gum, mangrove, beech, sandal-wood, and many others. There are also specimens of the famous eucalyptus, said to be a specific against malaria; and in one district it is said there are no fewer than 200 different varieties of woods available for every purpose, from cabinet-making to ship-building. Many of these are on exhibition. Owing to its vast area and the great diversity of its soil, climate and altitude, there is a greater variety of indigenous trees in Queensland than in the rest of the Australian colonies, and perhaps more than could be found in the same extent of country in any other part of the world. The specimens of woods exhibited are from a collection that was easily procured, and were chiefly chosen for their economic value. They do not, however, include one-fourth of the species existing in the colony. It is believed that with regard to some of these woods a higher value would be put upon them in America than that received in Queensland, which, being a young colony, has found very little time to experiment in them, and the consequence is that timbers probably of a superior quality are neglected, or used only as fire-wood.

The value of some varieties of the Australian eucalyptus for building or railway purposes has for some time past been fully recognized, and the number of species is greater in Queensland than in other parts of the continent. Inasmuch as the most of the available woods grow on the coasts and on the banks of rivers, it is not difficult or expensive to transport them. Several articles made from Queensland wood are exhibited, including hogsheads, tallow-casks, sugar-vats, and ax and pick-handles.

Of skins shown there are the kangaroo, wallaby, wallaroos, seal, etc. There is also a case with the tusk and teeth of a dugong, a dugong calf in spirits, samples of dugong oil, a hunting saddle, bridle, breastplate and pouch; trapper's saddle and bridle; stockman's saddle and bridle; pack-saddles, saddle-bags, and leggins. There are two life-size photographs of Australian natives, a species by no means numerous even in the unoccupied portions of the country. In the settled districts they are fast sharing the fate of the American Indian.

Tasmania is the next section, a country so remarkably healthy in its climate that it is the recognized sanitarium of Australia. The estimated population of Tasmania at the end of 1874 was 104,176. The revenue of the colony for that year was £327,925, and the expenditures £318,278. The value of imports was £1,257,785, that of exports £925,325.

Education in Tasmania is compulsory, and there is scarcely a remote district in which there is no school.

Tin, gold and silver are mined, and iron and coal to some extent. There is one remarkable feature distinguishing Tasmania from all other countries, which is the small mor-

tality among children, particularly those under one year of age. The principal animals are the kangaroo, wallaby, opossum and bandicoot, with the devil and Tasmanian tiger, which are formidable beasts that frequently make great havoc among the flocks. Of birds 171 species have

been preserved, but only 20 of these are supposed to be peculiar to Tasmania.

The exhibits in the Main Building begin with a display of rugs and skins, including the black and gray opossum, native cat-skins, ring-tail opossum, kangaroo, tiger-skins,

tery for household use. The cloth goods consist of blankets, shawls, dyed woolen cloth, dyed Angora goods, and fleece; there are specimens of silk in the raw material and worked on Brussels-net. Some ornaments made from fish-scales, pipes and roulette-boxes of *myall* wood are also

NATIONAL WOOD-MANUFACTURING CO.'S EXHIBIT, IN THE MAIN BUILDING.

sealskins, skins of the albatross, pelican and penguin, and those of the platypus, tiger-cat, kangaroo, red flying-squirrel, devil, wombat and bandicoot. Curiosities are a carved ivory and wood egg and cruet-stand, a spinning-jenny made of Tasmanian myrtle, an ornamental table-top with Tasmanian flowers painted on top by Miss Blythe, of Hobart Town, another by Miss Mary Hope, of Hobart Town, and one of Tasmanian woods by Mrs. John Wood-cock Graves. A handsome show of Tasmanian shells is made, and a fine display of the fleece of the merino sheep, bales of wool, etc.

Marble, limestone, salt, tin in ingots, gold in quartz, bismuth and tin ore, are displayed among the minerals, and there are a number of exhibits of grain and seeds, as also cubes of Tasmanian woods, including the blue-gum, pep-permint-gum, he and she oak, King William pine, myrtle, musk, tea-tree, eucalyptus, swamp-gum, stringy-bark, Huon pine, etc. The exhibition closes with charts and maps, meteorological tables, photographic views, photo-graph of the East Tasmanian aboriginal man, Billy Lanney, and other portraits of aborigines.

Tasmania is held to be a good country for emigrants, government lands to the extent of 320 acres for each indi-vidual being sold at £1 per acre, payable in 14 years, while land orders are issued to emigrants who pay the full cost of their families' passage out to the value of £18 for each member of the family above 15 years, and £9 for each member above 12 months and under 15 years of age, these land orders being receivable by the Government for pay-ment for any crown lands which the emigrant may buy after his arrival. The death rate of Tasmania in 1869 was less than 13 to 1,000 of the population. The black aboriginal population is reduced to one woman about 76 years old, whose photographic portrait is exhibited. Hobart Town, the chief city, has a population of about 20,000 inhabitants.

New South Wales was discovered by Captain Cook in 1770, and first settled 18 years afterward; but its real his-tory begins with the beginning of the nineteenth century, at about which time the introduction of merino sheep laid the basis of Australian commerce. In 1851 the southern districts were formed into the colony of Victoria, and in 1859 the northern districts into the colony of Queensland, leaving New South Wales in the centre. The popula-tion of the colony is at present over 600,000. Education is under a department of the state, and all schools supported by the state are under Government inspection. Every town and considerable village has its state primary school, and itinerant teachers are appointed to visit families of settlers scattered through the bush. The fee for tuition is a shilling a week; but where this cannot be met there is no charge.

Sidney, the capital, has a university, which was established and endowed in 1851. There are more than a hundred journals printed in the colony. Wages and profits are high, life and property are secure, and the means of living easy and manifold. The imports of New South Wales in 1874 amounted to £11,293,739; the exports £12,345,603. About £2,000,000 imports, and some £700,000 exports of this cover the trade with the United States. The city of Sidney is about four miles long by three miles broad. Its population is over 160,000.

The colony's pas-toral wealth is es-timated at about £40,000,000; the to-tal area leased at less than three farthings an acre for pastoral purposes is nearly 150,000,000, the leases varying in size from 5,000 to 100,000. There are many men in the colony, who began as simple shepherds, who have realized wealth and afflu-ence; while several of the squatters possess more than 100,000 sheep. Llamas and alpacas have been naturalized, and there are several flocks of angoras in the colony. The annual increase of stock is enormous. Tobacco, maize and sugar-cane are grown there, as well as all the fruits of northern and southern Europe. There are orange-groves as magnificent as may be seen in Spain and Portugal. As many as 10,000 oranges have been obtained from indi-vidual trees. The potato thrives well. Barley, oats, etc., are grown chiefly for fodder. Cotton also thrives, and grass-cloth is made from flax, which flourishes.

New South Wales abounds in minerals. The auriferous districts of this colony are as large as any in Australia. Up to 1870 only alluvial washings were carried on; yet besides coining millions of pounds sterling, she exported gold to the value of £40,000,000. The gold-fields extend, with short intervals, the entire length of the colony, and over a

breadth of 200 miles, comprising an area of 13,656 square miles; while all the great gold-fields of the west are within two days' journey of the capital. The authority to dig for gold costs only ten shillings a year, and entitles its pos-sessor to take up ground upon any gold-field to the extent of 60 x 60, to 114 x 114 feet, according to the class of mining. The export of gold in 1873 was £2,600,000.

The coal-beds of New South Wales extend from the 29th to the 35th parallel of latitude, Sidney being the centre of the coal basin; coal having been traced about 100 miles to the north, to the south and to the west. The value of the mineral raised in 1874 was about £800,000. Copper and tin are found in many parts of the colony, and also dia-monds, pearls, rubies, and other gems. The number of diamonds found up to 1874 was estimated at between 5,000

J. L. MOTT IRON-WORKS EXHIBIT. — IRON FOUNTAIN IN THE RENAISSANCE STYLE.

and 6,000, the largest having been one of five and three-quarter carats.

In manufactures, the colonists are able to compete with those of Europe in the supply of many local requirements. Wine-making is a settled industry. There were made in 1874, 684,258 gallons, and 859 gallons of brandy. There were also in that year 31 breweries turning out beer of ex-cellent quality. Large quantities of tobacco are manufac-tured, Virginia-leaf being imported for the purpose, and one of the largest manufactories of tobacco in the old State has set up extensive buildings in Sidney.

The preserved meats of New South Wales have acquired reputation in the markets of the world, and more than £100,000 worth were exported in 1874. The manufacture of cloths is being rapidly and profitably developed, as is also that of bricks and encaustic tiles, drain-pipes and other descriptions of pottery. The eight-hour system of labor applies in New South Wales, and the mechanics at that rate get from 8 to 12 shillings sterling per day, while the cost of lodging and board is 15 shillings per week.

The display of minerals, of building-stones and mining

products in the New South Wales section is very large and complete, including all the native minerals and iron ore, auriferous quartz, copper ore, tin and tin ore, galena and antimony. There is also a collection of the chief charac-teristic fossils of New South Wales exhibited by the Department of Mines, Sidney; samples of auriferous quartz, tailings from several of the gold fields, and 411 specimens of lode tin exhibited by the New South Wales Commis-sioners. The collection of minerals from New South Wales includes tourmaline and topaz, serpentine, smoky quartz, crystal, chalcedony, hornblende, diamonds, etc. Then there are coals, both semi-bituminous and bituminous, marble, sandstone, and kaolin. Finally, there is a gilt block in the form of an enormous cube, bearing the following inscrip-tion: "This model represents the quantity of gold ob-tained in New South Wales from 1851 to 1874; weight 8,205,232 ounces; value £30,536,246 10s. 6d."

In manufactures there are aerated waters and cordials, various yeast and baking-powders, soap, kerosene oil and stearine candles, paints, indigo, etc. In ceramic-ware there are a number of jars, bottles, galley-pots, etc.; and in glass a stained-glass staircase window, having for its subject, "Captain Cook." Some doors and window-sashes are shown, manufactured of native woods. There are also a number of mats and matting made of cocoa fibre, iron manufactured by the aborigines of New South Wales, and some artificial flowers are shown, made of wool and copied from Australian native flowers.

The furs and skins include the stuffed platypus, with a traveling-rug made from the skin of the same peculiar creature, which is the *Ornithorhyncus paradoxus*, or "beast with a bill." There is also a set of collerettes and cuffs of the same skin, with a rug of wallaby skin, and furs and skins of the opossum, platypus, wallaby and kangaroo, all tanned. The platypus is about 17 inches long, with rather short and dense fur, generally colored a dusky brown. The male is armed with spurs on the hind legs. This interesting crea-ture has excited, perhaps, more attention than any other Australian mammal. The question concerning this bird or animal is, whether it produces its young living, or by means of eggs. The platypus lives in bushes on the borders of rivers and creeks, these bushes varying from 10 to 40 feet in length. Its food consists of minute insects and pond-snails. The skins are much prized when cured, and are made into cloaks, bed-covers, muffs, wristlets and tippets.

Among the exhibits is the *mojo*, or stone-hatchet, of the aborigines, together with other flint implements. There are also boomerangs, clubs, etc.

The specimens of natural history, including the platypus, swamp-tiger and tiger-cat, wal-laby and kangaroo, water-rat and flying-squirrel, are exhibited by the Trustees of the Australian Museum at Sidney. A specimen of a duck-billed platypus in spirits, as also the Australian hedge-hog, is shown, with a large number of Australian birds exhibited by the New South Wales Commissioners and the Australian Museum.

A very large number of photographs, parti-cularly of public buildings in and around Sidney, with views from the interior, portraits of abori-gines, etc., are to be seen upon the walls. These include fine views of scenery.

There is a fine show of wool, with woolen cloths, shawls, etc.; speci-mens of seeds, wines, and an extra-ordinary exhibition of native woods; with seeds, nuts, bark, roots, and various specimens of grains, plants and beans.

One curious exhibit is the *Biche-de-mer*, or edible bird's nest, from the Fiji Islands. Condensed milk is shown by a Sidney inventor, and specimens of native fruit preserved in brine and syrup. Sugars, raw and refined, are exhibited, as also confectionery made of New South Wales sugar by a Sidney manufacturer. The native wines are both red and white, light and full-bodied, and include hermitage, mus-catel, burgundy, cawarra, claret, muscat, shiraz, pinean and malbec.

THE UNITED STATES.

The exhibition of articles in the Main Building from the United States includes all that portion of the building lying east of the centre transept and south of the nave, and on the north side of the building, the space extend-ing from the Mexican section to the eastern end, including in all 189,231 feet. The display made includes every variety of objects which would not come properly under the head of the Art Exhibition, or in Machinery or Agricultural Hall, and is five times as large in extent as the exhibition of

Great Britain, which stands next in size. A peculiar feature of this important portion of the Exhibition is the noticeable frequency with which one meets exhibits from Philadelphia houses; and that this fact has not been unobserved by the Philadelphia Press is made obvious by the complacent commentary of one of the papers in that city that "fully two-thirds of the best American exhibits are the result of the well-known energy and enterprise of Philadelphians." Without contesting or criticising this statement, we may not improperly draw attention to the general prevalence of Philadelphia in the Main Building; and whatever may explain the circumstance, there is no doubt that much energy is displayed. All her goods are of an exceedingly rich and attractive character, and her exhibition is vastly commendable.

New York City stands next in the extent and importance of her display, which, however, is scarcely fully representative or up to the possibilities of the metropolis. It should be observed, also, that New England looms up in this section in most admirable fashion, her exhibits comparing favorably with those of any other section; while in respect to manufactured goods and her educational representation she surpasses all the rest. With regard to New York, however, it may be remarked that the Empire State furnishes more than 1,550 of the 11,000 exhibitors in the Centennial from the United States, or more than one-seventh of the entire American contributions. Notwithstanding this, there has been much deficiency in important industries which might have been filled to greater advantage, had better preparation been made, and had there been more agreement among the exhibitors concerned. This is particularly the case in the matter of silks. It is a fact that in sewing silks America, and especially New York, leads the world; yet in this department the exhibition is nothing like what it ought to have been.

The glove trade is another New York industry, several manufacturers from New York City exhibiting, and one from Gloversville, in Fulton County, a little town which is entirely devoted to this industry. American kid gloves are notoriously as brilliant in color as the French, and more durable and shapely. Carpet-making, though represented in a slight degree only by New York exhibits, makes, nevertheless, a good display. Shirtings, which are represented by ten New York City houses, and other cotton goods, are also exhibited from that city in favorable examples. The display of stuff-goods, alpacas, mohairs and woolen goods from Cohoes and Auburn and other manufacturing places in the State, is large and fully representative. In furniture New York is prominent, being represented by more than forty exhibitors, with examples of styles, from the most costly to the most simple. In the latter classes other sections offer an improved quality of goods, but in first-class furniture New York City is unrivaled. Concerning furniture, also, it should be observed that superior instances of cabinet-making are presented by New York firms in a number of the superb pavilions, and in showcases containing goods in the Main Building.

The south wall of the building, north of the nave, is devoted to such of the mineral exhibits as are not contained in the annexes constructed for this particular class of exhibits. Here the different States are represented, sometimes in collective exhibits designed to fairly display the peculiarities of the State, as is the case with certain sections of Ohio, Pennsylvania and New Jersey, which exhibit their native ores and their minerals with some view to classification. The Wyoming Historical and Geological Society of Wilkesbarre, Pa., makes an interesting exhibit of fossils from the anthracite coal region of the Wyoming Valley. The minerals of the Pacific States and Territories, as well as those of Mexico, Central and South America, China and Japan, have a brilliant presentation in a collection exhibited by John Hatch, of San Francisco, California—himself the most peculiar, original and interesting exhibit of his collection. What with his microscopic gems, his large specimens of minerals, his own glib tongue and comprehensive and common-sense declamation, his exhibit has been a rare attraction; and this not to depreciate the value of his minerals, which were certainly most interesting and have doubtless inclined many to the pursuit which evidently forms the hobby of their exhibitor. Here are likewise found some hematite ores from Johnstown, Lake Superior, Lake Champlain and Iron Mountain; nickel ores from Camden, New Jersey; a collection of minerals and salts exhibiting a specialty brought hither by a Philadelphian chemist; and numerous fine specimens of minerals and ores from Tennessee, which certainly in this exhibition has made a most creditable and important display of

MESSRS. TIFFANY AND CO.'S EXHIBIT IN THE MAIN BUILDING.
THE BRYANT TESTIMONIAL VASE.

her mineral wealth. From an interior town in the State of New York, Mumford, we have a collection of petrified wood, leaves, flowers, etc., found on the premises of the exhibitor, Oliver Allen. Kentucky displays largely in the direction of iron ores, and a Rhode Island exhibitor furnishes a collection of minerals from Wyoming Territory. Pennsylvania, of course, is fully represented in this department, not only in metals but in coals, limestone, etc. Missouri exhibits specimens of her soil, and nickel, iron, lead, zinc, copper and other ores. Delaware sends building-stones, clays and natural woods; Michigan, bituminous and cannel coal, building-stones, marbles and slates; Maine, granite; and Vermont, marble. Quincy, Massachusetts, is represented by granite pedestals.

In manufactured stone there are mantels, columns, table and bureau-tops, pilasters, pedestals, etc., from Philadelphia, articles in artificial stone from Boston, and mill-stones from New York.

Next come metallurgical products, and here, too, as a matter of course, Pennsylvania is prominent; and we find Philadelphia and Pittsburgh displaying everything in metals, from gold and silver-leaf and bronze powder to pig, bloom, bar and muck and rail-iron, Bessemer steel, crucible cast-steel, boiler-plate, and all other manufactures in these metals. West Virginia has exhibits in this line, and from as far south as Alabama we have specimens of wire-rods, charcoal pig-iron and other similar exhibits. Nickel goods are displayed by a New Jersey house; copper products from New York, Michigan and other States; and the Edgemoor Iron Company, of Delaware, exhibits the wrought and cast-iron work of the Main Exhibition Building.

Finally, mining engineering is illustrated by maps and models from different exhibitors, representing coal, iron, and even gold mines. It is a gratifying feature of this part of the Exhibition to find mineral and metallurgical products and manufactures exhibited to so considerable an extent from the Southern States, such as Virginia, Tennessee, Georgia and Alabama. It is doubtful whether these States can be equaled in the variety of their iron ores, while it is an agreeable feature of the geological formation where these are found, that everything else necessary to change them from their crude state to merchantable purposes is found in close proximity to them, including coal, limestone, etc. Among the remarkable specimens of these minerals, and different grades of iron made from them, is a collection from the Woodstock Company of Anniston, Alabama, which is so classified and arranged as to make a presentment of great value to the student and practical and thinking man. Such exhibits as these give reason for hopeful confidence that the South will be ere long regenerated in an industrial sense, and present effectual evidence of her capacity and intention in this regard.

A pretty exhibit of graphite from one of the New England States is a handsome fountain in the nave near the centre of the building, which consists of a mass of rock, rough-hewn, and covered with holly, four feet high, surmounted with a cross, bearing the motto, "Ho, every one that thirsteth!" in answer to which water trickles from the foot of the cross below.

Rhode Island exhibits more than 200 specimens of her minerals, besides a variety of relics of the Narragansett Indians. A mineralogical curiosity is an immense quartz crystal from the hot springs of Arkansas. Another curiosity of a different kind is a steel rail exhibited by a Pittsburg shop, which is 130 feet long and weighs 3,480 pounds, said to be the largest in the world. The display of iron, copper and brass wire from Worcester, Massachusetts; that of brass and copper rivets from Connecticut; screws from Providence, Rhode Island; and zinc from New York and Illinois, have attracted particular attention.

The display of medicinal preparations and chemicals is very large, and in this department Philadelphia takes the lead, though one New York firm dates back as far as 1770. The quantity of sugar-coated pills, fluid extracts, gelatine-coated pills, and elixirs and tinctures, and other medicinal preparations of all kinds on exhibition, is inconceivable. Between sulphate of quinine, sugar-of-lead, and pyroligneous acid, one is in doubt as to which is the most poisonous; and to the layman, whether lacto-phosphate of lime is a manure or a milk offers a difficult conundrum. Acids and salts, dye-stuffs, white and red, paints, colors and oils, saccharated pepsin—these are some of the more simple articles contained in this department. Others, not so noticeable by their simplicity, are royalith, hydrastine, Girondin disinfectant and bromo-chloralum. It rests one, while wandering through these exhibits, to come upon baking yeast-powder, cod-liver oil, sugar of lemons, and scouring soap, and know, too, that these are also chemical. New York displays largely in coloring materials and varnishes, and Pennsylvania also. The ink exhibits are also numerous and varied, and include all the well-known old houses.

Finally, soaps make a lavish display, one exhibit in this line being a large model of the old bell of Independence, with its crack, motto, etc., all complete.

After the chemicals we have terra-cotta and other pottery, porcelain, etc., represented by about fifty exhibitors, of which the larger number are from Philadelphia and from New Jersey. An Ohio manufacturer exhibits some very pretty white granite work in what are termed "Centennial" and "Cable" patterns. The tops of the covered dishes are finished with round-shaped knobs with fluted sides. The shapes of the articles are graceful, and the tint clear and pure.

A collective exhibit made by glass-manufacturers west of the

MESSRS. TIFFANY & CO.'S EXHIBIT.—THE DIAMOND FEATHER.

Alleghanies is a very handsome display. A Rochester house shows a specialty in tumblers. A Pittsburg glass-manufacturer displays lamps, crystal and porcelain, glass-vases, and a very handsome display of flint-glassware and white porcelain-ware in tea-sets, bread-plates, etc. Some of the bread-plates have mottoes in raised letters, and ornamentation in gold and colors, which have attracted much admiration. Another Pittsburg house exhibits crystal covered dishes, fruit-stands, preserve-dishes, etc., of the most delicate manufacture. Here is also to be seen a Centennial plate, having in the centre medallion and views of Bunker Hill Monument in raised work, surrounded with patriotic mottoes, and the rim containing the names of Warren, Putnam, Stark and Prescott, and the dates 1776, 1876. Pittsburg comes out stronger than any other section in the matter of glass, for which her manufacturers are celebrated. The fine glass of the O'Hara works is particularly beautiful. Another house shows a tea-service in crystal, richly decorated with gold vines and leaves; and still another displays sets of Centennial ware, with the cracked Independence Bell, *ad libitum*. Altogether, the show of glass-ware in the United States section, if not so delicate and beautiful as that of Bohemia, is nevertheless delicate and beautiful enough, and very creditable to the progress and improved condition of the art in this country.

A great deal of terra-cotta ware is exhibited by Philadelphia and Trenton manufacturers, including statuary, vases, pedestals, fountains, flower-pots, garden edging and other articles, many of which are very artistic and handsome. Trenton, too, makes a good display in porcelain and Parian, and generally in crockery-ware. From Cincinnati, Ohio, we have an interesting exhibit of such ware. Philadelphia, which is noted for chemicals and drugs, is also a centre of druggists' and perfumers' glass-ware, and makes a considerable exhibit in this line. The display of chandeliers in the United States section is large and very gorgeous, presenting, besides numerous patterns obviously derived from French models, many which are plainly original, and in some instances quite beautiful.

Massachusetts makes a brilliant display of glass-ware, three establishments being represented by specimens which have received high commendation, and bear comparison with any similar exhibits except the unapproachable display from Bohemia. The ground and cut-glass articles are of the finest design and workmanship, including all kinds of table-ware, from the finest thin, ornamental wineglasses to the largest preserve-dishes. A massive punch-bowl, the mate of one formerly owned by Daniel Webster, is a prominent article in this collection. One establishment displays some exquisite specimens of paintings upon opaque glass, portraits of Charles Sumner and Longfellow being among them. The entire Massachusetts exhibition of table-services, toilet-sets, lamps and chandeliers need not fear examination side by side with either those of England or France. A curiosity in the Massachusetts glass exhibit is the first pressed-glass tumbler ever made. This was the result of the inventive powers of Deming Jarvis, of Sandwich, Mass., and was made in 1827. It is related that the success of the inventor so infuriated glass-blowers that Mr. Jarvis was forced to conceal himself, for fear of personal violence.

Near the exhibits of glass-ware are those of Britannia, plated and silver-ware, led by the great establishment of Tiffany & Co., of New York; the Gorham Manufacturing Company, of Providence, R. I.; Reed & Barton, Taunton, Mass.; and the Meriden Britannia Company, of West Meriden, Conn. The exhibits of diamonds and other precious stones, of jewelry and of silver-ware made by Messrs. Tiffany & Co., have been a centre of attraction during the Exhibition, the handsome court on the nave in which these were displayed having been constantly crowded. Here were to be seen numerous solid silver pieces designed and executed by this house, as prizes for yacht races or for gifts to public personages, and in such cases loaned by the owners. The magnificent Bryant memorial vase, presented to the great poet by a number of his admirers, may be particularly mentioned in this connection. One diamond necklace exhibited by this firm is

valued at $117,000; and the entire value of their exhibits verged upon half a million dollars.

The largest and most costly silver piece exhibited is said to have been the "Century" vase of the Gorham Company, which contains two thousand ounces of solid silver, and is valued at $25,000. This superb art-work was designed by George Wilkinson and J. Pierpont, and is five feet and two inches in height. While massive in the extreme, it is so graceful in its proportions, and so delicate in its decorations, as to present no appearance of unwieldiness. These decorations are emblematical of the progress of Western civilization, and of the growth toward perfection of the American Republican Government, and are appropriate and artistic. The "Hiawatha" barge is another beautiful exhibit from this house, and the "Aurora" epergne, valued at $3,500, is still another. Messrs. Reed & Barton display an exquisite ornamental vase, in whose emblematic ornamentation is finely delineated the progress of America, as illustrated by contrast of the present high state of civilization with the savage condition which obtained at the period of the discovery by Columbus. A superb fruit and flower-stand exhibited by this house is another of the notable works of art, and an embossed tea-set, plated on white metal, deserves special mention as discovering peculiar originality of decoration.

The amount of furniture exhibited by American exhibitors

ELKINGTON EXHIBIT IN THE MAIN BUILDING. — METAL PLAQUE OR PLATE, "THE POMPEIAN TOILETTE."

is enormous, and comprises every imaginable article of this class. As has been already indicated, there is a tendency toward display and gaudiness in our first-class furniture, which is to be deprecated. Philadelphia and New York houses, however, have exhibited articles of furniture which are to be commended for artistic elaboration of design and execution without extravagance. Library and dining-room furniture in the styles in vogue during the reigns of Henri II. and Louis XIV. and Louis XV., attest how dependent modern structural art—in furniture, at least—is on French taste of some period or other. Richly carved cabinets and buffets in the "Italian style—fifteenth century," are an occasional relief from this sameness, but "Renaissance" and "Louis Quatorze" seem to be the rule in furniture-building, save where enterprising Yankees come down upon us with novel inventions in "rockers"; or Connecticut wanders from style to material for a "strong hold," as in her exhibits of "Charter Oak" furniture, which are noteworthy. A Boston manufactory exhibits chamber and parlor sets made of rich, dark olive-wood, set off pleasingly with artistic mountings, highly polished, and displaying some fine carving. Worcester, Mass., contributes a large number of folding, arm and rocking-chairs, some of the designs being original and very clever. A curiosity here is a Centennial chair, in which flint-lock muskets and continental soldiers, carved in black walnut, are made to do double duty—as supports for the chair and as patriotic

memorials of "the days that tried men's souls." But besides the costly house-furniture, there are exhibited many rich articles of semi-religious character, being devised for use and ornament in churches. There are also specimens of rattan furniture, settees, reclining-chairs, leather-work in lambrequins and window-curtains, extension-tables of all woods and patterns, "combination" articles, which may include everything from a sofa-bedstead to a secretary, and finally, from the Mount Lebanon, N. Y., manufactories, "Shaker" chairs and other articles, which are as interesting in some respects as any other exhibits. When it is remembered that under the comprehensive title, "furniture," we are to include all household articles in wood or metal, it will be seen that we cannot even partially represent the nature of the exhibition.

In fabrics and woven goods of all classes, we find the chief exhibits are from Maine, New Hampshire and Massachusetts—Fall River, Lowell, Manchester and Nashau, of course, leading off.

The Silver Spring Bleaching and Dyeing Company, of Providence, R. I., display a large and costly case of bleached goods of the best manufacture. The Lowell cotton manufactories exhibit in combination in an elaborately finished case made of black walnut with plate glass in the form of a Maltese cross. This is an object which has attracted constant attention, both for its merit as a structure and for the magnificent show of plain and printed cotton goods illustrating the great Lowell mills. Among the fabrics displayed from Lowell is a most interesting collection of fine and coarse wire articles. Lawrence, Mass., also looms up prominently in the cotton department, exhibiting in one case, in an enormous pavilion, in which is included every kind of cotton cloth manufactured at the mills exhibiting, besides, all varieties of flannels, of every imaginable color and texture. Ware, Mass., exhibits also a fine display of flannels and a large and elegant assortment of other woolens, tastefully arranged. The Lawrence and Chicopee mills have a number of show-cases, designed in a novel and pleasing fashion, containing other exhibits. The Burlington Woolen Company, of Winooski, Vermont, and the Weybosset Mills, of Providence, R. I., make also a fine display of fabrics; while Rockville, Conn., exhibits a novelty in fancy cassimers of beautiful patterns.

The display of cotton and woolen goods, however, is by no means confined to the New England manufactories. Wilmington, Del., exhibits the celebrated Brandywine Mills ticking; Baltimore, Md., cotton duck for sails, tents and awnings; New York, brown cottons, drills and nankeens, brown and bleached sheetings, carpet warps, and jute bagging; New Jersey, lamp-wicks and cotton yards; Ohio and Mississippi, cottons and yarns; Philadelphia, shirtings, cambrics, silesias, umbrella cloths, hollands, ginghams, mourning goods, calicos, prints, etc. In woolen goods we have from Philadelphia, knitting cotton and Germantown wool; from Chester, Pa., cassimeres and doeskins; from New York, felt skirts, embroidered, and Italian cloth skirts, trimmed and quilted, fancy cassimeres, woolen shawls and fine white blankets.

The American carpet display is in some instances quite equal to the exhibits from European manufacturers, and includes Axminsters, tapestry-Brussels, ingrain, rag carpets from Philadelphia, Venetian carpets from Philadelphia, moquette, Brussels and Wilton carpets, rugs and mats from Clinton, Mass., etc. The carpet companies of New England in general are represented fully in a large and commodious pavilion, divided into eight sections, in which the Lowell Carpet Company and others are conspicuous in very fine and showy exhibits.

In clothing, traveling equipments and furs, we have exhibits from 235 exhibitors, including all the principal manufacturers of the country, and covering every variety of dress goods, gentlemen's and ladies' underwear, knit goods and embroideries, theatre costumes, military, naval, fire, baseball, boating and yachting equipments, and a full display of small articles, such as collars and cuffs, besides hats of every material and style, both for ladies and gentlemen; and this brings us to the book trade exhibit.

The book trade display was organized by a committee appointed by the Convention of the American Book Trade Association, held at Niagara Falls in the Summer of 1875, when a committee was appointed comprising the following gentlemen: J. B. Lippincott, John A. Black, George Remsen, Robert Porter, George Wood, H. W. Coates, Robert Lindsay, Presley Blakiston, and B. Griffiths. After due consultation this committee was successful in bringing together a display certainly most commendable, and particularly so in the judicious arrangement of the articles exhibited.

The American Book Trade structure occupied a full section close to the southeastern corner of the Main Building. By means of a two-story pavilion—the only one in the building—the difficulty of want of space was got over in a very satisfactory manner. A structure 117 by 34 feet in dimensions was built on a plan of three platforms, each supported by 16 light iron pillars and connected by two bridge platforms. The second story of this, 12 feet above the floor, was reached by two stairways. The cost of the structure proper was about $5,000, borne by the leading publishers occupying space up-stairs. This structure contained exhibits from 90 different exhibitors, each in his own division, and with special and appropriate cases and small pavilions, erected in accordance with individual taste.

Of course, it is impossible to do more than to refer to certain of the more prominent houses and special exhibits in our limited space.

Beginning with the Appletons, whose cases occupied a commanding position on the upper floor of the section, an interesting exhibit was made of the various medals awarded to this house, including those of the New York Industrial Exhibition of 1853, Vienna, 1873, and the silver medal presented by the Pope, in recognition of a copy of the fine work published by this house, known as "Picturesque America." Here was also shown the only copy known to be in existence of the first book published by the Appletons, a little volume about two inches by three, written by W. Mason, and entitled "Crumbs from the Master's Table; or, Selected Sentences, Doctrinal, Practical and Experimental," dated 1831. Here were also to be seen superb copies of the "American Encyclopedia," the new edition shown in four styles of binding—vellum, tree calf, morocco and crushed Levant; as also a magnificent specimen of the "Picturesque America," a work which may fairly be placed in competition with the best publications of the French houses in the line of costly illustrative works—the present copy being bound in brown Levant, inlaid in red and blue, lined with brown watered silk and richly tooled.

The bindings shown by the Appletons are all made under the supervision of the well-known binder, Matthews, formerly the proprietor of an establishment of his own at New York, but now for many years in charge of the binding department of the Appletons' manufacturing establishment in Williamsburgh.

A large pile of Webster's spelling-books was an interesting exhibit, as suggesting to those who are acquainted with the history of this extraordinarily successful book what grand and unexpected results may arise from small beginnings.

The educational display by the Appletons included 350 volumes, bound in uniform half vellum, and besides being a handsome and attractive exhibit, was representative of one of the most important items of the Exhibition.

Messrs. A. S. Barnes & Co. exhibited largely in educational works, while their miscellaneous publications included "One Hundred Years of American Independence," a fine illustrated work, and Mrs. Lamb's "History of New York," which is beginning to be an authority. The bibliographical exhibit of Mr. John Russell Bartlett should be mentioned, being a catalogue of the library of John Carter Brown, of Providence, compiled by him. It is in four volumes, handsomely illustrated, and printed in the best style of the celebrated Riverside Press.

The Bible Societies made a fine display in a very artistic case, wherein they were enabled to exhibit the Bible in 200 languages. The Bible case, made of ash, in what is known as the Eastlake fashion, was in itself one of the ornaments of the Main Building. As to the Bibles, there should be mentioned of them the Bible of 1476, the Douay Bible of 1610, Tyndall's 1525 edition, the King James of 1611, and other early publications. It may be mentioned here that the Pennsylvania Bible Society exhibited in a separate building, just south of Horticultural Hall.

N. W. Harding exhibited quarto albums in various elegant styles of binding, among which was the "Thousand Picture Album," the largest fairly imaginable.

Messrs. Harper & Bros. displayed in an open case what was scarcely a representative collection of the publications of this important house. Here were full sets of the Harpers' periodical publications, handsomely bound, and editions of the English classics and other works in different styles.

Messrs. Hurd & Houghton made one of the best exhibits in the collection, in the ornamental and elegant case upon which artists have displayed elaborately their talents, with the design of beautifying the framework inclosing the publications of this house. Here were to be seen specimens of printing and binding, the work of the Riverside Press, which can probably not be excelled by the publications of any other establishment in the country, if elsewhere. The large-paper Webster, Mrs. Clements's "Legendary and Mythological Art," and a glorious copy of Bacon's Works on India paper, bound in crushed Levant, were special exhibits by this house, besides the more strictly representative works, such as Dickens, Macaulay, etc.

Ivison, Blakeman, Taylor & Co. made a fine exhibition of school-books in plain and fine binding, and their division was chiefly notable for a specimen of Spencerian penmanship exhibited, and which was inclosed in an elegant frame six feet by eight, and included the Declaration of Independence, with signatures in fac-simile, besides ornamentation of various kinds, and portraits of Washington and the Generals of the Revolution.

STATUE, "SOAP BUBBLES."

Messrs. J. B. Lippincott & Co., of Philadelphia, exhibited, apart from the general display of the book trade, in a case said to have cost about $2,000, being 12 feet square and 20 feet high, ornamented with bronze busts of Shakespeare, Milton, Byron and Scott. On one side of this case was a handsome show of Bibles, including a very large and richly bound Bible valued at $250. Other exhibits were a fine show of the works of fiction published by this house, "Lippincott's Magazine" and "Chambers's Encyclopedia."

J. R. Osgood & Co., of Boston, well known as the publishers of the leading English and American poets and essayists, displayed their fine edition of the British Poets, and the works of Emerson, Lowell, Longfellow, Hawthorne, Agassiz and others, besides a very pleasing exhibit of their heliotype work and book illustrations.

T. B. Peterson & Brothers, of Philadelphia, exhibited their publications, works by the well-known authors, Mrs. Southworth, Mrs. Stephens, Lever, T. S. Arthur, Dickens, Dumas, etc., in various bindings.

Messrs. Porter & Coates, of Philadelphia, had three fine cases, ornamented by bronze busts of Shakespeare, Milton and Scott, and included in their publications exhibited new editions of Shakespeare, the works of Jules Verne, and Wilson's magnificent "American Ornithology." G. P. Putnam's Sons were represented by the works of Washington Irving, Tuckerman, Bayard Taylor and John P. Kennedy; the bindings being noticeable for excellence of taste.

Scribner, Armstrong & Co. made a handsome show of Guyot's well-known wall maps, the important works of Curtius, Mommsen, and Max Muller, besides specimens of fine illustrated works imported by this house through their London agency.

In connection with the book display should be mentioned the stationery exhibits of the leading American stationery houses, including departments of artists' materials, ink, mucilage, etc., gold pens, pencils, penholders, lead-pencils, paper and general stationery. A number of the principal exhibits in this line have been already illustrated and described in the HISTORICAL REGISTER. Some of the cases are themselves deserving of special commendation for artistic and appropriate structure and ornamentation. There is, perhaps, no class of articles more generally interesting to the ordinary observer than those comprised under the general title of "stationery." There is something exceedingly attractive both in the uses and the workmanship of all matters pertaining to the desk and the writing-table; and since never before, perhaps, have such articles been shown under similar favorable circumstances, and with such peculiarly interesting surroundings of taste, it follows that this department of the Main Building exhibition has throughout been one which has attracted attention.

The devices to attract the interest of spectators have been innumerable and successful. Here, for instance, a fine show of artists' colors includes a curious feature in the representation of the old Liberty Bell, constructed of broken paints, and in the design of the American flag—the top forming the Union with white stars, and the bottom being built in alternate stripes. Here, too, is seen a basin filled with quicksilver, and having floating upon its surface an iron cannon-ball. It may be mentioned that the costly and beautiful color, vermilion, is made from quicksilver. The house which exhibits these interesting articles is 106 years old—that of C. T. Raynolds & Co., of New York; and still another curious and interesting article in the collection is an original invoice issued by the founder of the house in 1774. The goods exhibited by this firm include water-colors, drawing materials, camel's-hair brushes, crayons, and all other articles necessary to the artist.

Messrs. Francis & Loutrel, of New York, made a fine display of their blank-book manufactures in Russia bindings. Charles A. Dickson & Co., of Philadelphia, exhibited specimens of copper and steel plate engraving, type printing, crests, monograms, etc. John Foley, of New York, and Mabie, Todd & Bard, also of New York, made fine exhibits of elaborate gold-plated and solid gold pencil-cases, ebony, ivory and pearl penholders, charm pencils, toothpicks, shoe-buttoners—some of these being set with diamonds or enameled, while others are made of onyx or agate—and two pen and pencil-cases, each with a diamond in its head, valued at over $200 each. Another gold pen house exhibited a large American eagle, built up of gold pens to the number of 3,000.

Thaddeus Davids & Co., whose exhibit has been already described, Carter, Dinsmore & Co., of New York, and George Mather's Sons, of New York, with the old house of Maynard & Noyes, of Boston, represented the ink trade; while in inkstands, including specimens of bronze, nickel plate, gold antique, and pressed and cut glass, Messrs. Brower Bros., of New York, had a handsome display.

Papers were exhibited by Hotchkiss & Sons, of Bridgeport, Conn., whose note-papers have attracted much attention; Chapin & Gould, of Springfield, Mass.; the Owen Paper Company, Housatonic; and the Mount Holly Paper Company, of Pennsylvania, and other manufacturers. In the exhibit of Jessup & Moore, of Philadelphia, was a roll of paper 80 inches high, said to weigh 1,900 pounds. The Whiting Paper Company, of Holyoke, Mass., exhibited a case 12 by 20 feet, and 14 feet high, of ebony and fine plate glass, estimated to have cost $5,000. In this case was exhibited a ream of paper 6 by 18 feet, weighing 2,000 pounds, called "The Monarch."

The stationery exhibition closed with a display of school furniture, slates and slate-pencils, cards and cardboard, mucilage, wedding and fancy stationery, blank-books, steel pens—the only American exhibit in this line being that of the Esterbrook Steel Pen Company, of Camden, New Jersey—a handsome display in four show-cases, 16 feet by 6, in which were to be seen pens in every stage of manufacture, including some mammoth pens 12 and 18 inches long, handsomely engraved.

The exhibition of firearms and hunting apparatus includes the names of all the leading manufacturers in the country, who exhibited specimens of their work, including the very latest improvements and patents. Prominent in this department was the magnificent case of the Messrs.

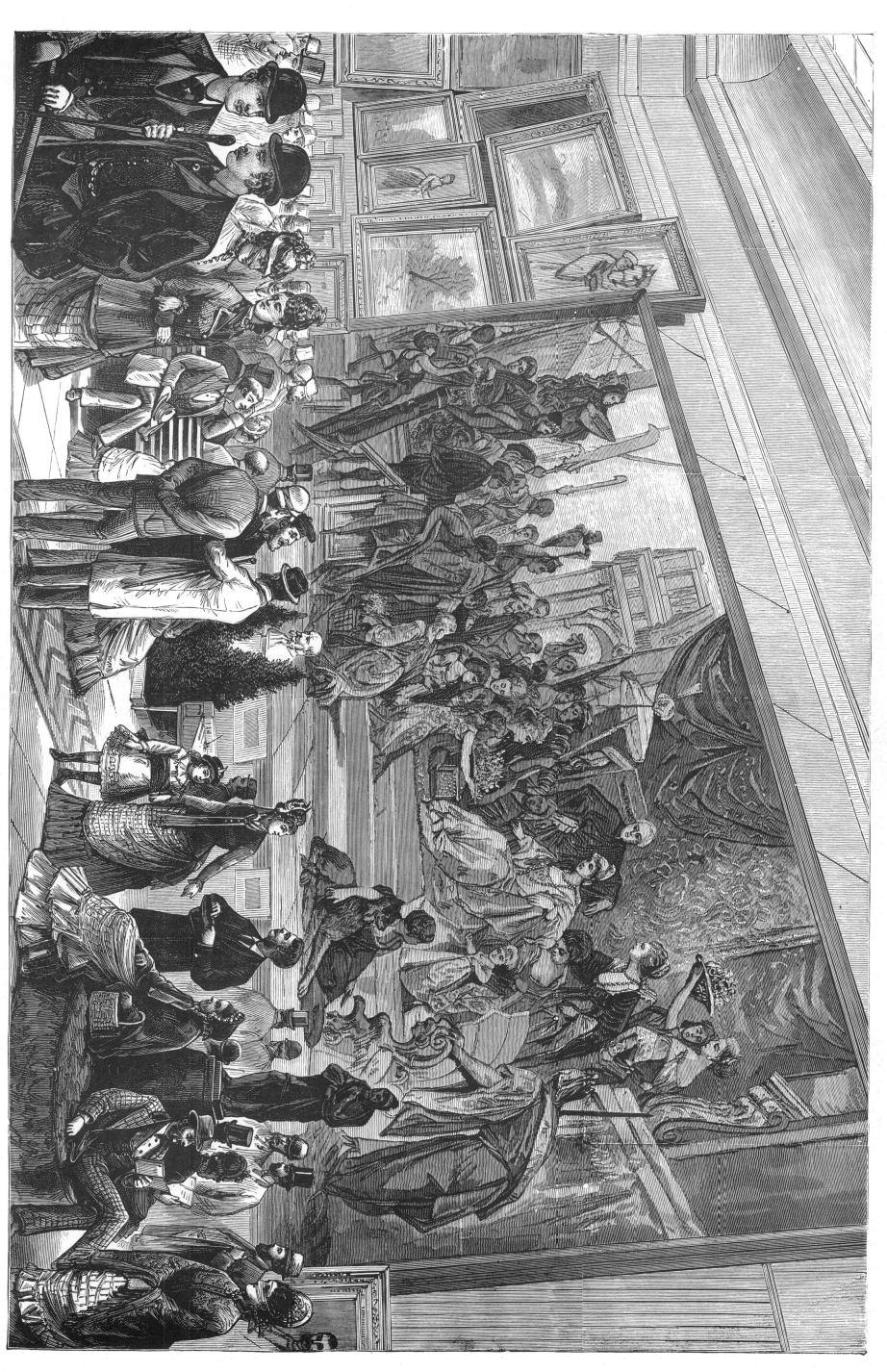

AUSTRIAN GALLERY, IN MEMORIAL HALL.

Remington & Sons, one of the most noticeable exhibits in passing up the nave of the Main Building from west to east. The Colt's Patent Firearms Manufacturing Company, Whitney Arms Company, Sharp's Rifle Company, Winchester Repeating Arms Company, Frank H. Snyder and Ames Manufacturing Company, were among the leading exhibitors, and displayed breech-loading firearms, revolving firearms, ammunition, military and pocket revolvers, small arms, shot-guns, magazine rifles, metallic shells, balls, wads, percussion caps, projectiles for rifled cannon, double-barrel breech-loading shot-guns, and all other arms or projectiles suitable for war or sport.

In the department of Medicine and Surgery there were exhibits of medicinal preparations, medical plants, a considerable display in homeopathic pharmacy, and a very large show of work in artificial limbs and articles designed for surgical cases; also surgical instruments, folding chairs, couches, invalid beds, etc.

The exhibition of artificial teeth, dental instruments and furniture, and the materials used in the manufacture of teeth, was comprehensive, and included all the different articles employed in this peculiarly American profession.

The exhibition of articles of hardware, edged tools, cutlery, etc., comprised 200 exhibitors, and included the leading houses in the country. These articles comprised everything known to this department, and are quite impossible to enumerate; tools of all kinds for all workers with tools—carpenters, shipwrights, machinists, bricklayers, plasterers, glaziers—in fact, mechanics of all sorts; also implements, including shovels, spades, picks, mattocks, etc.

Watchmakers' tools were shown by the Elgin Watch Company, of Elgin, Illinois, and by the American Watch Company of Waltham, Mass. Skates, razor-strops, oil-stones, grindstones, polishing implements, etc., were among the miscellaneous hardware. Cast-steel tools, sledges, hatchets, augers, planes, saws, and finally, entire tool-chests, either for amateurs or mechanics, included the customary and well-known articles of this character. Then we had all sorts of cutlery: butchers' knives, hunters' knives, druggists' knives, cast-steel scissors and shears, pruning shears, and everything else in this line. Then fire-grates, fenders, fire-places, fire-irons, fancy coal-boxes, iron culinary-ware, plain and ornamental bronze figures, etc., brass kettles, water-coolers, Japanned tinware, and, finally, locks and padlocks, from the ordinary door-lock to the wonderfully complicated and intricate bank-lock; time locks, cabinet locks, spring padlocks and car-locks, and a great quantity of nails, spikes, screws, gimlets, tacks, brass and other small wares. In materials manufactured into fabrics, we had woven and braided goods, brooms, brushes, cordage, twines, sash-cord, ship-riggings, regalias, flags, banners, bunting in very large quantities; articles made from paper—such as paper barrels, household ware, chamber sets, cuspadores, etc.; articles of rattan, baskets, etc.; Ja-

panese paper-ware, galvanized iron goods, zinc and other metallic work; pipe railings, wire work, cornices, architectural ornaments; packages for volatile liquids made of paper; casket trimmings, burial robes and dresses, coffin trimmings, etc., etc.

We may mention here the display of umbrellas, parasols and canes, of which, perhaps, the best exhibits were made by Philadelphia firms; and in the same connection those of whips, tortoiseshell goods, hard-rubber goods, including surgical and photographic articles, drinking-flasks, etc., and the exhibits of wax flowers, materials and sheet wax, leaves, shells, fruit, etc., which were included in the department of fancy articles to which the others above-mentioned belonged.

The exhibition of scientific and philosophical instruments made by United States exhibitors was very full, and displayed great improvement and considerable originality and invention in this direction. Here were seen philosophical and nautical instruments, and machinery for drawing instruments, models for scientific schools, automatic machines for grinding and polishing diamonds, for dividing units into equal parts and other minute work, specimens of aerographs or storm-writers for predetermining storms, thermometers, ellipsographs for describing ellipses, astronomical and other scientific instruments, portable instruments, ships' logs, and finally, clocks and watches without number; special attention being directed to the exhibits of the American Watch Company of Waltham, Mass., including watches and watch movements, gold and silver cases and watch materials; to the Waterbury Clock Company of Waterbury,

Conn., and other well-known American watch and clock manufactories.

In pianofortes and organs a large number of exhibits were made, covering about eighty exhibitors, and comprising all the principal American names, such as Hallet, Davis & Co., Boston; Mason & Hamlin Organ Company; Meyer, Conrad & Sons, Philadelphia; Hazelton Bros., Steinway and Sons, Decker Bros., Albert Weber, New York; William Knabe & Co., Baltimore; Chickering & Sons, Boston; and H. L. Roosevelt, of New York, who exhibited, in the north gallery of the transept, the magnificent organ whose music never failed to draw a large, appreciative and delighted audience.

In the article of pianos, the exhibition demonstrated that the United States need not fear competition with the manufacturers of any other country whatsoever. The full display of instruments, covering every improvement and all the numerous attachments, was one of the chief ornaments of the Main Building, as well as a demonstration of the peculiar adaptability of American mechanics in regard to the development of work requiring a combination of art with mechanism.

Here we may close our brief consideration of the United States department in the Main Building, and with it the present account of the Main Building itself. More than in any other part of the Exhibition, it has been here that comparison could be made which, while encouraging to those who emerged from it successfully, could not be otherwise than useful and advantageous, educationally, to those who were less fortunate. While the artists, mechanics and manufacturers of America are certainly not the equals of those of Europe and Asia in certain special branches of art and manufacture, it will be found, on consideration, that such is the case only with regard to the departments of effort toward which our attention has never been fully directed, and in which we have heretofore had neither opportunity for education nor comparison. Already our silks vie with those of the Lyons looms in certain most important qualities, our carpets compare favorably with the best English, French and Belgian make, while even in *repoussé* work we have been able to exhibit some specimens fit to compete with those shown by foreign experts in this line. It is scarcely expecting too much to believe that should the attention of our capitalists be turned in those directions it will not require another hundred years to develop our taste and capacity for execution in an equal degree in the departments of bronzes, faïence, or even lacquer-work.

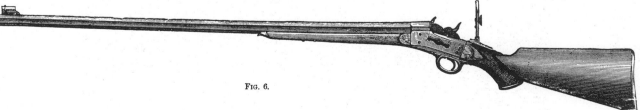

Fig. 1. Double-barreled Breech-loading Gun, showing working parts.   Fig. 2. Sectional view of the Rifle.   Fig. 3. Sectional view of Remington Target Rifle, showing breech action with Vernier Sights; also Wind-gauge Sights.   Fig. 4. Sectional view of Remington Rifle, open to receive the cartridge.   Fig. 5. Remington Breech-loading Single-barreled Gun.   Fig. 6. Remington "Creedmoor" Long Range Breech-loading Rifle.

PORTION OF E. REMINGTON & SONS' EXHIBITS.

PARIS RESTAURANT AUX TROIS FRERES PROVENCAUX.

EDUCATIONAL DEPARTMENT.

NOT confining ourselves in this connection to the Main Building, we desire to present a succinct view of the subject of education as illustrated in the entire Exposition by the different countries exhibiting. Beginning with Great Britain, we found numerous important articles representative of the work of British Sunday-schools, including books, magazines, cards, reward - tickets, Sunday-school registers, roll-books, minute-books, Sunday-school newspapers, etc., presenting a fair view of this important institution as conducted in the country where it first originated in its present form. The material and methods for promoting the education and employment of the blind were likewise displayed, and common-school education was represented in maps, atlases, globes, editions of the classics, and other educational works; and collaterally by means of engravings, photographs, blocks used for wood-engraving, specimens of type, and copies of illustrated and other newspapers, besides a very considerable number of scientific and other instruments.

The educational department of Victoria, at Melbourne, sent photographic views of the State School in Victoria, and the Victorian Asylum and School for the Blind exhibited a number of articles made by pupils of the institution, such as baskets, portmanteaus, trunks, mats, fancy wool-work; while the commissioners furnished official reports, school-books and other educational works, as well as philosophical instruments.

The exhibits from Canada have been already mentioned briefly. As heretofore stated, an important feature of these was comprised in the ingenious models of school-buildings and public institutions generally, a number of which were exhibited in the Woman's Pavilion.

The general educational exhibit of Ontario, of which a separate catalogue has been issued, included reports of the different schools in the Province, with copies of the laws governing them. There were also photographs of the educational institutions and other public buildings, including the University of Toronto; the Victoria Methodist University of Cobourg; Institution for the Blind Brantford; and Institution for the Deaf and Dumb, Belleville. The normal and model schools, collegiate institutions, high schools and public schools of Ontario were exhibited in reports, models and plans. Of school-fittings and furniture there were shown a number of desks, model of gymnasium, map-stands, blackboards, and school implements of all kinds. In school-work

the exhibits consisted of maps, pencil and scientific drawing, and penmanship. A number of these were from the model schools for girls and boys in Toronto.

The various text-books in use in Canada were exhibited; also books relating to the profession of teaching, and those employed in the examination of teachers. The Kindergarten system and object-teaching were illustrated, and a large collection of books used for prizes, drawing materials and models and music, was included. Geography and astronomy were fully illustrated in terrestrial and celestial globes, atlases, maps, charts, planetariums and diagrams. Natural history was presented in sets of fossils, minerals, geological specimens, models of flowers, botanical charts, stuffed specimens of mammalia, birds, reptiles and fishes. Anatomy and physiology, chemistry and mechanical science, electri-

SILK WEAVING IN LOG CABIN.

city and mechanics, had their appropriate apparatus. The Canadian educational department was the most important feature of the exhibits of the Dominion.

FRANCE makes no distinctive educational exhibit, but the Department of Public Education of Paris sent books, catalogues and reports; and a number of the educational societies and schools of France were represented by the work of pupils and by reports; while school-furniture and materials and educational books were profusely shown.

GERMANY made no special educational exhibits.

AUSTRIA illustrated her educational institutions by photographs of objects pertaining to them, and by collections of objects of natural history and models of schools, sent from Prague. The Austrian method of instructing the blind was illustrated; scientific and philosophic instruments were displayed, and the department of the Press in Vienna was illustrated by a representation covering the years between 1750 and 1876.

SWITZERLAND, where every child between five and eight years of age is compelled to attend school, sent a complete exhibit of her school system, each canton being represented by its Board of Education in collections of laws and regulations, books, maps, plans, reports, prospectuses, school apparatus and models. The drawings and other school-work of pupils presented a most pleasing and attractive showing, and especially the work of the blind and the deaf and dumb. A curious portion of this exhibition was found in a collection of large blank-books, in which were inserted specimens of all kinds of needlework, from babies' socks to elaborately constructed dresses. A number of Swiss organizations of a scientific or educational character were represented: such as the Swiss Geological Commission, the Swiss Statistical Society, Swiss Historical Society, Swiss Alpine Club, and the Societies for the Advancement of Natural Philosophy located in the different cantons. A fine collection of scientific and philosophical instruments was also exhibited, including drawing instruments, leveling instruments, and others.

Education in BELGIUM was presented in a school-house in the Belgian section in the Main Building, comprising three rooms, so hidden by the important articles exhibited around it, as to be difficult to find. The primary school, sent as a specimen, included a wash-room, a well-supplied gymnasium, model schoolroom lighted, warmed and ventilated on a scientific system, and desks and seats well adapted to their uses and graduated

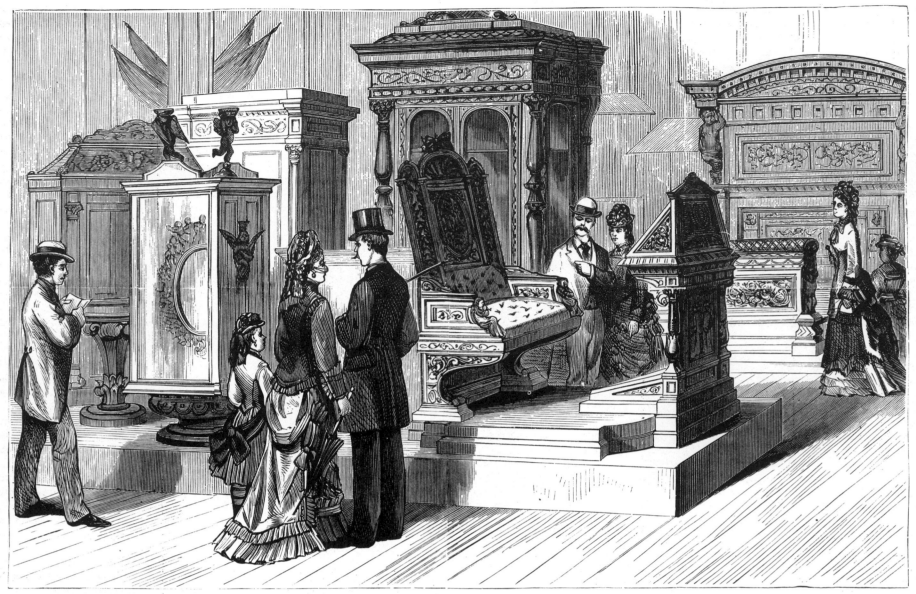

ITALIAN FURNITURE.

to the height of the pupils. Here were shown, also, as means of instruction, pictures, instruments, stuffed birds and animals, geometric forms, statistical tables, books, models, and many other articles designed for the improvement of the mind.

The KINGDOM OF THE NETHERLANDS is represented in its educational system by no special exhibit, but offered a collection of school-books, drawings and designs of work of pupils, besides a curious writing apparatus designed for the use of cripples.

The school system of SWEDEN, which is in many respects the best in the world, was fully displayed in the Exhibition, the Swedish schoolhouse, already illustrated and described in this work, being especially representative, and having formed an object which received considerable attention during the existence of the Exhibition. According to Swedish law, the school board of every county determines the age when education shall commence, providing that this shall not be postponed until after the ninth year of the child's age. This latter contingency seldom occurs except in localities where the hard climate renders it impracticable for very small children to attend school. Generally speaking, the school-life commences with their seventh year and continues until the fourteenth; but after nine years of age education is compulsory, and all who are not instructed in private schools, or at home by permission of the legal school board, must attend the public schools. Children whose parents are unable to clothe and feed them during the school period are assisted by a public fund. At the end of the year 1873 the number of children in Sweden between the ages of nine and fourteen was 734,165, or 17 per cent. In that year nearly 83 per cent. of all the children were instructed in the national schools. Of children who, on account of natural defects, had been without instruction, there were in the kingdom 2,678, and of those who for other reasons received no instruction, 16,121—although it is not stated whether this lack of instruction extended beyond the year given. Industrial schools for boys exist in many places, particularly in towns; while in most of the girls' schools they have opportunities for learning industries. In some of the larger towns opportunities are given to girls for practicing common household vocations, such as baking, washing and ironing, in institutions denominated "School for Housekeepers," and established for that purpose.

An important provision, by special royal enactment made in the year 1866, establishes a pension fund for the benefit of teachers, this being sustained by the communities. The full pension is paid to a teacher if he has served thirty years and attained sixty years of age, and also if he be afflicted with an incurable disease at that point of life when his age and term of service together amount to ninety years. Under certain other circumstances a small pension

is granted, the full pension amounting to something over $200 gold per annum.

Among the articles exhibited by Sweden in her educational department were specimens of the work of pupils in the different classes of schools, maps, models of schoolhouses, gymnastic apparatus, herbariums, drawings, and a collective exhibition of the technical elemental schools in six different cities and towns of Sweden.

NORWAY had no educational exhibits beyond a collection of materials for the free school, models of hand-writing, books and maps.

ITALY offered specimens of penmanship, maps in relief, books and newspapers, and some preparations in pathological anatomy and microscopy.

THE ARGENTINE REPUBLIC is the only South American country which had any educational exhibit, this including a few native school-books, educational statistics of certain of the provinces, annals of education, reading cards, statistics of certain schools and libraries—not including a general collection of books and periodicals, charts, maps, and plans, which was quite large and important.

JAPAN was represented by every article of importance used in the instruction of the Japanese youth, including text-books, cases of stuffed animals, skeletons, pressed plants and leaves, illustrations of the Kindergarten system, gymnasium, slates, school libraries, and the weekly and monthly

IMPROVED PRISMOIDAL RAILWAY FOR RAPID TRANSIT. REAR VIEW.

reports of several Japanese schools. It is stated, on the authority of a Japanese Commissioner, that while, five years ago, the Government found it advisable to send young men and women to Europe and America to receive full education, now it is unnecessary, since Japan has schools of the highest grade, equal to those of any other country

In the educational department the exhibits of the UNITED STATES were divided into States, viz., Indiana, Michigan, Wisconsin, Ohio, Rhode Island, New Hampshire, Illinois, Maine, Iowa, Tennessee, Massachusetts, New Jersey, New York—and the State of Pennsylvania, as presented in the handsome special education building devoted to the exhibits of that State. Among these, the State of Massachusetts made the largest, most comprehensive and most representative exhibition, including every article used in school education under the Massachusetts system, which is generally admitted to be the most practical as well as most scientific in use. The collection included plans of State normal schools, with stereoscope and stereoscopic views, drawings from high schools and academies, photographs of high schools in different towns, architectural drawings, photographs from Harvard University, Amherst College, Tuft's College, and other universities and colleges; reports, documents and views illustrating the various female seminaries and military schools, specimens of drawing, painting and modeling from the art schools, materials for instruction in industrial drawing, books, models in wood and plaster, anatomical preparations, books and apparatus illustrating the processes in use at the institutions for the blind and the deaf and dumb, annual reports of the Board of Education and the school committees of 18 cities and 323 towns in the commonwealth; and, finally, a large collection of text-books and miscellaneous works, pamphlets and periodicals, reports, public documents, plans and photographs, having reference in one way or another to the subject of education.

In the Pennsylvania Building, which was a circular structure divided into sections or alcoves by a corridor, with an open hall in the centre, we had exhibits from special schools, illustrating, in a curious and interesting manner, the progress of education. Thus, one alcove showed the old-time school-room with its appurtenances; an old hat and coat hanging on the wall; a clumsy desk spotted with spilled ink, a leather strap, suggestive of castigation; an antique-looking bucket, with a gourd for a drinking cup; an old-fashioned stove; old, dog's-eared books; and the generally dilapidated appearance common to the school-room of a generation since.

Next to this alcove was a section representing the school-room of the present. Here everything is new—new desks, maps, books, all the modern paraphernalia. In the space in the centre of the building were representations of the latest improvements in school-desks. Two sections were devoted to the work of soldier's orphans in different schools. The normal schools and colleges were represented by their students' work, with models of the colleges and school-buildings. A school of design for women exhibited some really artistic and interesting work. The Kindergarten system was displayed, and Pittsburgh had a special representation of the work of her mechanical night-schools. The school for the blind had a special representation. Finally, the Pennsylvania Sunday-schools made a full display, illustrating their methods of education.

Returning to the Main Building exhibition, it may be mentioned that Maryland exhibited models of her public schools, with specimens of school-furniture; New Hampshire was notable for the exhibit of a large relief map of White Mountain scenery; the Michigan University offered a fine collection of stuffed birds, shells, and specimens of natural history, besides a complete representative display of the public schools of the State; Wisconsin showed pictures of its school-buildings and a series of its text-books; Connecticut made a fine display, offering new styles of desks, maps, pictures of Yale College, with its halls, library, art gallery and other buildings; representations of schools of the different large towns, and a library of books written by Yale graduates, and other interesting objects.

New Jersey public schools were represented by the work of pupils. Ninety-six per cent. of her teachers have exhibited. Rhode Island illustrated evening school-work, and the Brown University. Iowa made a fine exhibit of school statistics. The education of the Freedmen, representing thirty-four schools and seminaries, was illustrated by a map on which was displayed the location of schools, also pictures of a normal labor school, and one representing the fine building, costing $100,000, erected by the Hampton Singers. Illinois was exhibited by her Industrial University, College of Engineering, the Chicago schools, and revolving cases showing examination papers and school-buildings. Here were photographs of school-buildings and volumes containing plans of school architecture. The Ohio and Indiana exhibits were complete, and in fact, the Western States made in education a remarkably full and interesting showing. It is to be recollected that the schools of the West had the advantage of a nine-million-dollar school fund, besides the benefit of Eastern experience. Ninety years ago they paid their teachers $2,000. Last year they paid them about $2,800,000. Indiana exhibited quite largely in mineral and chemical specimens, besides fishes, zoological specimens and native woods; all of which were collected and prepared by pupils of the different schools. Models of ward and high-school buildings at Indianapolis, Fort Wayne and Terre Haute were exhibited, and, what was a considerable curiosity, the model of a log school-house, the first built in Delaware County, Indiana, and which cost $25 in 1825. This work, taken in comparison with the Indiana schools of the present day, some of which cost as high as $75,000, was an interesting exhibit. A specialty in this collection comprised banners exhibiting the school system, statistics, and distribution of school-houses in the different communities.

The exhibit of the State of Tennessee included reports of the different schools exhibited by the State and County Superintendents; photographs of the Colored Training School at Jonesboro; examination manuscripts and geographical drawings from Memphis and Nashville, and photographs of prominent Tennessee educators. New York exhibited drawing instruments, models and machinery for scientific schools, text-books, school-books, slates, blackboards, maps, terrestrial and celestial globes, books, charts, and modern school material, desks and school furniture; and in fact, all the appurtenances which go to illustrate the New York public school system.

MINERAL ANNEX No. 2.*

THIS building, which, like No. 1, was an annex to the Main Building, was devoted chiefly to large masses of minerals and of their manufacture. It commenced with a novelty in the shape of concentrated anthracite fuel, made in bricks and composed of coal-dust held together by some new process, and afterward modeled into form. It is contended that this fuel is at last a successful effort to utilize coal-waste. Here also were numerous specimens of bituminous

* For Mineral Annex No. 1, see page 215.

and gas coals, and next, a large show of firebrick and a complete system of retorts from a Philadelphia establishment. Near by were some specimens of minerals taken from Howe's Cave, Schoharie County, New York, and these were followed by samples of coke, bituminous coal, a form of kaolin, and a large show of firebrick. Some galvanized sheet-iron came next, and then some very pretty monuments of small size made from native Pennsylvania marble. These were followed by specimens of porous drain-tile, and then came a full and comprehensive exhibition of Virginia and Kentucky minerals, arranged in good order, and labeled in a manner similar to those in Annex No. 1.

A few curious stuffed animals were exhibited by the Museum of Mount Union College, Lyons, Ohio. They included the gorilla, kangaroo, a large bat, and a Brazilian ant-eater. This building concluded with a collection of Tennessee minerals. The Kentucky mineral display was a remarkably fine one, and deserving of special notice.

In fact, the mineralogical exhibits from the Western and Southern States proved quite a surprise even to scientists, who probably did not expect to find the newer portions of the country so enthusiastic with regard to minerals, or so rich in the matter of collections.

RECEPTION OF LORD DUFFERIN AT ST. GEORGE'S HALL.

OUR ILLUSTRATIONS.

PLAYING-CARDS EXHIBIT OF A. DOUGHERTY.

A VERY pretty little case in the southeastern end of the American department of the Main Building contained an exhibit portrayed in our illustration, representing the playing-card manufactory of A. Dougherty, No. 80 Centre Street, New York. The packs of cards were arranged in ornamental fashion, displaying the special merits of these in texture, enamel, etc. A peculiar feature of the exhibit was the patent triplicate card—the difference between this card and all others consisting in its having itself reproduced in miniature in each corner, so that the value of the card may be seen at a glance by the player, without examining the whole face.

CENTENNIAL GLASS WORKS.

Certainly one of the most constantly attractive centres on the Centennial Grounds was the building where was exhibited the beautiful art of glass manufacturing in all its branches, and which was erected at the extreme southeastern end of the grounds, near the saw-mill. This building was put up by Messrs. Gillender & Sons, of the Franklin Flint Glass Works, whose manufactory in Philadelphia

covers a space of 237 feet by 156 feet. The founder of this house commenced business in Philadelphia in 1860, and all the various processes of his trade were daily exhibited in the pretty and ornamental miniature establishment on the Centennial Grounds. A single one-storied structure of considerable extent, unbroken by wall or pillar, containing a tall tower tapering in form from the bottom up, and a furnace, comprised the principal portion of the glass-works. Besides the main melting-furnace, other smaller furnaces supplied the necessary melting appurtenances of the establishment. About these red-hot furnaces could be seen continually in constant movement a large force of men and boys engaged in stirring up the hot metal within the main furnace, carrying to the various artificers balls of the red mass on the end of their metal sticks, and performing other duties involved in the mysteries of glass-making. Here, a workman was engaged in molding glass into various shapes while in its melted condition by pouring it into a matrix, from which it was withdrawn a completed lamp, tumbler, goblet, or what not; there, boys were running about with the newly-made article still at a red heat, carried on the top of a stick, to be placed on a board and undergo the annealing process in two ovens, each sixty feet in length—this latter important process being performed by tempering the glass, as it were, from a high to a low condition of heat, the articles placed on pans being carried by means of movable iron trucks over the space of sixty feet at a very slow speed, and emerging at the further end cool and annealed, an operation consuming altogether twelve hours.

At one side of the building men were engaged in frosting, cutting and engraving, by means of wheels, grindstones and tools, the various pieces of glass-ware designed to be so treated. In some cases, designs of flowers, letters, or other devices, were transferred to glass by means of little copper wheels; in other instances, articles were engraved, "Centennial, 1876," and also with the names or initials desired by the purchasers. Among such articles sold in enormous quantities during the Centennial Exposition in this building were very pretty little glass slippers, paper-weights of different kinds, delicate wine-glasses and tumblers, flower-holders, pitchers, and numerous other pleasing souvenirs. Altogether, there were probably no outside exhibitions at the Centennial which attracted so much attention, or perhaps conveyed so much information, as that of the Messrs. Gillender.

WOMEN'S DAY AT THE CENTENNIAL.

On November 7th, the ladies who had charge of the Women's Pavilion, led by Mrs. E. D. Gillespie on behalf of the Women's Centennial Executive Committee, of which she was the President, gave a reception; and this being election day, it was naturally noticeable that a very much larger assemblage of ladies than of gentlemen was present on the grounds. In preparation for the event of the day, a stage, ornamented with flags and banners, had been erected in the northern wing of the Women's Pavilion, facing the fountain, while other flags in large numbers, representing the different nations, were hung from the base of the rotunda and all around the building. The Girard College band occupied the eastern gallery, and this, too, was completely festooned with flags.

Previous to the reception, the exhibitors in the Pavilion presented a number of handsome bronze souvenirs to the ladies of the Executive Committee, and the articles were received with appropriate acknowledgments. The reception proper commenced at noon; and from that time for several hours Mrs. Gillespie and the other ladies of the Committee were engaged in receiving guests, who thronged to the pavilion in large numbers. At the conclusion of the reception, Mrs. Gillespie addressed the crowd of ladies and gentlemen present, welcoming them to the Women's Department of the Centennial, and thanking them for their generous response to the call for the Women's Day.

The Women's Centennial Committee was organized in February, 1873, and added $126,000 to the treasury of the Board of Finance, besides erecting their pavilion at a cost of $35,000, and supplying it with a handsome display illustrative of female labor. The organization existed in thirty-two States, and concluded to continue itself until the close of the Exposition, under the name of the Women's National Centennial League. One special instance of enterprise and success in this connection has been the publication of a weekly paper during the Exhibition, called *The New*

EXHIBIT OF MESSRS. R. HOE & CO., IN MACHINERY HALL.—THE HOE PRESS, PRINTING BOTH SIDES FROM THE ROLL, WITH FOLDING MACHINE ATTACHED.

Century for Women, which was entirely completed by women's labor—publisher, editors, contributors and type-setters being all of that sex.

WOMEN'S ART GALLERY.

The collection of pictures in the Women's Pavilion was not concluded upon until after the building had been constructed, and no proper space for the exhibition was included in the original design. A large number of paintings, drawings and statues were comprised in the exhibition, and, as might be expected, where but little discrimination was exercised, a majority of those works of art were not up to the standard of the other articles of women's work exhibited in the building. There were, however, some most creditable efforts, and our artist has wisely selected, in presenting his sketch, that portion of the gallery which contained certain articles of statuary, and the admirable pen-and-ink sketches exhibited by Miss Greatorex and Miss Clark.

"THE MOHAWK DUTCHMAN."

Mr. McChesney, known by his title of "The Mohawk Dutchman," will be remembered as the wood-sawyer in Machinery Hall, whose curious costume caused him to be constantly surrounded by an admiring crowd. This costume comprised an oval hat-frame of inlaid woods, having a small windmill at top; a pair of inlaid spectacles of quaint structure; a collar of different kinds of wood about his throat; around his waist a belt of red, white and blue, clasped with a six-inch buckle of wood; bracelets made of wood containing jewels; and apron of the American colors reaching from his shoulders to his feet—all these articles of clothing, so to speak, comprised the costume of this unique figure.

Mr. McChesney's immediate uses at the Centennial were to produce by means of his saw different articles of furniture cut very rapidly from a solid block of wood and without the use of mark-line measurement. These articles comprised rocking-chairs, sewing-chairs, sofas, footstools, sleighs, hobby-horses, etc., all of which he claimed to make from original designs. The wood-sawyer is a manufacturer of patent models by profession, has himself produced several patents, and is said to be a scientific and practical mechanic. He was certainly clever in his handiwork, and was one of the greatest attractions of Machinery Hall.

ROYAL BAKING POWDER PAVILION.

A point of interest in Agricultural Hall was the pavilion of the Royal Baking Powder Company of New York City. It was constantly surrounded by a crowd of interested spec-

tators witnessing the processes of manufacture carried on, involving the use of the celebrated Baking Powder; the large pavilion was fitted up with gas-stoves, ovens, and all appliances for baking, and with a practical baker on hand, there were constantly produced very beautiful and delicious specimens of articles illustrative of bread-making, which were dealt out to the eager crowd constantly in attendance. It is said that three millions of hot buttered biscuit and rolls, and more than two millions of griddle and buckwheat cakes, were thus dispensed during the continuance of the Exhibition. The manufactory where this powder is made is the largest establishment of the kind in the world.

W. J. PHILLIPS, TELEGRAPH DIRECTOR OF THE CENTENNIAL.

A most important part of the running mechanism of the Centennial management was the Telegraph Bureau, situated adjoining the Bureau of Public Comfort. Here a large number of instruments were constantly in use, while a complete corps of messenger-boys was in readiness at all hours during the day. From this point telegraphic dispatches could be sent to any part of the world, at present united with the grand telegraphic systems which do so much to facilitate the operations of civilization. Naturally for the conduct of this large and material portion of the business of the Centennial Exposition there was selected the best possible talent accessible, and this was found in the person of Mr. W. J. Phillips, President of the American District Telegraph Company of Philadelphia.

Mr. Phillips was one of the original House Printing operators, and was instrumental in erecting the first line worked on this patent between New York and Philadelphia, and of which he was manager. He also superintended the

construction of the Police and Fire Alarm Telegraph of Philadelphia, of which he is still in charge, while his official management of the District Telegraph Company, to whose Presidency he has recently been appointed, has gained for him the friendship and esteem of the entire mercantile population of that city. In his conduct of telegraphic matters at the Centennial, Mr. Phillips has still further developed the value and importance of his services, while the courtesy and kindliness of his personal manners have been noteworthy and appreciated.

As evidence of the amount of business done in Centennial telegraphy, it may be mentioned that in two months more than 40,000 dispatches were sent off and 15,000 received.

COLONEL MYER ASCH, SECRETARY OF THE CENTENNIAL COMMISSION.

Necessarily in so large an organization as was comprised in the Centennial management, there were many officials who, though performing onerous and continuous duties, were nevertheless in the background, as it were, and the value of their labors unrecognized save by those with whom they came more particularly in contact. This was especially the case with Colonel Asch, who, by his relations with the Director-General and through the authority of his own position, was brought into more immediate correspondence with the Foreign Commissioners than any other Centennial officer.

Colonel Asch was born in Philadelphia, and there graduated from the High School. The early years of his life were passed in Europe in completing his education; but at the breaking out of the war he returned to the United States to accept a Lieutenant's commission in the First New Jersey Cavalry. He soon rose to the position of Adjutant-General on the staff of Major-General Pope, and served with that officer during the campaign in Virginia. Later, he was Adjutant-General of Kurtz's Cavalry Division, of the Army of the James, and finally rose to the full rank of Colonel. During six months of the war Colonel Asch was imprisoned at Libby, Danville and Salisbury. Colonel Asch's war experience included one Indian campaign with General Pope; and at the close of the Rebellion he was tendered a commission in the United States Regular Army.

On the organization of the Centennial Commission, the important appointment of Secretary was the first one made, and this position was offered at once to Colonel Asch. As we have already mentioned, the duties of this office included all the correspondence and negotiations with foreign countries, and in the conduct of this delicate and serious business, and in effecting the

THE WALTER PRESS, PRINTING BOTH SIDES FROM THE ROLL, WITH CALENDERING APPARATUS.

necessary relations with the Foreign Commissioners, it is to be observed that Colonel Asch displayed singular tact and discretion and delicate courtesy.

The combination of qualities required in the exceptionally difficult position have found their best exponent in all particulars in Colonel Asch, who has thus deserved a niche in our gallery of portraits of gentlemen who have distinguished themselves in the direction and management of the United States Centennial Exposition.

"VICTOR" ROCK-DRILL.

This most ingenious machine, which was exhibited in Machinery Hall, is the invention of W. Weaver, of Phœnixville, Pa., who is the patentee. It has a capacity for drilling holes from half an inch to six inches in diameter, and at any depth and angle required, at the rate of two inches per minute, employing only one man to run it. It will be seen that this invention is a most important addition to rock-drilling machinery. A novelty in its making is the double-gouge bit. The simplicity and perfect success with which this rock-drill accomplished its purpose were so obvious, that its operations were constantly watched by the scientific, curious and interested observers.

OHIO AND PHILADELPHIA DAYS.

Thursday, November 2d, having been decided upon as the Ohio Day, Governor Hayes consented to be present, and it was estimated that over 100,000 persons were attracted by the occasion. The usual official formalities were gone through with, the Governor of Ohio being presented to the assembled citizens of his own and other States, and the proper and customary addresses were made by gentlemen designated for that purpose. In fact, the State Days resembled each other greatly in their general features, though affording an opportunity to those not otherwise interested for gaining a correct impression of the ethnological differences between the people of the different States.

On the following Thursday, November 9th, being the day before the close of the Exhibition, occurred what was denominated as Philadelphia Day. About 175,000 visitors were present, and with their gathering closed the series of pleasant State festivities of the Centennial.

THE CENTENNIAL CHIMES.

To most of the visitors to the Centennial Exposition a very pleasant diversion was found in listening to the chimes of the bells in the northeastern tower of Machinery Hall. These were heard three times each day—sunrise, noon and sunset; and it is quite certain that never were chimes heard which interpreted so volubly and so munificently the airs most favored by the American people. The bells were thirteen in number, representing the original thirteen States. Their aggregate weight was 21,000 pounds, that of the largest being 3,600 pounds, and that of the smallest 350 pounds. They were cast in Baltimore by McShane & Co., and it is claimed that the chime is the finest in this country.

During the existence of the Exposition the bells were operated by Professor Widdows, who was formerly in charge of the chimes at the Metropolitan Church in Washington. These bells were immovably suspended from a huge horizontal square frame, on the top floor of the tower. Each bell had two hammers, one heavy, the other light; the latter being muffled to produce a soft tone whenever desired. On the floor below, in the centre of the room, were twenty-six triangular levers, pivoted at one angle, being so arranged that a pull or depression on the outer arm caused the hammer to touch and strike a bell. The outer arms were connected by

means of long, elastic strips of wood, running through the ceiling, with an apparatus situated beneath the bells. There were two sets of levers, upper and lower, working the muffled and heavy hammers. These twenty-six levers were connected with the triangular levers above and the pump levers below, by means of leather straps. These were operated by hand, or, if desired, could be disconnected from the upright strips.

It is stated that Professor Widdows possessed a *répertoire* containing no fewer than 1,000 pieces. To those who ventured to ascend to the locality of his ministrations, a novel and curious sight would be presented. A short, stout gentleman, partially bald, whiskered in the British fashion, and with a round, good-humored face, would be seen springing from side to side of the room, pressing down the levers as rapidly and with the same facility as an expert pianist exhibits in his performances; and during the hot Summer days showing plainly that this was no child's play, but exceedingly energetic labor. Our illustration in another portion of this work exhibits the Professor in the act of manipulating his peculiar instrument.

THE BULLOCK PRESS, PRINTING FROM THE ROLL, EXHIBITED IN MACHINERY HALL.

MACHINERY HALL.

A VIEW of the interior of Machinery Hall, while in process of construction, will be found at pages 24 and 25 of the REGISTER, and a description of the building at page 21. It contained machines for working in metal, wood, glass, clay, stone, fibre, paper and gum, besides exhibits of motors, such as steam, air, gas and electrical engines. On the south side of the main body of Machinery Hall, extending from the centre, was the hydraulic annex, 208 by 210 feet, with a tank 60 by 106 feet, around which were the pumps and other exhibits in this department. At the south end of this annex was the "Cascade," 36 feet in breadth, heretofore described.

Eight main lines of shafting were provided for the machinery in the avenues and halls of Machinery Hall, the larger portion being kept up to 120 revolutions per minute, and one line, used principally for wood-working machines,

to 240 revolutions per minute. The entire length of shafting is estimated at 10,400 feet, each main line of 650 feet transmitting 180-horse-power to the various machines connected with it. The floor room in this building included 510,960 square feet, and it is an evidence of the economy with which the structure was erected that this space cost only $1 55 per square foot.

In the interior arrangement of Machinery Hall and the allotment of space, the foreign countries were located at the eastern end; these countries included Austria, the German Empire, Canada, France, Spain, Great Britain, Belgium, Sweden, Denmark, Russia, Brazil, Italy, and Switzerland.

On entering the edifice at the western end, a view was obtained which was at once picturesque and impressive. Here nearly every kind of machine, from a locomotive to a paper-folder, was exhibited, and nearly all of them in active operation. Of course, the central object of interest was the magnificent Corliss Engine, which we have already fully described, and which supplied all necessary steam-power. The machinery exposed presented all the latest patents and inventions, and was of a most ingenious and varied description. Here were apparatus used in mining, working in wood and stone; machines for spinning, weaving, felting, paper-making; in sewing and manufacture of clothing; type-setting, printing, stamping, embossing, book-making, and paper-working; in producing and transmitting power; in pumping, hoisting and lifting by hydraulic and pneumatic force; in manufacturing locomotives and railway stock; in preparing agricultural implements, and in aerial and marine transportation. Here were witnessed during the Exhibition the processes of rock-drilling, of well-boring, of coal-cutting, electro-plating; of planing, sawing, veneering, carving, cutting and stamping; of drilling, turning, punching; of shaping and polishing; of rolling iron, grinding glass, casting metals, and riveting, nailing, bolting and tacking by steam; the processes employed in the manufacture of silk, wools, cotton and linen goods, rope and twine, paper and felting, india-rubber goods, mixed fabrics and wire-cloth; mechanism used in making clocks and watches; pipes for smoking; printing, embossing and lithographing; type-casting and stereotyping, book-binding and paper-folding; generating power by boilers, water-wheels, hydraulic rams, steam, air, gas and electro-magnetic engines, with the means for transmitting it by shafting, pulleys, cables, etc., in lifting and moving liquids and solids, expanding or compressing air or gas; engines for extinguishing fire, and apparatus for escaping from it; mechanisms for manufacturing soda-water, bottling it and corking the bottles; diving apparatus for the recovery of sunken treasures; derricks, buffers, snow-plows, street-railways and horse-cars; grinding grist; refining sugar, making candy; preparing tobacco, oil, spices, and fancy goods; for brewing beer and liquids; for transporting cables; and finally, for the transportation of telegraph cables and railway trains, and propelling ships and steamboats.

GREAT BRITAIN.

This country occupied much the largest space in Machinery Hall devoted to foreign exhibitors, comprising 35,725 feet. This space began at the eastern end of the nave and ran south to the south wall and north to the first avenue. In this department 103 exhibitors were found represented, the contributions embracing various applications of steam, as steam traction engines, steam-pumps, sugar-mills with engines and centrifugal turning machine, steam boilers, steam coal mining machine and steam-driven hydraulic press. In machines for working in fibre, carding machines, and spinners, Jacquard loom, knitting-machines for socks, etc., calico-printing machines and

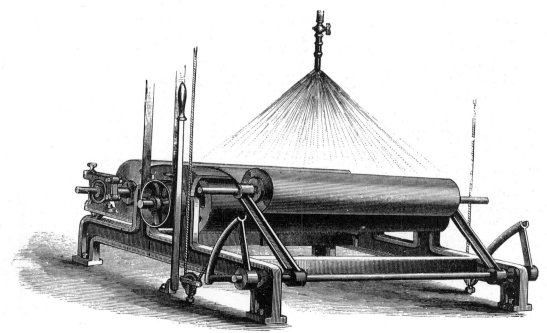

MACHINE FOR DAMPING PAPER, FOR BULLOCK PRESS.

JAPANESE SCREEN.

there was an eight-color machine exhibited by Thomas Gad, of Manchester, who also sent a combined engraving and punching-machine, a varnishing and ruling machine, engraver's block and lathe, and other interesting pieces of mechanism.

The exhibit of armor plate by C. Campbell & Co. always attracted a crowd. Most of the specimens had been used as targets, and were badly torn and crushed by the shot. Among these was a piece of the thickest plate ever rolled, being 21⅔ inches thick; and the manufacturers of this plate say they can roll very much thicker ones if necessary. One of the most curious as well as instructive exhibits by the English was a water-heater for steam boilers, consisting of a large number of vertical pipes, having machinery at their tops which run a number of scrapers up and down the pipes to prevent soot from collecting. The fire is made under the boiler; all the products of combustion which would otherwise escape up the chimney are passed in between the pipes, which are filled with water, and thus made to absorb the waste heat and heat the water before it passes into the boiler. By keeping the soot from the pipes it is claimed that fully 25 per cent. saving in fuel is effected. A sugar manufacturer in Philadelphia has adopted one of these heaters, having ten miles of pipe, through which the water passes before it reaches the boilers.

Great Britain also exhibited a beautiful model of a pumping engine made in that country for Ferrara, Italy. It had a pair of compound surface condensing engines, with patent centrifugal beam, and had a capacity for 2,000 tons of water a minute.

The weakness of Great Britain, however, in departments in which she ought to have been ready to compete with the world, was very manifest. In steam engines, she offered nothing in comparison with the great Corliss Engine, although the engine-builders of England have a reputation which is world-wide. Cotton-spinning, which represents so vast an amount of the wealth and industry of England, was displayed here only in one machine exhibited by H. Booth & Co., of Preston, Lancashire. Leeds sent a machine for tying in warps in looms, and Paisley a spooling-machine and thread-winding machine, as also machinery for carding, preparing and spinning jute. A self-acting machine for painting Venetian blinds, laths, and hoop-iron was exhibited by a Liverpool inventor; and from Sheffield an exhibit of anvils, vises and hammers is made by Messrs. Brooks & Cooper. There were also shown diving apparatus for divers, and the figure of a diver in his suit, with helmet and apparatus complete. A model of a turret and life-saving apparatus was shown; a model of a four-oared racing boat, designed to take to pieces for convenience of transportation; models of life-boats and salvage-boats, floating and other docks, and finally, a model of Her Majesty's turret ram *Alexandra*. The Midland Davy Lamp Works, of Birmingham, sent specimens of miner's safety lamps.

The methods for getting out coal, as employed in the English collieries, were exhibited by a London engineer through the means of three classes of machines: 1. rock and coal perforators; 2. machines for under-cutting coal; 3. weights for breaking down coal; and in this same line, cast-steel picks were exhibited by a Sheffield manufacturer, the picks being interchangeable and detachable from their shafts or handles. Archer's stone-breaking

and ore-crushing machinery was exhibited by the Dunston Engine Works Company, of Durham. B. & G. Massey exhibited steam-hammers for heavy forge work, smith-work, cutlery and light work, stamps for forging in dies at one blow, and models for steam-hammers. The machine exhibited by Duncan Mackenzie, engineer, London, the self-acting reeder for the Jacquard loom, is adapted for all kinds of ornamental figured fabrics. It is founded on the principle of arithmetical progression and geometrical exactness. It dispenses with skilled labor of adults, and places the manipulations and the operations of the reeder under the control of juvenile hands. One of his machines exhibited a combination of mechanism of a new construction, having a compound parallel and perpendicular movement applicable to a variety of other purposes, such as ruling paper, doing two sides of the sheet at the same time without change of pens.

A manufacturer of hosiery machinery in Leicester exhibited a large circular machine, having twelve feeders designed for making Cardigan jackets, and fitted with an adjustable machine to make the plain ribbed work. A small circular machine for making Cardigan jacket-sleeves, with welt and cuff complete, was also exhibited. Among the sewing-machines exhibited by four exhibitors were the "Queen Mab," "Express," "Queen of Scots," "Cleopatra," "Princess of Wales," "England's Queen," "Europa," "Queen of Hearts," and "Little Dorrit," displaying an amount of sentiment in the matter of sewing-machine nomenclature scarcely to be expected. These machines were mostly of the Wheeler & Wilson and Singer class, having, however, new attachments and special movements.

From Dublin we had an exhibit of a lithographer's manifold transfer machine for the reproduction of printed matter in enlarged or reduced dimensions from that of the original, used for the multiplication of printed books of various sizes, reproduced by the Typo-Relievo etching process for printing. A curious exhibit was found in the thermo-electric batteries, worked by gas, charcoal, coke or mineral oils, in their nature approaching the principle of the gas stove. Mrs. Henrietta Vansittart, of Twickenham,

JAPANESE SCREEN.

sewing-machines from London and Glasgow, there was considerable display. There were plate and bar shears, armor plating from 2 to 21⅔ inches thick, hot blast furnaces, mill lathes, the Walter web printing-press, felt roofing from Belfast. tobacco-spinning machine and railway safety apparatus.

Among the more remarkable articles in this section were a number of Aveling & Porter's road and farm steamers for hauling heavy loads, plowing, and doing farm-work of all kinds. They were said to draw six or seven heavily loaded wagons over rough roads or drag six plows at about four miles an hour, requiring only 600 or 700 pounds of coal a day, and one man or boy to run them. Where the land has never been cultivated, these do very well for plowing; but after the ground has once been broken it is stated they cannot be made to run upon it to any advantage. These steamers were very large and heavy, and cost from $3,200 to $4,000, gold. Some description has already been given of them in the account of the contents of the Agricultural Building.

A sewing-machine for sails was exhibited from Glasgow, being the largest in the Exhibition. This one had the traveling bed shortened so as to save space; but in the factory the bed is 60 feet in length, to enable the machine to sew seams of that length continuously. A splendid machine was that of a sugar-mill and engine of Murlees, Tait & Watson, Glasgow, consisting of a valveless engine working an air-pump for vacuum pan and for driving centrifugal machines. The steam cranes from England exhibited by Appleby Bros., London, have attracted considerable attention, being put in practical use. The Walter printing-machine, which is used by the London *Times*, the London *Daily News* (where eight "Walters" are employed), by many other English and foreign newspapers, and by the New York *Times*, was exhibited by John Walter, of London, its maker, and has given opportunity for comparison with our Hoe and other printing machines. A ribbon-weaving Jacquard loom exhibited from Coventry, England, was displayed in operation, weaving portraits of Shakespeare, Washington, John Wesley, Queen Victoria, Lincoln, Spurgeon, Grant, and others. In calico-printing, exhibited her screw propeller system in what is called the the Lowe-Vansittart Curved Line or Three Pitched Wave Line, Non-vibrating, full backing, Economical Screw Propeller, as fitted in the British Navy and Merchant Service by Mrs. Henrietta Vansittart, who is the daughter of Mr. Lowe, the inventor of the screw propulsion.

The buoy or turret system of life-preservation in case of shipwreck, already alluded to, was exhibited in a model. The principle of the system is easily explained. A compartment distinct and detached from the ship is built within her, large enough to contain provisions for the voyage and all the voyagers, if required. Should the vessel go down, the compartment floats, and all on board take refuge in it. This is simplicity itself. The model of the system for the prevention of railroad collisions and accidents exhibited, displays : 1st, railway signals and the model of a junction, with switches and signals interlocked on the English preventive system ; 2d, railway switches, model of apparatus for securing the proper fastening of switches and their immovability during the passing of trains over them ; 3d, railway level crossing gates, model arrangement for working gates simultaneously and interlocking them, and signals for securing safe passage on road and rail.

The Mirlees sugar-mill makes from 5,000 to 6,000 pounds of sugar per hour ; and this firm exhibited a smaller mill, designed to make from 200 to 300 pounds per hour. The

improved patent copper lightning conductors for the protection of ships and buildings from damage by lightning. In the matter of screw propulsion we had another exhibit by William Hewitt, of Bristol, who sent a model of a feathering screw propeller. The same exhibitor offered an improved gun-carriage and improved breech-loading gun.

GERMAN EMPIRE.

The section allotted to the German Empire comprised the extreme southeastern corner of Machinery Hall, next to that of Great Britain, and included 10,098 feet of space, besides about 800 feet in the pump annex. Germany made only 46 exhibits in all, of which certainly the most important and attractive were the Krupp guns, from the great works of this manufacturer, Friederich Krupp, at Essen, which were established in 1810 for the manufacture of axles, tires, wheels, bands, springs, rollers, steel for tools and springs and cannons, and received premiums at the London Exhibitions of 1851 and 1862, Paris 1867, and a diploma of honor at the Vienna Exhibition of 1873. The largest of the Krupp cannon was probably, after the Corliss Engine, the most striking article exhibited in Machinery Hall. This huge gun has a calibre of 1 1-6 feet, is 26¼ feet long, the bore extending 22½ feet, its weight 126,750 pounds. The bore has 80 parallel grooves of a uniform twist, of twice the whole length of the gun. To load the latter with a steel

extinguishing apparatus, and other similar machinery comprised the exhibits in the pump annex. Altogether, the German machinery exhibition, always excepting the Krupp guns, has not been particularly remunerative in the way of educational effect.

FRANCE.

The space occupied by France in Machinery Hall comprised 11,119 feet in the extreme northeast corner of the building. As is the case with the foreign sections in general, that of France gave no just idea of the condition of science and mechanical industry in that country. Many of the leading manufacturers of France, well known the world over for the quality of their work, and which should properly have found a place in Machinery Hall, were absent. Among the interesting articles on exhibition, the fine chromo-lithographic press of Aleuzet was especially noticeable. Another important collection was that of mining lamps, exhibited by M. Dubrulles, comprising all the varieties of this article, from the open air lamp to the last perfected model originating in the Davy lamp, and which by an ingenious combination of glass and metallic network reaches the maximum of illumination with the maximum of security. An admirable peculiarity of these lamps is that they are not only a protection to the miner against the gas which so often causes the most terrible catastrophes, but are also a protection against himself. It is well known that

THE JAPANESE BAZAAR.

patent tobacco-spinning machines previously mentioned are designed for spinning all descriptions of twist or rolled tobacco, from one-eighth to two inches in diameter, and were shown with samples of twist tobacco spun in various places in Europe.

The Inman Steamship Company exhibited a full-rigged model of the Royal Mail Steamer *City of Berlin*, built by Messrs. Laird & Co., Greenock, in 1875 ; length 523 feet, breadth 44 feet, depth 36 feet, gross tonnage 5,490 tons, net tonnage 3,140 tons, indicated horse-power, 5,000 horses, nominal power 950 horses, speed 15 knots. She made the fastest passage then on record, from Queenstown to New York, in September, 1875, in 7 days, 18 hours, 2 minutes ; and from New York to Queenstown in 7 days, 18 hours, 48 minutes.

A model of an iron lifeboat, under full sail, which is said to be non-capsizable, was exhibited. It contained covered accommodation for females and children, arrangements for water-saving, mail-box, and required no lowering-apparatus. It represented a 36 feet life-saving boat to be run overboard with hawsers, and was lateen-rigged. A London engineer and machinist exhibited a new improved ship's rudder which was represented by several models showing its application to a man-of-war, to an American river steamer, and to a sailing vessel. Sanderson & Proctor, of London, exhibited their patent fire-extinguisher for mills and all buildings where steam is used ; also their

or chilled-iron shell, 275 pounds of powder are required, the shell itself weighing over 1,150 pounds. The entire gun, carriage and slide, weighs over 200,000 pounds. Altogether, it is said to be the largest steel gun ever cast. The second cannon weighs 34,700 pounds, has a calibre of about 9½ inches, and a total length of 18 feet.

In Krupp's exhibit were five other guns, all the seven being made of crucible steel.

From Leipsic was exhibited a candle-making machine ; from Dortmund, a model of a drill, spinning-machinery and carders ; from Saxony and Berlin, a considerable show of nails ; from Aix-la-Chapelle, a collective exhibit of sewing-machines was made by different manufacturers, also from Dresden, Leipsic, Hamburg, Munich, Aix-la-Chapelle, and Altenburg ; the latter being a special machine for making gloves. In book-work there were three exhibits : one being of presses from Leipsic, a ruling-machine from Darmstadt, and some lithographic machinery from Offenbach-on-the-Main. Some armor plate and heavy driving-wheels were among the list of German exhibits, as also a huge pyramid of spiegeleisen mineral used in the manufacture of Bessemer steel. Rubber straps and belting were sent from Eibergen ; india-rubber exhibits, from Frankfort-on-the-Oder ; from Bremerhaven, we had a gun used among the safety mechanism for shipwrecks, and the Hamburg American Joint Steamship Company, of Hamburg, sent the model of a mail steamship. Siphon pumps, rotary pumps, fire-

frequently explosions occur through the imprudence of the miners in opening their lanterns in the midst of an inflammable atmosphere. With the Dubrulles lamp this danger is obviated, since it is so constructed that on being opened it is immediately extinguished.

Another French machine, simple but important, was the domestic motor of Fontaine. This is a small steam-engine which can be applied readily to sewing-machines, pumps, ventilators, or to other household purposes, being used with facility and without possibility of danger. Among the articles exhibited were machinery and tools for goldsmiths, others for working in wood, portable forges, crucibles, furnaces, and gas apparatus. From Lyons, we had silk weaving-looms, besides weaving machines and looms from Paris ; as also from the latter city, a machine for the manufacture of fishing-nets, and another for sewing straw hats. Gas motors, electro-magnetic machines, and other apparatus for utilizing power were seen in considerable number in the French section. The wine manufacture was represented by siphons, wine-presses, machines for charging wines with gas, soda-water machines and bottling machines. Railway apparatus comprised car-brakes, automatic clutch, forged iron wheels for locomotives and cars, and wheels manufactured by hydraulic pressure. Soap and chocolate machines made an important exhibit from Paris, chiefly from the house of Beyer Bros. Finally, the Transatlantic Company, of Paris, exhibited a model of the steamship

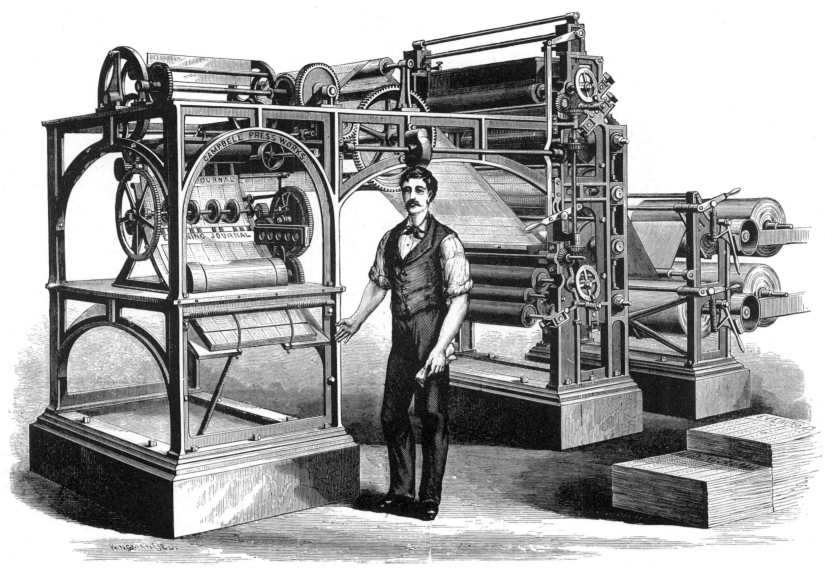

CAMPBELL'S NEW ROTARY PERFECTING-PRESS.

Pereire. A tapestry loom and a joint exhibit of brass and copper completed all that was noticeable in the French exhibition in Machinery Hall.

BELGIUM, THE NETHERLANDS, SWEDEN, NORWAY, ITALY, BRAZIL, AND THE ARGENTINE REPUBLIC.

Belgium had only 23 exhibits in Machinery Hall, one of which, curiously enough, was a Corliss Engine; the idea in sending it being to compliment the distinguished manufacturer. The further exhibits of mechanism included a drilling-machine for mines and tunnels, with models of plans and shafts sunk in Belgium, safety lamps and wicks for miners, models of a trip-hammer and of steam shears, machinery for making bolts, well-cleaning machines, festooning and embroidering-machines, sewing-machines, some wooden printing types, car-wheels, railway-brakes, a fire-engine, some pumps, and specimens of belting.

The Netherlands sent a sewing-machine from Utrecht, belting and leather straps, fire-extinguishers, railroad switches, coffee-mills, and a model of an engine for deepening rivers.

From Sweden, we had a machine for making bricks, gas apparatus, cork-cutting machines, sewing-machines, machine for turning veneer, mechanism for the manufacture of metal cartridges, emery wheel, a few sewing-machines, and paper-cutting machinery. Among the railway material exhibited will be remembered the locomotive "Nyhammer," which was put in use on the railroad track within the Centennial Grounds, and attracted considerable attention; model of a torpedo boat, a steamboat, and a fire-engine from Stockholm, which completed the Swedish list.

Norway exhibited some pumps, fire-engines and rotating steam-engine, some models and drawings of sailing vessels, and a mechanical mangle from Christiania.

From Italy we had a few furnaces and one or two other pieces of mechanism.

Then a few models and drawings from Brazil; a number of very good models of ironclads, casemate and monitor ships, steam launches and corvettes sent from Rio de Janeiro, models of engines for small vessels, models of fire-engines, and a steam-engine to be used as motor at the Pyrotechnical Laboratory at Rio de Janeiro, which exhibited fuses for artillery. A mounted rifle-gun and casemate, brass mortars, breech-loading rifle and sword, and cartridge-boxes for military service, were also exhibited.

The Argentine Republic sent a weaving-loom, some specimens of printing-types and electrotypes, and a few models of rafts and vessels, including pleasure steam yacht, steam lighter and propeller.

The exhibits of Austria included model of a glass milling furnace, models and apparatus for the arrangement of brushes, Jacquard machines, petroleum and steam engines, boilers, an invention for guarding against locomotives' sparks, and machines used for the manufacture of candy.

Switzerland has two exhibits in the pump annex: one a model of a new system of reversing gear for valve engines, and another an apparatus for heating railway-carriages. The machines pertaining to watch-making were exhibited in the Swiss section of the Main Building.

CANADA.

The space occupied by Canada was between the sections of Germany and France at the eastern end of the building, and on both sides of the nave comprised 4,300 feet. Canada had a very creditable display. A steam drill which works in any direction, a wood-working machine, a gold-quartz crusher, and some planers of iron and wood, were among the more notable exhibits. The quartz-crushing machine, by-the-way, came from Halifax, Nova Scotia—Nova Scotia being essentially a gold-producing country, although the business is so quietly conducted that Americans know very little about it. The wood-work machinery comprised a barrel-making machine, sash-making machine, a turning lathe, planing and notching-machine, chiefly from Ontario. A self-acting hand-loom, and a combing-machine for brush-makers were all there were exhibited in the way of mechanism for working fibrous materials. Quite a number of sewing-machines and needles were sent from Quebec and from Ontario. In motors and apparatus for the generation and transmission of power we had steam-boilers and steam-engines, water-wheels, gas-engines, rotary engines, a miniature steam-engine from Dartmouth, Nova Scotia, screw propeller, etc., from different sections of the Dominion. Quite a number of pumps of all kinds were exhibited, besides hydraulic elevator, hydraulic motor, a steam fire-engine, fire-escape, fire-extinguishers, diving apparatus, and submarine armor. Manufactures in the interest of railroads included all sorts of appurtenances to locomotives and cars, as well as safety switches, railway and telegraphic signals. Machines for agricultural uses comprised two or three tobacco-machines and cutters, lozenge-machine, cracker-machine, and mill-stones. A few models of ships and boats were exhibited; and exhibits were also made of various parts of a ship, wheels, windmills, capstan, etc.

UNITED STATES.

Excepting the allotments of space already enumerated as given to foreign countries exhibiting in Machinery Hall, the United States exhibitors occupied all the remainder of the building—that is to say, about four-fifths of the entire space. Of course it would be utterly useless, as well as being to a great extent

METAL-MELTING FURNACE AND MOLD FOR CASTING CURVED STEREOTYPED PLATES.

CAMPBELL PRINTING-PRESS AND MANUFACTURING CO.'S EXHIBIT.

uninteresting, to attempt to give anything like a categorical description of the American machinery exhibition, besides which the space remaining for the completion of the present work would be quite inadequate to the proper prosecution of such a task. It is only practicable to refer briefly to such special exhibits as would seem to demand particular consideration; and that, rather for the purpose of suggestion than description.

We have already described and illustrated the Corliss Engine, certainly the most important article in Machinery Hall, both as an exhibit and for its practical use. An incident occurred having some connection with this stupendous engine which is worth recording. A gentleman who gave his name as Levy Taylor, of Indianola, Indiana, stepped up to the engine one day, when as usual it was surrounded by a crowd of gazers, and taking from his pocket a small tin case, opened it and removed therefrom a tiny piece of mechanism, including a lamp, which he lighted, after which he placed his machine on the platform of the great engine. This proved to be a perfect steam engine complete in all its parts, the entire apparatus weighing only seven grains, while the engine proper weighed but three grains. It was made of gold, steel and platinum, its foundation being a 25 cent gold piece, and many of its parts being so small that they could not be seen without a magnifying glass. The fly-wheel was one quarter of an inch in diameter, the stroke three-quarters, and the cut-off one-sixty-fourth of an inch. The gentleman disappeared with his engine, and nothing was ever heard of it afterward.

Before proceeding further with Machinery Hall, we will give a little space to the Saw-mill Building, erected near the western end of the grounds. Here were exhibited saws and saw-mills from the Lane Manufacturing Company, of Montpelier, Vermont; Sterns Manufacturing Company, of Erie, Pa.; Harper & Co., of Philadelphia; Chase Turbine Manufacturing Company, of Orange, Mass.; Wells Balance Engine Company, of New York; W. P. Powers, La Crosse, Wis.; Harvey Easton, Lockhaven, Pa.; C. H. Watrous, Brantford, Ontario; E. P. Allis, Milwaukee, Wis.; Lane & Bodley Company, Cincinnati; Eau Claire Lumber Company, Wisconsin; Charles H. Brown, Fitchburg, Mass.; Hugh Young, New York City, and others. The exhibits included circular saw-mills, log-rollers, stave and box-board machines, a machine from California for cutting logs, lathe-machine, swaging-machine, reciprocating diamond saw-mill, and other machines of the same character. The stone saw-mill, with its 64-inch circular saw armed with 84 diamonds, attracted a great deal of attention. This is a Missouri invention, and is called "The Stone Monarch." The 64-inch saw makes 600 revolutions per minute, and cuts solid stone from 6 inches to 2 feet per minute; while the smaller saw, 20 inches in diameter, makes 2,200 revolutions per minute, being used for cutting or trimming stone, marble or fire-brick. One very heavy saw-mill, built principally for the heavy lumbering interest, contained numerous improvements: one being a manner of lubricating and cooling the entire surface of the saw on both sides, by means of water passing from the arbor to the periphery; and another, the method of adjusting the guide so as to avoid all danger to the operator. A switching-machine was the well-known Hinchley, the only switching-machine which does the work on the under side of the saw-tooth.

Returning to Machinery Hall and recognizing the fact that in such a description as is proposed here one can begin anywhere, we will commence by referring to a machine for the purpose of displaying the process of printing wall-paper. The frame of the machine is about 16 feet long, and about the same in height. Midway an iron cylinder six feet in diameter revolves. This is covered with cotton, and an endless rubber blanket, making a cushioned surface to receive the imprint of the

THE MATRIX MACHINE.

printing-rollers as they revolve against it. For printing-material, wood is generally employed, though blocks of metal are now being introduced. The design being sketched on the roller, it is outlined with brass driven firmly into the wood, and this is filled-in with compact filling. This is called raised or surface printing. Each printing-roller being set against the cylinder, is supplied with the color which it is to print on the paper by means of an endless woolen sieve cloth run over the brass rollers, against the upper part of which the printing-roll revolves, the lower part being in contact with another roller in a box or pan filled with the color which that roller is to imprint on the paper. By this machinery, besides being printed, the paper is cut into sixteen yard pieces, which are afterward rolled into the ordinary rolls of the shops.

Near the Corliss Engine, a dozen young ladies were constantly engaged, during the Exhibition, in making the finest portions of mechanism employed in the manufacture of watches by the Waltham Watch Company. These parts are so small and so exact, that the machinery for their construction is necessarily delicate and perfect, and the process of manufacture is one of the curiosities of American mechanics.

New England was particularly strong in tools, and the exhibition in this line was most instructive, and was viewed with unflagging interest by foreign visitors. The manufactures of the Pratt & Whitney Company, of Hartford, Conn., were specially worthy of notice, and their machine tools have a world-wide reputation. Recently this company has fitted up for the German Government three large armories—those of Erfurt, Dantzig, and Spandau. Among their machines on exhibition was one for rifling

gun-barrels, the only piece of this character in the department, and certainly a most ingenious and important piece of mechanism. Other machines were those for screw-making, milling-machines, a profiling-machine, lathes of all sizes, bolt-cutting machines, a boring mill, a press and die-sinking machine, and many others.

The Putnam Machine Company, of Fitchburg, Mass., also made a striking display, chiefly on account of the beautiful finish of their work. Their exhibits included engine-lathes, boring, bolt-cutting and tapping machines, drilling-machines, iron-planers, and a remarkably fine horizontal engine. In this the frame was novel and of a new pattern, cylindrical in form and remarkably strong. One of the lathes exhibited was designed for turning car and locomotive axles, and displayed remarkable power. Near this lathe was a very powerful vertical car-wheel borer. The planer exhibited was one of 56 different sizes manufactured by this company, and which run from 5 feet tables 24 inches wide up to 24 feet tables 80 inches wide. It is an interesting fact that the Putnam Company furnished the machine-tools for the first machine-shops erected in China and Japan.

The Ames Manufacturing Company, of Chicopee, Mass., is another well-known New England Company, which was fully represented in the Exhibition. Their principal tools exhibited were lathes and drills. One engine-lathe, of 36 inch swing and 12 feet bed, is made upon an entirely new pattern and provided with all the latest improvements. Other exhibits were their 7¼-inch lathe and screw-cutting engine-lathe.

The Brainard Company, of Boston, Mass., displayed a number of milling-machines, in the making of which they have reached perfection. A head-set screw-machine of a novel design for molding screws directly from a bar of iron without forging, and improved steel bar vises for machinists' use, were among the exhibits of this company.

A fine collection of presses was exhibited by the Stiles & Parker Press Company, of Middletown, Conn., among which a new press for tin-work was a novelty. This company supplies with their tools the armories of Prussia, Austria, Sweden, Egypt, and other countries.

The Nicholson File Company exhibited near the Corliss Engine, their factory being in Providence, R. I. Their exhibit included more than 1,000 varieties of work, finished and in process, showing the different stages from the ore or raw material as it comes from the mine, with every description of work upon which files can be used. The files made by this company are distinguished by peculiarities in the dispensation and spacing of the teeth, and various modifications are found necessary in the arrangement are found necessary in the manufacture of files for different kinds of work, so that it would almost appear that these were regulated by mathematical laws. These modifications include, for instance, the element of irregularity, by which the teeth are distributed in groups.

Another Providence firm is the Brown & Sharp Manufacturing Company, who manufacture the Willcox & Gibbs sewing-machines, of which it is said they have made nearly 300,000. This firm are the inventors of the machinery by which the most perfect instruments are furnished to draughtsmen and others. Their weighing-scales turn upon the accession of the thousandth part of a pound, their measuring-scales determine the thickness to the thousandth part of an inch. They exhibited the Ames Universal Squares, patent hardened cast-steel try-squares, the American Standard Wire Gauge, and a great variety of steel and box-wood rules and scales, and other small tools for machinists', draughtsmen's and wood-workmen's use. Besides these, their manufacture embraces milling-machines, grinding, screw and tapping-machines, screw-finishing and polishing machines, assorters, scales and testers for cotton and woolen manufacturers'

THE CURVED PLATE FINISHING MACHINE.

CAMPBELL PRINTING-PRESS AND MANUFACTURING CO.'S EXHIBIT.

use, patent cutters for gear-wheels, irregularly formed sewing-machines, besides trimming and stamping machines for cotton-mills, printworks, bleachers, etc.

Machinery Hall presented a rich and varied display of mining, quarrying and tunneling drills, perspective drills, steam or compressed air rock-drilling machines, machinery for boring artesian wells—some of these, outside of the building, were seen in operation—a coal-cutting machine, worked by compressed air, exhibited by an Indiana firm; machines for crushing ores and stones, and separating and washing machines for iron ore; as also stamping machines, such as are used in gold and silver mining. The manufacture and utilizing of gas was fully illustrated in the Exhibition: gas meters, registers, gaugers, gas regulators, portable gas generators, portable gas machines, dry gasometers, presses for removing naphthaline, and photometers for measuring and testing gas.

In wood-working machinery, besides the saw-mills and their mechanism already mentioned, we had mortising machines, planing and polishing machines, scroll saws, cork-cutting machines, cork-tapering machines, planers, lathes, carving machines, molding machines, paneling and concave cutters, planing, tonguing and grooving machines, wood-bending machinery, dove-tailing machinery, machines for cutting spools, mechanism for making kegs, barrels, staves and shooks, machines for sawing shingles and barrel-heads, machines for planing spokes, paneling machines, sand-paper machines, machines for making half-round hoops for barrels, and many others.

In metal-working machinery, there were mechanisms for nail-cutting, tack-making, machines for casting medals, tags and emblems, steam hammer, drop hammer, lathes for engraving precious stones and glass, automatic knife-grinders, portable pipe and bolt-cutting machines, and machines for tinware, drilling machines, screw machinery, power-punching press, machinery for making upholstery and springs, portable punches for punching spike-holes in rails, and so on. In metal-working tools Philadelphia was most prominent.

The great cost of moving heavy machinery prevented the exhibition of any of the largest steam hammers. Quite a number were exhibited, however, of various patterns and weights, double and single form. The Sellers Planing Machine, of 81 tons weight, having a bed weighing 15 tons and a traverse of 44 feet, was the largest machine tool exhibited. Next to the Corliss Engine, the largest shown was the blowing engine of J. P. Morris, of Philadelphia, of 750-horse-power. Of course a great deal of space was occupied by a variety of machinery for book and newspaper making, including type, paper and ruling machines, bookbinders', stereotyping machinery, and printers' tools in general. Seventy different exhibitors sent articles in this class, including Gordon, Bullock, and Hoe printing-presses; the celebrated house of George Bruce's Son & Co., in printing type; and exhibits in book-sewing, book-binding, folding-machines for books and newspapers, chromo-printing presses, automatic paper-feeders, and amateur printing-presses.

The Hoe printing-machines in Machinery Hall included the latest improvements in every department of printing, represented by seven or eight different descriptions of presses. The rotary press invented by Colonel Hoe has been in a measure superseded by the "web" printing machine, which was invented by Colonel Hoe and one of his partners, Mr. S. D. Tucker. This press works a roll of paper which is reeled off by machinery, the roll being a continuous sheet 4¼ miles long, and running through the machine at the rate of 750 feet per minute, or more, and as it passes through the press it is printed on both sides, and afterward cut and delivered, six papers at a time. This machine prints on both sides 15,000 copies per hour of an eight-page paper, or double that number of a four-page paper, the latter being worked off in Machinery Hall to illustrate the running of the machine; the paper selected being the Philadelphia *Times*. In this press the roll of paper is suspended upon an axle over the first pair of cylinders. To one of these are affixed the curved electrotype plates which constitute the form, the other being the impression cylinder. The paper passing between these is printed on one side, when it goes between the second type and impression cylinders and is printed on the other side. It is stated that twenty-three of these are now in operation, nine in this country. The London *Daily Telegraph*, *Standard*, *Lloyd's Weekly*,

and the Glasgow *Herald* are printed from these presses, while two of them are in use in Australia.

In the manufacture of clothing all the well-known sewing-machines were represented in operation, specimens of each being shown in different styles, some of them being elaborately ornamented, and making a very handsome display. Among these may be mentioned the Howe, Wilson, Willcox & Gibbs, Beckwith, Singer, Domestic, Wheeler & Wilson; besides the American button-hole machine, Franz & Pope knitting-machine, Lamb knitting-machine, the corset-weaving power loom, the United States Corset Company, and loom for manufacturing suspenders, exhibited by the National Suspender Company, of New York; a stocking-knitter, by the Home Knitter Company, of Ohio; and other mechanism for clothing and hat manufacture.

The most important exhibits of scales were those of the Fairbanks Company, displayed in 23 foreign departments in the Main Building, having 28 exhibits in all. The Fairbanks Company, it is stated, gives employment to nearly 900 men. The shops cover a flooring of 7½ acres. Ninety-three tenement houses have been built for the use of the employés. 4,000 tons of coal, 5,000 tons of iron, 2,000,000 feet of lumber, and large quantities of copper, tin, nails and screws are annually consumed. Their yearly freightage is 20,000 tons,

TERRA-COTTA FOUNTAIN IN THE ITALIAN EXHIBIT, "OUT IN THE RAIN."

and they make 50,000 scales yearly. They hold 28 patents. The factory is at St. Johnsbury, Vermont.

Besides the Fairbanks scales, scales were exhibited by the Howe Scale Company, Brandon, Vt.; the Brandon Manufacturing Company; the Buffalo Scale Company, Buffalo, N. Y.; the Chicago Scale Company, Chicago; Cleveland Scale Works Company, Automatic Scale Company, Harrisburg, Pa.; National Scale Company, Philadelphia, and others.

The Brandon Manufacturing Company, of Brandon, Vermont, made a handsome exhibition, including over 100 different varieties, and others of the improved Howe Standard Scales. A number of the scales exhibited by this firm were finished in the most elaborate manner: the woodwork being of rosewood, bird's-eye-maple, satin-wood, tulip, mahogany and other costly woods; and the iron work plated in silver and gold. About the centre of this exhibit a large, solid marble table from the Rutland (Vt.) quarries was placed, upon which was a patent drop-lever scale finished in black-and-gold plating, one of the handsomest articles in this line ever manufactured. Other scales were post-office and counter scales, in which the working parts were inclosed in a patent frame protecting them from dust and oil; portable warehouse platform scales with patent self-adjusting bearing, and arranged so that no direct

weight is brought on the sharp pivots. The Howe patent drop-lever scale and patent fish-scales were also improved varieties of the article.

Another excellent exhibit of scales was that made by the Philadelphia Scale and Testing Machine Works, in which there was one scale of 40 tons' capacity, designed to weigh railroad cars, and in which strength is nicely combined with accuracy of record. Heavy rolling-mill scales were also exhibited by this company, one of these having a weighing capacity of 12,000 pounds, the machine itself weighing over a ton. A compound beam for weighing heavy castings up to 30,000 pounds was exhibited by a Manchester firm, as also were four distinct machines which are improved pieces of mechanism. One of these has a capacity of 75 tons, another of 40,000 pounds. New machines for testing cements and for wire fibres, etc., were in this exhibit. The Buffalo Scale Company exhibited every variety of scales, from the smallest chemical laboratory balance to the enormous railroad and track scales. A peculiarity of this make is the patent combination beam, which does away with loose weights, and is peculiarly accurate in indicating. Applied to grain-weighing, it indicates bushels as well as pounds, and prevents all liability to err in computation. This manufacture was represented by New York in the exhibits of Chatillon & Co., who displayed spring-scales for weighing meats and poultry, and their Eureka self-adjusting scale. Messrs. Becker & Sons, also of New York, exhibited very handsome scales designed for the more delicate work of assaying United States bullion, druggists, and for scientific purposes.

In reference to the American Watch Company, of Waltham, Mass., to which we have already alluded in speaking of its exhibit of watch-making machinery in Machinery Hall, it is proper to state that the product of the factory is over 400 watches per day, and that at the close of the current year the entire number of its manufacture will be 1,000,000. In this manufacture the excellence obtained is due entirely to the wonderful accuracy of the machinery, which is so delicate that any deviation to the thousandth part of an inch can be detected by it. Accordingly, any part of a watch made by this company can be replaced at any time, the parts as manufactured being exactly and mathematically alike. Occupying one of the most conspicuous points in Machinery Hall, the working of the watch machinery employed in making wheels, jewels and screws, just as it is done at the great factory at Waltham, was witnessed by throngs of curious and interested visitors.

The display of fire-engines and other apparatus for preventing conflagration was large and exceedingly interesting, including fire-engines of all sorts, hook-and-ladder apparatus, hose-carts, hand and portable engines, and fire-extinguishers—all manufactured in the highest style of art. Among other exhibitors were the Silsby Manufacturing Company, of Seneca Falls, N. Y., with rotary steam fire-engines, and horse and hand hose-carts; E. A. Straw, Manchester, New Hampshire, who exhibited a steam fire-engine put to use on the grounds; C. Schanz, of Philadelphia, exhibiting a hook-and-ladder truck; the Champion Fire-Extinguisher Company, of Louisville, Kentucky, showing chemical engines with hook-and-ladder attachments; the Babcock Manufacturing Company, with their fire-extinguishers and chemical engines; Wm. T. Vose, of Boston, Mass., who exhibited a hydraulic engine; a Burlington Manufacturing Company, exhibiting a steam fire-engine in the pump annex; and other firms exhibiting hand hose-carriages, fire-hose, fire-box, hand fire-engines, rubber-hose, fire-escapes; the Paterson Steam Fire-engine Works, and J. N. Dennison, of Newark, New Jersey, both exhibiting steam fire-engines, etc.

Mr. H. P. N. Birkinbine, of Philadelphia, exhibited, for extinguishing fire, stationary machinery, consisting of three short sections of 10-inch water-pipes: one, representing the line of pipes conveying the water from the pumping apparatus to the reservoir; another, the pipe distributing the water from the reservoir into the net-work of pipes in the streets; and the third, a pipe connecting these two lines. By means of this invention, the entire pumping machinery of the water-supply of a city or town may be converted into a gigantic fire-engine, and that, in the smallest possible time by the manipulation of simple parts of the mechanism. In our large cities the telegraphic signals which give notice of a fire can be made to cause the

necessary change of valves which brings the entire system of the works into service. By this means the supply of water can be sent in any direction at a moment's notice.

Of course, the hydraulic or pump annex, with its great waterfall and surprising curiosities in the way of blowers and powerful pumps, was an immense attraction to visitors. The great tank, holding nearly 500,000 gallons of water, the numerous streams pouring into it, varying between an inch in diameter and the great cataract itself, 1¼ feet wide—these proved most interesting features of the display in Machinery Hall. The volume of water passing into the great tank from the smaller tank above, by way of the cataract, amounted to from 30,000 to 32,000 gallons every minute. This water was raised into the tank by means of two 15-inch centrifugal pumps with 15-inch suction pipes, the pumps being driven by two oscillating engines with 20-inch cylinders and 15-inch strokes. The power of these engines was about 125-horse-power each; and this power being transmitted to the pumps by angular belting, gave the latter about twice the number of revolutions of the engines. Immediately adjoining the pumps, and constructed by the same firm, Messrs. Andrews & Brothers, of New York, was the elevator employed for carrying up visitors to a platform running around three sides of the iron frame-work of the cataract, and presenting a most interesting bird's-eye view of the hydraulic annex, the great Corliss Engine, and other leading features. The same firm exhibited smaller pumps of a similar construction in full operation, discharging powerful streams into the main tank. It is said that these pumps are largely used for reclaiming low lands in countries like Holland.

The importance of the steam-pumping apparatus in mining cannot be overrated. In fact, without them the vast mining interests in this country, such as those of Nevada, for instance, could not be conducted. In this connection the exhibits of the Knowles Steam-pump Works of New York were especially interesting. These pumps are much used in iron mines. Combining the steam-engine and pump in one, they are particularly advantageous. Some of them have to be made of brass or gun-metal, they become so corroded by the gathering of sulphurous acid in coal mines, if made of iron. Special exhibits of pumps for copper and lead mines were shown; also those in use in gold and silver mining. A fine specimen of a pumping-engine, such as is used in silver mines, was exhibited, having two plungers working into opposite ends of the cylinder or working-barrel. It was of great power, and intended for use in a mine 600 feet deep. This will deliver water 10 inches in diameter from the bottom of the mine of the above depth to the surface. Such engines are in use to-day in the best silver mines in the West.

Other machinery exhibited by this company was for the purpose of pumping water into the mines for the uses of the stamp mills. One such in Utah delivers 2,000 gallons of water per hour to a height of 700 feet, and at a distance of three miles from the source of supply. The power rotary pumps of the Gould Manufacturing Company also deserve notice. These pumps have two *cams*, constructed so as to mesh into one another with the most perfect unity, with the minimum amount of friction. One of these discharges 2½ gallons at each revolution. A small hand rotary pump and a hydraulic ram, with glass air-chambers, in operation, were included in this exhibition. The Norwalk Steam Pump, the Niagara Pump, and the Duplex Fire-engine Pump, of Crane Bros., Chicago, were still other

important hydraulic exhibits. This latter has a capacity of 1,200 gallons of water a minute. Besides these, there were exhibits of the Valley Machine Company, of Hampton, Mass., in bucket engines; the Union Manufacturing Company, of New Britain, Conn., engines, pumps, etc.; the La France Company, of Elmira, N. Y., rotary pumps and fire-engines, the curious pulsometer steam-pump exhibited by J. S. Grosvenor, of Jersey City, New Jersey, which is operated by a pressure of the steam on the surface of the water; White, Clark & Co., of Baldwin, N. Y., centrifugal pump; Hydrostatic and Hydraulic Company, of Philadelphia, compound propeller pump for quarries and mines; and other firms exhibiting bilge-pumps for vessels, force-pumps, blowers, air-compressing engines, filtering apparatus, and other similar machinery.

The exhibits of locomotives and railway apparatus in general included nearly 75 names of exhibitors, and comprised locomotive engines and tenders, power-brakes, model cars, railway-station indicators, snow-plows, automatic brakes, car-couplings, steam and air brakes, railroad car and engine wheels, tires and castings, and spiral springs for cars and locomotives. A most important exhibit in locomotives was made by the Baldwin Locomotive Works, of Philadelphia, which exhibited six out of the fourteen locomotives shown in the United States section. To all those

who examined these gigantic mechanical structures it has been demonstrated that in them grace and beauty of manufacture were not sacrificed for power; and that while gigantic in size, they are in no instance unwieldy or clumsy. The Baldwin Locomotive Works turn out over 500 locomotives a year, although it takes several months to build one. A freight locomotive was exhibited which has cylinders 20 inches in diameter, with a stroke of piston 24 inches. Four pairs driving-wheels 50⅜ inches in diameter and a two-wheeled pony-truck have in these machines taken the place of three pair driving-wheels and four-wheeled truck, which were formerly used. One of the Baldwin locomotives on exhibition was constructed for the Dom Pedro Secundo Railroad, in Brazil, to run on a broad-gauge road five feet three inches in width, and to burn bituminous coal.

Next to the Baldwin exhibit came that of the Rogers Works, Paterson, N. J. This had a handsome freight locomotive, having a 16-inch cylinder with 24-inch stroke and a driving-wheel 56 inches in diameter. It was built for the Mobile and Montgomery Railroad, and will be principally used for hauling cotton, burning pine-wood for fuel. Another Paterson firm, the Danforth Locomotive and Machine Company, exhibited a large passenger engine, the "Vulcan," and a small narrow-gauge engine. In the former, the diameter of the driving-wheel is 62 inches, and the engine weighs 35 tons. The three-feet narrow-gauge engine was built for a sugar plantation in Central America. It has driving-wheels 26 inches in diameter. Three locomotives were exhibited by the Dickson Manufacturing

Co., of Wilkesbarre and Scranton. The first of these was a passenger, anthracite-burning engine; the second, a three-foot narrow-gauge engine, also for passenger traffic, burning anthracite, and having 42-inch driving-wheels; and the third was a remarkably well-constructed four-wheeled tank engine for a three-foot narrow-gauge track.

The Philadelphia & Reading Railroad Company exhibited a locomotive from the Reading shops which possessed peculiar interest in the fact that it was entirely constructed by shop apprentices, while there was nothing about it to indicate that it was not the work of skilled mechanics. Porter, Bell & Co., of Pittsburg, had on exhibition a small passenger engine, whose cylinder is about 11 by 16 inches, with 40-inch driving-wheels, making a very pretty exhibit.

A prominent and important exhibit was the apparatus for refining sugar of Messrs. Calwell & Bro., of New York. This apparatus consisted of a large closed vessel or vacuum pan, which was erected on lofty iron columns, in three divisions. From this vessel the air was exhausted by one of Blake's circulating pumps. In the interior of the pan were four spiral tubes, made of copper, representing in the aggregate about 600 square feet of heating surface. These tubes were connected by means of suitable valves and pipes with the steam-boilers, and with a vessel called the "steam recipient," into which all the steam in the various pumps was exhausted. By this arrangement all the spiral tubes could be operated at once with steam direct from the boilers, or separately; various other combinations by the use of steam being practicable with them. The ordinary method of manufacturing sugar is first to express the juice from the cane by means of heavy iron rollers, coupled together by suitable gearing, and driven by a powerful steam-engine. The juice is then taken to large iron or copper vessels, sometimes called "kettles," or "double-bottoms," the steam being admitted between the inner and outer bottoms, and the juice treated with lime; the latter is brought to a temperature as high as 200° Fahrenheit. Next, it is taken to what is called a "Jamaica-train," which generally consists of five open kettles, graduating in size from 200 to 600 gallons. A fire is kept up under the smallest—the last one in the train—and the others are heated by the gases passing under them. The cane-juice being first put into the largest kettle, is emptied into each one in succession, being boiled down by this process until it reaches in the least what is called the "finishing-point." It is then transferred to large iron tanks, where it is allowed to crystallize. After this has occurred, it is taken out with shovels and placed in hogsheads having perforated heads. These hogsheads are placed over gutters, by means of which the molasses draining through the perforators from the sugar is conducted to the proposed receptacle for it. This process usually takes three weeks between the time the juice is expressed and the time when it is ready for the market, while a large amount of sugar is lost to the planter in the molasses. But by the use of the vacuum-pan described above, the sugar is obtained and packed in hogsheads on the same day that the juice is expressed from the cane, instead of the process occupying three weeks, while there is little or no loss of sugar. A pan of nine feet in diameter, such as was exhibited in Machinery Hall, will produce in a single operation, only extending over three hours, no less than 2,000 pounds, or about 15 hogsheads, of sugar.

REED & BARTON MANUFACTURING CO.'S EXHIBIT OF GOLD AND SILVER WARE.

The barrel-making machinery of E. & B. Holmes, of Buffalo, was another valuable and interesting piece of mechanism. By this machine, through the medium of a wheel, fitted with self-acting knives, and which turns at the rate of 1,500 revolutions a minute, rough staves are first cut to a smooth surface, and then beveled so that when put into their proper position, they will make an exact barrel. The staves, thus prepared, are set into a strong iron hoop, a thick wire rope, which is attached to a windlass, being thrown about them; the windlass being started, the staves are drawn together by the rope, another very strong iron-hoop is dropped over them, the two middle hoops are then applied in the same manner, and the rope is released. Next, the jointings are tightened by pressure in another machine, so that the barrel cannot leak. This, which is called a "truss-machine," tightens 4,500 barrels a day, and employs only a boy to put the barrel in and another to take it out. The next process is to take the barrels to the machine which cuts the beveled edge on the inside of the ends of the staves, and the groove into which the head of the barrel is fitted.

The head is composed of pieces of the same wood as the staves, joined together, forming a circle. It is placed in a cutting-machine, which gives it a double bevel by one motion, leaving an edge which fits neatly into the grooves cut into the end of the barrel. The barrel having been coopered with ordinary wooden hoops, the iron hoops are removed, and the head is placed in position at either end by removing the hoop nearest to the end, thus allowing the staves to spring outward sufficiently to allow the head being placed in a position to enter the grooves, when the top-hoop is replaced. By these barrel-making machines, three thousand finished barrels a day can be turned out.

The silk-machinery exhibited by the Danforth Manufacturing Company, of Paterson, New Jersey, was interesting and striking. It included a spinner, winder, doubling-and-twister. Raw silk is wrapped around winders and transferred to bobbins, which then go through doubling-machines, on which from 3 to 10 threads are wound together. Whenever a thread breaks, the machine instantly stops. The bobbins are next taken from the doubling-machine and adjusted on the spinner, which in unwinding makes a strand. From here the bobbins go to the twisting-machines, where machine-twist is manufactured from three bobbins, and sewing-silk from two. After being twisted, the silk is rewound into skeins and washed in strong soapsuds. Then it is tied and stretched. From this it goes through the dyeing process, and is then wound for the purpose of spooling. One spooling-machine winds 100 dozen spools a day.

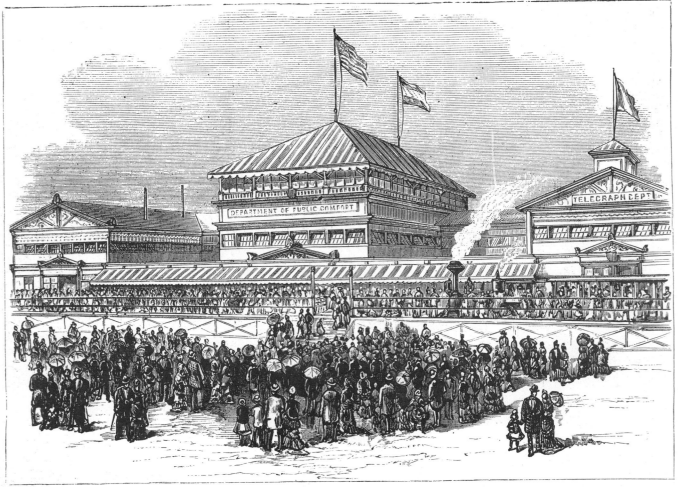

EXTERIOR OF THE BUILDING.

CHINESE CORNER.

SALES-COUNTER FOR CANES, UMBRELLAS, ETC.

THE PUBLIC COMFORT BUILDING.

The machinery for the manufacture of india-rubber goods has attracted much attention for its ingenuity and the novelty of its operations. A lump of crude rubber is first put into a machine, consisting of two corrugated iron rollers, about 12 inches long and 18 inches in diameter. As these wheels revolve, a stream of water is poured on the rubber, the result being that in a short space of time the solid cake of rubber, weighing from 10 to 12 pounds, is converted into a narrow sheet about 12 feet in length. For two weeks this is hung up in a drying-room, where it is dried thoroughly. The next process is that of vulcanizing the rubber with the chemical ingredients employed for the purpose, it being run through a grinder or mixer, from which it emerges in a condition somewhat similar to that of dough. Vulcanizing is combining sulphur with rubber, and subjecting the mixture to great heat. From the grinder the rubber passes through another machine, from which it comes in a thin sheet, which is impressed by the rollers through which it passes with the figure of the upper part of a shoe; then by another process with the sole of the shoe. These stamped sheets of rubber are now wound over glazed lining to prevent their adhering. The next machine consists of three chilled iron rollers, placed one above the other. One roller is covered with a thin coating of rubber fed in from above. Cloth to be coated is introduced through the lower rollers, and as it passes through receives an even and uniform coating of rubber. These coated sheets are now carried to work-tables, where women cut out the various parts of an overshoe, and stick them together. When complete, the shoe is varnished, and after varnishing the vulcanizing process is finished, a batch of shoes being placed on a car and run into a brick oven, whose temperature is about 270 or 280 Fahrenheit, where they remain for several hours. One woman will put together 60 pairs of rubber shoes a day, and one set of machinery will make 500 pairs.

The spool-winding machine exhibited by the George A. Clarke Thread Company, of Newark, N. J., is a most ingenious piece of mechanism. It is self-acting and winds eight spools at once, taking them up from the hoppers and discharging them with 200 yards of cotton thread wound upon each into troughs on the other side, the attendant merely keeping machines supplied with spindles of cotton, and the hoppers with spools, and removing the spools when wound. When the machine is started the cotton begins to wind on the spool with the regularity and convenience which is peculiar to the article. When the last round is finished the action of the machine ceases automatically, a chisel descends and cuts a nick in the spool, the end

THE RENDEZVOUS.

of the thread is drawn into the nick and severed by a cutter; the spool is dismissed and a new one is commenced upon.

Want of space will prevent our entering into any further details as to the machinery exhibited by the United States in Machinery Hall. Very much of this is familiar to our readers, and it is the gathering together of so many thousand separate specimens of ingenuity and invention within the limits of one space that is remarkable and interesting, rather than the articles themselves in their technical description, which can scarcely be made entertaining on paper. It is, however, in our

in its application to international exhibitions, or indeed to public gatherings of any kind in its entirety, found its home in the handsome building lying just northwest of the western end of the Main Building. This building was 264 feet by 112 in dimensions, cornering on the Avenue of the Republic and Agricultural Avenue, and consisting of a two-story frame structure, containing a reception-room, a ladies' parlor, barber-shop, coat and baggage-room, lunch-counter, etc. It was managed by an organization termed "The Department of Public Comfort Company (limited)," of which W. Marsh Casson, of Philadelphia, was chairman. In this building the public comfort was so thoroughly considered, that by means of small sales-counters, every imaginable article likely to be wanted by visitors could be readily purchased, and at fair and even low rates. In the open body of the main room large numbers of chairs were placed, and these, as will be remembered, were occupied daily from about the hour of noon by crowds of visitors who came there to lunch, either bringing with them materials for this repast or obtaining these at the lunch-counter or restaurant. Here might be seen groups of from three to a dozen, either families or large parties, sitting in circles, discussing the viands before them and commenting upon the Exhibition. Here was the established rendezvous

for parties who separated on entering the grounds to meet at appointed hours after the inspection of various buildings. A package-room gave convenience for leaving valises, satchels and small parcels, these being checked for delivery on being called for. At the sales-counters could be obtained not only umbrellas, canes and other articles of use or necessity, but numerous little souvenirs in the way of small jewelry, lacquer-boxes, fans, etc., all of which were held at reasonable rates. As an illustration of the success of this business, it may be stated that one party who kept a counter in the Public Comfort Build-

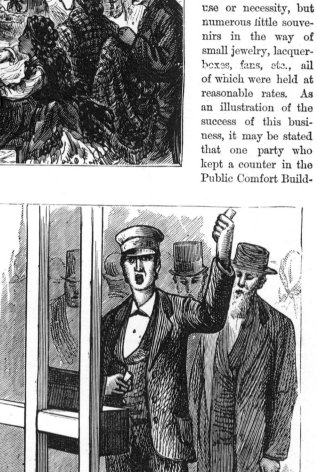

THE TICKET-OFFICE.

BUILDING FOR REST.

THE LUNCH.

exhibits of machinery that we have shown the foreign world represented at the great Centennial Exposition the impossibility of competing with us with any hope of success. No such gathering of ingenious inventions has previously been made, and while undoubtedly failing in the competition with other nations in articles of beauty and elegance, the United States can fearlessly point to its display of original machinery and labor-saving mechanism, and alike defy criticism and competition.

Here we close our consideration of Machinery Hall, and with it, that of the buildings and prominent exhibits of the Exposition proper. The remainder of this work will be devoted to some account of the progress of certain States of the Union as exemplified at Fairmount; to descriptions of certain minor buildings heretofore not considered; and, finally, to an examination and presentment of the statistics of the Exposition, and such collateral facts as are likely to be of interest to the reader.

DEPARTMENT OF PUBLIC COMFORT.

Of all the millions of visitors to the Centennial, whatever memory of the Exhibition each may have carried away, and whatever detail may have been forgotten or escaped notice, there is probably not one who will fail to recollect the Department of Public Comfort. This institution, so purely American and so unquestionably original

ing cleared over $10,000 on his business during the season. Annexed to the main rooms of the department were conveniences for boot-polishing and gents' lavatories. The American District Telegraph Company was close at hand; rolling-chairs were within immediate call; an office for the securing of seats in the theatres and places of amusement in Philadelphia existed in the building, and a post-office department distributed promptly letters addressed to the care of "Public Comfort." The department was thoroughly organized, having efficient superintendents over each division, with nearly 500 employés, uniformed and wearing badges. Special attention was paid to the care of lost articles, of which large numbers were returned to the rightful owners. The number of visitors to the building during the Exposition was more than a million and a quarter, the daily average being 8,000, and the largest number on any one day (Pennsylvania Day) was 20,000. Although thousands of parcels were received and checked, the only article lost up to October 1st was a lady's parasol. The sales of newspapers, stationery, etc., at the stands which were scattered about the grounds and in the buildings, amounted to as much as $5,000 per week. The supplies for the numerous lunch-counters in the buildings cost about $5,000 per week, and 300 hands were employed in this department. The furniture and table-ware cost over $10,000, and the entire expense before opening was $60,000. Finally, as an Exposition of democratic

THE PUBLIC COMFORT BUILDING,

institutions and the theory of republican equality, the Department of Public Comfort has never been equaled. Many made use of its facilities absolutely without expense ; while those who were desirous of investing their superfluous cash could here find numerous opportunities. Altogether, this institution was a positive boon to visitors to the Exposition.

HAYDEN'S U. S. GEOLOGICAL SURVEY.

Dr. Hayden, of the U. S. Geological Survey, is a native of Massachusetts, who emigrated to the West early in his life, and graduated at Oberlin College, Ohio. Subsequently he devoted his attention to geology, making several trips to the Far West, whence he brought back a large collection of specimens. In 1865 he was elected Professor of Geology and Mineralogy in the University of Pennsylvania, which position he continued to hold until 1872. The United States Geological Survey owes its origin to the following facts : In 1867, when

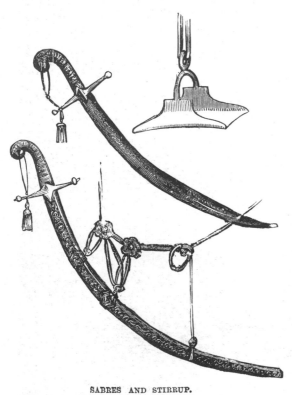

SABRES AND STIRRUP.

Nebraska was admitted as a State, Congress set apart the unspent balance of the appropriation for the legislative expenses of the Territory for the geological survey of the new State. This sum amounted to $5,000, and with its expenditure commenced the Geological Survey of the United States.

In 1868, another appropriation was made, and the work carried westward into Wyoming Territory, the report of the surveys for these two years being made to the Commissioner General of the Land Office in 1869. The survey was put under the supervision of the Secretary of the Interior, and an increased appropriation made for the reconnoissance along the eastern edge of the Rocky Mountains, from Cheyenne, Wyoming Territory, to Santa Fé, New Mexico. The following year an additional sum was appropriated and devoted to the slope of a portion of Wyoming Territory, including a belt of country bordering the line of the Union Pacific Railroad.

In 1871 and 1872 the field of operations was extended to

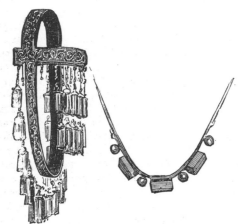

CAMEL HARNESS.

the country at the head-waters of the Yellowstone and Missouri, the region of the hot springs and geysers. One of the results of the work in that section was the reserving of the Yellowstone region as a national park. In 1873, the work of the survey was transferred to Colorado, where it has been carried on ever since. The survey made an exhibit in the United States Government Building which was one of the

SHIELD, DAGGER AND SCABBARD.

most remarkable of its character, perhaps, ever offered. It comprised models, maps, photographs, publications, sketches, pictures in water-colors and chromos. The models were divided into two classes : one, representing the geological structure ; and the other, the ancient ruins of Southwestern Colorado and adjacent portions of Utah and Arizona. Naturally, these latter were the most interesting exhibits to the majority of sight-seers.

Little is known by the generality of Americans concerning the race of people known as the Mound-builders of the Mississippi Valley, and in New Mexico and Arizona, by a more advanced condition of civilization. The Mound-builders left the peculiar structures — to which they are indebted for the only proper name by which we know them — all down through the Valley of the Mississippi, and along many of its tributary streams. Within the single State of Ohio there are immense numbers of these mounds, large and small. They are not made of earth alone, for some of them show brick-work and stone-work here and there, though earth is always the chief material. Some of them have chambers, and sometimes charred wood is found on top, as if fires had been kindled there.

THE FEZ.

In Central America similar mounds exist, having on their tops the remains of stone temples and palaces. All the earthworks of the Mound-builders show more or less of engineering skill. They vary greatly in shape, appearing sometimes in squares, and at others in circles and octagons. Sometimes all these figures are combined in one series of works, but it is noticeable that the circle is always a true circle and the square a true square ; and further, that in many cases the squares measure exactly 1,080 feet on a side, showing that the mound-builders had some definite

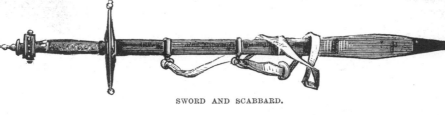

SWORD AND SCABBARD.

standard of measurement. Within these mounds have been found tools and ornaments, made from copper, silver, and valuable stones. They are axes, chisels, knives, bracelets and beads, pieces of thread and of cloth, sometimes gracefully ornamented vases and pottery. The Mound-builders knew how to mold in clay a variety of objects, such as birds, quadrupeds, and human faces. They practiced farming, though they had no domestic animals to help them. They mined for copper near Lake Superior, where the deserted mines may still be seen. In one of these mines there was a mass of copper weighing nearly six tons partly raised from the bottom, and supported by wooden logs now nearly decayed, and the stone and

THE SADDLE AND PILLION.

EGYPTIAN SADDLERY AND ARMS.

copper tools were lying about as if these men had just gone away. The only evidence that we have as to the age of the mounds consists in the fact that at the mouth of the mine just mentioned there are trees nearly 400 years old, growing on earth which was thrown out in digging the mine. On a mound at Marietta, Ohio, there are trees nearly 800 years old. The mounds must, of course, be as old as that, and nobody knows how much older. In the Mineral Annex of the Main Building, as has already been stated, there were on exhibition thousands of articles manufactured by these Mound-builders, including arrow-heads, ax-heads, copper tools, etc. The various expeditions which have crossed the Continent through New Mexico and Arizona have always found relics which indicate the former existence in these Territories of a vast population, whose character we can only conjecture. Some think that the present Moqui, Pueblo and Zuni Indians are the descendants of this ancient race, judging from the fact that the remains of some of their dwellings indicate the same style of structure, etc., which is observed among the American tribes of to-day ; but these are very different from those of Mound-builders.

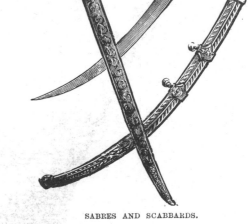

SABRES AND SCABBARDS.

The Pueblo Indians of New Mexico live in vast stone buildings, holding sometimes as many as 5,000 people. These buildings are usually placed on the summits of hills, and have walls so high as only to be reached by ladders. The Pueblo Indians dress neatly, live in families, practice various arts, and are utterly different from the roving tribes further north ; yet they are essentially unlike the Mound-builders, for the latter do not seem to have erected stone buildings, nor do the Pueblo Indians build lofty mounds. It is certain that some among the Mound-builders had reached the sea in their travels, for on some of their carved pipes there are representations of the seal and of the manatee or sea-cow, animals which they could only have seen by traveling to the ocean.

One of the models exhibited in the United States Government Building represented a two-story cliff-house, found in a cañon of the Rio Mancos, of Colorado. It is built in the crevice of a rock 800 feet above the sea, and is almost inaccessible. Another model represents the ruins of a double-walled tower, a building which seems to have been very common among those ancient people.

Returning to the subject of geology, we find two models of the Elk Mountain Range of Colorado, in which the boundaries of various formations are marked out in colors : one, being cut into sections showing the internal structure of the mountains ; another, is of the Yellowstone National Park, exhibiting its mountains, lakes and streams, and the hot-spring localities. Among the maps are some representing the geyser basins ; others, portions of Idaho and Montana, and of the Snake River ; a relief map of the Elk Mountains, maps of various portions of Colorado, and a contour map of Colorado, in six sheets, unfinished. The geological maps included one, six feet square, of Colorado, on which the geological structure of the "Centennial State" was represented in colors. There was also a map of the Yellowstone region,

SWINGING VASE.

MEXICAN SECTION, IN THE MAIN BUILDING.

and one of the region about the sources of the Snake River. The photographic portion of the exhibit included transparencies or photographs on glass, showing picturesque scenery of the Rocky Mountains, the geysers, hot springs, the ruins of Southwest Colorado, and adjacent parts of Arizona, Utah, and the homes of American Indians. There were also panoramic views of mountains, and two large volumes filled with photographs of Western scenery and representatives of the Indian tribes of the West. One case on exhibition contained a complete set of the publications of the survey, including the annual reports, profusely illustrated; maps and sections, bulletins, miscellaneous publications, and reports upon zoology and paleontology. A number of water-color sketches were also exhibited, showing the beautiful color of the hot springs of the Yellowstone and the centre of Colorado; while two large cases contained fine specimens from the geysers and hot springs, and fragments of pottery, arrow-heads, stone axes, chisels, etc., from the ancient races inhabiting this region.

NEVADA QUARTZ MILL.

An important exhibit in the mining interest was the quartz mill shown in active operation at the Exhibition, a most appropriate representation sent from Nevada. This mill cost $20,000, the entire expense being covered by an appropriation of the Nevada Legislature. By a mutual arrangement, material to keep the mill in operation had been furnished by four mines: the Consolidated Virginia, the California, the Ophir, and the Belcher; the product being kept separate, and sold for the benefit of the respective owners. The quartz, which had been furnished in sacks holding about a bushel each, was supplied to the stamps by means of a self-feeding hopper, coming out of the process in the form of a powder dissolved in a small stream of water which ran through a trough into the amalgamator, which was a large, round sheet-iron box, heated by steam. Quicksilver was here

added to the mixture, and this then passed into another circular tank, where it was kept in constant movement by revolving arms. The affinity of quicksilver for silver caused it to seize upon the latter, with which it amalgamated; after which, the two mixed metals were placed in iron pans and heated in a retort, when the mercury passed off in fumes, being afterward condensed and collected again and

PULPIT, BY F. & H. SCHROEDER.

again, to serve the same purpose. This mill will be remembered as standing back of Machinery Hall, a little west of the hydraulic annex. Besides displaying the crushing and amalgamating machinery, its contents also numbered all kinds of mining implements, while, from the pure silver furnished by the mills, medals were made at the Philadelphia Mint bearing appropriate devices and containing $1.29 of silver, these being sold at $2 each, as souvenirs of the Centennial Exposition.

METEORITES.

Among the natural curiosities which were exhibited at the Centennial Exposition, the meteorites were certainly the most remarkable, and probably to a large majority of visitors the least known. Four such specimens were exhibited: one from Chihuahua, Mexico, in the Mexican department of the Main Building; one from Ovifak, Greenland, to be seen at one of the entrances on the northern side of the Main Building; and two in the Government Building—one from Tucson, Arizona, and one known as the "Blake," from Tennessee. Of the existing collections of meteorites, that of the British Museum ranks first in importance, that of Vienna second, the Paris collection third, and that of Prof. Charles Hugh Shepard, of Amherst, Mass., fourth. In the last-named collection no less than 254 meteorites are represented, the total weight of the collection being about 1,200 pounds; the heaviest specimen weighing 438 pounds, and the lightest half an ounce. The largest meteoric stone in the Professor's collection weighs 57½ pounds, and is from Waconda, Kansas. Other important collections in the United States are those of the Academy of Natural Science of Philadelphia, Yale College, and that of Professor Smith, of Louisville, Kentucky. The Ovifak (Greenland) meteorite already mentioned, and the heaviest specimen on exhibition at the Centennial, weighs 6 20-100 tons; it is one of the group of iron meteorites discovered upon the shores of Greenland, by Professor Nordenskjold, the celebrated mineralogist and Arctic explorer, and one of the Judges in Group No. 1 at the Exhibition. This meteorite was discovered in 1870, at Ovifak, on Disco Island, upon the open coast, and at a place almost inaccessible in even a moderately rough sea. Here were found meteorites of various dimensions, which were supposed to have fallen during the Tertiary period of the world's history, and which have become imbedded in the strata of the Miocene period. The cliffs of this locality rise to a height of 2,000 feet above the sea level, the upper portion being formed of basalt. The meteorites were found at the base of these cliffs, within an area of about 50 square yards. In 1871 the Swedish Government fitted out an expedition comprising two naval vessels, to proceed to Disco and procure these masses of meteoric iron, constituting twelve large specimens and many small ones. One of these is now in the Museum at Copenhagen, and another in the British Museum. The Signet meteorite, sometimes called "The Signet Meteorite," located in the Smithsonian Department in the Government Building, was found in the early part of the last century in the Sierras, near Tucson, Arizona Territory, where there is a tradition among the old residents that there was a shower of meteorites in the mountains some 200 years ago. For a long time this meteorite remained in the town of Tucson, where it was used as a kind of public anvil by the people. It is now the property of the National Museum at Washington. "The Blake Meteorite" in the Government Building is a new and interesting specimen, weighing about 300 pounds, brought by General Wilder from Tennessee. It was discovered in 1875, about 10 miles from Greensville, Cocke County, by a farmer, who, after breaking two plows upon it, dug it out. It is a compact mass of iron. When found it was standing at an angle of about 45 degrees, the top being about 8 inches below the surface. It is one of a number of interesting specimens from the private collection of Professor W. P. Blake, the able director of the Mineral Department of the Smithsonian Institute. The Mexican or Chihuahua meteorite is a compact mass of iron, weighing 4,000 pounds, one of the several found at Chihuahua.

SKETCH OF G. W. CHILDS.

A COPY of the *Public Ledger* lies before us, dated March 25, 1836, and being the first number of that paper, now in its forty-first year. It is a little sheet of 15 by 13 inches in dimensions, but is important for several reasons.

In the first place, as being the type of the earliest issues of penny papers in America, and in the second place as having been the foundation of the fortune of the gentleman, some particulars concerning whose life we propose to offer in this place.

George W. Childs was born in Baltimore in 1829, and even in his earliest years gave token of the earnestness, perseverance and industry which have served to build up and sustain both his character and his fortune. When only thirteen years of age he entered the United States Navy, in which service he only remained fifteen months, gaining, however, it is probable, through this experience, that sense of order and that spirit of discipline which have marked both his own conduct and his direction of affairs ever since. When fifteen years old young Childs went from Baltimore to Philadelphia. He was at this time penniless, and, so far as Philadelphia was concerned, friendless. He was successful in obtaining a situation in a publishing-house, where he so proved himself to his employer as possessing not only the attributes we have mentioned, but sagacity and good judgment as well, that he was specially deputed, as a portion of his duty, to attend auction sales and purchase books for the house with which he was concerned. After a time the face of young Childs grew to be familiar to booksellers throughout the country as representing this establishment at the annual trade sales in New York. At the end of four years the young man started in business for himself in a small room of the building then occupied by the *Public Ledger* of Philadelphia. Here he was both industrious and successful, and growing by this time to be known and to make friends, he was presently offered a partnership in the house of R. E. Peterson & Co., publishers, the firm becoming thereafter Childs & Peterson. In his new and responsible position Mr. Childs did not fail to make the most excellent use of the good qualities which had thus far so materially aided in his advancement in life. Endowed with an intuitive taste and

apparently instinctive judgment in the selection of works for publication, his choice in this direction fell upon some of the most salable and profitable books which have ever been published in the United States, and which went far to establish the fortunes of the firm of Childs & Peterson. Among such may be named, "Dr. Kane's Arctic Explorations," and a book by Parson Brownlow. The work called "Familiar Science," compiled by Mr. Peterson, was, through Mr. Childs's energy and tact, pushed to a sale of 200,000 copies, gaining a footing in schools which it has held even up to the present time. For a dozen years or more Mr. Childs continued in the publishing business, the house issuing during this period such important works as "Bouvier's Law Dictionary," and "Institutes of American Law," "Fletcher's Brazil," and, most important of all, Dr. S. A. Allibone's "Dictionary of English and American Authors," which, with special courtesy and a due sense of appreciation, was dedicated by its distinguished author to Mr. Childs himself.

It would appear, from what we can learn both of Mr. Childs's own assertions and those of his friends from boyhood upward, that his first and last material ambition was to own and control a daily newspaper in a

JAPANESE CABINET.

capital city. The Philadelphia *Public Ledger*, which had now existed for twenty-eight years, had by 1864 reached and passed the turning-point of its existence. For many years a successful and still a valuable journal, circumstances had brought about a material change in its affairs, to that extent that at the time to which we allude it was in the market. Against the advice of his friends, Mr. Childs purchased the *Ledger*. His first move in its conduct was a revolutionary one. Despite the change in prices and values which the progress of events, and the War of the Rebellion among them, had brought about, the proprietors of the *Ledger* had held their paper at the same rates both for subscription and advertising under which it had been published for so many years. Latterly, they had been losing money with frightful rapidity, and it was naturally considered a rash and dangerous step, when, on entering into the proprietorship of this journal, Mr. Childs at once doubled the price of his paper and advanced the rates of advertising to what he deemed just compensation for the advantages which he offered. The immediate result of this action was, of course, to drive away in some measure both subscribers and advertisers; but, as the course of the paper under its new management became indicated, these came back to it, bringing in their train others, until there opened an influx of monetary success, which has continued up to the

present time without varying, and which promises to continue in the future.

The policy of the *Ledger*, to which we have referred, has been of a character to be described in a very few words. In the first place, it has been undeviatingly high-toned in its character, scorning the low moral standard which so widely obtains among the press of the United States, with a straightforward integrity of purpose that is characteristic of its proprietor. Again, it has striven to treat such subjects, and such only, as were within the line which divides the real interest of the public from that which is factitious. Finally, in its method of handling the questions of the day, it has followed the plan of treating each of these on its own merits, and without bias, or regard for personal opinion or criticism.

In its interior management, Mr. Childs has never failed to introduce into the *Ledger* establishment all improvements and inventions which, in his judgment, were calculated either to facilitate the business of his paper, or to advance the comfort and interests of his employés. On June 20, 1867, the *Public Ledger* took possession of a building especially constructed for its purposes, standing at the southwest corner of Sixth and Chestnut Streets, Philadelphia. Erected and fitted under his own personal direction, this building became a model printing-house; probably in all respects the most perfect and complete establishment of the kind in the world. Here, where Mr. Childs had full direction and control in carrying out his own plans, he devoted himself to arrangements calculated to enable those in his employment to work in a manner the most agreeable and most healthful to themselves, as well as with a proper consideration for the prosecution of the duties which should devolve upon them in advancing his own interests and those of the important journal in his charge.

Thus far, we have considered Mr. Childs in his accumulative capacity alone. It will become us now to look upon him in his character of a man of large wealth, with a view to seeing in what light he presents himself in his employment thereof. We are told in the proverb that "Sweet are the uses of adversity." This is a proposition which need not be gainsaid, yet with what added sweetness should become the uses of *prosperity* to those who have gained unto themselves its many possible advantages! In this country, where, according to one of its most distinguished political economists, "the rich are growing richer while the poor are growing poorer," we do not meet so frequently as would be desirable those of the one class who avail themselves of their advantages for the benefit of the other. And since it is in this light that the life of George W. Childs most becomes him, it is fitting that the good which possession of wealth has been made, through his generosity, to yield to the poor and unfortunate, should be set forth in any account of his life. In the direction of the many hundred persons in his employment, it is a matter of public notoriety in the city where he lives that Mr. Childs has dispensed a generosity which is as boundless as it is appreciative. It is not every newspaper publisher who presents his employés with life insurance policies, deals out festivals and amusement to them unsparingly on each recurring holiday, regards their health and welfare as he expects them to regard their duty during their lifetime, and when they die, supplies them with a burial-place. Yet these things are precisely what Mr. Childs has been accustomed to do for those employed in the office of the Philadelphia *Ledger*. These are, to be sure, benefits, a knowledge of which may readily be widespread, and of course, not to the disadvantage of the one who confers them; but not alone by this method of benevolence has Mr. Childs distinguished himself. In the matter of personal charity, and under circumstances where publicity was the last thing that could be expected, if it were hoped for, Mr. Childs has a reputation among those who know him best which is without parallel.

As to the ordinary ways of appropriating money for charitable purposes, probably no man in the country receives nearly so many applications as he, and it is seldom that he rejects or refuses any. For devising original methods of gratifying those who are seldom gratified he is no less noted. By sending entire charitable institutions on pleasure excursions, by throwing open to those who are poor and unaccustomed to them, amusements, the memory of which proves perhaps the brightest reflection in their lives—by a thousand and one such devices, Mr. Childs has made his name honorably known, not only in the city where he lives and where naturally the most of his wealth is dispensed, but throughout the country, and even abroad.

But there are more ways of dispensing wealth to public advantage than by charity alone. By freely opening his elegant residence in hospitality to visitors from foreign lands, Mr. Childs has doubtless done much for the credit

DAVIS TOWER-BASKET.

of his country in this particular, while he has brought about associations among distinguished personages which could scarcely fail to inure to the public benefit in some way. Probably no such gathering of distinguished and notable people was ever collected together in the parlors of a private citizen in this country as met by invitation at Mr. Childs's residence on the evening of May 10th, 1876, the day of the opening of the Centennial Exhibition in Philadelphia. On this occasion there were present the President of the United States, with his wife; all the members of the Cabinet, with their wives; the Chief Justice and Associate Justices of the Supreme Court of the United States and their wives; the Emperor and Empress of Brazil; the Diplomatic representatives of Great Britain, France, Spain, Austria, Prussia, Russia, Italy, Belgium, Turkey, Japan, China, and other Powers of Europe and Asia; the Governors of Maine, New Hampshire, Massachusetts, Rhode Island, Kentucky, Pennsylvania, New Jersey, Delaware and Maryland, with their staff officers; leading members of the United States Senate and House of Representatives; Generals Sherman, Sheridan, Hancock, McDowell; Admirals Porter, Rowan, Scott, Lardner, Turner, Jenkins and Alden; Centennial Judges and Commissioners from foreign countries and the United States; famous military and naval officers, eminent judges, leading lawyers, prominent divines, presidents of colleges, authors, journalists, artists; in fact, men famous in every branch of professional and private life. And this instance, except in the remarkable comprehensiveness of its scope, as to the guests, merely illustrates the rule in Mr. Childs's social life. Scarcely a prominent visitor from abroad arrives in this country who is not furnished with letters of introduction to Mr. Childs and feted by him. Compare such generous courtesy to the representatives of foreign aristocracy, wealth, and intelligence with the refinement

of delicate appreciation which induced Mr. Childs, during the continuance of the Centennial, to furnish with the means to visit the Great Fair not only numbers of poor women who would otherwise not have seen it, but also as many as two thousand children who, through Mr. Childs's liberality, were sent happy-hearted to the wonderful Exhibition at Fairmount and furnished with good dinners while there enjoying the show. Children of the Philadelphia Deaf and Dumb Asylum and those of other public institutions of that city were thus favored, and in the case of the House of Refuge, it illustrates the peculiar quality of his thoughtfulness that he made a special request that its inmates should be permitted to lay off the uniform which is their badge, while visiting the Exposition, and wear new suits to be supplied and paid for by him. It is in his peculiarly happy faculty for discrimination in the awarding of his benefits and in his methods of distribution, as much as in the lavishness with which he yields up to public and private uses such a material portion of his fortune, that Mr. Childs is specially distinguished. Not an unsuitable illustration of this characteristic, possibly, was his gift of a memorial window in Westminster Abbey in honor of the poets George Herbert, Charles Wesley and William Cowper. This munificent gift was merely occasioned by the receipt on the part of Mr. Childs of a circular from the committee of English gentlemen who had the matter in hand.

In considering this instance of the refinement of generosity, it should be remembered that it illustrates the patriotism of the man, no less than his liberal impulses. The placing of a memorial window in Westminster Abbey—the shrine of all the memories that by the English-speaking population of the world are held dearest—was a truly graceful act, associating the American people with their English brethren in a most generous and most fitting tribute to names the world delights to honor.

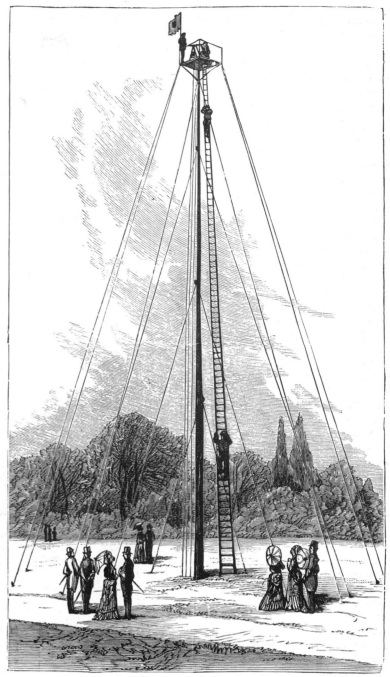

DAVIS ELEVATING SIGNAL-TOWER.

DAVIS SIGNAL—THE WAGON.

At the time of the appointment of its official representatives at the Centennial Exposition, the British Government honored Mr. Childs by designating him to the service referred to in the following highly complimentary acknowledgment on the part of the Duke of Richmond and Gordon, Lord President of the Council:

[Copy.]

4th January, 1877.

SIR,—I have heard with much pleasure from Colonel Sandford of the valuable and important assistance you have rendered me, as one of the Honorary Commissioners for Great Britain, her Colonies and Dependencies, at the Philadelphia International Exhibition of 1876.

It will gratify you to know that Her Majesty's Government have expressed their highest approval of the administration of the British section, towards the success of which in America you have been good enough so much to contribute.

I have the honor to be, Sir, your obedient servant,

(Signed) RICHMOND AND GORDON.

GEORGE W. CHILDS, ESQ.,
Honorary Commissioner for the United Kingdom.

As to the sentiment with which Mr. Childs is regarded abroad, Colonel John W. Forney says of him: "When I carried letters from him to Europe in 1867, his name was a talisman, and it was pleasant to see how a nobleman like the Duke of Buckingham honored the endorsement of an American who thirty years before was a poor boy." To be thus esteemed at home and abroad; to be regarded as a benefactor by the poor, and valued as a friend by the rich; to wield

LAYING THE TELEGRAPH.

GOVERNMENT TELEGRAPH AT THE CENTENNIAL GROUNDS.

generously, and with vivid appreciation of the relations which obtain in this life, the influences of vast and increasing wealth; to do all this while one lives is to rear certainly the most enduring and possibly the most satisfactory monument of fame which it is given to men to exhibit before posterity. It is said of Mr. Childs that while still young he set before himself as the intention and ambition of his future, "the accumulation of riches, not for himself alone, but to make others happy during and after his life." At the age of forty-seven Mr. Childs sees one-half of this scheme of his life completed, and the other half so far advanced toward accomplishment that it needs only to conclude it after its author's intention, the final seal and inscription which are set upon every man's doings, and which, it is to be hoped in the interests of humanity, may be long ere they come to George W. Childs.

THE SILK INDUSTRY
IN AMERICA.

PATERSON, New Jersey, gains, perhaps, its chief importance from its position as the leading centre of the silk industry in America. It claims, and not improperly, he title of the Lyons of America on this account; and a brief sketch of silk manufacturing in this locality may be properly inserted here.

Paterson lies among the foothills of the Ramapo range of mountains, distant only 20 miles by rail from New York City. Here the Passaic River furnishes a romantic as well as useful feature of the landscape, plunging suddenly downward at this point in a fall of 50 feet, and then rushing between perpendicular cliffs in a more gradual fall of 22 feet further to the level of the plain.

By reference to a previous article in this work it will be seen that the manufacture of silk was carried on in different States up to the beginning of the present century. From that time, however, the industry declined until, about 1830, when it began to be revived; and when the *Morus multicaulis* excitement commenced, which lasted until 1839, when the mania exploded. Early in 1830 the Chamber of Commerce at Lyons, France, published a report concerning American silk, in which it was stated that a sample reeled in Philadelphia was assayed by an assayer and declared to be of an extraordinary quality and admirably adapted to the uses of manufacture; that it was fine, regular, clean, of a fine color, and all that could be desired. Its value was estimated at 26 francs, a little over $5, per pound.

The first silk mill in Paterson appears to have been started by Christopher Colt, Jr., son of Christopher Colt, of Hartford, President of the Silk Manufacturing Company during its existence, which continued while the excitement lasted, between 1835 and 1839. Christopher Colt, Jr., was the nephew of Samuel Colt, the inventor of the revolving pistol. The silk mill of Paterson occupied the fourth story of Samuel Colt's factory for making revolvers. It was not successful, and, in a year, was offered for sale to Mr. G. W. Murray, of Northampton, Mass., who bought it for $3,200, including all the machinery. Mr. Murray put in charge of the factory Mr. John Ryle, a practical silk manufacturer, of Macclesfield, England, who had recently come out to America. This was the foundation of the silk manufacture of Paterson, which was then a town of 7,000 inhabitants. At the expiration of the three years' contract between Murray and Ryle, these two formed a partnership; and three years later, in 1846, Mr. Ryle was assisted by his brothers in England to buy out Mr. Murray's interest. For nearly twelve years from its foundation the silk mill of Mr. Ryle had no rival in Paterson. A fair specimen of the capacity of his establishment at this period was the manufacture of the large flag which waved over the Crystal Palace during the Exhibition at New York in 1853. In 1854 Mr. Ryle built the Murray Mill, covering 15,000 square feet with a two-story building, then one of the largest, and perhaps most thoroughly equipped, of the silk factories in America.

But, by 1854, competitors in the Paterson silk manufacture had begun to establish themselves, although at first on a small scale; and from that time the industry continued to increase in magnitude and importance, until, in 1875, it furnished the following interesting statistics: Number of firms and corporations engaged in the silk manufacture, 32; dyeing establishments, in addition to the private dye-houses of manufacturers, 5; number of operatives, nearly 8,000; proportion of female operatives, two-thirds; proportion of operatives under 16

ELEVATOR.

years of age, one-fourth; amount of wages paid during the year, $2,664,993; amount of capital employed and invested in the manufacture, $5,926,804; number of power looms, 730; number of hand looms, 563; number of braiding spindles, 23,445; number of pounds of silk dyed, 550,000.

In 1864, the Dale Silk Mills were commenced, this vast structure having finally cost half a million dollars. In 1867, the firm of Dexter, Lambert & Co. transferred their manufactory from Boston to Paterson, and built a large mill to accommodate their business, which began with ladies' dress trimmings and ribbons, and has since been developed in all sorts of fancy silks, handkerchiefs, etc. In the following year, Wm. Strange & Co. left Williamsburgh, N. Y., and started a ribbon factory at Paterson. Here, too, they make fancy goods, silk handkerchiefs, etc., employing 700 operatives. In 1871, Schoharie sent Frederick Barre to Paterson, where he established the Barre Silk Manufacturing Company. It is claimed that under the low tariff there was no competition in the silk manufacture at Paterson for nearly twelve years, and that it was not until the passage of the tariff of 1861 that this town became the centre of the great silk industry. If this be the case, it is certainly an argument in favor of protection, as far as it goes. Paterson has, however, been specially favored in many ways, particularly in the possession of abundant water-power, proximity to a great commercial port, and excellent facilities for transportation. While great power is not required for the silk mill—and it is a fact that steam is almost as economical as water for driving light machinery—pure water is required in large quantity in the processes of silk manufacture, especially in cleansing the silk by repeated washings, to bring out its natural lustre.

Cheap labor was another necessity to the silk industry; and at an early period Paterson appears to have drawn together a laboring population. The men were employed in machine-shops, and on heavy work, and their wives and children needed employment. Although this was afforded by the cotton mills, the operatives objected to it as being too confining and hard. The silk-mill afforded a welcome relief. Its work re-

quired care and dexterity, instead of protracted effort, and was clean and wholesome.

It is stated that the year 1875 was the most prosperous which the silk industry in America has ever experienced. Particularly has the increase in the business taken place in Paterson, N. J., and a marked feature of the improvement to the community has been the immigration of a number of master silk-weavers from France and England. These own their looms, which in many instances they have brought with them, carrying on the weaving at their homes, one or more rooms being fitted up for the purpose; and, as business increases, they employ weavers. The import of raw silk in 1874 was 1,330,482 pounds, the largest ever known. The total value of the products manufactured in America was about $27,815,071. Of this New Jersey furnished about $10,930,035, the balance being divided between 14 States, New York and Connecticut together supplying about as much as New Jersey alone. The value of capital invested in this industry in the United States amounts to $18,000,000, the number of operatives employed being 18,017. The number of females engaged in the silk business, April 26th, 1876, was 279.

The American silk exhibition at the Centennial was situated at the eastern entrance of the Main Exhibition Building, occupying a space of 117 feet along the central avenue or nave. It included 28 exhibitors, of whom 6 were from Pater-

ELEVATOR.

son, N. J. Besides these, there were exhibits of machines for the manufacture of silk goods in Machinery Hall, three of which were from Paterson, N. J.; in the Women's Pavilion, exhibits from two exhibitors; and in Agricultural Hall, one exhibit from San Francisco, of California raw silk cocoons, silkworms feeding, silk reeling, etc.

The following figures of comparison will be interesting in the consideration of the silk industry. They are for 1874: In that year the production of manufactured silk in France amounted to $116,400,000; in Germany, $38,000,000; in Switzerland, $16,000,000, and in all other countries less. In the United States, the production in 1874 was $21,120,428. In the same year the importation of manufactured silk into France, was $12,693,570; into Great Britain, $49,276,320; into the United States, $23,996,782.

INDUSTRIAL PROGRESS OF STATES.

OHIO.

WE have already briefly described the Ohio State Building, but a portion of the contents of that structure deserves a more extended notice. The building itself was constructed of stone from thirty Ohio quarries, all the fittings and furniture of the several departments being of Ohio material and workmanship. Among the curiosities exhibited was the masonic apron worn by General Washington, presented by him to Captain McClair, of Western Virginia, an officer of his staff, from whom it passed into the possession of a citizen of Ohio, and thence into that of Tiffin Lodge of Freemasons, from whose possession it was forwarded for exhibition. This apron, which is of white satin, is profusely ornamented with masonic emblems, and surrounded by a blue border very neatly worked. Another interesting exhibit is a series of photographs taken in 1860 of those who then survived of the victors in the naval battle of Lake Erie. None of them are now living. The portraits are inclosed by a frame made from the wood of the flagship *Lawrence*. A very handsome collection of iron, stone, and china from East Liverpool was also exhibited in the State Building.

In the Agricultural Hall, Ohio made a prominent display, too, of its great staples, wool and Indian corn, as also agricultural machinery, implements being exhibited from most of the leading Ohio manufacturers. In the Main Building and the Mineral Annex, Ohio was represented by a fine display of specimens of her wonderful mineral wealth, and its manufacture and results.

The Cleveland Iron and Coal Company made a magnificent showing of their manufacture, from the crude ore to threads of steel wound upon spools, so flexible that it could almost be used for sewing purposes. A curiosity in this display was a Bessemer steel rail. It

CARVED ELEPHANT TUSKS, SIAM.

ENGLISH PHAETON.

was rolled in 1868 by this company, and has outlasted 34 good iron rails. It has been run over 766,500 times by locomotives, and by 6,387,500 cars, while over it have been carried 143,080,000 tons of freight. All this showing of friction has left the rail in appearance in as good a condition as ever. Ohio displayed the largest block of coal in the Exhibition, being 12 feet 8 inches thick, and weighing 15,360 pounds. It was taken from a seam in Perry County. It is stated that the first furnace erected in the United States for the purpose of smelting iron with bituminous coal was at Lowell, Mahoning County, Ohio. The annual production of coal here exceeds 1,225,000 tons, much of which is shipped to Cleveland and Ashtabula, and thence, by the lakes, North. This coal is peculiarly adapted for the manufacture of iron for Bessemer steel. Six quarries of Ohio were represented in specimens of building-stones; and from the town of Pomeroy an exhibit of bromine was sent, that locality, it is stated, supplying more than half of all the article used throughout the world.

A century ago that portion of country lying between the Alleghany and the Rocky Mountains was a wilderness, inhabited only by wild beasts and Indians. The only white men who had penetrated so far westward were the Jesuit and Moravian missionaries. In 1785, Congress passed an ordinance for the survey of public territory, and two years later the "Northwestern Territory" was organized. Fifteen years after that, the State of Ohio was admitted into the Union. Already in 1803 the tide of emigration had begun to flow over the Alleghanies into the Valley of the Mississippi, and the heavy emigrant-wagon was to be seen pursuing its way toward the wilds of Kentucky and the plains of Ohio; as at a later date it traversed the desert land between Missouri and California. Ohio forms the one-sixth part of the Northwestern Territory, 40,000 square miles. It has 200 miles of navigable waters in the Ohio River, and a citizen of Ohio may pursue his navigation through 42,000 miles, all in his own country, and all within navigable reach of his own State. Possessing more than three times the surface of Belgium, and one-third of the whole of Italy, Ohio has more natural sources in proportion than either, and is capable of ultimately supporting a larger population than any country of equal surface in Europe. And while upon the hills and plains the grass and the forest trees grow abundantly, beneath the surface, and easily accessible, lie 10,000 square miles of coal and 4,000 square miles of iron.

The first settlement of Ohio was made by a colony from New England, at the mouth of the Muskingum. Of this settlement, Washington said: "No colony in America was ever settled under such favorable auspices as that which has just commenced at the Muskingum. Information, property and strength will be its characteristics. I know many of the settlers personally, and there never were men better calculated to promote the welfare of such a community." The subsequent settlements on the Miami and Scioto Rivers were made by citizens of New York and Virginia. In 1810 Ohio had 45,365 population. In 1870 its population was 2,655,260. At present it is estimated at 3,000,000 of people, a half a million more than the thirteen States in 1776. The aggregate amount of grain and potatoes produced in Ohio in 1874 was 157,323,597 bushels, the largest aggregate amount raised of any State but one, Illinois, which produces a larger amount per square mile than any other State in the country. In 1870 Ohio had 8,818,000 domestic animals; Illinois, 6,925,000; New York, 5,283,000; Pennsylvania, 4,443,000; and other States less. It is stated, further, that Ohio produces one-fifth of all the wool raised in the United States; one-seventh of all the cheese; one-eighth of all the corn; and one-tenth of all the wheat; and yet Ohio has but one-fourteenth part of the population and one-eightieth part of the surface of this country. The money value of the export product of the State is equal to $100,000,000 per annum, and to a solid capital of $15,000,000 after all the sustenance of the people has been taken out of the annual crop. About one-fifth of the bituminous coal region, which descends the western slopes of the Alleghanies, lies in Ohio. It occupies wholly or in part 36 counties. Ohio as an iron district extends from the mouth of the Scioto to a point north of the Mahoning River, in Trumbull County. The whole length is nearly 200 miles, and the breadth 20 miles. The iron in this district is of various qualities, and is manufactured into bars and castings. There are here 100 furnaces, 44 rolling-mills and 15 rail-mills, being the largest number of any State in the Union except Pennsylvania. By the census statistics of 1870, Ohio is the third State in the production of iron and iron manufactures. In 1874 its product of pig-iron was 420,000 tons. A large section of the southeastern portion of the State produces salt without limit. The production of the State in 1874 was 3,500,000 bushels, being one-fifth of the entire production of the country; the salt section being exceeded only by those of Syracuse, N. Y., and Saginaw, Mich.

The aggregate value of the products of manufactures, exclusive of mining, in 1870, was $269,713,000, being more than four times that of 1850, while in 1875 the estimated value reached $400,000,000. Ohio has a large number of sail, steam, and all kinds of vessels, which have been built at the ports of Cleveland, Toledo, Sandusky and Cincinnati, during the last twenty years. The annual trade of Ohio exceeds $700,000,000.

The progress of Ohio in education forms an important episode in the educational history of the country. The ordinance of Congress, passed in 1785, for the survey of public lands in the Northwestern Territory, provided that one-sixth part should be reserved for the maintenance of the public schools in each township. As the State of Ohio contained a little more than 25,000,000 of acres, this, together with two special grants of three townships to the universities, amounted to the dedication of 740,000 acres of land to the maintenance of schools and colleges. It was, however, sixteen years after the passage of this ordinance, in 1803, when Ohio entered the Union, that legislation upon this grant became possible. The Constitution of the State then declared that "schools and the means of education shall for ever be encouraged by legislative provision." A general school system was established in 1825, which was enlarged and increased by future legislation, until the State possessed a broad, liberal and efficient plan of public instruction. In 1874, the amount raised by taxation for school purposes was $7,452,135, and the number enrolled of the requisite age for schooling was 70 per cent., or 707,943. With regard to collegiate education, it is shown by the report of the Bureau of Education for 1874 that there are more collegiate institutions in Ohio than in all New England, and a greater number of college teachers. There are also a greater number of college students than either in Pennsylvania or New York. The number of schools in Ohio, in 1875 was 14,868, of which 450 were high schools and 14,414 common. The total enrollment of pupils in the same year was 712,129, being about 30 per cent. less than the enumeration. The number of teachers employed was 22,492, and their total expense for salaries, $4,787,963. The total common school fund of Ohio in 1875 was about $3,534,826. As has been already stated, the settlement of Ohio began in 1788, and in 1790 a school of young boys and girls was established at Belpre—the first school for white children opened in Ohio, the Moravian missionaries having established Indian schools at different missions in the State several years before this.

The nature of the schools and of education in Southwestern Ohio in these pioneer times was characteristic of the institutions throughout the West at the period of settlement. The few schools established were taught by cripples, worn-out old men and women, physically unable or constitutionally too lazy to scotch hemp or spin flax. The teacher was regarded as a kind of pensioner; his presence was tolerated only because county infirmaries were not then in existence. The capacity to teach was not a reason for employing him, but the fact that he could do nothing else was a satisfactory one. The popular demand for education was fully met when the scholar could write a tolerably legible hand, could read the Bible, and was able to calculate the value of a load of farm produce. This condition, however, is not a picture of that which existed in the section of Ohio peopled with settlers from New England.

At an early day the schools on the Western Reserve were in a thriving condition. Among the pioneers were found men who had received a liberal culture in schools and colleges second to none in the Union. Meanwhile the social condition of the teacher was far better than in the southern part of the State, while his qualifications were generally such as to command respect. In those days the teacher found board and lodging in the houses of his patrons; his evenings were spent with the family; and he thus became intimately acquainted with the habits and peculiarities of his pupils, and was enabled to turn his knowledge of their traits of character to good use in following out his plan of education. The system upon which the schools were arranged and organized was simple but original. The teacher was accustomed to draw up an article of agreement, binding himself to teach a school in some specified locality for a term of 13 weeks—6 days per week and 8 hours per day—for which he was paid a

POMPEIAN VASE.

EGYPTIAN VASE.

stipulated sum by his patrons, ranging from one to two dollars for each scholar, one-half payable perhaps in wheat at 50 cents per bushel, and the balance in money at the close of the term. The text-books in use included "Murray's English Reader," "The Columbian Orator," "Dillworth's Speller," "Pike's Arithmetic," and "Webster's Easy Standard Pronunciation," with Testaments, almanacs, and other miscellaneous works for general reading. Spelling and reading were made specialties and were regarded as the chief tests of scholarship. Spelling-matches were held frequently, usually at night, and were attended by old and young. A ride, or, more frequently, a walk of six miles was an obstacle easily surmounted by persons wishing to enjoy the competition in school and observe its last champion "spelled down." The schoolhouses of the day were crude enough. The vacant cabin which had been hastily constructed by some pioneer and removed from as soon as he had built a better one, or had left the settlement to seek a more favorite locality, sometimes served as a schoolhouse. At others, settlers would exercise their ingenuity and architectural skill in building what they deemed a suitable edifice for the purpose. This was formed of logs, sometimes roughly hewed, and was generally about

lying upon the ground instead of upon "sleepers." Others had clay floors. In some cases light was obtained by cutting out an entire log and pasting oiled-paper over the opening. The school-furniture was in keeping with the exterior and interior appearance of the building. By splitting the log 6 inches in diameter and 15 feet in length into halves and mounting these on four legs, flat side up, solid if not comfortable seats were made. In Winter immense logs blazed in the open fire-place, which occupied a great part of one end of the building. A wall of rough stone against the side of the house formed a foundation upon which the chimney rested, the chimney itself being made of sticks placed upon each other, chinked with mortar and thickly coated internally with the same material. Such was the style and condition of the schools of Ohio prior to the passage of the first school law in 1821. And this, indeed, may be considered a fair representation of the pioneer schools of the entire country. All of these were supported by the voluntary contributions of the people, until the system of school taxation had been authorized by the General Assembly. Even as late as 1825 there were no public schools, properly speaking, in Cincinnati. And in 1829, the whole amount of money apportioned to the directors of the rural districts

education in the high schools and have been appointed to their positions as a reward for continuing long enough in school to complete the prescribed course of study, and for making a good record for scholarship and deportment. The compensation allowed women ranges from $250 to $1,000 per annum, that of men $600 to $1,500 per annum. It is a fact which will doubtless be a surprise to many that the proportion of youths in Ohio attending school in comparison to the population, places it as the first State in the Union in this regard, and that the States west of the Alleghanies and north of Ohio, have more youths in school, proportionably, than New England and New York. Thus the proportion in Ohio is one in 4 2-10; Illinois, one in 4 3-10; Pennsylvania, one in 4 8-10; New York, one in 5 2-10; Connecticut, one in 8 7-10. Still another astounding fact is that in the State of Ohio there are a larger number of churches than in any other State of the Union, the figures being 6,488 for Ohio, 5,627 for New York, 5,984 for Pennsylvania, and 4,298 for Illinois.

The educational exhibit in the south gallery of the Main Building of the Centennial included historical sketches of the schools of Ohio, historical sketches of the higher educational institutions, photographs of school-buildings,

SPECIMEN OF BROCADE SILK.   JAPANESE SWORDS.   SPECIMEN OF BROCADE SILK.

18 feet wide by 24 long. The caves were about 10 feet from the ground, and the house was covered with rows of clapboards held in place by long poles running lengthwise. The openings between the logs were chinked with pieces of wood, stone, or any other convenient material, and plastered with mortar made from the ground near by. This work was called "mud-house." The directors generally attended to this branch of affairs every Fall, as the rains of Spring and Summer washed away the mortar, especially if straw or hay had not been used in fixing it. The door was made of rough boards, hung with wooden hinges, and fastened by means of a wooden latch, to which a string was attached, passing through a small hole above it into the open area. Access to the building was obtained by pulling a string by which the latch was lifted, and the door opened by muscular force.

The pioneers secured their houses from surreptitious entrance by pulling in the string. Thus it became that the "latch-string-out" was a sign of hospitality. Tardy pupils, who found no string outside of the schoolhouse door, knew that the master was "at prayers" within, and waited silently and solemnly around the door until the latch-string appeared. Some houses had rough floors laid with thick slabs or planks split from large logs and hewed on one side, being from three to four inches thick, and often

for the maintenance of free schools rarely exceeded $10. In 1837 a State School Department was established and a State Superintendent appointed. The plan of grading public schools was not adopted in the early history of popular education in Ohio, owing chiefly to the want of sufficient and suitable school buildings. The first schools opened in cities and towns were held in such rented rooms as could be obtained at the lowest possible expense. The furniture was made or furnished by common mechanics. It was not until 1836 that in Cincinnati the first public school buildings were erected. Ten of these were built and opened in that year, the houses being each 40 by 60 feet, two stories high, with two apartments in each story. From this time the system of grading and classification in Ohio continued to be made, until the establishment in 1847 of a high school completed the introduction of a system which had already been in use for some time in New York, Boston, Providence and Philadelphia.

In the years 1849 and 1850 the system of graded schools began to be extended to townships and small villages. Teachers' associations were formed and educational periodicals issued, and by the close of the year 1855 the formation of the graded system was permanently established throughout the State. About 90 per cent. of the teachers in Ohio are women, two-thirds of whom have received their academic

drawings and bound volumes of examination manuscripts from the several grades of the schools of Cincinnati, Cleveland, Columbus, Dayton, Sandusky, Toledo and other cities; crayon drawings and designs for frescoes, illuminations, etc., from the School of Design of the Cincinnati University; photographs of the principal colleges, seminaries and school-buildings, and charts illustrative of the condition and progress of education. The other exhibits of Ohio included a fine display of iron ores and manufactured iron from the different mines and foundries; fire-clay, coals, limestone, salt and other minerals, and a large and full representative and collective exhibit of building-stone. The archæological display of Ohio in the Mineral Annex No. 1 has been already considered in this work. It included contributions from the State Archæological Association of Ohio at Columbus; the Western Reserve Historical Society, of Cleveland; the Firelands Historical Society at Norwalk; Ohio Agricultural and Mechanical College, of Columbus; Western Reserve College of Hudson, and from forty other contributors, comprising stone, field implements and ornaments, pottery, shell ornaments, copper implements, articles from the mounds of Ohio, casts, photographs and drawings of the mounds, stone images and implements, pipes, etc. In manufactures Ohio exhibited chemicals, lard, tallow, grease, oil, candles, glycerine,

MERIDEN BRITANNIA CO.'S EXHIBIT, IN THE MAIN BUILDING.

ink, paints, matches, woven fabrics, fancy leather-ware, soap-stone articles, paper, etc. One remarkable exhibit was that of A. B. Griffin, of Ravenna, who sent a box and pyramid made of the woods of the world, containing 9.865 pieces.

In scientific and philosophical instruments there were exhibited electro-galvanic plates for medical purposes, telegraphic instruments, indicators, fire and burglar alarms, pianos, etc. In furniture and domestic articles, Ohio exhibited largely; Cincinnati in particular sending a fine display of household furniture, and East Liverpool adding materially to the value and interest of the American Exhibition of china-ware and pottery, as has been already remarked.

In Machinery Hall, Ohio made a good presentation, including many important pieces of mechanism of very original design. Among these were a patent wood-cutting machine, stave-sawing machine, automatic shingle-machine, sawing and grooving machine, automatic gas-machine, drills, automatic knitting-machine, sewing-machine, stocking-knitters, wash-machines, machine for making paper-boxes, meat-chopping machine, vertical portable engine, wood pumps, safety-lock for elevators, patent universal wood-workers, planing and match machines, band and scroll saws, etc.

The display in the Women's Pavilion was also very full, and, as has been already remarked, the work of the Ladies' School of Design of the University of Cincinnati, and other ladies of that city, in carving, china painting, etc., was elaborate, comprehensive, and in the highest degree artistic and creditable. Indeed, in the matter of wood-carving it is only fair to say that the display of Cincinnati has probably never been equaled. The articles exhibited included a carved grand piano of rosewood, a carved walnut bedstead, carved oak door, carved dining-room mantel, painted and slate panels, carved walnut cabinet with silver-and-bronze panels, carved oak secretary, cabinet with original metal-work, and carved mahogany hanging-cabinet from an old piano, a family relic 100 years old; wall-pockets, flower-stands, bread-plates, brackets, carved frames, card-receivers, etc. The porcelain-painting showed fine artistic taste and refinement in selection, the execution being in many instances elaborate and beautiful.

The display of agricultural implements from Ohio in Agricultural Hall was full, and indicated much original talent and inventive power. Here also were

exhibited specimens of fine wools from 17 contributors, a large show of Cincinnati specialties in hams, shoulders, lard, breakfast-bacon, pork, etc., and an admirably comprehensive display of cereals, carefully and judiciously arranged. In fact, there was no department or building at the Centennial where Ohio did not make a reputable presentment.

ILLINOIS.

From the address upon the history and resources of Illinois, delivered in the building of the State on the Centennial Grounds by Rev. Charles H. Fowler, we abstract a few important facts of interest in connection with the exhibit made by this State. The orator said that nearly four-fifths of the entire State is underlaid with a deposit of coal more than 40 feet thick on an average. Indeed,

THE CHILIAN MINERAL EXHIBIT.

recent surveys estimated it at 70 feet in thickness. Compared with the coal-fields of other countries, we have the following : Great Britain has 12,000 square miles of coal ; Spain, 3,000 ; France, 1,519 ; Belgium, 578. Illinois has about twice as many square miles as all these combined ; Virginia has 20,000 ; Pennsylvania, 16,000 ; Ohio, 12,000 ; Illinois, 41,000. One-seventh of all the known coal on this continent is in Illinois. Concerning the products and manufactures of the State, Dr. Fowler observed that grain and flour were imported from the East to Chicago until as late as 1837. The first exportation was in 1839, and the exports did not exceed the imports until 1842. The Chicago Board of Trade was organized in 1848, and at that time grain was purchased by the wagon-load in the street. Now the Chicago elevators will hold 15,000,000 bushels of grain, the cash value of the grain handled in a year weighing 7,000,000 tons, or 700,000 car-loads, worth about $215,000,000. One-tenth of all the wheat in the United States is handled in Chicago. Even as early as 1853 the receipts of grain in Chicago exceeded those of St. Louis, and in 1854 the exports from Chicago exceeded those of New York and those of St. Petersburg, Archangel or Odessa, the largest grain-markets in Europe. Meanwhile, the manufacturing interests of Chicago have not remained quiescent. In 1873 the manufactories employed 45,000 operatives, and in 1876, 60,000. The manufactured products in 1875 were estimated at $177,000,000.

INDIANA.

The State Building of Indiana contained one feature which was peculiar and original. This was a series of panels, upon which were displayed at a glance the leading statistical facts of interest in reference to each county in the State, including the date of settlement, mineral wealth, geographical position, present population, etc. The State appropriation for the Centennial was $5,000, but to this was added, in subscriptions by schools and individuals, a supplementary sum of nearly $20,000. In front of the building were displayed specimens of the mineral products of the State, among these being several cuttings of block coal, averaging from 7 to 12 feet in thickness. Samples of deposits of bituminous coal, ranging from 15 to 20 feet, were also shown, and besides several specimens of building-stones, the limestone rock of Decatur County being specially noticeable. The mineral display of Indiana, however, was best seen in the Mineral Annex of the Main Building, and has been already described. The

INTERIOR OF HORTICULTURAL HALL.

coal-fields of Indiana embrace an area of 6,500 square miles. Over this area there are distributed from three to four seams of coal, with a combined thickness of from 20 to 30 feet, three seams of block coal from 12 to 15 feet, and one seam of cannel coal, 4½ to 6 feet in thickness. The Indiana block coal has an extensive reputation as a fuel for metallurgical purposes. The building-stones from Decatur County and Jennings County have been used in the foundation of some of the finest and most costly public buildings in Indianapolis, and in the abutments of bridges that span the Ohio River at Cincinnati and Louisville. The oolite limestone is quarried in blocks from 10 to 12 feet thick, and is used in the most costly private and public buildings in the State. A recent discovery, of which specimens were on exhibition, is a deposit of porcelain clay, to which the State Geologist has given the name of "Indianite." This has been used at the various potteries of Ohio, and is found to be an excellent clay for manufacturing fine grades of chinaware.

MICHIGAN.

The exhibition of products of Michigan at the Centennial Exposition included specimens of native woods, native trees and other plants, to the number of some 1,500 varieties, including grasses, specimens of Lake Superior copper

and iron, and of iron from the Marquette iron district in the upper peninsula of Michigan, and samples of manufactured iron from the Wyandot Rolling Mills, made from the Lake Superior ores. There were also specimens of

SHIELDS.

salt from different districts, and the collection of nearly 500 articles of stone and copper, being Indian relics found in various localities in the State. The collection illustrating the forestry of the State included cross sections of trunks, native trees, and indistinct species; a collection of about 140 blocks and twigs, not over 6 inches in diameter by about 6 inches in length, mostly having the bark on them; a collection of boards 8 by 16 inches and half an inch in thickness, and some specimens not uniform. Also samples of seeds and cones representing about 50 species. Among the rare trees in the State are pawpaw, the Ohio buckeye, the striped maple and mountain maple, the elder, Kentucky coffee-tree, honey-locust, and some others. These are only occasionally found, while the yellow-pine, white and black spruce, cypress and red cedar are scarce, and the chestnut and white birch are confined to special localities. Among the more common trees of the State are the beech and sugar maple, white oak, white ash, black

walnut, white pine, white elm, and shagbark hickory. As to tall trees, some have been cut, furnishing spars 200 feet long. The largest tree known was a black walnut in Allegan County, which was 11 feet in diameter; a cotton-wood 10 feet in diameter was found at Almont. Two sections of a large cotton-wood tree were exhibited in the Centennial: one, near the ground, 10 feet across; the other, 50 feet above it, over 3 feet in diameter. This tree was 140 feet high. A specimen of white-wood or tulip-tree was exhibited, the tree having furnished 5,060 feet of lumber. It is stated that a single walnut tree in Potterville, Mich., sold for $1,000, and a black-walnut tree, 7 feet through, in Brookfield, was sold for nearly $1,200, to be cut up into veneering. Still another, a blister-walnut, very dark in color, which lay for some years exposed to the weather near Grand Rapids, was cut into veneering by the owner for his own use after he had refused $2,000 for it.

It is stated of a certain black-cherry tree at Grand Rapids, that it was shipped to Central America, and from there shipped back to this country as good mahogany. Some curiosities in tree-nuts were exhibited, and an oak having a deer's antler imbedded in it was among the curiosities. Michigan is now the great headquarters for valuable lumber. Two-thirds of the best markets—New York,

BRONZE MODEL OF A POMPEIIAN LAMP.

MAJOLICA VASE.

Philadelphia and Boston—go from this State. Some of it is sent to Germany and Great Britain. Michigan supplies immense quantities of lumber to the prairies southwest. As a matter of comparison, it may be observed that Oregon has 95,274 square miles of land, and Michigan only 56,243; and the former has but 10 species of trees natives of her soil, while Michigan has about 9 species.

The specimens of copper exhibited by Michigan include native metallic copper, crystallized native copper in spar, copper and silver, crystallized copper and quartz, malachite, sandstone, red oxide of copper, etc. The iron exhibits comprised specular slate ore, granular and specular ore, brown iron ore, soft hematite, hard hematite, granular and magnetic ore, manganiferous ore, steel, magnetic, ore and samples of Bessemer pig-iron.

The salt exhibited came from East Saginaw, Saginaw City, Carrolton, Portsmouth, Bay City, Winona, White Rock, etc., and included steam salt, solar salt, brine, pan salt, salt crystal, cattle salt, packer's salt, and dairy salt.

The archæological exhibits included stone, spades, axes, hatchets, pestals, a war hatchet in the school of Young, near Detroit, Indian stone gouches, hammers and Indian flute, Indian totums, pipes, the red, black and gray stone, stone lance-heads and ornaments, stone spear-point and stone gimlet, two perforated Indian skulls, stone arrow-heads and knives, Indian war-clubs, chisels, skinners, Indian spearhead with fossil shell on one side, Indian fish spear head; copper articles comprising awls, files, needles, knives, spades, axes, spears, arrow-heads, and numerous miscellaneous articles from the mounds, including shells, vases, pipes, etc.

The State of Michigan was first settled by the French, missionaries being said to have visited Detroit as early as 1620. Under the French and British dominion the territory was politically associated with Canada, but became a part of the territory of Virginia at the close of the War of Independence, although it was formally occupied by the United States until 1796, becoming a part of the "Northwest Territory," the first seat of whose government was at Chillicothe, in the present State of Ohio. Out of this territory have grown the five States of Ohio, Indiana, Illinois, Michigan and Wisconsin. Michigan was admitted in tothe Union in 1837. The lake shore line of the State is 1,620 miles in length, and there are also within its bounds over 5,000, the smaller lakes having an area of 712,864 acres. The population of the State in 1874 was 1,384,031. Along the eastern shore the descendants of the French colonists are quite numerous. From 1830 to 1840 the influx was chiefly from the Eastern States, New York furnishing the greater proportion. Later, large numbers of Irish entered the State, while from 1840 to 1850 there were numerous emigrants from Holland, the principal centre being the Holland Colony, of which Holland City, in Ottowa County, is the location. There are also a great many Germans in the State, though this class of emigration has been checked during the past four or five years by the depression in finance and business. The only lands held by the State in any considerable quantity are the Primary School, Agricultural College and swamp lands. The minimum price of the school lands is $4 per acre for farm land, 50 per cent. of which is payable at the time of purchase, the balance at the option of the purchaser with interest at 7 per cent., payable annually. As to the agricultural capacity, it is found that the soil of Michigan produces every variety of crops which flourish in the temperate zone. In cereals and fruits, the State is remarkably rich. The total number of farms in Michigan in 1870 was nearly 100,000. In 1873 the yield of wheat was more than 15,000,000 bushels, an increase of more than one-third in ten years. The average per acre was 13 62-100 bushels; 21,000,000 bushels of corn were harvested in the same year, and of all other grains, more than 3,000,000 bushels, or nearly one-third of the grain in 1870.

The wool-clip of Michigan in 1873 was 7,729,071 pounds. Over 15,000,000 pounds of pork were marketed, and the manufacture of butter and cheese, cider and maple-sugar, was reported large and increasing.

There were in Michigan in 1874, 281,394 horses, 3,906 mules, 321,732 milch cows, 401,719 swine over six months old, and 1,651,899 sheep over six months old. The value of fruit and garden vegetables grown in 1873 was something over $3,000,000. The cut lumber in 1874 was in all 3,000,000,000 feet, and the value of that trade in the same year approximated $40,000,000.

With regard to the mining interests, it is an interesting fact that in a work published in Paris, in 1636, the existence of mines of copper on Lake Superior was reported. It was not, however, until 1731 that a copper company was formed in England and mining operations were commenced in the State. The date of the iron discovery is quite uncertain. And indeed, it was as late as 1844 before it was officially established that iron ore existed in the upper peninsula of Michigan in considerable quantities. Copper mining on Lake Superior commenced in 1845, prior to which date copper had been obtained throughout the world in the form of sulphuret, the discoveries of Lake Superior being of native copper, a novelty in copper mining. It is a peculiarity of the Lake Superior native copper that it is in no instance contaminated with alloys of other metal. In 1873 a local paper published a list of 117 copper companies, whose aggregate assessments since the commencement of operations in 1875 amounted to about $17,296,500. The dividends declared for the same time were $11,910,000. Many of the companies are practically out of existence. The dividend paying mines do not exceed 8 or 10 in number. The yield of copper in 1875 was 17,625 tons. Curiosities of copper-finding are frequently mentioned, one being the discovery in 1830 of a mass weighing over 3,000 pounds. This is at present in Washington, having been claimed by the United States. The largest mass of pure copper found weighed 446 tons. Other masses weighing from 50 to 250 tons are of not infrequent occurrence. The evidences of ancient mining by a

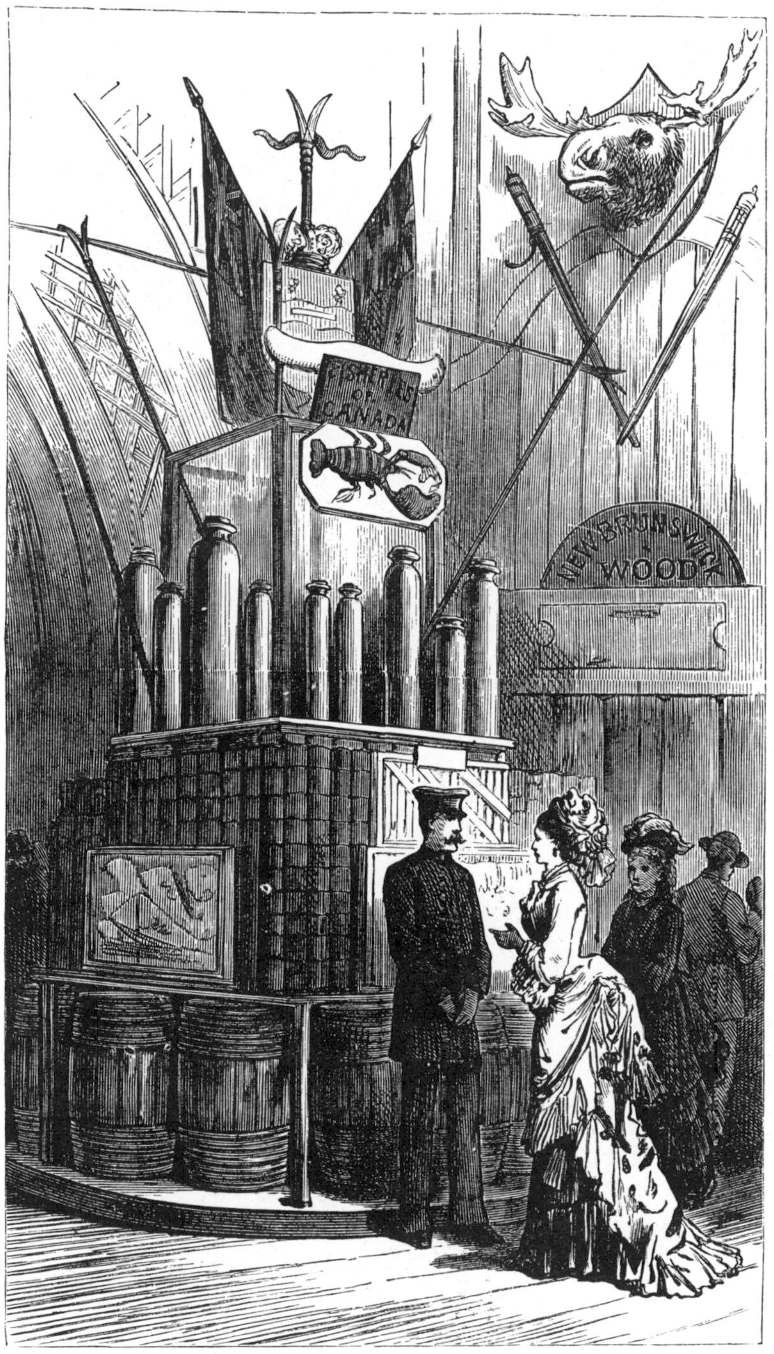

CANADIAN FISHERIES EXHIBIT.

primitive and unknown race are notable of the Lake Superior mines. Stone hammers are found weighing from 10 to even 30 pounds, and samples of mass copper are unearthed having marks of the hammer upon their surface. The practical working of the iron mines commenced about 1845. The iron ores of the Marquette region are mostly in open excavations, the process being closely allied to quarrying. Indeed, no considerable amount of ore has been mined underground in that region. The product of the Marquette mines in 1870 was about 825,000 gross tons of ore, yielding, on the average, 62½ per cent. of pig-iron in the furnace. About one-fifth of the pig-iron produced in this country was that from the Lake Superior ore. The total shipments of ore from 1856 to 1875, amounted to 8,500,000 tons.

The manufacture of salt is a large interest in Michigan, the first successful experiments having been made in 1859, in the Saginaw Valley. The salt product of 1875 was 1,081,865 barrels. In 1874 the amount of the capital invested in this business was $2,600,000 and the value of the product in that year was about $2,225,000. Slate, coal, plaster and building-stone are prominent among the partial development of the mineral resources of the State. The returns from these interests amount to about $700,000 annually.

The fisheries form another important branch of the Michigan interests, in which the investment in 1871 was estimated at about $500,000, the number employed being about 2,000. The catch for 1873 was estimated at 107,710 barrels.

In manufactures there were represented foundries and machine-shops, wagon, carriage and sleigh factories; agricultural implement works, planing and turning mills; sash, door and blind factories; furniture and chair factories; barrel, keg, pail and tub factories; breweries, wool and cotton factories; wooden-ware manufactories; brick and tile manufactories; tanneries, paper-mill, and tobacco and cigar factories, besides flouring mills. The quantity of flour manufactured in 1873 was 2,612,070 barrels, the value being a little over $20,000,000. The value of the other manufactures just named in the same year was about $30,000,000. The entire income, or the entire valuation of all manufactures in the State for 1873 was about $123,000,000. In 1875 the number of miles of railway in Michigan was 3,315.

Wisconsin.

The Legislature of Wisconsin did not determine that the State should be represented at the Centennial Exhibition until near the close of the session in the Spring of 1876, but after that time considerable energy was displayed in collecting specimens, it being particularly desired that the mineral resources of the State should be well represented, a result which it was difficult to obtain, owing to the unfavorable season of the year. The scientific collection exhibited was quite full. It comprised nearly a thousand specimens of rocks, ores, minerals and fossils, mainly from the extensive collection of Dr. J. A. Lapham, of Milwaukee. This cabinet, which Dr. Lapham was many years in collecting, was purchased by the State and donated to the University. That portion of the collection which appertains especially to the geology of the State was permitted by the University authorities to be exhibited in Philadelphia during the Exposition. Other specimens were exhibited by the Wisconsin Academy of Sciences, by the State Geological survey, and from private sources. The archæological exhibit, included with the mineral, consisted of nearly 3,000 porphyritic and copper implements. It was loaned from the State Historical Society of Wisconsin. Among the mineral specimens are granites, jasper, porphyritic greenstone, kaolin, red pipe-stone, fire-bricks, crystals, quartz, magnite, graphite, specular iron ore, native copper, sandstone, galena, millstone, marble, red sandstone, shale, malachite, fossil iron ore, chalcedony, lithographic, limestone, red porphyry, agates, carnelians, peat, clay, bog-iron ore, fossil-wood, portions of mastodon's tooth, and a vertebra of a mastodon, stalactite, besides iron, lead, zinc, and other ores. The archæological display of Wisconsin has been already considered in the description of the Mineral Annex. It is owned by the Wisconsin Historical Association, and was exhibited in two upright cases, each 8 feet long, 5 feet high and 6 inches deep. Two thousand four hundred and twenty stone spears and arrow-points were exhibited; 164 grooved axes, 152 ungrooved axes, chisels, etc.; 20 mauls, pestals, etc.; 52 spherical stones; 27 stone pipes, 2 mortars, 1 galena; 3 spades, or hoes about a foot in length, being spear-shaped; 39 fragments of pottery; a number of miscellaneous specimens of copper implements. There were 58 spear-points with sockets for the insertion of the handle, 10 chisels or wedges, 22 arrow or spear-points, 12 axes, 2 adzes, 17 fish-spears, drills and awls; 14 lance-shape implements, one of which contains a small mass of native silver; 2 pieces of copper showing hammer-marks, and a few miscellaneous articles; most of the implements showing evidence of having been hammered into the present shape. By chemical analysis the copper implements have been found to consist of pure metallic copper.

The agricultural exhibit of Wisconsin in Agricultural Hall comprised specimens of wheat, rye, buckwheat, oats, clover-seed, barley, cucumber-seed, tobacco, corn, peas, beans, grass-seed, grain in the head, and a collection of Wisconsin woods.

Wisconsin was the fifth State formed from the Northwest Territory admitted into the Union, this latter event happening in 1848. The population of the State in 1875 was 1,236,729. The agricultural interest is the leading one in Wisconsin, as in the southern and western portions of the State the whole country, being mostly prairie or oak opening, is susceptible of cultivation. The prairies are not so large as they are in Illinois or some other States, nor so flat. They are generally what are known as rolling prairies, and the soil is very rich and productive, capable of producing almost any crop. In the southern part of the State tobacco is raised in large quantities and of good quality. Hops are also produced in great abundance in this State.

The agricultural statistics of Wisconsin as late as 1876

show the production in wheat to be 1,613,932 bushels; oats, 909,153; corn, 840,882; barley, 187,423; rye, 128,935; hops, 10,932; tobacco, 3,296. The production of grass in the meadow-lands has not been returned; but it is large, as there is more stock-raising and less raising of grain than formerly. The State is becoming largely interested in the dairy business. It is a very fine cattle-raising country, and the stock thrives well. Cheese factories have recently become quite numerous, and Wisconsin cheese ranks high in the market, large quantities being exported. Butter is also made in large quantities, and is of superior quality. It is stated that at the June exhibit of butter and cheese, at the Centennial Exhibition, Wisconsin had the best show. Much attention is given to the raising of fine stock, and there are many blooded horses in the State, and a large number of herds of cattle. Sheep also do remarkably well.

The mineral resources of Wisconsin are extensive in lead, zinc, iron and copper ores; the manipulation of which are a source of great wealth to the people of the State. The lumber interest is among the most important in the country. It is estimated that there are 8,000,000 acres of pine land in the State, besides a large amount of hard wood and timber. Black-walnut, maple, ash, butternut, etc., are found in many places in the northern and central parts of the State. The amount of lumber manufactured in 1875 was 1,097,443,681 feet.

The State buildings of Wisconsin are numerous and important, including the capital at Madison, institutions for the deaf and dumb, blind and insane, State prisons, orphan asylums, industrial schools, etc. all of these institutions having been erected and sustained without the creation of a debt. In manufactures Wisconsin is not yet greatly advanced. The first cotton cloth made in the State was manufactured in 1875. At Beloit, Racine, La Crosse, Fond du Lac and Oshkosh there are manufacturing establishments, chiefly in agricultural implements and household wares. The first railroad in Wisconsin, a direct route from Lake Michigan to the Mississippi River, was built in 1857. The length of Wisconsin railroads is about 4,000 miles.

NEW JERSEY.

The population of New Jersey, in 1875, was 1,019,413. In 1870 the entire lands, improvements, and personal property in the State were assessed at $941,000,000, or $833 to each individual. In 1870 there were in the State, under cultivation, 23,000,000 acres, the value of her products being $43,000,000, averaging $14.30 per acre. In 1874 the school property of the State amounted to $66,000,000.

New Jersey is 160 miles long, and in breadth varies between 70 and 75 miles. Its area is 7,576 square miles. On leaving the Pennsylvania borders, the country is generally barren, as also those parts extending about 100 miles along the sea-coast. In the interior parts, however, and among the mountains, the soil is fertile. It is thoroughly cultivated, and the State abounds with pretty villages and large and thriving towns; and, inasmuch as it forms a great thoroughfare between the Northern and Southern States, it possesses much greater importance than is generally

ascribed to it. Its orchards are equal to those of any other State in the Union, and in peaches it has no rival. Small fruits—cranberries in particular—may be said to be staple articles of production, while in garden produce it is especially rich, furnishing both New York and Philadelphia.

Two of its principal towns—Newark and Paterson—rank high in their manufacturing interests; and the latter town in particular, as being the chief centre of the silk industry of the country, and also for its extensive manufactories of locomotive engines.

The first business of the population of New Jersey appears to have been farming; but the manufacture of iron was begun as early as 1682. Mining on an extensive scale was carried on many years before the Revolution, and a direct trade with the West Indies and Europe was established at several places.

A. B. DANIELL & SON'S (OF LONDON, ENGLAND) POTTERY EXHIBIT IN THE MAIN BUILDING.

This is the thirty-third State in size, the seventeenth in population, and the eighth in wealth. In manufacturing products it is the seventh, in its mining products the eleventh, and in the products of agriculture the twentieth. The price of farm lands in New Jersey has increased from year to year, and at present is said to be higher than in any other State in the Union. The yield of the iron-mines has had a steady increase for many years past, and in 1873 no less than 665,652 tons of iron ore were mined. The aggregate annual value of the clay product, for fire-brick, pottery, and other uses, is estimated at one million dollars, and the manufactured articles from it at an equal sum.

All the larger geological formations of the United States, except that of coal, are found in New Jersey. They occur in parallel belts or zones, usually some miles in breadth, traversing the State in a northeast and southwest direction;

and they are so regular in this respect that a person may travel on a northeast and southwest road from one side of the State to the other and see a single geological formation; while, on the other hand, he may travel from Barnegat, on the Atlantic coast, northwest to Port Jervis, on the Delaware, and he would cross every such formation in the State. The geological structure of New Jersey was largely exhibited at the Centennial in specimens comprising every rock and mineral known to the State. These included gneiss, cyanite, granite, crystalline limestone, sandstone, quartzite, slate, magnesian limestone, fossiliferous limestone, Labrador rock, coralline limestone, fossils, flagging-stone, lignite, trap-rock, all the varieties of clay, kaolin, marl, fossil oyster-shells, infusorial earth, beachpebbles, and beach-sand. Some of the more prominent minerals were garnets, calimine, sapphires, white quartz, asbestos, native copper, malachite, and mica. Specimens of marble and brownstone were among the building-stones, as also lime and cement. A number of fine specimens of magnetic iron-ore were exhibited.

There are 16 blast-furnaces in the State, and the mines now opened number nearly 200, capable of supplying a million tons annually.

The manufacture of iron was begun by Lewis Morris, in Monmouth County, in 1682, and forges for working the magnetic ore of Morris County into bar-iron were built about 1710.

Glass-sand formed an important exhibit of New Jersey, the localities where it is found being nearly all in the southern part of the State. It is reported that one-third of the window-glass and a large part of the hollow-ware manufactured in the United States are made at the several works in this State. Miscellaneous exhibits of New Jersey in this direction included peat, spiegeleisen, spelter, firebrick, flower-pots, glass and glassware, and a very fair display of fossils. A fine collecton of geological, topographical, mine, and drainage-maps was also shown, and a columnar section giving the order of succession in the geological series of New Jersey. This State made a very good display of native woods, this being the first effort made in the direction. The exhibit included white, yellow, pitch and spruce-pine; hemlock; black spruce; white cedar; a number of varieties of oak; chestnut; black walnut; several varieties of elm, ash, and birch; the tulip-tree; poplar; several species of gum, bass-wood, and button-wood; four varieties of hickory; wild-cherry; four varieties of maple; dog-wood; box; ailanthus; locust; sassafras; magnolia; and various fruit-trees.

Locomotives.—Returning to the two more important manufacturing industries of New Jersey—locomotive engines and silk—we may not improperly refer briefly to the history of the locomotive from the time of its invention.

Although steam, in its application to navigation, had been progressing rapidly, and even as early as 1807 attained such a degree of usefulness as to cause it to be looked upon as a fixed fact, yet its application in facilitating intercommunication upon the land had not been developed during a quarter of a century afterward. The first actual model of a steam-engine of which we have a written account was constructed by a Frenchman named Cuquot, who exhibited it in 1763. This inventor in 1769 built an engine to run on common roads, at the expense of the French monarch. This was the first steam-carriage of which we have any written account. It was put in motion by the impulsion of two single-acting cylinders, the piston of which acted alternately on the single front wheels. It traveled about three or four miles an hour, and carried four persons; but, from the smallness of its boiler, it would not continue to work more than twelve or fifteen minutes without stopping to get up steam.

A second engine by the same maker, made several successful trials in the streets of Paris, exciting much interest.

which he completed in the same year, to run upon these roads. This was tried upon a railway in South Wales, when it succeeded in drawing after it several wagons containing 10 tons of iron at the rate of five miles an hour. Here we have the first attempt to adapt the locomotive to service upon a railroad, of which we have any written account. Various other experiments were tried, including one in 1813, to make a machine which was to go upon legs like a horse. This one never got beyond the experimental state, for on one of its trials it blew up, killing and wounding several bystanders; and it was put aside as one of the failures of the time. One engine made by a Mr. Blackett, proved comparatively successful in being capable of drawing eight or nine wagons loaded with coal, although it

and succeeded in drawing eight loaded wagons of thirty tons weight at about four miles an hour on an ascending grade of one in 450 feet, being the most successful engine which had ever been constructed up to this period. Stephenson, however, soon discovered numerous defects in his work, and in 1815 patented a second effort in the same direction. Finally, in 1822, the Hatton colliery road in Durham having been altered into a locomotive railroad, Mr. Stephenson placed upon the road five engines, each of which drew 17 wagons, loaded, averaging 64 tons, at the rate of four miles an hour.

It was not until 1825 that the first passenger car was put upon a railroad. Finally, in 1829, a prize having been offered for a locomotive which should perform certain

SPANISH BRONZES.

It, however, met with an accident one day when running at a speed of about three miles an hour; and being considered dangerous, was locked up in the arsenal. This locomotive is still to be seen in the Museum of the Conservatory of Arts, in Paris.

The first English model of a steam carriage was made in 1784 by William Murdock. It was successful in its working, but was never brought into practical use. In 1802 a patent was taken out in England for a steam-carriage to run on common roads, by one Richard Trevithick, a foreman in a Cornish tin mine. This was the first successful high-pressure engine constructed on the principle of moving a piston by the elasticity of steam against the pressure of the atmosphere, and without a vacuum.

By this time tramroads or railways were in general use in England, and in 1804 Trevithick commenced a machine,

took nearly six hours to go five miles. This was soon abandoned.

All of this experimental work led up to the success of George Stephenson, who was born June 9th, 1781, in the colliery village of Wylam, on the River Tyne. Stephenson commenced his active life by herding cows at two pence per day, being next promoted to work in the mines in the capacity of a picker, and so on until he was placed in charge of the pumping-machine, in which position he made himself acquainted with the nature of the engine in his charge. He displayed considerable original mechanical talent, and as he was enthusiastic in studying as well as working, he soon became recognized as a capable engineer.

When Stephenson was about 26 years of age he set about the construction of a locomotive engine. His first attempt was completed in 1814. It was called "Blucher,"

specified duties, Mr. Stephenson constructed his engine, the "Rocket," which competed with three others by different makers, and which, having performed all the conditions, received the prize.

The first railroad built in the United States was three miles in length, extending from the granite quarries of Quincy, Mass., to the Neponset River. In 1828 the Delaware and Hudson Canal Company constructed a railroad from their coal mines to Honesdale, and the Baltimore and Ohio Railroad and the South Carolina Railroad were commenced in the same year. The competitive trial in England in which the "Rocket" was successful had been witnessed by certain American engineers who went thither expressly for this purpose. One of these was Horatio Allen, Esq., who purchased for the Delaware and Hudson Canal and Railroad Company three locomotives. The first

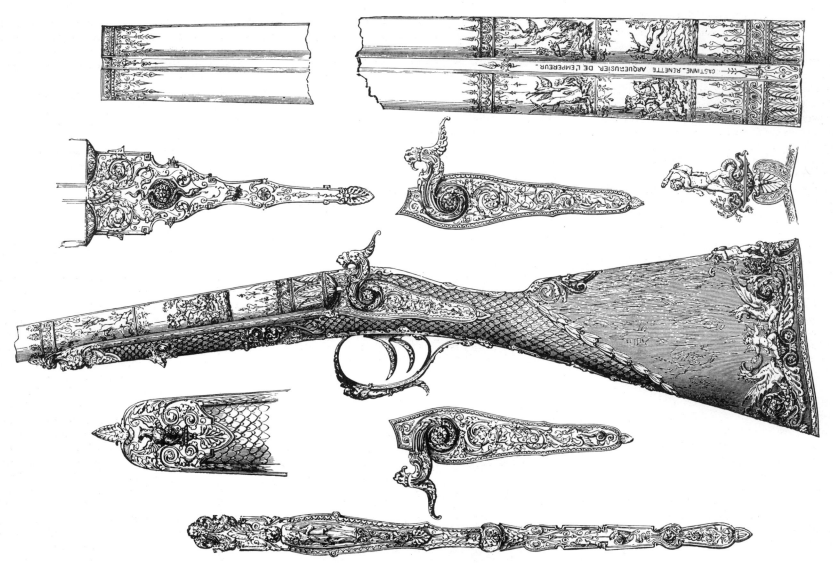

ELEGANT FOWLING-PIECE AT THE FRENCH EXHIBIT.

of these arrived in New York City at the foot of Beach Street, on the ship *John Jay*, about the middle of May, 1829. It was called the "Stourbridge Lion." Finally, on the 8th day of August, 1829, this locomotive, the "Stourbridge Lion," made its initial trial trip, being the first locomotive ever placed upon a road on the American Continent.

The first locomotive built, adapted to a curved road, was constructed by Mr. Peter Cooper, of New York, founder of the Cooper Institute of that city. This was constructed at the St. Clair Works, near Baltimore, and was run upon the Baltimore and Ohio Railroad, in the Summer of 1829. The Baltimore and Ohio Railroad was the pioneer railroad of any extent built with reference to trade and commerce in America. Previous to 1826 no railroad, even in England, had been constructed for the convenience of passengers or merchandise to be carried between two distant points, but solely for local purposes, such as conveyance of coal or ores from mines to points of shipment. Mr. Cooper's engine, although, as he terms it, "a very small and insignificant affair," made its trial trip of 13 miles, over an average ascending grade of 18 feet to the mile, in 1 hour and 12 minutes, and the return trip in 57 minutes. In this engine the boiler was tubular and upright in position, not more than 20 inches in diameter, and perhaps from 5 to 6 feet high. There was a single cylinder, $3\frac{1}{4}$ inches in diameter, $14\frac{1}{4}$ inches stroke, connected with its piston-rod, so as to take hold of the stroke by direct action. The fuel was anthracite coal. This was the original American locomotive.

The first locomotives ever ordered and made in the United States for regular railroad traffic were designed and built by Horatio Allen, at the West Point Foundry, in New York. In 1831 the directors of the Baltimore and Ohio Railroad offered a premium of $4,000 for the best American locomotive. This offer brought out many competitors, and introduced to notice several locomotive constructors, among these being Colonel Stephen H. Long and the late Mathias W. Baldwin, who in 1831 received an order from the Germantown Railroad Company for the construction of a locomotive engine to run on their road. Only one mechanic in America had yet succeeded in erecting a locomotive which could draw more than its own weight on a horizontal track, and the success of Mr. Baldwin, who six months after receiving the order placed the "Ironsides" on the road, was most creditable. Before the close of 1834 he had completed 5 engines. In 1835, 14 were built; in 1836, 40; in 1837, 45. Finally, the Baldwin Locomotive Works reached the distinction of being the most extensive locomotive establishment in the world, and from the capacity of one small engine, attained that of one per day, or over 300 of the most powerful and complete railroad locomotives in a year. The Baldwin Works are in Philadelphia; but the Rogers Locomotive Works, and others, in Paterson, N. J., entitle that town and State to consideration in this connection.

The iron industry in Paterson commenced as early as 1809, when a small factory was built in that town, where machinery was made and where the wool brought in by the country-people in the vicinity was carded. The locomotive manufacture was commenced here in 1837, and the first engine built in Paterson, the "Sandusky City," for the Mad River and Lake Erie Railroad, was finished in October, 1837, at the works of Rogers, Ketcham & Grosvenor. This firm continued in existence until 1856, when, on the death of the senior partner, a company was formed under the name of the Rogers Locomotive and Machine Works. This company continued to build cotton-machinery as well as locomotives until 1867, when they discontinued the former department of their manufacture, and have ever since devoted their entire works to the building of locomotives. In an article published in 1839 the locomotive works of this establishment was described as a main building 200 feet long and 3 stories high, and another of equal length, containing nearly 50 forges, being under the direction of this company. In the year 1838 seven engines were turned out, after which the production was gradually increased each year until 1854, in which year 103 were built. Its present capacity for building locomotives is equal to one a day.

In 1873 the locomotive shops of Paterson were turning out 40 engines per month, 480 in a year. The rolling-mill made and shipped 6,000 tons of merchants' iron and beams in a year, and 720 tons of rivets. The Steam Fire-Engine Company made from 8 to 12 engines a year. All the shops of Paterson employed about 5,300 hands, and paid out for labor more than $63,000 per week. In 1875 there were in Paterson 23 establishments engaged in the iron industry, making locomotives, stationary engines, steam fire-engines, cotton, silk, flax, hemp, jute, and other machinery, merchants' iron, angle iron, beams, files, bolts, rivets, spikes and switches.

The condition of the cotton industry in Paterson, according to the latest figures, is as follows: Production of cotton yarn, 300,000 pounds per year; cotton converted into yarn, 750 bales per year; hands employed in spinning yarn, 60. In the production of musquito-netting, buckram and crown lining alone, there are employed over 400 hands, using 400 looms and 26,000 spindles. The three shirt factories of the town produce 800 dozen shirts per week. The first cotton factory was finished in 1794, and was 90 feet long, 40 feet wide, and 4 stories high.

The water-power system of Paterson is quite remarkable. The Falls of the Passaic have an extraordinary water-shed of over 800 square miles. The minimum supply in the dry season is 50 square feet. The height of the fall allows three race-ways, the water being used successively that number of times. The great bulk of the water-power is the property of the Society for Establishing Useful Manufactures, one of the earliest incorporated manufacturing firms in the country, possessing a charter dated 1791. The total water supply belonging to this company equals about 2,108 horse-power, 1,700 being now in use.

MINNESOTA.

Minnesota, one of the Northwest States of the American Union, was the 19th admitted under the Federal Constitution. Its area is 52,005,760 acres. Lying nearly at the centre of the continent, Minnesota occupies the summit of the interior plain of North America formed by the basins of the Mississippi, St. Lawrence, and the rivers flowing into Lake Winnebago, and incloses the head-waters of the three great rivers of the continent. With the exception of a few hills, in no case higher than 1,700 feet above the level of the sea, or 600 feet above the average elevation of the country, the surface is generally an undulating plain, having an average elevation of only a few feet above the sea, and presenting a succession of small rolling prairies or table-lands, all dotted with timber. The Winters are cold, but clear and dry, and the fall of snow is light. The Summers are warm, with breezy nights, during which occur usually rains. The general salubrity of the climate recommends it to invalids. The country is well timbered with pine, birch, maple, ash and elm. A large forest of hardwood, covering an area of about 4,000 square miles, extends over the central portion of the State, west of the Mississippi.

Until the year 1845 Minnesota was occupied by the Chippewas and Sioux, the only representatives of civilization within the territory being the trappers and traders, the lumbermen on the St. Croix, and a few missionaries. The population of Minnesota in 1870 was 440,067, of which 738 were blacks and mulattoes, 1,528 Indians and half-breeds, natives 279,941, and foreign 160,126, of whom

MOORISH PADLOCK.

two-thirds were Germans and Scandinavians. The quantity of land under tillage in 1850 was 1,900 acres. Twenty years later it was 1,863,316 acres. The agricultural existence, however, of Minnesota may be considered to have commenced in 1859, that being the first year in which a surplus was produced over home consumption. The total number of farms in 1870 was 46,256. As to crops, there were 1,006,007 acres in wheat, producing over 17,000,000 bushels; 278,407 acres in oats, with a product of 10,500,000 bushels; 147,587 acres in corn, with a product of 4,500,000 bushels. The hay product of 1869 was 601,312 tons. There were 316,552 apple-trees growing. Of tobacco, about 12,000 pounds were produced, and the value of garden products was estimated at $312,000. The value of agricultural products in their entirety in 1869 was about $30,000,000. The returns of live-stock for 1870 show horses, 91,556; mules and asses, 2,381; milch cows, 120,271; working oxen, 42,643; other cattle, 144,609; sheep, 129,525; swine, 137,136. The entire estimated value of live-stock was $18,000,000.

The city of St. Paul, Minnesota, was first settled in the Summer of 1838 by a Canadian *voyageur* named Pierre Parrant, the site having been pitched upon by this adventurer as a good spot to sell whisky to the inhabitants of the fort near by without coming within reach of the rules in force against this traffic. In 1875 the population of the city was 33,000, its taxable property assessed at $27,000,000, the city being handsomely laid out with solid business blocks, public buildings and palatial mansions, having a well-arranged system of sewerage, important river commerce, eight railroads, with nearly 100 trains arriving and departing daily, manufacturers' warehouses, banking-houses, churches, hotels, public schools, charitable institutions, libraries—all this is presented as the accomplishment of thirty years of history in a north-west inland State in the energetic and prolific American Continent.

Tennessee.

The remarkably fine mineral exhibit made by Tennessee renders apology unnecessary for considering to some extent the character and resources of that State.

The area of Tennessee is about 27,000,000 acres, and it possesses the peculiarity of touching eight States on its borders—a greater number than is touched by the borders of any other State in the Union except Missouri. The Mississippi washes its western border, and the Tennessee and Cumberland, sweeping through the most valuable portions of the State, furnish a cheap mode of transportation for its products.

The political divisions of the State are three: East Tennessee, comprising all the territory from the North Carolina line to about the centre of the Cumberland table-land; Middle Tennessee, from the dividing line of the Cumberland table-land to the Tennessee River; and West Tennessee, from the Tennessee River to the Mississippi. In by far the larger portion of the State the climate is salubrious, the malarious districts being very limited. The mean temperature of the year averages between 57 and 59 degrees Fahrenheit. The average length of the growing season in Middle Tennessee is 189 days. Every variety of soil may be found within the limits of the State. Even the tops of the mountains afford fine pasture-ground for stock-herders, and buckwheat yields with remarkable fecundity. The acreage in timber is 13,268,789, only three States in the Union having more wooded land. Here nearly every variety of timber grows which is found in the United States—oak, ash, beech, birch, red-cedar, chestnut, cotton-wood, cypress, fir, gum, hickory, locust, sugar-maple, red-mulberry, poplar, sassafras, sycamore, and black-walnut growing in different sections. As a corn-growing State Tennessee ranks sixth in the Union. In 1840 it stood first. Its average annual production of this cereal is about 50,000,000 bushels. About one million acres are sown in wheat, and yield between five and ten million bushels. The product of oats is about 5,000,000 bushels. Tennessee stands third as a tobacco-growing State, Kentucky being first and Virginia second. The annual product of this staple varies between twenty and twenty-five million pounds, or between thirteen and twenty-two thousand hogsheads. It is said that in Tennessee, by careful management, a skillful tobacco-raiser can often realize from $150 to $200 per acre. Much of the yield is exported to French and Spanish markets, and some of it to Italy and Germany.

Cotton is one of the great staple products of Tennessee, the number of acres devoted to it in 1873 being 613,267, the best cotton being grown in the southern half of West Tennessee, where the staple is long and heavy, and the average yields of the best lands from 1,000 to 1,200 pounds of seed-cotton per acre. It is said that at the London Exposition in 1851 the cotton raised by Colonel John Pope, of the County of Shelby, received the medal for the best cotton known to the world. The entire yield of the State was, in 1870, 181,142 bales.

About 90,000 acres of land in Tennessee are used for the raising of hay, yielding about 110,000 tons, the crop being valued at nearly $2,000,000. Rye is not a staple crop, and the average devoted to barley is only 5,000 acres. The annual yield of sweet potatoes is 1,200,000 bushels, and that of Irish potatoes is only about the same quantity, averaging about one bushel to each inhabitant. Peanuts are an important product of the State, the quantity produced reaching, in 1872, 680,000 bushels. There are also grown in particular localities hemp, broom-corn, flax, and garden vegetables in abundance. Fruits of all kinds also grow well. Considerable enterprise is being displayed in the raising of grapes in vineyards of all sizes, from one to forty acres, which are being planted in every division of the State.

Tennessee ranks ninth in population in the States, the number of her inhabitants being 1,258,520, by the last census. She also ranks ninth in point of the value of her live-stock, which is estimated at $55,000,000.

ARMS AND IMPLEMENTS FROM SOUTH SEA ISLANDS.

The Appalachian coal-field crosses Tennessee, ending near Tuscaloosa, in Alabama. Of its 80,000 square miles of area, something over 5,000 lie in Tennessee. The report of the monthly product of coal in the various mines in operation in Tennessee in July, 1874, showed a return of about 821,000 bushels, or 10,000,000 bushels annually. The iron product of Tennessee in 1875 amounted to 28,311 tons. The iron lies in four distinct veins, covering, in whole or in part, 44 counties. Copper is found in Polk County, in an elevated mountain basin 2,500 feet above the level of the sea, and covers about 40 square miles. This region is mined by two companies, and the entire yield in 1872 was valued at $500,000.

The marble of Tennessee has gained, by its beautifully variegated appearance and fine polishing qualities, a high fame throughout the United States. Several varieties are found in the State, including black, gray, fawn-colored, conglomerate, and breccia. On Shoal Creek, in Lawrence County, 18 miles south of Lawrenceburg, and extending 15 miles each way, is a bed, 40 feet in thickness, of fine colored marble with fleecy clouds of green. A short distance below Manchester there is a bluish vein which is greatly admired. In Rutherford County a bed occurs of pale-yellowish color, with serpentine veins of red and dots of black. This has not been worked, and specimens have only been polished for paper-weights and other small articles.

Roofing-slates, mill-stones, gray hydraulic-rock, potter's-clay, and fire-clay are found in various parts of the State; lead, zinc, and black oxide of manganese are also frequently met with. Petroleum has been found at various points in the State, but the business of boring has not proven profitable.

Finally, Tennessee challenges comparison with any other portion of the United States in the number, variety, excellence, and medicinal value of its mineral waters. Many of these springs have a high reputation for their curative properties. Especially in East Tennessee and on the Cumberland table-land watering-places have been established, which are favorite Summer resorts.

PHILADELPHIA IN THE OLDEN TIME.

To THOSE who visited the Centennial, and who scarcely took the opportunity to see something of the Quaker City itself, a few words upon the appearance of that city one hundred years ago will not be without interest. At that time Market Street, the central avenue of the city, was called High Street. It obtained its change of name on the erection of eight or ten squares of market-houses directly in the centre of the open street. The streets running parallel with Market, and north of it, were then named Mulberry, Sassafras, and Vine; those south of it were Chestnut, Walnut, Spruce, Pine, and Cedar. These eight squares of blocks comprised the northern and southern limits of the city one hundred years ago. Now fifty streets are laid out and built upon north of Market Street, and almost an equal number south of it, the most of these being lined with substantial brick edifices from the Delaware to the Schuylkill. In the course of time Mulberry Street became Arch Street, and Sassafras Race Street—the latter name being given on account of the horse-races contantly taking place upon the street. For many years the racing was on the street line from below Fourth to Broad; and as early as 1726 the Grand Jury made a presentment to the effect "that, since the city has become so very populous, the usual custom of horse-racing at fairs in Sassafras Street is very dangerous to life; also, it is an evil that they who erect the booths, etc., in that street, at the fairs, do sell all sorts of liquors, etc." This custom of racing was continued until the commencement of the Revolutionary War. Cock-fighting was also exceedingly popular with all classes; and it is related that some of the leading citizens were in the habit of taking their fighting-cocks under their arms, and walking out to enjoy themselves an hour or so in witnessing the contest between their game chickens. Bull-baiting with dogs was also a fashionable amusement in the early days of the Quaker City.

Liberty Bell.

No symbol has, perhaps, ever become so popular anywhere as has the Liberty Bell, in the numerous forms in which it was sold and worn during the Centennial year. Some account of this national object of veneration will not be out of place here.

In 1752 the bell was imported for Philadelphia, and hung up in the steeple of the State House in that year. On the first trial-ringing after its arrival it cracked, and, under the direction of Isaac Morris, of Philadelphia, it was recast in the following year. This is the bell upon which is the inscription, "Proclaim Liberty throughout the Land, and unto all the Inhabitants thereof."

Its proclamation of liberty happened in this wise: On the 2d of July, 1776, the representatives of the thirteen rebellious colonies were assembled in the State House, discussing the question of the Declaration of Independence. It had been previously arranged that, in the event of an affirmative decision of this question, the bell in the steeple should be made to ring out the tidings; and for this the old bell-man was at his post, while a large and anxious crowd was gathered in the street awaiting the deliberation of the assemblage. Independence Square and the streets adjoining were densely packed with men with careworn and anxious faces, who remained for hours with their faces lifted toward the bell, the while they spoke in whispers, and wondered if their representatives would possess the courage to declare for liberty and independence. At length the door of the chamber opened, and John Nixon stepped to the threshold, having the Declaration of Independence in his hand. At the same moment a messenger hurried up the stairs to the belfry, and as Nixon proceeded to read the first sentence of the immortal document, the tones of the bell burst upon the silent and waiting city. A cheer rose from the multitude assembled, cannon pealed, and drums beat in a general chorus; and for two hours the sound of Liberty Bell was heard in the air, proclaiming freedom to the nation.

This bell was afterward taken down and replaced by a new one. Meanwhile the original has been seen by hundreds of thousands during the Centennial year, in its place in the room of the State House where the Declaration of Independence was written and signed.

STAR-SPANGLED BANNER.

OUR beautiful and patriotic national song was composed by Francis S. Key, Esq., a prominent citizen of Maryland, in 1814, under the following circumstances:

The gentleman had left Baltimore with a flag of truce

BORDER OF SPANISH LACE SHAWL.

for the purpose of getting released from the British fleet a friend who had been captured at Marlboro'. He went as far as Patuxent, and was not allowed to return. He was brought up the bay to the mouth of the Patapsco, and compelled to witness the bombardment of Fort McHenry, which the admiral had boasted he would carry in a few hours. During the day, with an anxiety better felt than described, he watched the flag of the fort until the darkness prevented him from seeing it. During the night he watched the bombshells, and at early dawn his eye was greeted again by the proudly floating flag of his country.

The Hon. Francis S. Key died in 1846. Besides the "Star-Spangled Banner," he also wrote several fugitive pieces of considerable merit.

AMERICAN SOCIETY FOR THE PREVENTION OF CRUELTY TO ANIMALS.

PROBABLY the first exhibition of this character ever made was the one in the Main Building, at the eastern end and a little south of the nave, and illustrative of the work which Mr. Henry Bergh, of New York, has accomplished in the way of relieving society of one of the worst features of cruelty which infest it. This exhibit was much more comprehensive than would be anticipated, and covered, in fact, the methods and implements by means of which cruelty to animals is accomplished, as well as illustrating the subject through the medium of stuffed specimens showing the effects of such cruelty. Thus, we had here appropriate specimens of game-cocks after the fight, as well as bulldogs taken from a pit at the close of battle. The cruelty of New York hack and car drivers was shown by the exhibition of the bones taken from the forelegs of a horse which was compelled to walk with these bones broken. Part of a horse's tongue was preserved, which was pulled out of the mouth of the animal by the inhuman driver, who had tied a cord about it for this purpose. The effects of improper shoeing in horses were shown by suitable representations of the nails as thus applied; and, finally, a large collection of instruments used to accelerate the speed or animate the spirits of weak or overworked animals was exhibited, including hammers, car-hooks, pick and hatchet-handles, boards, whips and sticks—the interesting feature of these articles being found in the fact that they were actually taken from parties whose names were appended to cards attached to them, and who used them for the purposes signified.

This exhibition was instructive and important in its representation of this most obnoxious feature of manners and

customs; and it is to be hoped will have done good service in inculcating the proper spirit of kindness toward our domestic animals and fowls.

OUR ILLUSTRATIONS.

EXHIBIT OF COATS'S COTTON.

NEAR the central entrance of Machinery Hall was exhibited the novel machinery used in the manufacture of

SPANISH FAN.

the cotton of Messrs. J. & P. Coats, of Paisley, Scotland. This machinery showed the entire manufacture from the time the thread leaves the bleachery. After this process, it is brought in the form of hanks to swifts, on which it is placed in skeins, and from these run off, or spooled, on large bobbins preparatory to winding. These large bobbins are placed on the winding-machine, and the thread on them

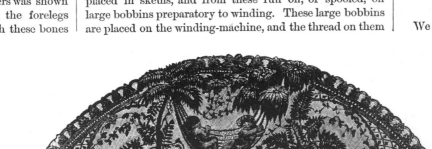

SPANISH FAN.

is wound off in lengths of 200 yards upon the small spools so familiar to all seamstresses.

This winding-machine, which is the invention of Mr. Hezekiah Conant, was one of the most interesting pieces of mechanism in Machinery Hall. It is self-adjusting, stopping when the spool is full, and as every number of thread has a different-sized spool, and every size of spool is gauged to hold just 200 yards of thread, the winder does not stop until the 200 yards are placed on the spool, unless the thread breaks, in which case the machine is immediately stopped by a falling lever, which is supported by the thread when the latter is unbroken. The machine is started again by the party

who runs it merely catching the end of the thread between the spool and spindle, passing it under the guide and starting the machine at exactly the place where it stopped, the centripetal force carrying the thread on the spool, while the guide lays it in even layers and puts the polish on the thread. The advantages of this binder are: First, that it places the thread evenly on the spool, and within the exact limits of the 200 yards; second, it breaks all knots at the point of contact between the guide and spool, and when the thread breaks no knot is tied in finishing the 200 yards on that spool, so that when running on sewing-machines, needles will not be bent or broken by the appearance of the knots; third, thread which has been rendered tender from chemical causes will not run on this machine, the tension being as strong as that on the sewing-machine, this resulting in the fact that any thread which runs smoothly on one of these winders is certain to run well on all sewing-machines. After winding, the thread undergoes careful inspection, imperfect spools being immediately rejected. The next process after inspection is ticketing the spools. Tickets being printed in sheets, are cut therefrom, and while held on the end of a lever are pasted and placed on the end of the spool, a different one on each end, and exactly in the centre.

Messrs. J. & P. Coats, who had already taken prizes at the exhibitions of London in 1862, Paris, 1867, and Vienna, 1873, crowned their successes by receiving a medal and diploma from the Centennial Commission, with commendation in the Judges' report for "superior strength and excellent quality in spool cotton."

WEBER'S PIANOFORTE EXHIBIT.

We have heretofore alluded, in our description of the Main Building, to the exhibit of pianofortes by 40 different exhibitors from the United States. Prominent among these was Mr. Albert Weber, of New York, whose department we illustrate. The Weber exhibit was more extensive than that of any other pianoforte manufacturer who contributed. It consisted of one magnificently inlaid concert grand, specially manufactured for the Centennial; one extra Centennial concert grand, rosewood; one regular concert grand, rosewood; one parlor grand, rosewood; one square grand piano, rosewood; one small upright, rosewood; one fancy case, black, gold-inlaid upright piano; one fancy case, rosewood, and gold-inlaid upright piano. The best popular contests of the pianos being indubitably furnished in the opportunity of hearing them—Mr. Weber got the start of his competitors at the outset by beginning a series of daily concerts immediately after the Exhibition opened, given by Mr. John W. Pattison, of New York, an artist well known to concert-goers throughout the country, and whose ability is universally confessed. Every day, at one o'clock, a crowd gathered around the Weber inclosure, and listened with delight until Mr. Pattison had finished his programme of four or five pieces, often good-naturedly supplemented by one or two others, at the request of persons in the audience. These recitals were kept up until the close of the Exhibition, and were a source of gratification to the thousands of visitors. It was certainly a severe test for a piano to be played in the midst of the noise caused by the movement of the thousands of people in the monster Main Building; and that the Weber "extra grand" displayed the power of making itself heard distinctly at a considerable distance, without harshness or stridency of tone, was certainly greatly to its credit. The tone of all of Mr. Weber's instruments is characterized by brilliancy of power. His upright pianos possessed many of the good qualities of the French and German uprights, with a more powerful tone. It is stated that the only reason for retaining so long the cumbersome square piano in this country after it had long been abandoned in Europe has been that American manufacturers either would not or could not make good and durable uprights. In the case of the Weber upright this objection has been utterly done away with. Its tone is in all respects as good as that in the square pianos. Meanwhile, his "grand" pianos have been warmly praised by such distinguished musicians as Parepa-Rosa, Nilsson, Lucca, De Murska, Wehli, Kellogg, Strauss, and many others.

As to the cases of these pianos, those of two uprights and one of the "grands" shown by Mr. Weber displayed admirable taste and skill in the inlaying of various woods upon ebony or walnut backgrounds, and were a surprise to many visitors, who were not prepared to find outside of the Italian and French sections such artistic work in this line. In a private interview one of the judges said: "Weber's pianos were unquestionably the best pianos on exhibition. Weber's grand piano was the most wonderful piano I ever touched or heard." The method of judgment as to the tone, quality, equality, and touch was by a range of figures, the highest being six, the lowest one. Each judge made his figures on these points, and these figures were the fundamental basis of all the awards. Thus the highest possible figure, adding up the numbers of each judge on each of the points, would be 24; or, if all the judges agreed, the highest possible number for any instrument would be 96, Weber's reaching 95.

THE BULLOCK PRINTING-PRESS COMPANY'S EXHIBIT.— SELF-FEED ROTARY PERFECTING PRINTING-PRESS.

The history of printing in America commences with the first printing-press in the American Colonies being set up at Cambridge, Mass., in 1639. It was procured, by subscription, from Amsterdam, and was given to the college, with a font of type of 49 pounds. On this press was printed, in 1683, the first edition of "Elliot's Indian Bible," which was wholly set up by an Indian, was three years going through the press, and was the first Bible printed in America. William Bradford established a press in Philadelphia in 1686, and in New York in 1692. One was in existence in Charleston, S. C., in 1730. Savannah, Ga., had one in 1762; Tennessee and Ohio in 1793; and the first printing west of the Mississippi was done at St. Louis, in 1808. But all of these presses were constructed on the old principle of the application of the screw, the first important modification of which was that devised by Earl Stanhope, which combined the screw with the bent lever, having a carriage for the form, which could be run in under the point of pressure and readily withdrawn. In 1790 Mr. William Nicholson, of England, took out a patent for a cylinder machine, which had also an ink

apparatus. This press was never brought into use, but furnished the suggestion for after constructors. The first cylinder press run by steam was built for the London *Times*, by Frederick König, of Saxony, and the number for November 28th, 1814, was worked by it at the rate of 1,100 impressions per hour. In 1827 Messrs. Applegath & Cowper constructed a press with four impression cylinders, the type being placed on the surface of the cylinder for the first time. The London *Times* was the first newspaper to adopt this improvement, and this was the beginning of all cylinder presses.

The web perfecting-press owes its origin to Sir Rowland Hill, chiefly famous for his advocacy of penny-postage in Great Britain, who obtained letters-patent in 1835 for a press of this character—that is, one capable of printing a roll of paper on both sides, and cutting and piling the

sheets. Difficulties, however, occurred in the management of this, due partly to inability to dispose of the printed sheets with sufficient rapidity; and it was not until 1853 that the successful web perfecting-presses became established, mainly through the invention of Victor Beaumont, of New York, who patented the serrated cutting blade, set lengthwise in one of the pair of cutting cylinders, having elastic surfaces inserted to hold the paper on each side of the cutting blade when the sheet is cut from the web. Finally a French inventor, about 1850, devised the process of flexible *papier-maché* matrices, rendering it practicable to cast the type-plates to fit the cylinders.

The invention of the press, to the illustration of which in the HISTORICAL REGISTER we would direct the attention of our readers, may be said to have completely revolutionized the printing art. In the year 1862 the printing-press had reached that stage when, by means of the important invention of Richard M. Hoe, of New York, a printed sheet could be laid down at each vibration of the machine. At this time, however, presses only printed one side of the sheet at a time, and had to be fed with the sheet by a separate attendant to each cylinder. The invention by William Bullock of his Self-feed Rotary Perfecting or Web Printing-press was the final step in the progress of construction, so far as these machines were concerned, beyond which no improvement has as yet been devised.

William Bullock was born in Greene County, N. Y., in 1813. At an early age he displayed a talent for mechanical construction. His understanding of the capacity of mechanism seems to have amounted to veritable genius—so much so that no machinery could come under his observation without an effort on his part—generally successful—to improve it. The consequence has been that he is the author of many inventions in various branches of mechanical construction other than that of the printing-press; and, indeed, his first attempt in this direction was the invention of an automatic sheet-feeder, which could be applied to the ordinary hand process. This was about fifteen years ago, and that improvement still sustains its position. At one time he was the editor and publisher of a weekly paper at Catskill, N. Y.; and, being forced to supply a printing-press for his establishment without having the necessary means to purchase one, he was able within a week, with the aid of local mechanics, to produce such a press as he needed, and issued his paper on the proper day of publication. This was his first press, and it was made entirely of wood, and mostly by his own hands—the bed, however, being of stone, and the impression being made by a wooden roller. Even in this press he developed a novel and original idea. It was a flat-bed press, having a series of impression cylinders, connected by an endless chain, by means of which they traversed over the form and around it continuously. It is an incident in the history of this, which he termed the Chain-running Press, that it was employed by Mr. Frank Leslie to print the edition of his *Illustrated Newspaper* which contained the first account of the fight between Heenan and Sayers, with the illustrations.

About the year 1860 Mr. Bullock commenced to develop

THE IRON TROPHY IN THE NORWEGIAN COURT.

the idea of the Rotary Self-feed or Web Perfecting-press, his object being to contrive a machine which should be fed from rolls of paper at both ends of the press, with such an arrangement of mechanism as should permit the sheets of paper to pass each other without interference while both were being printed, each end making its own delivery. This conception advanced, however, only to the construction of a large working model, which is still in existence, and the idea was abandoned for a form more simple and practical, and which resulted in the construction of a machine for the Cincinnati *Times*, about the year 1861, which was a success so far as its operation was concerned. A difficulty, however, occurred in the construction of this and several succeeding machines which were improvements upon it, in the fact that they lacked strength and solidity. Mr. Bullock now went to New York, and for a few years continued his efforts in the same direction, having always in view his original design, only a portion of which he had thus far succeeded in perfecting. By 1865, however, he had produced a press which answered to his original intention; and, having formed a company for its manufacture, he exhibited a completed machine in Philadelphia in 1867, built by him for a newspaper in that city. During its exhibition Mr. Bullock unfortunately met with an accident, receiving a serious injury, from the effects of which he died on the 15th of April, in the same year, in the 55th year of his age.

The death of the inventor did not, however, interfere with the successful prosecution of his purpose. The manufacture of his invention was fortunately in the hands of a company of gentlemen possessing energy, integrity, and the necessary means for advancing its interests. One by one the leading newspapers of the United States adopted the Bullock Press, and the New York *Herald*, on the 10th of February, 1875, comparing this machine with that which they had used previous to its adoption, stated that, "While their previous press had excited wonder and admiration from the rapidity and accuracy with which it turned out printed sheets by the hour, the performance of even so modern an invention is surpassed by that of the Improved Bullock Self-feeding Press, which performs double the work. It prints a quadruple sheet of the *Herald* at one impression, and needs the attendance of three men only." The preceding one had required fifteen men to work it effectively. The *Herald* remarked, further: "The Bullock Press is fed from a wide and endless roll, the sheet is printed on both sides, and is deposited on the receiver a perfect *Herald*. Every portion of the machinery is under the eye of the pressman, who can easily detect and correct any irregularity, and the delivery of the printed sheets is perfected with a precision not attained in any other press." With regard to its application to the necessities of the *Herald*, it may be remarked that each roll of paper used in that office is upward of three miles long, and on an average 30 of these rolls are used for each edition of the paper. The average production of the Bullock machine is 30,000 per hour, the machine printing and cutting two copies for each delivery on the receiving-tables. The New York *Sun*, which adopted the Bullock Press in substitution for the one previously used, commended it by saying: "When our seven Bullock Presses are working, we can turn off, without extravagant assertion, 210,000 copies an hour."

More than fifty of these presses are now in use in the newspaper offices of the principal cities of the United States. The papers employing them include the New York *Herald*, *Sun*, and German Press Association; Brooklyn *Argus*; Boston *Herald*; Philadelphia *German Demokrat* and *Press*; Chicago *Times* and *Tribune*; Indianapolis *Journal*; Cincinnati *Enquirer*; San Francisco *Post*; Baltimore *News*; Louisville *Courier-Journal*; Chicago *Inter-Ocean*; and the Government Printing Office at Washington. The New York *Herald* and *Sun* have each in use eight of the Bullock machines.

The Bullock Press, being composed entirely of cylinders, and having no reciprocating motion, is capable of being run at the highest possible speed consistent with safety. In feeding it, rolls of paper containing thousands of sheets are employed—these resting either on the press or being placed so near to it as to be drawn by slight tension into it, when the paper, passing between the feeder and the impression cylinders, is printed on one side. Immediately thereafter the unprinted side is met and printed by

another pair of similar cylinders—which operation completes the printing of the entire sheet, which is then separated by cutting-cylinders into two complete copies of the newspaper, and thus delivered on the receiving-table or fly-board. This press is only 12 feet long by 5½ high, occupying about one-quarter of the space required by its immediate predecessor. It does double the work which that one did; and, by reducing the staff of workmen which that required from 15 to 3, it effects an enormous saving of expense. Another important feature in the absolute value of this press is, that it is the simplest of all printing machines, is without difficulty kept in good working order, and, considering the severe strain upon it, is remarkably durable. Some of them in use twelve years are still in active operation and working efficiently.

The Bullock Press was the forerunner of its class, and the model which all others that have since appeared have followed, without improving upon it. There is, in fact, no possibility of improving upon it by any invention in the same direction. To effect this, it would be necessary for an invention to be made radically different in its conception and construction.

The engravings which we give illustrating the Bullock

NEW ZEALAND TROPHY OF GOLD.

Printing-press will be readily understood by those familiar with the article. These include, first, a view of the press itself; second, the sprinkler, used for damping the paper before this has passed into the impression-cylinder to be printed. On page 272 is presented the metal-melting furnace and mold for casting curved stereotype plates; and on page 273 is the matrix-machine, and also the curved-plate finishing machine, which reduces the stereotype plates to the requisite thickness and to proper conformity with each other, so as to correspond in their respective surfaces presented on the periphery of the type-cylinder for reception by the impression-cylinder. Had not our space for this subject been limited we should have noticed several other novel mechanical contrivances in connection with fast printing-presses. Mr. Bullock's invention has been honored by the medals of the Franklin Institute, of Philadelphia, and other institutions, including the Elliott Crasson Gold Medal—a most honorable testimonial.

THE LYALL POSITIVE MOTION LOOM.

MESSRS. J. & W. LYALL, of New York, made a most interesting and important display in their exhibit of their "Positive Motion Loom System." The principal feature of this invention is found in the positive and self-regulating motion of the shuttle, to which have been added by the

inventors other novel movements in mechanical combinations, which vastly increase the value of their machines. Five of these looms were on exhibition in Machinery Hall, and views of these seen from different positions are given on page 304. The other machinery exhibit comprised a bag-loom, which weaves four small bags in one operation; the carpet loom having a capacity of 100 yards of carpet per day; the ten-quarter cotton-loom, which is used by the New York Mills and the Wamsutta Mills in the manufacture of their celebrated sheetings and fabrics of great width, and the loom for making oil-cloth of 8 yards width and 40 yards length in 10 hours. It is stated that this latter machine could in a little more than six months produce enough oil-cloth to cover the entire vast area of Machinery Hall.

The advantages of the Lyall system are numerous and obvious, an important one being that the looms can be adapted to any material from the finest silk to the heaviest carpet. Another is, that smaller power is required in running them, and that the necessary operatives are reduced to a minimum, one girl being sufficient to conduct the weaving of fabrics of the greatest width and the heaviest body. The Judges' award for this mechanism gave a medal and diploma: First, for the invention of a positive motion; second, for its wide range of applicability; third, fitness for the purpose intended; fourth, excellence of design, construction and working; fifth, variety, extent and importance of the looms exhibited; sixth, utility and economy.

THE LYALL SEWING-MACHINE.

In the section in Machinery Hall devoted to the exhibits of Messrs. James & W. Lyall was presented a fine display of their improved sewing-machine. This machine, while it resembles the ordinary article in many respects, is very different in some of its most important particulars, having been so improved as to work at a remarkably high rate of speed, this being one of its special features. Other improvements are the dispensing with the different angular working parts, the number of working parts being considerably reduced, and those being retained so arranged as to require but little oil, and to be easily accessible to the operator. It is stated that on account of its similarity of structure, and the fact that it is manufactured of the very best materials, this machine can be run by skillful operators three times faster than any other shuttle machine, costing less to keep it in repair, and lasting very much longer than any other in the market. At the exhibition in Machinery Hall they were seen in operation, the work for which they were employed being that of edging corsets.

BIRD-CAGES.

A very remarkable piece of workmanship in bird-cage manufacture was exhibited in Agricultural Hall by the Osborne Manufacturing Company, of New York. This was an aviary or manufactured bird-cage, designed in imitation of Horticultural Hall. It was of metallic finish, nickel-plated under the Osborne patent, and received a diploma of award and medal from the Judges. The advantage of the Osborne patent in the construction of bird-cages consists in the neatness of result, its vermin-proof qualities, and its workmanship, in which are combined elegance, durability and safety to the inmate. Numerous devices for feeding, swinging and perching are original inventions, resulting from the experience of skilled workmen.

UNITED STATES CORSET COMPANY'S EXHIBIT.

Up to 1861 the corsets used in America were imported chiefly from Germany, where they were woven by hand-looms. During the Rebellion the prices of these goods became so high that few could wear even the commoner qualities of the imported article. For this reason, sewed corsets came into general use on account of cheapness, but failed to become satisfactory to consumers to the extent which would characterize the woven goods previously used. After the war the demand for foreign and woven goods continued to increase largely and steadily, until the United States Corset Company of New York, through the use of the patent wonderful positive motion loom, were enabled to manufacture corsets which were deemed to be more perfect in fit, durability and shape than imported ones, and at rates one-third less than these cost.

This company exhibited in Machinery Hall, and our illustration on page 305 displays a corset-loom in operation, where it stood west of the Corliss Engine. We also give a representation of the exhibit of the Company's corsets as displayed in the Main Building and Machinery Hall. The corset-loom is a combination of positive motion, the power-loom with Jacquard apparatus, combining three of the greatest inventions ever made to facilitate the art of weaving. The webs with every gusset and gore are woven by one operation, the article leaving the loom in a finished condition. In olden times five corsets per day was the capacity of the hand-loom of the German weaver, but by this machine 84 can be produced in the same time, and of infinitely superior quality.

Biscuit and Cracker Exhibit in Agricultural Hall.

Among the numerous exhibits of crackers, that of Messrs. E. J. Larrabee & Co., of Albany, New York, in Agricultural Hall, was one of the most attractive, including as it did nearly 300 different styles of fancy biscuit and cracker, all manufactured by this firm, and a part of their regular stock. One species exhibited was so small as to require 1,200 to make a pound. These received the name of "Centennial Dot." The Oswego biscuit, manufactured from the Oswego prepared corn, a recently introduced article, was also exhibited, and has become deservedly popular. The charcoal biscuit, in which charcoal is used, on account of its beneficial effects in dyspepsia, although medicinal in its uses, is also most palatable. This establishment claims to use nothing but the very best flour, carefully excluding all inferior and impure substances. Its manufacture gained a medal and diploma for "extent, variety and skill in manufacture."

The Portuguese Pavilion.

The headquarters of the Portuguese Commission stood on the Lansdowne drive, east of the Agricultural Hall Avenue, near the Restaurant Lafayette, and opposite the Swedish schoolhouse. It was a modest and very picturesque structure, formed in what the architects call the Renaissance pavilion style, and was 50 feet square by 14 in height. It was constructed under the immediate supervision of Mr. Edward Sayres, Portuguese Consul at Philadelphia, and was ornamented by porches around three sides of the building, its shape being octagonal, crowned with a dome and tower. The porch to the south gave admittance to the main parlor, an octagonal arm of 26 by 36, the entrance to the centre being by a double door. The cost of the building was $3,000, and it was elegantly carpeted and furnished.

Centennial Display of Live-stock—Sheep and Swine.

Our illustration of the display of sheep and swine in the live-stock exhibition at the Centennial includes the following animals:

Sheep.

No. 1. A merino ram, over 2 years old, from Paterson's Mills, Pennsylvania.

No. 2. The ram "Stub," from Bridport, Vt., 3 years and 5 months old.

No. 3. A merino ewe, name "Six Ewes," also from Bridport, Vt., 1 year old.

No. 4 is a Cotswold ram from Gloucestershire, England, 3 years and 8 months old, now owned by Dr. H. Howe, of Rhode Island.

No. 5 is a South-Down ewe, one of the several exhibited by Samuel J. Sharpless, of Philadelphia.

No. 6, also another by Mr. Sharpless, is a South-Down ram, named "Prince Arthur," white, 2 years old, bred by Lord Walsingham, of Merton, England.

Nos. 7 and 8 are Oxford-Down ram and ewe, "Duke of Oxford," imported, 2 years old, in pen with four ewes.

No. 9 is a South-Down ram, lambed in 1874, from Richmond Hill, Ontario.

No. 10 is a Shireling South-Down ewe, bred from imported stock in Ontario.

Swine.

No. 1. Suffolk boar, "Tom Bush," from Cheltenham, Ontario, farrowed March, 1875.

No. 2 is the Suffolk sow "Maggie," of Canada, farrowed March, 1874.

No. 3. Berkshire sow "Belladonna," 3 years old, bred at Hounslow, England.

No. 4 is a Berkshire boar, "Gloucester of Liverpool," 1 year and 7 months old, bred by exhibitor, of Burlington, New Jersey.

No. 5 in our illustration of swine is the Berkshire (England) boar "Collier," 10 months old, black with white points.

No. 6 is the small Yorkshire sow "Princess," 2 years and 5 months old, white, imported from Manchester, England.

No. 7. Small Yorkshire boar "King William," white, 13 months old, bred at Bristol, England.

No. 8. Pair of Chester fat white swine, 4 years old; male, 1,000 pounds; female, 800; from Willistown, Pennsylvania.

No. 9. Chester white sow, "Betts," 17 months old, with litter, from West Chester, Pennsylvania.

The National Wood Manufacturing Company's Exhibit.

This company, whose establishment is located at 950 Broadway, New York, made a fine exhibit of its peculiar manufacture in the Main Building of the Centennial, selections from which we present among our illustrations. This is an article of wood carpeting, an invention the result of a desire for some improvement in the appearance of wood floors without resorting to costly inlaid woods in marquetry and mosaic patterns. Hard-wood finish having of late years been generally employed in the interior construction of the better class of dwellings, the fashion conforming the style of floor-covering to this has not unnaturally followed. To bring this within the means of ordinary purses, some such invention as the one we are considering was necessary, and that of the National Wood Manufacturing Company has, after several years' test, proven its capacity to answer the requirements of durability, beauty and economy.

The wood-carpeting is manufactured from woods one-quarter of an inch in thickness, backed with canvas, and can be produced in ornamental designs of every description and to suit every taste. It is found to possess all the

NEW SOUTH WALES TROPHY.

advantages of hard-wood floors, without presenting any of their defects, and may be laid to advantage in parlors, drawing-rooms and libraries. It is susceptible of being used in connection with Persian rugs or Turkish carpets, either by having one of these laid in the centre and an ornamental border of wood-carpeting from 24 to 30 inches wide surrounding it, or the entire floor wood-carpeted and rugs placed upon it as furniture. It is also especially adapted for covering stairs, being readily laid, and, with ordinary care, very durable. For wainscoting purposes it is secured to the wall with moldings, where it appears to great advantage, giving a highly ornamental appearance to that portion of the interior of the room. It may also be used for panelings upon walls, or indeed in any situation where a wood finish is desirable.

The title wood-carpeting is appropriately applied to these inlaid wood floorings, since they produce the effect of carpets of the most esteemed patterns now in use in Europe and America. They, however, are a decided improvement upon carpets of any kind in durability, and particularly in the readiness with which they can be kept clean. Another advantage which these coverings possess over carpets will at once approve itself to every housekeeper. This is the fact that they are not affected either by moth or other deterioration from dust and other similar causes.

The wood-carpeting is made in three-quarter and yard wide sizes, the principal woods employed being walnut, ash, oak, maple and cherry. For fancy floors there are used rosewood, amaranth, holly, mahogany, tulip and ebony. In laying this covering the sections are accurately fitted together and secured with fine wire nails, the surface being afterwards covered with wax, or oil and shellac. This company is also manufacturing hard-wood floors, one inch or more in thickness, in which the difficulty of shrinkage is entirely avoided, a solid, heavy floor being laid, which is neither affected by moisture or furnace heat, both which influences are found to be injurious to the imported *parquet* floors. In houses already built, however, it is found desirable to use the wood-carpeting, whose thickness—quarter-inch—does not interfere with the doors, and forms an even surface with the centre carpet or rug.

The Hoe Printing-press.

The first two-cylinder press in this country was constructed by Robert Hoe, with his partner, Sereno Newton; and to the inventive genius of Messrs. Hoe is largely due the advance to almost absolute perfection of this species of mechanism. Richard M. Hoe, who inherited the ability and energy of his father, continued the business and opened a new era in the manufacture of printing-presses. "The Hoe Double-cylinder Press" was followed by Hoe's Lightning Press; then other, larger and better machines followed in quick succession, until Hoe's eight and ten-cylinder presses were used in nearly all the great newspaper offices of this country, and in many of those abroad. The most recent invention of Messrs. Hoe is a perfecting press (see page 268), capable of printing 15,000 copies per hour of an eight-page newspaper, or 28,000 or 30,000 copies of a duplicated four-page newspaper, from a roll of paper 52 inches wide and several miles in length. The sheets of either an eight or four-page newspaper are delivered from the press folded. The great advantage of this machine over the Hoe lightning rotary press are such as rapidly to displace the use of the latter by substituting this new masterpiece of the Messrs. Hoe's ingenuity.

A notable feature of this press is the fact of the absence of noise or vibration even when the machine is running at a high speed. This is due, doubtless, to the peculiarity of its construction. The first side of the paper is printed on the first pair of cylinders, consisting of one type and one impression-cylinder, over which hangs the roll of paper. The second side is printed by the second pair, which comprises likewise one type and one impression-cylinder—the latter, however, being larger than the former, and situated beneath it. This is so in order that the set-off from the fresh ink shall not fall continually on the same surface of the blanket. The result of this arrangement is that only every fourth sheet touches the same part of the blanket, giving this, therefore, time to dry. The combination includes a movable tympan, which can be changed if it gets too black or becomes defective. From the second pair of cylinders the sheet passes to the third pair, which act as the cutting-cylinders—the lower one having inserted rubber jaws with which to receive the edge of the knife provided in the upper roller, and operated by a cam movement, which projects the blade when it is necessary to perform its cutting duty, and withdraws it for the rest of the revolution. In the cutting process there are left upon the sheet small portions, each about a quarter of an inch wide, which are uncut, thus affording just enough strength to hold the paper together until it is taken hold of by the tapes, which conduct it to the first folding-cylinder, where each paper is folded lengthwise. During the passage of the paper from the first to the second folding-rollers it is, for single sheets, cut across the width of the newspaper. Between the first and the second the sheets are divided alternately between the upper and lower rollers by means of a simple spear-shaped switch, leaving two papers to the lower and two to the upper. By this means the folder runs at but half the speed of the press, thus equalizing the capacity of the latter with the folding-machine. To place the lower form-inking rollers in their proper location in the press, a small traveling carriage is provided. The distributing-rollers are operated laterally by a triple thread-worm movement, the ink being taken from them by two six-inch form-rollers. A register, or counter, is fixed to the former press, and is operated from the cutting-cylinders by a beveled gearing and worm movement. This press stands so low upon the floor that every part of it can be overlooked by the pressman. Another important feature is that the plates, rollers, and smaller parts can be abstracted from the press at the sides without ascending any steps, which is a decided advantage to the printer. The workmanship throughout is of the highest quality. The shafts of the impression-rollers, type-rollers, and folding-cylinders are of steel, and in every part durability as well as adaptability is insured. It is to this press, with its important improvements upon others which have preceded it, that America largely owes its reputation for producing the best printing-presses in the world.

Messrs. Elkington & Co.'s Exhibit.

Our illustration represents the *plaque* entitled, "The Pompeiian Toilette," a specimen of the manufacture of Messrs. Elkington & Co., manufacturing silversmiths in Birmingham, England, with establishments in London, Liverpool, and Manchester. The specialties of this firm include *repoussé* works of art in silver and iron, gold and silver damascened articles, *cloissonné* and *champlevé* enamels on silver and copper, bronze statuary, etc. Some account of the Elkington exhibits in the Main Building will be found in its proper place in this work: the "Pompeiian Toilette" deserves further consideration. This elaborate and beautiful *plaque*, or plate, was designed and made expressly for the Centennial Exposition, by the designer of the celebrated "Helicon Vase" and "Milton Shield," being the latest work in *repoussé* by this artist. The subject is one which has become somewhat famous to us of late years through the artistic efforts of Alma-Tadema, Coomans, and other contemporary painters. In the adoption of a Pompeiian scene, however, for the subject of his work, the present artist has drawn his inspiration from his own conception, guided, of course, by what has been discovered in reference to the manners and customs of Pompeii through the excavations and reproductions of Zahn, Gell, and others.

The scene chosen by him presents a Pompeiian lady engaged in the performance of her toilet and surrounded by her assistants, each of whom has in her charge some office appertaining to the important duty in hand. The locality depicted represents a court in that portion of a Pompeiian house allotted to women. In the background are to be seen columns, about which are wreathed masses of creeping vines; while between them artistic vases, containing a gorgeous array of flowers, produce the effect almost of a conservatory. Statues and other ornaments are scattered about the apartment. In the foreground, reclining upon a couch, covered with rich drapery, with a tiger or leopard skin at her feet, is the beautiful Pompeiian maiden who is the subject of the work. The figure is nude to the waist, and is displayed holding in one hand a small mirror. About her arms are bracelets in the form of serpents, and around her neck a rich necklace of gems. One slave at her feet adjusts her sandals, another stands waiting with some portion of her dress, while the third arranges the ornaments in her hair. Of the dwellings which have been brought to light in Pompeii, the most important are those of Sallust, Pansa, Castor and Pollux, and M. Lucretius, all of which were found to be very rich in pictures, mosaics, vases, bronzes and other ornaments. It is a curious fact that in the investigations among the ruins of Pompeii no buildings indicating poverty in their occupants have been discovered, and it is doubtful if the city had any population except the wealthy. It is only recently that Pompeiian subjects have been utilized in art, although it is more than a century since considerable excavations were made there, and important treasures brought to light. The application of this class of subjects to plastic and metal work is evidence of excellent judgment and taste. The present specimen has perhaps not been surpassed either in the beauty and originality of design as applied to this material, or in the delicacy of its handling.

Messrs. Mitchell, Vance & Co.'s Exhibit of Chandeliers.

The exhibit of Messrs. Mitchell, Vance & Co., of 597 Broadway, New York, in the Main Building, included chandeliers, gas-fixtures, bronze ornaments and fine clocks.

Our illustrations represent specimens of their wares, and fairly display their attractive and artistic character. It is unquestionable that these exhibits were quite the handsomest in their line. They were located near the centre of the Main Building, at N 49, and attracted general attention and commendation. When we consider that gas for illumination is an affair of little more than half a century, we are surprised at the extent of the application of art ideas to the implements and processes connected with its use.

DEPARTMENT OF PROTECTION.

Gas was, in fact, introduced into London in 1814; Paris, 1820; Boston, 1822; New York, 1827; and Philadelphia, 1835. From its first employment, however, the inventive and mechanical spirit of the age has been utilized in its behalf, and the result has been to improve the methods of using it, and to combine with its application to public and domestic employment the most ingenious, original and ornamental and attractive surroundings. In the present Exhibition, as in those of the past, there was considerable competition in this direction, and it is the highest praise which can be given to the firm of Mitchell, Vance & Co., to say that in this last competitive display they have undoubtedly borne away the palm for beauty, excellence and completeness of work. One of their exhibits was a gas chandelier, designed in the early Greek form of ornamentation, the main stem consisting of a tapering pedestal, ornamented with female figures in low relief, supporting a gracefully designed Greek vase, garlanded with laurel wreaths. From the top of the vase the stem is richly ornamented, and is crowned with a canopy formed by a succession of lions' heads in high relief, holding gilt curb-rings in their jaws. Four fluted columns, resting upon ornamental bases, surround the stem and support a dome-like structure, upon which are perched four winged animals, impossible to describe. Between the columns are seated four griffins upon pedestals, from which spring the arms, which terminate in burners, representing antique lamps, of chaste and elegant pattern. The chandelier is finished in the style known as verd-antique, relieved by gilding. It has eight lights, and is one of the most elaborate works of the kind ever designed or executed in this country.

A very graceful seven-light slide library chandelier, in the Neo Grec style, is ornamented with medallions, representing Music, Poetry and History, and has a centre sliding light with an argand burner. These centre lights, in combination with a chandelier made to slide, are a great advantage for use near a reading-table. In this particular manufacture the points of excellence are length of slide, strength in the double rods, freedom from heat and smoke, and from the effects of these in soiling the chandeliers. Other advantages consist in operating the balance-weights, and the ease with which the gas may be shut off and the slide taken out, should it become necessary, while the chandelier itself may remain in use. A design for a Newell standard with cluster lights presents an American subject in the figure of an Indian warrior with bow, tomahawk and scalping-knife, sustaining the upright on which the lights are placed. Hanging candelabra standards and other ornamental methods for applying gas to illuminating purposes were among the exhibits of this manufacture.

The immense factories and foundries of Messrs. Mitchell, Vance & Co. are situated on Twenty-fourth and Twenty-fifth Streets and Tenth Avenue, New York City.

E. Remington & Son's Breech-loading Arms.

Probably none of the millions who visited the Main Building will have failed to see the magnificent exhibit of Messrs. Remington, on the north side of the building, near the transept. The artistic manner in which the grouping of their various arms was combined, so as to effect a picture, was so novel as to be one of the features of the Exhibition.

The Remington system, as applied to breech-loaders, made its first public appearance before a Board of United States Army Officers convened at Springfield, Mass., in January, 1865. At this competition 65 different guns were represented, among them the well-known Peabody, the Roberts, the Sharp and Burnside, the former with a record at least as old as 1850, and several other models of recognized merit.

The system of the Remington carbine tried at Springfield was only a suggestion of the wonderful improvements which have since been embodied in this arm, and applied to all their various manufactures. By 1866 this system was perfected, and in 1869 a Board of Officers, convened to examine and test the best systems of breech-loading firearms, indorsed the Remington in preference to all others. Finally a commission of United States Army officers convened in 1870, and declared the Remington to be "the best system for the army of the United States." This report likewise recommended the adoption of the single-barreled Remington pistol, and from this time, in all trials, the Remington arms distanced all competitors. Our illustrations display the peculiar mechanical construction of the breech system of the Remington arm. The simplicity of the system, the largeness of its parts, and the natural operation, do away with all necessity for a more elaborate and distinct illustration. The operation of the arm is specially simple. To load the piece, the hammer is first brought to full cock, and the breech-piece swung back by pressing the thumb-piece with the thumb of the right hand, the backward motion of the breech-block withdrawing the discharged shell from the chamber. The fresh cartridge is then inserted, and the breech closed in one continuous motion. The arm is then ready to fire. The tests for strength to which this system has been subjected by the various military commissions, which have very carefully examined it, abundantly demonstrated its solidity. In no case has it failed. For convenience of manipulation and cleaning its

DEPARTMENT OF PROTECTION—INTERIOR OF COURT-ROOM.

THE CHINESE POTTERY EXHIBIT.

advantages are palpable. This is particularly the case in target-shooting, inasmuch as one can look entirely through the barrel from breech to muzzle, and see that the bore is perfectly clean—particularly at the end of the chamber. All Remington single-barreled breech-loading guns, whether rifle or shot, have been made upon this system—the same which has been used in the construction of over 900,000 military rifles for various governments. Two sizes are made—one for rifles weighing from $5\frac{1}{2}$ to 8 pounds, and the other for rifles weighing from $8\frac{1}{2}$ to 15 pounds. With the 22-rifle a practice of half an hour a day for a short time, combined with an ordinary amount of steadiness of nerve, is sufficient to make a first-rate off-hand shot. By the use of the centre-fire ammunition with this arm, it is practicable to use as heavy a charge of powder as is desired without danger to the shell. The late General Custer, in a letter written to Messrs. Remington, in 1873, describes the results obtained with the Remington arm during a hunting expedition, and comments in the highest terms upon the success met with in using this rifle; saying that he was "more than ever impressed with the many superior qualities possessed by the system of arms manufactured by this firm."

For the "Creedmoor Rifle," new long-range front and rear sights have been arranged—the front sight having a wind-gauge adjustment, and being provided with spirit-level and extra disks of the forms in use, when so ordered. The rear-sight is hinged to a base-piece secured to a tang on the frame, and is provided with a screw-adjustment and vernier for reading the elevations to single minutes. All this is seen in our illustrations. The rear sight is graduated into degrees and minutes by means of the vernier scale. To adjust it the eye-piece is first loosened; then, after a sight is properly set by means of a screw, the eye-piece is tightened, and holds the slide firmly, irrespective of the screw, which is intended only for convenience in adjusting the eye-piece. "The Creedmoor Rifle," so called, is that used by Dakin, Fulton, Bodine, Hepburn, Coleman, Farwell, Canfield, Hyde, Rathbone, Crouch, Sandford, and Weber. At the match between the American and Irish teams at Creedmoor, in 1874, the Remington breech-loader scored 478, the highest figure reached by any arm. At the match at Dollymount it shot closer and made more bull's-eyes than any other.

Bouche Fils & Co.'s Exhibit of Friedrichshall Bitter Water in Agricultural Hall.

The recent introduction of the Friedrichshall bitter water in this country has proved a veritable boon. This medicinal water is imported from Germany, and is not only greatly favored and frequently prescribed by physicians, but is being generally adopted by the public. As it has been recommended by such high scientific authorities as Sir Henry Thompson and Baron Von Liebig, it is evident that there are good grounds for its popular acceptation. Our illustration displays the pretty and attractive form in which the exhibit was made of this water in Agricultural Hall.

Exhibit of the Society for the Prevention of Cruelty to Animals.

An account of this noble and remarkable exhibit will be found in another portion of the HISTORICAL REGISTER. The space occupied by the articles exhibited was situated at the extreme eastern end of the north side of the Main Building, and was prominently indicated by a painted banner, 25 feet by 20, suspended from the iron rafters of the roof, and containing the names of the States and Territories where laws exist for the prevention of cruelty to animals. The wall space of the section was covered with photographs illustrating particular cases of cruelty. Besides the articles mentioned heretofore, there were exhibited the following:

A knife, used by Patrick Coyle to cut a horse, out of revenge to the owner; three months in the penitentiary.

A brick, used by August Sann, who was arrested for striking a horse on the body, breaking two of its ribs. The horse had to be destroyed. Offender fined $25, and one month in the penitentiary.

A hammer, used by William Starvey, who struck his horse several blows on its body; fined $25.

VENETIAN GLASS MIRROR.

Part of horse's leg, broken by getting caught in a street railroad track.

An iron pike, used on the traces of a team of coach-horses to make the animals "run wide."

A horse's hoof, rotted off from the effects of a nail, driven into the sensitive laminæ of the foot by an ignorant blacksmith.

The skull of a celebrated fighting dog, son of "Brandy," captured at Centreville, Long Island.

A pair of steel gaffs, captured on a game-cock found fighting in a cockpit at Harry Baxter's, East Eighty-sixth Street, New York; 28 men arrested; fines imposed, $280, and an aggregate imprisonment of nine months.

A horse's eye, knocked out with the butt-end of a whip, by Thomas Eley; fined $25 and 10 days in the city prison.

A bale-stick, used by F. B. Lance to beat his horse over the body; fined $25.

Two steel gaffs captured at a cock-pit, at Hunter's Point, L. I.; 12 men arrested.

A car-hook, used by a car-driver on the Belt line to beat a horse over the body; fined $10, and one month in the penitentiary.

A portion of a horse's hoof, wrenched off by being caught in a street railroad track, Centre Street, New York.

A dog-fighter's kit, being the contents of a bag belonging to a notorious dog-fighter, left in a dog-pit at Fort Hamilton, October 1st, 1874, when he escaped; also a muzzle and blanket belonging to the celebrated fighting-dog "Danger," captured on the same occasion.

A hatchet, used by Peter Trainor, who struck a horse over the head, cutting through the skull; one month in the penitentiary.

Steel gaffs, captured on birds fighting in a cock-pit, at John Mulholland's; 32 men arrested; fines $620.

A portion of a horse's tongue, which was torn off with a piece of whip-cord by James Ross; fined $25 and one month's imprisonment.

A wooden burr, taken from the trace between a team of Third Avenue Railroad car-horses—used to make horses "run wide."

Blacksmith's twitch, used by Patrick Dugan, a blacksmith, who knocked a horse's eye out by striking it on the head; fined $25.

Bit burrs, specimens of over 300, captured in New York and Brooklyn, used to "torture and torment" horses, attached to fashionable carriages. These bit-burrs are full of sharp-pointed tacks, and are placed on either side of the horse's mouth, and fastened to the bit.

Pick-handle, used by Thomas Carey to beat an overloaded horse; one month in the penitentiary.

A blacksmith's iron creasing-punch, used by Anton Buckhardt to beat his horse over the head and ribs; fined $20 and five days in the city prison.

Calculus, or lumps of adulterated horse-feed, composed of plaster-of-paris, bone-dust, etc., mixed by feed-dealers to make fine feed weigh heavy, and deceive the buyer. The lumps on exhibition were found in the stomach of a horse who died from the effects of the food eaten.

During the Exhibition over 20,000 pamphlets were distributed by the Society to visitors.

The above curiosities are now on permanent exhibition at the headquarters of the Society, Twenty-second Street and Fourth Avenue, New York.

Postal Telegraphy.

The art of telegraphing in fac-simile has for some time given good promise of coming to working perfection. Mr. W. E. Sawyer, an American electrician, is the inventor of the machine we illustrate, upon which there are seven

FURNITURE OF THE TURKISH HOUSE.

patents, and which gives good reason to suspect that before long postal telegraphy will be *un fait accompli.* In order to utilize this invention, the United States Postal Telegraph Company has been organized under the laws of the State of New York, for the purpose of constructing lines, and operating them under Mr. Sawyer's patents. This company starts with a capital stock of $2,000,000, with power to extend to $10,000,000. Since its organization it has chiefly been engaged in arranging for the construction of instruments. Such a complete revolution in telegraphy as this instrument contemplates requires that all the appliances should be perfect in their construction and exactly adapted to the uses for which they are designed.

The following are the officers of the Company : *President,* John R. Cecil, of New York ; *Vice-President,* A. M. Allerton, of New York ; *Secretary,* Geo. R. Williamson, of New York ; *Treasurer,* C. A. Kettle, of New York ; *General Superintendent,* James T. Smith, of Hackensack, N. J.; *Electrician,* W. E. Sawyer, of New York.

The peculiarity of this instrument consists in the fact that by its use a person's own handwriting or drawing can be transmitted by telegraph in perfect *fac-simile.* This is effected in the following manner, by means of the instrument which we have illustrated. The person desiring to communicate by this means writes upon ordinary white paper. This message is laid upon a metallic plate and passed between two friction-rollers, which exert sufficient pressure to transfer the lines of writing from the paper to the plate. The metallic plate containing the transferred lines of writing being placed upon the semi-cylindrical car shown in the engraving, which runs upon a railway, the instrument is set in motion. The operation of transferring the message and getting the plate upon the instrument, and the instrument in motion, occupies less than a quarter of a minute. The metallic plate is a conductor of electricity. The lines of writing, however, are non-conductors. Over the cylinder are carried metallic contact-points upon the revolving arms. Whenever a point is upon the metallic surface the electric current passes through the car to the line. When a point comes upon a line of writing the connection is broken, and a dot is made upon the receiving instrument upon chemically prepared paper placed upon this cylindrical car—the dot being made from a metallic point upon the revolving arms, at whatever place upon the chemical paper the record-point may be resting at the moment when the current is broken at the transmitting instrument. The two instruments operate synchronously—that is to say, the point passing over the cylindrical surface in one instrument is followed exactly by the point passing over the cylindrical surface in the other instrument—both recording and transmitting points always being at the same relative point upon both cars, no matter how distant the two instruments may be from each other at the same time. This is accomplished by an electro-magnetic detent, which checks the motion of the instruments at every half-revolution, but starts them both as soon as both have arrived at

the same relative point, so that one instrument can never gain upon the other at the same time that the points are passing over the cylindrical car. The car is moved longitudinally under them, so that they trace fine spiral lines over the blanks, and thus ultimately cover the entire surface of the cars. The synchronous motion is very rapid and perfect. It is made so by the peculiar employment of the electro motor shown in the engraving, with appropriate governing arrangements; the motor making 16 revolutions to one revolution of the transmitting or recording points. Thus any irregularity in the revolutions of the motor balance-wheel is reduced at the transmitting and receiving points to one-sixteenth of what it originally was, and hence perfect regularity is obtained. The motor is never stopped or checked in the transmission of a message, but continues its motion and storing up of power in the balance-wheel at the same time that the electro-magnetic detent may be holding the cars and revolving arms at a stand-still. This is accomplished by a friction-spring connection between the shaft carrying the arms and car and the gearing communicating with the motor. Herein, and in the principle of the motor application, as well as the peculiar operation of the magnetic detent, consists the value of the invention.

An important fact calculated to contribute to the popularity of this method of telegraphing is its capacity to

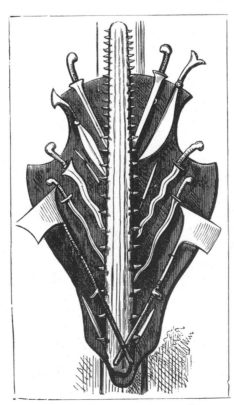

ARMS AND WEAPONS OF THE PHILIPPINE ISLANDS.

send a message which is written upon ordinary paper by running the instruments in opposite directions. The rate of speed of transmission varies according to the closeness of the writing ; but for ordinary writing it writes from sixty to one hundred words per minute. The received message appears in close, deep-blue dotted lines upon a white blank. A great advantage in time is gained by the fact that in this system there need be no delays at the sending station through counting of words, but in less than fifteen seconds after the message leaves the hands of the writer it may be forwarded to the receiver. The plan to be adopted in arranging the system for public use will be to charge a certain sum of money for whatever is written upon the blank, and this, whether five words or fifty words, will be sent for one price; since it is of no consequence to the Company how many words are written upon a blank of a certain size. A great merit of this invention is the impossibility of its transmitting an error, since the machine cannot send one word for another. Besides handwriting, there can be transmitted by this means drawings, maps, sketches of scenes or pieces of machinery ; in fact, everything that can be made with the pen upon paper. The fact that the machines operate automatically, and the transmission of the message is dependent upon no man's judgment, fidelity, or accuracy, is an assurance which cannot possibly be given by the ordinary telegraph system. Should this system come into general use, as it is to be hoped it speedily will, business men will doubtless find it greatly to their advantage to employ it, since those to whom messages are sent will receive them in the handwriting of the senders without delay, and with absolute accuracy. Further, messages can be sent by this means in all languages, without the necessity for translating. Again, by means of ciphers or stenographic writing, from 100 to 200 words can be sent by this same method as cheaply as a lesser number, space being the measure for estimating the proper charge for the transmission of any message. In fact, the many excellent advantages of the invention will at once approve themselves to the reader. During the continuance of the Centennial Exposition one of these instruments was constantly at work in the Signal Service Department of the United States Government Building. By special arrangement it was employed to transmit *fac-simile* copies of the weather maps from Washington, charts being presently reproduced by the officers of the service in the building, and afterward given away to visitors. Instruments employed for this purpose differ somewhat from the one we illustrate, improvements having been made since its first invention which very much add to its usefulness. Many of our readers will doubtless remember witnessing the operation of receiving the maps by telegraph, as it was exhibited in the United States Government Building.

THE BAILEY MITRAILLEUSE.

The idea of the machine-gun is claimed to be entirely American, and to have been conceived by Dr. R. J. Gatling, of Indianapolis, Indiana, in 1862, whose first American patent bears date November 4th of that year. The conception of this gun had occurred to Dr. Gatling in 1861, and his first constructed realization of it was exhibited and fired repeatedly in 1862, in the presence of thousands of persons, discharging 200 shots a minute. From the Gatling Gun, it is alleged, was derived the mitrailleuse, which played so important a part in the Franco - German war. The principle upon which machine-guns are constructed consists in a series of barrels secured upon the main shaft. The gun is fed either by a man standing beside it or automatically from a feed-case filled with cartridges. It is exploded by turning a crank, which, by the agency of certain gearing, revolves the main shaft, carrying with it lock-cylinder, barrels, and locks. As the gun is rotated the cartridges are carried along to a point where the operation of a hammer comes into play, when each cartridge is exploded in turn. The latest improvement on the Gatling Gun is by Mr. Bailey, of Indianapolis, and possesses the advantages of simplicity, rapidity of fire, extent of range, capacity for continuous firing, and economy. This arm was exhibited during the Centennial Exposition, in the Indiana State Building, on the Centennial Grounds. It is supplied with one lock, made in two pieces, which operates all the barrels, and the total number of pieces in the gun is less than that of any other mitrailleuse. It can be taken apart and refitted by any person of common intelligence, and in less time than any other arm; with one revolution of the crank it can be so exposed that every part can be cleaned with perfect ease. There is also less exposure of the parts to the enemy's fire than in any other gun. In rapidity of fire it is claimed that the Bailey Gun exceeds that of any other arm of the same character, while its range is equal to that of any other. To produce continuous firing, a special cartridge-case or belt is employed, by which continuance is secured so long as ammunition is supplied. Owing to the small number of its parts and the simplicity of the arm, the cost of this gun is much less in comparison with other arms. Finally, as the Bailey Mitrailleuse can

PHILIPPINE ISLANDS' CURIOSITIES.

be disabled by the extraction of the lock in ten seconds, so that its capture by an enemy would be of no advantage to him, an additional and important property presents itself as inherent in this gun.

AUCTION SALE OF CERAMICS AND BRIC-A-BRAC.

Our illustration presents a scene which was quite common in New York and Philadelphia after the close of the Centennial, when all sorts of Centennial articles—particularly in ceramics and bric-a-brac generally—were offered at public auction, and eagerly purchased by the public, whose taste for this class of ware had been developed by means of the Centennial itself. According to an English writer, bric-a-brac is "an elastic expression, made to cover everything, good, bad, or indifferent, in the most remote degree, relative to art, that has fallen into its second-hand stage, or, in other words, passed out of the hands of commerce into the fluctuations of chance." Thus bric-a-brac appears in public and private museums, and in art sales-rooms, in the form of ceramics, bronze armor, wood-carvings, antique or *rococo* jewelry, and, in fact, in every conceivable article wherein art, taste, or capacity has been displayed, and which has become rare by age or scarcity.

Within a few years auction sales of this class of wares have become very frequent, and quite a mania for collection has begun to grow among our cultivated people. It is probable that we shall now draw largely upon the collections of Europe, and, as private museums are dispersed, their contents will fall into the hands of collectors, to be immediately transmitted to this country, where a more lucrative market is certain to offer itself.

L. P. JUVET'S TIME GLOBE.

An interesting scientific article, which was exhibited both in the Main Building and the United States Government Building at the Centennial, was the Time Globe, invented by Mr. L. P. Juvet, of Glen's Falls, N.Y. This curious piece of mechanism exhibits a miniature representation of the diurnal motions of the earth, the globe which answers for the earth being made to revolve once in twenty-four hours, by means of concealed machinery. This invention is designed to facilitate instruction relative to the true character of the motion of the earth, and while performing this function reveals likewise the time of the various meridans or localities, this being indicated on a large dial at the equator, a small dial recording in the meantime the locality where the invention is used. By means of a sliding Vernier scale, divided into 360 degrees, the latitude of any locality can be readily ascertained, as also the degrees of any part of the earth or any of the planets. Moreover, every portion of this comprehensive instrument is utilized, the base being used to display a barometer, thermometer, and compass, altogether separate from the clock. The Time Globe will stand in any position, will run eight days, and is a stem-winder. It deserves being brought to the notice of educators as an excellent and fully adequate means for informing students in an important but little understood branch of instruction, while it is also calculated to prove practically useful in the library, the office or the counting-room.

DOM PEDRO AND THE EMPRESS OF BRAZIL.

Among the distinguished foreign visitors to the Centennial, the Emperor and Empress of Brazil were of all the

DOULTON POTTERY EXHIBIT, IN THE MAIN BUILDING—THE PULPIT.

SELLING CERAMIC BY AUCTION AFTER THE CLOSE OF THE EXHIBITION.

most notable and the most observed. The assiduity and perseverance with which Dom Pedro made himself acquainted with the character of the Exhibition and the nature of its contents recommended him constantly to those under whose observation he came, the possessor of these peculiarly American qualities being naturally an object of interest in this country. We present portraits of the Emperor and his wife, who were married on September 4, 1843. Dom Pedro II. was born in Rio Janeiro, December 2, 1825. He was crowned Emperor, July 18, 1841. The Empress was Adona Theresa Christiana Maria, daughter of the late Francis I., King of the Two Sicilies. The line of descent of the family has been continued through the marriage of the Emperor's daughter to Louis, Count d'Eu, son of the Duke of Nemours, who had a son born in 1875, who is the heir-apparent of the Imperial Crown of Brazil. Since the accession of Dom Pedro to the throne of Brazil that country has been steadily increasing in power and usefulness. The Emperor possesses literary and scientific acquirements, is a just and liberal sovereign, and enjoys the warm affection of his people. His acquaintance with scientific subjects is quite remarkable, and he is a member of the French Academy of Sciences. Dom Pedro arrived in this country in the month of April, 1876, spending a few days with his wife in the City of New York, being in the meantime actively occupied in visiting its various public institutions. It was his custom while in New York to start out very early in the morning on an investigating tour, in order to avoid publicity as much as possible. When in New York harbor, on board of the ship in which he came, a number of prominent men from the city proceeded to the steamship for the purpose of paying him their respects and escorting him to the city; but he failed to gratify their wishes, making a positive announcement that it was his desire to be treated as a private citizen, inasmuch as he came simply upon a tour of observation, and for no other purpose. Soon after his arrival he made a rapid trip to California, returning in time to be present at the opening of the Centennial Exhibition on the 10th of May, when he, in conjunction with President Grant, may be said to have set in motion that colossal enterprise. From that time until the latter part of the Summer the Emperor traveled through various parts of the country, investigating our resources, manners and customs, and public institutions, displaying an interest in our political and social economy which would scarcely be expected of any foreigner, and least of all by a crowned head. Dom Pedro became generally recognized by the public, and achieved a popularity in the United States which has seldom been reached by any of the foreign visitors. On leaving this country he went to Europe, and continued his travels into Egypt, Palestine and Syria, visiting the Suez Canal and other noted places in that section of the world. It is his intention to continue his touring expedition until the beginning of the year 1878, at which time he expects to take the reins of power in hand again, and bring the results of his observations to play, hoping thereby to put the Empire of Brazil upon a footing equal in civilization and advancement of art to that of any country he had occasion to visit. So far as this country could assist the Emperor to carry out his object, he could not have selected a more opportune time, for the Centennial Exposition presented, so to speak, in a comparatively small space, the position of the United States in the arts and industries as compared with all the other countries that were represented.

Concerning the Empress of Brazil, it is related that she is amiable, intelligent, charitable, and a most excellent helpmate for her husband. She is most popular and highly esteemed in her own country, and while in the United States was the recipient of many kind and well-meant attentions. She is small of stature as compared with the Emperor, and though in general good health, was apparently unequal to the rapid movements of Dom Pedro, she not accompanying him in all his travels. While he was taking his hasty trip to San Francisco, she remained in New York, at the Fifth Avenue Hotel.

While sojourning in the United States, their Majesties

THE OCEAN CHALLENGE CUP, MADE BY TIFFANY & CO., NEW YORK.

were the recipients, from several private individuals, of courtesies which were suitably acknowledged by the presentation of valuable souvenirs.

BARTHOLDI'S STATUE.

We present an illustration representing the right arm and hand, holding a torch, belonging to the illuminated statue of "Liberty Enlightening the World," designed by the celebrated Bartholdi. This fragment of the statue was erected on the Centennial grounds, a few rods south of Frank Leslie's Pavilion, and was observed with interest by visitors. The statue is designed to be placed, when completed, upon Bedloe's Island, or some other commanding point in New York Harbor. It originated with the people of France, who subscribed liberally for its construction, and, being completed by American subscriptions, will

BENT-WOOD TABLE-GLASS.

doubtless become a prominent object on our Atlantic seaboard. A committee, under the chairmanship of Hon. William M. Evarts, having appealed to the country for subscriptions—in amounts between ten cents and one hundred dollars—the work, when finished, will be representative of the liberality of the two friendly nations who unite to carry out the project.

ITALIAN STATUARY.

The exhibits of the Italian sculptors, in Memorial Hall and the Art Annex, have been already considered in this work, on pages 174 and 176, and 198 and 199, besides in short

notices of special subjects. We desire to refer at present more particularly to our illustrations, in No. IX. of the HISTORICAL REGISTER, of this department, including the pieces of sculpture entitled, "Vanity," "Soap-Bubbles," "Out in the Rain"—a charming work in terra-cotta, in the Main Building—"Blind-Man's-Buff," and "The Birth of Cupid"—an amusing little piece representing the small god emerging from an egg. To those who remember these works sincere pleasure will doubtless be experienced on having them recalled to mind more vividly through the medium of our illustrations. "Vanity," by Bottinelli, is a most graceful figure, fully displaying the idea designed to be interpreted in the marble. The "Soap-Bubble" subject will doubtless recall early experiences, being a representation possessing real force, and a close copy after nature. It will be well for the reader to turn to pages 180 and 183, and to 222 and 223, where will be found other representations of Italian sculpture, which are in all respects equal to those we have named, both in the merit of their design and that of their execution.

J. L. MOTT EXHIBIT.—FOUNTAIN.

This fountain, constructed most elaborately in the Renaissance style, will be remembered as having stood in the Main Building, where its artistic excellence and the bold breadth of its conception aroused considerable enthusiastic comment. As an ornate and beautiful piece of workmanship, in a rather difficult material to handle with ease and accuracy, this is a most commendable effort on the part of the exhibitors.

Hon. JOHN W. FORNEY.

The subject of this sketch, a portrait of whom will be found elsewhere in the HISTORICAL REGISTER, a distinguished journalist, was born at Lancaster, Pa., September 30, 1817. He was early apprenticed to the printing business, in the office of the Lancaster Journal. In 1837 he became editor and joint proprietor of the Lancaster Intelligencer, which in 1840 he consolidated with the Journal. In 1845 he removed to Philadelphia, and shortly after became one of the editors of the Pennsylvanian and a leading spirit in the Democratic Party, of which that paper was the organ. From 1851 to 1855 he was Clerk of the House of Representatives at Washington. In 1852–53 he relinquished his connection with the Pennsylvanian and became one of the editors of the Union, a Democratic organ at Washington, and labored earnestly and effectively to secure the election of Mr. Buchanan as President in 1856. In 1857 Mr. Forney was the Democratic candidate in Pennsylvania for the United States Senate, but was defeated by General Cameron, and in August of that year founded the Press as an Independent Democratic daily journal in Philadelphia, which became the organ of the Northern or Douglas wing of the Democracy.

Mr. Forney's opposition to Mr. Buchanan's administration grew out of the refusal of the President to allow the people of Kansas to vote on the question of slavery in that Territory without interference, a policy to which he had solemnly pledged himself before his election.

Mr. Forney was again elected Clerk of the National House of Representatives in the Thirty-sixth Congress, and served from 1859 to 1861. At the opening of the Civil War he took strong grounds in favor of its vigorous prosecution. In July of 1861 he was chosen Secretary of the United States Senate, and held this office until 1868, when he resigned. While proprietor and corresponding editor of the Press during those years, he started in Washington, and personally edited, a weekly paper entitled the Chronicle, which he converted into a daily in 1862. In 1867 Mr. Forney made an extensive tour in Europe, and on his return collected his letters to the Press and Chronicle, under the title of "Letters from Europe" (1869). In 1870 he disposed of his property in the Washington Chronicle, and has since confined himself to the Philadelphia Press. Shortly after Mr. Forney's return to his editorial chair in Philadelphia, General Grant tendered him the important position of the collector of customs at that port, a position which he accepted with much reluctance, owing to his earnest desire to have nothing to do with political appointments, and therefore, at the end of eleven months, having proved himself an admirable officer, he returned the commission to the President with warm thanks for the honor

BENT-WOOD CHAIR.

BENT-WOOD TABLE.

THONET BROS. VIENNA EXHIBIT OF BENT-WOOD FURNITURE.

extended to him. Since then he has devoted himself constantly and exclusively to his newspaper, varying his labors by periodical lectures on different subjects.

In July of 1874 Mr. Forney visited Europe for the second time, before leaving being appointed Commissioner by the Centennial authorities at Philadelphia, to invoke the attendance at the International Exhibition of the various foreign Powers. It is unnecessary to state that he performed this task with an ability that secured the highest praise from men of all parties, but it is not generally known that in discharging the duty he paid all his own expenses, simply receiving from the Commission the expense of the persons he had to employ to assist him in his great work. He not only paid his own way, but steadily refused to receive any compensation when he returned home.

Col. Forney is one of the few examples of generous, disinterested and enthusiastic devotion to the journalistic guild, perferring his editorial duties to any of the offices his party may have to bestow. With all this, he is an advanced Republican. His newspaper, while sternly avoiding all personalities, and ever ready to treat his peculiar opponents liberally, is a vigorous partisan, and acts upon the principle which is the Colonel's constant declaration, that

the Centennial representatives of European art, which possessed qualities differing from, and in some respects improvements on, the manufacture in this country. Already the result of the influence of foreign workmanship is being seen in our home manufacture, and it has been stated by a prominent artificer in silver and silver plate that in his opinion the effect upon American industrial art of this character occasioned by the Centennial Exhibition will not fall short of the influence exerted upon English art by the London Exhibition of 1851.

A brief account of the progress of the manufacture we are considering will not be inappropriate in this place. In manufacturing solid silver into articles of show, or for domestic purposes, an alloy is used, varying according to the peculiar process adopted by each manufacturer. The standard silver of England consists of 925 parts of silver and 75 of copper in a thousand parts; and in that country all vessels of silver are required to be stamped by the Goldsmiths' Company, who are authorized to search the shops of silversmiths and seize the articles which do not bear the Hall mark of the company. The company makes a charge of one shilling and sixpence per ounce on the weight of the object for the assay thereof and the impression of the

plating, consisted in the application of thin leaves of silver to finished brass articles. The part to be plated was heated to a point just below that at which the metal changes color. Silver-leaf was then laid on, and the adhesion produced by burnishing resulted in a fine polish. By another process the metal was first produced in sheets plated each one on both sides, and the goods then manufactured from these sheets; while another process consisted in laying the silver upon the metal to be plated, and pressing this upon the latter, cold. The improvement of this manufacture through the medium of electro-plating originated in the fact that, when a voltaic current is passed through a metallic solution decomposition takes place; the metal, in a revived form, attaches itself to the negative pole or electrode, while the acid or alkali goes to the positive pole. Although this fact is nearly coeval with the discovery of the voltaic pile, yet it was not until about the year 1839 that it occurred to any one to turn it to practical account in electro-metallurgic processes. From the first introduction of electro-plating the metallic basis selected, for the reason of its nearest approach in hue to silver, was that which has been extensively employed in the manufacture of spoons, forks, etc., and known as "German-silver," "nickel," "albata," and by

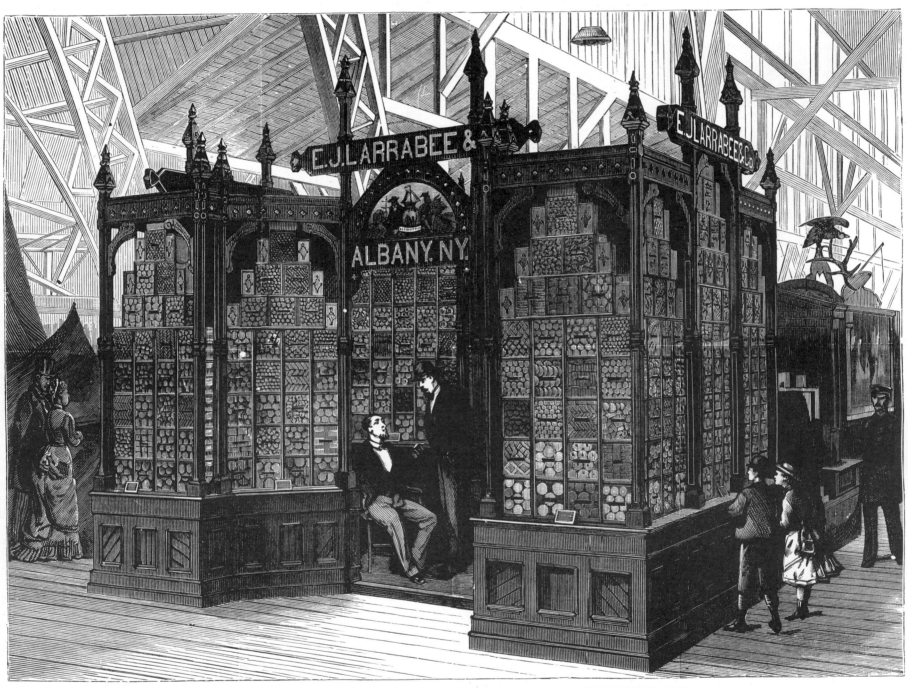

E. J. LARRABEE & CO.'S CRACKER AND BISCUIT EXHIBIT IN AGRICULTURAL HALL.

he believes the Republican organization, with all its errors, the best we have, and therefore entitled to his consistent and conscientious support. In addition to his quoted letters from Europe in 1869, he has since then published a volume, "Anecdotes of Public Men," and last year another, "A Centennial Commissioner in Europe." These three books have been largely circulated, and generally commended for their fairness and moderation.

SILVERWARE AND ELECTRO-PLATE EXHIBITS OF THE GORHAM COMPANY, AND REED & BARTON.

The exhibits of silver and electro-plated ware at the Centennial demonstrated, doubtless to the surprise of everybody, the capacity of American manufacturers to compete almost on equal grounds with the best ability in this line in Europe. Elsewhere will be found a description of the now celebrated "Century Vase," manufactured by the Gorham Manufacturing Company, of New York, and also of the monster piece of silver-plated ware named "Progress," exhibited by Messrs. Reed & Barton, of New York, and of Taunton, Mass. Satisfactory as the situation of this manufacture in relation to the industrial art of America must be, it is perhaps not less so that advantage is being taken in different directions of the examples furnished by

stamp. A larger portion of this sum is paid over to the Government as a tax, a small deduction being made for the assay. In France the alloy used for plate consists of $9\frac{1}{2}$ parts silver to half a part of copper; and for small articles of silver, such as those used for ornaments, it consists of 8 parts silver to 2 of copper. The addition of a small proportion of copper increases the hardness of silver in a remarkable degree, without diminishing its whiteness a great deal. An alloy of 7 parts silver and 1 of copper has a decidedly white color, although less pure than that of virgin silver. Even with even weights of the two metals the alloy is white. The maximum of hardness is attained when the copper amounts to one-fifth of the silver. Articles formed of alloyed silver are subjected to a process called whitening, which has the effect of removing the baser metal from the surface. The article to be whitened is heated nearly to redness, and plunged while still hot into water acidulated with nitric or sulphuric acid, by which means the oxide of copper, formed by heating the surface in contact with air, is immediately removed. German-silver is an alloy of copper, zinc, and nickel, which is cast and rolled in the same manner as sheet-brass, but is a more difficult metal to work, and requires greater care and skill. The original method of plating, long known as French

other names. The alloy, most difficult to work, is said to have been 40 parts of copper, 20 parts of spelter, and 20 parts of nickel; and to this mixture English manufacturers still adhere. The composition of the alloy, however, is always the secret of the manufacturer, and varies according to judgment derived from experience.

The first practical experiment in galvano-plastic was the simple one of transferring by its means the image and superscription of a copper coin to a copper deposit. In 1839 a Russian announced his ability to produce, by means of galvanism, a copy of any line, however fine, engraved in copper, and almost simultaneously an Englishman described processes which he had provided for electrotyping. Finally, as the new art developed, it was brought into use for the purpose of the reproduction of the most beautiful works of art, and also to substitute comparatively inexpensive, handsome and durable plated articles in lieu of the work which had hitherto been used. In the processes of electro-metallurgy the silver solution is usually composed of the double salts of cyanide of silver and potassium. All the sheets of silver in the bath are connected with one pole of a magneto-electro machine, and the objects to be plated are connected with the positive pole; the liquid, being an efficient conductor of electricity, follows the electric current and an interchange of elements in the solution takes place. The articles are suspended in the vats by means of wires on metal rods, and so arranged in each compartment as to expose an equal amount of surface to receive the deposit of silver or gold. The operation of plating is so nicely regulated that the rate at which the precious metal is being deposited can be exactly ascertained, and twenty-four ounces of silver can, so to speak, be veneered on to the surface of the metal, perfectly smooth and extremely hard, in the course of one hour. When the article has been in the bath a sufficient length of time, it is taken out, rinsed in cold water, and dried. In the manufacture of raised or *repoussé* work the operation is performed by means of a hammer, under various circumstances more or less complicated, though works in low relief are produced by means of dies of hardened steel or hard brass. Ornamental details of raised work, such as escutcheons, fluting, etc. are usually attached after the vessel or article has received its general form, as is also the case with regard to chasing and other ornamentation.

The Gorham Manufacturing Company are silversmiths, their business being the working of sterling silver, and their success in this manufacture having given them their name. In the early times of manufacturing silverware, coin was the basis of the best, but the Gorham Company use a standard which is twenty-five one-thousandths higher than coin. This company have manufactured solid silverware for more than thirty years. Their works are at Providence, R. I., where they employ about 450 hands. Here they have an entire block of buildings, filled with shafting and belting from steam engines of the largest size, connected by steam elevators with foundries for casting in iron, brass, gold, silver, and other metals; machine-shops, shops for wood-work, blacksmith-shops, rolling-mills, planing-machines, molding and refining furnaces, apartments for electro-plating and gilding, etc.

Besides the "Century Vase" (see page 261), there was exhibited at the Centennial a massive silver salver, ornamented with an elegant fretwork border several inches in breadth, exhibiting an appropriate design in the style of Benvenuto Cellini, which was purchased by a gentleman of New York for $3,000. Among other articles exhibited, were a bridal outfit and silver service of 320 pieces, and numerous complete sets, of great richness. An important feature in this manufacture is that comprised in the beauty of the cases made to contain the superb works in silver constructed by this company. These cases, many of them, are formed of inlaid wood lined with satin, or comprise massive oaken chests ornamented with silver corner-pieces and handles. All these are manufactured at the works of the company. In addition to their manufacture in solid silver, this company have introduced electro-plating into their work, and are widely known for their heavily plated ware called the "Gorham Ware." The resemblance of this to genuine silver is so close, that marks have to be resorted to for indication. Besides their factory in Providence, the Gorham Company have a wholesale sales' establishment in Bond Street, and a magnificent retail store at 37 Union Square, New York City.

The firm of Reed & Barton, who manufacture fine electro-plated ware, was established in 1824, and has its factory at Taunton, Mass.—a grand establishment, covering four or five acres, and employing 500 hands. Their salesroom in New York is at No. 686 Broadway—a large and handsome store, 40 by 130 feet, with basement, where are constantly displayed the most elegant and original works in the line of electro-plated work. The manufacture of this house includes not only the finer and more costly class of goods, but also articles less expensive and more suitable to the demands of the economical middle classes; and in these may be found the same beauty of design and the same delicate finish which have given a reputation to the more costly and elaborate pieces produced by this manufactory.

Taunton, Mass., is a thriving manufacturing centre, at the junction of the Old Colony and Taunton Branch Railroads, a location affording excellent facilities for access both to Boston and New York. The business of Messrs. Reed & Bar-

VENETIAN GLASS FLOWER-STAND.

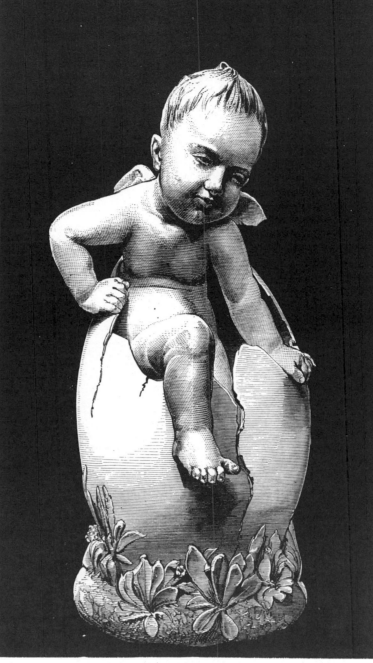

"THE BIRTH OF CUPID."

ton was founded here by Messrs. Babbitt & Crossman, who were directly succeeded by the present firm, whose head has been connected with the business since its establishment. As specimens of the high valuation set upon some of the articles manufactured by this house, it may be mentioned that they exhibited epergnes valued at $750 each, while a dessert-set may be seen costing $2,500. The capacity of the house to furnish the best silver-plated ware at as low price as goods of the same grade can be afforded elsewhere is unquestionable, and it is a fact that the trade-mark of Reed & Barton is accepted throughout the United States as a sufficient guarantee of both material and workmanship. The set which we illustrate in the HISTORICAL REGISTER is a fair specimen of the class of goods manufactured by this house, for which there is a constant demand, and the articles may be considered as samples of the material and workmanship usually employed.

THE BRYANT VASE.

One of the most noteworthy exhibits of American art at the Centennial Exhibition was the Bryant Testimonial Vase, the work of Messrs. Tiffany & Co., of New York, who exhibited it. This vase was the result of a subscription of $5,000 by the friends of William Cullen Bryant in the City of New York, who desired to offer some tribute of respect to the poet on the occasion of his reaching his eightieth year. It was presented to Mr. Bryant on June 20th, 1876, at a meeting of the subscribers and others interested, held at Chickering Hall, in New York. The ceremonies of presentation included music, the reception of the commemorative vase of the makers by the committee, its presentation to Mr. Bryant, with an address by the chairman, and a responsive address by Mr. Bryant. In presenting the vase to the chairman, a gentleman of the committee having the matter in charge—Mr. James H. Whitehouse, its designer, representing the firm of Tiffany & Co.—made an address, in which he explained the intention and character of the design and ornamentation which he had conceived and embodied in this beautiful work of art. Mr. Whitehouse was followed by Dr. Samuel A. Osgood, on behalf of the committee, who, in most suitable terms, offered the thanks of those gentlemen for the admirable manner in which their wishes had been carried out by the firm which had undertaken the task. After the musical interlude, Dr. Osgood addressed Mr. Bryant, congratulating him upon the ripe age he had reached, reminding him of the important periods in history covered by his long and useful life, and saluting him equally as the representative of American literature and the culture of the age.

Mr. Bryant received the gift thus pleasantly and appropriately offered in a few words of thanks, in which he characterized the vase as a product of genius both in the design and execution. His closing remarks, though amusing, are scarcely likely to be sustained by the fact of the future estimate of his genius. They were as follows:

"Hereafter some one may say, 'This beautiful vase was made in honor of a certain poet, whose name it bears, but whose writings are forgotten. It is remarkable that so much pains should have been taken to illustrate the life and writings of one whose works are so completely unknown at the present day.'"

It is hardly probable that the time will ever come, while the English language remains spoken and read, when the works of William Cullen Bryant, who may justly be termed the Wordsworth of America, will be either forgotten, neglected or misinterpreted.

The illustration of the Bryant Vase which we offer in the HISTORICAL REGISTER is especially appropriate to this work, both on account of its position among the art exhibits of the Centennial and because also of its being equally a representative work of American art, and a testimonial of America's greatest poet, happily presented in the Centennial Year. Some account of the peculiarities of the elaborate design of this work will be appropriate, and doubtless interesting both to those who have seen the vase and those who are only able to judge of its character by our representation of it. In considering the best method of illustrating the life and work of Mr. Bryant in the required vase, the artist necessarily devoted much contemplation to the characteristics which he wished to illustrate. Viewing Mr. Bryant's life as a symmetrical and rounded, although fortunately not completed, whole, Mr. Whitehouse was naturally struck with two prominent features which had, as it were, entwined themselves alike with the character and labors of the poet. These features the artist sought to perpetuate and embody, first, in the classical outline of the vase, and second, in the wealth and exuberance of nature's symbolism, which he introduced into its ornamentation. Thus the Greek form adopted symbolizes at once the combined simplicity and force of the poet's life, and also the character of his crowning work, the translation of Homer's "Iliad" and "Odyssey," accomplished when past seventy years of age. The elaborate application of the attributes of nature to the ornamentation of the work gives it at first sight a somewhat crowded and over-luxuriant aspect in this particular; but as we devote to the matter some degree of analysis, we find that there is a harmonious union of reason and sensibility involved in the selection made, and its just adaptation to the purpose indicated, which relieve it of this suggestion. Mr. Bryant, more than all other American poets, and perhaps more than all other poets whatsoever, excepting Wordsworth, is the poet of nature. It is, therefore, most proper and sympathetic, so to speak, that the field which he has chosen for his literary effort should be lavishly drawn upon in illustration of the latter.

The vase is made of oxidized silver, is 30 inches in height, and entirely covered with a fretwork, the chased lines of which are composed of forms simulating the apple branch with its blossoms, this tree in all its stages of growth, from the bud to the fruit, having always been a favorite with the poet, and suggestive to him of the moral of the beginning and the fullness of life. Interwoven with this fretwork are to be seen other flowers: the eglantine, which symbolizes the spirit of truth and poetry, and the amaranth, the flower that never fades, signifying immortality, being chiefly prominent. On one side of the vase is a medallion head of Mr. Bryant, admirable in its likeness, and on the reverse, one of similar size, representing Poetry contemplating Nature. Surrounding the work are other medallions in low relief, illustrative of various episodes in Mr. Bryant's life. In the first of these we see the child being instructed in the art of versification by his father, who indicates Homer as a suitable model. The second presents the poet as a young man walking in the woods, and reminds us at once of the beautiful

JAPANESE WARE.

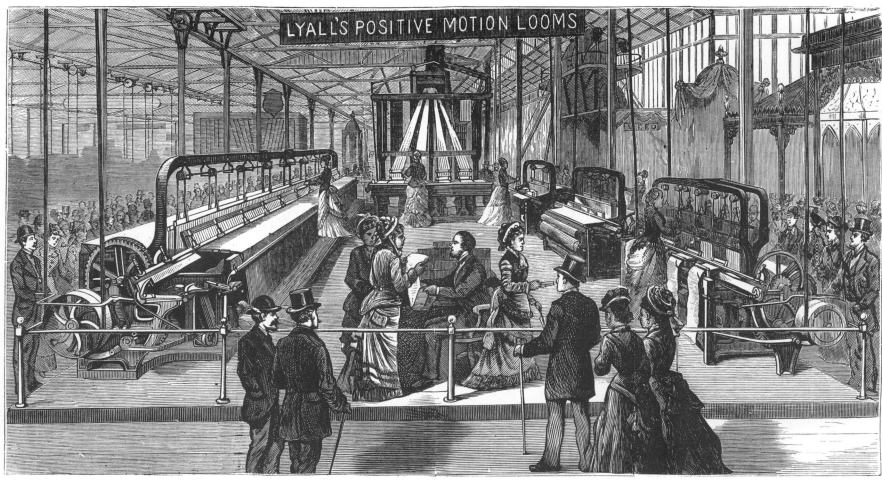

LYALL'S POSITIVE MOTION LOOMS, IN MACHINERY HALL.

lines from Thanatopsis," one of the most charming of Mr. Bryant's poetic effusions :

> " To him who, in the love of Nature, holds
> Communion with her visible forms, she speaks
> A various language."

The third medallion presents a representative scene from the life of Mr. Bryant as an editor, and the fourth shows him just rising from his chair after concluding his translation from Homer. Above the head of the poet we observe the lyre—significant of his poesy; and beneath it a view of the printing-press in its most primitive form—indicating his career as a journalist. Beneath this, occupying a prominent position, is a water-fowl. This last is introduced not merely to indicate Bryant's poem bearing that name, but also as emblematic of the religious faith which has ever been a special characteristic of Mr. Bryant :

> " He who from zone to zone
> Guides through the boundless sky his certain flight
> In the long way I must tread alone,
> Will lead my steps aright."

On the reverse of the vase, and immediately opposing the symbol we have just named, are seen the Bible and the lily, with " Matthew vi. 28th," reminding one of Christ's lesson in faith, commencing, " Consider the lilies of the field." The cup of the vase prominently displays the great staples of America—the Indian corn and cotton, significant of the nationality of the poet ; while its base is bordered with the water-lily—the emblem of eloquence—offering testimony of Mr. Bryant's achievements and reputation as an orator. The handles still further suggest America, through maize and cotton ; while here too is seen the bobolink, which is purely an American bird, and which reminds the observer of Mr. Bryant's humorous verse, and particularly the poem called " Robert of Lincoln." Around the lower neck of the vase are seen the primrose, representing early youth, and the ivy, symbolizing age, forming a border, while the lines running up from these are composed of the stems of field-flowers, which spread into blossoms. Above, there is seen the gentian, of which, in allusion to its always pointing to heaven, the poet says

> " I would that thus when I shall see
> The hour of death draw near to me,
> Hope blossoming within my heart,
> May look to Heaven as I depart."

In an ornamental border, near the top of the vase is the famous line :

> " Truth crushed to earth will rise again."

On the base supporting the vase are seen the lyre, and the broken shackles, in recognition of the poet's service in the cause of emancipation. This completes the design.

It is not unjustly claimed for this work of art by its designer that if by some convulsion of nature it were lost to humanity until all record of its existence, save that which it furnishes itself, were blotted out, its nature and intention could be readily gathered by the archæologist through the character of its design and the symbolical method of its ornamentation. Thus the head and the lyre would indicate a poet of renown, while the Indian corn and cotton would signify clearly his nationality. The wealth of floral decoration would announce him as a lover and exponent of Nature : the meaning of the chosen symbols indicating that his teachings must have been imbued with religious faith and fervor. The lilies would bespeak him an orator, while the old printing-press would set him down in his final character as a member of the respectable guild of journalists.

As we have already stated, the cost of this vase was $5,000. Messrs. Tiffany & Co. have succeeded in manufacturing an electrotype copy, which is positively wonderful in its excellence of imitation, and of which examples are offered for sale—*fac-similes* of the original—at $500 each.

PRISMOIDAL RAILROAD.

This novel style of road, which we illustrate on page 266 of the HISTORICAL REGISTER, consists of one rail—prism-shaped—the cars and engine running upon this by means of two wheels each, one at the front and another at the rear. Our readers will remember the car which crossed the ravine on the Centennial Grounds, known as Belmont Ravine, and which was liberally patronized by persons going to Lauber's Restaurant. This was called the "Safety Elevated Railway," and was designed by Roy Stone, and first erected at Phœnixville, Pa. Having been examined and fully approved by eminent engineers, it was taken to the Centennial Grounds under a concession to the West End Railroad Company, where it was placed as an exhibit for the conveyance of passengers. The system has been devised for rapid transit in cities, or for a cheap country railroad. Last November (1876), a road of $3\frac{1}{2}$ miles long was built in California on this plan, extending from Norfolk in the direction of Sonoma. The cost of this road, including that of the road-bed, was about $4,500 per mile.

CENTENNIAL ELEVATORS.

Our illustrations represent the two towers containing elevators, which were prominent objects in connection with the Centennial Exposition. From their lofty summits a magnificent view was presented in all directions, including the Schuylkill and Delaware Rivers, the mountains in the distance, the magnificent city of Philadelphia, and immediately beneath, Fairmount Park, in all its natural beauty, with the marvelous architectural and horticultural effects of the Centennial Grounds as the crowning glory of the scene.

AMERICAN PAINTINGS.

Of the American paintings—which have been fully considered in their proper place—we give illustrations representing certain of the more prominent works by well-known artists. Among these are "Moonrise at Sunset," by De Haas ; "Bison at Bay," a forcible representation, by the late W. J. Hays, one of the leading animal-painters of his time ; "Curling," by Brown, a clever representation of the popular Scotch game ; Shattuck's "White Hills" ; Boughton's "Normandy Girl in a Shower" ; and Beard's comical transfer of human frailty to brute life, entitled, "Out all Night."

The American exhibition of paintings was, in all, very fairly representative, including illustrations of the entire

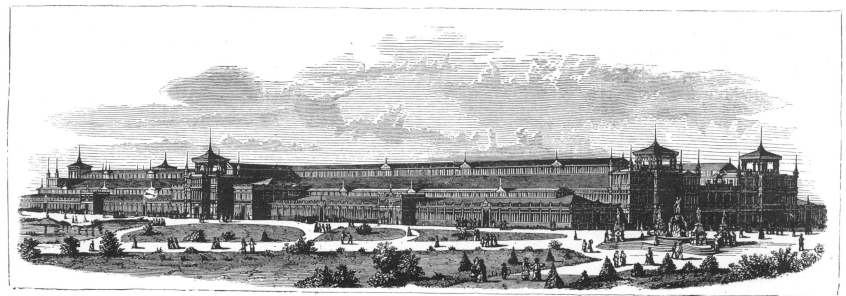

MACHINERY HALL.

period from Benjamin West to F. E. Church, and our engravings will serve to recall some of the more pleasing works in the collection.

Reception of Lord Dufferin at St. George's Hall.

We illustrate the cordial reception given to Lord Dufferin on the occasion of his visit to the Centennial Exposition, and which took place at St. George's Hall, the headquarters of the British Commission. The Earl of Dufferin succeeded to the title in 1841, and was for some years a lord-in-waiting on the Queen. He made his noted yacht voyage to Iceland in 1859, and in 1860 was sent out as British Commissioner to Syria. Later he was Under-Secretary of State for India, and Under-Secretary for War; and in 1872 was appointed Governor-General of the Dominion of Canada. Lord Dufferin has proven a most excellent administrator of affairs in the Dominion, where he is deservedly popular. His writings have been quite numerous, including several works of fiction, besides *brochures* on important political and social subjects.

Thonet Bros. Vienna Exhibit of Bent-Wood Furniture.

The bent-wood furniture in the Austrian Department of the Main Building was exhibited by Messrs. Thonet Bros., of Vienna, one member of the firm — Mr. Francis Thonet — being also honored by an appoint-

THE UNITED STATES CORSET COMPANY'S EXHIBIT IN THE MAIN BUILDING.

ment as one of the judges in Group VII., "Furniture, upholstery, etc."

The manufacture of this graceful class of household-ware will be found fully described on page 234 of the HISTORICAL REGISTER. The articles which we illustrate include a rocking-chair, table and table-glass—selections which give a fair representation of the character of the exhibit, and will remind the reader of the fine display made by the house to which we allude in the Austrian department.

Sir George Ferguson Bowen.

The subject of this sketch—whose portrait will be found elsewhere—was born in the North of Ireland, in 1821, and educated at the Charter-house School and Trinity College, Oxford, graduating from the latter university in 1844 as B. A. and first-class in classics. He was elected to a fellowship of Brasenose College, and from 1847 to 1851 was President of the University of Corfu, being appointed Chief Secretary to the Government of the Ionian Islands in 1854,

---

THE UNITED STATES CORSET COMPANY'S LOOM NO. 7, IN MACHINERY HALL.

a position which he held until 1859. In the latter year Sir George Bowen was appointed Captain-General and Governor-in-chief of the Colony of Queensland, in Australia; in 1867 he succeeded Sir George Grey as Governor of New Zealand, and in 1873 he was gazetted Governor of Victoria, a position which he still holds. In 1875 Sir George Bowen made an extended tour through Europe, and visited the United States, where he remained a considerable time, receiving the hospitalities of some of our most distinguished personages, and acquainting himself with the locality and scope of the proposed International Exposition, to which the colony under his government has since so creditably contributed. Sir George Bowen is the author of several important works, descriptive of his various travels in Europe.

The Ocean Challenge Cup.

This cup was made by Messrs. Tiffany & Co., of New York, for James Gordon Bennett, and by him presented to the New York Yacht Club. The design is highly appropriate for a yacht prize; the handles are formed of the prows of vessels winged with plumes suggestive of speed, and at the foot is the dolphin that follows in the wake of lucky vessels. The picture on the front is hammered from a smooth surface with a tool and hammer held in the hands of the skillful artisan, and by what is known as the *repoussé* process. It represents a scene from Longfellow's "Wreck of the *Hesperus*."

> "The skipper he stood beside his helm
> His pipe was in his mouth;
> And he watched how the veering flaw did blow
> The smoke, now west, now south."

The surmounting figure represents Columbus with the globe he traversed at his feet, and pointing with his index finger to the fair land that he first discovered.

The Centennial Race Cup of the New York Jockey Club.

The Centennial Race Cup of the New York Jockey Club connects the two subjects of patriotism and horses in a most appropriate manner for

THE "WHITEHILL" SEWING-MACHINE IN MACHINERY HALL.

---

the Centennial Year, by illustrating Washington's well-known love for fine stock, and representing him as a raiser of horses. This piece of metal sculpture attracted much attention at the Exhibition, where it occupied a prominent place in Messrs. Tiffany & Co.'s court.

The gentle firmness of Washington's character is shown to have won the confidence of the beautiful mare, and even the timid colt reaches shyly forward to receive a caress.

In the bas-relief here shown, horse and rider are represented in the heat of battle, and on the reverse side of the pedestal, another bas-relief shows Washington's triumphant entry into Trenton, and his reception by the people.

Meriden Britannia Company.

The exhibit of the Meriden Britannia company was located at N 43 in the Main Building, and consisted of a magnificent display of silver-plated goods, with ornamented work and articles of *vertu*. This company has manufactured plated ware only until recently, and has held a high position in the production of this class of goods. All this company's plated articles are stamped with its trade-marks, which —like that of the Goldsmiths' Company of London—give assurance of the genuineness of the manufacture and of the excellence of its quality. Recently the Meriden Company has begun to manufacture in bronze,

THE UNITED STATES CORSET COMPANY'S EXHIBIT IN MACHINERY HALL.

and has met with marked success. A peculiar method of triple-plating knives and forks is a specialty of this company, as is also their porcelain-lined ware, such as ice-pitchers, pie and pudding-dishes, etc. The Meriden Company's factory is at Meriden, Conn., and its New York sales' establishment in the fine building at No. 550 Broadway.

International Poultry Show.

The international display of poultry was held in the Pomological Building, an annex of Agricultural Hall, and continued from October 27th to November 6th. This exhibition was the finest ever held in the United States; and in the matter of pigeons, is said to be the largest and most comprehensive which has ever occurred anywhere.

The display of poultry proper comprised Asiatics, Hamburgs, Spanish, Dorkings, French, Polish, American, bantams, turkeys, geese, ducks, besides eight cages of canary-birds. There were, also, in the classes "ornamental" and "sundry," white

Guinea fowls, pea fowl; silver, golden, and English ring-necked pheasants; American quails; prairie chickens; rabbits, and Guinea pigs. All of the exhibits mentioned thus far were American. Next to these came pigeons, including carriers, pouters, pygmy pouters and fantails. There were also tumblers, Jacobins, turbits, Antwerps, and trumpeters; fifteen specimens of African owls, two Chinese owls and twenty-seven English owls, besides nineteen exhibits of swallows and seventeen of magpies. After these come nuns, runts, archangels, barbs, etc.

To go back to fowls proper, there were sixteen exhibits of light Brahmas over one year, and forty-five under one year, twenty-two of dark Brahmas, forty-two of partridge Cochins, fourteen of buff Cochins, eighteen of white Cochins, eight of black Cochins, and nine of other varieties. In games, there were seventy coops, chiefly from Pennsylvania and New Jersey. There were sixty-eight coops of Hamburgs, eighty-two of Spanish, eighteen of Dorkings, twenty-one of French, fifteen Polish, forty-six American, and one hundred and three bantams. The turkeys included light-bronze, dark-bronze, white Holland, slate, and three exhibits of wild turkeys. Altogether, there were twenty-eight coops. Of geese there were also nine coops, including Toulouse, white China, Hong-Kong, wild geese, and Egyptian. The ducks numbered forty-six coops, comprising Aylesbury, Cayuga, Rouen, Pekin white and colored, Muscovy white, crested and wood.

Great Britain furnished three exhibits of game fowl, and five coops of Hamburgs. Canada had sixteen coops of Asiatics, nineteen of games, eighteen Hamburgs, thirteen Spanish, eight Dorkings, ten French, sixteen Polish, and thirty-two coops of bantams; also four coops of geese, including white and bronze China and Brahma; thirteen coops of ducks, and thirty-six coops of pigeons.

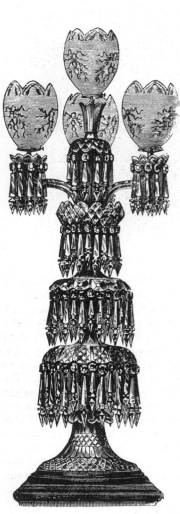

CRYSTAL STANDARD.

The Pomological Building, a structure 182 by 192 feet in dimensions, constructed of wood, one story high, and situated east of Agricultural Hall, was crowded to its fullest capacity with the coops of poultry ranged on tables. During the continuance of the Poultry Exhibition the Pomological Building was constantly filled with spectators. The display attracted much attention, and was evidently very gratifying.

THE CENTENNIAL POP-CORN.

An enterprising pop-corn man, who, it is said, secured the exclusive privilege of manufacturing pop corn on the Exhibition Grounds for a large sum of money, made good use of his concession, for he had several of these curious and attractive furnaces and selling-booths all over the Grounds. We illustrate the process of roasting corn over a fire—the women selling the flimsy but attractive grain prepared in this way, the men roasting, the piles of baskets filled with the round, red-and-white balls of the much-sought-after pop-corn. The booth in Machinery Hall was crowded all day, and thus showed the attractiveness of the exhibitor's peculiar wares and machinery.

DAMASCENED FOWLING-PIECE AND MOORISH PADLOCK.

On page 290 we illustrate specimens of ancient and modern damascened-work, as applied to firearms, etc. The musket is of Spanish origin, having been first used about 1520, though portable firearms of various patterns were in use in Europe about the middle of the fifteenth century. No sooner had fire-

THIRTY-LIGHT CRYSTAL CHANDELIER.

arms become portable than art was applied to their decoration. The barrels of arquebuses and pistols were encircled with delicate engraving and other ornamentation, inlaying in gold, silver, and ivory, etc. Damascening, or Damascus bronzing, is that in which dark and bright lines run through the brown ground. To produce this steel surface is rubbed over with diluted aquafortis and vinegar, mixed with a solution of sulphate of copper. It is then washed and dried, and rubbed with a hard brush to remove any scales of copper. Damascening is, in fact, a method of reproducing the peculiar appearance which characterized the original "Damascus blades," whose manufacture is a lost art.

SPANISH LACE AND FANS.

On page 292 will be found illustrations of the peculiar Spanish lace and Spanish fans, which have attained, and justly, to a world-wide reputation. Point lace reached a higher point of excellence of manufacture in Italy and Spain than in any other country, and even at the present day—as will have been seen by those who examined the Spanish Department in the Main Building—Spanish lace may defy competition as to its own peculiar characteristics.

Spanish fans are so well known as a distinctive belonging of the Spanish character, as illustrated in its costumes and ornamentation, that we need scarcely to refer to the fact. From the most ancient periods of Spanish history fans adorned with feathers have been in common use; at a later period the fashion of painting upon such articles national scenes, such as dances, feasts, and the like, became prominent. In the Spanish section of the Centennial Exposition there were exhibited most beautiful specimens, illustrating the point to which the art of adorning fans has reached in that country.

EX-GOVERNOR WILLIAM BIGLER.

The subject of this sketch was born at Shermansburg, Cumberland County, Pa., in December, 1813. His father being a farmer, and not very successful in that avocation, young Bigler received but a meagre common-school education, though he fortunately drifted into a printing-office, which stood for him in place of *alma mater.* About 1833 he commenced the publication of a political paper, writing editorials, setting type, working the press, and in fact comprising in himself his entire staff. In 1836 Mr. Bigler married, and shortly after sold out his paper and started in the lumber business. He had, however, addicted himself strenuously to politics, and becoming popular among the people with whom he was associated, he was elected to the State Senate in 1841. Ten years later Mr. Bigler was elected Governor of the State of Pennsylvania, being then only thirty-eight years of age.

ECCLESIASTICAL STANDARD.

The administration of Governor Bigler was characterized by the exhibition of virtues which we are accustomed to hear of as commonly attributed only to "the good old times," but which have regulated his conduct in every department of the affairs of life in which he has been engaged. These were rigid economy and strict accountability in the use of public moneys. In 1855 Governor Bigler was elected President of the Philadelphia and Erie Railroad Company, and in the same year to the United States Senate, where he served for six years. In 1857 he made himself prominent in the Kansas-Nebraska troubles, traveling over the greater part of Kansas, advocating a Free State policy. After the election of Mr. Lincoln, Governor Bigler was untiring in his efforts in the direction of a peaceful solution of the pending troubles. He was a member of the Charleston Convention of 1860, opposing Judge Douglas in that body. In 1864 he was temporary Chairman of the Democratic Convention, and voted for the nomination of Gen. George B. McClellan to the Presidency. Since 1868 Governor Bigler has lived in retirement at Clearfield, Pa., but was again brought prominently before the public in connection with the Centennial Board of Finance, on the formation of that body in 1872. In the specially important and responsible capacity of "financial agent" of the Bureau of Revenue, Governor Bigler labored very assiduously and judiciously toward effecting such a gathering of funds as should promise success to the

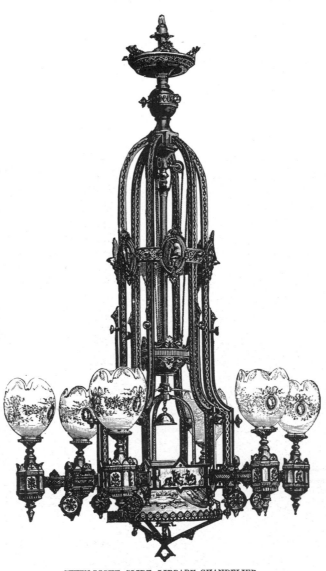

SEVEN-LIGHT SLIDE LIBRARY CHANDELIER.

MESSRS. MITCHELL, VANCE & CO.'S EXHIBIT OF CHANDELIERS, IN THE MAIN BUILDING.

EMPIRE TRANSPORTATION COMPANY'S EXHIBIT—MODEL OF OIL WELLS.

great object to which he now devoted all his time and efforts. Enthusiastic in his own confidence in the prospects of the Centennial Exhibition, he infused a similar belief into the minds of all with whom he came in contact, and by constant correspondence and personal solicitation was largely instrumental in advancing the interests of the Centennial at a time when even many of its strongest friends held back, dismayed at the formidable opposition which it so generally encountered.

As financial officer of the Centennial direction, the task of obtaining an appropriation from Congress was intrusted to Governor Bigler. In view of the contest between the United States Government and the Centennial Board of Finance, it is only fair to state that had the original bill passed as it was framed by Governor Bigler, the Government would have received $800,000 without a contest, since by that bill it was defined as a creditor on the same basis as the stockholders. But by means of an amendment framed by the opponents of the bill, a definition was given to the relations between the Government and the Centennial direction, which was so bunglingly constructed as to leave the former without any legal claim for anything. Governor Bigler fought this amendment earnestly, and no reason exists for charging him with any of the responsibility for the final conclusion.

In two letters which lie before us, written, respectively, to Senators Davis and Morrill in 1874, Governor Bigler foreshadowed the results

of the international character of the Exhibition with a precision that is positively remarkable.

Governor Bigler is a man of dignified yet genial appearance, affable, courteous and obliging; determined and energetic in any course of procedure which he adopts, and qualified by integrity of purpose and largeness of understanding to sustain and advance any movement with which he allies himself. He is, in fact, typical of the highest stamp of pronounced American manhood.

United States Field Telegraph Train.

The exhibit of the United States Signal Service, which we illustrate, consisted of a field telegraph train, with battery, wire-wagon, lance-trucks, running-gear, a portable signal-tower, and other signal appliances. It was

placed on State Avenue, on the Centennial Grounds, facing the New York State and British Government Buildings. The lance-wagon is 17 feet 7 inches long, and has a tool-box on each side, 7 feet long and 7 inches wide. The running-gear included a pole 9 feet long, and wheels 3 feet 4 inches and 4 inches in diameter. The wire-wagon has sills 8 feet 3 inches long, is all open at the back, and all its framework is made of white oak, ash, and poplar. The battery-wagon has a body of the same dimensions as the wire-wagon, and has three battery-boxes on each side, 2 feet 7 inches long, 7 inches wide and deep. It is supplied with a black canvas top and white duck curtains. Besides these appurtenances, there is a reel for the wire-wagon. The measurements of the signal tower are not at hand, and we are indebted to the United States Signal Service Department for the full schedule of dimensions, a portion of which only we are enabled to find space for in the HISTORICAL REGISTER.

Miscellaneous Objects.

Among the many articles which we illustrate, a large number will be found fully described in the remarks upon the sections of buildings where they were placed. Such are the statues "Flying Time" and "Love's Messenger"—the former appears on page 229, the latter on page 233. The Ségur exhibit of *paté de foie gras* was made by Messrs. Ségur & Obier, Périgueux, Dordogne, France, and was in Agricultural Hall. The Belgian Carved Pulpit and Belgian Furniture, of

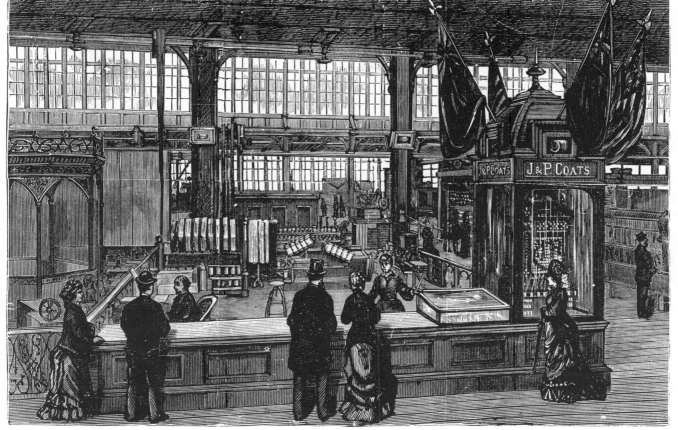

SPOOL COTTON EXHIBIT OF MESSRS. J. & P. COATS, OF PAISLEY, SCOTLAND, IN MACHINERY HALL.

THE MICHIGAN STATE BUILDING.

which we give illustrations, were in the Belgian section of the Main Building, and attracted constant attention from those who delight in carved furniture. A Japanese Vase and Sandwich Island Boat are each illustrative of the industry of the country represented. The Blowing Machinery, in Machinery Hall, will be remembered by all who experienced its wonderful force, and has been fully noticed elsewhere. Brewers' Hall is fully described on pages 158 and 159. The exhibit of the "Society for the Prevention of Cruelty to Animals" is considered at length in another portion of this work; while the illustration of an American Carriage, and those of the English Cutter, Sportsman's Carriage, and Phaeton, will be recognized as representing articles which were displayed in the Carriage-Annex to the Main Building. The illustrations of the exhibits of the Empire Transportation Company will be found described at length in the article entitled, American Freight Building, on page 147 of the REGISTER, and the views of the Arkansas State Building may be considered in connection with the descriptive article on page 167. The Washington State Carriage was in the Carriage-Annex, and was undoubtedly the actual vehicle in which the Father of his Country was accustomed to make his journeys in those days when railroads were not, and in it he very possibly traveled from his home in Virginia to New York on the occasion of his inauguration. Our illustration of the Baily Gun, an improvement on the Gatling and mitrailleuse, by an inventor who claims to have originated this class of artillery, represents the piece of ordnance which, in the latter days of the Centennial, was to be seen in the Indiana State Building; it is described on page 298. On page 250 is an engraving of the Russian Hut, and on page 97 we refer our readers for an account of the Russian exhibits in Agricultural Hall; and for descriptions of the Weber Pianoforte, Juvet's Time Globe, the Chilian Minerals, and Daniell's Pottery Exhibits, to the articles upon the American,

Chilian, and British sections in the Main Building. The Wisconsin and Illinois State Buildings are briefly referred to on page 169.

For description of the Bryant Testimonial Vase our readers are referred to page 303. Our second illustration of the exhibits of Messrs. Tiffany & Co., of New York, represents the superb ornament in the form of a feather, studded with diamonds, which has been so greatly admired by those who were privileged to see it.

CALIFORNIA AND ITS RESOURCES.

EXTENDING from latitude 22 deg. 20 min., its southern limit, northward to the 42d parallel, and between 114 deg. and 124 deg. west longitude, California has a coast-line of about 750 miles, with an average breadth of 230 miles, and comprises within its limits an area of 154,116 square miles, or nearly twice the extent of Great Britain. The general character of California is mountainous, and a remarkable feature of the State is the existence of two great mountain ranges running northwest and southeast—the Sierra Nevadas and the Coast Range Mountains. Near the northern boundary of the State is a latitudinal range, in which stands the grand and majestic Mount Shasta, 14,442 feet above the sea-level, its summit being within the limits of everlasting snow. The average height of the Coast Range is 23,000 feet above the sealevel, and it is intersected by numerous long, fertile, and narrow valleys—namely: Los Angelos, Salinas, Santa Clara, Sonoma, Napa, and Russian River Valley. The Sierra Nevada Mountains of California are clothed with valuable forests, while beneath are stores of incalculable mineral wealth. Between the two ranges of the mountains lie the extensive and productive valleys of San Joaquin and Sacra-

mento, extending from north to south a distance of about 500 miles in length, and from 50 to 60 in breadth. The principal rivers in the State are also named the Sacramento and San Joaquin. The former takes its rise near the lofty Mount Shasta, and the latter in the Sierra Nevadas. They are each about 350 miles in length. The climate of California is varied, differing greatly in different counties. The year is divided into two seasons, the wet and dry season. The latter season commences in the month of May and continues until about the middle of November, when the wet season commences and lasts until April or May. California is undoubtedly one of the most productive countries in the world. Entire counties are completely covered with wild oats, and are invaluable grazing grounds for numberless herds during the dry season. The soil does not require cultivation and manuring, as is usual in older countries.

THE IOWA STATE BUILDING.

From 15,000,000 to 25,000,000 bushels of wheat are produced annually in the State, the average yield being about 17 bushels per acre, although the best wheat-producing counties exceed 30 bushels per acre. In addition to wheat, barley, oats, rye, buckwheat, and Indian corn are extensively raised. The yield of agricultural products in the year 1873 was: wheat, about 25,000,000 bushels; barley, 8,000,000; oats, 1,200,000; rye, 16,000; maize, 1,000,000; buckwheat, 10,000; potatoes, 1,400,000; hay, 350,000 tons; butter, 5,000,000 pounds; honey, 500,000 pounds, and cheese, 3,000,000 pounds. The wheat-growing farms are of an immense size, ranging from 500 to 13,000 acres. The entire agricultural products for 1873 are valued at $100,000,000. During 1873 there were manufactured in California 85,000,000 cigars, consuming nearly 3,000,000 pounds of leaf-tobacco. Cotton has been grown on a constantly improving scale for several years. During the year 1873 about 2,000 acres were under cultivation, the quality being superior. Garden-produce of all descriptions is largely raised in the State, a peculiar feature being the enormous size of the fruit and vegetables. Pumpkins have been grown weighing 250 pounds; squashes, 200 pounds; a single beet weighed 118 pounds, and carrots have been raised weighing 30 pounds. The fig, olive, and pine-apple-trees grow luxuriantly in the southern gardens of the State. All varieties of European fruits and vegetables are produced to sell; in the southern

TIFFANY & CO.'S EXHIBIT.—THE CENTENNIAL RACE CUP OF THE NEW YORK JOCKEY CLUB, PRESENTED BY MR. AUGUST BELMONT.

counties tropical fruits, such as the plantain and banana, come to perfection. The most important of the native fruits is the grape, there being over 30,000,000 of vines planted in the State. The great grape-vine of Santa Barbara, a portion of which was on exhibition in Agricultural Hall at the Centennial, was planted forty-six years ago. In 1874 it measured 12 inches in diameter at 4 feet from the ground. At 2 feet higher the stem was divided, and its branches, supported by a rude trellis, formed a splendid bower, which covered an area of 10,000 square feet. It commonly produces about 12,000 pounds of grapes, the bunches weighing 6 or 7 pounds each, and being from 15 to 18 inches long. The next growth in value and importance is the orange, the culture of which has been confined almost entirely to the southern counties, the chief orange-producing locality being Los Angelos. There are about 25,000 orange - trees in the State. Of other fruits there are supposed to be 10,000 of mulberry-trees, 1,120,000 apple-trees, 1,000,000 peach, 40,000 quince, 52,000 apricot, 33,000 fig, 4,000 lemon, 20,000, olive, 7,000 prune, 25,000 almond, and millions of vines and bushels of small fruits. The forests of California are noted throughout the world, and the big trees of Mariposa and Calaveras rank among the natural curiosities of the United States. The sugar-pine grows about 300 feet in height, and measures 12 feet in diameter. The red-wood grows only on the coast, within 30 miles of the Pacific Ocean, and there is a giant plant of this species in Santa Cruz County, 275 feet high, and 19 feet in diameter 6 feet above the ground. Near the Klamath River there is said to be one as much as 30 feet in diameter, and one hollow red-wood stump is mentioned which is 38 feet in diameter, and in which 33 pack-mules were corraled at one time. The laurel is one of the most beautiful trees of the coast valleys. The madrona is another striking tree, while others are the juniper, yew, nutmeg, coast cypress, manzanita, etc.

California is a great stock-raising country. Formerly all the cattle were of pure Spanish blood, but for the last ten years this stock has been decreasing. Sheep-raising is one of the most important as well as profitable avocations in the State, and the business of wool-growing one of the most valuable. In 1873 the clip of wool was 36,000,000 pounds, and there are over 5,000,000 head of sheep in the State. There are from 20,000 to 30,000 common goats, and from 10,000 to 15,000 cashmere goats. Gold and silver form the chief mineral wealth, although extensive deposits of copper exist in some counties, and several kinds of iron ore are to be found in the Coast Range. There are also three or four beds of coal of the variety called lignite. Gold was discovered in a mill-race erected by General Sutter in 1848, and in a few months thousands of adventurous emigrants were on their way to the new El Dorado. In 1849 the product was nearly $5,000,000; in the following year it was five times as much, and by 1856 it had increased to $58,000,000. Since that time the gold yield has been gradually decreasing, and for the past five years the agricultural product of

the State has been greater than that of its mines by millions of dollars. Silver exists in large and extensive deposits in the counties east of the Sierra Nevadas.

The first railroad in California was constructed between Sacramento and Folsom, a distance of 22 miles, and was opened in 1856. The Central Pacific Railroad Company filed their certificate of incorporation June 28, 1861, and was incorporated with the Union Pacific Railroad Company two years after. The Central Pacific broke ground January 8th, 1863; the Union Pacific on the 2d December following; the first at Sacramento and the other at Omaha. In May, 1869, this line was opened.

The total population of California at the end of 1874 was about 700,000. Of these a large number are Chinese, the Chinese population in 1870 having been estimated at about 60 000. From 1852 to 1870, 90,000 Chinese

MAMMOTH JAPANESE BRONZE VASE.

emigrants arrived at San Francisco. Naturally the advent of so many Chinese in California suggested tea, and it is a fact that the cultivation of the tea-plant has grown to be quite an industry.

CENTENNIAL BUREAU OF PROTECTION.

THE Police arrangements of the Centennial were organized with wise forethought and judgment, and completely subserved the purpose for which they were designed. A sufficient force of Centennial Guards patrolled the Grounds during the day and night, and were stationed at all times in the different buildings. The men were under perfect military discipline, living in barracks on the Grounds, and being entirely devoted to the objects of their appointment. Court-rooms and other buildings for the distribution of

justice and the punishment of offense were also a portion of the surroundings of this Bureau, and these we illustrate on page 296 of the HISTORICAL REGISTER. It was gratifying to recognize at the close of the Exhibition the fact that the Bureau of Protection had had so little to do in the strict line of its duty as was the case. The visitors to the Exposition were orderly, good-humored and well-behaved, quite beyond precedent, and the arrests were very few in actual number, and comparatively unimportant.

POTTERY AND PORCELAIN.

THE numerous and beautiful exhibits of pottery and chinaware in the Main Building of the Centennial attracted so much attention, and awakened so much interest in the whole subject, that some examination of the history of the ceramic art will not be inappropriate in this place. The word "ceramic," by-the-way, comes from a Greek word signifying "potter's earth," the corresponding descriptive word from the Latin being "fictile," from *fingo*, "to form." The fashioning of utensils and the claying and baking of them, either in the sun or by fire, is unquestionably one of the earliest arts applied by humanity, evidences of this coming down to us from the remotest periods. By the ancient Egyptians the art was attributed to the gods, which shows that its origin must have been of a date preceding their records. Frequent allusions are made to it in the Old Testament, and among the articles of the different Eastern countries, as well as those of ancient nations which people America, relics are found illustrating this manufacture. Among the Egyptians, vases or jars appear to have been the prevailing utensils for a great variety of purposes. They were of all sizes, from several feet in height down to scarcely an inch, some being water-jars with wide necks, others peculiarly shaped, being made to contain wine, oil, honey, milk, drugs, ointments, and numerous other articles. These vases were made in terra cotta or in glazed common ware, the color being red, and some of the finer articles appearing to have been polished by some mechanical process. The date of these goes back to from 2,000 to 3,000 years before Christ. The glaze used appears to have been formed of pulverized silex and soda, and colored by various metallic oxides. The blue tint discovered and used at this early period retains its lustre to the present time, and is unsurpassed by the productions of modern art. The specimens of Eastern pottery which have been preserved to us are for the most part bricks, tiles, cylinders, etc. Among the Babylonian relics were bas-reliefs in terra-cotta, generally produced in molds representing figures of men and animals.

In Europe the most ancient pottery worthy of notice was that of the Etruscans. As far back as the seventh and eighth centuries before Christ, their vases—of course dark-brown ware—in great variety of sizes, ornamented with figures in relief, were produced in forms of such perfection and beauty as to entitle them to the rank of works of art,

At a later period the effect of intercourse with the Greeks changed the native style to imitations of the Hellenic. The Etruscan relics of this class are chiefly vases of black and brown metal, and terra-cotta, the most of which have been found in the sepulchres. From the fifth to the third century before Christ the pottery manufacture was important in Greece, and included a great variety of articles finished in the highest style of art. At Athens and in other Grecian cities there were at times public exhibitions of these works, by means of which a spirit of competition was incited. Among the relics of this manufacture have been found vases and small terra-cotta figures, small modern plaster casts, these being painted in appropriate colors by artists specially devoting themselves to this avocation. Lamps, also, of delicate construction, are found, many of these being readily referred to the period of the Roman dominion. Vases called "*amphoræ*" were universally employed for the storing and transportation, and other commodities, as well as for different domestic purposes. Ornamental vases are very numerous, in which are imitated the figures of animals, heads of Bacchantes, and others, highly decorated with figures in relief and elaborately colored. From the third century, B. C., the ceramic art declined in Greece, the introduction by Alexander the Great of metallic vases having led to the substitution of these for the better varieties of pottery. The finished specimens of Greek vases are found in Etruria, and were the work of Grecian artists removed thither, or were the work of Etruscan artists educated in Greece. In Roman pottery vases were the most numerous and useful products of the art, and these were far inferior to the Grecian manufacture of the same period. The finest ware known is from the potteries of Samos and Aretium, and about the second or third century, A.D. Chinese pottery dates back to the second century, B. C., and in that country porcelain is used not merely for domestic utensils, but for slabs and tiles. Marco Polo, in the latter part of the thirteenth century, was struck with the extent of the porcelain manufacture in China and the extraordinary cheapness of the ware, eight cups of which could be purchased for a Venetian groat. The finest articles were not exported, and the process of manufacture was kept secret. Upon the American continent numerous illustrations of ancient pottery have been discovered; the wares of the ancient Peruvians testifying to a high degree of skill in this art. The paste used is usually red or yellow, ornamented with figures of black, red, white, and yellow. Many flasks are beautifully formed, with long, delicate necks; and others are heads of animals—the jaguar—or have the forms of birds or of native fruits. The Mexicans also early attained a high degree of perfection in their pottery—that of the Tlascalans being unsurpassed in its excellence by any in Europe, while that of the Cholulans was extremely delicate, rivaling in beauty the Florentine manufacture. About the ruins of New Mexico and Chihuahua relics of this character are found in the greatest abundance, and for miles around certain ruins in that country the surface of the ground is found strewn with broken pottery of fine quality. The colors are red, black, and white, and many articles are painted on the inside, while modern Indian and Mexican wares are painted on the outside. After the decline of the Roman Empire pottery, as a decorative art, was lost in Europe. The Arabs introduced it into Spain on their conquest of that country, and also into Sicily in the next century. They confined their productions, however, chiefly to tiles for pavements and for the decoration of the walls of buildings, in which they have never been equaled. The Alhambra and the great mosque at Palermo, in Sicily, remain as illustrations of their facility in this art. Gradually the manufacture spread into Italy, and by the fourteenth century was improved by native invention and by the introduction of Grecian processes from Byzantium. In Pesara at this period was practiced what may be regarded as the basis of the majolica ware.

The ordinary pottery which constituted the common groundwork, after being partially baked was covered by immersion with a thin coating of pure white clay, with which were intermixed oxides of lead and tin. The baking was then completed in a kiln. This style was gradually perfected by the Robias, to whose labors we have referred in a previous article. For two centuries the finest ware in pottery was that of majolica, characterized by its peculiar lustres, and named, it is supposed from the island of Majolica, where similar ware has been produced by the Moors. Urbina, Gubio, Castel-Duronte and Faenza were places especially famous for this ware, and the word "faience," by which also it is designated, was probably derived from the last named city. In the sixteenth century this class of pottery manufacture was introduced in Nuremberg, Germany, and Navarre, France, and was practiced with great success by Bernard de Palissy, "the Potter." The Dutch have been famous from the fifteenth century for their colored tiles and other pottery produced at Delft and its vicinity. From that period they continued to be largely introduced into England for churches and expensive mansions, and in the sixteenth century their dishes for dinner service were well known throughout Europe. The Dutch appear to have copied from the old porcelain of Japan, with which their extensive Eastern commerce made them early acquainted. Chinese porcelain was imported into Europe by the Portuguese in the early part of the sixteenth century, and was known as "China." The Dutch and English afterward brought the ware from the East, and as it became known every attempt was made to ascertain the secret of its beautiful translucency, and to produce the same ware in European countries. The nature of the material was first discovered by Bätcher, an apothecary's assistant at Berlin, and a refugee in Saxony on account of being reputed as an alchemist, who succeeded in producing in 1709 a genuine white porcelain of natural clay, with old metallic fluxes. The Elector, Frederick Augustus, was so much pleased with this that he established a manufactory at Meissen, of which Bätcher was made director. Works for manufacturing this ware were established in 1735 at Chantilly, and ten years later at Vincennes. In 1754 by royal sanction the works were removed to Sèvres. Porcelain was made in England in the middle of the last century, first at Chelsea, under the patronage of George II., and afterward at Worcester and other places. The works at Worcester have been styled since 1786, "The Royal Porcelain Works." Staffordshire is also an important seat of the porcelain manufacture. There are in England the most extensive potteries, established upon the same spots which were occupied for the same purpose by the potteries during the period of Roman occupation. The so-called "Queen's-ware" was originated by Josiah Wedgewood, who was born in 1730, and who thirty years later produced specimens of this peculiar cream-colored ware. By means of his chemical acquirements and extraordinary skill, Wedgewood succeeded in imitating in porcelain for himself, cameos and antiques, and even the wonderful Portland vases of which he produced fifty copies, which were scarcely surpassed in beauty by the original itself.

GORHAM MANUFACTURING CO.'S EXHIBIT.—THE CENTURY VASE.

In Norway the manufacture of the finer grades of pottery—fine faience and porcelain—is not carried on to any very great extent, since an ample supply can be obtained from Sweden, where the native material is excellent, and where there are large factories, producing ware of superior quality. Only a small Norwegian exhibit was made of pottery, including a few painted porcelain articles, whose quality, however, was very good, the glaze upon some of the dinner services being quite rich and brilliant, but the painting in imitation of natural flowers was rather crude and inartistic. Certain specimens exhibited were ornamented after the Japanese fashion, with grotesque figures of men and dragons in black and red colors, and Japanese characters in black dotted over the intervening surface. The glaze in the Norwegian pottery is exceedingly brilliant, and it has attained to remarkable excellence in gilding. The King of Sweden, however, made, as has been already observed in the proper place, a very varied and interesting exhibit in ceramic wares. Indeed, the manufacture of pottery in its varied forms is one of the principal industries of the Swedish nation. At present this manufacture is carried on in two china and two faience factories at Rorstrand, established in 1726, and Gustaffsberg, established in 1830, both being close to Stockholm. There is also a recently established faience factory at Malmo, an earthenware factory at Hoganas, and a great number of factories and workshops for the manufacture of stone, inferior faience and common earthenware in different parts of the country. At the two principal—Rorstrand and Gustaffsberg—almost all sorts of earthenware are made, from the real feldspar porcelain to fine faience. These two factories are nearly equal in size, employing together about 1,200 persons, and the value of their manufactures in 1874 was about $750,000 gold, the greater part of this being sold in Sweden, but there being also a considerable quantity exported to Norway, Denmark and Russia. The Rorstrand exhibit of majolica and Bernard de Palissy ware was one of the most notable exhibits in the Swedish court. It comprised a great variety in vases, plaques, figure subjects, etc., the designs being spirited and highly artistic. The prevailing color was a rich, clear green, the largest pieces, such as jardinières, on pedestals, and the hollow vases, being particularly fine. One of these, representing a cupid sitting on a dolphin, and another a winged dragon, coiling up and around a tree trunk, were exceptionally excellent. Among the smaller pieces of majolica was a fine vase, supported at the base by thin, broad lily-leaves, in which the shades of green were beautifully blended. A favorite and rather pleasing style of decoration consisted of faience and delicate leaves in very low relief on a ground of gray, modeled with blue. A very beautiful piece of manufacture was a ewer with a snake handle, and lizard, flowers and bees in relief on the body. Rorstrand faience, plain and decorated, bisque ware and Parian, and useful ornamental china and porcelain were all of superior quality and artistic excellence. There were some vases and plaques exhibited, covered with a brilliant black or dark-blue glaze, with raised designs of flowers and ferns in white, which were most interesting and beautiful specimens. A pair of small vases with gilt figures was exhibited, in imitation of the ivory porcelain of Japan. A pair of deep covered dishes were ornamented with sprays of roses, which were arranged so ingeniously that the stems were often entirely detached from the body of the piece, against which the flower-stand leaves rested in imitation of nature.

The use of the Japanese ideas of decoration was exemplified again in a very pretty set of dessert-plates, which were ornamented with Japanese figures on a white ground, the borders being painted with butterflies and flowers on grounds of different colors. The largest vases were very rich in decoration, the colors being brilliant, and effectively and ingeniously combined. Biscuit figures of a basket pattern were quite numerous, in which the flower ornamentation was especially noticeable. The quality of the material permits of the most delicate manipulation, and the modeling of the pinks and delicate grasses may be claimed as a triumph of the ceramic art. One rare and remarkable specimen was a small vase, ornamented with flowers and grass, the whole piece—flowers and grass—afterward being covered with a transparent glaze. In Europe the forming of collections of pottery has long been an object of interest not only to numerous wealthy amateurs but also to the governments of states. In England this has been properly the case, the rage for ceramics having at times risen to the height of mania. In Dresden, at the Japanese palace, founded by the Elector Frederick Augustus I., is the magnificent national collection. In it the Oriental china alone occupies thirteen large rooms, the progress of the Dresden manufacture being represented by a great variety of well-selected pieces. The museum of the porcelain of Sevres was commenced in 1812, for the purpose of illustrating the progress of the ceramic art from the manufacture of reduced ware to that of the finest porcelain, including also the geography and chronology of the art. This manufacture affords an eminent instance of the value imparted to worthless materials by skill and science. Single vases of the Sèvres china, 12 to 15 inches high, have repeatedly sold for $5,000; majolica plate for $500; Chinese kyolins, or antique vases, for $1,500; and the prices at which some of these articles were valued at the Centennial were a further illustration of the estimation in which they are held. The preparation of the crude materials for manufacturing articles of pottery is a work of labor and time. In the first place, there are said to be no less than 167 different varieties of clay, the purest kinds of which are derived directly from the decomposition of the granitic rocks, which may be considered the original source of clays. Clay has the peculiarity of being gradually heated, or of parting with its water and diminishing in bulk without cracking, when heated to redness. It forms a solid mass when cooled in water and allowed to absorb this into its pores. Kaolin, or China clay, was originally known as a Chinese clay, and was so named from the Chinese word "Kaoling," referring to the name of a hill in China where this mineral is obtained. This clay is met with near Meissen, in Saxony; it is also found in Bavaria; near Limoges, in France; at Devonshire, in England; and other places in Europe. Such clays are also obtained in this country, an excellent material being found in Brunswick, Maine, and also at Haddam, Conn. In collecting the kaolin for the manufacture of pottery, vats are placed where the washing of the decomposition of the granitic rocks can collect and settle, passing from one to another. The water being drawn off, the fine sediment left is taken out of these in blocks and exposed to the weather for a few months, when it is crushed and packed in casks for the potteries. It is then an impalpable white powder, consisting of 60 parts of alumina and 20 of silica. The mixtures for true porcelain consist of kaolin and ground feldspar, with a little carbonate of lime introduced. These materials are ground to very fine powder, and are then mixed by stirring them in water in large cisterns; the surplus water is afterward removed until the composition is reduced to the consistency of dough, when it is worked over by kneading, etc. The porcelain paste requires lengthened working, and after this it is stored away for a long time, to go through what is called "the molding process," by which its plastic capacity is increased. Finally it is cut into lumps by a brass wire, and these are again incorporated by slapping them together. Form is given to the articles either by a potter's wheel or in molds. The former of these implements was used in Egypt 2,000 years B. C., and has been very little changed in appearance since. Handles, spouts and ornamental pieces are separately molded, and attached afterward. Great pains are taken to guard against distortion in the drying of the pieces, these being put upon shelves, and slightly dried by the sun and artificial heat. The application of glaze to porcelain bisque, which is done after a preparatory firing, is made by dipping the vessels into tubs containing the glaze composition.

The firing is conducted in tall, cylindrical kilns, like glass furnaces. The articles to be baked are carefully placed in drum-shaped clay vessels, which when filled are piled upon each other, forming columns filling the kilns. The heat required for firing varies in different places for different wares, but French porcelain usually takes from 25 to 30 hours. When this is completed, the kiln is closed up and left so from five to eight days, in order that the ware may anneal. When it is removed, about one-fourth is usually found to be misshapen and ruined, while all the pieces require a final revision and dressing with a stone grinding-wheel, etc. The pigments used for painting porcelain consist of flux; the coloring ingredient is commonly a metallic oxide. Those colors which withstand the high heat of the kiln are termed "refractory colors," and are applied before glazing. The others are applied after baking, and therefore involve an additional process. Gold is applied with the brush, and after firing the gilding is brought out by burnishing.

SPECIAL MEETINGS AT THE CENTENNIAL.

The Oddfellows' Celebration.

During the continuance of the Exhibition a great many organizations made it convenient to hold their special or regular meetings at the grounds, while also a considerable number of visits were made to Fairmount by gatherings organized for the purpose. Without pretending to enumerate or describe all of these, some reference to them will doubtless be found interesting to the general reader as well as to those who participated in them.

Probably one of the largest and most important and interesting of these meetings was that which occurred at the Oddfellows' Centennial celebration, when a grand parade of the Order took place in Philadelphia. The procession was divided into twenty grand divisions, these being subdivided into smaller divisions, each under proper officers. The formation took place in Broad Street, the headquarters of the Grand Marshal being located at the Forrest Mansion. The Grand Lodge of Pennsylvania met at the National Guard Hall, Race Street, below Sixth. The first Grand Division was formed on Broad Street, the right resting on Spruce, and the remaining divisions extended as far north as Columbia Avenue. After being properly formed, the procession marched over the prescribed route to the Grand Stand near the Main Building, where the concluding ceremonies took place.

The ceremonies were of a most imposing and attractive character. Four stands were erected near the eastern end of the Main Building, and from each of them orations were delivered. The programme was opened with instrumental music, when the Handel and Haydn Society sang a festival hymn. This was followed by prayer, and an ode sung by the Handel and Haydn Society, after which orations were delivered from the four different prescribed points by William Ellison, Past Grand Sire of Massachusetts, representing the East; Wilmot G. de Saussure, Past Grand Sire of South Carolina, representing the South; Nathan Porter, Grand Representative of California, representing the West; and John A. Jackson, Past Grand Representative of Minnesota, representing the North. These orations combined a consideration both of the growth of the country and that of the institution of Oddfellowship. They were all eloquent and comprehensive. The ceremonies concluded by singing the Doxology, and the pronouncing of the benediction by the Grand Chaplain.

The Order of Oddfellowship is purely an American institution. It was established in Baltimore on the 26th day of April, 1819, by Thomas Wildey, John Welsh, John Duncan, John Cheatam and Richard Rushworth, who met in a poor room of a small, unattractive building in an unfrequented street near the docks of Baltimore. Here they organized the first lodge recognized by the Order of the present day, which they called Washington Lodge No. 1. The founders were all foreigners. At the end of ten years the Order had been planted in Maryland, Pennsylvania, New York, Massachusetts and the District of Columbia, but its condition was comparatively feeble. About 1830, however, it began to spring into a more vigorous state, and from that period progressed with unparalleled rapidity. In 1834 it was introduced into Missouri; in 1836, into Mississippi and Illinois; in 1837, into Alabama and Texas; in 1839, into Arkansas and Connecticut; in 1840, into Tennessee and South Carolina; in 1841, into North Carolina and Florida; in 1842, into Georgia; in 1843, into Maine, New Hampshire and British America; in 1844, into Vermont, Michigan, Iowa, Great Britain and New South Wales; in 1846, into the Sandwich Islands; in 1849, into Minnesota and California; in 1851, it was established in New Mexico; in 1852, in Oregon; in 1855, in Nebraska and Washington Territory; in 1857, in Kansas and Nevada; in 1865, in Utah; in 1867, in Montana; in 1868, in Kentucky and Australia; in 1870, in Germany. The Order now numbers in the United States nearly half a million members.

GORHAM MANUFACTURING CO.'S EXHIBIT.—THE YACHT PRIZE CUP.

National Spelling Reform Convention.

A very interesting occasion was the meeting at the Atlas Hotel, opposite the Centennial Grounds, of from 60 to 80 educators and others interested in the revision of English orthography, embracing representatives of Brazil, Sweden, Australia, England, and all sections of the United States —the delegate from Virginia being a colored man, J. B. Town, of the Freedman's School.

The meeting was held under the auspices of the National Institute, and the proceedings were opened with prayer, after which Professor S. S. Haldeman, of the University of Pennsylvania, presiding officer, upon taking the chair, spoke concerning the importance of the phonetic movement. According to him, we should take as the basis of the new orthography the original powers of the letters, so far as we could find them, and form a scheme which should tend so far as possible to express those powers, in place of the system of spelling now in vogue, and which is, in his opinion, corrupt. The gentleman gave several illustrations of the misuse of letters, comparing the English with other languages.

At the permanent organization, the following gentlemen were elected officers: *President*, Professor S. S. Haldeman, of the University of Pennsylvania; *Vice-President*, Edward Jones, B. A., Liverpool, England; *Secretary*, Melville Demay, Amherst College; *Treasurer*, Hon. B. F. Burnham, President of the Massachusetts Tachygraphic Society.

Several of the subjects were then presented in papers read by the members, and in resolutions adopted by the American Philological Association at a previous meeting in New York, and were discussed. Of these papers, Professor F. A. March, of Lafayette College, Pennsylvania, presented one on the "Improvement of the Reading Machinery of the English Language and Spelling." Comparing the English with other systems of spelling, he stated that while this required three years to learn, the French and German took only 18 months. The speaker advocated a necessity for phonetic spelling. Mr. Edward Jones quoted Mr. Gladstone, Bishop Thirlwall, Earl Malmesbury and W. Hepworth Dixon against the present system of English spelling. The Convention adopted the resolutions of the American Philological Association as its views. The Convention lasted two or three days, and the subjects under consideration were discussed in full by the members.

Swiss Assemblage at the Centennial.

On August 26th and 27th, a large gathering of the various Swiss societies throughout the United States took place in Philadelphia. The first of these days was selected on account of its commemorating an important epoch in Swiss history, the anniversary of one of the decisive struggles by which the free institutions of their fathers were secured and perpetuated. The visiting societies were received in Philadelphia by the Swiss Maennerchor, and were called to order by the Swiss Consul in Philadelphia, who had charge of the arrangements for the demonstration. The assemblage afterward marched to the Exhibition Grounds, through which they paraded to Judges' Hall, where a meeting was held under the direction of the President of the Swiss Association in America, Gen. John A. Sutter, of California.

The congratulatory address of the Swiss to America upon the 100th anniversary of American independence was delivered by John A. Felwell, of Baltimore, and was highly eloquent. The speaker said: "Our native home, Switzerland, is the oldest Republic now existing. In 1307, 569 years ago, a small number of our ancestors vowed to each other, at the risk of their lives and fortunes, to throw off oppression, tyranny and insult, under which they were suffering, and to be once more independent, as their fathers were. Around the small nucleus, consisting of the three fairest cantons, one by one clustered other cantons, all holding tenaciously together, until we find in the beginning of this century the present confederation of 22 cantons, their entire number being, since 1848, happily united under a strong federal constitution. The earliest record of a Swiss coming to this country is that of one Conrad Gross, in the year 1660. Newbern, N. C., was early founded by the Swiss, in honor of the present Swiss capital. In 1720, Swiss immigrants founded Purisburg, the first town on the Savannah River; though the principal emigration from Switzerland to the United States is confined to the last forty or fifty years." The speaker then referred in complimentary terms to Gen. Sutter, a native Swiss, the pioneer gold-finder of California. A response to the eloquent orator was made by United States Senator Howe, of Wisconsin, after which the gathering dispersed to view the attractions of the Exhibition.

In the evening the Swiss societies proceeded to Schutzen Park, whose grounds were beautifully illuminated with Chinese lanterns. Here a banquet was enjoyed, and speeches, songs and recitations prolonged the festivities until a late hour. On the following day the festival was continued at Schutzen Park, a prominent feature of the exercises being the singing of a number of the singing societies of different States. Finally, a committee was appointed to form a combined organization of the Swiss Associations for benevolent purposes.

Various Meetings.

On August 17th, a yacht club called the "Innocents Abroad," composed of department officers and clerks, of Washington, D. C., arrived at Philadelphia, in their schooner yacht *Commerce*, and visited the Fairmount Exhibition. On the same day, the members of the National Maltsters' Convention, about 75 in number, visited Brewers'

Hall on the grounds, arriving there in carriages from the meeting-place of the Convention at St. George's Hall. The party were addressed by Wm. Massay; H. Rute, President of the National Brewers' Association; Mr. Katzenmeyer, Secretary of the same; D. A. Lynde, President of the National Maltsters' Association; John O'Byrne, and others.

On August 21st, 80 Chinese boys left Hartford, Conn., for Philadelphia, to attend the Exhibition. They were joined by about 35 others. These students are being educated in this country, under the superintendence of the Chinese Educational Commission. They were accompanied to Philadelphia by a native interpreter, native teacher, Professor D. E. Bartlett, of the American Asylum, Hartford, Professor J. N. Carleton, of the State Normal School, Professor E. B. Northrop, and others. On the 24th these young students assembled in Judges' Hall to listen to addresses from Gen. Hawley and other prominent gentlemen.

On August 30th, the New York Press Association visited Philadelphia, to attend the Exhibition. The entire party numbered 205, and after examining the various buildings on the grounds, they made an excursion by way of the Northern Pennsylvania R. R. to Washington. At about the same time, three excursions from Toronto and Hamilton, Canada, numbering over 3,000 persons, arrived at the Exhibition, and on August 28th, a delegation of the New York State National Guard arrived from Troy, N. Y., numbering 85 men, and accompanied by a fine band. On the same day, a delegation of fifty-two workmen, sent out by the French Government, arrived at the Exhibition and visited the different buildings, afterward inspecting the principal industrial establishments of Philadelphia. Among the delegates were representatives of the Société d'Agriculture, at Aix, the Typographical Mutual Benevolent Union in Paris, the Municipal Council at Besançon, the Municipal Council of Toulouse, and others. On August 28th there also visited the Exhibition a select party of prominent merchants and representative men of New York; and on the following day a grand Knights Templars' Centennial Excursion from Canada was added to the number of special visitations.

On September 9th, a reunion of Californians took place at the Pacific Coast Centennial Hall at Philadelphia. The occasion was the twenty-sixth anniversary of the admission of California into the Union, the address being delivered by the Hon. Rodman M. Price, ex-Governor of New Jersey, who participated with Commodore Slote in raising the American flag at Monterey in 1846. The National Agricultural Congress assembled at the grounds, September 14th, when an address on "Southern Agriculture" was delivered by Colonel Thomas Clayborne, after which the Congress adjourned to visit the Colorado and Kansas Building. The first annual meeting of the American Forestry Association took place September 15th, in the Judges' Pavilion. President John A. Warner, of Ohio, occupied the chair, and Mr. McAffee acted as Secretary. Two gentlemen from Spain were present, and two from the Forest Council. After the opening address by the President, Franklin S. Hough read an elaborate paper on the subject of Forestry. Addresses were also made by Bernard Laundreth and Professor McAffee. A committee was appointed to confer with the American Forest Council, and effect a union for mutual improvement in the art of Forestry.

Finally, Messrs. Steinway & Sons, pianoforte manufacturers, of New York, took their employés and friends on an excursion to the Centennial Exhibition, engaging a special train for the occasion. The members of the New York Liederkranz Society also visited the Exhibition, in company with the members of the Germania Maennerchor of Baltimore. A delegation of school-teachers from Ontario, Canada, visited the Exhibition on the 16th of September, and remained there a week. On September 24th, President and Mrs. Grant, accompanied by Mr. Sartoris, Secretary Borie, Secretary Fish and Mrs. Fish, visited the Exhibition and lunched at the residence of the British Commissioner. The President and family, however, visited the Centennial Exhibition several times informally, and spent some time in careful examination of the various objects displayed—seeming to be especially interested in the contents of Machinery Hall.

The Grangers.

The Grangers of the West came early to the conclusion that the cost of accommodation in Philadelphia during the continuance of the Centennial Exhibition was not likely to suit either their tastes or their pockets. They decided that they did not care to pay 50 cents to a transfer company for transportation to and from the grounds, nor $2.50 per day for one of the coupons of the Philadelphia Boarding-house Agency, limited. They therefore determined to provide accommodations for themselves; and accordingly those of the Order in Pennsylvania met in State Convention and placed the arrangement of matters in the hands of Mr. R. H. Thomas, the Secretary of the Order in that State.

By affiliating with the Pennsylvania Central R. R. Co., Mr. Thomas was enabled to obtain for the use of the Grangers an extensive tract of land at Elm Station, about six miles from the station at West Philadelphia, and four and a half miles from the Centennial depot. He also contracted with the road on the basis of 15 cents for transportation both ways to each individual Granger, or one way for 10 cents. Contracts were next entered into with builders for the erection of wooden sheds or huts to accommodate 2,400 people, a billiard saloon, bowling saloon, newspaper room, etc., a lecture room which should serve for church on Sundays, and for literary amusement on other days. The locality selected stood upon high ground, occupying, in fact, the first considerable hill from Philadelphia. There were numerous fine springs in the vicinity, rows of trees, and other attractions for the gratification of Summer visitors.

The construction of the Grangers' hostelry was peculiar. It consisted of long buildings, each containing 92 rooms, there being 46 on each side of a broad central corridor. These rooms were about twelve feet deep by eight feet broad, having sloping roofs. The schedule of prices adopted comprised 50 cents for lodging and 50 cents for each meal. Cold lunches were also prepared, ready packed, and sold to the Grangers at low prices. The organization and establishment of this institution was an entire success, as it was crowded throughout the continuance of the Exhibition. Shortly after the close of the latter, the Grangers' buildings took fire and were burned to the ground.

HIS MAJESTY DOM PEDRO II., EMPEROR OF BRAZIL.

Typical Buildings.

Among the structures erected at the Centennial grounds, designed either to illustrate modes of construction in use in different countries or to typify the manners and customs of ancient times, may be mentioned the Japanese, the buildings occupied by the English Commissioners, built in the Elizabethan style of architecture, the Swedish School-house, the Moorish Pavilion, the Tunisian Café, the Canadian Log-house, the Turkish Café, and New England Kitchen. Besides these, there were two which deserve more special description.

One of these was the model Palestine camp, which was pitched upon a beautiful lawn skirting the western side of Belmont Avenue, beyond Machinery Hall. This consisted of three gracefully shaped canvas tents, lined with fine blue cloth, embroidered in white and red, with Egyptian designs representing the branches of the palm-trees, with mottoes in Arabic, referring chiefly to the pleasures of travel. The largest tent, which was used for dining purposes, contained a long board table, capable of accommodating twenty persons. The floor was carpeted with mats. The sleeping tent, for two persons, was much smaller, and furnished with washstand, cot beds and easy-chairs. The third tent, used as a kitchen, was also made of canvas. The cooking was done on a long, low range, which could be folded up like a jack-knife for transportation, the fuel used being coal-oil. The entire encampment could be packed on four or five mules; but as tourists generally travel in parties of ten or more, the baggage and camp together generally require fifteen to twenty mules. The usual plan in journeying through the Holy Land is to send these by a short route to the point at which the party desire to stop over night, so that by the time the tourists have examined the places of interest on the way, the dragomans, cooks and waiters will have the tents pitched in readiness for their guests. The necessity of using tents and traveling in this fashion arises from the fact that from Jerusalem to Damascus there are no hotels, and only one building, that at Nazareth, where tourists can find shelter over night. In crossing the Jordan and traveling through Moab, tents are constantly needed. The Palestine camp on the Centennial grounds exhibited with its other attractions a fully costumed Syrian dragoman and cook.

Another most interesting and characteristic building of the sort we are describing, typical as distinctly of the West as the Palestine tents are of the East, was the log cabin which stood behind the Woman's Pavilion. The originator of the idea illustrated in this building was Miss Emma Southwick, of Boston, Mass. Miss Southwick visited the Vienna Exposition, and being greatly interested in the representation of peasant life in Hungary and Tyrol which she found there, conceived the idea of reproducing American pioneer life of a hundred years ago, at the Centennial Exposition. She accordingly procured the construction of this cabin, which consisted of several rooms, a loft at the back, and a veranda extending along one side, from which the dinners were served. The cabin was built of logs, and had small plots of ground on either side of the main entrance, fenced off with a plain low picket-fence. The interior room at the left had a wide, low fireplace, in which a fire was kept burning. Fire-irons occupied one side, the bellows stood in a corner. Strips of pumpkin were hung in strings from the ceiling, and other characteristic indications would be recognized by the old-time New Englander. This front room was what is known as the "living room." Back of this was the bedroom A little behind, across a narrow alleyway, was the kitchen, and back of that the veranda. The rooms were filled with ancient articles collected by Miss Southwick in various Massachusetts towns, and comprised many things especially interesting on account of their history as well as their antiquity.

Here was the first clock brought into Andover, four hundred years old; a chair belonging to Governor Hancock, more than hundred years old; another chair two hundred years old, and a wooden cradle which came over in the *Mayflower*, and in which was rocked little Peregrine White, the first child born in New England. He was of English parents, and was born on board the *Mayflower*, in the harbor of Boston, on December 20, 1620. He died in Marshfield, July 20, 1704. He was the son of William and Susannah White, and received, on account of his birth, two hundred acres of land from the General Court. He filled various civil and military offices, and is said to have been vigorous and of a comely aspect to the last. In his cradle in the log cabin were exhibited two dolls: one, a modern fine lady; the other, an antique body, which had evidently outlived many mistresses. On the walls were hung various wooden trenchers, and in one place there was an old-fashioned bonnet, having a broad straight brim, and trimmed with a pale-blue ribbon with white plaits, and having a long white vail hanging down behind. In the back room was an old bedstead, and on the bed were sheets of spun linen, two hundred years old, from Danvers, Mass., and a chintz coverlid, ornamented with figures of Liberty crowning the heroes of the Revolution. In a small old cupboard high up against the wall were some pieces of old china and antique Venetian glass. There was also a heavy shaving-glass, one hundred and twenty years old, used by the Rev. Samuel Hopkins; a little desk used by

John Alden, which came over from Manchester; a quantity of old blue crockery, and various other curious articles.

THE CENTENNIAL EXPOSITION.

CONTINUATION OF ITS HISTORY.

We resume the historical portion of our consideration of the Centennial Exposition at the point where that concluded with the ceremonies of the opening on May 10th, 1876, as presented in the Historical Register ending on page 78. Having laid before our readers, as far as was practicable in the space allotted, a panorama of the completed exhibitive effort at Fairmount, having described the numerous buildings and their contents, having made such a statement of the statistics and progress of the empires, kingdoms and states there represented as seemed necessary to the full elucidation of the world's enterprise, energy and result as represented in the Centennial, we proceed now to complete our work with such a continuation of the history of the Exposition, aided by a presentation of its statistics and other incidents, as shall furnish a fitting conclusion and enable our readers to acquaint themselves fully with the rise, progress and results of the most stupendous and successful competitive exhibition that the world ever saw.

Summary.

In order to enable the reader to obtain at a glance a just view of the more prominent features and incidents connected with the history of the Centennial, we will recapitulate these here.

On March 3d, 1871, Congress passed an Act providing for the celebration of the one hundredth anniversary of American independence by holding an International Exhibition of arts, manufactures and products of the soil and mine in the City of Philadelphia during the year 1876. This Act created the United States Centennial Commission, consisting of two delegates from each State and Territory, the Commissioners being duly appointed by the President of the United States on the nomination of the Governors of the respective States and Territories. On June 1st, 1872, Congress created the Centennial Board of Finance, consisting of two members from each Congressional district and four from each State and Territory at large, empowered to secure subscriptions of capital stock to an amount not exceeding $10,000,000. On July 3d, 1873, President Grant issued a proclamation declaring that the Exhibition should be opened on the 19th of April, 1876, and close on the 19th of October in the same year. These dates were afterward changed to May 10th and November 10th, 1876.

On January 23d, 1874, the President appointed a Board composed of a representative from each of the executive departments of the Government except the Department of State and that of the Attorney-General, and including the Department of Agriculture and the Smithsonian Institution, which was charged with the duty of perfecting a collective exhibition illustrating the functions and administrative faculties of the Government in time of peace, and its resources in time of war. On June 18th, 1874, Congress passed an Act providing that all articles imported for the Exhibition should be admitted without duty, provided that all of them sold in this country or withdrawn from the Exhibition for consumption here should be subject to the duties in force at the date of importation.

In July, 1874 the grading of the 240 acres comprised in the grounds intended for the Exhibition was begun. The reception of articles for the Exhibition was fixed to begin January 5th, and end May 1st, 1876; and it was resolved that all exhibits should be removed by December 31st. Thirty-eight foreign nations responded favorably to the President's invitation to co-operate in the Exhibition. Thirty-nine States and Territories took measures for the representation of their industries and resources, and appointed advisory boards to take charge of this duty. The following States and municipal governments made the appropriations mentioned to the stock of the Board of Finance:

Philadelphia, $1,575,000; Pennsylvania, $1,000,000; New Jersey, $100,000; Connecticut, $10,000; New Hampshire, $10,000; Delaware, $10,000; Wilmington, Delaware, $5,000; total, $2,710,000. To this sum is to be added the Congressional appropriation of $1,500,000.

Twenty States and Territories made appropriations toward the representation of their natural and protective interests to the amount of $234,000. These were as follows:

Massachusetts, $50,000; New York, $25,000; Nevada, $20,000; West Virginia, $20,000; Connecticut, $15,000; Arkansas, $15,000; Ohio, $15,000; New Jersey, $10,000; New Hampshire, $10,000; Illinois, $10,000; Delaware, $10,000; Michigan, $7,500; Arizona, $5,000; Indiana, $5,000; Kansas, $5,000; Montana, $5,000; Colorado, $4,000; Wisconsin, $3,000; Oregon, $1,000; Minnesota, $500.

The Women's Centennial Executive Committee, under the Presidency of Mrs. E. D. Gillespie, was organized through twenty-seven States, and collected subscriptions to the stock of the Board of Finance, besides providing $35,000 for the erection of the special building to contain an international exhibition of women's work. There were appointed 250 judges, one-half foreigners and the other half citizens of the United States, divided into twenty-eight groups, each assigned to a particular class of exhibits. The American judges were appointed by the United States Commission, and the foreign judges by the Foreign Commission.

On May 10th the Exhibition was opened at the appointed hour by the President of the United States, in the presence of distinguished officials of foreign countries and the representatives of the United States, State and Municipal Governments, the public Press, and a concourse of about 200,000 people. The number of paying admissions on May 10th was 76,172. The number of free admissions has been variously estimated at from 150,000 to 200,000.

SIR GEORGE BOWEN, GOVERNOR GENERAL OF VICTORIA, NEW SOUTH WALES.

A special feature was the appointment of certain days for the particular reception of visitors from the States, by whose name these days became respectively known. The statistics of admissions on these days are as follows:

States.	Date.	Free.	Cash.	Total.
New Jersey	Aug. 24	10,727	56,325	67,052
Connecticut	Sept. 7	10,985	64,059	75,044
Massachusetts	Sept. 14	12,073	85,795	97,868
New York	Sept. 21	12,585	122,003	134,588
Pennsylvania	Sept. 28	17,750	257,169	274,919
Rhode Island	Oct. 5	11,886	89,060	109,046
New Hampshire	Oct. 12	13,681	101,541	115,422
Delaware and Maryland	Oct. 19	15,052	161,355	176,407
Ohio	Oct. 26	13,361	122,300	135,661

Besides the ceremonies connected with the celebrations on the State days enumerated, Centennial addresses were delivered illustrative of the history of Arizona, Arkansas, Colorado, Dakota, Idaho, Illinois, Maine, Mississippi, Michigan, Missouri, Montana, Nevada, Tennessee, Texas, Utah, Vermont, Washington Territory and West Virginia. Other celebrations and occurrences took place as follows: May 23d, the Knights Templars of Pennsylvania assembled; May 24th, the Judges of Award were initiated with speeches and toasts; May 29th, the bankers of the United States assembled to open their special building; June 1st, the Knights Templars of the United States held a reunion and grand parade; June 7th, the brewers opened Brewers' Hall and held a convention therein; June 12th, Women's International Temperance Convention began; June 15th, the Sons of Temperance of America convened and dedicated a free ice-water fountain on the Grounds; June 27th, the West Point Cadets began a ten days' encampment on the Grounds; June and July, the international trial of reapers, mowers, and other agricultural machines and implements, was held near Schenck's Station, on the N. J. R. R.; July 2d, a Congress of Authors held in Independence Hall; July 4th, German citizens dedicated a monument to Humboldt in Fairmount Park, and 10,000 of the Pennsylvania National Guard, who had been encamped in Fairmount Park, paraded; July 16th, the Columbus, Ohio Cadets encamped on the Grounds; August 22d, International Regatta began on the Schuylkill, continuing two weeks thereafter; on this date, also, the Knights of Pythias of America paraded; August 28th, a reunion and parade of Swiss citizens was held; September 1st, the International display of Live Stock opened, and continued during the remainder of the Exhibition; September 2d, 500 of the Connecticut National Guard encamped near the Grounds; September 4th, the International Medical Congress began; September 6th, the Volunteer Firemen paraded; September 10th, the Associated Pioneers of California held a reunion; September 20th—the Independent Order of Oddfellows of America paraded; October 12th, the Italian citizens dedicated a marble statue of Columbus on the Grounds; October 13th, the Cadets of the Virginia Military Institute encamped on the Grounds; October 26th the American Merchants held a reunion on the Grounds; November 2d, the Colored Citizens dedicated a monument to Bishop Allen; November 7th, Mrs. E. D. Gillespie, President of the Women's Centennial Executive Committee, held a reception in the Women's Department; November 9th, the United States Centennial Commission and Board of Finance gave a farewell reception and banquet to the Foreign Commissioners, and an International Pyrotechnic contest between Professor Brock, of London, and Professor Jackson, of Philadelphia, was held at the Grounds; November 10th, the Exhibition closed.

In addition to the foregoing, an International Rifle Contest was held in September at Creedmoor, Long Island, in which five teams were represented: the Scotch, Irish, Australian, Canadian and American. The American team won the palm.

Close of the Exposition.

On Thursday evening, November 9th, 1876, the Foreign Commissioners to the Centennial Exhibition were entertained at a grand banquet at St. George's Hall by the members of the Centennial Commission and the members of the Board of Finance. The hall was tastefully decorated for the occasion, and covers were laid for upwards of 400. President Grant presided, supported on the right by General Hawley and Sir Edward Thornton, the British Minister, and on the left by Mr. John Welsh, of the Board of Finance, and Director-General Goshorn. The first toast was, "The President of the United States," and the second "The Foreign Commissioners." To the latter the various Commissioners responded in alphabetical order, the last to speak being Sir Edward Thornton, who read the following telegram, just received by him:

"London, November 9th.

"The Lord President requests you to offer, in his name, to the American authorities hearty congratulations on the successful result of their great labors, with best thanks for the attention paid to all his Grace's wishes in business matters, and for the cordial reception given to the British Staff."

The following was also read:

(*From his Grace the Duke of Richmond to Colonel Sanford.*)

"October 22, 1876.

"My Dear Colonel Sanford—Being the Minister in attendance to the Queen, I have had an opportunity to learn Her Majesty's wishes concerning the presentation of St. George's House to the City of Philadelphia. I am happy to say that it meets with Her Majesty's entire approval. Her Majesty considers it an excellent idea, and is very glad that St. George's House will remain in Philadelphia as a memorial of the part Great Britain took in the Exhibition this year.

"I am also glad to find that the British section, under your able guidance, should have been a success. As I have taken great interest in the proceedings, I take the opportunity of thanking you for what you have done. Believe me, yours truly,

"Richmond and Gordon."

This communication was in reference to the fact that a free gift had been made by the British Commissioners

INTERIOR OF THE SHOE AND LEATHER BUILDING.

of the English building known as St. George's Hall to the city of Philadelphia.

On the same evening, November 9th, the International Contest of Fireworks took place on the Centennial Exhibition Grounds, between Messrs. C. T. Brock & Co., of London, and Professor Samuel Jackson, of Philadelphia. This display attracted an immense number of persons to the Grounds. The programme was commenced by the Messrs. Brock, with a grand salute of aerial pieces. This was followed by an illumination of all the buildings and the park, covering an area of over 200 acres, during which 100 large rockets, 50-inch shells and six large magnesium balls were used; the whole forming an imposing picture. The entire number of pyrotechnic exhibits by the Messrs. Brock was eighteen, including large rockets, shells, magnesium stars, enormous set pieces, golden fountains, colored Roman candles, etc.

At its close Professor Jackson commenced his display with an ascension of 6 gas-balloons filled with fires and shooting stars, which were followed by rockets ascending to the height of 3,000 feet, where 13 stars were liberated, emblematical of the original thirteen States of the Union. Grand flights of signal rockets, batteries of bombshells and patriotic pieces followed; the whole being concluded by a grand display, covering an area of 10,000 feet. This commenced with a spirited bombardment, after which an immense pyric temple appeared, supporting a dome studded with 38 stars, surrounding the seal of the United States. Upon the apex appeared Liberty pointing to the American Eagle, soaring aloft with the starry banner in his beak, while rockets and bombs lighted up the entire area; the temple being flanked at the right and left by two gorgeous fountains, pouring out streams of golden fire. As to the competition between the two distinguished experts in pyrotechny, it was generally concluded that while Professor Jackson excelled in his production of large combination pieces, his English competitor had exhibited more brilliant rockets, bombs, etc., and displayed a greater variety of coloring.

November 10th opened gloomily, and throughout the day the descent of rain was continuous and increasing. Yet the unfortunate fact did not deter the public from making an early presentment of themselves at the gates of the Centennial Grounds, through which a steady stream of humanity flowed from eight o'clock until noon. As the time approached for the closing ceremonies of the Exhibition, the downpour of rain became a positive deluge; yet the open space between Machinery Hall and the Main Building was crowded with spectators, male and female, little of whom could be seen except the umbrellas with which they sought to shield themselves from the elemental rage.

It had been designed that the official ceremonies should take place in front of the western end of the Main Building; and for this purpose a platform had been erected capable of holding about 2,000 persons, while the space in front, as far as the Bartholdi Fountain, had been filled up with benches and settees, and preserved by chains and ropes from the pressure of the crowd. The inclemency of the weather, however, changed the plans of the Commissioners, and it was hastily concluded to devote Judges' Hall to the final exercises. Entrance to the hall was only obtained by ticket, and few of the vast masses who had gathered in the open air and the various buildings were aware of the change in the programme until the latter had been completely effected. Yet Judges' Hall was crowded to that extent that some fears were felt and expressed as to the stability of the structure and its capacity to sustain the immense pressure to which it was forced to submit under the circumstances.

Inasmuch as the most important act of the opening ceremonies had taken place in Machinery Hall, being that of setting in motion the Corliss engine, thousands of persons believed that the existence of the Exposition would cease by stoppage of this magnificent machine under similar circumstances. These, therefore, gathered near the colossal engine and waited patiently.

In front of the Judges' Pavilion a broad passageway was kept open by two long lines of the Centennial Guard, effectually barring the entrance of any one unprovided with a properly authenticated card of admission. In the gallery Theodore Thomas's grand orchestra had been hastily gathered, while on the platform were assembled the various dignitaries who were to officiate on the occasion. Here sat President Grant, on whose right were General Hawley, Director-General Goshorn, Secretary of War Cameron, and George W. Childs, Esq. To the left were Commissioner Daniel J. Morrell, Secretary of State Hamilton Fish, Rev. J. H. Seiss, John Welsh, and General Robert Paterson. Behind were Governor Hartranft of Pennsylvania, Governor Rice of Massachusetts, Governor Bedle of New Jersey, Governor Cochran of Delaware, Chief Justice Waite, Associate Justices Davis and Bradley, and Mayor Stokely. Here were also Sir Edward Thornton, in court dress, General N. P. Banks, Thomas A. Scott, Bishop Simpson, Asa Packer, the millionaire and philanthropist, U. S. Grant, Jr., Aristarche Bey, the Turkish Minister, members of the staffs of Governors, distinguished Army and Navy Officers, and finally, the Centennial Commissioners, the members of the Board of Finance, and members of the Diplomatic Corps, including the Ministers from Brazil and Japan, and the Hon. D. Chadwick and Hon. Alexander Macdonald, of the British Parliament, and Hon. George Brown, of the Canadian Parliament. Another prominent guest was Sarah Smith Stafford, of Trenton, daughter of Lieutenant James Bayard Stafford, who was with Commodore Paul Jones on the *Bon Homme Richard* in the latter's engagement with the *Serapis*, and who, when the flag was shot from the mast, rescued it, and received a severe gash in the left shoulder from a sword in the hands of a British officer. In 1784 the Marine Commissioners presented this flag to the Lieutenant as a reward for his bravery. Miss Stafford, its present owner, is seventy-four years of age.

Just before the exercises commenced, a pleasant incident occurred. Mrs. Gillespie, President of the Women's Centennial Commission, was seated on the right between Colonel Thomas A. Scott and Bishop Simpson, but a message came to the Master of Ceremonies, and she was conducted to a place of honor in the front rank on the platform beside Mr. Welsh.

EX-GOVERNOR WILLIAM BIGLER.

The Presidential procession entered the hall at two o'clock, immediately after which Thomas's Orchestra performed the "Centennial March," written by the great German composer, Wagner, for the opening ceremonies of the Exhibition. On the cessation of the music, General Hawley, President of the Centennial Commission, who acted as the presiding officer, introduced the Rev. Joseph A. Seiss, who offered a fervent prayer.

As the prayer was concluded, the orchestra began a chorale and fugue from Bach, closing with a grand combination of rich tones, which offered a cheerful introduction to the more formal subdivisions of the exercises.

Hon. D. J. Morrell, United States Centennial Commissioner from Pennsylvania, Chairman of the Executive Committee, was then presented, and after the hearty applause which greeted his appearance, spoke substantially as follows:

"On the 9th day of March, 1870, it was my privilege to introduce in Congress a Bill to provide for holding in the city of Philadelphia the Exhibition which this day brings to a close. On the 3d of March, 1871, that Bill became a law, not without opposition and amendments, which took from it all the advantages for carrying out the purposes contemplated by the Act itself. On the 4th of March, 1872, the Centennial Commission met and organized, and the labor of preparing for the Exhibition was commenced in the face of obstacles such as were never encountered in a similar undertaking.

"The Government had refused aid. Local jealousies were powerful. The newspapers of the country, with few exceptions, were lukewarm or openly hostile, and the mass of the people could not be interested in a thing which some feared for in the future. During the first year of the life of the Commission, doubt everywhere prevailed; and I am ashamed to say I shall strive to forget, and I hope history will not record, how few had faith in the success of our enterprise, and how many wise and eminent citizens rendered a hesitating support, or refused to commit themselves to what seemed a hopeless case. In this state of gloom, the city of Philadelphia was not afraid to charge itself with the expenses incident to the organization and labors of the Commission; and in this and all other official acts our municipal authorities have shown courageous liberality.

"The creation of the Board of Finance was the turning-point in the fortunes of the Centennial Exhibition. From that moment its prospects brightened; and though that Board was met with financial panic, its executive officers moved forward in the confidence which 'knows no such word as fail.' By slow and laborious stages public interest was aroused. The Women's Centennial Commission labored with zeal and energy. Money from private subscriptions to the stock of the Board of Finance went into the treasury. The State of Pennsylvania made liberal appropriations for the uses of the Exhibition, of which a memorial will remain to future Centennials, and when success was assured the National Congress recognized its duty and gave us material aid.

* * * * * * *

"It is but just, however, in speaking of the Executive Officers of the Commission, that I should point to the future historians of the Exhibition the great difficulties which have been encountered and overcome, and claim from them a charitable criticism. In comparing this work with others, I beg to note that this has been accomplished by the voluntary agents of a free people, clothed with no official or titular prestige or distinction, and without governmental support. The members of the Commission and of the Board of Finance have recognized that they were on exhibition as fully as any material object inclosed within these Grounds, that thousands of eyes would scan their every act.

* * * * *

"And I shall estimate above the praises of any, a word from that higher group of judges which represents the conscience of the world, that this work which we to-day commit to history is free from taint, that good men shall say it is honest. The managers of future Centennial celebrations to be held on these Grounds will see and do things more wonderful than our wildest dreams, and the remnants of our finest things may be exhibted by them as proofs of the rudeness of early days; but the records we have made, the full measure of our manhood, will go down to them untouched by the gnawing tooth of Time.

"Of the Exhibition, now to be numbered with the things of the past, it is difficult to speak. The nations are here. They have made this great spectacle what it is, and they deserve the gratitude of the American people. While they have taught much, they have also learned something; and they have seen in the crowds of American citizens of all occupations and conditions of life who have thronged these Grounds a polite, orderly, self-respecting and self-governing people. So far as their representatives have entered into our social life, we will hope they have found that what may be lacking in form is made up in substance; that the simplicity of republican manners is dignified by the sentiment of 'good-will to men.'

"The Exhibition was opened by starting in motion the Corliss engine, that giant of wonder to all, which for six months, with equal pulse, without haste, without rest, has propelled an endless system of belts and wheels. Silent and irresistible, it affects the imagination as realizing the fabled powers of genii and afrite in Arabian tales, and like them it is subject to subtle control. When these our ceremonies here are ended, the President of the United States by the motion of his hand will make the lightning his messenger to stop the revolution of its wheels, and at the same instant to tell the world that the International Exhibition, which marked the Centennial of American national life, is closed."

As Mr. Morrell ceased, Theodore Thomas gave the signal to the Centennial Chorus in the western balcony; and as the members rose, the orchestra began a soft, gentle prelude to Dettingen's "Te Deum." This musical introduction preluded the more striking phases of the theme soon to follow; and as the last of these was rendered, 400 well-trained voices united in the glorious harmonies of the stately "Te Deum." The next speaker was the President of the Centennial Board of Finance, Mr. John Welsh, who, after a graceful and eloquent presentation of the results, comparative and competitive, of the Exposition, was followed by General Goshorn and General Hawley.

At the conclusion of General Hawley's address the audience and chorus united in singing "My Country, 'tis of Thee," the blended voices being accompanied by Thomas's Orchestra. During the performance of this anthem the original flag of the American Union, to which we have already referred as first displayed by Commodore Paul Jones, on the *Bon Homme Richard*, was unfurled from a window above the platform by Miss Stafford. This incident was the signal for loud and long-continued enthusiasm. At the same moment a salute of forty-seven guns, one for each State and Territory, was fired from George's Hill by the Keystone Battery, and simultaneously from the United States steamer *Plymouth*, in the harbor. As this exciting scene terminated, President Grant arose and said: "Ladies

MAIN BUILDING.—MAIN AVENUE, LOOKING EAST.

THOMAS A. SCOTT, PRESIDENT OF THE PENNSYLVANIA RAILROAD COMPANY.

and gentlemen, I have now the honor to declare the Exhibition closed." The President then turned to the left and waved his hand to the operator at the telegraph instrument to give the signal for stopping the Corliss Engine and the machinery in the Hall. The operator touched the key of the instrument, and the characters "7—6" were signaled to the main telegraph office. The same current caused the hammer to strike the special gong stationed beside the Corliss Engine, which was the signal to stop; and at the moment all the gongs in the Machinery Hall experienced the effect of the electric current, and gave notice to the exhibitors that the Exhibition had been declared closed. Simultaneously in the main telegraph office the following dispatch was placed on the wires and sent to London, Liverpool, Paris, and the principal cities of Europe, the United States, and Canada:

"INTERNATIONAL CENTENNIAL EXHIBITION GROUNDS,
PHILADELPHIA, November 10, 1876.
"The President has this moment closed the International Exhibition; 3:37 P. M. W. J. PHILLIPS,
"Telegraph Director, U. S. International Exhibition."

The ceremonies closed by all present singing the long-meter Doxology to the words:

"Be Thou, O God! exalted high,
And as Thy glory fills the sky,
So let it be on earth displayed,
Till Thou art here as there obeyed."

While the ceremonies just described were progressing in the Judges' Hall, the location immediately surrounding the Corliss Engine had been gradually filling with people, and by two o'clock not less than 15,000 persons were gathered there, under the impression that the President would personally arrest the movement of the engine, in the same manner as he had started it on the 10th of May. By three o'clock a vast sea of upturned faces looked in the direction of the iron and steel engine which controlled the ceaseless revolving wheels, the whirring belts, and the operation of the labyrinth of mechanism. Just before four o'clock, two engineers took their position near the lever of the engine, with their eyes resting on the gong, which was to notify them when to apply the touch which should end the working of the machinery, the signal of the closing of the Centennial. A moment later the peal of the gong, attached by an electric wire, gave the signal, and an instant after the Corliss Engine had ceased its labors and rested, in company with the 23 miles of shafting and 40 odd miles of belting which, for six months, had moved the innumerable pieces of mechanism which had so charmed and delighted the visitors to Machinery Hall. Although the Exposition was now officially closed, the Grounds were suffered to remain open to the public on payment of the regular fee for admission. A considerable number of persons continued to avail themselves of the last remaining opportunity of visiting the Grounds and Buildings for a considerable period. On the day following the closing of the Exhibition there were 15,000 admissions. On Sunday the Grounds were opened, free, to the public, the buildings being closed. During the following week visitors continued to apply for admission, to the number of several thousand daily, gradually dwindling down, as the cold weather came on, to a few hundred. In the meantime, or from immediately after November 10th, the exhibitors in the different buildings proceeded to fence off their departments and pack their goods, preparatory to the removal of the latter. A large number of articles in the various sections had been already sold to visitors, delivery to take place after the close of the Exhibition. Such articles were in many instances duplicated to a very large extent, and for weeks those in charge of the various exhibits were fully employed in importing goods to answer the demands of purchasers.

THOMAS A. SCOTT.

NOT the least in importance, certainly, among the remarkable events connected directly and indirectly with the progress of the Centennial Exposition, is the fact that nearly the entire attendance at Fairmount Park found transportation over one system of railroads, owned by one company, and directed by one master mind; and that this vast movement of humanity occurred with no grave accident from first to last, and with a degree of accuracy quite unexampled in railroading experience.

It is, therefore, entirely pertinent and proper that we should include among our portraits illustrating phases of Centennial history that of Thomas A. Scott, President of the Pennsylvania Railroad Company.

Mr. Scott was born in Franklin County, Pennsylvania, December 28th, 1825, and was educated simply, amid all the customary disadvantages of ordinary district schools. In 1844 he became a clerk in the Collector's office at Columbia, Pa., and remaining there until 1847, was then transferred to the Collector's office at Philadelphia, where he staid three years, becoming then first connected with the Pennsylvania Railroad. Two years later, his remarkable energy and administrative capacity having attracted attention, Mr. Scott was appointed Superintendent of the Western Division, which position was followed in 1858 by that of General Superintendent of the road; and that in 1860, by the Vice-Presidency, from which it was an easy and natural step for such a man to the office of President of the road.

In the Fall of 1861 Mr. Scott was called by President Lincoln to assume the onerous and responsible position of Assistant Secretary of War. In this station it fell to his duty to supervise the transportation of our vast armies, than which it would be difficult to devise another more arduous, or more surrounded by difficulties. Prompt in action, and sustained by peculiar clearness of perception, Mr. Scott became recognized as an officer whose special fitness for a situation requiring these qualities was seldom matched. In the Fall of 1862 Mr. Scott returned to his railroad duties, and as these increased with the marvelous growth of the interests in his charge, he brought to bear upon his work those characteristics which have elevated him to the highest rank among those men—peculiarly the growth of our American civilization—who are qualified to grasp and control the complicated mechanism which goes to make up our comprehensive and intricate railroad system.

SOCIETY OF THE CINCINNATI.

THE fact that a meeting of the Society of the Cincinnati took place during the Centennial is a sufficient reason for giving some historical account of this organization, whose origin and history are probably not generally known to our readers. At the close of the Revolutionary contest with Great Britain, the cantonments of the American Army were on the Hudson. The veterans were now about to be disbanded, to return to their homes, many of them sick and destitute, and most of them dubious as to the future which might be before them. It was at this time that General Knox proposed the formation of a Society, which should serve to perpetuate the friendships which had been formed, and accomplish the purpose of cherishing the mutual feelings of patriotism and benevolence which had been created by a common experience of the hardships encountered in achieving the freedom of the country and establishing its rank among the nations of the earth. On the 10th of May, 1783, a meeting of the general officers, and one officer from the line of each regiment, was held, Baron Steuben presiding, when proposals for organizing the Society were considered. The question was referred to a committee consisting of Major-General Knox, Brigadier-General Hand, Brigadier-General Huntington, and Captain Shaw. Three days later, this committee made a report, which was unanimously accepted, and which is said to have been drafted by General Knox, and to be still in existence.

The preamble refers to the separation of the Colonies from Great Britain after a bloody conflict of eight years, and proceeds: "To perpetuate, therefore, as well the remembrance of this vast result, as the mutual friendships, which have been formed under the pressure of common danger and in many instances cemented by the blood of the parties, the Officers of the American Army do hereby in the most solemn manner associate, constitute and combine themselves into one society of friends, to endure as long as they shall endure, or any of their eldest posterity, and in failure thereof the collateral branches who may be judged worthy of becoming its supporters and members." Several distinguished officers in the war were men of cultivated minds, with whom the ancient classical history and literature were favorite reading. And it was doubtless for this reason that the Society adopted for their designation the name of the illustrious Roman, Lucius Quintus Cincinnatus. The propriety of this selection will not be questioned when it is remembered that this illustrious Roman patriot, Consul about 460 B. C., and twice afterward Dictator, delivered the Republic from her domestic and foreign enemies with the skill of a statesman and soldier, and retired to his farm on completing his task, refusing thereafter

HON. JOHN W. FORNEY.

THE FINAL CEREMONIES IN JUDGES' HALL.—MR. JOHN WELSH, PRESIDENT OF THE BOARD OF FINANCE, DELIVERING HIS CLOSING ADDRESS.

all recompense. The choice, in fact, was a delicate compliment to the immortal Washington himself.

In its organization the Society of the Cincinnatus held these principles to be immutable : "Incessant attention to preserve inviolate those exalted rights and liberties of human nature for which they have fought and bled, and without which the high rank of rational being is a curse instead of blessing ; an unalterable determination to promote and cherish that union of the respective States, and the national honor so essential to their happiness, and the future dignity of the American empire ; to render permanent the cordial affection subsisting among the officers. This spirit will promote brotherly kindness in all things, and particularly extend substantial acts of beneficence, according to the ability of the Society, toward those officers and their families who unfortunately may be under the necessity of receiving it." Appropriate emblems were devised for badges and ornaments, including the eagle, and uniting the blue and white, in compliment to the combined arms by which the successful result had been effected ; and the Society directed that one of its medals, suitably inscribed, should be sent to each of the distinguished characters among our French allies, namely: His Excellency Chevalier de la Luzerne ; His Excellency Sieur Gerard ; the Count d'Estaing ; the Count de Grasse ; the Count de Barras ; the Chevalier de Touches ; His Excellency the Count de Rochambeau, and the colonels and generals of his army ; also directing that they may be acquainted that the Society did itself the honor to consider them members. A committee was appointed, including Gen. Heath, Baron Steuben and Gen. Knox, to wait upon Gen. Washington and request him to honor the Society by placing his name at its head. At a meeting held on the 19th of June, 1783, the Commander-in-Chief was made President ; Major-General McDougall, Vice-President, and Major-General Knox, Secretary. The first meeting after the disbanding of the army took place at the City Tavern, Philadelphia. In May, 1784, Washington was again chosen President ; Major-General Gates, Vice-President, and Major-General Knox, Secretary. Prior to this meeting the civilians of the Revolution attacked the Society with great vigor, under the leadership of Jefferson, Jay, John and Samuel Adams, Elbridge Gerry and Franklin. The occasion of this opposition was the introduction of the hereditary principle of membership into the Society, this being, it was feared, likely to create in time a Society which would lead to the overthrow of the institutions of the country. So fiercely was this feature of the organization opposed, that it was finally thought

best to omit entirely any provision for a continuance of the institution beyond the period of its founders.

Washington would have been willing even to sacrifice the existence of the Society had it not been for its relation to the foreign officers enrolled in it. In order to relieve the Society from any imputation of its being hereditary, it was determined that he should accept the office of President-General, to which he had been invited. A compromise was, however, effected, and Washington continued to hold the office of President as long as he lived. After his death the institution was assumed to remain in its original position, and from this time greater regard was paid to the former leading idea of inheritable succession, and some certain lineal relation between the members and original founders became an established principle of the institution. In the absence of any positive rule, the membership has always been renewed by election, which has become so settled by usage as to be the normal organic law of the institution. The great French orator, Mirabeau, was one of the opponents of the Society, and in 1784 issued a pamphlet against it. In this he said : "It is an institution which must shortly undermine the public weal, their liberty and their country ; strip the middle and lower ranks of life of all influence and all importance, and consign them to the most palpable contempt, and reduce them to the completest nullity, or at best to the sad privilege of murmuring when it will be too late to remedy the evil." Even Franklin, writing from Passy, January 26, 1784, to his daughter, Mrs. Bache, sneers somewhat at the Society, and comments in the following terms upon the adoption of the "bald eagle" as the representative of his country : "For my part I wish the bald eagle had not been chosen as the representative of our country. He is a bird of bad moral character ; he does not get his living honestly. You may have seen him perched on some dead tree, where, too lazy to fish for himself, he watches the labors of the fishing-hawk, and when that diligent bird has at length taken a fish and is bearing it to his nest for the support of his mate and young ones, the bald eagle pursues him and takes it from him. With all this injustice he is never in good case, but like those among men who live by sharping and robbing, he is generally poor and often very lousy. Besides, he is a rank coward. The little king-bird, not bigger than a sparrow, attacks him boldly and drives him out of the district. He is therefore by no means a proper emblem of the brave and honest Cincinnati of America, who have driven all the *king-birds* from our busy country, though exactly fit for that order of knights which the French call *chevaliers d'industrie.*"

It is amusing now to read the various protests against this Society, whose whole existence has been modest and unassuming, without a shadow of political or social power, and the very names of whose present members are scarcely known to one in ten thousand out of their own immediate circle ; yet at the time of its origin it was esteemed a diabolical association, whose dangers the Governor of South Carolina pointed out in a speech to the Assembly, and which a committee of Massachusetts declared "dangerous to the peace, liberty and safety of the Union."

STATISTICS OF THE EXHIBITION.

Admissions.

THE total admissions to the Exhibition, from May 10th to November 10th, amounted to 9,892,625, of which 8,004,214 were cash admissions, and 1,888,411 free. The total cash receipts at the gates amounted to $3,819,497. The monthly receipts were as follows :

Month.	Paid.	Free.	Total.	Receipts.
May..	378,980	305,969	684,949	$189,490 35
June	695,666	307,159	1,200,825	347,833 40
July	636,513	269,929	906,447	318,199 25
August	908,684	266,630	1,175,314	415,659 25
September	2,130,991	308,698	2,439,689	928,056 00
October	2,334,530	229,340	2,663,879	1,160,811 50
November	918,894	115,637	1,034,531	459,447 25
	8,004,263	1,853,362	9,857,625	$3,819,497 00

The Exhibition was open 159 days, during which the daily average attendance of paid visitors was 49,986 ; average attendance of free admissions, 11,952 ; average total admissions, 61,938 ; average receipts, $23,807.50. The largest attendance on any one day was on Pennsylvania Day, September 28th, when the total admissions numbered 274,919. The attendance on the various State days was as follows :

State.	Date.	Paid.	Free.	Total.	Receipts.
New Jersey	Aug 24	56,325	10,727	67,052	$28,063 25
Connecticut	Sept. 7	64,059	10,985	75,044	30,853 75
Massachusetts	Sept. 14	85,795	12,073	97,868	41,193 00
New York	Sept. 21	122,003	12,585	134,588	59,986 00
Pennsylvania	Sept. 28	257,169	17,750	274,919	118,673 75
Rhode Island	Oct. 5	89,060	13,881	115,422	50,536 00
Delaware & Maryland	Oct. 19	161,355	15,052	176,407	80,367 50
Ohio	Oct. 26	122,300	13,361	135,661	61,094 50

The attendance compared with other Exhibitions shows the following :

PLACE.	YEAR.	No. OF VISITORS.	RECEIPTS.	OPEN DAYS.
London	1851	6,039,195	$2,530,000	141
Paris............	1855	5,162,330	600,500	200
London.........	1862	6,211,103	2,300,000	171
Paris...........	1867	10,000,000	2,822,932	210
Vienna	1873	7,254,687	2,000,000	186
Philadelphia ...	1876	9,857,625	3,819,497	159

From this it will appear that while the daily average of attendance at Philadelphia was 61,938, at London, in 1851, it was 49,923 ; at Paris, in 1855, it was 25,811 ; at London, in 1862, it was 36,320 ; at Paris, in 1867, it was 47,619 ; and at Vienna, in 1873, it was 39,003.

The following table gives the number of persons registering at the State Buildings :

STATE.	No. REGISTERING	LARGEST DAY.		AVERAGE.
Arkansas	989	Sept. 28...	633	11
California............	2,100	Sept. 29...	204	23
Illinois..............	20,750	July 1....	1,475	148
Tennessee	35,000	....		37
Kansas	61,060	Sept. 23...	128	59
Wisconsin............	10,357	....	200	85
Michigan............	19,771	Sept. 18...	1,311	187
Massachusetts	19,840	....	..	560
Delaware.............	20,930	....	560	180
New Jersey..........	74,793	Aug. 24...	1,796	699
Iowa	11,355	Sept. 16...	276	111
West Virginia........	33,902	....	..	213
Pennsylvania.........	34,541	Sept. 23...	3,067	331
Virginia	30,500	....	..	255
Colorado	37,500	Sept 7 ...	950	312

The Centennial Exhibition had the largest attendance ever known in a single month, or in a single week, or on a single day, besides the largest aggregate attendance. The following table shows the comparative attendance on the largest day of different Exhibitions :

PLACE.	YEAR.	DAYS.	LARGEST DAY.
London....................	1851	144	109,915
Paris.....................	1855	200	123,017
London	1862	171	67,891
Paris	1867	217	173,923
Vienna....................	1873	186	100,000
Philadelphia...............	1876	159	274,919

TRANSPORTATION.

The question of transportation has been one of the most important to be considered in connection with the great Exhibitions of the world. It has, in every instance, been surrounded with difficulties ; and both at Paris and Vienna those difficulties interfered materially with the success of the enterprise. In Philadelphia this subject was taken in hand at the earliest moment practicable, under the direction of Captain Dolphus Torrey, Chief of the Bureau of Transportation, whose railroad experience and natural administrative capacity insured every possible advantage being taken to secure rapidity, care and certainty, both in the delivery and passage of the goods. Captain Torrey commenced his duties early in 1875, and, by a series of circulars to the exhibitors, which clearly explained the necessary action to be taken by them in the premises, opened the way for delivering goods never before equaled in promptness and care. It has been estimated that the number of cases and packages transported to the Centennial numbered between 40,000 and 50,000, with an aggregate weight of about 26,000 tons. It is gratifying to know that the Foreign Commissioners have recognized the admirable management of this department by an unanimous expression of their satisfaction. In regard to the passenger-transportation, as early as July 5th, 1876, Captain Torrey made an experiment to test the carrying capacity of the railroads running into Philadelphia, and also that of the city passenger-roads. The result of this experiment proved that there was at that time a carrying capacity equal to 150,000 persons, as that number were taken to the Centennial Grounds without difficulty on that day. The most extraordinary feature in passenger-delivery occurred on "Pennsylvania Day," when nearly 275,000 persons were transported to and from the Centennial ; the larger number being delivered in a period of time not exceeding three hours. In addition to this it is to be remembered that there was an average delivery of from forty to fifty thousand persons per day, and that without a single accident during the entire six months. It is believed that the transportation of passengers on the Pennsylvania Railroad alone, to and from the Centennial Depot, aggregated as much as 4,000,000. The regularity of the arrival and departure of trains, the system, and method, and celerity with which passengers were deposited and taken away by this railroad, occasioned the most favorable notice on the part of foreign correspondents. Meanwhile it is estimated that as many as 1,000,000 additional arrived at the Pennsylvania Depot at West Philadelphia,

Kensington, and Camden, making a total of 5,000,000 persons received in and taken away from Philadelphia during the period of six months. The largest number on one day arriving at the Centennial Depot was on the 19th of October, when 33,919 were safely deposited within a few hours' time. On the Philadelphia and Reading R. R. the transportation figures are as follows : May, 1876, 169,296 ; June, 307,503 ; July, 306,081 ; August, 388,970 ; September, 801,819 ; October, 810,000 ; total, 2,783,669. The largest number delivered by this road was on Pennsylvania Day, and amounted to 185,800. The large extent of the Grounds occupied by the U. S. International Exhibition, and the distance from one building to another, rendered it necessary to secure some convenient method of transportation, and a narrow-gauge railroad was adopted. The track was laid so as to conveniently reach all buildings, and, with the sidings, was little less than seven miles in length. The number of daily trains upon this road was eight. The number of trips per train, fourteen ; the number of persons carried was as follows : From May 15th to 31st, 125,363 ; in June, 505,704 ; July, 460,558 ; August, 589,334 ; September, 1,054,465 ; October, 1,048,718 ; total to November 1st, 3,784,142. The largest number were carried on Pennsylvania Day, viz., 68,273. The general approximate total of all arrivals and departures may be estimated as follows : By railroads, 10,000,000 ; horse-cars, 4,000,000 ; all other conveniences, 2,000,000 ; on foot, 4,000,000 ; total, 20,000,000.

MEDICAL SERVICE.

The Bureau of Medical Service was organized in anticipation of the accidents which might occur during the erection and removal of the Exhibition buildings, as well as for the relief of visitors taken sick while in the Exhibition Grounds. It may be mentioned that there was an average of 1,531 persons, including the guard, members of the Fire Department, and others, domiciled within the Grounds. The Bureau of Medical Service was under the charge of a director, aided by a staff consisting of seven physicians, one of whom constantly resided upon the Grounds, while the others were on duty in rotation, two doctors being constantly in service—the organization of this department comprising Dr. William Pepper, Dr. Theodore Herbert (Resident Physician), and the following medical officers in attendance : Dr. Jacob Roberts, Dr. Horatio C. Wood, Jr., Dr. Samuel W. Gross, Dr. Rowland J. Curtin, Dr. Milton Osgood, Dr. De Forrest Willard, Dr. Harrison Allen, besides a skilled nurse and five attendants. The department was provided with a comfortable building, furnished as a

THE CLOSING CEREMONIES ON FRIDAY, NOVEMBER 10TH. — THE CROWD WAITING FOR THE ARRIVAL OF THE OFFICIAL GUESTS.

hospital and dispensary, including a waiting-room. The officers were furnished with a supply of medicines and surgical appliances and dressings, and the male and female wards were each provided with a bath and every necessary convenience. Stretchers were kept at various points throughout the Exhibition and the Grounds, while an ambulance was in constant readiness at the hospital. During the Exhibition the Department treated 6,016 persons, up to October 31st. A few cases were serious, though, as a rule, the complaints were of a trifling nature, such as are commonly incident to large assemblies. It was demonstrated by the Medical Director that, although the heat of the Summer was of almost unprecedented severity, and although Philadelphia had constantly during the time an enormous floating population added to her inhabitants, the average healthfulness of the city was maintained.

GROSS RECEIPTS OF THE CENTENNIAL.

During the progress of the Exhibition there were received by the managers the following sums : From admission fees, $3,819,497 ; from concessions, $290,000 ; from per centages and royalties, $205,010.75 ; total, $4,314,507.75. The gross amount ($290,000) of the concession contracts were divided as follows among the parties purchasing privileges :

NAME.	AMOUNT.
Centennial Catalogue Company	$100,000
Restaurants	36,000
Flemming, Tobacconist	18,000
Rolling Chair Company	13,000
Soda Water Venders	20,000
Department of Public Comfort	8,500
Centennial Photographic Company	3,000
Centennial Guide-book Company	5,000
Dairymen's Association	3,000
Virginia Tobacco Manufacture (Machinery Hall)	3,000
Vienna Bakery	3,000
Proprietor of Popcorn Stands	8,000
Gillender & Sons, Glassworks	3,000
Whitman's Confectionery Stands	5,000
Centennial National Bank	5,000
Globe Hotel	10,000
California Wine-booth	5,000
Safe Deposit in Main Building	5,000
Cut Flower Stands	3,000
American Fusee Company	1,000
Cafes	2,950
Confectionery	2,900
Miscellaneous	26,650

In addition to these, the Pacific and Atlantic Telegraph Company paid to the Commission 20 per cent. of their receipts for messenger service, and 50 per cent. of all other receipts ; and the American District Telegraph Company paid 10 per cent. of its receipts for messenger service. Including the royalties on beer and soda-water, the percentage on sales and other business, the total receipts of the Committee on Concessions amounted to $500,000.

CONCLUSION.

Here we close our chronicle of the Centennial Exposition.

Commenced at a period when public affairs were embarrassed to an extent to seemingly preclude the possibility of success, this vast undertaking was faithfully conducted to a conclusion of glorious triumph.

FRANK LESLIE'S HISTORICAL REGISTER has sought to display before its readers the history of this magnificent enterprise, not only in its own immediate details, but with such added resource of collateral illustration and description as should best indicate its promised results, as well as its intention. If this purpose be fulfilled in the present work, the design of its projector will have been effected.

THE CLOSE OF THE EXPOSITION.—FINAL CEREMONIES IN JUDGES' HALL, NOVEMBER 10TH—SCENE AT THE UNFURLING OF THE PAUL JONES FLAG.

Index.

LITERATURE.

ENGRAVINGS.

A facsimile of Frank Leslie's
   illustrated historical
   register of the Centennial